TEACHER'S EDITION

HOLT McDOUGAL

1 uno ¡Avancemos!

AUTHORS

Estella Gahala | Patricia Hamilton Carlin

Audrey L. Heining-Boynton | Ricardo Otheguy | Barbara Rupert Mondloch

HOLT McDOUGAL

HOUGHTON MIFFLIN HARCOURT

Cover Photography

Front cover Palacio Nacional at night, Mexico City, Mexico ©2010 Nino H. Photography/Getty Images; Inset: Charro mexicano, H. Sitton/zefa/Corbis

Back cover

Level 1a: View toward La Fortaleza, San Juan, Puerto Rico, Steve Dunwell/The Image Bank/Getty Images
Level 1b: View of Buenos Aires through the Puente de la Mujer, Joseph Rodriguez/Gallery Stock Limited
Level 1: Palacio Nacional at night, Mexico City, Mexico ©2010 Nino H. Photography/Getty Images
Level 2: Cibeles Fountain and Palacio de Comunicaciones at night, Madrid, Spain, Doug Armand/Getty Images
Level 3: Plaza de la Constitución at night, Santiago, Chile, David Noton Photography
Level 4: Antigua, Guatemala ©Michel Renaudeau/age fotostock/Robert Harding Photo Library

Photography

Title page H. Sitton/zefa/Corbis; **T12** *top right* ©Hemis/Alamy Images; **T12** *top center* ©Images & Stories/Alamy Images; **T12** *left* ©National Geographic Image Collection/Alamy Images; **T12** *bottom right* Houghton Mifflin Harcourt; **T13-T15** *all* Houghton Mifflin Harcourt; **T30** *bottom left* Jorge Albán/Holt McDougal/Houghton Mifflin Harcourt; **T30** *top right* ©Danny Lehman/Corbis; **T31** *top left* ©PhotoObjects/Jupiterimages; **T31** *rest* Jorge Albán/Holt McDougal/Houghton Mifflin Harcourt; **T32** *top left* ©Pep Roig/Alamy Images; **T32** *top center* Jorge Albán/Holt McDougal/Houghton Mifflin Harcourt; **T32** *top right* ©Corbis; **T32** *bottom right* ©Nik Wheeler/Corbis; **27a** Jorge Albán/Holt McDougal/Houghton Mifflin Harcourt; **81a** Vince Bucci/AFP/Getty Images; **135a** Jorge Albán/Holt McDougal/Houghton Mifflin Harcourt; **189a** Ken Walsh/age fotostock; **297a** Claudio Cruz/AP Images; **297b** Cesar Mullix/www.USlatino.com; **351a** *top* Jorge Albán/Holt McDougal/Houghton Mifflin Harcourt; **405a** Mitch Diamond/Alamy.

Illustration

243a Kenneth Batelman.

Printed in the U.S.A.

ISBN 978-0-547-87202-5

6 7 8 9 10 0868 20 19 18 17 16 15 14

4500482769 A B C D E F G

Contents

Teacher Reviewers

Teacher's Edition

Sue Arandjelovic
Dobson High School
Mesa, AZ

Shaun A. Bauer
Olympia High School, *retired*
Orlando, FL

Hercilia Bretón
Highlands High School
San Antonio, TX

Maria Fleming Alvarez
The Park School
Brookline, MA

Fatima Hicks
Suncoast High School, *retired*
Riviera Beach, FL

Robin C. Hill
Warrensville Heights High School
Warrensville Heights, OH

Pam Johnson
Stevensville High School
Stevensville, MT

Kristen M. Lombardi
Shenendehowa High School
Clifton Park, NY

Debbe Tomkinson
Madison Middle School
Titusville, FL

Ronie R. Webster
Monson Junior/Senior High School
Monson, MA

Student Text

Susan K. Arbuckle
Mahomet-Seymour High School
Mahomet, IL

Kristi Ashe
Amador Valley High School
Pleasanton, CA

Sheila Bayles
Rogers High School
Rogers, AR

Robert L. Bowbeer
Detroit Country Day Upper School
Beverly Hills, MI

Hercilia Bretón
Highlands High School
San Antonio, TX

Adrienne Chamberlain-Parris
Mariner High School
Everett, WA

Mike Cooperider
Truman High School
Independence, MO

Susan B. Cress
Sheridan High School
Sheridan, IN

Michèle S. de Cruz-Sáenz, Ph.D.
Strath Haven High School
Wallingford, PA

Lizveth Dague
Park Vista Community
High School
Lake Worth, FL

Parthena Draggett
Jackson High School
Massillon, OH

Rubén D. Elías
Roosevelt High School
Fresno, CA

Phillip Elkins
Lane Tech College Prep High School
Chicago, IL

Michael Garber
Boston Latin Academy
Boston, MA

Marco García
Derry University Advantage Academy
Chicago, IL

David Gonzalez
Hollywood Hills High School
Hollywood, FL

Raquel R. González
Odessa Senior High School
Odessa, TX

Neyda Gonzalez-Droz
Ridge Community High School
Davenport, FL

Becky Hay de García
James Madison Memorial
High School
Madison, WI

Robin C. Hill
Warrensville Heights High School
Warrensville Heights, OH

Gladys V. Horford
William T. Dwyer High School
Palm Beach Gardens, FL

Richard Ladd
Ipswich High School
Ipswich, MA

Patsy Lanigan
Hume Fogg Academic Magnet
High School
Nashville, TN

Kris Laws
Palm Bay High School
Melbourne, FL

Elizabeth Lupafya
North High School
Worcester, MA

David Malatesta
Niles West High School
Skokie, IL

Patrick Malloy
James B. Conant High School
Hoffman Estates, IL

Brandi Meeks
Starr's Mill High School
Fayetteville, GA

Kathleen L. Michaels
Palm Harbor University High School
Palm Harbor, FL

Linda Nanos
Brook Farm Business Academy
West Roxbury, MA

Nadine F. Olson
School of Teaching and Curriculum Leadership
Stillwater, OK

Pam Osthoff
Lakeland Senior High School
Lakeland, FL

Nicholas Patterson
Davenport Central High School
Davenport, IA

Carolyn A. Peck
Genesee Community College
Lakeville, NY

Daniel N. Richardson
Concord High School, *retired*
Concord, NH

Rita E. Risco
Palm Harbor University High School
Palm Harbor, FL

Miguel Roma
Boston Latin Academy
Boston, MA

Nona M. Seaver
New Berlin West Middle/High School
New Berlin, WI

Susan Seraphine-Kimel
Astronaut High School
Titusville, FL

Mary Severo
Thomas Hart Middle School
Pleasanton, CA

Clarette Shelton
WT Woodson High School, *retired*
Fairfax, VA

Maureen Shiland
Saratoga Springs High School
Saratoga Springs, NY

Lauren Schultz
Dover High School
Dover, NH

Irma Sprague
Countryside High School
Clearwater, FL

Mary A. Stimmel
Lincoln High School
Des Moines, IA

Karen Tharrington
Wakefield High School
Raleigh, NC

Alicia Turnier
Countryside High School
Clearwater, FL

Roberto E. del Valle
The Overlake School
Redmond, WA

Todd Wagner
Upper Darby High School, *retired*
Drexel Hill, PA

Ronie R. Webster
Monson Junior/Senior High School
Monson, MA

Cheryl Wellman
Bloomingdale High School
Valrico, FL

Thomasina White
School District of Philadelphia
Philadelphia, PA

Jena Williams
Jonesboro High School
Jonesboro, AR

Program Advisory Council

Louis G. Baskinger
New Hartford High School
New Hartford, NY

Linda M. Bigler
James Madison University
Harrisonburg, VA

Jacquelyn Cinotti-Dirmann
Duval County Public Schools
Jacksonville, FL

Flora Maria Ciccone-Quintanilla
Holly Senior High School
Holly, MI

Desa Dawson
Del City High School
Del City, OK

Robin C. Hill
Warrensville Heights High School
Warrensville Heights, OH

Barbara M. Johnson
Gordon Tech High School, *retired*
Chicago, IL

Ray Maldonado
Houston Independent School District, *retired*
Houston, TX

Karen S. Miller
Friends School of Baltimore
Baltimore, MD

Dr. Robert A. Miller
Woodcreek High School
Roseville Joint Union High School District
Roseville, CA

Debra M. Morris
Wellington Landings Middle School
Wellington, FL

Maria Nieto Zezas
West Morris Central High School
Chester, NJ

Rita Oleksak
Glastonbury Public Schools
Glastonbury, CT

Sandra Rosenstiel
University of Dallas, *retired*
Grapevine, TX

Emily Serafa Manschot
Northville High School
Northville, MI

1a

Theme	Vocabulary	Grammar	Recycling
Preliminar — ¡Hola!	**Nueva York**		
	Greetings; Introductions; Saying where you are from; Numbers from 1 to 10; Exchanging phone numbers; Days of the week; The weather; Classroom phrases	The Spanish alphabet	
Unidad 1 — Un rato con los amigos	**Estados Unidos**		
1 ¿Qué te gusta hacer?	After-school activities; Snack foods and beverages	Subject pronouns and **ser**; **Gustar** with an infinitive	Weather expressions
2 Mis amigos y yo	Describing yourself and others	Definite and indefinite articles; Noun-adjective agreement	**Ser**; Snack foods; **Gustar** with an infinitive; After-school activities
Unidad 2 — ¡Vamos a la escuela!	**México**		
1 Somos estudiantes	Daily schedules; Telling time; Numbers from 11 to 100	The verb **tener**; Present tense of **-ar** verbs	After-school activities
2 En la escuela	Describing classes; Describing location; Expressing feelings	The verb **estar**; The verb **ir**	Class subjects; Adjective agreement; Telling time
Unidad 3 — Comer en familia	**Puerto Rico**		
1 Mi comida favorita	Meals and food; Asking questions	**Gustar** with nouns; Present tense of **-er** and **-ir** verbs	**Gustar** with an infinitive; Snack foods; The verb **estar**; Telling time
2 En mi familia	Family; Giving dates; Numbers from 200 to 1,000,000	Possessive adjectives; Comparatives	The verb **tener**; Numbers from 11 to 100; After-school activities; Describing others
Unidad 4 — En el centro	**España**		
1 ¡Vamos de compras!	Clothing; Shopping	Stem-changing verbs: **e → ie**; Direct object pronouns	Numbers from 11 to 100; The verb **tener**; After-school activities
2 ¿Qué hacemos esta noche?	Places and events; Getting around town; In a restaurant	Stem-changing verbs: **o → ue**; Stem-changing verbs: **e → i**	Present tense of **-er** verbs; The verb **ir**; Direct object pronouns; **Tener** expressions

1b

Theme	Vocabulary	Grammar	Recycling
Repaso — Antes de Avanzar			
	This unit reviews most of the vocabulary in Units 1–4.	This unit reviews most of the grammar in units 1–4.	This unit recycles most of the vocabulary and grammar in units 1–4.
Unidad 5 — Bienvenido a nuestra casa	**Ecuador**		
1 Vivimos aquí	Describing a house; Household items; Furniture	**Ser** or **estar**; Ordinal numbers	Stem-changing verbs: **o → ue**; Location words; Colors; Clothing
2 Una fiesta en casa	Planning a party; Chores	More irregular verbs; Affirmative **tú** commands	**Tener que**; Interrogative words; Expressions of frequency; Direct object pronouns
Unidad 6 — Mantener un cuerpo sano	**República Dominicana**		
1 ¿Cuál es tu deporte favorito?	Sports	The verb **jugar**; **Saber** and **conocer**; The personal a	Numbers from 200 to 1,000,000; **Gustar** with nouns; Comparatives
2 La salud	Staying healthy; Parts of the body	Preterite of regular **-ar** verbs; Preterite of **-car, -gar, -zar** verbs	**Gustar** with nouns; Stem-changing verbs: **o → ue**; Telling time
Unidad 7 — ¡Una semana fenomenal!	**Argentina**		
1 En el cibercafé	Sending e-mails; Talking about when events occur	Preterite of regular **-er** and **-ir** verbs; Affirmative and negative words	Affirmative **tú** commands; Telling time; Foods and beverages; Preterite of regular **-ar** verbs;
2 Un día en el parque de diversiones	Making a phone call; Places of interest	Preterite of **ir, ser,** and **hacer**; Pronouns after prepositions	Noun-adjective agreement; Places around town; Stem-changing verbs: **o → ue**
Unidad 8 — Una rutina diferente	**Costa Rica**		
1 Pensando en las vacaciones	Daily routines; Vacation plans	Reflexive verbs; Present progressive	Preterite of **hacer**; Direct object pronouns; Parts of the body; Chores; Houses; Telling time
2 ¡Vamos de vacaciones!	Discussing vacation and leisure activities	Indirect object pronouns; Demonstrative adjectives	Family; Numbers from 200 to 1,000,000; **Gustar** with an infinitive; Present progressive; Classroom objects

	Theme	Vocabulary	Grammar	Recycling
Preliminar	**¡Hola!** — **Nueva York**			
		Greetings; Introductions; Saying where you are from; Numbers from 1 to 10; Exchanging phone numbers; Days of the week; The weather; Classroom phrases	The Spanish alphabet	
Unidad 1	**Un rato con los amigos** — **Estados Unidos**			
	1 ¿Qué te gusta hacer?	After-school activities; Snack foods and beverages	Subject pronouns and **ser**; **Gustar** with an infinitive	Weather expressions
	2 Mis amigos y yo	Describing yourself and others	Definite and indefinite articles; Noun-adjective agreement	**Ser**; Snack foods; **Gustar** with an infinitive; After-school activities
Unidad 2	**¡Vamos a la escuela!** — **México**			
	1 Somos estudiantes	Daily schedules; Telling time; Numbers from 11 to 100	The verb **tener**; Present tense of **-ar** verbs	After-school activities
	2 En la escuela	Describing classes; Describing location; Expressing feelings	The verb **estar**; The verb **ir**	Class subjects; Adjective agreement; Telling time
Unidad 3	**Comer en familia** — **Puerto Rico**			
	1 Mi comida favorita	Meals and food; Asking questions	**Gustar** with nouns; Present tense of **-er** and **-ir** verbs	**Gustar** with an infinitive; Snack foods; The verb **estar**; Telling time
	2 En mi familia	Family; Giving dates; Numbers from 200 to 1,000,000	Possessive adjectives; Comparatives	The verb **tener**; Numbers from 11 to 100; After-school activities; Describing others
Unidad 4	**En el centro** — **España**			
	1 ¡Vamos de compras!	Clothing; Shopping	Stem-changing verbs: **e** → **ie**; Direct object pronouns	Numbers from 11 to 100; The verb **tener**; After-school activities
	2 ¿Qué hacemos esta noche?	Places and events; Getting around town; In a restaurant	Stem-changing verbs: **o** → **ue**; Stem-changing verbs: **e** → **i**	Present tense of **-er** verbs; The verb **ir**; Direct object pronouns; **Tener** expressions
Unidad 5	**Bienvenido a nuestra casa** — **Ecuador**			
	1 Vivimos aquí	Describing a house; Household items; Furniture	**Ser** or **estar**; Ordinal numbers	Stem-changing verbs: **o** → **ue**; Location words; Colors; Clothing
	2 Una fiesta en casa	Planning a party; Chores	More irregular verbs; Affirmative **tú** commands	**Tener que**; Interrogative words; Expressions of frequency; Direct object pronouns
Unidad 6	**Mantener un cuerpo sano** — **República Dominicana**			
	1 ¿Cuál es tu deporte favorito?	Sports	The verb **jugar**; **Saber** and **conocer**; The personal **a**	Numbers from 200 to 1,000,000; **Gustar** with nouns; Comparatives
	2 La salud	Staying healthy; Parts of the body	Preterite of regular **-ar** verbs; Preterite of **-car, -gar, -zar** verbs	**Gustar** with nouns; Stem-changing verbs: **o** → **ue**; Telling time
Unidad 7	**¡Una semana fenomenal!** — **Argentina**			
	1 En el cibercafé	Sending e-mails; Talking about when events occur	Preterite of regular **-er** and **-ir** verbs; Affirmative and negative words	Affirmative **tú** commands; Telling time; Foods and beverages; Preterite of regular **-ar** verbs;
	2 Un día en el parque de diversiones	Making a phone call; Places of interest	Preterite of **ir, ser,** and **hacer**; Pronouns after prepositions	Noun-adjective agreement; Places around town; Stem-changing verbs: **o** → **ue**
Unidad 8	**Una rutina diferente** — **Costa Rica**			
	1 Pensando en las vacaciones	Daily routines; Vacation plans	Reflexive verbs; Present progressive	Preterite of **hacer**; Direct object pronouns; Parts of the body; Chores; Houses; Telling time
	2 ¡Vamos de vacaciones!	Discussing vacation and leisure activities	Indirect object pronouns; Demonstrative adjectives	Family; Numbers from 200 to 1,000,000; **Gustar** with an infinitive; Present progressive; Classroom objects

Scope and Sequence

	Theme	Vocabulary	Grammar	Recycling
Preliminar	**Mis amigos y yo**	**Florida**		
		Saying who you are; Personality characteristics; Daily activities and food; Places in school and around town; Saying how you feel; Daily routine; Making plans	Definite and indefinite articles; Subject pronouns and **ser;** Adjectives; The verb **tener;** The verb **gustar;** **Ir** + **a** + place; **Ser** or **estar;** Regular present-tense verbs; Stem-changing verbs	
Unidad 1	**¡A conocer nuevos lugares!**	**Costa Rica**		
	1 ¡Vamos de viaje!	Going on a trip	Direct object pronouns; Indirect object pronouns	Possessions; Prepositions of location; Places around town; Daily activities
	2 Cuéntame de tus vacaciones	On vacation	Preterite of **-ar** verbs; Preterite of **ir, ser, hacer, ver, dar**	Interrogatives; Food; Days of the week; Parties
Unidad 2	**¡Somos saludables!**	**Argentina**		
	1 La Copa Mundial	Sports and health	Preterite of **-er** and **-ir** verbs; Demonstrative adjectives and pronouns	Food; Sports equipment; Colors; Clothing; Classroom objects
	2 ¿Qué vamos a hacer?	Daily routines	Reflexive verbs; Present progressive	**Pensar;** Parts of the body; Telling time; Places in school and around town
Unidad 3	**¡Vamos de compras!**	**Puerto Rico**		
	1 ¿Cómo me queda?	Clothes and shopping	Present tense of irregular **yo** verbs; Pronouns after prepositions	**Gustar;** Clothing; Expressions of frequency
	2 ¿Filmamos en el mercado?	At the market	Preterite of **-ir** stem-changing verbs; Irregular preterite verbs	Family; Chores; Food
Unidad 4	**Cultura antigua, ciudad moderna**	**México**		
	1 Una leyenda mexicana	Legends and stories	The Imperfect tense; Preterite and imperfect	Expressions of frequency; Weather expressions; Daily activities
	2 México antiguo y moderno	Past and present	Preterite of **-car, -gar, -zar** verbs; More verbs with irregular preterite stems	Daily activities; Arts and crafts
Unidad 5	**¡A comer!**	**España**		
	1 ¡Qué rico!	Preparing and describing food	**Usted/ustedes** commands; Pronoun placement with commands	Staying healthy; Chores
	2 ¡Buen provecho!	Ordering meals in a restaurant	Affirmative and negative words; Double object pronouns	Prepositions of location; Pronoun placement with commands
Unidad 6	**¿Te gusta el cine?**	**Estados Unidos**		
	1 ¡Luces, cámara, acción!	Making movies	Affirmative **tú** commands; Negative **tú** commands	Daily routines; Telling time
	2 ¡Somos estrellas!	Invitations to a premiere	Present subjunctive with **ojalá;** More subjunctive verbs with **ojalá**	Spelling changes in the preterite; School subjects; Vacation activities; Sports
Unidad 7	**Soy periodista**	**República Dominicana**		
	1 Nuestro periódico escolar	The school newspaper	Subjunctive with impersonal expressions; **Por** and **para**	Present subjunctive; Events around town
	2 Somos familia	Family and relationships	Comparatives; Superlatives	Clothing; Family; Classroom objects
Unidad 8	**Nuestro futuro**	**Ecuador**		
	1 El mundo de hoy	The environment and conservation	Other impersonal expressions; Future tense of regular verbs	Expressions of frequency; Vacation activities
	2 En el futuro...	Careers and professions	Future tense of irregular verbs	Clothing; Telling time; Daily routine

Theme	Vocabulary	Grammar	Recycling
Preliminar — Una vida ocupada	**Estados Unidos**		
	Talking about yourself and your friends; Saying what you know how to do; Talking about people and places you know; Describing your daily routine; Making comparisons	Verbs like **gustar**; Present tense of regular verbs; Present tense of irregular verbs; Present tense of **yo** verbs; Stem-changing verbs; The verbs **decir, tener,** and **venir; Saber** or **conocer; Ser** or **estar;** Reflexive verbs	
Unidad 1 — Nos divertimos al aire libre	**México**		
1 Vamos a acampar	Camping; Nature	Preterite tense of regular verbs; Irregular preterites	Irregular present tense
2 Vamos a la playa	Family relationships; At the beach	Imperfect tense; Preterite vs. imperfect	**Saber** and **conocer**
Unidad 2 — ¡Es hora de ayudar!	**Estados Unidos**		
1 ¡Todos para uno y uno para todos!	Volunteer activities and projects	**Tú** commands; Other command forms	Irregular preterite; Family relationships; Describing a camping trip; Beach activities; **Ir a** + infinitive
2 ¿Cómo nos organizamos?	Requests and recommendations; Media	Pronouns with commands; Impersonal expressions + infinitive	Preterite vs. imperfect; Beach activities; Volunteer activities
Unidad 3 — ¡El futuro de nuestro planeta!	**Centroamérica**		
1 ¿Cómo será el futuro?	Environmental concerns	Future tense; **Por** and **para**	**Ustedes** commands; **Ir a** + infinitive; Media vocabulary
2 Por un futuro mejor	Social awareness; Presenting and supporting opinions	Present subjunctive of regular verbs; More subjunctive verb forms	**Ustedes** commands; Impersonal expressions; Future tense
Unidad 4 — Así quiero ser	**El Caribe**		
1 ¿Quién te inspira?	Describing others; Professions	Future tense; Subjunctive with verbs of influence	**Ser** vs. **estar**; Future tense
2 ¿Quiénes son los héroes?	Expressing positive and negative emotions; More professions; Supporting opinions	Subjunctive with doubt; Subjunctive with emotion	Describing people; Superlatives; Family relationships; **-ísimo**
Unidad 5 — ¿Cómo te entretienes?	**Los países andinos**		
1 Comuniquémonos entre naciones	Travel preparations; Computers; Requirements and conditions	Subjunctive with conjunctions; Subjunctive with the unknown	Commands with **tú**; Professions vocabulary
2 Nuevos amigos, nuevas oportunidades	Participating in a group discussion; Leisure activities	Conditional tense; Reported speech	Preterite; Computer vocabulary
Unidad 6 — ¿Dónde vivimos?	**España**		
1 La vida en la ciudad	Around the neighborhood; An apartment in the city	Past participle as adjectives; Present perfect tense	Preterite; Direct object pronouns
2 Fuera de la ciudad	Traveling by train; Describing a cultural excursion	Past perfect tense; Future perfect tense	Present perfect; **Tú** commands; Places in the neighborhood; Past participles as adjectives
Unidad 7 — Tu pasado y tu futuro	**Venezuela y Colombia**		
1 Recuerdos	Planning for the future; School activities and events; Part-time jobs	Imperfect subjunctive; Subjunctive of perfect tenses	Present perfect; Subjunctive with doubt; Impersonal expressions
2 Nuevos principios	Pursuing a career	**Si** clauses; Sequence of tenses	Subjunctive with impersonal expressions; Conditional future; Architectural structures
Unidad 8 — Hablemos de literatura	**Cono Sur**		
1 Cuentos y poesía	Discussing and critiquing literature	Past progressive; Conjunctions	Preterite vs. imperfect; Professions
2 El drama	Reading and interpreting plays	**Se** for unintentional occurrences; Uses of the subjunctive	**Si** clauses; Literary vocabulary

Scope and Sequence

	Theme	Vocabulary	Grammar	Recycling
Unidad 1	**El mundo del trabajo**			
	1 En busca de trabajo	Job searches and different jobs	**Ser** vs. **estar**; Direct and indirect object pronouns	Demonstrative adjectives; Preterite vs. imperfect
	2 Comunicándose en el trabajo	Workplace communication and tasks	Reflexive pronouns; Verbs with prepositions	Conditional; Preterite; Present perfect
Unidad 2	**Ejercicio y diversión**			
	1 Ejercicio al aire libre	Outdoor sports	Preterite vs. imperfect; Verbs that change meaning in the preterite	Adverbs; Reflexive pronouns
	2 Diversión bajo techo	Indoor sports and games	Comparatives; The gerund	**Ir a** + infinitive
Unidad 3	**La aventura de viajar**			
	1 ¿Adónde vamos de vacaciones?	Vacation plans and hotels	Past participle; Present perfect and past perfect	Preterite vs. imperfect; Preterite
	2 Viajemos en avión	Airplane travel	Future and conditional; Future and conditional of probability	**Ir a** + infinitive
Unidad 4	**¿Cómo es nuestra sociedad?**			
	1 Familia, sociedad y problemas sociales	Family, society, and social problems	Present subjunctive in noun and adjective clauses; Present subjunctive in adverbial clauses	Verbs with prepositions; Present progressive; Future
	2 Educación universitaria y finanzas	College education and finances	Present perfect subjunctive; Imperfect subjunctive	Direct and indirect object pronouns
Unidad 5	**¡Hablemos de arte!**			
	1 Arte a tu propio ritmo	Painting and music	Future perfect and conditional perfect; Relative pronouns	Present perfect
	2 A crear con manos y palabras	Sculpture and literature	Passive voice, passive **se** and impersonal **se**; **Se** for unintentional occurrences	Future tense; Imperfect
Unidad 6	**Ver, divertirse e informarse**			
	1 ¿Qué hay en la tele?	Television programming and advertising	Imperfect subjunctive in adverbial clauses; More uses of the imperfect subjunctive	Comparatives; Preterite vs. imperfect
	2 El mundo de las noticias	News coverage, media, and current events	Past perfect subjunctive; Sequence of tense	Past perfect indicative

Easy Articulation

One complete program for middle school through Level 4

or

Levels 1a & 1b are designed with middle school learners in mind. They include more practice, more games and more appropriate visuals for your middle school students. These books prepare students for *¡Avancemos!* level 2.

Level 1 introduces students to the culture and language of the Spanish-speaking world in eight manageable units. To provide flexibility and pacing options, the material taught in units 7 and 8 is fully spiraled in level 2.

Level 2 begins with a thorough review of core level 1 content. Seamless articulation continues, as material taught in units 7 and 8 of level 2 is spiraled into level 3.

Level 3 reviews core content from levels 1 and 2 before students move on to more advanced language skills.

Level 4 reviews and expands upon the content from the first three levels, as students go on to master more advanced language skills.

¡Avancemos!

¡Avancemos! transports students beyond the classroom on an exciting journey through the diverse Spanish-speaking world. The perfect blend of culture, instruction and interaction enables and motivates students to succeed.

Language takes you there

Remarkable Culture

Vivid, inspiring, and focused culture goes beyond the textbook with on-site videos, Cultura interactiva, **News + Networking** and more!

Relevant Instruction

Multi-tiered differentiation in presentation, practice, assessments, and in SPANISH InterActive Reader create a truly personalized learning environment.

Real Interaction

Students show what they know with **performance space**, a virtual one-to-one environment that allows students to record spoken and written responses.

Digital Resources

For the Teacher

Teacher One Stop
Resources available on DVD and at my.hrw.com
- All Print Resources
- Interactive Teacher Edition
- Calendar Planner
- Projectable Transparencies
- Lesson Plans
- TPRS

Interactive Whiteboard Lessons
- Ready-made presentations
- Interactive practice and games for the whole class

Online Assessment
Robust differentiated assessment
- ExamView® on Teacher One Stop
- HOAP Assessment
- Generate Success Rubric Generator

For the Student

eEdition Online
Fully interactive student edition
- Scorable activities
- Performance Space
- Audio and Video

eTextbook
Available for delivery on a variety of devices

Virtual Culture
- *Cultura interactiva*
- *WebQuests*

Online Practice
- @Home Tutor
- Animated Grammar
- Online Review

Conjuguemos.com

Holt McDougal Spanish Apps

Digital performance space

Practice and Assess Performance In this Virtual Environment!

- Teacher Dashboard to Manage Student Responses
- Student Dashboards to Track Completion and Feedback

News + Networking

- High-interest articles at appropriate levels of difficulty
- Current cultural and newsworthy videos
- Monitored blogs

SPANISH InterActive Reader

- Authentic texts
- Reading in the Content Areas
- Leveled for Difficulty

Video and Audio

Downloads available at my.hrw.com

- *AvanzaRap* Video (Animations of songs with Karaoke track, Teaching Suggestions, Activity Masters, Video Scripts and Answers)
- *¡Avancemos!* Video Program (Vocabulary, *Telehistoria,* Cultural Comparison)
- Audio Program (Student Text, Workbook, Assessment, Heritage Learners, *Lecturas para todos*)

For the Student

Cuaderno: práctica por niveles

- 3 levels of practice: A, B, C
- Vocabulary, Grammar
- Integrated skills
- Listening, Reading, Writing
- Culture

AvanzaCómics

High-interest stories with vocabulary students will know. Create-your-own version available.

Lecturas para todos

Encourages development of strong reading skills and strategies. Audio CD available.

For the Teacher

Unit Resource Books

- Reteaching & Practice Copymasters
- Practice Games
- Video Activities
- Video Scripts
- Audio Scripts
- Map/Culture Activities
- Fine Art Activities
- Family Letters
- Family Involvement Activities
- Absent Student Copymasters

Especially for Heritage Learners

Cuaderno para hispanohablantes

Heritage Learners Assessment

Lecturas para hispanohablantes

Differentiated Assessment Program

On-level, Modified, Pre-AP and Heritage Learner Assessments

- Vocabulary, Grammar, and Culture quizzes (on-level only)
- Lesson tests
- Unit tests
- Midterm Exam
- Final Exam

Best Practices Toolkit

- Strategies for Effective Teaching including Pre-AP and International Baccalaureate *

*International Baccalaureate is a registered trademark of the International Baccalaureate Organization.

Celebrate Culture!

The *Celebraciones* section of ***¡Avancemos!*** includes twelve mini cultural lessons about holidays and celebrations, one for each month of the year.

News + Networking
my.hrw.com
provides high-interest articles, cultural videos and monitored blog!

Cultura Interactiva my.hrw.com
See these pages come alive!

febrero

News + Networking

¡Carnaval!

Carnaval marks a period of festivity prior to the beginning of Lent. Lent was, and for some still is, a 40-day period of solemnity and fasting with the removal of meat from the diet being a key feature. You can see the word *carne* (meat) in *Carnaval*; traditionally, this was the last chance to eat meat before the Lenten fast. Today, *Carnaval* often resembles a lively, multi-day party.

Falling in either February or March, *Carnaval* is typically celebrated during the five days that precede Ash Wednesday, the first day of Lent. In some countries, *Carnaval* lasts longer, overlapping other local celebrations. In many regions, traditions such as throwing water and eggs can start over a month before the actual holiday. The planning for the next year's parades, parties, and dance groups often starts as soon as the current *Carnaval* ends!

España

Disfraces Elaborate costumes are central to the *Carnaval* celebration. This costume, entitled "África soy yo," appeared in Las Palmas, in the Canary Islands.

Paraguay

Carnaval Revelers dance in Encarnación, site of the largest celebration in Paraguay.

México

Cascarones Breaking *cascarones* on the heads of friends and other party-goers is a *Carnaval* tradition. The sprinkling of confetti from these hollowed-out eggs is said to bring good luck, as seen here in Mazatlán.

Bolivia

Máscaras are a *Carnaval* tradition dating back to medieval Spain. This masked dancer is from the parade in Oruro, where some 40,000 folkloric dancers and musicians participate.

Bailarines folklóricos Dancers from the Mestizaje dance group perform in Barranquilla. The Colombian government proclaimed this city's *Carnaval* celebration, which combines indigenous, African, and European traditions, a National Cultural Heritage. UNESCO declared it a "Masterpiece" for its cultural uniqueness.

Colombia

Vocabulario para celebrar

los bailarines	dancers
la banda	musical band
Carnaval	Carnival
los cascarones	confetti-filled eggs
el disfraz	costume
las máscaras	masks

Comparación cultural

1. The ways in which *Carnaval* is celebrated in the Spanish-speaking world differ depending on the region. Why do you think the celebrations have evolved differently?
2. Compare the traditions of *Carnaval* to any holiday that you celebrate. Which one(s) are similar? How are they similar?

C14 Celebraciones

Celebraciones C15

- *Cultura Interactiva* features can be viewed in English or Spanish online!

- The *Celebraciones* mini cultural lessons are also available online with the added benefit of *Cultura Interactiva*. Just click on any photo and watch the celebration come to life!

¡Cultura auténtica!

Each unit includes two thematic lessons that present a manageable amount of material.

- Each unit is set in a location that provides the cultural backdrop for real-life themes.
- Experience authentic culture online at my.hrw.com!

UNIDAD 4

España

En el centro

Lección 1
Tema: ***¡Vamos de compras!***

Lección 2
Tema: ***¿Qué hacemos esta noche?***

«¡Hola! Somos Maribel y Enrique. Vivimos en Madrid, la capital.»

Población: 40.491.052
Área: 194.897 millas cuadradas
Capital: Madrid
Moneda: el euro (comparte con otros 11 países)
Idiomas: castellano (español), catalán, gallego, vasco
Comida típica: tortilla española, paella, gazpacho
Gente famosa: Carmen Amaya (bailaora), Francisco de Goya (artista), Ana María Matute (escritora), Severo Ochoa (bioquímico)

Paella

CULTURA Interactiva my.hrw.com *See these pages come alive!*

Aficionados del fútbol Official songs, or **himnos oficiales,** are an important part of the Spanish soccer experience. Fans of the Real Madrid team sing **¡Hala Madrid!** *(Let's go, Madrid!)*, especially during games against rival team FC Barcelona, known as **El Barça.** *What teams have sports rivalries where you live?*

Un jugador de fútbol del Real Madrid

El arte y la literatura Pablo Picasso, one of the 20th century's greatest artists, portrayed traditional Spanish themes in his work. He made this print of fictional characters Don Quijote and Sancho Panza exactly 350 years after Cervantes wrote his famous novel, *El ingenioso hidalgo Don Quijote de la Mancha. What other works of Picasso are you familiar with?*

Don Quijote *(1955)*, *Pablo Picasso*

Las costumbres regionales During the **Feria de Abril** celebration, girls wear Seville's traditional costume, **el traje de sevillana. Sevillanas** are similar to **flamenco,** which involves singing, dance, and guitar as well as rhythmic clapping or foot taps. *What type of music and dress would be considered typically American?*

Bailarinas de flamenco en Sevilla

190 ciento noventa

España ciento noventa y uno 191

- Students get a quick look at important facts and figures about the target country.
- Meet the *Telehistoria* characters who will accompany you and your students through the unit.

- ***¡Avanza!*** lets your students know what they will learn and why.
- **Lessons** are based on themes that are relevant to students.
- **Digital Spanish** delivers what your students need to be engaged and successful.

- ***Compara con tu mundo*** helps students see the relevance of cultural information by asking them to compare the target culture with their own. Look for this feature throughout the unit.

Presentación de vocabulario

Vocabulary is presented in context; Interactive Whiteboard activities provide a great way to get the whole class involved.

- Look for the green recycling sign and *¿Recuerdas?* throughout the unit to see the wealth of review.
- *¡Avanza!* provides a clear goal to let students know what is new and what is review.

Presentación de VOCABULARIO

¡AVANZA! **Goal:** Learn about the clothes Enrique and Maribel like to wear. Then practice what you have learned to talk about clothes and how much they cost. ***Actividades 1–2***

¿Recuerdas? Numbers from 11 to 100 p. 87

VIDEO DVD

AUDIO

A ¡Hola! Me llamo Enrique. Voy de compras al centro comercial con mi amiga, Maribel. Queremos comprar ropa nueva. A Maribel le gusta ir a todas las tiendas.

B Voy a comprar una camisa y unos jeans. Cuestan treinta euros. El vestido de Maribel cuesta veinte euros. Es un buen precio.

En España se dice...
In Spain the word for *jeans* is **los vaqueros.** They also use **los tejanos.**

Más vocabulario

cerrar *to close*
¿Cuánto cuesta(n)? *How much does it (do they) cost?*
el dólar *dollar*
empezar *to begin*
entender *to understand*
preferir *to prefer*
tener suerte *to be lucky*

Expansión de vocabulario p. R5

C Me gusta llevar ropa blanca, roja y marrón. A Maribel le gusta llevar una camiseta verde y unos pantalones cortos azules.

D Maribel piensa que el vestido es un poco feo. Ella tiene razón; no es muy bonito. Ella compra otro vestido que le gusta más.

E En España hay cuatro estaciones. Maribel siempre tiene calor durante el verano. Me gusta el invierno, pero siempre tengo frío.

HOME TUTOR my.hrw.com Interactive Flashcards

¡A responder! Escuchar

Escucha las siguientes descripciones de ropa. Levanta la mano si llevas la ropa que escuchas. *(Listen to the following descriptions of clothes. Raise your hand if you are wearing that item.)*

Unidad 4 España
194 ciento noventa y cuatro

Lección 1
ciento noventa y cinco 195

- **Blue words** help students know what to study.
- A **listening** activity provides a quick comprehension check.
- Students practice online at their own level and their own pace.

Fun and visually engaging activities provide meaningful practice.

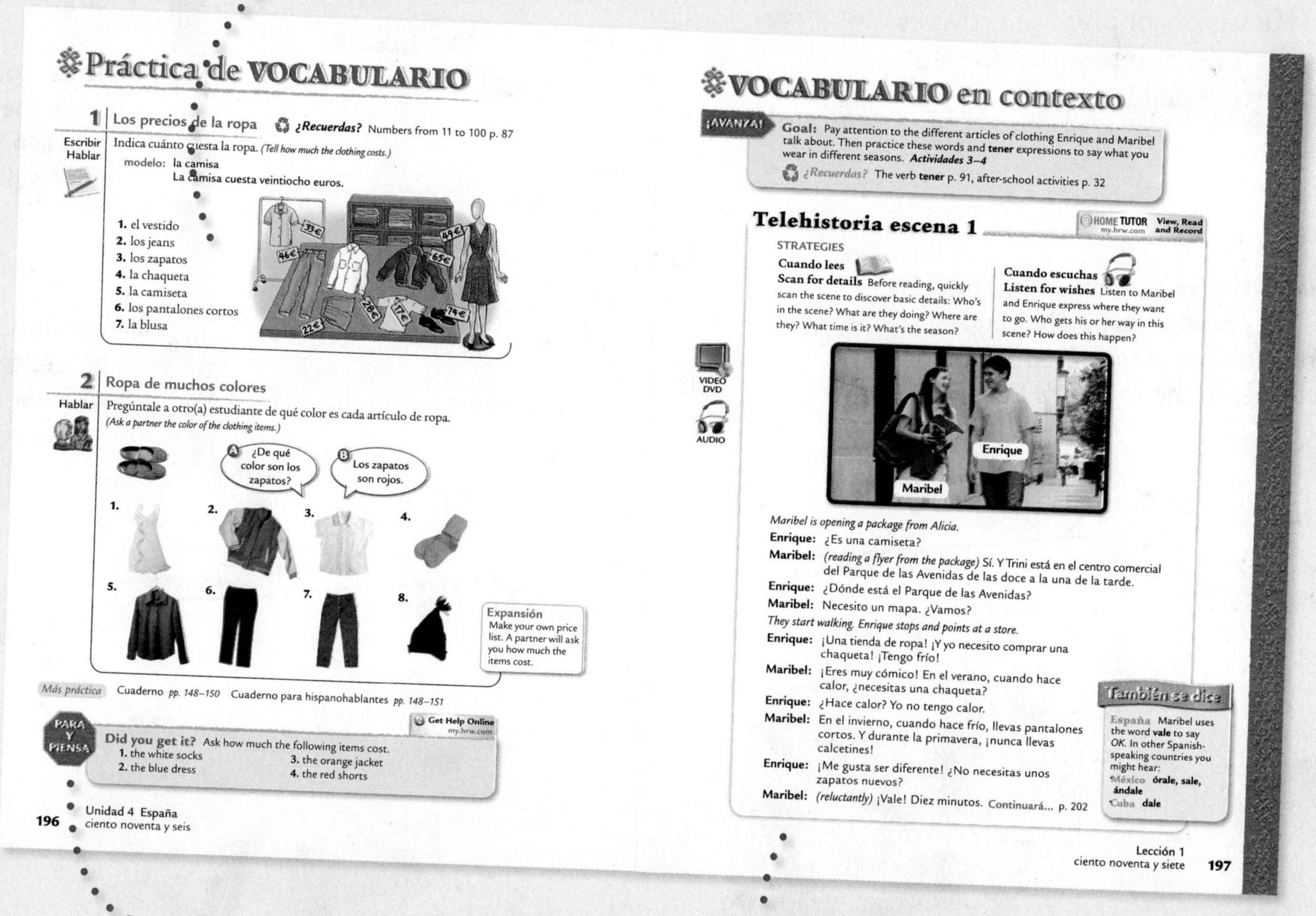

Práctica de VOCABULARIO

1 Los precios de la ropa ¿*Recuerdas?* Numbers from 11 to 100 p. 87

Escribir Hablar

Indica cuánto cuesta la ropa. *(Tell how much the clothing costs.)*

modelo: la camisa
La camisa cuesta veintiocho euros.

1. el vestido
2. los jeans
3. los zapatos
4. la chaqueta
5. la camiseta
6. los pantalones cortos
7. la blusa

2 Ropa de muchos colores

Hablar

Pregúntale a otro(a) estudiante de qué color es cada artículo de ropa. *(Ask a partner the color of the clothing items.)*

A ¿De qué color son los zapatos?

B Los zapatos son rojos.

1. 2. 3. 4. 5. 6. 7. 8.

Expansión
Make your own price list. A partner will ask you how much the items cost.

Más práctica Cuaderno *pp. 148–150* Cuaderno para hispanohablantes *pp. 148–151*

PARA Y PIENSA

Get Help Online my.hrw.com

Did you get it? Ask how much the following items cost.

1. the white socks
2. the blue dress
3. the orange jacket
4. the red shorts

196 Unidad 4 España
ciento noventa y seis

VOCABULARIO en contexto

¡AVANZA! **Goal:** Pay attention to the different articles of clothing Enrique and Maribel talk about. Then practice these words and **tener** expressions to say what you wear in different seasons. ***Actividades 3–4***

¿*Recuerdas?* The verb **tener** p. 91, after-school activities p. 32

Telehistoria escena 1

HOME TUTOR my.hrw.com View, Read and Record

STRATEGIES

Cuando lees
Scan for details Before reading, quickly scan the scene to discover basic details: Who's in the scene? What are they doing? Where are they? What time is it? What's the season?

Cuando escuchas
Listen for wishes Listen to Maribel and Enrique express where they want to go. Who gets his or her way in this scene? How does this happen?

VIDEO DVD

AUDIO

Maribel is opening a package from Alicia.

Enrique: ¿Es una camiseta?

Maribel: *(reading a flyer from the package)* Sí. Y Trini está en el centro comercial del Parque de las Avenidas de las doce a la una de la tarde.

Enrique: ¿Dónde está el Parque de las Avenidas?

Maribel: Necesito un mapa. ¿Vamos?

They start walking. Enrique stops and points at a store.

Enrique: ¡Una tienda de ropa! ¡Y yo necesito comprar una chaqueta! ¡Tengo frío!

Maribel: ¡Eres muy cómico! En el verano, cuando hace calor, ¿necesitas una chaqueta?

Enrique: ¿Hace calor? Yo no tengo calor.

Maribel: En el invierno, cuando hace frío, llevas pantalones cortos. Y durante la primavera, ¡nunca llevas calcetines!

Enrique: ¡Me gusta ser diferente! ¿No necesitas unos zapatos nuevos?

Maribel: *(reluctantly)* ¡Vale! Diez minutos. Continuará... p. 202

También se dice

España Maribel uses the word **vale** to say *OK.* In other Spanish-speaking countries you might hear:
México **órale, sale, ándale**
Cuba **dale**

Lección 1
ciento noventa y siete 197

Para y piensa helps students know if they "got it."

High interest storyline video incorporates new vocabulary and motivates students to keep watching to see what happens next.

Presentación de gramática

A wide variety of practice activities keeps students interested. Careful sequencing builds success.

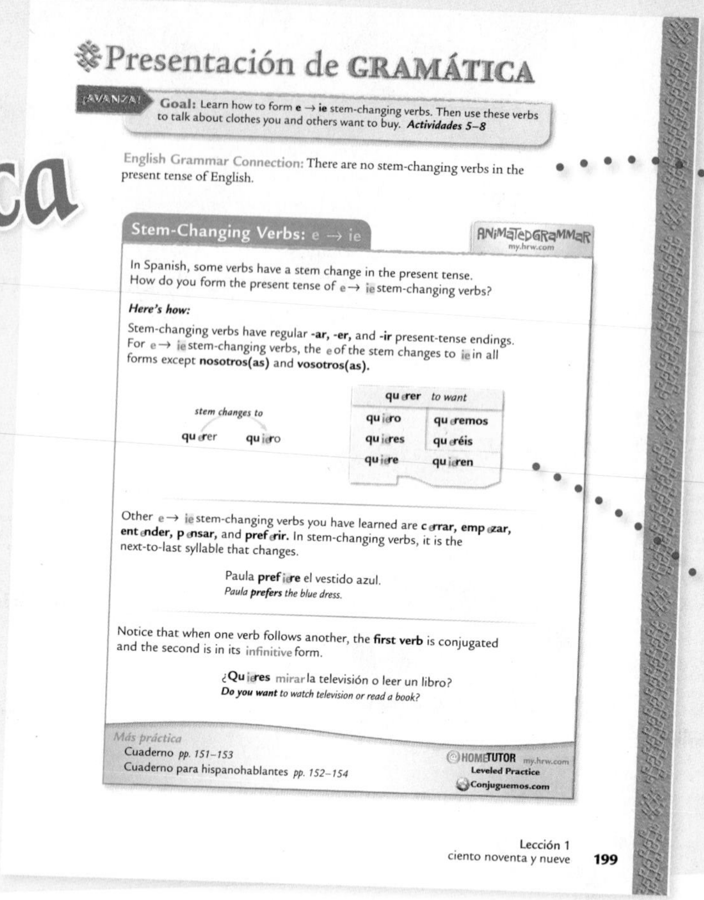

Presentación de GRAMÁTICA

¡AVANZA! **Goal:** Learn how to form **e → ie** stem-changing verbs. Then use these verbs to talk about clothes you and others want to buy. *Actividades 5–8*

English Grammar Connection: There are no stem-changing verbs in the present tense of English.

Stem-Changing Verbs: e → ie

In Spanish, some verbs have a stem change in the present tense. How do you form the present tense of e → ie stem-changing verbs?

Here's how:

Stem-changing verbs have regular **-ar, -er,** and **-ir** present-tense endings. For e → ie stem-changing verbs, the e of the stem changes to ie in all forms except **nosotros(as)** and **vosotros(as).**

stem changes to
qu**e**rer → qu**ie**ro

qu**e**rer *to want*	
qu**ie**ro	qu**e**remos
qu**ie**res	qu**e**réis
qu**ie**re	qu**ie**ren

Other e → ie stem-changing verbs you have learned are **c**e**rrar, emp**e**zar, ent**e**nder, p**e**nsar,** and **pref**e**rir.** In stem-changing verbs, it is the next-to-last syllable that changes.

Paula **pref**ie**re** el vestido azul.
*Paula **prefers** the blue dress.*

Notice that when one verb follows another, the **first verb** is conjugated and the second is in its infinitive form.

¿**Qu**ie**res** mirar la televisión o leer un libro?
***Do you want** to watch television or read a book?*

Más práctica
Cuaderno *pp. 151–153*
Cuaderno para hispanohablantes *pp. 152–154*

HOMETUTOR my.hrw.com Leveled Practice
Conjuguemos.com

Lección 1
ciento noventa y nueve **199**

- **English Grammar Connection** helps students make the link between Spanish and English.
- **Grammar presentations** are clear and easy to follow.
- ***Expansión*** provides enrichment for the students who need an extra challenge. There are additional *Expansión* options for many activities in the Teacher's Edition.

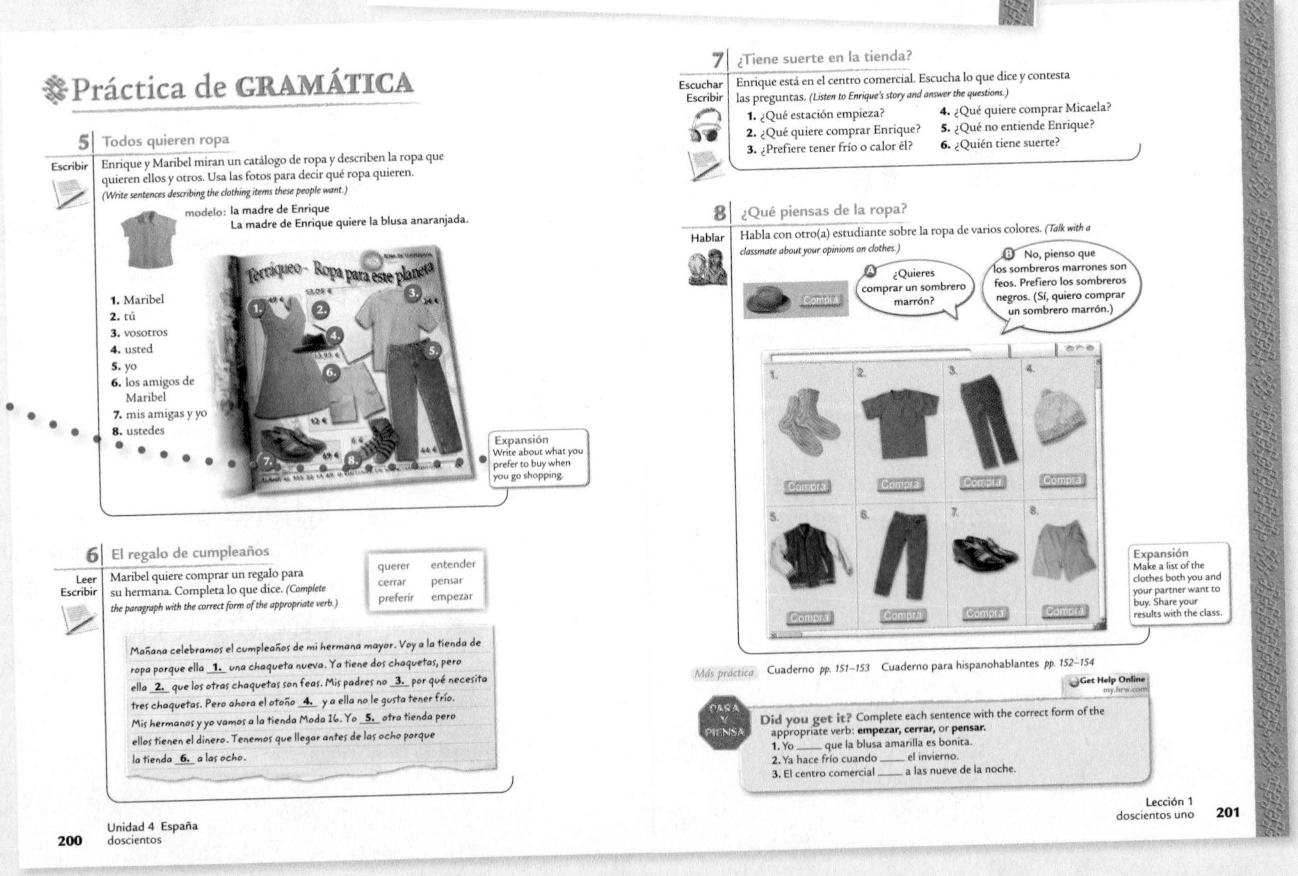

Práctica de GRAMÁTICA

5 Todos quieren ropa

Escribir

Enrique y Maribel miran un catálogo de ropa y describen la ropa que quieren ellos y otros. Usa las fotos para decir qué ropa quieren. *(Write sentences describing the clothing items these people want.)*

modelo: la madre de Enrique
La madre de Enrique quiere la blusa anaranjada.

1. Maribel
2. tú
3. vosotros
4. usted
5. yo
6. los amigos de Maribel
7. mis amigas y yo
8. ustedes

Expansión
Write about what you prefer to buy when you go shopping.

6 El regalo de cumpleaños

Leer
Escribir

Maribel quiere comprar un regalo para su hermana. Completa lo que dice. *(Complete the paragraph with the correct form of the appropriate verb.)*

querer	entender
cerrar	pensar
preferir	empezar

Mañana celebramos el cumpleaños de mi hermana mayor. Voy a la tienda de ropa porque ella __1.__ una chaqueta nueva. Ya tiene dos chaquetas, pero ella __2.__ que las otras chaquetas son feas. Mis padres no __3.__ por qué necesita tres chaquetas. Pero ahora el otoño __4.__ y a ella no le gusta tener frío. Mis hermanos y yo vamos a la tienda Moda 16. Yo __5.__ otra tienda pero ellos tienen el dinero. Tenemos que llegar antes de las ocho porque la tienda __6.__ a las ocho.

Unidad 4 España
200 doscientos

7 ¿Tiene suerte en la tienda?

Escuchar
Escribir

Enrique está en el centro comercial. Escucha lo que dice y contesta las preguntas. *(Listen to Enrique's story and answer the questions.)*

1. ¿Qué estación empieza?
2. ¿Qué quiere comprar Enrique?
3. ¿Prefiere tener frío o calor él?
4. ¿Qué quiere comprar Micaela?
5. ¿Qué no entiende Enrique?
6. ¿Quién tiene suerte?

8 ¿Qué piensas de la ropa?

Hablar

Habla con otro(a) estudiante sobre la ropa de varios colores. *(Talk with a classmate about your opinions on clothes.)*

A: ¿Quieres comprar un sombrero marrón?

B: No, pienso que los sombreros marrones son feos. Prefiero los sombreros negros. (Sí, quiero comprar un sombrero marrón.)

Expansión
Make a list of the clothes both you and your partner want to buy. Share your results with the class.

Más práctica Cuaderno *pp. 151–153* Cuaderno para hispanohablantes *pp. 152–154*

Get Help Online my.hrw.com

PARA Y PIENSA **Did you get it?** Complete each sentence with the correct form of the appropriate verb: **empezar, cerrar,** or **pensar.**
1. Yo ____ que la blusa amarilla es bonita.
2. Ya hace frío cuando ____ el invierno.
3. El centro comercial ____ a las nueve de la noche.

Lección 1
doscientos uno **201**

New language skills are practiced in a wide variety of contexts.

- **Strategies** for reading and listening give you options for presenting the *Telehistoria* and strengthen your students' skills.

GRAMÁTICA en contexto

¡AVANZA! **Goal:** Listen to the **e → ie** stem-changing verbs that Enrique and Maribel use while they are shopping for clothes. Then use the stem-changing verbs to talk about your clothing preferences. *Actividades 9–10*

Telehistoria escena 2

HOMETUTOR my.hrw.com View, Read and Record

STRATEGIES

Cuando lees
Look for color words In this scene, Enrique and Maribel discuss colors and types of clothing. Which color words do you find?

Cuando escuchas
Disregard stereotypes Who wants to keep looking at clothes and who is worried about being late? Is this expected? Why or why not?

VIDEO DVD

AUDIO

Maribel: Tenemos que estar en el centro comercial a las doce, ¿entiendes?
Enrique: Sí, entiendo. Dos minutos más. ¿Prefieres los vaqueros negros o los pantalones verdes?
Maribel: Prefiero ir al centro comercial, ¡ahora!
Enrique: Quiero la camisa blanca.
Vendedora: Tenemos camisas en color azul y en verde. ¿Queréis ver?
Maribel: *(to the clerk)* No, gracias. *(to Enrique, frustrated)* Pero Enrique, ¿una tienda de ropa? ¿No prefieres ir de compras al centro comercial?
Enrique: No. No quiero comprar la ropa en el centro comercial. Los precios no son buenos. *(still shopping)* ¿Te gustan los pantalones cortos azules?
Maribel: *(rushing him)* Sí, sí. Y me gustan los calcetines rojos, la camisa amarilla y los zapatos marrones...
Enrique: No, no, no. ¿Rojo, amarillo y marrón? No, no me gustan.

Continuará... p. 207

202 Unidad 4 España
doscientos dos

9 *Comprensión del episodio* En la tienda de ropa

Escuchar Leer

¿Quién prefiere las siguientes cosas, Maribel o Enrique? *(Who prefers the following things—Maribel or Enrique?)*

1. ir de compras en una tienda de ropa
2. la camisa amarilla
3. la camisa blanca
4. los calcetines rojos
5. los zapatos marrones
6. ir al centro comercial temprano

10 La ropa y las estaciones

Hablar

Habla con otro(a) estudiante de lo que prefieres llevar y no llevar durante cada estación. *(Talk about what you prefer to wear and not wear during each season.)*

A ¿Qué prefieres llevar durante el verano?

B Prefiero llevar pantalones cortos. Nunca llevo chaqueta durante el verano.

Expansión Describe what your partner is wearing.

Comparación cultural

El arte surrealista de España

How might dreams influence an artist's work? Artist Salvador Dalí from **Spain** is well known...

13 Unos modelos cómicos

Hablar

Maribel y Enrique van a una tienda y combinan ropa de muchos colores. Pregúntale a otro(a) estudiante quién lleva la ropa que describes. *(Ask a partner about Maribel's and Enrique's clothing.)*

modelo: gorro

A ¿Quién lleva **el gorro verde**?

B Enrique **lo** lleva.

1. zapatos
2. camisa
3. chaqueta
4. pantalones cortos
5. jeans
6. ¿ ?

14 ¿Qué llevas en julio?

Hablar

Comparación cultural

Climas diferentes

How does geography affect a country's climate? Countries near the equator have rainy and dry seasons, but have warm temperatures year-round. Countries in the northern and southern hemispheres have opposite seasons. For example, in **Spain,** July is a summer month and the weather is often hot, but in **Chile** it is a winter month. Chile's varied terrain, from beaches to mountains, and length (over 2,600 miles) create many different climates.

Compara con tu mundo *How does the geography of your area affect the climate?*

Barcelona, España

Los Andes en Chile

En julio, tú y otro(a) estudiante van a **Chile, México, España, Puerto Rico, Argentina** y **Nueva York.** Pregúntale qué ropa lleva. *(Ask a partner what he or she wears in these places in July.)*

A ¿Llevas una camiseta en Chile en julio?

B No, no la llevo. Llevo una chaqueta y...

Más práctica Cuaderno *pp. 154–156* Cuaderno para hispanohablantes *pp. 155–158*

Get Help Online my.hrw.com

PARA Y PIENSA

Did you get it? In each sentence, use the correct direct object pronoun.
1. Luisa quiere los pantalones blancos. Ella ____ compra.
2. No quiero la blusa nueva. ¿ ____ quieres tú?
3. Nosotros preferimos las camisas azules. ____ compramos.

206 Unidad 4 España
doscientos seis

- The continuing *Telehistoria* motivates students to find out what happens next and reinforces the grammar they have just learned.

- *Comparaciones culturales* highlight the variety of cultures within the Spanish-speaking world.

¡Todo junto!

Todo junto brings together everything students have learned so they can show what they know.

performance space

Helps students prove their capabilities.

Students can view and respond to video independently with @HOMETUTOR my.hrw.com

Todo junto

¡AVANZA! **Goal:** ***Show what you know*** Listen to Maribel and Enrique talk to the salesclerk about what Enrique wants to buy. Then use **e → ie** stem-changing verbs and direct object pronouns to talk about clothing preferences. ***Actividades 15–19***

Telehistoria completa

@HOMETUTOR my.hrw.com **View, Read and Record**

STRATEGIES

Cuando lees
Discover what's forgotten Enrique forgets something in this scene. Find out what he forgot. How does this create a problem?

Cuando escuchas
Take the "emotional temperature" Find out who has the greatest intensity of feeling by listening to voices. Who is the most upset and why?

Escena 1 *Resumen*
Maribel tiene que ir al centro comercial porque necesita el autógrafo de Trini. Pero Enrique quiere ir de compras en una tienda.

Escena 2 *Resumen*
Enrique y Maribel están en una tienda, y Enrique quiere comprar mucha ropa. Maribel prefiere ir al centro comercial.

VIDEO DVD

AUDIO

Escena 3

Maribel: Enrique, tienes que pagar. Son las once y media.
Enrique: Un gorro verde. ¡Lo quiero comprar! ¡Tengo que comprarlo!
Maribel: Enrique, ¡pero tú ya tienes un gorro verde!
Enrique: Sí, pero nunca lo llevo.
Maribel: Quieres una chaqueta, ¿no?
Enrique: Tienes razón. La chaqueta... la necesito. *(to the salesclerk)* ¿Vende chaquetas?
Vendedora: ¿En verano? No. Las vendo en el otoño.
Enrique: ¿Cuánto cuesta todo?
Vendedora: Los pantalones cuestan treinta euros, la camisa cuesta veinticinco, y el gorro, quince. Son setenta euros.
Enrique: ¡Mi dinero! ¡No lo tengo!
Maribel: ¡No te entiendo! ¿Quieres ir de compras y no tienes dinero?
Enrique: Está en mi mochila. ¿Dónde está mi mochila? ¿Tienes dinero? En el centro comercial yo compro la comida.
Maribel: ¿Con qué piensas pagar? No tienes dinero.

Lección 1
doscientos siete **207**

The ¡Avancemos! **Video Program** includes Vocabulary Presentation videos, Ongoing *Telehistoria*, and *Comparación cultural* videos. Optional Spanish captions.

Show the whole *Telehistoria* or simply view scene three!

- Each activity is labeled so you and your students know exactly which **skill** to focus on.
- Students read, listen, and speak using theme-related prompts. ***Integración*** prepares students for the AP® Language test.

15 *Comprensión de los episodios* ¿Cierto o falso?

Escuchar / Leer

Lee las oraciones y di si son ciertas o falsas. Corrige las oraciones falsas. *(Read the sentences and say if they are true or false. Correct the false statements.)*

1. Enrique piensa que los precios son buenos en el centro comercial.
2. Maribel prefiere llegar al centro comercial a las doce.
3. Maribel necesita comprar una chaqueta.
4. Enrique tiene setenta euros para comprar su ropa.
5. A Maribel le gusta ser diferente.
6. Enrique prefiere llevar una chaqueta en el invierno.
7. Enrique compra una chaqueta en la tienda de ropa.

16 *Comprensión de los episodios* Analizar la historia

Escuchar / Leer

Contesta las preguntas sobre los episodios. *(Answer the questions about the episodes.)*

1. ¿Qué estación es?
2. ¿Dónde quiere comprar ropa Enrique?
3. ¿De qué color es el gorro?
4. ¿Cuánto cuestan los pantalones? ¿La camisa? ¿El gorro?
5. ¿Qué problema tiene Enrique?

Expansión
Write a summary of what happens in the Telehistoria.

17 ¡A jugar! Un juego de quién

Digital performance space

Hablar

STRATEGY **Hablar**
Prepare and don't stress out Create a list of useful questions and possible answers. Include various types of clothes. Review your verb endings. Then just talk!

Da una pista sobre una persona de la clase. Las otras personas de tu grupo te van a hacer preguntas para adivinar quién es. Sigue el modelo. *(Give a clue about someone in your class. The other members of your group will ask you yes/no questions to identify who it is.)*

A: Lleva jeans azules.
B: ¿Tiene el sombrero verde?
A: Sí, lo tiene. (No, no lo tiene.)
C: ¿Lleva zapatos blancos?
A: Sí, los lleva. (No, no los lleva.)
B: ¿Es David?
A: Sí, ¡tienes razón! (No, no tienes razón.)

18 Integración

Digital performance space

Leer / Escuchar / Hablar

Lee el cupón de descuentos (*discounts*) y escucha el anuncio de la tienda. Describe qué ropa quieres comprar para tus amigos(as) y cuánto cuesta. *(Describe four items you want to buy for your friends and how much each item costs.)*

Fuente 1 Cupón

Fuente 2 Anuncio

Listen and take notes
- ¿Qué venden en la tienda?
- ¿Cuánto cuesta la ropa?

modelo: Quiero comprar un vestido verde para Emily. Cuesta...

19 Un poema de la estación

Digital performance space

Escribir

Escribe un poema sobre una de las estaciones. Incluye los siguientes elementos. *(Write a poem that talks about one of the seasons by including the following elements.)*

Para organizarte: — modelo:
- *el nombre de la estación* → verano
- *dos colores que describen la estación* → verde, azul
- *tres cosas que quieres* → quiero zapatos, helado, camisetas
- *cuatro actividades que prefieres hacer* → prefiero jugar, pasear, leer, descansar
- *una descripción de cómo estás* → tengo calor

Writing Criteria	Excellent	Good	Needs Work
Content	Your poem includes all of the elements.	Your poem includes some of the elements.	Your poem includes a few of the elements.
Communication	Most of your poem is easy to follow.	Parts of your poem are easy to follow.	Your poem is hard to follow.
Accuracy	Your poem has very few mistakes in grammar and vocabulary.	Your poem has some mistakes in grammar and vocabulary.	Your poem has many mistakes in grammar and vocabulary.

Expansión
Display your poem on a visual that reflects what you have expressed.

Más práctica Cuaderno *pp. 157–158* Cuaderno para hispanohablantes *pp. 159–160*

Get Help Online my.hrw.com

PARA Y PIENSA

Did you get it? Answer each question based on the Telehistoria with **sí**, using direct object pronouns.
1. ¿Necesita Enrique la chaqueta?
2. ¿Prefiere Enrique el gorro verde?
3. ¿Quiere comprar Enrique la comida?

- Frequent **recycling** helps students remember previously taught material.
- **An open-ended writing activity** provides a model and a rubric so students know exactly what they have to do to succeed. Teachers may use Generate Success to customize their rubrics.

¡Lecturas auténticas y culturales!

SPANISH InterActive Reader

This online reader provides additional authentic and content-area readings at a variety of levels of difficulties. Available at my.hrw.com

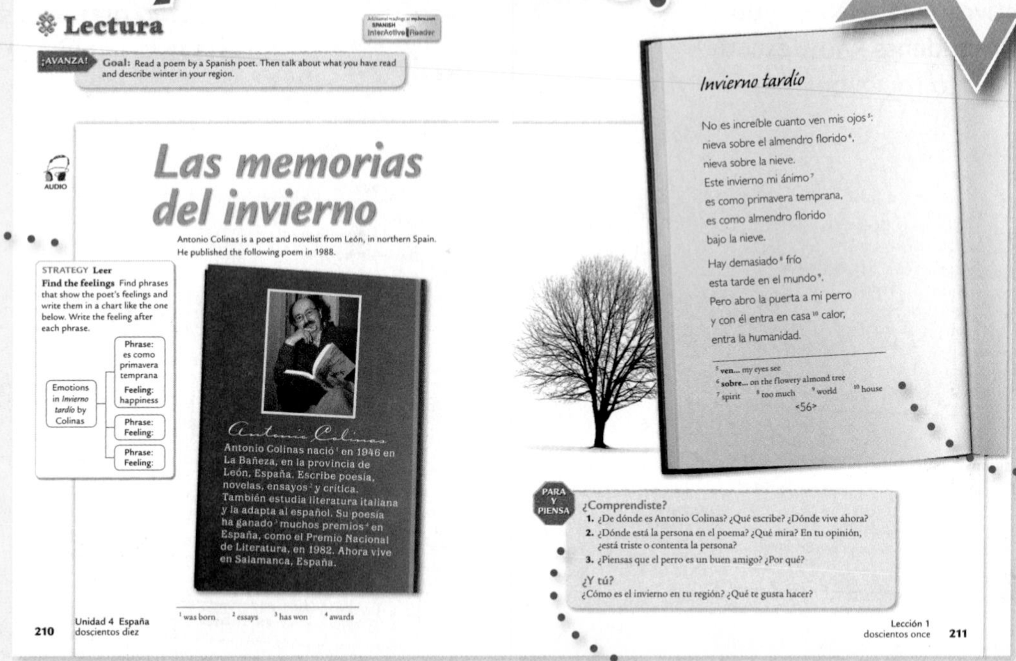
Lectura

¡AVANZA! Goal: Read a poem by a Spanish poet. Then talk about what you have read and describe winter in your region.

Las memorias del invierno

Antonio Colinas is a poet and novelist from León, in northern Spain. He published the following poem in 1988.

STRATEGY Leer
Find the feelings Find phrases that show the poet's feelings and write them in a chart like the one below. Write the feeling after each phrase.

Emotions in *Invierno tardío* by Colinas	Phrase: es como primavera temprana / Feeling: happiness
	Phrase: / Feeling:
	Phrase: / Feeling:

Antonio Colinas nació[1] en 1946 en La Bañeza, en la provincia de León, España. Escribe poesía, novelas, ensayos[2] y crítica. También estudia literatura italiana y la adapta al español. Su poesía ha ganado[3] muchos premios[4] en España, como el Premio Nacional de Literatura, en 1982. Ahora vive en Salamanca, España.

[1] was born [2] essays [3] has won [4] awards

Invierno tardío

No es increíble cuanto ven mis ojos[5]:
nieva sobre el almendro florido[6],
nieva sobre la nieve.
Este invierno mi ánimo[7]
es como primavera temprana,
es como almendro florido
bajo la nieve.
Hay demasiado[8] frío
esta tarde en el mundo[9].
Pero abro la puerta a mi perro
y con él entra en casa[10] calor,
entra la humanidad.

[5] ven... my eyes see [6] sobre... on the flowery almond tree [7] spirit [8] too much [9] world [10] house

<56>

PARA Y PIENSA
¿Comprendiste?
1. ¿De dónde es Antonio Colinas? ¿Qué escribe? ¿Dónde vive ahora?
2. ¿Dónde está la persona en el poema? ¿Qué mira? En tu opinión, ¿está triste o contenta la persona?
3. ¿Piensas que el perro es un buen amigo? ¿Por qué?
¿Y tú?
¿Cómo es el invierno en tu región? ¿Qué te gusta hacer?

210 Unidad 4 España doscientos diez

Lección 1 doscientos once 211

- Reading strategies help students become successful readers.
- Authentic readings spark students' interest!
- *Lectura cultural* highlights cultural diversity. Each reading presents a topic and compares how practices, products, and perspectives are the same or different in two countries.
- Comprehension questions encourage students to apply the information they have learned from the reading.

Lectura cultural

¡AVANZA! Goal: Read about weekend activities in Spain and Chile. Then talk about what each city offers and compare these activities with what you do on weekends.

Comparación cultural

El fin de semana en España y Chile

STRATEGY Leer
List attractions and places Use a table like the one below to list attractions and the places where they can be found.

	conciertos	zoológico	botes
Madrid	Parque del Buen Retiro		
Santiago de Chile			

Los habitantes de Madrid, España, y Santiago de Chile hacen muchas actividades en el fin de semana. Van a parques, restaurantes, teatros, cines y otros lugares divertidos. También van de compras.

En Madrid hay muchos lugares interesantes para pasar los fines de semana. La Plaza Mayor tiene muchos cafés y restaurantes. Hay un mercado de sellos[1] los domingos. El Parque del Buen Retiro es un lugar perfecto para descansar y pasear. En este parque hay jardines[2], cafés y un lago[3] donde las personas pueden alquilar botes. Hay conciertos allí en el verano. Otro parque popular es la Casa de Campo. Hay un zoológico, una piscina[4], un parque de diversiones[5] y un lago para botes.

Hay muchas tiendas en el centro. El almacén[6] más grande es El Corte Inglés: allí los madrileños[7] pueden comprar ropa, comida y mucho más.

[1] mercado... stamp market [2] gardens [3] lake [4] swimming pool [5] parque... amusement park [6] department store [7] people of Madrid

España

El Parque del Buen Retiro en Madrid

En Santiago de Chile las personas pasan los fines de semana en muchos lugares. Siempre hay mucha actividad en la Plaza de Armas, la parte histórica de Santiago. Hay conciertos allí los domingos.

El parque del Cerro Santa Lucía es perfecto para pasear. Los santiaguinos[8] pueden ver jardines y el panorama de Santiago. El Cerro San Cristóbal en el Parque Metropolitano es un lugar favorito para comer, correr y montar en bicicleta. Hay jardines, piscinas, un zoológico, cafés y restaurantes en el parque.

Los santiaguinos van a tiendas en el centro y a centros comerciales como Alto Las Condes. En el Mercado Central pueden comprar pescado y frutas y comer en restaurantes con precios baratos[9].

[8] people of Santiago, Chile [9] inexpensive

La Plaza de Armas

Chile

Cerro San Cristóbal

PARA Y PIENSA
¿Comprendiste?
1. ¿Qué hay en la Plaza Mayor y la Plaza de Armas los domingos?
2. ¿A qué parques van los madrileños y los santiaguinos?
3. ¿Dónde pueden ir de compras los habitantes de Madrid y Santiago?
¿Y tú?
¿Cuál(es) de estos lugares en Madrid y Santiago quieres visitar? ¿Adónde vas los fines de semana donde vives? ¿Qué haces allí?

234 Unidad 4 España doscientos treinta y cuatro

Lección 2 doscientos treinta y cinco 235

¡Conexiones y Proyectos!

- Students use Spanish to learn more about other disciplines in *Conexiones.*
- **Fun projects** offer a variety of opportunities for students to explore new topics.

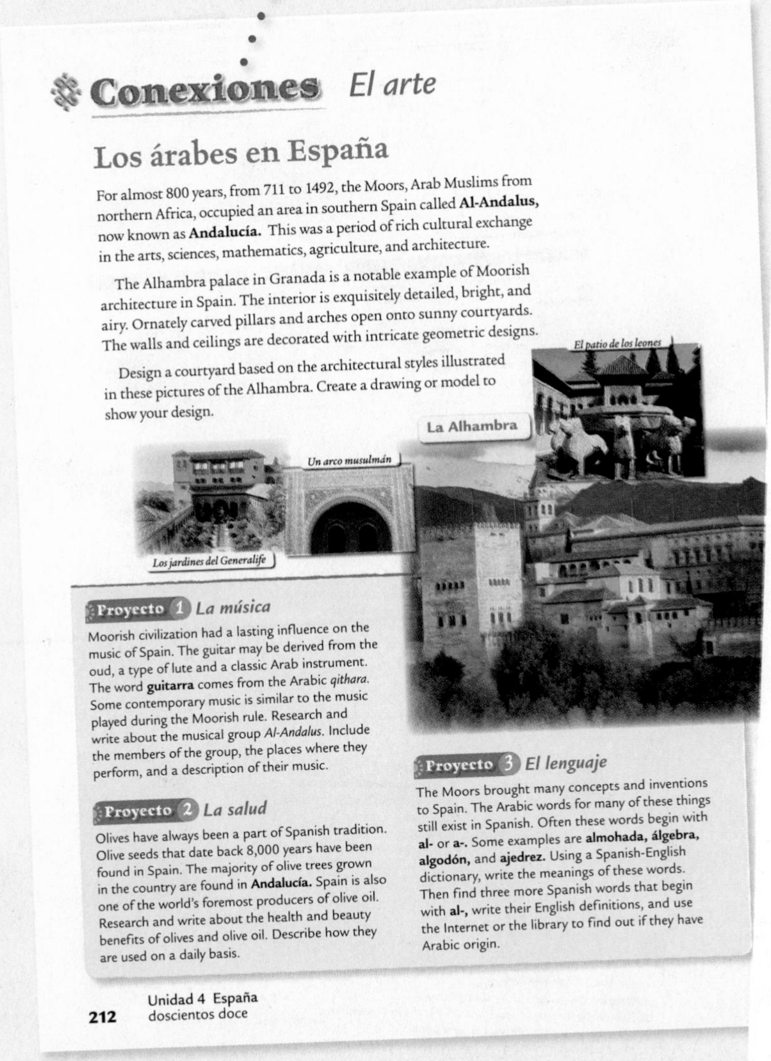

Conexiones *El arte*

Los árabes en España

For almost 800 years, from 711 to 1492, the Moors, Arab Muslims from northern Africa, occupied an area in southern Spain called **Al-Andalus,** now known as **Andalucía.** This was a period of rich cultural exchange in the arts, sciences, mathematics, agriculture, and architecture.

The Alhambra palace in Granada is a notable example of Moorish architecture in Spain. The interior is exquisitely detailed, bright, and airy. Ornately carved pillars and arches open onto sunny courtyards. The walls and ceilings are decorated with intricate geometric designs.

Design a courtyard based on the architectural styles illustrated in these pictures of the Alhambra. Create a drawing or model to show your design.

El patio de los leones

La Alhambra

Un arco musulmán

Los jardines del Generalife

Proyecto 1 *La música*

Moorish civilization had a lasting influence on the music of Spain. The guitar may be derived from the oud, a type of lute and a classic Arab instrument. The word **guitarra** comes from the Arabic *qithara.* Some contemporary music is similar to the music played during the Moorish rule. Research and write about the musical group *Al-Andalus.* Include the members of the group, the places where they perform, and a description of their music.

Proyecto 2 *La salud*

Olives have always been a part of Spanish tradition. Olive seeds that date back 8,000 years have been found in Spain. The majority of olive trees grown in the country are found in **Andalucía.** Spain is also one of the world's foremost producers of olive oil. Research and write about the health and beauty benefits of olives and olive oil. Describe how they are used on a daily basis.

Proyecto 3 *El lenguaje*

The Moors brought many concepts and inventions to Spain. The Arabic words for many of these things still exist in Spanish. Often these words begin with **al-** or **a-.** Some examples are **almohada, álgebra, algodón,** and **ajedrez.** Using a Spanish-English dictionary, write the meanings of these words. Then find three more Spanish words that begin with **al-,** write their English definitions, and use the Internet or the library to find out if they have Arabic origin.

212 Unidad 4 España
doscientos doce

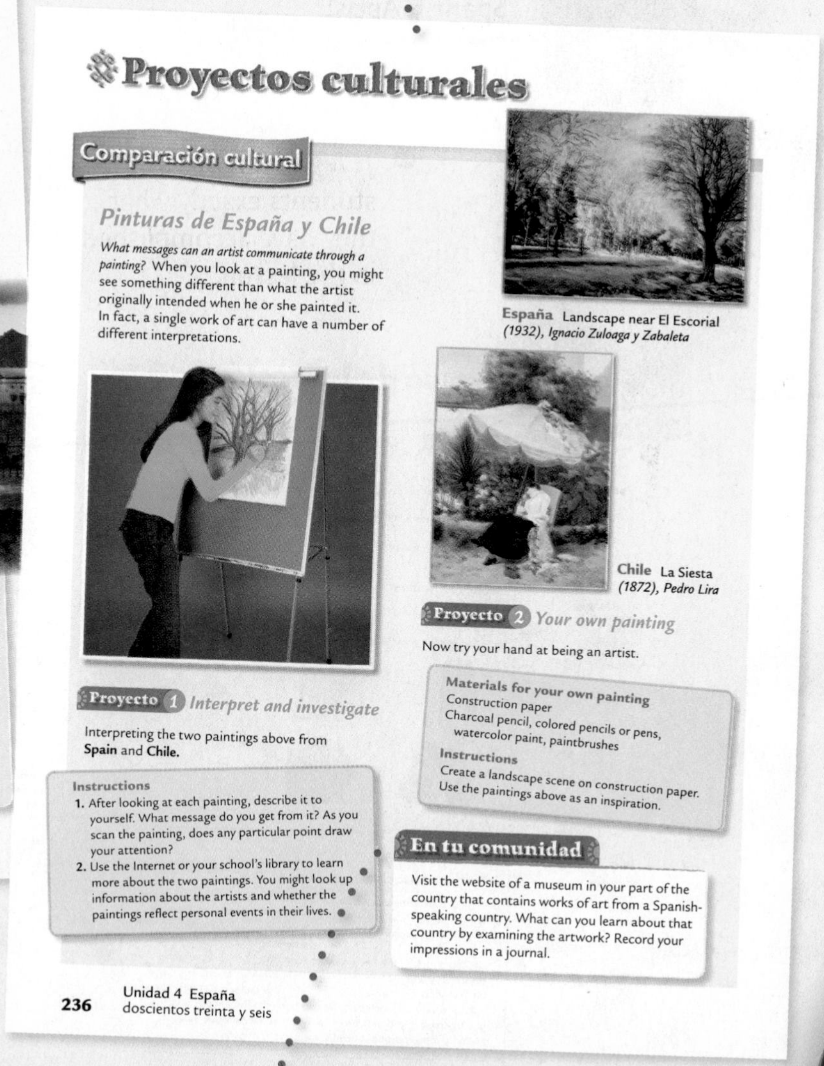

Proyectos culturales

Comparación cultural

Pinturas de España y Chile

What messages can an artist communicate through a painting? When you look at a painting, you might see something different than what the artist originally intended when he or she painted it. In fact, a single work of art can have a number of different interpretations.

España Landscape near El Escorial *(1932), Ignacio Zuloaga y Zabaleta*

Chile La Siesta *(1872), Pedro Lira*

Proyecto 1 *Interpret and investigate*

Interpreting the two paintings above from **Spain** and **Chile.**

Instructions

1. After looking at each painting, describe it to yourself. What message do you get from it? As you scan the painting, does any particular point draw your attention?
2. Use the Internet or your school's library to learn more about the two paintings. You might look up information about the artists and whether the paintings reflect personal events in their lives.

Proyecto 2 *Your own painting*

Now try your hand at being an artist.

Materials for your own painting
Construction paper
Charcoal pencil, colored pencils or pens, watercolor paint, paintbrushes

Instructions
Create a landscape scene on construction paper. Use the paintings above as an inspiration.

En tu comunidad

Visit the website of a museum in your part of the country that contains works of art from a Spanish-speaking country. What can you learn about that country by examining the artwork? Record your impressions in a journal.

236 Unidad 4 España
doscientos treinta y seis

- ***En tu comunidad*** opens the door for students to use Spanish in their community.

¡Repaso!

Review with Online Interactive Flashcards and Holt McDougal Spanish Apps!

- The all-inclusive review page highlights essential vocabulary and grammar from the lesson.

Lección 1 En resumen
Vocabulario y gramática

ANIMATEDGRAMMAR Interactive Flashcards my.hrw.com

Vocabulario

Talk About Shopping			
el centro comercial	shopping center, mall	el dólar	dollar
¿Cuánto cuesta(n)?	How much does it (do they) cost?	el euro	euro
Cuesta(n)...	It costs... (They cost...)	ir de compras	to go shopping
el dinero	money	pagar	to pay
		el precio	price
		la tienda	store

Expressions with tener	
tener calor	to be hot
tener frío	to be cold
tener razón	to be right
tener suerte	to be lucky

Describe Clothing			
la blusa	blouse	nuevo(a)	new
los calcetines	socks	los pantalones	pants
la camisa	shirt	los pantalones cortos	shorts
la camiseta	T-shirt	la ropa	clothing
la chaqueta	jacket	el sombrero	hat
feo(a)	ugly	el vestido	dress
el gorro	winter hat	los zapatos	shoes
los jeans	jeans		
llevar	to wear		

Discuss Seasons	
la estación (pl. las estaciones)	season
el invierno	winter
el otoño	autumn, fall
la primavera	spring
el verano	summer

Colors			
amarillo(a)	yellow	marrón (pl. marrones)	brown
anaranjado(a)	orange	negro(a)	black
azul	blue	rojo(a)	red
blanco(a)	white	verde	green

Other Words and Phrases	
durante	during
cerrar (ie)	to close
empezar (ie)	to begin
entender (ie)	to understand
pensar (ie)	to think, to plan
preferir (ie)	to prefer
querer (ie)	to want

Gramática

Nota gramatical: tener expressions p. 198

Stem-Changing Verbs: e → ie

For e → ie stem-changing verbs, the e of the stem changes to ie in all forms except **nosotros(as)** and **vosotros(as)**.

querer *to want*	
quiero	queremos
quieres	queréis
quiere	quieren

Direct Object Pronouns

Direct object pronouns can be used to replace direct object nouns.

Singular		Plural	
me	me	nos	us
te	you (familiar)	os	you (familiar)
lo	you (formal), him, it	los	you, them
la	you (formal), her, it	las	you, them

Practice Spanish with Holt McDougal Apps!

Lección 1 doscientos trece 213

- *¡Llegada!* reminds students exactly what they have accomplished in the lesson.

Lección 1 Repaso de la lección

HOMETUTOR my.hrw.com

¡LLEGADA!

Now you can
- talk about what clothes you want to buy
- say what you wear in different seasons

Using
- **tener** expressions
- stem-changing verbs: **e → ie**
- direct object pronouns

To review
- stem-changing verbs: **e → ie** p. 199
- direct object pronouns p. 204

1 Listen and understand

AUDIO

Escucha a Paula hablar de la ropa. Para cada artículo de ropa, indica si quiere comprarlo o no. Usa pronombres de objetos directos. *(Listen to Paula and indicate whether she wants to buy each article of clothing or not. Use direct object pronouns.)*

To review
- stem-changing verbs: **e → ie** p. 199

2 Talk about what clothes you want to buy

Fernando va de compras con sus padres. ¿Qué dice? *(Tell what Fernando says about his shopping experience.)*

preferir	cerrar	entender
empezar	pensar	querer

Las clases __1.__ el lunes y necesito ropa. Yo __2.__ comprar unas camisetas y unos pantalones pero no tengo mucho dinero. Yo __3.__ las camisetas a las camisas. Yo no __4.__ por qué una camiseta cuesta más en el centro comercial que en otras tiendas. Mi amiga Carla __5.__ que hay ropa más bonita y menos cara en la tienda Moda Zaragoza. Necesito ir hoy porque la tienda __6.__ los domingos.

214 Unidad 4 España doscientos catorce

To review
- **tener** expressions p. 198
- stem-changing verbs: **e → ie** p. 199

3 Talk about what clothes you want to buy

Indica si estas personas tienen calor o tienen frío basado en lo que piensan comprar. *(Indicate if these people are hot or cold based on what they are thinking about buying.)*

modelo: Ana / blusa de verano
Ana piensa comprar una blusa de verano porque tiene calor.

1. Juan y yo / gorros
2. yo / pantalones cortos
3. tú / chaqueta
4. Laura y Carlos / camisetas de verano
5. ustedes / calcetines de invierno
6. Pilar / vestido de primavera

To review
- direct object pronouns p. 204

4 Say what you wear in different seasons

Escribe oraciones para decir quién prefiere llevar la ropa. *(Tell who prefers to wear these clothing items.)*

modelo: los zapatos negros (Juan)
Juan los prefiere llevar. (Juan prefiere llevarlos.)

1. los pantalones cortos (Rosa)
2. las camisas azules (ellas)
3. el sombrero rojo (yo)
4. la camiseta anaranjada (Carlos)
5. el gorro negro (ellos)
6. la blusa amarilla (nosotros)
7. los calcetines blancos (ustedes)
8. la chaqueta marrón (tú)
9. los zapatos marrones (usted)
10. el vestido verde (Amanda)

To review
- **Sevillanas** p. 191
- Comparación cultural pp. 203, 206
- Lectura pp. 210–211

5 Spain and Chile

Comparación cultural

Answer these culture questions.

1. What are the characteristics of **sevillanas**?
2. How do the climates of Spain and Chile differ in July and why?
3. What are some characteristics of surrealist art?
4. What season is represented in Antonio Colinas' poem? How does the speaker of the poem feel and why?

Más práctica Cuaderno pp. 159–170 Cuaderno para hispanohablantes pp. 161–170

Get Help Online my.hrw.com

Lección 1 doscientos quince 215

- **Diagnostic review** helps students prepare for the test.

Generate Success

Create rubrics to evaluate students' performance with this online rubric generator.

Comparación cultural integrates reading and writing skills with cultural information.

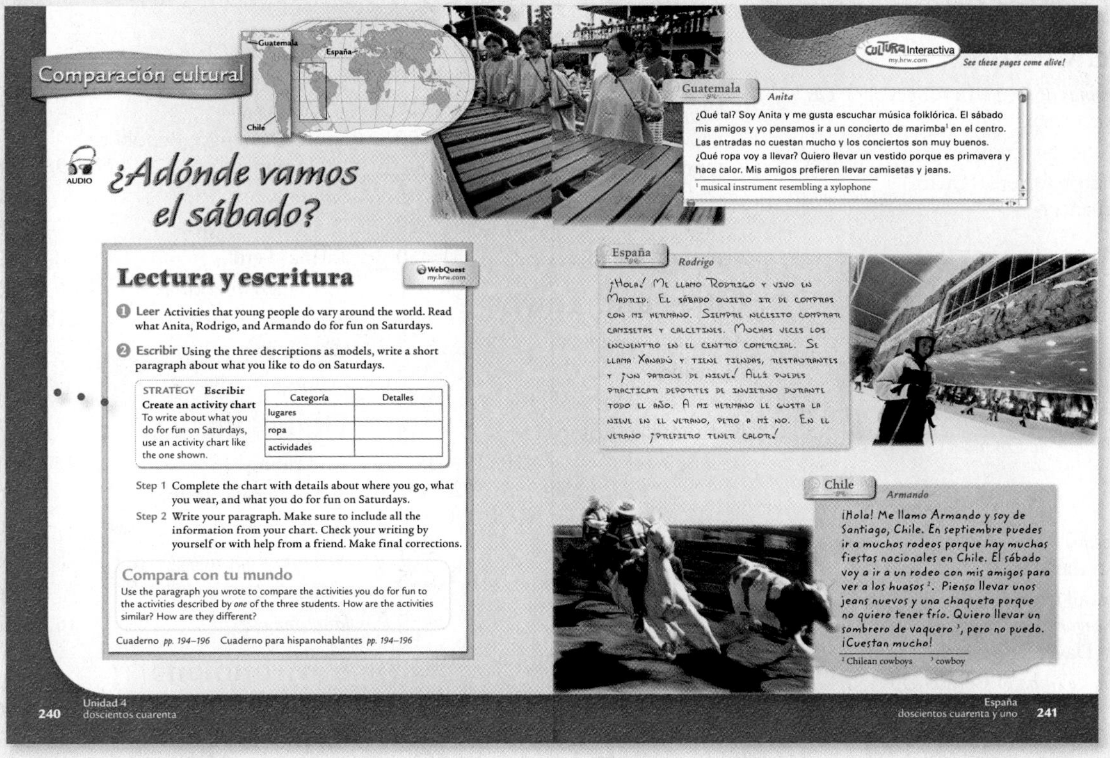

Comparación cultural

¿Adónde vamos el sábado?

AUDIO

Lectura y escritura

WebQuest my.hrw.com

1 Leer Activities that young people do vary around the world. Read what Anita, Rodrigo, and Armando do for fun on Saturdays.

2 Escribir Using the three descriptions as models, write a short paragraph about what you like to do on Saturdays.

STRATEGY Escribir
Create an activity chart
To write about what you do for fun on Saturdays, use an activity chart like the one shown.

Categoría	Detalles
lugares	
ropa	
actividades	

Step 1 Complete the chart with details about where you go, what you wear, and what you do for fun on Saturdays.

Step 2 Write your paragraph. Make sure to include all the information from your chart. Check your writing by yourself or with help from a friend. Make final corrections.

Compara con tu mundo
Use the paragraph you wrote to compare the activities you do for fun to the activities described by *one* of the three students. How are the activities similar? How are they different?

Cuaderno *pp. 194–196* Cuaderno para hispanohablantes *pp. 194–196*

CULTURA Interactiva my.hrw.com *See these pages come alive!*

Guatemala — *Anita*

¿Qué tal? Soy Anita y me gusta escuchar música folklórica. El sábado mis amigos y yo pensamos ir a un concierto de marimba[1] en el centro. Las entradas no cuestan mucho y los conciertos son muy buenos. ¿Qué ropa voy a llevar? Quiero llevar un vestido porque es primavera y hace calor. Mis amigos prefieren llevar camisetas y jeans.

[1] musical instrument resembling a xylophone

España — *Rodrigo*

¡Hola! Me llamo Rodrigo y vivo en Madrid. El sábado quiero ir de compras con mi hermano. Siempre necesito comprar camisetas y calcetines. Muchas veces los encuentro en el centro comercial. Se llama Xanadú y tiene tiendas, restaurantes y ¡un parque de nieve! Allí puedes practicar deportes de invierno durante todo el año. A mi hermano le gusta la nieve en el verano, pero a mí no. En el verano ¡prefiero tener calor!

Chile — *Armando*

¡Hola! Me llamo Armando y soy de Santiago, Chile. En septiembre puedes ir a muchos rodeos porque hay muchas fiestas nacionales en Chile. El sábado voy a ir a un rodeo con mis amigos para ver a los huasos[2]. Pienso llevar unos jeans nuevos y una chaqueta porque no quiero tener frío. Quiero llevar un sombrero de vaquero[3], pero no puedo. ¡Cuestan mucho!

[2] Chilean cowboys [3] cowboy

240 Unidad 4 doscientos cuarenta

España doscientos cuarenta y uno 241

Writing strategies help students organize their ideas.

performance space

Performance Space and ¡AvanzaRap! give sudents opportunities to show off their skills.

UNIDADES 1-4

Repaso inclusivo
Options for Review

¡AvanzaRap! DVD Sing and Learn
Digital performance space

1 Listen, understand, and compare

Escuchar — Listen to Mrs. Estrada and her son, Carlitos, order a meal at a restaurant. Then answer the questions.

1. ¿Qué tiene ganas de comer Carlitos?
2. ¿Qué pide para empezar? ¿Y de plato principal?
3. ¿Qué plato pide la señora Estrada para empezar?
4. ¿Qué no sirven hoy en el restaurante?
5. ¿Qué van a beber ellos?

Which order most resembles what you like to eat? What foods and drinks do you order when you go to restaurants?

2 Present a family outing

Hablar — Prepare a presentation about a family outing to a restaurant. Bring in a photo of your own or one from a magazine. Talk about the clothes each person is wearing, what food the restaurant serves, what each person orders, and how much it costs. You should talk for at least three minutes.

3 Compare school days

Hablar — Interview a partner about his or her day at school. Ask about the classes your partner prefers, what he or she eats for lunch and at what time, and what he or she is going to do after school today. Finish by comparing your days. Your conversation should be at least four minutes long.

4 Make a flier

Escribir — As president of the Spanish club, you have been put in charge of a booth at the upcoming international food fair. You have decided to serve breakfast dishes from Spain and Mexico. Use the Internet to learn about Spanish and Mexican cuisine. Create a flier to advertise what food and beverages you will serve, at what time you will be serving them, and how much the tickets cost. Your flier should have illustrations and describe in detail each dish.

5 Help find a lost child

Hablar — Role-play a situation in which you are a mall employee in customer service. Your partner is shopping at the mall with a younger cousin, but can't find him or her. Interview your partner to find out as much descriptive information as possible, including age, physical characteristics, and clothing. Your conversation should be at least three minutes long.

6 Create a fashion show

Hablar Escribir — Work in a group of five. Individually, write a detailed description of the clothes you are wearing. Include color, where the clothes are from, where you can buy each item, how much they cost, and in what season(s) you can wear them. Your description should have at least eight sentences. Then perform the fashion show for the class, reading each other's descriptions as each "model" walks down the runway.

7 Plan a weekend with family

Leer Escribir — You are studying in Barcelona, Spain, for the summer and your parents are coming to visit. Read this newspaper supplement to find out about the weekend's events. Then write an e-mail to your parents, and suggest what you can do and where you can go together or separately during the weekend. Keep in mind everyone's likes and dislikes. Your e-mail should have at least six suggestions.

Suplemento especial – fin de semana

GUÍA DEL OCIO - BARCELONA

VIERNES
Cena especial
Comida española típica, con música de flamenco.
Restaurante Casals (de las 21.30 a las 23.30 h)
Concierto
Los hermanos Pujols tocan música rock.
Plaza Cataluña (a las 14.30 h)

SÁBADO
Películas
Terror en el centro
Hollywood. Película de terror. Dos chicos de Nueva York van en autobús cuando llegan unos extraterrestres horribles.
Cines Maremagnum (a las 16.00 y 18.30 h)
Mi tía loca
España. Película cómica. La historia de una chica y su tía favorita.
Cine Diagonal Mar (a las 13.30 y 21.00 h)
Comprar y pasear
La calle que lo tiene todo: libros, ropa, comida ¡y más!
Las Ramblas (todo el día)

DOMINGO
Eliminar el cáncer
Puedes pasear y donar dinero para combatir el cáncer.
Parque Güell (a las 10.00 h)
Compras
Los mejores precios del verano en las tiendas de ropa.
Centro Comercial Barcelona Glorias (de las 10.30 a las 20.30 h)
Concierto de Beethoven
La orquesta de Barcelona toca música clásica. Un concierto para toda la familia.
Teatro Liceu (a las 20.00 h)

242 Unidad 4 doscientos cuarenta y dos

España doscientos cuarenta y tres 243

Repaso inclusivo provides options for cumulative review.

Activities focus on integrating language taught in previous units.

Cultural References

Cultural References

Pastimes, Sports, and Entertainment

People

Points of Interest

Publications

Shopping

Spanish Speakers

Traditions

Traditional Clothing

HOLT McDOUGAL

1 uno ¡Avancemos!

AUTHORS

Estella Gahala | Patricia Hamilton Carlin

Audrey L. Heining-Boynton | Ricardo Otheguy | Barbara Rupert Mondloch

HOLT McDOUGAL

HOUGHTON MIFFLIN HARCOURT

Cover Photography

Front cover
Palacio Nacional at night, Mexico City, Mexico ©2010 Nino H. Photography/Getty Images
Inset: Charro mexicano, H. Sitton/zefa/Corbis

Back cover
Level 1a: View toward La Fortaleza, San Juan, Puerto Rico, Steve Dunwell/The Image Bank/ Getty Images
Level 1b: View of Buenos Aires through the Puente de la Mujer, Joseph Rodriguez/Gallery Stock Limited
Level 1: Palacio Nacional at night, Mexico City, Mexico ©2010 Nino H. Photography/Getty Images
Level 2: Cibeles Fountain and Palacio de Comunicaciones at night, Madrid, Spain, Doug Armand/Getty Images
Level 3: Plaza de la Constitución at night, Santiago, Chile, David Noton Photography
Level 4: Antigua, Guatemala ©Michel Renaudeau/age fotostock/Robert Harding Photo Library

Printed in the U.S.A.

ISBN: 978-0-547-87191-2

1 2 3 4 5 6 7 8 9 10 XXXX 21 20 19 18 17 16 15 14 13 12

4500000000 A B C D E F G

1
uno

HOLT McDOUGAL

¡Avancemos!

Celebraciones

Cultura Interactiva **Explora las celebraciones del mundo hispano**

El Día de los Muertos, Santiago Sacatepéquez, Guatemala

New Year's Eve, Madrid, Spain

DIGITAL SPANISH my.hrw.com

Cultura Interactiva *pp. C2–C3, C4–C5, C6–C7, C8–C9, C10–C11, C12–C13, C14–C15, C16–C17, C18–C19, C20–C21, C22–C23, C24–C25*

LECCIÓN PRELIMINAR Nueva York

¡Hola!

Cultura

PARA Y PIENSA **Did you get it?**

Student Self-Check

pp. 5, 9, 11, 15, 17, 19, 21, 24

¡AvanzaRap! DVD

Sing and Learn

A performer wearing the colors of the Puerto Rican Flag

Dominican dancers in colorful costumes

UNIDAD 1 Estados Unidos

Un rato con los amigos

Una playa de Miami Beach, Miami Beach, Florida

Paseo del Río, San Antonio, Texas

Lección 2

Tema: *Mis amigos y yo* 54

¡AvanzaRap! DVD
Sing and Learn

UNIDAD 2

México

¡Vamos a la escuela!

Cultura

- **Explora México** *p. 82*
- **Uniformes escolares** *p. 92*
- **Los murales en México** *p. 97*
- **Una escuela internacional** *p. 102*

¿Recuerdas?

- after-school activities *p. 93*
- days of the week *p. 95*

PARA Y PIENSA **Did you get it?**

Student Self-Check
pp. 88, 90, 93, 95, 98, 101

DIGITAL SPANISH my.hrw.com

CULTURA Interactiva	ANIMATED GRAMMAR	@HOMETUTOR VideoPlus
pp. 82–83 132–133	*pp. 91, 96, 105 115, 120, 129*	*pp. 89, 94, 99 113, 118, 123*

Video/DVD

Vocabulario
pp. 86–87, 110–111
Telehistoria
pp. 89, 94, 99 113, 118, 123

La fuente de San Miguel en el Zócalo, Puebla, México

El patio de una escuela secundaria, México

Lección 2

Tema: *En la escuela*

¡AvanzaRap! DVD
Sing and Learn

UNIDAD 3

Puerto Rico

Comer en familia

Cultura

- **Explora Puerto Rico** *p. 136*
- **La cocina criolla** *p. 146*
- **La Plaza de Colón** *p. 152*
- **¡A comprar y a comer!** *p. 156*

¿Recuerdas?

- **gustar** with an infinitive *p. 142*
- snack foods *p. 144*
- the verb **estar** *p. 151*
- telling time *p. 154*

PARA Y PIENSA **Did you get it?**

Student Self-Check

pp. 142, 144, 147, 149, 152, 155

DIGITAL SPANISH my.hrw.com

Cultura Interactiva	Animated Grammar	@HomeTutor VideoPlus
pp. 136–137 186–187	*pp. 145, 150, 159 169, 174, 183*	*pp. 143, 148, 153 167, 172, 177*

Video/DVD

Vocabulario
pp. 140–141, 164–165
Telehistoria
pp. 143, 148, 153 167, 172, 177

La Plaza de Colón en el Viejo San Juan, San Juan, Puerto Rico

Una familia come en casa, San Juan, Puerto Rico

Lección 2

Tema: *En mi familia* . . . 162

Cultura

¿Recuerdas?

PARA Y PIENSA

Did you get it?

Student Self-Check *pp. 166, 168, 171, 173, 176, 179*

UNIT 3 WRAP-UP

¡AvanzaRap! DVD

Sing and Learn

UNIDAD 4

España

En el centro

Una tienda de ropa, Madrid, España

El Teatro de la Comedia en la calle Príncipe, Madrid, España

Lección 2

Tema: *¿Qué hacemos esta noche?* 216

Cultura

¿Recuerdas?

PARA Y PIENSA **Did you get it?**

Student Self-Check

¡AvanzaRap! DVD
Sing and Learn

UNIDAD 5

Ecuador

¡Bienvenido a nuestra casa!

Cultura

- **Explora Ecuador** *p. 244*
- **Casas ecuatorianas** *p. 255*
- **Sitios geográficos** *p. 260*
- **Vivir en Ecuador** *p. 264*

¿Recuerdas?

- stem-changing verbs: **o → ue** *p. 250*
- location words *p. 254*
- colors *p. 255*
- clothing *p. 259*

PARA Y PIENSA **Did you get it?**

Student Self-Check

pp. 250, 252, 255, 257, 260, 263

DIGITAL SPANISH my.hrw.com

CULTURA Interactiva	ANIMATED GRAMMAR	@HOMETUTOR VideoPlus
pp. 244–245 294–295	*pp. 253, 258, 267 277, 282, 291*	*pp. 251, 256, 261 275, 280, 285*

Video/DVD

Vocabulario
pp. 248–249, 272–273

Telehistoria
pp. 251, 256, 261 275, 280, 285

Una casa tradicional con jardín, Quito, Ecuador

Una fiesta de cumpleaños, Quito, Ecuador

Lección 2

Tema: *Una fiesta en casa*

Cultura

- **Fiestas de Quito** *p. 278*
- **Los textiles de Otavalo** *p. 284*
- **Bailes folklóricos de Ecuador y Panamá** *p. 288*
- **Arte textil de Ecuador y Panamá** *p. 290*
- **¡Así celebramos!** *p. 294*

¿Recuerdas?

- **tener que** *p. 276*
- interrogative words *p. 279*
- expressions of frequency *p. 281*
- direct object pronouns *p. 283*

PARA Y PIENSA

Did you get it?

Student Self-Check
pp. 274, 276, 279, 281, 284, 287

UNIDAD 6

República Dominicana

Mantener un cuerpo sano

Un partido en la escuela, Santo Domingo, República Dominicana

Un día en la Playa Caribe, Juan Dolio, República Dominicana

Lección 2

Tema: *La salud* 324

Cultura

- **La artista y su estilo** *p. 332*
- **El Festival del Merengue** *p. 338*
- **Dos atletas de alta velocidad** *p. 342*
- **Gestos y refranes** *p. 344*
- **Deportes favoritos** *p. 348*

¿Recuerdas?

- **gustar** with nouns *p. 330*
- stem-changing verbs **o → ue** *p. 330*
- telling time *p. 332*

PARA Y PIENSA **Did you get it?**

Student Self-Check

pp. 328, 330, 333, 335, 338, 341

UNIDAD 7

Argentina

¡Una semana fenomenal!

Cultura

- **Explora Argentina** *p. 352*
- **El lunfardo** *p. 362*
- **Las playas de Mar del Plata** *p. 368*
- **Un cuestionario sobre las computadoras** *p. 372*

¿Recuerdas?

- affirmative **tú** commands *p. 360*
- telling time *p. 362*
- foods and beverages *p. 363*
- preterite of regular **-ar** verbs *p. 368*

PARA Y PIENSA **Did you get it?**

Student Self-Check
pp. 358, 360, 363, 365, 368, 371

DIGITAL SPANISH my.hrw.com

CULTURA Interactiva	ANIMATED GRAMMAR	@HOMETUTOR VideoPlus
pp. 352–353 402–403	*pp. 361, 366, 375 385, 390, 399*	*pp. 359, 364, 369 383, 388, 393*

Video/DVD

Vocabulario
pp. 356–357, 380–381
Telehistoria
pp. 359, 364, 369 383, 388, 393

xviii

La Casa Rosada, Buenos Aires, Argentina

El Parque de la Costa, El Tigre, Argentina

Lección 2

Tema: *Un día en el parque de diversiones* . . . 378

Cultura

¿Recuerdas?

PARA Y PIENSA

Did you get it?

Student Self-Check

UNIT 7 WRAP-UP

¡AvanzaRap!
DVD
Sing and Learn

UNIDAD 8

Costa Rica

Una rutina diferente

Una familia habla de las vacaciones, San José, Costa Rica

Una tienda de artesanías y recuerdos, San José, Costa Rica

Lección 2

¡AvanzaRap! DVD

Sing and Learn

Recursos

¡Avancemos!

About the Authors

Estella Gahala

Estella Gahala received degrees in Spanish from Wichita State University, French from Middlebury College, and a Ph.D. in Educational Administration and Curriculum from Northwestern University. A career teacher of Spanish and French, she has worked with a wide variety of students at the secondary level. She has also served as foreign language department chair and district director of curriculum and instruction. Her workshops and publications focus on research and practice in a wide range of topics, including culture and language learning, learning strategies, assessment, and the impact of current brain research on curriculum and instruction. She has coauthored twelve basal textbooks. Honors include the Chevalier dans l'Ordre des Palmes Académiques and listings in *Who's Who of American Women*, *Who's Who in America*, and *Who's Who in the World*.

Patricia Hamilton Carlin

Patricia Hamilton Carlin completed her M.A. in Spanish at the University of California, Davis, where she also taught as a lecturer. Previously she earned a Master of Secondary Education with specialization in foreign languages from the University of Arkansas and taught Spanish and French at the K–12 level. Patricia currently teaches Spanish and foreign language/ESL methodology at the University of Central Arkansas, where she coordinates the second language teacher education program. In addition, Patricia is a frequent presenter at local, regional, and national foreign language conferences. In 2005, she was awarded the Southern Conference on Language Teaching's Outstanding Teaching Award: Post-Secondary. Her professional service has included the presidency of the Arkansas Foreign Language Teachers Association and the presidency of Arkansas's DeSoto Chapter of the AATSP.

Audrey L. Heining-Boynton

Audrey L. Heining-Boynton received her Ph.D. in Curriculum and Instruction from Michigan State University. She is a professor of Education and Romance Languages at The University of North Carolina at Chapel Hill, where she teaches educational methodology classes and Spanish. She has also taught Spanish, French, and ESL at the K–12 level. Dr. Heining-Boynton served as the president of ACTFL and the National Network for Early Language Learning. She has been involved with AATSP, Phi Delta Kappa, and state foreign language associations. In addition, she has presented both nationally and internationally and has published over forty books, articles, and curricula.

Ricardo Otheguy

Ricardo Otheguy received his Ph.D. in Linguistics from the City University of New York, where he is currently professor of Linguistics at the Graduate Center. He is also director of the Research Institute for the Study of Language in Urban Society (RISLUS) and coeditor of the research journal *Spanish in Context*. He has extensive experience with school-based research and has written on topics related to Spanish grammar, bilingual education, and Spanish in the United States. His work has been supported by private and government foundations, including the Rockefeller Brothers Fund and the National Science Foundation. He is coauthor of *Tu mundo: Curso para hispanohablantes*, and *Prueba de ubicación para hispanohablantes*.

Barbara Rupert Mondloch

Barbara Rupert Mondloch completed her M.A. at Pacific Lutheran University. She has taught Level 1 through A.P. Spanish and has implemented a FLES program in her district. Barbara is the author of CD-ROM activities for the *¡Bravo!* series. She has presented at many local, regional, and national foreign language conferences. She has served as president of both the Pacific Northwest Council for Languages (PNCFL) and the Washington Association for Language Teaching, and was the PNCFL representative to ACTFL. In 1996, Barbara received the Christa McAuliffe Award for Excellence in Education, and in 1999, she was selected Washington's "Spanish Teacher of the Year" by the Juan de Fuca Chapter of the AATSP.

John DeMado, Creative Consultant

John DeMado has been a vocal advocate for second-language acquisition in the United States for many years. He started his career as a middle/high school French and Spanish teacher, before entering the educational publishing profession. Since 1993, Mr. DeMado has directed his own business, John DeMado Language Seminars. Inc., a company devoted exclusively to language acquisition issues. He has authored numerous books in both French and Spanish that span the K–12 curriculum. Mr. DeMado wrote and performed the *¡AvanzaRap!* songs for Levels 1 and 2.

Carl Johnson, Senior Program Advisor

Carl Johnson received degrees from Marietta College (OH), the University of Illinois, Université Laval, and a Ph.D. in Foreign Language Education from The Ohio State University, during which time he studied French, German, Spanish, and Russian. He has been a lifelong foreign language educator, retiring in 2003 after 27 years as a language teacher (secondary and university level), consultant, and Director of Languages Other Than English for the Texas Department of Education. He has completed many publications relating to student and teacher language proficiency development, language textbooks, and nationwide textbook adoption practices. He also served as president of the Texas Foreign Language Association, Chair of the Board of the Southwest Conference on Language Teaching, and president of the National Council of State Supervisors of Foreign Languages. In addition, he was named Chevalier dans l'Ordre des Palmes Académiques by the French government.

Rebecca L. Oxford, Learning Strategy Specialist

Rebecca L. Oxford received her Ph.D. in educational psychology from The University of North Carolina. She also holds two degrees in foreign language from Vanderbilt University and Yale University, and a degree in educational psychology from Boston University. She leads the Second Language Education and Culture Program and is a professor at the University of Maryland. She has directed programs at Teachers College, Columbia University; the University of Alabama; and the Pennsylvania State University. In addition, she initiated and edited *Tapestry*, a series of student textbooks used around the world. Dr. Oxford specializes in language learning strategies and styles.

Contributing Writers

Louis G. Baskinger
New Hartford High School
New Hartford, NY

Jacquelyn Cinotti-Dirmann
Duval County Public Schools
Jacksonville, FL

Teacher Reviewers

Sue Arandjelovic
Dobson High School
Mesa, AZ

Susan K. Arbuckle
Mahomet-Seymour High School
Mahomet, IL

Kristi Ashe
Amador Valley High School
Pleasanton, CA

Shaun A. Bauer
Olympia High School, *retired*
Orlando, FL

Sheila Bayles
Rogers High School
Rogers, AR

Robert L. Bowbeer
Detroit Country Day Upper School
Beverly Hills, MI

Hercilia Bretón
Highlands High School
San Antonio, TX

Adrienne Chamberlain-Parris
Mariner High School
Everett, WA

Mike Cooperider
Truman High School
Independence, MO

Susan B. Cress
Sheridan High School
Sheridan, IN

Michèle S. de Cruz-Sáenz, Ph.D.
Strath Haven High School
Wallingford, PA

Lizveth Dague
Park Vista Community High School
Lake Worth, FL

Parthena Draggett
Jackson High School
Massillon, OH

Rubén D. Elías
Roosevelt High School
Fresno, CA

Phillip Elkins
Lane Tech College Prep High School
Chicago, IL

Maria Fleming Alvarez
The Park School
Brookline, MA

Michael Garber
Boston Latin Academy
Boston, MA

Marco García
Derry University Advantage Academy
Chicago, IL

David Gonzalez
Hollywood Hills High School
Hollywood, FL

Raquel R. González
Odessa Senior High School
Odessa, TX

Neyda Gonzalez-Droz
Ridge Community High School
Davenport, FL

Becky Hay de García
James Madison Memorial
High School
Madison, WI

Fatima Hicks
Suncoast High School, *retired*
Riviera Beach, FL

Gladys V. Horford
William T. Dwyer High School
Palm Beach Gardens, FL

Pam Johnson
Stevensville High School
Stevensville, MT

Richard Ladd
Ipswich High School
Ipswich, MA

Patsy Lanigan
Hume Fogg Academic Magnet
High School
Nashville, TN

Kris Laws
Palm Bay High School
Melbourne, FL

Kristen M. Lombardi
Shenendehowa High School
Clifton Park, NY

Elizabeth Lupafya
North High School
Worcester, MA

David Malatesta
Niles West High School
Skokie, IL

Patrick Malloy
James B. Conant High School
Hoffman Estates, IL

Brandi Meeks
Starr's Mill High School
Fayetteville, GA

Kathleen L. Michaels
Palm Harbor University High School
Palm Harbor, FL

Linda Nanos
Brook Farm Business Academy
West Roxbury, MA

Nadine F. Olson
School of Teaching and Curriculum
Leadership
Stillwater, OK

Pam Osthoff
Lakeland Senior High School
Lakeland, FL

Nicholas Patterson
Davenport Central High School
Davenport, IA

Carolyn A. Peck
Genesee Community College
Lakeville, NY

Daniel N. Richardson
Concord High School, *retired*
Concord, NH

Rita E. Risco
Palm Harbor University High School
Palm Harbor, FL

Miguel Roma
Boston Latin Academy
West Roxbury, MA

Nona M. Seaver
New Berlin West Middle/High School
New Berlin, WI

Susan Seraphine-Kimel
Astronaut High School
Titusville, FL

Lauren Schultz
Dover High School
Dover, NH

Mary Severo
Thomas Hart Middle School
Pleasanton, CA

Clarette Shelton
WT Woodson High School, *retired*
Fairfax, VA

Maureen Shiland
Saratoga Springs High School
Saratoga Springs, NY

Irma Sprague
Countryside High School
Clearwater, FL

Mary A. Stimmel
Lincoln High School
Des Moines, IA

Karen Tharrington
Wakefield High School
Raleigh, NC

Alicia Turnier
Countryside High School
Clearwater, FL

Roberto E. del Valle
The Overlake School
Redmond, WA

Todd Wagner
Upper Darby High School, *retired*
Drexel Hill, PA

Ronie R. Webster
Monson Junior/Senior High School
Monson, MA

Cheryl Wellman
Bloomingdale High School
Valrico, FL

Thomasina White
School District of Philadelphia
Philadelphia, PA

Jena Williams
Jonesboro High School
Jonesboro, AR

Program Advisory Council

Louis G. Baskinger
New Hartford High School
New Hartford, NY

Linda M. Bigler
James Madison University
Harrisonburg, VA

Flora Maria Ciccone-Quintanilla
Holly Senior High School
Holly, MI

Jacquelyn Cinotti-Dirmann
Duval County Public Schools
Jacksonville, FL

Desa Dawson
Del City High School
Del City, OK

Robin C. Hill
Warrensville Heights High School
Warrensville Heights, OH

Barbara M. Johnson
Gordon Tech High School, *retired*
Chicago, IL

Ray Maldonado
Houston Independent School District
Houston, TX

Karen S. Miller
Friends School of Baltimore
Baltimore, MD

Dr. Robert A. Miller
Woodcreek High School
Roseville Joint Union High School District
Roseville, CA

Debra M. Morris
Wellington Landings Middle School
Wellington, FL

Maria Nieto Zezas
West Morris Central High School
Chester, NJ

Rita Oleksak
Glastonbury Public Schools
Glastonbury, CT

Sandra Rosenstiel
University of Dallas, *retired*
Grapevine, TX

Emily Serafa Manschot
Northville High School
Northville, MI

La Telehistoria

VIDEO
DVD

Hi! My name is Alicia. My family and I live in Miami, Florida. My favorite thing to do is play soccer. At the Pan-American Youth Games, my team took second place. I made a lot of great friends from all over the world. I also met Trini Salgado, the best soccer player ever!

I got a T-shirt like hers, but I never got her to autograph it. She is always traveling to different countries, so maybe I can send my shirt to some of my soccer friends to try to get it signed.

Follow along in the ¡Avancemos! Telehistoria to find out what happens to Alicia's T-shirt as it travels from country to country.

1
San Antonio

Sandra

2
Mexico

Pablo

3
Puerto Rico

Rodrigo

4
Spain

Maribel

5
Ecuador

Manuel

6
Dominican Republic

Mario

7
Argentina

Florencia

8
Costa Rica

Jorge

Key Words to Know

el autógrafo autograph
la camiseta T-shirt
el jugador (la jugadora) de fútbol soccer player

Why Study Spanish?

Discover the world

Deciding to learn Spanish is one of the best decisions you can make if you want to travel and see the world.

More than 400 million people around the globe speak Spanish. After Chinese, English and Spanish are tied as the two most frequently spoken languages worldwide. Spanish is now the third most-used language on the Internet. In Europe, Spanish is the most popular foreign language after English. People who speak both Spanish and English can communicate with people from all around the globe, no matter where they find themselves.

xxx

Explore your community

Inside the United States, Spanish is by far the most widely spoken language after English.

There are currently over 30 million Spanish speakers in the U.S. When you start to look and listen for it, you will quickly realize that Spanish is all around you—on the television, on the radio, and in magazines and newspapers. You may even hear your neighbors speaking it. Learning Spanish will help you communicate and interact with the rapidly growing communities of Spanish speakers around you.

Experience a new perspective

Learning a language is more than just memorizing words and structures.

When you study Spanish, you learn how the people who speak it think, feel, work, and live. Learning a language can open your eyes to a whole new world of ideas and insights. And as you learn about other cultures, you gain a better perspective on your own.

Create career possibilities

Knowing Spanish opens many doors.

If you speak Spanish fluently, you can work for international and multinational companies anywhere in the Spanish-speaking world. You can create a career working as a translator, an interpreter, or a teacher of Spanish. And because the number of Spanish speakers in the U.S. is growing so rapidly, being able to communicate in Spanish is becoming important in almost every career.

What is Vocabulary?

Building Your Spanish Vocabulary

Vocabulary is a basic building block for learning a foreign language. By learning just a few words, you can start to communicate in Spanish right away! You will probably find that it is easier to understand words you hear or read than it is to use them yourself. But with a little practice, you will start to produce the right words in the right context. Soon you will be able to carry on conversations with other Spanish speakers.

xxxii

How Do I Study Vocabulary?

First Steps

- Read all of the new words in **blue** on the Vocabulary presentation page in your textbook.
- Point to each word as you say it out loud.

Be Creative

- Make flashcards with your new vocabulary words. You could also draw pictures of the words on the back of the flashcards.
- Group vocabulary words by theme. Add other words that fit the categories you've learned.
- Imagine a picture of the word.
- Create a rhyme or song to help you remember the words.

Make It Personal

- Use vocabulary words to write original sentences. Make them funny so you'll be sure to remember!
- Label everyday items in Spanish.
- Create reminders for difficult words. Put note cards inside your locker door, or on your mirror at home.
- See it, and say it to yourself! For example, if you are learning colors and clothing words, think of the Spanish word to describe what your friends are wearing.

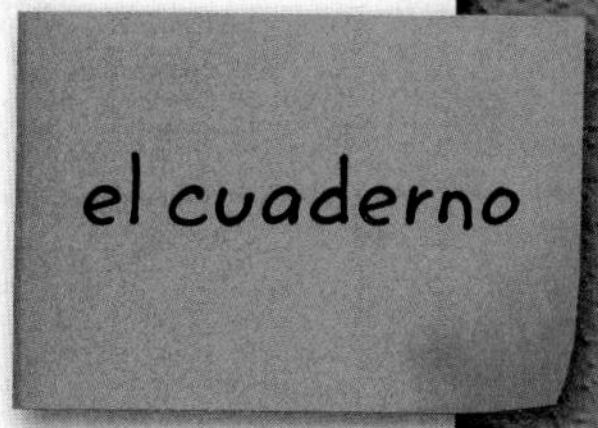

Practice Makes Perfect

- Say your vocabulary words out loud and repeat each word several times.
- Write each word five times, keeping its meaning in mind.
- Use Spanish words with your classmates outside of class—if you're having lunch in the cafeteria, use the words you know for food. Greet your classmates in the hallway in Spanish!

Create Your Own System

- Practice a little bit every day. Many short sessions are better than one long one.
- Focus on the words that are the hardest for you.
- Find a buddy. Quiz one another on the vocabulary words.
- Keep a vocabulary notebook and update it regularly.
- Use the study sheets in the back of your workbook to review vocabulary.

xxxiii

What is Grammar?

Some people think of grammar as the rules of a language, rules that tell you the "correct" way to speak a language. For instance, why do you say *big red house,* not *red big house*? Why do you say *how much money do you have* instead of *how many money*? If English is your first language, you probably don't think about the rule. You make the correct choice instinctively because it *sounds right.* Non-native speakers of English have to learn the rules. As you begin your study of Spanish, you will need to learn the grammar rules of Spanish.

xxxiv

Why Should I Study Grammar?

Grammar helps you to communicate.

For instance, using the past tense or future tense makes it clear when something happens. (*I did my homework* versus *I will do my homework.*) Using subject pronouns lets you know who is performing the action. (*I gave the book to her* versus *She gave the book to me.*) Using correct grammar when speaking Spanish will help you communicate successfully with native speakers of Spanish.

How Do I Study Grammar?

Read the English Grammar Connection before each grammar explanation.

Think about how you use the same type of grammar in English. Understanding your own language will help you to better understand Spanish.

> **English Grammar Connection:** A **verb tense** is the form of the verb that shows *when* an action is happening. The **present tense** shows that an action is happening *now.* The Spanish present-tense verb form **estudiamos** can be expressed in English in three different ways: *we study, we are studying,* or *we do study.*
>
> We **study** Spanish. → present-tense verb
>
> **Estudiamos** español. → present-tense verb

Practice the new forms that you are learning.

Completing the practice activities in your student book and workbook will help you to learn the correct way to say things.

Use the Spanish you know as often as you can.

After all, that's how you learned to speak English, by hearing and speaking it every day.

xxxv

What Is Culture?

To communicate with people from Spanish-speaking countries in a meaningful way, you need to know something about their culture. Vocabulary and grammar will help you learn what words to say and how to put them together, but culture will give you a better understanding of "how, when, and why to say what to whom."

What exactly is culture?

xxxvi

Culture includes . . .

Art
History
Traditions
Relationships
Music
Holidays
Food
Architecture
Pastimes

and more!

How can I learn about another culture?

- Read the **Comparación cultural** information to find out more about the cultures that you are studying.
- Think about the answers to the questions in the **Comparación cultural.**
- Think about the perspectives and practices that shape and influence the culture.
- Compare your own culture with the cultures you are studying.

El mundo

OCÉANO ÁRTICO
Mar de Siberia Oriental
Mar de Beaufort
Bahía de Baffin
GROENLANDIA (DINAMARCA)
RUSIA
Alaska (EE.UU.)
Mar de Bering
Bahía de Hudson
Mar del Labrador
CANADÁ
ESTADOS UNIDOS
OCÉANO ATLÁNTICO
REP. DOMINICANA
ISLAS BAHAMAS
PUERTO RICO (EE.UU.)
SAN CRISTÓBAL Y NEVIS
Golfo de México
HAITÍ
ANTIGUA Y BARBUDA
Islas Hawai (EE.UU.)
CUBA
GUADALUPE (FRANCIA)
MÉXICO
JAMAICA
DOMINICA
BELICE
Mar Caribe
MARTINICA (FRANCIA)
SANTA LUCÍA
SAN VICENTE Y GRANADINAS
ISLAS MARSHALL
GUATEMALA
GRANADA
BARBADOS
OCÉANO PACÍFICO
EL SALVADOR
PANAMÁ
TRINIDAD Y TOBAGO
HONDURAS
VENEZUELA
NICARAGUA
COSTA RICA
GUAYANA FRANCESA (FRANCIA)
COLOMBIA
NAURU
KIRIBATI
Islas Galápagos (Ecuador)
ECUADOR
GUYANA
ISLAS TUVALU
SURINAM
ISLAS SALOMÓN
PERÚ
BRASIL
SAMOA
Samoa Americana (EE.UU.)
VANUATÚ
BOLIVIA
FIDJI
TONGA
NUEVA CALEDONIA (FRANCIA)
PARAGUAY
CHILE
URUGUAY
NUEVA ZELANDA
ARGENTINA
Islas Malvinas (R.U.)

OCÉANO ÁRTICO
Mar de Kara
Mar de Laptev
Mar de Barents
Mar de Noruega
ANDIA
SUECIA
FINLANDIA
NORUEGA
RUSIA
1 DINAMARCA
2 HOLANDA
3 BÉLGICA
4 LUXEMBURGO
5 SUIZA
6 REPÚBLICA CHECA
7 ESLOVAQUIA
8 HUNGRÍA
9 ESLOVENIA
10 CROACIA
11 BOSNIA Y HERZEGOVINA
12 SERBIA Y MONTENEGRO
13 ALBANIA
14 MACEDONIA
15 BULGARIA
ESTONIA
LETONIA
LITUANIA
REINO UNIDO
Mar del Norte
Mar Báltico
IRLANDA
BIELORRUSIA
ALEMANIA
POLONIA
UCRANIA
Lago Baikal
Mar de Ojotsk
60°N
KAZAKSTÁN
MOLDAVIA
AUSTRIA
FRANCIA
ANDORRA
RUMANIA
Mar de Aral
MONGOLIA
Mar Negro
GEORGIA
UZBEKISTÁN
KIRGUISTÁN
ESPAÑA
ITALIA
Mar Caspio
PORTUGAL
TURQUÍA
TURKMENISTÁN
COREA DEL NORTE
Mar de Japón
ARMENIA
TADJIKISTÁN
GRECIA
ALTAR (R.U.)
MALTA
AZERBAIYÁN
COREA DEL SUR
JAPÓN
SIRIA
CHINA
TÚNEZ
Mar Mediterráneo
CHIPRE
MARRUECOS
LÍBANO
IRAQ
IRÁN
AFGANISTÁN
Canarias (Esp.)
BHUTÁN
KUWAIT
ISRAEL
30°N
ARGELIA
LIBIA
JORDANIA
QATAR
PAQUISTÁN
NEPAL
EGIPTO
BAHREIN
BANGLADESH
SAHARA OCCIDENTAL
E.Á.U
Trópico de Cáncer
ARABIA SAUDITA
OMÁN
INDIA
TAIWÁN
Mar Rojo
MYANMAR
OCÉANO PACÍFICO
MAURITANIA
LAOS
MALÍ
NÍGER
ERITREA
CHAD
TAILANDIA
VIETNAM
FILIPINAS
GUAM (EE.UU.)
SENEGAL
YEMEN
SUDÁN
BURKINA FASO
BENIN
JIBUTI
Mar Arábigo
Golfo de Bengala
CAMBOYA
Mar de China
GUINEA
COSTA DE MARFIL
NIGERIA
MICRONESIA
ETIOPÍA
TOGO
REP. CENTRO-AFRICANA
SRI LANKA
BRUNEI
PALAU
GHANA
CAMERÚN
LIBERIA
ISLAS MALDIVAS
SOMALIA
MALAYSIA
UGANDA
SIERRA LEONA
GUINEA ECUATORIAL
CONGO
KENIA
Ecuador 0°
GABÓN
REP. DEM. DEL CONGO
RUANDA
SINGAPUR
PAPUASIA NUEVA GUINEA
SANTO TOMÉ Y PRÍNCIPE
CABINDA (ANGOLA)
BURUNDI
TANZANÍA
SEYCHELLES
INDONESIA
COMORES
TIMOR ORIENTAL
ANGOLA
ZAMBIA
MALAWI
MOZAMBIQUE
NAMIBIA
ZIMBABWE
MADAGASCAR
MAURICIO
OCÉANO ÍNDICO
Trópico de Capricornio
BOTSWANA
AUSTRALIA
SUAZILANDIA
30°S
SUDÁFRICA
LESOTHO
N
O
E
S
0
1,000
2,000 millas
0
1,000
2,000 kilómetros
60°S
ANTÁRTIDA

xxxix

México y Centroamérica

El Caribe
ESTADOS UNIDOS
OCÉANO ATLÁNTICO
Nassau
ISLAS BAHAMAS
Estrecho de Florida
25°N
Trópico de Cáncer
La Habana
Santa Clara
CUBA
Nueva Gerona
Camagüey
Holguín
ISLAS DE TURCOS Y CAICOS (R.U.)
Manzanillo
Guantánamo
Santiago de Cuba
REPÚBLICA DOMINICANA
20°N
ANTILLAS MAYORES
HAITÍ
La Española
Arecibo
San Juan
Mayagüez
Puerto Príncipe
Santo Domingo
Ponce
Humacao
PUERTO RICO
JAMAICA
Kingston
Mar Caribe
HONDURAS
15°N
NICARAGUA
Aruba (Hol.)
Curaçao (Hol.)
Bonaire (Hol.)
San José
Caracas
10°N
COSTA RICA
Panamá
PANAMÁ
VENEZUELA
Golfo de Panamá
OCÉANO PACÍFICO
N
O
E
S
5°N
Bogotá
COLOMBIA
0
150
300 millas
0
150
300 kilómetros

Sudamérica

Mar Caribe
Barranquilla
Cartagena
Maracaibo
Lago Maracaibo
Caracas
TRINIDAD Y TOBAGO
Puerto España
10°N
Río Orinoco
VENEZUELA
Georgetown
Paramaribo
GUYANA
Cayena
SURINAM
GUAYANA FRANCESA (FRANCIA)
OCÉANO ATLÁNTICO
Medellín
Manizales
Bogotá
COLOMBIA
Cali
Otavalo
Quito
ECUADOR
Guayaquil
Cuenca
Ecuador 0°
Río Negro
Río Amazonas
Río Madeira
Río Tapajós
Río Xingú
Río Tocantins
Río São Francisco
PERÚ
Trujillo
CORDILLERA DE LOS ANDES
BRASIL
10°S
Callao
Lima
Lago Titicaca
BOLIVIA
La Paz
Cochabamba
Santa Cruz
Sucre
Brasilia
20°S
OCÉANO PACÍFICO
Bogotá
COLOMBIA
Islas Galápagos (Ecuador)
Quito
ECUADOR
PERÚ
0 200 400 millas
0 200 400 kilómetros
GRAN CHACO
PARAGUAY
Trópico de Capricornio
Asunción
Salta
CHILE
San Miguel de Tucumán
Resistencia
30°S
Córdoba
Valparaíso
Mendoza
Rosario
URUGUAY
Santiago
Buenos Aires
OCÉANO PACÍFICO
ARGENTINA
La Plata
Montevideo
OCÉANO ATLÁNTICO
Concepción
PAMPAS
Mar del Plata
Temuco
Bahía Blanca
40°S
PATAGONIA
N
O
E
S
0 250 500 millas
0 250 500 kilómetros
Estrecho de Magallanes
Islas Malvinas (R.U.)
50°S
Tierra del Fuego
Cabo de Hornos
100°O
90°O
80°O
70°O
50°O
40°O
30°O
20°O

España

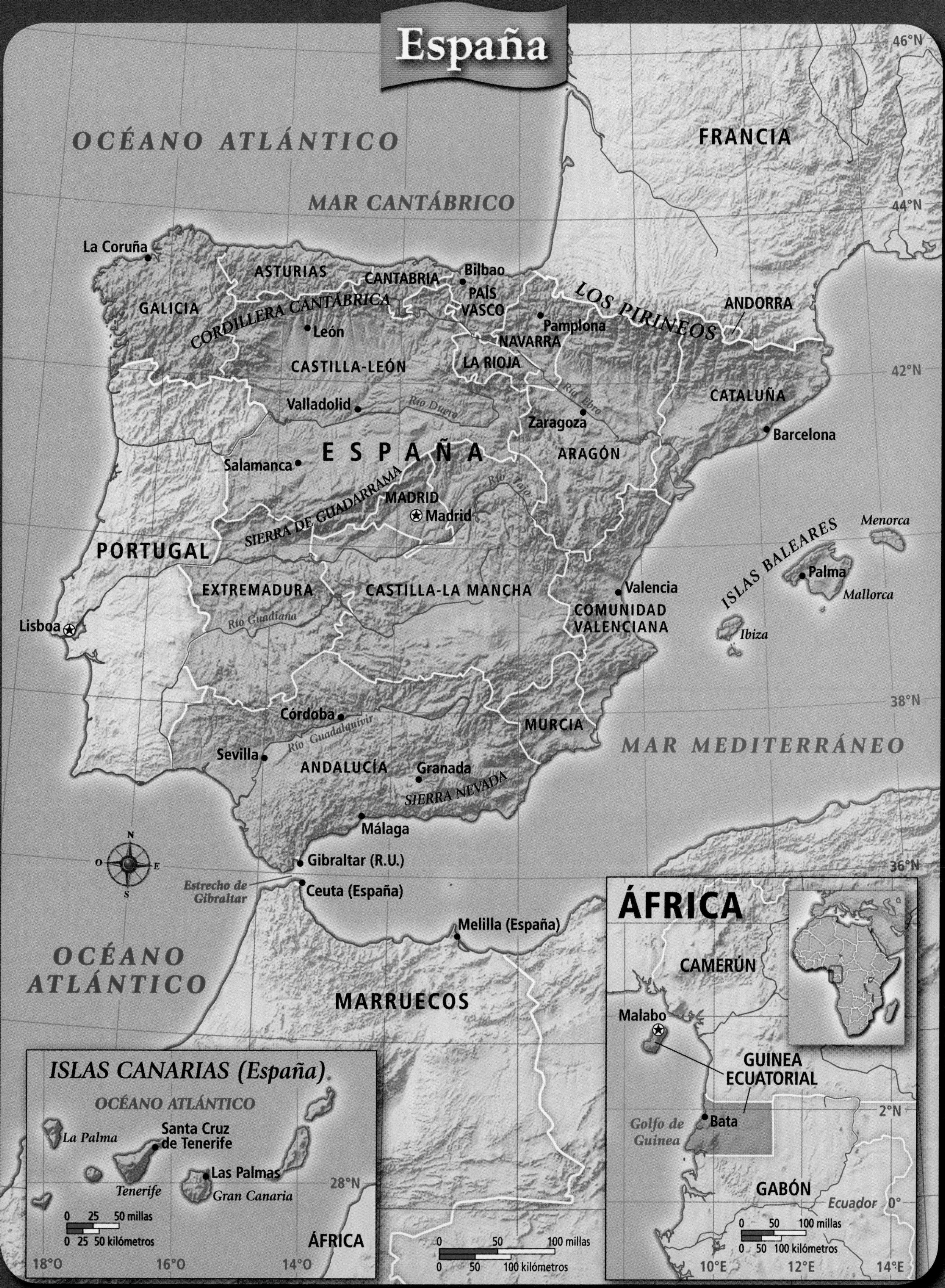

46°N
OCÉANO ATLÁNTICO
FRANCIA
MAR CANTÁBRICO
44°N
La Coruña
ASTURIAS
CANTABRIA
Bilbao
PAÍS VASCO
GALICIA
CORDILLERA CANTÁBRICA
LOS PIRINEOS
ANDORRA
León
Pamplona
NAVARRA
CASTILLA-LEÓN
LA RIOJA
42°N
CATALUÑA
Valladolid
Río Duero
Río Ebro
Zaragoza
Barcelona
ESPAÑA
ARAGÓN
Salamanca
SIERRA DE GUADARRAMA
MADRID
Madrid
Río Tajo
Menorca
ISLAS BALEARES
PORTUGAL
Palma
Mallorca
Valencia
EXTREMADURA
CASTILLA-LA MANCHA
COMUNIDAD VALENCIANA
Río Guadiana
Lisboa
Ibiza
38°N
Córdoba
MURCIA
MAR MEDITERRÁNEO
Sevilla
Río Guadalquivir
ANDALUCÍA
Granada
SIERRA NEVADA
Málaga
N
O
E
S
Gibraltar (R.U.)
36°N
Estrecho de Gibraltar
Ceuta (España)
Melilla (España)
OCÉANO ATLÁNTICO
MARRUECOS
0 50 100 millas
0 50 100 kilómetros
ISLAS CANARIAS (España)
OCÉANO ATLÁNTICO
La Palma
Santa Cruz de Tenerife
Las Palmas
Tenerife
Gran Canaria
28°N
0 25 50 millas
0 25 50 kilómetros
ÁFRICA
18°O
16°O
14°O
ÁFRICA
CAMERÚN
Malabo
GUINEA ECUATORIAL
Golfo de Guinea
Bata
2°N
GABÓN
Ecuador 0°
0 50 100 millas
0 50 100 kilómetros
10°E
12°E
14°E

Las celebraciones

The following lessons about holidays are provided for your personal enjoyment. You may choose to read them on your own, or your teacher may present them throughout the year.

Countries in the Spanish-speaking world often share the same celebrations and holidays. The celebrations are a result of a long history of traditions that reflect the mix of primarily Spanish, indigenous, and African cultures. Holidays celebrating religious events and beliefs are often similar between countries. Other holidays commemorate events or people that are important to a particular region. Many holidays, though celebrated on the same day, have traditions and customs that differ between countries.

As you read the pages of Celebraciones, you will discover how the Spanish-speaking world celebrates important holidays and how they compare to your own traditions.

Contenido

Feria de Málaga

Objectives

- Provide background for the topic: Feria de Málaga
- Familiarize students with the origin of the Feria de Málaga and its traditions.

Presentation Strategies

20-minute lesson

- Ask students to locate Spain and Málaga on a map.
- Have students read the pages about Feria de Málaga.
- Have small groups discuss the Comparación cultural questions.

50-minute lesson

- Complete 20-minute lesson.
- Have students preview the pictures to identify ways Feria de Málaga is celebrated. (music, food, dancing, rides)
- Introduce the Vocabulario para celebrar and pronounce the English and Spanish terms.
- Ask students to use math to determine how many years ago Ferdinand and Isabella entered Málaga. (Subtract 1487 from the present year.)
- Ask the groups to summarize their discussions for the class.

STANDARDS

2.1 Practices and perspectives
2.2 Products and perspectives
4.2 Compare cultures

Connections

Social Studies

Use a world map or map of the Mediterranean area (pp. xxxviii–xxxix, xliii).

- Help students locate the country of Spain and the city of Málaga on the map, pointing out that Málaga is a coastal city on the Mediterranean Sea.
- Tell students that Málaga is the capital city of the province (similar to an American state) also named Málaga.
- Explain that Málaga is an important port city. Encourage students to investigate the goods exported from and imported to the city.

News + Networking

FERIA DE MÁLAGA

La Feria de Málaga celebrates King Ferdinand and Queen Isabella's triumphant entrance into the coastal city of Málaga on August 19, 1487. The pair claimed the city for the crown of Castile, an event this Spanish city has been celebrating for over 500 years. The *Feria de Málaga* now lasts for nine days and takes place in two parts of the city. Each day at noon the downtown fills with fairgoers. In the *Real,* a separate fairground, participants in *flamenco* dress or riding clothes ride on horseback or in horse-drawn carriages, or stroll, in a tradition known as *el paseo.* This daytime *feria* unfolds against a backdrop of music, singing, and dancing and ends at 6:00 p.m., when everyone goes home to rest. The celebration starts again at night in the *Real* and continues into the early morning hours. For this nightly *feria,* people gather in public and private *casetas,* to enjoy concerts, theatrical presentations, music, dance, and food. The last night of the *feria* ends with a city-sponsored concert followed by a spectacular fireworks display.

Feria de caballos More than a thousand riders and over a hundred horse-drawn carriages and carts participate in *el paseo.*

Música callejera Musicians play in the streets during the *feria.* Here a *panda,* or group, plays *verdiales,* traditional music that features guitars, tambourines, and tiny cymbals.

Bridging Cultures

Heritage Language Learners

Regional Variations Some words in this mini-lesson have multiple or regional meanings. For example, **feria** can mean *small change* in Mexico and *tip* or *gratuity* in Central America. Help students identify the meaning of the word as used in the mini-lesson by providing several context sentences in which they insert the word. Do this for words such as **real** and **feria.**

English Learners

Increase Interaction Many of the English terms in the lesson may be unfamiliar to students. Encourage groups to find or draw pictures to illustrate the terms. Have them post each picture on a card and write the English term it illustrates. Have students work with partners to review the vocabulary using the cards.

CULTURA Interactiva my.hrw.com *See these pages come alive!*

Una entrada a la feria Riders pass in front of one of the decorative entrances to a street in the historic downtown of Málaga.

Una caseta offers free samples of *paella,* a rice and seafood dish that is a regional specialty from the coastal cities of Spain.

Bailando flamenco Fairgoers perform folkloric dances such as *flamenco* and *sevillanas* in the streets, plazas, and *casetas,* wherever there is music.

Vocabulario para celebrar

los caballos	horses
las carretas	horse-drawn carriages
las casetas	small houses or tents
la feria	fair
el paseo	a walk, stroll, or ride

Comparación cultural

1. Does your town or city celebrate its beginnings or inauguration as a community, or is there a special "town day"? What events take place during the celebration?
2. What events in your community or region are similar to those of the *Feria de Málaga?* Describe them and then compare them to the *Feria de Málaga.*

Enrichment

Arts and Crafts

Entranceway Decoration Have students examine the photograph of the entranceway on page C3. Tell students to imagine they are on a committee in charge of designing an entranceway for a holiday and a city of their choosing. Have them work in small groups to create the design. Have them post their designs on a bulletin board.

Music

Sevillanas and Flamenco Play traditional sevillanas or flamenco music and have students describe the music. You might arrange for a video demonstration of these folk dances. Encourage students to learn several steps and perform them as you play the music.

Feria de Málaga

Culture

About the Photos

Entranceway Encourage students to analyze the left-hand photograph on page C3. Point out that the entranceway depicts important parts of the culture of Málaga. Encourage students to list soccer ball, fans, guitar, fish, and flowers and relate them to the culture. Point out the name Picasso. If necessary, explain that Picasso was one of the most important artists of the 1900s. Ask students to infer why Picasso would be mentioned on the entranceway and to do research to verify their inference. (Picasso was a native son of Málaga, born on October 25, 1881.)

Gratis Have students read the sign in the top, right-hand photograph and the caption. Have students find, share, and compare recipes for paella. Explain that there are many variations on the recipe but most include seafood and rice.

Comparación cultural

Possible Answers

1. Students' communities may not celebrate their own historical beginnings, but they may have a special community festival each year or celebrate a national holiday. Encourage students to compare these celebrations to the Feria de Málaga. Students are likely to identify music and food as activities common to both celebrations.
2. The events may include parades, street festivals, carnivals, musical performances, and street dances.

Día de la Independencia

Objectives

- Provide background for the topic: Día de la Independencia.
- Familiarize students with Independence Day celebrations in Latin American countries.

Presentation Strategies

20-minute lesson

- Use a map to locate Mexico, the Central American countries, and Chile.
- Have students read aloud the pages about Día de la Independencia.
- Conduct a class discussion of the Comparación cultural questions.

50-minute lesson

- Complete 20-minute lesson.
- Display the national flags or pictures of the flags of the countries identified in the lesson. Encourage students to note similarities and differences in the flags.
- Have students reenact the commemoration activity of the Mexican president. Students might also role-play the president giving an Independence Day speech.

STANDARDS

2.1 Practices and perspectives
3.1 Knowledge of other disciplines
4.2 Compare cultures

News Networking

Día de la Independencia

El Día de la Independencia falls in September for many of the Spanish-speaking countries in the Americas. Mexico celebrates on September 15 and 16, with the *Grito de la Independencia,* music, fireworks, and parades. The first *Grito* occurred at dawn on September 16, 1810, when Padre Miguel Hidalgo y Costilla called to the people of Dolores to rise up against the Spanish crown. That rebellion led to the Mexican War of Independence.

Just two days later, on September 18, 1810, Chile declared its independence from Spain. Today Chile celebrates the date during a week of *fiestas patrias* that include parades, rodeos, dance competitions, and special foods.

Eleven years later, on September 15, 1821, a large part of Central America also proclaimed its independence from Spain, becoming El Salvador, Nicaragua, Guatemala, Costa Rica, and Honduras. These countries celebrate their independence on the 14 and 15 with a focus on students: parades, assemblies, and sports competitions.

México

El Grito de la Independencia On the night of September 15, the president of Mexico commemorates *el Grito* by ringing a bell, proclaiming *¡Que viva México!*, and waving the Mexican flag from a balcony above the Zócalo. Crowds gather below to participate in the *Grito*.

Bridging Cultures

Heritage Language Learners

Support What They Know Students may have participated in independence celebrations themselves or their family members may recall celebrations in their homeland. Encourage students to share their experiences to enrich the cultural understandings of all students. They might share songs, costumes, dance steps, or traditional foods.

English Learners

Increase Interaction Have partners of differing abilities read the mini-lesson together. The more proficient student can read the lesson aloud in English and summarize it in simpler language. A student might also provide a summary in Spanish. He or she might ask the English learner questions about the reading and have him or her answer them in simple English.

CULTURA Interactiva my.hrw.com *See these pages come alive!*

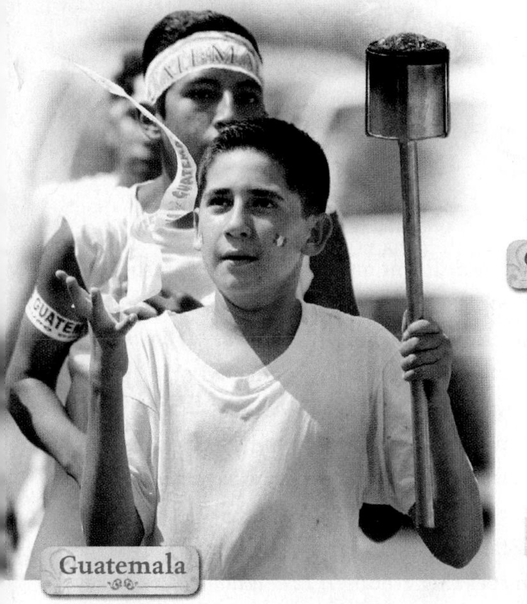

Guatemala

El recorrido de la antorcha Runners carrying a flaming torch start in Guatemala and end in Costa Rica. All along the route, uniformed schoolchildren wait expectantly for the torch to pass.

Fiestas patrias Costa Rican schoolchildren, dressed in colors of their country, dance in a parade.

Costa Rica

Vocabulario para celebrar

la antorcha	torch
la banda	band
las fiestas patrias	patriotic holidays
el grito	shout
el recorrido	run, journey
proclamar	to declare

Comparación cultural

1. Compare the way your town or city celebrates Independence Day with the celebrations in Mexico and Central America. How are they similar? Are there any differences?
2. How do you celebrate Independence Day? Do you participate in community events or have a special tradition?

Día de la Independencia

Culture

About the Photos

Mexico Explain that on the morning of September 16, 1810, Miguel Hidalgo rang the church bell to gather the people of Dolores, Mexico, together. He then called on the people to rebel against the Spanish, who ruled Mexico. Ask students why the president of Mexico rings a bell as part of today's independence celebration.

Guatemala Ask why the torch is carried from Guatemala to Costa Rica as part of the independence celebration.

Costa Rica Have students read the caption and study the picture to help them identify the colors of the national flag of Costa Rica. (red, white, and blue)

Enrichment

Timeline

Sequencing Independence Have students research information about the independence efforts of the countries mentioned in the mini-lesson as well as the United States. They can then make a timeline identifying important dates leading up to independence. For example, Mexico called for independence in 1810 but did not gain it until 1821. Both of these dates would be placed on the timeline.

Music

National Anthem Every nation has a national anthem that reflects the history or culture of the nation. Assign each country to a pair of students. Have students find the lyrics and music for the country's national anthem. Ask them to research the history of the anthem—its origins or what it stands for. Have students present their research and play or sing the national anthem.

Comparación cultural

Possible Answers

1. Students may find more similarities in activities such as parades, dances, and fireworks than differences in activities, such as student competitions or rodeos.
2. Students may suggest family events such as picnics or community events such as parades or fireworks.

Objectives

- Familiarize students with the origin of El 12 de Octubre and the differing ways people celebrate the holiday.
- Trace the route of Columbus's first voyage.

Presentation Strategies

20-minute lesson

- Ask students to locate Spain, the Canary Islands, Cuba, and Hispaniola on a map.
- Have students read the pages about El 12 de Octubre.
- Discuss the Comparación cultural questions as a class.

50-minute lesson

- Complete 20-minute lesson plan.
- Have students note the different names for October 12 celebrations. Discuss why different cultures might view the holiday differently.
- Introduce the Vocabulario para celebrar and pronounce the English and Spanish terms.
- Have students work in groups to develop a map showing Columbus' route, labeling the indigenous groups who lived in each location he visited.

STANDARDS

2.1 Practices and perspectives
4.2 Compare cultures

Connections

Social Studies

Columbian Exchange Encourage students to research information about the exchange of goods, people, and ideas that resulted from Columbus' arrival in the Americas and Spanish colonization.

- Provide examples of foods found in the Americas that were previously unknown in the rest of the world: chocolate, sweet potatoes, white potatoes, corn, peanuts, hot peppers, and tomatoes.
- Identify examples of plants and animals introduced in the Americas as part of the Columbian Exchange: wheat, rice, cattle, horses, and bees. Talk about how horses changed the lives of some Native Americans on the Plains.

El 12 de Octubre

El 12 de Octubre has many different meanings in the Spanish-speaking world. For some people it is *el Día de Colón,* the day Christopher Columbus arrived in the Americas. For some, it is *el Día de la Hispanidad,* a day to celebrate one's connection with all other Spanish-speaking people, regardless of their country. And for others, it is *el Día de la Raza,* a day when indigenous people come together as a community and celebrate their heritage. Other Spanish speakers celebrate their mixed heritage of indigenous, African, and European cultures. How you celebrate depends very much on you and your family's origin and on the community where you live. For all Spanish-speaking groups, *el 12 de octubre* marks a key turning point in the lives and cultures of the people in Spain and those living in the Americas.

Vocabulario para celebrar

Cristóbal Colón	Christopher Columbus
el Día Nacional	National Day
la hispanidad	the cultural community of Spanish speakers
la raza	race

Día de la Raza Indigenous groups gather in Mexico City dressed in their community's traditional outfits, some wearing pre-Columbian clothing and headdresses.

Bridging Cultures

Heritage Language Learners

Regional Variations Encourage students to consider reasons for the different views of October 12. For many indigenous people, it signaled the end of their traditional way of life. For others, it meant the pursuit of riches and opportunity. Have students identify and list the different names of the holiday in different places. Encourage them to give the English and Spanish translation of the holiday names.

English Learners

Provide Comprehensible Input English terms such as *indigenous* in the lesson may be unfamiliar to many students. Have students skim the lesson for words that are unfamiliar to them. They can make a chart giving the word, a dictionary pronunciation, and a definition. Have students refer to the chart as they read.

CULTURA Interactiva my.hrw.com *See these pages come alive!*

Chile

Día de la Raza A woman from the Pehuenche indigenous community gathers with other indigenous groups in downtown Santiago.

Nueva York

Día de la Hispanidad High school students carry flags representing all the American countries as they march in a parade down Fifth Avenue.

España

Día Nacional de España The Spanish government celebrates with a parade in Madrid.

Comparación cultural

1. How do you celebrate October 12 in your community or school? Is it similar to or different from the celebrations in Spanish-speaking countries? How so?
2. What does October 12 mean to you? Which of the Spanish names for the holiday has the most meaning for you? How would you rename the holiday to celebrate your heritage?

Culture

About the Photos

Have students note the names of the celebrations in each place. All celebrate the same day but focus on different meanings to the communities.

México Ask students which photograph shows someone in pre-Columbian costume.

Nueva York Ask students to identify the nations represented by the flags carried by the students.

Chile Ask why different indigenous groups might meet to celebrate their own identities.

Enrichment

Language Arts

Columbus Day Poetry Have students locate and read poems about Christopher Columbus and 1492. One classic poem is *In 1492*. Another is Emma Lazarus's poem *1492*. Help students read and summarize the poems. Have them compare and contrast the viewpoints of the poems.

Timeline and Maps

Columbian Voyages Columbus returned to the Americas three times after the first voyage. Ask students to draw a timeline and a map showing events related to Columbus' explorations.

Comparación cultural

Possible Answers

1. Celebrations may depend on students' heritage and cultural identity. Some communities may host parades and festivals; others may not plan any special activities.
2. Students should provide reasons for their preferences, which may be based on their heritage or personal identity. Their renaming of the holiday should reflect their opinion about the Columbian Exchange.

Objectives

- Familiarize students with Día de los Muertos celebrations in Mexico, the United States, Central America, and South America.
- Locate Mexico, the United States, Guatemala, and Ecuador on a map.

Presentation Strategies
20-minute lesson

- Use a map to locate the United States, Mexico, Guatemala, and Ecuador.
- Have students read aloud the pages about Día de los Muertos, including the picture captions.
- Conduct a class discussion of the Comparación cultural questions.

50-minute lesson

- Complete 20-minute lesson.
- Pronounce the Vocabulario para celebrar and ask students to use the terms in sentences about Día de los Muertos.
- Use a Venn diagram to compare and contrast Día de los Muertos celebrations from different nations or to compare and contrast Halloween and Día de los Muertos celebrations.

STANDARDS

2.1 Practices and perspectives
4.2 Compare cultures

Long-term Retention

Critical Thinking

Many Latino families have immigrated to the United States and no longer live close to the cemeteries and gravesites of their deceased family members. Ask students how these families might honor deceased family members if they cannot visit the gravesites to leave flowers.

News Networking

¡Día de los Muertos!

Estados Unidos

Las mojigangas People parade through the Pilsen-Little Village neighborhood of Chicago. Some carry *mojigangas*, giant papier-mâché puppets typically carried in Mexican processions.

On Día de los Muertos families visit the cemeteries and gravesites of their loved ones. They clean the sites and leave flowers and candles and, in many countries, they bring entire meals with special drinks and traditional breads to share with the deceased. Displays are set up next to the gravesite that include flowers, hand-crafted skeletons, colorful paper cutouts, candy skulls, personal items, and photos. Family members pass the night sharing food and conversation as they keep vigil for their ancestors.

The celebration of *Día de los Muertos* spans two days, November 1 and 2. Also known as *Día de los Difuntos*, the traditions originate in the centuries-old religious holiday *Día de Todos los Santos*. In the Americas, this holiday coincided with pre-Columbian festivals that celebrated the harvest, the new year, and honored the dead. The mix of cultures and traditions resulted in the celebration *Día de los Muertos*.

México

Las calaveras A display of dressed-up skulls and skeletons on a street in Mexico City

Bridging Cultures

Heritage Language Learners

Support What They Know Some families may associate deep religious meaning with Día de los Muertos whereas others enjoy it as a time for festivities. Encourage students to respect the differences. Suggest that students ask their families how Día de los Muertos was celebrated in their homelands. Discuss the similarities and differences in the way it is celebrated by families here.

English Learners

Provide Comprehensible Input Have a native English-speaking student tape record the lesson. Be sure he or she records the picture captions, vocabulary, and questions, as well as the paragraphs. Play the tape for students, stopping at the end of each paragraph. Ask students to verbally summarize the paragraph.

Cultura Interactiva my.hrw.com *See these pages come alive!*

¡Día de los Muertos!

Ecuador

El pan de muertos This bread is made only for *Día de los Muertos*. In Ecuador, these breads are called *guaguas de pan*. *Guagua* is the Quechua word for "baby" and refers to the bread's shape. The *guaguas* are served with *colada morada,* a warm, purple-colored drink made from blueberries and raspberries.

México

El papel picado These tissue paper cutouts are a common holiday decoration. To celebrate *Día de los Muertos,* the cutouts form images of skeletons.

Guatemala

Los barriletes Guatemalans celebrate by flying *barriletes,* or colorful kites, to which they attach messages for the deceased. The town of Santiago Sacatepéquez celebrates with a *barrilete* contest.

Vocabulario para celebrar

las calaveras	skulls
el cementerio	cemetery
los difuntos	deceased
el esqueleto	skeleton
el pan de muertos	special bread made for *Día de los Muertos*
el papel picado	paper cutouts
los santos	saints

Comparación cultural

1. Does your family or community have a special day or specific traditions to remember the deceased? How are they similar to or different from the traditions of *Día de los Muertos*?
2. Centuries ago in Europe, the night of October 31, before All Saint's Day, was known as "All Hallows Eve." According to ancient beliefs, on this night the dead join the world of the living. Today we call this night Halloween. How would you compare the celebrations of Halloween and *Día de los Muertos*?

Culture

About the Photos

Estados Unidos Find Chicago on a map of the United States. Point out that the Pilsen-Little Village section of the city has a large immigrant Latino population. Ask students to discuss why immigrants tend to move to the same neighborhoods.

México Encourage students to observe and comment on the fact that the skulls and skeletons shown on page C8 look friendly, rather than frightening.

Ecuador Tell students that Quechua is a native language spoken in Peru, Argentina, Bolivia, Chile, and Ecuador.

Guatemala Point out the city name Santiago Sacatepéquez on the kite in the foreground. Then ask students to identify the other word on the kite and its meaning. (paz meaning "peace") Ask why this might be a good word for a Día de los Muertos celebration.

Enrichment

Arts and Crafts

El pan de muertos Have students use molding clay rather than bread dough to fashion **guaguas de pan**. They can use the handle end of a paintbrush to carve designs into the clay. They can also use paints to draw faces and other details for the **guaguas de pan**. Alternatively, students might make paper cutouts of skeletons.

Projects

Family Have every student choose a deceased ancestor to commemorate. Ask students to write a brief biography of the individual. If photographs are available, a student could include those in the biography. Ask the student to plan a way to remember the individual through a **Día de los Muertos** activity.

Comparación cultural

Possible Answers

1. The traditions for remembering deceased loved ones may differ from culture to culture or family to family.
2. Students may find that in many places Halloween celebrations no longer relate to the original meaning of the holiday. Many Día de los Muertos celebrations continue to emphasize the traditional meanings and purpose of the holiday.

Objectives
- Familiarize students with the differing ways people celebrate las Navidades.
- Identify foods enjoyed during the holiday.
- Locate the countries mentioned on a map.

Presentation Strategies
20-minute lesson
- Ask students to locate the countries of Mexico, Panama, Peru, Argentina, Dominican Republic, Paraguay, and Spain.
- Have students read pp. C10–C11.
- Have students discuss the Comparación cultural questions in pairs.

50-minute lesson
- Complete 20-minute lesson plan.
- Have students summarize the content.
- Ask students to find these cities on a map: Panama City, Panama; Oaxaca, Mexico; Buenos Aires, Argentina; Madrid, Spain.
- Introduce the Vocabulario para celebrar and discuss the meaning of the terms.
- Have students list the foods identified in the text. Ask them to describe the foods.
- Ask a member from each pair to summarize their discussion.

STANDARDS
2.1 Practices and perspectives
2.2 Products and perspectives
4.2 Compare cultures

Connections
Language Arts
An **idiom** is a phrase or sentence with a meaning that does not have exactly the same meaning as the individual words. Write the phrase **contar muchas navidades** (to count many Christmases) on the board. Discuss the meaning of the individual words. Then discuss the meaning of the phrase (to be old). Encourage students to keep a log of English and Spanish idioms.

News Networking

Las Navidades

Las Navidades are celebrated throughout the Spanish-speaking world with family gatherings and special meals. Celebrations start in mid-December and, in some countries, extend to January 6.

Many families gather the night of December 24, or *la Nochebuena,* to share a special meal of traditional foods and drinks that vary depending on the country. *Tamales, empanadas,* and *buñuelos* are served in many countries. In Spain, there is turkey, or *pavo,* and *turrón.* In Argentina and Chile, where it is summer, people eat cold foods and salads.

The tradition of giving and receiving gifts also forms a part of *las Navidades.* In some countries, families exchange gifts at midnight on *la Nochebuena,* while in others children receive gifts the morning of December 25, and in other countries the gifts appear the morning of January 6. Often gifts are given primarily to children.

Panamá

Un desfile navideño The holiday parade in Panama City takes place in mid-December.

México

La noche de rábanos On the night of December 23, elaborate carvings made from radishes, or *rábanos,* are on display in Oaxaca's central plaza. The figures include people, animals, and even entire scenes. This unique tradition has been celebrated for over 100 years.

Argentina

Las empanadas Dancers dress as *empanadas* in Buenos Aires. These meat-filled pies are especially enjoyed during *las Navidades.*

Bridging Cultures

English Learners
Increase Interaction Have students learning English read the pages with an English-speaking student. Ask the pair to construct several true/false questions that they can use to quiz other students on lesson content. Pairs can take turns asking and answering each other's questions.

Heritage Language Learners
Support What They Know Encourage students to talk about Las Navidades celebrations. Have them ask family or friends whether the way the holidays are celebrated here differ from the way they are celebrated in their country of origin. Talk about reasons why people might adapt their celebrations when they move to a new place.

CULTURA Interactiva my.hrw.com *See these pages come alive!*

Perú

El Día de los Reyes Magos In Peru and in many other Spanish-speaking countries, Argentina, the Dominican Republic, Paraguay, and Spain, children receive presents on January 6 from *los Reyes Magos*. In anticipation, children leave out a snack for the Three Kings, carrots or grass for the camels, and a pair of empty shoes for the gifts.

España

Un desfile navideño Circus elephants take part in Madrid's holiday parade on January 5. In Spain, parades on January 5 or 6 celebrate the arrival of *los Reyes Magos*.

Vocabulario para celebrar

la Nochebuena	Christmas Eve
los Reyes Magos	Three Kings
la rosca de reyes	sweet bread eaten on January 6
el turrón	almond nougat candy
los villancicos	seasonal Christmas songs

Comparación cultural

1. Do you and your family celebrate a holiday in December? If so, compare the traditions of your family to the traditions of *las Navidades*.
2. What special meals and foods do you associate with certain holidays? Describe the foods you traditionally enjoy on a holiday you celebrate.
3. What time of the year do you give or receive gifts and for what reason?

Enrichment

Arts and Crafts

Piñatas The tradition of **las posadas** is a strong one in many Mexican communities. Each evening from December 16 through December 24, families gather at a different neighbor's home for a party. Each party ends with the breaking of a piñata. Although traditionally made from pottery, piñatas today may be papier-mâché covered in crepe paper. Have groups of students make piñatas.

Food

Holiday Drinks As part of the holidays, some Mexican families prepare special drinks. These include **rompope** (eggnog), **chocolate caliente** (hot chocolate), and spicy cider. Ask students to find a recipe for Mexican hot chocolate. Work with students to prepare the beverage in class. Provide cups so students can enjoy the tasty drink.

Culture

About the Photos

Panamá Help students use context to conclude that the Spanish word **desfile** has the same meaning as the English word *parade*.

México Point out that the radishes carved are much larger than the little red radishes found in the grocery store.

Argentina In Argentina, empanadas are pastries that may be filled with ground beef, olives, onions, eggs, and raisins. They might also be filled with other meats, cheese, tuna, corn, or spinach. There are also dessert empanadas.

Perú According to tradition, the Three Kings followed a star to bring gifts to a newborn child. Children receive gifts on January 6 from the kings in memory of this event.

España Children and other onlookers watch a circus elephant perform during the parade that celebrates the arrival of the Three Kings.

Comparación cultural

Possible Answers

1. Many families celebrate religious and nonreligious holidays in December. Christmas is on December 25. Hanukah occurs in December, and Eid al-Adha can fall in December too. Kwanzaa, an African American holiday, begins on December 26.
2. Students may associate specific foods with specific holidays, such as turkey and Thanksgiving. Encourage students to name at least three foods and tell when they enjoy them.
3. Students may exchange gifts on birthdays, at New Year, or on other special days. Some students may not have gift-giving traditions.

Objectives

- Familiarize students with Año Nuevo celebrations.
- Locate on a map the countries featured in the lesson.

Presentation Strategies

20-minute lesson

- Use a map to locate Peru, Spain, Colombia, and Guatemala.
- Have small groups read pages C12–C13 and respond to the Comparación cultural questions.

50-minute lesson

- Complete 20-minute lesson.
- Review the vocabulary in the Vocabulario para celebrar and ask students to pronounce and define the terms.
- Ask students to present summaries of the group discussion to the class and tally the number of individuals who participate in each kind of celebration mentioned.

STANDARDS

2.1 Practices and perspectives
4.2 Compare cultures

Long-term Retention

Critical Thinking

Different cultures have different traditional calendars. For example, the Chinese calendar is a lunar calendar and the New Year begins sometime between January 19 and February 21. Yet, most Chinese as well as other people celebrate the January 1 New Year holiday. Ask students why it is important for countries around the world to use the same calendar.

News Networking

¡Año Nuevo!

Perú

La buena suerte In Lima, people believe touching a Chinese Lion brings happiness, good luck, and prosperity in the New Year. Ten percent of Peru's population is of Chinese descent.

El Año Nuevo celebrates the arrival of the New Year and *la Nochevieja* says goodbye to the old. In much of the Spanish-speaking world, traditions include making a toast, exchanging a kiss or hug, or eating twelve grapes—one for each stroke of midnight—to ensure your wishes come true for the New Year. Other good luck traditions include wearing yellow or red, eating a tablespoon of lentils, or carrying a suitcase around the block if you hope to take a trip. To wish someone a happy New Year, say *¡Feliz año nuevo!* or *¡Próspero año nuevo!*

On *Nochevieja,* there are also traditions for saying goodbye to the old year. Some people dress in masks representing *el año viejo.* Others build satirical figures called *los años viejos* that represent famous people or politicians. Adorned with poems or messages that poke fun at *el año viejo,* and filled with shavings and firecrackers, these figures are lit on fire at midnight, to burn and explode on street corners, as a final *despedida,* or farewell, to the old year.

España

La medianoche In Madrid, people gather in the Puerta del Sol, holding bags of 12 grapes as they wait for the 12 strokes of midnight from the Puerta del Sol clock, the city's official timekeeper.

Bridging Cultures

Heritage Language Learners

Regional Variations Spanish has several ways of saying New Year's Eve. **La noche vieja, la víspera de año nuevo,** and **noche de uvas** all mean *New Year's Eve.* Have students find out from their families their most common way of referring to New Year's Eve.

English Learners

Build Background English learners may find it helpful to record Spanish terms with their English meanings that are not defined in Vocabulario para celebrar. Suggest that they alphabetize the Spanish terms. They can use the log to find the English meaning of Spanish terms easily.

Cultura Interactiva my.hrw.com *See these pages come alive!*

Colombia

Paseo de los años viejos In Popayán, families and neighbors take their *año viejo* figures out for a final ride before the *Nochevieja* celebration. Later on, at midnight, they will burn the figures.

Guatemala

Baile de los Gigantes In Antigua, people celebrate the New Year with the folkloric "Dance of the Giants." These giant heads, or *cabezudos,* are similar to costumes used since the medieval period in Spain.

Vocabulario para celebrar

el Año Nuevo	New Year
el brindis	toast
las doce uvas	twelve grapes
las lentejas	lentils
la medianoche	midnight
la Nochevieja	New Year's Eve

Comparación cultural

1. How do you celebrate the New Year? Does your family or community have any special traditions? Are any of the traditions similar to the ones in Spanish-speaking countries? How are they similar or different?
2. If you were to build an *año viejo* representing the past year, what figure or event would you portray? Explain your choice.

Culture

About the Photos

Perú Lima is Peru's capital city. It is located just off the Pacific Coast. Have students locate Lima on a map of Peru.

España Puerta del Sol is in the middle of historic Madrid. Prominently displayed there is a statue of an upright bear eating fruit from a tree.

Colombia Popayán is located south of Cali. Have students find this colonial town on a map of Colombia. An earthquake in the 1980s destroyed much of its historic architecture.

Guatemala For about 200 years until the late 1770s, Antigua served as the seat of Spanish government in Central America. This city sits in the shadow of an extinct volcano, west of the present-day capital city Guatemala City. Have students find the city on a map of Guatemala.

Enrichment

Social Studies

Current Events Have students choose a nation and do research to find out what current events took place in the past year. Have students write a brief description of one of the events. Ask them to draw satirical figures of the people involved in the events. Post their written descriptions and drawings on a bulletin board.

Music

Holiday Songfest Encourage students to find English and Spanish lyrics to the well-known New Year song "Auld Lang Syne." Discuss the meaning of the lyrics. Then help students learn the song in both Spanish and English. They can perform both versions for another class.

Comparación cultural

Possible Answers

1. Students should identify New Year's celebrations that they have participated in or observed. They might use a Venn diagram to compare and contrast celebrations.
2. Students' responses should identify the figure or event and cite reasons for their choices.

Objectives
- Familiarize students with Carnaval and its varied celebrations.
- Identify the traditional meaning of Carnaval and when it is held.

Presentation Strategies
20-minute lesson
- Ask students to find the Canary Islands, Paraguay, Mexico, Bolivia, and Colombia on a map.
- Read pages C14–C15 and discuss the photographs.
- Assign the Comparación cultural questions as homework.

50-minute lesson
- Complete 20-minute lesson.
- Introduce the Vocabulario para celebrar, pronounce the terms, and discuss their meanings.
- Discuss the word origin of **carnaval** and identify words in English and Spanish with the same origin.
- Have groups of students discuss the Comparación cultural questions. Students might use a Venn diagram to compare holidays.

STANDARDS
2.1 Practices and perspectives
2.2 Products and perspectives
4.2 Compare cultures

Connections
Social Studies
Help students find the Canary Islands off the coast of northwestern Africa. Also have students locate the islands in relationship to the mainland of Spain.

News Networking

¡Carnaval!

Carnaval marks a period of festivity prior to the beginning of Lent. Lent was, and for some still is, a 40-day period of solemnity and fasting with the removal of meat from the diet being a key feature. You can see the word *carne* (meat) in *Carnaval*; traditionally, this was the last chance to eat meat before the Lenten fast. Today, *Carnaval* often resembles a lively, multi-day party.

Falling in either February or March, *Carnaval* is typically celebrated during the five days that precede Ash Wednesday, the first day of Lent. In some countries, *Carnaval* lasts longer, overlapping other local celebrations. In many regions, traditions such as throwing water and eggs can start over a month before the actual holiday. The planning for the next year's parades, parties, and dance groups often starts as soon as the current *Carnaval* ends!

España

Disfraces Elaborate costumes are central to the *Carnaval* celebration. This costume, entitled "África soy yo," appeared in Las Palmas, in the Canary Islands.

Carnaval Revelers dance in Encarnación, site of the largest celebration in Paraguay.

Paraguay

Bridging Cultures

Heritage Language Learners
Support What They Know **Carnaval** is derived from the Latin words meaning removal of meat. Many Spanish and English words include the base *carn-* meaning *flesh* or *meat.* Encourage students to list Spanish and English words with this base. For example, the Spanish word **carnicería** means *butcher shop* and the English word *carnivore* means *an animal that eats meat.*

English Learners
Increase Interaction Many terms in this lesson may be unfamiliar to English learners. Have students work with native English-speaking partners. Together they can identify, pronounce, and define terms such as *solemnity, typically,* and *current,* that may present problems for English learners.

CULTURA Interactiva my.hrw.com *See these pages come alive!*

México

Cascarones Breaking *cascarones* on the heads of friends and other party-goers is a *Carnaval* tradition. The sprinkling of confetti from these hollowed-out eggs is said to bring good luck, as seen here in Mazatlán.

Bolivia

Máscaras are a *Carnaval* tradition dating back to medieval Spain. This masked dancer is from the parade in Oruro, where some 40,000 folkloric dancers and musicians participate.

Bailarines folklóricos Dancers from the Mestizaje dance group perform in Barranquilla. The Colombian government proclaimed this city's *Carnaval* celebration, which combines indigenous, African, and European traditions, a National Cultural Heritage. UNESCO declared it a "Masterpiece" for its cultural uniqueness.

Colombia

Vocabulario para celebrar

los bailarines	dancers
la banda	musical band
Carnaval	Carnival
los cascarones	confetti-filled eggs
el disfraz	costume
las máscaras	masks

Comparación cultural

1. The ways in which *Carnaval* is celebrated in the Spanish-speaking world differ depending on the region. Why do you think the celebrations have evolved differently?
2. Compare the traditions of *Carnaval* to any holiday that you celebrate. Which one(s) are similar? How are they similar?

Culture

About the Photos

España Ask students to translate the name of the costume **África soy yo.** Encourage discussion of what these words mean and why the costume was given this name.
Paraguay Encarnación is in southeastern Paraguay. It was founded in the early 1600s as a mission. Its Carnaval features parades, dancing, and a king and queen of the festival.
México Mazatlán is a popular Carnaval destination in Mexico. The celebration there even features a literary contest.
Bolivia In addition to parades, water fights are a popular Carnaval activity in Oruro. Spectators can join the dance groups in the parade.
Colombia Barranquilla in northern Colombia has a Carnaval filled with dancing, music, and theater that displays its diverse cultural heritage.

Enrichment

Arts and Crafts

Los cascarones Have students make their own cascarones with adult supervision. First they make a hole in an egg, shake out its contents, and use hot water to wash the egg, inside and out. Be sure they wash their hands thoroughly afterwards. They can use paints, wax pencils, glitter, and other supplies to decorate the eggs, fill them with confetti and tissue paper to seal them.

Research

UNESCO UNESCO is an acronym for United Nations Educational, Scientific, and Cultural Organization. Have students do research focused on this agency of the United Nations. Ask them to identify its goals and its history.

Comparación cultural

Possible Answers

1. The different ways of celebrating **Carnaval** may have evolved because of the different cultural heritage of the people.
2. Students should name a specific holiday that they or their community celebrates. They might use a chart to identify the celebrations that are similar to and different from **Carnaval** festivities.

Objective
- Familiarize students with an unusual holiday celebration in Valencia, Spain.

Presentation Strategies
20-minute lesson
- Locate Valencia on a map of Spain.
- Have students take turns reading aloud paragraphs in the lesson.
- Discuss the Comparación cultural questions in small groups.

50-minute lesson
- Complete 20-minute lesson.
- Review the vocabulary in the Vocabulario para celebrar, asking students to pronounce and define the terms.
- Discuss the text, photographs, and captions.
- Have a volunteer from each group summarize its discussion for the class.

STANDARDS
2.1 Practices and perspectives
2.2 Products and perspectives
4.2 Compare cultures

Long-term Retention

Critical Thinking
Fireworks, firecrackers, and bonfires are important parts of the **Las Fallas** celebration. This presents serious risks to the city. Ask students how they think the community protects the buildings and people from potential damage. What steps do they think firefighters and other safety personnel take to help protect the people and the buildings of Valencia?

News + Networking

Las Fallas

Las Fallas is a weeklong festival in March that engulfs the city of Valencia, Spain. Tens of thousands of visitors from all over the world come to the city to experience *Las Fallas,* a week of pageants, music, flowers, and creative displays. Each day, the deafening explosions of thousands of firecrackers, *la mascletà,* fills the city at 2:00 p.m. and each night's celebration ends in fireworks.

The main characters of the celebration are the *ninots,* gigantic figures built of wood, plaster, and cardboard. The largest are up to several stories tall. Neighborhood organizations build these enormous figures during the preceding year. Then, during the week of *Las Fallas,* they display them in intersections, parks, and plazas throughout the city. The public visits the more than 400 *fallas* and votes for their favorite one. On the last night at midnight, all but the favorite are burned in enormous bonfires. Then one final, brilliant display of fireworks explodes over the city.

Los ninots These gigantic figures poke fun at well-known people or current events from the preceding year.

Las falleras During the festival, women dress in traditional outfits that include lace dresses, veils, jewelry, and colorful sashes.

Bridging Cultures

Heritage Language Learners
Support What They Know Although **Las Fallas** is a well-known celebration throughout Spain, it is unique to Valencia. Ask students to discuss with family members any celebrations in their homelands that may be unusual or unique. Provide time for students to give a brief summary of the celebration.

English Learners
Increase Interaction English learners may benefit from reading the lesson in small groups. Encourage group members to read the paragraphs aloud, stopping to summarize sentences or to define terms as they read.

CULTURA Interactiva my.hrw.com See these pages come alive!

Las Fallas

La Cremà At midnight on the last night, the *fallas* are burned throughout the city. At the same time there are huge displays of colorful fireworks, which include explosions of roman candles and thousands of firecrackers.

Una falla iluminada Thousands of visitors come at night to see the illuminated *fallas.* This display was entered into a special contest, *la Sección Especial,* where a committee judges the *fallas* for creativity, gracefulness and charm, originality, and lighting.

Vocabulario para celebrar

La Cremà	burning of the *fallas*
las fallas	displays of figures
los falleros	celebrants of *Las Fallas*
los fuegos artificiales	fireworks
la mascletà	rhythmic explosion of large and small firecrackers
los ninots	large papier-mâché figures
quemar	to burn

Comparación cultural

1. Fireworks are a major part of *Las Fallas*. Does your community or region have fireworks displays? When and for what reasons?
2. Are there any other traditions in the festival of *Las Fallas* that are similar to traditions you follow in your community? What are they? Are they part of a specific celebration or season?

Culture

Expanded Information

Ninots The ninots are built by groups throughout Valencia. Many take up to six months to build and cost thousands of dollars. Most **ninots** are burned on the last day of **Las Fallas.** Those that have won prizes are the last to be burned. Only the favorite ninot is saved from destruction. It is displayed in a museum.

Mascletà The **mascletà** takes place every day at two in the afternoon. Firecrackers of different sizes are exploded in a plaza.

Celebration **Las Fallas** festivities include processions, concerts, dances, and street vendors.

Enrichment

Social Studies

Travel Arrangements Valencia, Spain's third largest city, is visited by thousands during the **Las Fallas** festival. Encourage students to find out about hotel accommodations and travel arrangements for a visit to Valencia in March for the festival. Have them prepare a brochure that an agent might use to promote the festival and discuss travel arrangements.

Arts and Crafts

Ninots and Fallas Have small groups of students brainstorm lists of past or present public celebrities. Ask each group to use cardboard and other art materials to make a ninot of one or more of the personalities on their list. They can create a scene in which to place their ninots as well. Have each group present its display to the class.

Comparación cultural

Possible Answers

1. Students may identify holidays such as July 4 and New Year's Day as days in which communities have fireworks displays.
2. Traditions that might be similar to those from **Las Fallas** will vary depending on the celebrations in the students' community.

Objectives

- Familiarize students with Semana Santa.
- Identify ways people in different countries celebrate Semana Santa.

Presentation Strategies

20-minute lesson

- Ask students to find Mexico, Ecuador, Peru, and El Salvador on a map.
- Have students read pp. C18–C19 together.
- Discuss the Comparación cultural questions.

50-minute lesson

- Complete 20-minute lesson.
- Discuss the photographs on pp. C18-C19.
- Introduce the Vocabulario para celebrar, pronounce the terms, and discuss their meanings.
- Discuss cognates such as **las procesiones** and *processions*.

STANDARDS

2.1 Practices and perspectives
2.2 Products and perspectives
4.2 Compare cultures

Long-term Retention

Critical Thinking

Summarize Have students work in pairs to write brief summaries of the reading and photo captions. Have them include as many Spanish words as possible.

News Networking

Semana Santa

La Semana Santa is one holiday during the year where in most Spanish-speaking countries entire towns, businesses, schools, and government close for at least four days, Thursday through Sunday. People that have relocated to other places often go back to their hometowns. Others take advantage of the long break to go to the countryside or beach. Entire communities come together for *Semana Santa* celebrations. In some places, religious processions fill the streets each day of the week from Palm Sunday to Easter; in others, Thursday and Friday are the most important days. Most *Semana Santa* traditions are hundreds of years old and originated in Spain, but many now have a unique twist due to the mix of cultures in each country.

Vestidos blancos Girls from San Miguel de Allende dress in white for the procession on *Viernes Santo.* In this town, the celebrations extend for two weeks, ending on *el Domingo de Pascua* with an explosion of papier-mâché figures in the center of town.

Alfombras de aserrín Rugs traditionally made of colored sawdust or sand, flowers, and fruits cover the streets where processions will pass in San Salvador. Artisans also now use modern industrial paints and sprays.

Bridging Cultures

Heritage Language Learners

Support What They Know For many people, **Semana Santa** is the most important religious holiday of the year. As students discuss their family traditions, remind them of the importance of respecting all religious and nonreligious observances of the week.

English Learners

Build Background The words **procesiones** and *processions* are cognates. Both the Spanish and the English terms are derived from Latin roots. Encourage students to identify any other related cognates. Remind them that knowing cognates can help them understand the meaning of the words in both languages.

CULTURA Interactiva my.hrw.com *See these pages come alive!*

Perú

Decoraciones de flores Flowers fill the city of Tarma for the *Semana Santa* celebrations. In preparation for the processions that begin on Thursday, arches and rugs made of flowers decorate the streets and remain on display until Sunday.

Ecuador

La fanesca Ecuadorians eat *fanesca,* a bean and grain soup with a fish base, only during *Semana Santa.* The soup is traditionally served with *bolitas de harina* (fritters), *plátano verde* (fried green plantain), fresh cheese, and *ají,* a spicy sauce.

Vocabulario para celebrar	
las alfombras	rugs
las flores	flowers
las procesiones	processions
Semana Santa	Holy Week

México

Una procesión Young boys carry streamers during the processions in Cadereyta.

Comparación cultural

1. What holidays do you celebrate with special parades or processions? What kinds of decorations do people use?
2. In what kind of event would most of the people in your community participate? Compare the event to *Semana Santa.*

Enrichment

Arts and Crafts

Carpets of Flowers or Sand Have students examine the sand and flower carpets shown in the pictures. Encourage students to design a pattern for their own sand or flower carpet to reflect a holiday of their choice. They can sketch their design, showing the colors they would use. If they have colored sand or can make paper flowers, they may wish to make a minirug of their design.

Foods

Fried Green Plantains With adult supervision, students can easily make fried green plantains. They simply peel and slice green plantains, which are similar to bananas. They then fry the plantains in a pan until golden; carefully remove and smash the plantains, sprinkle them with salt, and refry them until they are crispy. They should drain the plantains and let them cool before eating.

Culture

About the Photos

México Throughout Mexico, girls in white dresses are among those who participate in processions on Good Friday. Boys carry streamers in a street parade as part of the Holy Week celebration.
El Salvador Artisans spend many hours making the detailed sand and flower rugs for the streets of Sonsonate, a city west of the national capital San Salvador.
Perú Tarma is a town northeast of Lima. The carpets of flowers are roped off so that people do not walk on them.
Ecuador Ecuadorian **fanesca** has a cod-based broth and is full of vegetables including corn, cabbage, beans, peas, and squash. It is garnished with hard-boiled eggs and grated cheese.

Comparación cultural

Possible Answers

1. Students may mention a variety of holidays such as Labor Day, Thanksgiving Day, and Fourth of July that include parades. Decorations include flags, banners, and flowers.
2. Different communities have different festivities or community activities. These may include food sampling festivities, carnivals, street sales, heritage days, or national celebrations. Some celebrations may be primarily religious as with Semana Santa and others may be non-religious or neighborhood celebrations.

News Networking

¡Cinco de Mayo!

Cinco de Mayo has become a popular celebration thoughout the United States. However, not everyone who celebrates this uniquely Mexican holiday knows its origin. To find the reason, you must travel back to the year 1862 in Mexico. On May 5, in the town of Puebla de los Ángeles, the Mexican army, joined by farmers and townspeople, fought against the French and forced them to retreat. The Mexicans were led by General Ignacio Zaragoza and the town was later renamed Puebla de Zaragoza in his honor. Although the French went on to occupy Mexico City and assume a short-lived role in Mexico's government, *Cinco de Mayo* became a national holiday symbolizing Mexican unity.

A *Cinco de Mayo* celebration in Mexico includes dancing, music, and reenactments of the battle. In many parts of the U.S. where there is a large Mexican or Mexican-American community, you will often find *Cinco de Mayo* celebrations.

Mariachis y bailarines Folkloric dancers and musicians perform throughout the day in the Plaza Olvera during the *Cinco de Mayo* celebrations.

Objectives

- Familiarize students with Cinco de Mayo.
- Differentiate Cinco de Mayo from Mexican independence celebrations.
- Identify Cinco de Mayo celebrations in the United States.

Presentation Strategies

20-minute lesson

- Remind students that Mexican independence is celebrated in September.
- Locate Puebla, Mexico; Los Angeles; and Washington, D.C., on a map.
- Read the lesson and discuss the holiday.
- Discuss the Comparación cultural questions in small groups.

50-minute lesson

- Complete 20-minute lesson.
- Review the vocabulary in the Vocabulario para celebrar.
- Discuss the text, photographs, and captions.
- Ask groups to summarize their discussions of the Comparación cultural questions for the class.

STANDARDS

2.1 Practices and perspectives
3.1 Knowledge of other disciplines
4.2 Compare cultures

Long-term Retention

Critical Thinking

Discuss reenactments as a means of commemorating events. How do reenactments differ from other kinds of celebrations? How are reenactments like plays? Would people involved in reenactments have to rehearse? Explain.

Bridging Cultures

Heritage Language Learners

Family Celebrations Encourage students of Mexican descent to discuss Cinco de Mayo celebrations with their families. Is the holiday celebrated in their hometowns in Mexico? If so, how? Students can share their findings with the class. Encourage students to bring in photographs, programs, or costumes of past Cinco de Mayo celebrations to share with the class.

English Learners

Increase Interaction Pair English learners with native English-speaking students. Have them read pp. C20–C21 aloud, alternating after every few sentences. Encourage English learners to correct their own pronunciation and to use their partner's pronunciation as a model.

CULTURA Interactiva my.hrw.com *See these pages come alive!*

México

Reconstrucción de la batalla A reenactment of the historic battle in Puebla commemorates Mexico's victory over the French.

Vocabulario para celebrar

los bailarines	dancers
la batalla	battle
el ejército	army
los franceses	French
los músicos	musicians
la reconstrucción	reenactment

Washington, D.C.

Bailarín folklórico A dancer performs in a traditional Mexican costume at the White House.

Comparación cultural

1. Do you know of a *Cinco de Mayo* celebration in your community or region? If so, how or where is it celebrated?
2. What important battles or historic events are celebrated in your community or state? How are they celebrated? Are they local or national holidays? Compare one of these holiday celebrations with the *Cinco de Mayo* celebrations.

¡Cinco de Mayo!

Culture

About the Photos

Los Ángeles Los Angeles, California, is the second largest city in the United States. It is home to a large Latino population. Plaza Olvera is part of Olvera Street, a historic section of Los Angeles.

México Puebla is southeast of Mexico City, the national capital. The May 5th celebration commemorates the defeat of the French army by the Mexican army. Despite the victory, the French went on to rule Mexico for a time. The French finally withdrew in 1867.

Washington, D.C. Cinco de Mayo celebrations take place around the United States, which has a large Mexican American population. It is a celebration of freedom that all can enjoy.

Enrichment

Social Studies

Cinco de Mayo in the News Have students prepare news reports detailing the events of Cinco de Mayo, 1862, in Puebla, Mexico. The news reports should provide background information as well as information about the Mexican victory. Students can present their reports in a modern television documentary format. Encourage them to use drawings and maps to visually support the report.

Arts and Crafts

Folk Dance Invite Mexican folk dancers to perform for the class. If possible, ask a member of the troupe to teach the students a simple dance routine. Students can practice and perform the dance for other classes.

Comparación cultural

Possible Answers

1. Cinco de Mayo celebrations include parades and theatrical performances. Large cities and even schools may have Cinco de Mayo events.
2. Celebrations of historic events in much of the United States are celebrated with parades, memorial services, fireworks, concerts, and more. Different communities celebrate community and national events in different ways.

Objectives

- Familiarize students with Inti Raymi.
- Differentiate between summer and winter solstices.

Presentation Strategies
20-minute lesson

- Locate Peru, Ecuador, and Bolivia on a world map or globe. Trace the equator and identify the Northern and Southern hemispheres.
- Have students take turns reading aloud pages C22–C23.
- Have groups of students discuss the Comparación cultural questions.

50-minute lesson

- Complete 20-minute lesson.
- Review the Vocabulario para celebrar.
- Discuss the summer and winter solstices and when they occur in the Northern and Southern hemispheres.
- Ask group representatives to present their group's answers to the class.

STANDARDS

2.1 Practices and perspectives
4.2 Compare cultures

News Networking

Inti Raymi

Inti Raymi, or the "Festival of the Sun," falls on June 21 or 22, the date of the southern hemisphere's winter solstice, the shortest day of the year. Indigenous communities throughout the Andean highland countries of South America celebrate the winter solstice with ceremonies designed to bring the Sun back and shorten the longest night. Incan in origin, *Inti Raymi* honored the sun as the source of light, heat, and life, and celebrated the start of a new planting season. The name *Inti Raymi* comes from the Quechua language: *inti* means "sun" and *raymi* means "festival." The largest festival takes place in Cuzco, Peru, the ancient capital of the Incan civilization and empire. In Cuzco, *Inti Raymi* has grown into a major tourist attraction. Thousands of people visit the city to enjoy the performances by folkloric groups and to watch the theatrical presentation of the Incan ceremony, the focal point of the celebration.

Perú

Presentación cultural de Inti Raymi In Cuzco, professional actors and actresses interpret the roles of the Incan emperor and others. *Above:* A woman carries offerings. *Right:* The Incan emperor passes through the streets of Cuzco to the ruins of the Incan fortress, Sacsayhuaman.

C22 Celebraciones

Bridging Cultures

Heritage Language Learners

Support What They Know The **Inti Raymi** celebration began as an Incan holiday. Have students with family members from South America ask about celebrations of the summer or winter solstice. Together students can make a chart identifying nations that celebrate the solstice and the types of celebrations enjoyed.

Heritage Language Learners

Indigenous Languages Both Spanish and Quechua are official languages of Peru. Although Quechua is spoken in Ecuador, it is not an official language. In Bolivia, Spanish, Quechua, and Aymara are official languages. Have students find out what languages family members from South and Central America speak. Do they speak an indigenous language as well as Spanish?

Cultura Interactiva my.hrw.com See these pages come alive!

Ecuador

Indígenas ecuatorianas A dance group from the Paktarinmi cultural organization forms a "sacred circle" with grains of corn, a pre-Incan rite. In Ecuador, which lies on the equator, this date is considered the summer solstice, rather than the winter.

Vocabulario para celebrar

el aymara	language of indigenous group from Bolivia and Peru
los incas	Incas, an ancient South American people
el quechua	language common to many South American indigenous groups and adopted and spread by Incas
el sol	sun

Bolivia

Los aymaras In the pre-Columbian ruins of Tihuanaku, an Aymara priest blows on a shell to celebrate the winter solstice, which marks the new year. The Aymara are one of two dominant indigenous groups in Bolivia, comprising 25 percent of the population. The other group, Quechua, makes up 30 percent.

Comparación cultural

1. In North America, June 21 is the summer solstice, or the longest day of the year, and December 21 is the winter solstice, or the shortest day of the year. What important holidays or events occur during this time of year?
2. In ancient civilizations, the appearance of the sun and moon were important events that helped mark the passing of time and the seasons. If you were to celebrate the winter or summer solstice, what would you include in your celebration?

Connections

Science

The different seasons of the year exist due to the tilt of the earth. In the Southern Hemisphere, the winter solstice is in June and the summer solstice is in December. When it is the winter solstice in the Southern Hemisphere, it is the summer solstice in the Northern Hemisphere. Have students note Ecuador's position in relationship to the equator. Discuss why Ecuadorians consider the June solstice their summer solstice.

Culture

About the Photos

Peru, Ecuador, and Bolivia were all part of the Inca empire.

Perú The fortress of Sacsayhuaman was largely destroyed by the Spanish. Its ruins with stones expertly fit closely together illustrate the building skills of the Incas.

Ecuador The equator runs through the capital city of Quito, Ecuador. The name of the country is the Spanish word for equator.

Bolivia Once ruled by the Aymara people, Bolivia became part of the Inca empire in the 1400s.

Enrichment

Science

Seasonal Changes Have students use drawings or models to demonstrate the solstices and equinoxes in the Southern Hemisphere. Have them provide an explanation of what happens on those days including facts such as the number of hours of sunlight.

Foods

Quinoa Have students make a quinoa salad. Quinoa is an ancient Peruvian grain. If quinoa is not available in an ethnic food store, substitute rice or another grain. To make the salad, seed and chop a jalapeño pepper, peel and chop a cucumber, and dice a tomato. Add these to four cups of the cooked grain. Add fresh mint as well. Make a salad dressing of olive oil, lime juice, and salt and pepper.

Comparación cultural

Possible Answers

1. Many communities enjoy winter festivals in December. Many holidays take place in late December, such as the African American celebration of Kwanzaa.
2. Students may identify seasonal outdoor objects, such as flowers, lightning bugs, snow, and ice, with the solstices. They should name the items and explain how they would use them.

Objectives

- Provide biographical data on Simón Bolívar.
- Familiarize students with Día de Simón Bolívar.

Presentation Strategies
20-minute lesson

- Read pages C24–C25.
- Identify the present-day nations of South America that made up Gran Colombia.
- Locate Venezuela, Panama, Colombia, Ecuador, Bolivia, and Peru on a map.
- Conduct a class discussion of the Comparación cultural questions.

50-minute lesson

- Complete 20-minute lesson.
- Review the vocabulary in the Vocabulario para celebrar.
- Identify the meaning of **el libertador** and explain why Simón Bolívar was called el Libertador.
- Discuss the text, photographs, and captions.

STANDARDS

2.1 Practices and perspectives
2.2 Products and perspectives
3.1 Knowledge of other disciplines
4.2 Compare cultures

Long-term Retention

Critical Thinking

Have students identify the historical leaders who are on the American one dollar (George Washington), five dollar (Abraham Lincoln), ten dollar (Alexander Hamilton), and twenty dollar (Andrew Jackson) bills. Then remind students who is depicted on the Venezuelan currency. Why are these people depicted on the money? What does it show about their contribution to the nation? Which leaders do you think are most like Simón Bolívar? Why?

News Networking

Día de Simón Bolívar

Simón Bolívar, known as *El Libertador,* envisioned a united South America, a union for which he fought, but never attained. Despite this, he was instrumental in bringing about much of South America's independence from Spain and became one of its most revered leaders. His birthday is a national holiday in Venezuela, Ecuador, and Bolivia, and many cities and towns have plazas or monuments in his honor.

Born on July 24, 1783, in Caracas, Venezuela, Simón Bolívar strongly believed in freedom from Spanish rule and worked toward that goal as a political leader, writer, and military commander. With his troops, he liberated present-day Venezuela, then Colombia. He was then named president of Gran Colombia, a federation comprised of what is now Venezuela, Colombia, Panama, and Ecuador. He went on to lead his troops into Peru, aiding in the final defeat of Spain. For two more years, Bolívar maintained his leadership, writing the constitution of Bolivia, a country named in his honor. By 1827, his dream of unification dissolved amidst growing rivalries between the South American military leaders. Three years later Bolívar died, on December 17, 1830.

Colombia

Monumento a Simón Bolívar This monument marks the location of the Battle of Boyacá, where Bolívar's forces defeated the Spanish resulting in the liberation of Gran Colombia. To celebrate the anniversary of the battle, students form the colors of the Colombian flag.

Bolívares Venezuela's currency carries both Bolívar's name and image.

Venezuela

Bridging Cultures

Heritage Language Learners

Support What They Know Students with South American roots might ask family members whether they celebrated Simón Bolívar Day as children. Encourage them to identify ways the day was celebrated.

English Learners

Increase Interaction Have students proficient in English read the pages with English learners. Encourage students to summarize each paragraph and caption in simple terms. Students should consult a dictionary when necessary to understand the meaning of terms such as *instrumental, amidst, crucial,* and *commemorates.*

Cultura Interactiva
my.hrw.com
See these pages come alive!

Ecuador

Líder de la Batalla de Pichincha Each year, the city of Quito commemorates the Battle of Pichincha, where Simón Bolívar sent troops under the command of Antonio José de Sucre to defeat the Spanish in one of the crucial battles in the fight for independence.

Simón Bolívar ***(1830), José Gil de Castro*** José Gil de Castro, renowned painter of Chilean society and of the independence leaders, painted this portrait of Bolívar in the early 1800s.

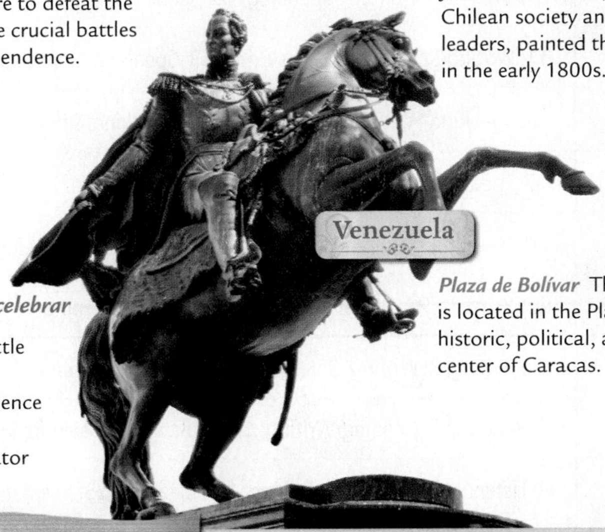

Venezuela

Plaza de Bolívar This statue of Bolívar is located in the Plaza Bolívar, the historic, political, and commercial center of Caracas.

Vocabulario para celebrar

la batalla battle
la independencia independence
El Libertador the liberator

Comparación cultural

1. What famous leader in U.S. history would you compare with Simón Bolívar? Why? What do both leaders have in common?
2. What U.S. holidays are in honor of famous leaders? How are they celebrated? What other ways do we honor our important leaders?

Culture

About the Photos

Colombia The Battle of Boyacá took place on August 7, 1819. It was a great victory for the independence movement.
Ecuador Antonio José de Sucre defeated the Spanish near Quito on May 24, 1822. He later served as Bolivia's first president.
Simón Bolívar (1830) José Gil de Castro also painted two other great South American liberators—Bernardo O'Higgins of Chile and José de San Martín of Argentina.
Venezuela In addition to the statue of Simón Bolívar in the center of the plaza, the Bolívar Plaza has statues in each of its four corners that represent the nations once part of Gran Colombia.

Enrichment

Arts and Crafts

Simón Bolívar Have students use clay or papier-mâché to make a miniature statue of Simón Bolívar. Alternatively, they might use markers or paints to do a portrait of the leader.

Timeline

Independence Many Central and South American nations gained their independence in the 1800s. Have students make a list of all the Central and South American nations and record their dates of independence. Students should then arrange the nations on a timeline to show the sequence of independence.

Comparación cultural

Possible Answers

1. Answers may vary, but students are likely to compare Simón Bolívar with George Washington. Both leaders commanded armed forces to help their countries gain freedom, and both served as presidents of new American nations.
2. Students might mention such holidays as Presidents' Day and Martin Luther King, Jr., Day. Celebrations include memorial services, speeches, and parades. Other ways of honoring leaders include writing and reading books about them and making movies about them.

Lesson Overview

Culture at a Glance

Topic & Activity	Essential Question
¡Hola! p. C26	How do Spanish-speaking people living in New York City celebrate their culture?
A mural in New York, p. 9	How can artists give back to their neighborhood through their work?

Practice at a Glance

	Objective	Activity & Skill
Vocabulary	Greetings	1: Reading; 2: Writing; 3: Speaking; 4: Reading; 5: Reading/Writing; 6: Speaking; 7: Speaking; Repaso 1: Listening/Speaking; Repaso 4: Writing
	Alphabet	8: Listening/Writing; 9: Speaking; 10: Speaking
	Countries	11: Writing/Speaking; 12: Speaking; 13: Speaking; Repaso 3: Writing
	Numbers from 0 to 10	14: Speaking/Writing; 15: Speaking; 16: Speaking; Repaso 3: Writing
	Days of the week	17: Speaking/Writing; 18: Listening; 19: Speaking
	Weather expressions	20: Listening; 21: Speaking; 22: Speaking; Repaso 2: Writing
	Classroom commands	23: Reading; 24: Writing/Speaking; Repaso 1: Listening
Communication	Greet people and say goodbye	1: Reading; 2: Writing; 3: Speaking; Repaso 1: Listening; Repaso 2: Writing
	Introduce yourself and others	4: Reading; 5: Reading/Writing; 6: Speaking; 7: Speaking; Repaso 2: Writing
	Ask and say how to spell names	8: Listening/Writing; 9: Speaking; 10: Speaking; 25: Speaking
	Say where you are from	11: Writing/Speaking; 12: Speaking; 13: Speaking; 22: Speaking; Repaso 3: Writing
	Exchange phone numbers	15: Speaking; 16: Speaking; Repaso 3: Writing; Repaso 4: Writing
	Say what day of the week it is	17: Speaking/Writing; 18: Listening; 19: Speaking; 25:Speaking
	Describe the weather	20: Listening; 21: Speaking; 22: Speaking; Repaso 2: Writing
	Respond to classroom instructions	23: Reading; 24: Writing/Speaking
	Pronunciation: The letter **h**	**Pronunciación: La letra h,** p. 5: Listening/Speaking
	Pronunciation: The vowels	**Pronunciación: Las vocales,** p. 11: Listening/Speaking

The following presentations are recorded in the Audio Program for ¡Avancemos!

- **¡A responder!** *pages 3, 7, 10, 13, 16, 18, 20, 23*
- **8: Lista** *page 11*
- **18: ¿Lógico o ilógico?** *page 19*
- **20: El tiempo** *page 21*
- **Repaso de la lección** *page 26*
  1: Listen and Understand

¡A responder!

TXT CD 1 track 2 page 3

1. Buenos días.
2. Hasta mañana.
3. Adiós.
4. ¿Qué tal?
5. Buenas tardes.
6. ¡Hasta luego!

TXT CD 1 track 5 page 7

1. Te presento a Sonia.
2. Hola. Me llamo Ricardo.
3. Me llamo Carolina. ¿Y tú?
4. Le presento a la señora Vargas.

TXT CD 1 track 7 page 10

1. ele
2. e
3. jota
4. eñe
5. pe
6. i
7. hache
8. be grande

TXT CD 1 track 11 page 13

1. Es de Costa Rica.
2. Es de Puerto Rico.
3. Es de Argentina.
4. Es de España.
5. Es de Ecuador.
6. Es de la República Dominicana.

TXT CD 1 track 13 page 16

a. ocho
b. cinco
c. nueve
d. seis
e. cuatro
f. uno
g. diez
h. siete

TXT CD 1 track 15 page 18

1. martes
2. domingo
3. lunes
4. miércoles
5. sábado
6. jueves

For **¡AvanzaRap!** scripts, see the **¡AvanzaRap! DVD.**

TXT CD 1 track 18 page 20

1. Hace viento.
2. Nieva.
3. Hace sol.
4. Llueve.
5. Hace frío.
6. Hace calor.

TXT CD 1 track 21 page 23

1. Abran los libros en la página 10.
2. Levanten la mano.
3. Cierren los libros.
4. Repitan: "buenos días".
5. Saquen una hoja de papel.

8 | Lista **TXT CD 1 track 8**

1. equis, i, eme, e, ene, a
2. ge, u, i, ele, ele, e, ere, eme, o
3. a, ele, e, jota, a, ene, de, ere, o
4. i griega, o, ele, a, ene, de, a
5. be grande, e, a, te, ere, i, zeta
6. jota, o, ese, e, efe, i, ene, a
7. hache, u, ge, o
8. te, o, eñe, o

18 | ¿Lógico o ilógico? **TXT CD 1 track 16**

1. Hoy es martes. Mañana es miércoles.
2. Hoy es jueves. Mañana es sábado.
3. Hoy es lunes. Mañana es viernes.
4. Hoy es sábado. Mañana es domingo.
5. Hoy es miércoles. Mañana es jueves.
6. Hoy es viernes. Mañana es martes.

20 | El tiempo **TXT CD 1 track 19**

1. Hace sol.
2. Llueve.
3. Hace viento.
4. Nieva.

Repaso de la lección **TXT CD 1 track 22**

1. Listen and understand

1. Te presento a Victoria. Es de España.
2. ¿Cómo se llama usted?
   Me llamo Rodrigo León.
   ¿Cuál es su número de teléfono?
   Cinco - dos - tres - siete - uno - nueve - cero.
3. Abran los libros en la página ocho.
4. Buenos días, señor. ¿Cómo está usted?

Resource List

Everything you need to ...

Plan

TEACHER ONE STOP

✓Lesson Plans
✓Teacher Resources
✓Audio and Video

Present

INTERACTIVE WHITEBOARD LESSONS

TEACHER ONE STOP WITH PROJECTABLE TRANSPARENCIES

POWER PRESENTATIONS

ANIMATEDGRAMMAR

Assess

ONLINE ASSESSMENT

✓ Assessments for on-level, modified, pre-AP, and heritage learners
✓ Create customized tests with the **Examview Assessment Suite**
✓ **performance space**
✓ *Generate Success* Rubric Generator

Print

Plan	Practice
URB 1 • Video Scripts p. 97 **Best Practices Toolkit**	**Differentiated Assessment Program** • *¡AvanzaCómics! SuperBruno y Nati,* Episodio 1 **URB 1** • Back-to-School Resources pp. 1–24 • Audio Scripts pp. 101–102

Projectable Transparencies (Teacher One Stop, my.hrw.com)

Culture	Classroom Management
• Atlas Maps 1–6	• Warm up Transparencies 22–25 • Student Book Answer Transparencies 34–45

Audio and Video

Audio	Video	¡AvanzaRap! DVD
• Student Book Audio CD 1 Tracks 1–22 • Heritage Learners Audio CD 3 Tracks 1–2 • Assessment Audio CD 1 Tracks 1–2 • Sing-along Songs Audio CD	• *Telehistoria Prólogo* DVD 1	• Video animations of all **¡AvanzaRap!** songs (with Karaoke track) • Interactive DVD Activities • Teaching Suggestions • **¡AvanzaRap!** Activity Masters • **¡AvanzaRap!** video scripts and answers

Online and Media Resources

Student	Teacher
Available online at my.hrw.com • Online Student Edition • News Networking • performance space • @HOMETUTOR • CULTURA Interactiva • WebQuests • Interactive Flashcards • Review Games • Self-Check Quiz **Student One Stop** **Holt McDougal Spanish Apps**	**Teacher One Stop (also available at my.hrw.com)** • Interactive Teacher's Edition • All print, audio, and video resources • Projectable Transparencies • Lesson Plans • TPRS • Examview Assessment Suite **Available online at my.hrw.com** *Generate Success* Rubric Generator and Graphic Organizers **Power Presentations**

Differentiated Assessment

On-level	Modified	Pre-AP	Heritage Learners
• On-level Preliminary Lesson Test pp. 1–6	• Preliminary Modified Lesson Test pp. 1–6	• Preliminary Pre-AP Lesson Test pp. 1–6	• Heritage Learners Diagnostic Test pp. 1–6 • Heritage Learners Preliminary Lesson Test pp. 7–12

Core Pacing Guide

50 Minute (9 Day)

	Objectives/Focus	Teach	Practice	Assess/HW Options
DAY 1	**Culture:** learn about the culture of Spanish-speaking people in New York City • Learn about greetings **5 min**	Lesson Opener pp. 0–1 **Hola, ¿qué tal?** pp. 2–5 • Read A–H • Play audio TXT CD 1 track 1 • *¡A responder!* TXT CD 1 track 2 • *Nota: ¿Cómo estás?* • *Pronunciación* TXT CD 1 track 3 **20 min**	**Hola, ¿qué tal?** pp. 2–5 • Acts. 1, 2, 3 **20 min**	**Assess:** *Para y piensa* p. 5 **5 min**
DAY 2	Learn about introductions • Warm Up OHT 22 **5 min**	**¡Mucho gusto!** pp. 6–9 • Read A–G • Play audio TXT CD 1 track 4 • *¡A responder!* TXT CD 1 track 5 • *Nota: ¿Cómo te llamas?* **15 min**	**¡Mucho gusto!** pp. 6–9 • Acts. 4, 5, 6 **20 min**	**Assess:** *Para y piensa* p. 9 **5 min**
DAY 3	Learn how to spell using the Spanish alphabet • Warm Up OHT 22, 23 • Learn how to say where people are from **5 min**	**El abecedario** pp. 10–11 • Read the alphabet • Play audio TXT CD 1 track 6 • *¡A responder!* TXT CD 1 track 7 • *Pronunciación:* TXT CD 1 track 9 **¿De dónde eres?** pp. 12–15 • Play audio TXT CD 1 track 10 • *¡A responder!* TXT CD 1 track 11 • Nota: *Asking questions* **20 min**	**El abecedario** pp. 10–11 • Act. 8 TXT CD 1 track 8 • Acts. 9, 10 **¿De dónde eres?** pp. 12–15 • Acts. 11, 12, 13 **20 min**	**Assess:** *Para y piensa* pp. 11, 15 **5 min**
DAY 4	Learn the numbers 0–10 and exchange phone numbers • Warm Up OHT 23 **5 min**	**Mi número de teléfono** pp. 16–17 • Read p. 16 • Play audio TXT CD 1 track 12 • *¡A responder!* TXT CD 1 track 13 **20 min**	**Mi número de teléfono** pp. 16–17 • Acts. 14, 15, 16 **20 min**	**Assess:** *Para y piensa* p. 17 **5 min**
DAY 5	Learn the days of the week • Warm Up OHT 24 **5 min**	**Los días de la semana** pp. 18–19 • Read A–B • Play audio TXT CD 1 track 14 • *¡A responder!* TXT CD 1 track 15 **15 min**	**Los días de la semana** pp. 18–19 • Acts. 17, 19 • Act. 18 TXT CD 1 track 16 **25 min**	**Assess:** *Para y piensa* p. 19 **5 min**
DAY 6	Learn to describe the weather • Warm Up OHT 24 **5 min**	**¿Qué tiempo hace?** pp. 20–21 • Read A–F • Play audio TXT CD 1 track 17 • *¡A responder!* TXT CD 1 track 18 **15 min**	**¿Qué tiempo hace?** pp. 20–21 • Act. 20 TXT CD 1 track 19 • Acts. 21, 22 **25 min**	**Assess:** *Para y piensa* p. 21 **5 min**
DAY 7	Learn classroom phrases • Warm Up OHT 25 **5 min**	**En la clase** pp. 22–24 • Read pp. 22–23 • Play audio TXT CD 1 track 20 • *¡A responder!* TXT CD 1 track 21 **15 min**	**En la clase** pp. 22–24 • Acts. 23, 24, 25 **25 min**	**Assess:** *Para y piensa* p. 24 **5 min**
DAY 8	**Review:** Lesson review • Warm Up OHT 25 **5 min**	**Repaso de la lección** pp. 26–27 **20 min**	**Repaso de la lección** pp. 26–27 • Act. 1 TXT CD 1 track 22 • Acts. 2, 3, 4 **20 min**	**Assess:** pp. 26–27 **5 min** **Homework:** *En resumen* p. 25
DAY 9	**Assessment**			**Assess:** Preliminary lesson test **50 min**

Core Pacing Guide 90 Minute (5 Day)

	Objectives/Focus	Teach	Practice	Assess/HW Options
DAY 1	**Culture:** learn about the culture of Spanish-speaking people in New York City • Learn about greetings 5 min	Lesson Opener pp. 0–1 **Hola, ¿qué tal?** pp. 2–5 • Read A–H • Play audio TXT CD 1 track 1 • *¡A responder!* TXT CD 1 track 2 • *Nota: ¿Cómo estás?* • *Pronunciación:* TXT CD 1 track 3 **20 min**	**Hola, ¿qué tal?** pp. 2–5 • Acts. 1, 2, 3 **15 min**	**Assess:** *Para y piensa* p. 5 @HomeTutor **5 min**
	Learn about introductions • Warm Up OHT 22 5 min	**¡Mucho gusto!** pp. 6–9 • Read A–G • Play audio TXT CD 1 track 4 • *¡A responder!* TXT CD 1 track 5 • *Nota: ¿Cómo te llamas?* **15 min**	**¡Mucho gusto!** pp. 6–9 • Acts. 4, 5, 6, 7 **20 min**	**Assess:** *Para y piensa* p. 9 **5 min**
DAY 2	Learn how to spell using the Spanish alphabet • Warm Up OHT 22 5 min	**El abecedario** pp. 10–11 • Read the alphabet • Play audio TXT CD 1 track 6 • *¡A responder!* TXT CD 1 track 7 • *Pronunciación:* TXT CD 1 track 9 **15 min**	**El abecedario** pp. 10–11 • Act. 8 TXT CD 1 track 8 • Acts. 9, 10 **15 min**	**Assess:** *Para y piensa* p. 11 **5 min**
	• Learn how to say where people are from 5 min	**¿De dónde eres?** pp. 12–15 • *¡A responder!* TXT CD 1 track 10 **20 min**	**¿De dónde eres?** pp. 12–15 • Acts. 11, 12, 13 **20 min**	**Assess:** *Para y piensa* p. 15 **5 min**
DAY 3	Learn the numbers 0–10 and exchange phone numbers • Warm Up OHT 23 5 min	**Mi número de teléfono** pp. 16–17 • Read p. 16 • Play audio TXT CD 1 track 12 • *¡A responder!* TXT CD 1 track 13 **15 min**	**Mi número de teléfono** pp. 16–17 • Acts. 14, 15, 16 **20 min**	**Assess:** *Para y piensa* p. 17 **5 min**
	Learn the days of the week 5 min	**Los días de la semana** pp. 18–19 • Read A–B • Play audio TXT CD 1 track 14 • *¡A responder!* TXT CD 1 track 15 **15 min**	**Los días de la semana** pp. 18–19 • Acts. 17, 19 • Act. 18 TXT CD 1 track 16 **20 min**	**Assess:** *Para y piensa* p. 19 **5 min**
DAY 4	Learn to describe the weather • Warm Up OHT 24 5 min	**¿Qué tiempo hace?** pp. 20–21 • Read A–F • Play audio TXT CD 1 track 17 • *¡A responder!* TXT CD 1 track 18 **15 min**	**¿Qué tiempo hace?** pp. 20–21 • Act. 20 TXT CD 1 track 19 • Acts. 21, 22 **25 min**	**Assess:** *Para y piensa* p. 21 **5 min**
	Learn classroom phrases 5 min	**En la clase** pp. 22–24 • Read pp. 22–23 • Play audio TXT CD 1 track 20 • *¡A responder!* TXT CD 1 track 21 **5 min**	**En la clase** pp. 22–24 • Acts. 23, 24, 25 **25 min**	**Assess:** *Para y piensa* p. 24 **5 min**
DAY 5	**Review:** Lesson review 5 min	**Repaso de la lección** pp. 26–27 **10 min**	**Repaso de la lección** pp. 26–27 • Act. 1 TXT CD 1 track 22 • Acts. 2, 3, 4 **20 min**	**Assess:** pp. 26–27 **5 min** **Homework:** *En resumen* p. 25
	Assessment **50 min**			**Assess:** Preliminary lesson test

Objectives

- Introduce lesson theme: **¡Hola!**
- **Culture:** Learn about New York City's Hispanic population and its cultural celebrations.

Presentation Strategies

- Ask students to study the photos on this spread, identify the city, and tell what they know about it.
- Ask students to talk about their initial impression of the city. Have them make a list of four important aspects of New York City.
- Have students talk about cultural celebrations in their own area and compare them to those in New York City.

STANDARDS

2.1 Compare practices and perspectives
4.2 Compare cultures

Comparación cultural

Exploring the Theme

Ask the following:

1. Is the architecture of the buildings seen here similar to buildings in your area?
2. Have you ever visited any area with this type of architecture? Do you like these buildings? Why or why not?
3. Think of the parades in the area where you live. What is the occasion for these celebrations? What do the people that participate in the parade wear? What do they do?

LECCIÓN PRELIMINAR

Nueva York

Tema:

¡Hola!

¡AVANZA! **Let's get started**

- greet people and say goodbye
- introduce yourself and others
- ask and say how to spell names
- say where you are from
- exchange phone numbers
- say what day of the week it is
- describe the weather
- respond to classroom instructions

A performer wearing the colors of the Puerto Rican flag

Dominican dancers in colorful costumes

Nueva York New York City has the largest Hispanic population of any city in the nation. During its annual Hispanic Day Parade, colorful floats, bands, costumed dancers, and flags from Spanish-speaking countries fill Fifth Avenue. *What cultural celebrations are there in your area?*

Differentiating Instruction

Multiple Intelligences

Visual Learners Students who are visual learners learn better when provided with visual input: photos, drawings, shapes, colors, etc. Encourage these students to create vocabulary flashcards with drawings, magazine cutouts, or color coding to help them remember the meanings of words.

Heritage Language Learners

Support What They Know Ask Spanish-speaking students to talk about their experiences attending a parade in their country of origin. What was the occasion for the parade? Where and when did it take place? Who participated in the parade? What did the participants wear? What were they doing? Were there floats? Who attended the parade?

DIGITAL SPANISH my.hrw.com
ONLINE STUDENT EDITION with...

- performance space
- News Networking
- @HOMETUTOR
- CULTURA Interactiva

- Audio and Video Resources
- Interactive Flashcards
- Review Activities
- WebQuest
- Conjuguemos.com

PRACTICE SPANISH WITH HOLT MCDOUGAL APPS!

A view of Lower Manhattan from the East River
New York, New York

Differentiating Instruction

English Learners

Build Background Students whose first language is not English may need extra support with the information on these pages. Inform them that New York is very diverse, meaning that people of many different backgrounds live there. Ask students what their images and impressions of this city are.

Slower-paced Learners

Personalize It Have students express their opinions about the photos.

DIGITAL SPANISH

TEACHER TOOLS
- Interactive Whiteboard Lessons
- Generate Success!

ALSO AVAILABLE...
- Online Workbook
- Spanish InterActive Reader

SPANISH ON THE GO!
- Performance Space
- Holt McDougal Spanish Apps
- ¡Avancemos! eTextbook

Using the Photo

Location Information

New York City lies about 100 miles south of Boston at the mouth of the Hudson River with more than eight million residents. It is divided into five boroughs. Most Americans are familiar with their names: the Bronx, Brooklyn, Queens, Staten Island, and Manhattan.

Expanded Information

Spanish-speaking Population Approximately one in eight people in the U.S. is of Latin American origin. New York City has the highest Spanish-speaking population of any U.S. city. Puerto Ricans make up almost 40 percent of the Latin American population in New York City. While Spanish-speaking people in the southwestern part of the U.S. primarily come from Mexico, New York City draws people from Puerto Rico, the Dominican Republic, and other areas of the Caribbean.

¡AVANZA! **Objectives**
- Present vocabulary: greetings and saying goodbye.
- Check for recognition.

Core Resource
- Audio Program TXT CD 1 tracks 1, 2

Presentation Strategies
- Tell students that the ¡Avanza! sets the goals for each segment and that the Para y piensa is a self-check to see if they have accomplished those goals.
- Ask students how they greet the following people: a friend, a teacher, a parent of a classmate.
- Have students look at the photos on pp. 2–3 and ask them to point out any similarities and differences they notice between greeting styles in Spanish-speaking cultures and those in English-speaking cultures.
- Point to each photo on the spread, and ask students to guess in English what the people are saying. Are the greetings casual? Are they formal? Do they take place in the morning? In the afternoon?
- Play the audio as students read A–H.

STANDARDS
1.2 Understand language

Communication
Pair Work

Students should go around the room and practice the mini-conversations on this spread with their classmates. They should shake hands or wave goodbye as they engage in conversation. After the mini-conversation, each one should raise his/her hand and switch partners with someone else who has a hand raised. Time this activity for five minutes to give students time to greet several classmates.

Students may be fearful of speaking a foreign language, so initially they should not be expected to produce the language in front of the entire class. Give them multiple opportunities for partner and group practice to help them feel more comfortable.

Hola, ¿qué tal?

¡AVANZA! **Goal:** Learn how various Spanish speakers greet each other. Then practice what you have learned to greet and say goodbye to others. ***Actividades 1–3***

AUDIO

B **Juan:** ¡Hola, Miguel! **¿Qué tal?**
Miguel: Hola, **¿qué pasa?**

C **Juan:** ¡**Hasta luego**, Ana!
Ana: Hasta luego.

D **Srta. Daza:** **Adiós.**
Sr. Ortega: Adiós, **señorita.**

Differentiating Instruction

English Learners

Build Background Explain to students whose native language is not English the different gestures English-speaking people use to say hello and goodbye. They wave, shake hands, hug, or give a kiss on the cheek. Ask students to share the common gestures associated with greetings in their culture. Are they the same or different from those shown on pp. 2 and 3?

Multiple Intelligences

Interpersonal Interpersonal learners enjoy interacting with people and are sensitive to other people's feelings. Have these students work with a partner to develop a short role-play. Partners should greet each other, ask each other how they are, and then say goodbye. Remind students to use appropriate gestures and facial expressions to support the meaning of their words.

E **Sr. Martínez:** Buenos días, señora Ramos. ¿Cómo está usted?
Sra. Ramos: Regular. ¿Y usted?
Sr. Martínez: Más o menos.

F **Juan:** Buenas tardes. ¿Cómo estás?
Esteban: Muy bien.

G **Sra. Acevedo:** Hola, buenas noches.
Diana: Buenas noches, señora.

H **Sr. García:** Buenas noches, Diana.
Diana: Hasta mañana, señor García.

¡A responder! Escuchar

Listen to these people greeting and saying goodbye. Wave toward the front of the room if you hear a greeting or toward the back of the room if you hear a goodbye.

LECCIÓN PRELIMINAR

Comparisons

English Language Connection

Buenos días Although **buenos días** literally translates as *good days,* it is primarily used for saying *good morning.* **Buenas tardes** is used for *good afternoon* and **buenas noches** for *good night, good evening.* After going over the expressions, have students give the appropriate greeting for the following times of day: **1.** 11:00 a.m.; **2.** 8 p.m.; **3.** 7 a.m.; **4.** 3 p.m. ; **5.** 11 p.m.; **6.** 1:30 p.m.

Answers: 1. Buenos días. 2. Buenas noches. 3. Buenos días. 4. Buenas tardes. 5. Buenas noches. 6. Buenas tardes.

Communication

Regionalisms

Young people in Spanish-speaking countries have informal ways of greeting each other. For example, in Mexico they say **¿Qué hubo?** and **¿Qué onda?** to express *What's up?* or *What's going on?* In Argentina, they use **Chau** to say *goodbye.*

Communication

Motivating with Music

To practice the concepts presented in the Lección preliminar, use the **¡AvanzaRap!** song found on the **¡AvanzaRap! DVD.** In addition to the animated rap video, you can also find interactive DVD activities, helpful teaching suggestions, and activity masters.

Differentiating Instruction

Inclusion

Clear Structure Create the following headings on the board: **Hola, ¿Cómo estás?** and **Adiós**. Review the meanings of these words and phrases. Then have students organize the vocabulary presented on pp. 2–3 into these three categories. Which words and phrases can be used to say hello, ask or tell how someone is, or say goodbye?

Heritage Language Learners

Support What They Know Ask students to share other greetings that they have heard or used. Are there words and phrases popular among teenagers to say *hi* and *bye*? Ask students to model these words and phrases for the group. Then have the whole group repeat. Encourage all students to practice these terms when they arrive at or leave Spanish class.

Answers Projectable Transparencies, P-34 and P-35

¡A responder! Audio Script, TE p. C25b

1. Students wave toward the front.
2. Students wave toward the back.
3. Students wave toward the back.
4. Students wave toward the front.
5. Students wave toward the front.
6. Students wave toward the back.

Objectives
- Practice greetings and saying goodbye.
- Practice familiar and formal greetings.
- Learn to say names in Spanish.
- Pronunciation: Learn about the letter **h** in Spanish.

Core Resource
- Audio Program: TXT CD 1 track 3

Practice Sequence
- **Activity 1:** Controlled practice: greetings and farewells
- **Activity 2:** Transitional practice: greetings and farewells
- **Activity 3:** Transitional practice: familiar and formal greetings
- **Pronunciation:** Oral comprehension and production of the letter **h**.

STANDARDS
1.1 Engage in conversation, Acts. 2–3
1.3 Present information, Acts. 2–3, PYP

Communication
Interpersonal Mode
Read aloud the list of Spanish names and have students repeat each name. Have each student select a Spanish name and create a name tag. Then have students go around the room and greet each other using their new names. Be sure to point out the correct pronunciation of **Me llamo**. It may be helpful to write a phonetic spelling on the board: /*may*//*yahmo*/.

Communication
Role-Playing and Skits
Divide students into groups of three or four. Have them prepare mini-dialogues to be presented to the rest of the class. Ask them to write on the board the time of day that the conversation occurs so that you, and classmates, can check to see if they are using the proper greetings. You may wish to assign the time of day to be sure that all greetings besides simply **hola** are used.

See Activity Answers on page 5.

1 Muy bien
Leer

Complete each expression.

1. ¿Cómo está...	**a.** tal?
2. Buenas...	**b.** mañana.
3. ¿Qué...	**c.** usted?
4. Muy bien...	**d.** tardes.
5. Hasta...	**e.** ¿Y usted?

2 ¿Cómo estás?
Escribir

Create a conversation to complete the speech bubbles of this cartoon strip.

Expansión
Write a conversation in which a teacher and student greet each other, ask how each other is doing, and say goodbye.

Manuel

Nombres de chicos		Nombres de chicas	
Alejandro	Juan	Alejandra	Juana
Andrés	Luis	Alicia	Luisa
Carlos	Manuel	Ana	María
Cristóbal	Mateo	Bárbara	Marta
Daniel	Miguel	Carmen	Natalia
David	Nicolás	Carolina	Patricia
Eduardo	Pablo	Cristina	Raquel
Esteban	Pedro	Diana	Rosa
Felipe	Ramón	Elena	Sofía
Guillermo	Ricardo	Emilia	Susana
Jaime	Roberto	Florencia	Teresa
Jorge	Tomás	Gabriela	Verónica
José	Vicente	Isabel	Yolanda

Isabel

Differentiating Instruction

Multiple Intelligences
Visual Learners Have students create a **¿Cómo estás?** poster. The poster should include possible answers to the question, such as **bien, muy bien, más o menos, regular,** and **mal**, as well as a drawing expressing the meaning of each. For example, students might draw a face with a big smile for **muy bien**, and a face with a big frown for **mal**. Display the posters in the classroom for reference.

Inclusion
Alphabetic/Phonetic Awareness Model for students the pronunciation of Spanish names. Point out that even though some names are spelled the same in English and Spanish, they are pronounced differently. Some examples would include **Daniel, David, Diana,** and **Verónica**. Invite students to choose names to use in class. They could be similar to or different from their English names.

Nota

¿Cómo estás? and **¿Cómo está usted?** both mean *How are you?*

¿Cómo estás? and **¿Y tú?** are familiar phrases used with:

- a person your own age
- a relative
- a person you call by his or her first name

Other familiar greetings: **¿Qué tal?** and **¿Qué pasa?**

¿Cómo está usted? and **¿Y usted?** are formal phrases used with:

- a person you don't know
- someone older
- a person to whom you want to show respect

3 Buenos días

Hablar

According to the time of day, greet your partner as if he or she were the following people. Use a formal greeting or a familiar greeting depending on whom you address.

modelo: Sr. (Sra.) Vargas / 7 a.m.

A Buenos días, señor (señora) Vargas. ¿Cómo está usted?

B Muy bien.

1. your best friend / 10 p.m.
2. the school principal / 2 p.m.
3. Sr. (Srta.) López / 7 p.m.
4. your mother/father / 9 a.m.
5. Sr. (Sra.) Santos / 4 p.m.
6. your brother/sister / 9 p.m.
7. your coach / 11 a.m.
8. your Spanish teacher / 10 a.m.

AUDIO

Pronunciación La letra h

In Spanish, the letter **h** is always silent.

Listen and repeat.

ha	**he**	**hi**	**ho**	**hu**
hace	**helado**	**hispano**	**hola**	**humano**

¡Hola, Hugo!

Hasta mañana, Héctor.

Get Help Online my.hrw.com

PARA Y PIENSA

Did you get it?
1. Tell a friend good morning.
2. Ask a friend how he or she is.
3. Say goodbye to your teacher.

Differentiating Instruction

Slower-paced Learners

Peer-study Support Have students work with their partners to create a script for each exchange in Activity 3. Instruct pairs to look at the person and time presented in the prompt, and then discuss the best greeting and response to use. Advise them to write each of their lines down before saying them aloud.

Inclusion

Alphabetic/Phonetic Awareness To teach students the sound of the Spanish letter **h,** write the following words on the board: **hola, helado, hilo, hombre, humano,** and **hispano.** Say each aloud, and have students repeat. Then ask students to describe what they notice about the *h* at the beginning of each word. Reinforce that the letter *h* is always silent in Spanish.

Nota

In some Spanish-speaking countries, people follow the custom of using formal speech to show respect to parents and grandparents. They are taught to use **usted** when addressing an older family member.

✓ Ongoing Assessment

Dictation After practicing the sounds under the pronunciation heading, dictate the following sentences and have students write them in their notebooks.

Hola, Hugo. Hasta luego. Hasta mañana. Hola, Héctor.

Get Help Online More Practice my.hrw.com

✓ Ongoing Assessment

PARA Y PIENSA

Quick Check The Para y piensa is a quick self-assessment tool that allows students to evaluate their understanding of the lesson's topic. If students have difficulty with the sentences in Para y piensa, ask them to review pp. 2–4.

Answers Projectable Transparencies, P-34 and P-35

Answers for Activities on pp. 4, 5.

Activity 1 **1.** c; **2.** d; **3.** a; **4.** e; **5.** b

Activity 2 Answers will vary.
Sample answers include:
A. Buenos días, Juan, **B.** Hola, Pablo. ¿Cómo estás?
A. Bien. ¿Y tú? **B.** Mal.
A. Hasta luego. **B.** Hasta mañana.

Activity 3 Answers to each question may include: Muy bien, regular, más o menos. ¿Y tú?

1. Buenas noches. ¿Cómo estás?
2. Buenas tardes, señor/señora ______. ¿Cómo está usted?
3. Buenas noches, señor/señorita López. ¿Cómo está usted?
4. Buenos días. ¿Cómo estás?
5. Buenas tardes, señor/señora Santos. ¿Cómo está usted?
6. Buenas noches. ¿Cómo estás?
7. Buenos días. ¿Cómo está usted?
8. Buenos días, señor/señorita ______. ¿Cómo está usted?

Para y piensa

1. Buenos días.
2. ¿Cómo estás?
3. Adiós/Hasta mañana/Hasta luego, señor/señora ______.

Objective
- Learn to make introductions.

Core Resource
- Audio Program: TXT CD 1 tracks 4, 5

Presentation Strategies
- Ask students how they introduce themselves to new people. What body language or gestures are used? Are there differences according to the age or status of the person?
- Assign students the roles of the people in A–G and have them read the conversations. Correct pronunciation and gestures as needed.
- Ask students to walk around the class introducing themselves and asking the other student's name: **Hola, me llamo Carlos. ¿Y tú? ¿Cómo te llamas?** Continue until each student has introduced himself or herself to five other students.
- Play the audio.

STANDARDS
1.2 Understand language

Warm Up
Projectable Transparencies, P-22

Verb llamar Complete each sentence with the correct form of the verb.

1. ¿Como se _____ ellos?
2. Yo me llamo Helena, ¿cómo te _____ tú?
3. Por favor, señor, ¿cómo se _____ usted?
4. Mucho gusto, yo me _____ Daniel.

Answers: 1. llaman; 2. llamas; 3. llama; 4. llamo

Communication
Group Work
Pass out name tags as students enter the room, some with first names only and others with names of teachers in your school preceded by the correct title–**Sr.** or **Sra.** Students are to walk around the room and give the appropriate greeting and ask how the other is doing. Model a greeting with a volunteer first to show appropriate formal and informal greetings. Always monitor students when doing group or pair work. Knowing that you will be stopping by to hear them encourages students to stay on task.

¡Mucho gusto!

¡AVANZA! **Goal:** Notice how certain speakers introduce themselves and others. Then practice what you have learned to make introductions. ***Actividades 4–7***

AUDIO

A **Esteban:** Hola. Me llamo Esteban. ¿Y tú? **¿Cómo te llamas?**
Diana: Me llamo Diana.
Esteban: **Encantado,** Diana.
Diana: **Igualmente.**

B **Diana:** **Te presento a** Esteban.
Ana: **Encantada.**
Esteban: Igualmente.

C **Srta. Machado:** **Perdón.** ¿Cómo se llama?
Srta. Daza: Me llamo Raquel Daza.

D **Srta. Machado:** **Le presento a** Ana Vega.
Sr. Ortega: **Mucho gusto.**
Ana: **El gusto es mío.**

Differentiating Instruction

Heritage Language Learners
Writing Skills Heritage language learners may need practice with punctuation, spelling, and grammar. Have students choose one of the photos on pp. 6, 7. Then invite them to write down an expansion of the conversation based on what they see in the photo. What else might these two or three people say to each other? Remind students to focus on using correct punctuation, spelling, and grammar.

Slower-paced Learners
Sentence Completion Copy one of the dialogues on the board replacing some of the words with blanks. For example:

Hola. Me llamo _____.
Me _____ Diana.
Encantado, Diana.
_____.

Then have volunteers fill in each blank with an appropriate word.

E

F

G **Rosa:** ¿Se llama Miguel?
Esteban: Sí. Se llama Miguel Luque.

¡A responder! Escuchar

Listen to four people make introductions. Point to yourself if you hear someone introducing themselves. Point to the person next to you if you hear someone introducing someone else.

Differentiating Instruction

English Learners

Build Background Discuss with students the different phrases used in different languages to tell someone your name. Point out that in English, you say *My name is...*, while in Spanish you say **Me llamo...**, or *I call myself...* Ask students to share how to tell someone your name in their first language. Have students practice saying **Me llamo...** in several different languages.

Slower-paced Learners

Yes/No Questions Use yes/no questions to help students practice saying their names, and the names of their classmates. Point to a student as you ask: **¿Se llama Isabel?** Students should answer **sí** or **no**. If it is the wrong name, they should follow up with an explanation. **No, se llama Natalia.**

Communication

Common Error Alert

Students may be confused with the **se llama** structures. Explain that **Me llamo** does not literally mean *My name is*. Instead, it is literally translated as *I call myself*. **Se llama** can mean *You (formal) call yourself* or *He/she calls himself/herself*. English speakers, of course, would be more likely to say *Your name is* or *His/her name is*. To avoid confusion with **se llama**, include the appropriate pronoun in the question. For example: **¿Cómo se llama usted?** *How do you call yourself? (What is your name?)*

Communication

Grammar Activity

Read the following sentences and have students write **tú** if the statement or question is familiar; have them write **usted** if the speaker is addressing someone formally.

1. Buenos días, señor. ¿Cómo está usted?
2. Hola. ¿Cómo te llamas?
3. Te presento a Felipe.
4. Le presento a María.
5. Me llamo Juan Carlos. ¿Cómo te llamas?
6. Muy bien. ¿Y usted?
7. ¿Cómo se llama, señora?

Answers: 1. usted; 2. tú; 3. tú; 4. usted; 5. tú; 6. usted; 7. usted

Communication

Role-Playing and Skits

Divide students into groups of three. Ask them to create a conversation between a teacher and two students (three students for a group of four). They should greet each other, ask names, perform introductions, and say goodbye.

Answers Projectable Transparencies, P-34 and P-35

¡A responder! Audio Script, TE p. C25b

1. Student points to person next to him or her.
2. Student points to himself or herself.
3. Student points to himself or herself.
4. Student points to person next to him or her.

Objectives

- Practice greetings, to make introductions.
- **Culture:** Discuss the murals of Manuel Vega.
- Ask someone's name.

Practice Sequence

- **Activity 4:** Controlled practice: introductions
- **Activity 5:** Controlled practice: greetings, introductions
- **Activity 6:** Transitional practice: introductions
- **Activity 7:** Transitional practice: introductions

STANDARDS

1.1 Engage in conversation, Acts. 6-7
1.3 Present information, Acts. 4-7, PYP
2.2 Products and perspectives, CC
4.2 Compare cultures, CC

Communication

Interpersonal Mode

Write a series of statements or questions on the board and ask student pairs to read them and provide a logical answer. For example, student reads and says: **¿Quién es?** (Student points to another student in the class). Partner answers: **Es Margarita.** Continue with the following examples:
1. Te presento a Miguel.
2. ¿Cómo te llamas?
3. Buenas tardes. ¿Cómo estás?
4. Encantada.

Check for use of correct rejoinder and pronunciation.

Communication

Role-Playing and Skits

Ask students to complete Activity 5 using their own names. Then have them repeat their lines until they have memorized them. Ask them to act out the scene in front of the class using appropriate gestures to accompany their lines.

See Activity answers on p. 9.

4 ¿Cómo te llamas?

Leer

Choose the correct response to each question or statement.

1. ¿Quién es?
a. Es Hugo.
b. Encantado.
c. Me llamo Carlos.

2. Encantada.
a. Le presento a Sergio.
b. ¿Y tú?
c. Igualmente.

3. Te presento a Joaquín.
a. ¿Cómo se llama?
b. Mucho gusto.
c. Igualmente.

4. ¿Cómo te llamas?
a. Perdón.
b. Me llamo Isabel.
c. Bien.

5. Me llamo Gabriel.
a. Igualmente.
b. Encantado.
c. El gusto es mío.

6. Mucho gusto.
a. Buenas tardes.
b. ¿Quién es?
c. El gusto es mío.

5 Conversación

Leer
Escribir

Complete the conversation with the correct words.

Carlos: Hola. Me __1.__ Carlos. ¿ __2.__ te llamas?
Beatriz: Me __3.__ Beatriz.
Carlos: __4.__, Beatriz.
Beatriz: __5.__.

6 Mucho gusto

Hablar

Work in a group of four. Introduce yourself to each member of the group.

Expansión
Introduce yourself to your teacher.

Differentiating Instruction

Inclusion

Metacognitive Support Help students to think how language is structured before they do Activity 4. Ask them to explain why some answers make sense, and why the others do not. The question in number 4 is **¿Cómo te llamas? Perdón** is a polite way of saying excuse me, but it doesn't answer the question. **Bien** answers the question **¿Cómo estás?** The correct answer is **Me llamo Isabel.**

Heritage Language Learners

Support What They Know Invite students to expand on the possibilities for their conversations in Activity 6. As part of the introduction, they might also talk about where they live, where they go to school, and some of their hobbies or interests.

Nota

¿Cómo te llamas? and **¿Cómo se llama?** both are used to ask *What is your name?*
Te presento a... and **Le presento a...** both mean *I'd like you to meet . . .*

¿Cómo te llamas? and **Te presento a...** are familiar phrases used with:

- a person your own age
- a relative
- a person you call by his or her first name

¿Cómo se llama? and **Le presento a...** are formal phrases used with:

- a person to whom you want to show respect
- a person you don't know
- someone older

7 Te presento a...

Hablar

Work in a group of three. Take turns introducing each other.

A: Te presento a Tomás.

B: Encantado(a), Tomás.

C: Igualmente.

Comparación cultural

Un mural en Nueva York

How can artists give back to their neighborhood through their work? Artist Manuel Vega moved with his family from Puerto Rico to **New York** at a young age. He grew up in East Harlem and his works often depict neighborhood scenes inspired by his childhood. Vega was commissioned to restore this image, originally created by Hank Prussing in 1973, on a multi-story building in East Harlem.

The Spirit of East Harlem, *Manuel Vega*

Compara con tu mundo *What childhood memory would you paint if you were creating a neighborhood mural? Compare it with the scene in Vega's mural.*

Get Help Online my.hrw.com

PARA Y PIENSA

Did you get it? Complete each statement.

1. Me llamo... a. a Maricela.
2. Te presento... b. gusto, señor.
3. Mucho... c. Walter.

Differentiating Instruction

Inclusion

Clear Structure Create two columns on the board. At the top of one, write **¿Cómo te llamas?** and **Te presento a...** At the top of the other, write **¿Cómo se llama?** and **Le presento a...** Then ask for volunteers to come add names to one column or the other. With whom would students use these phrases?

Multiple Intelligences

Visual Learners Give students the opportunity to paint or draw a scene depicting people in their own neighborhood. Then have them use their artwork to practice naming and introducing people. Have them point out and introduce characters in their paintings. **Te presento a ... Se llama...**

Comparación cultural

Essential Question

Suggested Answer Artists can give back to their neighborhood by depicting its landscape, people, and activities in their work. This can give residents a sense of pride in their community and themselves.

Background Information

Manuel Vega, or Manny as he is called, grew up in the Bronx. His work is not limited to painting. He also designs mosaics and prints and has been active in creating and restoring murals in New York City. He often involves the youth of the city in the mural restoration projects. African, Latino, and Caribbean influences can be seen in his art. He has been named the Artist in Residence at New York's Guggenheim Museum.

✓ Ongoing Assessment

Get Help Online
More Practice
my.hrw.com

Peer Assessment Have pairs of students read aloud the sentences in Para y piensa and correct each other.

Answers Projectable Transparencies, P-34 and P-35

Answers for Activities on pp. 8, 9.

Activity 4
1. a; **2.** c; **3.** b; **4.** b; **5.** b; **6.** c

Activity 5
1. llamo; **2.** Cómo; **3.** llamo;
4. Mucho gusto/Encantado; **5.** El gusto es mío/Igualmente

Activity 6 Answers will vary. Suggested answers include:
A. Hola, me llamo Debbie.
B. Encantado. Me llamo Luis.

Activity 7 Answers will vary. Sample answers include:
A. Te presento a Margarita. **B.** Mucho gusto, Margarita. **C.** El gusto es mío.

Para y piensa **1.** c; **2.** a; **3.** b

Objectives

- Learn and say the Spanish alphabet.
- Practice spelling words in Spanish.
- Practice pronouncing the Spanish vowels **a, e, i, o, u.**

Core Resource

- Audio Program: TXT CD 1 tracks 6, 7, 8, 9

Presentation Strategies

- Say the Spanish alphabet and have students repeat after you.
- Point out the letter **ñ** and reinforce the difference between the pronunciation of **n** and **ñ.**
- Say a Spanish alphabet letter and the word that starts with it. **Jota: jabón.** Have students repeat after you. Continue with the rest of the alphabet.
- Play the audio as students follow the script in their text.

Practice Sequence

- **Activity 8:** Vocabulary recognition: spelling words
- **Activity 9:** Vocabulary production: spelling words
- **Activity 10:** Vocabulary production: spelling words
- **Pronunciation:** Oral comprehension and production of the vowels.

STANDARDS

1.1 Engage in conversation, Acts. 9–10
1.2 Understand language, Act. 8
1.3 Present information, Acts. 8-10, PYP
4.1 Compare languages, Pronunciación

Warm Up Projectable Transparencies, P-22

Familiar vs. Formal Have students read the following sentences and write **Familiar** or **Formal** depending on whom they address.

1. ¿Cómo está usted?
2. Señor Ortega, le presento a Ana Vega.
3. ¿Qué tal? ¿Cómo estás?
4. Te presento a Carolina.
5. Perdón. ¿Cómo se llama?

Answers: 1. Formal; 2. Formal; 3. Familiar; 4. Familiar; 5. Formal

Answers Projectable Transparencies, P-34 and P-35

¡A responder! Audio Script, TE p. C25b
Students should write and hold up the following letters.
1. L; **2.** E; **3.** J; **4.** Ñ; **5.** P; **6.** I; **7.** H; **8.** B.

El abecedario

¡AVANZA! **Goal:** Learn to say the Spanish alphabet. Then practice how to say the letters to spell different things. ***Actividades 8–10***

AUDIO

¡A responder! Escuchar

Listen to letters of the Spanish alphabet. Write each letter that you hear on a piece of paper and hold it up.

Differentiating Instruction

Multiple Intelligences

Musical/Rhythmic Musical learners are sensitive to music and rhythm. To appeal to these students, lead them in a version of the traditional ABC song, using the Spanish alphabet. Point out that there are two additional letters in Spanish that will need to be incorporated into the song.

Inclusion

Multisensory Input/Output Whenever possible, present topics both orally and visually. Help students remember the letters of the Spanish alphabet through this activity.

1. Say a letter aloud. Have students repeat.
2. Have students point to the letter on p. 10.
3. Have students write the letter on a separate piece of paper.

8 Lista

Escuchar
Escribir

Listen to someone dictate an invitation list for a party. Write down each name as it is spelled.

modelo: You hear: de, a, ene, i, e, ele
You write: Daniel

Audio Program
TXT CD 1 Track 8
Audio Script, TE p. C25b

9 Me llamo...

Hablar

Work in a group of three. Ask each person his or her name and write down the name as he or she spells it.

A ¿Cómo te llamas?

B Me llamo Shawna, S - H - A - W - N - A. (ese, hache, a, doble uve, ene, a)

Expansión
Continue the activity with your last name.

10 ABC

Hablar

Spell aloud the following things for a partner. He or she will write the word. Then verify that your partner spelled the word correctly.

your middle name	your favorite singer	the name of your town
the name of your school	your favorite sports team	¿ ?

Pronunciación Las vocales

AUDIO

In Spanish, the vowels are **a, e, i, o,** and **u.** Each vowel is always pronounced the same way. Spanish vowels are always short and crisp.

Listen to and repeat these words.

a → as in *father*	**encantada**	**mal**	**mañana**
e → as in *hey*	**menos**	**señor**	**presento**
i → sounds like *meet*	**igualmente**	**adiós**	**bien**
o → as in *woke*	**hola**	**noches**	**cómo**
u → sounds like *boot*	**usted**	**mucho**	**tú**

Get Help Online
my.hrw.com

PARA Y PIENSA

Did you get it? Recite the Spanish alphabet.

Differentiating Instruction

Multiple Intelligences

Visual Learners Invite students to create a name poster of their original or Spanish name. The poster should include each letter of the name written as a character and as a word. For example, **J-jota, U-u, A-a, N-ene.** It should also include a picture of something that starts with each letter. Refer students back to the chart on page 10 for ideas.

Inclusion

Alphabetic/Phonetic Awareness Ask students to write the vowels, **a, e, i, o,** and **u** on small pieces of paper. Review with students the sound represented by each of these letters. Then say a one-syllable word aloud, such as **tú** or **mal.** Have students hold up the letter whose sound they hear. Continue the activity with two-syllable words, and have students hold up the two vowels they hear.

Communication

Common Error Alert

Explain to students that there is generally only one sound for each Spanish vowel. Have students write down phonetic spellings for the vowels: /ah/; /ay/; /ee/; /oh/; /oo/. Model their pronunciation and have students repeat.

Long-term Retention

Personalize It

Give students the opportunity to make what they've learned their own. Ask them to illustrate their own examples of alphabet letters and display them in the classroom. They can use vocabulary from the glossary if they run out of word ideas.

✓ Ongoing Assessment

Get Help Online
More Practice
my.hrw.com

PARA Y PIENSA

Alternative Strategy Prepare in advance a randomized alphabet list and ask students to take turns saying the letters.

Answers Projectable Transparencies, P-34 and P-35

Activity 8
1. Ximena
2. Guillermo
3. Alejandro
4. Yolanda
5. Beatriz
6. Josefina
7. Hugo
8. Toño

Activity 9 Answers will vary. Sample answers: **A.** ¿Cómo te llamas? **B.** Me llamo Thomas, T-H-O-M-A-S. (te, hache, o, eme, a, ese)

Activity 10 Answers will vary. Sample answers:
Middle name: be grande, e, ene, jota, a, eme, i, ene
Name of school: de, a, ye; hache, i, ge, hache; ese, ce, hache, o, o, ele
Favorite singer: eme, a, ere, i, a hache; ce, a, ere, e, i griega
Favorite sports team: jota, e, te, ese
Name of your town: te, a, eme, pe, a

Para y piensa Students should recite the Spanish alphabet.

Objectives
- Learn the names of countries in the Spanish-speaking world
- Learn to say where someone is from.

Core Resource
- Audio Program: TXT CD 1 tracks 10, 11

Presentation Strategies
- Read aloud the text on p. 12 and have students repeat after you.
- Ask students yes/no questions about the people in the text. For example: **¿Es Pablo de Costa Rica?** (No.) **¿Es Marisol de Puerto Rico?** (Sí).
- Point to **Los países hispanohablantes** on p. 13, say the countries, and have students repeat them. Correct pronunciation as needed.
- Point to a country on the map on p. 12, and ask individual students to identify it, using the list on p. 13.
- Play the audio as students follow in their texts.

STANDARDS
1.2 Understand language

Warm Up
Projectable Transparencies, P-23

Spelling Have students spell the following words in Spanish.

1. zapato
2. encantado
3. helado
4. bate
5. usted

Answers: 1. zeta, a, pe, a, te, o; 2. e, ene, ce, a, ene, te, a, de, o; 3. hache, e, ele, a, de, o; 4. be grande, a, te, e; 5. u, ese, te, e, de

Communication

Pair Work
Have students practice asking each other **¿De dónde eres?** and answering with **Soy de ____**.

¿De dónde eres?

¡AVANZA! **Goal:** Look at the Spanish-speaking world and how Spanish speakers say where someone is from. Then practice what you have learned to ask where people are from. ***Actividades 11–13***

AUDIO

Differentiating Instruction

Slower-paced Learners
Yes/No Questions Ask students yes or no questions about the people presented on pages 12 and 13. Here are a few possibilities:
¿Es Fernando de Ecuador? (sí)
¿Es Marisol de Costa Rica? (no)

Heritage Language Learners
Support What They Know Invite students with a personal or family connection to one of the countries listed to share something about that country with the group. Encourage students to give a general description of the place, its culture and people. Also, encourage them to share memories or impressions of the place.

Enrique es de **España.**

¡A responder! Escuchar

For each statement you hear, point to the person in the photo to whom it refers.

Culture

Teaching with Maps

Have the students draw or trace the map on p. 12. Have them label and color each Spanish-speaking country in bright colors. The countries that are not Spanish-speaking should be colored a neutral color such as gray. Students should not use the same color for two countries that border each other. Have the students glue their colored maps on construction paper. You may wish to laminate them to preserve the surface.

Communication

Group Work

As students enter the classroom, give them a sheet with a Spanish name and a country. For example, one card may be **Diego/Venezuela.** Have them locate that country on a map. They will introduce themselves to each other and show each classmate the country on the map. For example: **Me llamo Diego. Soy de Venezuela. Y tú, ¿cómo te llamas? ¿De dónde eres?**

Long-term Retention

Critical Thinking

Ask students to look at the map and the list on pp. 12–13 and count in English the number of countries where Spanish is spoken. Based on this information, have them discuss why it is important to learn Spanish.

Differentiating Instruction

Inclusion

Alphabetic/Phonetic Awareness Model for students the pronunciation of country names in Spanish. Point out that even though some names are spelled the same in English and Spanish, they are pronounced differently. Some examples would include **Panamá, Chile, México**, and **Cuba**.

Pre-AP*

Expand and Elaborate Ask students to choose one of the countries presented on p. 13, say the name, and share with the class what they know about that country. Allow them time to do some research, and then report to the class something about the country.

* Pre-AP is a registered trademark of the College Entrance Examination Board, which was not involved in the production of and does not endorse this product.

Answers Projectable Transparencies, P-34 and P-35

¡A responder! Audio Script, TE p. C25b
Students should point to the following people.

1. Susana
2. Marisol
3. Mariano
4. Enrique
5. Fernando
6. Isabel

Objectives

- Practice saying where someone is from and asking others where they are from.
- Identify the countries in a map of Latin America.

Practice Sequence

- **Activity 11:** Controlled practice: identifying countries on a map, telling where a person is from
- **Activity 12:** Controlled practice: asking and telling where someone is from
- **Activity 13:** Transitional practice: asking and telling where someone is from

STANDARDS

1.1 Engage in conversation, Acts. 12–13
1.3 Present information, Acts. 11–13, PYP

Culture

Teaching with Maps

Have students write the name of the northernmost country from each pair.

1. Chile/Ecuador
2. Panamá/Paraguay
3. Argentina/Venezuela
4. Perú/Cuba
5. Puerto Rico/Honduras
6. Bolivia/Guatemala
7. El Salvador/Estados Unidos

Answers: 1. Ecuador 2. Panamá 3. Venezuela 4. Cuba 5. Puerto Rico 6. Guatemala 7. Estados Unidos

Long-term Retention

Study Tips

When memorizing the location of countries on a map, it may be helpful for some students to create a mnemonic device. For example, when trying to remember the placement of the islands in the Caribbean, students may create a sentence such as *Charlie Really Digs Purple Rice.* Have students come up with their own sentences.

See Activity answers on p. 15.

11 Es de...

Escribir Hablar

Indicate where each person is from, according to the number on the map.

modelo: Guillermo / (7)

Guillermo es de **Uruguay.**

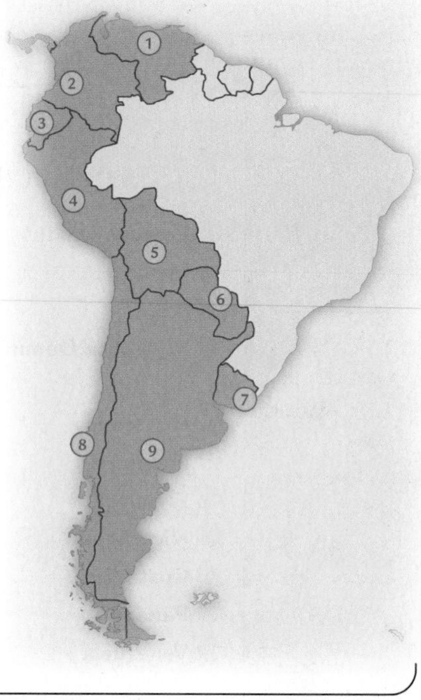

1. Andrea / (5)
2. Tomás / (8)
3. Nicolás / (4)
4. Sofía / (2)
5. Verónica / (3)
6. Mateo / (9)
7. Consuelo / (1)
8. Pablo / (6)

12 ¿De dónde eres?

Hablar

Ask a partner where he or she is from. Your partner will answer with the country listed.

modelo: Colombia

1. Venezuela
2. Panamá
3. México
4. Uruguay
5. España
6. Estados Unidos
7. El Salvador
8. Nicaragua

Expansión
Ask a partner the same questions, using formal address.

Differentiating Instruction

Inclusion

Cumulative Instruction Ask students to work in pairs. Then instruct partners to read their answers to Activity 11 aloud to each other. Tell students to spell out the names of the people and countries for their partner. **Guillermo: ge-u-i-ele-ele-e-ere-eme-o.**

Multiple Intelligences

Interpersonal Have students work with a partner to develop a short role-play. Partners should greet each other, ask each other their names and where they are from, and then say goodbye. Remind students to use appropriate gestures and facial expressions to support the meaning of their words. Give each pair the chance to present their exchange to the class.

Nota

When you are speaking, one way to change a statement into a question is to simply raise the intonation of your voice.

Beto es de Paraguay. **¿Beto es de Paraguay?**

Answer simple yes/no questions with **sí** (*yes*) or **no** (*no*).

¿Eres de California? No. **Soy de Nueva York.**

In written Spanish, all questions begin with an upside-down question mark (¿) and end with a question mark (?).

13 ¿Eres de Honduras?

Hablar

Ask a partner if he or she is from the country indicated. He or she will answer according to the number.

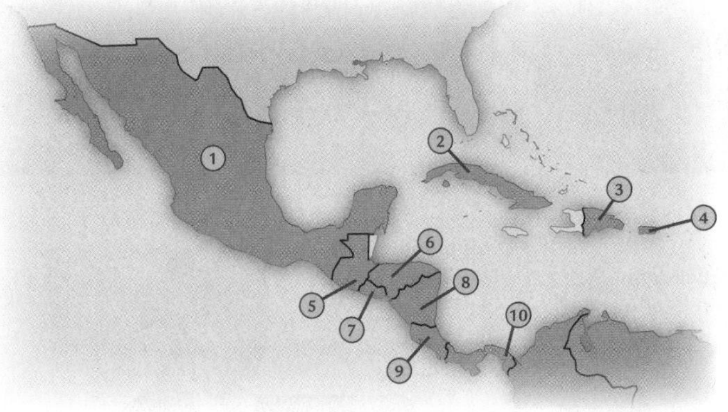

modelo: ① / ⑩

A ¿Eres de **México**?

B No. Soy de **Panamá**.

Estudiante A		Estudiante B	
1. ⑨	4. ⑩	1. ③	4. ⑩
2. ④	5. ⑤	2. ④	5. ⑤
3. ⑥	6. ⑧	3. ②	6. ⑦

Get Help Online my.hrw.com

PARA Y PIENSA

Did you get it? Match each question with the correct response.

1. ¿De dónde eres?
2. ¿De dónde es Hugo?
3. ¿Eres de México?

a. Es de Puerto Rico.
b. Soy de Colombia.
c. Sí, soy de México.

Long-term Retention
Recycle

Have students work in small groups to create chain stories. The first student says hello; the next introduces himself or herself and a Spanish-speaking friend. The next student says where he or she is from.

Communication
TPR Activity

Using a large wall map, play a game by dividing students into two groups. They will line up, relay style, behind a marked line. Give a fly swatter to the first student in each line. Call out a country name. The first student to hit that country with the fly swatter scores a point for his or her team. He or she then goes to the back of the line and it is the next student's turn.

Ongoing Assessment

Get Help Online
More Practice
my.hrw.com

Alternative Assessment Cover the questions 1–3 in Para y piensa and have students say the questions that go with each response.

Differentiating Instruction

Heritage Language Learners

Writing Skills Review with students the different punctuation marks used to indicate a question versus a sentence. Have students write down five sentences. Then have them convert each sentence into a question by changing the punctuation and/or word order.

Slower-paced Learners

Personalize It Have students answer the question **¿De dónde eres?** supplying information about themselves. They might respond with the name of their neighborhood, city, state, or country.

Answers Projectable Transparencies, P-34 and P-35

Answers for Activities on p. 14.

Activity 11

1. Andrea es de Bolivia.
2. Tomás es de Chile.
3. Nicolás es de Perú.
4. Sofía es de Colombia.
5. Verónica es de Ecuador.
6. Mateo es de Argentina.
7. Consuelo es de Venezuela.
8. Pablo es de Paraguay.

Activity 12

A. ¿De dónde eres? **B.** Soy de + *country*.

Activity 13

1. A. ¿Eres de Costa Rica? **B.** No, soy de la República Dominicana.
2. A. ¿Eres de Puerto Rico? **B.** Sí, soy de Puerto Rico.
3. A. ¿Eres de Honduras? **B.** No, soy de Cuba.
4. A. ¿Eres de Panamá? **B.** Sí, soy de Panamá.
5. A. ¿Eres de Guatemala? **B.** Sí, soy de Guatemala.
6. A. ¿Eres de Nicaragua? **B.** No, soy de El Salvador.

Para y piensa 1. b; 2. a; 3. c

Mi número de teléfono

¡AVANZA! **Goal:** Learn how to say the numbers from zero to ten and how to exchange phone numbers. Then use what you have learned to say your home (or cellular) phone number. ***Actividades 14–16***

AUDIO

¡A responder! Escuchar

Listen to these numbers. If you hear an even number, raise your right hand. If you hear an odd number, raise your left hand.

Objectives
- Say the numbers from zero to ten.
- Exchange phone numbers.

Core Resource
- Audio Program: TXT CD 1 tracks 12, 13

Presentation Strategies
- Say the numbers from zero to ten and have students repeat after you.
- Call on students at random and ask them to say their phone number. **¿Cuál es tu número de teléfono? Es 2-2-3-5-4-9-2.**
- Point out the formal and familiar ways of asking for someone's phone number.
- Play the audio.

Practice Sequence
- **Activity 14:** Controlled practice: numbers and math
- **Activity 15:** Transitional practice: phone numbers
- **Activity 16:** Transitional practice: phone numbers

STANDARDS
1.1 Engage in conversation, Acts. 15-16

Warm Up
Projectable Transparencies, P-23

Names of countries Have students complete the names of the following countries.

1. _ O _ O M _ I _
2. B _ _ I _ I _
3. _ H _ L E
4. _ I C _ R _ _ U A
5. _ _ N _ U R _ S

Answers: 1. Colombia; 2. Bolivia; 3. Chile; 4. Nicaragua; 5. Honduras

Answers
Projectable Transparencies, P-34 and P-35

¡A responder! Audio Script, TE p. C25b

a. Student should raise their right hand.
b. Student should raise their left hand.
c. Student should raise their left hand.
d. Student should raise their right hand.
e. Student should raise their right hand.
f. Student should raise their left hand.
g. Student should raise their right hand.
h. Student should raise their left hand.

Differentiating Instruction

Inclusion
Metacognitive Support Point out to students that when asking for someone's phone number in Spanish, the question word **cuál** is used. The direct translation of the question would be *Which is your phone number?* as opposed to the English phrasing *What is your phone number?*

Multiple Intelligences
Visual Learners Invite students to create a number poster of the numbers **uno** through **diez**. The poster should include each number written as a numeral and as a word. It should also include a picture to represent each number, such as an octopus next to the word **ocho**.

14 Matemáticas

Hablar
Escribir

Give the answers to the following math problems using words.

modelo: 2 + 4
seis

1. 8 − 3 **2.** 4 + 4 **3.** 3 + 6 **4.** 7 − 7 **5.** 1 + 9 **6.** 5 − 2 **7.** 6 − 5 **8.** 7 + 0 **9.** 10 − 8 **10.** 1 + 3

Expansión
Say each completed problem, using **más** (*plus*) and **menos** (*minus*).

15 Teléfono

Hablar

Work in a group of five. Whisper a phone number to the person at your right. He or she will repeat it to the person at his or her right, and so on. Verify that the phone number you gave was repeated accurately.

A Mi número de teléfono es cinco - dos - uno - nueve - ocho - siete - uno.

B Cinco - dos - uno - nueve - ocho - siete - uno.

C Cinco - dos - uno...

16 ¿Quién es?

Hablar

Work with a partner. Look at this Buenos Aires phone directory and read a phone number at random. Your partner will say whose phone number it is.

Santander Gemma
Lauerbach 3472 Pb 11- Capital Federal
Ciudad de Buenos Aires.................... 4301-9203

Santander Genoveva
Löschner 244- Capital Federal
Ciudad de Buenos Aires.................... 4921-4808

Santander Geraldo
López de Padilla 12 Pb 4- Capital Federal
Ciudad de Buenos Aires.................... 4704-5960

Santander Giancarlo
Filippozzi 9903 Pb Casa- Capital Federal
Ciudad de Buenos Aires.................... 4638-3123

Santander Gianmarco
Filippozzi 1099- Capital Federal
Ciudad de Buenos Aires.................... 4303-8740

Santander Gregorio
Sta Marta 374 Pb 7- Capital Federal
Ciudad de Buenos Aires.................... 4941-7819

A Cuatro - tres - cero - tres - ocho - siete - cuatro - cero.

B Gianmarco Santander.

Get Help Online
my.hrw.com

PARA Y PIENSA

Did you get it? Say these phone numbers.
1. 6251-4209 **2.** 3708-9263 **3.** 4185-2760

Differentiating Instruction

Pre-AP

Expand and Elaborate Invite students to brainstorm other numbers they use and can say in Spanish. These may include numbers in addresses, classroom numbers, or their school's phone number. Ask for volunteers to write a number on the board, and then read it aloud.

Multiple Intelligences

Logical/Mathematical Point out to students that the symbol + is read as **más** in Spanish, while the symbol – is read as **menos**. Then invite students to create their own simple math problems on the front of an index card. Have students exchange cards with a partner, read the problems aloud, and find the answers.

Communication

TPR Activity

Have students create flashcards with the numerals 1-10 on each—the numbers should be large enough for you to see. They may use both sides of the paper, such as having 1 on one side and 2 on the other. Call out numbers at random in Spanish and have students hold up the correct numeral.

Communication

Group Work

Pronounce the numbers for the students and have them repeat. Then have them write the numeral as you say them in random order. For example: 7, 9, 4, 2, 10, 1, 8, 6, 5, 3. Have them check each other's papers as you call out the correct answers.

✓Ongoing Assessment

Get Help Online
More Practice
my.hrw.com

PARA Y PIENSA **Peer Assessment** Have pairs of students say the phone numbers in Para piensa aloud and correct each other.

Answers Projectable Transparencies, P-34 and P-35

Activity 14 **1.** cinco; **2.** ocho; **3.** nueve; **4.** cero; **5.** diez; **6.** tres; **7.** uno; **8.** siete; **9.** dos; **10.** cuatro

Activity 15 Answers will vary. Sample answers:
A. Mi número de teléfono es cinco-cinco-cinco-dos-nueve-tres-siete. **B.** Cinco-cinco-cinco-dos... **C.** Cinco-cinco...

Activity 16 Answers will vary. Sample answers:
A. cuatro-tres-cero-uno-nueve-dos-cero-tres
B. Gemma Santander
A. cuatro-nueve-dos-uno-cuatro-ocho-cero-ocho
B. Genoveva Santander

Para y piensa
1. seis-dos-cinco-uno-cuatro-dos-cero-nueve
2. tres-siete-cero-ocho-nueve-dos-seis-tres
3. cuatro-uno-ocho-cinco-dos-siete-seis-cero

Los días de la semana

¡AVANZA! **Goal:** Learn to talk about the days of the week. Then practice what you have learned to say what day of the week it is. ***Actividades 17–19***

AUDIO

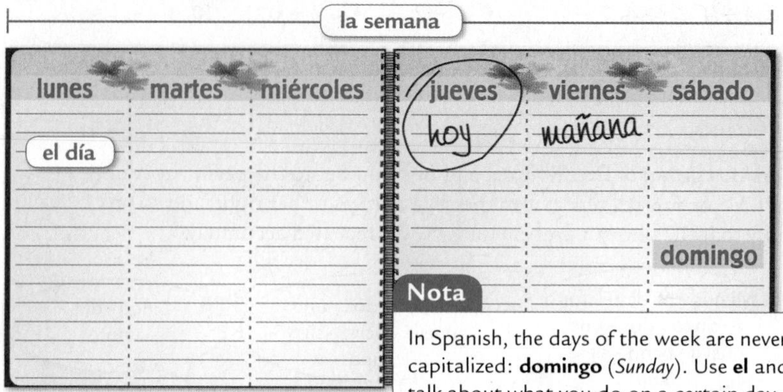

Nota

In Spanish, the days of the week are never capitalized: **domingo** (*Sunday*). Use **el** and **los** to talk about what you do on a certain day or days.

el lunes	*on Monday*
los lunes	*on Mondays*

A **Ana:** ¿Qué día es hoy?
Rosa: **Hoy** es **jueves.**

B **Juan:** ¿Hoy es viernes?
Esteban: No. **Mañana** es viernes.

¡A responder! Escuchar

Listen to the days of the week. If you hear a day that you have Spanish class, stand up. If you hear a day that you don't have Spanish class, remain seated.

Objective
- Learn and practice the days of the week.

Core Resource
- Audio Program: TXT CD 1 tracks 14, 15, 16

Presentation Strategies
- Show students the agenda from p. 18. Explain that in most Spanish-speaking countries, the week starts with Monday.
- Prompt students to ask you **¿Qué día es hoy?** Respond and point to the day at the top of the agenda. Then ask students **¿Qué día es mañana?**
- Play the audio.

Practice Sequence
- **Activity 17:** Controlled practice: days of the week
- **Activity 18**: Controlled practice: days of the week
- **Activity 19:** Transitional practice: days of the week

STANDARDS
1.1 Engage in conversation, Act. 19
1.2 Understand language, Act. 18
1.3 Present information, Acts. 17-19, PYP

Warm Up
Projectable Transparencies, P-24

Numbers Have students write the missing number(s) in each sequence.

1. uno, ____, ____, cuatro
2. dos, ____, seis, ____, diez
3. tres, ____, nueve
4. ____, cinco, ____, nueve

Answers 1. dos, tres; 2. cuatro, ocho; 3. seis; 4. tres, siete

Answers
Projectable Transparencies, P-34 and P-35

¡A responder! Audio Script, TE p. C25b

a. Student should raise their right hand.
b. Student should raise their left hand.
c. Student should raise their left hand.
d. Student should raise their right hand.
e. Student should raise their right hand.
f. Student should raise their left hand.
g. Student should raise their right hand.
h. Student should raise their left hand.

Differentiating Instruction

Slower-paced Learners
Memory Aids Have students create a chart to help remember the names of the days of the week in Spanish. Encourage students to start each class by talking about the name of the day, and which day will follow. **Hoy es lunes. Mañana es martes.**

Slower-paced Learners
Yes/No Questions Write the names of the days of the week on the board. Circle the current day, and write the word **hoy** below it. Then ask students yes or no questions about the days of the week. **¿Hoy es jueves? ¿Mañana es domingo? ¿Mañana es lunes?** Continue the questions by changing the day that is today.

17 Los días

Hablar / Escribir

Complete each list with the missing day of the week.

1. lunes, ____, miércoles, jueves
2. viernes, ____, domingo, lunes
3. ____, martes, miércoles, jueves
4. lunes, martes, miércoles, ____
5. ____, jueves, viernes, sábado
6. domingo, ____, martes, miércoles
7. sábado, ____, lunes, martes
8. martes, miércoles, jueves, ____

18 ¿Lógico o ilógico?

Escuchar

Listen to these statements about the days of the week. Write **L** if the statement you hear is **lógico** (*logical*) or **I** if it is **ilógico** (*not logical*).

modelo: You hear: Hoy es viernes. Mañana es domingo.
You write: I

Audio Program
TXT CD 1 Track 16
Audio Script, TE p. C25b

19 ¿Qué día es?

Hablar

Ask a partner what day of the week it is. He or she will tell you what day of the week today is and what tomorrow is.

modelo: 6

A ¿Qué día es hoy?

B Hoy es **martes.** Mañana es **miércoles.**

1. 2
2. 12
3. 28
4. 15
5. 18
6. 3
7. 20
8. 16

SEPTIEMBRE

L	M	M	J	V	S	D
			1	2	3	4
5	6	7	8	9	10	11
12	13	14	15	16	17	18
19	20	21	22	23	24	25
26	27	28	29	30		

Get Help Online
my.hrw.com

PARA Y PIENSA

Did you get it?
1. Tell someone that today is Monday. Hoy es ____.
2. Ask what day tomorrow is. ¿Qué día es ____?

Differentiating Instruction

Inclusion

Alphabetic/Phonetic Awareness Remind students of phonetic points related to talking about the days of the week. Here are a few examples:
- The **h** at the beginning of **hoy** is silent.
- The **ñ** in **mañana** sounds like *ny* in *canyon*.
- The **es** at the end of each day's name sounds similar to the English *ace*.

Multiple Intelligences

Intrapersonal Have students create a diary of a typical week. Instruct them to write the name of each day of the week, and draw pictures of activities they do on each day. As students learn new vocabulary for everyday activities, have them return to these diaries to add the words and phrases they have learned.

Communication

Group Work

Have students repeat the days of the week after you. Tell them you will say a day of the week. They are to say what the next day of the week would be. **martes → miércoles.** Continue with the other days of the week.

Communication

Class Work

Game Using numerals 0–10, the days of the week, and the words **semana, hoy, mañana, día, qué**, have students create a Bingo grid with sixteen squares. They are to write one word or numeral in each square. They will not use all of the words as there are 23 in the list. Call out the English word or the Spanish number. The first student to get four in a row wins.

✓ Ongoing Assessment

Get Help Online
More Practice
my.hrw.com

PARA Y PIENSA **Peer Assessment** Have student pairs say their sentences and correct each other.

Answers Projectable Transparencies, P-34 and P-35

Activity 17 **1.** martes; **2.** sábado; **3.** lunes; **4.** jueves; **5.** miércoles; **6.** lunes; **7.** domingo; **8.** viernes

Activity 18 **1.** L; **2.** I; **3.** I; **4.** L; **5.** L; **6.** I

Activity 19
1. ¿Qué día es hoy? Hoy es viernes.Mañana es sábado.
2. ¿Qué...? Hoy es lunes. Mañana es martes.
3. ¿...? Hoy es miércoles. Mañana es jueves.
4. ¿...? Hoy es jueves. Mañana es viernes.
5. ¿...? Hoy es domingo. Mañana es lunes.
6. ¿...? Hoy es sábado. Mañana es domingo.
7. ¿...? Hoy es martes. Mañana es miércoles.
8. ¿...? Hoy es viernes. Mañana es sábado.

Para y piensa
1. lunes; **2.** mañana

Objective
- Learn and practice weather expressions.

Core Resource
- Audio Program: TXT CD 1 tracks 17, 18, 19

Presentation Strategies
- Point to the map on p. 20 and ask **¿Qué tiempo hace?** Read each of the weather descriptions and have students repeat.
- Assign students the roles of the teens in A–F and ask them **¿Qué tiempo hace?** Students respond according to their role.
- Play the audio.

Practice Sequence
- **Activity 20:** Vocabulary recognition: weather expressions
- **Activity 21:** Vocabulary production: weather expressions
- **Activity 22:** Vocabulary production: weather expressions, tell where someone is from

STANDARDS
1.1 Engage in conversation, Acts. 21–22
1.2 Understand language, Act. 20
1.3 Present information, Acts. 20–22, PYP

Warm Up Projectable Transparencies, P-24
Days of the Week Unscramble the days of the week.
1. absodá
2. senul
3. seléimroc
4. tmraes
5. ogniodm

Answers: 1. sábado; 2. lunes; 3. miércoles; 4. martes; 5. domingo

Answers Projectable Transparencies, P-34 and P-35
¡A responder! Audio Script, TE p. C25b
Students should point to the following students.
1. Diego
2. Mariana
3. Natalia
4. Jorge
5. Andrea
6. Luis

¿Qué tiempo hace?

¡AVANZA! **Goal:** Learn how to describe the weather. Then practice what you have learned to describe a sunny day, a rainy day, and a windy day.
Actividades 20–22

¡A responder! Escuchar
Listen to weather descriptions. Point to the photo of the person that corresponds to the description you hear.

Differentiating Instruction

Slower-paced Learners
Yes/No Questions Use yes/no questions to help students practice talking about the weather. Point to one of the people on p. 20 as you ask: **¿Hace viento?** or **¿Hace calor?** Students should answer **sí** or **no**. If the answer is **no**, they should follow up with an explanation. **No, no hace calor. Hace frío.**

Inclusion
Cumulative Instruction Use the pictures on p. 20 to help students review skills they have learned so far in the lesson. Here are a few possibilities:
- Ask someone their name.
- Ask someone where they are from.
- Spell out the name of a person or place.

20 El tiempo

Escuchar

Listen to four meteorologists describe the weather in their region. Write the letter of the photo that corresponds to the weather description you hear.

a.  **b.**  **c.**  **d.** 

Audio Program
TXT CD 1 Track 19
Audio Script, TE p. C25b

21 ¿Hace calor o hace frío?

Hablar

Work with a partner. Say whether it is cold or hot, according to the temperature given.

modelo: 32°F / 0°C
Hace frío.

1. 15°F / -9°C
2. 94°F / 35°C
3. 20°F / -6°C
4. 4°F / -16°C
5. 88°F / 32°C
6. 104°F / 40°C

Expansión
Say whether you think it is raining or snowing at these temperatures.

22 ¿Qué tiempo hace?

Hablar

Tell what city you are from, and ask a partner what the weather is like. He or she will give you the weather conditions for that city.

A Soy de la Ciudad de México. ¿Qué tiempo hace?

B Hace viento.

Get Help Online
my.hrw.com

PARA Y PIENSA

Did you get it? Match each question with the correct response.

1. ¿Qué tiempo hace?
2. ¿Hace calor?
3. ¿Llueve?

a. No. Hace frío.
b. Hace viento.
c. No. Hace sol.

LECCIÓN PRELIMINAR

Communication
Common Error Alert

Because **hace** is used with so many weather expressions, students tend to use it with **nieva** and **llueve**. Explain to students that **hace** is a verb and is only needed with nouns such as **calor, frío, viento. Nieva** and **llueve** are verbs that express complete thoughts and do not require the use of **hace.**

Communication
TPR Activity

Instruct students to draw a picture that reflects the weather condition as you say it in Spanish.
1. Hace sol. 2. Nieva. 3. Hace viento.
4. Hace calor. 5. Llueve. 6. Hace frío.
Send volunteers to the board to draw pictures. Have them write the weather expression underneath each.

Ongoing Assessment

Get Help Online
More Practice
my.hrw.com

PARA Y PIENSA **Quick Check** If students have problems matching the questions and responses from Para y piensa, refer them to p. 20.

Differentiating Instruction

Multiple Intelligences

Naturalist Have students work in small groups to create a weather chart. Their charts should include words to describe different types of weather, as well as a picture to represent each phrase. Start each class by having students update their charts and talk about the day's weather.

Slower-paced Learners

Personalize It Ask students to write a few sentences about the weather in their own city or a place they have visted. When they finish writing, ask them to read their sentences aloud.

Answers Projectable Transparencies, P-34 and P-35

Activity 20
1. b; **2.** a; **3.** d; **4.** c

Activity 21
1. Hace frío; **2.** Hace calor; **3.** Hace frío; **4.** Hace frío; **5.** Hace calor; **6.** Hace calor.

Activity 22
A. Soy de Buenos Aires. ¿Qué tiempo hace?
B. Hace sol. Hace calor.
A. Soy de Bogotá. ¿Qué...? **B.** Hace viento.
A. Soy de Madrid. ¿...? **B.** Llueve. Hace frío.
A. Soy de Nueva York. ¿...? **B.** Nieva. Hace frío.

Para y piensa
1. b; **2.** a; **3.** c

Objective
- Learn useful classroom phrases.

Core Resource
- Audio Program: TXT CD 1 tracks 20, 21

Presentation Strategies
- Remind students that this material is to help them understand recurring Spanish phrases used in class.
- Read aloud the phrases for En la clase and Otras instrucciones on pp. 22–23 and use gestures whenever possible to clarify meaning.
- Review these phrases often and post them in the classroom until students are comfortable using them.
- Play the audio. Practice the phrases with sample situations.

STANDARDS
1.2 Understand language

Warm Up
Projectable Transparencies, P-25

Vocabulary Unscramble the weather.
1. ¿Qué tiempo hace? Hace r c l a o
2. ¿Qué tiempo hace? Hace e n o v t i
3. ¿Qué tiempo hace? Hace l o s
4. ¿Qué tiempo hace? L u v e l e
5. ¿Qué tiempo hace? N a v e i

Answers: 1. calor; 2. viento; 3. sol; 4. Llueve; 5. Nieva

Communication
TPR Activity

Go over the expressions on p. 22 and add the expression **Levántense** *Stand up,* on the board. Model two of the commands and have students imitate what you do. Then say the commands and have students obey them. Gradually add more commands as they master two at a time. Sample script: **Levántense. Levanten la mano. Siéntense. Levanten la mano. Levántense. Siéntense. Abran los libros. Levanten la mano. Cierren los libros. Levántense. Siéntense. Abran los libros. Saquen una hoja de papel. Cierren los libros.**

En la clase

¡AVANZA! **Goal:** Learn some useful phrases used by teachers and students. Then practice what you have learned to use classroom phrases with others. ***Actividades 23–25***

AUDIO

En la clase

Abran los libros (en la página...)	*Open your books (to page . . .)*
Cierren los libros.	*Close your books.*
¿Cómo se dice...?	*How do you say . . .?*
Se dice...	*You say . . .*
¿Cómo se escribe (tu nombre)?	*How do you spell (your name)?*
Se escribe...	*It is spelled . . .*
¿Comprendes?	*Do you understand?*
Levanten la mano.	*Raise your hand.*
Más despacio, por favor.	*More slowly, please.*
No sé.	*I don't know.*
¿Qué quiere decir...?	*What does . . . mean?*
Quiere decir...	*It means . . .*
Repitan, por favor.	*Please repeat.*
Saquen una hoja de papel.	*Take out a piece of paper.*
Siéntense.	*Sit down.*
¿Tienen preguntas?	*Do you have questions?*
¿Verdad?	*Right?*

Differentiating Instruction

Inclusion
Multisensory Input/Output Model for students how to follow important commands from the list on p. 22. For example, say **abran los libros** as you open a book. Say **levanten la mano** as you raise your hand. Have students find and point to each phrase on p. 22, and then practice following the command.

Multiple Intelligences
Interpersonal Have students work in groups of three to develop a short role-play. One student will play the part of the teacher, and the others will be students. The scene should involve a classroom situation. The teacher might ask the students questions, such as **¿Cómo te llamas?** or give the students instructions, such as **Siéntense**.

En el libro

Completa la conversación.	*Complete the conversation.*
Contesta las preguntas.	*Answer the questions.*
Escoge la palabra / la respuesta...	*Choose the word / answer . . .*
Escribe...	*Write . . .*
Escucha...	*Listen . . .*
Explica...	*Explain . . .*
Indica si es cierto o falso.	*Indicate whether it is true or false.*
Lee...	*Read . . .*
Pregúntale a otro(a) estudiante.	*Ask another student.*
Trabaja con otro(a) estudiante.	*Work with another student.*
Trabaja en un grupo de...	*Work in a group of . . .*

¡A responder! Escuchar

Listen to each classroom instruction and respond appropriately.

Differentiating Instruction

English Learners

Build Background Ask students to share information about teachers, students, and classrooms in their country of origin. What are some phrases that might be heard in a typical classroom? Are they similar to or different from the phrases listed on pp. 22 and 23?

Slower-paced Learners

Memory Aids Have students create a set of flashcards to help practice vocabulary related to common classroom phrases. Using index cards, have them write the vocabulary word or phrase on one side, and draw a simple picture on the other. Encourage students to use their cards individually or with a partner.

Communication

Group Activity

Divide students into two groups to act out the expressions on pp. 22–23. The other students will try to guess which classroom command they are demonstrating.

Communication

Pair Work

Before students arrive to class, write isolated words and phrases from the classroom commands on index cards. For example, write **Pregúntale** on one card and **a otro(a) estudiante** on another. They should find their match to create the correct phrase. They will then take turns reading and demonstrating the expressions to the class.

Communication

Pair Work

Have students work with a partner to give the commands on pp. 22–23. Each should give five commands for the other to follow before switching roles.

Long-term Retention

Study Tips

Ask student pairs to go through the list and note the items that each of them has difficulty remembering. Partners then devise a way to help each other remember (flashcards, drawings, graphic organizers) according to their preferred learning style.

Answers Projectable Transparencies, P-34 and P-35

¡A responder! Audio Script, TE p. C25b

1. Students open their books to page 10.
2. Students raise their hand.
3. Students close their books.
4. Students repeat: "Buenos días."
5. Students take out a sheet of paper.

Objective

- Practice classroom phrases.

Practice Sequence

- **Activity 23:** Vocabulary recognition: classroom phrases
- **Activity 24:** Vocabulary production: classroom phrases.
- **Activity 25:** Vocabulary production: classroom phrases, greetings, days of the week, weather

STANDARDS

1.1 Engage in conversation, Act. 25
1.3 Present information, Acts. 24–25, PYP

Get Help Online
More Practice
my.hrw.com

✓ Ongoing Assessment

PARA Y PIENSA **Peer Assessment** Before writing the correct answers on the board, have students exchange papers and correct each other's statements.

Answers Projectable Transparencies, P-34 and P-35

Activity 23 **1.** d; **2.** c; **3.** b; **4.** a

Activity 24

1. Muchas gracias.
2. Más despacio, por favor.
3. ¿Cómo se dice *book*?
4. ¿Qué quiere decir **página**?
5. No sé.
6. ¿Comprendes?

Activity 25

1. A. ¿Cómo se dice *Spanish*? B. Se dice español. A. ¿Cómo se escribe español? B. Se escribe: e, ese, pe, a, eñe, o, ele.
2. A. ¿Cómo se dice *week*? B. Se dice semana. A. ¿Cómo se escribe semana? B. Se escribe: ese, e, eme, a, ene, a.
3. A. ¿Cómo se dice *Thank you very much*? B. Se dice Muchas gracias. A. ¿Cómo se escribe Muchas gracias? B. Se escribe: eme, u, ce, hache, a, ese, ge, ere, a, ce, i, a, ese.
4. A. ¿Cómo se dice *male teacher*? B. Se dice maestro. A: ¿Cómo se escribe maestro? B: Se escribe: eme, a, e, ese, te, ere, o.
5. A. ¿Cómo se dice *See you later*? B. Se dice Hasta luego. A. ¿Cómo se escribe Hasta luego? B. Se escribe hache, a, ese, te, a, ele, u, e, ge, o.
6. A. ¿Cómo se dice *Friday*? B. Se dice viernes. A. ¿Cómo se escribe viernes? B. Se escribe uve, i, e, ere, ene, e, ese.
7. A. ¿Cómo se dice *It's raining*? B. Se dice Llueve. A. ¿Cómo se escribe Llueve? Se escribe ele, ele, u, e, uve, e.

Para y piensa

1. ¿Cómo se dice *please*? **2.** ¿Comprendes?

23 Instrucciones

Leer

Match each picture with the correct instruction.

a. Abran los libros en la página 7.
b. Levanten la mano.
c. Repitan, por favor.
d. Siéntense.

24 ¿Qué dices?

Escribir
Hablar

Indicate what you would say in each situation. Refer to the expressions on pages 22–23.

1. You want to thank your Spanish teacher.
2. Your teacher is speaking too fast.
3. You want to know how to say *book* in Spanish.
4. You want to know what **página** means.
5. You must admit that you don't have the answer to a question.
6. You wonder if your friend understands the lesson.

25 ¿Cómo se dice?

Hablar

Ask a partner to say the following words in Spanish and how to spell them.

modelo: Tuesday

1. Spanish
2. week
3. Thank you very much.
4. male teacher
5. See you later.
6. Friday
7. It's raining.

A ¿Cómo se dice *Tuesday*?
B Se dice *martes*.
¿Cómo se escribe *martes*?
Se escribe eme, a, ere, te, e, ese.

Expansión
Continue this activity with four more words of your choosing.

Get Help Online
my.hrw.com

PARA Y PIENSA **Did you get it?** 1. Ask how to say the word *please*.
2. Ask a friend if he or she understands.

Differentiating Instruction

Multiple Intelligences

Kinesthetic Help students review common classroom instructions by playing a modified Simon Says game. Give students a command, such as **Levanten la mano**. Direct all students to follow the command as quickly as possible. Continue with other commands, such as **Abran los libros**. After a few rounds, give volunteers the chance to act as the leader.

Heritage Language Learners

Support What They Know Partner students with a non-heritage language learner for Activity 25. Have the other students use their partner as a resource to ask about additional words and phrases they are interested in.

A: ¿Cómo se dice *play the piano*? **B: Se dice** *tocar el piano*. **A: ¿Cómo se escribe** *piano*? **B: Se escribe** *pe-i-a-ene-o*.

En resumen
Vocabulario

¡AvanzaRap! DVD Sing and Learn

Vocabulario

Greet People and Say Goodbye

Greetings

Buenos días.	*Good morning.*
Buenas tardes.	*Good afternoon.*
Buenas noches.	*Good evening.*
Hola.	*Hello./Hi.*

Say Goodbye

Adiós.	*Goodbye.*
Buenas noches.	*Good night.*
Hasta luego.	*See you later.*
Hasta mañana.	*See you tomorrow.*

Say How You Are

¿Cómo estás?	*How are you? (familiar)*
¿Cómo está usted?	*How are you? (formal)*
¿Qué tal?	*How is it going?*
Bien.	*Fine.*
Mal.	*Bad.*
Más o menos.	*So-so.*
Muy bien.	*Very well.*
Regular.	*Okay.*
¿Y tú?	*And you? (familiar)*
¿Y usted?	*And you? (formal)*
¿Qué pasa?	*What's up?*

Make Introductions

¿Cómo se llama?	*What's his/her/your (formal) name?*
Se llama...	*His/Her name is . . .*
¿Cómo te llamas?	*What's your (familiar) name?*
Me llamo...	*My name is . . .*
Te/Le presento a...	*Let me introduce you (familiar/formal) to . . .*
El gusto es mío.	*The pleasure is mine.*
Encantado(a).	*Delighted./Pleased to meet you.*
Igualmente.	*Same here./Likewise.*
Mucho gusto.	*Nice to meet you.*
¿Quién es?	*Who is he/she/it?*
Es...	*He/She/It is . . .*

Say Which Day It Is

¿Qué día es hoy?	*What day is today?*
Hoy es...	*Today is . . .*
Mañana es...	*Tomorrow is . . .*
el día	*day*
hoy	*today*
mañana	*tomorrow*
la semana	*week*

Days of the week *p. 18*

Exchange Phone Numbers

¿Cuál es tu/su número de teléfono?	*What's your (familiar/ formal) phone number?*
Mi número de teléfono es...	*My phone number is . . .*

Numbers from zero to ten *p. 16*

Other Words and Phrases

la clase	*class*
el (la) maestro(a) de español	*Spanish teacher (male/female)*
el país	*country*
Perdón.	*Excuse me.*
por favor	*please*
(Muchas) Gracias.	*Thank you (very much).*
De nada.	*You're welcome.*
el señor (Sr.)	*Mr.*
la señora (Sra.)	*Mrs.*
la señorita (Srta.)	*Miss*
sí	*yes*
no	*no*

Describe the Weather

¿Qué tiempo hace?	*What is the weather like?*
Hace calor.	*It is hot.*
Hace frío.	*It is cold.*
Hace sol.	*It is sunny.*
Hace viento.	*It is windy.*
Llueve.	*It is raining.*
Nieva.	*It is snowing.*

Say Where You Are From

¿De dónde eres?	*Where are you (familiar) from?*
¿De dónde es?	*Where is he/she from?*
¿De dónde es usted?	*Where are you (formal) from?*
Soy de...	*I am from . . .*
Es de...	*He/She is from . . .*

Spanish-speaking countries *p. 13*

Practice Spanish with Holt McDougal Apps!

Differentiating Instruction

Inclusion

Cumulative Instruction Write the headings **Preguntas** and **Respuestas** on the board. Review the meaning of these terms with students. Then ask students to list as many questions as they can that they learned in the lesson. After each question, have students brainstorm as many possible responses as possible.

Multiple Intelligences

Visual Learners Have students create a comic strip involving two or three characters. The characters should greet each other, ask each other two or three questions, and then say goodbye. Advise students to use word bubbles to show the characters' dialogue. Give students the opportunity to share their comic strips with the whole group.

LECCIÓN PRELIMINAR

Objective
- Review lesson vocabulary.

DIGITAL SPANISH

TEACHER TOOLS
- Interactive Whiteboard Lessons
- Generate Success!

ALSO AVAILABLE...
- Online Workbook
- Spanish InterActive Reader

SPANISH ON THE GO!
- Performance Space
- Holt McDougal Spanish Apps
- ¡Avancemos! eTextbook

Communication
Role-Playing and Skits

Divide students into groups of three or four. They should create a skit in which they greet each other, make introductions, ask how each other is doing, ask where each other is from, and say goodbye. Have them present in front of the class.

Long-term Retention
Critical Thinking

Categorize Have students group vocabulary from En resumen into questions and answers for easy recall. Students should write a question on one side of an index card and the corresponding answer(s) on the other side using different color markers.

1. Te presento a Victoria
Es de España.
2. ¿Cómo se llama Ud?
Me llamo Rodrigo León.
3. ¿Cuál es tu número de tel
523-7190
3. Abran los libros en
la p. 8
4. Buenos días, señor
¿Cómo está Ud?

Objective
- Review lesson vocabula

Core Resource
- Audio Program: TXT C

Presentation Str
- Draw students' attentic
- Before starting the audi ask students to listen ca conversation and pay sp expressions that tie in w
- Before doing Activity 2, look at the word bank a words that refer to gree refer to introductions, a to the weather.
- Review numbers by saying one number and asking students to say the next number. For example, say **ocho**. Students say **nueve.**
- Before doing Activity 4, review the meaning of question words by saying a statement and asking students to choose the correct question from the ones in the activity. For example: **Me llamo Luis Aguirre.** Students respond: **¿Cómo te llamas?**

STANDARDS
1.2 Understand language, Act. 1
1.3 Present information, Acts. 1–4

Warm Up Projectable Transparencies, P-25

Vocabulary Complete the sentences with the correct word.

presento mañana gusto dónde día

1. ¿Qué _____ es hoy?
2. Te _____ a Matilde.
3. ¿De _____ eres?
4. Hasta _____.
5. Mucho _____.

Answers: 1. día; 2. presento; 3. dónde; 4. mañana; 5. gusto

Answers Projectable Transparencies, P-34 and P-35

Activity 1 **1.** d; **2.** a; **3.** c; **4.** b

Activity 2 **1.** Hola; **2.** Cómo; **3.** llamo; **4.** Soy; **5.** Hoy; **6.** calor; **7.** tiempo; **8.** Hace; **9.** Adiós

LECCIÓN

Repaso de la lección

@HOMETUTOR my.hrw.com

¡LLEGADA!

Now you can
- greet people and say goodbye
- introduce yourself and others
- ask and say how to spell names
- say where you are from
- exchange phone numbers
- say what day of the week it is
- describe the weather
- respond to classroom instructions

Audio Program
TXT CD 1 Track 22
Audio Script, TE p. C25b

Listen and understand

You will hear four separate conversations. Put the drawings in order according to what you hear.

a.

b.

c.

d.

To review
- greet people pp. 2–3
- introductions pp. 6–7
- weather p. 20

2 Introduce yourself and others

Complete Enrique's e-mail message to his new e-pal.

Adiós	Hace	Hoy
calor	Hola	Soy
Cómo	tiempo	llamo

1. ,
¿ **2.** estás? Me **3.** Enrique. **4.** de Panamá. **5.** es sábado y hace **6.** . ¿Qué **7.** hace en Estados Unidos?
¿ **8.** frío?
9. ,
Enrique

Differentiating Instruction

Slower-paced Learners

Read Before Listening Before students listen to the conversations in Activity 1, have them preview the pictures. Direct them to brainstorm possible words and phrases related to each picture. For example, in picture **a.**, what might the two characters be saying to each other? Have students write their ideas on a separate piece of paper, and refer to their notes as they listen.

Heritage Language Learners

Writing Skills Ask students to imagine they are writing to a new e-pal. Have them draft a message in which they introduce themselves, ask questions about where their e-pal lives, and talk about their own interests, and where they live. Remind students to use proper punctuation to differentiate questions from statements.

To review
- origin pp. 12–13
- numbers p. 16

3 Say where you are from

Look at these students' ID cards from the International Club. Then complete the sentences that follow.

1. ____ es de España.
2. El número de teléfono es ocho - nueve - ocho - uno - cero - tres - cinco. Se llama ____.
3. Se llama Cristina. El número de teléfono es ____.
4. La señorita de Chile se llama ____.
5. Se llama Guillermo. El número de teléfono es ____.
6. ____ es de México.

To review
- alphabet p. 10
- numbers p. 16
- days of the week p. 18

4 Answer personal questions

Answer these questions using complete sentences.

1. ¿Cómo te llamas?
2. ¿Cómo se escribe tu nombre?
3. ¿De dónde eres?
4. ¿Cuál es tu número de teléfono?
5. ¿Quién es el (la) maestro(a) de español? ¿De dónde es?
6. ¿Cómo se llama el libro de español?
7. ¿Qué día es mañana?
8. ¿Qué tiempo hace hoy?
9. ¿Cómo se dice *country* en español?

Get Help Online my.hrw.com

Differentiating Instruction

Multiple Intelligences

Linguistic/Verbal Model introducing yourself in Spanish, then have students follow your model: **Hola, buenos días, me llamo... Yo soy de...** Then ask volunteers to introduce themselves and expand the introduction. For example, **Hola, me llamo Carlos, soy de Puerto Rico. En Puerto Rico hace sol.**

Slower-paced Learners

Peer-study Support Organize students into pairs to check their answers for Activity 4. Have partners take turns reading the questions aloud. Both partners should then read or say their responses aloud. Encourage partners to give each other constructive feedback when appropriate.

Get Help Online
More Practice
my.hrw.com

✓ Ongoing Assessment

Intervention and Remediation If students achieve less than 80% accuracy with the activities, direct them to pp. 2-3, 6-7,10, 12-13, 16, 18, 20, 22-23 and to get help online at my.hrw.com.

✓ Ongoing Assessment

Alternative Strategy After doing Activity 2 in class, have students write a letter to a classmate. You may wish to assign partners or have them draw names. They will tell their names, where they're from, what day of the week it is and what the weather is like. They may add additional information. They should include at least two questions to be answered by the receiver.

✓ Ongoing Assessment

Peer Assessment Have student pairs exchange answers for Activity 4, and correct each other's work.

Answers Projectable Transparencies, P-34 and P-35

Activity 3
1. Guillermo Morales
2. Alejandro Cruz
3. dos-cuatro-uno-cero-nueve-siete-seis
4. Yolanda Hoyos
5. cuatro-seis-cero-uno-ocho-cinco-tres
6. Alejandro Cruz

Activity 4 Answers will vary. Sample answers include:
1. Me llamo George.
2. Se escribe ge-e-o-ere-ge-e.
3. Soy de Nueva York.
4. Mi número de teléfono es cinco-siete-siete-tres-dos-nueve-cero.
5. El(la) maestro(a) de español es el señor (la señora) Ramos. Es de Miami.
6. El libro de español se llama *¡Avancemos!*
7. Mañana es jueves.
8. Hace calor.
9. Se dice país.

Proyectos adicionales

Art Project

Create a mosaic. Have students look at the maps found on pages xxxviii–xliii of their text. Work with students to generate a list of Spanish-speaking countries and write them on the board. Ask students to select six countries. Bring students to the library where they can research various flags and make notes about color, and so forth.

1. Hand out pieces of cardboard and have students fold it into a cube.
2. On each side, have students create mosaic images of six of the flags they choose.They can tear colored construction paper into very small pieces and paste it onto the outer surface of the box. Each side should have a different flag representing one of the various countries.
3. Ask for volunteers to talk about their mosaic. Students should say which countries their mosaic represents, where the countries are located, and what the weather is like there.
4. Make a small hole in one corner of each box and tie string or fishing line on them in order to hang the mosaics from the ceiling.

PACING SUGGESTION: One 50-minute class period.

21st CENTURY **Creativity and Innovation**

(Virtual) Bulletin Board

¿Qué me gusta hacer? Ask students to look through magazines and newspapers, to draw, or to go online to find three things that they like to do in their free time and/or during a particular season of the year. Be sure they identify who they are, and what they like to do. After you've created the bulletin board, go around the classroom and ask each student to tell the class what they like to do and why. As a tech alternative, you may wish to have students create their projects on a class wiki page.

PACING SUGGESTION: One 50-minute class period.

21st CENTURY **Communication**

Web Research

Cities online. Find out about different Spanish-speaking cultures in the U.S. Pair students up and assign them one of the following cities: Miami, San Antonio, Los Angeles.

Encourage students to provide the following information:

- tell where the majority of the population comes from (e.g., Miami–Cuba etc.)
- describe any cultural practices and/or typical foods that can be found in the community
- have students imagine they live in one of the cities and describe three things they would do there in their free time.

Students report what they have learned. Encourage them to print out interesting things they found online or to provide a drawing of things they would like to do in the particular city.

Search Key Words: "Little Havana," "the Greater Miami Chamber of Commerce," "San Antonio," "the Los Angeles Visitors Bureau." Also visit **my.hrw.com** for more information.

PACING SUGGESTION: Two-day project for one 50-minute class. One-day project for one 90-minute class.

21st CENTURY **Technology Literacy**

Games

Diez

Have students stand up at their desks. Begin in one corner of the room. The first student starts with number **"Uno"** and has the option to name up to three numbers in sequence. (For example, the student who begins has the option to say **"Uno," "Uno, Dos," or "Uno, Dos, Tres."**) The next student continues, and again may name up to three sequential numbers, following from where the first student left off. The student who arrives at the point where he or she must say **"Diez"** is automatically out and has to sit down. The game then starts again at **"Uno"** and continues as long as there are players left standing.

PACING SUGGESTION: Twenty minutes of classtime.

Espalda con espalda

Select a student to be "it." Have him/her sit on a chair at the front of the class blindfolded. Have another student also sit on a chair at the front of the class. One-by-one, the rest of the class provides clues describing the second student to the blindfolded student. The blindfolded student gets one guess after each clue. When correct, the student who provided the last clue is the next one to be "it." Play continues until a predetermined time limit is reached. To keep hesitations to a minimum, keep a reference vocabulary list available for students.

PACING SUGGESTION: Twenty minutes of classtime.

¿Quién es?

Alternatively, hand out 3x5 index cards. Ask students to provide the following information:

- where they are from
- a short description of what they look like
- two adjectives to describe themselves
- what they like to do in their free time

Collect the cards. Then either read the descriptions and have students guess who is who or distribute the cards to various students to read aloud (make sure they don't read their own). Students guess who is who.

PACING SUGGESTION: Thirty minutes of classtime.

Recipe

Guacamole is the second most popular dip in the southwestern U.S. (after salsa). It is generally served with fried corn chips, tostadas, but can also be served with flour tortillas cut into strips. With your students, try this quick-and-easy recipe for Olé Guacamole.

Olé Guacamole

Ingredientes

6 aguacates bien maduros
1 tomate: pelado, sin semillas y en trozos pequeños
1/4 taza de cebolla bien picada
1/4 taza de hojas de cilantro picadas
8 cdas. de jugo fresco de limón verde
sal a gusto

Instrucciones

Cortar los aguacates por la mitad, quitar la semilla y sacar la pulpa. Pisar la pulpa con un tenedor; añadir el tomate, la cebolla, el cilantro, el jugo de limón verde y la sal a gusto. Refrigerar cubierto con papel de plástico por 1/2 hora. Servir con tortillas.

(Sirve a 6-8.)

Tiempo de preparación 40 minutos
Tiempo total 90 minutos

Music

Pop music. Both Spanish and English speakers in the U.S. enjoy Spanish language music. Some popular singers are Gloria Estefan, Jennifer Lopez, and Marc Anthony. Have students go to an online music store and find out the names of other Spanish-speaking singers and groups. Play some of the music they research. Discuss what music they like and why. Samples can be heard on music sites.

¡AvanzaRap! DVD

- Video animations of all **¡AvanzaRap!** songs (with Karaoke track)
- Teaching Suggestions
- **¡AvanzaRap!** Activity Masters
- **¡AvanzaRap!** Video Scripts and Answers

Also available on the **Teacher One Stop**

UNIT THEME
Time with friends

UNIT STANDARDS

COMMUNICATION
- Talk about activities
- Say what you like and don't like to do
- Tell where you are from
- Describe yourself and others
- Identify people and things

CULTURES
- *Los Premios Juventud*
- Art of Xavier Cartada
- Favorite activities of Florida teenagers
- Mexican and Tex-Mex food
- Los cascarones

CONNECTIONS
- Geography: Cities—old and new
- Mathematics: Calculate distances
- Language: Places in the U.S. with Spanish names
- Music: Tex-Mex

COMPARISONS
- Florida beaches, places students go in their free time.
- Famous performers and athletes
- The Spanish **p, t,** and **ñ,** the English *p, t,* and /*ny*/ sound
- Representing communities in art
- Paseo del Río, places of interest
- Restaurants with foods from other countries
- Family traditions
- Places of interest in San Antonio and Miami
- Traditional dishes of Mexico and Cuba
- Personal descriptions

COMMUNITIES
- Restaurants with food from Spanish-speaking countries

UNIDAD 1

Estados Unidos

Un rato con los amigos

Lección 1
Tema: ***¿Qué te gusta hacer?***

Lección 2
Tema: ***Mis amigos y yo***

«¡Hola!
Nosotras somos Alicia y Sandra. Somos de Estados Unidos.»

Población: 304.059.724

Población de ascendencia hispana: 43.168.000

Ciudad con más latinos: Nueva York (más de 2.000.000)

Ciudad con mayor porcentaje de latinos: El Paso, Texas (77%)

Comida latina: el sándwich cubano, burritos, fajitas

Gente famosa: Sandra Cisneros (escritora), Gloria Estefan (cantante), Eva Mendes (actriz), Eloy Rodríguez (bioquímico)

El sándwich cubano

Cultural Geography

Setting the Scene
- Where are we? South America or North America? (North America)
- What are the girls' names? (Alicia and Sandra)
- Which city has a larger Latino population, Boston or New York? (New York)

Teaching with Maps
- Which countries have borders with the United States? (Mexico and Canada)
- The United States has coasts along which bodies of water? (Pacific Ocean, Atlantic Ocean, Gulf of Mexico)

Cultura Interactiva my.hrw.com *See these pages come alive!*

Hispanic friends gather for a celebration in New York City

La ascendencia hispana The over 40 million Hispanics living in the United States trace their roots to more than 20 nations. From September 15 to October 15, Hispanic Heritage Month celebrates the diverse backgrounds and cultures of these Americans. *Do you know anyone from a Spanish-speaking country?*

La comunidad cubana de Miami The Cuban American community thrives in Miami's Little Havana. **Calle Ocho** is known for its Cuban restaurants, cafés, and shops, and the nearby Freedom Tower houses the Cuban American Museum. *How have people from other countries shaped your community?*

Miami's Freedom Tower, home to the Cuban American Museum

Dancers in traditional dress during the ***Fiesta San Antonio***

Las celebraciones San Antonio is proud of its unique multicultural history. The **Fiesta San Antonio,** a ten-day celebration with food, music, and parades, honors the heroes of the Alamo and the Battle of San Jacinto. La Villita, the city's oldest neighborhood, hosts many of the festival events. *How do people celebrate history and culture where you live?*

Cultura Interactiva my.hrw.com

Send your students to my.hrw.com to explore authentic Latin culture in the United States. Tell them to click on Cultura interactiva to see these pages come alive!

Culture

About the Photos

- The photo of the teens shows a diverse group of people. According to the 2000 U.S. Census, the term *Hispanic* refers to Spanish-speaking people in the U.S. of any race.
- The Freedom Tower's octagonal shape was inspired by the Cathedral Tower at Sevilla Cathedral in Seville, Spain.
- The Fiesta San Antonio grew out of the Battle of the Flowers (1891). A group of women adorned horse-drawn carriages, paraded in front of the Alamo, and bombarded each other with flower blossoms—as homage to the heroes of the Alamo and San Jacinto.

Expanded Information

- Hispanic Heritage Month begins on the anniversary of independence of five Latin American countries—Costa Rica, El Salvador, Guatemala, Honduras, and Nicaragua.
- La Villita is home to a thriving arts and crafts community.

Video Character Guide

Alicia and Sandra are friends from the U.S. Alicia lives in Miami. She likes to ride her bike, play soccer, and skateboard.

Bridging Cultures

Heritage Language Learners

Support What They Know If there are students from Spanish-speaking countries in class, ask them to talk about where their families are from. Encourage them to share some traditions they celebrate in their countries, typical foods, famous people, and so forth.

English Learners

Build Background Encourage students to think about other cities with large Latino communities (New York, El Paso) and list them on the board. Organize students into groups and have them select a city that interests them. Ask them to create an almanac similar to the one on p. 28, based on the information they find about their communities.

Lesson Overview

Culture at a Glance

Topic & Activity	Essential Question
Beaches in Florida pp. 30-31	Where do teenagers go during their free time in Florida?
Youth awards show p. 41	How have Latino performers and athletes affected popular culture in the United States?
Art in Miami p. 44	How would being Cuban American influence an artist's work?
What teens like to do pp. 48-49	What are the favorite activities of teens in a dual-language school in Florida?
Culture review p. 53	What Latino cultural elements exist in San Antonio and Miami?

COMPARISON COUNTRIES — Estados Unidos — Colombia — México

Practice at a Glance

	Objective	Activity & Skill
Vocabulary	Activities	1: Reading/Writing; 3: Listening/Reading; 4: Speaking; 5: Writing/Speaking; 13: Writing; 14: Speaking; 15: Listening/Writing; 17: Listening/Reading; 18: Listening/Reading; 19: Speaking; 20: Reading/Listening/Speaking; 21: Writing; Repaso 1: Listening; Repaso 2: Writing; Repaso 4: Writing
Vocabulary	Foods and beverages	2: Writing/Speaking; 4: Speaking; 20: Reading/Listening/Speaking; Repaso 1: Listening; Repaso 2: Writing
Grammar	Using subject pronouns and **ser**	6: Writing; 7: Reading/Writing; 8: Writing; 9: Speaking; 10: Listening/Reading; 11: Reading/Speaking; 12: Speaking; 17: Listening/Reading; 19: Speaking; 21: Writing; Repaso 1: Listening; Repaso 3: Writing
Grammar	Using **de** to describe where you are from	8: Writing; 9: Speaking; 10: Listening/Reading; 11: Reading/Speaking; 12: Speaking; 17: Listening/Reading; 19: Speaking; 21: Writing; Repaso 1: Listening
Grammar	Using **gustar** with an infinitive	2: Writing/Speaking; 3: Listening/Reading; 4: Speaking; 5: Speaking; 13: Writing; 14: Speaking; 15: Listening/Writing; 16: Speaking; 17: Listening/Reading; 18: Listening/Reading; 19: Speaking; 20: Reading/Listening/Speaking; 21: Writing; Repaso 1: Listening; Repaso 2: Writing; Repaso 4: Writing
Communication	Talk about activities	4: Speaking; 5: Writing/Speaking; 14: Speaking; 16: Speaking; 19: Speaking; 20: Reading/Listening/Speaking; 21: Writing
Communication	Tell where you are from	9: Speaking; 11: Reading/Speaking; 12: Speaking; 19: Speaking; 20: Reading/Listening/Speaking; 21: Writing
Communication	Say what you like and don't like to do	2: Writing/Speaking; 4: Speaking; 5: Writing/Speaking; 14: Speaking; 16: Speaking; 19: Speaking; 20: Reading/Listening/Speaking; 21: Writing
Communication	Pronunciation: The letters **p** and **t**	*Pronunciación: Las letras p y t,* p. 43: Listening/Speaking
Recycle	Weather expressions	4: Speaking

The following presentations are recorded in the Audio Program for *¡Avancemos!*

- **¡A responder!** *page 33*
- **15: Las actividades** *page 44*
- **20: Integración** *page 47*
- **Repaso de la lección** *page 52*
  1: Listen and understand

For **¡AvanzaRap!** scripts, see the **¡AvanzaRap! DVD.**

¡A responder! TXT CD 1 track 24

1. beber
2. descansar
3. hablar por teléfono
4. comer
5. tocar la guitarra
6. leer un libro
7. jugar al fútbol
8. dibujar

15 Las actividades TXT CD 1 track 28

Hola. Me llamo Mariana. Hoy es sábado. A mis amigos Jorge y Federico y a mí nos gusta descansar. A Federico le gusta pasear pero a Jorge no. Me gusta pasear pero hoy no hace sol. Me gusta más tocar la guitarra. A ellos les gusta escuchar música pero no les gusta tocar la guitarra. A los dos les gusta mirar la televisión. A mí no me gusta mirar la televisión.

20 Integración TXT CD 1 tracks 30, 31

¡Hola, Vanessa! Me llamo Carmen. Soy de Carolina, Puerto Rico. Después de las clases, me gusta practicar deportes, hacer la tarea o estudiar. No me gusta escuchar música. Y no me gusta mirar la televisión. Los sábados y domingos me gusta pasar un rato con los amigos. Me gusta comer pizza o papas fritas y descansar.

Repaso de la lección TXT CD 1 track 33

1 Listen and understand

Pablo: Me llamo Pablo. Soy de Miami. Después de las clases me gusta andar en patineta y escuchar música. Sara es de Puerto Rico. Sara, ¿qué te gusta hacer después de las clases? ¿Te gusta andar en patineta y escuchar música?

Sara: ¿Andar en patineta? No, no me gusta andar en patineta. Pero me gusta escuchar música. También me gusta comer frutas.

Pablo: ¡Uy! ¡No me gusta comer frutas! Me gusta comer helado.

Sara: A mí también. A nosotros nos gusta comer helado. Mmmmmm...

Resource List

Everything you need to ...

Plan	Present	Assess
TEACHER ONE STOP ✓Lesson Plans ✓Teacher Resources ✓Audio and Video	INTERACTIVE WHITEBOARD LESSONS TEACHER ONE STOP WITH PROJECTABLE TRANSPARENCIES POWER PRESENTATIONS ANIMATEDGRAMMAR	ONLINE ASSESSMENT ✓ Assessments for on-level, modified, pre-AP, and heritage learners ✓ Create customized tests with the **Examview Assessment Suite** ✓ **performance space** ✓ *Generate Success* Rubric Generator

Print

Plan	Present	Practice	Assess
URB 1 • Video Scripts pp. 97–98 • Family Letter p. 123 • Absent Student Copymasters pp. 125–132 **Best Practices Toolkit**	**URB 1** • Video Activities pp. 79–86	• *Cuaderno* pp. 1–23 • *Cuaderno para hispanohablantes* pp. 1–23 • *Lecturas para todos* pp. 108–112 • *Lecturas para hispanohablantes* • *¡AvanzaCómics! SúperBruno y Nati,* Episodio 1 **URB 1** • Practice Games pp. 57–64 • Audio Scripts pp. 103–107 • Map/Culture Activities pp. 113–114 • Fine Art Activities pp. 117–118	**Differentiated Assessment Program** **URB 1** • Did you get it? Reteaching and Practice Copymasters pp. 29–38

Projectable Transparencies (Teacher One Stop, my.hrw.com)

Culture	Presentation and Practice	Classroom Management
• Atlas Maps 1–6 • U.S. Map 7 • Fine Art Transparencies 8, 9	• Vocabulary Transparencies 12, 13 • Grammar Presentation Transparencies 16, 17	• Warm Up Transparencies 26–29 • Student Book Answer Transparencies 46–49

Audio and Video

Audio	Video	¡AvanzaRap! DVD
• Student Book Audio CD 1 Tracks 23–33 • Workbook Audio CD 1 Tracks 1–10 • Heritage Learners Audio CD 1 Tracks 1–4, CD 3 Tracks 3–4 • Assessment Audio CD 1 Tracks 3–4 • *Lecturas para todos* Audio CD1 Track 1, CD 2 Tracks 1–6 • Sing-along Songs Audio CD	• Vocabulary Video DVD 1 • *Telehistoria* DVD 1 Escena 1 Escena 2 Escena 3 Completa	• Video animations of all **¡AvanzaRap!** songs (with Karaoke track) • Interactive DVD Activities • Teaching Suggestions • **¡AvanzaRap!** Activity Masters • **¡AvanzaRap!** video scripts and answers

Online and Media Resources

Student	Teacher
Available online at my.hrw.com • Online Student Edition • News + Networking • performance space • @HOMETUTOR • CULTURA Interactiva • WebQuests • Interactive Flashcards • Review Games • Self-Check Quiz **Student One Stop** **Holt McDougal Spanish Apps**	**Teacher One Stop (also available at my.hrw.com)** • Interactive Teacher's Edition • All print, audio, and video resources • Projectable Transparencies • Lesson Plans • TPRS • Examview Assessment Suite **Available online at my.hrw.com** *Generate Success* Rubric Generator and Graphic Organizers **Power Presentations**

Differentiated Assessment

On-level	Modified	Pre-AP	Heritage Learners
• Vocabulary Recognition Quiz p. 11 • Vocabulary Production Quiz p. 12 • Grammar Quizzes pp. 13–14 • Culture Quiz p. 15 • On-level Lesson Test pp. 16–22	• Modified Lesson Test pp. 11–17	• Pre-AP Lesson Test pp. 11–17	• Heritage Learners Lesson Test pp. 17–23

Core Pacing Guide

50 Minute (9 Day)

	Objectives/Focus	Teach	Practice	Assess/HW Options
DAY 1	**Culture:** Learn about Hispanic culture in the U.S. **Vocabulary:** activities, what you like to do • Warm Up OHT 26 **5 min**	Unit Opener pp. 28–29 Lesson Opener pp. 30–31 **Presentación de vocabulario** pp. 32–33 • Read A–F • View video DVD 1 • Play audio TXT CD 1 track 23 • *¡A responder!* TXT CD 1 track 24 **25 min**	Lesson opener pp. 30–31 **Práctica de vocabulario** p. 34 • Acts. 1, 2 **15 min**	**Assess:** *Para y piensa* p. 34 **5 min** **Homework:** *Cuaderno* pp. 1–3 @HomeTutor
DAY 2	**Communication:** talking about activities, saying what you like to do • Warm Up OHT 26 • Check Homework **5 min**	**Vocabulario en contexto** pp. 35–36 • *Telehistoria escena 1* DVD 1 **20 min**	**Vocabulario en contexto** pp. 35–36 • Act. 3 TXT CD 1 track 25 • Acts. 4, 5 **20 min**	**Assess:** *Para y piensa* p. 36 **5 min** **Homework:** *Cuaderno* pp. 1–3 @HomeTutor
DAY 3	**Grammar:** subject pronouns, **ser, ser de** • Warm Up OHT 27 • Check Homework **5 min**	**Presentación de gramática** p. 37 • Subject pronouns and **ser** **Práctica de gramática** pp. 38–39 • *Nota gramatical:* **ser de** **20 min**	**Práctica de gramática** pp. 38–39 • Acts. 6, 7, 8, 9 **20 min**	**Assess:** *Para y piensa* p. 39 **5 min** **Homework:** *Cuaderno* pp. 4–6 @HomeTutor
DAY 4	**Communication:** using **ser de** to talk about where people are from • Warm Up OHT 27 • Check Homework **5 min**	**Gramática en contexto** pp. 40–41 • *Telehistoria escena 2* DVD 1 **15 min**	**Gramática en contexto** pp. 40–41 • Act. 10 TXT CD 1 track 26 • Acts. 11, 12 **25 min**	**Assess:** *Para y piensa* p. 41 **5 min** **Homework:** *Cuaderno* pp. 4–6 @HomeTutor
DAY 5	**Grammar:** using **gustar** to talk about what people like to do • Warm Up OHT 28 • Check Homework **5 min**	**Presentación de gramática** p. 42 • **Gustar** with an infinitive **Práctica de gramática** pp. 43–44 • *Pronunciación* TXT CD 1 track 27 **Culture:** *El arte de Miami* **15 min**	**Práctica de gramática** pp. 43–44 • Acts. 13, 14, 16 • Acts. 15 TXT CD 1 track 28 **25 min**	**Assess:** *Para y piensa* p. 44 **5 min** **Homework:** *Cuaderno* pp. 7–9 @HomeTutor
DAY 6	**Communication:** Culmination: what you like to do, **ser, ser de, gustar** • Warm Up OHT 28 • Check Homework **5 min**	**Todo junto** pp. 45–47 • *Escenas 1, 2: Resumen* • *Telehistoria completa* DVD 1 **15 min**	**Todo junto** pp. 45–47 • Acts. 17, 18 TXT CD 1 tracks 25, 26, 29 • Act. 20 TXT CD 1 tracks 30, 31 • Acts. 19, 21 **25 min**	**Assess:** *Para y piensa* p. 47 **5 min** **Homework:** *Cuaderno* pp. 10–11 @HomeTutor
DAY 7	**Reading:** What do you like to do? **Connections:** Geography • Warm Up OHT 29 • Check Homework **5 min**	**Lectura** pp. 48–49 • *¿Qué te gusta hacer?* TXT CD 1 track 32 **Conexiones** p. 50 • *La geografía* **20 min**	**Lectura** pp. 48–49 • *¿Qué te gusta hacer?* **Conexiones** p. 50 • *Proyectos* 1, 2, 3 **20 min**	**Assess:** *¡Interpreta! ¿Y tú?* p. 49 **5 min** **Homework:** *Cuaderno* pp. 15–17 @HomeTutor
DAY 8	**Review:** Lesson review • Warm Up OHT 29 **5 min**	**Repaso de la lección** pp. 52–53 **15 min**	**Repaso de la lección** pp. 52–53 • Act. 1 TXT CD 1 track 33 • Acts. 2, 3, 4, 5 **20 min**	**Assess:** *Repaso de la lección* pp. 52–53 **10 min** **Homework:** *En resumen* p. 51; *Cuaderno* pp. 12–14, 18–23 (optional) Review Games Online @HomeTutor
DAY 9	**Assessment**			**Assess:** Lesson 1 test **50 min**

Core Pacing Guide 90 Minute (5 Day)

Day	Objectives/Focus	Teach	Practice	Assess/HW Options
DAY 1	**Culture:** learn about Hispanic culture in the U.S. **Vocabulary:** activities, what you like to do • Warm Up OHT 26 **5 min**	Unit Opener pp. 28–29 Lesson Opener pp. 30–31 **Presentación de vocabulario** pp. 32–33 • Read A–F • View video DVD 1 • Play Audio TXT CD 1 track 23 • *¡A responder!* TXT CD 1 track 24 **20 min**	Lesson Opener pp. 30–31 **Práctica de vocabulario** p. 34 • Acts. 1, 2 **20 min**	**Assess:** *Para y piensa* p. 34 **5 min** @HomeTutor
	Communication: talking about activities, saying what you like to do **5 min**	**Vocabulario en contexto** pp. 35–36 • *Telehistoria escena 1* DVD 1 **15 min**	**Vocabulario en contexto** pp. 35–36 • Act. 3 TXT CD 1 track 25 • Acts. 4, 5 **15 min**	**Assess:** *Para y piensa* p. 36 **5 min** **Homework:** *Cuaderno* pp. 1–3 @HomeTutor
DAY 2	**Grammar:** subject pronouns **ser, ser de** • Warm Up OHT 27 • Check Homework **5 min**	**Presentación de gramática** p. 37 • Subject pronouns and **ser** **Práctica de gramática** pp. 38–39 • *Nota gramatical:* **ser de** **20 min**	**Práctica de gramática** pp. 38–39 • Acts. 6, 7, 8, 9 **15 min**	**Assess:** *Para y piensa* p. 39 **5 min**
	Communication: using **ser de** to talk about where people are from **5 min**	**Gramática en contexto** pp. 40–41 • *Telehistoria escena 2* DVD 1 **20 min**	**Gramática en contexto** pp. 40–41 • Act. 10 TXT CD 1 track 26 • Acts. 11, 12 **15 min**	**Assess:** *Para y piensa* p. 41 **5 min** **Homework:** *Cuaderno* pp. 4–6 @HomeTutor
DAY 3	**Grammar:** using **gustar** to talk about what people like to do • Warm Up OHT 28 • Check Homework **5 min**	**Presentación de gramática** p. 42 • **Gustar** with an infinitive **Práctica de gramática** pp. 43–44 • *Pronunciación* TXT CD 1 track 27 **Culture:** *El arte de Miami* **15 min**	**Práctica de gramática** pp. 43–44 • Acts. 13, 14, 16 • Act. 15 TXT CD 1 track 28 **20 min**	**Assess:** *Para y piensa* p. 44 **5 min**
	Communication: Culmination: what you like to do, **ser, ser de, gustar** **5 min**	**Todo junto** pp. 45–47 • *Escenas 1, 2: Resumen* • *Telehistoria completa* DVD 1 **10 min**	**Todo junto** pp. 45–47 • Acts. 17, 18 TXT CD 1 tracks 25, 26, 29 • Act. 20 TXT CD 1 tracks 30, 31 • Acts. 19, 21 **25 min**	**Assess:** *Para y piensa* p. 47 **5 min** **Homework:** *Cuaderno* pp. 7–11 @HomeTutor
DAY 4	**Reading:** What do you like to do? • Warm Up OHT 29 • Check Homework	**Lectura** pp. 48–49 • *¿Qué te gusta hacer?* • TXT CD 1 track 32 **15 min**	**Lectura** pp. 48–49 • *¿Qué te gusta hacer?* **15 min**	**Assess:** *Para y piensa* p. 49 **5 min**
	Review: Lesson review **5 min**	**Repaso de la lección** pp. 52–53 **20 min**	**Repaso de la lección** pp. 52–53 • Act. 1 TXT CD 1 track 33 • Acts. 2, 3, 4, 5 **25 min**	**Assess:** *Repaso de la lección* pp. 52–53 **5 min** **Homework:** *En resumen* p. 51; *Cuaderno* p. 12–23 (optional) Review Games Online @HomeTutor
DAY 5	**Assessment**			**Assess:** Lesson 1 test **45 min**
	Connections: Geography **5 min**	**Conexiones** p. 50 • *La geografía* **10 min**	**Conexiones** p. 50 • *Proyectos* 1, 2, 3 **30 min**	

¡AVANZA! **Objectives**
- Introduce lesson theme: **¿Qué te gusta hacer?**
- **Culture:** Compare everyday activities.

Presentation Strategies
- Introduce characters' names: Alicia, Teresa, Miguel, Sandra.
- Ask students to make a list of their favorite activities and foods.
- Ask students to talk about beaches they know.

STANDARDS
2.2 Products and perspectives
4.2 Compare cultures
21st Century **Critical Thinking and Problem Solving,** Pre-AP

Warm Up Projectable Transparencies, 1-26

Numbers Write the names of the following numbers:

0. _____	6. _____
1. _____	7. _____
2. _____	8. _____
3. _____	9. _____
4. _____	10. _____
5. _____	

Answers: 0. cero; 1. uno; 2. dos; 3. tres; 4. cuatro; 5. cinco; 6. seis; 7. siete; 8. ocho; 9. nueve; 10. diez

Comparación cultural

Exploring the Theme
Ask the following:
1. How might the activities the students enjoy in the photo differ from activities you enjoy?
2. Which activities do you think they prefer?
3. Which climate do you think they prefer? Why?
4. What are some kinds of activities that are more easily done in their preferred climate?

¿Qué ves? Possible answers include:
- It is sunny and warm.
- They are friends.
- The boy likes to play soccer and the girl likes to draw.

UNIDAD 1
Estados Unidos

Lección 1

Tema:
¿Qué te gusta hacer?

¡AVANZA! **In this lesson you will learn to**
- talk about activities
- tell where you are from
- say what you like and don't like to do

using
- subject pronouns and **ser**
- **de** to describe where you are from
- **gustar** with an infinitive

¿Recuerdas?
- weather expressions

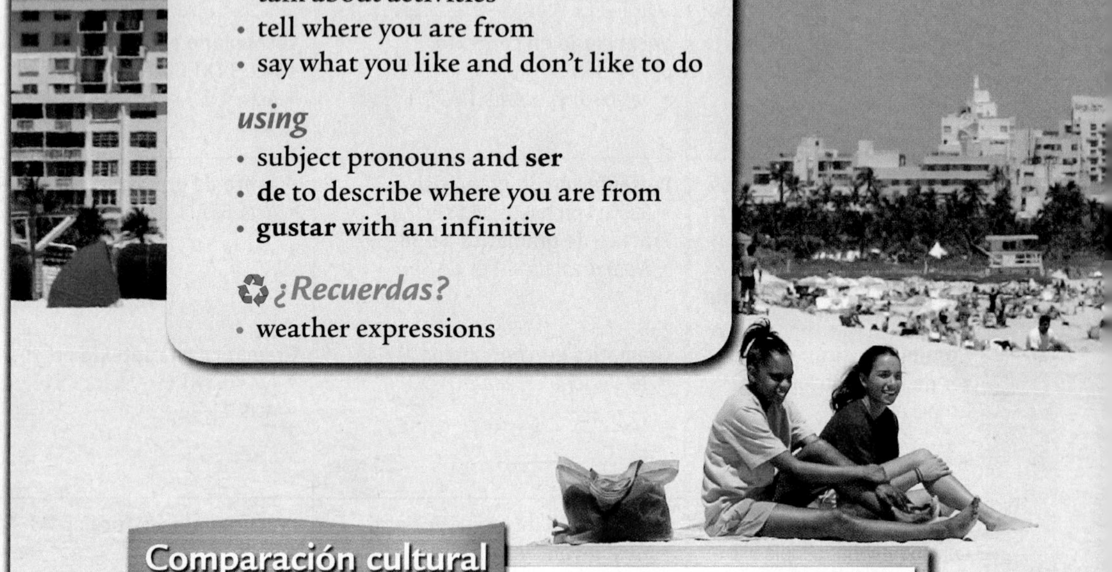

Comparación cultural

In this lesson you will learn about
- *Los Premios Juventud,* an awards show in Miami
- Cuban-American artist Xavier Cortada
- free-time activities of students at a Florida school

Compara con tu mundo
This group of teenagers is spending the day at a beach. In southern Florida, beaches are open year-round and are popular places to do many different activities. *Where do you like to go with your friends in your free time? What do you like to do?*

¿Qué ves?
Mira la foto
What is the weather like?
Do you think that these teenagers are friends?
What activities do they like to do?

Differentiating Instruction

Multiple Intelligences
Visual Learners After viewing and discussing the opening photo, ask students to illustrate their ideal vacation spot—real or imaginary. Students can create a drawing or a collage by cutting pictures from magazines. Be sure the drawings illustrate people engaged in some of their favorite activities. Have them share their work with the class.

Pre-AP
Draw Conclusions Using a map, point out the city of Miami. Ask students to think about why Miami is so greatly influenced by Latin culture. Why does its location and neighbors make this a logical conclusion? Point out the Spanish-speaking countries that are close to Miami, such as Cuba, the Dominican Republic, and so on.

DIGITAL SPANISH my.hrw.com
ONLINE STUDENT EDITION with...

performance space
News + Networking
@HOMETUTOR
CulTura Interactiva

- Audio and Video Resources
- Interactive Flashcards
- Review Activities
- WebQuest
- Conjuguemos.com

PRACTICE SPANISH WITH HOLT MCDOUGAL APPS!

Una playa de Miami Beach
Miami Beach, Florida

DIGITAL SPANISH

TEACHER TOOLS
- Interactive Whiteboard Lessons
- Generate Success!

ALSO AVAILABLE...
- Online Workbook
- Spanish InterActive Reader

SPANISH ON THE GO!
- Performance Space
- Holt McDougal Spanish Apps
- ¡Avancemos! eTextbook

Using the Photo

Location Information

Miami Beach The photo shows Miami Beach, Florida; downtown Miami can be seen in the background. Miami's 35-mile stretch of sand and sea offers ample space for jogging, surfing, kite flying, volleyball, and swimming.

Expanded Information

South Beach, located at the southern end of Miami Beach, has a mix of first-class hotels, youth hostels, cafés, and trendy Latin and Caribbean restaurants.

Population Since the 2000 U.S. Census for Miami-Dade County, non–Cuban Latins have outnumbered the more than 650,000 people of Cuban descent. The Mexican population was up by 65 percent and the Colombian population grew 31 percent.

Differentiating Instruction

Heritage Language Learners

Expand and Elaborate Ask students to share what they know about the city of Miami. Students might mention:
- Miami is the most populous city in the state of Florida.
- Nearly 60 percent of Miami residents are of Latin origin.
- Miami is the only city in the United States founded by a woman, Julia Tuttle.

Multiple Intelligences

Naturalist Have students study the photo and write down the elements that indicate what kind of physical environment is shown (clothing, sand, ocean, etc.). Students can then compare and contrast the area pictured with their local area.

Long-term Retention

Interest Inventory

If you need more information on what students like to do after school, ask them now and list their responses on the board. Read the list aloud and have students raise their hands to indicate their favorite things. Record their responses so students with similar interests can work together.

¡AVANZA! Objectives

- Present vocabulary about daily activities, snack foods, and likes and dislikes.
- Check for recognition.

Core Resources

- Video Program: DVD 1
- Audio Program: TXT CD 1 tracks 23, 24

Presentation Strategies

- Draw students' attention to the ¡Avanza! which shows objectives that begin each section, and the Para y piensa, which ends each section and shows what students will be able to do at the end of each section.
- Play the audio as students read A–F.
- Show the video.

STANDARD

1.2 Understand language

Communication

TPR Activity

After modeling the terms below, select students to act out the following activities as you say them aloud:

- hablar por teléfono
- leer un libro
- tocar la guitarra
- dibujar
- andar en patineta
- jugar al fútbol

Comparisons

English Language Connection

Cognates are words in Spanish that resemble English. **Bicicleta,** for example, is a cognate of the English word *bicycle*. Scan the two pages for other cognates. Possible answers include: **la pizza** = *pizza;* **teléfono** = *telephone.*

Presentación de VOCABULARIO

¡AVANZA! **Goal:** Learn about what Alicia and her friends like to do. Then use what you have learned to talk about activities. ***Actividades 1–2***

VIDEO DVD

AUDIO

A ¡Hola! Me llamo Teresa. **Después de las clases, me gusta pasar un rato con los amigos.** Me gusta **escuchar música o tocar la guitarra.**

Miguel Teresa Alicia

B ¡Hola! Me llamo Miguel. A mí me gusta **hablar por teléfono, dibujar y estudiar.** Me gusta **pasear, pero me gusta más correr.** A ti, **¿qué te gusta hacer?**

C ¡Hola! Me llamo Alicia. A mí me gusta **montar en bicicleta y jugar al fútbol. También** me gusta **andar en patineta.**

Differentiating Instruction

Multiple Intelligences

Mathematical/Logical Create a Venn diagram on the board. Label one circle "Indoors" and the other "Outdoors." Have students brainstorm a list based on the activities on pp. 32–33. Volunteers come to the board and place each activity in the appropriate circle. There might be overlapping activities.

Slower-paced Learners

Yes/No Questions Ask students yes/no questions to help reinforce new vocabulary. Use gestures to support the meaning of each question. **¿Te gusta dibujar? ¿Te gusta jugar al fútbol?** Instruct students to point to the picture of the activity in each question, and then answer **sí** or **no**.

D Hoy hace calor en Miami. **Antes de practicar deportes** me gusta **comprar agua.**

E Me gusta **beber** agua o **jugo** pero no me gusta beber **refrescos.**

Más vocabulario

la actividad *activity*
alquilar un DVD *to rent a DVD*
aprender el español *to learn Spanish*
la escuela *school*
hacer la tarea *to do homework*
Expansión de vocabulario p. R2

F No me gusta **trabajar** los sábados y domingos. Me gusta **escribir correos electrónicos** y **descansar.** También me gusta **mirar la televisión.** ¿Te gusta pasar un rato con los amigos?

@HOMETUTOR my.hrw.com Interactive Flashcards

¡A responder! Escuchar

Escucha la lista de actividades. Mientras escuchas, representa las actividades. *(Act out the activities as you hear them.)*

TEACHER to TEACHER

Matt Cavanaugh
Rye, New York

Tips for Presenting Vocabulary

I choose five to eight words from the vocabulary list that are most easily illustrated by dramatic gestures. I display the target words on the board and point to each one. The class repeats them several times as they imitate my gestures. I repeat the drill, mixing up the order of the words and gradually erasing the words as students master them. The presentation is complete when students can produce the words upon seeing the gestures as easily as they can act out their meanings when they hear or read them.

Go online for more tips!

Communication — Common Error Alert

- In Spanish there is more than one verb that means *to play*. **Jugar** means *to play a game*, and **tocar** means *to play an instrument*.
- Point out as well that although the noun **agua** is feminine, it's always preceded by the masculine article **el**.

Communication — Regionalisms

Explain to students that there are regional variations for some of the words and phrases in this spread, for example: **montar en bicicleta** (México); **andar en bicicleta** (España); **patineta** (Argentina); **monopatín** (México); **el refresco** (México); **la gaseosa** (España); **el jugo** (Latinoamérica); **el zumo** (España).

Differentiating Instruction

Pre-AP

Communicate Preferences Make a list of ten activities mentioned on pp. 32–33 and write it on the board. Have students copy the list on a separate piece of paper and rate the activities from 1 to 10. Call on individual students to read their list in order of preference.

Inclusion

Alphabetic/Phonetic Awareness Have students divide a piece of paper into two columns, **Acciones** and **Objetos.** Students should list the new vocabulary words on pp. 32–33 in the appropriate column. Point out phonetic differences between Spanish and English, such as the silent **h** at the beginning of **helado** and **hablar,** or the pronunciation of the **ll** in **galletas.**

Answers Projectable Transparencies, 1-46

¡A responder! Audio Script, TE p. 29b
Students should act out the following.
1. beber (to drink)
2. descansar (to rest)
3. hablar por teléfono (to talk on the phone)
4. comer (to eat)
5. tocar la guitarra (to play the guitar)
6. leer un libro (to read a book)
7. jugar al fútbol (to play soccer)
8. dibujar (to draw)

Práctica de VOCABULARIO

Objectives
- Practice vocabulary: daily activities and likes and dislikes.
- State preferences about favorite activities.

Core Resource
- *Cuaderno,* pp. 1–3

Practice Sequence
- **Activity 1:** Vocabulary recognition: everyday activities, stating preferences
- **Activity 2:** Vocabulary production: stating preferences

STANDARDS
1.1 Engage in conversation, Act. 2
1.2 Understand language, Act. 1
1.3 Present information, Acts. 1–2, PYP

1 El sábado

Leer
Escribir

Miguel, Teresa y Alicia hablan de las actividades que les gusta hacer. Completa la conversación con las palabras apropiadas. *(Complete the conversation about what they like to do.)*

Alicia: Miguel, ¿te gusta escuchar __**1.**__ los sábados?
Miguel: Sí, pero me gusta más practicar __**2.**__ . Teresa, ¿te gusta montar en __**3.**__ ?
Teresa: No, no me gusta. Me gusta más leer __**4.**__ .
Alicia: Teresa, ¿te gusta hacer __**5.**__ los sábados?
Teresa: ¿Los sábados? No, sólo me gusta preparar __**6.**__ , alquilar __**7.**__ y descansar.

un libro
un DVD
bicicleta
deportes
la comida
música
la tarea

Expansión:
Teacher Edition Only
Ask groups of students to read aloud Alicia, Teresa, and Miguel's dialogue.

2 ¿Te gusta?

Escribir
Hablar

Explica si te gusta o no te gusta comer o beber estas comidas y bebidas.
(Tell whether you like or don't like to eat or drink these foods and beverages.)

modelo: beber
(No) Me gusta beber refrescos.

1. comer

2. beber

3. comer

4. comer

5. beber

6. comer

Expansión
Compare your answers with a classmate's.

Más práctica Cuaderno *pp. 1–3* Cuaderno para hispanohablantes *pp. 1–4*

Get Help Online
my.hrw.com

PARA Y PIENSA

Did you get it?
1. Tell someone that you like to listen to music. Me gusta ____ .
2. Ask a friend if he or she likes to do homework. ¿Te gusta ____ ?

Long-term Retention
Personalize It

Use Expansión de vocabulario on p. R14. Encourage students to list words and phrases used for after-school activities. Have them use their list to answer questions about the activities they like and dislike.

Ongoing Assessment

Get Help Online
More Practice
my.hrw.com

Quick Check These activities are self-checks. If students have trouble completing them, they can practice online. For additional practice, use Reteaching & Practice Copymasters URB 1, pp. 29, 30.

Answers Projectable Transparencies, 1-46

Activity 1
1. música **4.** un libro **6.** la comida
2. deportes **5.** la tarea **7.** un DVD
3. bicicleta

Activity 2 Answers will vary. Sample answers include:
1. (No) Me gusta comer galletas.
2. (No) Me gusta beber jugo.
3. (No) Me gusta comer helado.
4. (No) Me gusta comer papas fritas.
5. (No) Me gusta beber agua.
6. (No) Me gusta comer fruta.

Para y piensa **1.** Me gusta escuchar música.
2. ¿Te gusta hacer la tarea?

Differentiating Instruction

Slower-paced Learners

Sentence Completion Before doing Activity 1, read aloud the dialogue. Invite volunteers to play the parts of Alicia, Miguel, and Teresa. As students read each sentence aloud, model gestures to support key vocabulary (e.g., pantomime putting on headphones for the word **escuchar**). Instruct students to point to the word in the list that they believe goes in each blank.

Heritage Language Learners

Support What They Know Have students share any additional information describing the foods presented in this activity. For example, someone from the Dominican Republic might call french fries something different than someone from Spain would. Generate a list on the board to compare similarities and differences.

VOCABULARIO en contexto

¡AVANZA! **Goal:** Listen to the words Alicia and Sandra use to talk about activities. Then practice what you have heard to talk about the activities you and others like to do. ***Actividades 3–5***

¿Recuerdas? Weather expressions p. 20

Telehistoria escena 1

@HOMETUTOR my.hrw.com View, Read and Record

STRATEGIES

Cuando lees
Search for clues Look for clues in the picture before starting to read. Who's in the photos? What are they doing?

Cuando escuchas
Listen for intonation The way people speak, not just what they say, often reflects how they feel. Listen for Alicia's intonation. How does she feel about the activities mentioned?

VIDEO DVD

AUDIO

Alicia: *(on phone, to Sandra, a friend in San Antonio, Texas)* En Miami, hace calor. ¿Te gusta andar en patineta?

Sandra: No, me gusta más pasear o montar en bicicleta. Los sábados me gusta hacer la tarea.

Alicia: ¿Sí? Los sábados me gusta pasar un rato con amigos... ¡y dibujar! Y los domingos, ¡jugar al fútbol! Los viernes me gusta alquilar un DVD y comer pizza.

Sandra: Sí, sí. Mmm. Me gusta comer pizza y hablar por teléfono.

Alicia: ¿Hablar por teléfono? No me gusta hablar por teléfono. *(Father gives a look of disbelief.)*

Continuará... p. 40

También se dice

Miami To talk about riding bicycles, Sandra uses the phrase **montar en bicicleta.** In other Spanish-speaking countries you might hear:
- **muchos países andar en bicicleta**

¡AVANZA! Objective
- Understand activity vocabulary in context.

Core Resources
- Video Program: DVD 1
- Audio Program: TXT CD 1 track 25

Presentation Strategies
- Draw students' attention to the ¡Avanza!
- Ask students to predict Alicia and Sandra's conversation.
- Show the video and/or play the audio.

STANDARDS
1.2 Understand language
Communication, Heritage Language Learners

Warm Up
Projectable Transparencies, 1-26

Vocabulary Choose a verb to complete each sentence: **mirar, escribir, escuchar, pasar, montar.**

1. Me gusta _____ música.
2. A mí me gusta _____ en bicicleta.
3. Los sábados me gusta _____ la televisión.
4. Después de las clases me gusta _____ un rato con los amigos.
5. No me gusta _____ correos electrónicos.

Answers: 1. escuchar; 2. montar; 3. mirar; 4. pasar; 5. escribir

Communication

Interpersonal Mode

Telehistoria Ask students to keep the following questions in mind:
1. Who likes to do homework on Saturdays?
2. Who likes to draw? Who likes to play soccer?
3. Who doesn't like to talk on the telephone?

Video Summary

@HOMETUTOR VideoPlus my.hrw.com

Alicia and Sandra, friends who met through playing soccer, talk about what they like to do in their free time. Alicia's father listens to her side of the conversation, and is very surprised to hear her say that she doesn't like to talk on the phone.

Differentiating Instruction

Inclusion

Clear Structure Write phrases from the Telehistoria on individual sentence strips (e.g., **Me gusta montar en bicicleta.**). Label one half of the board Alicia, and the other Sandra. Have students read each sentence aloud and post it under the name of the character who said it. If both girls enjoy an activity, they should post the sentence in the center.

Heritage Language Learners

Increase Accuracy With a partner, have students create their own short dialogue, describing what they like to do in their free time. They should use the Telehistoria as a model. Invite volunteers to act out their conversations in front of the class after they have had a chance to practice.

Objectives

- Practice using vocabulary in context.
- Recycle: weather expressions.
- Practice using **gustar** + infinitive.

Core Resource

- Audio Program: TXT CD 1 track 25

Practice Sequence

- **Activity 3:** Telehistoria comprehension
- **Activity 4:** Vocabulary production: **gustar;** Recycle: weather expressions
- **Activity 5:** Vocabulary production: **gustar**

STANDARDS

1.1 Engage in conversation, Acts. 4–5; PYP
1.2 Understand language, Act. 3
1.3 Present information, Acts. 4–5; PYP
21st Century **Creativity and Innovation,** Slower-paced Learners

✓ Ongoing Assessment

Get Help Online
More Practice
my.hrw.com

PARA Y PIENSA **Dictation** Have students read aloud the sentences in the Para y piensa then have them write the sentences as you dictate them. For additional practice, use Reteaching & Practice Copymasters URB 1, pp. 29, 31, 38.

3 *Comprensión del episodio* A Alicia y a Sandra les gusta...

Escuchar Leer

Indica si lo que dicen Alicia y Sandra es cierto o falso. Si es falso, corrige la oración. *(Tell if what Alicia and Sandra say is true or false. Correct the false statements.)*

modelo: **Alicia:** Los viernes no me gusta comer pizza.
Falso. Los viernes me gusta comer pizza.

1. **Alicia:** Llueve en Miami.
2. **Sandra:** Me gusta correr los sábados.
3. **Alicia:** Me gusta pasar un rato con los amigos.
4. **Sandra:** Me gusta hacer la tarea los domingos.
5. **Alicia:** Los sábados me gusta alquilar un DVD.
6. **Sandra:** Me gusta hablar por teléfono.

Expansión:
Teacher Edition Only
Have students write an activity they like to do for each day of the week.

4 ¡Hace frío! *¿Recuerdas?* Weather expressions p. 20

Hablar

Habla con otro(a) estudiante de qué te gusta hacer en cada situación. *(Tell a partner what you like to do in each situation.)*

beber agua	leer un libro	pasear
correr	jugar al fútbol	mirar la televisión
descansar	montar en bicicleta	¿ ?

modelo: Hace viento.

A: Hace viento. ¿Qué te gusta hacer?
B: Me gusta mirar la televisión o descansar.

1. Hace frío y llueve.
2. Hace sol.
3. Hace viento y hace frío.
4. Hace calor.
5. Nieva y hace sol.
6. Llueve y hace calor.

Expansión
Write what you don't like to do for each weather expression.

5 ¡Me gusta!

Escribir Hablar

Escribe una lista de tus actividades después de las clases. Luego compara las actividades con las de otros(as) estudiantes. *(Write a list of your after-school activities and compare them with other students'.)*

– escribir correos electrónicos
– practicar deportes
– dibujar
– andar en patineta

A: ¿Te gusta pasear después de las clases?
B: Sí, me gusta pasear.
C: No, me gusta pasear antes de las clases.

Expansión:
Teacher Edition Only
Have students write their list of activities in order of preference.

Get Help Online
my.hrw.com

PARA Y PIENSA **Did you get it?** Fill in Alicia's sentences with the appropriate vocabulary word.

1. Me gusta ____ al fútbol.
2. ¿Te gusta escuchar ____ ?
3. También me gusta ____ pizza.

Answers Projectable Transparencies, 1-46

Activity 3
1. Falso. Hace calor en Miami.
2. Falso. Me gusta pasear o montar en bicicleta.
3. Cierto.
4. Falso. Me gusta hacer la tarea los sábados.
5. Falso. Los viernes me gusta alquilar un DVD.
6. Falso. No le gusta hablar por teléfono.

Activity 4 Answers will vary. Sample answers should follow this pattern:
1. **A:** Hace frío y llueve.¿Qué te gusta hacer?
B: Me gusta leer un libro.
2. ... Me gusta jugar al fútbol.
3. ... Me gusta descansar.
4. ... Me gusta beber agua.
5. ... Me gusta pasear.
6. ... Me gusta correr.

Answers continue on p. 37.

Differentiating Instruction

Slower-paced Learners

Memory Aids Divide students into groups to create posters illustrating each of the weather phrases listed in Activity 4. Instruct each group to write the weather phrase in large letters and draw a picture illustrating that specific weather condition. Keep the posters displayed to assist in daily discussions of the weather.

Pre-AP

Expand and Elaborate Have Pre-AP students ask and answer questions regarding their activity preferences. For example, Student A may ask **¿Te gusta más practicar deportes o mirar la televisión?** and Student B may answer **Me gusta más practicar deportes.**

Presentación de GRAMÁTICA

¡AVANZA! **Goal:** Learn how to use subject pronouns and the verb **ser.** Then practice the forms of **ser** with **de** to talk about where you and others are from. *Actividades 6–9*

English Grammar Connection: **Pronouns** are words that take the place of nouns. **Subject pronouns** indicate who is being described or who does the action in a sentence.

We are friends. — Nosotros somos amigos.

Subject Pronouns and ser

ANIMATEDGRAMMAR my.hrw.com

Ser means *to be*. Use **ser** to identify a person or say where he or she is from. How do you use this verb with **subject pronouns**?

Here's how:

	Singular			Plural			
	yo	soy	*I am*	nosotros(as)	somos	*we are*	
familiar	tú	eres	*you are*	vosotros(as)	sois	*you are*	*familiar*
formal	usted	es	*you are*	ustedes	son	*you are*	
	él, ella	es	*he, she is*	ellos(as)	son	*they are*	

Yo **soy** de Buenos Aires.
I am *from Buenos Aires.*

Ellas **son** de Venezuela.
They are *from Venezuela.*

Singular

Use **tú** with
- a friend
- a family member
- someone younger

Use **usted** with
- a person you don't know
- someone older
- someone to whom you want to show respect

Plural

- Use **vosotros(as)** with friends, family, and younger people only in Spain.
- Use **ustedes** with people you don't know, older people, and people for whom you want to show respect in Spain; use it in Latin America with any group of people.
- Use **nosotras, vosotras,** and **ellas** when all the people you are talking about are female.

Más práctica
Cuaderno *pp. 4–6*
Cuaderno para hispanohablantes *pp. 5–7*

@HOMETUTOR my.hrw.com
Leveled Practice
Conjuguemos.com

Differentiating Instruction

Slower-paced Learners

Personalize It Have students fold a piece of paper in half lengthwise. Instruct them to label one column **tú,** and the other column **usted.** Then tell students to list the names of people in their own lives whom they would address using these pronouns. Possible names in the **tú** column: friends and family members. Names in the **usted** column: teachers, principals, and other adults.

Heritage Language Learners

Regional Variations Encourage students to share a sentence describing their family's country or region of origin. **Yo soy de Venezuela. Yo soy de Madrid.** Then ask students to discuss whether they are more familiar with the pronoun **vosotros** or **ustedes.** How does this relate to their country or region of origin?

¡AVANZA! **Objective**
- Present subject pronouns and **ser.**

Core Resource
- *Cuaderno,* pp. 4–6

Presentation Strategies
- Present forms and uses of subject pronouns and **ser.** Check understanding: one student gives a pronoun and another student gives the corresponding verb form.
- Discuss uses of formal and familiar forms.

STANDARDS
4.1 Compare languages

Warm Up Projectable Transparencies, 1-27

Vocabulary Copy the sentences onto a separate piece of paper and number them according to the sequence in which they appear on the Telehistoria on p. 35. The first one is done for you.

__1.__ En Miami hace calor.
_____ No, me gusta más pasear o montar en bicicleta.
_____ No me gusta hablar por teléfono.
_____ ¿Te gusta andar en patineta?
_____ Me gusta comer pizza y hablar por teléfono.
_____ Los sábados me gusta hacer la tarea.

Answers: 3; 6; 2; 5; 4

Communication
Common Error Alert

Unlike English, subject pronouns can often be omitted in Spanish because the verb form indicates the subject: **Soy de Venezuela.**

Answers Projectable Transparencies, 1-46

Answers continued from p. 36.

Activity 5 Answers will vary. Sample answers include:
A. ¿Te gusta escuchar música? **B.** Sí, me gusta escuchar música. **C.** No, me gusta más andar en patineta.

A. ¿Te gusta ver la televisión? **B.** Sí, me gusta ver la televisión. **C.** No, me gusta más alquilar un DVD.

Para y piensa **1.** jugar; **2.** música; **3.** comer

Objectives
- Practice using subject pronouns.
- Use **ser de** + location to tell where someone is from.

Core Resource
- *Cuaderno,* pp. 4–6

Practice Sequence
- **Activity 6:** Controlled practice: subject pronouns
- **Activity 7:** Controlled practice: **ser de**
- **Activity 8:** Transitional practice: **ser de**
- **Activity 9:** Open-ended practice: subject pronouns and **ser de**

STANDARDS
1.1 Engage in conversation, Act. 9
1.3 Present information, Acts. 6–8
4.1 Compare languages, Acts. 7–9
21st Century **Creativity and Innovation,** Pre-AP

Communication
Common Error Alert
Give students names, as well as combinations of names and subject pronouns. Have them provide the appropriate pronoun. For example: **Marcos y yo = nosotros.**

Comparisons
English Language Connection
Plural subject pronouns in Spanish corresponding to *we, you* (familiar), and *they* have feminine and masculine forms: **nosotros/nosotras, vosotros/vosotras, ellos/ellas.**

Answers Projectable Transparencies, 1-46

Activity 6

1. ellos	**3.** yo	**5.** nosotras
2. ella	**4.** él	**6.** ellas

Activity 7

1. somos	**4.** son	**7.** es
2. soy	**5.** son	**8.** eres
3. es	**6.** es	

Práctica de GRAMÁTICA

6 ¿Quién?

Escribir

Escribe el pronombre que corresponde. *(Write the corresponding pronoun.)*

modelo: ella

1.

2.
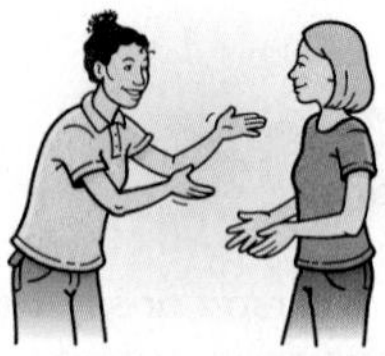
3.

4.

5.

6.

Expansión:
Teacher Edition Only
Have student groups use TPR to demonstrate personal pronouns. One student says a personal pronoun, the other points to the appropriate person(s).

Nota gramatical
Use **de** with the verb **ser** (p. 37) to talk about where someone is from.

Daniela y Sonia **son de** Miami.	Martín **es de** Honduras.
*Daniela and Sonia **are from** Miami.*	*Martín **is from** Honduras.*

7 ¿De dónde son?

Leer
Escribir

Los amigos y maestros de Lucía son de diferentes lugares. Escribe la forma correcta de **ser** para saber de dónde son. *(Write the correct form of **ser**.)*

Hola, me llamo Lucía. Mi amigo Andrés y yo **1.** de la República Dominicana. Yo **2.** de Santo Domingo y él **3.** de San Pedro de Macorís. La señora Muñoz y el señor Vázquez **4.** de Puerto Rico. Son mis maestros favoritos. Mis amigas Laura y Ana **5.** de Colombia. Laura **6.** de Bogotá y Ana **7.** de Cartagena. Y tú, ¿de dónde **8.** ?

Expansión
Write an e-mail message telling where at least five of your teachers and friends are from.

Differentiating Instruction

Inclusion
Frequent Review/Repetition Before doing Activity 6, have students go through the activity orally. Instruct them to point to each picture as they say aloud the corresponding pronoun. Then reverse the activity. Say a pronoun aloud, and have students point to the corresponding picture. After students have written their answers, ask them to share their responses aloud once again.

Heritage Language Learners
Writing Skills Have students use the text in Activity 7 as a model to draft an e-mail message to a friend. Remind students to capitalize proper nouns. If students have questions regarding the spelling of place names, refer them to a dictionary or atlas. Once students have drafted their e-mails, have them exchange papers to peer-edit each other's work.

8 Los amigos de Alicia

Escribir

Alicia tiene muchos amigos y vas a conocerlos en los próximos capítulos. Escribe de dónde son. *(Alicia has many friends that you will meet. Write where they are from.)*

modelo: Maribel y Enrique / España
Maribel y Enrique son de España.

1. yo / Miami

2. Claudia y Pablo / México

3. Marisol / Puerto Rico

4. papá y yo / Miami

5. Fernando / Ecuador

6. Mario / la República Dominicana

Expansión:
Teacher Edition Only
Ask students to name three famous people and tell where they are from.

9 De muchos países

Hablar

Pregúntale a otro(a) estudiante de dónde son los amigos de Miguel. Usa los pronombres. *(Ask another student where Miguel's friends are from. Use pronouns.)*

modelo: Luis: Bolivia

A ¿De dónde es Luis?

B Él es de Bolivia.

1. Leticia: Perú
2. Álvaro y Linda: Nicaragua
3. Isabel y Ángela: California
4. Andrés y Jorge: Uruguay
5. Ana Sofía y Elena: Panamá
6. Y tú, ¿ ?

Expansión:
Teacher Edition Only
Have students replace the name in each question with its corresponding subject pronoun. For example: **¿De dónde es Luis? = ¿De dónde es él?**

Más práctica Cuaderno *pp. 4–6* Cuaderno para hispanohablantes *pp. 5–7*

Get Help Online
my.hrw.com

PARA Y PIENSA

Did you get it? Match the phrases to make a complete sentence.

1. Cristóbal y yo
2. Tomás
3. Yo

a. soy de México.
b. somos de Honduras.
c. es de la República Dominicana.

Differentiating Instruction

Multiple Intelligences

Visual Learners Direct students to find each of the countries, states, and cities mentioned on p. 39 on a map or in an atlas. For the cities and states mentioned, have students identify the country. For each country mentioned, have students name some of its major cities. Invite students to add this information as they talk about **Los amigos de Alicia**.

Pre-AP

Expand and Elaborate Give students the opportunity to create a simple scrapbook showing where their friends are from. Have students choose five or six of their friends to write about. Direct them to model their sentences after those in Activities 8 and 9. Students might use a photo of each friend or draw a picture to illustrate each page. **Isabella es de California. Jorge es de Denver.**

Connections
Geography

Activities 8 and 9 Have students use a map to locate the places mentioned in the activities. Then have them create a table with the headings **América del Norte, América del Sur, América Central, El Caribe,** and **Europa.** Have them list the places mentioned under the appropriate heading.

Communication
Common Error Alert

Be sure that students understand that questions asked with one pronoun may require a different pronoun in the answer. For example: **¿tú/usted? yo, ¿vosotros/ustedes? nosotros,** and so on.

Ongoing Assessment

Get Help Online
More Practice
my.hrw.com

PARA Y PIENSA **Intervention** Have student pairs practice asking each other where they are from and where their parents are from. For additional practice, use Reteaching & Practice Copymasters URB 1, pp. 32, 33.

Answers Projectable Transparencies, 1-47

Activity 8
1. Yo soy de Miami.
2. Claudia y Pablo son de México.
3. Marisol es de Puerto Rico.
4. Papá y yo somos de Miami.
5. Fernando es de Ecuador.
6. Mario es de la República Dominicana.

Activity 9
1. ¿De dónde es Leticia? Ella es de Perú.
2. ¿De dónde son Álvaro y Linda? Ellos son de Nicaragua.
3. ¿De dónde son Isabel y Ángela? Ellas son de California.
4. ¿De dónde son Andrés y Jorge? Ellos son de Uruguay.
5. ¿De dónde son Ana Sofía y Elena? Ellas son de Panamá.
6. ¿De dónde eres tú? Yo soy de (city or country).

Para y piensa **1.** b; **2.** c; **3.** a

¡AVANZA! Objectives

- Practice **ser** in context.
- **Culture:** discussion of a well-known Latino award show in Miami.
- Practice names of Latin American countries.

Core Resources

- Video Program: DVD 1
- Audio Program: TXT CD 1 track 26

Presentation Strategies

- Ask students to scan the Telehistoria script before watching the video.
- Show the video. Point out gestures/intonations and uses of **ser de.**
- Play audio.

Practice Sequence

- **Activity 10:** Telehistoria comprehension
- **Activity 11:** Transitional practice: **ser de**
- **Activity 12:** Open-ended: **ser de**

STANDARDS

1.1 Engage in conversation, Act. 11
1.2 Understand language, Acts. 10–12
2.2 Products and perspectives, Act. 11
4.1 Compare languages, Act. 12
21st Century **Collaboration,** Inclusion; **Creativity and Innovation,** Heritage Language Learners

Warm Up Projectable Transparencies, 1-27

Pronouns Match the letter of the pronoun to its corresponding subject.

1. Sr. Ruiz _____	**a.** ella
2. Mi amigo Miguel y yo _____	**b.** ustedes
3. Tú y Marta _____	**c.** ellas
4. Sandra _____	**d.** él
5. Alicia y Teresa _____	**e.** nosotros

Answers: 1. d; 2. e; 3. b; 4. a; 5. c

Video Summary

HOMETUTOR VideoPlus my.hrw.com

Alicia, Teresa, and Miguel run into Mr. Costas, a Spanish teacher. Alicia introduces her friends to him, and Mr. Costas tries to guess where they are from. In turn, Teresa and Miguel try to guess where Mr. Costas is from. The friends are surprised to find out that Mr. Costas is from Florida.

GRAMÁTICA en contexto

¡AVANZA! **Goal:** Notice how Alicia and her friends say where they are from. Then use **ser** with **de** to tell where people are from. ***Actividades 10–12***

Telehistoria escena 2

HOMETUTOR my.hrw.com View, Read and Record

STRATEGIES

Cuando lees
Scan for details Quickly look ahead for certain details before you read the scene. Scan for names and people. What do you think this scene is about?

Cuando escuchas
Listen for guesses Listen as Mr. Costas guesses where Teresa and Miguel are from. What does he guess? What does Miguel guess about where Mr. Costas is from?

VIDEO DVD

AUDIO

Alicia: ¡Hola! Señor Costas, le presento a dos amigos... Teresa y Miguel. Ellos son de...

Mr. Costas stops her because he wants to guess.

Sr. Costas: Tú eres de... ¿Puerto Rico? ¿Panamá? ¿Costa Rica?

Teresa: No, yo soy de...

Mr. Costas interrupts and gestures toward Miguel.

Sr. Costas: ¿Él es de México? ¿El Salvador? ¿Colombia?

Miguel: No, nosotros somos de *(pointing to himself)* Cuba y *(pointing to Teresa)* de Honduras. Y usted, ¿de dónde es?

Sr. Costas: Soy de...

Miguel: ¿Argentina? ¿Chile? ¿Cuba?

Sr. Costas: Soy de la Florida.

Continuará... p. 45

Differentiating Instruction

Slower-paced Learners

Read Before Listening Have students preview the text of the Telehistoria before listening to it. Instruct them to raise their hands when they come across the name of a state or country. Assign one student to write it on the board. Model for students how to pronounce each place name, and have them repeat after you.

Heritage Language Learners

Writing Skills Invite students to write their own script for an original scene based on the Telehistoria. Tell them that their scenes will have a similar theme, but can use different characters and place names. Point out the punctuation used in the Telehistoria script. Remind students to use question marks correctly to make their script easy to read.

10 Comprensión del episodio Los orígenes

Escuchar
Leer

Contesta las preguntas. *(Answer the questions.)*

1. Teresa y Miguel son los amigos de
   a. Alicia.
   b. el señor Costas.
   c. el señor Díaz.
2. ¿De dónde es Miguel?
   a. Es de Puerto Rico.
   b. Es de Cuba.
   c. Es de la República Dominicana.
3. ¿De dónde es Teresa?
   a. Es de Puerto Rico.
   b. Es de Costa Rica.
   c. Es de Honduras.
4. ¿Quién es de la Florida?
   a. Miguel
   b. el señor Costas
   c. Teresa

Expansión:
Teacher Edition Only
Ask students to write one additional question about the Telehistoria followed by three answer options.

11 Los famosos en Miami

Leer
Hablar

Comparación cultural

Los Premios Juventud

How have Latino performers and athletes affected popular culture in the United States? Los Premios Juventud is an awards show held in **Miami** and broadcast on Spanish-language television. Teens vote for their favorite stars in music, film, and sports. Past nominees include: Shakira and Juanes (Colombia), Paulina Rubio and Gael García Bernal (Mexico), Miguel Cabrera (Venezuela), and Jennifer Lopez (New York).

Juanes

Paulina Rubio

Compara con tu mundo *Who are your favorite figures in music, film, and sports, and why?*

Pregúntale a otro(a) estudiante sobre el origen de los famosos nominados para un Premio Juventud. *(Talk with a partner about where the nominees are from.)*

A ¿De dónde es Juanes?

B Juanes es de Colombia.

12 ¿De dónde somos?

Hablar

Pregúntales a otros(as) estudiantes de dónde son. *(Ask other students where they are from.)*

A Nora, ¿de dónde eres?

B Soy de Miami. ¿Y tú?

A También soy de Miami.

Expansión
As a class, compile the results into a chart to show where everyone is from.

Get Help Online
my.hrw.com

PARA Y PIENSA

Did you get it? Create sentences to tell where the people are from.

1. el Sr. Costas / la Florida
2. Alicia / Miami
3. Teresa y Miguel / Honduras y Cuba

Comparación cultural

Essential Question

Suggested Answer Since Latinos became the largest ethnic minority in the United States, there has been a massive growth in Spanish media, music, art, and literature, which in turn is having an increasingly dramatic effect on American culture.

Background Information

Premios Juventud gives awards in 22 unconventional subcategories such as: **¡Qué actorazo!** (Can He Act or What?); **Actriz que se roba la pantalla** (She Steals the Show); **Voz del momento** (All Over the Dial); **Novato del año** (Rookie that Rocks). Shakira, Juanes, and Paulina Rubio are all musicians (pop/rock). Gael García Bernal is an actor and Miguel Cabrera is a professional baseball player. Jennifer Lopez is a singer/actress.

✓ Ongoing Assessment

Get Help Online
More Practice
my.hrw.com

PARA Y PIENSA **Peer Assessment** Have pairs of students read aloud the sentences and correct each other.

For additional practice, use Reteaching & Practice Copymasters URB 1, pp. 32, 34.

Answers Projectable Transparencies, 1-47

Activity 10
1. a; **2.** b; **3.** c; **4.** b

Activity 11 Answers will vary.
¿De dónde es Shakira? Shakira es de Colombia.
¿De dónde es Paulina Rubio? Paulina Rubio es de México.

Activity 12 Answers will vary but should follow the format: (Name), ¿de dónde eres? Soy de (name of city or country).

Para y piensa
1. El Sr. Costas es de la Florida.
2. Alicia es de Miami.
3. Teresa y Miguel son de Honduras y Cuba.

Differentiating Instruction

Inclusion

Alphabetic/Phonetic Awareness In groups, have students compile a list of the place names they find on pp. 40–41. Have the groups organize their lists in alphabetical order. Then invite volunteers to read the names from their lists. Model the Spanish pronunciation of names that may be spelled the same, but pronounced differently in English. Examples include **México, Miami,** and **Puerto Rico.**

Slower-paced Learners

Personalize It Write the following headings on the chalkboard or chart paper: **Música** (music), **Cine** (movies), **Deportes** (sports). Explain to students the meanings of these words. Then ask for volunteers to add names of their own favorite stars under each heading and say where they are from. Point out stars who are from Spanish-speaking countries or of Hispanic origin.

¡AVANZA! **Objectives**
- Present **gustar** + infinitives.
- Present personal **a** + noun/pronoun.

Core Resource
- *Cuaderno*, pp. 7–9

Presentation Strategies
- Ask students what an infinitive is.
- Point out the verb form **gusta** and the pronouns that identify the people that like the activity.

STANDARDS
4.1 Compare languages

Warm Up Projectable Transparencies, 1-28

Gustar Complete the following sentences with **mí**, **ti**, **me**, or **te**.

1. A _____ te gusta correr.
2. A mí _____ gusta montar en bicicleta.
3. ¿A ti _____ gusta hablar por teléfono?
4. A _____ me gusta descansar los domingos.
5. A mí me gusta comer helado pero a _____ no.

Answers: 1. ti; 2. me; 3. te; 4. mí; 5. ti

Comparisons
English Grammar Connection

Gustar does not literally mean **to like**, but rather to be pleasing. **Me gusta** = *It is pleasing to me*. Use indirect object pronouns **me, te, le, nos, os, les** to indicate to whom an activity is pleasing. Place the indirect object pronoun immediately before the conjugated form of **gustar**. To say that someone does not like something, **no** is used directly before the indirect object pronoun.

Verbs Students Know

Keep in mind that students have studied the meanings of the following infinitives:

alquilar	**dibujar**	**montar (en bicicleta)**
andar (en patineta)	**escribir**	**pasar (un rato)**
aprender	**escuchar**	**pasear**
beber	**hacer (la tarea)**	**practicar**
comer	**hablar**	**preparar**
comprar	**jugar**	**tocar (un instrumento)**
correr	**leer**	**trabajar**
descansar	**mirar**	

Presentación de GRAMÁTICA

¡AVANZA! **Goal:** Learn how to express what people like to do using the verb **gustar.** Then use **gustar** to say what you and others like to do. ***Actividades 13–16***

English Grammar Connection: An **infinitive** is the basic form of a **verb,** a word that expresses action or a state of being. In English, most infinitives include the word *to*. In Spanish, infinitives are always one word that ends in **-ar, -er,** or **-ir.**

I like to run. → **infinitive** (to run)
Me gusta correr. → **infinitive** (correr)

Gustar with an Infinitive

ANIMATEDGRAMMAR my.hrw.com

Use gustar to talk about what people like to do.

Here's how: Use phrases like me gusta + **infinitive.**

Me gusta **dibujar.**	*I like to draw.*
Te gusta **dibujar.**	*You (familiar singular) like to draw.*
Le gusta **dibujar.**	*You (formal singular) like to draw. He/She likes to draw.*
Nos gusta **dibujar.**	*We like to draw.*
Os gusta **dibujar.**	*You (familiar plural) like to draw.*
Les gusta **dibujar.**	*You (plural) like to draw. They like to draw.*

When you want to really emphasize or identify the person that you are talking about, add a + **noun/pronoun.**

A Sonia le gusta **leer.** *Sonia likes to read.*
A ella le gusta **leer.** *She likes to read.*

These are the pronouns that follow a.

A mí me gusta dibujar.	A nosotros(as) nos gusta dibujar.
A ti te gusta dibujar.	A vosotros(as) os gusta dibujar.
A usted le gusta dibujar.	A ustedes les gusta dibujar.
A él, ella le gusta dibujar.	A ellos(as) les gusta dibujar.

Más práctica
Cuaderno *pp. 7–9*
Cuaderno para hispanohablantes *pp. 8–11*

@HOMETUTOR my.hrw.com
Leveled Practice

Differentiating Instruction

Inclusion

Clear Structure Create the following four-column chart on the chalkboard or chart paper and write an example under each column head.

A + name(s)/pronoun + **le/les gusta** + activity
A Ana y a Adela les gusta comer helado.

Have students complete the chart with examples of their own. Help students organize their sentences in the correct order.

Heritage Language Learners

Support What They Know Invite students to share a short paragraph explaining what they, their family members, and their friends like to do. Encourage students to use gestures or picture clues to clarify vocabulary that may not be familiar to all.

Práctica de GRAMÁTICA

13 ¿Les gusta o no?

Escribir Escribe lo que a estas personas les gusta o no les gusta hacer. *(Write what these people like and don't like to do.)*

modelo: a Luisa / preparar la comida ☹
No le gusta preparar la comida.

1. a nosotros / comer pizza ☺
2. a ustedes / estudiar ☹
3. a ti / montar en bicicleta ☹
4. a Alicia y a Miguel / aprender el español ☺
5. a mí / escuchar música ☺
6. a usted / trabajar ☹

Expansión:
Teacher Edition Only
Have students tell you that someone else has the opposite opinion of the activity indicated. For example: A **nosotras nos gusta comer helado.** A **ti no te gusta comer helado.**

14 ¿Qué les gusta hacer?

Hablar Con otro(a) estudiante, di lo que a Alicia y a otros les gusta hacer, según las fotos. *(Tell what Alicia and others like to do.)*

Teresa

A ¿Qué le gusta hacer a Teresa?

B Le gusta leer un libro.

1. Alicia

2. ella

3. él

4. Alicia y Miguel

5. Teresa

6. ustedes

Expansión
For each person pictured, write a sentence stating what they don't like to do.

AUDIO

Pronunciación Las letras p y t

When you pronounce the **p** and **t** in English, a puff of air comes out of your mouth. In Spanish, there is no puff of air. Listen and repeat.

pasar	**por favor**	**Puerto Rico**	**fruta**	**televisión**	**practicar**
pizza	**pero**	**papas**	**tocar**	**estudiar**	**tarea**

Pepe prepara las papas fritas.

¿Te gusta montar en bicicleta?

Objectives
- Encourage students to state likes and dislikes with **gustar** + infinitives.
- Compare pronunciation of the letters **p** and **t** in Spanish and English.

Core Resource
- Audio Program: TXT CD 1 track 27

Practice Sequence
- **Activity 13:** Controlled practice: **gustar** + infinitive
- **Activity 14:** Transitional practice: **gustar** + infinitive
- **Pronunciation:** Oral comprehension and production of the letters **p** and **t**

STANDARDS
1.1 Engage in conversation, Act. 14
1.3 Present information, Acts. 13–14
4.1 Compare languages, Pronunciación
21st Century **Productivity and Accountability,** Multiple Intelligences

Comparisons
English Language Connection
Infinitives In English, an infinitive consists of *to* + *verb* (to sing); in Spanish an infinitive is one word, a verb ending in **-r** (**dibujar**).

Answers Projectable Transparencies, 1-46 thru 1-49

Activity 13
1. A nosotros nos gusta comer pizza.
2. A ustedes no les gusta estudiar.
3. A ti no te gusta montar en bicicleta.
4. A Alicia y a Miguel les gusta aprender el español.
5. A mí me gusta escuchar música.
6. A usted no le gusta trabajar.

Activity 14
1. **A.** ¿Qué le gusta hacer a Alicia?
   B. Le gusta escribir correos electrónicos.
2. **A.** ¿Qué le gusta hacer a ella?
   B. Le gusta andar en patineta.
3. **A.** ¿Qué le gusta hacer a él?
   B. Le gusta comprar frutas.
4. **A.** ¿Qué les gusta hacer a Alicia y a Miguel?
   B. Les gusta pasear.
5. **A.** ¿Qué le gusta hacer a Teresa?
   B. Le gusta tocar la guitarra.
6. **A.** ¿Qué les gusta hacer a ustedes?
   B. Nos gusta pasar un rato con los amigos.

Differentiating Instruction

Slower-paced Learners
Sentence Completion Before students discuss their responses to Activity 14, provide them with the following template on the chalkboard or chart paper:
Estudiante A: ¿Qué ____ gusta hacer a ____?
Estudiante B: ____ gusta ____.
Have students draft their responses by filling in the blanks with the appropriate pronoun, name, and activity.

Multiple Intelligences
Intrapersonal Invite students to keep their own personal Spanish-language journals. Encourage them to make entries about themselves and their own lives. At this point, they might include information about where they and their friends are from, and some of their favorite activities.

Objectives

- Practice **gustar** + infinitives.
- **Culture:** Miami's artwork.

Core Resources

- *Cuaderno,* pp. 7–9
- Audio Program: TXT CD 1 track 28

Practice Sequence

- **Activity 15:** Transitional practice: **gustar** + infinitives
- **Activity 16:** Open-ended practice: **gustar** + infinitives

STANDARDS

1.1 Engage in conversation, Acts. 15–16
1.2 Understand language, Act. 15
1.3 Present information, Act. 15
2.2 Products and perspectives, CC
3.1 Knowledge of other disciplines, CC
4.2 Compare cultures, CC

Comparación cultural

Essential Question

Suggested Answer A Cuban-American artist might create art depicting themes that mix elements of both American and Cuban cultures.

About the Artist

Xavier Cortada is active in his community and has created a variety of public artwork in Miami. This piece, *Music,* was created for Festival Miami 2005, a music festival at the University of Miami (Cortada's alma mater).

✓ Ongoing Assessment

Get Help Online
More Practice
my.hrw.com

PARA Y PIENSA **Remediation** If students have problems saying the sentences in Para y piensa, have them review p. 42 and repeat Activities 13 and 14 on p. 43. For additional practice, use Reteaching & Practice Copymasters URB 1, pp. 35, 36.

Answers Projectable Transparencies, 1-46 thru 1-49

Activity 15

1. ...le gusta descansar, mirar la televisión y escuchar música.
2. ...le gusta descansar, pasear y tocar la guitarra.

Answers continue on p. 45.

15 Las actividades

Escuchar Escribir

Copia esta tabla en una hoja de papel. Escucha la descripción de lo que a Mariana y a sus amigos les gusta hacer los sábados y completa la tabla con **sí** o **no.** Luego contesta las preguntas. *(Copy this chart on a piece of paper. Listen to Mariana's description and complete your chart with **sí** or **no.** Then answer the questions.)*

¿Le gusta...?	descansar	pasear	mirar la televisión	tocar la guitarra
● A Mariana	sí			
A Jorge		no		
A Federico				

1. ¿Qué le gusta hacer a Jorge?
2. ¿Qué le gusta hacer a Mariana?
3. ¿Qué le gusta hacer a Federico?
4. ¿Qué no le gusta hacer a Mariana?
5. ¿Qué no les gusta hacer a Jorge y a Federico?
6. ¿Qué les gusta hacer a los tres amigos?

Audio Program
TXT CD 1 Track 28
Audio Script, TE p. 29b

Expansión
Write a list of the "top five" activities you like to do and the "bottom five" that you don't like to do. Compare with a classmate's.

16 A mi amigo(a) le gusta

Hablar

Habla con otro(a) estudiante para saber qué le gusta y qué no le gusta hacer los sábados y domingos. Luego dile a la clase. *(Ask a classmate what he or she likes to do on weekends. Tell the class.)*

Comparación cultural

El arte de Miami

How would being Cuban American influence an artist's work? Growing up in **Miami,** artist Xavier Cortada learned about his Cuban heritage through his family and community around him. Many of his paintings reflect his identity as a Cuban American. His colorful painting *Music* presents a variety of instruments found in traditional Cuban music *(son, rumba, mambo, Afro-Latin jazz)* as well as American music. How many instruments can you identify?

Music (2005), Xavier Cortada

Compara con tu mundo *What would you paint to represent your community?*

Más práctica Cuaderno *pp. 7–9* Cuaderno para hispanohablantes *pp. 8–11*

Get Help Online
my.hrw.com

PARA Y PIENSA

Did you get it? Complete each sentence with the correct **gustar** phrase.

1. _____ correr. (a ella)
2. ¿_____ andar en patineta? (a ti)
3. _____ tocar la guitarra. (a nosotros)

Differentiating Instruction

Inclusion

Frequent Review/Repetition Have students add the names of three classmates to the bottom of the chart for Activity 15. Then have them repeat questions 1 through 6, inserting the names of their peers. **¿Qué le gusta hacer a Miguel? ¿Qué le gusta hacer a Adriana?** Review with students the questions they will have to ask to get this information. **Miguel, ¿te gusta descansar los sábados?**

Multiple Intelligences

Visual Learners Have students create their own paintings or murals to express the things they like to do. Provide materials such as poster boards, colored pencils, or markers. Have students title their paintings. They may wish to present or exhibit their artwork to the rest of the class.

Todo junto

¡AVANZA! **Goal:** ***Show what you know*** Pay attention to Alicia and her friends as they describe the activities they like to do. Then use **ser** and **gustar** to say where you are from and what you like to do. ***Actividades 17–21***

Telehistoria completa

@HOMETUTOR my.hrw.com **View, Read and Record**

STRATEGIES

Cuando lees
Unlock the main idea Find repeated phrases that can unlock the overall meaning. Find all the phrases that contain the verb **gustar.** What is this scene about?

Cuando escuchas
Listen for cognates A cognate is a Spanish word that sounds like an English word and means the same thing. For example, *telephone* and **teléfono.** In the video, listen for at least three cognates.

Escena 1 *Resumen*
A Alicia y a Sandra les gusta hacer muchas actividades. Les gusta dibujar, comer pizza y más.

Escena 2 *Resumen*
Miguel es de Cuba y Teresa es de Honduras. El señor Costas es de la Florida.

Escena 3

VIDEO DVD

AUDIO

Alicia: ¿Qué les gusta hacer?
Miguel: Me gusta mirar la televisión.
Teresa: No me gusta mirar la televisión. Me gusta más tocar la guitarra o escuchar música.
Miguel: Me gusta comer.
Teresa: Sí, me gusta comer.
Alicia: ¡Nos gusta comer!

They stand to go eat.
Alicia: ¿Qué les gusta comer? ¿Pizza? ¿Les gusta comer helado? ¿Fruta? ¿Beber jugos?
Both say no, and they all sit. Teresa shows them the paper.
Alicia: ¿Trini Salgado? ¿En San Antonio? *(She quickly takes out her cell phone.)* ¡Sandra!

Differentiating Instruction

Slower-paced Learners

Yes/No Questions Ask students yes/no questions to reinforce their understanding of Escena 3 of the Telehistoria. **¿A Miguel le gusta mirar la televisión? ¿Sí o no? ¿A Teresa le gusta mirar la televisión?** Encourage students to point to the place in the text where they found their information.

English Learners

Provide Comprehensive Input Explain to students that cognates are words that are similar in spelling and have the same meaning in two languages. For example: **música** and *music.* Ask students to share words in their own language that are English cognates. Ask students to find Spanish/English cognates in the Telehistoria.

¡AVANZA! **Objective**
· Integrate lesson content.

Core Resource
· Audio Program: TXT CD 1 track 29

Presentation Strategies
· Ask students what they remember about the Telehistoria so far.
· Show the video and/or play the audio.

STANDARDS
1.2 Understand language
4.1 Compare languages

Warm Up Projectable Transparencies, 1-28

Gustar + infinitive Unscramble the following sentences.
1. le gusta/a Mariana/beber jugos
2. mirar la televisión/nos gusta/a nosotros
3. no/a mí/preparar la comida/me gusta
4. les gusta/a Federico y a Jorge/descansar

Answers: 1. A Mariana le gusta beber jugos.
2. A nosotros nos gusta mirar la televisión.
3. A mí no me gusta preparar la comida.
4. A Federico y a Jorge les gusta descansar.

Video Summary

@HOMETUTOR **VideoPlus** my.hrw.com

Alicia, Teresa, and Miguel are trying to decide what to do. They all agree that they like to eat, but then disagree on what to eat or drink. Teresa points to a story in the newspaper about Trini Salgado. Alicia decides to send her Trini Salgado T-shirt to Sandra.

Answers Projectable Transparencies, 1-48

Answers continued from p. 44.
3. ...le gusta descansar, pasear, mirar la televisión y escuchar música.
4. ...no le gusta mirar la televisión.
5. ...no les gusta tocar la guitarra. A Jorge no le gusta pasear.
6. ...les gusta descansar.

Activity 16
Answers will vary. Sample answers include:
¿Qué te gusta hacer los sábados y domingos?
A: ¿Qué no te gusta hacer?
B: Me gusta pasear y tocar la guitarra. No me gusta hacer la tarea.

Para y piensa
1. le gusta; **2.** te gusta; **3.** nos gusta

Objective
- Practice using and integrating lesson vocabulary and grammar.

Core Resources
- *Cuaderno,* pp. 10–11
- Audio Program: TXT CD 1 tracks 25, 26, 29, 30, 31

Practice Sequence
- **Activities 17, 18:** Telehistoria comprehension
- **Activity 19:** Transitional practice: speaking
- **Activity 20:** Open-ended practice: reading, listening, and speaking
- **Activity 21:** Open-ended practice: writing

STANDARDS
1.1 Engage in conversation, Acts. 19–20
1.2 Understand language, Acts. 17–18
1.3 Present information, Acts. 17, 20–21
21st Century **Communication,** Act. 19/ Heritage Language Learners

17 *Comprensión de los episodios* ¿Quiénes son?

Escuchar Leer

Escribe el nombre de cada persona, según las descripciones. *(Write names according to the descriptions.)*

1. No le gusta andar en patineta.
2. Es de Honduras.
3. Les gusta comer.
4. Es de la Florida.
5. Le gusta tocar la guitarra.
6. Es de San Antonio, Texas.
7. Le gusta hablar por teléfono.
8. Le gusta escuchar música.

Expansión
Write clues for another character from the Telehistoria and have a partner guess who it is.

18 *Comprensión de los episodios* Los amigos

Escuchar Leer

Contesta las preguntas según los episodios. *(Answer the questions according to the episodes.)*

1.
- **a.** ¿Cómo se llama?
- **b.** ¿Qué le gusta hacer?
- **c.** ¿Qué no le gusta hacer?

2.
- **a.** ¿Cómo se llama?
- **b.** ¿De dónde es?
- **c.** ¿Qué le gusta hacer?

Expansión:
Teacher Edition Only
Have students write one additional detail about Alicia and Miguel.

19 Nuevos amigos

Digital performance space

Hablar

STRATEGY Hablar
Boost your "speaking self-confidence" with positive statements To increase your speaking self-confidence, say something positive to yourself like: *I learn from my mistakes. I can say things now that I couldn't say last week.* Create your own positive statement. Say it to yourself before the speaking activity below.

Eres un(a) estudiante nuevo(a) en la escuela. Di a otros(as) estudiantes de dónde eres y lo que te gusta y no te gusta hacer. Haz una lista de las cosas que tienen en común. *(Talk with a group of students about where you are from and what you like and don't like to do. Make a list of things you have in common.)*

A Hola, me llamo Víctor. Soy de Chicago. Me gusta escuchar música y correr.

B Hola, me llamo Carolina y soy de Chicago también. No me gusta escuchar música pero me gusta practicar deportes.

C Hola. Me llamo Alex...

Expansión:
Teacher Edition Only
Have students write a list of the things they don't have in common.

Answers Projectable Transparencies, 1-46 thru 1-49

Activity 17

1. Sandra
2. Teresa
3. Alicia, Teresa y Miguel
4. el Sr. Costas
5. Teresa
6. Sandra
7. Sandra
8. Teresa

Activity 18

1. a. Alicia. **b.** A Alicia le gusta dibujar y pasar un rato con amigos. **c.** A Alicia no le gusta hablar por teléfono.

2. a. Miguel. **b.** Miguel es de Cuba. **c.** Le gusta mirar la televisión y comer.

Answers continue on p. 47.

Differentiating Instruction

Slower-paced Learners

Read Before Listening Have students read aloud the questions in Activity 18 before listening to the episodes. Discuss what kind of information they should listen for to answer each question. For example, to answer the question **¿Cómo se llama?,** students should listen for the name of a person.

Multiple Intelligences

Interpersonal After students introduce themselves in Activity 19, have them choose a partner and repeat their introductions to each other. Next have students introduce their partner to the group. Teach how to change the sentences they have heard. For example, **Me llamo Carolina** becomes **Se llama Carolina.**

20 Integración

Digital performance space

Leer
Escuchar
Hablar

Lee el correo electrónico de Vanessa. Después escucha a Carmen y toma apuntes. ¿Qué les gusta hacer a las dos chicas? *(Read the e-mail from Vanessa, then listen to Carmen. Say what both of them like and don't like.)*

Fuente 1 Correo electrónico

¡Hola, Carmen! Soy Vanessa. Soy de Morelos, México. Me gusta mucho practicar deportes. También me gusta andar en patineta. No me gusta escuchar música. Después de las clases me gusta pasar un rato con los amigos y comer pizza. Los sábados y domingos no me gusta hacer la tarea. Me gusta más alquilar un DVD o descansar. ¿Y a ti? ¿Qué te gusta hacer?

Fuente 2 Escucha a Carmen

Listen and take notes
- ¿Qué le gusta hacer a Carmen?
- ¿Qué no le gusta hacer?

modelo: A las chicas les gusta...

Audio Program
TXT CD 1 Tracks 30, 31
Audio Script, TE p. 29b

21 Un correo electrónico

Digital performance space

Escribir

Vas a escribirle un correo electrónico a un(a) nuevo(a) amigo(a) en Puebla, México. Preséntate y explica de dónde eres y qué te gusta y no te gusta hacer. También escribe tres preguntas. *(Write your new e-pal, introducing yourself and telling him or her where you're from and what you like and don't like to do. Ask three questions.)*

modelo: Hola, Eva. Me llamo Ana, y soy de la Florida. Me gusta leer un libro, pero no me gusta mirar la televisión. ¿Te gusta hablar por teléfono?

Writing Criteria	Excellent	Good	Needs Work
Content	Your e-mail includes a lot of information and questions.	Your e-mail includes some information and questions.	Your e-mail includes little information and not enough questions.
Communication	Most of your e-mail is organized and easy to follow.	Parts of your e-mail are organized and easy to follow.	Your e-mail is disorganized and hard to follow.
Accuracy	Your e-mail has few mistakes in grammar and vocabulary.	Your e-mail has some mistakes in grammar and vocabulary.	Your e-mail has many mistakes in grammar and vocabulary.

Expansión:
Teacher Edition Only
Ask students to work in pairs to write a few simple sentences saying what they both like to do.

Más práctica Cuaderno *pp. 10–11* Cuaderno para hispanohablantes *pp. 12–13*

Get Help Online
my.hrw.com

PARA Y PIENSA

Did you get it? Tell where these people are from and what they like to do, based on the Telehistoria.

1. Teresa / Honduras / tocar la guitarra
2. Alicia / Miami / comer
3. Miguel / Cuba / mirar la televisión

Differentiating Instruction

Heritage Language Learners

Writing Skills Have students expand on the e-mail they write for Activity 21 by including information about their heritage countries. For example, students may want to describe in detail a city or region of their country, write about foods and dishes, or discuss in more detail the types of activities one can do.

Slower-paced Learners

Peer Study Support Review with the students the writing rubric that accompanies Activity 21. After students have completed their e-mail messages, have them exchange papers with a partner. Each student reads his or her partner's work and applies the rubric. Model for students how to give constructive criticism to help their partners improve their writing.

Long-term Retention

Pre-AP Integration

Activity 20 Have students make a chart. Label the columns with the girls' names and the rows as **Le gusta** or **No le gusta.** Ask them to make notes as they read the e-mail and listen to the audio.

✓ Ongoing Assessment

Rubric Activity 20

Listening/Speaking

Proficient	Not There Yet
Student takes detailed notes and names most or all the activities that both girls like and dislike.	Student takes few notes and only names some of the activities that both girls like and dislike.

To customize your own rubrics, use the ***Generate Success*** *Rubric Generator and Graphic Organizers.*

✓ Ongoing Assessment

Get Help Online
More Practice
my.hrw.com

PARA Y PIENSA **Intervention** If students have difficulty completing the Para y piensa sentences, refer them to the Telehistorias on pp. 35, 40, and 45. For additional practice, use Reteaching & Practice Copymasters URB 1, pp. 36, 37.

Answers Projectable Transparencies, 1-48 and 1-49

Answers continued from p. 46.

Activity 19 Answers will vary. Sample answers include: Hola, me llamo María. Soy de Costa Rica. Me gusta montar en bicicleta y dibujar.

Activity 20 Answers will vary. Sample answers include: A las chicas les gusta comer pizza y pasar un rato con los amigos.

Activity 21 Answers will vary. Sample answers include: Hola, Juan. Me llamo Pedro y soy de Puerto Rico. Me gusta comer pizza, pero no me gusta preparar la comida. ¿Te gusta mirar la televisión? Hasta luego.

Para y piensa
1. Teresa es de Honduras y le gusta tocar la guitarra.
2. Alicia es de Miami y le gusta comer.
3. Miguel es de Cuba y le gusta mirar la televisión.

¡AVANZA! Objectives

- Use surveys to talk about favorite activities.
- **Culture:** learn what students in a dual-language school in Florida like to do in their free time.
- Interpret information recorded in a bar graph about favorite activities.
- Compare favorite activities of teens.

Core Resource

- Audio Program: TXT CD 1 track 32

Presentation Strategies

- Ask students: What are the activities listed on the survey and graph? Which activity is your favorite? Create a conversation about those activities.
- Explain how to interpret the information in the bar graph.
- Ask students what activities they would list in their own survey or graph.

STANDARDS

1.1 Engage in conversation
1.2 Understand language
2.1 Practices and perpectives
4.2 Compare cultures
21st Century **Communication,** Pair Work: Oral Presentation; **Critical Thinking and Problem Solving,** ¡Interpreta!

Warm Up Projectable Transparencies, 1-29

Ser de and gustar Write an appropriate question for each statement.

1. Nos gusta dibujar.
2. Soy de Costa Rica.
3. A Trini le gusta escuchar música.
4. A Jorge y a Federico no les gusta pasear.
5. Ana y yo somos de San Antonio.

Answers: 1. ¿Qué les gusta hacer a ustedes?; 2. ¿De dónde eres?; 3. ¿Qué le gusta hacer a Trini?; 4. ¿Qué no les gusta hacer a Jorge y a Federico?; 5. ¿De dónde son ustedes?

Culture

Background Information

Explain that dual-language programs allow students to develop proficiency in two languages by learning academic subjects in both languages.

Lectura

Additional readings at my.hrw.com SPANISH InterActive Reader

¡AVANZA! Goal: Read about what students in a dual-language school in Florida like to do in their free time. Then compare the activities they like to do with what you like to do.

AUDIO

¿Qué te gusta hacer?

This is a survey about what students like to do in their free time. It was conducted among students at a dual-language school in Florida.

STRATEGY Leer
Use a judgment line Draw a line like this one with *least popular* on the left and *most popular* on the right. On the line, list all the activities in the survey according to their popularity.

leer estudiar ... dibujar
least popular ... most popular

Una encuesta en la escuela

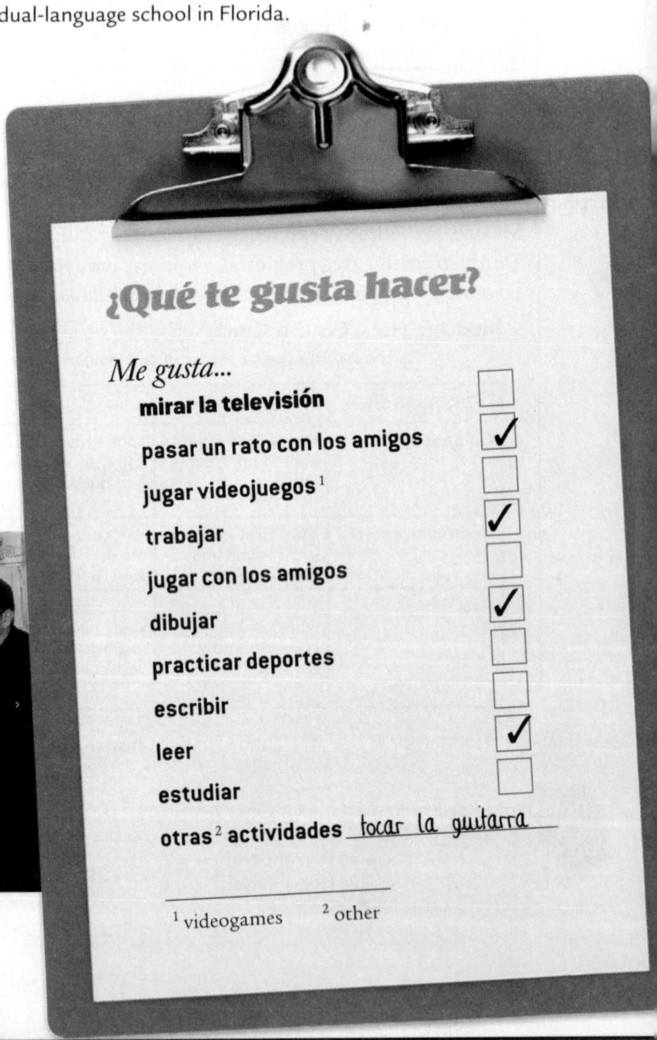

Differentiating Instruction

Heritage Language Learners

Support What They Know Ask students to share any knowledge or experience they have with dual-language schools or programs. Have they, their friends, or family members ever participated in such a program? Encourage students to discuss the advantages of attending a dual-language school. Do they see any disadvantages? Have students express and support their opinions on this topic.

Multiple Intelligences

Interpersonal Have students brainstorm activities they like to do in their free time. For example, **Me gusta dibujar.** Ask a volunteer to write his/her responses on the board in a survey chart similar to the one on p. 48. Have another volunteer tally the results. Call on students to report which are the most popular and least popular activities.

Resultados de la encuesta[3]

25 estudiantes respondieron[4] a las 11 categorías o actividades.

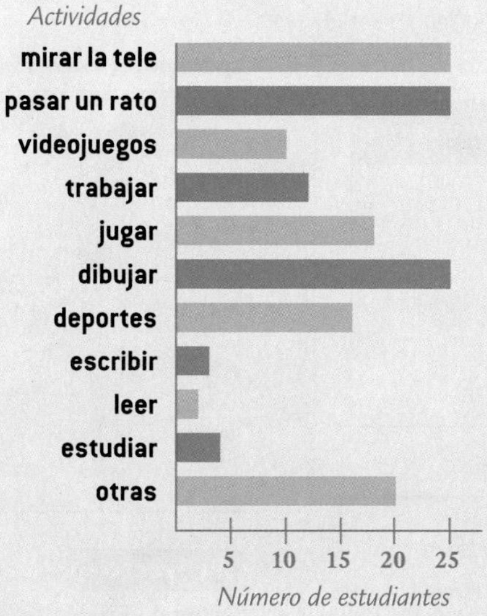

[3] survey [4] replied

PARA Y PIENSA

¡Interpreta!

Based on the chart and survey, answer the following questions.

1. How many students took the survey?
2. What are the three most popular activities and the three least popular activities?
3. Would you get the same results if you used the survey with your classmates? Give specific reasons why or why not.

¿Y tú?

Record your answers to the survey on the previous page and compare them to the results of these students.

Connections

Mathematics

Before working on Para y piensa, remind students that a bar graph shows the relationship between different things. Also remind them that percentages show the proportion of something or the number of parts in every hundred.

Communication

Pair Work

Oral Presentation Have student pairs ask each other whether they like or dislike each activity on the bar graph. Have pairs share conclusions in a presentation to the class.

Communication

Pair Work

Have students pairs ask each other which activities from the survey they like more. For example: **A: ¿Qué te gusta más, jugar o dibujar? B: Me gusta más jugar.** After three exchanges, have them switch roles.

Differentiating Instruction

Slower-paced Learners

Personalize It Direct students' attention to the bar graph. Ask for volunteers to read aloud the different activities listed along the y-axis. Then ask students to point to their favorite activity on the graph. Ask how many students in the survey chose that same activity. Repeat the discussion having students point to their second and third favorite activities.

Inclusion

Cumulative Instruction In order to interpret the results of the bar graph in Spanish, review with students the names for numbers one through twenty. Then ask a series of questions that students must use numbers to answer. If necessary, give two possible choices for students to choose from. **¿A cuántos estudiantes les gusta leer? ¿A dos estudiantes o a veinte estudiantes?**

Answers Projectable Transparencies, 1-46 thru 1-49

Para y piensa

¡Interpreta!

1. Twenty-five students took the survey.
2. The three most popular activities are watching television, spending time with friends, and drawing. The least popular activities are writing, reading, studying.
3. Answers will vary. Sample answer: No, because we have different interests. For example, very few students in my class like to draw.

¿Y tú? Answers will vary. Sample answer will follow this format:
Estudiante A: ¿Te gusta escribir o te gusta leer o practicar deportes?
Estudiante B: Me gusta escribir.

Objectives

- Read about Hernando de Soto's exploration of the southeastern U.S.
- Calculate geographical distances.
- Find places in the U.S. with Spanish names.
- Describe Tex-Mex music.

Presentation Strategies

- Ask students if they know any places that have Spanish names. Do they know why the names are in Spanish? Do they know what the names mean?
- Point out on a map the area Hernando de Soto explored. Ask students to name the states that currently form that area.
- Tell students that the areas explored by the Spaniards were often populated by Native Americans. Ask students how they think the two cultures might have interacted.

STANDARDS

2.2 Products and perspectives
3.1 Knowledge of other disciplines
21st Century Social and Cross-Cultural Skills, Multiple Intelligences

Connections
La historia

Ask students to write a brief historical biography in English of an explorer of their choice. Their bio should include the explorer's birthplace and the regions he explored. Suggest names of explorers, such as Hernando de Soto, Francisco Pizarro, Hernán Cortés, and Francisco de Orellana.

Answers Projectable Transparencies, 1-46 thru 1-49

Conexiones
Ucita: Tampa, FL; Casqui: Parkin, AR; Mabila: Mobile, AL; Anhayca: Tallahassee, FL

Proyecto 1
Ucita to Anhayca: 58 leguas; Anhayca to Mobila: 64 leguas; Mabila to Casqui: 99 leguas

Proyecto 2
Students should be able to come up with some just by looking at a map of the U.S. Other Spanish place names may be found by using online search engines. Possible Answers:
Nevada—snowy　Arizona—arid zone
Colorado—colored　Puerto Rico—rich port
Montana—from montaña (mountain)

Proyecto 3
Answers will vary. Common instruments in Tex/Mex include the accordion, guitar, drums, bass, and saxophone.

Conexiones *La geografía*

La expedición de Hernando de Soto

Hernando de Soto

The map below shows one account of the expedition of Hernando de Soto, a sixteenth-century Spanish explorer. It is believed that de Soto's team traveled through ten present-day U.S. states, and through many Native American villages. The following table gives the latitude and longitude of four U.S. cities, as well as the villages that were close to these locations. Use the coordinates to find the city that corresponds to each Native American village.

NATIVE AMERICAN VILLAGE	LOCATION OF CITY	NAME OF CITY
Ucita	27° 56' N 82° 27' O	
Casqui	35° 15' N 90° 34' O	
Mabila	30° 41' N 88° 02' O	
Anhayca	30° 26' N 84° 16' O	

La expedición (1539–1543)

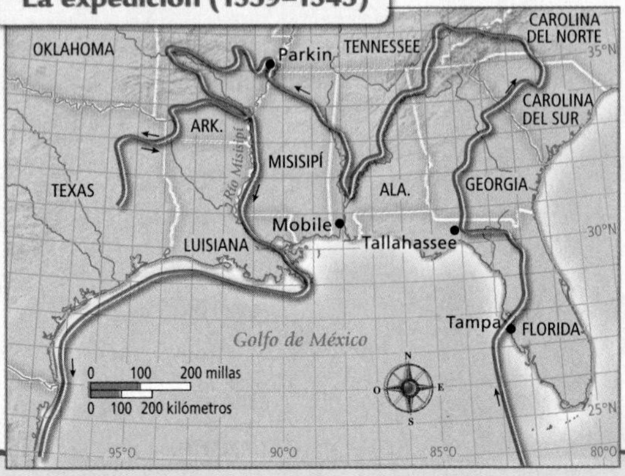

Proyecto 1 *Las matemáticas*

A common form of measurement during the time of de Soto was the league (**legua**). A league was based on the distance an average person could walk in an hour: 3.5 miles. Calculate what these distances would be in leagues.

Ucita to Anhayca:	204 miles
Anhayca to Mabila:	224 miles
Mabila to Casqui:	347 miles

Proyecto 2 *El lenguaje*

Many places in the United States have Spanish names. **Florida,** for instance, means *full of flowers.* Use an atlas or the Internet to find three places in the United States with Spanish names. Then write the meaning of each place.

Proyecto 3 *La música*

The term "Tex-Mex" also describes music that blends elements of Mexico and the southwestern U.S. Most Tex-Mex music features the accordion, brought to Texas in the 1890s by German immigrants. Find an example of Tex-Mex music—such as Selena or Los Tigres del Norte—and listen to it. Then write a paragraph describing the instruments and the music and list the Spanish names of the instruments.

Los Tigres del Norte

Differentiating Instruction

Multiple Intelligences

Logical/Mathematical Most Spanish-speaking countries around the world use the metric system of measurement. Have small groups of students research the Spanish names of both the standard and metric units (**millas, leguas**) for measuring distance, and then ask them to create tables showing the conversions between these units.

English Learners

Check Comprehension Read **La expedición de Hernando de Soto** aloud with students. Stop after each sentence to ask follow-up questions and gauge their comprehension. During each pause, ask *who, what, where,* and *when* questions to help students identify the key ideas in each sentence. For example, after the second sentence you might ask, *Who* is this sentence about? *What* did they do?

Lección 1

En resumen

Vocabulario y gramática

ANIMATED GRAMMAR
Interactive Flashcards
my.hrw.com

Objective

- Review lesson vocabulary and grammar.

Vocabulario

Talk About Activities

alquilar un DVD	*to rent a DVD*	hacer la tarea	*to do homework*
andar en patineta	*to skateboard*	jugar al fútbol	*to play soccer*
aprender el español	*to learn Spanish*	leer un libro	*to read a book*
		mirar la televisión	*to watch television*
beber	*to drink*	montar en bicicleta	*to ride a bike*
comer	*to eat*		
comprar	*to buy*	pasar un rato con los amigos	*to spend time with friends*
correr	*to run*		
descansar	*to rest*	pasear	*to go for a walk*
dibujar	*to draw*	practicar deportes	*to practice / play sports*
escribir correos electrónicos	*to write e-mails*	preparar la comida	*to prepare food / a meal*
escuchar música	*to listen to music*	tocar la guitarra	*to play the guitar*
estudiar	*to study*	trabajar	*to work*
hablar por teléfono	*to talk on the phone*		

Snack Foods and Beverages

el agua (fem.)	*water*
la fruta	*fruit*
la galleta	*cookie*
el helado	*ice cream*
el jugo	*juice*
las papas fritas	*French fries*
la pizza	*pizza*
el refresco	*soft drink*

Say What You Like and Don't Like to Do

¿Qué te gusta hacer?	*What do you like to do?*	Me gusta...	*I like . . .*
¿Te gusta...?	*Do you like . . . ?*	No me gusta...	*I don't like . . .*

Other Words and Phrases

la actividad	*activity*
antes de	*before*
después (de)	*afterward, after*
la escuela	*school*
más	*more*
o	*or*
pero	*but*
también	*also*

Gramática

Nota gramatical: **de** to describe where you are from *p. 38*

Pronouns and ser

Ser means *to be.* Use **ser** to identify a person or say where he or she is from.

Singular		Plural	
yo	soy	nosotros(as)	somos
tú	eres	vosotros(as)	sois
usted	es	ustedes	son
él, ella	es	ellos(as)	son

Gustar with an Infinitive

Use **gustar** to talk about what people like to do.

A mí me gusta dibujar.
A ti te gusta dibujar.
A usted le gusta dibujar.
A él, ella le gusta dibujar.
A nosotros(as) nos gusta dibujar.
A vosotros(as) os gusta dibujar.
A ustedes les gusta dibujar.
A ellos(as) les gusta dibujar.

Practice Spanish with Holt McDougal Apps!

DIGITAL SPANISH

Interactive Flashcards Students can hear every target vocabulary word pronounced in authentic Spanish. Flashcards have Spanish on one side, and a picture or a translation on the other.

Review Games Matching, concentration, hangman, and word search are just a sampling of the fun, interactive games students can play to review for the test.

performance space
News Networking
@HOMETUTOR
CULTURA Interactiva

- **Audio and Video Resources**
- **Interactive Flashcards**
- **Review Activities**
- **WebQuest**
- **Conjuguemos.com**

Communication

Group Work

Game Bring a small ball to class. Write on the board the following vocabulary categories in Spanish: **Comidas** (Foods), **Bebidas** (Beverages), **Acciones** (Actions.) Call out a category and toss a ball to a student. The student says a word that belongs to that category and tosses the ball to another student who names another word in that category. When a student cannot come up with a word, he or she is out of the game.

Long-term Retention

Study Tips

Help students think of categories for the different activities listed in the Vocabulario. For example: Activities to do at home and Activities to do outside, Activities I do alone and Activities I do with friends. Have them write the activities under the categories they have chosen.

Differentiating Instruction

Slower-paced Learners

Memory Aids Give students the opportunity to create their own flashcards to review the words and phrases in the "Talk about activities" and "Snack Foods and Beverages" lists. Instruct students to write the word or phrase on one side of the card, and draw or paste a picture from a magazine on the other side. Have students work in pairs to use their flashcards.

Inclusion

Frequent Review/Repetition With a partner, have students study each group of vocabulary words. One partner goes down the list and tries to give the meaning of each word while covering the English definition. The other partner checks his or her partner's work. If students cannot recall a word's meaning, or offer the wrong meaning, have the partners study the word together, and try again.

Objective
- Review lesson grammar and vocabulary.

Core Resources
- *Cuaderno,* pp. 12–23
- Audio Program: TXT CD 1 track 33

Presentation Strategies
- Direct students' attention to the ¡Llegada!
- As students listen to Activity 1, instruct them to pay special attention to the uses of **gustar** + infinitive.
- Before doing Activity 4, ask students to identify the activities in the photos.
- Review forms of **ser** by saying a subject pronoun and asking students to provide the correct form of **ser.**
- Ask students to generate three questions to ask their classmates based on the Comparación cultural.

STANDARDS
1.2 Understand language, Acts. 1,3
1.3 Present information, Acts. 2, 4
4.1 Compare languages, Act. 3
4.2 Compare cultures, Act. 5
21st Century **Creativity and Innovation,** Multiple Intelligences; **Technology Literacy,** Heritage Language Learners

Warm Up Projectable Transparencies, 1-29
Vocabulary Complete the sentences with the correct word from the group below.

beber más helado pero hablar

1. Me gusta dibujar, _____ no me gusta leer.
2. ¿Qué te gusta _____, escuchar música o mirar la televisión?
3. A Marta le gusta _____ por teléfono.
4. Hoy hace calor. Me gusta _____ agua.
5. Mmm. Me gusta comer _____.

Answers: 1. pero; 2. más; 3. hablar; 4. beber; 5. helado

✓Ongoing Assessment
Get Help Online
More Practice
my.hrw.com

Intervention/Remediation If students achieve less than 80% accuracy on each activity, direct them to the review pages and to get help online at my.hrw.com.

See Activity answers on p. 53.

Lección 1

Repaso de la lección

@HOMETUTOR my.hrw.com

¡LLEGADA!

Now you can
- talk about activities
- tell where you are from
- say what you like and don't like to do

Using
- subject pronouns and **ser**
- **de** to describe where you are from
- **gustar** with an infinitive

To review
- **gustar** with an infinitive p. 42
- **de** to describe where you are from p. 38

Audio Program
TXT CD 1 Track 33
Audio Script, TE p. 29b

1 Listen and understand

AUDIO

Escucha a Pablo y a Sara hablar de sus actividades. Empareja las descripciones con el (los) nombre(s). *(Match according to what Pablo and Sara say about their activities.)*

1. Es de Puerto Rico.
2. Es de Miami.
3. Le gusta escuchar música.
4. No le gusta andar en patineta.
5. No le gusta comer frutas.
6. Le gusta comer helado.

a. Pablo
b. Sara
c. Pablo y Sara

To review
- **gustar** with an infinitive p. 42

2 Say what you like and don't like to do

Escribe oraciones para describir las actividades que te gusta y no te gusta hacer. *(Write sentences describing the activities you like to do and don't like to do.)*

modelo: alquilar un DVD
(No) Me gusta alquilar un DVD.

1. beber refrescos
2. preparar la comida
3. hacer la tarea
4. descansar
5. escribir correos electrónicos
6. pasar un rato con los amigos
7. practicar deportes
8. trabajar
9. comprar libros
10. comer pizza

Differentiating Instruction

Slower-paced Learners
Read Before Listening Before students listen to the script in Activity 1, have them read aloud the sentences in the left-hand column. Discuss which key words they should be listening for and ask them if that is a good key word. For example, for sentence 6, you might ask, Is **le** a good key word to listen for? What about **gusta**? What about **helado**?

Inclusion
Metacognitive Support Read aloud the **modelo** in Activity 2. Point out the order in which the parts of the sentence are put together. Have them write these components on three separate index cards: Card 1: **A Sonia** Card 2: **le gusta** Card 3: **hablar por teléfono**. Then have them put their cards together to form the complete sentence. Repeat this for every item.

To review
- subject pronouns and **ser** p. 37
- **de** to describe where you are from p. 38

3 Tell where you are from

Completa el mensaje con **ser.** *(Complete the e-mail with the appropriate form of **ser.**)*

```
Hola, me llamo Eduardo. Yo __1.__ de Miami. Y tú, ¿de
dónde __2.__? Mis amigos y yo __3.__ de diferentes países.
Roberto __4.__ de Chile y Yolanda __5.__ de Perú. Nosotros
__6.__ estudiantes. El señor Santana y la señora Zabala
__7.__ maestros. Ellos __8.__ de Cuba.
```

To review
- **gustar** with an infinitive p. 42

4 Talk about activities

Indica qué actividades les gusta hacer a estas personas según las fotos. *(Tell what activities these people like to do, according to the photos.)*

modelo: a José
A José le gusta tocar la guitarra.

1. a Sonia

2. a ellos

3. a usted

4. a nosotras

5. a ustedes

6. a ti

To review
- Miami's Freedom Tower p. 29
- Fiesta San Antonio p. 29
- Comparación cultural pp. 41, 44

5 United States

Comparación cultural

Answer these culture questions.

1. What is inside Miami's Freedom Tower?
2. What occurs during Fiesta San Antonio?
3. Who votes for the winners of **Los Premios Juventud**?
4. What is Xavier Cortada's heritage?

Más práctica Cuaderno *pp. 12–23* Cuaderno para hispanohablantes *pp. 14–23*

Get Help Online
my.hrw.com

Differentiating Instruction

Heritage Language Learners

Writing Skills Have students draft their own e-mail messages based on the model in Activity 3. Instruct them to explain where they, their friends, family, and teachers are from. Encourage them to give a short description of each of the places they are familiar with. If possible, have students send their e-mail messages to other classmates or pen pals.

Multiple Intelligences

Musical/Rhythmic Have students create a short poem or song describing who they are and the things they like to do. Since many of the action verbs have similar sounds (**comer/correr, descansar/trabajar**), students may find it easy to create verses that rhyme. Invite students to read their poems to the class.

✓ Ongoing Assessment

Peer Assessment **Activity 3** Have student pairs exchange the completed e-mail messages and check each other's work.

✓ Ongoing Assessment

Alternative Strategy **Activity 4** Have students combine sentences by using such words as **más, pero,** and **también.** For example, a student may combine the first two sentences and write **A ella le gusta hablar por teléfono y también le gusta escuchar música.**

Answers Projectable Transparencies, 1-46 thru 1-49

Answers for Activities on pp. 52, 53.

Activity 1

1. b **3.** c **5.** a
2. a **4.** b **6.** c

Activity 2

1. (No) Me gusta beber refrescos.
2. (No) Me gusta preparar la comida.
3. (No) Me gusta hacer la tarea.
4. (No) Me gusta descansar.
5. (No) Me gusta escribir correos electrónicos.
6. (No) Me gusta pasar un rato con los amigos.
7. (No) Me gusta practicar deportes.
8. (No) Me gusta trabajar.
9. (No) Me gusta comprar libros.
10. (No) Me gusta comer pizza.

Activity 3

1. soy
2. eres
3. somos
4. es
5. es
6. somos
7. son
8. son

Activity 4

1. A Sonia le gusta hablar por teléfono.
2. A ellos les gusta jugar al fútbol.
3. A usted le gusta leer.
4. A nosotra s nos gusta correr.
5. A ustedes les gusta pasar un rato con los amigos.
6. A ti te gusta montar en bicicleta.

Activity 5

1. The Cuban-American Museum is inside Miami's Freedom Tower.
2. During Fiesta San Antonio, there is a ten days celebration with food, music, and parades to honor the heroes of the Álamo, and Battle of San Jacinto.
3. Teens vote for the winners of Los Premios Juventud.
4. Javier Cortada is of Cuban heritage.

Lesson Overview

Culture at a Glance

Topic & Activity	Essential Question
The Paseo del Río pp. 54-55	What do teenagers do at the Paseo del Río and where you live?
Mexican and Tex-Mex food p. 60	How does local environment affect the food that people eat?
Free time activities pp. 72-73	What kinds of things are there to do in San Antonio, Miami, and where you live?
Traditional dishes of Mexico and Cuba p. 74	Why do traditional dishes change when they are brought from one country to another?
Culture review p. 77	What are some leisure activities and traditional foods in San Antonio and Miami?

COMPARISON COUNTRIES Estados Unidos Colombia México

Practice at a Glance

	Objective	Activity & Skill
Vocabulary	Adjectives	1: Reading; 2: Writing/Speaking; 3: Listening/Reading; 4: Reading/Speaking; 5: Reading; 8: Speaking/Writing; 12: Reading; 13: Writing; 14: Writing/Speaking; 15: Speaking; 17: Listening/Reading; 18: Writing/Speaking; 19: Reading/Listening/Speaking; 20: Writing; Repaso 1: Listening; Repaso 2–4: Writing
Vocabulary	Nouns for identifying people	5: Reading; 8: Speaking/Writing; 11: Speaking; 14: Writing/Speaking; 15: Speaking; 16: Listening/Reading; 18: Writing/Speaking; 20: Writing; Repaso 1: Listening; Repaso 2,3: Writing
Grammar	Using **ser** to describe what someone is like	5: Reading; 8: Speaking/Writing; 12: Reading; 13: Writing; 14: Writing/Speaking; 15: Speaking; 16: Listening/Reading; 17: Listening/Reading; 18: Writing/Speaking; 19: Reading/Listening/Speaking; 20: Writing; Repaso 1: Listening; Repaso 2–4: Writing
Grammar	Using definite and indefinite articles	5: Reading; 6: Listening/Writing; 7: Speaking/Writing; 8: Speaking/Writing; 11: Speaking; 15: Speaking; Repaso 2: Writing
Grammar	Practicing noun-adjective agreement	12: Reading; 13: Writing; 14: Writing/Speaking; 15: Speaking; 16: Listening/Reading; 18: Writing/Speaking; 19: Reading/Listening/Speaking; 20: Writing; Repaso 1: Listening; Repaso 2–4: Writing
Communication	Describe yourself and others	2: Writing/Speaking; 4: Reading/Speaking; 8: Speaking/Writing; 14: Writing/Speaking; 15: Speaking; 18: Writing/Speaking; 19: Reading/Listening/Speaking; 20 Writing
Communication	Identify people and things	7: Speaking/Writing; 8: Speaking/Writing; 11: Speaking; 14: Writing/Speaking; 18: Writing/Speaking
Communication	Pronunciation: The letter **ñ**	**Pronunciación:** *La letra* **ñ**, p. 65: Listening/Speaking
Recycle	**Ser, gustar** with an infinitive	1: Reading; 2: Writing/Speaking; 9: Speaking
Recycle	Snack foods, after-school activities	7: Speaking/Writing; 11: Speaking

Student Text Audio Scripts

The following presentations are recorded in the Audio Program for ***¡Avancemos!***

- **¡A responder!** *page 57*
- **6: La lista de Sandra** *page 62*
- **19: Integración** *page 71*
- **Repaso de la lección** *page 76*
  1 Listen and understand
- **Repaso inclusivo** *page 80*
  1 Listen, understand, and compare

For **¡AvanzaRap!** scripts, see the **¡AvanzaRap! DVD.**

¡A responder! TXT CD 1 track 35

1. pelirroja
2. atlético
3. organizada
4. cómico
5. grande
6. perezoso
7. joven
8. trabajador

6 | La lista de Sandra TXT CD 1 track 37

Me gusta comprar libros, DVDs, frutas, helados, papas fritas, jugo, galletas y pizza.

19 | Integración TXT CD 1 track 42

¡Hola! Soy Alejandro. Tengo pelo rubio. No soy muy alto pero no soy bajo. Soy simpático y tengo muchos amigos. Me gusta escribir correos electrónicos. ¿Y tú? ¿Cómo eres? ¿Qué te gusta hacer?

¡Hola! Me llamo Édgar. ¿Y tú? ¿Cómo te llamas? ¿De dónde eres? A mí me gusta escuchar música. También me gusta escribir correos electrónicos y hablar por teléfono. ¡Hasta luego!

Repaso de la lección TXT CD 1 track 44

1 Listen and understand

Hola. Me llamo Carlos. Soy estudiante de español. Soy alto, pero no soy muy grande. Tengo pelo rubio. Soy un chico cómico, pero soy estudioso. Me gusta aprender el español. La maestra de español es la señora Pérez. Ella es muy buena. También es organizada y trabajadora. Es una mujer pequeña. Es baja y tiene pelo castaño. Le gusta dibujar porque es muy artística.

Repaso inclusivo TXT CD 1 track 46

1 Listen, understand, and compare

Buenos días. Yo soy Magdalena Canseco. Después de las clases, a los estudiantes de Miami les gusta pasar un rato con los amigos. Son muy estudiosos pero les gusta más practicar deportes. Les gusta montar en bicicleta y jugar al fútbol. Los estudiantes de Miami son muy atléticos.

Yo soy Magdalena Canseco, Radio Sol, Miami. David...

Gracias, Magdalena. Soy David Guzmán. En San Antonio, los estudiantes también son atléticos. Les gusta correr y jugar al fútbol. Pero hoy hace Pero hoy hace calor. Les gusta más leer o descansar. Pero no son perezosos. Los estudiantes de San Antonio son muy trabajadores.

Yo soy David Guzmán, Radio Sol, San Antonio.

Resource List

Everything you need to ...

Plan

TEACHER ONE STOP

✓Lesson Plans
✓Teacher Resources
✓Audio and Video

Present

INTERACTIVE WHITEBOARD LESSONS

TEACHER ONE STOP WITH PROJECTABLE TRANSPARENCIES

POWER PRESENTATIONS

ANIMATEDGRAMMAR

Assess

ONLINE ASSESSMENT

✓ Assessments for on-level, modified, pre-AP, and heritage learners
✓ Create customized tests with **Examview Assessment Suite**
✓ **performance space**
✓ *Generate Success* Rubric Generator

Print

Plan	Present	Practice	Assess
URB 1 • Video Scripts pp. 99–100 • Family Involvement Activity p. 124 • Absent Student Copymasters pp. 133–143 **Best Practices Toolkit**	**URB 1** • Video Activities pp. 87–94	• *Cuaderno* pp. 24–49 • *Cuaderno para hispanohablantes* pp. 24–49 • *Lecturas para todos* pp. 113–117 • *Lecturas para hispanohablantes* • *¡AvanzaCómics! SuperBruno y Nati*, Episodio 1 **URB 1** • Practice Games pp. 65–72 • Audio Scripts pp. 108–112 • Fine Art Activities pp. 119–120	**Differentiated Assessment Program** **URB 1** • Did you get it? Reteaching and Practice Copymasters pp. 39–50

Projectable Transparencies (Teacher One Stop, my.hrw.com)

Culture	Presentation and Practice	Classroom Management
• Atlas Maps 1–6 • U.S. Map 7 • Fine Art Transparencies 10, 11	• Vocabulary Transparencies 14, 15 • Grammar Presentation Transparencies 18, 19 • Situational Transparencies and label overlay 20, 21 • Situational Student Copymasters pp. 1, 2	• Warm Up Transparencies pp. 30–33 • Student Book Answer Transparencies 50–53

Audio and Video

Audio	Video	¡AvanzaRap! DVD
• Student Book Audio CD 1 Tracks 34–46 • Workbook Audio CD 1 Tracks 11–20 • Heritage Learners Audio CD 1 Tracks 5–8, CD 3 Tracks 5–8 • Assessment Audio CD 1 Tracks 5–8 • *Lecturas para todos* Audio CD 1 Track 2, CD 2 Tracks 1–6 • Sing-along Songs Audio CD	• Vocabulary Video DVD 1 • *Telehistoria* DVD 1 Escena 1 Escena 2 Escena 3 Completa • Culture Video DVD 1	• Video animations of all **¡AvanzaRap!** songs (with Karaoke track) • Interactive DVD Activities • Teaching Suggestions • **¡AvanzaRap!** Activity Masters • **¡AvanzaRap!** video scripts and answers

Online and Media Resources

Student	Teacher
Available online at my.hrw.com • Online Student Edition • **News** + Networking • **performance space** • @HOMETUTOR • CULTURA Interactiva • WebQuests • Interactive Flashcards • Review Games • Self-Check Quiz **Student One Stop** **Holt McDougal Spanish Apps**	**Teacher One Stop (also available at my.hrw.com)** • Interactive Teacher's Edition • All print, audio, and video resources • Projectable Transparencies • Lesson Plans • TPRS • Examview Assessment Suite **Available online at my.hrw.com** *Generate Success* Rubric Generator and Graphic Organizers **Power Presentations**

Differentiated Assessment

On-level	Modified	Pre-AP	Heritage Learners
• Vocabulary Recognition Quiz p. 28 • Vocabulary Production Quiz p. 29 • Grammar Quizzes pp. 30–31 • Culture Quizzes p. 32 • On-level Lesson Test pp. 33–39 • On-level Unit Test pp. 45–51	• Modified Lesson Test pp. 23–29 • Modified Unit Test pp. 35–41	• Pre-AP Lesson Test pp. 23–29 • Pre-AP Unit Test pp. 35–41	• Heritage Learners Lesson Test pp. 29–35 • Heritage Learners Unit Test pp. 41–47

Core Pacing Guide

50 Minute (9 Day)

	Objectives/Focus	Teach	Practice	Assess/HW Options
DAY 1	Culture: learn about Hispanic culture in the United States Vocabulary: describe yourself and others, identify people and things • Warm Up OHT 30 **5 min**	Lesson Opener pp. 54–55 **Presentación de vocabulario** pp. 56–57 • Read A–F • View video DVD 1 • Play audio TXT CD 1 track 34 • *¡A responder!* TXT CD 1 track 35 **Práctica de vocabulario** p. 58 • *Nota gramatical:* ser **25 min**	Lesson Opener pp. 54–55 **Práctica de vocabulario** p. 58 • Acts. 1, 2 **15 min**	**Assess:** *Para y piensa* p. 58 **5 min** **Homework:** *Cuaderno* pp. 24–26 @HomeTutor
DAY 2	**Communication:** describing yourself and others • Warm Up OHT 30 • Check Homework **5 min**	**Vocabulario en contexto** pp. 59–60 • *Telehistoria escena 1* DVD 1 Culture: *La comida mexicana y Tex-Mex* **20 min**	**Vocabulario en contexto** pp. 59–60 • Act. 3 TXT CD 1 track 36 • Act. 4 **20 min**	**Assess:** *Para y piensa* p. 60 **5 min** **Homework:** *Cuaderno* pp. 24–26 @HomeTutor
DAY 3	Grammar: definite and indefinite articles • Warm Up OHT 31 • Check Homework **5 min**	**Presentación de gramática** p. 61 • Definite and indefinite articles **20 min**	**Práctica de gramática** pp. 62–63 • Acts. 5, 7, 8, 9 • Act. 6 TXT CD 1 track 37 **20 min**	**Assess:** *Para y piensa* p. 63 **5 min** **Homework:** *Cuaderno* pp. 27–29 @HomeTutor
DAY 4	**Communication:** using definite and indefinite articles to talk about people • Warm Up OHT 31 • Check Homework **5 min**	**Gramática en contexto** pp. 64–65 • *Telehistoria escena 2* DVD 1 • *Pronunciación* TXT CD 1 track 39 **15 min**	**Gramática en contexto** pp. 64–65 • Act. 10 TXT CD 1 track 38 • Act. 11 **25 min**	**Assess:** *Para y piensa* p. 65 **10 min** **Homework:** *Cuaderno* pp. 27–29 @HomeTutor
DAY 5	Grammar: noun-adjective agreement, using adjectives to describe people • Warm Up OHT 32 • Check Homework **5 min**	**Presentación de gramática** p. 66 • Noun-adjective agreement **15 min**	**Práctica de gramática** pp. 67–68 • Acts. 12, 13, 14, 15 **25 min**	**Assess:** *Para y piensa* p. 68 **5 min** **Homework:** *Cuaderno* pp. 30–32 @HomeTutor
DAY 6	**Communication:** Culmination: describing people, definite and indefinite articles, descriptive adjectives • Warm Up OHT 32 • Check Homework **5 min**	**Todo junto** pp. 69–71 • *Escenas 1, 2: Resumen* • *Telehistoria completa* DVD 1 **20 min**	**Todo junto** pp. 69–71 • Acts. 16, 17 TXT CD 1 tracks 36, 38, 40 • Act. 19 TXT CD 1 tracks 41, 42 • Acts. 18, 20 **20 min**	**Assess:** *Para y piensa* p. 71 **5 min** **Homework:** *Cuaderno* pp. 33–34 @HomeTutor
DAY 7	Reading: Greetings from San Antonio and Miami Review: Lesson review • Warm Up OHT 33 • Check Homework **5 min**	**Lectura cultural** pp. 72–73 • *Saludos desde San Antonio y Miami* • TXT CD 1 track 43 **Repaso de la lección** pp. 76–77 **15 min**	**Lectura Cultural** pp. 72–73 • *Saludos desde San Antonio y Miami* **Repaso de la lección** pp. 76–77 • Act. 1 TXT CD 1 track 44 • Acts. 2, 3, 4, 5 **20 min**	**Assess:** *Para y piensa* p. 73; *Repaso de la lección* pp. 76–77 **10 min** **Homework:** *En resumen* p. 75; *Cuaderno* pp. 35–49 (optional) Review Games Online @HomeTutor
DAY 8	**Assessment**			**Assess:** Lesson 2 test or Unit 1 test **50 min**
DAY 9	**Unit Culmination** **5 min**	**Comparación cultural** pp. 78–79 • TXT CD 1 track 45 • View culture video DVD 1 **Repaso inclusivo** pp. 80–81 **15 min**	**Comparación cultural** pp. 78–79 **Repaso inclusivo** pp. 80–81 • Act. 1 TXT CD 1 track 46 • Acts. 2, 3, 4, 5, 6, 7 **25 min**	**Homework:** *Cuaderno* pp. 41–43 **5 min**

Core Pacing Guide 90 Minute (5 Day)

	Objectives/Focus	Teach	Practice	Assess/HW Options
DAY 1	**Culture:** learn about Hispanic culture in the United States **Vocabulary:** describe yourself and others, identify people and things • Warm Up OHT 30 5 min	Lesson Opener pp. 54–55 **Presentación de vocabulario** pp. 56–57 • Read A–F • View video DVD 1 • Play audio TXT CD1 track 34 • *¡A responder!* TXT CD 1 track 35 **Práctica de vocabulario** p. 58 • *Nota gramatical:* ser **20 min**	Lesson Opener pp. 54–55 **Práctica de vocabulario** p. 58 • Acts. 1, 2 **20 min**	**Assess:** *Para y piensa* p. 58 **5 min**
	Communication: describing yourself and others 5 min	**Vocabulario en contexto** pp. 59–60 • *Telehistoria escena 1* DVD 1 **Culture:** *La comida mexicana y Tex-Mex* **15 min**	**Vocabulario en contexto** pp. 59–60 • Act. 3 TXT CD 1 track 36 • Act. 4 **15 min**	**Assess:** *Para y piensa* p. 60 **5 min** **Homework:** *Cuaderno* pp. 24–26 @HomeTutor
DAY 2	**Grammar:** definite and indefinite articles • Warm Up OHT 31 • Check Homework 5 min	**Presentación de gramática** p. 61 • Definite and indefinite articles **20 min**	**Práctica de gramática** pp. 62–63 • Acts. 5, 7, 8, 9 • Act. 6 TXT CD 1 track 37 **15 min**	**Assess:** *Para y piensa* p. 63 **5 min**
	Communication: using definite and indefinite articles to talk about people 5 min	**Gramática en contexto** pp. 64–65 • *Telehistoria escena 2* DVD 1 • *Pronunciación* TXT CD 1 track 39 **20 min**	**Gramática en contexto** pp. 64–65 • Act. 10 TXT CD 1 track 38 • Act. 11 **15 min**	**Assess:** *Para y piensa* p. 65 **5 min** **Homework:** *Cuaderno* pp. 27–29 @HomeTutor
DAY 3	**Grammar:** noun adjective agreement, using adjectives to describe people • Warm Up OHT 32 • Check Homework 5 min	**Presentación de gramática** p. 66 • Noun-adjective agreement **15 min**	**Práctica de gramática** pp. 67–68 • Acts. 12, 13, 14, 15 **20 min**	**Assess:** *Para y piensa* p. 68 **5 min**
	Communication: Culmination: describing people, definite and indefinite articles, descriptive adjectives 5 min	**Todo junto** pp. 69-71 • *Escenas 1, 2: Resumen* • *Telehistoria completa* DVD 1 **15 min**	**Todo junto** pp. 69–71 • Acts. 16, 17 TXT CD 1 tracks, 36, 38, 40 • Act. 19 TXT CD 1 tracks 41, 42 • Acts. 18, 20 **20 min**	**Assess:** *Para y piensa* p. 71 **5 min** **Homework:** *Cuaderno* pp. 30–34 @HomeTutor
DAY 4	**Reading:** Greetings from San Antonio and Miami **Projects:** Traditional Mexican and Cuban Dishes • Warm Up OHT 33 • Check Homework 5 min	**Lectura cultural** pp. 72–73 • *Saludos desde San Antonio y Miami* • TXT CD 1 track 43 **Proyectos culturales** p. 74 • *Platos tradicionales de México y Cuba* **15 min**	**Lectura cultural** pp. 72–73 • *Saludos desde San Antonio y Miami* **Proyectos culturales** p. 74 • *Proyecto 1, 2* **15 min**	**Assess:** *Para y piensa* p. 73 **10 min**
	Review: Lesson review 5 min	**Repaso de la lección** pp. 76–77 **15 min**	**Repaso de la lección** pp. 76–77 • Act. 1 TXT CD 1 track 44 • Acts. 2, 3, 4, 5 **20 min**	**Assess:** *Repaso de la lección* pp. 76–77 **5 min** **Homework:** *En resumen* p. 75; *Cuaderno* pp. 35–46 (optional) @HomeTutor
DAY 5	**Assessment**			**Assess:** Lesson 2 test or Unit 1 test **45 min**
	Unit Culmination 5 min	**Comparación cultural** pp. 78–79 • TXT CD 1 track 45 **Repaso inclusivo** pp. 80–81 **10 min**	**Comparación cultural** pp. 78–79 **Repaso inclusivo** pp. 80–81 • Act. 1 TXT CD 1 track 46 • Acts. 2, 3, 4, 5, 6, 7 **20 min**	**Homework:** *Cuaderno* pp. 47–49 **5 min**

¡AVANZA! Objectives

- Introduce lesson theme: **Mis amigos y yo.**
- **Culture:** Learn about activities teens enjoy in the U.S. and in Spanish-speaking countries.

Presentation Strategies

- Introduce the characters' names: Sandra, Ricardo and Alberto.
- Ask students to look at the photo on pp. 54–55.
- Ask students to identify the city, tell what they know about it, and have them identify what they see in the photo.
- Have students make a list of what they would like to do if they were to visit that city.

STANDARDS

2.1 Practices and perspectives
4.2 Compare cultures
21st Century **Communication,** ¿Qué ves?; **Information Literacy,** Pre-AP; **Social and Cross-Cultural Skills,** Compara con tu mundo

Warm Up Projectable Transparencies, 1-30

Ser Complete the sentences with the correct form of **ser.**

1. Juan, ¿de dónde _____ tú?
2. Yo _____ de Costa Rica.
3. Y Ana y María, ¿de dónde _____ ellas?
4. Ana _____ de Panamá y María de Honduras.
5. Pablo y yo _____ de Uruguay.

Answers: 1. eres; 2. soy; 3. son; 4. es; 5. somos

Comparación cultural

Exploring the Theme

Ask the following:

1. Are there places in your neighborhood that sell Mexican and/or Tex-Mex food?
2. Have you tried any Mexican and/or Tex-Mex food? Can you name some examples?

¿Qué ves? Possible answers include:

- Sí, son amigos.
- Les gusta pasar un rato con amigos, hablar, pasear, comer.
- Hace sol. Hace mucho sol.

UNIDAD 1

Estados Unidos

Lección 2

Tema:

Mis amigos y yo

¡AVANZA! In this lesson you will learn to

- describe yourself and others
- identify people and things

using

- **ser** to describe what someone is like
- definite and indefinite articles
- noun-adjective agreement

¿Recuerdas?

- snack foods, after-school activities
- **ser, gustar** with an infinitive

Comparación cultural

In this lesson you will learn about

- Latin-American and Tex-Mex food
- the tradition of making **cascarones**
- after-school activities in Miami and San Antonio
- students from Miami, Colombia, and Mexico

Compara con tu mundo

These Texas teens are exploring the Paseo del Río, one of San Antonio's main attractions. In this refreshing city retreat, people eat in restaurants, ride riverboats, or stroll along the river. *Does your city or town have a park or place of interest? What do people do there?*

¿Qué ves?

Mira la foto
¿Son amigos?
¿Qué les gusta hacer?
¿Llueve o hace sol?

Differentiating Instruction

Multiple Intelligences

Naturalist Brainstorm with students to create a list of natural resources in your region or state. Then have students draft a design for an outdoor space that would allow the public access to, and enjoyment of, one of these natural resources. Encourage students to use San Antonio's **Paseo del Río** as one possible model.

Slower-paced Learners

Yes/No Questions Ask students yes or no questions about what they see in the photo on pp. 54–55. Point to the appropriate item in the photo for each question. **¿Hace frío? ¿Les gusta pasar un rato con amigos? ¿Les gusta practicar deportes?**

DIGITAL SPANISH my.hrw.com
ONLINE STUDENT EDITION with...

performance space
News + Networking
@HOMETUTOR
CULTURA Interactiva

- Audio and Video Resources
- Interactive Flashcards
- Review Activities
- WebQuest
- Conjuguemos.com

PRACTICE SPANISH WITH HOLT MCDOUGAL APPS!

Paseo del Río
San Antonio, Texas

DIGITAL SPANISH

TEACHER TOOLS
- Interactive Whiteboard Lessons
- Generate Success!

ALSO AVAILABLE...
- Online Workbook
- Spanish InterActive Reader

SPANISH ON THE GO!
- Performance Space
- Holt McDougal Spanish Apps
- ¡Avancemos! eTextbook

Using the Photo

Location Information

Paseo del Río The **Paseo del Río** shown in the photo is in San Antonio, a city located in south-central Texas. It is a walkway that borders the San Antonio River. Around 1986, this area of the city became a popular tourist attraction. It has a large mall, shops, restaurants, open-air cafés, and an amphitheater.

Expanded Information

San Antonio Native Americans first called the place that is now San Antonio *Yanaguana,* which means refreshing waters. San Antonio is approximately 150 miles from Mexico.

The Alamo San Antonio is home to the famous Alamo, the first Spanish mission established in the area.

Differentiating Instruction

Heritage Language Learners

Support What They Know Display photos of historical places in Texas and a map of San Antonio. Invite students who have visited or have relatives in Texas to share what they know about the state. Based on the information they have given, ask students what places they would like to visit and why. What type of food would they eat there?

Pre-AP

Expand and Elaborate San Antonio is a city rich in history and culture. Have students use the library or Internet to research one aspect of the city's history. Some key words for their search could include: **historia**/history of San Antonio. Then give students the opportunity to share what they have learned with the rest of the group.

Long-term Retention

Connect to Previous Learning

Review weather vocabulary from Lección Preliminar and **ser** and **gustar** from Unidad 1, Lección 1 by having students generate questions and answers about the photo: **¿Qué tiempo hace? Hace sol; ¿De dónde son los amigos? Son de San Antonio.**

¡AVANZA! **Objective**
- Present vocabulary: adjectives to describe yourself and friends.

Core Resources
- Video Program: DVD 1
- Audio Program: TXT CD 1, tracks 34, 35

Presentation Strategies
- Have students look at pp. 56–57 and repeat each vocabulary word after you.
- Ask **sí/no** questions to verify comprehension. For example: **¿Laura es alta? (no) ¿Rosita es joven? (sí)**
- Play the audio as students read A–F.
- Show the video.

STANDARDS
1.2 Understand language
21st Century **Creativity and Innovation,** Multiple Intelligences

Comparisons
English Language Connection

Point out that the verb **tener,** *to have,* is also used to talk about the features a person has: **tiene pelo castaño.**

Long-term Retention
Study Tips

Introduce students to the practice of learning new adjectives and their opposites. Have them write an adjective on index cards and its opposite from the vocabulary, for example: **trabajador/perezoso; bueno/malo; organizada/desorganizada.**

Communication
Regionalisms

Explain to students that in Cuba and Puerto Rico, **guapo(a)** also means bold, daring, or defiant.

Presentación de VOCABULARIO

¡AVANZA! **Goal:** Learn how Sandra describes herself and her friends. Then practice what you have learned to describe yourself and others.
Actividades 1–2
¿Recuerdas? **ser** p. 37

VIDEO DVD
AUDIO

A ¡Hola! Soy Sandra. Soy **artística** y **tengo pelo castaño.** A mi **amigo** Ricardo le gusta practicar deportes **porque** es **atlético.**

B Alberto es **trabajador** y **estudioso.** Le gusta estudiar. David es **un poco perezoso.** No es **un estudiante muy bueno.** No le gusta trabajar.

Más vocabulario

bonito(a) *pretty*
guapo(a) *good-looking*
malo(a) *bad*
Expansión de vocabulario p. R2

C Soy **una persona** muy **organizada.** Mi **amiga** Ana es **inteligente** pero un poco **desorganizada.**

Differentiating Instruction

Inclusion

Multisensory Input/Output Say one of the featured vocabulary words aloud as you write it on the board. Then have students copy the word onto a small slip of paper as they repeat it aloud. After students have written all of the words, say each aloud again. This time, have students place their slips of paper on top of the appropriate photo in the text.

Multiple Intelligences

Intrapersonal Invite students to reflect on their own traits and personalities by creating a personality page. On their pages students might include a photo, a self-portrait, or other drawing of things they like. They should also include adjectives that describe themselves. **Soy organizada. No soy muy alta.**

D Rafael es muy **alto,** pero Laura es **baja.** Manuel es **grande,** pero Francisco es **pequeño.** La señora Santa Cruz es un poco **vieja,** pero Rosita es **joven.**

E La señora Guardado es **pelirroja** y el señor Guardado **tiene** pelo castaño. Marco y Laura son **chicos** muy buenos. Marco tiene **pelo rubio** y Laura tiene pelo castaño.

F Yo soy un poco **seria,** pero mi amigo Alberto es muy **cómico. Todos** mis amigos son muy **simpáticos.** ¿Y tú? **¿Cómo eres?**

@HOMETUTOR my.hrw.com Interactive Flashcards

¡A responder! Escuchar

Escucha estas descripciones de Sandra y sus amigos. Indica la persona en la foto que corresponde a cada descripción. *(Point to the person on these pages who matches each description you hear.)*

TEACHER to TEACHER

Roberto E. del Valle
Redmond, WA

Tips for Presenting Vocabulary

Vocabulary Bingo *I have students fill a 4 X 4 grid (16 squares) with new vocabulary words (one per square). I then describe the word without using it or miming it. When students figure out the word, I ask them to put an X on the word in the square. When 4 words in a row are Xed, a student shouts* **¡Lo tengo!** *To claim the prize students need to use one word in a sentence. I also vary the rules: only vertical, or horizontal or diagonal, only the 4 in the middle, and so forth can win.*

Go online for more tips!

Communication
Common Error Alert

Often, students forget to use the definite article before the titles **señor (Sr.), señora (Sra.),** and **señorita (Srta.).** Remind students to use **el** or **la** before these titles except when addressing a person directly. For example: **Hola, Sr. Sánchez. Le presento a la Sra. García.**

Communication
Regionalisms

Explain to students that in Argentina and Mexico, the word **grande** means "big" but is also used when referring to an older person. For example, **Él es un señor grande.** Meaning he is an old man. Instead of using the word **viejo** (old), they use **grande** (big).

Differentiating Instruction

Pre-AP

Expand and Elaborate Have students choose three people from the photos. Ask them to describe those people using as many details as possible. For example: **La mujer pelirroja se llama Sra. Guardado. Ella es bonita y simpática. Le gusta tocar la guitarra y dibujar.**

Heritage Language Learners

Regional Variations Ask students to discuss other words they know and use that mean the same as the words presented on pp. 56–57. For example, other words that mean the same thing as **chico(a)** are **muchacho(a)** and **niño(a)** in many Latin American countries; **chaval(a)** in Spain; **chavo(a)** in Mexico, and **pibe(a)** in Argentina.

Answers Projectable Transparencies, 1-50

¡A responder! Audio Script, TE p. 53b

Students should point to:

1. La señora Guardado	**5.** Manuel
2. Ricardo	**6.** David
3. Sandra	**7.** Rosita
4. Alberto	**8.** Alberto

Objectives
- Practice vocabulary: adjectives, likes and dislikes.
- Recycle: **ser** to describe people.

Core Resource
- *Cuaderno,* pp. 24-26

Practice Sequence
- **Activity 1:** Vocabulary recognition: descriptive adjectives, opposites
- **Activity 2:** Vocabulary production: associating preferences with characteristics

STANDARDS
1.2 Understand language, Act. 1
1.3 Present information, Act. 2

✓ Ongoing Assessment

Get Help Online
More Practice
my.hrw.com

PARA Y PIENSA **Quick Check** Say the following adjectives aloud and ask students to say the opposite: **bueno, pequeño, viejo, cómico, organizado. Answers:** malo; grande; joven; serio; desorganizado
For additional practice, use Reteaching & Practice Copymasters URB 1, pp. 39, 40.

Answers
Projectable Transparencies, 1-50

Activity 1
1. b **3.** c **5.** f
2. d **4.** a **6.** e

Activity 2
1. A Ricardo le gusta hacer la tarea porque es estudioso.
2. ... le gusta dibujar porque es artístico.
3. A Alberto no le gusta ser cómico porque es serio.
4. ... le gusta correr porque es atlético.
5. ... no le gusta ser perezoso porque es trabajador.
6. ... no le gusta ser organizado porque es desorganizado.

Para y piensa
1. Juan es bajo.
2. David es artístico.
3. Carlos es serio.

Práctica de VOCABULARIO

1 Los opuestos

Leer

Sandra describe a sus amigos pero Ricardo dice lo opuesto. Empareja la descripción de Sandra con la respuesta de Ricardo. *(Sandra describes her friends but Ricardo says the opposite. Match Sandra's description with Ricardo's response.)*

Sandra	Ricardo
1. Marco es pequeño.	**a.** No, es bueno.
2. Luisa es trabajadora.	**b.** No, es grande.
3. Pablo es organizado.	**c.** No, es desorganizado.
4. Joaquín es malo.	**d.** No, es perezosa.
5. Anabel es joven.	**e.** No, es serio.
6. Francisco es cómico.	**f.** No, es vieja.

Expansión:
Teacher Edition Only
Ask students to write other examples of a description and its opposite.

Nota gramatical ¿Recuerdas? **ser** p. 37

Use **ser** to describe what people are like.

La mujer **es** alta.
*The woman **is** tall.*

Los chicos **son** organizados.
*The boys **are** organized.*

2 Porque...

Escribir
Hablar

Explica por qué a Ricardo y a Alberto les gusta o no les gusta hacer estas actividades. *(Explain why Ricardo and Alberto like or don't like the following activities.)*

serio	desorganizado
atlético	estudioso
artístico	trabajador

modelo: A Ricardo le gusta practicar deportes porque es atlético.

1. A Ricardo le gusta hacer la tarea.
2. A Ricardo le gusta dibujar.
3. A Alberto no le gusta ser cómico.
4. A Alberto le gusta correr.
5. A Alberto no le gusta ser perezoso.
6. A Alberto no le gusta ser organizado.

Expansión
Draw, cut out pictures, or use clip art to illustrate all of the adjectives in the word bank.

Más práctica Cuaderno *pp. 24–26* Cuaderno para hispanohablantes *pp. 24–27*

Get Help Online
my.hrw.com

PARA Y PIENSA **Did you get it?**
1. Say that Juan is short.
2. Say that David is artistic.
3. Say that Carlos is serious.

Differentiating Instruction

Slower-paced Learners
Yes/No Questions Have students bring in photos of sports teams, family members, or friends. Create yes/no questions about physical and personal traits of the people represented in each photo and have the class respond **sí** or **no.** For example: **John es atlético. (sí) La maestra es vieja. (no)**

Pre-AP
Expand and Elaborate Have students write a paragraph about their favorite celebrity. They may include information about where this person is from, what he or she likes to do and why, and a description. Have students read their paragraph to the class and have the class guess the identity of the celebrity.

VOCABULARIO en contexto

¡AVANZA! **Goal:** Notice how Sandra and her friends describe themselves and each other. Then practice these words to describe others. ***Actividades 3–4***

Telehistoria escena 1

@HOMETUTOR my.hrw.com **View, Read and Record**

STRATEGIES

Cuando lees
Skim Find the main idea by skimming (rapidly glancing over) the text before reading it carefully. What is the main idea of the scene below?

Cuando escuchas
Find the humor Humor makes a scene fun and memorable. Listen for exaggeration, teasing, and jokes. What are some examples of humor in the following scene?

VIDEO DVD

AUDIO

Sandra, speaking to Alicia via webcam, holds up Alicia's T-shirt.

Sandra: Es bonita. Pero te gusta más con el autógrafo de Trini Salgado, ¿no?

Alberto and Ricardo join Sandra.

Sandra: Alicia, te presento a mis amigos: Alberto y Ricardo.

Alberto: Hola, Alicia. Me llamo Alberto. Soy alto... no soy muy alto. Tengo pelo castaño, y soy muy trabajador. Pero me gusta mirar la televisión y escuchar música. *(He pulls CDs from his backpack.)*

Sandra: No, él no es perezoso pero es un poco desorganizado.

Ricardo: Hola, Alicia. ¿Qué tal? Me llamo Ricardo. Soy inteligente, simpático y estudioso. Me gusta practicar deportes porque soy atlético. Y me gusta dibujar porque soy muy artístico.

Sandra shows one of Ricardo's drawings that is not very good.

Sandra: Sí. Él es muy artístico.

Ricardo: Ella es cómica, ¿no?

Alberto: Ella no es muy seria.

Sandra: OK, OK. Adiós, Alicia. Hasta luego.

Continuará... p. 64

¡AVANZA! **Objective**
- Understand vocabulary in context: descriptive words.

Core Resources
- Video Program: DVD 1
- Audio Program: TXT CD 1, track 36

Presentation Strategies
- Ask students to predict what Sandra, Alberto, and Ricardo are talking about.
- Show the video with books open, then with books closed. Encourage students to find examples of humor in the scene.
- Play audio while students follow the script in the text.

STANDARDS
1.2 Understand language

Warm Up Projectable Transparencies, 1-30

Vocabulary Match each adjective with its appropriate like or dislike.

1. perezoso	**a.** le gusta dibujar
2. estudiosa	**b.** le gusta correr
3. artística	**c.** le gusta leer y estudiar
4. atlético	**d.** no le gusta trabajar

Answers: 1. d; 2. c; 3. a; 4. b

Communication
Interpretive Mode

Telehistoria Ask students to keep the following questions in mind:
1. **¿Cómo son Alberto y Ricardo?**
2. **¿Qué le gusta hacer a Alberto?**
3. **¿Qué le gusta hacer a Ricardo?**

Video Summary
@HOMETUTOR VideoPlus my.hrw.com

At River Walk Café, Sandra sets up her laptop and Web cam. She contacts her friend Alicia, who has sent her a T-shirt with Trini Salgado's autograph. Sandra is joined by her friends, Alberto and Ricardo, who introduce themselves to Alicia via the Web cam. Each boy describes himself favorably in a humorous way. Sandra rolls her eyes.

Differentiating Instruction

Inclusion

Frequent Review/Repetition Organize students into groups of three. Give them the opportunity to read through the Telehistoria four times. The first time, instruct students to read the script silently. The second time, have each group member read the part of one character. Then have students change roles, and read through the script twice more. Each student should get a chance to play each role.

Pre-AP

Identify Main Idea Write the following words on individual index cards: **trabajador, desorganizado, inteligente, simpático, estudioso, atlético.** Then create two concept webs on the board, one for **Ricardo,** and the other for **Alberto.** Invite volunteers to post each word around the appropriate name. Have students point to the place in the text where they found their information and read the text.

Objectives
- Practice using vocabulary in context.
- **Culture:** Compare Mexican and Tex-Mex food.

Core Resource
- Audio Program: TXT CD 1 track 36

Practice Sequence
- **Activity 3:** Telehistoria comprehension
- **Activity 4:** Vocabulary production: descriptive adjectives; **gustar** + infinitive

STANDARDS
1.1 Engage in conversation, Act. 4
1.2 Understand language, Acts. 3–4
1.3 Present information, Acts. 3–4
2.2 Products and perspectives, CC
21st Century **Creativity and Innovation,** Act. 4: Expansión

Get Help Online
More Practice
my.hrw.com

✓ Ongoing Assessment
PARA Y PIENSA **Quick Check** Play a word association game before students do the Para y piensa. You say an activity and students supply an appropriate adjective. For example: **Le gusta correr. Es atlético.** For additional practice, use Reteaching & Practice Copymasters URB 1, pp. 39, 41.

Comparación cultural
Essential Question
Suggested Answer Local agriculture often dictates the foods people eat. For example, many Mexican foods contain corn and chile peppers because those crops grow abundantly in Mexico's climate.

3 *Comprensión del episodio* Las características
Escuchar Leer

Copia el diagrama Venn en una hoja de papel para comparar a Ricardo y Alberto. Escribe sus diferencias debajo de sus nombres. En el centro escribe lo que tienen en común. *(Copy the Venn diagram and use it to compare Ricardo and Alberto. Write their differences below their names. In the center, write what they have in common.)*

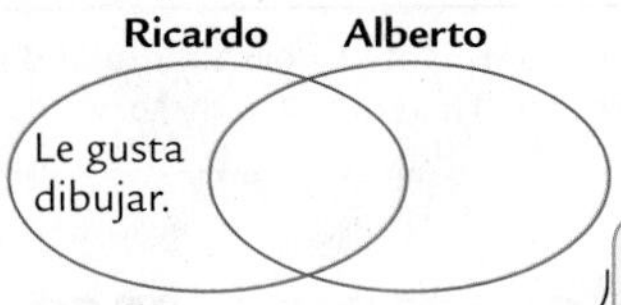

Expansión:
Teacher Edition Only
Ask students to compare two people they know using a Venn diagram.

4 Una entrevista
Leer Hablar

Lee la entrevista con Raúl López, un joven futbolista famoso. Después, habla con otro(a) estudiante sobre el artículo. Usa por lo menos tres adjetivos para hacerle preguntas. *(Work with another student to talk about the article. Ask him or her questions using at least three adjectives.)*

A ¿Es Raúl perezoso?

B No, es trabajador porque le gusta estudiar.

ENTREVISTA
¡ESTRELLA DEL FUTURO!

Revista Estrella: Raúl, ¿cómo eres?
Raúl: Soy muy atlético. Me gusta mucho jugar al fútbol y practicar deportes. Pero también me gusta descansar.
Revista Estrella: Y eres un estudiante serio, ¿no?
Raúl: Sí, me gusta leer libros y estudiar.
Revista Estrella: ¿Te gusta escuchar música?
Raúl: Sí, me gusta escuchar música, pero me gusta más tocar la guitarra. También me gusta dibujar.

Expansión
Write an interview between you and your favorite actor or actress. Ask them what they are like and what they like to do.

Comparación cultural

Unas fajitas

La comida mexicana y Tex-Mex
How does local environment affect the food that people eat? Tex-Mex is a regional cuisine that combines styles of cooking from **Mexico** and **Texas.** Did you know that *nachos,* crispy tacos, tortilla chips with salsa, *fajitas,* and *chili con carne* are all Tex-Mex dishes? Common Tex-Mex ingredients include flour tortillas, yellow cheese, refried beans, and beef. In the interior of Mexico, traditional ingredients are corn tortillas, white cheese, black beans, chicken, seafood, and pork.

Compara con tu mundo *What are some restaurants in your community that serve foods from other countries?*

Get Help Online
my.hrw.com

PARA Y PIENSA **Did you get it?** Fill in the appropriate adjective.
1. Alberto es trabajador. No es ____ .
2. A Ricardo le gusta practicar deportes. Es ____ .
3. A Ricardo le gusta hacer la tarea. Es ____ .

Answers Projectable Transparencies, 1-50
Activity 3 Answers will vary. Possible answers include:

Activity answers continue on p. 61.

Differentiating Instruction

Slower-paced Learners
Personalize It Ask students to talk about experiences they have had with Tex-Mex cuisine. Perhaps it was at a restaurant, a friend's house, or at home. Perhaps it was a recipe they prepared themselves. Encourage students to talk about their personal preferences in Spanish. **Me gusta comer el chile con carne. Me gusta comer las fajitas.**

Pre-AP
Support Ideas with Details Write the following adjectives describing Raúl López on the board: **atlético, estudioso, artístico.** Then ask students to find details in the interview to support each of these ideas. For example, under **atlético** you might add **le gusta jugar al fútbol** and **le gusta practicar deportes.**

Presentación de GRAMÁTICA

¡AVANZA! **Goal:** Learn about definite and indefinite articles. Then practice using these articles to identify people and things. ***Actividades 5–9***

¿Recuerdas? Snack foods p. 33, **gustar** with an infinitive p. 42

English Grammar Connection: **Definite articles** (in English, *the*) are used with nouns to indicate *specific* persons, places, or things. **Indefinite articles** (*a, an*) are used with nouns to indicate *nonspecific* persons, places, or things.

The boy is a friend.		El chico es un amigo.	
definite article (The)	**indefinite article** (a)	**definite article** (El)	**indefinite article** (un)

Definite and Indefinite Articles

ANIMATEDGRAMMAR my.hrw.com

In Spanish, articles match nouns in gender and number.

Here's how: All Spanish nouns, even if they refer to objects, are either **masculine** or **feminine.**

- Nouns ending in **-o** are usually **masculine.**
- Nouns ending in **-a** are usually **feminine.**

		Definite Article	Noun	Indefinite Article	Noun
Masculine	Singular	el *the*	chico *boy*	un *a*	chico *boy*
Masculine	Plural	los *the*	chicos *boys*	unos *some*	chicos *boys*
Feminine	Singular	la *the*	chica *girl*	una *a*	chica *girl*
Feminine	Plural	las *the*	chicas *girls*	unas *some*	chicas *girls*

matches *matches*

Los **libro**s son para la **maestr**a. ***The** books are for **the** teacher.*

To form the **plural** of a noun, add **-s** if the noun ends in a vowel. Add **-es** if the noun ends in a consonant.

vowel estudiante → estudiant**es** *consonant* mujer → muj**eres**

Más práctica

Cuaderno *pp. 27–29*

Cuaderno para hispanohablantes *pp. 28–30*

@HOMETUTOR my.hrw.com **Leveled Practice**

Differentiating Instruction

English Learners

Provide Comprehensible Input Have students fold a piece of paper in half lengthwise. Tell them to label the left column **Singular** and the right column **Plural**. Then invite students to create a list of ten things that they see in the classroom. Tell them to write the singular form of each word on the left, and the plural form on the right. Allow students to read their lists aloud for the group.

Inclusion

Metacognitive Support Direct students to the chart within the grammar box that explains *Definite and Indefinite Articles.* Ask students to describe the patterns they notice within the information presented. For example, they might point out that all plural articles end in **s,** or that there are four ways to say *the* in Spanish.

¡AVANZA! **Objective**

- Present definite and indefinite articles.

Core Resource

- *Cuaderno,* pp. 27–29

Presentation Strategies

- Check students' understanding of definite and indefinite articles by saying a noun and asking them to provide the correct article. For example: **el chico**.
- Say a singular noun and ask students to provide the corresponding indefinite article: **un niño.** Repeat with plural nouns: **unos niños.**
- Check formation of plural nouns by saying a singular noun and asking students to provide the plural noun. **mujer/mujeres**

STANDARDS

4.1 Compare languages

Warm Up Projectable Transparencies, 1-31

Vocabulary Complete the sentences using the correct word.

mujer chicos hombre chica pelo

1. Marco y Lauro son_____ muy buenos.
2. Marco tiene el _____ rubio.
3. La señora Díaz es una _____ joven.
4. El señor Roldán es un _____ alto.
5. Sara es una _____ muy simpática.

Answers: 1. chicos; 2. pelo; 3. mujer; 4. hombre; 5. chica

Answers Projectable Transparencies, 1-50

Activity answers continued from p. 60.

Activity 4 Answers will vary. Sample answers include:

¿Es Raúl atlético? Sí. Le gusta mucho jugar al fútbol.

¿Es Raúl un estudiante serio? Sí. Le gusta leer libros.

¿Es Raúl viejo? No. Es joven.

Para y piensa

Alberto: No es perezoso; Ricardo: Es atlético; Ricardo: Es trabajador/estudioso.

¡AVANZA! Objectives

- Practice using definite and indefinite articles.
- Recycle: snack foods; **gustar** + infinitives.

Core Resources

- *Cuaderno,* pp. 27–29
- Audio Program: TXT CD 1 track 37

Practice Sequence

- **Activity 5:** Controlled practice: definite articles
- **Activity 6:** Transitional practice: definite and indefinite articles
- **Activity 7:** Transitional practice: indefinite articles; Recycle: snack foods
- **Activity 8: ser** + indefinite articles
- **Activity 9:** Open-ended practice: definite and indefinite articles; Recycle: **gustar** + infinitives

STANDARDS

1.1 Engage in conversation, Act. 9
1.3 Present information, Acts. 5–8
4.1 Compare languages, Act. 7; PYP
21st Century **Creativity and Innovation,** Act. 8: Expansión

Communication
Grammar Activity

Before doing Activity 5, divide students into four groups. One group writes **el** on an index card. The other group writes **la** on another index card. The third group writes **los**, and the last group writes **las**. Read aloud the nouns from the Activity at random, and have groups take turns raising the corresponding card. For example you say: **Chico**, group one raises the card with **el**.

✓ Ongoing Assessment

Alternative Strategy Have students practice when to ask **¿Qué es?** and when to ask **¿Qué son?** using the illustrations from Activity 7.

Answers Projectable Transparencies, 1-50

Activity 5

1. Las	3. Los	5. Las	7. Las	9. Los
2. La	4. El	6. El	8. Las	10. La

Activity answers continue on p. 63.

Práctica de GRAMÁTICA

5 ¿Cómo son las personas en la oficina?

Leer

Miguel describe a varias personas en la oficina de la escuela. Completa sus oraciones con **el, la, los, las.** *(Complete the sentences with the correct definite article.)*

1. ____ chicas son atléticas.
2. ____ maestra es inteligente.
3. ____ amigos son simpáticos.
4. ____ chico es pelirrojo.
5. ____ mujeres son artísticas.
6. ____ hombre es guapo.
7. ____ personas son organizadas.
8. ____ amigas son jóvenes.
9. ____ estudiantes son bajos.
10. ____ mujer es cómica.

Expansión
Choose three of the sentences and illustrate them.

6 La lista de Sandra

Escuchar
Escribir

A Sandra le gusta comprar muchas cosas. Escucha y escribe una lista de lo que le gusta comprar, usando **el, la, los, las.** *(Listen and write a list of what Sandra likes to buy, using definite articles.)*

Audio Program
TXT CD 1 Track 37
Audio Script, TE p. 53b

7 ¿Qué es? ¿Recuerdas? Snack foods p. 33

Hablar
Escribir

Identifica las comidas, usando **un, una, unos, unas.** *(Identify these foods using indefinite articles.)*

modelo: Son unas galletas.

1. 
2. 
3. 
4. 
5. 
6. 
7. 
8. 

Expansión:
Teacher Edition Only
Ask students to write another sentence for each picture. They can say if they like to eat each food or not.

Differentiating Instruction

Inclusion

Alphabetic/Phonetic Awareness Before students complete Activity 5, have them copy it on a separate sheet of paper. Have them circle the letters in each noun that will help them determine whether it is masculine or feminine, singular or plural. For example, in item 1, students circle the **-as** in **chicas.** This indicates the noun is feminine and plural and requires the article **las.**

Multiple Intelligences

Visual Learners Divide students into two teams to play a "Draw and Guess" game. In advance, copy a number of familiar nouns onto index cards. Have one player choose a card, and draw a picture of the noun for his or her team. The teammates need to guess the item using an indefinite article. **¡Es un teléfono! ¡Son unas chicas!**

8 ¿Son estudiosos?

Hablar
Escribir

Describe a estas personas usando el verbo **ser** y **un, una, unos, unas.** *(Describe these people using **ser** and the correct indefinite article.)*

modelo: chico cómico
Daniel es un chico cómico.

1. chicas estudiosas
2. chicos serios
3. amigas trabajadoras
4. chico desorganizado
5. chica alta
6. chico alto
7. estudiante pelirroja
8. chico grande

Expansión
Choose one of the students from the picture and invent a complete description of him or her.

9 ¿Qué te gusta más?

¿Recuerdas? **gustar** with an infinitive p. 42

Hablar

Pregúntale a otro(a) estudiante qué le gusta hacer más. *(Ask a partner what he or she likes to do more.)*

modelo: comprar / fruta / papas fritas

A ¿Te gusta más comprar una fruta o unas papas fritas?

B Me gusta más comprar una fruta.

1. leer / libro / correos electrónicos
2. hablar con / chicos / chicas
3. pasar un rato con / amigos / maestro
4. comer / galletas / pizza
5. beber / jugo / refresco
6. comprar / DVDs / libro

Expansión:
Teacher Edition Only
Have students work in pairs to ask and answer each other's questions about what they like to buy.

Más práctica Cuaderno *pp. 27–29* Cuaderno para hispanohablantes *pp. 28–30*

Get Help Online
my.hrw.com

PARA Y PIENSA

Did you get it?
Match the article to its corresponding noun.

1. la	a. libro
2. unas	b. hombres
3. el	c. televisión
4. unos	d. frutas

Differentiating Instruction

Slower-paced Learners

Personalize It Have students replace the names in Activity 8 with names of their own classmates. Who among their friends could be described as **chicas estudiosas, buenas amigas,** or **un chico alto**?

Inclusion

Sequential Organization For Activity 9, have students write a subject (male or female), the verb form **es,** the articles **un** and **una** + noun, and adjectives they know on separate index cards. Use the cards to practice forming sentences using the correct word order. Use color coding to reinforce sentence pattern. For example: blue = subject, yellow = verb, and so on.

Long-term Retention

Recycle

Activity 8 Remind students that to make a sentence negative, they must place the word **no** before the verb. **Las chicas no son estudiosas.** Expand Activity 8 by having students make all the sentences negative.

✓ Ongoing Assessment

Get Help Online
More Practice
my.hrw.com

PARA Y PIENSA **Alternative Strategy** After completing Activity 9, each student should report to the class some of his or her partner's preferences using: **A él (ella) le gusta más...** For additional practice, use Reteaching & Practice Copymasters URB 1, pp. 42, 43, 48, 49.

Answers

Projectable Transparencies, 1-50 and 1-51

Answers for Activities on pp. 62, 63.

Activity 6
los libros; los DVDs; las frutas; los helados; las papas fritas; el jugo; las galletas; la pizza

Activity 7
1. Son unas papas fritas.
2. Es un refresco.
3. Es una galleta.
4. Es un helado.
5. Es una pizza.
6. Son unos helados.
7. Son unas frutas.
8. Es un jugo.

Activity 8
1. Sara y Laura son unas chicas estudiosas.
2. Óscar y Justino son unos chicos serios.
3. Sara y Laura son unas amigas trabajadoras.
4. Daniel es un chico desorganizado.
5. Diana es una chica alta.
6. Óscar es un chico alto.
7. Sara es una estudiante pelirroja.
8. Justino es un chico grande.

Activity 9 Answers will vary. Student must use the following structure in their responses: **¿Te gusta más?** + infinitive +indefinite article + nouns.
Me gusta más + infinitive + sentence.
For example: **¿Te gusta más leer un libro o unos correos electrónicos? Me gusta más leer unos correos electrónicos.**

Para y piensa **1.** c; **2.** d; **3.** a; **4.** b

¡AVANZA! **Objectives**

- Practice definite and indefinite articles in context.
- **Culture:** Compare regional variations: foods.
- Recycle: after-school activities.
- Pronunciation: the letter **ñ** and its /ny/ sound.

Core Resources

- Video Program: DVD 1
- Audio Program: TXT CD 1, tracks 38, 39

Presentation Strategies

- Have students read the script.
- Show the video and/or play the audio.
- Ask who the people in the picture are.
- Ask what interests Ricardo and Alberto.

Practice Sequence

- **Activity 10:** Telehistoria comprehension
- **Activity 11:** Transitional practice: definite and indefinite articles; descriptive adjectives; Recycle: after-school activities

STANDARDS

1.1 Engage in conversation, Act. 11
1.2 Understand language, Acts. 10–11
1.3 Present information, Act. 11
4.1 Compare languages, Pronunciación
21st Century **Creativity and Innovation,** Slower-paced Learners

Warm Up Projectable Transparencies, 1-31

Indefinite Articles Write the appropriate indefinite article for the following.

1. _____ chico
2. _____ mujeres
3. _____ galleta
4. _____ amigas
5. _____ refresco
6. _____ hombres

Answers: 1. un; 2. unas; 3. una; 4. unas; 5. un; 6. unos

Video Summary @HOMETUTOR VideoPlus my.hrw.com

Ricardo, Alberto, and Sandra are at the café. The boys inquire about a girl, Ana who is sitting with a group of girls from Mrs. García's class. Sandra tells them what she knows about Ana, and the boys become more interested. Sandra signals that it is time to leave and the boys follow. Alberto almost bumps into Ana. Sandra, once again, rolls her eyes.

GRAMÁTICA en contexto

¡AVANZA! **Goal:** Listen to the conversation between Sandra and her friends. Then use definite and indefinite articles to talk about people. ***Actividades 10–11***

¿Recuerdas? After-school activities p. 32

Telehistoria escena 2

@HOMETUTOR my.hrw.com **View, Read and Record**

STRATEGIES

Cuando lees
Answer questions related to context Knowing the context helps you understand the meaning. Ask yourself: Where is the action taking place?

Cuando escuchas
Listen for unstated wishes People often reveal their wishes without saying them out loud. How do Alberto and Ricardo make it obvious that they want to meet Ana?

VIDEO DVD

AUDIO

Ricardo: Un helado.
Alberto: Unas papas fritas y un refresco.
Sandra: Un jugo y una pizza. *(Alberto looks over at another table.)*
Alberto: ¿Son las chicas de la clase de la señora García?
Ricardo: Sí, son Marta, Carla y...
Sandra: Ana.
Both boys look interested.
Alberto: ¿Quién es ella?
Sandra: Ella es la amiga de Carla. Es muy inteligente. Le gusta leer y tocar la guitarra.
Alberto: Me gusta escuchar música. Ana, ¿no?
Sandra: Sí. Y le gusta practicar deportes.
Ricardo: Yo soy atlético. Soy muy bueno.
Sandra: ¡Ay, los chicos! *(Leaving, Alberto trips and lands in the seat next to Ana and her friends.)*
Alberto: Uh... hola. Perdón.

Continuará... p. 69

También se dice

San Antonio Alberto says **unas papas fritas** to talk about French fries. In other Spanish-speaking countries you might hear:
- **España** **las patatas fritas**
- **Colombia, México** **las papitas**

To talk about juice, Sandra says **un jugo.** In other Spanish-speaking countries you might hear:
- **España** **el zumo**

Differentiating Instruction

Multiple Intelligences

Interpersonal Invite three volunteers to play the parts of Ricardo, Alberto, and Sandra. As these students read through the script, encourage them to emphasize the facial expressions appropriate to each character's emotions. When Sandra says, **¡Ay, los chicos!** what might her expression be?

Slower-paced Learners

Memory Aids Have students create their own "Snack Bar Menus" to help remember active vocabulary. Menus should include the name of each item preceded by the appropriate definite article and an illustration or photo from a magazine. Display the menus for future reference.

10 Comprensión del episodio A corregir

Escuchar Leer

Todas estas oraciones son falsas. Corrige los errores. *(Correct the errors.)*

1. Las chicas se llaman Marta, Beatriz y Ana.
2. Ana es la amiga de Sandra.
3. A Ricardo le gusta escuchar música.
4. Ana no es inteligente.
5. A Alberto le gusta tocar la guitarra.
6. Ricardo no es atlético.

Expansión
Write three false statements about the Telehistoria and ask a partner to correct them.

11 En el parque

¿Recuerdas? After-school activities p. 32

Hablar

Escoge una persona o un grupo de personas de los dibujos. Según el modelo, dale pistas a otro(a) estudiante. Él o ella va a adivinar quién es o quiénes son. Túrnense para describir a todas las personas.
(Choose a person or a group of people from the drawings. Follow the model to give clues to another student, who will guess the people you describe. Change roles and describe everyone.)

A: Es una chica. Le gusta tocar la guitarra.

B: Es la chica de San Antonio.

Expansión:
Teacher Edition Only
Have students work in pairs. One student gives clues about a person who both students know, following the **modelo.** The other student guesses who that person is.

AUDIO

Pronunciación La letra ñ

The ñ sounds like the /ny/ of the word *canyon*. The letter ñ does not exist in English, but the sound does. Listen and repeat.

señor **España** **mañana** **pequeño** **castaño**

La señora es española. **El señor es de España y tiene pelo castaño.**

PARA Y PIENSA

Get Help Online my.hrw.com

Did you get it? Change the article to be more or less specific.
1. Ricardo es el amigo de Alberto.
2. Marta y Carla son las chicas de la clase de la clase de español.
3. Ana es la chica muy inteligente.

Differentiating Instruction

Multiple Intelligences

Visual Learners Give students the opportunity to create their own illustrations similar to those in Activity 11. Encourage them to include two different people engaged in two different activities and a place name. Suggest that students review the vocabulary they have learned so far when making their choice of who and what to draw. Have students describe their illustrations.

Inclusion

Alphabetic/Phonetic Awareness Say each of the following words: **señora, España, Antonio, uno, mañana, organizado, pequeño, castaño.** Have students raise a hand when they hear a word with the /ny/ sound and ask them to pronounce it.

Communication
Role-Playing and Skits

Turn the class into a café in Madrid. Bring in a tablecloth and ask one student to be the waiter. Place a napkin on his or her arm. Have students practice the first six lines of the Telehistoria. Remind them that they are now in a café in Madrid and must use the terms **zumo** and **patatas fritas** when they order their food.

Ongoing Assessment

Get Help Online
More Practice
my.hrw.com

PARA Y PIENSA **Dictation** Read aloud the sentences below as students copy what you say. Have students make the necessary corrections in spelling.
1. **Soy de España, no de San Antonio.**
2. **Me gusta la clase de español porque es pequeña.**
3. **Hasta mañana, señor Salgado.**
4. **¿Tiene el señor Costas pelo castaño?**

For additional practice, use Reteaching & Practice Copymasters URB 1, pp. 42, 44, 50.

Answers Projectable Transparencies, 1-51

Activity 10
1. Las chicas se llaman Marta, Carla y Ana.
2. Ana es la amiga de Carla.
3. A Alberto le gusta escuchar música.
4. Ana es inteligente.
5. A Ana le gusta tocar la guitarra.
6. Ricardo es atlético.

Activity 11 Answers will vary. Students must follow this structure: **Es/Son** + indefinite article + noun. **Le/Les gusta** + infinitive + noun. **Es/Son** + definitive article + noun + de + name of place. For example: **Es un chico. Le gusta escuchar música. Es el chico de Bogotá.**

Para y piensa
1. Ricardo es un amigo de Alberto.
2. Marta y Carla son unas chicas de la clase de español.
3. Ana es una chica muy inteligente.

¡AVANZA! Objective

- Present noun-adjective agreement.

Core Resource

- *Cuaderno,* pp. 30–32

Presentation Strategies

- Say or write expressions with noun-adjective agreement **La chica bonita. El chico alto.**
- Ask students to note the changes according to the gender and number of the nouns in the expressions.

STANDARDS

4.1 Compare languages

Warm Up Projectable Transparencies, 1-32

Definite articles Write the appropriate definite article for the following words:

1. _____ pelo
2. _____ guitarra
3. _____ hombre
4. _____ chicos
5. _____ mujeres

Answers: 1. el; 2. la; 3. el; 4. los; 5. las

Communication

Common Error Alert

In Spanish, when an adjective describes a group that contains both masculine and feminine forms, the masculine plural form of the adjective is used: **Tengo un amigo y una amiga. Son muy serios.**

Adjectives Students Know

Students have learned the following adjectives whose masculine singular forms end in **-o** and whose feminine singular forms end in **-a**:

alto(a)	**cómico(a)**	**pequeño(a)**
artístico(a)	**desorganizado(a)**	**perezoso(a)**
atlético(a)	**estudioso(a)**	**rubio(a)**
bajo(a)	**guapo(a)**	**serio(a)**
bonito(a)	**malo(a)**	**simpático(a)**
bueno(a)	**organizado(a)**	**viejo(a)**
castaño(a)	**pelirrojo(a)**	

Presentación de GRAMÁTICA

¡AVANZA! **Goal:** Learn how to use adjectives with nouns. Then practice using adjectives to describe people. ***Actividades 12–15***

English Grammar Connection: Adjectives are words that describe **nouns.** In English, the adjective almost always comes before the noun. In Spanish, the adjective usually comes after the noun.

before the noun — the **serious students**
after the noun — los **estudiantes serios**

Noun-Adjective Agreement

ANIMATEDGRAMMAR my.hrw.com

In Spanish, adjectives match the gender and number of the nouns they describe.

Here's how:

	Singular	Plural
Masculine	el chic**o** alt**o** *the tall boy*	los chic**os** alt**os** *the tall boys*
Feminine	la chic**a** alt**a** *the tall girl*	las chic**as** alt**as** *the tall girls*

- Adjectives that end in **-e** match both genders. — el maestr**o** inteligent**e** / la maestr**a** inteligent**e**
- Many adjectives that end in a **consonant** match both genders. — el amig**o** jove**n** / la amig**a** jove**n**
- Some adjectives that end in a **consonant** add **-a** to form the feminine singular. These exceptions have to be memorized. — el chic**o** trabajado**r** / la chic**a** trabajado**ra**
- To make an adjective plural, add **-s** if it ends in a **vowel;** add **-es** if it ends in a **consonant.** — las chicas trabajador**as** / los chicos trabajador**es**

Más práctica
Cuaderno *pp. 30–32*
Cuaderno para hispanohablantes *pp. 31–34*

@HOMETUTOR my.hrw.com
Leveled Practice

Differentiating Instruction

English Learners

Build Background Review with English learners the terms *noun* and *adjective.* Remind students that a *noun* is a person, place, or thing, and that an *adjective* describes a noun. Model a few sample phrases in English, such as *the tall girl* or *the serious boy.* Write the phrases on the board, and ask for volunteers to underline the adjective, and circle the noun in each.

Inclusion

Metacognitive Support Create a Venn diagram. Label one side **English,** and the other **Español.** Ask students to think about the similarities and differences between nouns and adjectives in the two languages. Similarity: Nouns and adjectives often appear next to each other; Difference: In English the adjective almost always precedes the noun, while in Spanish the adjective usually follows the noun.

Práctica de GRAMÁTICA

12 Un correo electrónico

Leer

Alicia le escribe un correo electrónico a Sandra con una adivinanza. Escoge las palabras apropiadas entre paréntesis. *(Help Sandra solve the puzzle in Alicia's e-mail by choosing the correct words in parentheses.)*

A: Sandra

Asunto: ¡Una persona famosa en Miami!

Hola, amiga. Te gusta jugar al fútbol y eres **1.** (inteligente / inteligentes), ¿no? ¿Quién es la persona famosa en Miami? No es un chico **2.** (grande / grandes). No es una chica **3.** (pequeño / pequeña). Tiene pelo **4.** (castaño / castaña) y es una persona **5.** (simpático / simpática). Es una mujer **6.** (serio / seria) pero le gusta pasar un rato con los amigos. Los amigos de ella son **7.** (atléticos / atlético) también y les gusta practicar deportes. Ella se llama Trini...

Alicia

Expansión: Teacher Edition Only
Have students write an e-mail describing themselves to a new friend.

13 Descripciones

Escribir

Escribe descripciones de las personas en el dibujo. *(Write descriptions of the people in the drawing.)*

alto(a)	desorganizado(a)
guapo(a)	serio(a)
atlético(a)	cómico(a)
estudioso(a)	¿ ?

Expansión
Choose a photo of people from a magazine. Describe the people in the photo.

Differentiating Instruction

Slower-paced Learners

Sentence Completion Organize students into pairs to complete Activity 12. Instruct partners to take turns reading sentences aloud. If necessary, tell them to try out both choices in the parentheses, and listen for which one "sounds right." Point out that **chica pequeña** sounds like it goes together, while **chica pequeño** is a mismatch.

Heritage Language Learners

Writing Skills Encourage students to elaborate on their descriptions in Activity 13. Ask them to add other appropriate adjectives that may not have been included in the lesson. Tell students to consult a dictionary for the accurate spelling of words they are unsure of. Remind students to pay attention to the agreement of articles, nouns, and adjectives.

Objectives

- Practice noun-adjective agreement.
- Practice using adjectives that describe people.

Practice Sequence

- **Activity 12:** Controlled practice: noun-adjective agreement
- **Activity 13:** Transitional practice: noun-adjective agreement

STANDARDS

1.3 Present information, Act. 13
4.1 Compare languages, Act. 12
Communication, Acts. 12: Expansión, 13: Expansión

Communication
Grammar Activity

Explain to students that in Spanish some adjectives are not masculine or feminine. Those adjectives are known as invariable in gender meaning they describe both masculine or feminine nouns. For example, **la chica es inteligente, el chico es inteligente** or **la maestra es joven, el maestro es joven.**

Answers Projectable Transparencies, 1-51

Activity 12
1. inteligente
2. grande
3. pequeña
4. castaño
5. simpática
6. seria
7. atléticos

Activity 13 Answers will vary. Sample answers include:
Mario es alto. Él es estudioso.
La señora de Silva es simpática. Ella es baja.
Mónica es atlética. Ella es guapa.
Rafael es cómico. Él es joven.

Objectives
- Practice noun-adjective agreement.
- **Culture:** Recognize or discuss the influence of cultural traditions.

Core Resource
- *Cuaderno,* pp. 30–32

Practice Sequence
- **Activity 14:** Open-ended practice: noun-adjective agreement
- **Activity 15:** Open-ended practice: descriptive adjectives

STANDARDS
1.1 Engage in conversation, Act. 15
1.2 Understand language, Act. 14
1.3 Present information, Acts. 14–15
2.1 Practices and perspectives, Act. 15
2.2 Products and perspectives, Act. 15
4.2 Compare cultures, Act. 15
21st Century **Communication,** Act. 14

Comparación cultural
Essential Question
Suggested Answer Many artists include in their work aspects of their culture such as family ritual activities including games, crafts, and foods. For the artist Carmen Lomas Garza, family is an important component in Mexican-American culture.

✓ Ongoing Assessment
Get Help Online
More Practice
my.hrw.com

PARA Y PIENSA **Remediation** If students have problems supplying the correct adjective endings in Para y piensa, have them review p. 66 and repeat Activities 12 and 13 on p. 67. For additional practice, use Reteaching & Practice Copymasters URB 1, pp. 45, 46.

See Activity answers on p. 69.

14 ¿Cómo son los amigos de clase?

Escribir
Hablar

Escribe descripciones de tres personas en la clase. Lee la descripción a otro(a) estudiante. Él o ella debe adivinar quién es. *(Write descriptions of three people in the class. Read the descriptions to a partner, who will guess the people being described.)*

A: Es un chico. Es alto, inteligente y atlético. Es un poco serio también. Tiene pelo castaño.

B: Es Felipe.

Expansión
Describe someone you know to a partner. Your partner will try to draw that person.

15 El arte tejano

Hablar

Comparación cultural

Fiesta San Antonio

El arte en Texas

How do cultural traditions influence an artist's work? *Cascarones* are painted eggs filled with confetti. They are popular at Easter and events such as parties or graduations. They are also a common sight during Fiesta San Antonio, an annual city-wide celebration that honors the history and culture of San Antonio, **Texas.** But *cascarones* are not meant for decoration. Children sneak up on their friends and try to crack the eggs over their heads. If a *cascarón* is broken over your head, it is supposed to bring you good luck! Artists are often influenced by traditions like these. Carmen Lomas Garza is a Mexican-American artist who depicts scenes of traditional celebration. In her 1989 painting *Cascarones,* Lomas Garza presents a family making the colorful eggs.

Compara con tu mundo *What are some traditions in your family and why are they important to you?*

Indica a una persona en la foto y pregúntale a otro(a) estudiante cómo es. Tu compañero(a) va a responder. Túrnense para describir a todas las personas. *(Point to a person in the photo and ask your partner what he or she is like. Change roles. Describe all the people in the photo.)*

A: ¿Cómo es la chica?

B: La chica es bonita.

Expansión:
Teacher Edition Only
Ask a student to describe one person in the photo and have another student point to the person being described.

Más práctica Cuaderno *pp. 30–32* Cuaderno para hispanohablantes *pp. 31–34*

Get Help Online
my.hrw.com

PARA Y PIENSA

Did you get it? Give the correct ending for each adjective.
1. una estudiante desorganizad ____
2. unos chicos simpátic ____
3. unas mujeres trabajador ____
4. un hombre grand ____

Differentiating Instruction

Multiple Intelligences
Visual Learners Ask students to paint or draw a depiction of one of their own family traditions. Once paintings or drawings are complete, have them describe the people they have depicted. **Es Gabriela. Es una chica pequeña.**

Heritage Language Learners
Support What They Know Ask students to discuss the traditions their families and communities practice during the holidays, at parties, or at graduations. Also, ask all students to talk about traditions in their cultures that are supposed to bring good luck. What kinds of things do people do, or not do, to bring good luck?

Todo junto

¡AVANZA! **Goal:** ***Show what you know*** Pay attention to how Sandra and her friends describe specific people. Then use definite and indefinite articles and adjectives to tell what someone is like. ***Actividades 16–20***

Telehistoria completa

@HOMETUTOR my.hrw.com View, Read and Record

STRATEGIES

Cuando lees
Discover a problem Scenes often reveal problems that the characters must solve. While reading the text below, search for a problem. What is it? Can it be solved?

Cuando escuchas
Listen for the parts Even a short scene can have parts, each with a somewhat different topic or action. These can be keys to meaning. How would you divide this scene?

Escena 1 *Resumen*
Alberto y Ricardo son amigos de Sandra. Alberto es un poco desorganizado. Ricardo es artístico.

Escena 2 *Resumen*
Ana es la amiga de Carla. A Ricardo y a Ana les gusta practicar deportes, y a Alberto y a Ana les gusta escuchar música.

VIDEO DVD

AUDIO

Escena 3

The group enters a store where Trini Salgado will be signing autographs.

Alberto: Ana es bonita, inteligente, simpática… y nosotros somos inteligentes y simpáticos, ¿no?

Sandra: Sí, sí, ustedes son inteligentes, atléticos, cómicos. Ricardo, tú eres estudioso y Alberto, tú eres cómico.

Ricardo notices a woman in the store.

Ricardo: ¿Es Trini Salgado?

Alberto: ¿Quién?

Ricardo: La mujer seria. Tiene pelo castaño.

Sandra: No es ella. Es un poco baja. Trini es alta y más joven.

Ricardo finds the sign announcing Trini Salgado and points to the date.

Sandra: Pero… es el sábado. Hoy es domingo.

Ricardo: Sí, el sábado en San Antonio y el lunes en México.

Sandra: ¿México? ¿Puebla, México? Pablo, un amigo muy simpático de Alicia, es de México.

Sandra thinks of a plan to send the T-shirt to Pablo.

¡AVANZA! Objectives

- Integrate lesson content.

Core Resources

- Video Program: DVD 1
- Audio Program: TXT CD 1, track 40

Presentation Strategies

- Ask students what they remember about the Telehistoria so far.
- Before showing the video or playing the audio, tell students to watch for the surprise ending and to be ready to talk about it.

STANDARDS

1.2 Understand language

Warm Up Projectable Transparencies, 1-32

Noun-Adjective Agreement Match the following nouns with their corresponding adjectives.

1. unos estudiantes	**a.** trabajadoras
2. unas señoras	**b.** alto
3. una amiga	**c.** serios
4. un chico	**d.** atlética

Answers: 1. c; 2. a; 3. d; 4. b

Video Summary

@HOMETUTOR VideoPlus my.hrw.com

The trio walks into a store where Trini Salgado will be signing autographs. Ricardo finds a sign that says that Trini signed autographs yesterday. The next stop on her tour is Puebla, Mexico. Sandra says she knows a friend of Alicia's in Puebla.

Differentiating Instruction

Slower-paced Learners

Read Before Listening Have students read the script before listening to the audio or viewing the video. Ask them to make a list of adjectives for each character, for example: **Ricardo: estudioso.** Have them refer to this list as they listen to audio or view the video.

Inclusion

Sequential Information Write sentences from the Telehistoria on individual sentence strips. Scramble the sentences. Have students arrange them in order based on what they read or hear.

Answers Projectable Transparencies, 1-51 and 1-52

Answers for Activities on p. 68.

Activity 14 Answers will vary. Students must use the structure: verb + adjective in their response. For example: **Es bonita.**

Activity 15 Answers will vary. Sample answers include:
A: ¿Cómo es la señora? **B:** La señora es bonita.
A: ¿Cómo es el señor? **B:** El señor es grande.

Para y piensa desorganizada; simpáticos; trabajadoras; grande

TODO JUNTO

Objective
- Practice using and integrating lesson vocabulary and grammar.

Core Resources
- *Cuaderno,* pp. 33–34
- Audio Program: TXT CD 1, tracks 36, 38, 40, 41, 42

Practice Sequence
- **Activities 16, 17:** Telehistoria comprehension
- **Activity 18:** Transitional practice: writing, speaking
- **Activity 19:** Open-ended practice: reading, listening, speaking
- **Activity 20:** Open-ended practice: writing

STANDARDS
1.1 Engage in conversation, Act. 18
1.2 Understand language, Acts. 16, 18
1.3 Present information, Acts. 17–20
21st Century **Collaboration,** Act. 17: Expansión; **Initiative and Self-Direction,** Pre-AP

✓ Ongoing Assessment

Rubric Activity 18

Speaking Criteria	Maximum Credit	Partial Credit	Minimum Credit
Content	The description is complete.	The description is partially complete.	The description is incomplete.
Communication	Description and pronunciation are easy to follow and clear.	Parts of the description and pronunciation are somewhat organized and clear.	Description and pronunciation are disorganized and unclear.
Accuracy	There are few mistakes in grammar and vocabulary.	There are some mistakes in grammar and vocabulary.	There are many mistakes in grammar and vocabulary.

Answers
Projectable Transparencies, 1-52

Activity 16
1. f; **2.** b; **3.** g; **4.** h; **5.** e; **6.** d; **7.** a; **8.** c

Activity 17 Answers will vary. Students must follow this structure: Name + **es** + adjective. For example: Alicia es inteligente y bonita. Alberto no es muy alto, tiene el pelo castaño.

Activity answers continue on p. 71.

16 *Comprensión de los episodios* ¿Cómo son?

Escuchar
Leer

Combina frases de las dos columnas para hacer oraciones sobre las personas en la Telehistoria. *(Combine phrases from the two columns to make sentences about the people in the Telehistoria.)*

1. Alberto y Ricardo son	**a.** un poco baja.
2. Sandra es	**b.** una amiga de Ricardo y Alberto.
3. Ana es	**c.** un amigo de Alicia.
4. Ricardo es	**d.** jóvenes.
5. Alberto es	**e.** alto y trabajador.
6. Todos los chicos son	**f.** cómicos.
7. La mujer seria es	**g.** inteligente y le gusta leer.
8. Pablo es	**h.** artístico y atlético.

Expansión:
Teacher Edition Only
Ask students to think of other characteristics of each person in the Telehistoria.

17 *Comprensión de los episodios* Los amigos

Escuchar
Leer

Escribe una descripción de los personajes de la Telehistoria según los tres episodios.
(Write descriptions of the Telehistoria characters.)

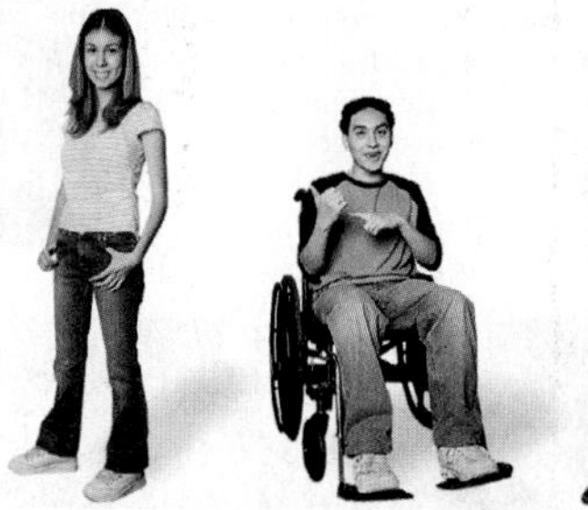

Expansión:
Teacher Edition Only
Have groups of students create a dialogue based on the Telehistoria that explains what might happen next.

18 Las personas famosas

Digital performance space

Escribir
Hablar

STRATEGY Hablar
Practice pronunciation To speak more fluently and accurately, practice the sounds of words you need to use in your descriptions. Paying attention to pronunciation will help you with cognates.

Escribe descripciones de tres personas famosas. Menciona lo que les gusta y no les gusta hacer. Lee tus descripciones a otro(a) estudiante.
(Write descriptions of three famous people, including what they like and don't like to do. Read the descriptions to a partner, who will guess the people being described.)

A Es un hombre. Tiene pelo rubio. Es muy atlético. Le gusta montar en bicicleta. No es muy joven y no es muy viejo. Es de Estados Unidos. ¿Quién es?

B Es Lance Armstrong.

Expansión
Pick another celebrity and have a partner ask five yes/no questions to find out who it is.

Differentiating Instruction

Multiple Intelligences
Interpersonal Invite students to expand on Activity 16 by describing their own friends and family. Direct students to substitute names of people they know in the first column, and then combine those names with appropriate phrases from the second column. Remind students to modify articles and adjective endings when necessary.

Heritage Language Learners
Support What They Know Ask students to name a famous person from their country of origin and describe that person using the vocabulary they have learned. For example: **Antonio Banderas es un actor de España. No es muy joven y no es muy viejo. Es alto y tiene pelo castaño. Es muy inteligente y le gusta leer.**

19 Integración

Digital performance space

Leer
Escuchar
Hablar

Lee la página Web y escucha los mensajes de los chicos. Describe a los dos chicos. *(Read the Web page and listen to the boys' messages. Describe the two boys.)*

Fuente 1 Página Web

Amigos por correspondencia

Buscar en la Web

Alejandro: ¡Hola! Soy de San José, Costa Rica. Soy un estudiante muy bueno. Soy inteligente y me gusta estudiar. Soy un poco serio pero también soy simpático.
¡Escucha!

Édgar: Soy de Colombia. Soy alto y tengo pelo castaño. Soy cómico y simpático. Soy inteligente pero no soy muy trabajador. No me gusta estudiar. ;-)
¡Escucha!

Fuente 2 Audio en Internet

Listen and take notes
- ¿Cómo es Alejandro? ¿Qué le gusta hacer?
- ¿Cómo es Édgar? ¿Qué le gusta hacer?

modelo: Alejandro es un poco serio, pero Édgar es cómico...

Audio Program
TXT CD 1 Tracks 41, 42 Audio Script, TE p. 53b

20 Un(a) amigo(a) perfecto(a)

Digital performance space

Escribir

Describe el (la) amigo(a) perfecto(a) para una página especial en el anuario. ¿Cómo es? ¿Qué le gusta hacer? ¿Por qué? *(Describe the perfect friend for the yearbook. What is this person like? What does he or she like to do? Why?)*

modelo: Ella se llama Megan. Es bonita, inteligente y artística. Es una chica muy simpática. Le gusta escuchar música y...

Writing Criteria	Excellent	Good	Needs Work
Content	Your description includes a lot of information.	Your description includes some information.	Your description includes little information.
Communication	Most of your description is organized and easy to follow.	Parts of your description are organized and easy to follow.	Your description is disorganized and hard to follow.
Accuracy	Your description has few mistakes in grammar and vocabulary.	Your description has some mistakes in grammar and vocabulary.	Your description has many mistakes in grammar and vocabulary.

Expansión: Teacher Edition Only
Have students describe another person that they like.

Más práctica Cuaderno *pp. 33–34* Cuaderno para hispanohablantes *pp. 35–36*

Get Help Online
my.hrw.com

PARA Y PIENSA

Did you get it? Create sentences with the following information.

1. Alberto / chico(a) / simpático(a)
2. Ricardo / estudiante / trabajador(a)
3. Sandra / persona / organizado(a)

Differentiating Instruction

Inclusion

Clear Structure Remind students to follow the steps of the writing process in order to create their descriptions in Activity 20. Have them brainstorm important vocabulary, draft complete sentences, revise, and then proofread before turning in their final drafts.

Pre-AP

Self-correct After students have completed their descriptions in Activity 20, encourage them to read their writing aloud. Remind them to listen for agreement between articles, nouns, and adjectives. If something does not sound right, tell students to take a closer look and confirm they have used the correct endings.

Long-term Retention

Pre-AP Integration

Activity 19 Have students work in pairs. Have one student write an e-mail describing himself/herself following the activity model. As that student reads the e-mail, his or her partner takes notes.

✓ Ongoing Assessment

Rubric Activity 19

Listening/Speaking

Proficient	Not There Yet
Student takes detailed notes and provides a complete description.	Student takes few notes and provides an incomplete description.

To customize your own rubrics, use the ***Generate Success*** *Rubric Generator and Graphic Organizers.*

✓ Ongoing Assessment

Get Help Online
More Practice
my.hrw.com

PARA Y PIENSA

Peer Assessment Have student pairs say the sentences out loud and correct each other. For additional practice, use Reteaching & Practice Copymasters URB 1, pp. 45, 47.

Communication

Motivating with Music

The **¡AvanzaRap!** song for this unit targets descriptions, likes and dislikes, and ages. To reinforce these concepts, play the **¡AvanzaRap!** animated video song and have students complete the Activity Master. Activity masters and teaching suggestions can be found on the **¡AvanzaRap! DVD.**

Answers Projectable Transparencies, 1-52

Activity 19 Sample answers include:

Alejandro es inteligente y un poco serio, pero también es simpático.

Activity 20 Answers will vary. Sample descriptions will follow this outline:

Él/Ella se llama... Es..., ... y..... Es un(a) chico/chica muy... Le gusta... y....

Para y piensa
1. Alberto es un chico simpático.
2. Ricardo es un estudiante trabajador.
3. Sandra es una persona organizada.

¡AVANZA! **Objectives**
- Learn about after-school activities in Miami and San Antonio.
- Build vocabulary with new terms for activities, food, and interesting places.

Core Resource
- Audio Program: TXT CD 1 track 43

Presentation Strategies
- Ask students to look at the photos on pp. 72 and 73. Ask quick comprehension questions: **¿Qué tiempo hace? ¿Qué le gusta hacer al chico en Miami?**
- Have students listen to the audio paying special attention to all activities mentioned.

STANDARDS
1.1 Engage in conversation
1.2 Understand language
2.1 Practices and perspectives
4.2 Compare cultures
21st Century **Critical Thinking and Problem** Solving, Strategy; **Information Literacy,** Heritage Language Learners

Warm Up Projectable Transparencies, 1-33

Noun-Adjective Agreement Fill in the blanks with the appropriate **-o/-a** ending.

1. Alejandro es un estudiante muy buen ____.
2. Él es un poco seri ____.
3. Megan es artístic ____.
4. Ella es una chica muy simpátic ____.

Answers: 1. bueno; 2. serio; 3. artística 4. simpática

Comparación cultural

Background Information

El Álamo The Álamo was named for the grove of cottonwood trees in which it stands. It was the chapel of the Mission San Antonio de Valero, founded in 1716. In December 1835, Texans were at war with Mexico, seeking independence. Members of the volunteer army captured the city of San Antonio, and occupied the Álamo. The leader of the Texas independence movement, Sam Houston, advised the volunteers to abandon the Álamo, but they refused. In February 1836, Mexican troops under the command of General Antonio López de Santa Anna began a seige of the Álamo.

Lectura cultural

Additional readings at my.hrw.com SPANISH InterActive Reader

¡AVANZA! **Goal:** Read about things to do in San Antonio and Miami. Then compare what teens do in those cities with what you like to do where you live.

Comparación cultural

AUDIO

Saludos desde[1] San Antonio y Miami

STRATEGY Leer
Make a comparison chart
Create a chart like the one below to compare San Antonio and Miami.

	San Antonio	Miami
sitios de interés		
actividades		
comida		

En San Antonio, Texas, hay[2] parques de diversiones[3], museos[4], el Paseo del Río y el Álamo. Después de las clases, a los chicos y a las chicas les gusta pasar un rato con los amigos en El Mercado, donde es posible escuchar música de los mariachis y comer comida típica mexicana.

[1] **Saludos...** Greetings from
[2] there are
[3] amusement parks
[4] museums

San Antonio

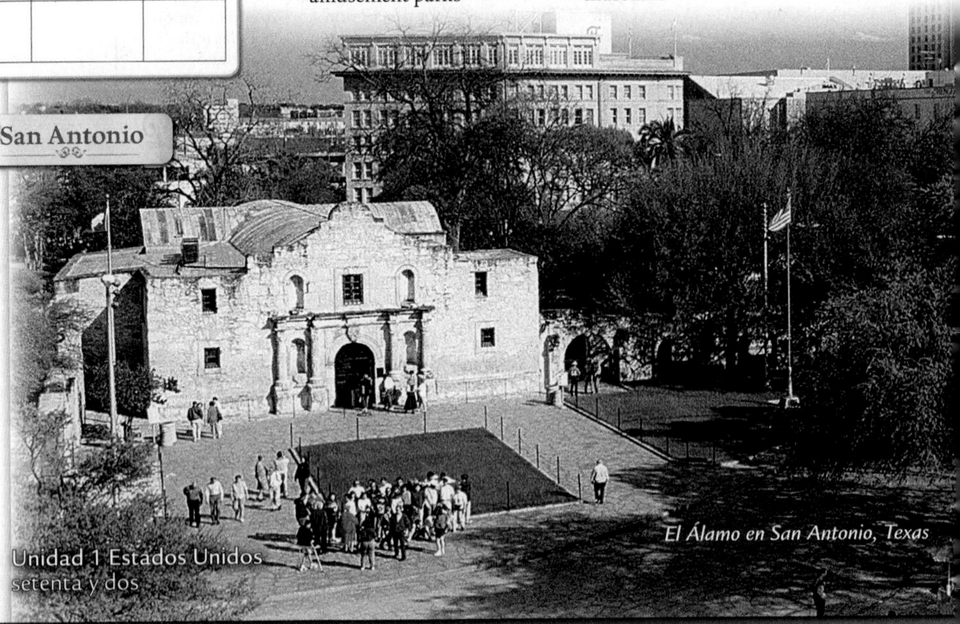

El Álamo en San Antonio, Texas

Differentiating Instruction

Multiple Intelligences

Interpersonal Have students form groups of three or four. Ask each group to discuss favorite after-school activities in their hometown. Are any the same as or similar to those of students in San Antonio or Miami? Ask each group to give an informal oral report to the class.

Heritage Language Learners

Writing Skills Have students do research about some of San Antonio's famous sites such as the Álamo, Paseo del Río, and La Villita. Have them use the information to write a short report to present to the class. Monitor correct spelling, pronunciation, and word usage.

En Miami, Florida, si[5] hace buen tiempo, a los chicos y a las chicas les gusta andar en patineta o montar en bicicleta. Después de las clases, a muchos chicos les gusta pasear con los amigos por la Calle Ocho, en la Pequeña Habana de Miami. ¡Es una pequeña Cuba en la Florida! Allí[6] es posible comer sándwiches cubanos y beber jugo de mango.

[5] if [6] There

Andar en patineta en Miami, Florida

PARA Y PIENSA

¿Comprendiste?

1. ¿Qué hay en San Antonio?
2. ¿Qué les gusta hacer a muchos chicos en Miami?
3. ¿Qué hay en la Pequeña Habana de Miami?

¿Y tú?

¿De dónde eres? ¿Qué te gusta hacer después de las clases?

Communication
Group Work

Organize students in groups of four to talk about activities they do on weekends with their families or friends. Have them discuss if their activities are similar or different to the activities young people do in San Antonio and Miami. Allow them to work by themselves and record their findings using a Venn diagram.

Comparisons
English Language Connection

Cognates Have students look for cognates in the reading. Ask them to write the words down, give their meanings in English, and then share the words with the class.

Long-term Retention
Personalize It

Ask students what activities they would like to do if they were in Miami or in San Antonio and explain why. For example, **En San Antonio me gusta pasar un rato en El Mercado porque me gusta escuchar música de los mariachis. En Miami me gusta pasear por la Calle Ocho porque me gusta comer sándwiches cubanos.**

Differentiating Instruction

Slower-paced Learners

Sentence Completion If students have trouble responding to the ¿Comprendiste? questions, ask them to complete sentences that begin with:
En San Antonio les gusta...
A muchos chicos les gusta pasear...
En la Pequeña Habana de Miami...

Pre-AP

Communicate Preferences After students have read the selection, ask them to discuss what they have read about San Antonio and Miami. For example: **¿Dónde te gusta pasear en Miami? ¿Qué te gusta hacer en San Antonio?** Have them share their preferences about places, activities, foods, and explain why.

Answers

Para y piensa

¿Y tú Comprendiste?

1. En San Antonio, hay parques de diversiones, museos, el Paseo del Río, el Álamo y El Mercado.
2. A muchos chicos les gusta andar en patineta, montar en bicicleta, pasear por la Calle Ocho.
3. La Calle Ocho está en la Pequeña Habana. Allí es posible comer sándwiches cubanos y beber jugo de mango.

¿Y tú?

Answers will vary. Sample answers will follow this format: **Soy de... Después de las clases me gusta...**

Objectives

- Read about traditional dishes from Mexico and Cuba.
- **Culture:** Discuss how traditional dishes change from one country to another.
- **Community:** Investigate sources of Latin American food in your community.

Presentation Strategies

- Ask students to describe Latin dishes they have tasted. Have they eaten **salsa fresca** or **sándwiches cubanos?**
- Have students read the two recipes. Assign two students to look up these words in an English-Spanish dictionary and come up with a list of ingredients in Spanish.
- Conduct a class survey to find out which dish the class prefers, and why.

STANDARDS

3.1 Knowledge of other disciplines
5.1 Spanish in the community
21st Century **Collaboration,** Heritage Language Learners

Comparación cultural

Essential Question

Suggested Answer Traditional dishes change because certain ingredients might not be available in other countries. For example, the abundance of wheat in the U.S. caused flour to become the basis for many Tex-Mex dishes instead of the corn meal used in Mexico.

Expanded Information

Mexican restaurants in the U.S. have followed the form and style of "Tex-Mex" food, a combination of Northern Mexican food with Texas farm and cowboy fare. Chili, which some consider Texas' state dish, was unknown in Mexico and derived from an ample supply of beef in Texas.

Communities

Spanish in the Marketplace

Have students visit a grocery store that sells traditional Latin American foods. Ask students to write down the names of Mexican and/or Cuban foods that are sold and report back to the class.

Proyectos culturales

Comparación cultural

Platos tradicionales de México y Cuba

Why do traditional dishes change when they are brought from one country to another? In the U.S. we enjoy foods from many different Spanish-speaking countries. In many parts of the U.S. you can easily find dishes from Mexico, the Caribbean, Central America, and South America. Yet you might be surprised that those dishes aren't exactly the same as they are in their countries of origin. Here are two traditional recipes. The original list of ingredients for both has been modified to include foods more readily available in the U.S. They also reflect the widespread cooking practices and tastes that were already in place when the recipes were brought to this country.

Proyecto 1 *Salsa fresca*

México This is a common sauce in Mexico and all Central America. It is made from scratch and can be eaten as a dip with tortilla chips.

Ingredients for salsa fresca
4–5 fresh tomatoes, diced
1 onion, diced
1 green chile, diced
1 clove of garlic, crushed
Juice of 1 fresh lime

Instructions
Combine the ingredients in a bowl. Cover and let stand for an hour in the refrigerator so that the flavors mix. Serve with tortilla chips.

Proyecto 2 *Sándwich cubano*

Cuba This is a traditional Cuban lunch dish found throughout Florida. The sandwich is pressed in a special grill or on a skillet.

Ingredients for sándwich cubano
1 long sandwich roll
Slices of roast pork, ham, turkey, or bacon
Slice of Swiss or monterey jack cheese
Mustard or mayonnaise
Olive oil

Instructions
First brush the outside of the roll with olive oil. Then split it open and lay meat, cheese, and mustard or mayonnaise as desired. Put the sandwich in a hot skillet, placing a small, heavy skillet on top and pressing lightly. Cook three minutes or until cheese melts and bread is toasted.

En tu comunidad

Check the Internet or your phone book for restaurants that serve foods from Mexico, Cuba, or other Spanish-speaking countries. Do any of the restaurants in your area serve **salsa fresca** or **sándwiches cubanos**?

Differentiating Instruction

Heritage Language Learners

Support What They Know Ask student pairs to cut from magazines or download from the Internet recipes from their country of origin. Have them present their recipe as if they were doing it in front of a TV audience. Have props available as needed. As one student reads the recipe, the other student pantomimes its preparation.

Multiple Intelligences

Logical/Mathematical Ask students to name multiple-ingredient sandwiches that are popular in their hometowns. They might be hoagies, submarines, po'boys, or grinders. Ask them to create tables that show how similar ingredients are used in Cuban sandwiches and other locally popular sandwiches.

Lección 2

En resumen

Vocabulario y gramática

ANIMATEDGRAMMAR
Interactive Flashcards
my.hrw.com

Vocabulario

Describe Yourself and Others

¿Cómo eres?	*What are you like?*

Personality

artístico(a)	*artistic*
atlético(a)	*athletic*
bueno(a)	*good*
cómico(a)	*funny*
desorganizado(a)	*disorganized*
estudioso(a)	*studious*
inteligente	*intelligent*
malo(a)	*bad*
organizado(a)	*organized*
perezoso(a)	*lazy*
serio(a)	*serious*
simpático(a)	*nice*
trabajador(a)	*hard-working*

Appearance

alto(a)	*tall*
bajo(a)	*short (height)*
bonito(a)	*pretty*
grande	*big, large; great*
guapo(a)	*good-looking*
joven (pl. jóvenes)	*young*
pelirrojo(a)	*red-haired*
pequeño(a)	*small*
viejo(a)	*old*
Tengo...	*I have . . .*
Tiene...	*He / She has . . .*
pelo rubio	*blond hair*
pelo castaño	*brown hair*

People

el (la) amigo(a)	*friend*
la chica	*girl*
el chico	*boy*
el (la) estudiante	*student*
el hombre	*man*
la mujer	*woman*
la persona	*person*

Other Words and Phrases

muy	*very*
un poco	*a little*
porque	*because*
todos(as)	*all*

Gramática

Nota gramatical: **ser** to describe what someone is like *p. 58*

Definite and Indefinite Articles

In Spanish, articles match nouns in gender and number.

		Definite Article	Noun	Indefinite Article	Noun
Masculine	Singular	el	chico	un	chico
	Plural	los	chicos	unos	chicos
Feminine	Singular	la	chica	una	chica
	Plural	las	chicas	unas	chicas

Noun-Adjective Agreement

In Spanish, adjectives match the gender and number of the nouns they describe.

	Singular	Plural
Masculine	el chico alto	los chicos altos
Feminine	la chica alta	las chicas altas

Practice Spanish with Holt McDougal Apps!

Differentiating Instruction

Multiple Intelligences

Interpersonal Using the Vocabulario, ask students to create poems that describe themselves. They may arrange the phrases creatively on colored paper and draw illustrations, borders, and other decorations.

English Learners

Build Background Ask students to draw pictures of their immediate families. Under the image of each family member, students should write the person's name and the appropriate term from the vocabulary for *People*.

Objective

- Review lesson vocabulary and grammar.

DIGITAL SPANISH

Interactive Flashcards Students can hear every target vocabulary word pronounced in authentic Spanish. Flashcards have Spanish on one side, and a picture or a translation on the other.

Review Games Matching, concentration, hangman, and word search are just a sampling of the fun, interactive games students can play to review for the test.

performance space
News Networking
@HOMETUTOR
CULTURA Interactiva

- **Audio and Video Resources**
- **Interactive Flashcards**
- **Review Activities**
- **WebQuest**
- **Conjuguemos.com**

Long-term Retention

Personalize It

Help students create personal Spanish-English dictionaries using two-column tables. They may illustrate the words as well as define them.

Long-term Retention

Study Tips

Ask students to list vocabulary terms that have English cognates, and create a mnemonic device that helps them remember the cognate pair.

Communication

Interpersonal Mode

Have students quiz each other on the vocabulary. One pantomimes an adjective and the other classmate guesses which word his/her partner is acting out.

¡AVANZA! **Objective**
- Review lesson content: vocabulary, definite and indefinite articles, noun-adjective agreement, the verb **ser**.

Core Resources
- *Cuaderno*, pp. 35–46
- Audio Program: TXT CD 1 track 44

Presentation Strategies
- Direct students' attention to the ¡Llegada!
- As students listen to the audio, instruct them to pay special attention to the endings of nouns and adjectives.
- Monitor correct use of **ser** and noun-adjective agreement as students do the activities.
- Go over the Comparación cultural with students and clarify any questions that arise.
- Review may be done in class or given as homework.
- You may want students to access the review online.

STANDARDS
1.2 Understand language, Acts. 1, 3
1.3 Present information, Acts. 2, 4
4.2 Compare cultures, Act. 5

Warm Up Projectable Transparencies, 1-33

Noun-Adjective Agreement Complete each phrase with the correct adjective form.
1. una chica _____ (alto)
2. un chico _____ (guapo)
3. las mujeres _____ (bajo)
4. los hombres _____ (viejo)
5. una maestra _____ (simpático)

Answers: 1. alta; 2. guapo; 3. bajas; 4. viejos; 5. simpática

Ongoing Assessment
Get Help Online
More Practice
my.hrw.com

Remediation If students achieve less than 80% accuracy with the activities, direct them to the review pages and to get help online at my.hrw.com.

Lección 2 Repaso de la lección

@HOMETUTOR my.hrw.com

¡LLEGADA!

Now you can
- describe yourself and others
- identify people and things

Using
- **ser** to describe what someone is like
- definite and indefinite articles
- noun-adjective agreement

¡AvanzaRap! DVD Sing and Learn

To review
- definite and indefinite articles p. 61
- **ser** to describe what someone is like p. 58
- noun-adjective agreement p. 66

1 Listen and understand

AUDIO

Escucha a Carlos hablar de él mismo y de su maestra. Escribe una descripción de Carlos y de la señora Pérez, según lo que dice Carlos. *(Listen to Carlos describe himself and his teacher. Write a description of Carlos and Mrs. Pérez, according to what Carlos says.)*

Audio Program
TXT CD 1 Track 44
Audio Script, TE p. 53b

To review
- definite and indefinite articles p. 61

2 Identify people and things

Identifica a las personas en el dibujo. *(Identify the people in the drawing.)*

modelo: señor viejo / hombre
El señor viejo es un hombre de Honduras.

México Honduras Uruguay Panamá Bolivia Argentina Estados Unidos

1. chica pelirroja / estudiante
2. hombre grande / maestro
3. chicos pelirrojos / amigos
4. mujer joven / maestra
5. señora alta / mujer
6. chico atlético / estudiante
7. chico desorganizado / persona
8. hombres simpáticos / amigos

Differentiating Instruction

Multiple Intelligences

Musical/Rhythmic After students have completed Activity 2, divide them into groups of four or five. In turn, ask groups to chant each of the sentences, tapping out a strong rhythm to keep time.

Inclusion

Multisensory Input/Output Ask students to draw a T-table in their notebooks. Ask them to write **Carlos** on one column, and **Sra. Pérez** on the other. As students listen to the audio, ask them to write the descriptions for Carlos and for Sra. Pérez under the appropriate headings.

REPASO DE LA LECCIÓN

To review
- noun-adjective agreement p. 66

3 Describe yourself and others

Lee este párrafo del diario de Alejandra. Completa la información con la forma correcta de la palabra entre paréntesis. *(Complete Alejandra's diary entry with the correct form of the word in parentheses.)*

> Lunes
>
> Todos mis amigos son muy **1.** (simpático). Miguel es un chico **2.** (inteligente) y muy **3.** (guapo). Beatriz es **4.** (bonito) y **5.** (estudioso). A Miguel y a Beatriz les gusta practicar deportes porque son **6.** (atlético). Carmen y yo no somos **7.** (atlético). Nosotras somos **8.** (artístico). Todos nosotros somos unos estudiantes **9.** (serio) y muy **10.** (bueno).

To review
- **ser** to describe what someone is like p. 58
- noun-adjective agreement p. 66

4 Describe yourself and others

Ramón y Ramona tienen características opuestas. Escribe oraciones para describirlos, según las descripciones. *(Ramón and Ramona are complete opposites. Write sentences describing them, based on the descriptions.)*

modelo: **Ramón es malo.**
Ramona es buena.

1. Ramón es viejo.
2. Ramona es seria.
3. Ramón es organizado.
4. Ramona es pequeña.
5. Ramón es perezoso.
6. Ramona es baja.

To review
- Comparación cultural pp. 54, 60, 68
- Lectura cultural pp. 72–73

5 United States

Comparación cultural

Answer these culture questions.

1. What can people do at San Antonio's Paseo del Río?
2. Give an example of a Tex-Mex dish and a Mexican dish.
3. When do people generally use **cascarones** and what do they do with them?
4. What can people do in San Antonio's El Mercado and Miami's Calle Ocho?

Más práctica Cuaderno *pp. 35–46* Cuaderno para hispanohablantes *pp. 37–46*

Get Help Online my.hrw.com

Differentiating Instruction

Slower-paced Learners

Read Before Listening Give students the script for Activity 1. First, ask them to read the script silently. Second, ask them to use their index fingers to track the text as you read it to them slowly. Then have them listen to the audio.

Multiple Intelligences

Visual Learners Ask students to choose three of the characteristics that describe Ramón and/or Ramona in Activity 4. Have students draw a picture of the fictional Ramón/Ramona illustrating these qualities and write three sentences describing the person. Example: **Ramona es seria. Ramona es organizada. Ramona es baja.**

✓ Ongoing Assessment

Alternative Strategy **Activity 2**
Have students make all sentences plural. For example: **Los señores viejos son unos hombres de Honduras.**

✓ Ongoing Assessment

Peer Assessment **Activity 3**
Have students exchange the complete paragraph and check each other's work.

Answers Projectable Transparencies, 1-52 and 1-53

Activity 1

Carlos es estudiante de español. Él es alto y tiene pelo rubio. Es cómico pero es estudioso. La señora Pérez es buena, organizada y trabajadora. Ella es baja y tiene pelo castaño. Ella es muy artística.

Activity 2

1. La chica pelirroja es una estudiante de Panamá.
2. El hombre grande es un maestro de Argentina.
3. Los chicos pelirrojos son amigos de Uruguay y Panamá
4. La mujer joven es una maestra de Bolivia.
5. La señora alta es una mujer de México.
6. El chico atlético es un estudiante de Uruguay.
7. El chico desorganizado es una persona de Estados Unidos.
8. Los hombres simpáticos son amigos de Uruguay y Argentina.

Activity 3

1. simpáticos; **2.** inteligente; **3.** guapo; **4.** bonita; **5.** estudiosa; **6.** atléticos; **7.** atléticas; **8.** artísticas; **9.** serios; **10.** buenos

Activity 4

1. Ramona es joven.
2. Ramón es cómico.
3. Ramona es desorganizada.
4. Ramón es grande.
5. Ramona es trabajadora.
6. Ramón es alto.

Activity 5

1. People can eat in restaurants, ride riverboats, or stroll along the river.
2. Chile con carne, tortillas with black beans, and chicken.
3. People use cascarones at Easter time; children crack them over their friends' heads.
4. In Calle Ocho people eat Cuban sandwiches and drink mango juice. In El Mercado people eat typical Mexican food and listen to mariachi music.

Objectives

- Read three personal accounts about personal descriptions and favorite activities.
- Compare favorite activities of teens with your favorite activities.
- Write a self-description.

Core Resources

- *Cuaderno,* pp. 47–49
- Audio Program: TXT CD 1 track 45
- Video Program: DVD 1

Presentation Strategies

- Ask students to read the headings on p. 78 and look at the photos on p. 79 and predict what they will read in the text. List their responses on the board.
- Have students listen to audio as they follow it in their text.
- Assign students to read each of the three accounts. Encourage them to say if they also like to do activities described by these young people.

STANDARDS

1.2 Understand language
1.3 Present information
2.1 Practices and perspectives
4.2 Compare cultures
21st Century **Flexibility and Adaptability,** Role-Playing and Skits; **Technology Literacy,** Multiple Intelligences

Communication
Role-Playing and Skits

Ask students to work in pairs to write and perform skits based on conversations between the following people: José Manuel and one of his teammates, Martina and María, and Mónica and Maite.

Comparación cultural

AUDIO

Me gusta...

Lectura y escritura

WebQuest
my.hrw.com

1 Leer Read how José Manuel, Martina, and Mónica describe themselves and state their favorite activities.

2 Escribir Using the three descriptions as models, write a short paragraph about yourself.

STRATEGY **Escribir**
Use a personal chart
Make a chart showing information about yourself. This will help you write your description.

Categoría	Detalles
país de origen	
descripción física	
personalidad	
actividades favoritas	
comidas favoritas	

Step 1 Complete the chart by adding details about where you are from, a physical description, personality, and favorite activities and foods.

Step 2 Write your paragraph, including all the information from your chart. Check your writing by yourself or with help from a friend. Make final corrections.

Compara con tu mundo

Use the paragraph you wrote to compare your personal description to a description by *one* of the three students. What similarities do you find? What differences?

Cuaderno *pp. 47–49* Cuaderno para hispanohablantes *pp. 47–49*

Differentiating Instruction

Inclusion

Clear Structure Lead a discussion about each of the categories described in step 2 Escribir. Use a discussion to help guide students in creating brainstorming webs as part of their prewriting strategy.

Multiple Intelligences

Naturalist Ask students to use an online weather information source to research weather conditions for the day in Bogotá, Mexico City, Miami, and their hometowns. Then ask them which activities mentioned in the Comparación cultural would be appropriate or inappropriate for the day's weather in each city.

CULTURA Interactiva my.hrw.com *See these pages come alive!*

Colombia *José Manuel*

Me llamo José Manuel. Soy de Bogotá. Soy cómico y un poco desorganizado pero también soy estudioso. Después de hacer la tarea me gusta jugar al fútbol con mis amigos en el parque El Tunal. También me gusta mirar el fútbol en la televisión.

Estados Unidos *Martina*

¡Hola! Me llamo Martina y soy de Miami. Soy inteligente, alta y atlética. Los domingos, me gusta montar en bicicleta. También me gusta preparar jugo de mango o de melón con mi amiga, María. Nos gusta beber mucho jugo porque en Miami hace calor.

México *Mónica*

¿Qué tal? Me llamo Mónica y soy de México, D.F. Tengo pelo castaño y soy seria. Mis amigas Maite y Alejandra también tienen pelo castaño y son muy simpáticas. Maite y yo somos artísticas. Nos gusta tocar la guitarra. También nos gusta dibujar.

Estados Unidos

Comparación cultural

Exploring the Theme

Soccer, or **fútbol**, has long been popular in Europe and Latin America, and has gained in popularity in the United States in the past 20 years. The sport originated with the Olmecs, who flourished in Mexico about 1200 BC. It was a ritual ball game played by all the peoples of Mexico and Central America. The ruins of almost every ancient city include a walled court for this sacred game. The ball used was small but extremely heavy because it was made of solid rubber. The Aztecs thought its movements during the ball game symbolized the sun's east-west journey across the sky. The players were not allowed to hit the ball with their hands and feet. They could use only their knees, hips and elbows.

✓ Ongoing Assessment

Quick Check Ask students quick comprehension questions about each of the three descriptions and write their responses on the board. For example: **¿Cómo se llama la chica de Estados Unidos? ¿Qué deporte le gusta jugar a José Manuel? ¿Quién tiene pelo rubio?**

✓ Ongoing Assessment

Rubric **Lectura y escritura**

Writing Criteria	Very Good	Proficient	Not There Yet
Content	Paragraph contains a lot of information.	Paragraph contains some information.	Paragraph lacks information.
Communication	Paragraph is organized and easy to follow.	Paragraph is fairly well organized and easy to follow.	Paragraph is disorganized and hard to follow.
Accuracy	Paragraph has few mistakes in vocabulary and grammar.	Paragraph has some mistakes in vocabulary and grammar.	Paragraph has many mistakes in vocabulary and grammar.

To customize your own rubrics, use the ***Generate Success*** *Rubric Generator and Graphic Organizers.*

Differentiating Instruction

Pre-AP

Expand and Elaborate Have students respond to three young people from Bogotá, Miami, and Mexico City by writing an e-mail to each one. In their e-mails they should take into account the information given by José Manuel, Martina, and Mónica and then write about their own likes and dislikes.

Slower-paced Learners

Yes/No Questions Check students' comprehension of the readings by asking yes/no questions. For example: **José Manuel es muy organizado, ¿verdad? (No.) ¿Mónica tiene pelo castaño? (Sí.) ¿A Martina le gusta montar en bicicleta? (Sí.)**

Objective
- Cumulative review.

Core Resource
- Audio Program: TXT CD 1 track 46

Review Options
- **Activity 1:** Listening
- **Activity 2:** Speaking
- **Activity 3:** Speaking
- **Activity 4:** Writing
- **Activity 5:** Speaking
- **Activity 6:** Speaking
- **Activity 7:** Reading

STANDARDS
1.2 Understand language, Acts. 1, 3, 5
1.3 Present information, Acts. 2–7
2.1 Practices and perspectives, Act. 1
4.2 Compare cultures, Act. 1
21st Century **Collaboration,** Act. 5; **Creativity and Innovation,** Act. 6; **Critical Thinking and Problem Solving,** Multiple Intelligences: Naturalist; **Flexibility and Adaptability,** Act. 3

Long-term Retention
Study Tips
Ask students to make flashcards with Spanish words on one side and English translations on the other. An alternate design for flashcards would be pictures drawn by students or clipped from magazines and pasted on the cards.

UNIDAD 1

Repaso inclusivo

Options for Review

¡AvanzaRap! DVD Sing and Learn

Digital performance space

1 Listen, understand, and compare

Escuchar

Listen to two teen radio reporters talk about typical after-school activities in Miami and San Antonio. Then answer the questions.

1. ¿Cómo son los estudiantes de Miami?
2. ¿Qué les gusta hacer a los estudiantes de Miami?
3. ¿Cómo son los estudiantes de San Antonio?
4. ¿Qué tiempo hace en San Antonio?
5. ¿Qué les gusta hacer a los estudiantes de San Antonio?

Are you and your friends like the students in Miami and/or San Antonio? Do you like to do the same kinds of activities?

Audio Program
TXT CD 1 Track 46
Audio Script, TE p. 53b

2 Oral presentation

Hablar

Your principal is making a video about your school and you are going to be a featured student. In a segment that lasts at least 30 seconds, introduce yourself, say where you are from, describe yourself, and talk about what you like to do after school.

3 Role-play conversation

Hablar

Role-play a conversation with a new student at your school. The new student, played by your partner, will introduce himself or herself and ask you what you are like and what you and your friends like to do. Answer the new student's questions and ask questions of your own to get to know him or her. Your conversation should be at least two minutes long.

4 Create a yearbook entry

Escribir

Bring in a photo of yourself and create a caption that could be used in a yearbook. Give your name, where you are from, what you are like, who you like to spend time with, and what activities you like to do.

Differentiating Instruction

Inclusion

Metacognitive Support Ask students to read all seven options for review. Hold a short discussion on the various options, and then ask students to think about which of the options would best help them, as individuals, review the material. Ask students to share their thoughts with the class. Finally, have the class vote on three or four different ways they will review the lesson.

Multiple Intelligences

Linguistic/Verbal After listening to the audio interview in "Listen, understand, and compare," ask students to write a short newspaper story based on the interviews. In addition to the audio interviews, students should interview a partner and include that information in their article.

Answers

Activity 1
1. Son muy estudiosos y atléticos.
2. Les gusta pasar un rato con los amigos, estudiar, practicar deportes, montar en bicicleta y jugar al fútbol.
3. Son atléticos y trabajadores.
4. Hace mucho calor.
5. Les gusta correr, jugar al fútbol, leer y descansar.

Activities 2–7 Answers will vary.

5 Do an interview

Hablar

Work in a group of four. Create a talk show program to get to know your classmates. One of the members of your group will be the host and the others will be the guests. The host should ask the guests questions about what they are like, where they are from, and what they like to do. The guests should greet the host, introduce themselves, answer questions, and ask the host at least one question each. Each person on the program should talk for at least two minutes.

6 Create a collage

Hablar

Work with a partner to create individual collages. Use magazine clippings, photos, or your own drawings. Use the collage to introduce yourself to your partner, say where you are from, and show some of the things you like to do. When you finish, exchange your collages and use them to introduce each other to the class.

7 Write a profile

Leer
Escribir

You are collecting information for this school's Web site. Read the questionnaire and write a profile of this student. Include his name, where he is from, and what he likes and doesn't like to do.

Escuela Secundaria Cuauhtémoc
Cuestionario estudiantil

Nombre: *Esteban Leñeros*

País de origen: *México*

ACTIVIDADES

¿Qué te gusta hacer? *practicar deportes, estudiar, comer enchiladas, escuchar música*

¿Qué no te gusta hacer? *andar en patineta, comer helado, dibujar*

Communication

Group Work

Ask students to think of an activity they like to do using the vocabulary from this unit. Select one student to go first, asking him or her to say the activity. That student should then ask another student who will describe his or her favorite activity. Continue until each student in the class has had a turn. Repeat the activity, asking students to share an activity they don't like.

✓ Ongoing Assessment

Integrated Performance Assessment
Rubric Oral Activities 2, 3, 5, 6
Written Activities 4, 7

Very Good	Proficient	Not There Yet
The student thoroughly develops all requirements of the task.	The student develops most requirements of the task.	The student does not develop the requirements of the task.
The student demonstrates excellent control of verb forms.	The student demonstrates good to fair control of verb forms.	The student demonstrates poor control of verb forms.
Good variety of appropriate vocabulary.	Adequate variety of appropriate vocabulary.	The vocabulary is not appropriate.
The pronunciation is excellent to very good.	The pronunciation is good to fair.	The pronunciation is poor.

To customize your own rubrics, use the ***Generate Success*** *Rubric Generator and Graphic Organizers.*

Differentiating Instruction

Multiple Intelligences

Naturalist Ask students to identify latitude and longitude for San Antonio, Miami, Bogotá, México, D.F., and their hometowns. Ask students to discuss how latitude could affect after-school activities. Ask them to use longitude to determine the time zone for each city. When their school day is over, what time is it in each of the other cities?

Slower-paced Learners

Memory Aids To adapt Activity 3, ask students to form pairs and discuss the questions they plan to ask each other, and the answers they want to give. Each pair should work together to create cue cards by writing the answers in enlarged print on 8″ x 10″ sheets of paper. They can read from the cue cards during the conversation.

Proyectos adicionales

Planning Ahead

Projects **Create a mural.** Have students work collaboratively to create a "public art" mural that represents their individuality and interests. Using large pieces of butcher paper, have each student create a nearly life-sized drawing of him- or herself doing one of his or her favorite activities. Students can use magic markers, or paint if time allows. Also, ask each student to create one or two items for the mural's background. These might include school items, a clock, or a window. Once the drawings are complete and the paint is dry, have students cut out their figures. Then have them work together to arrange and display their characters and objects on a classroom or hallway wall.

After the mural is complete, distribute two index cards to each student. On one card, instruct students to write as much as they can about their own figure in the mural. On another card, have them choose a friend's figure and write as much as they can about that. Post these cards next to or underneath their corresponding figures in the mural.

PACING SUGGESTION: Upon completion of **Lección 2** to review vocabulary related to school, activities, emotions, and personal traits.

21st Century **Collaboration; Creativity and Innovation**

(Virtual) Bulletin Board

Create a bulletin board with the following title: **¿A qué hora?** Using a large cardboard circle and two cardboard "hands," create a large clock on the bulletin board. Attach the hands with a brass brad or paper fastener so that they can be moved into different positions. You can use the clock to help students talk about time, as well as to play different games. Here's one. Write a number of different school activities on separate index cards. Place these in an envelope and attach it to the bulletin board. Have volunteers come choose a card and then set the clock at the right time for that activity. **La clase de ciencias es a la una y veinte.** As a tech alternative, you may wish to have students create their projects on a class wiki page.

PACING SUGGESTION: Before **Lección 1** to preview telling time, and throughout the lesson for reinforcement as time allows.

21st Century **Critical Thinking and Problem Solving**

Web Research

Go online to connect with a pen pal in Mexico. There are many Web sites that can help students connect with a pen pal. A simple search of the words "Mexico" and "pen pal" will lead you to many potential sites. Some examples include **penpalsnow.com** and **mylanguageexchange.com.**

Begin by having students work together to brainstorm ideas for their first message. Advise them to include some kind of greeting, an introduction, a description of their family, a description of their school, and an explanation of their daily schedule of activities. Once students have finished brainstorming ideas, have them draft their own e-mail messages on a separate piece of paper. Once students have identified potential recipients, have each student send his or her message. Alternately, you could draft one message for the whole class, and send it as a group.

Hopefully, students will receive a response. Give students the opportunity to share the messages they receive, and to discuss what they will write about next.

PACING SUGGESTION: Upon completion of **Lección 1,** and throughout **Lección 2** as messages arrive.

21st Century **Technology Literacy**

Games

¿Tienes?

This game is similar to Go Fish. Begin by having students create the cards for the game. Have students draw on index cards the classroom items presented on p. 110. There should be four index cards for each item.

To play, organize students into groups of three or four. Each group needs one deck of cards. One student deals each player five cards, then places the remaining cards face down. The goal is to get matching pairs. The dealer begins by asking whether another player has a card: **¿Tienes un lápiz?** If the player has the card, he or she responds affirmatively and gives the card to the dealer. The dealer than sets the pair aside and takes another turn. If the player doesn't have the card, the dealer must draw one from the pile and the next player takes a turn. The game ends when one player puts down or gives away the last card. The player with the most pairs wins.

PACING SUGGESTION: After vocabulary is presented in **Lección 2** to reinforce classroom items. Can be replayed using different sets of cards.

Tengo... Estoy...

Before playing, collect a number of classroom items, such as those listed on p. 110. Have a group of five or six students sit in a circle. The first player chooses one of the items, and tells the player to his or her right, **Tengo una pluma.** That player responds with a question: **¿Tienes una pluma?** The first player repeats his or her assertion: **Sí, tengo una pluma.** The second player then takes the item, stating, **No, *yo* tengo la pluma.** The conversation then begins again between this player and the player to his or her right. Allow the item to travel all the way around the circle. Then repeat with a new item. For a variation, the game can also be played using emotion words. Have the first player begin: **Estoy cansado(a).** Encourage students to act out an appropriate facial expression. The next player responds with the question: **¿Estás cansado(a)?** The first player repeats his or her assertion: **Sí, estoy cansado(a).** The second player then imitates the face, stating, **Yo estoy cansado(a) también.**

For an added challenge, don't wait for the item or emotion to travel all the way around the circle before introducing the next one.

PACING SUGGESTION: Upon completion of **Lección 2.**

Recipe

Natilla is an easy-to-make Mexican dessert. It is very similar to a basic **flan,** another traditional custard dessert served across the Spanish-speaking world.

Natilla

Ingredientes

- 4 huevos separados
- 1 taza de leche
- 1/8 cucharadita de sal
- 1/4 taza de harina
- 3/4 taza de azúcar
- 1 cucharadita de nuez moscada

Instrucciones

En una fuente, hacer una pasta con las yemas de los huevos, la harina y 1/2 taza de leche. En una cacerola mediana, añadir el azúcar y la sal a la leche sobrante y escaldar a temperatura mediana. Añadir la mezcla de yemas a la leche escaldada y continuar cociendo a temperatura mediana hasta que cobre una consistencia cremosa. Retirar la cacerola del fuego y enfriar. Cuando esté fría, ponerle la nuez moscada por encima.

Music

Mexican music is diverse and ever-changing. Some traditional styles include **mariachi, ranchera, norteña,** and **banda.** Some contemporary styles combine these traditions with rock and hip-hop. Have a student go to a music store or to an online music store such as iTunes or MP3.com to find examples of traditional and modern Mexican music. Play some of the music they research. Discuss what music they like and why. Samples can be heard on music sites online.

¡AvanzaRap! DVD

- Video animations of all **¡AvanzaRap!** songs (with Karaoke track)
- Teaching Suggestions
- **¡AvanzaRap!** Activity Masters
- **¡AvanzaRap!** Video Scripts and Answers

Also available on the **Teacher One Stop**

UNIT THEME
Let's go to school

UNIT STANDARDS

COMMUNICATION
- Talk about daily schedules
- Ask and tell time
- Say what you have and have to do
- Say what you do and how often
- Describe classes and classroom objects
- Say where things are located
- Say where you are going
- Talk about how you feel

CULTURES
- School uniforms
- Diego Rivera and Frida Kahlo
- The National Museum of Anthropology

CONNECTIONS
- History: Reading historical maps
- Art: Creating maps and symbols
- Social Studies: Technology in education
- Health: Health benefits of cacti

COMPARISONS
- Meeting places in Spanish-speaking countries and in the U.S.
- School uniforms in Mexico, the Dominican Republic, and the U.S.
- Public artwork in Mexico and the U.S.
- The Spanish **ch** and **d** and the English *ch* and *d*
- School years in Mexico and the U.S.
- Ancient artifacts and future artifacts
- Self-portraits of Frida Kahlo
- Favorite classes of Mexican and Dominican students
- A culture's view of the natural world reflected in art
- School schedules in Mexico, the Dominican Republic, and Paraguay
- Huichol yarn painting, Taino rock art

COMMUNITIES
- Arts and crafts influenced by Spanish-speaking cultures in a local store

UNIDAD 2

México

¡Vamos a la escuela!

Lección 1
Tema: ***Somos estudiantes***

Lección 2
Tema: ***En la escuela***

«¡Hola!
Somos Pablo y Claudia. Somos de México.»

Población: 109.955.400
Área: 761.606 millas cuadradas
Capital: México, D.F. (Ciudad de México)
Moneda: el peso mexicano
Idiomas: español, maya y otras lenguas indígenas; el país con más hispanohablantes del mundo
Comida típica: tortillas, tacos, enchiladas
Gente famosa: Carlos Fuentes (escritor), Salma Hayek (actriz), Mario Molina (químico), Thalía (cantante)

Chocolate

82 ochenta y dos

Cultural Geography

Setting the Scene
- What is the currency of Mexico? (peso)
- What are the colors of Mexico's flag? (red, white, green)
- What is the boy's name? (Pablo) What is the girl's name? (Claudia)

Teaching with Maps
- Mexico shares a border with which country to the north? (United States)
- Chichén Itzá is located in which peninsula? (Yucatán)

CULTURA Interactiva
my.hrw.com
See these pages come alive!

Jóvenes en el Jardín Principal de San Miguel de Allende

◀ **Un rato con familia y amigos** In San Miguel de Allende, people of all ages go to the **Jardín Principal,** a tree-lined park in the center of town, to stroll, listen to live music, and spend time with family and friends. *When you want to spend time outside, where do you go?*

Las ruinas de Chichén Itzá The ruins of the ancient Mayan city of Chichén Itzá include structures built for worship, sports, and studying astronomy. The pyramid of **Kukulcán** was used as a temple. *What are some important buildings in your area used for?* ▶

La estatua de Chac-Mool y la pirámide de Kukulcán

◀ **Una universidad con mucha historia y arte La Universidad Nacional Autónoma de México (UNAM)** is one of the oldest universities in the Americas, and the largest public university in Mexico, with over 270,000 students. The library's mosaic mural depicts moments in the cultural history of Mexico. *What are some well-known universities in your area?*

La biblioteca de la UNAM con el mural mosaico

Bridging Cultures

Heritage Language Learners

Support What They Know Invite students, with a personal or family connection to Mexico, to add to the information presented on pp. 82 and 83. What are their memories and/or impressions of Mexico? How would they compare schools and students in Mexico with those in the United States?

English Learners

Build Background Direct students to read p. 83 in order to identify the main idea of each paragraph. Remind them that the title and topic sentence can be good clues toward finding the main idea. After students have defined the main idea, ask them to draw connections between these elements of Mexican life and those in their own home country. Are there any similarities?

CULTURA Interactiva
my.hrw.com

Send your students to my.hrw.com to explore authentic Mexican culture. Tell them to click on Cultura interactiva to see these pages come alive!

Culture

About the Photos

- Music is an ever-present feature of the Jardín Principal. Saturday afternoons and evenings are the liveliest times, when both mariachis and amateur musicians meander around the central square.
- **Kukulcán** is the Mayan name for the Plumed Serpent, a deity frequently shown in Central American art. The Spanish name for the pyramid is **El Castillo de la Serpiente Emplumada,** or The Castle of the Plumed Serpent.
- The Mexico City campus of the university boasts a number of architecturally impressive buildings. One of them bears the university's coat of arms, with the motto **Por mi raza hablará el espíritu** (For my race the spirit will speak).

Expanded Information

- San Miguel de Allende is a charming tourist town that draws many artists, artisans, and musicians every year. In its network of narrow streets are brightly painted red, orange, and yellow buildings that house tiny shops, eateries, and art galleries.
- Chichén Itzá was once a great Mayan city, complete with a plaza, marketplace, athletic fields, and numerous temples. Between A.D. 700 and A.D. 1200, it was the Yucatán's seat of power for government, religion, and the military.
- The university, founded over 500 years ago, has been attended by dozens of Mexico's presidents, statesmen, scientists, writers, and artists.

Video Character Guide

Pablo and Claudia are classmates. They are both good students.

Lesson Overview

Culture at a Glance

Topic & Activity	Essential Question
Town Squares or Plazas pp. 84–85	Does your city or town have a main square?
School Uniforms p. 92	How does the way students dress reflect a culture?
Mexican Murals p. 97	How does society affect public artwork?
Culture Review p. 107	What is Chichén Itzá and what can you find there?

COMPARISON COUNTRIES México · República Dominicana · Paraguay

Practice at a Glance

	Objective	Activity & Skill
Vocabulary	Numbers from 11 to 100	2: Speaking
Vocabulary	School subjects, classroom activities	2: Speaking; 3: Listening, Reading; 4: Writing; 5: Writing; 6: Listening, Writing; 10: Speaking, Writing; 11: Speaking, Writing; 13: Speaking; 18: Speaking; 19: Reading, Listening, Writing
Vocabulary	Adverbs of frequency	7: Speaking; 9: Writing; 11: Speaking, Writing; 14: Speaking; 15: Writing, Speaking; 19: Reading, Listening, Writing
Grammar	The verb **tener** and **tener que**	5: Writing; 6: Listening, Writing; 10: Speaking, Writing; 12: Reading, Writing; 13: Speaking; 17: Listening, Reading; 18: Speaking
Grammar	Present tense of **-ar** verbs	9: Writing; 10: Speaking, Writing; 11: Speaking, Writing; 12: Reading, Writing; 14: Speaking; 16: Listening, Reading; 18: Speaking
Communication	Talk about daily schedules	1: Writing, Speaking; 3: Listening, Reading; 4: Writing; 5: Writing; 10: Speaking, Writing; 11: Speaking, Writing; 12: Reading, Writing; 13: Speaking; 14: Speaking; 16: Listening, Reading; 19: Reading, Listening, Writing; 20: Writing
Communication	Ask and tell time	1: Writing, Speaking; 10: Speaking, Writing; 19: Reading, Listening, Writing
Communication	Say what you have and have to do	6: Listening, Writing; 7: Speaking; 8: Listening, Reading; 9: Writing; 10: Speaking, Writing; 11: Speaking, Writing; 12: Reading, Writing; 17: Listening, Reading; 18: Speaking; 19: Reading, Listening, Writing
Communication	Say what you do and how often you do things	7: Speaking; 9: Writing; 10: Speaking, Writing; 11: Speaking, Writing; 12: Reading, Writing; 14: Speaking; 19: Reading, Listening, Writing
Communication	Pronunciation: The sound **ch**	*El sonido* **ch** p. 98: Listening
Recycle	After-school activities	7: Speaking
Recycle	Days of the week	9: Writing

The following presentations are recorded in the Audio Program for ***¡Avancemos!***

- **¡A responder!** *page 87*
- **6: ¿Qué tienen que hacer?** *page 92*
- **19: Integración** *page 101*
- **Repaso de la lección** *page 106*
  1: Listen and understand

For **¡AvanzaRap!** scripts, see the **¡AvanzaRap! DVD.**

¡A responder! TXT CD 2 track 2

1. la clase de matemáticas es a las siete.
2. la clase de español es a la una y media.
3. la clase de arte es a las doce menos diez.
4. la clase de inglés es a las diez y cuarto.
5. la clase de historia es a las doce y media.
6. la clase de ciencias es a las ocho y diez.

6 | ¿Qué tienen que hacer?

TXT CD 2 track 4

Hola, me llamo Pablo. Mis amigos y yo tenemos mucho que hacer.
Claudia tiene un examen mañana. Son las ocho y tiene que estudiar.
Me gusta escribir correos electrónicos. Son las diez menos cuarto y tengo que usar la computadora.
Pepe tiene que hacer la tarea porque son las cuatro y diez.
Es la una y media. Laura y Diana tienen que tocar la guitarra.
Hoy es lunes. Son las seis y cuarto y Carlos tiene que trabajar.
Son las once menos veinte. Manuel y yo tenemos que leer un libro para la clase de historia.

19 | Integración TXT CD 2 tracks 8, 9

Atención, estudiantes. Mañana los maestros tienen una reunión y el horario de clases es diferente. Todos los estudiantes tienen que llegar 45 minutos después de la hora normal a las clases de la mañana y 15 minutos después de la hora normal a las clases de la tarde. Repito. Mañana el horario de clases es diferente. Todos los estudiantes tienen que llegar 45 minutos después de la hora normal a las clases de la mañana y 15 minutos después de la hora normal a las clases de la tarde. Gracias.

Repaso de la lección TXT CD 2 track 11

1 Listen and understand

Martín: Hola, Lupe.
Lupe: ¡Martín! ¿Cómo estás?
Martín: Regular. ¿Qué hora es?
Lupe: Son las diez y cuarto.
Martín: Tengo la clase de historia a las diez y media. Me gusta llegar temprano porque necesito sacar una buena nota.
Lupe: ¿Ustedes tienen que tomar muchos apuntes?
Martín: Sí. Tomamos apuntes todos los días. También tomamos muchos apuntes en la clase de inglés, y contestamos preguntas. ¡Hay muchas preguntas!
Lupe: Yo tengo la clase de ciencias a las diez y media. La maestra es joven y es muy buena. De vez en cuando usamos la computadora. También tenemos que contestar muchas preguntas.
Martín: ¡Uy! Es la hora de clase, ¿no?
Lupe: Sí. Casi son las diez y media. Hasta luego.
Martín: Adiós.

Resource List

Everything you need to ...

Plan

TEACHER ONE STOP

✓Lesson Plans
✓Teacher Resources
✓Audio and Video

Present

INTERACTIVE WHITEBOARD LESSONS

TEACHER ONE STOP WITH PROJECTABLE TRANSPARENCIES

POWER PRESENTATIONS

ANIMATEDGRAMMAR

Assess

ONLINE ASSESSMENT

✓ Assessments for on-level, modified, pre-AP, and heritage learners
✓ Create customized tests with **Examview Assessment Suite**
✓ **performance space**
✓ *Generate Success* Rubric Generator

Print

Plan	Present	Practice	Assess
URB 2 • Video Scripts pp. 67–68 • Family Letter p. 90 • Absent Student Copymasters pp. 92–99 **Best Practices Toolkit**	**URB 2** • Video Activities pp. 49–56	• *Cuaderno* pp. 50–72 • *Cuaderno para hispanohablantes* pp. 50–72 • *Lecturas para todos* pp. 12–16 • *Lecturas para hispanohablantes* • *¡AvanzaCómics! SuperBruno y Nati*, Episodio 1 **URB 2** • Practice Games pp. 29–36 • Audio Scripts pp. 71–74 • Map/Culture Activities pp. 81–83 • Fine Art Activities pp. 85–86	**Differentiated Assessment Program** **URB 2** • Did you get it? Reteaching and Practice Copymasters pp. 1–10

Projectable Transparencies (Teacher One Stop, my.hrw.com)

Culture	Presentation and Practice	Classroom Management
• Atlas Maps 1–6 • Map: Mexico: 1 • Fine Art Transparencies 2, 5	• Vocabulary Transparencies 6, 7 • Grammar Presentation Transparencies 10, 11	• Warm up Transparencies 16–19 • Student Book Answer Transparencies 24–27, 32–39

Audio and Video

Audio	Video	¡AvanzaRap! DVD
• Student Book Audio CD 2 Tracks 1–11 • Workbook Audio CD 2 Tracks 21–30 • Heritage Learners Audio CD 1 Tracks 9–12, CD 3 Tracks 9–10 • Assessment Audio CD 1 Tracks 9, 10 • *Lecturas para todos* Audio CD 1 Track 3, CD 2 Tracks 1–6 • Sing-along Songs Audio CD	• Vocabulary Video DVD 1 • *Telehistoria* DVD 1 *Escena 1* *Escena 2* *Escena 3* *Completa*	• Video animations of all **¡AvanzaRap!** songs (with Karaoke track) • Interactive DVD Activities • Teaching Suggestions • **¡AvanzaRap!** Activity Masters • **¡AvanzaRap!** video scripts and answers

Online and Media Resources

Student	Teacher
Available online at my.hrw.com • Online Student Edition • News + Networking • performance space • @HOMETUTOR • CULTURA Interactiva • WebQuests • Interactive Flashcards • Review Games • Self-Check Quiz **Student One Stop** **Holt McDougal Spanish Apps**	**Teacher One Stop (also available at my.hrw.com)** • Interactive Teacher's Edition • All print, audio, and video resources • Projectable Transparencies • Lesson Plans • TPRS • Examview Assessment Suite **Available online at my.hrw.com** *Generate Success* Rubric Generator and Graphic Organizers **Power Presentations**

Differentiated Assessment

On-level	Modified	Pre-AP	Heritage Learners
• Vocabulary Recognition Quiz p. 57 • Vocabulary Production Quiz p. 58 • Grammar Quizzes pp. 59–60 • Culture Quiz p. 61 • On-level Lesson Test pp. 62–68	• Modified Lesson Test pp. 47–53	• Pre-AP Lesson Test pp. 47–53	• Heritage Learners Lesson Test pp. 53–59

Core Pacing Guide

50 Minute (9 Day)

	Objectives/focus	Teach	Practice	Assess/HW Options
DAY 1	**Culture:** Learn about Mexican culture **Vocabulary:** daily schedules • Warm Up OHT 16 **5 min**	**Presentación de vocabulario** pp. 86–87 • Read A–D • View video DVD 1 • Play audio TXT CD 2 track 1 • *¡A responder!* TXT CD 2 track 2 **20 min**	**Práctica de vocabulario** p. 88 • Activities 1, 2 • *Nota gramatical* **20 min**	**Assess:** *Para y piensa* p. 88 **5 min** **Homework:** *Cuaderno* pp. 50–52 @HomeTutor
DAY 2	**Communication:** talking about daily schedules • Warm Up OHT 16 • Check Homework **5 min**	**Vocabulario en contexto** pp. 89–90 • *Telehistoria escena 1* DVD 1 • *Nota gramatical* **20 min**	**Vocabulario en contexto** pp. 89–90 • Act. 3 TXT CD 2 track 3 • Act. 4 **20 min**	**Assess:** *Para y piensa* p. 90 **5 min** **Homework:** *Cuaderno* pp. 50–52 @HomeTutor
DAY 3	**Grammar:** the verb **tener** • Warm Up OHT 17 • Check Homework **5 min**	**Presentación de gramática** p. 91 • The verb **tener** **Práctica de gramática** p. 92 **20 min**	**Práctica de gramática** pp. 92–93 • Activities 5–7 • *Nota gramatical* **20 min**	**Assess:** *Para y piensa* p. 93 **5 min** **Homework:** *Cuaderno* pp. 53–55 @HomeTutor
DAY 4	**Communication:** using **tener** to talk about daily schedules • Warm Up OHT 17 • Check Homework **5 min**	**Gramática en contexto** pp. 94–95 • *Telehistoria escena 2* DVD 1 **20 min**	**Gramática en contexto** pp. 94–95 • Activity 8 TXT CD 2 track 5 • Activities 9–10 **20 min**	**Assess:** *Para y piensa* p. 95 **5 min** **Homework:** *Cuaderno* pp. 53–55 @HomeTutor
DAY 5	**Grammar:** present tense form of **-ar** verbs • Warm Up OHT 18 • Check Homework **5 min**	**Presentación de gramática** p. 96 • Present tense of **-ar** verbs • **Práctica de gramática** pp. 97–98 • *Pronunciación* TXT CD 2 track 6 **Culture:** *Mexico's Murals* **15 min**	**Práctica de gramática** pp. 97–98 • Activities 11–15 • *Pronunciación* TXT CD 2 track 6 **25 min**	**Assess:** *Para y piensa* p. 98 **5 min** **Homework:** *Cuaderno* pp. 56–58 @HomeTutor
DAY 6	**Communication:** Culmination: use **tener** and **-ar** verbs to talk about daily activities • Warm Up OHT 18 • Check Homework **5 min**	**Todo junto** pp. 99–101 • *Escenas 1, 2: Resumen* • *Telehistoria completa* DVD 1 **15 min**	**Todo junto** pp. 99–101 • Activities 16, 17 TXT CD 2 tracks 3, 5, 7 • Activity 19 TXT CD 2 tracks 8, 9 • Activities 18, 20 **25 min**	**Assess:** *Para y piensa* p. 101 **5 min** **Homework:** *Cuaderno* pp. 59, 60 @HomeTutor
DAY 7	**Reading:** An International School in Mexico • Strategy: use word families and context • Warm up OHT 18 • Check Homework **5 min**	**Lectura** pp. 102–103 • *Una escuela internacional en México* • *TXT CD 2 track 10* **Conexiones** p. 104 • *El pueblo de Zempoala* **15 min**	**Lectura** pp. 102–103 • *Una escuela internacional en México* **Conexiones** p. 104 • *Proyectos* 1, 2, 3 **25 min**	**Assess:** *Para y piensa* p. 103 **5 min** **Homework:** *Cuaderno* pp. 64–66 @HomeTutor
DAY 8	**Review:** Lesson Review • Warm Up OHT 19 **5 min**	**Repaso de la lección** pp. 106–107 **15 min**	**Repaso de la lección** pp. 106–107 • Act. 1 TXT CD 2 track 11 • Acts. 2, 3, 4, 5 **25 min**	**Assess:** *Repaso de la lección* **5 min** **Homework:** *En resumen* p. 105, *Cuaderno* pp. 61–63, 67–72 (optional) Review Games Online @HomeTutor
DAY 9				**Assess:** Lesson 1 Test **50 min**

Core Pacing Guide 90 Minute (5 Day)

	Objectives/focus	Teach	Practice	Assess/HW Options
DAY 1	**Culture:** learn about Mexican culture **Vocabulary:** daily schedule • Warm Up OHT 16 **5 min**	Unit Opener pp. 82–83 Lesson Opener pp. 84–85 **Presentación de vocabulario** pp. 86–87 • Read A-D • View video DVD 1 • Play audio TXT CD 2 track 1 • *¡A responder!* TXT CD 2 track 2 **20 min**	Lesson Opener pp. 84–85 **Práctica de vocabulario** p. 88 • Acts. 1, 2 • *Nota gramatical* **20 min**	**Assess:** *Para y piensa* p. 88 **5 min** @HomeTutor
	Communication: talking about daily schedules **5 min**	**Vocabulario en contexto** pp. 89–90 • *Telehistoria escena 1* DVD 1 • *Nota gramatical* **15 min**	**Vocabulario en contexto** pp. 89–90 • Activity 3 TXT CD 2 track 3 • Activity 4 **15 min**	**Assess:** *Para y piensa* p. 90 **5 min** **Homework:** *Cuaderno* pp. 50–52 @HomeTutor
DAY 2	**Grammar:** the verb **tener** • Warm Up OHT 17 • Check Homework **5 min**	**Presentación de gramática** p. 91 • The verb tener **Práctica de gramática** pp. 92–93 • *Nota gramatical:* expressions of frequency **20 min**	**Práctica de gramática** pp. 92–93 • Acts. 5, 6, 7 **15 min**	**Assess:** *Para y piensa* p. 93 **5 min**
	Communication: using **tener** and **tener que** to talk about what you have to do **5 min**	**Gramática en contexto** pp. 94–95 • *Telehistoria escena 2* DVD 1 **20 min**	**Gramática en contexto** pp. 94–95 • Act. 8 TXT CD 2 track 5 • Activities 9, 10 **15 min**	**Assess:** *Para y piensa* p. 95 **5 min** **Homework:** *Cuaderno* pp. 53–55 @HomeTutor
DAY 3	**Grammar:** present tense form of **-ar** verbs • Warm Up OHT 18 • Check Homework **5 min**	**Presentación de gramática** p. 96 • Present tense of **-ar** verbs **Práctica de gramática** pp. 97–98 • *Pronunciación* TXT CD 2 track 6 **Culture:** *Los murales en México* **15 min**	**Práctica de gramática** pp. 97–98 • Acts. 11, 12, 13, 14, 15 • *Pronunciación* TXT CD 2 track 6 **20 min**	**Assess:** *Para y piensa* p. 98 **5 min**
	Communication: Culmination: use **tener** and **–ar** verbs to talk about daily activities **5 min**	**Todo junto** pp. 99–101 • *Escenas 1 & 2: Resumen* • *Telehistoria completa* DVD 1 **15 min**	**Todo junto** pp. 99–101 • Activities 16, 17, 18 • Activity 19 TXT CD 2 tracks 8, 9 • Activity 20 **20 min**	**Assess:** *Para y piensa* p. 101 **5 min** **Homework:** *Cuaderno* pp. 56–58 @HomeTutor
DAY 4	**Reading:** An International School in Mexico • Warm Up OHT 19 • Check Homework **5 min**	**Lectura** pp. 102–103 • *Una escuela internacional en México* • TXT CD 2 track 10 **15 min**	**Lectura** pp. 102–103 • *Una escuela internacional en México* **15 min**	**Assess:** *Para y piensa* p. 103 **5 min**
	Review: lesson review **5 min**	**Repaso de la lección** pp. 106–107 **15 min**	**Repaso de la lección** pp. 106–107 • Activity 1 TXT CD 2 track 11 • Activities 2, 3, 4, 5 **25 min**	**Assess:** *Repaso de la lección* pp. 106–107 **5 min** **Homework:** *En resumen* p. 105; *Cuaderno* pp. 61–69 (optional) Review Games Online @HomeTutor
DAY 5	**Assessment**			**Assessment:** Lesson 1 Test **45 min**
	Connections: History **5 min**	**Conexiones** p. 104 • *La historia* **10 min**	**Conexiones** p. 104 • *Proyecto 1, 2, 3* **30 min**	

¡AVANZA! Objectives

- Introduce lesson theme: **Somos estudiantes.**
- **Culture:** Different schools and schedules.

Presentation Strategies

- Introduce the characters' names: Claudia and Pablo.
- Have students make a list of their daily schedule.
- Have students talk about places to visit in their city.

STANDARDS

2.1 Practices and perspectives
4.2 Compare cultures
21st Century **Flexibility and Adaptability,** Multiple Intelligences; **Information Literacy,** Heritage Language Learners; **Social and Cross-Cultural Skills,** Exploring the Theme

Warm Up Projectable Transparencies, 2-16

Vocabulary Have students write *Carlos* if the sentence describes a boy. Have them write *Carla* if the sentence describes a girl.

1. Es inteligente y estudioso.
2. Es cómico y un poco artístico.
3. Es alta y seria.
4. Es bonita y tiene el pelo castaño.
5. Es joven y atlética.

Answers: 1. Carlos 2. Carlos 3. Carla 4. Carla 5. Carla

Comparación cultural

Exploring the Theme

Ask the following:

1. Does your town have a central or town square?
2. How is it different from the one in this photo? How is it similar?
3. What historical buildings do you know of in your town?

¿Qué ves? Possible answers include:

- Hace sol.
- Es lunes.
- El estudiante es guapo, simpático, alto y joven. La estudiante es bonita, baja y simpática.

UNIDAD 2

México

Lección 1

Tema:

Somos estudiantes

¡AVANZA! In this lesson you will learn to

- talk about daily schedules
- ask and tell time
- say what you have and have to do
- say what you do and how often you do things

using

- the verb **tener** and **tener que**
- expressions of frequency
- present tense of **-ar** verbs

¿Recuerdas?

- after-school activities
- days of the week

Comparación cultural

In this lesson you will learn about

- what students wear to school
- Mexican muralists
- courses in a school in Mexico

Compara con tu mundo

These Mexican students are walking to school through a **zócalo,** or a town square. These are very common in Mexico and other Spanish-speaking countries, where they are also called **plazas.** *Does your city or town have a main square? If not, is there a central meeting place?*

¿Qué ves?

Mira la foto
¿Hace sol?
¿Es domingo o lunes?
¿Cómo es el estudiante? ¿Y la estudiante?

84 ochenta y cuatro

Differentiating Instruction

English Learners

Build Background Ask students to share experiences they have had attending schools in other countries. What are the similarities and differences? For example, do they have to wear school uniforms? What is their school year calendar?

Slower-paced Learners

Personalize It Explain to students that a **zócalo** is similar to a town square. Ask students to name locations in their own town or city that might be referred to as a **zócalo.** What features do these areas have? Why do people congregate there?

DIGITAL SPANISH my.hrw.com
ONLINE STUDENT EDITION with...

performance space
News + Networking
@HOMETUTOR
CULTURA Interactiva

- Audio and Video Resources
- Interactive Flashcards
- Review Activities
- WebQuest
- Conjuguemos.com

PRACTICE SPANISH WITH HOLT MCDOUGAL APPS!

La fuente de San Miguel en el Zócalo
Puebla, México

DIGITAL SPANISH

TEACHER TOOLS

- Interactive Whiteboard Lessons
- Generate Success!

ALSO AVAILABLE...

- Online Workbook
- Spanish InterActive Reader

SPANISH ON THE GO!

- Performance Space
- Holt McDougal Spanish Apps
- ¡Avancemos! eTextbook

Using the Photo

Location Information

Puebla, Mexico Puebla, established in 1531, is the most European of Mexico's colonial cities. The town square, **El Zócalo**, is in the heart of the historic district that includes architecture dating to the 17th century.

History El **Cinco de Mayo** is a celebration of the Mexican victory over French invaders at Puebla on May 5, 1862. It is not to be confused with Mexico's Independence Day from Spain celebrated September 16. In the early hours of this day in 1810, Father Hidalgo, followed by other Mexican patriots, rang the bell of his church calling all Mexicans to fight for their independence from Spain. The war lasted 10 years. Today, just like the 4th of July in the United States, Mexicans celebrate September 16th with a big **fiesta** with fireworks and the Mexican flag is displayed in every house and building.

Differentiating Instruction

Heritage Language Learners

Support What They Know Divide a piece of chart paper into two columns. First, invite students to share what they know about the country of Mexico. Record their responses in the left-hand column. Then ask students to share questions that they have about Mexico. Record these questions in the right-hand column. Invite students to choose one question to research and report back on.

Multiple Intelligences

Kinesthetic Assign two students to play the roles of the students in the photo. Have them create a dialogue about the weather, what they like to do, and what their friends are like.

Long-term Retention

Connect to Previous Learning

Remind students that they have learned words and phrases to describe primarily after-school and extracurricular activities. Explain that in this lesson they will be able to describe their time spent at school. Ask them to share Spanish words and phrases already learned about what would take place during a typical school day. Write them on the board.

¡AVANZA! **Objectives**
- Present vocabulary: time, school and class schedules, numbers, school subjects, classroom activities.
- Check for recognition..

Core Resources
- Video Program: DVD 1
- Audio Program: TXT CD 2 tracks 1, 2

Presentation Strategies
- Say the vocabulary words on pp. 86-87 and have students repeat after you.
- Play the audio as students read A-D.
- Show the video.

STANDARDS
1.2 Understand language
21st CENTURY **Communication,** Pre-AP; **Creativity and Innovation,** Multiple Intelligences: Intrapersonal

Comparisons
English Language Connection

Cognates Remind students that there are many Spanish words that look similar to their English meanings and that these are called "cognates." Discuss some of the cognates seen on pp. 86-87. Point out that **nota** as used on p. 86 is a false cognate. It does not mean *note*; in this case, it means *grade.*

Long-term Retention
Connect to Previous Learning

Mention that neither school subjects nor languages are capitalized in Spanish. Ask them what other words they have learned that are not capitalized in Spanish although they are in English. Answers include the days of the week, the months of the year, and the subject pronoun **yo.**

Presentación de VOCABULARIO

¡AVANZA! **Goal:** Learn about Pablo's school and class schedule. Then practice what you have learned to talk about daily schedules. ***Actividades 1–2***

VIDEO DVD
AUDIO

A ¡Hola! Me llamo Pablo. Mi amiga es Claudia. Somos estudiantes **en** Puebla, México. Me gusta **llegar** a clase **temprano.** Claudia, **¿qué hora es?**

el horario

B ¿A qué hora son mis clases? Tengo **muchas** clases.

las matemáticas

La clase de **matemáticas** es **a las siete de la mañana.**

las ciencias

La clase de **ciencias** es **a las ocho y diez** de la mañana.

el inglés

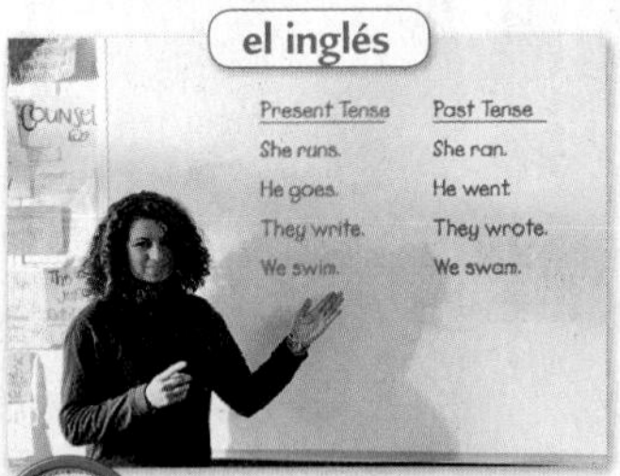

La clase de **inglés** es **a las diez y cuarto** de la mañana.

el arte

La clase de **arte** es **a las doce menos diez** de la mañana.

la historia

La clase de **historia** es **a las doce y media de la tarde.**

el español

La clase de **español** es **a la una y media** de la tarde.

Differentiating Instruction

Inclusion

Cumulative Instruction Before introducing the vocabulary on pp. 86-87, review with students the numbers 1 through 10. Write a number on the board, and have students call out its name in Spanish. Then invite volunteers to the board to write down a number whose name you say aloud. Preview the list of numbers 11 to 100 on p. 87 by reading each aloud, and having students repeat.

Multiple Intelligences

Intrapersonal Invite students to create a sample page from a daily planner that represents their own daily schedule. The page should include the time and name of each class, and a symbol or picture representing each class. Give students the opportunity to practice reading their schedules aloud. Have them model their sentences after the examples on p. 86.
La clase de arte es a las ocho de la mañana.

C Son **las** ocho y diez y tengo la clase de ciencias. A Claudia **siempre** le gusta **contestar** las preguntas del maestro. Ella es muy inteligente. Yo **tengo que** estudiar **mucho** y **tomar apuntes** en clase.

Más vocabulario

de vez en cuando *once in a while*
muchas veces *often, many times*
nunca *never*
todos los días *every day*
casi *almost*
difícil *difficult*
fácil *easy*
hay... *there is, there are...*
la hora *hour; time*
el minuto *minute*
¿Cuántos(as)...? *How many...?*
Expansión de vocabulario p. R3

D Tengo que **sacar una buena nota** en la clase de inglés. A Claudia y a mí nos gusta estudiar a las ocho **de la noche.** Es un poco **tarde** pero **necesito** estudiar. ¡No me gusta **sacar una mala nota**!

Numbers from 11 to 100

11	once	**25**	veinticinco
12	doce	**26**	veintiséis
13	trece	**27**	veintisiete
14	catorce	**28**	veintiocho
15	quince	**29**	veintinueve
16	dieciséis	**30**	treinta
17	diecisiete	**31**	treinta y uno
18	dieciocho	**40**	cuarenta
19	diecinueve	**50**	cincuenta
20	veinte	**60**	sesenta
21	veintiuno	**70**	setenta
22	veintidós	**80**	ochenta
23	veintitrés	**90**	noventa
24	veinticuatro	**100**	cien

@HOMETUTOR my.hrw.com Interactive Flashcards

¡A responder! Escuchar

Saca dos hojas de papel. En una escribe **la mañana,** y en la otra escribe **la tarde.** Escucha el horario de Pablo y levanta la hoja que indica cuándo tiene cada clase. *(On separate pieces of paper, write the words **la mañana** and **la tarde.** Listen to Pablo describe his schedule. Hold up the paper that indicates when he has each class.)*

TEACHER to TEACHER

Rosa Jacks
Mountain Lakes, New Jersey

Tips for Presenting Vocabulary

Whenever I teach time, I bring a large plastic clock or one made from a paper plate with movable hands. I say a time on the hour, half hour, and quarter hour. Then I call on one student to come up and move the hands to those times. I hold the clock up to the class, and say the time three times. I repeat the process with several more students.

Go online for more tips!

Communication

Interpretive Mode

Telehistoria Have students keep the following questions in mind:

1. Where are Pablo and Claudia students?
2. What time is **las diez y cuarto de la mañana?**
3. What time is **las siete de la mañana?**
4. What time is **la una y media de la tarde?**
5. Who likes to answer the teacher's questions?

Answers: 1. Puebla, México; 2. 10:15 A.M.; 3. 7:00 (A.M.); 4. 1:30 (P.M.); 5. Claudia

Communication

Pair Work

Ask students to write the order in which they
pañol, la
ticas. Next
he time at
they finish
e.

Retention

hat photos
tand what
nding every
g a new
theme of
ne photos.

3/7

Differentiating Instruction

Pre-AP

Communicate Preferences Ask students to talk about the classes they do and do not like and explain why. **¿Te gusta la clase de ciencias? Sí, me gusta la clase de ciencias porque no es difícil. ¿Te gusta la clase de historia? No, no me gusta la clase de historia porque tengo que tomar muchos apuntes.**

Multiple Intelligences

Visual Learners Give students a p
drawing paper. Then instruct them
one of the vocabulary words from p
87 to draw. For example, they migh **la computadora** or a scene from **la clase de inglés.** Have students share their completed drawings with a group. The rest of the group must name the vocabulary word or phrase represented.

Answers
Projectable Transparencies, 2-24

¡A responder! Audio Script, TE p. 83b

1. la mañana **2.** la tarde **3.** la mañana **4.** la mañana **5.** la tarde **6.** la mañana

Objectives
- Practice vocabulary: time and class schedules.
- Practice numbers, school subjects.

Core Resource
- *Cuaderno,* pp. 50–52

Practice Sequence
- **Activity 1:** Vocabulary recognition: time, school subjects
- **Activity 2:** Vocabulary production: practice numbers, school subjects

STANDARDS
1.1 Engage in conversation, Act. 2; PYP
1.2 Demonstrate understanding of written and spoken language
1.3 Present information, Act. 1
4.1 Compare languages, Nota

✓ Ongoing Assessment

Get Help Online
More Practice
my.hrw.com

PARA Y PIENSA **Peer Assessment** Before writing the correct answers on the board, have students exchange papers and read their partners' sentences making corrections as needed. For additional practice, use Reteaching & Practice Copymasters URB 2, pp. 1, 2.

Nota gramatical
Expanded Information Numbers always replace the articles when they come before the noun. **Veintiuno** adds an accent mark when the *o* is dropped: **veintiún**. However, no accent mark is needed when writing **treinta y un, cuarenta y un**, and so on.

Answers Projectable Transparencies, 2-24
Activity 1
1. A las once menos cuarto Claudia tiene la clase de inglés.
2. A las siete y media Claudia tiene una clase de ciencias.
3. A las doce Claudia tiene una clase de historia.
4. A las nueve menos veinte Claudia tiene una clase de arte.
5. A las nueve y cuarto Claudia tiene una clase de matemáticas.
6. A las dos y media Claudia tiene una clase de música.

Answers continue on p. 89.

Práctica de VOCABULARIO

1 Las clases de Claudia

Escribir Hablar

Identifica las clases de Claudia según la hora. *(Identify Claudia's classes according to the time.)*

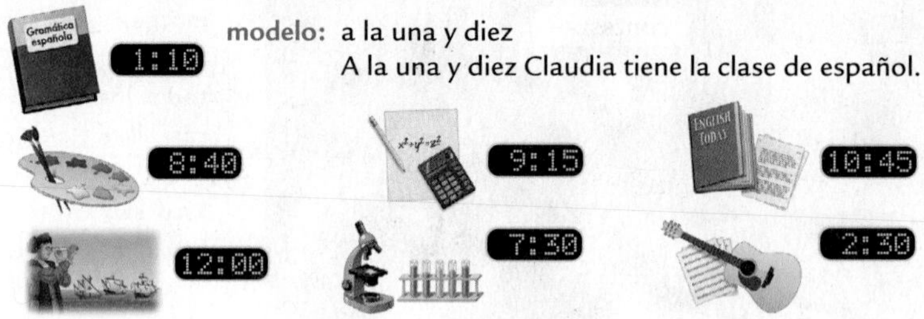

modelo: a la una y diez
A la una y diez Claudia tiene la clase de español.

1. a las once menos cuarto
2. a las siete y media
3. a las doce
4. a las nueve menos veinte
5. a las nueve y cuarto
6. a las dos y media

Expansión:
Teacher Edition Only
For each of the times listed, have students name the activities they like to do during the weekend at that time.

Nota gramatical
For the numbers **21, 31,** and so on, use **veintiún, treinta y un,** and so on before a masculine noun and **veintiuna, treinta y una,** and so on before a feminine noun.

Hay **veintiún** maestros en la escuela. *There are **twenty-one** teachers in the school.*

Hay **treinta y una** personas en mi clase. *There are **thirty-one** people in my class.*

2 ¿Cuántas personas?

Hablar

Habla con otro(a) estudiante sobre el número de personas en estas clases. *(Talk with a partner about the number of people in these classes.)*

modelo: chicos / historia y arte (29)

A ¿Cuántos chicos hay en las clases de historia y arte?

B Hay veintinueve chicos en las clases de historia y arte.

1. chicas / matemáticas (16)
2. estudiantes / inglés y arte (58)
3. chicos / historia y ciencias (27)
4. estudiantes / historia y arte (62)
5. chicas / música y español (33)
6. estudiantes / arte (40)
7. chicas / todas las clases (71)
8. chicos / todas las clases (74)

Expansión
Tell how many people are in your other classes.

Más práctica Cuaderno *pp. 50–52* Cuaderno para hispanohablantes *pp. 50–53*

Get Help Online
my.hrw.com

PARA Y PIENSA **Did you get it?**
1. Tell someone you like to draw in art class.
2. Say that there are 23 boys in math class.

Differentiating Instruction

Inclusion
Synthetic/Analytic Support Help students break down, and then put together, the names of numbers greater than twenty. Write a two-digit number on the board, such as 43. Then break the number down by writing 40 + 3. Have students repeat the name of each component. Point to the 40 as you say **cuarenta**; point to the + as you say **y**; and point to the 3 as you say **tres**. Repeat with other examples.

Pre-AP
Expand and Elaborate Write the words **hay, hoy,** and **hora** on the board. Read them aloud, and have students repeat. Then circle the *h* at the beginning of each word. Ask students to describe what they notice about this letter. Elicit that the *h* in each word is silent. Ask students to brainstorm other words they know that begin with *h*. Examples might include **hola, historia,** and **horario.**

VOCABULARIO en contexto

¡AVANZA! **Goal:** Listen to how Pablo and Claudia talk about at what time they will study. Then practice these words to ask and tell time. ***Actividades 3–4***

Telehistoria escena 1

@HOMETUTOR my.hrw.com **View, Read and Record**

STRATEGIES

Cuando lees
Focus on time Read for expressions of time like **hoy** or **a las ocho.** How many can you find in this scene? What do they mean?

Cuando escuchas
Listen for questions Listen to find all the questions in this scene. Who asks most of the questions? What does that person ask about?

VIDEO DVD

AUDIO

Claudia: Pablo, hay examen de ciencias mañana, ¿no?
Pablo: Sí... Me gusta la clase de ciencias, pero... sacar una buena nota, un 90 o un 100, ¡es difícil!
Claudia: Necesitas estudiar una o dos horas... ¿Te gusta estudiar con amigos?
Pablo: Sí... pero hoy no. ¡Hay fútbol! ¿Mañana?
Claudia: Sí. ¿En la escuela?
Pablo: Sí. ¿A las ocho de la mañana? ¿O más temprano?
Claudia: A las siete de la mañana. ¿Está bien?
Pablo: ¡Sí!
The bell rings, and they part ways for class.
Pablo: Hmmm... Hay chicas muy inteligentes en la escuela...

Continuará... p. 94

Differentiating Instruction

Multiple Intelligences

Logical/Mathematical Before listening to the Telehistoria, have students preview the text silently. Tell them to look specifically for numbers or number words. Then have two volunteers read the roles of Claudia and Pablo aloud. Instruct students to raise their hands when they hear a number. Discuss what each number refers to: a grade, an amount, or a time of day.

Slower-paced Learners

Sentence Completion Provide students with sentence starters related to the Telehistoria. Instruct students to find the place in the script that gives them the information, and then have them complete each sentence. Here are a few examples:

- **Claudia y Pablo tienen un examen de _____.**
- **Sacar una buena nota es _____.**
- **A Pablo le gusta estudiar con _____.**

¡AVANZA! Objective

- Understand activity vocabulary in context.

Core Resources

- Video Program: DVD 1
- Audio Program: TXT CD 2 track 3

Presentation Strategies

- Have students look at the photo and ask quick comprehension questions such as, **¿Es de mañana o es de noche? ¿Cuántos chicos hay en la foto?**
- Show the video with books open; then with books closed.
- Play audio while students follow the script in the text.

STANDARDS

1.2 Understand language

Warm Up
Projectable Transparencies, 2-16

Numbers Write the correct number in Spanish.

1. 11 cuadernos
2. 21 maestros
3. 31 mochilas
4. 71 estudiantes
5. 57 clases

Answers: 1. once; 2. veintiún; 3. treinta y una; 4. setenta y un; 5. cincuenta y siete

Video Summary

@HOMETUTOR VideoPlus my.hrw.com

Claudia and Pablo are classmates discussing a science test they have tomorrow. Pablo likes getting good grades, but today he wants to play soccer instead of studying for the test. They make plans to meet at school tomorrow at 7AM to study, although Pablo would prefer to arrive at 8:00.

Answers
Projectable Transparencies, 2-24

Answers continued from p. 88.

Activity 2 Answers should follow the format: **¿Cuántos/Cuántas + people + hay en la/las clase/clases de + class? Hay + number + people + en la/las clase/clases de + class.**

Para y piensa
1. Me gusta dibujar en la clase de arte.
2. Hay veintitrés chicos en la clase de matemáticas.

Objectives
- Practice using vocabulary in context.
- Practice telling time.

Core Resource
- Audio Program: TXT CD 2, track 3

Practice Sequence
- **Activity 3:** Telehistoria comprehension
- **Activity 4:** Vocabulary production: time, class schedules, school subjects

STANDARDS
1.1 Engage in conversation, Act. 4
1.2 Understand language, Act. 3; PYP
1.3 Present information, Act. 4
4.1 Compare languages, Nota
Communication, Ongoing Assessment

✓ Ongoing Assessment

Get Help Online
More Practice
my.hrw.com

Alternative Strategy Have students practice saying at what time and day of the week they like to do their favorite activity. For example, **Me gusta patinar los sábados a las tres y treinta de la tarde.** For additional practice, use Reteaching & Practice Copymasters URB 2, pp. 1, 3.

Answers Projectable Transparencies, 2-24 and 2-25

Activity 3
1. Falso. Hay un examen en la clase de ciencias.
2. Cierto
3. Cierto
4. Cierto
5. Falso. La clase de ciencias es difícil.

Activity 4
La clase de historia es a las siete de la mañana.
La clase de matemáticas es a las ocho y cuarto/quince de la mañana.
La clase de inglés es a las nueve y treinta/media de la mañana.
La clase de arte es a las diez y cuarenta y cinco/once menos cuarto de la mañana.
La clase de ciencias es a la una y cinco de la tarde.
La clase de español es a las dos y diez de la tarde.

Para y piensa
1. a las diez y cuarto/quince.
2. las ocho y veinte.
3. a las siete de la noche.

3 *Comprensión del episodio* Planes para estudiar

Escuchar
Leer

¿Es cierto o falso? Si es falso, di lo que es cierto. *(True or false? If it is false, say what is true.)*

1. Hay un examen en la clase de español mañana.
2. A Pablo le gusta estudiar con amigos, pero hoy no.
3. A Pablo le gusta la clase de ciencias.
4. Hay fútbol hoy.
5. La clase de ciencias es fácil.

Expansión: Teacher Edition Only
Ask students to make two more true statements based on the dialogue.

Nota gramatical
- Use **Es la una** to say that it is one o'clock; use **Son las...** for any other time.
  Son las cinco. *It is 5:00.*
- Use y + **minutes** for the number of minutes after the hour (up to 30).
  Son las dos y **diez.** *It is 2:10.*
- Use menos + **minutes** for the number of minutes before the hour.
  Es la una menos **veinte.** *It is 12:40.*
- Use y or **menos cuarto** for a quarter of an hour and **y media** for half an hour.
- To say at what time something happens, use **a la(s)...**
  La clase de arte es **a la** una y la clase de inglés es **a las** dos.

4 El horario de clases

Escribir

Escribe a qué hora son las clases de Marisol. *(Write the times of Marisol's classes.)*

modelo: La clase de historia es a las siete de la mañana.

MARISOL AGUILAR

HORA	LUNES
7:00	HISTORIA
8:15	MATEMÁTICAS
9:30	INGLÉS
10:45	ARTE
1:05	CIENCIAS
2:10	ESPAÑOL

Expansión
Draw five clocks showing different times. Point to each one and ask a partner what time it is.

PARA Y PIENSA

Get Help Online
my.hrw.com

Did you get it? Complete each sentence with the appropriate time.
1. El jueves Claudia tiene que llegar a la escuela ____ . (10:15)
2. Son ____ . (8:20)
3. A Pablo le gusta hacer la tarea ____ de la noche. (7:00)

Differentiating Instruction

English Learners
Build Background Use a model clock to review the terms *before* and *after* with English language learners. Also, remind them of other English terms that can be used with time, such as *past, until,* or *to.* Set a time on the model clock, and ask students to read it aloud in English and Spanish. ***It's twenty past two.* Son las dos y veinte.**

Inclusion
Metacognitive Support Read with students the information presented in **Nota gramatical.** Then ask them to reflect on the aspects of telling time in Spanish that differ from English. For example, in Spanish you use an article, **la** or **las,** before the number. And whereas you might say *three-fifty* in English, in Spanish you would say **las cuatro menos diez.**

Presentación de GRAMÁTICA

¡AVANZA! **Goal:** Learn how to form the verb **tener.** Then use this verb to say what people have and have to do and how often. ***Actividades 5–7***

¿Recuerdas? After-school activities p. 32

English Grammar Connection: **Conjugating** is changing the forms of a verb to indicate who is doing the action. For example, the English verb *to have* is conjugated as *I have, you have, he/she/it has, we have, they have.*

Claudia **has** a computer. → **conjugated verb**

Claudia **tiene** una computadora. → **conjugated verb**

The Verb tener

ANIMATEDGRAMMAR my.hrw.com

Use the verb **tener** to talk about what you have. How do you conjugate this verb?

Here's how:

tener *to have*			
yo	tengo	nosotros(as)	tenemos
tú	tienes	vosotros(as)	tenéis
usted, él, ella	tiene	ustedes, ellos(as)	tienen

Tenemos clase el lunes.
***We have** class on Monday.*

¿**Tienes** una bicicleta?
***Do you have** a bike?*

Tener + **que** + **infinitive** is used to talk about what someone has to do.

Tengo que estudiar.
***I have to** study.*

Miguel **tiene que leer** un libro.
*Miguel **has to** read a book.*

Más práctica
Cuaderno *pp. 53–55*
Cuaderno para hispanohablantes *pp. 54–56*

@HOMETUTOR my.hrw.com
Leveled Practice
Conjuguemos.com

¡AVANZA! **Objective**
- Present the verb **tener.**

Core Resource
- *Cuaderno,* pp. 53–55

Presentation Strategies
- Present forms of the verb **tener.**
- Tell students that they can use the verb **tener** to denote possession, and also as an equivalent of the expression *have to + verb.*

STANDARDS
4.1 Compare languages

Warm Up Projectable Transparencies, 2-17

Writing Comprehension Ask students to fill in the times.

1. Tengo que estudiar ____. (11:00)
2. Tenemos la clase de ciencias ____. (12:30)
3. Tienes la clase de matemáticas ____. (2:15)
4. Tengo la clase de inglés ____. (8:00)
5. Tienen que llegar a la escuela ____. (6:40)

Answers: 1. a las once; 2. a las doce y treinta; 3. a las dos y quince; 4. a las ocho; 5. a las seis y cuarenta

Nota gramatical

The word **que** has several meanings but is not translated into English when used with **tener.** However, it is essential in Spanish when telling what someone has to do. **Tienes que llegar temprano.** (You have to arrive early.)

Comparisons
English Language Connection

Tell students that in some countries in Central America, people might use **a la(s)** to say the time. For example, **un cuarto a las cinco** or **veinte a las cuatro,** which in English would be a *quarter to five* or *twenty to five.*

Differentiating Instruction

Inclusion

Multisensory Input/Output Say a form of the verb **tener** aloud as you write it on the board. For example, **Yo tengo.** Have students copy the phrase, as they repeat it aloud. After you have gone through all of the forms, repeat the exercise. This time, only provide students with the pronoun. They must provide the correct form of the verb.

Pre-AP

Timed Answer Create two sets of cards. The first set will have pronouns: **yo, tú, él,** etc. The second set will have familiar nouns: **una computadora, una bicicleta,** etc. Invite a volunteer to choose one card from each set. Based on the pronoun and noun chosen, the student has fifteen seconds to create a complete sentence using the verb **tener.**

Objectives
- Practice **tener,** lesson vocabulary, and expressions of frequency.
- **Culture:** Compare school uniforms.
- Recycle: after school activities.

Core Resources
- *Cuaderno,* pp. 53–55
- Audio: TXT CD 2 track 4

Practice Sequence
- **Activity 5:** Controlled practice: **tener**
- **Activity 6:** Transitional practice: time and **tener que**
- **Activity 7:** Open-ended practice: **tener que;** Recycle: after-school activities

STANDARDS
1.1 Engage in conversation, Act. 1; PYP
1.2 Understand language, Act. 2
1.3 Present information, Acts. 5–6
2.1 Practices and perspectives, CC
2.2 Products and perspectives, CC
4.1 Compare languages, Act. 5; Nota
4.2 Compare cultures, CC
21st Century **Initiative and Self-Direction,** Inclusion; **Social and Cross-Cultural Skills,** Compara con tu mundo

Comparación cultural

Essential Question
Suggested Answer Most schools in Spanish-speaking countries require students to wear uniforms. Often times, students are even required to wear a certain kind of shoes. Wearing uniforms prevents students from feeling pressure to dress a certain way, or to be influenced by advertising and trends.

Expanded Information
In many Latin American high schools, students do not change classrooms as they do in the United States. Except for physical education and art, students remain in the same classroom, while the teachers come to them. In many schools, it is common to have as much as fifteen minutes between each class. During their break, students often play **fútbol** or have a snack.

See Activity answers on p. 93.

Práctica de GRAMÁTICA

5 Las clases

Escribir

Escribe qué clases tienen estas personas, usando formas de **tener.**
*(Write what class these people have, using forms of **tener.**)*

1. yo

2. nosotros

3. Claudia y Pablo

4. tú

5. Claudia

6. ustedes

Expansión:
Teacher Edition Only
Have students make up sentences using **tener** and their schedule of classes.

6 ¿Qué tienen que hacer?

Escuchar
Escribir

Escucha la descripción de lo que Pablo y sus amigos tienen que hacer. Luego escribe oraciones para indicar qué hora es y quién tiene que hacer estas actividades. *(Listen and write sentences saying what time it is and who has to do the following activities.)*

1. estudiar
2. usar la computadora
3. hacer la tarea
4. tocar la guitarra
5. trabajar
6. leer un libro

Audio Program
TXT CD 2 Track 4
Audio Script, TE p. 83b

Expansión
Tell what you and your friends have to do today.

Comparación cultural

Uniformes escolares
How does the way students dress reflect a culture? In **Mexico,** it is common for students to wear uniforms in both public and private schools. The type and color of the uniforms can vary depending on the individual school. Most students in the **Dominican Republic** also wear uniforms. Public schools have the same uniforms, while private school uniforms may vary.

Compara con tu mundo *Why do some schools require uniforms? Are they common in your community?*

Estudiantes en México y la República Dominicana

Differentiating Instruction

Slower-paced Learners
Read Before Listening Have students copy the words and phrases from Activity 6 onto a separate piece of paper. Then tell them to draw a simple picture next to each word or phrase to help recall its meaning. As students listen to Pablo's description, have them take notes on their own page, recording each person's name next to the proper picture.

Pre-AP
Relate Opinions Ask students to share their personal opinions on the topic of school uniforms. Do they think they are a good or bad idea? What do they see as some of the benefits and drawbacks of having a school uniform? Ask students to imagine and discuss what their school would be like if it did, or did not have uniforms. Generate some of the vocabulary they will need.

Nota gramatical

The expressions of frequency **siempre** and **nunca** are usually placed before the verb.

Antonio **siempre** toma apuntes.	*Antonio **always** takes notes.*
Rafael **nunca** llega a clase tarde.	*Rafael **never** arrives late to class.*

Mucho is usually placed after the verb.

Raquel estudia **mucho.**	*Raquel studies **a lot.***

De vez en cuando, muchas veces, and **todos los días** are usually placed at the beginning or the end of the sentence.

Todos los días Jaime trabaja.	*Jaime works **every day.***
Jaime trabaja **todos los días.**	

7 Las obligaciones

¿Recuerdas? After-school activities p. 32

Hablar

Pregúntales a otros(as) estudiantes si tienen que hacer estas actividades. Ellos van a responder usando una expresión de frecuencia. *(Ask other students whether they have to do these activities. They will respond using an expression of frequency.)*

A ¿Tienen que tomar apuntes ustedes?

B Sí, tengo que tomar apuntes muchas veces.

C Sí, tengo que tomar apuntes de vez en cuando.

1. 
2. 
3. 
4. 
5. 
6. 

Expansión
Write three or four sentences about the activities you and your friends never have to do.

Más práctica Cuaderno *pp. 53–55* Cuaderno para hispanohablantes *pp. 54–56*

Get Help Online
my.hrw.com

PARA Y PIENSA

Did you get it? Answer each question with the word(s) in parentheses.
1. ¿Tiene que preparar la comida Juan? (nunca)
2. ¿Cuándo tenemos la clase de inglés? (todos los días)
3. ¿Tienes que usar la computadora? (siempre)

Differentiating Instruction

Multiple Intelligences

Interpersonal Write the expressions of frequency outlined on p. 93 on the board. Then ask students questions about their own classmates using vocabulary phrases from the lesson. **¿Llega Diana a la clase tarde? ¿Usa Javier la computadora?** Tell students to use the most appropriate expression of frequency in their answers. **Diana nunca llega a la clase tarde. Javier usa la computadora de vez en cuando.**

Inclusion

Frequent Review/Repetition As students answer each other's questions in Activity 7, advise them to refer to the Nota gramatical after each response. Have students confirm that they used the expression of frequency in the correct place in the sentence. If they did not, have them rearrange the sentence, and repeat their answers as many times as necessary.

Communication

Grammar Activity

Activity 7 Give a blank sheet of paper to the first person in each row. The first student will write a subject pronoun; the student after him/her will write the correct form of **tener que** next to it. The third person will supply a different subject pronoun and pass the paper to the fourth person for that form of **tener que.** Continue to the end of the row. If there are any errors, return the paper to the beginning of the row for corrections. The first row to conjugate all forms correctly is the winning row.

✓ Ongoing Assessment

Get Help Online
More Practice
my.hrw.com

PARA Y PIENSA

Quick Check Ask students if any of the expressions of frequency can be placed both at the beginning or at the end of the sentences. For additional practice, use Reteaching & Practice Copymasters URB 2, pp. 4, 5, 10.

Answers Projectable Transparencies, 2-25

Answers for Activities on p. 92.

Activity 5
1. Yo tengo la clase de matemáticas.
2. Nosotros tenemos la clase de inglés.
3. Claudia y Pablo tienen la clase de ciencias.
4. Tú tienes la clase de arte.
5. Claudia tiene la clase de historia.
6. Ustedes tienen la clase de español.

Activity 6
1. Son las ocho y Claudia tiene que estudiar.
2. Son las diez menos cuarto y Pablo tiene que usar la computadora.
3. Son las cuatro y diez y Pepe tiene que hacer la tarea.
4. Es la una y media, y Laura y Diana tienen que tocar la guitarra.
5. Son las seis y cuarto y Carlos tiene que trabajar.
6. Son las once menos veinte, y Manuel y Pablo tienen que leer un libro.

Activity 7 Answers should follow this format:
¿Tienen que + activity?
Sí/No, tengo que + activity + expression of frequency.

Para y piensa
1. Juan nunca tiene que preparar la comida.
2. Tenemos la clase de inglés todos los días.
3. Siempre tengo que usar la computadora.

¡AVANZA! Objectives

- Practice **tener** in context.
- Recycle: Days of the week.

Core Resources

- Video Program: DVD 1
- Audio Program: TXT CD 2 track 5

Presentation Strategies

- Have students read the script and talk about what they say when they answer the phone.
- Show the video or play the audio.

Practice Sequence

- **Activity 8:** Telehistoria comprehension
- **Activity 9:** Transitional practice: **tener que;** Recycle: days of the week
- **Activity 10:** Open-ended practice: **tener;** telling time, **tener** + **que**

STANDARDS

1.2 Understand language, Act. 8
1.3 Present information, Acts. 9–10; PYP
4.1 Compare languages
21st Century **Creativity and Innovation,** Heritage Language Learners

Warm Up
Projectable Transparencies, 2-17

Tener Write the correct form of the verb **tener** for each pronoun.

1. yo _____
2. tú _____
3. ella _____
4. nosotros _____
5. ustedes _____
6. ellos _____

Answers: 1. tengo; 2. tienes; 3. tiene; 4. tenemos; 5. tienen; 6. tienen

Communication
Regionalisms

Point out to students that in Colombia the word for grades is **calificaciones.**

Video Summary
@HOMETUTOR VideoPlus my.hrw.com

Claudia calls Pablo to remind him of their plans to meet at school at 7:00 to study for a science test. As they walk to class the next morning, Claudia gently reminds Pablo that he likes to get good grades and should study more.

GRAMÁTICA en contexto

¡AVANZA! **Goal:** Notice how Pablo and Claudia use the verb phrase **tener que** to talk about what they have to do at school. Then use **tener** and **tener que** to say what you and others have and have to do. ***Actividades 8–10***

¿Recuerdas? Days of the week p. 18

Telehistoria escena 2

@HOMETUTOR my.hrw.com View, Read and Record

STRATEGIES

Cuando lees
Find the "tag questions" This scene contains the "tag question" **¿no?** Where are the tag questions in a sentence? How do they differ from questions like **¿Quién es?**

Cuando escuchas
Weigh the motive Listen for Pablo's reasons for not studying for the test. What are his reasons? Do they sound credible to you? Have you ever used them?

VIDEO DVD
AUDIO

Pablo's cell phone rings.

Pablo: Hola... ¿Quién es? ¡Claudia! ¿Qué tal?... Sí, sí, a las siete. ¡Tenemos que estudiar mucho!

The next morning, Claudia and Pablo walk to class.

Claudia: Pablo, tienes que estudiar más, ¿no?

Pablo: Sí. Tenemos mucha tarea y los exámenes son muy difíciles.

Claudia: Pero te gusta sacar buenas notas, ¿no?

Pablo: Sí. Tenemos que estudiar más.

Continuará... p. 99

También se dice

México Pablo uses the word **tarea** to talk about homework. In other Spanish-speaking countries you might hear:
- **muchos países los deberes**

Differentiating Instruction

Pre-AP

Draw Conclusions Have students reread Pablo's side of the cell phone conversation in the Telehistoria. Based on what Pablo says, have students draft the lines for Claudia to say in between. For example, after Pablo asks **¿Quién es?** Claudia might say, **Es Claudia.** What might Claudia be asking before Pablo says, **Sí, sí, a las siete.**

Heritage Language Learners

Writing Skills Have students copy the following story starter on a piece of paper: **Tengo que estudiar más, pero...** Then have students create an imaginary excuse explaining why they can't study more. Encourage students to be as creative as possible. Give students the opportunity to read their work to the rest of the group.

8 Comprensión del episodio Un examen importante

Escuchar
Leer

Contesta las preguntas. *(Answer the questions.)*

1. ¿Qué tienen que hacer Pablo y Claudia?
- **a.** Tienen que descansar mucho.
- **b.** Tienen que estudiar.
- **c.** Tienen que enseñar.

2. ¿A qué hora tienen que estudiar?
- **a.** a las siete
- **b.** a las siete y media
- **c.** a las ocho

3. ¿Qué tienen Pablo y Claudia?
- **a.** muchos libros
- **b.** un poco de tarea
- **c.** mucha tarea

4. ¿Qué le gusta hacer a Pablo?
- **a.** Le gusta estudiar.
- **b.** Le gusta llegar tarde.
- **c.** Le gusta sacar buenas notas.

Expansión:
Teacher Edition Only
Have students write a fourth answer to each question.

9 Las responsabilidades

¿Recuerdas? Days of the week p. 18

Escribir

Tienes que hacer muchas actividades esta semana. Escribe un correo electrónico para explicar cinco cosas que tienes que hacer durante la semana. *(Write an e-mail about five things you have to do after school this week.)*

modelo:

```
Hola, Jeff.
Tengo mucho que hacer. El lunes tengo que practicar
la guitarra. El martes tengo que hacer la tarea...
```

Expansión
Talk with your classmates and find out how many people have to do the same activity.

10 ¿Y tú?

Hablar
Escribir

Contesta las preguntas. *(Answer the questions.)*

1. ¿Qué clases tienes? ¿Son fáciles o difíciles?
2. ¿A qué hora tienes la clase de español?
3. ¿Tienes que tomar apuntes? ¿En qué clases?
4. ¿Qué tienes que hacer todos los días?
5. ¿Qué tienes que hacer todos los sábados y domingos?
6. ¿Qué nunca tienes que hacer?
7. ¿Tienes que trabajar? ¿A qué hora?
8. ¿A qué hora necesitas llegar a la escuela?

Expansión:
Teacher Edition Only
Have students add two more questions, with their answers, about things they have to do.

Get Help Online
my.hrw.com

PARA Y PIENSA

Did you get it? **¿Tener** or **tener que?** Complete each sentence based on the Telehistoria with the correct form of the verb or expression.
1. Pablo y Claudia _____ mucha tarea.
2. Pablo _____ estudiar mucho.
3. Ellos _____ un examen en la clase de ciencias.

Communication
Common Error Alert

Remind students not to use **en** when saying on Monday, on Tuesday. They should use **el: el lunes, el martes**. When saying on Mondays, on Tuesdays, the **el** changes to **los.**

Ongoing Assessment

Get Help Online
More Practice
my.hrw.com

PARA Y PIENSA

Peer Assessment After students have completed the sentences, each student should compare answers with two other students and correct each other's work. For additional practice, use Reteaching & Practice Copymasters URB 2, pp. 4, 6.

Differentiating Instruction

Slower-paced Learners

Read Before Listening Provide scripts to students before listening to the audio and doing Activity 8. Then go over each of the choices given to make sure students understand their meaning.

Inclusion

Clear Structure Remind students of the elements of a sentence to draft their answers for Activity 10.
1. Record ideas for the answer in words or phrases.
2. Underline the words in the question that you'll need in the answer.
3. Conjugate the verb to the correct form.
4. Put the pieces of the sentence together.

Answers Projectable Transparencies, 2-25 and 2-26

Activity 8
1. b **2.** a **3.** c **4.** c

Activity 9 Answers will vary. Sample answers include:

Hola Carla:
Tengo muchas cosas que hacer. El lunes tengo que ir a la biblioteca. El martes tengo que llegar temprano al examen. El miércoles tengo que usar la computadora. El jueves tengo que estudiar inglés. El viernes tengo que ir a una fiesta.

Activity 10 Answers will vary. Sample answers include:
1. Tengo las clases de matemáticas, español, historia y ciencias.
2. Tengo la clase de español a las once de la mañana.
3. Sí, tengo que tomar apuntes todos los días. Tengo que tomar apuntes en las clases de ciencias e historia.
4. Tengo que usar la computadora todos los días.
5. Tengo que ir a hacer deportes los sábados y domingos.
6. Nunca tengo que preparar la comida.
7. Sí, tengo que trabajar todas las tardes. Tengo que trabajar a las tres de la tarde.
8. Tengo que llegar a la escuela a las ocho de la mañana.

Para y piensa
1. tienen **2.** tiene que **3.** tienen

¡AVANZA! Objectives
- Present the present tense of regular **-ar** verbs.
- Compare English equivalencies.

Core Resource
- *Cuaderno,* pp. 56–58

Presentation Strategies
- Introduce the present tense of regular **-ar** verbs.
- Reassure students that the pattern of **-ar** verb conjugations in Spanish is very predictable.

STANDARDS
4.1 Compare languages

Warm Up Projectable Transparencies, 2-18

Tener que Create sentences using the following phrases and the correct form of **tener que** + pronoun in parentheses.

1. escuchar música (yo)
2. montar en bicicleta (ellos)
3. dibujar (nosotras)
4. hablar por teléfono (tú)
5. tocar la guitarra (ustedes)

Answers: 1. Tengo que...; 2. Tienen que...; 3. Tenemos que...; 4. Tienes que...; 5. Tienen que...

Verbs Students Know

Students have learned the following **-ar** verbs, which are all regular in the present tense:

alquilar	**escuchar**	**pasar**
andar	**estudiar**	**pasear**
comprar	**hablar**	**practicar**
contestar	**llegar**	**sacar**
descansar	**mirar**	**tomar**
dibujar	**montar**	**trabajar**
enseñar	**necesitar**	**usar**

Note that the verb **jugar** is not regular; its conjugation will be taught in Unit 6.

Answers Projectable Transparencies, 2-26

Answers for Activities on p. 97.

Activity 11 Answers will vary. Sample answers include:

1. Yo siempre escucho en clase.
2. Pablo siempre toma apuntes.
3. Nosotros nunca sacamos malas notas.
4. Claudia y Pablo siempre estudian.
5. Tú siempre contestas preguntas.
6. Diego y yo nunca llegamos a clase tarde.
7. Lorena nunca mira la televisión.
8. Ustedes siempre sacan buenas notas.

Answers continue on p. 97.

Presentación de GRAMÁTICA

¡AVANZA! **Goal:** Learn the forms of **-ar** verbs. Then practice using the verbs to say what people do. ***Actividades 11–15***

English Grammar Connection: A **verb tense** is the form of the verb that shows *when* an action is happening. The **present tense** shows that an action is happening *now*. The Spanish present-tense verb form **estudiamos** can be expressed in English in three different ways: *we study, we are studying,* or *we do study.*

We study Spanish. → **present-tense verb** (study)

Estudiamos español. → **present-tense verb** (Estudiamos)

Present Tense of -ar Verbs

ANIMATEDGRAMMAR my.hrw.com

Many infinitives in Spanish end in **-ar.** How do you form the present tense of these verbs?

Here's how: In Spanish, the present tense is formed by changing the ending of the verb.

To form the present tense of a regular verb that ends in **-ar**, drop the **-ar** and add the appropriate **ending.**

habl~~ar~~ ◄ **o, as, a, amos, áis, or an**

hablar *to talk, to speak*			
yo	**hablo**	nosotros(as)	**hablamos**
tú	**hablas**	vosotros(as)	**habláis**
usted, él, ella	**habla**	ustedes, ellos(as)	**hablan**

Hablo inglés.
I speak *English.*
I am speaking *English.*
I do speak *English.*

¿**Hablan** español?
Do they speak *Spanish?*
Are they speaking *Spanish?*

Más práctica
Cuaderno *pp. 56–58*
Cuaderno para hispanohablantes *pp. 57–60*

@HOMETUTOR my.hrw.com
Leveled Practice
Conjuguemos.com

Differentiating Instruction

Slower-paced Learners

Memory Aids Have students create their own set of verb reference cards. On an index card, have students copy the forms of the verb **hablar** as presented on p. 96. Then have them recall the forms of the verb **tener,** and create a card for this verb. Each time students encounter a new verb, have them take the time to create a new verb card.

Inclusion

Metacognitive Support Ask students to think about why subject pronouns are not always necessary in Spanish. Why, for example, does **hablo inglés** suffice in Spanish, while the pronoun would be necessary to express the same phrase in English? Point out that verb endings help to indicate the subject pronoun.

Práctica de GRAMÁTICA

11 Somos buenos estudiantes

Hablar
Escribir

Pablo, Claudia y sus amigos son buenos estudiantes. Explica si siempre o nunca hacen lo siguiente. *(Tell whether good students always or never do the following.)*

modelo: Claudia / llegar a clase temprano
Claudia **siempre** llega a clase temprano.

1. yo / escuchar en clase
2. Pablo / tomar apuntes
3. nosotros / sacar malas notas
4. Claudia y Pablo / estudiar
5. tú / contestar preguntas
6. Diego y yo / llegar a clase tarde
7. Lorena / mirar la televisión
8. ustedes / sacar buenas notas

Expansión
Say how often you do these things.

12 El fin de semana

Leer
Escribir

A Sandra le gusta pasar un rato con los amigos. Completa el párrafo con la forma correcta del verbo apropiado. *(Complete the paragraph with the correct form of the appropriate verb.)*

escuchar	pasar
tocar	montar
alquilar	dibujar
estudiar	practicar

Nosotros __1.__ en bicicleta después de las clases. Amy y Rosa __2.__ deportes y yo __3.__ la guitarra. A mi amigo Eduardo no le gusta descansar. Él __4.__ inglés o __5.__ para la clase de arte. Es muy artístico. Si llueve, nosotros __6.__ música en un café o __7.__ un DVD. ¿Dónde __8.__ tú un rato con los amigos?

Expansión:
Teacher Edition Only
Have students rewrite the paragraph using different subjects so they can practice different present tense forms.

13 ¿Qué estudias?

Hablar

Con otro(a) estudiante, habla de tu horario y lo que estudias. *(Talk with a partner about your schedule and what you study.)*

A ¿Estudias ciencias?

B Sí, tengo la clase de ciencias a las once.

Comparación cultural

Los murales en México

How does society affect public artwork? From the 1920s to the 1950s, the Mexican government commissioned artists to paint the walls of public buildings. Diego Rivera, José Orozco and David Alfaro Siqueiros were the three most notable muralists. Their art promoted their political and social views on Mexican history and government, education, social security, class structure, and technology.

Compara con tu mundo *What would you paint in a mural representing your community?*

Detalle de Por una seguridad completa para todos los mexicanos (1952–1954)

Objectives

- Practice present tense regular **-ar** verbs.
- **Culture:** Society's effect on public artwork.
- Practice lesson vocabulary.

Practice Sequence

- **Activity 11:** Controlled practice: **-ar** verbs
- **Activity 12:** Transitional practice: Present tense of **-ar** verbs
- **Activity 13:** Transitional practice: **tener**

STANDARDS

1.3 Present information, Acts. 11, 12
2.1 Practices and perspectives, Act. 13
2.2 Products and perspectives, Act. 13
3.1 Knowledge of other disciplines, Act. 13
4.1 Compare languages, Acts. 11, 13
21st Century **Information Literacy,** Heritage Language Learners

Comparación cultural

Essential Question

Suggested Answer There are situations in society that inspire artists to reproduce them in artwork. Those situations could be related to education, industrialization, or historical events happening at a certain time.

Differentiating Instruction

Heritage Language Learners

Literacy Skills Encourage students to use the library or Internet to research other murals created by the artists mentioned above. Then ask students to explain how the name of the work and the content are related. Give students the opportunity to present their findings to the whole group.

Inclusion

Clear Structure Have students copy the paragraph in Activity 12 onto a separate sheet of paper. Instruct them to break Activity 12 into smaller steps. For example, for the first blank: 1. Circle a key word: **bicicleta;** 2. Choose the correct verb: **montar;** 3. Underline the pronoun: **nosotros;** 4. Write the correct form of the verb on the blank: **montamos.**

Answers Projectable Transparencies, 2-26

Answers continued from p. 96.

Activity 12

1. montamos
2. practican
3. toco
4. estudia
5. dibuja
6. escuchamos
7. alquilamos
8. pasas

Activity 13 Answers will vary. Sample answers include: ¿Estudias matemáticas? Sí, tengo la clase de matemáticas a las ocho. ¿Estudias historia? Sí, tengo la clase de historia a la una.

Objectives
- Practice the present tense of regular **–ar** verbs.
- Practice using expressions of frequency.
- Practice pronouncing the **ch** combination.

Core Resources
- *Cuaderno,* pp. 56–58
- Audio Program: TXT CD 2, track 6

Practice Sequence
- **Activity 14:** Open-ended practice: Present tense **–ar** verbs; expressions of frequency
- **Activity 15:** Open-ended practice: Present tense **–ar** verbs.
- Pronunciation: oral comprehension and the **ch** sound.

STANDARDS
1.1 Engage in conversation, Acts. 14–15
1.3 Present information, Act. 15
4.1 Compare languages, Pronunciación; PYP
21st Century **Communication,** Pre-AP

✓ Ongoing Assessment
Get Help Online
More Practice
my.hrw.com

PARA Y PIENSA **Dictation** After students finish doing the Para y piensa, dictate the same sentences with the correct answers. Then, check student's spellings. For additional practice, use Reteaching & Practice Copymasters URB 2, pp. 7, 8.

Answers
Projectable Transparencies, 2-26

Activity 14 Answers will vary. Sample answers include:
1. ¿Estudias en la escuela? Sí, siempre estudio en la escuela.
2. ¿Escuchas música? No, nunca escucho música.
3. ¿Compras refrescos? Sí, compro refrescos de vez en cuando.
4. ¿Practicas deportes? Sí, siempre practico deportes.
5. ¿Tocas la guitarra? No, nunca toco la guitarra.
6. ¿Pasas un rato con los amigos? Sí, paso buenos ratos con los amigos.

Activity 15 Answers will vary. Sample answers include: Siempre estudio en la biblioteca. Muchas veces descanso un rato. Nunca trabajo los fines de semana.

Para y piensa
1. usamos; **2.** preparo; **3.** dibujan; **4.** Necesitas

14 ¿En la escuela?

Hablar

Pregúntale a otro(a) estudiante si hace estas actividades en la escuela. Usa expresiones de frecuencia. *(Ask another student if he or she does these activities at school. Use expressions of frequency.)*

modelo: dibujar

A ¿Dibujas en la escuela?

B No, nunca dibujo en la escuela.

1. estudiar
2. escuchar música
3. comprar refrescos
4. practicar deportes
5. tocar la guitarra
6. pasar un rato con los amigos

Expansión
Say how often you do these activites on Sundays.

15 Un sábado típico

Escribir
Hablar

Describe lo que haces los sábados y con qué frecuencia. Usa los verbos de la lista. Luego compara tus actividades con las de otros(as) estudiantes.
(Use verbs from the list to describe what you do on Saturdays and how often you do it. Then compare your activities with other students'.)

alquilar	estudiar	escuchar	trabajar
comprar	descansar	usar	¿ ?

modelo: Siempre hablo por teléfono los sábados. Muchas veces paso un rato con las amigas. Nosotras alquilamos un DVD...

Expansión:
Teacher Edition Only
Have students use two additional verbs in their descriptions.

AUDIO

Pronunciación El sonido ch

In Spanish, the **ch** sounds like the *ch* of the English word *chip.*

Listen and repeat.

cha	**che**	**chi**	**cho**	**chu**
mucha	**noche**	**chico**	**dieciocho**	**churro**

Muchas chicas escuchan música de Pancho Sánchez.

Más práctica Cuaderno *pp. 56–58* Cuaderno para hispanohablantes *pp. 57–60*

Get Help Online
my.hrw.com

PARA Y PIENSA

Did you get it? Complete each sentence with the correct form of the verb in parentheses.
1. Nosotros _____ la computadora mucho. (usar)
2. Yo _____ la comida de vez en cuando. (preparar)
3. Los chicos _____ en la clase de arte. (dibujar)
4. ¿ _____ tú sacar una buena nota? (necesitar)

Differentiating Instruction

Pre-AP
Expand and Elaborate After students complete Activity 15, have them reread their descriptions. Encourage them to add a sentence after each existing sentence. This new sentence should elaborate upon the one preceding it. **Siempre hablo por teléfono los sábados. Me gusta hablar mucho con mi amiga Melissa.**

Inclusion
Alphabetic/Phonetic Awareness Write **mucha** and **noche** on the board leaving out the letter **ch** in each word, and placing a blank in its place. Say each word aloud, stressing the /ch/ sound. Have students repeat. Then ask for volunteers to come add the missing letters to each word.

Todo junto

¡AVANZA! **Goal:** ***Show what you know*** Pay attention to how Pablo and Claudia use **tener** and **-ar** verbs to talk about their test and what they do after school. Then use these verbs to say what you and others do during and after school. ***Actividades 16–20***

Telehistoria completa

@HOMETUTOR my.hrw.com **View, Read and Record**

STRATEGIES

Cuando lees
Look for the unexpected As you read, look for two surprises involving Pablo. What are they? Why are they unexpected? What did you expect to happen?

Cuando escuchas
Listen for cognates Listen for cognates like **examen** (exam, test). What cognates do you hear? What English word(s) do they sound like? What do they mean?

Escena 1 *Resumen*
Pablo y Claudia necesitan estudiar porque tienen un examen de ciencias.

Escena 2 *Resumen*
Pablo y Claudia hablan por teléfono. Tienen que estudiar más.

VIDEO DVD

AUDIO

Escena 3

Pablo: ¡Claudia! En el examen de ciencias, tengo... ¡un 90!
Claudia: ¡Y yo, un 100!
Pablo: ¿Estudiamos, tú y yo, todos los días?
Claudia: Sí... pero tú necesitas tomar buenos apuntes, ¿no? *(Pablo grins.)* ¿A qué hora practican fútbol?
Pablo: Muchas veces practicamos a las cinco. Mañana practicamos temprano, a las tres y media. ¿Y tú? ¿Qué necesitas hacer mañana?
Claudia: ¿Mañana? Estudiar y hacer la tarea de ciencias.
Claudia says goodbye and leaves. As his friend Roberto walks up, Pablo distractedly pulls Alicia's T-shirt out of his bag and puts it on.
Roberto: ¡Ay, Pablo, qué interesante!
Pablo, embarrassed, takes the shirt off quickly.

¡AVANZA! Objective
- Integrate lesson content.

Core Resources
- Video Program: DVD 1
- Audio Program: TXT CD 2, track 7

Presentation Strategies
- Ask students what they remember about the Telehistoria so far.
- Show the video or play the audio.
- Students may read to practice the strategy.

STANDARDS
1.2 Understand language
4.1 Compare language
21st Century **Collaboration,** Group Work; **Critical Thinking and Problem Solving,** Pre-AP

Warm Up
Projectable Transparencies, 2-18

-ar verbs Write on a separate piece of paper all forms of the verb **pasear. yo..., tú..., usted/él/ella..., nosotros..., vosotros..., ustedes/ellos/ellas...**

Answers: paseo; paseas; pasea; paseamos; paseáis; pasean.

Communication

Group Work

Telehistoria Ask students to work in groups and write a summary of the dialogue in Spanish, using Pablo and Claudia as the subjects of the sentences instead of **yo, tú,** or **nosotros.**

Video Summary

@HOMETUTOR VideoPlus my.hrw.com

Pablo is not happy because Claudia got a higher grade on her science test than he did. She tells him that he has to take better notes. Claudia asks Pablo what time he has soccer practice tomorrow and he asks her what she's doing tomorrow. She tells him that she is going to study and do her science homework. Pablo is going to soccer practice early. As he walks away, he puts on Alicia's T-shirt and Roberto teases him about the T-shirt.

Differentiating Instruction

Pre-AP

Summarize Direct students to review Escena 1 on p. 89 and Escena 2 on p. 94. Then ask them to summarize each of these scenes in their own words. They might begin by brainstorming important words or phrases, and then drafting a summarizing sentence. After students have given their own summaries, have them read those presented on p. 99. How do they compare?

Multiple Intelligences

Interpersonal Invite three volunteers to play the parts of Pablo, Claudia, and Roberto. As these students read the script, encourage them to emphasize the facial expressions appropriate to each character's emotions. When Pablo says **tengo... ¡un 90!,** what emotion might he be feeling? When Roberto says **¡Ay, Pablo, qué interesante!,** what might Pablo's expression be?

TODO JUNTO

Objective

- Practice and integrate lesson vocabulary and grammar.

Core Resources

- *Cuaderno,* pp. 59–60
- Audio Program: TXT CD 2, tracks 3, 5, 7, 8, 9

Practice Sequence

- **Activity 16:** Controlled practice: listening, reading
- **Activity 17:** Transitional practice: listening, writing
- **Activity 18:** Transitional practice: speaking
- **Activity 19:** Open-ended practice: reading, listening, speaking
- **Activity 20:** Open-ended practice: writing

STANDARDS

1.1 Engage in conversation, Act. 18
1.2 Understand language, Act. 16
1.3 Present information, Acts. 17, 19–20
4.1 Compare languages, PYP
21st Century **Communication,** Acts. 18, 20

✓ Ongoing Assessment

Rubric **Activity 18**

Speaking Criteria	Maximum Credit	Partial Credit	Minimum Credit
Content	Dialogue includes all the information.	Dialogue includes some of the information.	Dialogue includes little information.
Communi-cation	Most of the informa-tion is well organized.	Parts of the informa-tion is well organized.	The message is disorga-nized.
Accuracy	There are few mistakes in grammar and vocabulary.	There are some mistakes in grammar and vocabulary.	There are many mistakes in grammar and vocabulary.

To customize your own rubrics, use the ***Generate Success*** *Rubric Generator and Graphic Organizers.*

Answers Projectable Transparencies, 2-26

Activity 16

1. Pablo tiene que practicar el fútbol.
2. Claudia y Pablo llegan a la escuela a las siete de la mañana.

Answers continue on p. 101.

16 Comprensión de los episodios ¿Quién es?

Escuchar Leer

¿A quién se refieren estas oraciones? ¿A Claudia, a Pablo o a los dos? Escribe el (los) nombre(s) y la forma correcta del verbo entre paréntesis. *(Do these sentences refer to Claudia, Pablo, or both? Write the name(s) and the correct form of the verb in parentheses.)*

Pablo

Claudia y Pablo

Claudia

1. ____ (tener) que practicar fútbol.
2. ____ (llegar) a la escuela a las siete de la mañana.
3. ____ (hablar) por teléfono.
4. ____ (necesitar) estudiar una o dos horas.
5. ____ (tener) un examen de ciencias.
6. ____ (sacar) una buena nota.
7. ____ (estudiar) para la clase de ciencias mañana.
8. ____ (practicar) a las tres y media mañana.

Expansión:
Teacher Edition Only
Have students make up other sentences about Claudio and Pablo from the Telehistoria.

17 Comprensión de los episodios ¿Qué hacen?

Escuchar Leer

Completa las oraciones con información de los episodios. *(Finish the sentences.)*

1. Pablo y Claudia tienen que...
2. A las siete Pablo y Claudia...
3. Mañana Claudia...
4. Pablo necesita tomar...
5. Claudia y Pablo sacan...

Expansión:
Teacher Edition Only
Ask students to write a summary of the Telehistoria.

18 ¿Qué tienes que hacer?

Digital performance space

Hablar

STRATEGY **Hablar**
Create a dialogue of your own Use the model question and substitute different school subjects. Use the model answer, but change verbs, or use multiple verbs in a single sentence. Bring in humor if you can.

Habla con otro(a) estudiante de lo que haces y qué tienes que hacer en tus clases. *(Talk with a partner about what you do and have to do in your classes.)*

A ¿Qué tienes que hacer en la clase de matemáticas?

B Tengo que tomar apuntes. Siempre escucho en clase...

Expansión:
Teacher Edition Only
Ask students to talk about things they have to do outside school.

Differentiating Instruction

Pre-AP

Expand and Elaborate After they complete Activity 16, pair students and have them change each sentence into a question to ask their partner. For example:

1. **¿Y tú? ¿Tienes que practicar el fútbol?**
2. **¿Y tú? ¿Llegas a la escuela a las siete de la mañana?**

If the partner answers no, they must provide an explanation. **No, tengo que hacer la tarea.**

Slower-paced Learners

Sentence Completion Help students complete the sentences in Activity 17 by providing two choices. For example, **Pablo y Claudia tienen que estudiar. Pablo y Claudia tienen que montar en bicicleta.** Have students repeat, and then write the correct choice. Also, help them locate the place in the text where the information for the correct answer is presented.

19 Integración

Leer
Escuchar
Hablar

Mañana los maestros tienen una reunión y el horario de clases es diferente. Lee el horario de Manuel y escucha el mensaje del director. Indica a qué hora necesita llegar Manuel a sus clases. *(Tell at what time Manuel needs to arrive at each of his classes.)*

Audio Program
TXT CD 2 Track 8, 9
Audio Script, TE p. 83b

Fuente 1 Horario de clases

Rojas, Manuel — Colegio Benito Juárez

HORA	CLASE	MAESTRO
7:10	ciencias	Sra. Burgos
8:30	arte	Sr. Rivera
9:50	inglés	Sr. Ortiz
11:10	historia	Sra. Sánchez
1:20	español	Sr. Acevedo
2:40	matemáticas	Sra. Gala

Fuente 2 Mensaje del director

Listen and take notes
- ¿Cuántos minutos después de la hora normal son las clases de la mañana? ¿Las clases de la tarde?

modelo: Manuel necesita llegar a la clase de... a las...

Expansión:
Teacher Edition Only
Ask students at what times their classes start when there is a morning assembly.

20 Tu horario

Digital performance space

Escribir

Describe tu horario en la escuela. ¿Qué clases tienes? ¿A qué hora? ¿Qué tienes que hacer todos los días? ¿Qué haces de vez en cuando? ¿Qué actividades nunca haces en las clases? *(Describe your school schedule. What classes do you have and at what times? What do you do and not do in your classes?)*

modelo: Tengo muchas clases en mi horario. Tengo la clase de español todos los días a las nueve menos cuarto. Llego a clase temprano...

Writing Criteria	Excellent	Good	Needs Work
Content	Your description includes a lot of information.	Your description includes some information.	Your description includes little information.
Communication	Most of your description is organized and easy to follow.	Parts of your description are organized and easy to follow.	Your description is disorganized and hard to follow.
Accuracy	Your description has few mistakes in grammar and vocabulary.	Your description has some mistakes in grammar and vocabulary.	Your description has many mistakes in grammar and vocabulary.

Expansión
Write about what your teachers do and have to do at school.

Más práctica Cuaderno *pp. 59–60* Cuaderno para hispanohablantes *pp. 61–62*

Get Help Online
my.hrw.com

PARA Y PIENSA

Did you get it? Write the correct form of **tomar, estudiar,** or **practicar.**

1. Claudia siempre _____ buenos apuntes.
2. Pablo tiene que _____ fútbol a las cinco.
3. Pablo y Claudia _____ todos los días.

Long-term Retention

Pre-AP Integration

Activity 19 Have each student present his/her answers to the class. Have the class correct the pronunciation and grade the presentation.

Ongoing Assessment

Rubric Activity 19

Listening/Speaking

Proficient	Not There Yet
Student takes detailed notes and relays the times correctly and in complete sentences.	Student takes few notes and does not relay the correct time in complete sentences.

Ongoing Assessment

Get Help Online
More Practice
my.hrw.com

PARA Y PIENSA

Peer Assessment Have students check each other's papers as you call out the correct answers. For additional practice, use Reteaching & Practice Copymasters URB 2, pp. 7, 9.

Answers Projectable Transparencies, 2-26 and 2-27

Answers continued from p. 100.

3. Claudia y Pablo hablan.
4. Pablo necesita estudiar.
5. Claudia y Pablo tienen.
6. Pablo y Claudia sacan.
7. Claudia y Pablo estudian.
8. Pablo practica.

Activity 17 Answers will vary. Sample answers include:
1. estudiar más.
2. estudian para el examen de ciencias.
3. tiene que estudiar y hacer la tarea de ciencias.
4. buenos apuntes.
5. buenas notas.

Activity 18 Answers will vary. Sample answers include: ¿Qué tienes que hacer en la clase de historia? Tengo que estudiar. Siempre tomo apuntes.

Activity 19
Manuel necesita llegar a la clase de ciencias a las 7:55... a la clase de arte a las 9:15... a la clase de inglés a las 10:35... a la clase de historia a las 11:55... a la clase de español a la 1:35... a la clase de matemáticas a las 2:55.

Activity 20 Answers will vary. Sample answers include: Tengo la clase de inglés los lunes. Tengo que tomar apuntes y escuchar a la maestra. A las diez tengo la clase de matemáticas.

Para y piensa
1. toma; **2.** practicar; **3.** estudian

Differentiating Instruction

Multiple Intelligences

Visual Learners Once students have completed Activity 19, give them the opportunity to create a new schedule for Manuel, based on their answers. Provide them with chart paper and colored pencils or pens. Students may want to present their schedules to the rest of the class.

Inclusion

Clear Structure Have students copy each of the prompt questions in Activity 20 onto a piece of paper. Then have them brainstorm the content for each response using only words, numbers and phrases. Once students have recorded the information they want to convey, have them start adding pronouns, articles, and verbs to create complete sentences.

¡AVANZA! Objectives

- Learn about an international school in Mexico.
- Learn about graduation requirements from an international school in Mexico.
- Compare these requirements with graduation requirements in U.S. schools.

Core Resources:

- Audio Program: TXT CD 2 track 10

Presentation Strategies:

- Ask students what they think might be the advantages of international schooling.
- Ask students if they would like to attend an international school and why or why not.
- Play the audio while students read the handbook and course requirements.

STANDARDS

1.2 Understand language
2.2 Practices and perspectives
4.2 Compare cultures
21st Century **Flexibility and Adaptability,** Pair Work; **Technology Literacy,** Multiple Intelligences

Warm Up Projectable Transparencies, 2-19

-ar Verbs Write the correct form of **sacar, llegar, dibujar,** or **necesitar.**

1. Nosotros _____ buenas notas en las clases.
2. Yo _____ a la escuela a las siete de la mañana.
3. Ustedes _____ en la clase de arte.
4. ¿ _____ tú tomar muchos apuntes?

Answers: 1. sacamos; 2. llego; 3. dibujan; 4. Necesitas

Culture

Background Information

The **bachillerato** is a three-year high-school program and students are usually between 15 and 18 years old. The objective of these schools is to prepare students for further study in a university. Although the course of study varies, all high schools (called **Preparatorias** in Mexico) have a curriculum of social studies, language, culture, science and technology. These schools are managed privately, by the nation, or occasionally housed within a university.

Lectura

Additional readings at my.hrw.com SPANISH InterActive Reader

¡AVANZA! Goal: Read about the requirements for graduating from an international school in Mexico. As you read these documents, compare them with the course requirements needed to graduate from your school.

AUDIO

Una escuela internacional en México

The following pages are from the student handbook for Colegio Internacional.

STRATEGY Leer
Use what you know As you read the graduation requirements of Colegio Internacional, use what you know. Find words that sound and look somewhat similar to those in English — cognates like **ciencias** or **matemáticas.** Then use the context and what you already know to guess what **desarrollo humano** and **optativas** mean.

MANUAL DEL ESTUDIANTE

Estudiantes en el Colegio Internacional

«A mí me gusta mucho el Colegio Internacional. Las clases son muy buenas. Los maestros son trabajadores y muy inteligentes. Y los estudiantes son súper simpáticos. Siempre tenemos que trabajar mucho, pero... ¡¿dónde no?! Y también en la escuela hay muchas actividades después de las clases. ¡Es una escuela excelente!»
–Marta Ramos, estudiante

COLEGIO INTERNACIONAL

Differentiating Instruction

Multiple Intelligences

Interpersonal Ask student pairs to visit the website of a bilingual or international school in Mexico. They can search using these key words: Bilingual Schools Mexico. Have them click on the home page of one of these schools to find additional information about school subjects offered, extracurricular activities and graduation requirements. Ask them to write a brief report in English and use it for class discussion.

Slower-paced Learners

Personalize It Ask students to look closely at the photo on the cover of the **Manual del Estudiante.** Ask them: What are the different groups of students doing? Do the students in the photo look as if they enjoy their school? Does this look like a school you'd like to attend?

Requisitos para graduarse de bachillerato

A continuación[1], los requisitos para graduarse con los dos certificados: el certificado mexicano y el certificado estadounidense.

Clase	Número de unidades
Inglés	4 unidades
Español	4 unidades
Matemáticas	4 unidades
Ciencias	4 unidades
Ciencias Sociales de México	1 unidad
Historia de México II	1 unidad
Geografía de México	1 unidad
Derecho[2]	1 unidad
Ciencias Sociales	3 unidades
Computación	0,5 unidades
Educación Física	0,5 unidades
Desarrollo Humano[3]	1 unidad
Optativas[4]	2 unidades
Total	**27 unidades**

COLEGIO INTERNACIONAL

[1] **A...** following are [2] Law
[3] Human Development [4] Electives

PARA Y PIENSA

¿Comprendiste?

1. ¿Cuántas clases necesitas para los dos programas?
2. ¿Cuántas unidades de matemáticas tienes que tomar?

¿Y tú?

¿Qué clases del Colegio Internacional hay en tu escuela? ¿Cómo son?

Differentiating Instruction

Heritage Language Learners

Writing Skills Ask students if anyone they know ever attended a bilingual or international school. If so, ask them to compare the bilingual or international school and their school. Write their opinions in two lists on the board. Have students use the lists to write their comparisons in paragraph form.

Pre-AP

Expand and Elaborate Ask students to work in groups to design a four-year curriculum for an international school based on the **Requisitos para graduarse de bachillerato**. How long would the day be? How long would each period be? What courses would they offer, and in what years?

Communication

Presentational Mode

Ask students to write their own statement for the cover of a **Manual del Estudiante** for their own school. Give them the following questions as a guide: **¿Cómo se llama tu escuela? ¿Cómo son las clases? ¿Cómo son los maestros? ¿Qué tienes que hacer en la escuela? ¿Qué actividades tienes después de las clases? ¿Cómo es la escuela?** Encourage them to add a photo or poster of their school to accompany their class presentation.

Communication

Pair Work

Assign students the roles of school admissions counselor in a Mexican school and prospective student. The student asks questions about the school, required subjects and graduation requirements. Encourage them to use the vocabulary from the **Manual del Estudiante** and the **Requisitos para graduarse de bachillerato.** Example:
A: ¿Cómo son los maestros de la escuela? B: Son muy simpáticos. A: ¿Cuántas unidades de ciencias sociales tengo que tomar? B: Tienes que tomar tres unidades.

Long-term Retention

Critical Thinking

Evaluate Play the audio once without pausing and then play it once again, stopping along the way to check comprehension. Make a list of difficult words on the board for review. Add a list of topics to help students evaluate the school**: las clases, los maestros, los requisitos, los números de unidades.** Possible answers: **Es una escuela muy difícil porque tienes que tomar muchas clases.**

Answers

Para y piensa ¿Comprendiste?
1. Necesitas trece clases para los dos programas.
2. Tienes que tomar cuatros unidades de matematicas.

¿Y tú? Answers will vary, but should follow the pattern: En mi escuela hay inglés, español, matemáticas, ciencias, ciencias sociales, computación, educación física, y las optativas.

Objectives

- Analyze an antique map over 400 years old to learn about an ancient Mexican city.
- Deduce the meaning of symbols in the map's key.

Presentation Strategies

- Ask students to think about as many different kinds of maps as they can, and list the responses on the board (weather maps, road maps, etc.).
- Ask them which maps they have used, and if they think it is helpful to have illustrations on maps.
- Ask them to think about the different purposes for maps.
- Tell them that in 1577, Spain asked for information about its territories in the New World, and received maps like the one on this page. Ask how they think the information on the map was used.

STANDARDS

1.3 Present information
3.1 Knowledge of other disciplines
3.2 Acquire information
21st Century **Critical Thinking and Problem Solving,** Pre-AP; **Information Literacy,** Proyecto 3 (Health Literacy)

Connections

La historia

The name Zempoala means *place of the 20 waters,* for the several rivers that converge near the site. At the time of the Conquest, Zempoala was the largest city on the Gulf of Mexico, with a population of about 30,000. The map on this page is part of a collection of maps called the **Relaciones Gráficas** Collection. Many of them are held at the Universty of Texas at Austin in the Benson Latin American Collection, and can be viewed online. The map is labeled in Nahuatl, the language of the Aztec empire, which is still spoken widely in Mexico.

Answers

Conexiones Historians are still trying to decipher the meanings of the symbols on this map. Students should write their opinion of what the symbols mean.

Answers continue on page 105.

Conexiones *La historia*

El pueblo de Zempoala

In 1577, the Spanish crown sent a questionnaire to Mexico to get information about its territories in the New World. The responses that were sent back included local maps drawn by indigenous mapmakers.

The map below depicts the town (**pueblo**) of Zempoala, located in the modern Mexican state of Hidalgo. Research Zempoala to learn more about the town and this map. Then choose three specific map symbols not listed in the legend (**leyenda**) and explain what you think they mean.

El mapa de Zempoala

Proyecto 1 *El arte*

Draw a map of your town or city similar to the one of Zempoala. Give information about people, buildings, roads, and vegetation. Use symbols like the ones in the map above and label them in Spanish.

Proyecto 2 *Las ciencias sociales*

In 1968, Mexico established a televised system of secondary schools called **Telesecundaria.** Today, educational video programs are broadcast via satellite to more than 15,000 schools. Write two paragraphs about the use of technology in education. How is it used in your school? Can you think of other ways it can be used in education?

Proyecto 3 *La salud*

The map of Zempoala shows a number of cacti. The cactus has been an important source of food and medicine for people in Mexico for many years. Make a list of different types of cacti found in Mexico and create a chart showing how people have used them for health and beauty purposes.

Un nopal con flores

Differentiating Instruction

Pre-AP

Draw Conclusions Point out that the Telesecundaria system of instruction is capable of transmitting 24 hours a day. Nowadays programs are more interactive. Lessons can be watched live on TV or can be recorded. Based on this information, ask students: **¿Es una buena idea tener clases 24 horas al día? ¿Por qué?**

English Learners

Increase Interaction Pair English learners with native English-speaking students to discuss the information on p. 104. Have them work together on the planning and creation of maps for Proyecto 1.

En resumen

Vocabulario y gramática

ANIMATEDGRAMMAR
Interactive Flashcards
my.hrw.com

Vocabulario

Tell Time and Discuss Daily Schedules

¿A qué hora es...?	*At what time is . . . ?*	la hora	*hour; time*
¿Qué hora es?	*What time is it?*	el horario	*schedule*
A la(s)...	*At . . . o'clock.*	menos	*to, before (telling time)*
Es la... / Son las...	*It is . . . o'clock.*		
de la mañana	*in the morning (with a time)*	el minuto	*minute*
		...y cuarto	*quarter past*
de la tarde	*in the afternoon (with a time)*	...y (diez)	*(ten) past*
		...y media	*half past*
de la noche	*at night (with a time)*		

Describe Frequency

de vez en cuando	*once in a while*
muchas veces	*often, many times*
mucho	*a lot*
nunca	*never*
siempre	*always*
todos los días	*every day*

Describe Classes

School Subjects

el arte	*art*
las ciencias	*science*
el español	*Spanish*
la historia	*history*
el inglés	*English*
las matemáticas	*math*

Classroom Activities

contestar	*to answer*
enseñar	*to teach*
llegar	*to arrive*
necesitar	*to need*
sacar una buena / mala nota	*to get a good / bad grade*
tomar apuntes	*to take notes*
usar la computadora	*to use the computer*

Other Words and Phrases

casi	*almost*
¿Cuántos(as)...?	*How many . . . ?*
difícil	*difficult*
en	*in*
el examen (*pl.* los exámenes)	*exam, test*
fácil	*easy*
hay...	*there is, there are . . .*
muchos(as)	*many*
tarde	*late*
temprano	*early*
tener que	*to have to*

Numbers from 11 to 100 *p. 87*

Gramática

Notas gramaticales: Numbers *p. 88*, Telling time *p. 90*, Expressions of frequency *p. 93*

The Verb tener

Use the verb **tener** to talk about what you have.

tener *to have*			
yo	tengo	nosotros(as)	tenemos
tú	tienes	vosotros(as)	tenéis
usted, él, ella	tiene	ustedes, ellos(as)	tienen

Tener + **que** + **infinitive** is used to talk about what someone has to do.

Present Tense of -ar Verbs

To form the present tense of a regular verb that ends in **-ar**, drop the **-ar** and add the appropriate **ending**.

hablar *to talk, to speak*			
yo	hablo	nosotros(as)	hablamos
tú	hablas	vosotros(as)	habláis
usted, él, ella	habla	ustedes, ellos(as)	hablan

Practice Spanish with Holt McDougal Apps!

Differentiating Instruction

Multiple Intelligences

Musical/Rhythmic Lead students in chanting **yo hablo, tú hablas, usted habla, él habla, ella habla, nosotros hablamos, vosotras habláis, ustedes hablan, ellos hablan, ellas hablan.** As they progress through the sequence, have them gesture to indicate about whom they are talking. Conduct this exercise first as a large group and then in pairs.

Inclusion

Synthetic/Analytic Support Ask students to make flashcards with the personal pronoun on one side and the correct form of **tener** on the other side. Ask students to work in pairs, taking turns as one student shows the pronoun and the other says the verb form, then one student shows the verb form and the other says the pronoun.

Objective

- Review lesson vocabulary and grammar.

DIGITAL SPANISH

Interactive Flashcards Students can hear every target vocabulary word pronounced in authentic Spanish. Flashcards have Spanish on one side, and a picture or a translation on the other.

performance space
News Networking
@HOMETUTOR
CULTURA Interactiva

- **Audio and Video Resources**
- **Interactive Flashcards**
- **Review Activities**
- **WebQuest**
- **Conjuguemos.com**

Long-term Retention

Study Tips

Have students study the first category of words in En resumen for 1 minute. Then tell them to close their books and write down as many words as they can remember in 2 minutes. They should then open their book and check their work. Continue with the other categories.

Answers

Answers continued from page 104.

(This is a continuation of the answer for main project) Possible answers include: The plant life may represent fields used for farming. The places where earth is shown could be hills or mountains. The buildings may represent the center of town.

Proyecto 1 Students should draw maps that incorporate similar images and orientations as the map of Zempoala.

Proyecto 2 Answers will vary. Sample answers include computers, the Internet, overhead projectors, TVs, VHS, DVDs.

Proyecto 3 Examples of cacti include maguey and nopal. Several parts of the nopal are eaten–the actual cactus leaves as well as the fruit that comes off it, called the prickly pear or **tuna** in Spanish. The fruit is also used to make juice. The maguey is used to produce soap, food, medicine, rope, fibers, furniture, and paper.

Objectives
- Review lesson grammar and vo[illegible]ulary.

Core Resources
- *Cuaderno,* pp. 61–72
- Audio Program: TXT CD 2[illegible]

Presentation Strat[illegible]
- Before listening to the aud[illegible]y 1, ask students to listen to it [illegible]ial attention to the subjects a[illegible] mentioned.
- Before doing Activity 2, review forms of tener and telling time with students.
- Review present forms of **-ar** verbs by saying a subject and an infinitive and asking students to supply the correct verb form. For example: **él/practicar: él practica.**
- Review expressions of frequency before doing Activity 4.
- Ask students to generate two questions to ask their classmates based on the Comparación cultural.

STANDARDS
1.2. Understand language, Act. 1
1.3 Present information, Acts. 2–5
4.2 Compare cultures, Act. 5
Critical Thinking and Problem Solving, Pre-AP

Warm Up
Projectable Transparencies, 2-19

Vocabulary Complete the sentences with the correct word.

difícil notas hora tarde apuntes

1. No me gusta sacar malas ____.
2. De vez en cuando, llego ____ a clase.
3. En la clase de historia tenemos que tomar muchos ____.
4. La clase de matemáticas no es ____.
5. ¿A qué ____ es la clase de arte?

Answers: 1. notas; 2. tarde; 3. apuntes; 4. difícil; 5. hora

Ongoing Assessment
Get Help Online
More Practice
my.hrw.com

Intervention and Remediation If students achieve less than 80% accuracy with the activities, ask them to review pages 83–84, 91–93, 96–97, and to get help on line at my.hrw.com.

Lección 1 Repaso de la lección

@HOMETUTOR my.hrw.com

¡LLEGADA!

Now you can
- talk about daily schedules
- ask and tell time
- say what you have and have to do
- say what you do and how often you do things

Using
- the verb **tener** and **tener que**
- expressions of frequency
- present tense of **-ar** verbs

To review
- the verb **tener** and **tener que** p. 91
- expressions of frequency p. 93
- present tense of **-ar** verbs p. 96

1 Listen and understand

AUDIO

Escucha a Martín y a Lupe hablar de sus clases y empareja la información. *(Match according to what you hear Martín and Lupe say about their activities.)*

1. ¿Qué hora es?
2. ¿A qué hora es la clase de historia?
3. ¿En qué clase tiene que sacar una buena nota Martín?
4. ¿En qué clases contestan muchas preguntas?
5. ¿Cómo es la maestra de ciencias?
6. ¿En qué clase usan la computadora?

a. joven
b. en la clase de ciencias
c. Son las diez y cuarto.
d. Es a las diez y media.
e. en las clases de inglés y ciencias
f. en la clase de historia

Audio Program
TXT CD 2 Track 11
Audio Script, TE p. 83b

To review
- the verb **tener** and **tener que** p. 91

2 Say what you have and have to do

Indica qué clases tienen Beto y sus amigos a estas horas y qué tienen que hacer. *(Tell what classes Beto and his friends have at these times and what they have to do.)*

8:00 **modelo:** Adela: arte / dibujar
Adela tiene la clase de arte a las ocho.
Tiene que dibujar.

1. 9:15 yo: historia / tomar muchos apuntes
2. 10:30 ustedes: matemáticas / estudiar los problemas
3. 11:45 tú: español / hablar español
4. 1:20 David y yo: inglés / contestar muchas preguntas
5. 2:15 Lilia: ciencias / usar la computadora
6. 3:30 Eva y Víctor: música / tocar la guitarra

Differentiating Instruction

Pre-AP
Draw Conclusions For Activity 1, ask students to discuss why Martín needs to take a lot of notes in history and why he has to answer many questions. Why does the history class differ from Martín's other classes?

Multiple Intelligences
Visual Learners To help visual learners with Activity 3, ask students to create a chart that shows Pati León's schedule. Direct them to use symbols or pictures as well as words to indicate what Pati will be doing on each day.

To review
- present tense **-ar** verbs p. 96

3 Talk about daily schedules

Lee la información sobre Pati León. Complétala con la forma correcta de los verbos entre paréntesis. *(Read the information about Pati León. Then complete the information with the correct form of the verbs in parentheses.)*

Mi horario es muy bueno. Yo __1.__ (trabajar) mucho los lunes, martes y miércoles. Los jueves Gustavo y yo __2.__ (andar) en patineta. Los viernes Gustavo __3.__ (descansar), pero yo __4.__ (montar) en bicicleta con Eloísa y Héctor. Ellos __5.__ (practicar) deportes casi todos los días. Los viernes nosotros __6.__ (comprar) una pizza y __7.__ (mirar) la televisión. ¿Y los sábados y domingos? Muchas veces mis amigos y yo __8.__ (pasear). ¿Y tú? ¿También __9.__ (pasar) un rato con los amigos los sábados y domingos?

To review
- expressions of frequency p. 93
- present tense of **-ar** verbs p. 96

4 Say what you do and how often you do things

Escribe oraciones para decir con qué frecuencia estas personas hacen las siguientes actividades. *(Tell how often these people do the following activities.)*

0 días	1 – 2 días	3 – 4 días	5 – 6 días	7 días
nunca	de vez en cuando	muchas veces	casi siempre	todos los días

modelo: nosotros / mirar un DVD (2 días)
Miramos un DVD de vez en cuando.

1. Roberta / contestar preguntas (0 días)
2. tú / hablar español (5 días)
3. Nicolás / practicar deportes (6 días)
4. yo / escuchar música (3 días)
5. Carlos y Pilar / estudiar historia (2 días)
6. nosotros / tocar la guitarra (4 días)
7. los maestros / usar la computadora (7 días)

To review
- Chichén Itzá p. 83
- Comparación cultural pp. 84, 92, 97

5 Mexico and the Dominican Republic

Comparación cultural

Answer these culture questions.

1. What is Chichén Itzá and what can you find there?
2. What are **zócalos**?
3. What do many students in Mexico and the Dominican Republic wear to school?
4. Who are three famous Mexican muralists?

Más práctica Cuaderno *pp. 61–72* Cuaderno para hispanohablantes *pp. 63–72*

Get Help Online my.hrw.com

Differentiating Instruction

Inclusion

Clear Structure Ask students to write a description of their school schedule. Encourage them to brainstorm ideas in these categories: class subjects and times, class activities, frequency of activities, lunch time, and after-school activities. Ask them to use a concept web to organize their ideas before they start writing. Make sure they write their schedule in chronological order.

Slower-paced Learners

Yes/No Questions Ask students yes/no questions about their school activities. Use frequency words, such as **de vez en cuando, muchas veces, casi siempre,** and **todos los días** in your questions. **¿Llegas de vez en cuando tarde a la escuela? ¿Usas la computadora muchas veces? ¿Escuchas música casi siempre?** Encourage students to add to their responses after answering **sí** or **no**.

✓ Ongoing Assessment

Peer Assessment Have students complete Activity 3 individually. Then ask pairs of students to read answers aloud and check each other's written work.

✓ Ongoing Assessment

Quick Check Ask students how often they do the activities listed in Activity 4. For example: **Carlos, ¿con qué frecuencia escuchas música? Peter y Alice, ¿con qué frecuencia usan la computadora?**

Answers Projectable Transparencies, 2-27

Activity 1 **1.** c; **2.** d; **3.** f, **4.** e; **5.** a; **6.** b

Activity 2
1. Yo tengo la clase de historia a las nueve y cuarto. Tengo que tomar muchos apuntes.
2. Ustedes tienen la clase de matemáticas a las diez y media. Tienen que estudiar los problemas.
3. Tú tienes la clase de español a las doce menos cuarto. Tienes que hablar español.
4. David y yo tenemos clase de inglés a la una y veinte. Tenemos que contestar muchas preguntas.
5. Lilia tiene la clase de ciencias a las dos y cuarto. Tiene que usar la computadora.
6. Eva y Víctor tienen la clase de música a las tres y media. Tienen que tocar la guitarra.

Activity 3 **1.** trabajo; **2.** andamos; **3.** descansa; **4.** monto; **5.** practican; **6.** compramos; **7.** miramos; **8.** paseamos; **9.** pasas

Activity 4
1. Roberta nunca contesta preguntas.
2. Tú hablas español casi siempre.
3. Nicolás practica deportes casi siempre.
4. Yo escucho música muchas veces.
5. Carlos y Pilar estudian historia de vez en cuando.
6. Nosotros tocamos la guitarra muchas veces.
7. Los maestros usan la computadora todos los días.

Activity 5
1. Chichén Itzá is an ancient Mayan city. You can find there the statue of Chac-Mool and the pyramid of Kukulcán.
2. A **zócalo** is a town square or **plaza.**
3. Many students in Mexico and the Dominican Republic wear uniforms to school.
4. Diego Rivera, José Orozco and David Alfaro Siqueiros are famous Mexican muralists.

Lesson Overview

Culture at a Glance

Topic & Activity	Essential Question
The school year pp. 108-109	How is the Mexican school year different or similar to yours?
The National Museum of Anthropology p. 116	What do ancient artifacts teach us about a culture?
Self-Portraits of Frida Khalo p. 122	What does a self-portrait reveal about an artist?
Favorite Classes of Mexican and Dominican students pp. 126-127	How would you talk about your favorite class?
Huichol yarn painting and Taino rock art p. 128	How does art reflect a culture's view of the natural world?
Culture Review p. 131	What are some Mexican and Dominican cultural elements?

COMPARISON COUNTRIES México · República Dominicana · Paraguay

Practice at a Glance

	Objective	Activity & Skill
Vocabulary	Classroom Objects	1: Speaking/Writing; 3: Speaking; 5: Speaking; 9: Speaking; 19: Speaking; 20: Reading/Listening/Speaking; 21: Writing
	Feelings	8: Speaking; 10: Listening/Reading; 11: Speaking; Repaso 2: Writing
	Places in school	2: Reading/Writing; 6: Speaking/Writing; 12: Speaking; 14: Listening/Writing; 15: Speaking; 18: Listening/Reading; 19: Speaking
Grammar	The verb **estar**	6: Speaking/Writing; 7: Speaking; 8: Speaking; 10: Listening/Reading; Repaso 4: Writing
	The conjugated verb before the subject to ask a question	8: Speaking; 12: Speaking
	The verb **ir**	13: Reading/Writing; 14: Listening/Writing; 15: Speaking; 16: Speaking/Writing; 19: Speaking; 20: Reading/Listening/Speaking; Repaso 3: Reading/Writing
Communication	Describe classes and classroom objects	1: Speaking/Writing; 3: Speaking; 4: Listening/Reading; 5: Speaking; 17: Listening/Reading; 19: Speaking; 20: Reading/Listening/Speaking; 21: Reading/Writing
	Say where things are located	6: Speaking/Writing; 7: Speaking; 9: Speaking; 10: Listening/Reading; Repaso 1: Listening; Repaso 4: Writing
	Say where you are going	13: Reading/Writing; 14: Listening/Writing; 15: Speaking; 16: Speaking/Writing; Repaso 1: Listening; Repaso 3: Reading/Writing
	Talk about how you feel	8: Speaking; 11: Speaking; Repaso 2: Writing
	Pronunciation: The letter **d**	*Pronunciación: La letra **d**,* p. 121: Listening/Speaking
Recycle	Class subjects	5: Speaking
	Telling time	19: Speaking

The following presentations are recorded in the Audio Program for ¡Avancemos!

- **¡A responder!** *page 111*
- **14: ¿Adónde van?** *page 121*
- **20: Integración** *page 125*
- **Repaso de la lección** *page 130*
  1: Listen and understand
- **Repaso inclusivo** *page 134*
  1: Listen, understand, and compare

For **¡AvanzaRap!** scripts, see the **¡AvanzaRap! DVD.**

¡A responder! TXT CD 2 track 13

1. enojado
2. nervioso
3. cansado
4. contento
5. deprimido
6. emocionado
7. tranquilo

14 | ¿Adónde van? TXT CD 2 track 16

Pablo: Hola, me llamo Pablo. ¡Me gusta practicar deportes! A las ocho de la mañana yo voy al gimnasio.

Hola, Claudia. ¿Adónde vas?

Claudia: ¡Hola, Pablo! Voy a la clase de inglés.

Pablo: Martín y Sara, ¿adónde van ustedes?

Sara: Son las doce y Martín y yo tenemos que comer. Vamos a la cafetería.

Pablo: Pero, ¿adónde va la maestra de inglés? La clase de inglés es a la una.

Claudia: ¡Ay, Pablo! Ella va a la biblioteca. Necesita un libro para la clase.

Pablo: María y Claudia, ¿qué tal? Ustedes van al gimnasio, ¿no?

Claudia: María y yo vamos a la clase de matemáticas.

Pablo: Sr. Treviño, ¿adónde va usted después de clase?

Sr. Treviño: Después de clase voy a la oficina de la directora. Necesito hablar con ella.

20 | Integración TXT CD 2 tracks 19, 20

Hola, Raquel. Soy yo, Mario. Tenemos el examen de historia mañana, a las tres menos cuarto. ¡Necesitamos estudiar! Vamos a la biblioteca mañana, ¿no? Voy a la clase de ciencias a las siete y media de la mañana. No tengo clase a las nueve menos veinte pero a las diez menos diez tengo la clase de matemáticas. A las doce necesito comer con Andrés. A las doce y media descanso. A la una y media estoy en la clase de inglés. ¡Estoy muy nervioso! ¿Cuándo estudiamos?

Repaso de la lección TXT CD 2 track 22

1: Listen and understand

Hola. ¿Dónde estás? Son las ocho de la mañana. Estoy delante de la clase de arte. Voy a la clase de español. Hasta luego.

Hola. Mmmm. No contestas. Son las diez y cuarto. Estoy en el pasillo. Del pasillo, voy a la clase de inglés. Adiós.

¿Qué pasa? ¿Dónde estás? Son las doce y media. Estoy en la cafetería. De la cafetería, voy a la clase de matemáticas. Hasta luego.

Hola. Soy yo... Ana. Son las tres menos cuarto de la tarde. Estoy en la oficina. De la oficina, voy a la clase de historia. Adiós.

¡Hola! ¡Hola! ¡Contesta, por favor! Son las cuatro y diez. Estoy en la biblioteca. De la biblioteca, voy al gimnasio. ¿Y tú? ¿Dónde estás? ¿Estás en el gimnasio?

Repaso inclusivo TXT CD 2 track 24

1: Listen, understand, and compare

Javier: Los maestros enseñan pero a ellos también les gusta hacer otras cosas. El señor Minondo enseña la clase de historia y después de las clases practica deportes con amigos.

Sr. Minondo: Soy estudioso y atlético también. Después de enseñar, voy al gimnasio con los amigos para jugar al fútbol... y estoy más tranquilo.

Javier: La señora Cruz es la directora de la escuela.

Sra. Cruz: Tengo que ser organizada y seria pero también soy artística. Después de un día difícil, voy a mi oficina y toco la guitarra.

Javier: Cuando estás en el pasillo después de las cuatro de la tarde y escuchas música, es la directora y ella está contenta. Los maestros y directores son muy interesantes.

Resource List

Everything you need to ...

Plan	Present	Assess
Teacher One Stop ✓Lesson Plans ✓Teacher Resources ✓Audio and Video	**Interactive Whiteboard Lessons** **Teacher One Stop with Projectable Transparencies** **Power Presentations** **AnimatedGrammar**	**Online Assessment** ✓ Assessments for on-level, modified, pre-AP, and heritage learners ✓ Create customized tests with **Examview Assessment Suite** ✓ **performance space** ✓ *Generate Success* Rubric Generator

Print

Plan	Present	Practice	Assess
URB 2 • Video Scripts pp. 69, 70 • Family Letter p. 90 • Family Involvement Activity p. 91 • Absent Student Copymasters pp. 100–110 **Best Practices Toolkit**	**URB 2** • Video Activities pp. 57–64	• *Cuaderno* pp. 73–95 • *Cuaderno para hispanohablantes* pp. 73–95 • *Lecturas para todos* pp. 17–21 • *Lecturas para hispanohablantes* • *¡AvanzaCómics! SuperBruno y Nati*, Episodio 1 **URB 2** • Practice Games pp. 37–44 • Audio Scripts pp. 75–80 • Map/Culture Activities pp. 81–82 • Fine Art Activities pp. 87–88	**Differentiated Assessment Program** **URB 2** • Did you get it? Reteaching and Practice Copymasters pp. 11–22

Projectable Transparencies (Teacher One Stop, my.hrw.com)

Culture	Presentation and Practice	Classroom Management
• Atlas Maps 1–6 • Map Mexico: 1 • Fine Art Transparencies 4, 5	• Vocabulary Transparencies 8, 9 • Grammar Presentation Transparencies 12, 13 • Situational Transparencies and label overlay 14, 15 • Situational Student Copymasters 1, 2	• Warm Up Transparencies 20–23 • Student Book Answer Transparencies 28–31

Audio and Video

Audio

- Student Book Audio CD 2 Tracks 12–24
- Workbook Audio CD 1 Tracks 31–40
- Heritage Learners Audio CD 1 Tracks 13–16, CD 3 Tracks 11–14
- Assessment Audio CD 1 Tracks 11–14
- *Lecturas para todos* Audio CD 1 Track 4, CD 2 Tracks 1–6
- Sing-along Songs Audio CD

Video

- Vocabulary Video DVD 1
- *Telehistoria* DVD 1
  - *Escena 1*
  - *Escena 2*
  - *Escena 3*
  - *Completa*
- Culture Video DVD 1

¡AvanzaRap! DVD

- Video animations of all **¡AvanzaRap!** songs (with Karaoke track)
- Interactive DVD Activities
- Teaching Suggestions
- **¡AvanzaRap!** Activity Masters
- **¡AvanzaRap!** video scripts and answers

Online and Media Resources

Student

Available online at my.hrw.com

- Online Student Edition
- News Networking
- performance space
- @HOMETUTOR
- CULTURA Interactiva
- WebQuests
- Interactive Flashcards
- Review Games
- Self-Check Quiz

Student One Stop

Holt McDougal Spanish Apps

Teacher

Teacher One Stop (also available at my.hrw.com)

- Interactive Teacher's Edition
- All print, audio, and video resources
- Projectable Transparencies
- Lesson Plans
- TPRS
- Examview Assessment Suite

Available online at my.hrw.com

Generate Success Rubric Generator and Graphic Organizers

Power Presentations

Differentiated Assessment

On-level

- Vocabulary Recognition Quiz p. 74
- Vocabulary Production Quiz p. 75
- Grammar Quizzes pp. 76–77
- Culture Quiz p. 78
- On-level Lesson Test pp. 79–85
- On-level Unit 2 Unit Test pp. 91–97

Modified

- Modified Lesson Test pp. 59–65
- Modified Unit 2 Unit Test pp. 71–77

Pre-AP

- Pre-AP Lesson Test pp. 59–65
- Modified Unit 2 Unit Test pp. 71–77

Heritage Learners

- Heritage Learners Lesson Test pp. 65–71
- Heritage Learners Unit 2 Unit Test pp. 77–83

Core Pacing Guide

50 Minute (9 Day)

	Objectives/focus	Teach	Practice	Assess/HW Options
DAY 1	**Vocabulary:** typical school day • Warm Up OHT 20 **5 min**	Lesson Opener pp. 108–109 **Presentación de vocabulario** pp. 110–111 • Read A-D • View video DVD 1 • Play Audio TXT CD 2 track 12 • *¡A responder!* TXT CD 2 track 13 **25 min**	Lesson Opener pp. 108–109 **Práctica de vocabulario** p. 112 • Activities 1, 2, 3 **15 min**	**Assess:** *Para y piensa* p. 112 **5 min** **Homework:** *Cuaderno* pp. 73–75 @HomeTutor
DAY 2	**Communication:** describing classes and classroom objects • Warm Up OHT 20 • Check Homework **5 min**	**Vocabulario en contexto** pp. 113–114 • *Telehistoria escena 1* DVD 1 **20 min**	**Vocabulario en contexto** pp. 113–114 • Activities 4, 5 **20 min**	**Assess:** *Para y piensa* p. 114 **5 min** **Homework:** *Cuaderno* pp. 73–75
DAY 3	**Grammar:** using the verb **estar** to talk about location and condition • Warm Up OHT 21 • Check Homework **5 min**	**Presentación de gramática** p. 115 • the verb **estar** **Práctica de gramática** pp. 116–117 • *Nota gramatical:* Asking a question **20 min**	**Práctica de gramática** pp. 116–117 • Activities 6, 7, 8, 9 **20 min**	**Assess:** *Para y piensa* p. 117 **5 min** **Homework:** *Cuaderno* pp. 76–78 @HomeTutor
DAY 4	**Communication:** **estar** to talk about emotions and locations • Warm Up OHT 21 • Check Homework **5 min**	**Gramática en contexto** pp. 118–119 • *Telehistoria escena 2* DVD 1 **15 min**	**Gramática en contexto** pp. 118–119 • Activity 10 TXT CD 2 track 15 • Acts. 11, 12 **25 min**	**Assess:** *Para y piensa* pp. 119 **5 min** **Homework:** *Cuaderno* pp. 76–78 @HomeTutor
DAY 5	**Grammar:** using the verb **ir** to say where you go during and after school • Warm Up OHT 22 • Check Homework **5 min**	**Presentación de gramática** p. 120 • the verb **ir** **Práctica de gramática** pp. 121–122 • *Pronunciación* TXT CD 2 track 17 **Culture:** *El autorretrato* **15 min**	**Práctica de gramática** pp. 121-122 • Activities 13, 15, 16 • Act. 14 TXT CD 2 track 16 • *Pronunciación* TXT CD 2 track 17 **25 min**	**Assess:** *Para y piensa* p. 122 **5 min** **Homework:** *Cuaderno* pp. 79–81 @HomeTutor
DAY 6	**Communication:** Culmination: use **ir** and **estar** • Warm Up OHT 22 • Check Homework **5 min**	**Todo junto** pp. 123–124 • *Escenas 1, 2: Resumen* • *Telehistoria completa* DVD 1 **15 min**	**Todo junto** pp. 123–124 • Activities 17, 18, TXT CD 2 tracks 14, 15, 18 • Activity 20 TXT CD 2 tracks 19, 20 • Activity 19, 21 **25 min**	**Assess:** *Para y piensa* p. 125 **5 min** **Homework:** *Cuaderno* pp. 82–83 @HomeTutor
DAY 7	**Reading:** My favorite class • Warm Up OHT 23 • Check Homework **Review:** Lesson Review • Warm Up OHT 23 **5 min**	**Lectura cultural** pp. 126–127 • *Mi clase favorita* TXT CD 2 track 21 **Proyectos culturales** p. 128 • *Arte de México y la República Dominicana* **Repaso de la lección** pp. 130–131 **20 min**	**Lectura cultural** pp. 126–127 • *Mi clase favorita* **Repaso de la lección** pp. 130–131 • Activity 1 TXT CD 2 track 22 • Activities 2, 3, 4, 5 **20 min**	**Assess:** *Para y piensa* p. 127; *Repaso de la lección* pp. 130–131 **5 min** **Homework:** *En resumen* p. 129 *Cuaderno* pp. 84–95 (optional) Review Games Online @HomeTutor
DAY 8	**Assessment**			**Assess:** Lesson 2 Test or Unit 2 Test **50 min**
DAY 9	**Unit Culmination** **5 min**	**Comparación cultural** pp. 132–133 • TXT CD 2 track 23 • View video DVD 1 **Repaso inclusivo** pp. 134–135 **20 min**	**Comparación cultural** pp. 132–133 **Repaso inclusivo** pp. 134–135 • Act. 1 TXT CD 2 track 24 • Acts. 2, 3, 4, 5, 6, 7 **25 min**	**Homework:** *Cuaderno* pp. 96–98

	Objectives/focus	Teach	Practice	Assess/HW Options
DAY 1	**Vocabulary:** typical school day • Warm Up OHT 20 **5 min**	Lesson Opener pp. 108–109 **Presentación de vocabulario** pp. 110–111 • Read A-D • View video DVD 1 • Play Audio TXT CD 2 track 12 • *¡A responder!* TXT CD 2 track 13 **20 min**	Lesson Opener pp. 108–109 **Práctica de vocabulario** p. 112 • Acts. 1, 2, 3 **20 min**	**Assess:** *Para y piensa* p. 112 **5 min**
	Communication: describing classes and classroom objects **5 min**	**Vocabulario en contexto** pp. 113–114 • *Telehistoria escena 1* DVD 1 **15 min**	**Vocabulario en contexto** pp. 113–-114 • Acts. 4, 5 **15 min**	**Assess:** *Para y piensa* p. 114 **5 min** **Homework:** *Cuaderno* pp. 73–75 @HomeTutor
DAY 2	**Grammar:** Using the verb **estar** to talk about location and condition • Warm Up OHT 21 • Check Homework **5 min**	**Presentación de gramática** p. 115 • the verb **estar** **Práctica de gramática** pp. 116–117 • *Nota gramatical:* Asking a question **20 min**	**Práctica de gramática** pp. 116–117 • Acts. 6, 7, 8, 9 **15 min**	**Assess:** *Para y piensa* p. 117 **5 min**
	Communication: estar to talk about emotions and locations **5 min**	**Gramática en contexto** pp. 118–119 • *Telehistoria escena 2 DVD 1* **20 min**	**Gramática en contexto** pp. 118–119 • Act. 10 TXT CD 2 track 15 • Acts. 11, 12 **15 min**	**Assess:** *Para y piensa* p. 119 **5 min** **Homework:** *Cuaderno* pp. 76–78 @HomeTutor
DAY 3	**Grammar:** Using the verb **ir** to say where you go during and after school • Warm Up OHT 22 • Check Homework **5 min**	**Presentación de gramática** p. 120 • the verb **ir** **Práctica de gramática** pp. 121–122 • *Pronunciación* TXT CD 2 track 17 **Culture:** *El autorretrato* **15 min**	**Práctica de gramática** pp. 121–122 • Act. 13 • Act. 14 TXT CD 2 track 16 • *Pronunciación* TXT CD 2 track 17 • Acts. 15–16 **20 min**	**Assess:** *Para y piensa* p. 122 **5 min**
	Communication: Culmination: • use **ir** and **estar** **5 min**	**Todo junto** pp. 123–124 • *Escenas 1, 2: Resumen Telehistoria completa DVD 1* **10 min**	**Todo junto** pp. 123–124 • Acts. 17, 18, TXT CD 2 tracks 14, 15, 18 • Act. 20 TXT CD 2 tracks 19, 20 • Acts. 19, 21 **25 min**	**Assess:** *Para y piensa* p. 125 **5 min** **Homework:** *Cuaderno* pp. 79–81 @HomeTutor
DAY 4	**Reading:** My favorite class **Projects:** The Art of Mexico and the Dominican Republic • Warm Up OHT 23 • Check Homework **5 min**	**Lectura cultural** pp. 126–127 • *Mi clase favorita TXT CD 2 track 21* **Proyectos culturales** p. 128 • *Arte de México y la República Dominicana* **15 min**	**Lectura cultural** pp. 126–127 • *Mi clase favorita* **15 min**	**Assess:** *Para y piensa* p. 127 **5 min**
	Review: Lesson Review **5 min**	**Repaso de la lección** pp. 130–131 **15 min**	**Repaso de la lección** pp. 130–131 • Activity 1 TXT CD 2 track 22 • Activities 2, 3, 4, 5 **25 min**	**Assess:** *Repaso de la lección* pp. 130–131 **5 min** **Homework:** *En resumen* p. 129, *Cuaderno* pp. 84–95 @HomeTutor
DAY 5	**Assessment**			**Assess:** Lesson 2 Test or Unit 2 test **45 min**
	Unit Culmination **5 min**	**Comparación cultural** pp. 132–133 • TXT CD 2 track 23 • View Video DVD 1 **Repaso inclusivo** pp. 134–135 **10 min**	**Comparación cultural** pp. 132–133 **Repaso inclusivo** pp. 134–135 • Act. 1 TXT CD 2 track 24 • Acts. 2, 3, 4, 5, 6, 7 **30 min**	

¡AVANZA! Objectives

- Introduce lesson theme: **En la escuela.**
- **Culture:** Discuss different school systems in the Spanish-speaking world.

Presentation Strategies

- Introduce characters' names: Pablo and Claudia
- Ask students to look at the photo on pp. 108–109.
- Have students talk about their school and their classes.
- Have students make a list of things in their classroom.

STANDARDS

4.2 Compare cultures

21st Century **Social and Cross-Cultural Skills,** Compara con tu mundo

Warm Up Projectable Transparencies, 2-20

-ar Verbs Write the form of **mirar** for each subject.

1. nosotros	**5.** Juan y Nicolás
2. Carla	**6.** tú
3. yo	**7.** María y yo
4. ustedes	**8.** usted

Answers: 1. miramos; 2. mira; 3. miro; 4. miran; 5. miran; 6. miras; 7. miramos; 8. mira

Comparación cultural

Exploring the Theme

Ask students the following:

1. Are all schools in the United States on the same yearly schedule?
2. School breaks are often set around important holidays. Why do you think schools in Mexico do not have a break at the end of November as we do?
3. Schools south of the equator, such as those in Chile and Argentina, are in session June through August while U.S. students are enjoying summer vacation. Why do you think this is so?

¿Qué ves? Possible answers include:

- Sí, hay una escuela en la foto.
- Pablo dibuja.
- Las chicas son atléticas. Practican el fútbol.

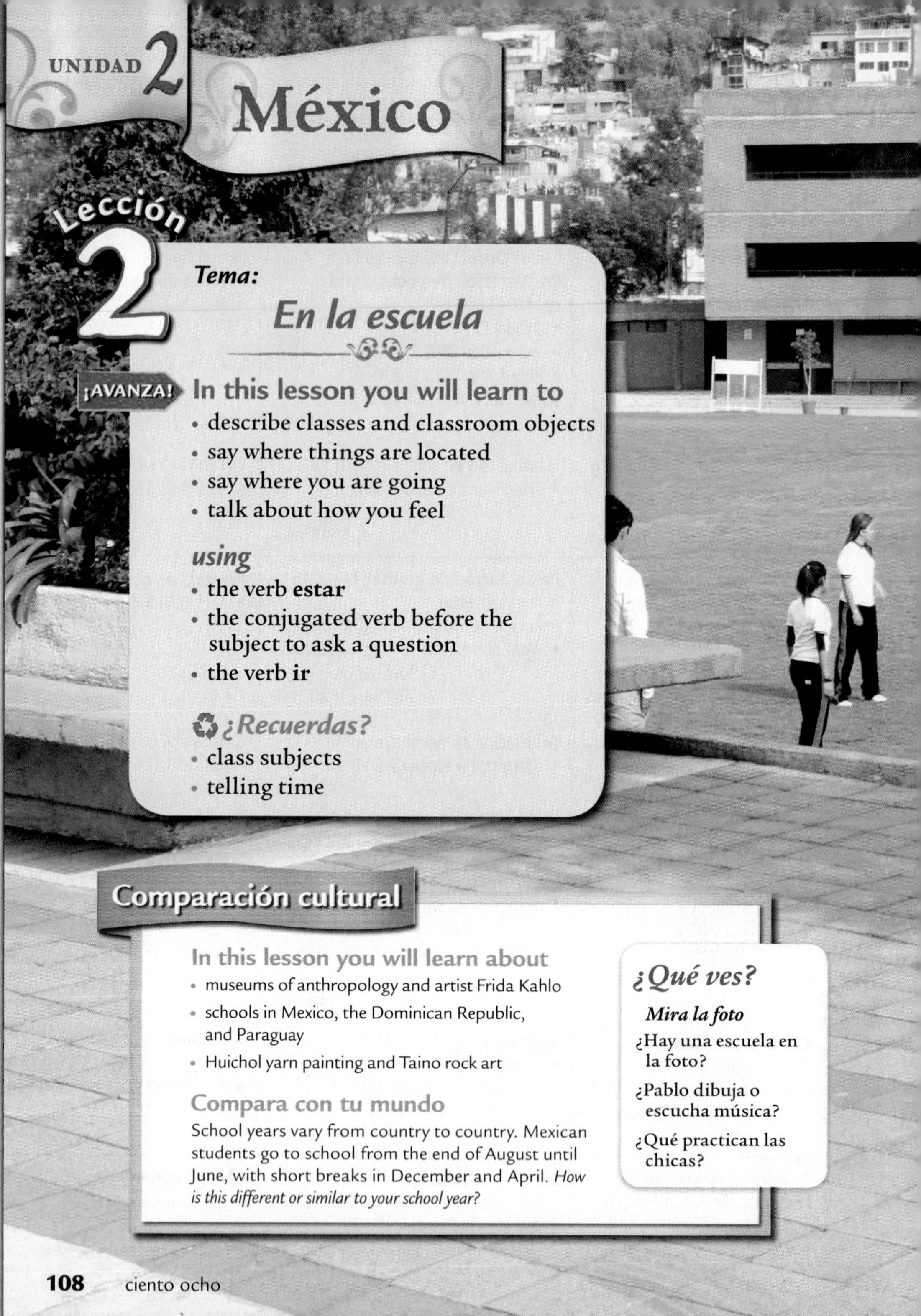

UNIDAD 2 México

Lección 2

Tema:

En la escuela

¡AVANZA! In this lesson you will learn to

- describe classes and classroom objects
- say where things are located
- say where you are going
- talk about how you feel

using

- the verb **estar**
- the conjugated verb before the subject to ask a question
- the verb **ir**

¿Recuerdas?

- class subjects
- telling time

Comparación cultural

In this lesson you will learn about

- museums of anthropology and artist Frida Kahlo
- schools in Mexico, the Dominican Republic, and Paraguay
- Huichol yarn painting and Taino rock art

Compara con tu mundo

School years vary from country to country. Mexican students go to school from the end of August until June, with short breaks in December and April. *How is this different or similar to your school year?*

¿Qué ves?

Mira la foto

¿Hay una escuela en la foto?

¿Pablo dibuja o escucha música?

¿Qué practican las chicas?

Differentiating Instruction

Multiple Intelligences

Visual Learners Have students work in small groups to create a floor plan of their ideal school. What would the school have both outside and inside? As students learn vocabulary related to school items and places, have them label the objects and rooms in their floor plan. Encourage students to use vocabulary from previous lessons where applicable.

Pre-AP

Communicate Preferences Discuss with students the information presented in the Comparación cultural. Which of the school year schedules presented do they prefer and why? Ask them to discuss some of the advantages and disadvantages of different school year models.

El patio de una escuela secundaria
México

DIGITAL SPANISH my.hrw.com
ONLINE STUDENT EDITION with...

performance space
News Networking
@HOMETUTOR
CULTURA Interactiva

- Audio and Video Resources
- Interactive Flashcards
- Review Activities
- WebQuest
- Conjuguemos.com

PRACTICE SPANISH WITH HOLT MCDOUGAL APPS!

Differentiating Instruction

Inclusion

Frequent Review/Repetition Have students create a list of words and phrases they already know that could be applied to the photo on pp. 108 and 109. Some examples might include **estudiantes atléticos, amigos,** or **fútbol.** After students finish, have them compare their lists with a partner and add any new words or phrases.

Slower-Paced Learners

Memory Aids Review the months of the year with students. Then have them create a chart to show the months in which they do and do not have school. Students can design their chart in any way that accurately represents the information.

DIGITAL SPANISH

TEACHER TOOLS
- Interactive Whiteboard Lessons
- Generate Success!

ALSO AVAILABLE...
- Online Workbook
- Spanish InterActive Reader

SPANISH ON THE GO!
- Performance Space
- Holt McDougal Spanish Apps
- ¡Avancemos! eTextbook

Using the Photo

Location Information

The School Yard Recess areas are usually very big in schools not only in Mexico, but also in Latin America.

Expanded Information

Recess In Mexico, recess lasts approximately thirty minutes. During this time students are permitted to buy refreshments, play a quick game of soccer, eat lunch together, or just sit around and relax.

Long-term Retention

Connect to Previous Learning

Read the following list of activities, and have students write **sí** if the activity is taking place in the photo, and **no** if it is not: **tocar la guitarra (no), hablar por teléfono (no), jugar al fútbol (sí), andar en patineta (no), hablar (sí), preparar la comida (no), hacer la tarea (sí), escribir (sí).**

Communication

TPR Activity

To ensure that students recognize words they've learned, play Simon Says by saying: **abran el libro, cierra el libro, levanten la mano,** etc.

¡AVANZA! **Objective**

- Present vocabulary: classroom objects, places in school, and adjectives.

Core Resources

- Video Program: DVD 1
- Audio Program: TXT CD 2, tracks 12, 13

Presentation Strategies

- Point to items in the classroom, say the word, and have students repeat after you.
- Play the audio as students read A–D.
- Show the video.

STANDARDS

1.2 Understand language

Communication

Common Error Alert

If you have told your students that most nouns that end in **-a** are feminine, they may question the word **el mapa.** Explain to them that many Spanish words that are masculine and that end in **-a** are of Latin/Greek origin. Students should learn nouns with the correct article in order to learn the gender of the nouns.

Long-term Retention

Recycle

Review adjectives by having students write the opposite adjective of those below. Caution them to be aware of masculine and feminine forms.

1. cómico
2. mala
3. trabajadora
4. pequeño
5. bajo
6. desorganizada
7. viejo
8. seria
9. alta

Communication

Pair Work

Ask students to create a list of activities. Exchange lists with a partner and have each person tell how he or she feels doing each activity. Introduce the expression **estoy** (*I am*) and remind female students to change the adjective endings to **-a.**

Presentación de VOCABULARIO

¡AVANZA! **Goal:** Learn about Pablo and Claudia's school and how they spend their day. Then practice what you have learned to talk about your school day. ***Actividades 1–3***

VIDEO DVD

AUDIO

A La clase de historia no es **aburrida** porque la maestra es **interesante.** La clase es **divertida** pero es difícil. **Cuando** una clase no es fácil, tengo que trabajar mucho. Necesito sacar buenas notas.

B En la escuela siempre tengo mi **mochila.**

En México se dice...

In Mexico the word for *chalk* is **el gis.**

Más vocabulario

¿(A)dónde? *(To) Where?*
¿Cuándo? *When?*
deprimido(a) *depressed*
emocionado(a) *excited*
ocupado(a) *busy*
el problema *problem*
la puerta *door*
Expansión de vocabulario p. R3

Differentiating Instruction

Heritage Language Learners

Regional Variations Ask students if they use any words different than those that appear on this page, but mean the same thing. For instance, in Argentina a pen is **la lapicera** and in Venezuela and Perú is **el lapicero.** A student's desk in Venezuela and Argentina is referred to as **el pupitre**. Remind students that many words are said differently in some countries, but they all have the same meaning.

Slower-paced Learners

Yes/No Questions Assess students' understanding of new vocabulary by walking around the room pointing at classroom items and asking **Sí/No** questions. For example: **¿Es un escritorio? Sí, es un escritorio. ¿Es el pizarrón? No, no es el pizarrón.** Put labels on classroom items to increase retention.

C Mi escuela es grande. Hay **una cafetería**, **un gimnasio** y **una biblioteca**.

la cafetería

el gimnasio

la biblioteca

el pasillo

los baños

la oficina del director

D Me gusta **pasar un rato** con Claudia en la biblioteca. Claudia **usa la computadora** pero yo **tengo que estudiar**.

cansado(a)

nervioso(a)

contento(a)

tranquilo(a)

enojado(a)

triste

@HOMETUTOR my.hrw.com Interactive Flashcards

¡A responder! Escuchar

Escucha la lista de adjetivos. Dibuja una cara para cada uno. *(Listen to the list of adjectives and draw a face representing each one.)*

TEACHER to TEACHER

Jorge Dominguez
Valley Stream, New York

Tips for Presenting Vocabulary

To present classroom vocabulary, I prepare in advance a transparency of two classrooms (labeled A and B) that are similar except for five or six details. I call on students to identify the objects that are similar and different in both pictures. For example: En el dibujo A y en el dibujo B hay un mapa. En el dibujo A hay dos ventanas, pero en el dibujo B hay una ventana. *These pictures can also be used later to practice prepositions of location. For example:* En el dibujo A el mapa está al lado de la ventana, pero en el dibujo B el mapa está debajo del reloj.

Go online for more tips!

Communication
TPR Activity

Write the names of different areas of your school (in English) on construction paper and place them around your classroom. Include places such as the hallway, the principal's office, the library, the cafeteria, the restrooms, and the gymnasium. Go to each sign and say the name of each area in Spanish. Have students go to each place as you give the command in Spanish. Explain that **ve** means **go.** For example: **Cindy, ve al gimnasio. Jason, ve a la cafetería,** etc. Choose a different group and make the sentences more difficult. For example: **Rolanda, ve a la biblioteca para leer un libro. Matt, ve al gimnasio para la clase de educación física.**

Long-term Retention
Study Tips

Have students prepare index cards with a picture of a school item on one side and the corresponding vocabulary word on the reverse side. Students can use the flash cards to test one another.

Answers Projectable Transparencies, 2-28

¡A responder! Audio Script, TE p. 107b
Students will draw faces representing the following adjectives:

1. angry
2. nervous
3. tired
4. happy
5. depressed
6. excited
7. calm

Differentiating Instruction

Inclusion

Multisensory Input/Output Collect examples of the school supplies shown on p. 110. Pass the items out to students, and then ask questions regarding who has what. Instruct students to hold their item up as they answer. **¿Quién tiene la pluma? Yo tengo la pluma.** After a few rounds, have students switch items. Then allow students to ask, as well as answer, the questions.

Multiple Intelligences

Kinesthetic Copy the names of rooms and emotion words onto index cards. Then invite a volunteer to choose one card to act out for the group. If it is a room in the school, the student might show the actions that people do there. If it is an emotion, the student can use facial expressions and gestures. The rest of the group must guess the word being portrayed.

Objective
- Practice vocabulary: classroom objects and places in school.

Core Resource
- *Cuaderno,* pp. 73–75

Practice Sequence
- **Activity 1:** Vocabulary recognition: classroom objects
- **Activity 2:** Vocabulary recognition: places in school
- **Activity 3:** Vocabulary production: classroom objects

STANDARDS
1.1 Engage in conversation

Communication
Common Error Alert
Before doing Activity 1, remind students that the plural of **lápiz** is **lápices.** Explain that the word **por** is used here to express how much for something: **5 plumas por 30 pesos.**

Ongoing Assessment
Get Help Online
More Practice
my.hrw.com

PARA Y PIENSA **Peer Assessment** Have students share their answers with a partner without looking at the textbook. Partners will listen to see if they can understand. They will then reverse roles. For additional practice, use Reteaching & Practice Copymasters URB 2, pp. 11, 12.

Answers Projectable Transparencies, 2-28

Activity 1
los lápices; la calculadora; los cuadernos; los borradores; la mochila; las plumas

Activity 2

1. baños	**4.** cafetería
2. gimnasio	**5.** oficina del director
3. biblioteca	**6.** clase

Activity 3 Answers will vary. Answers should follow format:
A ¿Cuántos/Cuántas... hay en la clase? B Hay... en la clase.

Para y piensa Answers will vary. Sample answers include:
1. la cafetería, la oficina del director, la clase
2. el escritorio, el lápiz, el cuaderno

Práctica de VOCABULARIO

1 Para la escuela

Hablar Escribir

¿Qué tienen en la Tienda Martínez? Nombra las cosas. *(Name the items at Tienda Martínez.)*

Expansión: Teacher Edition Only
Have students list other items with their prices, that could be sold in Tienda Martínez.

2 ¿Qué lugar es?

Leer Escribir

Claudia habla de varios lugares en la escuela. Completa las oraciones con la palabra apropiada. *(Complete the sentences with the appropriate place word.)*

biblioteca	cafetería
gimnasio	baños
oficina del director	clase

En el gimnasio hay dos __1.__ , uno para chicas y uno para chicos. Tenemos que correr y practicar deportes en el __2.__ . Hay muchos libros en la __3.__ . Nos gusta comer pizza y pasar un rato con los amigos en la __4.__ . Hablamos con el director en la __5.__ . Hay escritorios y pizarrones en la __6.__ .

Expansión: Teacher Edition Only
Have students pick a place word and write an additional sentence for it.

3 ¿Cuántos hay en la clase?

Hablar

Habla con otro(a) estudiante sobre lo que hay en la clase. *(Talk with another student about objects in the classroom.)*

pizarrón	puerta	tiza
mapa	escritorio	¿ ?
ventana	reloj	

modelo: mapa

A ¿Cuántos mapas hay en la clase?

B Hay tres mapas en la clase.

Expansión
Tell what objects aren't in your room.

Más práctica Cuaderno *pp. 73–75* Cuaderno para hispanohablantes *pp. 73–76*

Get Help Online
my.hrw.com

PARA Y PIENSA
Did you get it?
1. Name three rooms in your school.
2. Name three objects you could find in your classroom.

Differentiating Instruction

Multiple Intelligences
Logical/Mathematical For Activity 1, assign students the roles of client and sales clerk at Tienda Martínez. The client asks for several of each item and the sales clerk tells how much the total cost is. Provide students with the following sample dialogue: **Necesito seis lápices./18 pesos, por favor.**

Heritage Language Learners
Writing Skills Have students write a paragraph about a particular class and classroom in as much detail as possible. They should include the time the class takes place, the subject, the items found in the classroom, the number of students, what the class is like, what the teacher is like, and why they like or don't like that class. Make sure they use correct spelling, grammar, and punctuation.

VOCABULARIO en contexto

¡AVANZA! **Goal:** Identify the words Pablo and Claudia use to talk about what they do after school. Then use the words you have learned to describe classes and classroom objects. ***Actividades 4–5***

¿Recuerdas? Class subjects p. 86

Telehistoria escena 1

@HOMETUTOR my.hrw.com View, Read and Record

STRATEGIES

Cuando lees
Look for exclamations Many sentences below are exclamations. Exclamations reveal emphasis, warning, or emotions. How many exclamation-type sentences can you find? Why is each one used?

Cuando escuchas
Listen for emotions What different emotions do Claudia and Pablo show? How do they express them? How would you feel in their place?

VIDEO DVD

AUDIO

A poster announces Trini Salgado's guest appearance in the school gym.

Maestro: Trini Salgado, ¿eh? ¿Y vas tú al gimnasio?

Pablo: ¡Sí!

Maestro: ¡Muy divertido! *(later on in science class...)* ¿Quién contesta la pregunta? ¿Pablo? Bueno, ¡al pizarrón!

Pablo tries, but gets the problem wrong. Claudia goes to the board and corrects it. The bell rings and they leave class together.

Claudia: Pablo, ¿vamos a la biblioteca? Estudiamos, hacemos la tarea y llegamos bien al gimnasio... ¡Trini Salgado, Pablo!

Pablo: ¡Sí! Necesito estudiar, ¡y tú enseñas muy bien! ¿Y tu mochila? *(He points to her backpack, which she has left in the classroom.)*

Claudia: ¡Gracias, Pablo!

Continuará... p. 118

También se dice

México The teacher uses the word **pizarrón** to call Pablo to the board. In other Spanish-speaking countries you might hear:
- **muchos países** **la pizarra**

Differentiating Instruction

Slower-paced Learners

Read Before Listening Before listening to the Telehistoria, have students preview the text silently. Instruct them to copy any unfamiliar words onto a separate piece of paper. Then have them refer to pp. 110 and 111 to review the meanings of the words on their list.

Heritage Language Learners

Writing Skills Have students draft their own versions of a short conversation between a teacher and two friends at school. Point out to students the punctuation that is used in the Telehistoria to indicate exclamations and questions. Advise students to proofread their own scripts for correct punctuation.

¡AVANZA! Objective

- Understand vocabulary in context: classroom objects and places in school.

Core Resources

- Video Program: DVD 1
- Audio Program: TXT CD 2, track 14

Presentation Strategies

- Have students skim the Telehistoria and identify uses of exclamation signs in Spanish.
- Show the video with books open, then with books closed.
- Play audio while students follow the script in the text.

STANDARDS

1.2 Understand language

Warm Up

Projectable Transparencies, 2-20

Vocabulary Complete the sentences with a correct word from the list below.

biblioteca tiza mochila aburrida cafetería

1. Necesito una ____ para escribir en el pizarrón.
2. No me gusta comer en la ____.
3. Hay muchos libros en la ____.
4. La clase de historia no es divertida, es ____.
5. Tengo tres cuadernos en mi ____.

Answers: 1. tiza; 2. cafetería; 3. biblioteca; 4. aburrida; 5. mochila

Communication

Pair Work

Have pairs of students take turns making statements and answering with the name of the person from the Telehistoria to which the statement applies. For example: **¡al pizarrón!/ Maestro.**

Video Summary

@HOMETUTOR VideoPlus my.hrw.com

Pablo and Claudia plan to go to the school's gym to see Trini Salgado. In science class, the teacher sends Pablo to the board to solve a problem, but he gets it wrong. After class, Claudia suggests that they go to the library to study and do homework. Pablo agrees. He notices that she doesn't have her backpack.

Objectives
- Practice using vocabulary in context.
- Recycle: class subjects.

Core Resource
- Audio Program: TXT CD 2 track 14

Practice Sequence
- **Activity 4:** Telehistoria comprehension
- **Activity 5:** Vocabulary production: descriptive adjectives; Recycle: class subjects

STANDARDS
1.1 Engage conversation
1.2 Understand language

Long-term Retention
Personalize It
Ask students to write sentences describing the classroom using numbers or prepositions of location. For example, their sentences may be: **Hay un mapa al lado de la puerta. Hay un pizarrón cerca de la ventana. Hay veinticinco escritorios.**

Get Help Online
More Practice
my.hrw.com

✓ Ongoing Assessment
PARA Y PIENSA **Quick Check** Ask students to write other activities that can be done in the library and the gym. For additonal practice, use Reteaching & Practice Copymasters URB 2, pp. 11, 13, 20.

Communication
Motivating with Music
The **¡AvanzaRap!** song for this unit targets school supplies and classes. To reinforce these concepts, play the **¡AvanzaRap!** animated video for students and have them complete the Activity Master. Activity masters and teaching suggestions can be found on the **¡AvanzaRap! DVD.**

Answers Projectable Transparencies, 2-28
Activity 4
1. e; **2.** a; **3.** d; **4.** c; **5.** b; **6.** f
Activity 5 Answers should follow this format:
A. ¿Cómo es la clase de + class?
B. Es + descriptive adjectives.
Para y piensa
1. la biblioteca; **2.** el gimnasio; **3.** la biblioteca

4 *Comprensión del episodio* En clase
Escuchar
Leer

Describe lo que pasa en el episodio. Empareja frases de cada columna.
(Describe what happens in the episode by matching phrases from each column.)

1. Pablo no contesta la pregunta	**a.** la pregunta en el pizarrón.
2. Después de Pablo, Claudia contesta	**b.** la mochila.
3. Pablo y Claudia necesitan ir	**c.** estudiar con Claudia.
4. Pablo necesita	**d.** a la biblioteca y al gimnasio.
5. Claudia no tiene	**e.** porque el problema es difícil.
6. Claudia enseña	**f.** muy bien.

Expansión:
Teacher Edition Onl
Have students take turns reading aloud the complete sentences they formed.

5 ¿Cómo son las clases? *¿Recuerdas?* Class subjects p. 86
Hablar

Describe las clases a otro(a) estudiante. *(Describe your classes to another student.)*

A ¿Cómo es la clase de español?
B Es divertida y fácil.

1. 
2. 
3. 
4. 
5. 
6. 

Expansión
Give reasons for two of your descriptions.

Get Help Online
my.hrw.com

PARA Y PIENSA **Did you get it?** Tell where Pablo and Claudia are going by writing **la biblioteca** or **el gimnasio.**
1. Pablo y Claudia tienen que estudiar.
2. Pablo necesita practicar fútbol.
3. Ellos necesitan un libro.

Differentiating Instruction

Slower-paced Learners
Sentence Completion Before students attempt Activity 5, write the following sentence on the board. **La clase de _____ es _____.** Ask students to list as many possibilities as they can for each of the blanks. Record these words underneath each blank. Then have students use this information as they converse during Activity 5.

Pre-AP
Expand and Elaborate As students talk about their classes in Activity 5, encourage them to follow up each statement with an explanation to support their statement. **La clase de ciencias es difícil. Tenemos muchos exámenes. Muchos estudiantes sacan malas notas.**

Presentación de GRAMÁTICA

¡AVANZA! **Goal:** Learn to use the verb **estar** to talk about location and condition. Then practice using **estar** to say and ask where things are located and how people feel. *Actividades 6–9*

English Grammar Connection: There are two ways to say the English verb *to be* in Spanish: **ser** and **estar.** You already learned **ser** (see p. 37).

The Verb estar

ANIMATEDGRAMMAR my.hrw.com

Use **estar** to indicate location and say how people feel.

Here's how:

estar *to be*			
yo	**estoy**	nosotros(as)	**estamos**
tú	**estás**	vosotros(as)	**estáis**
usted, él, ella	**está**	ustedes, ellos(as)	**están**

Pedro **está** en la cafetería. *Pedro **is** in the cafeteria.*

Use **estar** with the following words of location.

al lado (de)	**debajo (de)**	**dentro (de)**	**encima (de)**
cerca (de)	**delante (de)**	**detrás (de)**	**lejos (de)**

Use the word **de** after the location word when a specific location is mentioned. When **de** is followed by the word **el,** they combine to form the contraction **del.**

La biblioteca **está al lado de la** cafetería.
*The library **is next to the** cafeteria.*

La tiza **está encima del** borrador.
*The chalk **is on top of the** eraser.*

Estar is also used with **adjectives** to say how someone feels at a given moment.

El maestro **está tranquilo.**
*The teacher **is** calm.*

Las chicas **están cansadas.**
*The girls **are** tired.*

¿Recuerdas? Adjectives agree in gender and number with the nouns they describe (see p. 66).

Más práctica
Cuaderno *pp. 76–78*
Cuaderno para hispanohablantes *pp. 77–79*

@HOMETUTOR my.hrw.com
Leveled Practice
Conjuguemos.com

Differentiating Instruction

Inclusion

Metacognitive Support Write the following sentences on the board. You can add additional examples as well. **Claudia _____ de Argentina. Pablo _____ nervioso. La clase _____ fácil. Mi pluma _____ en mi mochila.** Then ask students to identify whether each sentence calls for the verb **ser** or the verb **estar,** and to explain why.

Multiple Intelligences

Kinesthetic Help students practice words of location by playing this game. Each student will need a pen. Place a pen on top of a desk, and ask **¿Dónde está la pluma?** Have students copy your action as they respond: **La pluma está encima del escritorio.** Change the relationship of the pen to the desk each time you ask the question.

¡AVANZA! **Objective**
- Present the uses of the verb **estar.**

Core Resource
- *Cuaderno,* pp. 76–78

Presentation Strategies
- Explain the different uses of the verb **estar.**
- Remind students that in Spanish adjectives need to agree in gender and number with the nouns they describe.

STANDARDS
1.2 Understand language
4.1 Compare languages

Warm Up Projectable Transparencies, 2-21

Vocabulary Write the location where each activity would take place:
1. practicar deportes
2. comer pizza y hablar con amigos
3. hablar con el director de la escuela
4. hacer la tarea o leer un libro

Answers: 1. el gimnasio; 2. la cafetería; 3. la oficina del director; 4. la biblioteca

Communication
Common Error Alert

The inclusion of the accent mark over the **a** in **estás, está,** and **están** is very important. The accent marks change the pronunciation of the words but in the case of **estás** and **está,** they also change the meaning. **Estas** means *these* and **esta** means *this.*

Comparisons
English Grammar Connection

Remind students that there are words that combine to form contractions in English; for example, *is* + *not* → *isn't.* English contractions use apostrophes.

Communication
Common Error Alert

Point out that **estar** is conjugated like other **-ar** verbs except for the **yo** form (**estoy**) and the accents on some of the other forms.

¡AVANZA! Objectives

- Practice using **estar.**
- **Culture:** artifacts and their impact on culture.
- Practice using adjectives to describe feelings.
- Practice using prepositions of place and vocabulary.

Core Resource

- *Cuaderno,* pp. 76–78

Practice Sequence

- **Activity 6:** Controlled practice: **estar**
- **Activity 7:** Open-ended practice: prepositions of place
- **Activity 8:** Open-ended practice: feelings using (descriptive) adjectives
- **Activity 9:** Open-ended practice: classroom objects and prepositions

STANDARDS

1.1 Engage in conversation
1.2 Understand language

Comparación cultural

Essential Question

Suggested Answer Ancient artifacts offer clues about earlier cultures. Often artifacts show whether a society was agrarian-based or depended on hunting for survival. Artifacts can also show how people constructed their homes and measured time.

Background Information

The **Piedra del Sol** has a diameter of just under 12 feet and a thickness of 3 feet. It was carved in 1479, during the reign of the sixth Aztec monarch, and was discovered in 1760, buried under the Zócalo of Mexico City. It was placed in the metropolitan cathedral until 1885, when it was moved to the National Museum of Anthropology.

Answers Projectable Transparencies, 2-28

Activity 6

1. Ustedes están en el gimnasio.
2. Yo estoy en la clase de ciencias.
3. Miguel y Alejo están en el pasillo.
4. Sergio está en el baño.
5. Claudia y yo estamos en la biblioteca.
6. Cristina y Sarita están en la cafetería.

Answers continue on p. 117.

Práctica de GRAMÁTICA

6 ¿Dónde están?

Hablar
Escribir

Di dónde están las personas según Pablo. *(Tell where people are, according to Pablo.)*

modelo: el señor Díaz
El señor Díaz está en la oficina.

1. ustedes

2. yo

3. Miguel y Alejo

4. Sergio

5. Claudia y yo

6. Cristina y Sarita

Expansión
Choose two places and name something you would find in each.

7 Las salas del museo

Hablar

Comparación cultural

El museo de antropología

What do ancient artifacts teach us about a culture? The National Museum of Anthropology in Mexico City contains artifacts from **Mexico's** many indigenous cultures. A main attraction is the *Piedra del Sol,* or Sun Stone, an Aztec calendar that weighs almost 25 tons. In **Paraguay,** the Andrés Barbero Museum of Ethnography in Asunción contains tools, musical instruments, and artwork from its indigenous cultures.

Piedra del Sol

Un plano de El Museo Nacional de Antropología en la Ciudad de México

Compara con tu mundo *What items might people find 1,000 years from now that give clues about life in the 21st century?*

Usa el plano para decirle a otro(a) estudiante dónde están las salas del museo. *(Tell your partner where the rooms are located in the museum.)*

A ¿Dónde está la Sala Tolteca?

B La Sala Tolteca está al lado de la Sala Teotihuacán.

Expansión:
Teacher Editio[n]
Only
Have student[s]
write sentenc[es]
using a subje[ct]
a form of est[ar]
and a room i[n]
the museum.

Differentiating Instruction

Pre-AP

Expand and Elaborate Encourage students to elaborate on their sentences in Activity 6. After expressing where each person is, have students describe that person's personality, activity or emotion. **El señor Díaz está en la oficina. Es trabajador.**

Heritage Language Learners

Literacy Skills Brainstorm with students a list of things they would be interested in learning about an ancient culture. Some topics might include food, clothing, tools, and music. Then have students choose one ancient culture to research, such as the Aztec or Maya. Give them the opportunity to report to the group what they learned about each topic.

Nota gramatical

You already know that you can use rising intonation to ask a yes/no question. You can also switch the position of the **verb** and the **subject** to form a question.

María tiene una patineta. *María has a skateboard.*	¿**Tiene María** una patineta? *Does María have a skateboard?*

8 Las emociones

Hablar

Habla con otro(a) estudiante de cómo están estas personas. *(Talk with another student about how these people are feeling.)*

modelo: el maestro / nervioso
el maestro 🙂

A: ¿Está nervioso el maestro?
B: No, está tranquilo.

Estudiante A	Estudiante B
1. Pablo / tranquilo	Pablo
2. Claudia / triste	Claudia
3. los maestros / cansado	los maestros
4. los amigos / enojado	los amigos
5. las amigas / emocionado	las amigas
6. tú / ocupado	yo ¿ ?

Expansión: Teacher Edition Only
Have students come up with two additional questions and answers about people they know.

9 ¿Qué es?

Hablar

Dale pistas a otro(a) estudiante sobre un objeto del dibujo. Él o ella tiene que adivinar el objeto. *(Give clues to another student. He or she has to guess the object.)*

A: Está encima del cuaderno. Está al lado del libro.
B: Es la calculadora.

Expansión
Give clues to your partner about objects that are in your classroom.

Más práctica Cuaderno *pp. 76–78* Cuaderno para hispanohablantes *pp. 77–79*

Get Help Online my.hrw.com

PARA Y PIENSA

Did you get it? 1. Tell someone that you are near the windows.
2. Ask Pablo if he is nervous.

Nota gramatical

Expanded Presentation When inverting the subject and verb to form a question, the subject may come immediately after the verb or at the end of the question. This is especially true when the subject contains more than one word. For example: **¿Tiene una mochila la chica pelirroja?** *Does the red-haired girl have a backpack?*

Comparison
English Language Connection

English speakers add words like *do* and *does* when asking questions. Spanish speakers do not. For example: *Does Juana have a pencil?* **¿Tiene Juana un lápiz?**

Get Help Online
More Practice
my.hrw.com

✓ Ongoing Assessment

PARA Y PIENSA **Peer Assessment** Ask students to write the answers to Para y piensa, exchange them with a partner, and check each other's work. For additional practice, use Reteaching & Practice Copymasters URB 2, pp. 14, 15.

Answers Projectable Transparencies, 2-28 and 2-29

Answers continued from p. 116.

Activity 7 Answers should follow this format:
¿Dónde está + room?
La/El + room + está + location + room.

Activity 8
1. ¿Está tranquilo Pablo? No, está nervioso.
2. ¿Está triste Claudia? Sí, está triste.
3. ¿Están cansados los maestros? Sí, están cansados.
4. ¿Están enojados los amigos? Sí, están enojados.
5. ¿Están emocionadas las amigas? No, están tristes.
6. ¿Estás ocupado(a) tú? Sí, yo estoy ocupado(a) or No, yo estoy (will vary).

Activity 9 Answers will vary. Sample answers include:
Está detrás del escritorio. Está detrás de la silla. Es el pizarrón.

Para y piensa
1. Estoy cerca de las ventanas.
2. Pablo, ¿estás nervioso?

Differentiating Instruction

Inclusion

Synthetic/Analytic Support Write the following words on index cards: **Pablo, está,** and **contento.** Discuss with students which of these words is a noun, verb, and adjective. Then color-code the cards by shading each with a different colored highlighter. Display the cards in the order to form a question. **¿Está contento Pablo?** Then ask for a volunteer to come change the order to create an answer. Repeat with other examples.

Multiple Intelligences

Intrapersonal Provide students with the following situations:
- **Cuando saco una mala nota...**
- **Cuando tengo un examen...**
- **Cuando paso un rato con los amigos...**

You can add additional examples as well. Ask students to reflect on how they feel in each of the situations presented. Students might record their responses in their journals.

GRAMÁTICA en contexto

¡AVANZA! **Goal:** Listen to how Pablo and Claudia use **estar** to talk about how Pablo feels. Then practice using **estar** to talk about emotions and locations. *Actividades 10–12*

Telehistoria escena 2

HOMETUTOR my.hrw.com View, Read and Record

STRATEGIES

Cuando lees
Read for motives behind actions This scene contains a physical action related to Pablo's complaints. What is the action, and what are his complaints? Are his complaints justified?

Cuando escuchas
Listen for feelings What feelings are mentioned in this scene? How does Pablo explain how he feels? Have you ever felt this way?

VIDEO DVD

AUDIO

Claudia: Eh, Pablo, ¿qué pasa? ¿Estás deprimido? ¿Estás enojado?

Pablo: No, no estoy enojado... Estoy nervioso... Tengo que estar en el gimnasio a las cinco pero tengo que hacer la tarea.

Pablo leaves the library. Later Claudia joins him outside.

Pablo: Ay, Claudia, nunca descanso... Me gusta pasar un rato con los amigos... Y ¡esta mochila!

Claudia: ¿Qué pasa?

Pablo starts swinging his backpack back and forth.

Pablo: Aquí tengo libros, cuadernos, plumas, calculadoras... ¡estoy cansado!

Suddenly Pablo lets go of his backpack.

Pablo: ¡Ay! ¿Dónde está mi mochila?

Claudia: ¡Pablo, tu mochila!

She points to his backpack, which is caught in a basketball hoop.

Continuará... p. 123

También se dice

México To say he has pens in his backpack, Pablo uses the word **plumas.** In other Spanish-speaking countries you might hear:
- **muchos países** el bolígrafo, el boli

¡AVANZA! Objective

- Practice **estar** in context.

Core Resources

- Video Program: DVD 1
- Audio Program: TXT CD 2, track 15

Presentation Strategies

- Ask students to describe the photo by asking quick comprehension questions.
- Have students read the script.
- Show the video and/or play the audio.

Practice Sequence

- **Activity 10:** Telehistoria comprehension
- **Activity 11:** Transitional practice: **estar** and emotions
- **Activity 12:** Open-ended practice: **estar** and places in school

STANDARDS

1.1 Engage in conversation
1.2 Understand language
21st Century **Communication,** Act. 11: Expansión/Heritage Language Learners

Warm Up Projectable Transparencies, 2-21

Estar and Words of Location Use the given pronoun and the location to write sentences with the correct form of the verb **estar:**

1. yo/biblioteca
2. tú/cafetería
3. nosotros/pasillo
4. él/cerca de la ventana.

Answers: 1. Estoy en la biblioteca; 2. Estás en la cafetería; 3. Estamos en el pasillo; 4. Él está cerca de la ventana.

Video Summary

HOMETUTOR VideoPlus my.hrw.com

Claudia asks Pablo if he is depressed or angry. He tells her he is nervous because he has to be at the gym at 5:00, but he also has to do homework. Later, Pablo complains that he never rests. He points out that his backpack is full of school supplies and begins to swing it back and forth. Pablo loses his grip on the backpack and it gets caught in a basketball net.

Differentiating Instruction

Multiple Intelligences

Interpersonal Divide students into two groups. Assign one group the role of Claudia, and the other the role of Pablo. Have the groups read their assigned parts chorally. As they do, instruct students to exaggerate the emotions and facial expressions of their character. Then have groups switch roles.

Slower-paced Learners

Read Before Listening Direct students to preview the Telehistoria silently. Tell them their goal is to locate all of the emotion words used in the conversation. Have students copy these words onto a separate piece of paper. Then ask them to draw a face to represent the emotion of each word in their list.

10 *Comprensión del episodio* El problema de Pablo

Escuchar Leer

Lee las oraciones y decide si son ciertas o falsas. Si son falsas, corrígelas. *(Decide if these sentences are true or false. Correct the false statements.)*

1. Claudia y Pablo están en la oficina.
2. Pablo está nervioso porque tiene que jugar al fútbol.
3. Claudia tiene que estar en el gimnasio a las cinco.
4. Pablo está enojado.
5. A Claudia y a Pablo les gusta pasar un rato con los amigos.
6. Pablo está deprimido porque tiene libros, cuadernos, plumas y calculadoras en la mochila.

Expansión: Teacher Edition Only
Have students expand the activity by asking each other about other emotions.

11 ¿Cuándo?

Hablar

Pregúntale a otro(a) estudiante cuándo tiene estas emociones. *(Ask another student when he or she feels these emotions.)*

A: ¿Cuándo estás triste?

B: Estoy triste cuando saco una mala nota.

Estudiante A

1. 2. 3. 4. 5. 6.

Estudiante B

sacar una buena / mala nota
escuchar música
practicar deportes
trabajar
estudiar
¿ ?

Expansión: Teacher Edition Only
Have students talk about their family's emotions when they get good grades and when they don't.

12 ¡A jugar! ¿Dónde estoy?

Hablar

Estás en varios lugares de la escuela. Da pistas y los otros estudiantes van a adivinar dónde estás. *(You are in various parts of the school. Give clues for other students to guess where you are.)*

A: Compro papas fritas y jugo. Paso un rato con los amigos. Estoy tranquilo.

B: ¿Estás en la cafetería?

Expansión
Describe where these places are located.

Get Help Online my.hrw.com

PARA Y PIENSA

Did you get it? Give three sentences about Pablo and Claudia using the verb **estar.** Use one of the following words in each sentence: **la biblioteca, nervioso(a), el gimnasio.**

Differentiating Instruction

Multiple Intelligences

Visual Learners Have students come up with additional emoticons. They can illustrate them and use a dictionary to help them translate the emotion into Spanish.

Heritage Language Learners

Support What They Know After students complete Activity 11, ask them to think about a specific time when they felt one of the emotions listed. Encourage students to share an anecdote about a time they felt sad, nervous, or angry. What was the situation, and why did it make them feel that way?

Communication

Interpersonal Mode

Play a simple memory game with each row of students by conjugating the verb **estar** + adjective of emotion. The first student in the row begins by saying, for example, **Estoy emocionado**. The second student says, **Él/Ella está emocionado(a)**. The third student could say **Ustedes están emocionados**, the next one would say **Nosotros estamos emocionados** and they continue until the present tense of the verb has been conjugated.

✓ Ongoing Assessment

Get Help Online More Practice my.hrw.com

PARA Y PIENSA **Peer Assessment** Allow students to work in pairs to correct each statement. For additional practice, use Reteaching & Practice Copymasters URB 2, pp. 14, 19.

Answers Projectable Transparencies, 2-29

Activity 10
1. Falsa: Pablo y Claudia están en la escuela.
2. Falsa: Pablo está nervioso porque tiene que estar en el gimnasio a las cinco pero tiene que hacer la tarea.
3. Falsa: Pablo tiene que estar en el gimnasio a las cinco.
4. Falsa: Pablo está nervioso.
5. Falsa: A Pablo le gusta pasar un rato con los amigos
6. Falsa: Pablo está cansado porque tiene libros, cuadernos, plumas y calculadoras en la mochila.

Activity 11 Answers should follow this format:
A. ¿Cuándo estás + emotion?
B. Estoy + emotion + cuando + reason.

Activity 12 Answers will vary. Sample answers include:
A. Estudio mucho. No hablo.
B. ¿Estás en la biblioteca?

Para y piensa Answers will vary. Sample answers include:
Pablo y Claudia están en la biblioteca.
Pablo está nervioso.
Pablo tiene que estar en el gimnasio a las cinco.

¡AVANZA! Objective

- Present the verb **ir.**

Core Resource

- *Cuaderno,* pp. 79–81

Presentation Strategies

- Practice using **ir** by conjugating the verb as a class.
- Explain to students the use of the words **a** and **adónde** to say or ask where someone is going.

STANDARDS

1.2 Understand language
4.1 Compare languages

Warm Up Projectable Transparencies, 2-22

Adjectives Look at the following emoticons below. Then write the corresponding emotion for each.

1. ☹
2. 😠
3. ☺
4. 😌

Answers: 1. triste; 2. enojado; 3. contento; 4. tranquilo

Comparisons

English Grammar Connection

Forms of **ir** can be translated as **go** or *am/is/are going,* depending upon the context of the conversation. Although **ir** looks nothing like **–ar** verbs, its forms are very similar. A helpful memorization technique is to learn the **yo** form—**voy**—and, for the rest of the forms, use the letter ***v*** + the regular **–ar** endings, except for the **vosotros** form, which has no accent.

Communication

Common Error Alert

In English, it is common to hear prepositions used at the end of questions and answers. *Where are you going to?* is very frequently heard. Spanish avoids this by combining the preposition **a** with **dónde** to create the word **adónde. Dónde** is used to ask where someone or something is; **adónde** is used to ask to where someone is going.

Presentación de GRAMÁTICA

¡AVANZA! **Goal:** Learn how to form the verb **ir** in order to say where you and others are going. Then practice using **ir** to say where you go during and after school. ***Actividades 13–16***

English Grammar Connection: Remember that **conjugating** is changing the forms of a verb to indicate who is doing the action (see p. 91). In English, *to go* is conjugated as *I go, you go, he/she/it goes, we go, they go.*

Pablo **goes** to the cafeteria at twelve. ↑ **conjugated verb**

Pablo **va** a la cafetería a las doce. ↑ **conjugated verb**

The Verb ir

ANIMATEDGRAMMAR my.hrw.com

Use **ir** to talk about where someone is going.
How do you form the present tense of this verb?

Here's how:

ir *to go*			
yo	**voy**	nosotros(as)	**vamos**
tú	**vas**	vosotros(as)	**vais**
usted, él, ella	**va**	ustedes, ellos(as)	**van**

Use **ir** with the word **a** to say that someone is going to a specific place.
When **a** is followed by the word **el,** they combine to form the contraction **al.**

Voy a la biblioteca.
***I'm going to the** library.*

Los estudiantes **van al** gimnasio.
*The students **are going to the** gym.*

To ask where someone is going, use **¿adónde...?**

¿Adónde vas?
*Where **are you going?***

Más práctica
Cuaderno *pp. 79–81*
Cuaderno para hispanohablantes *pp. 80–83*

@HOMETUTOR my.hrw.com
Leveled Practice
Conjuguemos.com

Differentiating Instruction

Slower-paced Learners

Memory Aids Have students copy the forms of the verb **ir** onto an index card. Instruct them to write a capital *I* in the upper right-hand corner of the card to indicate that **ir** is an *irregular* verb. Then have students add this card to their collection of verb cards. Have them add an *I* for irregular, or *R* for regular to each verb card they have already created.

Pre-AP

Timed Answer Have pairs of students take turns reciting the conjugated verb forms as the partners call out the different subject pronouns. Partners can time themselves to see who can recite the conjugated forms the fastest.

Práctica de GRAMÁTICA

13 ¿Un estudiante serio?

Leer
Escribir

Claudia y Pablo hablan en la escuela. Completa la conversación con formas de **ir.** *(Complete the conversation, using forms of* ***ir.****)*

Claudia: ¡Tengo mucha tarea en la clase de inglés! Yo ___1.___ a la biblioteca... ¿___2.___ tú y yo?
Pablo: No, yo no ___3.___ a la biblioteca hoy.
Claudia: ¿No ___4.___ tú a la biblioteca? ¡Tienes que hacer la tarea!
Pablo: Sí, pero necesito comprar pizza y un refresco. Mis amigos y yo ___5.___ a la cafetería. Después yo ___6.___ al gimnasio y ellos ___7.___ a la clase de matemáticas.
Claudia: ¿___8.___ Carlos al gimnasio?
Pablo: No, él ___9.___ a la biblioteca.
Claudia: ¡Ay, Pablo! Tú también necesitas ir. ¿___10.___ tú y Carlos mañana?
Pablo: Sí, todos nosotros ___11.___ mañana.

Expansión:
Teacher Edition Only
Have pairs of students ask each other where they are going.

14 ¿Adónde van?

Escuchar
Escribir

¿Adónde van Pablo y las otras personas? Escucha la descripción y escribe oraciones para decir adónde van estas personas. *(Listen to the description and write sentences to tell where these people are going.)*

la cafetería	la clase de inglés
el gimnasio	la clase de matemáticas
la biblioteca	la oficina de la directora

1. Pablo
2. Claudia
3. Martín y Sara
4. la maestra de inglés
5. María y Claudia
6. el señor Treviño

Audio Program
TXT CD 2 Track 16
Audio Script, TE p. 107b

AUDIO

Pronunciación La letra d

In Spanish, the letter **d** has two sounds. At the beginning of a sentence, after a pause, or after the letters **l** or **n,** the **d** sounds like the English *d* in *door.* In all other cases, the **d** sounds like the *th* of the word *the.*

Listen and repeat, paying close attention to the two sounds of **d.**

comida	**divertido**	**¿Dónde está David?**
adiós	**falda**	**Daniel está al lado de la puerta.**
lado	**grande**	**¿Adónde vas con mi cuaderno?**

Objectives
- Practice using **ir.**
- Practice naming places in school.
- Practice pronouncing the different sounds of the letter **d.**

Core Resource
- Audio Program: TXT CD 2, tracks 16, 17

Practice Sequence
- **Activity 13:** Controlled practice: **ir** and places in school
- **Activity 14:** Transitional practice: **ir** and places in school
- Pronunciation: Oral comprehension of the letter **d** sound.

STANDARDS
1.1 Engage in conversation
1.2 Understand language
4.1 Compare languages

Communication

Reluctant Speakers
Have students repeat the forms of **ir** as a group. Then ask them, as a group, to supply the missing verb form after you say a subject, or hold up a flashcard with a subject written on it.

Differentiating Instruction

Multiple Intelligences
Linguistic/Verbal Organize students into a circle. The first student asks the student on his or her right **¿Adónde vas?** That student gives an answer. **Voy a la oficina.** The first student then reports the answer to the group. **Él/Ella va a la oficina.** The second student then asks the question of the next in line. **¿Adónde vas?**

Inclusion
Clear Structure Instruct students to break Activity 13 into smaller steps. First, have them circle the noun or pronoun near the blank. Second, have them choose the correct verb form. Third, ask them to read the sentence aloud. Remind students that two pronouns together have a different meaning than each separately. For example, **tú y yo** means **nosotros.**

Answers Projectable Transparencies, 2-29 and 2-30

Activity 13
1. voy
2. Vamos
3. voy
4. vas
5. vamos
6. voy
7. van
8. Va
9. va
10. van (vais)
11. vamos

Activity 14
1. Pablo va al gimnasio.
2. Claudia va a la clase de inglés.
3. Sara y Martín van a la cafetería.
4. La maestra de inglés va a la biblioteca.
5. María y Claudia van a la clase de matemáticas.
6. El señor Treviño va a la oficina de la directora.

Objectives

- Practice using **ir** and lesson vocabulary.
- **Culture:** The importance of self-portraits in an artist's work.

Core Resource

- *Cuaderno,* pp. 79–81

Practice Sequence

- **Activity 15:** Open-ended practice: **ir** and lesson vocabulary
- **Activity 16:** Open-ended practice: **ir** and answering questions

STANDARDS

4.2 Compare cultures

Comparación cultural

Essential Question

Suggested Answer In addition to capturing what the artist looks like, self-portraits reveal something about the artist's personality, feelings, and lifestyle.

About the Artist

Frida Kahlo, a native of Mexico City, was stricken with polio as a child and suffered throughout her life, both emotionally and physically. She was married to the Mexican muralist Diego Rivera, but her art was very different from that of her husband's. She died in 1954 at the age of 47.

✓ Ongoing Assessment

Get Help Online
More Practice
my.hrw.com

PARA Y PIENSA **Peer Assessment** Exchange with a partner and check each other's answers. Ask for a show of hands as to how many made no mistakes. For additional practice, use Reteaching & Practice Copymasters URB 2, pp. 17, 18.

Answers Projectable Transparencies, 2-30

Activity 15 Answers should follow this format:
¿Cuándo vas al/a la + place?
Voy al/a la + place + cuando + reason.

Activity 16 Answers will vary but will include these elements:

1. Voy a la escuela a las ______.
2. Vamos a la cafetería a las ______.

Answers continue on p. 123.

15 ¿Cuándo vas a...?

Hablar

Pregúntale a otro(a) estudiante cuándo va a estos lugares. *(Ask a partner when he or she goes to these places.)*

A: ¿Cuándo vas a la oficina?

B: Voy a la oficina cuando tengo problemas.

modelo: la oficina

Estudiante A

1. el gimnasio	**4.** la biblioteca
2. la oficina	**5.** la cafetería
3. la escuela	**6.** la clase de...

Estudiante B

tengo (que)
necesito
hay
¿ ?

Expansión
Tell the class when your partner goes to the places in the activity.

16 ¿Y tú?

Hablar
Escribir

Contesta las preguntas. *(Answer the questions.)*

1. ¿A qué hora vas a la escuela?
2. ¿Cuándo van tú y tus amigos(as) a la cafetería?
3. ¿Adónde vas después de la clase de español?
4. ¿Vas mucho a la oficina del (de la) director(a)?
5. ¿Adónde vas cuando tienes que estudiar?
6. ¿Qué hay dentro de tu mochila?

Expansión:
Teacher Edition Only
Have students use question 6 to conduct a brief survey about the contents of their backpacks.

Comparación cultural

El autorretrato

What does a self-portrait reveal about an artist? Mexican artist Frida Kahlo painted many self-portraits, including *Autorretrato con collar.* She was influenced by the indigenous cultures of **Mexico** in both her style of painting and style of clothing. She often wore traditional native clothing, as depicted in the photograph. How do you think she depicted herself in her self-portraits?

Compara con tu mundo *What would you include in a portrait of yourself and why?*

Una fotografía de Frida Kahlo (1941), Nickolas Muray

Más práctica Cuaderno *pp. 79–81* Cuaderno para hispanohablantes *pp. 80–83*

Get Help Online
my.hrw.com

PARA Y PIENSA

Did you get it? Tell where the following people are going.

1. Teresa / la cafetería
2. los estudiantes / la oficina del director
3. nosotros / el gimnasio
4. yo / la clase de matemáticas

Differentiating Instruction

Pre-AP

Self-correct After students complete Activity 16, have them read their answers aloud to a partner. Remind students to listen for the correct form of the verb **ir,** as well as appropriate word order. If an answer does not sound correct, have the partners analyze the problem.

Multiple Intelligences

Visual Learners Give students the opportunity to create a sketch of a self-portrait. They might depict themselves engaged in a favorite activity, or just show their face. Have students create five sentences describing themselves based on their sketches. Sentences might describe fixed traits. **No soy muy alta.** Or they might describe current emotions. **Estoy tranquilo.**

Todo junto

¡AVANZA! **Goal:** ***Show what you know*** Notice how Pablo and Claudia use **ir** to talk about where they are going, and **estar** to say where things are. Then use **ir** and **estar** to talk about your own schedule. ***Actividades 17–21***

¿Recuerdas? Telling time p. 90

Telehistoria completa

@HOMETUTOR my.hrw.com View, Read and Record

STRATEGIES

Cuando lees
Read for locations This scene mentions specific places people are going. What are those places? Alicia's T-shirt is now located in a specific place. Where is it?

Cuando escuchas
Notice the problems In this scene, Pablo's problems go from bad to worse. What are the problems? How does he react?

Escena 1 *Resumen*
Pablo no contesta la pregunta en la clase de ciencias porque el problema es difícil. Claudia contesta la pregunta.

Escena 2 *Resumen*
Pablo no está contento porque tiene mucho que hacer y no tiene la mochila con la camiseta de Alicia.

VIDEO DVD

AUDIO

Escena 3

Roberto approaches, holding a poster.

Roberto: ¿Qué pasa?

Claudia: Vamos al gimnasio. Bueno, Pablo va al gimnasio, yo voy a la cafetería...

Pablo: ¡Necesito ir al gimnasio a las cinco, y son las cinco menos cuarto!

Claudia: ¡Y necesita la mochila! Dentro está la camiseta de Alicia.

Pablo: A las cinco Trini Salgado va al gimnasio, y yo...

Roberto: No, no. ¡A las cuatro!

Pablo: No... ¡A las cinco!

Roberto: Mira... a las cuatro.

He shows his autographed poster to Pablo. It says four o'clock.

Pablo: *(dejectedly)* No...

Differentiating Instruction

Inclusion

Frequent Review/Repetition Organize students into pairs. Ask each pair to use **ir** in a sentence to say places they go with their families or at school, for example, **Yo voy a...**, or **Vamos a...**, using as many vocabulary words as possible. Have other pairs correct pronunciation or add other words to the sentences.

Slower-paced Learners

Peer-study Support Have students work in pairs to draft a question about the Telehistoria. Have them write the question on an index card. Then have each pair switch cards with another group. Tell students to read the question they received, and discuss the answer with their partner. Repeat the activity with each pair getting a new question each time.

¡AVANZA! Objective

- Integrate lesson content.

Core Resources

- Video Program: DVD 1
- Audio Program: TXT CD 2 track 18

Presentation Strategies

- Ask students what they remember about the Telehistoria so far.
- Before showing the video or playing the audio tell students to watch for the surprise ending and to be ready to talk about it.

STANDARDS

1.2 Understand language

Warm Up Projectable Transparencies, 2-22

Ir Write the corresponding form of the verb for each pronoun.

1. yo ____. **4.** nosotros ____.
2. tú ____. **5.** vosotros ____.
3. él ____. **6.** ustedes ____.

Answers: 1. voy; 2. vas; 3. va; 4. vamos; 5. vais; 6. van

Video Summary

@HOMETUTOR VideoPlus my.hrw.com

Pablo and Claudia meet a friend, Roberto, who has a poster. Pablo is in a hurry as it is 4:45 and he has to be at the gym at 5:00. Claudia says he needs the backpack because Alicia's shirt is inside of it. Roberto tells Pablo that Trini Salgado was at the gym at 4:00 instead of 5:00 and points it out on the poster that has been autographed by Trini Salgado.

Answers Projectable Transparencies, 2-30

Answers continued from p. 122.

3. Voy a la (al) ____ después de la clase de español.
4. No, no voy (Sí, voy) a la oficina del (de la) director(a) mucho.
5. Voy a la (al) ____ cuando tengo que estudiar.
6. En mi mochila hay ____.

Para y piensa
1. Teresa va a la cafetería.
2. Los estudiantes van a la oficina del director.
3. Nosotros vamos al gimnasio.
4. Yo voy a la clase de matemáticas.

TODO JUNTO

Objective
- Practice using and integrating lesson vocabulary and grammar.
- Recycle: Telling time

Core Resources
- *Cuaderno,* pp. 82–83
- Audio Program: TXT CD 2, tracks 14, 15, 18, 19, 20

Practice Sequence
- **Activities 17, 18:** Telehistoria comprehension
- **Activity 19:** Transitional practice: speaking; Recycle: telling time
- **Activity 20:** Open-ended practice: reading, listening, speaking
- **Activity 21:** Open-ended practice: writing

STANDARDS
1.1 Engage in conversation
1.2 Understand language
1.3 Present information
21st Century **Creativity and Innovation,** Multiple Intelligences; **Flexibility and Adaptability,** Heritage Language Learners

✓ Ongoing Assessment

Rubric Activity 19

Speaking Criteria	Maximum Credit	Partial Credit	Minimum Credit
Content	Numerous words from previous lessons as well as words from this unit.	Few words from previous lessons and unit.	Words are limited to this lesson and unit.
Communication	Easy to understand good pronunciation.	Can be understood. Some errors in pronunciation.	Hard to understand. Many errors in pronunciation.
Accuracy	Few mistakes in grammar and vocabulary.	Some mistakes in grammar and vocabulary.	Many mistakes in grammar and vocabulary.

To customize your own rubrics, use the ***Generate Success*** *Rubric Generator* and *Graphic Organizers.*

Answers Projectable Transparencies, 2-30 and 2-31

Activity 17 The correct order for the sequence of events is as follows: 5; 3; 4; 1; 2

Answers continue on p. 125.

17 *Comprensión de los episodios* ¡A organizar!

Escuchar
Leer

Pon las oraciones en orden para describir los episodios. *(Put the events in order to describe the episodes.)*

1. La camiseta está en la mochila y Pablo no tiene la mochila.
2. Pablo y Claudia hablan con Roberto.
3. Claudia y Pablo van a la biblioteca y estudian.
4. Pablo está nervioso; tiene que ir al gimnasio a las cinco.
5. Pablo va a la clase de ciencias y no contesta la pregunta.

Expansión:
Teacher Edition Only
Have students add dialogue to their desriptions.

18 *Comprensión de los episodios* ¡A describir!

Escuchar
Leer

Describe lo que pasa en estas fotos. Incluye dónde están y cómo están las personas en las fotos. *(Describe what is happening in the photos.)*

modelo: Pablo está en la clase de ciencias. Va al pizarrón porque tiene que contestar una pregunta. Está nervioso.

1. 
2. 
3. 

Expansión:
Teacher Edition Only
Ask students to look through all photos in their books and discuss the emotions of the characters.

19 ¿Adónde vamos?

¿Recuerdas? Telling time p. 90

Digital performance space

Hablar

STRATEGY Hablar
Make it lively Keep the discussion interesting! Add as many details about your classes as possible. Don't just talk about your classes; include other places in your school.

Habla con otros(as) estudiantes sobre adónde van y a qué hora. *(Talk with other students about schedules.)*

A: ¿A qué hora van ustedes a la cafetería?
B: Voy a la cafetería a las doce y media.
C: Voy a la cafetería a la una.

Expansión
Write a summary of the classes that you have in common with other members of your group.

Differentiating Instruction

Pre-AP
Expand and Elaborate Have volunteers share their descriptions of the photos in Activity 18. Then challenge the group to add more information to each description. For example, the following might be added to the model. **Pablo está nervioso. La clase de ciencias es muy difícil.**

Inclusion
Clear Structure Before students discuss Activity 19, have them create a two-column chart. Tell them to write the heading **¿adónde?** at the top of the left-hand column, and **¿a qué hora?** at the top of the right. Then have students brainstorm places in school on the left, and record the appropriate time for each on the right. Encourage students to use their charts as they ask and answer questions.

20 Integración

Digital performance space

Leer
Escuchar
Hablar

Raquel y Mario necesitan estudiar en la biblioteca. Lee la agenda de Raquel y escucha el mensaje de Mario. Luego indica cuándo van a la biblioteca y explica por qué no estudian a las otras horas mencionadas. *(Tell when Raquel and Mario will go to the library to study. Explain why they won't go at the other times mentioned.)*

Fuente 1 Agenda personal

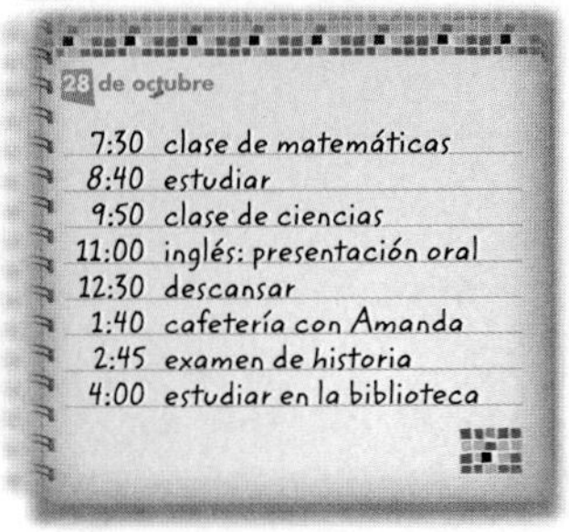

Fuente 2 Un mensaje por teléfono

Listen and take notes
- Escribe qué hace Mario y a qué hora.

modelo: Ellos van a la biblioteca a las... No estudian a las siete y media porque...

Audio Program
TXT CD 2 Tracks 19, 20
Audio Script, TE p. 107b

Expansión:
Teacher Edition Only
Have students expand Raquel's schedule to include her activities for the rest of the afternoon and the evening.

21 El periódico escolar

Digital performance space

Escribir

Tú tienes que escribir un artículo para el periódico escolar sobre tu día típico en la escuela. Explica a qué clases vas, cómo son y qué usas en cada clase. *(Write an article for the school paper about your typical school day.)*

modelo: Yo siempre estoy muy ocupado. A las siete y media voy a la clase de matemáticas. La clase es muy divertida. Usamos calculadoras, pero no es fácil. A las ocho y cuarto...

Writing Criteria	Excellent	Good	Needs Work
Content	Your article includes a lot of information.	Your article includes some information.	Your article includes little information.
Communication	Most of your article is organized and easy to follow.	Parts of your article are organized and easy to follow.	Your article is disorganized and hard to follow.
Accuracy	Your article has few mistakes in grammar and vocabulary.	Your article has some mistakes in grammar and vocabulary.	Your article has many mistakes in grammar and vocabulary.

Expansión
Interview your teacher and write about a typical day for him or her.

Más práctica Cuaderno *pp. 82–83* Cuaderno para hispanohablantes *pp. 84–85*

Get Help Online
my.hrw.com

PARA Y PIENSA

Did you get it? Complete each sentence with the correct forms of **estar** and **ir + a.**

1. A la una Pablo____ en la clase de arte, pero a las dos _____la cafetería.
2. ¿Dónde _____Roberto y Claudia? Ellos _____la cafetería.
3. Claudia _____nerviosa porque _____la oficina de la directora.

Differentiating Instruction

Multiple Intelligences

Musical/Rhythmic Have students create a poem or song based on the schedule shown in Activity 20. Students may want to read their poems or sing their songs for the rest of the class.

Heritage Language Learners

Writing Skills After students have completed their articles for Activity 21, organize them into groups of three. Provide each student with copies of the three articles. Tell students that they will each play the part of the writer, editor, and editor-in-chief. The writer reads his or her article aloud. The editor reads along, suggesting revisions and proofreading. The editor-in-chief checks the editor's work.

Long-term Retention

Pre-AP Integration

Activity 20 Ask students to work in pairs to write a short script about what they do during the day and at what time. Ask them to follow the time schedule given in Activity 20, and use **estar, ir** and contractions **al, del.** When they finish, ask them to read aloud their scripts and the other students to correct the pronunciation.

✓ Ongoing Assessment

Rubric Activity 20
Listening/Speaking

Proficient	Not There Yet
Student correctly uses **estar** and **ir + a** in all three sentences.	Student correctly uses **estar** and **ir + a** in two or fewer sentences.

✓ Ongoing Assessment

Get Help Online
More Practice
my.hrw.com

PARA Y PIENSA **Quick Check** Ask students to read aloud the completed sentences and ask the class to correct their pronunciation. For additional practice, use Reteaching & Practice Copymasters URB 2 p. 17, 19

Answers Projectable Transparencies, 2-30 and 2-31

Answers continued from p. 124.

Activity 18
1. Claudia está en la clase de ciencias. Contesta la pregunta.
2. Pablo y Claudia están delante de la escuela. Hablan. Pablo está nervioso porque tiene que estar en el gimnasio a las cinco y tiene que hacer la tarea.
3. Pablo y Roberto están delante de la escuela. Hablan de Trini Salgado.

Activity 19 Sample answer: **A.** ¿Qué van a hacer a la una? **B.** Yo voy a la biblioteca. **C.** Yo voy a las clase de español.

Activity 20 Ellos van a la biblioteca a las nueve menos veinte. No estudian a las siete y media porque Mario tiene la clase de ciencias. No estudian a las diez menos diez porque Mario tiene la clase de matemáticas. ...las doce porque Mario necesita comer con Andrés. ...a las doce y media porque Mario descansa. ...a la una y media porque Mario tiene la clase de inglés.

Activity 21 Answers will vary. Sample answer: Yo voy a la escuela a las ocho de la mañana. Tengo examen de ciencias. Tengo que estudiar...

Para y piensa **1.** está, va a; **2.** están, van a; **3.** está, va a

¡AVANZA! Objectives

- Read two compositions about **Mi clase favorita.**
- Compare ways of explaining and talking about favorite classes.
- **Culture:** Learn how students in Mexico and the Dominican Republic plan to prepare for their careers.

Core Resource

- Audio Program: TXT CD 2 track 21

Presentation Strategies

- Ask students to name their favorite classes.
- Review the classes listed in both compositions.
- Lead a discussion on how students will prepare for the careers they want. Point out how their favorite classes may help them in their career planning.

STANDARDS

1.2 Understand language
4.2 Compare cultures
21st Century **Collaboration,** Group Work; **Critical Thinking and Problem Solving,** Multiple Intelligences

Warm Up Projectable Transparencies, 2-23

Ir Complete the sentences with the correct form of **ir.**

1. Yo _____ a la biblioteca.
2. Pablo _____ a la cafetería.
3. ¿Adónde _____ ustedes?
4. Nosotros _____ al gimnasio.
5. Y tú, ¿adónde _____?

Answers: 1. voy; 2. va; 3. van; 4. vamos; 5. vas

Comparación cultural

Background Information

Graduation Requirements in Dominican Schools A minimum of 25 credits must be earned in Grades 9–12. Eight semesters of successful full-time attendance in high school are required. Students must maintain an academic GPA of 2.0 (70%). Required courses include a modern language, social studies, mathematics, science, Spanish, physical and health education, fine arts and computer technology.

Lectura cultural

Additional readings at my.hrw.com SPANISH InterActive Reader

¡AVANZA! Goal: Read the excerpts from the essays of two students from Mexico and the Dominican Republic. Then compare the descriptions of their favorite classes and talk about your favorite class.

Comparación cultural

AUDIO

Mi clase favorita

STRATEGY Leer

Use the title The title *Mi clase favorita* helps you anticipate the contents of the reading. Write down the things that you would expect to find, then search for them.

Expected contents	Actual contents
El (La) maestro(a)...	
La clase...	
Más información:	

Below are compositions by two finalists who entered the essay contest called "Mi clase favorita."

Tomás Gutiérrez Moreno
Colegio de la Providencia
Guadalajara, México

Mi nombre es Tomás Gutiérrez Moreno. Soy de Guadalajara, México. Estudio en el Colegio de la Providencia.

La historia es muy interesante; es mi clase favorita. Me gusta mucho estudiar el pasado[1] de México. Soy estudioso y siempre saco buenas notas en la clase.

En la universidad deseo[2] estudiar historia. Deseo ser maestro y enseñar historia mexicana en Guadalajara.

[1] past [2] I wish to

México

Mural en la Biblioteca Central de la Universidad Nacional Autónoma de México en la Ciudad de México

Differentiating Instruction

Heritage Language Learners

Writing Skills Ask students to write a composition about their favorite class. Instruct them to use pp. 126–127 as a model. Provide them with the following questions as a guide: **¿Cómo te llamas? ¿De dónde eres? ¿Dónde estudias? ¿Qué te gusta estudiar?** Check for correct spelling, punctuation, and grammar.

Multiple Intelligences

Linguistic/Verbal Explain that people reveal a great deal about themselves through their writing. Ask half the class to reread Tomás's essay and the other half to reread María's. Ask students to write short reflections in Spanish in which they explain how much they can tell about the personalities of María and Tomás; then ask students to share their reflections with the rest of the class.

María González
Colegio San Esteban
San Pedro de Macorís, República Dominicana

Me llamo María González. Soy de la República Dominicana. Estudio en el Colegio San Esteban.

Tengo dos clases favoritas: el inglés y el español. Deseo estudiar idiomas[3] en Santo Domingo, la capital, y después, trabajar en mi país.

El turismo es muy importante para[4] la economía de la República Dominicana. Deseo trabajar en un hotel, en las famosas playas[5] de Punta Cana o de Puerto Plata.

[3] languages [4] for [5] beaches

Mural en la Universidad Nacional en Santo Domingo, República Dominicana

República Dominicana

PARA Y PIENSA

¿Comprendiste?

1. ¿Dónde estudia Tomás?
2. ¿Cómo es Tomás?
3. ¿De dónde es María?
4. ¿Qué le gusta estudiar más a María?

¿Y tú?

¿Cuál es tu clase favorita? ¿Cómo es?

Communication

Presentational Mode

Ask students to write a summary of one of the two compositions and present it to the class. The summary should be given in third person. For example: **Tomás Gutiérrez Moreno es de Guadalajara. Estudia en el Colegio de la Providencia. Le gusta estudiar historia.**

Comparisons

English Language Connection

Cognates and False Cognates Have half the class search the reading for cognates and list them. Ask the other half to search for false cognates (words that look the same but have different meanings) and list them (**gustar** and *gusto,* **colegio** and *college,* **idioma** and *idiom,* **nota** and *note*). Ask both groups to share their words with the class.

Communication

Group Work

Divide the class into small groups to come up with a description of the ideal school. Ask them to brainstorm for ideas about the following: **el horario perfecto, las clases favoritas, los maestros más interesantes.** Assign one student from each group to take notes. Each group will present their description of the ideal school to the rest of the class.

Differentiating Instruction

Slower-paced Learners

Personalize It Organize students into pairs. Then have partners ask each other questions based on the content of both compositions. Instruct students to answer from their own perspective.

Estudiante A: ¿Te gusta la clase de inglés?
Estudiante B: Sí, me gusta la clase de inglés.
Estudiante A: ¿Sacas buenas notas en inglés?
Estudiante B: Sí, saco buenas notas.

Inclusion

Metacognitive Support Teach students how to use context clues to find the meanings of words they don't know. Have them skim the two compositions on pp. 126–127. Then ask them to look at the glossed words without looking at the English translation and guess their meaning. For example, students read that Tomás's favorite class is history, which provides them with the context clue to the word **el pasado** (the past).

Answers

Para y piensa

¿Comprendiste?

1. Tomás estudia en el Colegio de la Providencia.
2. Tomás es estudioso.
3. María es de la República Dominicana.
4. A María le gusta más estudiar el inglés y el español.

¿Y tú? Answers will vary but should follow the model: **Mi clase favorita es...**

Objectives
- Read about yarn painting in Mexico and rock drawing in the Dominican Republic.
- **Culture:** Compare the art of two indigenous cultures: the Huichol of Mexico and the Taino of the Greater Antilles.
- **Community:** Investigate sources of arts and crafts influenced by Spanish-speaking cultures in the community.

Presentation Strategies
- Ask students to look at the illustrations on this page and identify similarities and differences between the two kinds of folk art.
- Have students tell about folk art traditions they have seen (beaded moccasins, hand-woven blankets, etc.) or may own.
- Bring in samples of indigenous art for students to see.
- Ask students to read the **proyectos** and choose the one they want to create.

STANDARDS
1.3 Present information
2.2 Products and perspectives
4.2 Compare cultures
5.1 Spanish in the community
21st Century Productivity and Accountability, Spanish in the Marketplace (Business Literacy)

Comparación cultural

Essential Question
Suggested Answer The natural world can be portrayed in various ways through art; realistic, idealistic, even fantastic. The type of portrayal can show how a culture thinks or feels about the natural world.

Expanded Information
The yarn paintings of the Huichol are still being made. Originally intended as religious offerings, these paintings describe the way the Huichol people saw the world they lived in and the way they saw the world they hoped for.

Communities
Spanish in the Marketplace
Ask students to visit local craft stores to search for supplies that are imported from Latin America. Ask them to keep records of what they find and where it comes from. In the classroom, have students combine their findings in a list of words and countries.

Proyectos culturales

Comparación cultural

Arte de México y la República Dominicana

How does art reflect a culture's view of the natural world? Many cultures use art to capture the beauty and wonder of their natural surroundings. Two indigenous groups whose art can still be appreciated are the Huichol of **Mexico** and the Taino of the Greater Antilles (including what is now known as the **Dominican Republic**).

Proyecto 1 *Yarn Painting*

México Some Huichol still live in the isolated mountains of western Mexico. They make yarn paintings of birds, flowers, and other natural shapes. Make your own Huichol-style yarn painting.

Materials for yarn painting
Cardboard
2–3 colors yarn
Glue

Instructions
1. On a piece of cardboard, draw a pencil outline of the design you'd like to make.
2. Place one strand of yarn along the outline's length. Glue the yarn to the cardboard.
3. Fill in the design by laying yarn just inside the outline you made, coiling the yarn around until the figure is filled.
4. Section off the background and fill it in the same way.

Proyecto 2 *Rock Drawing*

República Dominicana The Taino lived in the islands of the Caribbean until the 16th century. Their rock art can still be seen in the caverns of the Dominican Republic. Try making your own rock art.

Materials for rock drawing
Rock
Pencil
Optional: Markers, pens, or chalk

Instructions
1. Begin by finding a smooth, oval rock about the size of your hand with an adequate surface for drawing.
2. Use a pencil to sketch the animal or design you'd like to make.
3. Then use a black felt tip pen to make it permanent. Add color by using colored felt tip pens or colored chalk.

En tu comunidad
Visit an arts and crafts store or a museum in your community. Look for any items that have been influenced by Spanish-speaking cultures.

Differentiating Instruction

Heritage Language Learners
Support What They Know Encourage students to bring in samples of folk art from their country of origin. Have students describe who makes them, where are they made, what they are made of, and if they are used for decoration or other purposes.

English Learners
Provide Comprehensible Input Provide English learners with extra illustrations of Huichol yarn paintings and Taino rock drawings. If possible, show them examples of other students' completed work. Model the processes for completing these **proyectos,** then encourage the student to make his or her own. Also be sure the student has a dual-language dictionary available for clarification.

Lección 2

En resumen

Vocabulario y gramática

ANIMATED GRAMMAR
Interactive Flashcards
my.hrw.com

Vocabulario

Describe Classroom Objects

el borrador	*eraser*	el pizarrón (*pl.* los pizarrones)	*board, chalkboard*
la calculadora	*calculator*	la pluma	*pen*
el cuaderno	*notebook*	la puerta	*door*
el escritorio	*desk*	el reloj	*clock; watch*
el lápiz (*pl.* los lápices)	*pencil*	la silla	*chair*
el mapa	*map*	la tiza	*chalk*
la mochila	*backpack*	la ventana	*window*
el papel	*paper*		

Describe Classes

aburrido(a)	*boring*
divertido(a)	*fun*
interesante	*interesting*

Places in School

el baño	*bathroom*
la biblioteca	*library*
la cafetería	*cafeteria*
el gimnasio	*gymnasium*
la oficina del (de la) director(a)	*principal's office*
el pasillo	*hall*

Say Where Things Are Located

al lado (de)	*next to*	dentro (de)	*inside (of)*
cerca (de)	*near (to)*	detrás (de)	*behind*
debajo (de)	*underneath, under*	encima (de)	*on top (of)*
delante (de)	*in front (of)*	lejos (de)	*far (from)*

Talk About How You Feel

cansado(a)	*tired*	nervioso(a)	*nervous*
contento(a)	*content, happy*	ocupado(a)	*busy*
deprimido(a)	*depressed*	tranquilo(a)	*calm*
emocionado(a)	*excited*	triste	*sad*
enojado(a)	*angry*		

Other Words and Phrases

¿(A)dónde?	*(To) Where?*
¿Cuándo?	*When?*
cuando	*when*
el problema	*problem*

Gramática

Nota gramatical: Conjugated verb before the subject to ask a question *p. 117*

The Verb estar

Use **estar** to indicate location and say how people feel.

estar *to be*			
yo	estoy	nosotros(as)	estamos
tú	estás	vosotros(as)	estáis
usted, él, ella	está	ustedes, ellos(as)	están

The Verb ir

Use **ir** to talk about where someone is going.

ir *to go*			
yo	voy	nosotros(as)	vamos
tú	vas	vosotros(as)	vais
usted, él, ella	va	ustedes, ellos(as)	van

Practice Spanish with Holt McDougal Apps!

Objective
- Review lesson vocabulary and grammar.

DIGITAL SPANISH

Interactive Flashcards Students can hear every target vocabulary word pronounced in authentic Spanish. Flashcards have Spanish on one side, and a picture or a translation on the other.
Review Games Matching, concentration, hangman, and word search are just a sampling of the fun, interactive games students can play to review for the test.

performance space
News Networking
@HOMETUTOR
CULTURA Interactiva

- **Audio and Video Resources**
- **Interactive Flashcards**
- **Review Activities**
- **WebQuest**
- **Conjuguemos.com**

Communication
Humor and Creativity

Ask students to write vocabulary words from En resumen on small slips of paper and place them, by category, in containers. One at a time, have students pull a word from each of three or four containers and put them together in a sentence. Possible combinations: **(Yo estoy) (debajo de) (la pluma).**

Long-term Retention
Study Tips

Ask students to sort the vocabulary into smaller categories of their choice. For example: **en la mochila, en la clase.** Have them use graphic organizers such as charts or word webs to do so. Ask them to share their work and discuss the reasons for assigning an item to a particular category.

Differentiating Instruction

Inclusion

Multisensory Input/Output First lead the class in creating facial expressions that match the Talk About How You Feel vocabulary. Then divide the class into pairs and ask each pair to quiz each other on the vocabulary words. One student will give the Spanish word, and the other will make the appropriate facial expression.

Multiple Intelligences

Visual Learners Give students two options: mapping their school or mapping their classroom. Ask them to draw detailed maps and label each space or item in Spanish.

Objective
- Review lesson grammar and vocabulary.

Core Resources
- *Cuaderno,* pp. 84–95
- Audio Program: TXT CD 2 track 22

Presentation Strategies
- Before playing the audio for Activity 1, ask students to listen to it carefully, especially to the times and the forms of **estar** and **ir.**
- Monitor correct use of **ser, estar,** and prepositions of location.
- Read the Comparación cultural with students and clarify any questions that arise.
- Review may be done in class or given as homework.
- Students can also access the review activities on line at my.hrw.com.

STANDARDS
1.2 Understand language, Act. 1
1.3 Present information, Acts. 1-5
4.2 Compare cultures, Act. 5
21st Century **Communication,** Pre-AP

Warm Up
Projectable Transparencies, 2-23

Vocabulary Complete the sentences with the correct word.

cafetería al lado divertida biblioteca tiza

1. En la _____ hay muchos libros.
2. No me gusta comer la pizza en la _____.
3. Necesito _____ para escribir en el pizarrón.
4. La clase de español es interesante y _____.
5. El reloj está _____ del mapa.

Answers: 1. biblioteca; 2. cafetería; 3. tiza; 4. divertida; 5. al lado

Ongoing Assessment
Get Help Online
More Practice
my.hrw.com

Intervention and Remediation If students achieve less than 80% accuracy with the activities, direct them to review pp. 108, 115–117, 120, 122, 126–127 and to get help online at my.hrw.com.

Lección 2 Repaso de la lección

@HOMETUTOR
my.hrw.com

¡AvanzaRap! DVD
Sing and Learn

¡LLEGADA!

Now you can
- describe classes and classroom objects
- say where things are located
- say where you are going
- talk about how you feel

Using
- the verb **estar**
- the conjugated verb before the subject to ask a question
- the verb **ir**

To review
- the verb **estar** p. 115
- the conjugated verb before the subject to ask a question p. 117
- the verb **ir** p. 120

1 Listen and understand

AUDIO

Copia esta tabla en una hoja de papel. Escucha los mensajes de teléfono y completa la tabla. Usa la información para escribir oraciones. *(Copy the chart. Listen to the phone messages and complete the chart. Write sentences using the information.)*

La hora	¿Dónde está Ana?	¿Adónde va Ana?
modelo: 8:00	delante de la clase de arte	clase de español
10:15		
12:30		
2:45		
4:10		

modelo: A las ocho Ana está delante de la clase de arte. Ella va de la clase de arte a la clase de español.

Audio Program
TXT CD 2 Track 22
Audio Script, TE p. 107b

To review
- the verb **estar** p. 115
- the conjugated verb before the subject to ask a question p. 117

2 Talk about how you feel

Escribe preguntas para verificar cómo están todos. *(Write questions to find out how these people are feeling.)*

modelo: Bárbara
¿Está emocionada Bárbara?

1. Jorge y Pilar
2. las maestras
3. la directora
4. usted
5. tú
6. ustedes

Differentiating Instruction

Multiple Intelligences
Intrapersonal Ask students to create a table like the one in Activity 1. The headings for columns in this table, though, should be **La hora, ¿Dónde estoy?** and **¿Adónde voy?** Have them fill out the table according to their own schedule.

Pre-AP
Expand and Elaborate Ask students to explain their class schedules to a partner, identifying the subjects they take, what time they meet, and how often they have them. For example: **Tengo inglés a las ocho de la mañana. Tengo inglés todos los días. A las nueve estoy en la clase de historia.** Then ask them to exchange schedules and explain the sequence of each other's classes.

REPASO DE LA LECCIÓN

To review
- the verb **ir** p. 120

3 Say where you are going

Lee el correo electrónico de Mario y complétalo con las formas correctas de **ir.** *(Read Mario's e-mail message and complete it with the correct forms of* ***ir.****)*

```
Hola, Luis. Yo __1.__ a la clase de ciencias en
quince minutos. Es una clase interesante, pero es
difícil. A las doce y media mis amigos y yo __2.__
a la cafetería. Después Inés __3.__ al gimnasio y
Jerónimo __4.__ a la oficina del director. A las cinco
ellos __5.__ a la biblioteca para estudiar. ¿Adónde
__6.__ tú después de las clases?
```

To review
- the verb **estar** p. 115

4 Say where things are located

Escribe oraciones para decir dónde están los borradores de la señora Romero. *(Write sentences telling where Mrs. Romero's students have put the erasers.)*

modelo: pizarrón (cerca / lejos)
Un borrador está cerca del pizarrón.

1. reloj (al lado / debajo)
2. silla (debajo / encima)
3. mochila (dentro / debajo)
4. ventana (delante / detrás)
5. escritorio (encima / delante)
6. maestra (lejos / detrás)

To review
- Comparación cultural pp. 108, 116, 122
- Lectura cultural pp. 126–127

5 Mexico and the Dominican Republic

Comparación cultural

Answer these culture questions.

1. When do Mexican students attend school?
2. How did indigenous cultures influence Frida Kahlo?
3. What can you find in Mexico City's National Museum of Anthropology?
4. Why is tourism important in the Dominican Republic?

Más práctica Cuaderno *pp. 84–95* Cuaderno para hispanohablantes *pp. 86–95*

Get Help Online my.hrw.com

✓ Ongoing Assessment

Alternative Assessment Activity 2 Ask students to draw their own emoticon faces and label them **cansado(a), contento(a), deprimido(a), emocionado(a), enojado(a), nervioso(a), ocupado(a), tranquilo(a),** and **triste.**

✓ Ongoing Assessment

Peer Assessment Activity 4 Ask students to take turns quizzing each other by taking an eraser and moving it around the room to the places indicated in Activity 4. Example: One student moves the eraser and the other says where it is. They should keep score of right and wrong answers.

Answers Projectable Transparencies, 2-31

Activity 1 A las diez y cuarto Ana está en el pasillo. Ella va del pasillo a la clase de inglés.

A las doce y media Ana está en la cafetería. Ella va de la cafetería a la clase de matemáticas.

A las tres menos cuarto Ana está en la oficina. Ella va de la oficina a la clase de historia.

A las cuatro y diez Ana está en la biblioteca. De la biblioteca, ella va al gimnasio.

Activity 2
1. ¿Están enojados Jorge y Pilar?
2. ¿Están cansadas las maestras?
3. ¿Está contenta la directora?
4. ¿Está usted nervioso?
5. ¿Estás tú triste?
6. ¿Están ustedes cansados?

Activity 3
1. voy
2. vamos
3. va
4. va
5. van
6. vas

Activity 4
1. Un borrador está debajo del reloj.
2. Un borrador está debajo de la silla.
3. Un borrador está dentro de la mochila.
4. Un borrador está delante de la ventana.
5. Un borrador está encima del escritorio.
6. Un borrador está detrás de la maestra.

Activity 5
1. Mexican students attend school from the end of August until June.
2. Indigenous cultures influenced Frida Kahlo's style of painting and style of clothing. She often wore traditional native clothing.
3. In Mexico City's National Museum of Anthropology I can find the *Piedra del Sol*, which is an Aztec calendar, as well as other artifacts from Mexico's indigenous cultures.
4. Tourism is very important to the economy of the Dominican Republic, particularly for the travel and hotel industries.

Differentiating Instruction

Slower-paced Learners

Yes/No Questions As an alternative to Activity 4, ask students questions following the model: **¿Está un borrador cerca del pizarrón?** Have them answer in complete sentences. **Sí, un borrador está cerca del pizarrón.** Continue asking about the other items in the picture.

Heritage Language Learners

Increase Accuracy Ask students to reply to Mario's e-mail in Activity 3. They should use forms of **ir** and **ser** to describe their school schedule. For example: **Hola, Mario. Yo voy a la clase de matemáticas en diez minutos. Es una clase difícil pero el maestro es muy bueno. A las doce, mis amigos y yo vamos a...** Correct common spelling mistakes such as **boy** and **siensas.**

Objectives
- Read personal narratives about school and classes in three different countries.
- Have students compare the favorite classes of the authors with their own favorite classes.
- Ask students to write about their school schedule.

Core Resources
- *Cuaderno,* pp. 96–98
- Audio Program: TXT CD 2, track 23
- Video Program: DVD 1

Presentation Strategies
- Ask students to look at the photos on pp. 132 and 133 and describe what they see.
- Instruct students to follow the text in the book as they listen to the audio.
- Tell students to think about their own class schedules while they are reading the three personal accounts.

STANDARDS
1.2 Understand language
1.3 Present information
2.1 Practices and perspectives
4.2 Compare cultures
Critical Thinking and Problem Solving, Pre-AP; **Social and Cross-Cultural Skills,** Compara con tu mundo

Communication
Group Work
Ask students to work in groups of three to write e-mail messages from Juan Carlos to Rafael, from Rafael to Andrea, and from Andrea to Juan Carlos. The subject of the e-mails should be school schedules.

Long-term Retention
Recycle
Review telling time by asking individual students to generate a list of activities. For example: **llegar a la escuela, ir a la cafetería, mirar la televisión, descansar.** Have them use the list to ask their partners when they do these activities. **A: ¿A qué hora llegas a la escuela? B: Llego a la escuela a las siete y cuarto.**

Comparación cultural

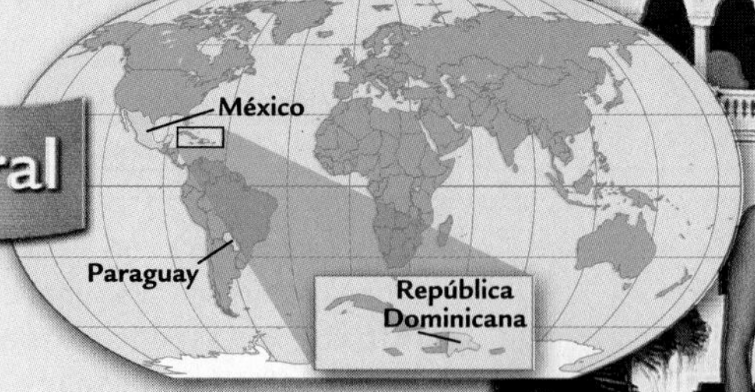

AUDIO

Horarios y clases

Lectura y escritura

WebQuest
my.hrw.com

1. **Leer** School subjects and daily schedules vary around the world. Read how Rafael, Andrea, and Juan Carlos spend a typical day at school.
2. **Escribir** Using the three descriptions as models, write a short paragraph about your daily schedule.

STRATEGY **Escribir**
Create a schedule Draw two large clocks, one for a.m. and the other for p.m. Write your school schedule on these clocks.

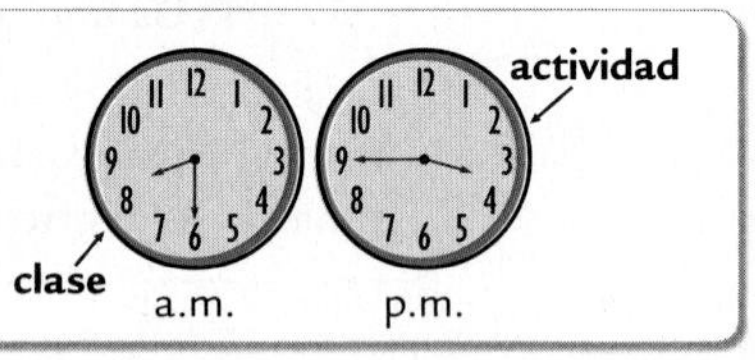

Step 1 Complete the two clocks by listing your classes and after-school activities. Use arrows to point to the correct times.

Step 2 Write your paragraph. Make sure to include all the classes, activities, and times. Check your writing by yourself or with help from a friend. Make final corrections.

Compara con tu mundo
Use the paragraph you wrote to compare your school schedule to the schedule of *one* of the three students. What are the similarities in the schedules? What are the differences?

Cuaderno *pp. 96–98* Cuaderno para hispanohablantes *pp. 96–98*

Differentiating Instruction

Multiple Intelligences
Naturalist Ask students to determine the time zone differences between Santo Domingo, Asunción, México, D.F., and their hometown. Have students write down what time it is where they live and in the other cities when Rafael leaves school. Then ask them to determine what they, Andrea, and Juan Carlos are doing at those times.

Inclusion
Read Before Listening Ask students to read the descriptions silently. Then read them aloud to the class, asking students to track your voice by tracing their index fingers along the printed words as you pronounce them.

Cultura Interactiva my.hrw.com *See these pages come alive!*

República Dominicana

Rafael

¡Hola a todos! Me llamo Rafael y estudio en una escuela en Santo Domingo. Tengo clases todos los días de las ocho de la mañana a la una de la tarde. A las diez tenemos un descanso de quince minutos. Luego, voy a la clase de historia. Es interesante y yo tomo muchos apuntes. En la tarde muchas veces paso un rato con los amigos.

Paraguay

Andrea

¿Qué tal? Me llamo Andrea y estudio en Asunción, Paraguay. Mis clases son en la tarde, de la una a las cinco. En la escuela los estudiantes tienen muchas clases. Todos los días, tengo clases de español, ciencias, historia y matemáticas. También tengo clase de guaraní[1]. Después de las clases, voy al gimnasio y practico deportes. De vez en cuando uso la computadora en la biblioteca.

[1] an indigenous language spoken in Paraguay

México

Juan Carlos

¡Hola! Soy Juan Carlos. Soy estudiante en México, D.F. En la escuela necesito trabajar mucho porque tengo nueve clases. Las clases son de las siete de la mañana a las dos de la tarde. ¡Tengo que llegar muy temprano! Mi clase favorita es la clase de matemáticas. Es interesante y divertida. Después de las clases mis amigos y yo estudiamos en la biblioteca.

Comparación cultural

Exploring the Theme

The Guarani language, which was being used in South America at the time the Spaniards explored the area, is one of the official languages of Paraguay. It is spoken by 94% of the population, and by many Paraguayans who have emigrated to other countries. The constitution of Paraguay is written in both Spanish and Guarani, and state-produced textbooks are printed with half the text in Spanish and half in Guarani. It is the second official language in the province of Corrientes in Argentina. The English words *tapioca, toucan,* and *jaguar* can be traced to Guarani roots.

✓ Ongoing Assessment

Quick Check Ask students yes or no questions to assess comprehension. For example: **¿Es Rafael de México?** (no)

✓ Ongoing Assessment

Rubric Lectura y escritura

Writing Criteria	Excellent	Good	Needs Work
Content	Paragraph contains a lot of information about daily schedule.	Paragraph contains some information about daily schedule.	Paragraph lacks information about daily schedule.
Communication	Paragraph is organized and easy to follow.	Paragraph is fairly well organized and easy to follow.	Paragraph is disorganized and hard to follow.
Accuracy	Paragraph has few mistakes in vocabulary and grammar.	Paragraph has some mistakes in vocabulary and grammar.	Paragraph has many mistakes in vocabulary and grammar.

To customize your own rubrics, use the ***Generate Success** Rubric Generator and Graphic Organizers.*

Differentiating Instruction

Pre-AP

Expand and Elaborate Have students scan the three descriptions on p. 133 and explain the different lengths of the students' school days and number of classes. Then ask students to express their opinion on the reasons for such differences.

Slower-paced Learners

Yes/No Questions Ask students yes or nor questions to assess their comprehension of the descriptions presented on p. 133. If the answer to a question is no, ask students to supply the correct information. For example:
¿Tiene Andrea clases en la mañana?
No, Andrea tiene clases en la tarde.

Objective
- Cumulative review

Core Resource
- Audio Program: TXT CD 2 track 24

Review Options
- **Activity 1:** Listening activity
- **Activity 2:** Speaking activity
- **Activity 3:** Speaking activity
- **Activity 4:** Writing activity
- **Activity 5:** Speaking activity
- **Activity 6:** Speaking and writing activity
- **Activity 7:** Reading and writing activity

STANDARDS
1.2 Understand language, Act. 1
1.3 Present information, Acts. 1-7
2.1 Practices and perspectives, Act. 1
4.2 Compare cultures, Act. 1
21st Century **Creativity and Innovation,** Act. 4/ Multiple Intelligences; **Flexibility and Adaptability,** Acts. 3, 6; **Initiative and Self-Direction,** Study Tips/Pre-AP

Long-term Retention
Study Tips
Ask students to think of new ways to organize vocabulary and grammar notes. This may include color-coding, alphabetizing, or sorting according to another set of categories the student proposes. Remind students that sorting is not the goal, but that organizing material should make it easier to remember.

Answers
Activity 1
1. El señor Minondo enseña la clase de historia.
2. El señor Minondo practica fútbol.
3. La señora Cruz es la directora de la escuela.
4. A la señora Cruz le gusta tocar la guitarra.
5. Los maestros son muy interesantes.

Activity 2–7 Answers will vary.

UNIDADES 1-2

Repaso inclusivo
Options for Review

¡AvanzaRap! DVD Sing and Learn

Digital performance space

1 Listen, understand, and compare
Escuchar

Javier interviewed teachers and administrators at his school for Teacher Appreciation Day. Listen to his report and answer the questions.

1. ¿Qué enseña el señor Minondo?
2. ¿Qué deporte practica el señor Minondo?
3. ¿Quién es la señora Cruz?
4. ¿Qué le gusta hacer a la señora Cruz?
5. ¿Cómo son los maestros?

Are your teachers and administrators like those at Javier's school? What kind of activities do your teachers like to do after classes?

2 Give a school orientation
Hablar

You are giving a talk at an orientation meeting for students who are new to your school. Greet the new students, introduce yourself, and give them some background information about yourself: what classes you have, what you like to do after school, etc. Then tell them where the gym, cafeteria, and other locations around the school are. Finish by describing some of the classes that are available and what they have to do in each class. Your talk should be at least two minutes long.

3 Talk with a school counselor
Hablar

Role-play a conversation with a school counselor. The counselor wants to know what your classes are like and what you like to do after classes. Answer your partner's questions, tell him or her what you do in each class, and ask a few questions of your own about the school. Your conversation should be at least two minutes long.

Differentiating Instruction

Pre-AP
Self-correct Have students audiotape their performances in Activities 2, 3, 5, and 6. Ask them to listen closely to themselves and identify errors or hesitations. Encourage students to write down and correct their errors. Then give them the opportunity to present the activity again, being mindful of correcting themselves as they speak.

Inclusion
Clear Structure Before students begin their interviews in Activity 5, have each pair of students draw a large concept web. First, have them write their topic in the center (**Entrevista**). Then have them record useful vocabulary around the web (**clases, actividades, horarios**). Advise students to refer to their webs as they talk.

4 Write a brochure

Escribir

Create a brochure about your school that would be helpful to a new student from a Spanish-speaking country. Include some of the following: places in the school, classes offered, school supplies needed, teachers, and extracurricular activities. Your brochure should have illustrations and at least six sentences.

5 Interview at a new school

Hablar

Role-play an interview in which you are seeking admission to a school in Mexico. Your partner is the interviewer at the school. The interviewer should ask you questions about your classes and activities. Answer his or her questions and ask a few of your own about the school. The interview should be at least two minutes long.

6 Hold a press conference

Hablar
Escribir

Hold a mock press conference. You and your classmates are reporters and have to ask your teacher questions about his or her school schedule and favorite activities. Use the answers to write a short profile of your teacher that could appear in a Spanish edition of the school newspaper. The profile should have at least five sentences.

7 Write a postcard

Leer
Escribir

You received the following postcard from your new pen pal in Mexico. Write back, answering all of your pen pal's questions and asking a few of your own. Your letter should have at least eight sentences.

PUEBLA

Hola. Me llamo Manuel Salazar. Soy de Puebla, México. Soy estudioso y atlético. Soy un estudiante organizado. Siempre saco buenas notas. ¿Cómo eres tú? ¿Cómo son tus clases? Tengo clases difíciles pero los maestros son muy simpáticos. Estudio mucho y también paso un rato con los amigos. Me gusta jugar al fútbol y andar en patineta. ¿Qué te gusta hacer con los amigos?

Tu amigo,

Manuel

Communication

Group Work

Assign students to work in groups in which there are a variety of learning styles/multiple intelligences. Ask each group to select a favorite part of the lesson. Within each group, ask each person to describe the favorite part according to his or her strength: to draw it, sing it, chart it, etc.

✓ Ongoing Assessment

Rubric Integrated Performance Assessment
Oral Activities 2, 3, 5, 6
Written Activities 4, 6, 7

Very Good	Proficient	Not There Yet
The student thoroughly develops all requirements of the task.	The student develops most requirements of the task.	The student does not develop the requirements of the task.
The student demonstrates excellent control of grammar.	The student demonstrates good to fair control of grammar.	The student demonstrates poor control of grammar.
Good variety of appropriate vocabulary.	Adequate variety of appropriate vocabulary.	The vocabulary is not appropriate.
The pronunciation is excellent to very good.	The pronunciation is good to fair.	The pronunciation is poor.

To customize your own rubrics, use the ***Generate Success*** *Rubric Generator and Graphic Organizers.*

Differentiating Instruction

Multiple Intelligences

Musical/Rhythmic Ask students to take information about their school, their schedules, and their classes, and use it as lyrics to create a song or a chant. Ask for volunteers to bring in musical instruments to play accompaniments.

Slower-paced Learners

Sentence Completion Write a list of classes on the board. For example: **la historia, la música, el arte, las ciencias.** Below the list, write the following sentence frame: **La clase favorita de _____ es _____**. Ask students to copy the sentence frame several times. Then ask them to fill in a person's name (a classmate) and a class for each sentence frame.

Proyectos adicionales

Planning Ahead

Projects **Create a calendar.** Have students create their own calendars for the next few months, or the entire year. Encourage them to be creative and original in their designs, and to use a theme related to Puerto Rico, such as Old San Juan, **la comida criolla,** or famous Puerto Ricans. Once their calendars are complete, have students label specific dates with special events, such as the birthdays of family members. Also, have students review vocabulary related to school activities to record upcoming events, such as specific classes, sports practices, or exams.

PACING SUGGESTION: Upon completion of **Lección 2** to review vocabulary related to dates, family members, school, and activities.

21st Century **Collaboration; Creativity and Innovation**

(Virtual) Bulletin Board

Create a bulletin board with the title **¡A comer!** Provide students with paper plates and a selection of cooking magazines. Instruct students to find favorite food items in the magazines, cut them out, and glue them onto their plates to create a favorite meal. Staple the completed plates to a bulletin board. Use these "dishes" to ask questions about what students see, as well as foods they like and don't like. As a tech alternative, you may wish to have students create their projects on a class wiki page.

PACING SUGGESTION: After **Lección 1** to reinforce food vocabulary and questions and answers using the verb **gustar.**

21st Century **Communication**

Create a bulletin board with the title **Nuestras familias.** Invite students to bring in photographs of one or more family members. Then have them create and decorate frames for their photos using construction paper, stickers, glitter, or other craft supplies. After displaying the photos on a bulletin board, use this "family album" to spark discussions about names, ages, birthdays, favorite foods, and favorite activities. As a tech alternative, you may wish to have students create their projects on a class wiki page.

PACING SUGGESTION: After **Lección 2** to reinforce vocabulary related to ages, birthdays, food, and favorite activities.

21st Century **Communication**

Projects **Play house.** Using large shoe boxes or boxes of similar size, have students create a miniature family dining room. They can create furniture out of clay or cardboard, and cut plates and food out of construction paper. They might bring in small dolls or action figures to serve as the family in their scenes, or use clay or paper to create their people. Encourage students to add a calendar to the wall in their scenes, as well as other objects for which they know the vocabulary. On different days, give students the opportunity to rearrange their scenes, and say something new about the people and objects in their "dining room." **Es el siete de diciembre. Es el cumpleaños de la hermana. La familia come pastel.**

PACING SUGGESTION: Throughout the unit as time allows.

21st Century **Creativity and Innovation**

Games

Dominós

Domino games are a common sight in the parks and plazas throughout Puerto Rico. Obtain several sets of dominos and have students learn how to play. Throughout the unit, hold an ongoing tournament. Keep track of the results on a grid so play can continue as time allows on different days.

Alternately, have students create their own domino sets using pieces of cardboard or index cards. Instead of dots, have students draw simple pictures of food items and family members. As students add to the "train" of tiles, have them name the item they are connecting with. **Tengo una hermana. Tengo un café.**

PACING SUGGESTION: For regular dominos, at any time during the unit. For vocabulary dominos, after vocabulary is presented in **Lección 1** and **2** to reinforce food items and family names. Can be replayed using different sets of tiles.

Music

Create a lyrics poster of the words to **La Borinqueña,** the Puerto Rican national anthem. You can find the lyrics on the Internet. To teach students the melody, locate a recording or download one from the Internet.

Also, invite interested students to research an aspect of Puerto Rican music, such as the musical styles **bomba** or **plena;** or international music stars from Puerto Rico, such as Danny Rivera, Ricky Martin, Chayanne, or the group Menudo.

¡AvanzaRap! DVD

- Video animations of all **¡AvanzaRap!** songs (with Karaoke track)
- Teaching Suggestions
- **¡AvanzaRap!** Activity Masters
- **¡AvanzaRap!** Video Scripts and Answers

Also available on the **Teacher One Stop**

Recipe

Piraguas are sold by **piragüeros** in the parks and on the streets of Puerto Rico. These refreshing treats are like snow cones with tropical fruit flavors. You can make them in your classroom using a blender.

Piraguas

Ingredientes

1 bolsa de hielo

3 o más latas de jugo concentrado de sabores tropicales (piña, mango, papaya, etc.)

Instrucciones

En un jarrón, diluir cada lata de jugo concentrado a 1/3 de lo que indican las instrucciones (usualmente una lata de agua en vez de tres). Triturar hielo en la licuadora y ponerlo en pequeños vasos de cartón. Verter el almíbar sobre el hielo y servir con una cucharita.

La comida criolla. Plan a Puerto Rican tasting day! Have students research recipes for traditional Puerto Rican dishes, such as **empanadillas, asopao, tostones,** or **arroz con pollo.** Organize volunteers to bring in their culinary creations, as well as paper plates, napkins, and plastic silverware. Invite each "chef" to speak about his or her dish, and then **¡Buen provecho!**

UNIT THEME
Eating with the family

UNIT STANDARDS

COMMUNICATION
- Talk about foods and beverages
- Ask questions
- Say which foods you like and don't like
- Talk about family
- Ask and tell ages
- Express possession
- Give dates
- Make comparisons

CULTURES
- Traditional cooking of Puerto Rico, El Salvador
- La Plaza de Colón in Old San Juan
- Grocery shopping
- Government elections in Puerto Rico
- Rafael Tufiño and Fernando Sayán Polo
- Instruments from Puerto Rico and Peru

CONNECTIONS
- Science: Researching severe weather
- Math: Calculating the speed of a storm
- History: Researching Caribbean hurricanes
- Geography: Tracking Hurricane Georges

COMPARISONS
- Hot weather foods and drinks
- Traditional Puerto Rican and Salvadoran dishes
- The Spanish letters **r** and **rr**; the letter **j** in Spanish and in English
- The **quinceañera** celebration in Peru and Puerto Rico
- Landmarks in Puerto Rico and the U.S.
- The **sobremesa,** and other mealtime traditions
- Elections in Puerto Rico and the U.S.
- Portraits by Rafael Tufiño (Puerto Rico) and Fernando Sayán Polo (Peru)
- The **quinceañera** celebration
- Instruments from Puerto Rico and Peru
- Sunday meals in El Salvador, Peru, Puerto Rico, the U.S.

COMMUNITIES
- Andean music and music of other countries in a local store

UNIDAD 3

Puerto Rico

Comer en familia

Lección 1
Tema: ***Mi comida favorita***

Lección 2
Tema: ***En mi familia***

«¡Hola!
Somos Marisol y Rodrigo.
Somos de Puerto Rico.»

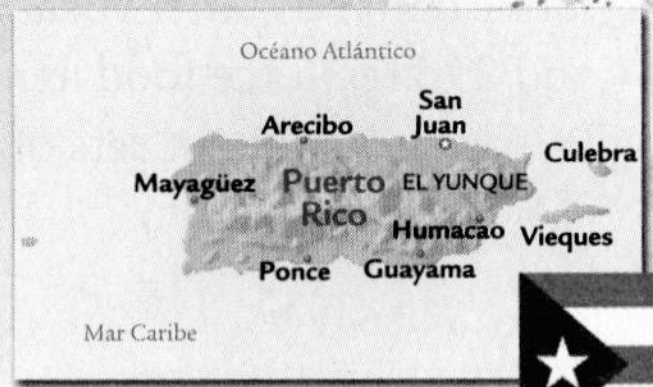

Población: 3.958.128
Área: 3.515 millas cuadradas
Capital: San Juan
Moneda: el dólar estadounidense
Idiomas: español, inglés (los dos son oficiales)
Comida típica: pasteles, arroz con gandules, pernil
Gente famosa: Julia de Burgos (poetisa), Roberto Clemente (beisbolista), Rosario Ferré (escritora), Luis Muñoz Marín (político)

Pasteles

136 ciento treinta y seis

Cultural Geography

Setting the Scene
- How many stars does the Puerto Rican flag have? (one)
- What are the two official languages of Puerto Rico? (Spanish, English)
- What is the currency of Puerto Rico? (U.S. dollar) Why? (Puerto Rico is a U.S. commonwealth.)

Teaching with Maps
- Which country is Puerto Rico's closest Spanish-speaking neighbor? (Dominican Republic)
- Where on the island is San Juan located? (the Northern coast)
- What are the names of two smaller islands that belong to Puerto Rico? (Culebra, Vieques)

CULTURA Interactiva my.hrw.com *See these pages come alive!*

Una familia come en la playa

◀ **Comidas al aire libre** Many Puerto Ricans enjoy informal gatherings at a beach or park, where families can spend the day together, barbecue, and listen to music. **Pinchos** (skewers of chicken or pork) are popular at barbecues and snack stands. *Where do people like to eat outdoors where you live?*

Casas de colores vivos San Juan is famous for its well-preserved colonial quarter, called **Viejo San Juan.** Its narrow streets are lined with brightly-colored houses with balconies. *What are some historic areas close to where you live?* ▶

Casas coloniales en el Viejo San Juan

La Cascada de la Coca en El Yunque

◀ **Un parque nacional** El Yunque is the only tropical rain forest in the care of the U.S. Forest Service. The park has many waterfalls, such as the Cascada de la Coca, and is home to the **coquí,** a tiny tree frog named for its distinctive song. *What are some features of other parks in the United States?*

CULTURA Interactiva my.hrw.com

Send your students to my.hrw.com to explore authentic Puerto Rican culture. Tell them to click on Cultura interactiva to see these pages come alive!

Culture

About the Photos

- The architecture of **Viejo San Juan** dates from the 16th century and mimics the majestic, yet charming, architecture of many southern Spanish cities. These well-preserved, pastel-colored buildings are the pride of the Old City.
- The waterfall pictured here is located in an ancient rain forest, just a short distance from San Juan. The forest offers a variety of trees, flowers, and wildlife.

Expanded Information

- Puerto Rican food, or **comida criolla,** has a distinctive taste, which comes from the herbs and spices that enhance it. A combination of local ingredients produces **sofrito,** the seasoning used in popular dishes such as **arroz con pollo.**
- Old San Juan has other centuries-old, historically important structures: El Morro Fortress, San Juan Cathedral, and the Dominican Convent.
- **El Yunque,** which lies in the Luquillo Mountain Range, was once considered a sacred place by Puerto Rico's native Taino people. The name **El Yunque** means *White Lands* and refers to the cloud-covered mountaintops in this part of the island.

Bridging Cultures

Heritage Language Learners

Support What They Know Invite those students who have a personal or family connection to Puerto Rico to enrich the information presented on pp. 136 and 137. What are their memories and/or impressions of this island? How would they compare family life and food in Puerto Rico with that of the United States? What are some of their favorite traditional Puerto Rican dishes?

English Learners

Build Background Encourage students to make connections with the information on p. 137. After reading each paragraph, ask the follow-up question in reference to their home country. Substitute the name of the country for the phrase *where you live.* For example: *Where do people like to eat outdoors in Korea? What are some historic areas in Haiti?*

Video Character Guide

Marisol and Rodrigo are friends who live in Puerto Rico. They both enjoy food, but disagree about what the best choices are when grocery shopping or eating.

Lesson Overview

Culture at a Glance

Topic & Activity	Essential Question
Hot weather foods and beverages pp. 138-139	What do you like to eat or drink during hot weather?
Traditional Cooking p. 146	How do historical influences affect the food that people eat?
Let's go grocery shopping! pp. 156-157	What are some of the food items that people from Puerto Rico buy on a regular basis?
Culture Review p. 161	What are some aspects of Puerto Rican and Salvadoran culture?

COMPARISON COUNTRIES Puerto Rico El Salvador Perú

Practice at a Glance

	Objective	Activity & Skill
Vocabulary	Food and beverages	1: Writing; 2: Speaking; 5: Reading/Writing; 7: Speaking; 8: Reading/ Speaking; 9: Writing/Speaking; 10: Listening/Reading; 11: Writing; 12: Speaking/Writing; 13: Writing/Speaking; 20: Reading/Listening/Speaking; Repaso 1: Listening; Repaso 2: Writing
	Interrogative words	3: Listening/Reading; 16: Speaking; 18: Listening/Reading; Repaso 3: Writing
Grammar	Using interrogative words	3: Listening/Reading; 18: Listening/Reading; Repaso 3: Reading/Writing
	Gustar with nouns	5: Reading/Writing; 7: Speaking; 8: Reading/Speaking; 9: Writing/Speaking; 10: Listening/Reading; 11: Writing; 12: Speaking/Writing; 21: Writing; Repaso 4: Writing
	Present tense of **-er** and **-ir** verbs	13: Writing/Speaking; 14: Writing/Speaking; 15: Listening/Writing; 16: Speaking; 19: Speaking; Repaso 2: Speaking
	The verb hacer	16: Speaking; 19: Speaking; Repaso 2: Writing
Communication	Talk about foods and beverages	1: Writing; 2: Speaking; 4: Speaking; 5: Reading/Writing; 7: Speaking; 8: Reading/Speaking; 9: Writing/Speaking; 10: Listening/Reading; 11: Writing; 12: Speaking/Writing; 21: Writing; Repaso 4: Writing
	Ask questions	2: Speaking; 7: Speaking; 8: Reading/Speaking; 12: Speaking/Writing; 16: Speaking
	Say which foods you like and don't like	5: Reading/Writing; 7: Speaking; 8: Reading/Speaking; 9: Writing/Speaking; 10: Listening/Reading; 11: Writing; 12: Speaking/Writing; 21: Writing; Repaso 4: Writing
	Pronunciation: the letters r and **rr**	Las letras ***r*** y ***rr***, p. 146: Listening/Speaking
Recycle	Gustar with an infinitive	2: Speaking
	Snack foods	4: Speaking
	The verb estar	14: Writing/Speaking
	Telling time	19: Speaking

The following presentations are recorded in the Audio Program for ***¡Avancemos!***

- **¡A responder!** *page 141*
- **15: Actividades en el almuerzo** *page 151*
- **20: Integración** *page 155*
- **Repaso de la lección** *page 160*
  1: Listen and understand

For **¡AvanzaRap!** scripts, see the **¡AvanzaRap! DVD.**

¡A responder! TXT CD 3 track 2

1. la hamburguesa
2. la leche
3. el pan
4. el sándwich de jamón y queso
5. el cereal
6. la sopa
7. el huevo
8. el café

15 | Actividades en el almuerzo

TXT CD 3 track 6

Marisol: ¡Hola! Soy Marisol. Antes del almuerzo, tengo la clase de inglés. Escribo en el cuaderno, pero es difícil porque tengo mucha hambre.

Rodrigo: Soy Rodrigo. Es la hora del almuerzo. Hmmm... la cafetería vende sopa, uvas y bananas.

Mateo: Me llamo Mateo. ¡Me gusta la comida nutritiva! Hoy Rodrigo y yo comemos uvas.

Carmen: Hola, me llamo Carmen. Ahora estoy en la cafetería. Bebo jugo de naranja porque tengo sed. ¡Es rico!

Raúl y David, ¿qué hacen ustedes? ¿Por qué no comen?

Raúl: Leemos un libro. Nos gustan los libros.

Laura: Hola, soy Laura. Hoy la cafetería no vende sándwiches. ¡Qué horrible! Pero mi amiga Diana tiene un sándwich y nosotras compartimos. Es una buena amiga.

20 | Integración TXT CD 3 tracks 8, 9

¿Tienes hambre? En Supermercado Econo vendemos todo para el desayuno: cereal, huevos y muchas frutas. También hay almuerzo todos los días en la cafetería dentro del supermercado. Vendemos hamburguesas muy ricas, sándwiches de jamón, sopas nutritivas y ¡más!

Repaso de la lección TXT CD 3 track 11

1 Listen and understand

Roque: Gracias por estar con nosotros, Lola.

Lola: El gusto es mío, Roque. Me gusta hablar de la comida.

Roque: Ah, ¿sí? ¿Qué te gusta comer más?

Lola: Las hamburguesas son muy ricas. En el desayuno como dos hamburguesas casi todos los días.

Roque: ¿Te gustan las hamburguesas en el desayuno? Interesante... ¿Y bebes café también?

Lola: No, el café es para la cena. Bebo café todas las noches.

Roque: ¿Qué te gusta comer en la cena?

Lola: Siempre como huevos y pan.

Roque: ¿Qué comes y bebes en el almuerzo?

Lola: Como cereal y una banana.

Roque: ¿Bebes leche?

Lola: Sí, bebo leche en el almuerzo porque es muy buena.

Roque: También bebes leche en el desayuno, ¿no?

Lola: No, me gusta más beber un refresco en el desayuno.

Roque: Gracias, Lola. Eres una persona muy interesante.

Resource List

Everything you need to ...

Plan

TEACHER ONE STOP

✓Lesson Plans
✓Teacher Resources
✓Audio and Video

Present

INTERACTIVE WHITEBOARD LESSONS

TEACHER ONE STOP WITH PROJECTABLE TRANSPARENCIES

POWER PRESENTATIONS

ANIMATEDGRAMMAR

Assess

ONLINE ASSESSMENT

✓ Assessments for on-level, modified, pre-AP, and heritage learners
✓ Create customized tests with **Examview Assessment Suite**
✓ **performance space**
✓ *Generate Success* Rubric Generator

Print

Plan	Present	Practice	Assess
URB 3 • Video Scripts pp. 69–70 • Family Letter p. 91 • Absent Student Copymasters pp. 93–100 **Best Practices Toolkit**	**URB 3** • Video Activities pp. 51–58	• *Cuaderno* pp. 99–121 • *Cuaderno para hispanohablantes* pp. 99–121 • *Lectura para todos* pp. 22–26 • *Lectura para hispanohablantes* • *¡AvanzaCómics! SúperBruno y Nati,* Episodio 2 **URB 3** • Practice Games pp. 31–38 • Audio Scripts pp. 73–77 • Map/Culture Activities pp. 83–84 • Fine Art Activities pp. 86–87	**Differentiated Assessment Program** **URB 3** • Did you get it? Reteaching and Practice Copymasters pp. 1–12

Projectable Transparencies (Teacher One Stop, my.hrw.com)

Culture	Presentation and Practice	Classroom Management
• Atlas Maps 1–6 • Map: Puerto Rico 1 • Fine Art Transparencies 2, 3	• Vocabulary Transparencies 6, 7 • Grammar Presentation Transparencies 10, 11	• Warm Up Transparencies 16–19 • Student Book and Workbook Answer Transparencies 24–27, 33–39

Audio and Video

Audio	Video	¡AvanzaRap! DVD
• Student Book Audio CD 3 Tracks 1–11 • Workbook Audio CD 2 Tracks 1–10 • Heritage Learners Audio CD 1 Tracks 17–20, CD 3 Tracks 15, 16 • Assessment Audio CD 1 Tracks 15, 16 • *Lecturas para todos* Audio CD 1 Track 5, CD 2 Tracks 1–6 • Sing-along Songs Audio CD	• Vocabulary Video DVD 1 • *Telehistoria* DVD 1 Escena 1 Escena 2 Escena 3 Completa	• Video animations of all **¡AvanzaRap!** songs (with Karaoke track) • Interactive DVD Activities • Teaching Suggestions • **¡AvanzaRap!** Activity Masters • **¡AvanzaRap!** video scripts and answers

Online and Media Resources

Student	Teacher
Available online at my.hrw.com • Online Student Edition • News + Networking • performance space • @HOMETUTOR • CULTURA Interactiva • WebQuests • Interactive Flashcards • Review Games • Self-Check Quiz **Student One Stop** **Holt McDougal Spanish Apps**	**Teacher One Stop (also available at my.hrw.com)** • Interactive Teacher's Edition • All print, audio, and video resources • Projectable Transparencies • Lesson Plans • TPRS • Examview Assessment Suite **Available online at my.hrw.com** *Generate Success* Rubric Generator and Graphic Organizers **Power Presentations**

Differentiated Assessment

On-level	Modified	Pre-AP	Heritage Learners
• Vocabulary Recognition Quiz p. 103 • Vocabulary Production Quiz p. 104 • Grammar Quizzes pp. 105–106 • Culture Quiz p. 107 • On-level Lesson Test pp. 108–114	• Modified Lesson Test pp. 83–89	• Pre-AP Lesson Test pp. 83–89	• Heritage Learners Lesson Test pp. 89–95

Core Pacing Guide

50 Minute (9 Day)

	Objectives/Focus	Teach	Practice	Assess/HW Options
DAY 1	**Culture:** learn about Puerto Rican culture **Vocabulary:** breakfast, lunch, and dinner foods and beverages • Warm Up OHT 16 **5 min**	Unit Opener pp. 136–137 Lesson Opener pp. 138–139 **Presentación de vocabulario** pp. 140–141 • Read A–D • View video DVD 1 • Play audio TXT CD 3 track 1 • *¡A responder!* TXT CD 3 track 2 **25 min**	Lesson opener pp. 138–139 **Práctica de vocabulario** p. 142 • Acts. 1, 2 **15 min**	**Assess:** *Para y piensa* p. 142 **5 min** **Homework:** *Cuaderno* pp. 99–101 @HomeTutor
DAY 2	**Communication:** identify question words, practice using them to ask questions and give answers • Warm Up OHT 16 • Check Homework **5 min**	**Vocabulario en contexto** pp. 143–144 • *Telehistoria escena 1* DVD 1 • *Nota gramatical:* interrogative words **20 min**	**Vocabulario en contexto** pp. 143–144 • Act. 3 TXT CD 3 track 3 • Act. 4 **20 min**	**Assess:** *Para y piensa* p. 144 **5 min** **Homework:** *Cuaderno* pp. 99–101 @HomeTutor
DAY 3	**Grammar: gustar** with nouns • Warm Up OHT 17 • Check Homework **5 min**	**Presentación de gramática** p. 145 • **Gustar** with nouns **Práctica de gramática** pp. 146–147 • *Pronunciación:* TXT CD 3 track 4 **20 min**	**Práctica de gramática** pp. 146–147 • Acts. 5, 6, 7, 8, 9 **20 min**	**Assess:** *Para y piensa* p. 147 **5 min** **Homework:** *Cuaderno* pp. 102–104 @HomeTutor
DAY 4	**Communication:** talk about likes and dislikes using **gustar** • Warm Up OHT 17 • Check Homework **5 min**	**Gramática en contexto** pp. 148–149 • *Telehistoria escena 2* DVD 1 **15 min**	**Gramática en contexto** pp. 148–149 • Act. 10 TXT CD 3 track 5 • Acts. 11,12 **25 min**	**Assess:** *Para y piensa* p. 149 **5 min** **Homework:** *Cuaderno* pp. 102–104 @HomeTutor
DAY 5	**Grammar:** present tense of **-er** and **-ir** verbs • Warm Up OHT 18 • Check Homework **5 min**	**Presentación de gramática** p. 150 • Present tense of **-er** and **-ir** verbs **Práctica de gramática** pp. 151–152 **Culture:** *La Plaza de Colón* • *Nota gramatical:* the verb **hacer** **15 min**	**Práctica de gramática** pp. 151–152 • Acts. 13, 14, 16 • Act. 15 TXT CD 3 track 6 **25 min**	**Assess:** *Para y piensa* p. 152 **5 min** **Homework:** *Cuaderno* pp. 105–107 @HomeTutor
DAY 6	**Communication:** Culmination: talk about eating healthy foods; using **-er** and **-ir** verbs • Warm Up OHT 18 • Check Homework **5 min**	**Todo junto** pp. 153–155 • *Escenas 1, 2: Resumen* • *Telehistoria completa* DVD 1 **20 min**	**Todo junto** pp. 153–155 • Acts. 17, 18 TXT CD 3 tracks 3, 5, 7 • Act. 20 TXT CD 3 tracks 8, 9 • Acts. 19, 21 **20 min**	**Assess:** *Para y piensa* p. 155 **5 min** **Homework:** *Cuaderno* pp. 108–109 @HomeTutor
DAY 7	**Reading:** Let's shop and eat! **Connections:** Science • Warm Up OHT 19 • Check Homework **5 min**	**Lectura** pp. 156–157 • *¡A comprar y a comer!* TXT CD 3 track 10 **Conexiones** p. 158 • *Las ciencias* **15 min**	**Lectura** pp. 156–157 • *¡A comprar y a comer!* **Conexiones** p. 158 • *Proyectos* 1, 2, 3 **25 min**	**Assess:** *Para y piensa* p. 157 **5 min** **Homework:** *Cuaderno* pp. 113–115 @HomeTutor
DAY 8	**Review:** *Lesson review* • Warm Up OHT 19 • Check Homework **5 min**	**Repaso de la lección** pp. 160–161 **15 min**	**Repaso de la lección** pp. 160–161 • Act. 1 TXT CD 3 track 11 • Acts. 2, 3, 4, 5 **25 min**	**Assess:** *Repaso de la lección* pp. 160–161 **5 min** **Homework:** *En resumen* p. 159; *Cuaderno* pp. 110–112, 116–121 (optional) Review Games Online @HomeTutor
DAY 9	**Assessment**			**Assess:** Lesson 1 test **50 min**

Core Pacing Guide 90 Minute (5 Day)

	Objectives/focus	Teach	Practice	Assess/HW Options
DAY 1	**Culture:** learn about Puerto Rican culture **Vocabulary:** breakfast, lunch, and dinner foods and beverages • Warm Up OHT 16 **5 min**	Unit Opener pp. 136–137 Lesson Opener pp. 138–139 **Presentación de vocabulario** pp. 140–141 • Read A–D • View video DVD 1 • Play audio TXT CD 3 track 1 • *¡A responder!* TXT CD 3 track 2 **25 min**	Lesson Opener pp. 138–139 **Práctica de vocabulario** p. 142 • Acts. 1, 2 **15 min**	**Assess:** *Para y piensa* p. 142 **5 min**
	Communication: identify question words, practice using them to ask questions and give answers **5 min**	**Vocabulario en contexto** pp. 143–144 • *Telehistoria escena 1* DVD 1 • *Nota gramatical:* interrogative words **15 min**	**Vocabulario en contexto** pp. 143–144 • Act. 3 TXT CD 3 track 3 • Act. 4 **15 min**	**Assess:** *Para y piensa* p. 144 **5 min** **Homework:** *Cuaderno* pp. 99–101 @HomeTutor
DAY 2	**Grammar: gustar** with nouns • Warm Up OHT 17 • Check Homework **5 min**	**Presentación de gramática** p. 145 • **Gustar** with nouns **Práctica de gramática** pp. 146–147 • *Pronunciación:* TXT CD 3 track 4 **15 min**	**Práctica de gramática** pp. 146–147 • Acts. 5, 6, 7, 8, 9 **20 min**	**Assess:** *Para y piensa* p. 147 **5 min**
	Communication: talk about likes and dislikes using **gustar** **5 min**	**Gramática en contexto** pp. 148–149 • *Telehistoria escena 2* DVD 1 **15 min**	**Gramática en contexto** pp. 148–149 • Act. 10 TXT CD 3 track 5 • Acts. 11, 12 **20 min**	**Assess:** *Para y piensa* p. 149 **5 min** **Homework:** *Cuaderno* pp. 102–104 @HomeTutor
DAY 3	**Grammar:** present tense of **-er** and **-ir** verbs • Warm Up OHT 18 • Check Homework **5 min**	**Presentación de gramática** p. 150 • Present tense of **-er** and **-ir** verbs **Práctica de gramática** pp. 151–152 • *Nota gramatical:* the verb **hacer** **Culture:** *La Plaza de Colón* **15 min**	**Práctica de gramática** pp. 151–152 • Acts. 13, 14, 16 • Acts. 15 TXT CD 3 track 6 **20 min**	**Assess:** *Para y piensa* p. 152 **5 min**
	Communication: Culmination: talk about eating healthy foods; using **-er** and **-ir** verbs **5 min**	**Todo junto** pp. 153–155 • *Escenas 1, 2: Resumen* • *Telehistoria completa* DVD 1 **15 min**	**Todo junto** pp. 153–155 • Acts. 17, 18 TXT CD 3 tracks 3, 5, 7 • Act. 20 TXT CD 3 tracks 8, 9 • Acts. 19, 21 **20 min**	**Assess:** *Para y piensa* p. 155 **5 min** **Homework:** *Cuaderno* pp. 105–109 @HomeTutor
DAY 4	**Reading:** Let's shop and eat! • Warm Up OHT 19 • Check Homework **5 min**	**Lectura** pp. 156–157 • *¡A comprar y a comer!* TXT CD 3 track 10 **15 min**	**Lectura** pp. 156–157 • *¡A comprar y a comer!* **20 min**	**Assess:** *Para y piensa* p. 157 **5 min**
	Review: Lesson review **5 min**	**Repaso de la lección** pp. 160–161 **15 min**	**Repaso de la lección** pp. 160–161 • Act. 1 TXT CD 3 track 11 • Acts. 2, 3, 4, 5 **20 min**	**Assess:** *Repaso de la lección* pp. 160–161 **5 min** **Homework:** *En resumen* p. 159; *Cuaderno* p. 110–121 (optional) Review Games Online @HomeTutor
DAY 5	**Assessment**			**Assess:** Lesson 1 test **45 min**
	Connections: Science **5 min**	**Conexiones** p. 158 • *Las ciencias* **10 min**	**Conexiones** p. 158 • *Proyectos 1, 2, 3* **30 min**	

¡AVANZA! Objectives

- Introduce lesson theme: **Mi comida favorita.**
- **Culture:** Learn about and compare foods from different countries.

Presentation Strategies

- Introduce the characters' names: Rodrigo and Marisol.
- Ask students to make a list of their favorite foods and beverages.
- Have students from other countries talk about foods and beverages typical of their countries.

STANDARDS

2.2 Products and perspectives
4.2 Compare cultures
21st Century **Social and Cross-Cultural Skills,** Heritage Language Learners

Warm Up Projectable Transparencies, 3-16

Ir Fill in the blanks with the appropriate form of **ir.**

1. Anita y Juan _____ a la cafetería a las doce.
2. Selena y yo _____ al gimnasio después de las clases.
3. ¿_____ ustedes a la biblioteca? Tengo que ir también.
4. ¿_____ tú al baño?
5. Yo _____ a la oficina.

Answers: 1. van; 2. vamos; 3. Van; 4. Vas; 5. voy

Comparación cultural

Exploring the Theme

Ask the following:

1. Do you buy food from street vendors?
2. Do you like to try new types of foods when you travel?
3. Are there any grocery shops where you live that sell foods from other countries?

¿Qué ves? Sample answers include:

- Sí, los chicos están contentos.
- Están delante del señor.
- A los chicos les gusta comer helado.

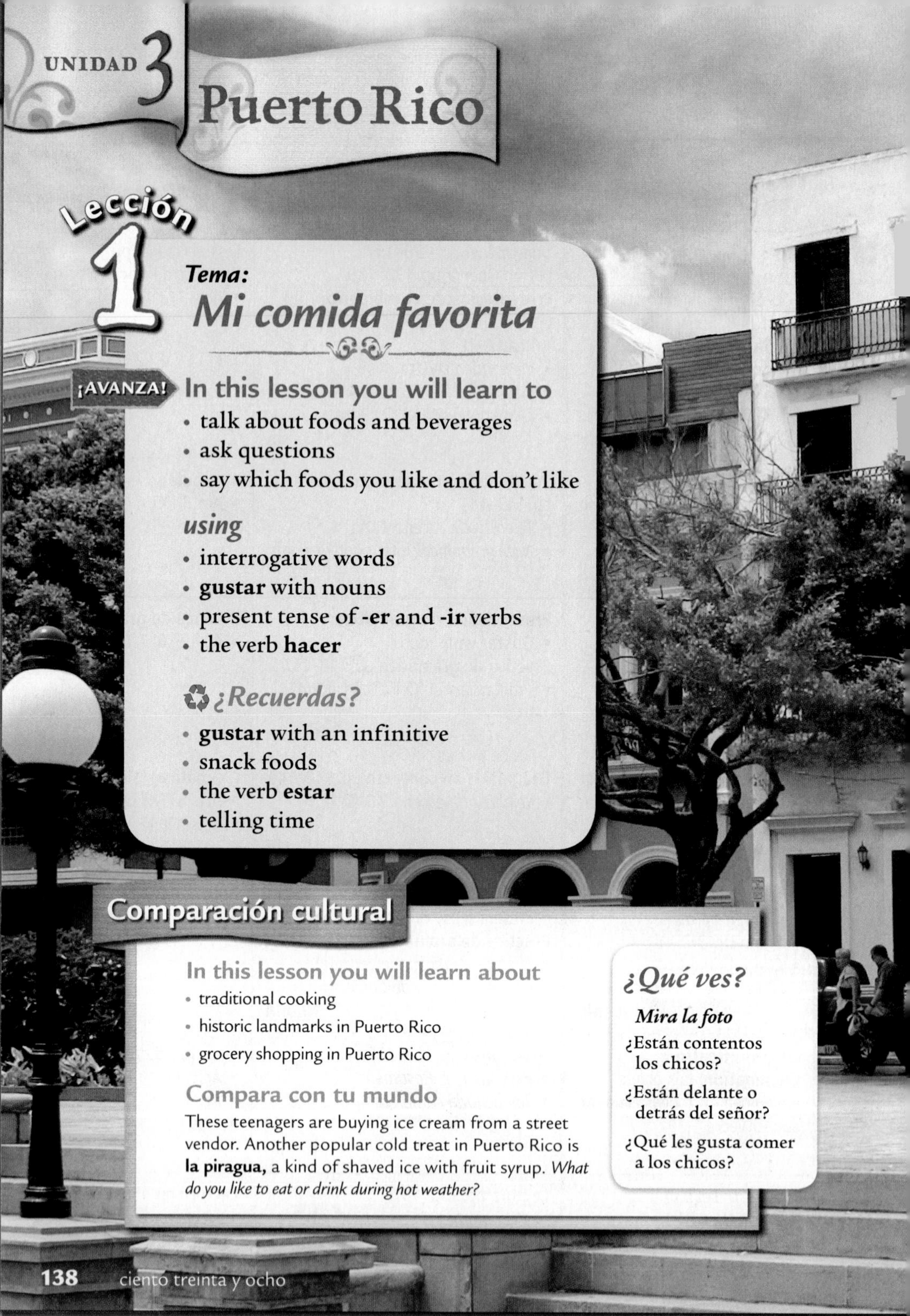

UNIDAD 3 Puerto Rico

Lección 1

Tema:

Mi comida favorita

¡AVANZA! In this lesson you will learn to

- talk about foods and beverages
- ask questions
- say which foods you like and don't like

using

- interrogative words
- **gustar** with nouns
- present tense of **-er** and **-ir** verbs
- the verb **hacer**

¿Recuerdas?

- **gustar** with an infinitive
- snack foods
- the verb **estar**
- telling time

Comparación cultural

In this lesson you will learn about

- traditional cooking
- historic landmarks in Puerto Rico
- grocery shopping in Puerto Rico

Compara con tu mundo

These teenagers are buying ice cream from a street vendor. Another popular cold treat in Puerto Rico is **la piragua,** a kind of shaved ice with fruit syrup. *What do you like to eat or drink during hot weather?*

¿Qué ves?

Mira la foto

¿Están contentos los chicos?

¿Están delante o detrás del señor?

¿Qué les gusta comer a los chicos?

Differentiating Instruction

Heritage Language Learners

Support What They Know Ask students what are some popular or typical dishes from their country of origin. What are the main ingredients, and how are they prepared? If you have students of Puerto Rican descent, ask them to share what they know about typical Puerto Rican cuisine. You can also have students research the topic at the library or via the Internet.

Inclusion

Cumulative Instruction Remind students that they already learned some vocabulary related to food in Unidad 1, Lección 1. Ask students to review this vocabulary by writing each familiar word and then drawing a corresponding picture. Then ask students to draw pictures of new food items for which they would like to learn the Spanish word.

DIGITAL SPANISH my.hrw.com
ONLINE STUDENT EDITION with...

performance space
News Networking
@HOMETUTOR
CULTURA Interactiva

- Audio and Video Resources
- Interactive Flashcards
- Review Activities
- WebQuest
- Conjuguemos.com

PRACTICE SPANISH WITH HOLT MCDOUGAL APPS!

La Plaza de Colón en el Viejo San Juan
San Juan, Puerto Rico

DIGITAL SPANISH

TEACHER TOOLS
- Interactive Whiteboard Lessons
- Generate Success!

ALSO AVAILABLE...
- Online Workbook
- Spanish InterActive Reader

SPANISH ON THE GO!
- Performance Space
- Holt McDougal Spanish Apps
- ¡Avancemos! eTextbook

Using the Photo

Location Information

Plaza de Colón, shown in the photo, is in the heart of San Juan's Old Town. Originally called **Plaza Santiago,** it was renamed in 1893 to honor the 400th anniversary of Columbus's arrival to that island. The plaza hosts several quaint cafés and ice-cream stands.

Expanded Information

Puerto Rico The island of Puerto Rico is 100 miles long, and only 35 miles wide. Both Spanish and English are official languages of Puerto Rico. Puerto Rico is not a country or a state. It is a self-governing commonwealth in association with the United States. Its official name is **Estado Libre Asociado de Puerto Rico.**

Differentiating Instruction

Pre-AP

Expand and Elaborate Have students write three to five things they know about Puerto Rico. Topics can include history, geography, daily life, climate, language, etc. Have them post this information around a map of Puerto Rico and call on volunteers to give a short description of the island.

Slower-paced Learners

Yes/No Questions Ask students yes/no questions about what they see in the photo on pp. 138 and 139. Point to the appropriate item in the photo when the answer is yes. **¿Hay dos chicos en la foto? ¿Hay un parque?** Use familiar vocabulary on other topics when the answer is no. **¿Hay una chica enojada? ¿Hay un gimnasio?**

Long-term Retention

Recycle

Have students write a list of snack foods or beverages that they enjoy eating or drinking. Then have them practice these words by using them in the following sentence: **Me gusta comer/beber _____.**

Objective
- Present vocabulary: food, meals.

Core Resources
- Video Program: DVD 1
- Audio Program: TXT CD 3, tracks 1, 2

Presentation Strategies
- Have students look at pp. 140–141 and present vocabulary.
- Ask **cierto/falso** questions to verify comprehension. For example: **La leche es una comida (Falso, es una bebida).**
- Play the audio as students read A–D.
- Show the video.

STANDARD
1.2 Understand language

Creativity and Innovation, Pre-AP; **Social and Cross-Cultural Skills,** English Learners

Comparisons
English Language Connection
Spanish often requires the use of **tener** rather than an English equivalent of the verb *to be* to express a condition. Note: **tener hambre** and **tener sed.** To say that one is very thirsty or very hungry, use **tener mucha sed** and **tener mucha hambre. Tener ganas de** + an infinitive means *to feel like.*

Long-term Retention
Personalize It
Read the names of the food items on pp. 140–141 and ask students to vote with a show of hands whether they are **rico/a/os/as** or **horrible(s).** Tally the votes on the board.

Communication
Regionalisms
In Spain and Mexico many people use **la comida** instead of **el almuerzo.** In the Southwest of the United States the preferred term is **el lonche.** In Spain **un sándwich** is called **un bocadillo** and in Mexico it is called **una torta.**

Presentación de VOCABULARIO

¡AVANZA! **Goal:** Learn about what Rodrigo and Marisol eat for breakfast, lunch, and dinner. Then practice what you have learned to talk about foods and beverages. ***Actividades 1–2***

¿Recuerdas? **gustar** with an infinitive p. 42

VIDEO DVD

AUDIO

A ¡Hola! Me llamo Rodrigo y ella es Ana. Son las ocho de la mañana. **Es importante** comer **un desayuno nutritivo** todos los días.

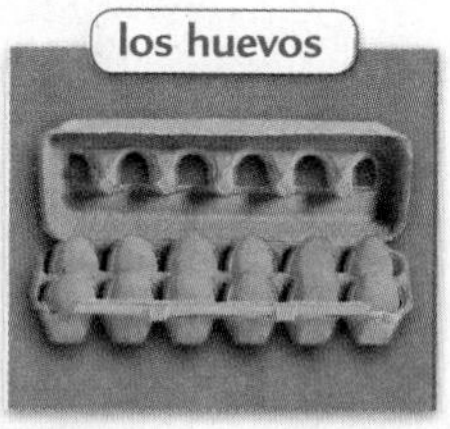

B Cuando **tengo hambre,** me gusta comer **huevos** y **pan.** Cuando **tengo sed,** bebo **jugo de naranja.** Me gusta mucho porque es **rico.** Nunca bebo **café** porque es **horrible.**

En Puerto Rico se dice...

In Puerto Rico the word for *orange juice* is **el jugo de china.** The word for *banana* is **el guineo.**

Más vocabulario

¿Cómo? *How?*	¿Quién(es)? *Who?*
¿Cuál(es)? *Which?*	compartir *to share*
¿Por qué? *Why?*	otro(a) *other*
¿Qué? *What?*	*Expansión de vocabulario* p. R4

Differentiating Instruction

English Learners
Build Background Before introducing the Spanish vocabulary on p. 140, give English learners the opportunity to familiarize themselves with the photos. Discuss the food items presented and whether similar items exist in their countries of origin. If items do not exist, is there something similar that people eat or drink?

Multiple Intelligences
Logical/Mathematical Say aloud the name of one of the breakfast foods presented on p. 140. Tell students to raise their hands if they had that item for breakfast that morning. Record the findings of your survey on the board. Then have students present the information in the form of a bar graph that represents which breakfast foods are most popular among their classmates.

C Es la una y **ahora** Marisol y yo comemos **el almuerzo.** En la cafetería **venden** muchas **comidas: sándwiches, hamburguesas** y **sopa.** También venden **bebidas: leche,** jugos y refrescos.

el sándwich de jamón y queso

el almuerzo

la hamburguesa

la sopa

D Marisol y yo compramos fruta **para** mi papá: **manzanas, bananas** y **uvas. La cena** es a las siete y **tengo ganas de** comer. Siempre como mucho cuando mi mamá prepara la comida.

las uvas

la manzana

la banana

la cena

@HOMETUTOR my.hrw.com Interactive Flashcards

¡A responder! Escuchar

En un papel escribe **desayuno** y en otro escribe **almuerzo.** Escucha la lista de comida. Para cada comida, levanta el (los) papel(es) correcto(s) para indicar cuándo la comes. *(Write **desayuno** and **almuerzo** on separate pieces of paper. Then hold up the correct paper[s] based on the foods you hear.)*

TEACHER to TEACHER

Ildaura D. Boreland
Orlando, Florida

Tips for Classroom Management

"I work in an inner city school in Orlando, and I like to give my students a sense of organization. Before class, I stand at the door and hand out worksheets, index cards or any other type of materials that contain information related to the lesson of the day. The students immediately know that there is work ahead to do. I also write the instructions on the overhead or the board for reinforcement."

Go online for more tips!

Comparisons

English Language Connection

Point out that in English a noun is often used to describe another noun: *orange juice, ham sandwich.* The describing noun comes first and the noun that's being described comes second. In Spanish the noun that's being described comes first and is followed by **de** + the describing noun: **jugo de naranja, sándwich de jamón.**

Communication

Humor/Creativity

Hold a contest in which students write and read aloud horrible combinations of foods and/or beverages. For example: **jugo de huevo, yogur de jamón,** and so on. The class can vote for the most horrible combination.

Differentiating Instruction

Pre-AP

Expand and Elaborate Have students bring empty food packages to class such as soup, milk, juice, and yogurt containers. Have them create short TV food ads for a fictitious food item brand and present them to the class. For example: **Cuando tengo hambre siempre como el cereal Nutrirrico porque es rico y nutritivo.**

Heritage Language Learners

Support What They Know In small groups, have students create a role-play based on the vocabulary presented on pp. 140 and 141. Have students pick one of the following settings: **en el desayuno,** or **en el almuerzo.** Then instruct them to write a short script wherein they each play a part. Give students the opportunity to perform their plays for the group.

Answers Projectable Transparencies, 3-24

¡A responder! Audio Script, TE p. 137b

Students will hold up the following pieces of paper:

1. almuerzo (la hamburguesa)
2. desayuno (la leche)
3. desayuno (el pan)
4. almuerzo (el sándwich de jamón y queso)
5. desayuno (el cereal)
6. almuerzo (la sopa)
7. desayuno (el huevo)
8. desayuno (el café)

Objectives
- Practice vocabulary: food, meals.
- Recycle: **gustar** with an infinitive.

Core Resource
- *Cuaderno,* pp. 99–101

Practice Sequence
- **Activity 1:** Vocabulary recognition: foods
- **Activity 2:** Vocabulary production: stating preferences; Recycle: using **gustar** with an infinitive

STANDARDS
1.1 Engage in conversation, Act. 2
1.3 Present information, Acts. 1–2, PYP

Get Help Online
More Practice
my.hrw.com

✓ Ongoing Assessment
PARA Y PIENSA **Alternative Strategy** Have students use whiteboards to complete the Para y Piensa. On the count of three, direct students to display their answers. For additional practice, use Reteaching & Practice Copymaster URB 3, pp. 1, 2, 10.

Answers Projectable Transparencies, 3-24
Activity 1
la sopa; el pan; el huevo; el yogur; el sándwich; las uvas; la manzana; la hamburguesa

Activity 2
1. ¿Te gusta más comer cereal o huevos? Me gusta más comer huevos/cereal.
2. ¿Te gusta más beber leche o jugo de naranja? Me gusta más beber leche/jugo de naranja.
3. ¿Te gusta más comer sopa o un sándwich de jamón y queso? Me gusta más comer sopa/un sándwich de jamón y queso.
4. ¿Te gusta más comer una hamburguesa o pizza? Me gusta más comer una hamburguesa/pizza.
5. ¿Te gusta más comer una manzana o una banana? Me gusta más comer una banana/una manzana.
6. ¿Te gusta más beber un refresco o un café? Me gusta más beber un refresco/un café.

Para y piensa Answers will vary. Sample answers include: **1.** huevos, cereal, yogur; **2.** hamburguesa, sopa, sándwich de jamón y queso

Práctica de VOCABULARIO

1 ¡A jugar! Busca, busca

Escribir

Busca y escribe las ocho comidas escondidas en este dibujo de una cafetería.
(Find and list the eight hidden foods.)

Expansión:
Teacher Edition Only
Have students create three sentences about the people in the picture and the food they like to eat.

2 ¿Qué te gusta más? ¿Recuerdas? gustar with an infinitive p. 42

¿Recuerdas? gustar with an infinitive p. 42

Hablar

Habla con otro(a) estudiante sobre qué te gusta comer o beber más.
(Tell what you like more.)

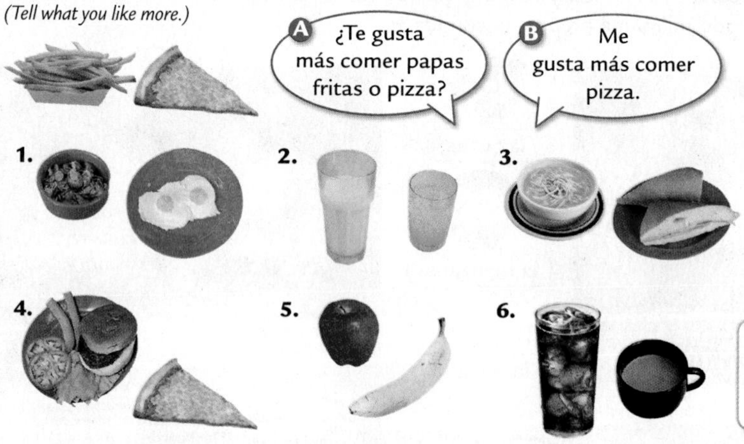

Expansión
Tell what items you like to eat or drink at dinner.

Más práctica Cuaderno *pp. 99–101* Cuaderno para hispanohablantes *pp. 99–102*

Get Help Online
my.hrw.com

PARA Y PIENSA **Did you get it?**
1. Name three breakfast foods. 2. Name three lunch foods.

Differentiating Instruction

Slower-paced Learners
Yes/No Questions In pairs, have students create a deck of food cards. Have them draw a sketch of each of the foods shown on p. 142 on an index card. Then have each partner choose two cards. Students must use yes/no questions to figure out which foods their partner is holding. **¿Tienes la manzana? No, no tengo la manzana. ¿Tienes la sopa? No, no tengo la sopa.**

Heritage Language Learners
Regional Variations Ask students to share the expressions that people in their country or region of origin use when food is really delicious. What do people say when a meal is not so good? Also, ask students to share the expressions people use before starting a meal or making a toast. What are some common phrases heard around the table?

VOCABULARIO en contexto

¡AVANZA! **Goal:** Identify the words Rodrigo and Marisol use to ask questions. Then practice these words to ask questions and give answers. ***Actividades 3–4***

¿Recuerdas? Snack foods p. 33

Telehistoria escena 1

@HOMETUTOR my.hrw.com View, Read and Record

STRATEGIES

Cuando lees

List the question words As you read, list the words that indicate questions, such as **Qué** in **¿Qué amiga?** Save the list so that you can add more question words as you encounter them.

Cuando escuchas

Think about motives In this scene, Marisol asks questions repeatedly. Think of possible reasons why she does this. Which reason seems the most probable to you?

VIDEO DVD

AUDIO

Rodrigo and Marisol walk to the grocery store. Rodrigo is counting his money.

Marisol: ¿A la escuela? ¿Por qué vas a la escuela hoy? Es sábado.

Rodrigo: Trini Salgado llega hoy y necesito un autógrafo en una camiseta. Es importante.

Marisol: ¿En una camiseta? ¿Qué camiseta?

Rodrigo: Tengo una amiga...

Marisol: *(teasing him)* ¿Una amiga? ¿Qué amiga? ¿Cómo se llama?

Rodrigo: Se llama Alicia.

Marisol: ¿De dónde es?

Rodrigo: Es de Miami. *(He loses count and starts over, sighing.)*

Marisol: ¿Cuándo tienes que estar en la escuela?

Rodrigo: A las cuatro de la tarde. *(Rodrigo loses count.)* ¡Y por favor! ¡No más preguntas! *(He starts to count again.)*

Marisol: Quince, veinte, cuarenta... Continuará... p. 148

También se dice

Puerto Rico Rodrigo uses the word **la camiseta** when he mentions Alicia's T-shirt. In other Spanish-speaking countries you might hear:

- **Argentina** la remera
- **Perú** el polo
- **Venezuela** la franela
- **México** la playera

¡AVANZA! Objective

- Understand vocabulary in context: interrogative words.

Core Resources

- Video Program: DVD 1
- Audio Program: TXT CD 3 track 3

Presentation Strategies

- Ask students to make a list of the question words they hear.
- Show the video with the books closed. Then show it again with the books open.
- Play the audio while students follow the script in the text.

STANDARD

1.2 Understand language

Warm Up Projectable Transparencies, 3-16

Asking Questions Match each question with its appropriate answer.

a. Es una bebida. **b.** Es una amiga.
c. Es nutritivo. **d.** porque no tengo ganas

1. ¿Cómo es el desayuno?
2. ¿Qué es el café?
3. ¿Quién es Ana?
4. ¿Por qué no comes?

Answers: 1. c; 2. a; 3. b; 4. d

Communication — Pair Work

Telehistoria Ask students to take on the role of Marisol or Rodrigo in the Telehistoria script. They should read their lines aloud several times. Walk around the room and correct students' pronunciation of words as you hear errors.

Differentiating Instruction

English Learners

Provide Comprehensible Input Before listening to the Telehistoria, have students preview the text for question words. Help them remember their meanings by providing an accompanying gesture for each. Say **¿dónde?** and look around the room pointing to different places. Say **¿cuándo?** and look at your watch or the clock. Say **¿qué?** as you hold your hands out and shrug your shoulders slightly.

Inclusion

Frequent Review/Repetition Provide student pairs with sentence starters related to the Telehistoria. Direct each pair to find the place in the text that gives them the information, and then complete each sentence. Here are a few examples:

Rodrigo va a ____.
Rodrigo necesita un autógrafo en ____.
La amiga de Rodrigo se llama ____.

Video Summary

@HOMETUTOR VideoPlus my.hrw.com

As Rodrigo counts his money on his way to the store, Marisol distracts him with several annoying questions. He tells Marisol that he is going to school to get Trini Salgado's autograph.

Objectives
- Practice using vocabulary in context.
- Recycle: snack foods.

Core Resource
- Audio Program: TXT CD 3 track 3

Practice Sequence
- **Activity 3:** Telehistoria comprehension
- **Activity 4:** Vocabulary production; Recycle: snack foods

STANDARDS
1.1 Engage in conversation, Act. 4
1.2 Understand language, Act. 1
1.3 Present information, Act. 4 PYP

✓ Ongoing Assessment

Get Help Online
More Practice
my.hrw.com

PARA Y PIENSA **Intervention** If students have problems completing the sentences in Para y piensa, have them repeat Activity 3. For additional practice, use Reteaching & Practice Copymasters URB 3 pp. 1, 3, 11.

Answers Projectable Transparencies, 3-24

Activity 3
1. Qué, c.
2. Cómo, d.
3. dónde, a.
4. Por qué, b.
5. Quién, e.

Activity 4 Answers will vary. Sample answers include:
1. ¿Cómo es la pizza? La pizza es rica.
2. ¿Cómo es el cereal? ...es nutritivo.
3. ¿Cómo es la sopa? ...es buena.
4. ¿Cómo es el sándwich de jamón y queso? ...es rico.
5. ¿Cómo es la banana? ...es horrible.
6. ¿Cómo es la hamburguesa? ...es mala.
7. ¿Cómo es el jugo de naranja? ...es bueno.
8. ¿Cómo es la galleta? ...es rica.

Para y piensa
1. ¿Quiénes son las amigas de Rodrigo?
2. ¿Cuándo llega Trini Salgado?
3. ¿Por qué necesita Rodrigo el autógrafo?

Nota gramatical

You learned interrogative words on p. 140. Use an **interrogative word** followed by a **conjugated verb** to ask a question. Notice that each interrogative has an accent.

¿**Cómo está** usted? *How are you?*
¿**Por qué estás** triste? *Why are you sad?*

3 *Comprensión del episodio* Muchas preguntas

Escuchar Leer

Completa las preguntas con la palabra interrogativa apropiada y escoge la respuesta correcta según el episodio. *(Complete the questions with the appropriate question word and choose the correct answer.)*

cómo	quién	qué
dónde	por qué	

1. ¿ _____ necesita Rodrigo?
2. ¿ _____ se llama la amiga de Rodrigo?
3. ¿De _____ es Alicia?
4. ¿ _____ va a la escuela Rodrigo?
5. ¿ _____ es Trini Salgado?

a. Es de Miami.
b. porque Trini Salgado está allí
c. un autógrafo
d. Alicia
e. una atleta famosa

Expansión
Write two more questions and answers about the Telehistoria.

4 ¿Cómo es? *¿Recuerdas?* Snack foods p. 33

Hablar

Habla con otro(a) estudiante para describir las siguientes comidas y bebidas en la cafetería. *(Describe the following foods and drinks in your school's cafeteria.)*

Ⓐ ¿Cómo es la leche?
Ⓑ La leche es buena.

Estudiante Ⓐ

Estudiante Ⓑ
nutritivo(a)
bueno(a)
malo(a)
horrible
rico(a)

Expansión:
Teacher Edition Only
Have students ask each other two more questions about other foods and drinks.

Get Help Online
my.hrw.com

PARA Y PIENSA

Did you get it? Choose the correct interrogative word.
1. ¿(Qué / Quiénes) son las amigas de Rodrigo?
2. ¿(Cuándo / Cuál) llega Trini Salgado?
3. ¿(Quién / Por qué) necesita Rodrigo el autógrafo?

Differentiating Instruction

Inclusion

Synthetic/Analytic Support Write these words on separate index cards: **cómo, dónde, quién, por qué, qué, es, está, tiene,** and **Rodrigo.** Display the words on the board at random. Invite volunteers to choose words to build a question. Remind them to start with a question word followed by a verb. They may add additional words, such as adjectives, if necessary.

Heritage Language Learners

Writing Skills Remind students that question words always have an accent. Point out, however, that **como, donde, quien, porque,** and **que** have different meanings. Have students write two sentences using each word, once as a question word, and once as a relative pronoun, adverb, or conjunction. **¿Qué tiene Alicia? Ella tiene la camiseta que tiene el autógrafo.**

Presentación de GRAMÁTICA

¡AVANZA! **Goal:** Learn how to use **gustar** with nouns. Then practice using this verb to express what foods you like and don't like. ***Actividades 5–9***

English Grammar Connection: In English, the phrase *I like* doesn't change. In Spanish, there are two ways to say it, depending on whether what you like is singular or plural. This is because the Spanish phrase **me gusta** literally means that something *is pleasing to me.*

Gustar with Nouns

ANIMATEDGRAMMAR my.hrw.com

¿Recuerdas? You have already learned to use **gustar** with infinitives to say what people like to do (see p. 42).

To talk about the things that people like, use **gustar** + **noun.**

Here's how:

If what is liked is singular, use the **singular** form **gusta.**

If what is liked is plural, use the **plural** form **gustan.**

Singular	Plural
me gusta **la sopa**	me gustan **los jugos**
te gusta **la sopa**	te gustan **los jugos**
le gusta **la sopa**	le gustan **los jugos**
nos gusta **la sopa**	nos gustan **los jugos**
os gusta **la sopa**	os gustan **los jugos**
les gusta **la sopa**	les gustan **los jugos**

matches singular noun

Me gusta **el cereal.**
***I like** cereal.*

matches plural noun

Me gustan **las uvas.**
***I like** grapes.*

Notice that the singular and plural forms of **gustar** match what is liked, not the person who likes it.

Más práctica
Cuaderno *pp. 102–104*
Cuaderno para hispanohablantes *pp. 103–105*

@HOMETUTOR my.hrw.com
Leveled Practice

Differentiating Instruction

Pre-AP

Relate Opinions Give students a list of food items. Have students circulate around the class and ask their classmates which items they like and dislike. For example: **¿Te gusta la pizza? Sí,/No, no me gusta la pizza.** Have students work in small groups to compile the opinions of their classmates. Have each group report their findings to the class.

Slower-paced Learners

Personalize It Show students a collection of photos or pictures of familiar foods. Then ask them to express their personal preferences using the verb **gustar.** Remind them to focus on whether the food word is singular or plural. **¿Te gustan las uvas? Sí, me gustan las uvas.**

¡AVANZA! Objectives

- Present **gustar** with nouns.
- Practice **gustar** to express what foods you like and don't like.

Core Resource

- *Cuaderno,* pp. 102–104

Presentation Strategies

- Present forms and uses of the verb **gustar** with nouns.
- Remind students that they can use **gustar** with infinitives to talk about things that people like to do.

STANDARD

4.1 Compare languages

Warm Up Projectable Transparencies, 3-17

Interrogative Words Read the following sentence: **José no va al gimnasio los lunes porque tiene que estudiar.** Now write four questions about the sentence using these interrogative words: **¿Quién? ¿Cuándo? ¿Por qué?** and **¿Qué?**

Possible Answers: ¿Quién no va al gimnasio? ¿Cuándo no va al gimnasio? ¿Por qué no va al gimnasio José? ¿Qué tiene que hacer José?

Long-term Retention

Connect to Previous Learning

Remind students that they are already familiar with the use of **gustar** with infinitives. Refer them back to **gustar** with infinitives on p. 42 of Unidad 1 to see which pronouns to use.

Communication

Common Error Alert

Tell students to use **gustan** when listing more than one singular noun. For example, **Me gustan la leche y el jugo de naranja.**

Objectives

- Practice **gustar** with nouns.
- **Culture:** compare traditional foods of Puerto Rico and El Salvador.
- Practice using **gustar** to express what foods you like and don't like.
- Pronunciation: the letters **r** and **rr**

Core Resources

- *Cuaderno,* pp. 102–104
- Audio Program: TXT CD 3 track 4

Practice Sequence

- **Activity 5:** Controlled practice: **gustar** with nouns
- **Activities 6 and 7:** Transitional practice: **gustar** with nouns
- **Activities 8 and 9:** Open-ended practice: **gustar** with nouns

STANDARDS

1.1 Engage in conversation, Acts. 6–8
1.2 Understand language, Pronunciación
1.3 Present information, Acts. 5–9, PYP
4.1 Compare languages, Pronunciación
21st Century Critical Thinking and Problem Solving, Personalize it

Comparación cultural

Essential Question

Suggested Answer Often times, historical influences affect the types of food we consume and the ways we prepare them. For example, the Spaniards brought olives and garlic to Puerto Rico. People of African descent influenced Puerto Rican cuisine by introducing plantains and coconuts.

Background Information

Many Puerto Rican recipes use **sofrito** which is a condiment mix based on onions, green bell peppers, red bell peppers, cilantro, and garlic. Meat is usually seasoned with **adobo** (seasoning salt) which is a mix of salt, onion powder, garlic powder, and ground black pepper.

See Activity answers on p. 147.

Práctica de GRAMÁTICA

5 En el supermercado

Leer
Escribir

Indica lo que les gusta o no les gusta a estas personas en el supermercado, según la descripción. *(Indicate what these people like and don't like.)*

modelo: El yogur es horrible. (a Rodrigo)
A Rodrigo no le gusta el yogur.

1. Las uvas son ricas. (a ti)
2. La sopa es buena. (a Marisol)
3. El cereal es malo. (a nosotros)
4. Los huevos son horribles. (a mí)
5. El café es muy bueno. (a usted)
6. Los jugos son nutritivos. (a ellos)

Expansión
Say whether you like each of the items listed.

6 Las comidas favoritas

Hablar

Comparación cultural

Tostones

La cocina criolla

How do historical influences affect the food that people eat?
Traditional cooking in **Puerto Rico,** known as *la cocina criolla,* combines Spanish, African, and indigenous influences. *Tostones* (fried plantains) are a common side dish. Popular snack foods are *alcapurrias* (fried plantains stuffed with meat) and *bacalaítos* (codfish fritters). In **El Salvador,** traditional cuisine blends indigenous and Spanish influences. A typical food is the *pupusa,* a corn tortilla filled with beans, pork, and cheese. *Pupusas* are often served with *curtido,* a spicy coleslaw. *Semita,* a sweet bread layered with pineapple marmalade, is also popular.

Pupusas

Compara con tu mundo *Which of these dishes would you most like to try and why?*

Usa la información para hablar sobre las comidas preferidas en Puerto Rico y El Salvador. *(Talk with a partner about food preferences in both countries.)*

A ¿A quiénes les gustan los tostones?

B A los chicos de Puerto Rico les gustan.

Expansión:
Teacher Edition Only
Ask students to mention all the foods they have learned about in this and in previous lessons.

Pronunciación Las letras r y rr

AUDIO

In Spanish, the letter **r** in the middle or the end of a word is pronounced by a single tap of the tongue against the gum above the upper front teeth. The letter **r** at the beginning of a word or **rr** within a word is pronounced by several rapid taps called a trill. Listen and repeat.

para	**cereal**	**beber**	**yogur**
rico	**rubio**	**horrible**	**pizarrón**

El cereal y el yogur son ricos; no son horribles.

Differentiating Instruction

Inclusion

Alphabetic/Phonetic Awareness Have students write the letter **r** on a card, and the letter **rr** on another card. Then say: **para, horrible, pizarrón, beber, cereal,** and **rico.** Emphasize the trill in the words containing **rr.** Tell students to hold up the appropriate card to show whether they are hearing the **r** or **rr** sound. Then have students repeat each word aloud.

English Learners

Build Background Ask students to talk about traditional dishes from their country of origin. What are the main ingredients? Is frying, baking, or boiling the preferred cooking method? How do those dishes compare to the **cocina criolla**? Encourage interested students to research a recipe of one of these dishes and bring it in to share with the group.

7 Opiniones

Hablar

Trabaja en un grupo de tres y hablen de las comidas y bebidas que les gustan y no les gustan. *(Talk in a group of three about what you like and don't like.)*

la pizza	el jugo de naranja
las manzanas	la leche
las uvas	¿ ?

A ¿A ustedes les gusta la pizza?

B A mí no me gusta la pizza. No me gusta el queso.

C Sí, a mí me gusta la pizza con jamón.

Expansión: Teacher Edition Only
Have students extend the dialogue using other foods and beverages.

8 El menú

Leer Hablar

Pregúntale a otro(a) estudiante qué comidas del menú le gustan más y por qué. *(Ask your partner questions about the foods he or she likes more and why.)*

A ¿Te gusta más el desayuno uno o el desayuno dos?

B Me gusta más el desayuno dos porque me gusta el cereal y no me gustan los huevos.

Restaurante Borinquen

Desayunos (de 8:00 a 11:00)
1. *Huevos fritos o revoltillo con jamón* *$4.00*
2. *Cereal frío y fruta* *$4.00*
3. *Frutas frescas (uvas, guineos, manzanas), yogur* *$3.50*

Bebidas incluidas: jugo de china, café o leche

Almuerzos (de 12:00 a 3:00)
1. *Hamburguesa americana, papas fritas* *$5.50*
2. *Sándwich de jamón y queso, con fruta* *$6.50*
3. *Pizza con jamón y queso* *$5.50*
4. *Asopao de vegetales (sopa tradicional de Puerto Rico)* *$4.00*

Bebidas incluidas: jugos, refrescos o café
Postres incluidos: helado, flan o pastel del día

Expansión: Teacher Edition Only
Have students work in groups to create a menu using foods and beverages they know.

9 ¿Y tú?

Escribir Hablar

Contesta las preguntas. *(Answer the questions.)*

1. ¿Qué comida te gusta cuando tienes mucha hambre?
2. ¿Qué bebida te gusta cuando tienes mucha sed?
3. ¿Cuál es una comida nutritiva?
4. ¿Qué comidas nutritivas te gustan y no te gustan?
5. ¿Qué comidas en la cafetería de la escuela te gustan?
6. ¿Qué comidas en la cafetería de la escuela no te gustan?

Expansión
Talk with a partner. Compare your answers in a Venn diagram.

Más práctica Cuaderno *pp. 102–104* Cuaderno para hispanohablantes *pp. 103–105*

Get Help Online my.hrw.com

PARA Y PIENSA

Did you get it?
1. Tell a friend you like eggs for breakfast.
2. Say that José likes pizza with ham.
3. Ask a friend why he or she doesn't like fruit.

Differentiating Instruction

Multiple Intelligences

Visual Learners Have students work in small groups to create a menu for a breakfast special. Instruct students to include choices in their special. For example, customers can choose **huevos, huevos con queso,** or **huevos con jamón.** They can choose **jugo de naranja, jugo de manzana,** or **jugo de uva.** Share each menu with the group, and ask volunteers to place their orders.

Heritage Language Learners

Support What They Know Tell students that in the northern part of Colombia **tostones** are called **patacones.** Also, that in Colombia and Venezuela, the **pupusa** is called **arepa. Arepas** can be mixed with cheese or filled with eggs or meat. Ask students if they know other names or variations of the foods mentioned on p. 146.

Long-term Retention

Personalize it

Have student groups poll their classmates regarding their favorite cafeteria foods. Have them create a graphic such as a chart or pie graph to report their findings, and write five sentences to accompany their visual.

✓ Ongoing Assessment

Get Help Online
More Practice
my.hrw.com

PARA Y PIENSA **Peer Assessment** Have student pairs say their sentences aloud and correct each other's pronunciation. For additional practice, use Reteaching & Practice Copymasters URB 3, pp. 4, 5.

Answers Projectable Transparencies, 3-25

Answers for Activities 5 and 6 on p. 146.

Activity 5
1. A ti te gustan las uvas.
2. A Marisol le gusta la sopa.
3. A nosotros no nos gusta el cereal.
4. A mí no me gustan los huevos.
5. A usted le gusta el café.
6. A ellos les gustan los jugos.

Activity 6 Answers will vary. Sample answers should follow the pattern:
¿Dónde les gustan las...? En... les gustan las...

Activity 7 Answers will vary. Sample answers should follow the pattern:
A: ¿A ustedes les gustan las manzanas?
B: No, a mí no me gustan las manzanas.
C: Sí, a mí me gustan las manzanas.

Activity 8 Answers will vary. Sample answers include:
A: ¿Te gusta más el desayuno dos o el desayuno tres?
B: Me gusta más el desayuno tres porque me gustan las frutas y no me gusta el cereal....

Activity 9 Answers will vary. Sample answers include:
1. Cuando tengo mucha hambre me gusta comer una hamburguesa.
2. Cuando tengo mucha sed me gusta beber un jugo de naranja.
3. El cereal es una comida nutritiva.
4. Me gusta el yogur. No me gustan los huevos.
5. Me gusta la sopa.
6. No me gusta el sándwich de jamón y queso.

Para y piensa
1. Me gustan los huevos en el desayuno.
2. A José le gusta la pizza con jamón.
3. ¿Por qué no te gusta la fruta?

¡AVANZA! Objectives

- Practice **gustar** with nouns.
- Practice using **gustar** to express what foods you like and don't like.

Core Resources

- Video Program: DVD 1
- Audio Program: TXT CD 3, track 5

Presentation Strategies

- Have students read the script.
- Ask who the people in the picture are.
- Point out the different breakfast foods mentioned in the script.
- Show the video and/or play the audio.

Practice Sequence

- **Activity 10:** Telehistoria comprehension
- **Activity 11:** Transitional practice: **gustar** with nouns; foods

Activity 12: Open-ended practice: **gustar** with nouns; foods

STANDARDS

1.1 Engage in conversation, Act. 12
1.2 Understand language, Act. 10
1.3 Present information, Acts. 11–12, PYP
21st Century **Communication,** Act. 11/Pre-AP

Warm Up Projectable Transparencies, 3-17

Gustar with Nouns Complete the sentences with **gusta** or **gustan.**

1. ¿Te _____ las frutas?
2. A mí no me _____ el queso.
3. A Teresa le _____ los helados.
4. ¿Les _____ la leche?
5. ¿A quién no le _____ el jugo de naranja?

Answers: 1. gustan; 2. gusta; 3. gustan; 4. gusta; 5. gusta

Video Summary

HOMETUTOR VideoPlus my.hrw.com

Rodrigo and Marisol are at a supermarket. They are talking about the kinds of foods they like for breakfast. Marisol says that she doesn't like to eat much for breakfast, but now she states that she's hungry. Rodrigo concludes that she's hungry because she doesn't eat much for breakfast.

GRAMÁTICA en contexto

¡AVANZA! **Goal:** Listen to how Marisol and Rodrigo use **gustar** to talk about what they like to eat. Then use **gustar** to talk about likes and dislikes. ***Actividades 10–12***

Telehistoria escena 2

HOMETUTOR my.hrw.com View, Read and Record

STRATEGIES

Cuando lees
Organize with a chart To keep thoughts organized, make a chart listing Rodrigo's and Marisol's likes and dislikes about breakfast foods. Are your preferences more like Rodrigo's or more like Marisol's?

Cuando escuchas
Use mental pictures to remember words Listen for names of foods. For each name you hear, picture the food mentally. Remember these words by repeatedly linking them to the mental pictures.

VIDEO DVD

AUDIO

Marisol: ¿Qué te gusta comer en el desayuno?
Rodrigo: Me gustan el cereal, el yogur, las frutas... Y a ti, Marisol, ¿qué te gusta comer en el desayuno?
Marisol: No me gusta el yogur y no me gustan los huevos.
Rodrigo: ¿Te gustan las frutas? ¿Las uvas, las manzanas?
Marisol: No me gusta comer mucho en el desayuno.
Rodrigo: ¡Tienes que comer bien en el desayuno! ¿Te gusta el pan? ¿O la leche?
Marisol: Me gustan las galletas. Tengo hambre.
Rodrigo: Sí. ¡Porque no te gusta comer mucho en el desayuno!

Continuará... p. 153

Differentiating Instruction

Inclusion

Metacognitive Support Have students read through the script of the Telehistoria in unison. After each sentence containing the verb **gustar,** ask students to explain why the verb appears as **gusta** or **gustan** in that particular context. For example, why does Marisol say **No me gusta el yogur y no me gustan los huevos.** Elicit that **yogur** is singular, while **huevos** is plural.

Slower-paced Learners

Yes/No Questions Ask students yes/no questions based on the topics discussed in the Telehistoria. Here are a few possibilities:

- **¿Te gustan las frutas?**
- **¿Te gustan los huevos?**
- **¿Te gusta el yogur?**

After answering **sí** or **no,** encourage students to follow up with a complete sentence. **Sí, me gustan las galletas.**

10 *Comprensión del episodio* ¿Un desayuno grande?

Escuchar
Leer

Contesta las preguntas sobre el episodio. *(Answer the questions.)*

1. ¿Qué le gusta comer a Rodrigo en el desayuno?
2. ¿A quién no le gustan los desayunos grandes?
3. ¿Qué le gusta comer a Marisol?
4. ¿Por qué tiene hambre Marisol?

Expansión:
Teacher Edition Only
Have students write one more question about the dialog between Rodrigo and Marisol and provide an answer.

11 En el desayuno y el almuerzo

Escribir

Escribe una descripción de qué comidas y bebidas te gustan y no te gustan en el desayuno y el almuerzo. *(Write a description of what foods and drinks you like and don't like for breakfast and lunch.)*

modelo: En el desayuno me gusta el pan. Para beber, me gusta el jugo de naranja. También me gustan las bananas. Es importante comer fruta. No me gustan los huevos. Son horribles. En el almuerzo...

Expansión:
Teacher Edition Only
Ask students to talk about the foods they like and don't like in the school cafeteria.

12 Una entrevista

Hablar
Escribir

Pregúntale a otro(a) estudiante qué le gusta y no le gusta en el almuerzo. Escribe sus respuestas. Luego compara lo que les gusta a los dos, usando un diagrama de Venn. *(Ask a classmate what he or she likes and doesn't like for lunch. Write the responses. Compare your likes and dislikes, using a Venn diagram.)*

modelo: A Nicolás le gustan los sándwiches de queso en el almuerzo. También le gusta la fruta. No le gusta la pizza...

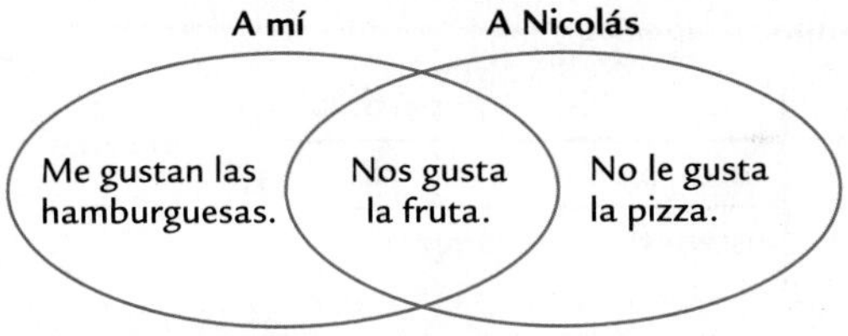

Expansión
Present your common likes and dislikes to the class.

Get Help Online
my.hrw.com

PARA Y PIENSA

Did you get it? Complete each sentence based on the Telehistoria with the correct form of **gustar.**

1. A Marisol no le ____ la comida nutritiva.
2. A Rodrigo le ____ el cereal.
3. A Marisol le ____ las galletas.

Differentiating Instruction

Pre-AP

Support Ideas with Details After completing Activity 11, have students copy their descriptions onto a separate piece of paper. Instruct them to leave a few blank lines in between each sentence. Then have students add a phrase of explanation after each sentence using the word **porque. En el desayuno me gusta el pan porque no me gusta un desayuno grande. Me gusta beber jugo de naranja porque es nutritivo.**

Heritage Language Learners

Writing Skills Have students use their Venn diagrams from Activity 12 for a Compare and Contrast essay. Essays should follow this format: *I. Introduction*—Explain what the essay will be about. *II. Compare*—Describe the foods you have in common. *III. Contrast*—Describe the foods you disagree on. *IV. Conclusion*—Sum up your findings.

Long-term Retention
Critical Thinking

Categorize Before doing Activity 11, ask students to draw a Venn diagram with one oval labeled **el desayuno** and the other **el almuerzo.** Have them write names of breakfast and lunch foods in the appropriate ovals. Use the overlapping area to write in items that fit both categories.

Communication
Role-Playing and Skits

Telehistoria Have students prepare a short dialogue based on the Telehistoria, changing the foods that are mentioned. Encourage them to use humor in their dialogue and gestures. Then have them present the dialogue to the class.

Communication
Common Error Alert

Some students may forget about gender agreement, particularly for nouns not ending in **-a** or **-o.** To avoid this problem, ask students to identify the foods in writing and to include the appropriate article. For example: **la leche, el sándwich, el cereal.**

Ongoing Assessment

Get Help Online
More Practice
my.hrw.com

PARA Y PIENSA **Peer Assessment** Have pairs exchange their answers and correct errors. For additional practice, use Reteaching & Practice Copymasters URB 3 pp. 4, 6.

Answers Projectable Transparencies, 3-25

Activity 10
1. Le gusta comer el cereal, el yogur y las frutas.
2. A Marisol no le gustan los desayunos grandes.
3. A Marisol le gusta comer galletas.
4. Tiene hambre porque no le gusta comer mucho en el desayuno.

Activity 11 Answers will vary. Answers should include the use of the verb **gustar** + names of foods and drinks.

Activity 12 Answers will vary. Sample answers will follow this outline:
(No) Me gusta(n)...
(No) Nos gusta(n)...
(No) Le gusta(n)...

Para y piensa **1.** gusta; **2.** gusta; **3.** gustan

¡AVANZA! Objective

- Present the present tense **-er** and **-ir** verbs.

Core Resource

- *Cuaderno,* pp. 105–107

Presentation Strategies

- Point out the differences in the endings of both **-er** and **-ir** verbs.
- Say sentences using **-er** and **-ir** verbs, asking students to note the endings in each form.

STANDARDS

4.1 Compare languages

Warm Up

Projectable Transparencies, 3-18

Gustar with Nouns Write what foods these people like.

1. a Jorge: las papas fritas
2. a mí: el cereal con fruta
3. a Marta y a Estela: los huevos con jamón
4. a nosotros: la pizza
5. a ti: las uvas

Answers: 1. A Jorge le gustan las papas fritas. 2. A mí me gusta el cereal con fruta. 3. A Marta y a Estela les gustan los huevos con jamón. 4. A nosotros nos gusta la pizza. 5. A ti te gustan las uvas.

Communication
Grammar Activity

Have students write the endings for **-er** and **-ir** verbs on index cards. Then have them say a sentence using an **-er** or **-ir** verb but leave the verb ending out. For example: **Yo escrib_.** Students should hold up the **-o** card and say in unison **escribo.**

Verbs Students Know

Students have already learned the following **-er** and **-ir** verbs. In the next Nota grammatical they will learn that **hacer** has an irregular **yo** form but otherwise follows the pattern for **-er** verbs.

-er verbs	*-ir verbs*
aprender	**compartir**
beber	**escribir**
comer	
correr	
hacer	
leer	
vender	

Presentación de GRAMÁTICA

¡AVANZA! **Goal:** Learn how to form **-er** and **-ir** verbs. Then use these verbs and **hacer** to talk about school activities and what you and others eat and drink. ***Actividades 13–16***

¿Recuerdas? The verb **estar** p. 115

English Grammar Connection: Remember that the **present tense** shows an action happening now (see p. 96).

Present Tense of -er and -ir Verbs

ANIMATED GRAMMAR my.hrw.com

Regular verbs that end in -er or -ir work a little differently than regular **-ar** verbs. How do you form the present tense of regular -er and -ir verbs?

Here's how:

The endings for -er and -ir verbs are the same except in the **nosotros(as)** and **vosotros(as)** forms. The letter change in these two forms matches the ending of the infinitive.

vender *to sell*			
yo	**vendo**	nosotros(as)	**vendemos**
tú	**vendes**	vosotros(as)	**vendéis**
usted, él, ella	**vende**	ustedes, ellos(as)	**venden**

-er verbs = **-emos**, **-éis**

Mario **vende** comida en la cafetería.
*Mario **sells** food in the cafeteria.*

compartir *to share*			
yo	**comparto**	nosotros(as)	**compartimos**
tú	**compartes**	vosotros(as)	**compartís**
usted, él, ella	**comparte**	ustedes, ellos(as)	**comparten**

-ir verbs = **-imos**, **-ís**

Compartimos las uvas.
***We are sharing** the grapes.*

Más práctica
Cuaderno *pp. 105–107*
Cuaderno para hispanohablantes *pp. 106–109*

@HOMETUTOR my.hrw.com
Leveled Practice
Conjuguemos.com

Differentiating Instruction

Multiple Intelligences

Visual Learners Ask students to illustrate the **-er** and **-ir** verbs they know: **beber, comer, compartir, correr, escribir,** and **vender.** Have them write a subject pronoun for each drawing. Ask them to exchange their drawing with another student. He or she should say what the people in the picture are doing.

Inclusion

Metacognitive Support Use Venn diagrams to help students see the similarities and differences between the endings of **-ar** and **-er** verbs. Have students recite and compare the endings for two verbs, such as **hablar** and **vender.** When the endings are the same, write the ending in the center of the circles. When the endings are different, write them on the appropriate side. Repeat with **-ar** and **-ir** verbs.

Práctica de GRAMÁTICA

13 ¿Comer o beber?

Escribir
Hablar

Indica lo que estas personas comen o beben. *(Tell what these people eat or drink.)*

modelo: Rodrigo (cereal)
Rodrigo come cereal.

1. Rodrigo y Marisol (uvas)
2. tú (refrescos)
3. ustedes (pan)
4. Marisol y yo (sopa)
5. Ana (hamburguesas)
6. usted (sándwiches)
7. yo (jugo de naranja)
8. los maestros (café)

Expansión:
Teacher Edition Only
Have students make up sentences about what they and their friends eat and drink.

14 ¿En la cafetería o en clase?

¿Recuerdas? The verb **estar** p. 115

Escribir
Hablar

Di qué hacen estas personas e indica dónde están ahora: en la cafetería o en clase. *(Tell what these people are doing and where they are right now.)*

modelo: Marisol / vender fruta
Marisol vende fruta. Ahora está **en la cafetería.**

1. yo / beber leche
2. ellas / leer un libro
3. tú / comer yogur
4. Rodrigo / aprender el español
5. ustedes / escribir en el pizarrón
6. tú y yo / compartir una pizza

Expansión
Tell who does these things at your school.

15 Actividades en el almuerzo

Escuchar
Escribir

Escucha las descripciones de Marisol y sus amigos y toma apuntes. Luego escribe oraciones para describir qué hacen. Usa elementos de cada columna. *(Listen to Marisol and her friends and take notes. Then write sentences saying who does what, using elements from each column.)*

Audio Program
TXT CD 3 Track 6
Audio Script, TE p. 137b

1. Marisol
2. la cafetería
3. Rodrigo y Mateo
4. Carmen
5. Raúl y David
6. Laura y Diana

Expansión:
Teacher Edition Only
Ask students to talk about what they eat for breakfast on the weekends.

Objectives

- Practice using the present tense of **-er** and **-ir** verbs.
- Practice lesson vocabulary: breakfast and lunch foods.
- Recycle: **estar.**

Core Resource

- Audio Program: TXT CD 3 track 6

Practice Sequence

- **Activity 13:** Controlled practice: present tense of **-er** and **-ir** verbs
- **Activity 14:** Controlled practice: present tense of **-er** and **-ir** verbs; Recycle: **estar**
- **Activity 15:** Transitional practice: present tense of **-er** and **-ir** verbs

STANDARDS

1.2 Understand language, Act. 15
1.3 Present information, Acts. 13–14

Long-term Retention
Study Tips

Activity 13 Before doing this activity, prepare an overhead transparency to review the sound of words with **r** and **rr.**

Differentiating Instruction

Heritage Language Learners

Increase Accuracy Write **Puerto Rico** on the board and read the words aloud. Have students talk about the two **r** sounds: In **Puerto** it sounds soft, and in **Rico** hard. Some students tend to replace the initial **r** sound for **j: Puerto Jico.** Remind them that **r** at the beginning of a word sounds like **rr.** Ask them to find words on p. 151 that have the **r** and **rr** sounds.

Slower-paced Learners

Read Before Listening Before students listen to the descriptions of Marisol and her friends in Activity 15, have them preview the words and pictures presented. Ask volunteers to say aloud each of the items pictured. As other students listen, tell them to point to each item and verb as they hear it.

Answers Projectable Transparencies, 3-25 and 3-26

Activity 13
1. Rodrigo y Marisol comen uvas.
2. Tú bebes refrescos.
3. Ustedes comen pan.
4. Marisol y yo comemos sopa.
5. Ana come hamburguesas.
6. Usted come sándwiches.
7. Yo bebo jugo de naranja.
8. Los maestros beben café.

Activity 14
1. Yo bebo leche. Ahora estoy en la cafetería.
2. Ellas leen un libro. Ahora están en clase.
3. Tú comes yogur. Ahora estás en la cafetería.
4. Rodrigo aprende el español. Ahora está en la clase de español.
5. Ustedes escriben en el pizarrón. Ahora están en clase.
6. Tú y yo compartimos una pizza. Ahora estamos en la cafetería.

Activity 15
1. Marisol escribe en el cuaderno.
2. La cafetería vende sopa, uvas y bananas.
3. Rodrigo y Mateo comen uvas.
4. Carmen bebe jugo de naranja.
5. Raúl y David leen un libro.
6. Laura y Diana comparten un sándwich.

Objectives
- Practice present tense of **-er** and **-ir** verbs.
- **Culture:** discuss La Plaza de Colón.
- Introduce the verb **hacer** and connect it to **-er** verbs.

Core Resource
- *Cuaderno,* pp. 105–107

Practice Sequence
Activity 16: Transitional practice: present tense of **-er** and **-ir** verbs

STANDARDS
1.1 Engage in conversation, Act. 16
1.3 Present information, Act. 16, PYP
4.2 Compare cultures, CC
21st Century **Creativity and Innovation,** Multiple Intelligences

Comparación cultural
Essential Question
Suggested Answer Some cities, such as old San Juan, have physical reminders of their colonial pasts. Old San Juan has colonial-style buildings. There is also a statue of Christopher Columbus.

Nota gramatical
Explain to students the conjugation for hacer. **Hago, haces, hace, hacemos, hacéis, hacen.** Ask students to say sentences using **hacer. Yo hago el almuerzo.**

✓ Ongoing Assessment
Get Help Online
More Practice
my.hrw.com

PARA Y PIENSA **Intervention** If students have problems completing the Para y piensa have them review p. 150, repeat Activities 13 and 14 on p. 151. For additional practice, use Reteaching & Practice Copymasters URB 3, pp. 7, 8, 12.

See Activity answers on p. 153.

Nota gramatical
The verb **hacer** is irregular in the present tense only in the **yo** form: **hago.** In the other forms, it follows the pattern for **-er** verbs. (See p. R19 for the complete conjugation.)

Hago un sándwich.	Carmen **hace** la tarea.
I am making *a sandwich.*	*Carmen* ***is doing*** *her homework.*

16 ¿Con quién?
Hablar

Pregúntale a otro(a) estudiante con quién hace las siguientes actividades.
(Ask a partner with whom he or she does the following activities.)

modelo: comer pizza

A ¿Con quién comes pizza?

B Como pizza con Alicia.

1. correr
2. compartir el almuerzo
3. hacer la tarea
4. comer ¿ ?
5. escribir correos electrónicos
6. beber ¿ ?

Expansión
Tell when and where you do each activity.

Comparación cultural

La Plaza de Colón

La Plaza de Colón
How do some cities reflect their historical colonial past? In Old San Juan you will find cobblestone streets, Spanish colonial buildings, and many plazas as part of Puerto Rico's Spanish heritage. The Plaza de Colón is popular with both tourists and locals. A statue of Christopher Columbus in the center of the square includes plaques commemorating the explorer's achievements.

Compara con tu mundo *What is a well-known landmark in your area? Why is it important?*

Más práctica Cuaderno *pp. 105–107* Cuaderno para hispanohablantes *pp. 106–109*

Get Help Online
my.hrw.com

PARA Y PIENSA

Did you get it? Complete each sentence with the correct form of the verb in parentheses.
1. ¿Qué ____ ellas? (hacer) Ellas ____ el desayuno. (comer)
2. ¿Qué ____ tú? (hacer) Yo ____ un libro. (leer)
3. ¿Qué ____ Rafael? (hacer) Rafael ____ un refresco. (beber)

Differentiating Instruction

Inclusion
Alphabetic/Phonetic Awareness Write the present tense forms of **hacer** on the board. Discuss with students how Spanish and English phonics differ using these words as an example. For example, how would the combination of letters **hace** be pronounced in English? Remind students that in Spanish, the **h** is silent, the **a** makes an *ah* sound, the **c** is soft, and the **e** makes an *ay* sound.

Multiple Intelligences
Visual Learners Have students work in small groups to create a tourist brochure of Old San Juan. Encourage them to use the Internet to find images and more information. Some possible features might include:
- **La Plaza Colón**
- **El Morro**
- **La Plaza de Armas**
- **La Puerta de San Juan**

Todo junto

¡AVANZA! **Goal:** ***Show what you know*** Pay attention to the **-er** and **-ir** verbs Rodrigo and Marisol use to talk about eating healthy food. Then practice these verbs and **gustar** to talk about lunchtime in the cafeteria. ***Actividades 17–21***

¿Recuerdas? Telling time p. 90

Telehistoria completa

@HOMETUTOR my.hrw.com View, Read and Record

STRATEGIES

Cuando lees

Find the twist There is sometimes a "twist," or something unexpected, toward the end of a story or scene. Find the twist in this scene. What is it? Why is it unexpected?

Cuando escuchas

Listen for attitude changes To understand the scene fully, notice people's attitudes. At the beginning of the scene, what are Marisol's and Rodrigo's contrasting attitudes? Whose attitude changes during the scene? Why?

Escena 1 *Resumen*
Rodrigo necesita el autógrafo de Trini Salgado para Alicia. Tiene que estar en la escuela a las cuatro de la tarde.

Escena 2 *Resumen*
Rodrigo compra comida. Le gusta la comida nutritiva. Marisol tiene hambre porque no le gusta comer mucho en el desayuno.

VIDEO DVD

AUDIO

Escena 3

Marisol stops to order an ice cream.

Rodrigo: ¿Helado? ¿En el almuerzo?

Marisol: Sí, tengo ganas de comer helado. ¿Compartimos?

Rodrigo: El helado no es nutritivo.

Marisol: ¡Pero es muy rico!

Rodrigo: ¿Qué comes en la cena? ¿Una hamburguesa con papas fritas?

Marisol: ¿Venden papas fritas?

Rodrigo: Tienes que comer comidas buenas.

Marisol: Sí, sí. Yo como comida nutritiva de vez en cuando.

Rodrigo: ¿Sí? ¿Qué comes?

Marisol: Me gusta la sopa.

Rodrigo: La sopa es muy buena.

Marisol: Necesito una bebida.

Marisol walks away. Rodrigo sneaks a taste of her ice cream.

Rodrigo: El helado es muy rico.

Differentiating Instruction

Pre-AP

Vary Vocabulary As students read Escena 3, have them substitute a different food for each food mentioned in the script. For example, they might say **yogur** in place of **helado,** and **un sándwich de jamón y queso** in place of **una hamburguesa.** Have students read the script with the new food items. Remind them to make necessary changes in articles and adjective endings.

Slower-paced Learners

Personalize It Ask students for their own answers to the questions raised by Rodrigo in the Telehistoria.

- **¿Comes helado en el almuerzo?**
- **¿Qué comes en la cena?**
- **¿Comes comida nutritiva de vez en cuando?**
- **¿Qué comes?**

¡AVANZA! **Objective**
- Integrate lesson content.

Core Resources
- Video Program: DVD 1
- Audio Program: TXT CD 3, track 7

Presentation Strategies
- Ask students what they remember about the Telehistoria so far.
- Before showing the video or playing the audio, tell students to watch for the surprise ending and to be ready to talk about it.

STANDARD
1.2 Understand language

Warm Up
Projectable Transparencies, 3-18

Hacer Match the questions and the answers.

1. ¿Qué haces en la biblioteca?
2. ¿Qué hacen ustedes en la cafetería?
3. ¿Qué hace Marisa en el gimnasio?

a. Comemos hamburguesas.
b. Escribo en el cuaderno.
c. Corre.

Answers: 1. b; 2. a; 3. c

Video Summary

@HOMETUTOR VideoPlus my.hrw.com

Marisol wants to buy an ice cream for lunch. Rodrigo continues to stress the importance of eating nourishing foods. Marisol leaves him for a moment, and while she's gone Rodrigo sneaks a taste of her ice cream.

Answers
Projectable Transparencies, 3-26

Answers for Activities from p. 152.

Activity 16 Answers will vary. Sample answers include:

1. ¿Con quién corres? Corro con mis amigos.
2. ¿Con quién compartes el almuerzo? Comparto el almuerzo con mi hermana.
3. ¿Con quién haces la tarea? Hago la tarea con mi mamá.
4. ¿Con quién comes papas fritas? Como papas fritas con mi familia.
5. ¿Con quién escribes correos electrónicos?
6. ¿Con quién bebes leche? Bebo leche con un amigo.

Para y piensa

1. ¿Qué hacen ellas? Ellas comen el desayuno.
2. ¿Qué haces tú? Yo leo un libro.
3. ¿Qué hace Rafael? Rafael bebe un refresco.

TODO JUNTO

Objective

- Practice using and integrating lesson vocabulary and grammar.

Core Resources

- *Cuaderno*, pp. 108–109
- Audio Program: TXT CD 3 tracks 3, 5, 7, 8, 9

Practice Sequence

- **Activity 17:** Telehistoria comprehension
- **Activity 18:** Transitional practice: listening, reading
- **Activity 19:** Open-ended practice: speaking
- **Activity 20:** Open-ended practice: reading, listening, speaking
- **Activity 21:** Open-ended practice: writing

STANDARDS

1.1 Engage in conversation, Acts. 18–19
1.2 Understand language, Acts. 17–19
1.3 Present information, Acts. 18–21, PYP
21st Century **Communication,** Pre-AP: Expand and Elaborate/Act. 21; **Creativity and Innovation,** Pre-AP: Integration

Answers Projectable Transparencies, 3-26

Answers for Activities on p. 155.

Activity 17

1. ...el autógrafo de Trini Salgado para Alicia.
2. ...Alicia.
3. ...cereal, yogur y frutas.
4. ...no le gusta comer mucho en el desayuno.
5. ...comer helado.
6. ...come el helado.

Activity 18 Answers will vary. Sample answers include:
Marisol es simpática. No le gusta comer mucho en el desayuno. Le gustan las galletas y las papas fritas. Come comida nutritiva de vez en cuando.

Activity 19 Answers will vary. Sample answers should follow this outline:
A: ¿A qué hora van a la cafetería? ¿Qué hacen?
B: Como en la cafetería a la(s)... Venden...
C: Como... y bebo... porque ...

Activity answers continue on p. 155.

17 *Comprensión de los episodios* ¡A completar!

Escuchar
Leer

Completa las siguientes oraciones, según los episodios. *(Complete the following sentences, based on the episodes.)*

1. Rodrigo necesita...
2. La amiga de Miami se llama...
3. En el desayuno Rodrigo come...
4. Marisol tiene hambre porque...
5. Marisol tiene ganas de...
6. Cuando Marisol compra una bebida, Rodrigo...

Expansión:
Teacher Edition Only
Have students make other sentences about Rodrigo and Marisol from the Telehistoria.

18 *Comprensión de los episodios* Organiza la información

Escuchar
Leer

Escribe un artículo sobre Marisol o Rodrigo. Organiza la información usando este mapa. *(Write an article about Marisol or Rodrigo using a map like this one to organize information.)*

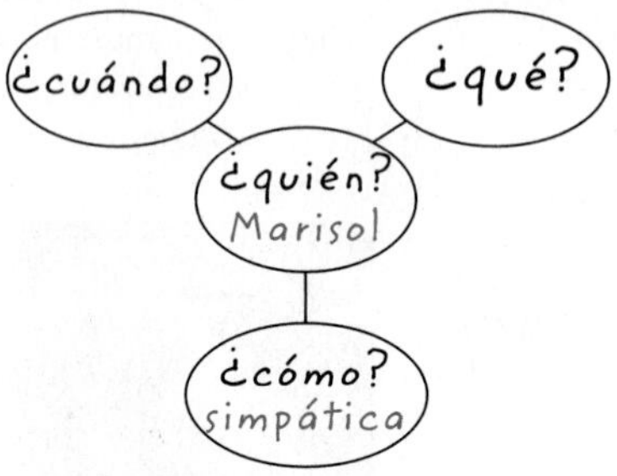

Expansión:
Teacher Edition Only
Have pairs of students write an article about what they do during lunch time.

19 ¿Qué hacen en la cafetería?

¿Recuerdas? Telling time p. 90

Digital performance space

Hablar

STRATEGY Hablar
Think and practice in advance First write down words or phrases you want to say. Then practice pronouncing them aloud. Say them in sentences several times and you will be ready for your conversation!

Trabaja en un grupo de tres. Habla con los otros estudiantes de lo que haces en la cafetería. Incluye a qué hora vas y qué venden allí. También explica qué comes y bebes, y por qué. *(Work in a group of three to talk about what you do in the cafeteria.)*

A ¿A qué hora van ustedes a la cafetería? ¿Qué hacen?

B Como en la cafetería a la una. Venden fruta, sándwiches, leche y otras bebidas. Los lunes como pizza y bebo jugo porque no me gusta la leche.

C Yo compro una manzana y leo un libro...

Expansión:
Teacher Edition Only
Ask students to talk about things they do at home and at what time they do each activity.

Differentiating Instruction

Inclusion

Frequent Review/Repetition Have students copy each of the sentence starters in Activity 17 onto a separate index card. Then direct students to reread each of the episodes. When students find the information needed to complete one of the sentences, have them copy the word or phrase onto the card.

Pre-AP

Expand and Elaborate Encourage students to expand their conversations in Activity 19 by adding an anecdote. Ask them to share a story about something that happens often in the school cafeteria. It could be something funny, surprising, or out of the ordinary.

20 Integración

Digital performance space

Audio Program
TXT CD 3 Tracks 8, 9. Audio Script, TE p. 137b

Leer Escuchar Hablar

Lee el anuncio del Supermercado Grande. Después escucha el anuncio de radio del Supermercardo Econo. ¿Qué comidas te gustan a ti y en cuál supermercado las venden? *(Read the newspaper ad and listen to the radio ad. Say what foods you like and where they sell them.)*

Fuente 1 Anuncio

Fuente 2 Anuncio de radio

Listen and take notes
- ¿Qué comidas venden en el Supermercado Econo?
- ¿Qué venden en la cafetería?

modelo: A mí me gustan las uvas. Venden uvas en el Supermercado Grande...

Expansión:
Teacher Edition Only
Ask volunteers to read the newspaper ad and have students say which items they like and don't like.

21 La cafetería de la escuela

Digital performance space

Escribir

Escríbele una carta al (a la) director(a) de la escuela para describir la cafetería. ¿Qué es bueno? ¿Qué es malo? ¿Por qué? ¿Tienes preguntas? *(Write a letter to your principal about your school cafeteria.)*

modelo: Sr. Hogan:
¿Cómo está usted? Me gusta la escuela pero no me gusta mucho la cafetería. No es muy grande y hay muchos estudiantes. ¿Por qué no venden...

Writing Criteria	Excellent	Good	Needs Work
Content	Your letter includes a lot of information.	Your letter includes some information.	Your letter includes little information.
Communication	Most of your letter is organized and easy to follow.	Parts of your letter are organized and easy to follow.	Your letter is disorganized and hard to follow.
Accuracy	Your letter has few mistakes in grammar and vocabulary.	Your letter has some mistakes in grammar and vocabulary.	Your letter has many mistakes in grammar and vocabulary.

Expansión
Write a reply letter from the principal to you that responds to your questions and comments.

Más práctica Cuaderno *pp. 108–109* Cuaderno para hispanohablantes *pp. 110–111*

Get Help Online my.hrw.com

PARA Y PIENSA

Did you get it? Complete the first sentence with a form of **gustar,** and the second sentence with the correct form of **compartir** or **beber.**
1. A Rodrigo le ____ la fruta. Él ____ jugo de naranja.
2. A Rodrigo y a Ana les ____ los sándwiches. Siempre ____ un sándwich.

Long-term Retention

Pre-AP Integration

Activity 20 Ask students to write a radio announcement for a supermarket. They can check the glossary at the end of the book, or use a dictionary to find additional food words. Have them tape their announcement and play it for the class.

✓ Ongoing Assessment

Rubric Activity 20

Listening/Speaking

Proficient	Not There Yet
Student uses correct forms of **vender** and vocabulary.	Student uses incorrect form of **vender** and does not use enough vocabulary.

To customize your own rubrics, use the ***Generate Success*** *Rubric Generator and Graphic Organizers.*

✓ Ongoing Assessment

Get Help Online More Practice my.hrw.com

PARA Y PIENSA **Peer Assessment** Have students exchange papers and make corrections. For additional practice, use Reteaching & Practice Copymasters URB 3, pp. 7, 9, 12

Differentiating Instruction

Slower-paced Learners

Peer-study Support Remind students of the strategy they learned in Activity 19—to think and practice in advance. Before doing Activity 20, organize them in pairs of strong/weak students. Ask them to write the words and phrases they want to use, then to create sentences, and finally, to put the sentences into a story. Ask them to share their story with the class.

Heritage Language Learners

Writing Skills Review the standard form of a business letter with students. Provide a model that shows proper placement of the heading: date, address, and return addresses. Also show the greeting, **Estimado Sr. Hogan:** and the closing, **Atentamente.** Remind students to tailor the tone of their language to their audience—the principal of their school.

Answers Projectable Transparencies, 3-26

Activity answers continued from p. 154

Activity 20 Answers will vary. Sample answers:
A mí me gusta la pizza de queso. Venden pizza en el Supermercado Grande.

Activity 21 Answers should include the use of lesson vocabulary and grammar.

Para y piensa
1. A Rodrigo le gusta la fruta. Él come manzanas en la cafetería.
2. A Rodrigo y a Ana les gustan los sándwiches. Siempre comparten en el almuerzo.

¡AVANZA! Objectives

- Learn about supermarkets in the Spanish-speaking world and the products they sell.
- Compare foods purchased by families in Puerto Rico with food products bought by students' families.
- Read a supermarket shopping list.

Core Resource

- Audio Program: TXT CD 3 track 10

Presentation Strategies

- Ask students to think about the ads they've seen from supermarkets.
- Ask students which items in the ad on pp. 156 and 157 look familiar.
- Ask which items seem to be typical of a Spanish-speaking country and why.
- Play the audio while students read the circular and shopping list.

STANDARDS

1.1 Engage in conversation
1.2 Understand language
2.1 Products and perspectives
4.2 Compare cultures
21st Century **Flexibility and Adaptability,** Multiple Intelligences: Kinesthetic; **Initiative and Self-Direction,** Pre-AP; **Productivity and Accountability,** Spanish in the Supermarket (Business Literacy)

Warm Up
Projectable Transparencies, 3-19

Estar and ir + a Complete the following sentences with the correct forms of **estar** and **ir + a.**

1. A las siete yo ____ en el gimnasio.
2. Esteban ____ la biblioteca a las tres.
3. ¿Por qué ____ tú nerviosa?
4. Nosotros ____ en la clase de ciencias.
5. Los estudiantes ____ la cafetería a la una.

Answers: 1. estoy; 2. va a; 3. estás; 4. estamos; 5. van a

Culture

Expanded Information

In Spanish-speaking countries, food flyers are often included in the weekly and Sunday editions of the local paper. Flyers list reduced items on particular days of the week.

Lectura

Additional readings at my.hrw.com SPANISH InterActive Reader

¡AVANZA! **Goal:** Read a section from a supermarket ad and then a shopping list. Compare this information with the foods and beverages you eat and drink.

AUDIO

¡A comprar y a comer!

The following is a supermarket ad from Supermercados La Famosa and a shopping list.

STRATEGY Leer
Don't translate; use pictures! Sketch and label pictures of the foods and beverages on the shopping list. Below each picture, write the brand or type of item you can buy at Supermercados La Famosa.

[1] onzas [2] libra

Differentiating Instruction

Pre-AP

Self-correct Ask students to add their favorite foods to the grocery list, and then work in pairs to read the new lists they've written to a partner. Tell students to think of corrections as they read their lists out loud. Then ask the partners to note points when self-corrections would have been appropriate but did not take place.

Multiple Intelligences

Logical/Mathematical Ask students to create charts organizing the food on the list. Students should come up with their own categories. Possibilities are dairy products, fruit, beverages, sandwich ingredients, etc. How many categories can each food belong to? Are there foods that only belong to one category?

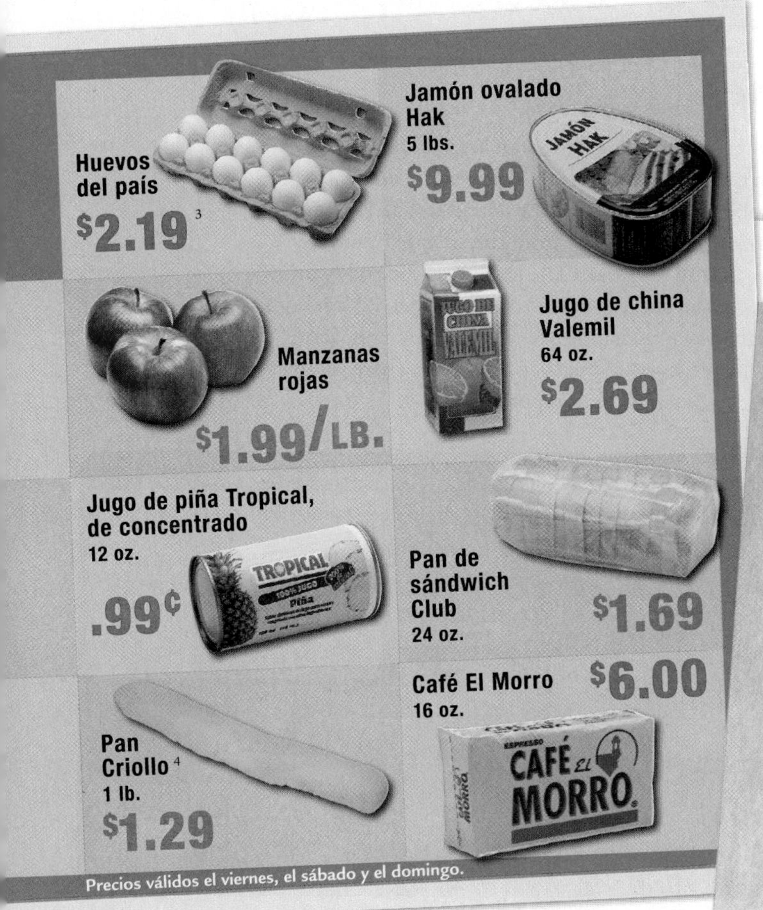

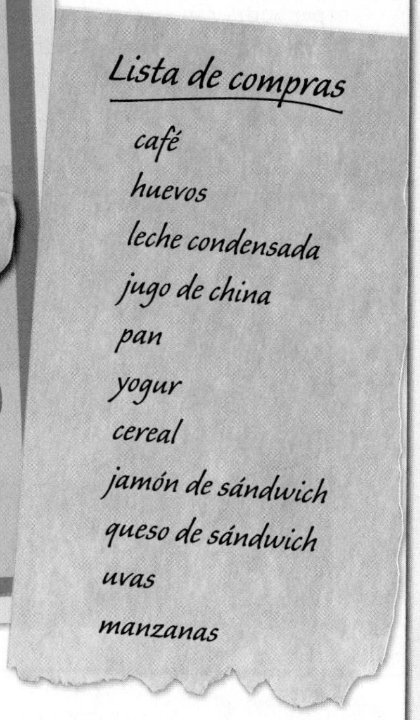

[3] En Puerto Rico usan dólares estadounidenses

[4] bread similar to French bread

PARA Y PIENSA

¿Comprendiste?

1. ¿Qué hay en la lista que no está en la circular?
2. ¿Qué venden en Supermercados La Famosa que no está en la lista?
3. ¿Qué frutas hay en la lista?

¿Y tú?

¿Qué comida en Supermercados La Famosa comes tú? ¿Qué bebes?

Differentiating Instruction

Multiple Intelligences

Kinesthetic Ask students to role-play a family eating breakfast and lunch. Ask them to take on the characters of different family members and discuss what they would like for the two meals. Students should choose names, decide which family members will ask for the food, and which family members will serve it.

Slower-paced Learners

Yes/No Questions Review names for the foods on the grocery list. Ask students to respond with **sí** or **no** to the question(s): **¿A ti te gusta la leche? ¿el café? ¿el pan? ¿A ti te gustan las uvas? ¿las manzanas?** Then ask students to repeat their classmates' preferences, using **sí** or **no** to questions like **¿A (name) le gustan las uvas?**

Communication

Pair Work

Have student pairs write their own **lista de compras** using items from the supermarket ad. They will need to learn the word **libra(s)** to say how many pounds of **jamón, uvas,** and **manzanas** they want. Next to each item, have them write the price indicated in the ad, and ask them to calculate the total cost of the food.

Comparisons

English Language Connection

Cognates Ask students to review all the food items on these pages and list cognates. Tell them to think of similarities in sound as well as spelling and to discuss the relationship between the beginning of words like **jamón** and *ham,* and **jugo** and *juice.*

Communities

Spanish in the Supermarket

Ask students to visit a Spanish market or the section of the supermarket that sells food items from Latin America or Spain. Ask them to make a list of the items they find, including the brand name, and to report their findings back to the class.

Communication

Regionalisms

Explain to students that there are regional variations for some of the words on the supermarket flyer. For example, sliced deli meat and cheese can be described as **...de sándwich** (Puerto Rico), **...en fetas** (Argentina), **...en tajadas** (muchos países), or **una lonja de...** (España).

Answers

Para y piensa ¿Comprendiste?

1. Cereal está en la lista, pero no está en la circular.
2. Venden hamburguesas, queso crema, jamón ovalado, jugo de piña.
3. Hay uvas y manzanas.

¿Y tú? Answers will vary. Sample answer: Yo como yogur, huevos, pan de sándwich y jamón de sándwich. Bebo jugo de piña y jugo de china.

Objectives

- Read about the conditions that contribute to the formation of hurricanes.
- Learn about Hurricane Georges and its effect on Puerto Rico.
- Use math skills and the metric system to analyze the path of **huracán Georges.**

Presentation Strategies

- Before reading, ask students what they know about hurricanes. How do they form? What types of weather do they cause?
- Ask for a volunteer to read the main paragraph.
- Ask students to recall the names of hurricanes they've seen on television.

STANDARDS

1.3 Present information
3.1 Knowledge of other disciplines
3.2 Acquire information
Critical Thinking and Problem Solving, English Learners; **Information Literacy,** Proyecto 2/Pre-AP

Connections

Las ciencias

The Saffir-Simpson Hurricane Scale is used to categorize hurricanes by the speed of their winds. There are five categories, ranging from 1 (winds from 74–95 mph) to 5 (winds greater than 155 mph). In the West Indies, for several centuries hurricanes were named after the saints on whose day the hurricane hit land. In the mid-twentieth century, hurricanes were given women's names, a practice discontinued in 1978. Today the World Meteorological Association uses a rotating list of names to identify hurricanes.

Answers

Conexiones Have students show their research in writing, in a 3-D model, or in a presentation.

Proyecto 1 The length of Puerto Rico (from Humacao to Mayagüez) is 179 kilometers.
179 km / 24 km per hour = 7.46 hours
Students should write out their calculations using the Spanish words for kilometers **(kilómetros)**, hours **(horas)**, per hour **(por hora)**, divided by **(entre)**, equals **(son)**.

Answers continue on p. 159.

Conexiones *Las ciencias*

Los huracanes

The Caribbean island of Puerto Rico is located in an area prone to hurricanes (**huracanes**). The word *hurricane* comes from the Taino word *hurákan*, which was used by the pre-Columbian inhabitants of the island to describe these storms (**tormentas**). Hurricanes draw energy from the surface of warm tropical waters and from moisture in the air. The extreme winds of 74 miles per hour or more can create storm surges—domes of water up to 20 feet high and 100 miles wide—and can spawn tornadoes, torrential rain, and floods. Research and write about the most severe weather condition where you live. Create a diagram or drawing to illustrate your report.

La ruta del huracán Georges

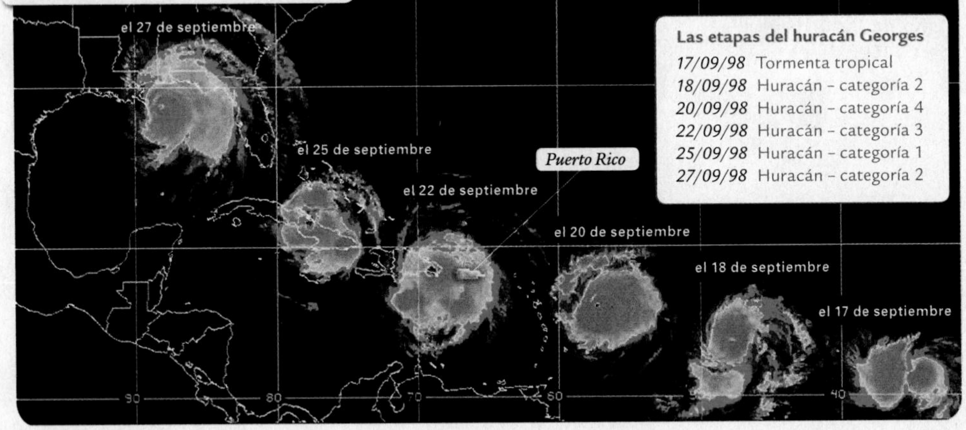

Proyecto 1 *Las matemáticas*

Hurricane Georges passed over Puerto Rico at a speed of about 24 kilometers per hour (**kilómetros por hora**). Find the distance from Humacao to Mayagüez in kilometers and calculate the time it took for the storm to move from one city to the other.

Proyecto 2 *La historia*

Research another major hurricane that has hit Puerto Rico in the past two decades. Draw a map showing the trajectory of the hurricane. Then write a paragraph describing the storm.

Proyecto 3 *La geografía*

Compare this map to the one on page xxxi to name three other countries that were hit by Hurricane Georges. Make a chart in Spanish showing the three countries, the dates of the storm, and the category of the hurricane at the time it hit.

La playa Ocean Park, Puerto Rico, durante el huracán Georges

Differentiating Instruction

English Learners

Build Background Ask students to read the text about hurricanes. After each line, check for comprehension and clarify any questions that arise. After students finish reading, ask them to explain in their own words how hurricanes form. Personalize the topic by asking them whether they have ever lived through a hurricane in their country of origin. If so, ask them to describe what happened.

Pre-AP

Expand and Elaborate Have students research hurricane-related topics such as: Different terminology for hurricanes in other parts of the world (Typhoon, Severe Tropical Cyclone, etc.); The Saffir-Simpson Hurricane Scale; Hurricane Watches and Forecasts; Hurricane Preparedness Guides; Storm Names. Ask students to give oral reports with visuals such as photos or charts.

Lección 1

En resumen
Vocabulario y gramática

ANIMATEDGRAMMAR
Interactive Flashcards
my.hrw.com

Objective
- Review lesson vocabulary and grammar.

DIGITAL SPANISH

Interactive Flashcards Students can hear every target vocabulary word pronounced in authentic Spanish. Flashcards have Spanish on one side, and a picture or a translation on the other.

Review Games Matching, concentration, hangman, and word search are just a sampling of the fun, interactive games students can play to review for the test.

performance space
News Networking
@HOMETUTOR
CULTURA Interactiva

- Audio and Video Resources
- Interactive Flashcards
- Review Activities
- WebQuest
- Conjuguemos.com

Vocabulario

Talk About Foods and Beverages

Meals

el almuerzo	*lunch*
la bebida	*beverage, drink*
la cena	*dinner*
compartir	*to share*
la comida	*food; meal*
el desayuno	*breakfast*
vender	*to sell*

For Breakfast

el café	*coffee*
el cereal	*cereal*
el huevo	*egg*
el jugo de naranja	*orange juice*
la leche	*milk*
el pan	*bread*
el yogur	*yogurt*

For Lunch

la hamburguesa	*hamburger*
el sándwich de jamón y queso	*ham and cheese sandwich*
la sopa	*soup*

Fruit

la banana	*banana*
la manzana	*apple*
las uvas	*grapes*

Describe Feelings

tener ganas de...	*to feel like . . .*
tener hambre	*to be hungry*
tener sed	*to be thirsty*

Ask Questions

¿Cómo?	*How?*
¿Cuál(es)?	*Which?; What?*
¿Por qué?	*Why?*
¿Qué?	*What?*
¿Quién(es)?	*Who?*

Other Words and Phrases

ahora	*now*
Es importante.	*It's important.*
horrible	*horrible*
nutritivo(a)	*nutritious*
otro(a)	*other*
para	*for; in order to*
rico(a)	*tasty, delicious*

Gramática

Notas gramaticales: Interrogative words *p. 144,* The verb **hacer** *p. 152*

Gustar with Nouns

To talk about the things that people like, use gustar + **noun.**

Singular	Plural
me gusta **la sopa**	me gustan **los jugos**
te gusta **la sopa**	te gustan **los jugos**
le gusta **la sopa**	le gustan **los jugos**
nos gusta **la sopa**	nos gustan **los jugos**
os gusta **la sopa**	os gustan **los jugos**
les gusta **la sopa**	les gustan **los jugos**

Present Tense of -er and -ir Verbs

vender *to sell*	
vendo	vendemos
vendes	vendéis
vende	venden

compartir *to share*	
comparto	compartimos
compartes	compartís
comparte	comparten

Practice Spanish with Holt McDougal Apps!

Communication
Interpersonal Mode

Ask student pairs to talk about what they like to eat and drink using **gustar** and the food vocabulary listed in En resumen. Responses should include a reason why they like that food item. For example: **¿Te gusta el jugo de naranja? Sí, me gusta porque es muy nutritivo.**

Differentiating Instruction

Inclusion

Frequent Review/Repetition Divide the class into two groups. Ask students to look at the singular and plural columns indicating the use of **gustar** with nouns. Lead one group in calling out **me gusta la sopa**, and the other group in responding **me gustan los jugos.** Then **te gusta la sopa**, and **te gustan los jugos.** Repeat this pattern until both groups have gone through the columns.

Multiple Intelligences

Intrapersonal Have students visualize a time when they are hungry, thirsty, or feel like doing something. Ask them to write a short journal entry, briefly describing the time, and expressing the feeling in Spanish. For example: **A las doce siempre tengo hambre y como una hamburguesa.**

Answers

Answers continued from p. 158.

Proyecto 2 Some major hurricanes include Hugo, Marilyn, Bertha, Hortense, and Lenny.

Proyecto 3 The students' charts should be in Spanish and should include country name, date, and category of the hurricane.

La República Dominicana: el veintidós de septiembre, categoría 3.

Cuba: el veinticinco de septiembre, categoría 1.

Estados Unidos: el veintisiete de septiembre, categoría 2.

Objectives

- Review lesson grammar and vocabulary.

Core Resources

- *Cuaderno,* pp 110–121
- Audio Program: TXT CD 3 track 11

Presentation Strategies

- Before starting the audio for Activity 1, ask students to listen to it carefully and pay special attention to what Lola eats and drinks for each meal.
- Before doing Activity 2, ask students to identify the foods in the pictures.
- Review question words by giving a statement and asking students to supply a corresponding question. For example: **El helado es rico. ¿Cómo es el helado?**
- Ask students to generate two questions to ask their classmates, based on the Comparación cultural.

STANDARDS

1.2 Understand language, Act. 1
1.3 Present information, Acts. 2–5
4.2 Compare cultures, Act. 5
21st Century **Communication,** Pre-AP

Warm Up Projectable Transparencies, 3-19

Vocabulary Decide whether the following statements are **cierto** or **falso.**

1. Cuando no tengo hambre como una hamburguesa, una pizza, papas fritas y un helado.
2. La manzana es una fruta.
3. La leche es una bebida muy nutritiva.
4. Comemos el desayuno en la noche.
5. Necesito pan para hacer un sándwich.

Answers: 1. falso; 2. cierto; 3. cierto; 4. falso; 5. cierto

Get Help Online
More Practice
my.hrw.com

✓ Ongoing Assessment

PARA Y PIENSA **Intervention and Remediation** If students achieve less than 80% accuracy with the activities, direct them to pp. 137–138, 144–146, 150, 152 and to get help online at my.hrw.com.

See Activity answers on p. 161.

Lección 1 Repaso de la lección

@HOMETUTOR
my.hrw.com

¡LLEGADA!

Now you can	Using
• talk about foods and beverages • ask questions • say which foods you like and don't like	• interrogative words • **gustar** with nouns • present tense of **-er** and **-ir** verbs • the verb **hacer**

To review
- **gustar** with nouns p. 145
- present tense of **-er** and **-ir** verbs p. 150

1 Listen and understand

AUDIO

Lola nunca come comidas tradicionales. Escucha la entrevista en la radio y escribe **el desayuno, el almuerzo** o **la cena,** según cuándo come o bebe cada cosa. *(Listen to the radio interview and write at what meal Lola eats and drinks each item.)*

1. huevos	**3.** leche	**5.** banana	**7.** pan
2. café	**4.** hamburguesas	**6.** refresco	**8.** cereal

Audio Program
TXT CD 3 Track 11
Audio Script, TE p. 137b

To review
- present tense of **-er** and **-ir** verbs p. 150
- the verb **hacer** p. 152

2 Talk about foods and beverages

Escribe lo que hacen estas personas en la cafetería. *(Write what these people are doing in the cafeteria.)*

modelo: Daniel / comer
Daniel come pan.

1. Irene / beber

5. yo / comer

2. ustedes / compartir

6. tú / hacer

3. yo / hacer

7. los estudiantes / beber

4. nosotros / vender

8. Trinidad y yo / compartir

Differentiating Instruction

Multiple Intelligences

Visual Learners Ask students to make a color code for the endings of **-er** and **-ir** verbs. Tell them to copy the tables showing the present tenses of **vender** and **compartir** on p. 159. Ask them to write the basic verb forms in black, but the endings in one of six colors. They should use the same color for the first person in both verbs, a second color for the second person familiar in both verbs, etc.

Pre-AP

Timed Answer Ask students what food and beverages they like for breakfast and lunch and to explain why they like or dislike them. **Para el desayuno, me gusta el jugo de naranja porque es nutritivo pero no me gusta el café porque es malo.** Tell students they must talk about their likes and dislikes for at least two minutes.

REPASO DE LA LECCIÓN

To review
- interrogative words p. 144

3 Ask questions

Gilberto es un nuevo estudiante. Es la hora de almuerzo y está en la cafetería con Julia. Completa la conversación con palabras interrogativas.
(Complete the conversation with interrogative words.)

modelo: ¿Cuál es el sándwich del día?
Es el sándwich de jamón y queso.

Gilberto: ¿ __1.__ está el yogur?
Julia: Está al lado de las frutas.
Gilberto: ¿ __2.__ no venden pizza?
Julia: Porque hoy no es viernes.
Gilberto: ¿ __3.__ venden los martes?
Julia: Venden hamburguesas.
Gilberto: ¿ __4.__ es la sopa?
Julia: Es muy rica.
Gilberto: ¿ __5.__ prepara la comida?
Julia: La señora Aguirre.
Gilberto: ¿ __6.__ personas trabajan en la cafetería?
Julia: Nueve o diez.
Gilberto: ¿ __7.__ compramos la bebida?
Julia: Ahora, con la comida.
Gilberto: ¿ __8.__ vamos después del almuerzo?
Julia: A la clase de inglés.

To review
- **gustar** with nouns p. 145

4 Say which foods you like and don't like

Estas personas están en el supermercado y hablan de comidas y bebidas. Escribe oraciones sobre lo que les gusta o no les gusta, según las opiniones.
(Write sentences about the foods these people like and dislike.)

modelo: la señora Medina: «El yogur es bueno.»
A la señora Medina le gusta el yogur.

1. ustedes: «No, el yogur es horrible.»
2. Adán y Susana: «Necesitamos manzanas. Son nutritivas.»
3. el señor Chávez: «El café es bueno.»
4. nosotros: «No, el café es malo.»
5. yo: «Tengo ganas de comer uvas.»
6. tú: «Las hamburguesas son ricas.»

To review
- El Yunque p. 137
- Comparación cultural pp. 138, 146, 152

5 Puerto Rico and El Salvador

Comparación cultural

Answer these culture questions.

1. What is El Yunque and what can you find there?
2. What is a popular cold treat in Puerto Rico?
3. What can you find in Plaza de Colón?
4. Describe some popular foods from Puerto Rico and El Salvador.

Más práctica Cuaderno *pp. 110–121* Cuaderno para hispanohablantes *pp. 112–121*

Get Help Online my.hrw.com

✓ Ongoing Assessment

Alternative Strategy To review the interrogative words in Activity 3, have students generate five questions to ask their classmates using **¿Cómo? ¿Dónde? ¿Por qué? ¿Quién? ¿Cuándo?** and **¿Qué?** Check for correct questions and answers.

✓ Ongoing Assessment

Peer Assessment Have student pairs exchange answers for Activity 4, and correct each other's work.

Answers Projectable Transparencies, 3-27

Answers for Activities on p. 160.

Activity 1 **1.** la cena; **2.** la cena; **3.** el almuerzo; **4.** el desayuno; **5.** el almuerzo; **6.** el desayuno; **7.** la cena; **8.** el almuerzo

Activity 2
1. Irene bebe jugo de naranja.
2. Ustedes comparten las uvas.
3. Yo hago un sándwich.
4. Nosotros vendemos manzanas.
5. Yo como cereal.
6. Tú haces sopa.
7. Los estudiantes beben leche.
8. Trinidad y yo compartimos una pizza.

Activity 3 **1.** Dónde; **2.** Por qué; **3.** Qué; **4.** Cómo; **5.** Quién; **6.** Cuántas; **7.** Cuándo; **8.** Adónde

Activity 4
1. A ustedes no les gusta el yogur.
2. A Adán y a Susana les gustan las mazanas.
3. Al señor Chávez le gusta el café.
4. A nosotros no nos gusta el café.
5. A mí me gustan las uvas.
6. A ti te gustan las hamburguesas.

Activity 5
1. **El Yunque** is a tropical rain forest. There you can find many waterfalls and a small frog called **coquí.**
2. A popular cold treat in Puerto Rico is **la piragua.**
3. In Plaza de Colón you can find a statue of Christopher Columbus.
4. Popular foods from Puerto Rico include **tostones** (fried plantains), **alcapurrias** (fried plantains stuffed with meat), and **bacalaítos** (codfish fritters). Typical foods from El Salvador include the **pupusa** (corn tortilla filled with beans, pork, and cheese) and a sweet bread layered with pineapple marmalade called **semita.**

Differentiating Instruction

Slower-paced Learners

Read Before Listening Before playing the audio for Activity 1, distribute copies of the script to the class and read it aloud. Tell them to track your voice by following the words with their index fingers as you say them.

Multiple Intelligences

Interpersonal Have students work with a partner to list the foods served in the school cafeteria that day or the day before. Partners should then take turns asking each other if they like each food or not. They may also emphasize their answers with gestures and facial expressions.

Lesson Overview

Culture at a Glance

Topic & Activity	Essential Question
Mealtime traditions pp. 162-163	Does your family have any traditions or customs involving mealtimes?
Elections in Puerto Rico p. 170	What do elections reveal about a culture?
Portraits by Rafael Tufiño and Fernando Sayán Polo p. 176	How do portraits represent the people in a country?
La quinceañera p. 180	How does a **quinceañera** celebration compare to a Sweet Sixteen celebration?
Culture Review Activity 5 p. 185	What are some cultural traditions in Puerto Rico and Peru?

COMPARISON COUNTRIES Puerto Rico El Salvador Perú

Practice at a Glance

	Objective	Activity & Skill
Vocabulary	Family members	1: Speaking/Writing; 2: Reading; 4: Speaking; 5: Reading; 6: Reading/Writing; 8: Speaking; 9: Listening/Reading; 11: Writing; 20: Writing; Repaso 1: Listening
	Months and numbers	3: Listening/Reading; 7: Speaking; 10: Speaking; Repaso 4: Writing
Grammar	Using **de** to show possession	2: Reading; 4: Speaking; 6: Reading/Writing; 19: Reading/Listening/Speaking; 20: Writing
	Possessive adjectives	5: Reading; 6: Reading/Writing; 8: Speaking
	Comparatives	5: Reading; 6: Reading/Writing; 12: Writing; 13: Writing/Speaking; 14: Listening/Writing; Repaso 3: Writing
Communication	Talk about family Ask and tell ages Express possession	1: Speaking/Writing; 2: Reading; 8: Speaking; 9: Listening/Reading; 11: Writing; 16: Listening/Reading; 17: Listening/Reading; 18: Speaking; 20: Writing; Repaso 2: Writing
	Give dates	3: Listening/Reading; 7: Speaking; 10: Speaking; Repaso 4: Writing
	Make comparisons	12: Writing; 13: Writing/Speaking; 14: Listening/Writing; 15: Writing; 18: Speaking; Repaso 3: Writing
	Pronunciation: the letter **j**	Pronunciación: *La letra **j***, p. 175: Listening
Recycle	The verb **tener,** Describing others	4: Speaking; 8: Speaking
	Numbers from 11 to 100	4: Speaking
	After-school activities	6: Reading/Writing

The following presentations are recorded in the Audio Program for ***¡Avancemos!***

- **¡A responder!** *page 165*
- **14: Capitán y Príncipe** *page 176*
- **19: Integración** *page 179*
- **Repaso de la lección** *page 184*
  1: Listen and understand
- **Repaso inclusivo** *page 188*
  1: Listen, understand, and compare

For **¡AvanzaRap!** scripts, see the **¡AvanzaRap! DVD.**

¡A responder! TXT CD 3 track 13

1. María y Cristóbal son los padres de Rodrigo.
2. Camila es la tía de Ana.
3. Rodrigo es el hermano de Ana.
4. Pablo es el hermano de Ester.
5. Camila y Pablo son los padres de Tito.
6. Ana y Ester son hermanas.
7. Tito es el hijo de María.
8. José es el padre de Ana.

14 | Capitán y Príncipe TXT CD 3 track 17

Mi familia y yo tenemos un perro y un gato. Nuestro perro se llama Capitán y nuestro gato se llama Príncipe. Capitán es tan simpático como Príncipe, pero también son diferentes. Príncipe es mucho más pequeño que Capitán. A Príncipe le gusta descansar tanto como comer. Capitán tiene tres años; Príncipe tiene ocho años. Capitán no hace mucho; es más perezoso que Príncipe.

19 | Integración TXT CD 3 tracks 19, 20

Hoy presentamos un perro muy especial.
Dino es un bóxer blanco. Él tiene cinco años y es muy bonito. Siempre está tranquilo. Le gusta más descansar que correr. Es un poco perezoso pero muy divertido. La actividad favorita de Dino es mirar la televisión. Es pequeño, inteligente y muy simpático. Si usted vive en San Juan, nuestro número de teléfono es 555-6346.

Repaso de la lección TXT CD 3 track 22

1 Listen and understand

Hola, me llamo Marcos. Tengo una foto de toda mi familia. Mi hermano se llama Pedro y mis hermanas se llaman Elena y Rosa. Detrás de nosotros, están nuestros padres. Nuestro padre se llama Julio y nuestra madre se llama Norma. Mi abuelo se llama Alberto. Al lado de mi abuelo están mis primos. Ellos se llaman Diego y Felipe. Detrás de mis primos está mi tía. Ella se llama Carmen. Mi familia es bonita, ¿no?

Repaso inclusivo TXT CD 3 track 24

1 Listen, understand, and compare

Esperanza: Hola, Diana, ¿qué problema tienes?

Diana: Bueno, yo soy más estudiosa que mi hermano. A él y a sus amigos les gusta tocar la guitarra toda la tarde. A mí me gusta escuchar música tanto como estudiar, pero yo tengo que estudiar mucho. Tengo muchos exámenes en la clase de ciencias.

Esperanza: Hmmm... ¿Óscar es mayor o menor que tú?

Diana: Es menor que yo. Yo tengo catorce años y él tiene diez.

Esperanza: ¡Ah! Diana, tienes que aprender a vivir con tu hermano.

Diana: Pero, ¿qué necesito hacer?

Esperanza: Necesitas hablar con Óscar. Tú estudias de las tres a las cinco de la tarde. Tu hermano y sus amigos tocan la guitarra de las cinco a las siete, y tú escuchas.

Diana: Está bien. ¡Gracias!

Resource List

Everything you need to ...

Plan

TEACHER ONE STOP

✓Lesson Plans
✓Teacher Resources
✓Audio and Video

Present

INTERACTIVE WHITEBOARD LESSONS
TEACHER ONE STOP WITH PROJECTABLE TRANSPARENCIES
POWER PRESENTATIONS
ANIMATEDGRAMMAR

Assess

ONLINE ASSESSMENT

✓ Assessments for on-level, modified, pre-AP, and heritage learners
✓ Create customized tests with **Examview Assessment Suite**
✓ **performance space**
✓ *Generate Success* Rubric Generator

Print

Plan	Present	Practice	Assess
URB 3 • Video Scripts pp. 71–72 • Family Involvement Activity p. 92 • Absent Student Copymasters pp. 101–111 **Best Practices Toolkit**	**URB 3** • Video Activities pp. 59–66	• *Cuaderno* pp. 122–147 • *Cuaderno para hispanohablantes* pp. 122–147 • *Lecturas para todos* pp. 27–31 • *Lecturas para hispanohablantes* • *¡AvanzaCómics! SúperBruno y Nati,* Episodio 2 **URB 3** • Practice Games pp. 39–46 • Audio Scripts pp. 78–82 • Fine Art Activities pp. 88–89	**Differentiated Assessment Program** **URB 3** • Did you get it? Reteaching and Practice Copymasters pp. 13–24

Projectable Transparencies (Teacher One Stop, my.hrw.com)

Culture	Presentation and Practice	Classroom Management
• Atlas Maps 1–6 • Map of Puerto Rico 1 • Fine Art Transparencies 4, 5	• Vocabulary Transparencies 8, 9 • Grammar Presentation Transparencies 12, 13 • Situational Transparencies and label overlay 14, 15 • Situational Student Copymasters pp. 1, 2	• Warm Up Transparencies 20–23 • Student Book Answer Transparencies pp. 28–31

Audio and Video

Audio	Video	¡AvanzaRap! DVD
• Student Book Audio CD 3 Tracks 12–24 • Workbook Audio CD 2 Tracks 11–20 • Heritage Learners Audio CD 1 Tracks 21–24, CD 3 Tracks 17–20 • Assessment Audio CD 1 Tracks 17–20 • *Lecturas para todos* Audio CD 1 Track 6, CD 2 Tracks 1–6 • Sing-along Songs Audio CD	• Vocabulary Video DVD 1 • *Telehistoria* DVD 1 Escena 1 Escena 2 Escena 3 Completa • Culture Video DVD 1	• Video animations of all **¡AvanzaRap!** songs (with Karaoke track) • Interactive DVD Activities • Teaching Suggestions • **¡AvanzaRap!** Activity Masters • **¡AvanzaRap!** video scripts and answers

Online and Media Resources

Student	Teacher
Available online at my.hrw.com • Online Student Edition • News Networking • performance space • @HOMETUTOR • Cultura Interactiva • WebQuests • Interactive Flashcards • Review Games • Self-Check Quiz **Student One Stop** **Holt McDougal Spanish Apps**	**Teacher One Stop (also available at my.hrw.com)** • Interactive Teacher's Edition • All print, audio, and video resources • Projectable Transparencies • Lesson Plans • TPRS • Examview Assessment Suite **Available online at my.hrw.com** *Generate Success* Rubric Generator and Graphic Organizers **Power Presentations**

Differentiated Assessment

On-level	Modified	Pre-AP	Heritage Learners
• Vocabulary Recognition Quiz p. 120 • Vocabulary Production Quiz p. 121 • Grammar Quizzes pp. 122–123 • Culture Quiz p. 124 • On-level Lesson Test pp. 125–131 • On-level Unit Test pp. 137–143	• Modified Lesson Test pp. 95–101 • Modified Unit Test pp. 107–113	• Pre-AP Lesson Test pp. 95–101 • Pre-AP Unit Test pp. 107–113	• Heritage Learners Lesson Test pp. 101–107 • Heritage Learners Unit Test pp. 113–119

Core Pacing Guide

50 Minute (9 Day)

	Objectives/Focus	Teach	Practice	Assess/HW Options
DAY 1	**Culture:** learn about Puerto Rican culture **Vocabulary:** family, months, numbers from 200 to 1,000,000 • Warm Up OHT 20 **5 min**	Lesson Opener pp. 162–163 **Presentación de vocabulario** pp. 164–165 • Read A–C • View video DVD 1 • Play Audio TXT CD 3 track 12 • *¡A responder!* TXT CD 3 track 13 **Práctica de vocabulario** p. 166 • *Nota gramatical:* possession with **de** **25 min**	Lesson opener pp. 162–163 **Práctica de vocabulario** p. 166 • Acts. 1, 2 **15 min**	**Assess:** *Para y piensa* p. 166 **5 min** **Homework:** *Cuaderno* pp. 122–124 @HomeTutor
DAY 2	**Communication:** identify family and birthday vocabulary, practice using them to ask and tell a person's age • Warm Up OHT 20 • Check Homework **5 min**	**Vocabulario en contexto** pp. 167–168 • *Telehistoria escena 1* DVD 1 • *Nota gramatical:* use **tener** to talk about age **20 min**	**Vocabulario en contexto** pp. 167–168 • Act. 3 TXT CD 3 track 14 • Act. 4 **20 min**	**Assess:** *Para y piensa* p. 168 **5 min** **Homework:** *Cuaderno* pp. 122–124 @HomeTutor
DAY 3	**Grammar:** possessive adjectives • Warm Up OHT 21 • Check Homework **5 min**	**Presentación de gramática** p. 169 • Possessive adjectives **Práctica de gramática** pp. 170–171 **Culture:** *Las elecciones en Puerto Rico* • *Nota gramatical:* writing the date **20 min**	**Práctica de gramática** pp. 170–171 • Acts. 5, 6, 7, 8 **20 min**	**Assess:** *Para y piensa* p. 171 **5 min** **Homework:** *Cuaderno* pp. 125–127 @HomeTutor
DAY 4	**Communication:** use possessive adjectives to talk about family and people's birthdays • Warm Up OHT 21 • Check Homework **5 min**	**Gramática en contexto** pp. 172–173 • *Telehistoria escena 2* DVD 1 **15 min**	**Gramática en contexto** pp. 172–173 • Act. 9 TXT CD 3 track 15 • Acts. 10, 11 **25 min**	**Assess:** *Para y piensa* p. 173 **5 min** **Homework:** *Cuaderno* pp. 125–127 @HomeTutor
DAY 5	**Grammar:** comparatives • Warm Up OHT 22 • Check Homework **5 min**	**Presentación de gramática** p. 174 • Comparatives **Práctica de gramática** pp. 175–176 • *Pronunciación:* TXT CD 3 track 16 **15 min**	**Práctica de gramática** pp. 175–176 • Acts. 12, 13, 15 • Act. 14 TXT CD 3 track 17 **25 min**	**Assess:** *Para y piensa* p. 176 **5 min** **Homework:** *Cuaderno* pp. 128–130 @HomeTutor
DAY 6	**Communication:** Culmination: use comparative words and possessive adjectives to describe your family and friends • Warm Up OHT 22 • Check Homework **5 min**	**Todo junto** pp. 177–179 • *Escenas 1, 2: Resumen* • *Telehistoria completa* DVD 1 **20 min**	**Todo junto** pp. 177–179 • Acts. 16, 17 TXT CD 3 tracks 14, 15, 18 • Act. 19, TXT CD 3 tracks 19, 20 • Act. 18, 20 **20 min**	**Assess:** *Para y piensa* p. 179 **5 min** **Homework:** *Cuaderno* pp. 131–132 @HomeTutor
DAY 7	**Reading:** The **quinceañera** celebration **Review:** Lesson review • Warm Up OHT 23 • Check Homework **5 min**	**Lectura Cultural** pp. 180–181 • *La quinceañera* TXT CD 3 track 21 **Repaso de la lección** pp. 184–185 **10 min**	**Lectura Cultural** pp. 180–181 • *La quinceañera* **Repaso de la lección** pp. 184–185 • Act. 1 TXT CD 3 track 22 • Acts. 2, 3, 4, 5 **25 min**	**Assess:** *Para y piensa* p. 181; *Repaso de la lección* pp. 184–185 **10 min** **Homework:** *En resumen* p. 183; *Cuaderno* pp. 133–144 (optional) Review Games Online @HomeTutor
DAY 8	**Assessment**			**Assess:** Lesson 2 test or Unit 3 test **50 min**
DAY 9	**Unit Culmination** **5 min**	**Comparación cultural** pp. 186–187 TXT CD 3 track 23 **Repaso inclusivo** pp. 188–189 **15 min**	**Comparación cultural** pp. 186–187 **Repaso inclusivo** pp. 188–189 • Act. 1 TXT CD 3 track 24 • Acts. 2, 3, 4, 5, 6, 7 **25 min**	**Homework:** *Cuaderno* pp. 145–147 **5 min**

	Objectives/Focus	Teach	Practice	Assess/HW Options
DAY 1	**Culture:** learn about Puerto Rican culture **Vocabulary:** family, months, numbers from 200 to 1,000,000 • Warm Up OHT 20 **5 min**	Lesson Opener pp. 162–163 **Presentación de vocabulario** pp. 164–165 • Read A–C • View video DVD 1 • Play Audio TXT CD 3 track 12 • *¡A responder!* TXT CD 3 track 13 **Práctica de vocabulario** p. 166 • *Nota gramatical:* showing posession with **de** **25 min**	Lesson Opener pp. 162–163 **Práctica de vocabulario** p. 166 • Acts. 1, 2 **15 min**	**Assess:** *Para y piensa* p. 166 **5 min**
	Communication: identify family and birthday vocabulary, practice using them to ask and tell a person's age **5 min**	**Vocabulario en contexto** pp. 167–168 • *Telehistoria escena 1* DVD 1 • *Nota gramatical:* use **tener** to talk about age **15 min**	**Vocabulario en contexto** pp. 167–168 • Act. 3 TXT CD 3 track 14 • Act. 4 **15 min**	**Assess:** *Para y piensa* p. 168 **5 min** **Homework:** *Cuaderno* pp. 122–124 @HomeTutor
DAY 2	**Grammar:** possessive adjectives • Warm Up OHT 21 • Check Homework **5 min**	**Presentación de gramática** p. 169 • Possessive adjectives **Práctica de gramática** pp. 170–171 **Culture:** *Las elecciones en Puerto Rico* • *Nota gramatical:* writing the date **15 min**	**Práctica de gramática** pp. 170–171 • Acts. 5, 6, 7, 8 **20 min**	**Assess:** *Para y piensa* p. 171 **5 min**
	Communication: use possessive adjectives to talk about family and people's birthdays **5 min**	**Gramática en contexto** pp. 172–173 • *Telehistoria escena 2* DVD 1 **15 min**	**Gramática en contexto** pp. 172–173 • Act. 9 TXT CD 3 track 15 • Acts. 10, 11 **20 min**	**Assess:** *Para y piensa* p. 173 **5 min** **Homework:** *Cuaderno* pp. 125–127 @HomeTutor
DAY 3	**Grammar:** comparatives • Warm Up OHT 22 • Check Homework **5 min**	**Presentación de gramática** p. 174 • Comparatives **Práctica de gramática** pp. 175–176 • *Pronunciación:* TXT CD 3 track 16 **15 min**	**Práctica de gramática** pp. 175–176 • Acts. 12, 13, 15 • Act. 14 TXT CD 3 track 17 **20 min**	**Assess:** *Para y piensa* p. 176 **5 min**
	Communication: Culmination: use comparative words and possessive adjectives to describe family and friends **5 min**	**Todo junto** pp. 177–179 • *Escenas 1, 2: Resumen* • *Telehistoria completa* DVD 1 **15 min**	**Todo junto** pp. 177–179 • Acts. 16, 17 TXT CD 3 tracks 14, 15, 18 • Act. 19, TXT CD 3 tracks 19, 20 • Acts. 18, 20 **20 min**	**Assess:** *Para y piensa* p. 179 **5 min** **Homework:** *Cuaderno* pp. 128–132 @HomeTutor
DAY 4	**Reading:** The **quinceañera** celebration • Warm Up OHT 23 • Check Homework **5 min**	**Lectura cultural** pp. 180–181 • *La quinceañera* TXT CD 3 track 21 **15 min**	**Lectura cultural** pp. 180–181 • *La quinceañera* **20 min**	**Assess:** *Para y piensa* p. 181 **5 min**
	Review: Lesson review **5 min**	**Repaso de la lección** pp. 184–185 **15 min**	**Repaso de la lección** pp. 184–185 • Act. 1 TXT CD 3 track 22 • Acts. 2, 3, 4, 5 **20 min**	**Assess:** *Repaso de la lección* pp. 184–185 **5 min** **Homework:** *En resumen* p. 183; *Cuaderno* pp. 133–144 (optional) Review Games Online @HomeTutor
DAY 5	**Assessment**			**Assess:** Lesson 2 test or Unit 3 test **45 min**
	Unit Culmination **5 min**	**Comparación cultural** pp. 186–187 TXT CD 3 track 23 **Repaso inclusivo** pp. 188–189 **15 min**	**Comparación cultural** pp. 186–187 **Repaso inclusivo** pp. 188–189 • Act. 1 TXT CD 3 track 24 • Acts. 2, 3, 4, 5, 6, 7 **20 min**	**Homework:** *Cuaderno* pp. 145–147 **5 min**

¡AVANZA! Objectives

- Introduce lesson theme: **En mi familia.**
- **Culture:** Learn about **la sobremesa** and compare mealtime traditions.

Presentation Strategies

- Introduce the characters' names: Rodrigo, Marisol, Sra. Vélez, Ana.
- Have students identify the people in the photo and tell what is happening.
- Have students talk about traditions and customs involving mealtime.

STANDARDS

2.1 Compare practices and perspectives
4.2 Compare cultures
21st Century **Collaboration,** Inclusion; **Social and Cross-Cultural Skills,** Compara con tu mundo

Warm Up Projectable Transparencies, 3-20

-er and -ir Verbs Write the correct form of each verb.

1. tú _____ (beber)
2. yo _____ (compartir)
3. ella _____ (escribir)
4. usted _____ (leer)
5. ellos _____ (compartir)

Answers: 1. bebes; 2. comparto; 3. escribe; 4. lee; 5. comparten

Comparación cultural

Exploring the Theme

Ask students the following questions:

1. Is this family eating inside or outside?
2. When do you think is a good time to eat outside the house?
3. What do you think people talk about when they are eating together?
4. Why do you think people in Puerto Rico find it convenient to eat outdoors?

¿Qué ves? Possible answers include:

- Sí, Rodrigo tiene sed.
- Los señores beben café.
- La chica es bonita, joven, seria. La chica tiene el pelo castaño.

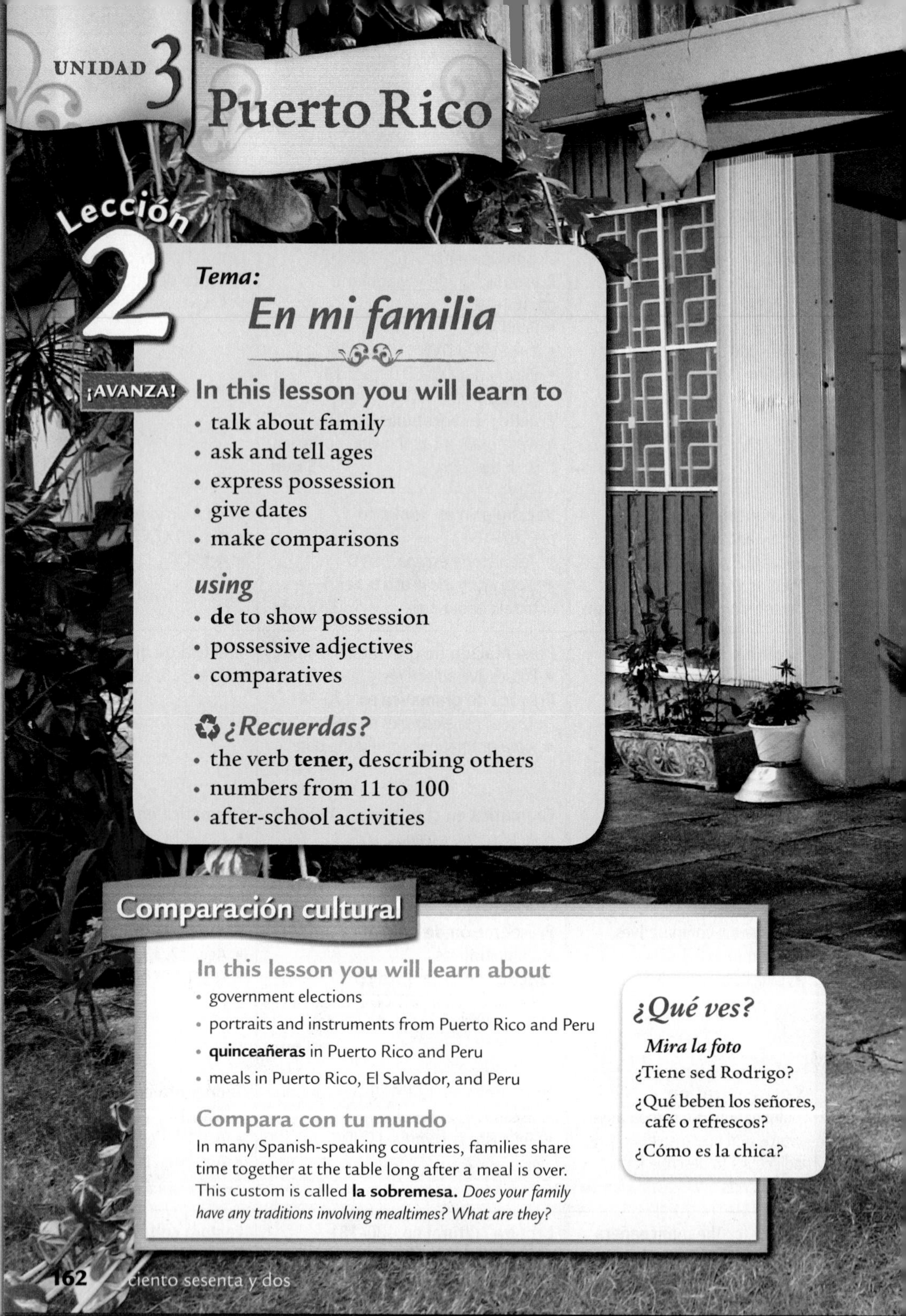

UNIDAD 3 **Puerto Rico**

Lección 2

Tema:
En mi familia

¡AVANZA! In this lesson you will learn to

- talk about family
- ask and tell ages
- express possession
- give dates
- make comparisons

using

- **de** to show possession
- possessive adjectives
- comparatives

¿Recuerdas?

- the verb **tener,** describing others
- numbers from 11 to 100
- after-school activities

Comparación cultural

In this lesson you will learn about

- government elections
- portraits and instruments from Puerto Rico and Peru
- **quinceañeras** in Puerto Rico and Peru
- meals in Puerto Rico, El Salvador, and Peru

Compara con tu mundo

In many Spanish-speaking countries, families share time together at the table long after a meal is over. This custom is called **la sobremesa.** *Does your family have any traditions involving mealtimes? What are they?*

¿Qué ves?

Mira la foto

¿Tiene sed Rodrigo?

¿Qué beben los señores, café o refrescos?

¿Cómo es la chica?

162 ciento sesenta y dos

Differentiating Instruction

Inclusion

Cumulative Instruction Organize students into small groups. Give each group a piece of poster board. Instruct students to write the heading **comer** at the top of their poster. Then have each group brainstorm as many words and phrases related to food and eating as they can remember from previous lessons. Encourage them to add pictures as well. Give each group the opportunity to share their poster.

Slower-paced Learners

Yes/No Questions Ask students yes or no questions about what they see in the photo. Point to the appropriate item in the photo for each question whose answer is yes. **¿Hay un refresco? ¿Hay un café? ¿Hay una chica?** Use vocabulary familiar to students when the answer is no. **¿Hay un cuaderno? ¿Hay un chico triste?**

DIGITAL SPANISH my.hrw.com
ONLINE STUDENT EDITION with...

performance space
News Networking
@HOMETUTOR
CULTURA Interactiva

- Audio and Video Resources
- Interactive Flashcards
- Review Activities
- WebQuest
- Conjuguemos.com

PRACTICE SPANISH WITH HOLT MCDOUGAL APPS!

Jna familia come en casa
an Juan, Puerto Rico

Puerto Rico
ciento sesenta y tres 163

Differentiating Instruction

Multiple Intelligences

Visual Learners Have students draw a picture of a typical family meal. Remind them to consider the question words **¿quién?, ¿dónde?, ¿qué?, ¿cuándo?, ¿cómo?** as they draw. Who is at the table? Where do they eat? What are they eating? When do they eat? How do people feel about the meal? Then, ask students to write a short sentence that answers each question.

Heritage Language Learners

Support What They Know Ask students to share expressions that might be heard around their family's table. What do people say when the meal is about to start? How do people in their family ask someone to pass a dish? How do they ask to be excused?

DIGITAL SPANISH

TEACHER TOOLS
- Interactive Whiteboard Lessons
- Generate Success!

ALSO AVAILABLE...
- Online Workbook
- Spanish InterActive Reader

SPANISH ON THE GO!
- Performance Space
- Holt McDougal Spanish Apps
- ¡Avancemos! eTextbook

Using the Photo

Location Information

Puerto Rico is the easternmost island of the Greater Antilles, lying approximately 1,000 miles southeast of Miami. The island itself is slightly smaller than three times the size of Rhode Island. Puerto Rico's interior terrain is mountainous.

Expanded Information

History and Education Puerto Rico was ruled by Spain from 1493 until the end of the Spanish-American War in 1898, when it was ceded to the United States. San Juan is its capital. Puerto Ricans were granted U.S. citizenship in 1917 but have chosen to remain a self-governing commonwealth of the U.S. Puerto Rican students are required to study English as a second language.

Long-term Retention

Recycle

Ask students to look at the photo and answer the following questions in Spanish:

1. ¿Qué tiempo hace?
2. ¿Puerto Rico está en América Central o en el Caribe?
3. ¿De dónde es la familia?
4. ¿Qué bebe Rodrigo?

Possible answers include: 1. Hace calor, sol. 2. Está en el Caribe. 3. La familia es de Puerto Rico (de San Juan). 4. Bebe agua.

¡AVANZA! Objectives

- Present vocabulary: family, numbers, months of the year.
- Check for vocabulary recognition.

Core Resources

- Video Program: DVD 1
- Audio Program: TXT CD 3 tracks 12, 13

Presentation Strategies

- Read the vocabulary words aloud and have students repeat after you. Check students' pronunciation.
- Play the audio as students read A–C.

STANDARD

1.2 Understand language

Communication

Interpersonal Mode

Based on Rodrigo's family tree, have student pairs ask and answer questions about the names of his family members and pets. For example: **¿Cómo se llama el abuelo? El abuelo se llama Cristóbal. ¿Cómo se llama el perro? El perro se llama Capitán.**

Communication

Common Error Alert

Point out that when a pet is a female, **la perra** and **la gata** may be used in place of **el perro** and **el gato.** Explain to the students that the meanings of the pet names on this page are *Captain* and *Prince*.

Sensitivity

Some students might not be comfortable discussing their family. Always give them the option of describing a fictitious family when answering personal questions.

Communication

Motivating with Music

After presenting the vocabulary, play the **¡AvanzaRap!** animated video and have students identify the family terms they can understand. If students struggle with this activity, play the version with subtitles. As a follow-up activity, have groups of students add one or two lines to the rap song. Ask volunteers to "perform" their added lyrics for the class.

Presentación de VOCABULARIO

¡AVANZA! **Goal:** Learn about Rodrigo's family. Then practice what you have learned to talk about families and express possession. ***Actividades 1–2***

VIDEO DVD

AUDIO

A Soy Rodrigo. **Vivo** en Puerto Rico con **mis padres.** Ellos tienen dos **hijos.** Yo soy **su hijo** y **mi hermana** Ana es su **hija.** Te presento a las otras personas en **nuestra familia.**

B **¿Cuántos años tienes** tú? Yo **tengo** quince **años.** Ana, mi hermana **menor,** tiene nueve años. Soy su **hermano mayor.**

Differentiating Instruction

Heritage Language Learners

Writing Skills Have students write a short paragraph about their family members. Ask them to include names, relationships, ages, and what they like to do. After students complete their writing have them review it for spelling and grammar.

Pre-AP

Expand and Elaborate Have students create a family tree similar to Rodrigo's on p. 164. Tell them to organize and record the names and relationships of their own family members. Ask for volunteers to share their family trees with the group.

C **¿Cuál es la fecha?** Hoy **es el primero de abril.** Es mi **cumpleaños.** ¿Cuándo es **tu** cumpleaños?

¡Feliz cumpleaños!

Numbers from 200 to 1,000,000

200	**doscientos(as)**	**700**	**setecientos(as)**
300	**trescientos(as)**	**800**	**ochocientos(as)**
400	**cuatrocientos(as)**	**900**	**novecientos(as)**
500	**quinientos(as)**	**1,000**	**mil**
600	**seiscientos(as)**	**1,000,000**	**un millón (de)**

Más vocabulario

la madrastra *stepmother* | **la fecha de nacimiento** *birth date*
el padrastro *stepfather* | **ya** *already*

Expansión de vocabulario p. R4

@HOMETUTOR my.hrw.com Interactive Flashcards

¡A responder! Escuchar

Escucha las oraciones sobre la familia de Rodrigo. Si la oración es cierta, levanta la mano izquierda; si es falsa, levanta la mano derecha.
(Listen to the sentences about Rodrigo's family. If the sentence is true, raise your left hand; if it is false, raise your right hand.)

Differentiating Instruction

Multiple Intelligences

Logical/Mathematical Write the months of the year on the board. Then ask students **¿Cuándo es tu cumpleaños?** Record each response by placing a tally mark under the appropriate month. Instruct students to use this data to create a bar graph. Encourage students to analyze and comment on their graphs. **Cinco estudiantes tienen cumpleaños en abril.**

Slower-paced Learners

Memory Aids Collect pretend hundred dollar bills from a board game, or create them out of construction paper. Show the bills to students as you count **doscientos, trescientos, cuatrocientos,** etc. Have students repeat each word after you say it. Then have students create their own bills writing a multiple of one hundred on each. Encourage students to practice counting and sequencing their bills.

TEACHER to TEACHER
Carmen Moreno
Rye, New York

Classroom Management

I often use transparencies for vocabulary spreads or grammar paradigms that appear on preceding pages so that students don't have to flip back and forth to do an activity related to that particular topic.

Go online for more tips!

Communication

Common Error Alert

Months are not capitalized in Spanish, just as days of the week are not capitalized. Be sure to point out that *first* is always expressed as **primero,** but that the cardinal (counting) numbers are used for all other dates.

Communication

Group Work

Have students write numbers in hundreds from 200 to 1,000 on index cards. Then have them work in small groups and practice saying the numbers out loud.

Long-term Retention

Recycle

Have students write a possible weather condition in your area for each date expressed in Spanish.

1. El veinte de julio
2. El primero de enero
3. El cinco de mayo
4. El primero de octubre

Possible answers: 1. hace calor, hace sol; 2. hace frío, nieva; 3. llueve, hace sol, hace viento; 4. hace viento, llueve, hace sol

Answers Projectable Transparencies, 3-28

¡A responder! Audio Script, TE p. 161b

Students will raise their left hand if the statement is true and their right hand if the statement is false.

1. Falsa	**5.** Cierta
2. Cierta	**6.** Falsa
3. Cierta	**7.** Falsa
4. Falsa	**8.** Cierta

Objectives
- Practice vocabulary: family members.
- Express possession using **de.**

Core Resource
- *Cuaderno,* pp. 122–124

Practice Sequence
- **Activity 1:** Vocabulary recognition: family members
- **Activity 2:** Vocabulary production: family members; possession using **de**

STANDARDS
1.2 Understand language, Act. 2
1.3 Present information, Acts. 1-2; PYP
4.1 Compare languages, Nota

✓ Ongoing Assessment
Get Help Online
More Practice
my.hrw.com

PARA Y PIENSA **Peer Assessment** Have students compare answers with a classmate. Then call on individuals for the answers. For additional practice, use Reteaching & Practice Copymasters URB 3, pp. 13, 14.

Práctica de VOCABULARIO

1 La familia de Rodrigo

Hablar
Escribir

Indica la relación de cada persona con Rodrigo. Usa el árbol genealógico de la página 164. *(Tell how each person is related to Rodrigo.)*

Expansión
Draw your own family tree or that of a famous family. Explain how the people are related.

Nota gramatical
In Spanish, **'s** is never used. To show possession, use **de** and the **noun** that refers to the owner/possessor.

el gato **de Marisa** *Marisa's cat*   los primos **de Juan** *Juan's cousins*

2 La familia de Marisol

Leer

Combina las frases para describir las relaciones entre las personas de la familia de Marisol. *(Match the descriptions.)*

1. El padre de mi madre es...	**a.** mi hermana.
2. Las hermanas de mi padre son...	**b.** mi madre.
3. La hija de mi padre es...	**c.** mis tías.
4. Los hijos de mis padres son...	**d.** mi abuelo.
5. Las hijas de mi tía son...	**e.** mis primas.
6. La hermana de mi tía es...	**f.** mis hermanos.

Expansión: Teacher Edition Only
Have students describe the relationship of two additional family members using **de** to show possession.

Más práctica Cuaderno *pp. 122–124* Cuaderno para hispanohablantes *pp. 122–125*

Get Help Online
my.hrw.com

PARA Y PIENSA

Did you get it? Fill in the blank with the correct vocabulary word.
1. El _____ de tus tíos es tu primo.
2. Los _____ de tus padres son tus abuelos.
3. Las _____ de tu madre son tus tías.

Answers Projectable Transparencies, 3-28
Activity 1
1. María es la abuela.
2. Tito es el primo.
3. Camila es la tía.
4. Cristóbal es el abuelo.
5. Celia es la madre.
6. Pablo es el tío.
7. Ana es la hermana.

Activity 2
1. d; 2. c; 3. a; 4. f; 5. e; 6. b

Para y piensa
1. hijo; 2. padres; 3. hermanas

Differentiating Instruction

Pre-AP
Circumlocution Remind students they can use words they know to talk around words they don't know. Write the following words on the board: *great-aunt, great-grandfather,* and *second cousins.* Ask students to think about other ways they could express these words using the vocabulary they've already learned. Possible answers: **La hermana de mi abuelo, El abuelo de mi padre, Los hijos del primo de mi madre.**

Heritage Language Learners
Regional Variations Ask students to share any regional terms that people use for family members in their country or region of origin. Do people always say **madre** and **padre,** or are there more familiar words that people use for mother and father? For example: **mamita, papito.** What are some terms of endearment that people use to address other family members?

VOCABULARIO en contexto

¡AVANZA! **Goal:** Identify the words Marisol and Rodrigo use to talk about birthdays and other family members. Then practice the words you have learned to ask and tell a person's age. ***Actividades 3–4***

¿Recuerdas? The verb **tener** p. 91, numbers from 11 to 100 p. 87

Telehistoria escena 1

@HOMETUTOR my.hrw.com **View, Read and Record**

STRATEGIES

Cuando lees
Analyze the scene This scene starts out calmly and ends with a problem. What do the characters talk about at the beginning? What is the problem, and whose problem is it?

Cuando escuchas
Remember, listen, and predict Before listening, remember why Rodrigo wanted Alicia's T-shirt. What happens to the T-shirt in this scene? After listening, predict what will happen next.

VIDEO DVD

AUDIO

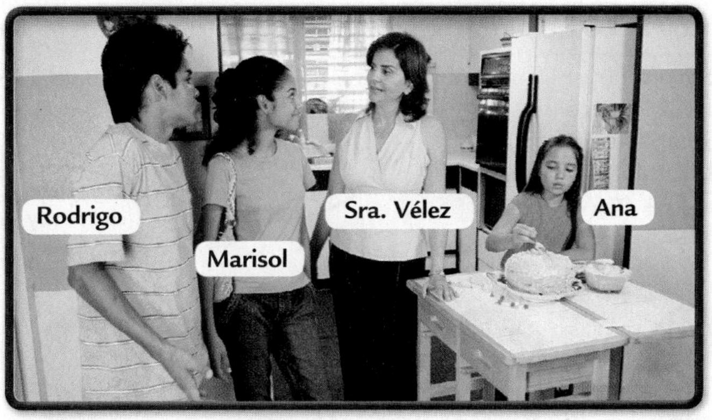

Rodrigo and Marisol arrive in Rodrigo's kitchen.

Marisol: Señora Vélez, ¿es su cumpleaños?
Sra. Vélez: No, es el cumpleaños de Ana.
Marisol: ¡Feliz cumpleaños! ¿Cuántos años tienes?
Ana: Hoy tengo nueve años. Mañana, ¡diez!
Marisol: ¿Mañana? ¿El veintiocho de febrero?
Rodrigo: No. El primero de marzo.
Marisol: El cumpleaños de mi abuela es el primero de marzo.
Ana: Ah, ¿sí? ¿Cuántos años tiene?
Marisol: Tiene sesenta y ocho años.
Rodrigo: Mamá, ¿dónde está la camiseta? Trini Salgado está en la escuela a las cuatro.

Continuará... p. 172

También se dice

Puerto Rico Marisol uses the word **abuela** to talk about her grandmother. In other Spanish-speaking countries you might hear:
- **Perú, Argentina** **la mamama**

¡AVANZA! Objective
- Understand activity vocabulary in context.

Core Resources
- Video Program: DVD 1
- Audio Program: TXT CD 3 track 14

Presentation Strategies
- Ask students to provide ideas about creating family trees.
- Show the video with the books closed.
- Play the audio while students follow the script in the text.

STANDARDS
1.2 Understand language
4.1 Compare languages
Critical Thinking and Problem Solving, Multiple Intelligences

Warm Up
Projectable Transparencies, 3-20

Vocabulary Complete the following sentences with the correct word.

abuelos perro prima fecha cumpleaños

1. La hija de mi tía es mi ____.
2. Mi ____ es el dos de enero.
3. Los padres de mi madre son mis ____.
4. Mi ____ se llama Rover.
5. El 5 de diciembre es mi ____ de nacimiento.

Answers: 1. prima; 2. cumpleaños; 3. abuelos; 4. perro; 5. fecha

Communication

Regionalisms

Spanish speakers use the diminutive endings **-ito** and **-ita** to express terms of endearment. For example, **abuelo** becomes **abuelito** and **abuela** becomes **abuelita.**

Differentiating Instruction

English Learners

Build Background Ask students if they know of any other words used in their country or place of origin to refer to grandparents or great-grandparents. Do they use a diminutive? Do they use special words to refer to the family members they like most? Ask them to say the word in their language or in English, and then repeat the word in Spanish.

Multiple Intelligences

Interpersonal Have students work in pairs to think about what might be causing Ana and Rodrigo to feel certain emotions. **¿Por qué está Ana contenta? ¿Por qué está Rodrigo nervioso?** Encourage students to explain their answers with information from the text.

Video Summary

@HOMETUTOR VideoPlus my.hrw.com

Marisol notices a cake and asks if it is Mrs. Vélez's birthday. She learns that the next day, March 1st, is Ana's 10th birthday. Marisol informs them that her grandmother's birthday is the same day, and that she'll be 68. Rodrigo asks his mother where the T-shirt is, and says that Trini Salgado is at the school at four.

Objectives
- Practice using vocabulary in context.
- Recycle: the verb **tener**, numbers from 11 to 100.
- Practice using **tener** to talk about one's age.

Core Resource
- Audio Program: TXT CD 3 track 14

Practice Sequence
- **Activity 3:** Telehistoria comprehension
- **Activity 4:** Vocabulary production: family members; Recycle: numbers from 11 to 100

STANDARDS
1.1 Engage in conversation, Act. 4
1.2 Understand language, Act. 3; PYP
1.3 Present information, Act. 4
4.1 Compare languages, Nota

✓ Ongoing Assessment
Get Help Online
More Practice
my.hrw.com

PARA Y PIENSA **Quick Check** Have pairs of students talk about the age of three family members. Check questions and answers. For additional practice, use Reteaching & Practice Copymasters URB 3, pp. 13, 15, 22, 23.

Answers Projectable Transparencies, 3-28

Activity 3
1. Falsa. Es el cumpleaños de Ana.
2. Falsa. Mañana es el primero de marzo.
3. Falsa. El cumpleaños de Ana es en el mes de marzo.
4. Cierta.

Activity 4
1. ¿Cuántos años tiene la hermana de Rodrigo? Tiene nueve años.
2. ¿... el primo de Rodrigo? Tiene diez años.
3. ¿... el abuelo de Rodrigo? Tiene sesenta y seis años.
4. ¿... la prima de Rodrigo? Tiene catorce años.
5. ¿... la tía de Rodrigo? Tiene treinta y ocho años.
6. ¿... la madre de Rodrigo? Tiene cuarenta y cinco años.
7. ¿... el tío de Rodrigo? Tiene treinta y nueve años.
8. ¿... la abuela de Rodrigo? Tiene sesenta y cuatro años.

Para y piensa
1. tiene catorce; 2. tiene ocho; 3. tienen cincuenta y dos

3 *Comprensión del episodio* Un cumpleaños

Escuchar
Leer

Indica si las oraciones son ciertas o falsas. Si es falsa, escribe lo que es cierto.
(Tell if the statements are true or false. Correct the false statements to make them true.)

1. Es el cumpleaños de la señora Vélez.
2. Mañana es el veintiocho de febrero.
3. El cumpleaños de Ana es en el mes de febrero.
4. El cumpleaños de la abuela de Marisol es el primero de marzo.

Expansión:
Teacher Edition Only
Have students write one additional false statement about the Telehistoria. Then have them switch papers to correct the errors.

Nota gramatical ¿Recuerdas? The verb **tener** p. 91

Use the verb **tener** to talk about how old a person is.

¿Cuántos años **tiene** tu amiga?
How old is your friend?

¿Violeta? **Tiene** quince años.
Violeta? She's fifteen years old.

4 ¿Cuántos años tienen? ¿Recuerdas? Numbers from 11 to 100 p. 87

Hablar

Habla con otro(a) estudiante sobre cuántos años tienen estas personas de la familia de Rodrigo. Si es necesario, usa el árbol genealógico de la página 164. *(Talk with a partner about the ages of the people in Rodrigo's family.)*

47 años

A ¿Cuántos años tiene el padre de Rodrigo?
B Tiene cuarenta y siete años.

1. 9 años

2. 10 años

3. 66 años

4. 14 años

5. 38 años

6. 45 años

7. 39 años

8. 64 años

Expansión
Say how old the members of your family are.

Get Help Online
my.hrw.com

PARA Y PIENSA

Did you get it? Give each age, using **tener** and the word for each number in parentheses.

1. Marisol _____ _____ años. (14)
2. El gato de la familia Vélez _____ _____ años. (8)
3. Los padres de Marisol _____ _____ años. (52)

Differentiating Instruction

Heritage Language Learners
Writing Skills Have students write a short paragraph about a favorite family member. They should include the name of the person, family relationship, physical description, age, date of birth, what he/she likes to do, and why he/she is their favorite relative. Make sure they review their paragraph for correct spelling and punctuation.

Inclusion
Cumulative Instruction Before talking about characters' ages in Activity 4, have students review the present-tense forms of the verb **tener.** If students are keeping verb cards, have them take out and review the card for this verb. Say each pronoun aloud, and ask students to supply the correct form of the verb.

Presentación de GRAMÁTICA

¡AVANZA! **Goal:** Learn to express possession. Then practice using possessive adjectives to talk about your family members and to give dates. ***Actividades 5–8***

¿Recuerdas? After-school activities p. 32, describing others p. 58

English Grammar Connection: Possessive adjectives tell you who owns something or describe a relationship between people or things. The forms of possessive adjectives do not change in English, but they do change in Spanish.

They are my cousins. Ellos son mis primos.

Possessive Adjectives

ANIMATEDGRAMMAR my.hrw.com

In Spanish, possessive adjectives agree in number with the nouns they describe.

Here's how:

Singular Possessive Adjectives	
mi *my*	nuestro(a) *our*
tu *your (familiar)*	vuestro(a) *your (familiar)*
su *your (formal)*	su *your*
su *his, her, its*	su *their*

Plural Possessive Adjectives	
mis *my*	nuestros(as) *our*
tus *your (familiar)*	vuestros(as) *your (familiar)*
sus *your (formal)*	sus *your*
sus *his, her, its*	sus *their*

Es mi tía.
*She is **my** aunt.*

Son mis tías.
*They are **my** aunts.*

Nuestro(a) and vuestro(a) must also agree in gender with the nouns they describe.

agrees
Nuestra **abuela** tiene 70 años.
***Our** grandmother is 70 years old.*

agrees
Nuestros **abuelos** viven en San Francisco.
***Our** grandparents live in San Francisco.*

Más práctica
Cuaderno *pp. 125–127*
Cuaderno para hispanohablantes *pp. 126–128*

@HOMETUTOR my.hrw.com
Leveled Practice

Differentiating Instruction

English Learners

Build Background Direct students to the grammar box explaining *Possessive Adjectives* on p. 169. Ask students to describe the facts and patterns they notice within the information presented. For example, they might point out that all plural possessive adjectives end in *s*, or that the word **su** has multiple meanings: *your, his, her, its,* and *their.*

Slower-paced Learners

Personalize It Ask questions about objects in the classroom that belong to different students. If necessary, model the correct possessive adjective. Here are a few examples: **¿Es la mochila de José? ¿Es su mochila? Sí, es su mochila. ¿Es tu cuaderno? Sí, es mi cuaderno. ¿Son los exámenes de ustedes? ¿Son sus exámenes? Sí, son nuestros exámenes.**

¡AVANZA! Objective

- Present possessive adjectives.

Core Resource

- *Cuaderno,* pp. 125–127

Presentation Strategies

- Explain when and how possessive adjectives are used.
- Remind students that all possessive adjectives agree in number with the nouns they describe.

STANDARD

4.1 Compare languages

Warm Up
Projectable Transparencies, 3-21

Vocabulary Write how old each person is using **tener...años.**

1. Luisa: 7
2. Mi hermano: 27
3. Mis abuelos: 75
4. Yo: 14
5. Tú: 12
6. Mis padres: 35

Answers: 1. Luisa tiene siete años. 2. Mi hermano tiene veintisiete años. 3. Mis abuelos tienen setenta y cinco años. 4. Yo tengo catorce años. 5. Tú tienes doce años. 6. Mis padres tienen treinta y cinco años.

Communication

Common Error Alert

Explain to students that possessive adjectives indicate possession, and that they are either singular or plural. Also explain that there should be agreement between the subject and the possessive adjective. For example, **mi hermano/mis hermanos, su prima/sus primas.**

Comparisons

English Grammar Connection

The possessive adjectives **su** and **sus** have multiple meanings. If the meaning is not clear from the context, one can replace the possessive adjective with the definite article and add **de** + a pronoun or the person's name to clarify its meaning. **Margarita estudia con su hermano. Margarita estudia con el hermano de ella.**

Objectives

- Practice possessive adjectives and lesson vocabulary.
- **Culture:** Discuss the election process in Puerto Rico.
- Practice saying birth dates.
- Recycle: after-school activities, describing others.

Core Resource

- *Cuaderno,* pp. 125–127

Practice Sequence

- **Activity 5:** Controlled practice: possessive adjectives
- **Activity 6:** Transitional practice: possessive adjectives; Recycle: after-school activities
- **Activity 7:** Open-ended practice: dates, months of the year, numbers
- **Activity 8:** Open-ended practice: possessive adjectives; Recycle: describing others

STANDARDS

1.1 Engage in conversation, Acts. 7–8; PYP
1.2 Understand language, Act. 5
1.3 Present information, Act. 6
2.1 Practices and perspectives, CC, PYP
4.1 Compare languages, Acts. 5–7; PYP; Nota
4.2 Compare cultures, CC
21st Century **Initiative and Self-Correction,** Pre-AP

Comparación cultural

Essential Question

Suggested Answer Elections can reveal the will of the majority of the people and the direction in which they want their country to go.

Expanded Information

Government The formal name in Spanish for Puerto Rico is **Estado Libre Asociado de Puerto Rico** (Free Associated State of Puerto Rico). The Executive power of this Commonwealth is exercised by the governor who leads a cabinet of 15 ministers.

See Activity answers on p. 171.

Práctica de GRAMÁTICA

5 Las familias

Leer

Marisol habla de las familias y sus animales. Escoge el adjetivo posesivo correcto para expresar lo que dice. *(Choose the correct possessive adjectives.)*

1. Nosotros tenemos tres primas. (Nuestros / Nuestras) primas son altas.
2. Ustedes tienen un abuelo. (Su / Nuestro) cumpleaños es el dos de abril.
3. Mi familia y yo tenemos una gata vieja. (Nuestra / Su) gata es Rubí.
4. Yo tengo dos hermanos mayores. (Mi / Mis) hermanos son estudiosos.
5. Mis abuelos tienen un perro. (Su / Mi) perro es perezoso.
6. ¡Feliz cumpleaños! Hoy tienes quince años. Es (tu / su) cumpleaños.

Expansión:
Teacher Edition Only
Have students redo the activity using a different subject in the first sentence and a different possessive adjective in the second.

6 ¿Qué hacen?

¿Recuerdas? After-school activities p. 32

Leer
Escribir

Usa un adjetivo posesivo y escribe qué actividades hacen estas personas. *(Restate the relationship with a possessive adjective and tell what activities these people do.)*

modelo: **La hermana de Alicia es inteligente. (sacar buenas notas)**
Su hermana saca buenas notas.

1. Los abuelos de nosotros no son muy serios. (escuchar música rock)
2. Los tíos de ustedes son trabajadores. (trabajar mucho)
3. La prima de Marisol no es perezosa. (hacer la tarea)
4. La madre de Rodrigo es atlética. (practicar deportes)
5. La hermana de nosotros es muy estudiosa. (leer muchos libros)
6. El padrastro de Luz es simpático. (pasar un rato con la familia)

Expansión
Write what these people don't do, based on the descriptions.

Comparación cultural

Las elecciones en Puerto Rico

What do elections reveal about a culture? **Puerto Rico** is a commonwealth of the United States. Puerto Ricans have U.S. citizenship and those living on the mainland can vote in presidential elections. On the island, Puerto Ricans vote for their governor and local legislature. Voter turnout is high, often over 80 percent. Puerto Rico has three main political parties: the *Partido Popular Democrático* favors the current political status, the *Partido Nuevo Progresista* wants Puerto Rico to become the 51st state, and the *Partido Independentista Puertorriqueño* supports independence from the U.S.

Compara con tu mundo *What issues would motivate you to vote when you are 18?*

Residencia y oficina del gobernador, Viejo San Juan

Differentiating Instruction

Pre-AP

Self-Correct Have students write sentences describing their favorite person. Ask them to use a possessive adjective from p. 169, and subject/adjective agreement. For example, possessive adjective: **Julia es *mi* amiga.** Subject/adjective agreement: ***Ella* es *simpática.*** Have students read aloud their sentences. Give them a clue when they make a mistake and allow them time to correct themselves.

Inclusion

Frequent Review/Repetition Provide student pairs the opportunity to review the two ways to express possession. Have each student write a list of at least 5 family members and a possession for each. Students exchange lists and create two sentences, one using possession with **de** and the other one using a possessive adjective. For example: **el primo/el gato: Es el gato de tu primo. Es su gato.**

Nota gramatical

To give the date, use the following phrase: **Es el** + **number** + **de** + **month.**

Hoy **es el diez de diciembre.** *Today is the* ***tenth of December.***

Only the first of the month does not follow this pattern.

Es el primero de diciembre. *It is* ***December first.***

The year is expressed in **thousands** and **hundreds.**

mil cuatrocientos noventa y dos *1492*

7 Unos puertorriqueños famosos

Hablar

Trabaja con otro(a) estudiante. Usa la línea cronológica para decir las fechas de nacimiento de estos puertorriqueños famosos. *(Use the timeline to give the birth dates.)*

A ¿Cuál es la fecha de nacimiento de Carlos Beltrán?

B Su fecha de nacimiento es el veinticuatro de abril de mil novecientos setenta y siete.

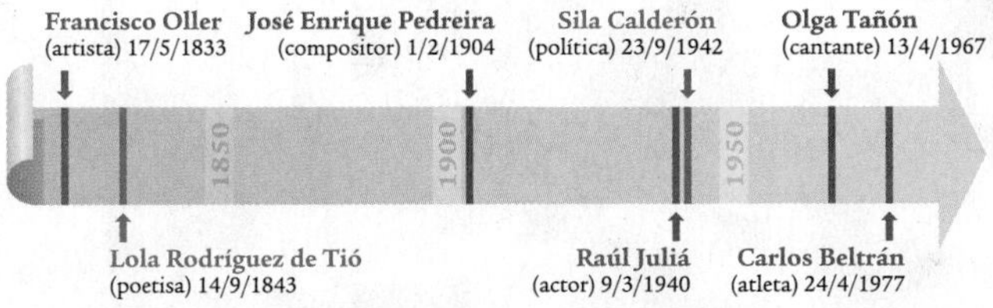

Expansión
Write six sentences about the birth dates of your family members and friends.

8 ¿Cómo son?

¿Recuerdas? Describing others p. 58

Hablar

Habla con otro(a) estudiante sobre las personas y animales domésticos en tu familia. *(Talk about your family and pets.)*

modelo: serio(a)

A ¿Hay una persona seria en tu familia?

B Sí, mi tío David es muy serio.

1. atlético(a)
2. cómico(a)
3. desorganizado(a)
4. inteligente
5. perezoso(a)
6. artístico(a)
7. simpático(a)
8. trabajador(a)
9. ¿ ?

Expansión:
Teacher Edition Only
Have students write a question and its answer, using a possessive adjective.

Más práctica Cuaderno *pp. 125–127* Cuaderno para hispanohablantes *pp. 126–128*

Get Help Online my.hrw.com

PARA Y PIENSA

Did you get it? Fill in the correct possessive adjective and dates.

1. El cumpleaños de _____ *(my)* madrastra es _____. (6/9)
2. El cumpleaños de _____ *(our)* hermano es _____. (25/1)
3. El cumpleaños de _____ *(his)* amigo es _____. (17/4)

Differentiating Instruction

Slower-paced Learners

Personalize It Write today's date in numbers on the board, for example 2/6. Read the date aloud in Spanish and have students repeat **dos de junio.** Then have students write their birth dates in numbers on a separate piece of paper. Invite volunteers to say their birth dates aloud in a sentence. **Mi cumpleaños es el veintiocho de marzo de...**

Multiple Intelligences

Logical/Mathematical Have students create a calendar in Spanish. Record each student's birth date. They should count to see which month has the most birth dates and which has the least. If possible, have the calendar permanently displayed in the classroom.

Nota gramatical

Point out that in Spanish-speaking countries dates are always written with the day first, then the month.

✓ Ongoing Assessment

Get Help Online More Practice my.hrw.com

PARA Y PIENSA **Peer Assessment** Have pairs of students say aloud their sentences and correct each other. For additional practice, use Reteaching & Practice Copymasters URB 3, pp. 16, 17, 24.

Answers Projectable Transparencies, 3-29

Answers for Activities on pp. 170, 171.

Activity 5
1. Nuestras; 2. Su; 3. Nuestra; 4. Mis; 5. Su; 6. tu

Activity 6
1. Nuestros abuelos escuchan música rock.
2. Sus tíos trabajan mucho.
3. Su prima hace la tarea.
4. Su madre practica deportes.
5. Nuestra hermana lee muchos libros.
6. Su padrastro pasa un rato con la familia.

Activity 7 Questions and answers should follow the pattern: **¿Cuál es la fecha de nacimiento de...? Su fecha de nacimiento es...**

¿Cuál es la fecha de nacimiento de Francisco Oller? Su fecha de nacimiento es el diecisiete de mayo de mil ochocientos treinta y tres.

¿... de Lola Rodríguez de Tío? ... es el catorce de septiembre de mil ochocientos cuarenta y tres.

¿... de José Enrique Pedreira? ... es el primero de febrero de mil novecientos cuatro.

¿... de Raúl Juliá? ... es el nueve de marzo de mil novecientos cuarenta.

¿... de Sila Calderón? ... es el veintitrés de septiembre de mil novecientos cuarenta y dos.

¿... de Olga Tañón? ... es el trece de abril de mil novecientos sesenta y siete.

Activity 8 Answers will vary. Questions and answers should follow the pattern:
1. ¿Hay una persona atlética en tu familia? Sí, mi abuela Marta es muy atlética.
2. ¿Hay una persona cómica...? Sí mi tío... cómico.
3. ¿Hay una persona desorganizada...? Sí, mi prima... desorganizada.
4. ¿Hay una persona inteligente...? Sí, mi madre... inteligente.
5. ¿Hay una persona perezosa...? Sí, mi gato... perezoso.
6. ¿Hay una persona artística...? Sí, mi abuela... artística.
7. ¿Hay una persona simpática...? Sí, mi hermano... simpático.
8. ¿Hay una persona trabajadora...? Sí, mi abuela... trabajadora.

Para y piensa 1. mi, el seis de septiembre; 2. nuestro, el veinticinco de enero; 3. su, el diecisiete de abril

¡AVANZA! Objectives

- Practice grammar in context.
- Practice using possessive adjectives, vocabulary for family members, and birth dates.

Core Resources

- Video Program: DVD 1
- Audio Program: TXT CD 3 track 15

Presentation Strategies

- Ask students to name the people in the photo. Ask comprehension questions: **¿Qué hace la señora Vélez? ¿Qué hace Rodrigo?**
- Play the audio and/or show the video.

Practice Sequence

- **Activity 9:** Telehistoria comprehension
- **Activity 10:** Transitional practice: birth dates, months of the year, numbers
- **Activity 11:** Open-ended practice: family members, possessive adjectives, numbers, expressions with **tener**

STANDARDS

1.1 Engage in conversation, Act. 10
1.2 Understand language, Act. 9
1.3 Present information, Act. 11; PYP
4.1 Compare languages, PYP
21st Century **Information Literacy,** Heritage Language Learners

Warm Up Projectable Transparencies, 3-21

Possessive Adjectives Rewrite the phrases with the correct possessive adjective.

1. el amigo de Roberto
2. los tíos de ustedes
3. la prima de nosotros

Answers: 1. su amigo; 2. sus tíos; 3. nuestra prima

Video Summary

@HOMETUTOR VideoPlus my.hrw.com

Rodrigo asks where the T-shirt is. Mrs. Vélez calls his cousins and eventually asks if one of them has it. While she is talking, Rodrigo and Marisol look at a family photo. Rodrigo explains to Marisol that his Aunt Camila is Ester and Tito's mother. He adds that his mother has two sisters and his father has one brother and one sister. Mrs. Vélez tells them that Tito has Alicia's T-shirt. Rodrigo then tells Marisol that he doesn't like his cousin's big dogs also shown in the photo.

GRAMÁTICA en contexto

¡AVANZA! **Goal:** Listen to the possesive adjectives Marisol and Rodrigo use to talk about the members of his family. Then use possessive adjectives to talk about your family and the birthdays of people you know. ***Actividades 9–11***

Telehistoria escena 2

@HOMETUTOR my.hrw.com View, Read and Record

STRATEGIES

Cuando lees
List and practice words While reading, list the words for family members, such as **madre.** Then practice! Say these words aloud several times. Say them in sentences and create questions with them.

Cuando escuchas
Track the people and actions While listening, identify the people involved and the actions. What does each one say? Who helps solve the key problem? What new problem arises?

VIDEO DVD

AUDIO

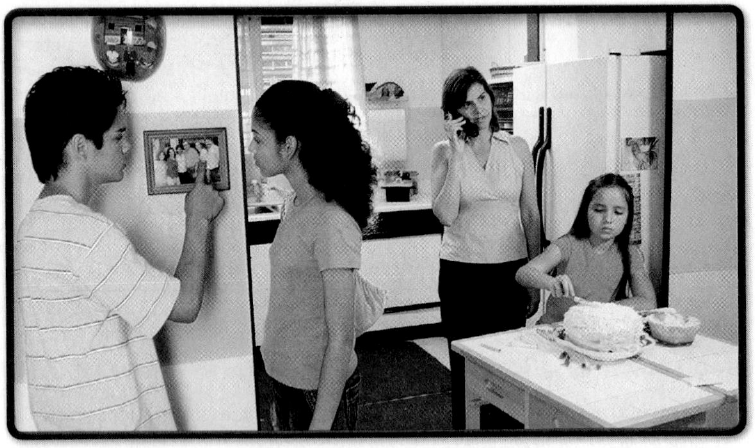

Rodrigo: ¿Dónde está la camiseta?
Sra. Vélez: ¡Ah, tus primos! *(She picks up the phone and dials.)*
Rodrigo: *(explaining to Marisol)* Ellos comen con nosotros todos los viernes. A nuestros primos les gusta jugar al fútbol.
Sra. Vélez: *(on the phone)* ¿Camila? Es Celia. Tengo una pregunta...
Rodrigo: Es mi tía Camila. La tía Camila es la madre de Éster y Tito. Mis primos tienen catorce y diez años.
Marisol: *(pointing to a family portrait)* ¿Es tu familia?
Rodrigo: Mi madre tiene dos hermanas: Inés y Mónica. Mi padre tiene un hermano, Sergio, y una hermana, Camila.
Sra. Vélez: Rodrigo, tu primo Tito tiene la camiseta de tu amiga Alicia.
Rodrigo: *(to Marisol)* Mi primo tiene perros muy grandes. ¡No me gustan los perros de Tito!

Continuará... p. 177

Differentiating Instruction

Slower-paced Learners

Read Before Listening Have students preview the Telehistoria in order to create a list of the characters' names mentioned. Then have students search the text to find the relationship of each character to Rodrigo. Write the appropriate word or phrase next to each name. For example: **Camila: la tía de Rodrigo; Celia: la madre de Rodrigo.**

Pre-AP

Draw Conclusions Write the names **Ester** and **Tito** in the center of a concept web. Then have students supply information regarding these characters based on what they learned in the Telehistoria. For example, **Les gusta jugar al fútbol.** Or **Tito tiene perros grandes.** Then have students draw conclusions to create additional sentences. **Los primos de Rodrigo son atléticos. A Tito le gustan los perros.**

9 Comprensión del episodio Una familia grande

Escuchar Leer

Completa las oraciones para describir el episodio. *(Complete the sentences.)*

1. La madre de Rodrigo
a. no tiene la camiseta.
b. no tiene hermanas.

2. Los primos de Rodrigo
a. comen en su casa todos los días.
b. comen en su casa todos los viernes.

3. A los primos de Rodrigo
a. les gusta jugar al fútbol.
b. les gusta hablar por teléfono.

4. La tía Camila
a. es la madre de Tito y Éster.
b. es la hermana de Inés y Mónica.

5. El padre de Rodrigo
a. tiene dos hermanas.
b. tiene una hermana.

6. A Rodrigo
a. no le gusta la camiseta.
b. no le gustan los perros.

Expansión:
Teacher Edition Only
Have students write one incomplete statement about the Telehistoria followed by two possible completions. Students exchange statements with a partner and choose the correct completion.

10 ¿Cuál es tu fecha de nacimiento?

Hablar

Pregúntales a ocho estudiantes cuáles son sus fechas de nacimiento. Haz una tabla con la información. Comparte los resultados con la clase. *(Find out the birth dates of eight classmates and make a chart. Share the results with the class.)*

A ¿Cuál es tu fecha de nacimiento?
B Mi fecha de nacimiento es el quince de enero de...

enero	febrero	marzo
Sandy 15/1/...	Lillian 24/2/...	
Doug 21/1/...		

Expansión:
Teacher Edition Only
Have students read aloud their charts to a partner and ask the partner to correct the speaker's pronunciation.

11 Tu familia

Escribir

Escribe un párrafo sobre tu familia. Incluye las respuestas a las siguientes preguntas. *(Write a paragraph about your family. Include the answers to the following questions.)*

- ¿Es grande o pequeña tu familia?
- ¿Cuántos hermanos y hermanas tienes?
- ¿Cómo son las personas de tu familia?
- ¿Cuántos años tienen las personas de tu familia?

modelo: Mi familia es grande. Tengo tres hermanos y una hermana. Mi madre tiene treinta y siete años. Es...

Expansión
Say what each family member likes to do on his or her birthday.

Get Help Online
my.hrw.com

PARA Y PIENSA

Did you get it? Using complete sentences, tell the birthdays of the following people.
1. Camila (12/6) **2.** Éster (1/10) **3.** Tito (28/3) **4.** Celia (17/1)

Differentiating Instruction

Inclusion

Frequent Review/Repetition Have students say their birth dates aloud in Spanish as they arrange themselves in a line in the order of their birthdays. They will have to say their birthdays repeatedly until the line is formed correctly.

Heritage Language Learners

Support What They Know Have students research and write down the names and dates of three important celebrations in their heritage countries. Give them the opportunity to describe the occasion and the festivities that take place during these celebrations. Check their written work for correct spelling. Allow students to check dates and other facts at a library or on the Internet, if necessary.

Communication

Grammar Activity

Write several dates on the board using numbers and have students tell you the corresponding date in Spanish. For example: **15/4: el quince de abril; 1/2 el primero de febrero.**

Communication

Common Error Alert

Reiterate to students the difference between English and Spanish when saying or writing dates. In Spanish, **de** or *of*, is always used to correctly say the month and the year. It is like saying *28* of *July* of *two thousand seven* which in Spanish is **28 *de* julio *de* dos mil siete.** Have students practice verbally saying dates in Spanish.

✓ Ongoing Assessment

Get Help Online
More Practice
my.hrw.com

PARA Y PIENSA **Dictation: Mis primos vienen a visitarnos el tres de noviembre. El veintesiete de junio tenemos que jugar al fútbol.** For additional practice, use Reteaching & Practice Copymasters URB 3, pp. 16, 18.

Answers Projectable Transparencies, 3-29 and 3-30

Activity 9
1. a **2.** b **3.** a **4.** a **5.** b **6.** b

Activity 10 Answers will vary. Sample answers include: ¿Cuál es tu fecha de nacimiento? Mi fecha de nacimiento es el diez de octubre.

Activity 11 Answers will vary. Sample answers include: Mi familia es grande. Tengo dos hermanos y una hermana. Mi hermano es inteligente y simpático. Mi hermana es muy desorganizada. Mis padres tienen cuarenta años. Mi hermano mayor tiene diecisiete años, mi hermana tiene seis años y mi hermano menor tiene diez años.

Para y piensa
1. El cumpleaños de Camila es el doce de junio.
2. El cumpleaños de Éster es el primero de octubre.
3. El cumpleaños de Tito es el veintiocho de marzo.
4. El cumpleaños de Celia es el diecisiete de enero.

¡AVANZA! **Objective**

- Present comparatives.

Core Resource

- *Cuaderno,* pp. 128–130

Presentation Strategies

- Point out different types of comparatives.
- Explain the use of the irregular comparative words **mayor, menor, mejor,** and **peor.**

STANDARD

4.1 Compare languages

21st Century **Creativity and Innovation,** Pre-AP

Warm Up Projectable Transparencies, 3-22

Dates Write the dates using numerals.

1. el trece de abril
2. el veintiuno de julio
3. el catorce de febrero
4. el primero de diciembre
5. el quince de enero

Answers: 1. 13/4; 2. 21/7; 3. 14/2; 4. 1/12; 5. 15/1

Comparisons
English Grammar Connection

When saying *more than/less than + number,* **de** is used instead of **que.** For example, **Tengo más de veinte primos.**

Mayor and **menor** are used to compare people's ages. **Yo soy mayor que mi hermano pero menor que mi hermana.**

Mejor and **peor** are the comparative forms of **bueno** and **malo. Ella es mejor estudiante que yo.**

Communication
Grammar Activity

Write a list of adjectives on the board: **viejo, joven, bonito, grande, pequeño, alto, bajo.** Ask students to compare two items in the classroom using the constructions: **más... que, menos... que, tan... como.**

Presentación de GRAMÁTICA

¡AVANZA! **Goal:** Learn to make comparisons. Then use them to describe your family, your friends, and yourself. ***Actividades 12–15***

English Grammar Connection: Comparatives are expressions used to compare two people or things. In English, comparative adjectives are formed by adding *-er* to the end of a word or by using *more, less,* and *as.*

Rodrigo is **taller** than his sister. Rodrigo es **más alto** que su hermana.

Comparatives

ANIMATED GRAMMAR my.hrw.com

There are several phrases in Spanish used to make comparisons.

Here's how: Use the following phrases with an **adjective** to compare two things. The adjectives agree with the first noun.

agrees

más... que *more . . . than*	Mi abuel**a** es **más artística que** mi padre. *My grandmother is **more** artistic **than** my father.*
menos... que *less . . . than*	La clase de ciencias es **menos divertida que** la clase de inglés. *Science class is **less** fun **than** English class.*
tan... como *as . . . as*	Tus hermanas son **tan serias como** la maestra. *Your sisters are **as** serious **as** the teacher.*

When a comparison does not involve an adjective, use these phrases.

más que... *more than . . .*	Me gusta ir a la biblioteca **más que** al gimnasio. *I like to go to the library **more than** to the gym.*
menos que... *less than . . .*	Me gustan las hamburguesas **menos que** los tacos. *I like hamburgers **less than** tacos.*
tanto como... *as much as . . .*	¿Te gusta hablar **tanto como** escuchar? *Do you like to talk **as much as** listen?*

There are a few irregular comparative words. They agree in number with the first noun.

mayor	menor	mejor	peor
older	*younger*	*better*	*worse*

agrees

Mis tío**s** son **mayores** que mi tía.
*My uncles are **older** than my aunt.*

Más práctica
Cuaderno *pp. 128–130*
Cuaderno para hispanohablantes *pp. 129–132*

@HOMETUTOR my.hrw.com Leveled Practice

Differentiating Instruction

Pre-AP

Expand and Elaborate Have students work in groups to create a fictitious family. Each student in the group will represent a family member. Ask them to select Spanish names, ages, and create personalities. Each member should describe himself/herself in complete sentences. For example, **Me llamo Mario. Tengo veintitrés años y soy el tío de Carmen. Soy alto y guapo.**

Multiple Intelligences

Linguistic/Verbal Assign groups of students to become experts in one category of comparisons: **más... que; menos... que; tan... como; más que...; menos que...; tanto como...** Have students say aloud several examples of their category and explain how it works to the rest of the class. **Él es más alto que yo. Yo soy tan grande como él.**

Práctica de GRAMÁTICA

12 Sus familias

Escribir

Completa las oraciones con **que** o **como** para describir a las familias de Rodrigo y Marisol. *(Complete the sentences with **que** or **como**.)*

1. Marisol es tan simpática ____ su madrastra.
2. Ana es menor ____ Rodrigo.
3. Marisol corre tanto ____ sus padres.
4. Rodrigo tiene menos hermanos ____ José.
5. El tío Pablo toca la guitarra mejor ____ la tía Camila.
6. Ester es mayor ____ Tito.

Expansión
Rewrite the sentences with another comparative.

13 Comparaciones

Escribir
Hablar

Mira los dibujos y haz comparaciones usando **más... que, menos... que, tan... como** o **tanto como.** *(Make a comparison for each drawing using the correct phrase.)*

modelo: Nicolás / grande / Sara
Nicolás es más grande que Sara.

1. Nora / alto(a) / Patricia

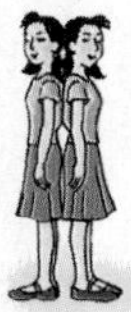

2. Marcos / serio(a) / José

3. Ana / perezoso(a) / Alí

4. Pablo / desorganizado(a) / Pedro

5. María / atlético(a) / David

6. A Elena / gustar / correr / escuchar música

Expansión:
Teacher Edition Only
Have students make additional comparisons reversing the subjects: **Sara es más pequeña que Nicolás.**

Pronunciación — La letra j

AUDIO

The **j** in Spanish sounds similar to the English *h* in the word *hello.*
Listen and repeat.

jamón **mujer** **dibujar** **joven** **junio** **hija**

La mujer pelirroja es joven. El cumpleaños del hijo es en julio.

Objectives
- Practice comparisons with **más... que, menos... que,** and **tan... como.**
- Practice lesson vocabulary.
- Practice pronunciation of the letter **j** in Spanish.

Core Resource
- Audio Program: TXT CD 3 track 16

Practice Sequence
- **Activity 12:** Controlled practice: comparatives
- **Activity 13:** Transitional practice: comparatives

STANDARDS
1.3 Present information, Act. 13
4.1 Compare languages, Act. 12; Pronunciación
21st Century **Critical Thinking and Problem Solving,** Pair Work

Communication — Pair Work
Bring in photos/clippings of famous people and have students make comparisons. Have students use these adjectives: **alto(a), bajo(a), serio(a), cómico(a).** To practice **mayor que** and **menor que,** ask each pair of students to compare the ages of the famous people.

Long-term Retention — Recycle
As students brainstorm a list of sports, have a volunteer write them on the board. Then, have students compare two of them at a time: **Me gusta nadar más que jugar al fútbol.**

Differentiating Instruction

Inclusion
Clear Structure Write the words **más, menos, tan,** and **tanto** on the board. Then ask students which word completes each phrase, **que** or **como.** Record their responses on the board. As students complete Activity 12, have them write in their notebooks the comparison word in each sentence. Tell them to refer to the board to choose the correct word to complete each phrase.

Heritage Language Learners
Increase Accuracy Monitor spelling of words with **j** and **h.** Write the word **hijo** on the board. Circle the letter **j,** and ask students to isolate its sound. Point out that the letter **j** in Spanish sounds like the letter **h** in English. Next, circle the letter **h.** Remind students that the **h** in Spanish is silent. Dictate words containing **h** and **j: Julio, jamón, hola, mejor, juntos.** Check students' spelling.

Answers Projectable Transparencies, 3-30

Activity 12

1. como 2. que 3. como
4. que 5. que 6. que

Activity 13

1. Nora es tan alta como Patricia.
2. Marcos es más serio que José.
3. Ana es más perezosa que Alí.
4. Pablo es menos desorganizado que Pedro.
5. María es más atlética que David.
6. A Elena le gusta correr tanto como escuchar música.

Objectives
- Practice using comparatives.
- **Culture:** Discuss the portraits of Rafael Tufiño and Fernando Sayán Polo.

Core Resources
- *Cuaderno,* pp. 128–130
- Audio Program: TXT CD 3 track 17

Practice Sequence
- **Activity 14:** Transitional practice: comparatives
- **Activity 15:** Open-ended practice: comparatives

STANDARDS
1.1 Engage in conversation, PYP
1.2 Understand language, Act. 14
1.3 Present information, CC
2.2 Products and perspectives, CC
3.1 Knowledge of other disciplines, CC

Comparación cultural

Essential Question

Suggested Answer Portraits can reflect the different groups of people of a country in terms of family, relationship, age, gender, ethnicity, and so on.

About the Artists

Rafael Tufiño, born in Brooklyn in 1922, is one of the central figures in the history of twentieth-century Puerto Rican art. **Fernando Sayán Polo** was born in Peru in 1947. The city of Cuzco is the root of his artistic motivation.

Ongoing Assessment

Get Help Online
More Practice
my.hrw.com

PARA Y PIENSA **Quick Check** Call on individual students to read their answers aloud and correct them if necessary. For additional practice, use Reteaching & Practice Copymasters URB 3, pp. 19, 20.

Answers Projectable Transparencies, 3-30

Activity 14

1. Falsa	**2.** Cierta	**3.** Cierta
4. Falsa	**5.** Falsa	**6.** Cierta

Activity 15 Sample answers include:
La mujer es tan interesante como la chica.
La chica es más simpática que la mujer.

Answers continue on p. 177.

14 Capitán y Príncipe

Escuchar Escribir

Ana habla de sus animales, Capitán y Príncipe. Escucha su descripción y decide si las siguientes oraciones son ciertas o falsas. *(Listen to the description and indicate whether the following sentences are true or false.)*

1. La familia de Ana tiene más perros que gatos.
2. Príncipe es tan simpático como Capitán.
3. Capitán es más grande que Príncipe.
4. A Príncipe le gusta comer más que descansar.
5. Príncipe es menor que Capitán.
6. Capitán es más perezoso que Príncipe.

Audio Program
TXT CD 3 Track 17
Audio Script, TE p. 161b

Expansión
Correct the false statements.

15 Compara a las personas

Escribir

Comparación cultural

Los retratos

How do portraits represent the people in a country? Rafael Tufiño was born in New York and moved to **Puerto Rico,** his parents' homeland, as a child. Much of his work reflects the people and culture of Puerto Rico. In addition to paintings like *Lavandera,* he painted many portraits of his mother, giving them the title *Goyita.* These portraits came to represent not just his mother, but Puerto Rican women overall. Fernando Sayán Polo, an artist from **Peru,** also reflects the people of his country through his artwork. His painting *Niña campesina sonriente* depicts a young girl wearing traditional Andean dress.

Lavandera *(1960),*
Rafael Tufiño

Niña campesina sonriente *(2005),*
Fernando Sayán Polo

Compara con tu mundo *If you had to paint a portrait of someone famous, which person would you choose and why? How would you portray him or her?*

Escribe cinco oraciones para comparar a las personas en los cuadros. *(Write five sentences comparing the two people in the paintings.)*

modelo: La mujer es mayor que la chica. La chica es más...

Expansión:
Teacher Edition O
Have students exchange their descriptions with partner and compare them.

Más práctica Cuaderno *pp. 128–130* Cuaderno para hispanohablantes *pp. 129–132*

Get Help Online
my.hrw.com

PARA Y PIENSA

Did you get it?
1. Say that your brother is taller than your father.
2. Say that you like apples as much as bananas.
3. Say that math class is better than art class.

Differentiating Instruction

Slower-paced Learners

Read Before Listening Before listening to Ana's description in Activity 14, have students copy the sentences on a piece of paper, then have them draw a sketch to represent each sentence. Have students refer to their pictures as they listen to see if the statements are true or false.

Heritage Language Learners

Literacy Skills Have students use the library or Internet to research the life of painter Rafael Tufiño. Tell them their goal is to find four important events in his life and the respective dates. Have students share their findings to create a group timeline of the artist's life and work.

Todo junto

¡AVANZA! **Goal:** ***Show what you know*** Notice the comparative words Marisol and Rodrigo use to talk about why Rodrigo doesn't like Tito's dogs. Then use comparative words and possessive adjectives to describe your family and friends. ***Actividades 16–20***

Telehistoria completa

@HOMETUTOR my.hrw.com View, Read and Record

STRATEGIES

Cuando lees
Work with comparisons This scene contains comparisons of animals and of people. How many comparisons do you see? Write down the "comparison words." Practice them in sentences.

Cuando escuchas
Remember, listen, and predict At the beginning of this scene, Marisol is calm. How does she change and why? Does this happen suddenly or slowly? How do you know?

Escena 1 *Resumen*
Mañana es el cumpleaños de Ana, la hermana de Rodrigo. Rodrigo está nervioso porque no tiene la camiseta de Alicia.

Escena 2 *Resumen*
Tito, el primo de Rodrigo, tiene la camiseta. A Rodrigo no le gustan los perros de Tito.

VIDEO DVD

AUDIO

Escena 3

Rodrigo and Marisol are walking to Tito's house.

Marisol: ¿No te gustan los perros? Son simpáticos.

Rodrigo: Me gustan más los gatos. Son más simpáticos que los perros.

Marisol: Los perros son menos perezosos que los gatos.

Rodrigo: Los perros de Tito son perezosos y muy grandes. ¡Son tan grandes como tú!

They stop outside the gate and look around. Tito appears, wearing Alicia's T-shirt, which is filthy.

Tito: ¡Hola, Rodrigo! Tu camiseta.

Suddenly the dogs begin growling. Rodrigo and Marisol run away frightened.

¡AVANZA! Objective

- Integrate lesson content.

Core Resources

- Video Program: DVD 1
- Audio Program: TXT CD 3 track 18

Presentation Strategies

- Ask students to identify the people in the photo. Ask: **¿Quién es mayor, Tito o Rodrigo?**
- Have students skim the Telehistoria paying special attention to comparison words.
- Show the video or play the audio.

STANDARD

1.2 Understand language

Warm Up Projectable Transparencies, 3-22

Comparisons Unscramble the following sentences.

1. más/Rosa/que/ baja/hermano/su/es
2. que/ soy/hermano/mi/mayor
3. como/es/nuestra/madre/alto/tan/él

Answers: 1. Rosa es más baja que su hermano. 2. Soy mayor que mi hermano. 3. Él es tan alto como nuestra madre.

Video Summary

@HOMETUTOR VideoPlus my.hrw.com

Marisol and Rodrigo are going to Tito's house to retrieve Alicia's T-shirt. Marisol asks him why he dislikes dogs. Rodrigo says that he likes cats better; they are nicer than dogs. Marisol says that dogs are less lazy than cats, but Rodrigo says that Tito's dogs are lazy and very big. When they arrive, Tito is wearing the T-shirt, which is very dirty. Then the dogs growl, and Rodrigo and Marisol run away.

Differentiating Instruction

Pre-AP

Expand and Elaborate Invite students to talk about their own pets. Begin by asking if students have a dog or a cat. **¿Tienes un gato? ¿Tienes un perro?** For the students who answer yes, have them share their pets' names. Then ask students to write a short paragraph that answers the questions: **¿Es simpático tu perro? ¿Es perezoso tu gato?**

Multiple Intelligences

Visual Learners Have students select one line from Escena 3 that includes a comparative expression to illustrate. For example, **Los perros son menos perezosos que los gatos,** they could show two sleeping cats and two busy dogs. Have students read the scene aloud. Tell them to hold up their drawing when the group comes to the line they have illustrated.

Answers Projectable Transparencies, 3-30

Answers continued from p. 176.

Para y piensa

1. Mi hermano es más alto que mi padre.
2. Me gustan las manzanas tanto como las bananas.
3. La clase de matemáticas es mejor que la clase de arte.

TODO JUNTO

Objective
- Practice using and integrating lesson vocabulary and grammar.

Core Resources
- *Cuaderno,* pp. 131–132
- Audio Program: TXT CD 3 tracks 14, 15, 18, 19, 20

Practice Sequence
- **Activities 16, 17:** Telehistoria comprehension
- **Activity 18:** Open-ended practice: speaking
- **Activity 19:** Open-ended practice: reading, listening, speaking
- **Activity 20:** Open-ended practice: writing

STANDARDS
1.1 Engage in conversation, Act. 18
1.2 Understand language, Acts. 16–17
1.3 Present information, Acts. 19–20; PYP
4.1 Compare languages, PYP

✓ Ongoing Assessment

Rubric Activity 18

Speaking Criteria	Maximum Credit	Partial Credit	Minimum Credit
Content	Opinions are well-expressed.	Opinions expressed are limited.	Opinions are poorly expressed.
Communi-cation	Pronuncia-tion is correct and easily understood.	Pronuncia-tion is fairly correct and understood.	Pronuncia-tion is difficult to understand.
Accuracy	There are few mistakes in grammar and vocabulary.	There are some mistakes in grammar and vocabulary.	There are many mistakes in grammar and vocabulary.

To customize your own rubrics, use the ***Generate Success*** *Rubric Generator and Graphic Organizers.*

Answers Projectable Transparencies, 3-30 and 3-31

Activity 16
1. Tito **2.** Tito **3.** Marisol
4. Rodrigo **5.** Tito **6.** Tito
7. Rodrigo **8.** Tito

Activity 17
1. ... es el primero de marzo.
2. ... a las cuatro.
3. A Rodrigo...
4. ... tienen catorce y diez años.
5. ... tiene dos hermanas.
6. Tito...

Answers continue on p. 179.

16 *Comprensión de los episodios* ¿Rodrigo, Marisol o Tito?

Escuchar
Leer

¿A quién de los tres se refiere cada oración? *(To whom does each sentence refer?)*

1. Pasa un rato con su tía Celia.
2. Tiene perros muy grandes.
3. El cumpleaños de su abuela es el primero de marzo.
4. Necesita la camiseta de su amiga Alicia.
5. Come con la familia de Rodrigo todos los viernes.
6. Es menor que Rodrigo.
7. No le gustan los perros.
8. Tiene la camiseta de Alicia.

Expansión:
Teacher Edition Only
Have students write three more statements about the people in the photos.

17 *Comprensión de los episodios* ¿Comprendiste?

Escuchar
Leer

Contesta las preguntas según los episodios. *(Answer the questions.)*

1. ¿Cuándo es el cumpleaños de Ana?
2. ¿A qué hora está Trini Salgado en la escuela?
3. ¿A quién le gustan más los gatos, a Rodrigo o a Marisol?
4. ¿Cuántos años tienen los primos de Rodrigo?
5. ¿Cuántas hermanas tiene la madre de Rodrigo?
6. ¿Quién tiene la camiseta de Alicia?

Expansión:
Teacher Edition Only
Have students write three more questions about the three episodes and then give the answers.

18 La familia ideal

Digital performance space

Hablar

STRATEGY **Hablar**
Consider your beliefs Before the conversation, consider your beliefs about families. What is an ideal family? Describe it on paper and then aloud. Do you know such a family?

Trabaja en un grupo de tres para expresar opiniones sobre la familia ideal. Incluye tus respuestas a las siguientes preguntas. *(Offer opinions about the ideal family. Include your answers to these questions.)*

Para organizarte
- ¿Es grande o pequeña la familia? ¿Dónde vive?
- ¿Cuántas personas hay en la familia?
- ¿Cómo son las personas de la familia? ¿Qué hacen?
- ¿Cuántos años tienen las personas de la familia?

A Una familia pequeña es buena.

B Una familia grande es mejor que una familia pequeña porque es más interesante.

C No, una familia cómica es mejor...

Expansión
Give a summary of your group's opinions.

Differentiating Instruction

Inclusion
Synthetic/Analytic Support Before answering the questions in Activity 17, have students write the question words for each in their notebooks. Discuss what kind of answer students should be listening for, based on the question word. For example, the answer to a question starting with **¿cuántos?** will be a number.

Inclusion
Clear Structure Before students discuss their beliefs in Activity 18, create on the board a concept web around the word **familia.** Help students brainstorm as many words and phrases as they can relate to the theme of family. Ask them to write these words on the board. They might include names of family members, adjectives that describe people, or activities that families do together.

19 Integración

Digital performance space

Leer
Escuchar
Hablar

Lee el cartel de una familia que busca una casa para su perro. Después escucha el anuncio de radio de una organización para la protección de animales. Empareja cada perro con un miembro de tu familia y explica tu decisión. *(Read the flyer and listen to the radio announcement. Match each dog to someone in your family and explain your choices.)*

Audio Program
TXT CD 3 Tracks 19, 20
Audio Script, TE p. 161b

Fuente 1 Cartel

Rayo
Labrador marrón.
Tiene un año.

Es tan inteligente como su madre y... ¡más activo!

Le gusta correr, nadar y jugar al fútbol. ¡Es más atlético que yo! ☺

Vamos a Nueva York en enero y Rayo no va con nosotros. ☹

Si necesitas un amigo, Rayo necesita una familia.

Llámanos: 555-8231

Fuente 2 Anuncio de radio

Listen and take notes
- ¿Cómo es Dino?
- ¿Qué le gusta hacer a Dino?

modelo: Rayo es un buen perro para mi primo Alberto. Rayo es menos tranquilo que Dino y a mi primo le gusta correr...

Expansión:
Teacher Edition Only
Have students match a cat to a family member and explain their decision.

20 Un amigo nuevo

Digital performance space

Escribir

Tu familia va a recibir a un(a) estudiante de Puerto Rico. Escríbele una carta para describir a los miembros de tu familia. Usa comparativos. *(Write a letter to an exchange student comparing members of your family.)*

modelo: ¡Hola! Te presento a mi familia. Tengo dos hermanos. Yo soy mayor que mis hermanos. Mi hermano Lance es menor que...

Writing Criteria	Excellent	Good	Needs Work
Content	Your letter includes a lot of information.	Your letter includes some information.	Your letter includes little information.
Communication	Most of your letter is organized and easy to follow.	Parts of your letter are organized and easy to follow.	Your letter is disorganized and hard to follow.
Accuracy	Your letter has few mistakes in grammar and vocabulary.	Your letter has some mistakes in grammar and vocabulary.	Your letter has many mistakes in grammar and vocabulary.

Expansión
Write comparisons of your friends.

Más práctica Cuaderno *pp. 131–132* Cuaderno para hispanohablantes *pp. 133–134*

Get Help Online
my.hrw.com

PARA Y PIENSA

Did you get it? Create sentences based on the Telehistoria using possessive adjectives and comparatives.
1. los perros (de Tito) / tan grande / Marisol
2. el primo (de Rodrigo) / menor / él
3. los perros (de Tito) / más perezoso(a) / los gatos

Differentiating Instruction

Slower-paced Learners

Sentence Completion If students have difficulty getting their stories started in Activity 19, provide them with two or three sentence starters. Here are a few possibilities:

Rayo es tan inteligente como...
Le gusta correr...
Rayo necesita...

Heritage Language Learners

Support What They Know Ask students to write a short e-mail comparing two of their friends in terms of age, physical characteristics, character, and preferred activities. They should use comparisons and state reasons for their opinion.

Long-term Retention

Pre-AP Integration

Activity 19 Use Activity 19 as a model for writing a short radio announcement about a pet adoption agency. It should include the name of the pet, what it looks like, what it likes to do, and why it would be an ideal pet for a family member. If time allows, record the announcements and have the class vote on the best one.

✓ Ongoing Assessment

Rubric Activity 19

Listening/Speaking

Proficient	Not There Yet
Student takes detailed notes, gives solid reasons, and shows good use of comparisons.	Student takes few notes and gives some good reasons and fair-to-poor use of comparisons.

To customize your own rubrics, use the ***Generate Success** Rubric Generator and Graphic Organizers.*

✓ Ongoing Assessment

Get Help Online
More Practice
my.hrw.com

PARA Y PIENSA **Quick Check** If students have difficulties creating the sentences, review pp. 169 and 174 with them. For additional practice, use Reteaching & Practice Copymasters URB 3, pp. 19, 21.

Answers Projectable Transparencies, 3-31

Answers for Activities on pp. 178, 179.

Activity 18 Answers will vary. Answers should demonstrate correct usage of comparatives: Una familia grande es mejor que una familia pequeña porque siempre hay muchas personas en casa para hablar y jugar.

Activity 19 Answer will vary. Sample answer should include: Dino es el mejor perro para mi tío Gustavo. Es tan tranquilo como Gustavo y a Gustavo le gusta mirar la televisíon.

Activity 20 Answers will vary. Sample answer should include: ¡Hola! Te presento a mi familia. Tengo tres hermanas menores que yo y un hermano mayor. Mi hermano John es el más cómico de la familia. Es mi hermano favorito.

Para y piensa
1. Sus perros son tan grandes como Marisol.
2. Su primo es menor que él.
3. Sus perros son más perezosos que los gatos.

¡AVANZA! Objectives

- Compare **quinceañera** celebrations in Peru and Puerto Rico.
- Compare fifteenth birthday parties in Latin America with similar celebrations in the United States.
- Find out what activities take place at a **quinceañera** celebration.

Core Resource

- Audio Program: TXT CD 3 track 21

Presentation Strategies

- Ask students to predict what **la quinceañera** is, based on what they have learned about birthdays, and the photos on these pages.
- Ask students to describe the activities that take place during a **fiesta de quinceañera,** based on the photos on pp. 180–181.

STANDARDS

1.2 Understand language
1.3 Present information
2.1 Practices and perspectives
4.2 Compare cultures
21st Century **Collaboration,** Group Work; **Social and Cross-Cultural Skills,** ¿Comprendiste?

Warm Up Projectable Transparencies, 3-23

Comparatives Create sentences using forms of **ser** and comparatives.

1. yo / menor / mi prima.
2. Carla / tan alto(a) / su padre
3. ellas / menos atléticos(as) / yo
4. Ana y Marta / tan perezosos(as) / Alberto
5. nosotros / más serios(as) / el maestro

Answers: 1. Yo soy menor que mi prima. 2. Carla es tan alta como su padre. 3. Ellas son menos atléticas que yo. 4. Ana y Marta son tan perezosas como Alberto. 5. Nosotros somos más serios que el maestro.

Comparación cultural

Background Information

The tradition of the **quinceañera** was first established during the years of Spanish colonization in Latin America. When a girl reached the age of fiteen, a party was celebrated where she was "presented to society." In some present-day celebrations, the girl dances a waltz with her father or her godfather.

Lectura cultural

Additional readings at my.hrw.com SPANISH InterActive Reader

¡AVANZA! **Goal:** Read about the **quinceañera** celebrations in Peru and Puerto Rico. Then compare the parties and talk about the activities at the birthday parties you go to.

Comparación cultural

AUDIO

La quinceañera

STRATEGY Leer
Compare and contrast Draw a Venn diagram like this one. Use it to compare the **quinceañera** celebrations of Peru and Puerto Rico.

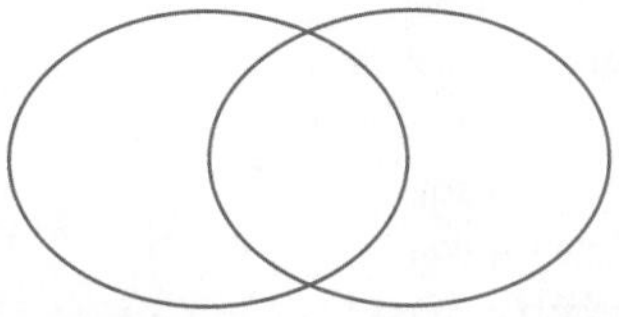

La fiesta[1] de quinceañera es muy popular en muchos países de Latinoamérica. Es similar al *Sweet Sixteen* de Estados Unidos. Muchas veces hay una ceremonia religiosa y una fiesta con banquete. En la fiesta hacen un brindis[2] en honor a la quinceañera y después todos bailan un vals[3].

La chica que celebra su cumpleaños también se llama la quinceañera. En Perú (y otros países) la quinceañera tiene catorce o quince damas de honor[4]: una por cada[5] año que tiene. No hay un menú especial de banquete, pero en Perú es común comer comida típica del país, bailar y escuchar música tradicional.

[1] party [2] toast [3] **bailan...** dance a waltz
[4] **damas...** maids of honor [5] **por...** for each

Perú

Comidas tradicionales: lomo saltado, chupe, mondongo y guiso

Differentiating Instruction

Multiple Intelligences

Linguistic/Verbal Ask students to work in pairs, with each taking turns offering descriptions of a **fiesta de quinceañera.** They should include words and expressions such as **banquete, damas de honor, una fiesta,** and **un vals,** as well as other important elements of the celebration.

Heritage Language Learners

Support What They Know If students have been to a **quinceañera** celebration, ask them to describe it. Where did it take place? Who was there? What food was served? What did people do during the celebration? What did the **quinceañera** wear? What music did they play? What gifts did she receive?

Una quinceañera en Puerto Rico con familia y amigos

Puerto Rico

En Puerto Rico, la celebración se llama el quinceañero. Muchas veces las chicas tienen la gran fiesta en su cumpleaños número dieciséis (por influencia del *Sweet Sixteen*) y no en el cumpleaños de los quince años.

En el banquete de una quinceañera de Puerto Rico es normal comer comida típica del país, como arroz con pollo[6]. Todos bailan y escuchan música del Caribe: salsa, merengue, reggaetón y el hip-hop cubano.

[6] chicken and rice dish

PARA Y PIENSA

¿Comprendiste?

1. ¿Qué fiesta en Estados Unidos es similar a la fiesta de quinceañera?
2. ¿Cuántas damas de honor tiene una quinceañera en Perú?
3. ¿Cuándo tienen la fiesta las chicas de Puerto Rico?

¿Y tú?

¿Te gustan las fiestas de cumpleaños? ¿Qué haces en las fiestas?

Communication

Group Work

Ask students to work in groups to write a short description of the ideal birthday party. They should include where the party takes place, in what month, how many people are going, and the activities. Provide additional vocabulary if needed.

Comparisons

English Language Connection

Cognates Ask students to read the Lectura cultural and list all the cognates they can find. The list should include, but not be limited to, **popular, similar, honor, ceremonia, religiosa, banquete, vals, menú, música, influencia, celebración, tradicional, típica,** and **común.**

Communication

Pair Work

Assign two students the roles of interviewer and **quinceañera.** The interviewer must prepare in advance a minimum of five questions to ask the **quinceañera.** Questions may be based on the reading or on related vocabulary students have learned. Example: **¿Vas a tener una fiesta con banquete? ¿Qué van a bailar? ¿Cuántas damas de honor tienes? ¿Hay un menú especial?**

Differentiating Instruction

English Learners

Build Background Ask students to describe birthday traditions with their families. How are they similar or different from the **quinceañera** celebrations shown on pp. 180–181?

Pre-AP

Sequence Information Ask students to write about an imaginary **quinceañera** party. Suggest that they brainstorm to generate as many details as they can on such topics as location, date, time and place, guests, type of food served, music, gifts. Ask students to write a short paragraph sequencing the information they have gathered.

Answers

Para y piensa ¿Comprendiste?

1. En Estados Unidos el *Sweet Sixteen* es similar a la fiesta de quinceañera.
2. Una quinceañera en Perú tiene catorce o quince damas de honor.
3. Muchas veces las chicas de Puerto Rico tienen la fiesta en su cumpleaños número dieciséis.

¿Y tú? Answers will vary but should follow the model:

A mí me gustan las fiestas de cumpleaños. En las fiestas de cumpleaños yo bailo, escucho música, como comida rica y paso un buen rato con los amigos.

Objectives
- Read about musical instruments of Puerto Rico and Peru.
- **Culture:** Learn about percussion instruments in Puerto Rico and the **zampoña** in Peru.
- **Community:** Investigate sources of Andean music in the community.

Presentation Strategies
- Ask students if they have ever heard traditional Andean music.
- Ask if anyone knows how to play a percussion or a wind instrument and ask him/her to identify it.
- If possible, bring CDs of Andean or Puerto Rican music for students to listen to in class.

STANDARDS
1.3 Present information
4.2 Compare cultures
5.1 Spanish in the community

Comparación cultural
Essential Question
Suggested Answer Some instruments played in certain regions have their origins in their history. For example, Andean people inherited a variety of wind instruments of all sizes and shapes, made of materials (such as wood and reeds) that grew in the area.

Communities
Spanish in the Marketplace
Andean music has gained in popularity throughout the world. Performers of this music are easily recognized by their typical Andean attire (ponchos or colorful sweaters). They can be found in squares, fairs, shopping malls, subway stations, and other public areas in the United States. Instruments commonly used in Andean music include the **quena,** a flute, **siku,** panpipes, and a small guitar. Most large music stores have a section dedicated to Andean music. Well-known groups include Inti Illimani, Viento de los Andes and Ecuador Manta.

Proyectos culturales

Comparación cultural

Instrumentos de Puerto Rico y Perú

How do certain instruments and music become associated with a particular region? Percussion instruments that produce strong beats and rhythms are the base of much of the music of **Puerto Rico.** In **Peru,** the **zampoña** is a wind instrument that adds a deep and distinctive sound to traditional Andean music.

Proyecto 1 *Percussion*
Puerto Rico Make your own rhythm on a homemade percussion instrument.

Materials for your own percussion instrument
An object that can be used as a "found" percussion instrument, such as:
- coffee or juice can
- yogurt cup with pebbles, sand or seeds, secured inside with a lid on top
- wooden, plastic, or metal spoons
- pan lid and long-handled brush
- upside-down basket

Instructions
Practice making a rhythm pattern you can repeat on your "found" percussion instrument. Try creating different tones by striking the instrument in different places or with different objects.

Proyecto 2 *Zampoña*
Perú Use these simple materials to create your own **zampoña.**

Materials for zampoña
4 or more plastic or glass bottles, all the same size
Water

Instructions
1. Bring to class four or more bottles (all the same size) and add water so that they all have different amounts, ranging from empty to two thirds full.
2. Put your mouth to the top of each bottle and blow as if playing the flute. Because each bottle contains a different amount of air and water, you should hear various pitches.
3. Add tape so that the bottles are connected in a row. Arrange the bottles according to their pitch, from low to high.

En tu comunidad
Find out if any Andean music groups play in your community, perhaps at a cultural heritage fair or at a local university. Share your findings with the class.

Differentiating Instruction

Heritage Language Learners
Support What They Know Ask students for the lyrics to a favorite Spanish-language song, preferably from Peru or Puerto Rico. Ask them to write them on poster board or chart paper. Encourage them to read the lyrics aloud for the class and explain unfamiliar vocabulary. If possible, have them bring a recording of a song so their classmates can listen and read along.

Pre-AP
Expand and Elaborate Ask students to write a short report in English about Andean music. The report should include:
- examples of typical percussion, wind, and string instruments
- origins of instruments
- types of music played

Ask students to share this information with the rest of the class.

Lección 2

En resumen

Vocabulario y gramática

ANIMATEDGRAMMAR
Interactive Flashcards
my.hrw.com

Vocabulario

Talk About Family

la abuela	*grandmother*	la madrastra	*stepmother*
el abuelo	*grandfather*	la madre	*mother*
los abuelos	*grandparents*	el padrastro	*stepfather*
la familia	*family*	el padre	*father*
la hermana	*sister*	los padres	*parents*
el hermano	*brother*	el (la) primo(a)	*cousin*
los hermanos	*brothers, brother(s) and sister(s)*	los primos	*cousins*
		la tía	*aunt*
		el tío	*uncle*
la hija	*daughter*	los tíos	*uncles, uncle(s) and aunt(s)*
el hijo	*son*		
los hijos	*son(s) and daughter(s), children*		

Give Dates

¿Cuál es la fecha?	*What is the date?*
Es el... de...	*It's the . . . of . . .*
el primero de...	*the first of . . .*
el cumpleaños	*birthday*
¡Feliz cumpleaños!	*Happy birthday!*
la fecha de nacimiento	*birth date*

Pets

el (la) gato(a)	*cat*
el (la) perro(a)	*dog*

Ask, Tell, and Compare Ages

¿Cuántos años tienes?	*How old are you?*	mayor	*older*
Tengo... años.	*I am . . . years old.*	menor	*younger*

Other Words and Phrases

vivir	*to live*
ya	*already*

Numbers from 200 to 1,000,000 *p. 165*

Months *p. 165*

Gramática

Notas gramaticales: de to express possession *p. 166*, **tener... años** *p. 168*, Giving dates *p. 171*

Possessive Adjectives

In Spanish, **possessive adjectives** agree in number with the nouns they describe. **Nuestro(a)** and **vuestro(a)** must also agree in gender with the nouns they describe.

Singular Possessive Adjectives

mi *my*	**nuestro(a)** *our*
tu *your (familiar)*	**vuestro(a)** *your (familiar)*
su *your (formal)*	**su** *your*
su *his, her, its*	**su** *their*

Plural Possessive Adjectives

mis *my*	**nuestros(as)** *our*
tus *your (familiar)*	**vuestros(as)** *your (familiar)*
sus *your (formal)*	**sus** *your*
sus *his, her, its*	**sus** *their*

Comparatives

Use the following phrases with an adjective to compare two things.

más... que
menos... que
tan... como

When a comparison does not involve an adjective, use these phrases.

más que...
menos que...
tanto como...

There are a few irregular comparative words.

mayor	**menor**	**mejor**	**peor**
older	*younger*	*better*	*worse*

Practice Spanish with Holt McDougal Apps!

Objective

- Review lesson vocabulary and grammar.

DIGITAL SPANISH

Interactive Flashcards Students can hear every target vocabulary word pronounced in authentic Spanish. Flashcards have Spanish on one side, and a picture or a translation on the other.

Review Games Matching, concentration, hangman, and word search are just a sampling of the fun, interactive games students can play to review for the test.

performance space
News Networking
@HOMETUTOR
CULTURA Interactiva

- Audio and Video Resources
- Interactive Flashcards
- Review Activities
- WebQuest
- Conjuguemos.com

Long-term Retention

Critical Thinking

Ask students to develop a chant that will emphasize the differences between singular and plural possessive adjectives in Spanish. It could be similar to a sing-song rendition of **Mi perro pero mis perros; mis perros pero mi perro.**

Communication

Group Work

Assign a family member name to each student. Begin by saying **la abuela,** at which point the student who is **la abuela** should say **¡Yo soy la abuela!** and call out another family member, and the student who is that relative should then call out another family member name. Continue until every student has spoken at least once.

Differentiating Instruction

Inclusion

Multisensory Input/Output Ask students to draw a real or imaginary family tree. Tell them to include names, ages, and birthdays. Have students exchange their family trees with a classmate and describe it to the rest of the class. For example: **La familia de Susana es pequeña. Ella tiene un hermano menor. Se llama Jorge y su cumpleaños es el 12 de noviembre. Ella no tiene hermanas.**

Multiple Intelligences

Linguistic/Verbal Divide the class into groups. In three minutes, see how many sentences students can make using at least two vocabulary words per sentence. The team with the largest number of grammatically correct sentences wins.

Objectives
- Review lesson vocabulary and grammar.

Core Resources
- *Cuaderno*, pp. 133–144
- Audio Program: TXT CD 3 track 22

Presentation Strategies
- Before playing the audio for Activity 1, ask students to listen to it carefully, especially to the relationships Marcos describes.
- Monitor correct use of numbers, possessive adjectives, and comparatives.
- Read the Comparación cultural with students and clarify any questions that arise.
- Review may be done in class or given as homework.
- Students can also access the review activities online at my.hrw.com.

STANDARDS
1.2 Understand language, Acts. 1, 3
1.3 Present information, Acts. 1–5
4.2 Compare cultures, Act. 5
21st Century **Collaboration,** Multiple Intelligences

Warm Up
Projectable Transparencies, 3-23

Vocabulary Complete the sentences with the correct word.

cumpleaños que perro tío mayor

1. Jorge tiene un gato, pero ahora quiere un _____.
2. El hermano de mi madre es mi _____.
3. El _____ de mi abuela es el 5 de marzo.
4. Mi hermana es _____ que yo.
5. Nosotros tenemos más primos _____ ellos.

Answers: 1. perro; 2. tío; 3. cumpleaños; 4. mayor; 5. que

✓ Ongoing Assessment
Get Help Online
More Practice
my.hrw.com

Intervention and Remediation If students achieve less than 90% accuracy with the activities, direct them to review pp. 162, 166, 169, 170, 174, 176, 180–181, and to get help online at my.hrw.com.

Lección 2

Repaso de la lección

@HOMETUTOR
my.hrw.com

¡LLEGADA!

¡AvanzaRap! DVD Sing and Learn

Now you can
- talk about family
- ask and tell ages
- express possession
- give dates
- make comparisons

Using
- **de** to express possession
- possessive adjectives
- comparatives

To review
- **de** to express possession p. 166
- possessive adjectives p. 169

1 Listen and understand

AUDIO

Marcos tiene una foto de su familia y explica quiénes son. Escucha a Marcos y luego indica su relación con las siguientes personas. *(Listen to Marcos describe a family photo and indicate each person's relationship to him.)*

modelo: Pedro
Pedro es el hermano de Marcos.

1. Elena y Rosa
2. Julio
3. Norma
4. Alberto
5. Diego y Felipe
6. Carmen

Audio Program
TXT CD 3 Track 2
Audio Script, TE p. 161b

To review
- possessive adjectives p. 169

2 Talk about family

Escribe oraciones para describir las relaciones de estas personas y sus edades. Usa adjetivos posesivos. *(Tell what family members these people have, and what their ages are. Use possessive adjectives.)*

modelo: yo / hermano menor (5 años)
Yo tengo un hermano menor. Mi hermano tiene cinco años.

1. Bárbara / hermana mayor (19 años)
2. tú / dos primos (7 y 11 años)
3. nosotros / abuelo (67 años)
4. Manuel y Óscar / padre (34 años)
5. yo / perro (5 años)
6. ustedes / madre (36 años)
7. tú y yo / dos tíos (48 y 44 años)
8. usted / abuela (81 años)
9. ellas / dos gatos (2 años)
10. yo / tía (30 años)

Differentiating Instruction

Slower-paced Learners
Sentence Completion Review family relationships by asking students to complete sentences with the correct information. Write on the board:

El padre de mi padre es mi _____. (abuelo)
Los hermanos de mi madre son mis _____. (tíos)
La hija de mi tía es mi _____. (prima)

Pre-AP
Summarize Ask students to explain the way dates are expressed verbally in Spanish, and how they are written numerically. Then ask them to say the dates for the following: **El Día de la Independencia de Estados Unidos; El Día de Año Nuevo; El Día de San Valentín (de los enamorados); el día de Halloween.**

REPASO DE LA LECCIÓN

To review
- comparatives p. 174

3 Make comparisons

Josefina describe a su gato, Memo, y a su perro, Sancho. Lee la descripción y escoge las palabras apropiadas. *(Read Josefina's description of her pets and choose the appropriate words.)*

Memo, mi gato, y Sancho, mi perro, viven con mi familia. Memo tiene diez años y Sancho tiene cinco. Memo es __1.__ (menor / mayor) que Sancho. Pero Sancho es __2.__ (tan / más) grande que Memo y come más __3.__ (como / que) él. Memo come __4.__ (mejor / menor) comida que Sancho porque come buena comida para gatos. Sancho come comida __5.__ (mayor / menos) nutritiva porque muchas veces come pizza y papas fritas. Memo y Sancho son muy perezosos. Memo es __6.__ (tanto / tan) perezoso como Sancho. Descansan mucho. A Memo le gusta descansar __7.__ (tanto / más) como a Sancho. Pero Memo y Sancho no son aburridos. También les gusta jugar un poco todos los días. Jugar con ellos es más divertido __8.__ (como / que) mirar la televisión.

To review
- **de** to express possession p. 166

4 Give dates

Escribe oraciones con las fechas de cumpleaños de estas personas. *(Write sentences giving these people's birthdays.)*

modelo: el señor Gómez: 13/4
El cumpleaños del señor Gómez es el trece de abril.

1. Berta: 23/12	**4.** Olga: 5/8	**7.** la maestra: 30/9
2. Emilio y Emilia: 1/2	**5.** Germán: 15/10	**8.** Luis: 27/3
3. la señora Serrano: 14/1	**6.** el director: 11/6	**9.** Víctor: 12/11

To review
- Comparación cultural pp. 162, 170, 176
- Lectura cultural pp. 180–181

5 Puerto Rico and Peru

Comparación cultural

Answer these culture questions.
1. What do people do during **la sobremesa**?
2. Which political positions do people vote for in Puerto Rico?
3. Who does Rafael Tufiño portray in *Goyita?*
4. What are some **quinceañera** traditions? Describe at least three.

Más práctica Cuaderno *pp. 133–144* Cuaderno para hispanohablantes *pp. 135–144*

Get Help Online my.hrw.com

Differentiating Instruction

Inclusion

Frequent Review/Repetition Ask each student to come to the board and write his or her birthday using numbers. When all the birthdays are on the board, lead the class in checking to make sure they are in the Spanish order. Then ask students to say them out loud in Spanish.

Multiple Intelligences

Interpersonal Have students work in pairs and plan a **quinceañera.** Have them create a chart in Spanish and write where and when it will take place, what activities they will do, what food they will eat, and which family members will be there. Students will use their charts and discuss their **quinceañera** with other pairs.

✓ Ongoing Assessment

Get Help Online More Practice my.hrw.com

Peer Assessment Have students read their completed description from Activity 3 to a partner, who will correct any errors.

Answers Projectable Transparencies, 3-31 and 3-32

Activity 1
1. Elena y Rosa son las hermanas de Marcos.
2. Julio es el padre de Marcos.
3. Norma es la madre de Marcos.
4. Alberto es el abuelo de Marcos.
5. Diego y Felipe son los primos de Marcos.
6. Carmen es la tía de Marcos.

Activity 2
1. Bárbara tiene una hermana mayor. Su hermana mayor tiene diecinueve años.
2. Tú tienes dos primos. Tus primos tienen siete y once años.
3. Nosotros tenemos un abuelo. Nuestro abuelo tiene sesenta y siete años.
4. Manuel y Óscar tienen un padre. Su padre tiene treinta y cuatro años.
5. Yo tengo un perro. Mi perro tiene cinco años.
6. Ustedes tienen una madre. Su madre tiene treinta y seis años.
7. Tú y yo tenemos dos tíos. Nuestro tíos tienen cuarenta y ocho y cuarenta y cuatro años.
8. Usted tiene una abuela. Su abuela tiene ochenta y un años.
9. Ellas tienen dos gatos. Sus gatos tienen dos años.
10. Yo tengo una tía. Mi tía tiene treinta años.

Activity 3
1. mayor; **2.** más; **3.** que; **4.** mejor; **5.** menos; **6.** tan; **7.** tanto; **8.** que

Activity 4
1. El cumpleaños de Berta es el veintitrés de diciembre.
2. ...de Emilio y Emilia es el primero de febrero.
3. ...de la señora Serrano es el catorce de enero.
4. ...de Olga es el cinco de agosto.
5. ...de Germán es el quince de octubre.
6. ...del director es el once de junio.
7. ...de la maestra es el treinta de septiembre.
8. ...de Luis es el veintisiete de marzo
9. ...de Víctor es el doce de noviembre.

Activity 5
1. During **la sobremesa,** families spend time together at the table long after a meal is over.
2. Puerto Ricans living on the island vote for their governor and local legislators.
3. Rafael Tufiño portrays his mother in *Goyita.*
4. Some **quinceañera** traditions include having a religious ceremony followed by a banquet, having maids of honor, and dancing a waltz.

Objectives
- Read three personal accounts about Sunday gatherings written by teens from Puerto Rico, El Salvador, and Peru.
- Compare Sunday meals with one of the three students in the text.
- Write a short essay about your typical Sunday meal.

Core Resource
- *Cuaderno,* pp. 145–147
- Audio Program: TXT CD 3 track 23
- Video Program: DVD 1

Presentation Strategies
- Draw students' attention to the photos on p. 187 and have them predict what the text will be about. Assign a student to list their responses on the board.
- Have students take turns reading each narration as their classmates follow it in the text.
- Play the audio.

STANDARDS
1.2 Understand language
1.3 Present information
2.1 Practices and perspectives
4.2 Compare cultures
21st Century **Creativity and Innovation,** Multiple Intelligences; **Social and Cross-Cultural Skills,** Compara con tu mundo

Long-term Retention
Personalize It
After students read the three narratives, conduct an informal survey by having students call out the foods they would like to have for their own Sunday meal. Assign one student to write on the board the food items mentioned and have another student read the items to the class. Students can reply with **sí** or **no** after each item is read.

Comparación cultural

AUDIO

¿Qué comemos?

Lectura y escritura

WebQuest my.hrw.com

1. **Leer** Meals vary for people around the world. Read how María Luisa, Silvia, and José enjoy a meal on Sundays.

2. **Escribir** Using the three descriptions as models, write a short paragraph about a typical Sunday meal.

STRATEGY **Escribir**
Make a mind map To write about a real or imaginary Sunday meal, make a mind map like the one shown.

La comida del domingo
¿Dónde? ¿Qué? ¿Con quién?

Step 1 Complete the mind map of your Sunday meal by adding details to the categories of place (where you eat), foods (what you eat), and people (with whom you eat).

Step 2 Write your paragraph. Make sure to include all the information from your mind map. Check your writing by yourself or with help from a friend. Make final corrections.

Compara con tu mundo
Use the paragraph you wrote to compare your Sunday meal to a meal described by *one* of the three students. In what ways is your meal similar? In what ways is it different?

Cuaderno *pp. 145–147* Cuaderno para hispanohablantes *pp. 145–147*

Differentiating Instruction

English Learners
Provide Comprehensible Input Explain that a mind map consists of a larger oval that contains the main topic and is linked to smaller ovals that contain questions related to the main topic. Ask students what the main topic of the paragraph is: *Sunday Meal.* Go over the meaning of the questions: *Where? What? With whom?* Check comprehension: *Where do you eat on Sundays? With whom do you eat?*

Heritage Language Learners
Support What They Know Ask students to describe to the class a typical Sunday meal gathering in their country of origin. Where does the meal take place? At what time? Who is invited? Who prepares the meal? What typical dishes are served? What dishes are his or her favorites?

CULTURA Interactiva
my.hrw.com
See these pages come alive!

El Salvador *María Luisa*

Hola, soy María Luisa. Yo soy de El Salvador. Los domingos, voy con mi hermana mayor y mi prima a Metrocentro[1]. Después de pasear unas horas, vamos a un café porque estamos cansadas y tenemos sed y hambre. En el café venden sándwiches, refrescos y jugos de papaya, mango, melón y otras frutas. A mí me gusta más la horchata[2]. Es una bebida muy rica.

[1] popular mall in San Salvador

[2] beverage made of rice, water, and milk

Perú *Silvia*

Yo soy Silvia y vivo en Lima, Perú. Todos los domingos comemos la cena con mis tíos. Mi tío Ricardo siempre prepara su comida favorita, el ceviche[3]. A mí me gusta más el ají de gallina[4] que hace mi abuela. ¡Es mejor que el ceviche de mi tío! Después de la cena, mis padres y mis tíos beben café y hablan. Mis primos y yo comemos helado y escuchamos música.

[3] fish marinated in lime juice [4] spicy chicken and potato dish

Puerto Rico *José*

¿Qué tal? Me llamo José. Vivo en San Juan, Puerto Rico. Todos los domingos, mi familia y yo comemos el almuerzo en un restaurante. Nos gusta comer carne asada[5]. Es muy, muy buena. También me gustan los tostones[6]. ¡Pero los tostones de mi madre son más ricos que los tostones en un restaurante!

[5] barbecued [6] fried plantains

Differentiating Instruction

Multiple Intelligences

Kinesthetic Divide the class into three groups, and assign each group to create a skit based on the descriptions José, María Luisa, and Silvia wrote about the time they spend with friends and family. Suggest that students bring in props to create a restaurant scene as well as write a script.

Pre-AP

Communicate Preferences Draw students' attention to the food preferences expressed by José, María Luisa, and Silvia. Ask students to research recipes for these dishes, try them if possible, and then explain why they like or don't like them.

Comparación cultural

Exploring the Theme

Horchata is a beverage made of ground almonds, rice barley, or tigernuts. The name comes from Valencian *orxata,* a barley-based beverage. Eventually the Spanish brought the *orxata* to Latin America, particularly Mexico, Ecuador, and El Salvador. In Mexico, **horchata** is a rice-based beverage that includes blanched almonds, sugar, cinnamon, vanilla, orange, or lime. In El Salvador, **horchata** is typically flavored with ground cocoa and cinnamon as well as sesame seeds.

✓ Ongoing Assessment

Quick Check Ask students quick comprehension questions about each of the three narrations and write their responses on the board. For example: **¿De dónde es María Luisa? ¿Adónde va los domingos? ¿Cuál es la comida favorita de Silvia? ¿Qué le gusta comer a José?**

✓ Ongoing Assessment

Rubric Lectura y escritura

Writing Criteria	Excellent	Good	Needs Work
Content	Paragraph contains a lot of information.	Paragraph contains some information.	Paragraph lacks information.
Communication	Paragraph is organized and easy to follow.	Paragraph is fairly well organized and easy to follow.	Paragraph is disorganized and hard to follow.
Accuracy	Paragraph has few mistakes in vocabulary and grammar.	Paragraph has some mistakes in vocabulary and grammar.	Paragraph has many mistakes in vocabulary and grammar.

To customize your own rubrics, use the ***Generate Success*** *Rubric Generator and Graphic Organizers.*

Objective
- Cumulative review.

Core Resource
- Audio Program: TXT CD 3 track 24

Review Options
- **Activity 1:** Listening
- **Activity 2:** Speaking
- **Activity 3:** Speaking
- **Activity 4:** Writing
- **Activity 5:** Speaking
- **Activity 6:** Speaking and writing
- **Activity 7:** Reading and writing

STANDARDS
1.1 Engage in conversation, Acts. 3, 5, 6
1.2 Understand language, Acts. 1, 7
1.3 Present information, Acts.2–7
21st Century **Creativity and Innovation,** Act. 6; **Critical Thinking and Problem Solving,** Act. 7; **Flexibility and Adaptability,** Acts. 3, 5

Communication
Presentational Mode
Have students bring to class a photo of their pet (real or imaginary). Ask them to present their pet, talk about its personality traits, favorite activities, and favorite foods. Encourage them to explain why this is the perfect pet for them.

Answers
Activity 1
1. Diana es estudiosa. Su hermano toca la guitarra toda la tarde y ella necesita estudiar.
2. Tiene que estudiar porque tiene muchos exámenes en la clase de ciencias.
3. A Diana le gusta escuchar música y estudiar. A Óscar le gusta tocar la guitarra.
4. Óscar es menor que Diana. Él tiene diez años y Diana tiene catorce.
5. Ella va a estudiar de tres a cinco y él va a tocar la guitarra de cinco a siete.

UNIDADES 1-3

Repaso inclusivo
Options for Review

¡AvanzaRap! DVD Sing and Learn

Digital performance space

1 Listen, understand, and compare
Escuchar

Listen to this episode from a call-in radio show giving advice to teens. Then answer the questions.

1. ¿Cómo es Diana? ¿Qué problema tiene?
2. ¿Por qué tiene que estudiar Diana?
3. ¿Qué le gusta hacer a Diana? ¿Y a Óscar?
4. ¿Óscar es mayor o menor que Diana? ¿Cuántos años tienen?
5. ¿Qué va a hacer Diana?

Audio Program
TXT CD 3 Track 24 Audio Script, TE p. 161b

Do you have siblings or cousins? Do you have a lot in common or are you very different? Explain.

2 Present a friend
Hablar

Bring in a photo or drawing of your best friend or a person you admire. Introduce the person to the class and talk about what personality traits, favorite activities, and favorite foods you have in common. Then mention your differences. Prepare to talk for at least three minutes.

3 Get to know a new student
Hablar

Role-play a conversation in which you are an exchange student from Puerto Rico, and your partner is your host brother or sister. Introduce yourself and ask about his or her classes, likes and dislikes, and what his or her family is like. Then answer his or her questions for you. Your conversation should be at least four minutes long.

4 Plan a family reunion
Escribir

Your family is hosting a reunion with all of your extended family members. You are in charge of organizing a breakfast for everyone. Create a seating chart, and label each seat with the person's name, age, and relation to you. Write what breakfast foods and drinks each person likes and doesn't like.

Differentiating Instruction

Pre-AP
Relate Opinions Have students write a brief paragraph stating some of the possible advantages and disadvantages of living with a large extended family. They should support their opinions with at least three reasons. For example: **Me gusta tener muchos hermanos porque es más divertido. No me gusta tener una familia grande porque siempre tengo que compartir.**

Inclusion
Multisensory Input/Output Ask one student to read aloud the information about Manolo from Activity 7 and another student to read the information about Martín while the class follows in their texts. Draw a Venn diagram on the board with the headings Manolo and Martín. Ask individual students to come to the board and fill in the diagram based on information they have just heard.

5 Talk with a nutritionist

Hablar

Work in a group of four. Three members of the group are siblings and the fourth is a nutritionist. The nutritionist should ask each family member's age, at what time they eat their meals, their food likes and dislikes, and what they do after school. The nutritionist should tell them what healthy foods they have to eat and the activities they have to do. Each person should talk for at least two minutes.

6 Display your family tree

Hablar
Escribir

Work with a partner to create a poster of your family tree or that of a TV family. Use photos or make drawings of each family member. Label each person's name, age, birthday, favorite activity, and favorite food. Use the family tree to describe your family to your partner, making comparisons between family members. Then present your partner's family to the class.

7 Compare twins

Leer
Escribir

Read this chart from a magazine article about Manolo and Martín Santos, twins that were recently reunited after being separated at birth. Then write a paragraph comparing the two men. Include at least six comparisons.

MUCHAS COINCIDENCIAS

Manolo

Nacimiento: 30/7, a las 2:20 de la tarde
Personalidad: serio, muy artístico
Profesión: Maestro de español. Enseña cuatro clases. Trabaja 45 horas en la semana.
Familia: dos hijos (Enrique y Arturo) y una hija (Rebeca)
Actividades: Le gusta practicar deportes: correr, montar en bicicleta, jugar al fútbol.

Martín

Nacimiento: 30/7, a las 2:22 de la tarde
Personalidad: cómico, muy artístico
Profesión: Maestro de español. Enseña seis clases. Trabaja 52 horas en la semana.
Familia: dos hijos (Eduardo y Ángel) y dos hijas (Rebeca y Rosa)
Actividades: Le gusta practicar deportes: andar en patineta, jugar al fútbol, jugar al golf.

La historia increíble de los hermanos Santos

✓ Ongoing Assessment

Integrated Performance Assessment Rubric **Oral Activities 2, 3, 5, 6**
Written Activities 4, 7

Use the following rubric to assess the student's progress. The last dimension applies only to the oral performance.

Excellent	Good	Needs Work
The student thoroughly develops all requirements of the task.	The student develops most requirements of the task.	The student does not develop the requirements of the task.
The student demonstrates excellent control of verb forms.	The student demonstrates good to fair control of verb forms.	The student demonstrates poor control of verb forms.
Good variety of appropriate vocabulary.	Adequate variety of appropriate vocabulary.	The vocabulary is not appropriate.
The pronunciation is excellent to very good.	The pronunciation is good to fair.	The pronunciation is poor.

To customize your own rubrics, use the ***Generate Success** Rubric Generator and Graphic Organizers.*

Differentiating Instruction

Slower-paced Learners

Read Before Listening Provide scripts of the audio for Activity 1 before playing it. Ask students to read the questions first, then the script. While they are reading the script, they should look for the answers. After students have read the script, have them put it away. Then play the audio and have students take notes as they listen.

Multiple Intelligences

Linguistic/Verbal Assign student pairs to write an article similar to the one in Activity 7, comparing two people. If possible, have them paste a photo above each description. Have students exchange articles with another pair. Each pair must then make at least five comparisons based on their classmates' article.

Proyectos adicionales

Planning Ahead

Create a city entertainment guide. In small groups, have students create a shopping and entertainment guide for the city of Madrid, or for their own hometown. Each group's guide should include the location and a short description of six different events going on around the city. These may include exhibits at museums, sales at stores, events at parks, concerts, or special menus at restaurants. The guides should also include information about transportation to each event. Advise students to look at examples of entertainment guides on the Internet or in their local newspaper. The events in their guides, however, can be fictional. Also, encourage students to include photos or drawings to show readers what the events will look like. Give each group the opportunity to present their guide to the whole class.

PACING SUGGESTION: Upon completion of **Lección 2** to review vocabulary related to shopping, places and events in town, types of transportation, and restaurants.

21st CENTURY **Creativity and Innovation**

(Virtual) Bulletin Board

Create a bulletin board with the title **¡A Madrid!** Provide students with poster board and magic markers. Instruct them to create a poster that might be found on the streets of Madrid. The poster might advertise a museum exhibit, a sale at the shopping center, or a new menu at a restaurant. Remind students that each poster should be attractive and interesting to look at. They should also include information about times, cost, and transportation to get to the place being advertised. As a tech alternative, you may wish to have students create their projects on a class wiki page.

PACING SUGGESTION: After **Lección 1** to reinforce vocabulary related to shopping and prices. After **Lección 2** to reinforce vocabulary related to places around town and transportation.

21st CENTURY **Creativity and Innovation**

Web Research

Go online to learn more about interesting places around the city of Madrid. Some examples might include:

- **El Prado**
- **La Plaza Mayor**
- **El Retiro**
- **Teatro de la Zarzuela**
- **Moda** Shopping Center

Begin by having students pick a place or type of place they are interested in learning about. Then have them conduct an Internet search to find more information. A simple search such as "Madrid and shopping" or "Madrid and museums" will yield many results. Once students have focused their research, instruct them to isolate four or five interesting facts or figures about their location. Have them record their information on an index card along with a drawing or photo of their locale. Give students the opportunity to share the information they find with the whole group. Then organize discussions between students who have researched the same type of location, such as theaters or parks. How are their specific places similar and different?

PACING SUGGESTION: Throughout the unit as time allows.

21st CENTURY **Technology Literacy**

Games

¿Me lo vendes?

Divide the class in half. Give half the students in the class a total of 100 euros each in play money. Give the other half pictures of clothing items to sell. Tell the sellers that they must establish a price for the item they are trying to sell. The sellers should try to get as much money for their items as possible, while the buyers should try to buy as many items as possible. Give students ten minutes to circulate and ask and answer each other's questions about prices. At the end of ten minutes, the seller with the most money, and the buyer with the most clothing items win. Then have students switch roles and play again.

PACING SUGGESTION: After vocabulary is presented in **Lección 1** to reinforce clothing items, colors, and shopping phrases.

Nuestra ciudad

In small groups, have students create a simple board game about their city or hometown. The spaces on the board should offer places or events to go to, such as concerts, stores, parks, restaurants, museums, schools, houses, or streets. The game pieces can be different modes of transportation, such as a car, bus, train, on foot, etc. Students should also prepare game cards that tell each player where to go with a word and picture.

Play the game by choosing a card and moving your vehicle to the place indicated. Once there, you should say something that might be said at that location, such as ordering from the menu at a restaurant, or buying a shirt at the store.

PACING SUGGESTION: Students can work on constructing their games at any time throughout the unit. They can play their games after vocabulary is presented in **Lección 2.**

Music

Have students create their own examples of traditional Spanish instruments, such as the Galician **gaita,** Basque **alboka,** or the rhythm instrument **la zambomba.** Organize students into small groups, and have each group choose one of these, or another traditional Spanish instrument. Advise them to find photos of the instrument, as well as information about its history and how it is played. Then have students use found materials to create their own example of their instrument. For example, to build their own **zambomba,** students might use a pot or box for the base, a piece of plastic to cover the top, and a long stick as the neck.

Recipe

Tortilla española is a popular dish that can be eaten at breakfast, as an appetizer, or as a light supper.

Tortilla española

Ingredientes

4 huevos
3 patatas
1 cebolla pequeña
1/2 taza de aceite de oliva
3/8 cucharadita de sal

Instrucciones

Corte las papas y las cebollas. Póngalas en una sartén y cocine las papas y la cebolla en el aceite de oliva hasta que estén levemente doradas. Bata bien los huevos. Viértalos sobre las papas y la cebolla. Cocínelos a fuego bajo hasta que el huevo esté firme. Ponga un plato encima de la sartén y dele vuelta a la tortilla encima del plato. Deslice nuevamente la tortilla en la sartén para que se cocine por el otro lado.

¡AvanzaRap! DVD

- Video animations of all **¡AvanzaRap!** songs (with Karaoke track)
- Teaching Suggestions
- **¡AvanzaRap!** Activity Masters
- **¡AvanzaRap!** Video Scripts and Answers

Also available on the **Teacher One Stop**

UNIT THEME
Downtown

UNIT STANDARDS

COMMUNICATION
- Talk about what clothes you want to buy
- Say what you wear in different seasons
- Describe places and events in town
- Talk about types of transportation
- Say what you are going to do
- Order from a menu

CULTURES
- Surrealism and Salvador Dalí
- Climates around the world
- Spanish poet and novelist Antonio Colinas
- Local markets in Spain and Guatemala
- *Las meninas,* by Velázquez and Picasso

CONNECTIONS
- Art: Designing a courtyard based on the architectural style of La Alhambra
- Music: Researching the musical group *Al-Andalus*
- Health: Learning about the health and beauty benefits of olives and olive oil
- Language: Tracing the Arabic origins of Spanish words that begin with **al-** or **a-**

COMPARISONS
- Shopping in Madrid
- The role of dreams in surrealism
- The Spanish **c** with **a, o, u** and with **e, i**
- Variations in geography and climate in Spain, Chile, and the U.S.
- Teatro de la Comedia and other weekend activities
- Handicrafts and collectibles in different local markets
- Two versions of the painting *Las meninas:* Velázquez and Picasso
- Weekend activities in Madrid and Santiago de Chile
- Art of Spain and Chile
- Leisure activities in Guatemala, Spain, Chile, and the U.S.

COMMUNITIES
- Art from Spain or a Spanish-speaking country in a nearby museum

UNIDAD 4

España

En el centro

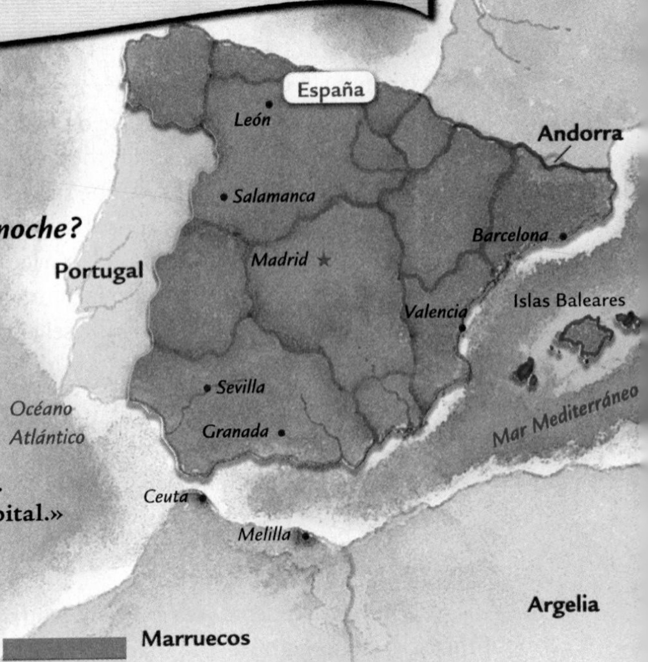

Lección 1
Tema: ***¡Vamos de compras!***

Lección 2
Tema: ***¿Qué hacemos esta noche?***

«¡Hola!
Somos Maribel y Enrique. Vivimos en Madrid, la capital.»

Población: 40.491.052

Área: 194.897 millas cuadradas

Capital: Madrid

Moneda: el euro (comparte con otros 11 países)

Idiomas: castellano (español), catalán, gallego, vasco

Comida típica: tortilla española, paella, gazpacho

Gente famosa: Carmen Amaya (bailaora), Francisco de Goya (artista), Ana María Matute (escritora), Severo Ochoa (bioquímico)

Paella

190 ciento noventa

Cultural Geography

Setting the Scene
- What is the capital of Spain? (Madrid)
- What is the currency of Spain? (the euro) It shares this currency with how many other countries? (11)
- What other languages besides **castellano** (Spanish) are spoken in Spain? **(catalán, gallego, vasco)**

Teaching with Maps
- Spain has borders with which other countries? (Portugal, Andorra, France)
- Which islands belong to Spain? (Baleares, Canarias)
- Spain has coasts on which bodies of water? (Atlantic Ocean, Mediterranean Sea)

CULTURA Interactiva my.hrw.com *See these pages come alive!*

Un jugador de fútbol del Real Madrid

◀ **Aficionados del fútbol** Official songs, or **himnos oficiales,** are an important part of the Spanish soccer experience. Fans of the Real Madrid team sing **¡Hala Madrid!** *(Let's go, Madrid!)*, especially during games against rival team FC Barcelona, known as **El Barça.** *What teams have sports rivalries where you live?*

El arte y la literatura Pablo Picasso, one of the 20th century's greatest artists, portrayed traditional Spanish themes in his work. He made this print of fictional characters Don Quijote and Sancho Panza exactly 350 years after Cervantes wrote his famous novel, *El ingenioso hidalgo Don Quijote de la Mancha. What other works of Picasso are you familiar with?* ▶

Don Quijote *(1955), Pablo Picasso*

Bailarinas de flamenco en Sevilla

◀ **Las costumbres regionales** During the **Feria de Abril** celebration, girls wear Seville's traditional costume, **el traje de sevillana. Sevillanas** are similar to **flamenco,** which involves singing, dance, and guitar as well as rhythmic clapping or foot taps. *What type of music and dress would be considered typically American?*

CULTURA Interactiva my.hrw.com

Send your students to my.hrw.com to explore authentic Spanish culture. Tell them to click on Cultura interactiva to see these pages come alive!

Comparación cultural

About the Photos

- Real Madrid has been called the best soccer team of the 20th century. Its home games are played at Madrid's Santiago Bernabéu stadium.
- Picasso (1881–1973), who started creating art when he was just a teenager, had a prolific career in which he did more than paint. He was also a sculptor, printmaker, and ceramic artist and is best known for innovating the cubist style.
- Visitors to Seville can enjoy a flamenco show at one of Seville's many theater boats. While the dancers perform with amazing accuracy, grace, and passion, their movements are enhanced by the musicians' guitar playing and voices.

Expanded Information

- Soccer was first played in Spain in the late 1800s. Today, it is a national passion appropriately called **El Deporte Rey,** or *The King of Sports.*
- Much of what Picasso produced in his 75-year career can be seen at the Picasso Museum in Barcelona. Apart from contributing to the evolution of art, Picasso also made many political and social statements through his work.
- Flamenco has its roots in Gypsy culture, but has been evolving for centuries, incorporating Moorish and Spanish influences.

Bridging Cultures

Heritage Language Learners

Support What They Know Ask students if they are familiar with any **himnos** from soccer or other sports. What do they say to cheer for their favorite team? Have students model these chants for the whole group to repeat. Or, have students make up new **himnos** for the sports teams at your school.

English Learners

Build Background Ask students questions to help them report on the information presented on pp. 190 and 191. Follow up each question by asking students to draw a connection to their country of origin. Here are a few examples: *What is the capital city of Spain? What is the capital of your home country? Name one typical Spanish dish. Is it similar to any dish in your culture?*

Video Character Guide

Maribel and Enrique are friends who both love clothes—looking at them, shopping for them, and wearing them. They talk about where to shop and what to buy.

Lesson Overview

Culture at a Glance

Topic & Activity	Essential Question
Let's go shopping! pp. 192-193	Where do you like to shop for clothes?
Surrealist Art in Spain p. 203	How might dreams influence an artist's work?
Different Climates p. 206	How does geography affect a country's climate?
A poem by Antonio Colinas pp. 210-211	How would you describe winter in your area?
Culture Review p. 215	What are some elements of Spanish or Chilean culture?

COMPARISON COUNTRIES España Chile Guatemala

Practice at a Glance

	Objective	Activity & Skill
Vocabulary	Shopping	1: Writing/Speaking; 7: Listening/Writing; 9: Listening/Reading; 15: Listening/Reading; 16: Listening/Reading
	Clothing	2: Speaking; 3: Listening/Reading; 4: Speaking; 5: Writing; 8: Speaking; 10: Speaking; 13: Speaking; 14: Speaking; 17: Speaking; 18: Reading/Listening/Speaking; Repaso 1: Listening; Repaso 4: Writing
Grammar	**Tener** expressions	5: Writing; 6: Reading/Writing; 8: Speaking; 9: Listening/Reading; 10: Speaking; Repaso 2: Writing
	Stem-changing verbs: **e → ie**	7: Listening/Writing; 17: Speaking; 19: Writing; Repaso 3: Writing
	Direct object pronouns	11: Reading; 12: Writing; 13: Speaking; 17: Speaking; Repaso 4: Writing
Communication	Talk about what clothes you want to buy	1: Writing/Speaking; 2: Speaking; 5: Writing; 6: Reading/Writing; 8: Speaking; 9: Listening/Reading; 15: Listening/Reading; 16: Listening/Reading; 18: Reading/Listening/Speaking; Repaso 1: Listening; Repaso 2: Writing
	Say what you wear in different seasons	3: Listening/Reading; 4: Speaking; 7: Listening/Writing; 10: Speaking; 14: Speaking; 19: Writing; Repaso 3: Writing; Repaso 4: Writing
	Pronunciation: The letter **c** with **a, o, u**	Pronunciación: La letra c con a, o, u, p. 205: Listening/Speaking
Recycle	Numbers from 11 to 100	1: Writing/Speaking
	After-school activities	4: Speaking

The following presentations are recorded in the Audio Program for *¡Avancemos!*

- **¡A responder!** *page 195*
- **7: ¿Tiene suerte en la tienda?** *page 201*
- **18: Integración** *page 209*
- **Repaso de la lección** *page 214*
  1: Listen and understand

For **¡AvanzaRap!** scripts, see the **¡AvanzaRap! DVD.**

¡A responder! TXT CD 4 track 2

1. una camiseta
2. una blusa
3. unos pantalones cortos
4. una camisa
5. unos calcetines
6. unos zapatos
7. unos jeans
8. un vestido

7 | ¿Tiene suerte en la tienda?

TXT CD 4 track 4

Enrique: El invierno empieza. Hoy voy de compras en el centro comercial. Quiero comprar un gorro nuevo. No me gusta tener frío; prefiero tener calor. Mi amiga Micaela también está en el centro comercial porque quiere comprar ropa. Yo prefiero un gorro azul, y Micaela quiere comprar un gorro negro. Pienso que el gorro azul cuesta diez euros. Hablo con la señora.

Vendedora: Cien euros, por favor.

Enrique: ¿Cien euros? ¿No cuesta diez euros? ¡No entiendo! Ah... el precio tiene otro cero. No quiero el gorro azul. Cuesta mucho. A Micaela le gusta el gorro negro; cuesta quince euros. Ella tiene suerte.

18 | Integración TXT CD 4 tracks 8, 9

Buenas tardes. Aquí en Alta Moda tenemos los mejores precios.
Para los chicos, los jeans cuestan 35 euros y los pantalones, 25 euros. Las chaquetas de otoño cuestan 44 euros. También vendemos calcetines que cuestan 8 euros.
Y chicas... tenemos buenos precios para ustedes también. Las blusas cuestan 29 euros y los vestidos cuestan 36. Los zapatos cuestan 60 euros. También vendemos sombreros muy bonitos... ¡18 euros!

Repaso de la lección TXT CD 4 track 11

1 Listen and understand

Hola, soy Paula. Voy de compras en el centro comercial porque necesito ropa nueva. Necesito jeans azules, pero todos los jeans cuestan 70 euros. No quiero pagar 70 euros.

Todos los días llevo una blusa a la escuela. Necesito una blusa nueva. La blusa blanca es muy bonita. ¡Y no cuesta mucho!

En una tienda hay un sombrero amarillo. No es feo, pero prefiero un sombrero negro.

Quiero comprar zapatos nuevos. Tengo suerte porque hay muchos zapatos que me gustan. Pienso que los zapatos negros son bonitos.

Necesito una chaqueta porque el otoño empieza. Me gusta la chaqueta anaranjada más que la chaqueta roja.

En otra tienda hay un vestido amarillo. Tiene un buen precio: 43 euros. Me gusta mucho.

Resource List

Everything you need to ...

Plan

TEACHER ONE STOP

- ✓ Lesson Plans
- ✓ Teacher Resources
- ✓ Audio and Video

Present

INTERACTIVE WHITEBOARD LESSONS

TEACHER ONE STOP WITH PROJECTABLE TRANSPARENCIES

POWER PRESENTATIONS

ANIMATEDGRAMMAR

Assess

ONLINE ASSESSMENT

- ✓ Assessments for on-level, modified, pre-AP, and heritage learners
- ✓ Create customized tests with **Examview Assessment Suite**
- ✓ **performance space**
- ✓ *Generate Success* Rubric Generator

Print

Plan	Present	Practice	Assess
URB 4 • Video Scripts pp. 69–70 • Family Letter p. 91 • Absent Student Copymasters pp. 93–100 **Best Practices Toolkit**	**URB 4** • Video Activities pp. 51–58	• *Cuaderno* pp. 148–170 • *Cuaderno para hispanohablantes* pp. 148–170 • *Lecturas para todos* pp. 138–142 • *Lecturas para hispanohablantes* • *¡AvanzaCómics! SúperBruno y Nati,* Episodio 2 **URB 4** • Practice Games pp. 31–38 • Audio Scripts pp. 73–76 • Map/Culture Activities pp. 83–84 • Fine Art Activities pp. 86–87	**Differentiated Assessment Program** **URB 4** • Did you get it? Reteaching and Practice Copymasters pp. 1–12

Projectable Transparencies (Teacher One Stop, my.hrw.com)

Culture	Presentation and Practice	Classroom Management
• Atlas Maps 1–6 • Map of Spain 1 • Fine Art Transparencies 2, 3	• Vocabulary Transparencies 6, 7 • Grammar Presentation Transparencies 10, 11	• Warm Up Transparencies 16–19 • Student Book Answer Transparencies 24–27

Audio and Video

Audio	Video	¡AvanzaRap! DVD
• Student Book Audio CD 4 Tracks 1–11 • Workbook Audio CD 2 Tracks 21–30 • Heritage Learners Audio CD 1 Tracks 25–28, CD 3 Tracks 21, 22 • Assessment Audio CD 1 Tracks 21–22 • *Lecturas para todos* CD 1 Track 7, CD 2 Tracks 1–6 • Sing-along Songs Audio CD	• Vocabulary Video DVD 1 • *Telehistoria* DVD 1 Escena 1 Escena 2 Escena 3 Completa	• Video animations of all **¡AvanzaRap!** songs (with Karaoke track) • Interactive DVD Activities • Teaching Suggestions • **¡AvanzaRap!** Activity Masters • **¡AvanzaRap!** video scripts and answers

Online and Media Resources

Student	Teacher
Available online at my.hrw.com • Interactive Online Student Edition • **News** + Networking • **performance space** • @HOMETUTOR • CULTURA Interactiva • WebQuests • Interactive Flashcards • Review Games • Self-Check Quiz **Student One Stop** **Holt McDougal Spanish Apps**	**Teacher One Stop (also available at my.hrw.com)** • Interactive Teacher's Edition • All print, audio, and video resources • Projectable Transparencies • Lesson Plans • TPRS • Examview Assessment Suite **Available online at my.hrw.com** *Generate Success* Rubric Generator and Graphic Organizers **Power Presentations**

Differentiated Assessment

On-level	Modified	Pre-AP	Heritage Learners
• Vocabulary Recognition Quiz p. 149 • Vocabulary Production Quiz p. 150 • Grammar Quizzes pp. 151–152 • Culture Quiz p. 153 • On-level Lesson Test pp. 154–160	• Modified Lesson Test pp. 119–125	• Pre-AP Lesson Test pp. 119–125	• Heritage Learners Lesson Test pp. 125–131

Core Pacing Guide

50 Minute (9 Day)

	Objectives/focus	Teach	Practice	Assess/HW Options
DAY 1	**Culture:** learn about Spain **Vocabulary:** clothing • Warm Up OHT 16 **5 min**	Unit Opener pp. 190–191 Lesson Opener pp. 192–193 **Presentación de vocabulario** pp. 194–195 • Read A–E • View video DVD 1 • Play Audio TXT CD 4 track 1 • *¡A responder!* TXT CD 4 track 2 **25 min**	Lesson Opener pp. 192–193 **Práctica de vocabulario** p. 196 • Acts. 1, 2 **15 min**	**Assess:** *Para y piensa* p. 196 **5 min** **Homework:** *Cuaderno* pp. 148–150 @HomeTutor
DAY 2	**Communication:** talking about clothes • Warm Up OHT 16 • Check Homework **5 min**	**Vocabulario en contexto** pp. 197–198 • *Telehistoria escena 1* DVD 1 **20 min**	**Vocabulario en contexto** pp. 197–198 • Act. 3 TXT CD 4 track 3 • Act. 4 **20 min**	**Assess:** *Para y piensa* p. 198 **5 min** **Homework:** *Cuaderno* pp. 148–150 @HomeTutor
DAY 3	**Grammar:** stem-changing verbs: **e → ie** • Warm Up OHT 17 • Check Homework **5 min**	**Presentación de gramática** p. 199 • stem-changing verbs: **e → ie** **Práctica de gramática** pp. 200–201 **20 min**	**Práctica de gramática** pp. 200–201 • Acts. 5, 6, 8 • Act. 7 TXT CD 4 track 4 **20 min**	**Assess:** *Para y piensa* p. 201 **5 min** **Homework:** *Cuaderno* pp. 151–153 @HomeTutor
DAY 4	**Communication:** use stem-changing verbs: **e → ie** to talk about your clothing preferences • Warm Up OHT 17 • Check Homework **5 min**	**Gramática en contexto** pp. 202–203 • *Telehistoria escena 2* DVD 1 **Culture:** *El arte surrealista de España* **15 min**	**Gramática en contexto** pp. 202–203 • Act. 9 TXT CD 4 track 5 • Act. 10 **25 min**	**Assess:** *Para y piensa* p. 203 **5 min** **Homework:** *Cuaderno* pp. 151–153 @HomeTutor
DAY 5	**Grammar:** direct object pronouns • Warm Up OHT 18 • Check Homework **5 min**	**Presentación de gramática** pp. 204–205 **• Direct object pronouns** **Práctica de gramática** pp. 205–206 • *Pronunciación* TXT CD 4 track 6 **15 min**	**Práctica de gramática** pp. 205–206 • Acts. 11, 12, 13, 14 **25 min**	**Assess:** *Para y piensa* p. 206 **5 min** **Homework:** *Cuaderno* pp. 154–156 @HomeTutor
DAY 6	**Communication:** Culmination: stem-changing verbs, direct object pronouns, clothing preference • Warm Up OHT 18 • Check Homework **5 min**	**Todo junto** pp. 207–209 • *Escenas 1, 2: Resumen* • *Telehistoria completa* DVD 1 **15 min**	**Todo junto** pp. 207–209 • Acts. 15, 16 TXT CD 4 tracks, 3, 5, 7 • Act. 18 TXT CD 4 tracks 8, 9 • Acts. 17, 19 **25 min**	**Assess:** *Para y piensa* p. 209 **5 min** **Homework:** *Cuaderno* pp. 157–158 @HomeTutor
DAY 7	**Reading:** *Las memorias del invierno* **Connections:** Art • Warm Up OHT 19 **5 min**	**Lectura** pp. 210–211 • *Las memorias del invierno* TXT CD 4 track 10 **Conexiones** p. 212 • *El arte* **20 min**	**Lectura** pp. 210–211 • *Las memorias del invierno* **Conexiones** p. 212 • *Proyectos* 1, 2, 3 **20 min**	**Assess:** *Para y piensa* p. 211 **5 min** **Homework:** *Cuaderno* pp. 162–164 @HomeTutor
DAY 8	**Review:** Lesson Review • Warm Up OHT 19 **5 min**	**Repaso de la lección** pp. 214–215 **15 min**	**Repaso de la lección** pp. 214–215 • Act. 1 TXT CD 4 track 11 • Acts. 2, 3, 4, 5 **20 min**	**Assess:** *Repaso de la lección* pp. 214–215 **10 min** **Homework:** *En resumen* p. 213 *Cuaderno* pp. 159–161, 165–170 (optional) Review Games Online @HomeTutor
DAY 9	**Assessment**			**Assess:** Lesson 1 Test **50 min**

	Objectives/focus	Teach	Practice	Assess/HW Options
DAY 1	**Culture:** learn about Spain **Vocabulary:** clothing • Warm Up OHT 16 5 min	Unit Opener pp. 190–191 Lesson Opener pp. 192–193 **Presentación de vocabulario** pp. 194–195 • Read A–E • View video DVD 1 • Play audio TXT CD 4 track 1 • *¡A responder!* TXT CD 4 track 2 20 min	Lesson Opener pp. 192–193 **Práctica de vocabulario** p. 196 • Acts. 1, 2 20 min	**Assess:** *Para y piensa* p. 196 5 min
	Communication: talking about clothes 5 min	**Vocabulario en contexto** pp. 197–198 • *Telehistoria escena 1* DVD 1 15 min	**Vocabulario en contexto** pp. 197–198 • Act. 3 TXT CD 4 track 3 • Act. 4 15 min	**Assess:** *Para y piensa* p. 198 5 min **Homework:** *Cuaderno* pp. 148–150 @HomeTutor
DAY 2	**Grammar:** stem-changing verbs: **e → ie** • Warm Up OHT 17 • Check Homework 5 min	**Presentación de gramática** p. 199 • stem-changing verbs: **e → ie** **Práctica de gramática** pp. 200–201 20 min	**Práctica de gramática** pp. 200–201 • Acts. 5, 6, 8 • Act. 7 TXT CD 4 track 4 15 min	**Assess:** *Para y piensa* p. 201 5 min
	Communication: use stem-changing verbs: **e → ie** to talk about your clothing preferences 5 min	**Gramática en contexto** pp. 202–203 • *Telehistoria escena 2* DVD 1 **Culture:** *El arte surrealista de España* 20 min	**Gramática en contexto** pp. 202–203 • Act. 9 TXT CD 4 track 5 • Act. 10 15 min	**Assess:** *Para y piensa* p. 203 5 min **Homework:** *Cuaderno* pp. 151–153 @HomeTutor
DAY 3	**Grammar:** direct object pronouns • Warm Up OHT 18 • Check Homework 5 min	**Presentación de gramática** p. 204 • Direct object pronouns **Práctica de gramática** pp. 205–206 • *Pronunciación* TXT CD 4 track 6 15 min	**Práctica de gramática** pp. 205–206 • Acts. 11, 12, 13, 14 20 min	**Assess:** *Para y piensa* p. 206 5 min
	Communication: Culmination: stem-changing verbs, direct object pronouns, clothing preference 5 min	**Todo junto** pp. 207–209 • *Escenas 1 & 2: Resumen* • *Telehistoria completa* DVD 1 10 min	**Todo junto** pp. 207–209 • Acts. 15, 16 TXT CD 4 tracks 3, 5, 7 • Act. 18 TXT CD 4 tracks 8, 9 • Acts. 17, 19 25 min	**Assess:** *Para y piensa* p. 209 5 min **Homework:** *Cuaderno* pp. 154–158 @HomeTutor
DAY 4	**Reading:** *Las memorias del invierno* • Warm Up OHT 19 • Check Homework 5 min	**Lectura** pp. 210–211 • *Las memorias del invierno* TXT CD 4 track 10 15 min	**Lectura** pp. 210–211 • *Las memorias del invierno* 15 min	**Assess:** *Para y piensa* p. 211 5 min
	Review: Lesson Review 5 min	**Repaso de la lección** pp. 214–215 15 min	**Repaso de la lección** pp. 214–215 • Act. 1 TXT CD 4 track 11 • Acts. 2, 3, 4, 5 25 min	**Assess:** *Repaso de la lección* pp. 214–215 5 min **Homework:** *Cuaderno* pp. 159–170 (optional) Review Games Online @HomeTutor
DAY 5	**Assessment**			**Assess:** Lesson 1 Test 45 min
	Connections: Art 5 min	**Conexiones** p. 212 • *El arte* 10 min	**Conexiones** p. 212 • *Proyectos 1,2,3* 30 min	

¡AVANZA! **Objectives**
- Introduce lesson theme: **¡Vamos de compras!**
- **Culture:** Discuss where people like to shop for clothing in different countries.

Presentation Strategies
- Introduce the characters' names: Enrique and Maribel.
- Ask students to compare the clothing in the store window with the type of clothing teens wear in their own community.
- Ask students to talk about shops and department stores in the area where they live.

STANDARDS
2.1 Practices and perspectives
4.2 Compare cultures
21st CENTURY **Social and Cross-Cultural Skills,** Heritage Language Learners

Warm Up
Projectable Transparencies, 4-16

Comparatives Complete the sentences with **que** or **como.**
1. Alicia es tan alta _____ su hermana.
2. Mi tío es menos atlético _____ yo.
3. El yogur es tan rico _____ el helado.
4. Patricia es más artística _____ su hermana.
5. Jorge toca la guitarra mejor _____ su padre.

Answers: 1. como; 2. que; 3. como; 4. que; 5. que

Comparación cultural

Exploring the Theme
Ask the following:
1. Is there a difference between the store windows in the photo and the store windows where you live?
2. What kind of clothing is shown in the store window? What season is it for? What clothing do you wear in that season?
3. Who do you see in the picture? Do you ever go clothes shopping with friends of the opposite gender?

¿Qué ves? Possible answers include:
- Sí, la chica está al lado del chico.
- El chico es más alto.
- Ellos están contentos y tranquilos.

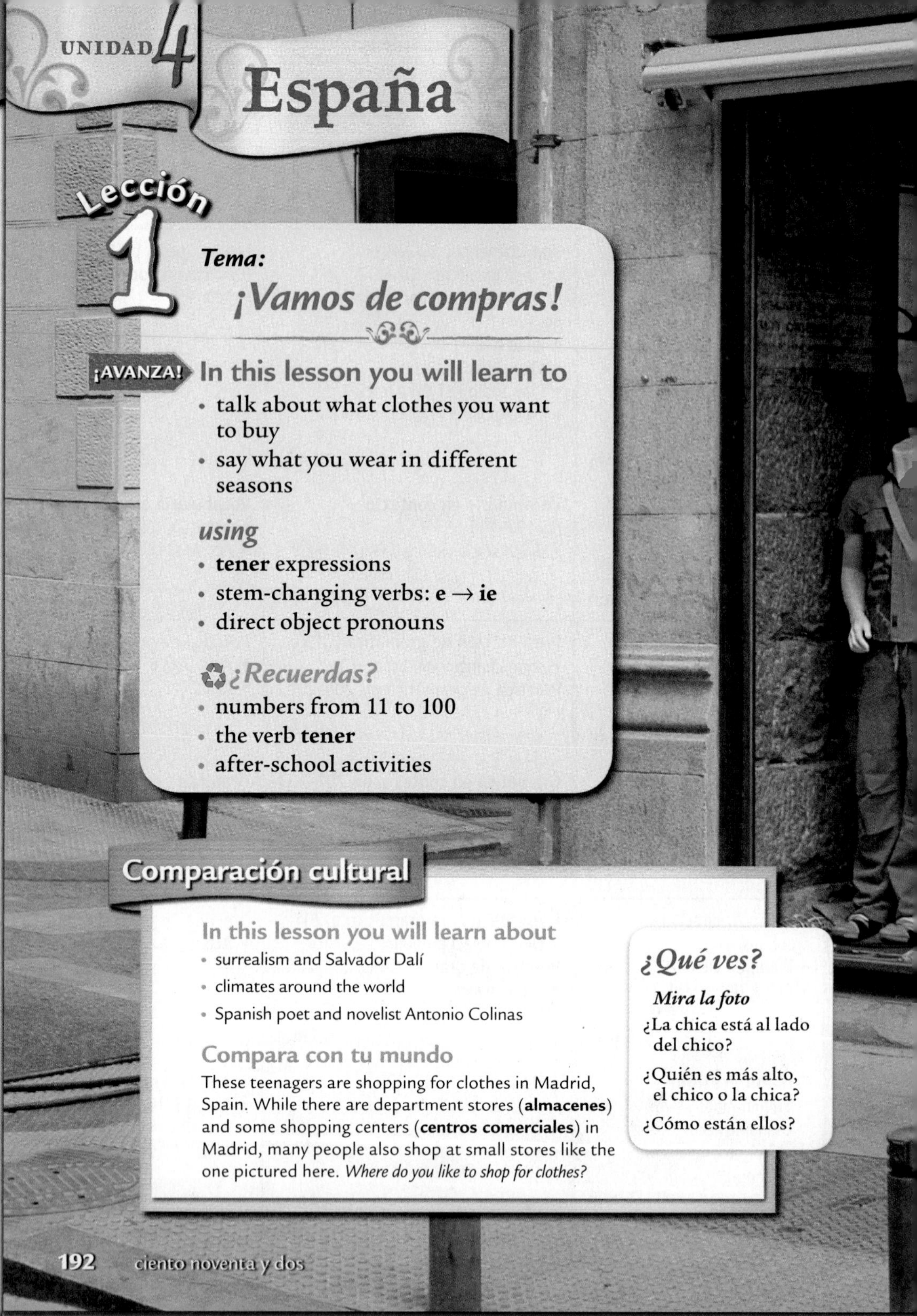

UNIDAD 4 España

Lección 1

Tema:

¡Vamos de compras!

¡AVANZA! **In this lesson you will learn to**
- talk about what clothes you want to buy
- say what you wear in different seasons

using
- **tener** expressions
- stem-changing verbs: **e → ie**
- direct object pronouns

¿Recuerdas?
- numbers from 11 to 100
- the verb **tener**
- after-school activities

Comparación cultural

In this lesson you will learn about
- surrealism and Salvador Dalí
- climates around the world
- Spanish poet and novelist Antonio Colinas

Compara con tu mundo
These teenagers are shopping for clothes in Madrid, Spain. While there are department stores (**almacenes**) and some shopping centers (**centros comerciales**) in Madrid, many people also shop at small stores like the one pictured here. *Where do you like to shop for clothes?*

¿Qué ves?
Mira la foto
¿La chica está al lado del chico?
¿Quién es más alto, el chico o la chica?
¿Cómo están ellos?

Differentiating Instruction

Heritage Language Learners
Support What They Know Ask students to share experiences or any knowledge they have of shopping customs in other countries. Do people typically shop at **tiendas** or in **un centro comercial?** Ask students if they know some common shopping expressions. How would they ask how much something costs? **¿Cuánto cuesta esto?**

Slower-paced Learners
Yes/No Questions Use yes or no questions about the photograph in the textbook to introduce students to some of the vocabulary related to clothing. You might ask what students see, like, or have themselves. Point to each item in the photo as you ask about it. Here are some possible questions: **¿Hay un vestido? ¿Te gusta la camiseta de la chica? ¿Tienes jeans?**

Una tienda de ropa
Madrid, España

DIGITAL SPANISH my.hrw.com
ONLINE STUDENT EDITION with...

- performance space
- News + Networking
- @HOMETUTOR
- CULTURA Interactiva

- Audio and Video Resources
- Interactive Flashcards
- Review Activities
- WebQuest
- Conjuguemos.com

PRACTICE SPANISH WITH HOLT MCDOUGAL APPS!

Differentiating Instruction

Pre-AP

Expand and Elaborate Have students brainstorm a list of questions about the city of Madrid and things to do there. Divide students into pairs or small groups to research one of the questions at the library or on the Internet. Ask each group to share what they learned. If possible, have them download images or maps of the areas they have chosen to accompany their presentation.

Multiple Intelligences

Visual Learners Give students two minutes to memorize the details of the photo on p. 193. Then have them close their books and draw the photo with markers or colored pencils. Ask them to write a brief description of their drawing in Spanish, identifying the people and their characteristics.

DIGITAL SPANISH

TEACHER TOOLS
- Interactive Whiteboard Lessons
- Generate Success!

ALSO AVAILABLE...
- Online Workbook
- Spanish InterActive Reader

SPANISH ON THE GO!
- Performance Space
- Holt McDougal Spanish Apps
- ¡Avancemos! eTextbook

Using the Photo

Location Information

Spain In Spain, lunch is the most important meal of the day. It is also the most important time to spend with family and friends, and a time to rest. Most shops, businesses, and schools close for two or three hours during lunchtime. This tradition is called the **siesta.** Due to global influences, however, customs are changing and today some stores remain open during lunchtime, especially in the big cities.

Long-term Retention

Critical Thinking

Predict Have students think about the lesson topics. Have them brainstorm possible vocabulary groups and related items. For example, clothing (pants, shirts, dresses) and colors (blue, green, red).

¡AVANZA! **Objectives**

- Present vocabulary: stores, clothes, colors, seasons.
- Check for recognition.

Core Resources

- Video Program: DVD 1
- Audio Program: TXT CD 4 tracks 1, 2

Presentation Strategies

- Ask students yes/no questions about what they are wearing: **¿Llevas una blusa? ¿Llevas unos jeans?**
- Ask students to take turns pointing to each of the illustrations on pp. 194–195 and reading the words aloud.
- Play the audio as students read A–E.
- Play the video.

STANDARD

1.2 Understand language

Communication, Interpersonal Mode (Financial Literacy)

Communication

Common Error Alert

Monitor correct writing of plural forms of **calcetín, estación, marrón.** Point out that these words do not carry an accent in their plural forms: **calcetines, estaciones, marrones.**

Culture

Expanded Information

The euro is the currency of twelve European Union countries, stretching from the Mediterranean to the Arctic Circle (namely Belgium, Germany, Greece, Spain, France, Ireland, Italy, Luxembourg, the Netherlands, Austria, Portugal, and Finland). Euro bills and coins have been in circulation since January 1, 2002 and are now a part of daily life for over 300 million Europeans living in the euro zone.

Presentación de VOCABULARIO

¡AVANZA! **Goal:** Learn about the clothes Enrique and Maribel like to wear. Then practice what you have learned to talk about clothes and how much they cost. ***Actividades 1–2***

¿Recuerdas? Numbers from 11 to 100 p. 87

VIDEO DVD

AUDIO

A ¡Hola! Me llamo Enrique. **Voy de compras** al **centro comercial** con mi amiga, Maribel. **Queremos** comprar **ropa nueva.** A Maribel le gusta ir a todas **las tiendas.**

B Voy a comprar **una camisa** y **unos jeans. Cuestan** treinta **euros.** **El vestido** de Maribel **cuesta** veinte euros. Es un buen **precio.**

En España se dice...

In Spain the word for *jeans* is **los vaqueros.** They also use **los tejanos.**

Más vocabulario

cerrar *to close*	**preferir** *to prefer*
¿Cuánto cuesta(n)? *How much does it (do they) cost?*	**tener suerte** *to be lucky*
el dólar *dollar*	
empezar *to begin*	
entender *to understand*	

Expansión de vocabulario p. R5

Differentiating Instruction

Slower-paced Learners

Memory Aids Provide each student with construction paper and a pair of scissors. Ask them to cut out models of different styles of clothing in different colors. Then have them label each item, for example, **la camisa amarilla, los jeans azules,** etc. Allow students to create and talk about different combinations of clothing.

Multiple Intelligences

Visual Learners Have students brainstorm a description of a person. Encourage them to include personal adjectives, emotion words, clothing and color words. For example: **Es una chica alta. Tiene pelo castaño. Es artística. Tiene una chaqueta verde y un gorro azul.** Then organize students into pairs. As one student reads his or her description, the other student must draw what he or she hears.

C Me gusta **llevar** ropa **blanca, roja** y **marrón.** A Maribel le gusta llevar **una camiseta verde** y **unos pantalones cortos azules.**

D Maribel **piensa** que **el vestido** es un poco **feo.** Ella **tiene razón;** no es muy bonito. Ella **compra** otro vestido que le gusta más.

E En España hay cuatro **estaciones.** Maribel siempre **tiene calor durante el verano.** Me gusta **el invierno,** pero siempre **tengo frío.**

@HOMETUTOR my.hrw.com Interactive Flashcards

¡A responder! Escuchar

Escucha las siguientes descripciones de ropa. Levanta la mano si llevas la ropa que escuchas. *(Listen to the following descriptions of clothes. Raise your hand if you are wearing that item.)*

TEACHER to TEACHER

Lourdes Casanova
Kissimmee, Florida

Tips for Teaching Vocabulary

I ask students to bring in some of their favorite clothing articles. The items are then classified by seasons and placed in booths around the classroom. The studnets then go shopping for a particular trip or vacation. Once students have selected their clothes, they describe their cchoices to the class.

Go online for more tips!

Communication

Interpersonal Mode

Give pages from a clothing catalogue to pairs of students. Have one student ask how much an item costs, and a second student answer based on the catalogue information. Remind students to use **¿Cuánto cuesta?** for one item and **¿Cuánto cuestan?** for several items.

Long-term Retention

Personalize It

Make a chart with the names of the four seasons. Complete the chart by asking students to write which items of clothing they would wear in each season.

Long-term Retention

Connect to Previous Learning

Review weather expressions with students. Then have them work in pairs to talk about what they are wearing according to the weather. For example: **Hace frío, ¿qué llevas hoy? Llevo una chaqueta, un gorro y pantalones.**

Differentiating Instruction

Inclusion

Frequent Review/Repetition Divide the board into two columns: **Sustantivos** and **Adjetivos**. Then have students brainstorm a list of nouns and adjectives based on the new vocabulary. For example, nouns: **blusa;** adjectives: **azul.** Using their lists as a guide, have students create simple sentences like, **La camisa es negra.** Remind them that the adjective's ending must agree with the noun.

Slower-paced Learners

Personalize It Have students use the verbs **tener** and **gustar** to talk about clothing that they have and like. Encourage each student to provide two sentences using the photos on pp. 194–195 as a guide. **Tengo una blusa roja. Me gustan los pantalones cortos.**

Answers Projectable Transparencies, 4-24

¡A responder! Audio Script, TE p. 191b

Answers will vary depending on what students are wearing.

Objectives
- Practice vocabulary: cost of items, clothing, colors.
- Recycle: numbers 11–100.

Core Resource
- *Cuaderno,* pp. 148–150

Practice Sequence
- **Activity 1:** Vocabulary recognition: cost of items, clothing, numbers; Recycle: numbers from 11 to 100
- **Activity 2:** Vocabulary production: clothing, colors

STANDARDS
1.1 Engage in conversation, Act. 2
1.3 Present information, Act. 1, PYP
21st Century **Communication,** Multiple Intelligences; **Critical Thinking and Problem Solving,** Pre-AP

✓Ongoing Assessment

Get Help Online
More Practice
my.hrw.com

PARA Y PIENSA **Quick Check** Have students describe the color of two items they are wearing. Check their responses. For additional practice, use Reteaching & Practice Copymasters URB 4 pp. 1, 2, 10.

Answers Projectable Transparencies, 4-24

Activity 1
1. El vestido cuesta cuarenta y nueve euros.
2. Los jeans cuestan cuarenta y seis euros.
3. Los zapatos cuestan setenta y cuatro euros.
4. La chaqueta cuesta sesenta y cinco euros.
5. La camiseta cuesta diecisiete euros.
6. Los pantalones cortos cuestan veintidós euros.
7. La blusa cuesta treinta y tres euros.

Activity 2
1. ¿De qué color es el vestido? El vestido es amarillo.
2. ¿De qué color es la chaqueta? La chaqueta es blanca y verde.
3. ¿De qué color es la blusa? La blusa es blanca.
4. ¿De qué color son los calcetines? Los calcetines son anaranjados.
5. ¿De qué color es la camisa? La camisa es azul.
6. ¿De qué color son los pantalones? Los pantalones son negros.
7. ¿De qué color son los jeans? Los jeans son azules.
8. ¿De qué color es el gorro? El gorro es negro.

Para y piensa
1. ¿Cuánto cuestan los calcetines blancos?
2. ¿Cuánto cuesta el vestido azul?
3. ¿Cuánto cuesta la chaqueta anaranjada?
4. ¿Cuánto cuestan los pantalones cortos rojos?

Práctica de VOCABULARIO

1 Los precios de la ropa

¿Recuerdas? Numbers from 11 to 100 p. 87

Escribir Hablar

Indica cuánto cuesta la ropa. *(Tell how much the clothing costs.)*

modelo: la camisa
La camisa cuesta veintiocho euros.

1. el vestido
2. los jeans
3. los zapatos
4. la chaqueta
5. la camiseta
6. los pantalones cortos
7. la blusa

Expansión: Teacher Edition Only
Have students rewrite the answers using adjectives to describe the col[or] of the items.

2 Ropa de muchos colores

Hablar

Pregúntale a otro(a) estudiante de qué color es cada artículo de ropa. *(Ask a partner the color of the clothing items.)*

A ¿De qué color son los zapatos?

B Los zapatos son rojos.

1. 
2. 
3. 
4. 
5. 
6. 
7. 
8. 

Expansión
Make your own pric[e] list. A partner will as[k] you how much the items cost.

Más práctica Cuaderno *pp. 148–150* Cuaderno para hispanohablantes *pp. 148–151*

Get Help Online
my.hrw.com

PARA Y PIENSA

Did you get it? Ask how much the following items cost.
1. the white socks
2. the blue dress
3. the orange jacket
4. the red shorts

Differentiating Instruction

Multiple Intelligences

Interpersonal Collect a number of real clothing items, and give each a price tag. In groups of three or four, have students role-play being in a store and asking about prices. Encourage students to use as much language as possible including greetings and explanations of why they need a certain item. **Hola. Necesito una chaqueta verde. ¿Cuánto cuesta la chaqueta?**

Inclusion

Metacognitive Support Remind students that it is important to think about expressions in a different language, and not just translate word-for-word. Point out, for example, that the phrase *How much?* in English is equivalent to the single question word **¿Cuánto?** in Spanish. And the question *What color?* in English requires a preposition in Spanish **¿De qué color?** or literally *Of what color?*

VOCABULARIO en contexto

¡AVANZA! **Goal:** Pay attention to the different articles of clothing Enrique and Maribel talk about. Then practice these words and **tener** expressions to say what you wear in different seasons. ***Actividades 3–4***

¿Recuerdas? The verb **tener** p. 91, after-school activities p. 32

Telehistoria escena 1

@HOMETUTOR my.hrw.com **View, Read and Record**

STRATEGIES

Cuando lees
Scan for details Before reading, quickly scan the scene to discover basic details: Who's in the scene? What are they doing? Where are they? What time is it? What's the season?

Cuando escuchas
Listen for wishes Listen to Maribel and Enrique express where they want to go. Who gets his or her way in this scene? How does this happen?

VIDEO DVD

AUDIO

Maribel is opening a package from Alicia.

Enrique: ¿Es una camiseta?

Maribel: *(reading a flyer from the package)* Sí. Y Trini está en el centro comercial del Parque de las Avenidas de las doce a la una de la tarde.

Enrique: ¿Dónde está el Parque de las Avenidas?

Maribel: Necesito un mapa. ¿Vamos?

They start walking. Enrique stops and points at a store.

Enrique: ¡Una tienda de ropa! ¡Y yo necesito comprar una chaqueta! ¡Tengo frío!

Maribel: ¡Eres muy cómico! En el verano, cuando hace calor, ¿necesitas una chaqueta?

Enrique: ¿Hace calor? Yo no tengo calor.

Maribel: En el invierno, cuando hace frío, llevas pantalones cortos. Y durante la primavera, ¡nunca llevas calcetines!

Enrique: ¡Me gusta ser diferente! ¿No necesitas unos zapatos nuevos?

Maribel: *(reluctantly)* ¡Vale! Diez minutos. **Continuará...** p. 202

También se dice

España Maribel uses the word **vale** to say *OK*. In other Spanish-speaking countries you might hear:
- **México** **órale, sale, ándale**
- **Cuba** **dale**

Differentiating Instruction

Slower-paced Learners

Read Before Listening Before listening to the Telehistoria, have students preview the text silently. Tell them to look specifically for clothing words, and to create a list of the words that they find. Then have students draw a quick sketch next to each clothing word to represent its meaning.

Pre-AP

Support Ideas with Details Write Enrique's line **¡Me gusta ser diferente!** on the board. Then ask for volunteers to add information from the text that supports this idea. For example: **Lleva pantalones cortos cuando hace frío.** Ask students to imagine other things Enrique might do. For example: **Lleva un gorro en el verano.**

¡AVANZA! **Objective**
- Understand clothing vocabulary in context.

Core Resources
- Video Program: DVD 1
- Audio Program: TXT CD 4 track 3

Presentation Strategies
- Ask students for what season Maribel and Enrique are dressed.
- Have students scan the dialogue and write the seasons mentioned in it.
- Show the video or play the audio.

STANDARD
1.2 Understand language

Warm Up
Projectable Transparencies, 4-16

Vocabulary Complete the following sentences with the correct word or expression.

fea	**pantalones cortos**
ir de compras	**estaciones**
precio	

1. Es un buen _____.
2. Los _____ son azules.
3. La chaqueta no es bonita. Es _____.
4. En España hay cuatro _____.
5. Me gusta _____ los sábados.

Answers: 1. precio; 2. pantalones cortos; 3. fea; 4. estaciones; 5. ir de compras

Video Summary

@HOMETUTOR **VideoPlus** my.hrw.com

Maribel has just received a package from her friend Alicia. The package contains a T-shirt and a flyer indicating that Trini will be at the Parque de las Avenidas mall between noon and 1:00 PM. Neither Enrique nor Maribel knows where the mall is. On their way, Enrique says he is cold and needs to buy a jacket. Maribel thinks it's funny that Enrique needs a jacket when it's warm in summer. Enrique says he likes to be different. Maribel agrees to go into the store with Enrique for ten minutes.

Objectives
- Practice using vocabulary in context.
- Recycle: **tener,** after-school activities.

Core Resource
- Audio Program: TXT CD 4 track 3

Practice Sequence
- **Activity 3:** Telehistoria comprehension
- **Activity 4:** Vocabulary production: clothing, the verb **llevar;** Recycle: after-school activities

STANDARDS
1.1 Engage in conversation, Act. 4
1.2 Understand language, Act. 3
1.3 Present information, Act. 4, PYP

Nota gramatical
Students have learned the following expressions with the verb **tener: tener que** in Unidad 1, Lección 2; **tener ganas de..., tener sed, tener hambre** in Unidad 3, Lección 1, and **tener... años** in Unidad 3, Lección 2.

Ongoing Assessment
Get Help Online
More Practice
my.hrw.com

PARA Y PIENSA **Quick Check** Ask students to write three sentences explaining what they would wear to be different from other students. For additional practice, use Reteaching & Practice Copymasters URB 4, pp. 1, 3, 11, 12.

Answers Projectable Transparencies, 4-24
Activity 3 **1.** d; **2.** e; **3.** f; **4.** a; **5.** c; **6.** b
Activity 4 Answers will vary. Sample answers:
1. ¿Qué ropa llevas cuando montas en bicicleta? Llevo jeans y un gorro.
2. ... tienes calor? Llevo pantalones cortos y una camiseta.
3. ... practicas deportes? Llevo una camiseta y pantalones.
4. ... tienes frío? Llevo un gorro y una chaqueta.
5. ... vas a la escuela? Llevo pantalones cortos y una camisa.
6. ... en verano? Llevo un vestido y zapatos blancos.

Para y piensa **1.** tiene frío; **2.** tiene calor; **3.** tiene frío

3 *Comprensión del episodio* La ropa apropiada
Escuchar Leer

Escoge la palabra o frase correcta para completar las oraciones, según el episodio. *(Complete the sentences by choosing the correct word or phrase, according to the episode.)*

1. Maribel tiene ____ .	**a.** pantalones cortos
2. Trini está en ____ .	**b.** diferente
3. Enrique necesita comprar ____ .	**c.** calcetines
4. Enrique lleva ____ en el invierno.	**d.** una camiseta
5. Enrique nunca lleva ____ en la primavera.	**e.** el centro comercial
6. A Enrique le gusta ser ____ .	**f.** una chaqueta

Expansión: Teacher Edition Only
Have students work in pairs. Each student writes two false statements about the episode and exchanges them with his/her partner to correct them.

Nota gramatical
¿Recuerdas? The verb **tener** p. 91

Tener is used to form many expressions that in English would use the verb *to be.*

tener **calor**	*to be hot*	tener **razón**	*to be right*
tener **frío**	*to be cold*	tener **suerte**	*to be lucky*

En el invierno **tengo frío,** y en el verano **tengo calor.**
In winter, I'm cold, and in summer, I'm hot.

4 ¿Qué ropa llevas?
¿Recuerdas? After-school activities p. 32

Hablar

Pregúntale a otro(a) estudiante qué ropa lleva en estas situaciones. *(Ask a partner what he or she wears in these situations.)*

A ¿Qué ropa llevas cuando paseas?
B Llevo pantalones, una camiseta y un sombrero.

Estudiante A	Estudiante B
1. montar en bicicleta	gorro
2. tener calor	pantalones cortos
3. practicar deportes	chaqueta
4. tener frío	camiseta
5. ir a la escuela	vestido
6. ¿ ?	¿ ?

Expansión
Choose three activities that you like to do with your friends and say what you wear.

Get Help Online
my.hrw.com

PARA Y PIENSA
Did you get it? Enrique likes to be different. Complete each sentence with the correct form of **tener calor** or **tener frío.**
1. En el verano, Enrique ____ y lleva una chaqueta.
2. En el invierno, él lleva pantalones cortos porque ____ .
3. Cuando Maribel tiene calor, Enrique ____ .

Differentiating Instruction

Pre-AP
Expand and Elaborate Once students have chosen the correct ending in Activity 3, encourage them to expand each sentence by providing details or an explanation, based on the Telehistoria. For example:
Enrique necesita comprar una chaqueta porque tiene frío.

Multiple Intelligences
Kinesthetic Ask students to write one expression with the **yo** form of the verb **tener** on a piece of paper and to keep the papers out of sight from other students: **Tengo hambre, tengo sed, tengo calor, tengo frío, tengo suerte,** etc. Ask volunteers to pantomime their phrases and have the class guess by saying the phrase aloud. Continue until all students have participated.

Presentación de GRAMÁTICA

¡AVANZA! **Goal:** Learn how to form **e → ie** stem-changing verbs. Then use these verbs to talk about clothes you and others want to buy. ***Actividades 5–8***

English Grammar Connection: There are no stem-changing verbs in the present tense of English.

Stem-Changing Verbs: e → ie

ANIMATEDGRAMMAR my.hrw.com

In Spanish, some verbs have a stem change in the present tense. How do you form the present tense of e → ie stem-changing verbs?

Here's how:

Stem-changing verbs have regular **-ar, -er,** and **-ir** present-tense endings. For e → ie stem-changing verbs, the e of the stem changes to ie in all forms except **nosotros(as)** and **vosotros(as).**

stem changes to

querer → quiero

querer *to want*	
quiero	**queremos**
quieres	**queréis**
quiere	**quieren**

Other e → ie stem-changing verbs you have learned are **cerrar, empezar, entender, pensar,** and **preferir.** In stem-changing verbs, it is the next-to-last syllable that changes.

Paula **prefiere** el vestido azul.
Paula ***prefers*** *the blue dress.*

Notice that when one verb follows another, the **first verb** is conjugated and the second is in its infinitive form.

¿**Quieres** mirar la televisión o leer un libro?
Do you want *to watch television or read a book?*

Más práctica
Cuaderno *pp. 151–153*
Cuaderno para hispanohablantes *pp. 152–154*

@HOMETUTOR my.hrw.com
Leveled Practice
Conjuguemos.com

Differentiating Instruction

Slower-paced Learners

Memory Aids Point out that **e → ie** stem-changing verbs are called boot verbs because if you outline the verb forms that have a stem change, the resulting shape forms a boot. Show an example on the board using **querer.** Ask: Which verb forms are outside the boot? Students should answer: **queremos, queréis.** Have students write a similar chart with the forms of **pensar**.

Inclusion

Metacognitive Support Ask a volunteer to read aloud the **e → ie** stem-changing verbs on p. 199 while you write on the board: **Mario _____ (querer) _____ (leer) un libro.** Ask students to say the missing verbs: **Mario quiere leer un libro.** Ask them to write other sentences using **querer, preferir,** and **pensar** followed by another verb.

¡AVANZA! **Objectives**

- Present stem-changing verbs: **e → ie.**
- Practice using stem-changing verbs to talk about clothes you and your friends want to buy.

Core Resource

- *Cuaderno,* pp. 151–153

Presentation Strategies

- Present forms and uses of stem-changing verbs: **e → ie.**
- Remind students that stem-changing verbs have regular **-ar, -er,** and **-ir** present-tense endings.

STANDARD

4.1 Compare languages

Warm Up Projectable Transparencies, 4-17

Expressions with tener Complete each sentence with the appropriate expression.

a. tenemos suerte **c.** tienes razón
b. tienes calor **d.** tiene frío

1. Liliana lleva un gorro porque _____.
2. Dos y dos son cinco, ¿verdad? No, no _____.
3. Compramos los pantalones más bonitos. _____.
4. Tú llevas pantalones cortos porque _____.

Answers: 1. d; 2. c; 3. a; 4. b

Communication

TPR Activity

Prepare in advance a list of ten sentences, some with regular verbs and some with **e → ie** stem-changing verbs and read them aloud. Have them clap once when they hear a sentence with a regular verb form. Have students clap twice when they hear a sentence with an **e → ie** verb. For example: **Hoy llevo zapatos negros.** (Clap once.) **Hoy quiero comprar zapatos marrones.** (Clap twice.)

Objective

- Practice **e → ie** stem-changing verbs and lesson vocabulary.

Core Resources

- *Cuaderno,* pp. 151–153
- Audio Program: TXT CD 4 track 4

Practice Sequence

- **Activity 5:** Transitional practice: **e → ie** stem-changing verbs; clothes
- **Activities 6, 7:** Transitional practice: **e → ie** stem-changing verbs, clothes, seasons
- **Activity 8:** Open-ended practice: **e → ie** stem-changing verbs, clothes, colors

STANDARDS

1.1 Engage in conversation, Act. 8
1.2 Understand language, Act. 7
1.3 Present information, Acts. 5–8, PYP
21st Century **Communication,** Act. 5/Role-Playing and Skits

Long-term Retention

Study Tips

Before doing Activity 6, have students skim the paragraph before completing it with forms of the appropriate verb.

Answers Projectable Transparencies, 4-25

Activity 5 Answers will vary. Sample answers:

1. Maribel quiere el vestido rojo.
2. Tú quieres la camiseta blanca.
3. Vosotros queréis la camisa amarilla.
4. Usted quiere el sombrero negro.
5. Yo quiero los jeans azules.
6. Los amigos de Maribel quieren los pantalones cortos verdes.
7. Mis amigas y yo queremos los zapatos marrones.
8. Ustedes quieren los calcetines anaranjados.

Activity 6

1. quiere
2. piensa
3. entienden
4. empieza
5. prefiero
6. cierra

Práctica de GRAMÁTICA

5 Todos quieren ropa

Escribir

Enrique y Maribel miran un catálogo de ropa y describen la ropa que quieren ellos y otros. Usa las fotos para decir qué ropa quieren. *(Write sentences describing the clothing items these people want.)*

modelo: la madre de Enrique
La madre de Enrique quiere la blusa anaranjada.

1. Maribel
2. tú
3. vosotros
4. usted
5. yo
6. los amigos de Maribel
7. mis amigas y yo
8. ustedes

Expansión
Write about what you prefer to buy when you go shopping.

6 El regalo de cumpleaños

Leer
Escribir

Maribel quiere comprar un regalo para su hermana. Completa lo que dice. *(Complete the paragraph with the correct form of the appropriate verb.)*

querer	entender
cerrar	pensar
preferir	empezar

Mañana celebramos el cumpleaños de mi hermana mayor. Voy a la tienda de ropa porque ella **1.** *una chaqueta nueva. Ya tiene dos chaquetas, pero ella* **2.** *que los otras chaquetas son feas. Mis padres no* **3.** *por qué necesita tres chaquetas. Pero ahora el otoño* **4.** *y a ella no le gusta tener frío. Mis hermanos y yo vamos a la tienda Moda 16. Yo* **5.** *otra tienda pero ellos tienen el dinero. Tenemos que llegar antes de las ocho porque la tienda* **6.** *a las ocho.*

Expansión:
Teacher Edition O
Have students ad two more sentenc to the paragraph.

Differentiating Instruction

Inclusion

Cumulative Instruction Before beginning Activity 5, help students review the verb forms and vocabulary they will need. Elicit the present tense forms of the verb **querer** and write them on the board. Then ask students to supply clothing and color words that they see in the catalogue. Create a list of each on the board. Encourage students to refer to these lists as they craft their responses.

Heritage Language Learners

Writing Skills Have students use the paragraph in Activity 6 as a model for their own writing. Direct them to start with the sentences: **Mañana es el cumpleaños de mi _____. Voy a la tienda de ropa porque _____.** Have them continue with their own narration. As an added challenge, instruct students to use each of the verbs presented in the box at least once in their paragraph.

7 ¿Tiene suerte en la tienda?

Escuchar
Escribir

Enrique está en el centro comercial. Escucha lo que dice y contesta las preguntas. *(Listen to Enrique's story and answer the questions.)*

1. ¿Qué estación empieza?
2. ¿Qué quiere comprar Enrique?
3. ¿Prefiere tener frío o calor él?
4. ¿Qué quiere comprar Micaela?
5. ¿Qué no entiende Enrique?
6. ¿Quién tiene suerte?

Audio Program
TXT CD 4 Track 4
Audio Script, TE p. 191b

8 ¿Qué piensas de la ropa?

Hablar

Habla con otro(a) estudiante sobre la ropa de varios colores. *(Talk with a classmate about your opinions on clothes.)*

A ¿Quieres comprar un sombrero marrón?

B No, pienso que los sombreros marrones son feos. Prefiero los sombreros negros. (Sí, quiero comprar un sombrero marrón.)

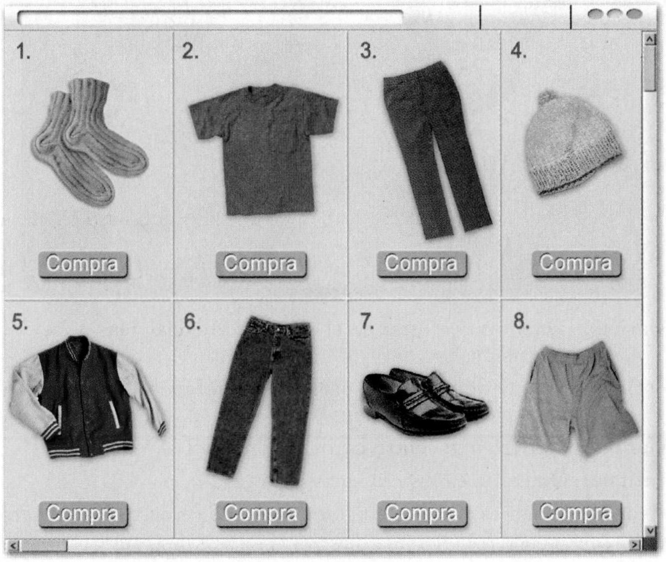

Expansión
Make a list of the clothes both you and your partner want to buy. Share your results with the class.

Más práctica Cuaderno *pp. 151–153* Cuaderno para hispanohablantes *pp. 152–154*

Get Help Online
my.hrw.com

PARA Y PIENSA

Did you get it? Complete each sentence with the correct form of the appropriate verb: **empezar, cerrar,** or **pensar.**
1. Yo _____ que la blusa amarilla es bonita.
2. Ya hace frío cuando _____ el invierno.
3. El centro comercial _____ a las nueve de la noche.

Differentiating Instruction

Slower-paced Learners

Read Before Listening Have students preview each question before listening to Activity 7. Ask them to write down a key word or phrase in each, and then brainstorm possible answers. For example:
¿Qué estación empieza? (circle **estación**)
Possible Answers: **invierno/primavera/verano/otoño**

Pre-AP

Relate Opinions Show an illustration of clothing, such as a green T-shirt. Review with students the different strategies they now have for expressing opinions about the item. They might begin with **Prefiero..., Quiero..., (No) Me gusta...,** or **Pienso que...** For example: **Quiero otro color de camiseta. Pienso que las camisetas verdes son feas.** Repeat the discussion with other clothing items.

Communication
Role-Playing and Skits

Bring in catalogues from well-known clothing stores. Assign student pairs the role of customer and telephone operator taking orders. For example: **A: Quiero comprar una camisa verde. El número del catálogo es 123 y el precio es $23.00. B: No tenemos más camisas verdes. ¿No quiere comprar una camisa azul? A: No, gracias, prefiero una camisa verde.**

✓ Ongoing Assessment

Get Help Online
More Practice
my.hrw.com

Intervention If students have difficulties completing the Para y piensa, have them review p. 199. For additional practice, use Reteaching & Practice Copymasters URB 4, pp. 4, 5.

Answers Projectable Transparencies, 4-25

Activity 7
1. El invierno empieza.
2. Enrique quiere comprar un gorro nuevo.
3. Enrique prefiere tener calor.
4. Micaela quiere comprar un gorro negro.
5. Enrique no entiende el precio del gorro azul.
6. Micaela tiene suerte.

Activity 8
Answers will vary. Sample answers include:
1. ¿Quieres comprar unos calcetines azules? Sí, quiero (No, no quiero) comprar unos calcetines azules.
2. ¿Quieres comprar una camiseta roja? Sí, quiero (No, no quiero) comprar una camiseta roja.
3. ¿Quieres comprar unos pantalones marrones? Sí, quiero (No, no quiero) comprar unos pantalones marrones.
4. ¿Quieres comprar un gorro anaranjado? Sí, quiero (No, no quiero) comprar un gorro anaranjado.
5. ¿Quieres comprar una chaqueta roja? Sí, quiero (No, no quiero) comprar una chaqueta roja.
6. ¿Quieres comprar unos jeans azules? Sí, quiero (No, no quiero) comprar unos jeans azules.
7. ¿Quieres comprar unos zapatos negros? Sí, quiero (No, no quiero) comprar unos zapatos negros.
8. ¿Quieres comprar unos pantalones cortos verdes? Sí, quiero (No, no quiero) comprar unos pantalones cortos verdes.

Para y piensa **1.** pienso; **2.** empieza; **3.** cierra

¡AVANZA! Objectives

- Practice **e → ie** stem-changing verbs and new vocabulary in context.
- **Culture:** Surrealist art in Spain.

Core Resources

- Video Program: DVD 1
- Audio Program: TXT CD 4 track 5

Presentation Strategies

- Ask students to identify the characters in the photo, tell where they are, and describe what they are doing.
- Have students preview the video activities before watching the video.
- Show the video and/or play the audio.

Practice Sequence

- **Activity 9:** Telehistoria comprehension
- **Activity 10:** Transitional practice: **e → ie** verbs, clothes, seasons

STANDARDS

1.1 Engage in conversation, Act. 10
1.2 Understand language, Act. 9
1.3 Present information, PYP
2.2 Products and perspectives, CC
4.2 Compare cultures, CC
21st Century **Communication,** Act. 10/ Interpersonal Mode

Warm Up Projectable Transparencies, 4-17

e → ie Stem-changing Verbs Complete each sentence with the correct verb form.

1. La tienda _____ a las ocho de la noche. (cerrar)
2. Los estudiantes no _____ ir de compras. (querer)
3. ¿ _____ Jaime la camisa blanca o la camisa amarilla? (preferir)

Answers: 1. cierra; 2. quieren; 3. Prefiere

Video Summary

@HOMETUTOR VideoPlus my.hrw.com

Maribel is eager to get to the shopping center at noon, but Enrique is busy shopping in the clothing store. Maribel wonders if Enrique wouldn't prefer to go shopping in the mall, but Enrique says the prices there are not good. To hurry Enrique along, Maribel points out items in the store she likes, but Enrique says he doesn't like those things.

GRAMÁTICA en contexto

¡AVANZA! **Goal:** Listen to the **e → ie** stem-changing verbs that Enrique and Maribel use while they are shopping for clothes. Then use the stem-changing verbs to talk about your clothing preferences. ***Actividades 9–10***

Telehistoria escena 2

@HOMETUTOR my.hrw.com **View, Read and Record**

STRATEGIES

Cuando lees
Look for color words In this scene, Enrique and Maribel discuss colors and types of clothing. Which color words do you find?

Cuando escuchas
Disregard stereotypes Who wants to keep looking at clothes and who is worried about being late? Is this expected? Why or why not?

VIDEO DVD

AUDIO

Maribel: Tenemos que estar en el centro comercial a las doce, ¿entiendes?
Enrique: Sí, entiendo. Dos minutos más. ¿Prefieres los vaqueros negros o los pantalones verdes?
Maribel: Prefiero ir al centro comercial, ¡ahora!
Enrique: Quiero la camisa blanca.
Vendedora: Tenemos camisas en color azul y en verde. ¿Queréis ver?
Maribel: *(to the clerk)* No, gracias. *(to Enrique, frustrated)* Pero Enrique, ¿una tienda de ropa? ¿No prefieres ir de compras al centro comercial?
Enrique: No. No quiero comprar la ropa en el centro comercial. Los precios no son buenos. *(still shopping)* ¿Te gustan los pantalones cortos azules?
Maribel: *(rushing him)* Sí, sí. Y me gustan los calcetines rojos, la camisa amarilla y los zapatos marrones...
Enrique: No, no, no. ¿Rojo, amarillo y marrón? No, no me gustan.

Continuará... p. 207

Differentiating Instruction

Heritage Language Learners

Regional Variations Ask students to comment on ways to say **los jeans.** Point out that the word **vaqueros** is used in Uruguay, Spain, and Argentina. Spaniards also use **los tejanos** for jeans. In recent years, **los jeans** seems to be the preferred term used in much of Latin America. In Puerto Rico, however, the preferred term is **los mahones.**

Slower-paced Learners

Memory Aids Have students create a drawing of each piece of clothing mentioned in the Telehistoria to help them remember vocabulary. Have students sketch each item on the same piece of paper. Then have students use their drawings to ask questions of their peers. **¿Prefieres la camisa blanca o los pantalones verdes? ¿Te gustan los zapatos marrones?**

9 Comprensión del episodio En la tienda de ropa

Escuchar
Leer

¿Quién prefiere las siguientes cosas, Maribel o Enrique?
(Who prefers the following things—Maribel or Enrique?)

1. ir de compras en una tienda de ropa
2. la camisa amarilla
3. la camisa blanca
4. los calcetines rojos
5. los zapatos marrones
6. ir al centro comercial temprano

Maribel

Enrique

Expansión: Teacher Edition Only
Have students write a statement that refers to either Maribel or Enrique and have their peers guess who the statement refers to.

10 La ropa y las estaciones

Hablar

Habla con otro(a) estudiante de lo que prefieres llevar y no llevar durante cada estación. *(Talk about what you prefer to wear and not wear during each season.)*

A: ¿Qué prefieres llevar durante el verano?

B: Prefiero llevar pantalones cortos. Nunca llevo chaqueta durante el verano.

Expansión
Describe what your partner is wearing.

Comparación cultural

El arte surrealista de España

How might dreams influence an artist's work? Artist Salvador Dalí from **Spain** is well known for his surrealist paintings. In surrealist art, the imagery reflects an artist's imagination and is often inspired by dreams. *La persistencia de la memoria,* considered one of Dalí's masterpieces, shows pocket watches that appear to be melting. Many interpret this painting as a commentary about the nature of time. What do you think Dalí's message is?

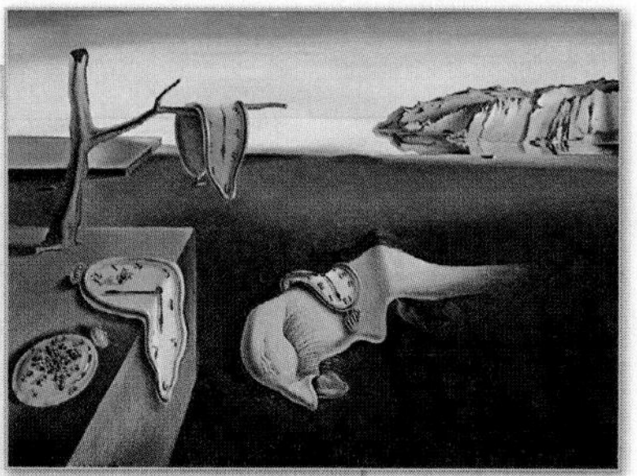
La persistencia de la memoria *(1931),* *Salvador Dalí*

Compara con tu mundo *Can you think of a dream you had that would make an interesting painting?*

Get Help Online
my.hrw.com

PARA Y PIENSA

Did you get it? Complete each sentence based on the Telehistoria with the correct form of the verb in parentheses.

1. Enrique _____ que van al centro comercial. (entender)
2. Maribel _____ ir al centro comercial. (preferir)
3. Enrique _____ comprar la camisa blanca. (querer)

Communication

Interpersonal Mode

Ask each student in the class to write a description of another student in the class in terms of what they are wearing. Collect the descriptions, then ask a student to read one description aloud. Ask another student to guess who is being described. Students should begin their descriptions with **La persona lleva...** so as not to reveal the gender.

Comparación cultural

Essential Question

Suggested Answer Dreams are part of the artist's subconscious imagination and can come out in an artist's work unintentionally. Some artists strive to depict images they have seen in dreams.

About the Artist

Salvador Dalí This painting is considered one of Salvador Dalí's masterpieces. The background of the painting shows Cape Creus, in the Catalonian region of Spain where Dalí grew up. The images in Dalí's surrealist paintings are confusing and startling, like those in dreams.

✓ Ongoing Assessment

Get Help Online
More Practice
my.hrw.com

PARA Y PIENSA

Intervention If students miss more than one item in the Para y piensa, have them review p.199 and repeat Activities 5 and 6 on p. 200. For additional practice, use Reteaching & Practice Copymasters URB 4, pp. 4, 6.

Differentiating Instruction

Pre-AP

Expand and Elaborate Ask student to research information about a well-known Spanish or Latin American surrealist painter using the encyclopedia or the Internet. Key words for research: Roberto Matta (Chile), Remedios Varos (Mexico), Óscar Domínguez (Spain), Joan Miró (Spain). Have students share their findings.

Multiple Intelligences

Visual Learners Have students create a drawing that illustrates different clothing items using surrealist techniques. Students present their drawings to the class and describe it in terms of items depicted, colors and techniques.

Answers Projectable Transparencies, 4-25

Activity 9
1. Enrique **2.** Maribel **3.** Enrique **4.** Maribel **5.** Maribel **6.** Maribel

Activity 10 Answers will vary. Sample answers include:
¿Qué prefieres llevar durante el otoño? Prefiero llevar unos pantalones y una camisa durante el otoño.
¿Qué prefieres llevar durante el invierno? Prefiero llevar unos jeans y un gorro durante el invierno.

Para y piensa
1. entiende; **2.** prefiere; **3.** quiere

¡AVANZA! **Objective**

- Present direct object pronouns.

Core Resource

- *Cuaderno,* pp. 154–156

Presentation Strategies

- Explain how direct object pronouns are used.
- Explain that when an infinitive follows the conjugated verb, the direct object pronoun can be placed before the conjugated verb or be attached to the infinitive.

STANDARD

4.1 Compare languages

Warm Up Projectable Transparencies, 4-18

Noun/Adjective Agreement Complete each sentence with the appropriate adjective.

amarilla blancos rojas negro

1. Eduardo lleva unos calcetines _____.
2. Gloria lleva un vestido _____.
3. Los niños llevan unas chaquetas _____.
4. Yo quiero comprar una camiseta _____.

Answers: 1. blancos; 2. negro; 3.rojas; 4. amarilla

Comparisons

English Grammar Connection

Note that unlike English, direct object pronouns are usually placed before the conjugated verb in Spanish.
I buy them. **Yo los compro.**
In Spanish, a direct object pronoun must reflect the number and gender of the noun it replaces.
Quiero la camisa. La quiero. Quiero los zapatos. Los quiero.

Communication

Common Error Alert

If the direct object pronoun comes before a conjugated verb, add **no** before the pronoun to make the sentence negative. **No la quiero. No la quiero comprar.** If the direct object pronoun is attached to an infinitive, add **no** before the conjugated verb to make the sentence negative. **No quiero comprarlos.**

Presentación de GRAMÁTICA

¡AVANZA! **Goal:** Learn how to use direct object pronouns. Then practice using them to talk about the clothes you wear and those you want to buy.
Actividades 11–14

English Grammar Connection: **Direct objects** receive the action of the verb in a sentence. They answer the question *whom?* or *what?* about the verb. The direct object can be a **noun** or a **pronoun.**

Luisa is buying the blouse. (noun) Luisa is buying it. (pronoun) Luisa compra la blusa. (noun) Luisa la (pronoun) compra.

Direct Object Pronouns

ANIMATEDGRAMMAR my.hrw.com

Direct object pronouns can be used to replace direct object nouns.

Here's how:

	Singular		Plural	
	me	*me*	nos	*us*
	te	*you (familiar)*	os	*you (familiar)*
masculine	lo	*you (formal), him, it*	los	*you, them* (*masculine*)
feminine	la	*you (formal), her, it*	las	*you, them* (*feminine*)

The direct object noun is placed *after* the **conjugated verb.**

The direct object pronoun is placed directly *before* the **conjugated verb.**

replaced by

Quiero la camisa azul. → La **quiero.**
I want the blue ***shirt.*** → *I want* ***it.***

When an infinitive follows the **conjugated verb,** the direct object pronoun can be placed *before* the **conjugated verb** or be *attached* to the infinitive.

replaced by

Quiero comprar zapatos negros. → Y los **quiero** comprar hoy.
I want to buy black ***shoes.*** *or* Y **quiero** comprarlos hoy.
And I want to buy ***them*** *today.*

Más práctica
Cuaderno *pp. 154–156*
Cuaderno para hispanohablantes *pp. 155–158*

@HOMETUTOR my.hrw.com
Leveled Practice

Differentiating Instruction

Multiple Intelligences

Kinesthetic Write on index cards each word of the following sentence: **Prefiero los zapatos negros, pero no los venden en la tienda.** Distribute the cards to different students and ask them to come to the front of the class and hold up the cards in scrambled order. Ask volunteers to arrange the students/cards in the correct order. Ask students to identify the direct object pronoun.

Slower-paced Learners

Yes/No Questions Use yes or no questions to provide students practice using direct object pronouns. Write each question and answer on the board. Circle each noun and pronoun, and draw a line connecting the two. **¿Quieres la blusa? Sí, la quiero. ¿Compras los jeans azules? Sí, los compro. ¿Prefieres las camisetas verdes? Sí, las prefiero.** Continue the activity using other questions.

Práctica de GRAMÁTICA

11 Ropa para una fiesta

Leer Maribel y su amiga hablan de la ropa que quieren comprar para la fiesta del sábado. Completa sus mensajes instantáneos con los pronombres correctos. *(Complete the instant messages by choosing the correct direct object pronouns.)*

mensajero instantáneo

pelirroja16: Quiero comprar un vestido azul pero no tengo mucho dinero. ¿ 1. (Lo/La) compro?

busco_rebaja: Mmm... 2. (me/te) entiendo. Bueno, ¿cuánto cuesta el vestido?

pelirroja16: Veintinueve euros. Y tú, ¿qué necesitas comprar? ¿Una blusa blanca?

busco_rebaja: Ya 3. (la/los) tengo. Necesito unos zapatos. Los zapatos negros son más elegantes. ¿ 4. (Me/Os) entiendes?

pelirroja16: Sí, tienes razón. Si quieres zapatos negros, 5. (nos/los) venden en la Tienda Betún.

busco_rebaja: ¡Vale! También venden vestidos azules. 6. (Nos/Los) tienen por veinte euros.

Expansión
Write what you and your friends prefer to wear to a party.

12 Lo que Enrique quiere

Escribir Identifica lo que Enrique quiere y no quiere comprar. Usa pronombres. *(Use direct object pronouns to tell what Enrique wants or doesn't want to buy.)*

modelo: No le gustan **los zapatos anaranjados.**
No **los** quiere comprar. (No quiere comprar**los.**)

1. Los pantalones son feos.
2. No le gusta la camiseta.
3. Le gustan mucho las camisas.
4. Prefiere los calcetines verdes.
5. El sombrero es horrible.
6. Prefiere los zapatos azules.
7. No necesita pantalones cortos.
8. Prefiere la chaqueta blanca.

Expansión:
Teacher Edition Only
Have students rewrite each answer, changing the placement of the direct object pronoun.

Pronunciación La letra c con a, o, u

AUDIO

Before **a, o,** or **u,** the Spanish **c** is pronounced like the /k/ sound in the English word *call.* Listen and repeat.

ca	→	**ca**misa	**ca**lor	to**ca**r	nun**ca**
co	→	**co**mprar	**co**rto	po**co**	blan**co**
cu	→	**cu**mpleaños	**cu**ando	**cu**aderno	es**cu**ela

Carmen compra pantalones cortos. Carlos tiene calor; quiere una camiseta.

Before a consonant other than **h,** it has the same sound: **clase, octubre.**

Objectives
- Practice direct object pronouns.
- Practice lesson vocabulary.
- Demonstrate pronunciation of the letter **c** with **a, o, u.**

Core Resource
- Audio Program: TXT CD 4 track 6

Practice Sequence
- **Activity 11:** Controlled practice: direct object pronouns
- **Activity 12:** Transitional practice: direct object pronouns
- **Pronunciation:** Oral comprehension and prediction of the letter **c** with **a, o, u**

STANDARDS
1.3 Present information, Acts. 11–12
4.1 Compare languages, Pronunciación

✓ Ongoing Assessment

Dictation Have students write the following dictation with the letter combinations **ca, co,** and **cu: Carolina Camacho es de Cúcuta, Colombia, pero ahora está en Cuenca, Ecuador.**

Differentiating Instruction

Pre-AP

Self-correct As students choose the correct direct object pronoun in Activity 11, encourage them to read both of the possible choices aloud. Advise students to listen for the pronoun that agrees with the noun being replaced, and also makes sense in the context of the sentence.

Inclusion

Alphabetic/Phonetic Awareness Inform students that the hard /k/ sound in Spanish is almost always spelled with the letter **c**. One exception would be words in the metric system that start with the prefix **kilo**. Write **ca co cu** on the board. Have them brainstorm words they have learned that have these sound combinations. Have them come to the board and write these words.

Answers Projectable Transparencies, 4-25

Activity 11

1. Lo **2.** te **3.** la **4.** Me **5.** los **6.** Los

Activity 12

1. No los quiere comprar. (No quiere comprarlos.)
2. No la quiere comprar. (No quiere comprarla.)
3. Las quiere comprar. (Quiere comprarlas.)
4. Los quiere comprar. (Quiere comprarlos.)
5. No lo quiere comprar. (No quiere comprarlo.)
6. Los quiere comprar. (Quiere comprarlos.)
7. No los quiere comprar. (No quiere comprarlos.)
8. La quiere comprar. (Quiere comprarla.)

Objectives
- Practice direct object pronouns.
- **Culture:** Compare different climates.

Core Resource
- *Cuaderno,* pp. 154–156

Practice Sequence
- **Activity 13:** Transitional practice: direct object pronouns
- **Activity 14:** Open ended practice: direct object pronouns, seasons

STANDARDS
1.1 Engage in conversation, Acts. 13, 14
1.3 Present information, Acts. 13, 14
2.1 Practices and perspectives, Act. 14
4.2 Compare cultures, Act. 14
Information Literacy, Comparación cultural/Multiple Intelligences; **Technology Literacy,** Pre-AP

Comparación cultural

Essential Question
Suggested Answer The physical features of our planet, such as mountains, valleys, rivers, lakes, oceans, desert, rain forests, etc., have a great impact on weather patterns.

Expanded Information
Spain is surrounded by the Atlantic Ocean and the Mediterranean Sea, while the country's interior is high and mountainous. These factors give Spain the most varied climate in Europe. **Chile** also has a varied climate. The country stretches 1,800 miles from north to south. It rises from the Pacific Ocean to the Andes mountains, which cover one third of the country.

✓ Ongoing Assessment
Get Help Online
More Practice
my.hrw.com

PARA Y PIENSA **Quick Check** Say five sentences starting with **Quiero...** followed by an item of clothing and have students repeat them replacing the direct object with a corresponding object pronoun. Example: **Quiero las camisetas. Las quiero.** For additional practice, use Reteaching & Practice Copymasters URB 4 pp. 7, 8.

See Activity answers on p. 207.

13 Unos modelos cómicos

Hablar

Maribel y Enrique van a una tienda y combinan ropa de muchos colores. Pregúntale a otro(a) estudiante quién lleva la ropa que describes.
(Ask a partner about Maribel's and Enrique's clothing.)

modelo: gorro

A ¿Quién lleva **el gorro verde**?

B Enrique **lo** lleva.

1. zapatos
2. camisa
3. chaqueta
4. pantalones cortos
5. jeans
6. ¿ ?

Expansión: Teacher Edition Only
Have students write a paragraph about going shopping for clothing.

14 ¿Qué llevas en julio?

Hablar

Comparación cultural

Climas diferentes
How does geography affect a country's climate? Countries near the equator have rainy and dry seasons, but have warm temperatures year-round. Countries in the northern and southern hemispheres have opposite seasons. For example, in **Spain,** July is a summer month and the weather is often hot, but in **Chile** it is a winter month. Chile's varied terrain, from beaches to mountains, and length (over 2,600 miles) create many different climates.

Compara con tu mundo *How does the geography of your area affect the climate?*

Barcelona, España

Los Andes en Chile

En julio, tú y otro(a) estudiante van a **Chile, México, España, Puerto Rico, Argentina** y **Nueva York.** Pregúntale qué ropa lleva. *(Ask a partner what he or she wears in these places in July.)*

A ¿Llevas una camiseta en Chile en julio?

B No, no la llevo. Llevo una chaqueta y...

Expansión: Teacher Edition Only
Ask students to work in pairs and ask each other questions about what to wear in the winter and summer where they live.

Más práctica Cuaderno *pp. 154–156* Cuaderno para hispanohablantes *pp. 155–158*

Get Help Online
my.hrw.com

PARA Y PIENSA

Did you get it? In each sentence, use the correct direct object pronoun.
1. Luisa quiere los pantalones blancos. Ella _____ compra.
2. No quiero la blusa nueva. ¿ _____ quieres tú?
3. Nosotros preferimos las camisas azules. _____ compramos.

Differentiating Instruction

Multiple Intelligences
Naturalistic Organize students into small groups, and assign each group one of the countries listed in Activity 14. Tell students to use their prior knowledge, information from the text, or other research to create a depiction of an outdoor scene in their country in the month of July. Have them write labels and captions in Spanish to describe the climate and what people wear.

Pre-AP
Expand and Elaborate Have students research the climate and geography of one of the countries mentioned in Activity 14 using an encyclopedia or the Internet. Students should include specific information such as the name of the continent where the country is located, longitude, latitude, topographical information, average annual temperatures, and average precipitation.

Todo junto

¡AVANZA! **Goal:** ***Show what you know*** Listen to Maribel and Enrique talk to the salesclerk about what Enrique wants to buy. Then use **e → ie** stem-changing verbs and direct object pronouns to talk about clothing preferences. ***Actividades 15–19***

Telehistoria completa

@HOMETUTOR my.hrw.com **View, Read and Record**

STRATEGIES

Cuando lees
Discover what's forgotten Enrique forgets something in this scene. Find out what he forgot. How does this create a problem?

Cuando escuchas
Take the "emotional temperature" Find out who has the greatest intensity of feeling by listening to voices. Who is the most upset and why?

Escena 1 ***Resumen***
Maribel tiene que ir al centro comercial porque necesita el autógrafo de Trini. Pero Enrique quiere ir de compras en una tienda.

Escena 2 ***Resumen***
Enrique y Maribel están en una tienda, y Enrique quiere comprar mucha ropa. Maribel prefiere ir al centro comercial.

Escena 3

VIDEO DVD

AUDIO

Maribel: Enrique, tienes que pagar. Son las once y media.

Enrique: Un gorro verde. ¡Lo quiero comprar! ¡Tengo que comprarlo!

Maribel: Enrique, ¡pero tú ya tienes un gorro verde!

Enrique: Sí, pero nunca lo llevo.

Maribel: Quieres una chaqueta, ¿no?

Enrique: Tienes razón. La chaqueta... la necesito. *(to the salesclerk)* ¿Vende chaquetas?

Vendedora: ¿En verano? No. Las vendo en el otoño.

Enrique: ¿Cuánto cuesta todo?

Vendedora: Los pantalones cuestan treinta euros, la camisa cuesta veinticinco, y el gorro, quince. Son setenta euros.

Enrique: ¡Mi dinero! ¡No lo tengo!

Maribel: ¡No te entiendo! ¿Quieres ir de compras y no tienes dinero?

Enrique: Está en mi mochila. ¿Dónde está mi mochila? ¿Tienes dinero? En el centro comercial yo compro la comida.

Maribel: ¿Con qué piensas pagar? No tienes dinero.

Differentiating Instruction

Heritage Language Learners

Support What They Know Ask students to recall the problem Enrique has at the end of the Telehistoria. Then encourage them to share an experience they've had in which they lost something important. Have them explain what they lost, why it was important, and what they did to resolve the situation.

Multiple Intelligences

Interpersonal Have students read through the Telehistoria twice silently. The first time, instruct them to read the script for meaning. The second time, tell them to read the script for emotion. Then have volunteers take turns reading lines aloud, emphasizing the emotional tone. Have students name the emotion expressed in each line.

¡AVANZA! **Objective**
- Integrate lesson content.

Core Resources
- Video Program: DVD 1
- Audio Program: TXT CD 4 track 7

Presentation Strategies
- Have students read the Resumen from Escena 1 and Escena 2 to review background information.
- Ask a few quick comprehension questions about the Escena 3 photo. ¿Quiénes están en la foto? ¿Qué tiene la vendedora?
- Show the video or play the audio.

STANDARD
1.2 Understand language

Warm Up Projectable Transparencies, 4-18

Direct Object Pronouns Complete each sentence with **lo, la, los** or **las.**

1. ¿La chaqueta azul? _____ quiero comprar.
2. ¿Unos jeans negros? No _____ compro.
3. ¿El vestido rojo? No _____ tengo.

Answers: 1. La; 2. los; 3. lo

Video Summary

@HOMETUTOR VideoPlus my.hrw.com

Although Maribel has her eye on the time and is eager to leave the clothing store, Enrique continues to look at different items and ask how much they cost. When it finally comes time to pay, Enrique realizes he does not have either his money or his backpack and asks Maribel if she has any money.

Answers Projectable Transparencies, 4-26

Answers for Activities on p. 206.

Activity 13
1. ¿Quién lleva unos zapatos marrones? Enrique los lleva.
2. ¿... una camisa roja? Enrique la lleva.
3. ¿... una chaqueta blanca? Enrique la lleva.
4. ¿... unos pantalones cortos azules? Maribel los lleva.
5. ¿... unos jeans negros? Enrique los lleva.
6. ¿Quién lleva ...?

Activity 14 Answers will vary. Sample answers include:
¿Llevas pantalones cortos en Argentina en julio? No, llevo una chaqueta y un gorro.

Para y piensa **1.** los; **2.** La; **3.** Las

TODO JUNTO

Objective
- Practice using and integrating lesson vocabulary and grammar.

Core Resources
- *Cuaderno,* pp. 157–158
- Audio Program: TXT CD 4 tracks 3, 5, 7, 8, 9

Practice Sequence
- **Activities 15, 16:** Telehistoria comprehension
- **Activity 17:** Open-ended practice: speaking
- **Activity 18:** Open-ended practice: reading, listening, speaking
- **Activity 19:** Open-ended practice: writing

STANDARDS
1.1 Engage in conversation, Acts. 17–18
1.2 Understand language, Acts. 15–16, Act. 18
1.3 Present information, Acts. 16–19, PYP

21st Century **Communication,** Act. 17/ Integration (Financial Literacy); **Creativity and Innovation,** Act. 19

✓ Ongoing Assessment

Rubric Activity 17

Speaking Criteria	Maximum Credit	Partial Credit	Minimum Credit
Content	Questions and answers include a variety of vocabulary. Clues are clear.	Questions and answers do not include enough vocabulary. Clues are somewhat clear.	Questions and answers are not complete. Clues are not clear.
Communi-cation	Easy to follow.	Somewhat easy to follow.	Hard to follow.
Accuracy	Few mistakes in grammar and vocabulary.	Some mistakes in grammar and vocabulary.	Many mistakes in grammar and vocabulary.

Answers Projectable Transparencies, 4-26

Activity 15
1. Falso. ... los precios no son buenos en el....
2. Cierto.
3. Falso. Enrique....
4. Falso. Enrique no tiene dinero.
5. Falso. A Enrique le gusta ser diferente.
6. Falso. ... una chaqueta en el verano.
7. Falso. ... Enrique compra unos pantalones...

Answers continue on p. 209.

15 *Comprensión de los episodios* ¿Cierto o falso?

Escuchar
Leer

Lee las oraciones y di si son ciertas o falsas. Corrige las oraciones falsas. *(Read the sentences and say if they are true or false. Correct the false statements.)*

1. Enrique piensa que los precios son buenos en el centro comercial.
2. Maribel prefiere llegar al centro comercial a las doce.
3. Maribel necesita comprar una chaqueta.
4. Enrique tiene setenta euros para comprar su ropa.
5. A Maribel le gusta ser diferente.
6. Enrique prefiere llevar una chaqueta en el invierno.
7. Enrique compra una chaqueta en la tienda de ropa.

Expansión: Teacher Edition Or[...]
Have students wr[...] two additional fa[...] statements about the three Episodi[...] exchange them w[...] their partners an[...] correct each othe[...] work.

16 *Comprensión de los episodios* Analizar la historia

Escuchar
Leer

Contesta las preguntas sobre los episodios. *(Answer the questions about the episodes.)*

1. ¿Qué estación es?
2. ¿Dónde quiere comprar ropa Enrique?
3. ¿De qué color es el gorro?
4. ¿Cuánto cuestan los pantalones? ¿La camisa? ¿El gorro?
5. ¿Qué problema tiene Enrique?

Expansión
Write a summary of what happens in the Telehistoria.

17 ¡A jugar! Un juego de quién

Digital performance space

Hablar

STRATEGY Hablar
Prepare and don't stress out Create a list of useful questions and possible answers. Include various types of clothes. Review your verb endings. Then just talk!

Da una pista sobre una persona de la clase. Las otras personas de tu grupo te van a hacer preguntas para adivinar quién es. Sigue el modelo. *(Give a clue about someone in your class. The other members of your group will ask you yes/no questions to identify who it is.)*

Expansión: Teacher Edition Only
Ask students t[...] write about th[...] color and type of clothing the[...] are wearing.

Differentiating Instruction

Slower-paced Learners

Sentence Completion Before students complete Activity 16, help them convert each question into the beginning of a sentence. Then have them find the information to complete the sentence. Here are a few examples:

¿Qué estación es? La estación es ____.
¿Dónde quiere comprar ropa Enrique?
Enrique quiere comprar ropa en ____.

Pre-AP

Expand and Elaborate Once students guess the correct person in Activity 17, ask them to take turns creating a descriptive sentence about the person in question. Remind students to use vocabulary related to clothing, as well as personal traits, favorite activities, and emotions. The goal is to keep the description going as long as possible.

18 Integración

Digital performance space

Leer
Escuchar
Hablar

Lee el cupón de descuentos (*discounts*) y escucha el anuncio de la tienda. Describe qué ropa quieres comprar para tus amigos(as) y cuánto cuesta. *(Describe four items you want to buy for your friends and how much each item costs.)*

Fuente 1 Cupón

Fuente 2 Anuncio

Listen and take notes
- ¿Qué venden en la tienda?
- ¿Cuánto cuesta la ropa?

modelo: Quiero comprar un vestido verde para Emily. Cuesta...

Audio Program
TXT CD 4 Tracks 8, 9
Audio Script, TE p. 191b

Expansión:
Teacher Edition Only
Have students talk about three items in the ad or the coupon that they don't want to buy.

19 Un poema de la estación

Digital performance space

Escribir

Escribe un poema sobre una de las estaciones. Incluye los siguientes elementos. *(Write a poem that talks about one of the seasons by including the following elements.)*

Para organizarte:	**modelo:**
• *el nombre de la estación* →	verano
• *dos colores que describen la estación* →	verde, azul
• *tres cosas que quieres* →	quiero zapatos, helado, camisetas
• *cuatro actividades que prefieres hacer* →	prefiero jugar, pasear, leer, descansar
• *una descripción de cómo estás* →	tengo calor

Writing Criteria	Excellent	Good	Needs Work
Content	Your poem includes all of the elements.	Your poem includes some of the elements.	Your poem includes a few of the elements.
Communication	Most of your poem is easy to follow.	Parts of your poem are easy to follow.	Your poem is hard to follow.
Accuracy	Your poem has very few mistakes in grammar and vocabulary.	Your poem has some mistakes in grammar and vocabulary.	Your poem has many mistakes in grammar and vocabulary.

Expansión
Display your poem on a visual that reflects what you have expressed.

Más práctica Cuaderno *pp. 157–158* Cuaderno para hispanohablantes *pp. 159–160*

Get Help Online my.hrw.com

PARA Y PIENSA

Did you get it? Answer each question based on the Telehistoria with **sí,** using direct object pronouns.
1. ¿Necesita Enrique la chaqueta?
2. ¿Prefiere Enrique el gorro verde?
3. ¿Quiere comprar Enrique la comida?

Long-term Retention

Pre-AP Integration

Activity 18 Have students write a list of the clothing items they would like to buy for their summer vacation.

✓ Ongoing Assessment

Rubric Activity 18 Listening/Speaking

Proficient	Not There Yet
Student takes detailed notes and correctly describes the items and how much they cost.	Student takes few notes and cannot describe the items and how much they cost.

To customize your own rubrics, use the ***Generate Success*** *Rubric Generator and Graphic Organizers.*

✓ Ongoing Assessment

Get Help Online More Practice my.hrw.com

PARA Y PIENSA **Remediation** If students have difficulty answering the Para y piensa questions, ask them to review the Telehistoria on p. 207. For additional practice, use Reteaching & Practice Copymasters URB 4, pp. 7, 9.

Answers Projectable Transparencies, 4-26 and 4-27

Answers continued from p. 208.

Activity 16
1. Es el verano.
2. Enrique quiere comprar ropa en una tienda.
3. El gorro es verde.
4. Los pantalones cuestan treinta euros. La camisa cuesta veinticinco euros. El gorro cuesta quince euros.
5. Enrique no tiene dinero.

Activity 17 Answers will vary. Sample answers:
Estudiante A: Lleva unos jeans azules.
Estudiante B: ¿Tiene una camiseta blanca?
Estudiante A: Sí, la tiene. (No, no la tiene.)
Estudiante C: ¿Lleva unos calcetines rojos?
Estudiante A: Sí, los lleva. (No, no los lleva.)
Estudiante B: ¿Es Justin?
Estudiante A: ¡Sí, tienes razón! (No, no tienes razón.)

Activity 18 Answers will vary. Sample answers:
Quiero comprar unos pantalones negros para Ramón. Cuestan veinte euros.

Activity 19 Answers should follow instructions in the modelo for writing the poem about the seasons.

Para y piensa
1. Sí, Enrique la necesita. 2. Sí, lo prefiere.
3. Sí, la quiere comprar. Sí, Enrique quiere comprarla.

Differentiating Instruction

Inclusion

Multisensory Input/Output Before doing Activity 18, have them read the script as they listen to the announcement. Help them take notes by listing first the items on sale for boys and next the items on sale for girls. Ask comprehension questions about what they have written. For example: **¿Qué ropa venden para chicos? ¿Qué ropa venden para chicas?** Use these same questions for the coupon.

Multiple Intelligences

Musical/Rhythmic As students compose their poems, remind them to consider the sound and rhythm of the words they choose. They might focus on similar beginning sounds: **verano, verde.** Or they might create a pattern with endings: **quiero jugar, pasear, descansar.** Perhaps they want to create contrast with the sounds and rhythms they choose. Allow them to read their poetry aloud.

¡AVANZA! Objectives

- Learn about Spanish poet Antonio Colinas.
- Discuss the poet's feelings about winter.
- Compare a description of winter in a poem with winter in your own region.

Core Resource

- Audio Program: TXT CD 4 track 10

Presentation Strategies

- Play the audio as students read and listen to the poem.
- Ask students to take turns reading the poem lines. Correct pronunciation as needed.
- Ask students to think about how Colinas uses nature (animals, plants, weather) to express his thoughts.

STANDARDS

1.2 Understand language
2.1 Practices and perspectives
4.1 Compare languages
4.2 Compare cultures

Warm Up Projectable Transparencies, 4-19

Direct Object Pronouns Complete the sentences by choosing the correct direct object pronoun.

1. Quiero la camiseta verde. ¿(Lo / La) compro?
2. ¿Quieres calcetines rojos? (Las / Los) venden en la Tienda Ramón.
3. No quiero el gorro. ¿(Me / Lo) quieres tú?
4. No (te / nos) entiendo. ¿No tienes el dinero?

Answers: 1. La; 2. Los; 3. Lo; 4. te

Culture

Background Information

El Premio Nacional de Literatura en la modalidad de Poesía is awarded annually in Spain to a poet whose work has been published in Spain in the year preceding the award. A panel of distinguished judges selects the winner, who receives 15,000 euros in addition to being honored with this prestigious title. It is comparable to the Pulitzer Prize in the U.S.

Lectura

Additional readings at my.hrw.com SPANISH InterActive Reader

¡AVANZA! **Goal:** Read a poem by a Spanish poet. Then talk about what you have read and describe winter in your region.

AUDIO

Las memorias del invierno

Antonio Colinas is a poet and novelist from León, in northern Spain. He published the following poem in 1988.

STRATEGY Leer

Find the feelings Find phrases that show the poet's feelings and write them in a chart like the one below. Write the feeling after each phrase.

Emotions in *Invierno tardío* by Colinas
- Phrase: es como primavera temprana / Feeling: happiness
- Phrase: / Feeling:
- Phrase: / Feeling:

Antonio Colinas

Antonio Colinas nació[1] en 1946 en La Bañeza, en la provincia de León, España. Escribe poesía, novelas, ensayos[2] y crítica. También estudia literatura italiana y la adapta al español. Su poesía ha ganado[3] muchos premios[4] en España, como el Premio Nacional de Literatura, en 1982. Ahora vive en Salamanca, España.

[1] was born [2] essays [3] has won [4] awards

Differentiating Instruction

English Learners

Increase Interaction Ask English learners to work on the strategy with native English speakers. Have them create a chart together and write the name of each feeling or emotion in English and the English learner's native language.

Heritage Language Learners

Literacy Skills Encourage students to expand their vocabulary by asking them to search in a Spanish dictionary for examples of words that belong to the same family as words in the poem. Ask: **¿Qué palabra es similar a tardío? (tarde) ¿A nieve o nieva? (nevar, nevada) ¿A florido? (flor) ¿A humanidad? (humano)**

Invierno tardío

No es increíble cuanto ven mis ojos[5]:
nieva sobre el almendro florido[6],
nieva sobre la nieve.
Este invierno mi ánimo[7]
es como primavera temprana,
es como almendro florido
bajo la nieve.

Hay demasiado[8] frío
esta tarde en el mundo[9].
Pero abro la puerta a mi perro
y con él entra en casa[10] calor,
entra la humanidad.

[5] **ven...** my eyes see
[6] **sobre...** on the flowery almond tree
[7] spirit [8] too much [9] world [10] house

<56>

PARA Y PIENSA

¿Comprendiste?

1. ¿De dónde es Antonio Colinas? ¿Qué escribe? ¿Dónde vive ahora?
2. ¿Dónde está la persona en el poema? ¿Qué mira? En tu opinión, ¿está triste o contenta la persona?
3. ¿Piensas que el perro es un buen amigo? ¿Por qué?

¿Y tú?

¿Cómo es el invierno en tu región? ¿Qué te gusta hacer?

Comparisons

English Language Connection

Cognates Ask students to search the poem for words that have English cognates, and to list the cognate pairs on the board. They should include: **increíble, humanidad.**

Communication

Pair Work

Cut the poem into separate lines. Present the poem in this fashion to pairs of students and ask them to order the lines. After they have finished and presented their work, then ask them to read the original version. Discuss the differences with the class.

Long-term Retention

Personalize It

Present to the class the concept of simile, a figure of speech expressing comparison by the use of the terms *like,* or *as*. Point to the word **como** in the poem and explain that without the accent this word means *like.* Ask students to find examples of similes in the poem. Then have them compose their own simile about winter starting with the following phrase. **Este invierno mi ánimo es como...**

Differentiating Instruction

Pre-AP

Summarize Ask students to write a brief summary of *Invierno tardío.* Encourage them to include as many details as possible, including what the poem is about, how the author feels, and how it makes them feel.

Multiple Intelligences

Naturalist Give students the following questions about flowering almond trees and ask them to research the answers. **¿Dónde hay almendros? ¿De qué color son?** Then ask them to choose a plant or flower in their region and describe what happens to it in winter.

Answers

Para y piensa
¿Comprendiste?

1. Antonio Colinas es de la provincia de León, España. Él escribe poesía, novelas, ensayos y crítica. Vive en Salamanca, España.
2. Está en casa. Mira el almendro y la nieve. Está contenta.
3. Sí, el perro es un buen amigo porque con él entra la humanidad en casa.

¿Y tú? Answers will vary. Sample answer: Hace mucho frío en el invierno en mi región. Me gusta estar en casa, descansar y mirar la televisión.

Objectives
- Learn about the history of the Moors in Spain.
- Read about the distinctive decorative styles of the Alhambra.
- Use perspectives from music, health, and language to better understand the Arab legacy in Spain.

Presentation Strategies
- Ask if students are aware of the relationship between Arab Muslims and Spain.
- Draw students' attention to the pictures, and ask them to reflect on the architectural style.

STANDARDS
1.3 Present information
3.1 Knowledge of other disciplines
3.2 Acquire information
21st Century **Technology Literacy,** Pre-AP

Connections
La historia
The *oud,* ancestor of the guitar, has an ancient history, and has been traced to 1600 B.C. in Mesopotamia. In the 9th century A.D., the instrument was used in healing, and it is believed that it was used this way in Arab Spain during the 11th century. It was thought to be invigorating, at the same time bringing harmony to the body and the heart.

Answers
Conexiones Students can create their design by drawing, building a model, or using computer software.

Proyecto 1 At the core of the group Al-Andalus are Tarik Banzi and Julia Banzi. Their music is inspired by the music of Moorish Spain from the 8th to 15th centuries. They play in various locations, including museums, concert halls, international festivals, embassies, and colleges. Examples: 1991 Portland Classical Guitar Festival, Smithsonian Institute, Embassy of Egypt in Washington, D.C.

Proyecto 2 Olive oil is used as a moisturizer by many. It is also considered a healthy cooking oil.

Proyecto 3
almohada – pillow; **álgebra** – algebra; **algodón** – cotton; **ajedrez** – chess; **alcachofa** – artichoke; **azúcar** – sugar.

Conexiones *El arte*

Los árabes en España

For almost 800 years, from 711 to 1492, the Moors, Arab Muslims from northern Africa, occupied an area in southern Spain called **Al-Andalus,** now known as **Andalucía.** This was a period of rich cultural exchange in the arts, sciences, mathematics, agriculture, and architecture.

The Alhambra palace in Granada is a notable example of Moorish architecture in Spain. The interior is exquisitely detailed, bright, and airy. Ornately carved pillars and arches open onto sunny courtyards. The walls and ceilings are decorated with intricate geometric designs.

Design a courtyard based on the architectural styles illustrated in these pictures of the Alhambra. Create a drawing or model to show your design.

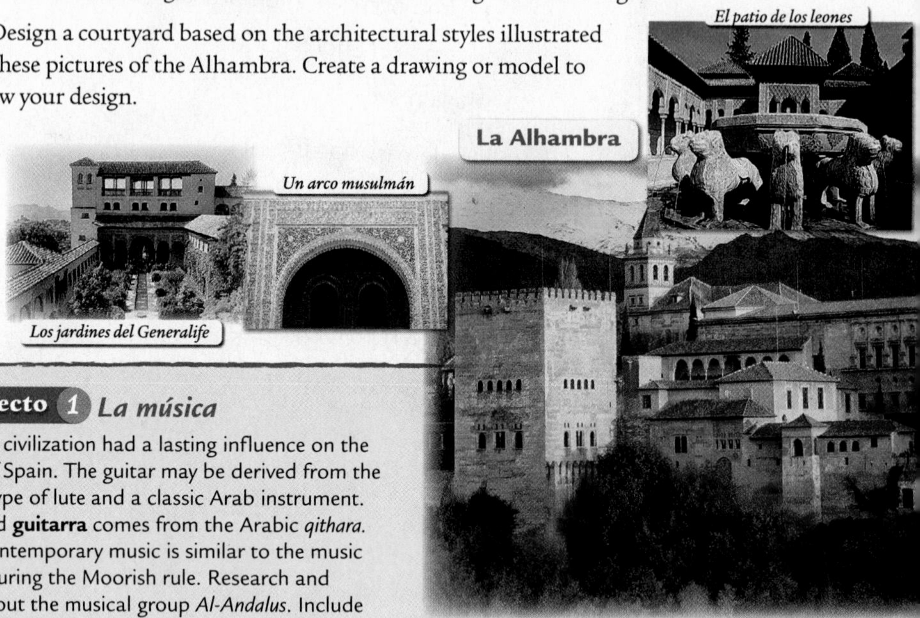

El patio de los leones
La Alhambra
Un arco musulmán
Los jardines del Generalife

Proyecto 1 *La música*
Moorish civilization had a lasting influence on the music of Spain. The guitar may be derived from the oud, a type of lute and a classic Arab instrument. The word **guitarra** comes from the Arabic *qithara.* Some contemporary music is similar to the music played during the Moorish rule. Research and write about the musical group *Al-Andalus.* Include the members of the group, the places where they perform, and a description of their music.

Proyecto 2 *La salud*
Olives have always been a part of Spanish tradition. Olive seeds that date back 8,000 years have been found in Spain. The majority of olive trees grown in the country are found in **Andalucía.** Spain is also one of the world's foremost producers of olive oil. Research and write about the health and beauty benefits of olives and olive oil. Describe how they are used on a daily basis.

Proyecto 3 *El lenguaje*
The Moors brought many concepts and inventions to Spain. The Arabic words for many of these things still exist in Spanish. Often these words begin with **al-** or **a-.** Some examples are **almohada, álgebra, algodón,** and **ajedrez.** Using a Spanish-English dictionary, write the meanings of these words. Then find three more Spanish words that begin with **al-,** write their English definitions, and use the Internet or the library to find out if they have Arabic origin.

Differentiating Instruction

English Learners
Increase Interaction Have students take turns reading the Conexiones aloud. After each paragraph, ask them to list any words that they don't understand and clarify their meaning. Then ask brief questions to check comprehension. For example: For how many years did the Moors occupy Spain? Where is **Andalucía?** Where is the Alhambra?

Pre-AP
Expand and Elaborate Ask students to work in groups to research on the Internet additional information about the Moors and their occupation of Spain and to construct a timeline starting with the year 711 and ending in 1492, listing additional important dates and significant events. Have them provide a brief description of what happened on each date. Search Key Words: Moors + Spain.

En resumen

Vocabulario y gramática

ANIMATEDGRAMMAR Interactive Flashcards my.hrw.com

Vocabulario

Talk About Shopping

el centro comercial	*shopping center, mall*	el dólar	*dollar*
¿Cuánto cuesta(n)?	*How much does it (do they) cost?*	el euro	*euro*
Cuesta(n)...	*It costs . . . (They cost . . .)*	ir de compras	*to go shopping*
el dinero	*money*	pagar	*to pay*
		el precio	*price*
		la tienda	*store*

Expressions with *tener*

tener calor	*to be hot*
tener frío	*to be cold*
tener razón	*to be right*
tener suerte	*to be lucky*

Describe Clothing

la blusa	*blouse*	nuevo(a)	*new*
los calcetines	*socks*	los pantalones	*pants*
la camisa	*shirt*	los pantalones cortos	*shorts*
la camiseta	*T-shirt*	la ropa	*clothing*
la chaqueta	*jacket*	el sombrero	*hat*
feo(a)	*ugly*	el vestido	*dress*
el gorro	*winter hat*	los zapatos	*shoes*
los jeans	*jeans*		
llevar	*to wear*		

Discuss Seasons

la estación (*pl.* las estaciones)	*season*
el invierno	*winter*
el otoño	*autumn, fall*
la primavera	*spring*
el verano	*summer*

Other Words and Phrases

durante	*during*
cerrar (ie)	*to close*
empezar (ie)	*to begin*
entender (ie)	*to understand*
pensar (ie)	*to think, to plan*
preferir (ie)	*to prefer*
querer (ie)	*to want*

Colors

amarillo(a)	*yellow*	marrón (*pl.* marrones)	*brown*
anaranjado(a)	*orange*	negro(a)	*black*
azul	*blue*	rojo(a)	*red*
blanco(a)	*white*	verde	*green*

Gramática

Nota gramatical: **tener** expressions *p. 198*

Stem-Changing Verbs: e → ie

For **e** → **ie** stem-changing verbs, the **e** of the stem changes to **ie** in all forms except **nosotros(as)** and **vosotros(as)**.

querer *to want*	
quiero	**queremos**
quieres	**queréis**
quiere	**quieren**

Direct Object Pronouns

Direct object pronouns can be used to replace direct object nouns.

Singular		Plural	
me	*me*	nos	*us*
te	*you (familiar)*	os	*you (familiar)*
lo	*you (formal), him, it*	los	*you, them*
la	*you (formal), her, it*	las	*you, them*

Practice Spanish with Holt McDougal Apps!

Objective

- Review lesson vocabulary and grammar.

DIGITAL SPANISH

Interactive Flashcards Students can hear every target vocabulary word pronounced in authentic Spanish. Flashcards have Spanish on one side, and a picture or a translation on the other.

Review Games Matching, concentration, hangman, and word search are just a sampling of the fun, interactive games students can play to review for the test.

performance space
News + Networking
@HOMETUTOR
CULTURA Interactiva

- **Audio and Video Resources**
- **Interactive Flashcards**
- **Review Activities**
- **WebQuest**
- **Conjuguemos.com**

Long-term Retention

Study Tips

Have students study the first category of words in En resumen for one minute. Then tell them to close their books and write down as many words as they can remember in two minutes. They should then open their book and check their work. Continue with the other categories.

Communication

Humor and Creativity

Ask students to make up their own skits using as many of the vocabulary terms and grammatical expressions from En resumen as they can. Divide the class into groups of three and have each group focus on a specific set of vocabulary. Assign shopping and clothing vocabulary to some groups; seasons, expressions with **tener,** and "other words and phrases" to other groups; and stem-changing verbs and direct object pronouns to the remaining groups.

Differentiating Instruction

Slower-paced Learners

Sentence Completion To help students put sentences together, provide them with the following sentence frame. **Durante el/la** (season) **cuando tengo... llevo** (clothing items) + (color). **Mi amigo(a) lleva** (clothing item) + color. Encourage them to use the En resumen vocabulary to find the correct words.

Multiple Intelligences

Visual Learners Give each student a blank sheet of paper and a black crayon or marker. Tell students to think of a color and draw a large object that they associate with that color. For example: **rojo** → an apple. Call on students to show their drawing as other students identify the color.

Objective
- Review lesson grammar and vocabulary.

Core Resources
- *Cuaderno,* pp. 159–170
- Audio Program: TXT CD 4 track 11

Presentation Strategies
- Before playing the audio for Activity 1, ask students to listen to it carefully and pay special attention to the articles of clothing she mentions.
- Before doing Activities 2–4 review stem-changing **e → ie** verbs by saying a subject followed by an infinitive and asking students to supply the correct verb form. For example: **tú: empezar → tú empiezas.**
- For Activity 3, remind students that the season often determines what you wear.
- Ask students to generate two questions to ask their classmates, based on the Comparación cultural.

STANDARDS
1.2 Understand language, Act. 1
1.3 Present information, Acts. 2-5
4.2 Compare cultures, Act. 5
21st Century **Media Literacy,** Heritage Language Learners

Warm Up Projectable Transparencies, 4-19

Querer Fill in the blanks with the appropriate forms of **querer.**

1. Nosotros _____ los pantalones cortos.
2. Yo _____ el gorro rojo.
3. Tú _____ la camiseta amarilla.
4. María _____ la chaqueta azul.
5. Ustedes _____ los calcetines verdes.

Answers: 1. queremos; 2. quiero; 3. quieres; 4. quiere; 5. quieren

✓ Ongoing Assessment
Get Help Online
More Practice
my.hrw.com

Remediation If students achieve less than 80% accuracy with the activities, direct them to review pp. 191, 198, 199, 203–204, 206, 210–211 and to get help online at my.hrw.com.

See Activity answers on p. 215.

Lección 1

Repaso de la lección

@HOMETUTOR my.hrw.com

¡LLEGADA!

Now you can
- talk about what clothes you want to buy
- say what you wear in different seasons

Using
- **tener** expressions
- stem-changing verbs: **e → ie**
- direct object pronouns

To review
- stem-changing verbs: **e → ie** p. 199
- direct object pronouns p. 204

1 Listen and understand

AUDIO

Escucha a Paula hablar de la ropa. Para cada artículo de ropa, indica si quiere comprarlo o no. Usa pronombres de objetos directos. *(Listen to Paula and indicate whether she wants to buy each article of clothing or not. Use direct object pronouns.)*

1. 
2. 
3. 
4. 
5. 
6. 

To review
- stem-changing verbs: **e → ie** p. 199

2 Talk about what clothes you want to buy

Fernando va de compras con sus padres. ¿Qué dice? *(Tell what Fernando says about his shopping experience.)*

preferir	cerrar	entender
empezar	pensar	querer

Las clases __**1.**__ el lunes y necesito ropa. Yo __**2.**__ comprar unas camisetas y unos pantalones pero no tengo mucho dinero. Yo __**3.**__ las camisetas a las camisas. Yo no __**4.**__ por qué una camiseta cuesta más en el centro comercial que en otras tiendas. Mi amiga Carla __**5.**__ que hay ropa más bonita y menos cara en la tienda Moda Zaragoza. Necesito ir hoy porque la tienda __**6.**__ los domingos.

Differentiating Instruction

Slower-paced Learners
Personalize It Ask students to adapt and rewrite Activity 2 by adding the names of people and stores they know, by using the name of their favorite mall, and by talking about clothing they have recently bought or plan to buy soon.

Pre-AP
Circumlocution Ask students to look up additional items of clothing in a Spanish-English dictionary. For example: **suéter** (sweater), **sandalias** (sandals), **tenis** (sneakers), etc. Ask them to describe the clothing in Spanish so that their classmates understand, and then refer to those items with pronouns. For example: **Las sandalias son zapatos. Las llevo en el verano.**

To review
- **tener** expressions p. 198
- stem-changing verbs: **e → ie** p. 199

3 Talk about what clothes you want to buy

Indica si estas personas tienen calor o tienen frío basado en lo que piensan comprar. *(Indicate if these people are hot or cold based on what they are thinking about buying.)*

modelo: Ana / blusa de verano
Ana piensa comprar una blusa de verano porque tiene calor.

1. Juan y yo / gorros
2. yo / pantalones cortos
3. tú / chaqueta
4. Laura y Carlos / camisetas de verano
5. ustedes / calcetines de invierno
6. Pilar / vestido de primavera

To review
- direct object pronouns p. 204

4 Say what you wear in different seasons

Escribe oraciones para decir quién prefiere llevar la ropa. *(Tell who prefers to wear these clothing items.)*

modelo: los zapatos negros (Juan)
Juan los prefiere llevar. (Juan prefiere llevarlos.)

1. los pantalones cortos (Rosa)
2. las camisas azules (ellas)
3. el sombrero rojo (yo)
4. la camiseta anaranjada (Carlos)
5. el gorro negro (ellos)
6. la blusa amarilla (nosotros)
7. los calcetines blancos (ustedes)
8. la chaqueta marrón (tú)
9. los zapatos marrones (usted)
10. el vestido verde (Amanda)

To review
- **Sevillanas** p. 191
- Comparación cultural pp. 203, 206
- Lectura pp. 210–211

5 Spain and Chile

Comparación cultural

Answer these culture questions.

1. What are the characteristics of **sevillanas**?
2. How do the climates of Spain and Chile differ in July and why?
3. What are some characteristics of surrealist art?
4. What season is represented in Antonio Colinas' poem? How does the speaker of the poem feel and why?

Más práctica Cuaderno *pp. 159–170* Cuaderno para hispanohablantes *pp. 161–170*

Get Help Online my.hrw.com

Differentiating Instruction

Heritage Language Learners

Support What They Know Ask students which fashion magazines in Spanish are popular among teens in their country of origin. If possible, ask them to bring magazines to share with their classmates and to use as a starting point to discuss fashion's latest trends.

Multiple Intelligences

Kinesthetic Tell students that they are going to have a fashion show. Bring to class several large-sized, colorful clothing items (or ask students to bring them). Students will put on these items over their clothes and model them for their classmates. Assign one student to be the presenter and describe the clothes being modeled.

REPASO DE LA LECCIÓN

✓ Ongoing Assessment

Alternative Strategy Have students redo Activity 4, replacing the verb **preferir** with **pensar** or **querer** and using different clothing items. For example: **los pantalones verdes (Juan)—Juan los piensa llevar. (Juan piensa llevarlos.)**

Answers Projectable Transparencies, 4-27

Answers continued from p. 214.

Activity 1
1. Ella no quiere comprarlos.
2. Ella quiere comprarla.
3. Ella no quiere comprarlo.
4. Ella quiere comprarlos.
5. Ella no quiere comprarla.
6. Ella quiere comprarlo.

Activity 2
1. empiezan
2. quiero
3. prefiero
4. entiendo
5. piensa
6. cierra

Activity 3
1. Juan y yo pensamos comprar unos gorros porque tenemos frío.
2. Yo pienso comprar unos... porque tengo calor.
3. Tú piensas comprar una... porque tienes frío.
4. ...piensan comprar unas... porque tienen calor.
5. ...piensan comprar unos... porque tienen frío.
6. ...piensa comprar un... porque tiene calor.

Activity 4
1. Rosa los prefiere llevar.
2. Ellas las prefieren llevar.
3. Yo lo prefiero llevar.
4. Carlos la prefiere llevar.
5. Ellos lo prefieren llevar.
6. Nosotros la preferimos llevar.
7. Ustedes los prefieren llevar.
8. Tú la prefieres llevar.
9. Usted los prefiere llevar.
10. Amanda lo prefiere llevar.

Activity 5
1. **Sevillanas** are similar to **flamenco**, which involves singing, dance, and guitar as well as rhythmic clapping or foot taps.
2. The climates of Spain and Chile differ in July because these countries are located in different hemispheres. In Spain July is a summer month, but in Chile it is a winter month.
3. In surrealist art, the imagery reflects an artist's imagination and is often inspired by dreams.
4. The season represented in Antonio Colinas' poem is winter. The speaker of the poem feels happy because it feels like early spring.

Lesson Overview

Culture at a Glance

Topic & Activity	Essential Question
Madrid's Teatro de la Comedia pp. 216–217	What do you like to do on weekends?
The local markets p. 225	How do local markets reflect the culture of an area?
Las meninas p. 230	Why might an artist create a version of another artist's masterpiece?
Weekends in Spain and Chile pp. 234–235	What are some of the weekend activities that people enjoy in Spain and Chile?
Paintings from Spain and Chile p. 236	What messages can an artist communicate through a painting?
Culture Review p. 239	What are some aspects of culture in Spain, Guatemala, and Chile?

COMPARISON COUNTRIES España Guatemala Chile

Practice at a Glance

	Objective	Activity & Skill
Vocabulary	In Town	1: Reading; 3: Listening/Reading; 6: Writing; 7: Speaking; 8: Speaking; 9: Listening/Reading; 10: Speaking; 15: Listening/Reading; 16: Listening/Reading; 18: Reading/Listening/Speaking; Repaso 3: Writing
Vocabulary	In a Restaurant	2: Speaking; 4: Speaking; 11: Writing/Speaking; 12: Writing/Speaking; 13: Listening/Writing; 14: Speaking; 17: Speaking; 19: Writing; Repaso 1: Listening; Repaso 4: Writing
Grammar	Stem-changing verbs: **o → ue**	5: Reading/Writing; 6: Writing; 7: Speaking; 8: Speaking; 10: Speaking; 18: Reading/Listening/Speaking; Repaso 3: Writing
Grammar	**Ir a** + infinitive	4: Speaking; 18: Reading/Listening/Speaking; Repaso 2: Writing
Grammar	Stem-changing verbs: **e → i**	11: Writing/Speaking; 12: Writing/Speaking; 13: Listening/Writing; 14: Speaking; 19: Writing; Repaso 4: Writing
Communication	Describe places and events in town	1: Reading; 2: Speaking; 3: Listening/Reading; 6: Writing; 9: Listening/Reading; 10: Speaking; 18: Reading/Listening/Speaking; Repaso 3: Writing
Communication	Say what you are going to do	4: Speaking; 7: Speaking; 18: Reading/Listening/Speaking; Repaso 2: Writing
Communication	Order from a menu	11: Writing/Speaking; 17: Speaking; Repaso 3: Writing; Repaso 4: Writing
Communication	Pronunciation: the letter **c** with **e, i**	La letra **c** con **e, i** p. 229: Listening
Recycle	Present tense of **-er** verbs	2: Speaking
Recycle	**Tener** expressions	14: Speaking
Recycle	Direct object pronouns	12: Writing/Speaking
Recycle	The verb **ir**	4: Speaking

The following presentations are recorded in the Audio Program for ***¡Avancemos!***

- **¡A responder!** *page 219*
- **13: ¿Qué sirven en el café?** *page 230*
- **18: Integración** *page 233*
- **Repaso de la lección** *page 238*
  1: Listen and understand
- **Repaso inclusivo** *page 242*
  1: Listen, understand, and compare

¡A responder! CD 4 track 13

1. la ensalada
2. el pescado
3. las patatas
4. el bistec
5. el pollo
6. las verduras
7. el arroz
8. el pastel

13 | ¿Qué sirven en el café?

TXT CD 4 track 17

Enrique: Hola, soy Enrique. Estoy en el Café Moderno. ¡Los camareros trabajan mucho hoy! Ahora sirven pollo y arroz.
Señor Fuentes, ¿qué sirve usted?

Sr. Fuentes: Sirvo bistec y patatas.

Enrique: Camarero, ¿vas a servir brócoli?

Camarero: Sí, lo sirvo ahora.

Camarera: Hola. Soy camarera. Ahora sirvo un pescado. Es muy rico.

Enrique: Luis y José, ¿qué servís vosotros?

Luis: Servimos verduras. Son muy nutritivas.

Enrique: Hola, Ana. ¿Qué sirves después de los platos principales?

Ana: De postre, sirvo un pastel de frutas. Es más nutritivo que un pastel de chocolate.

18 | Integración TXT CD 4 tracks 19, 20

Hay muchas actividades hoy en el centro. Si quieres ver una película en inglés, hay películas de Estados Unidos en el Cine Ábaco. Pero, si te gustan las películas de España, puedes ir a la Biblioteca Nacional. Hoy en el Restaurante Oberón sirven paella y pescado. En el Café Almagro hay pasteles y café. También puedes pasear en el Parque del Buen Retiro. O, si prefieres escuchar música rock, hay un concierto en la Plaza de la Moncloa. Hay otro concierto, de música clásica, en el Teatro Marquina. ¡Ah! Otra actividad... puedes ir de compras en el centro comercial. Pero necesitan volver al hotel a las seis, ¿vale?

For **¡AvanzaRap!** scripts, see the **¡AvanzaRap! DVD.**

Repaso de la lección TXT CD 4 track 22

1 Listen and understand

Raúl: Una mesa para dos.

Camarero: ¿Para dos? Por aquí, por favor. En el menú ustedes van a ver los platos principales. Todos son ricos.

Raúl: Mmmm. Me gusta mucho el bistec. Voy a pedir el bistec con arroz. Y para beber, quiero un refresco.

Camarero: Muy bien. ¿Y para usted, señorita?

Tere: Prefiero el pescado con una ensalada. Y para beber, un jugo, por favor.

Camarero: ¿Van a pedir postre después?

Raúl: Sí, pero no encuentro los postres en el menú... Ah, aquí están. De postre quiero el pastel de manzana.

Tere: Yo prefiero el helado.

Camarero: El pastel para el señor y el helado para la señorita. Vuelvo en un minuto.

Repaso inclusivo TXT CD 4 track 24

1 Listen, understand, and compare

Camarero: Buenas tardes. ¿Ustedes van a pedir ahora?

Carlitos: Sí. Tengo ganas de comer papas fritas.

Sra. Estrada: No, no. Hoy no vas a comerlas.

Camarero: ¿Quieren empezar con sopa? También servimos unas ensaladas muy ricas.

Carlitos: Bueno... Empiezo con sopa, y de plato principal, pollo con papas fritas.

Sra. Estrada: Está bien. Yo tengo mucha hambre. Quiero empezar con una ensalada de tomates. Y de plato principal... el pescado.

Camarero: Perdón, señora, hoy no lo servimos. ¿Prefiere otro plato?

Sra. Estrada: Bueno... yo también pido el pollo, pero con frijoles.

Camarero: ¿Y para beber?

Carlitos: Un refresco.

Sra. Estrada: Y yo voy a beber agua.

Camarero: Muy bien. Vuelvo en un minuto con las bebidas.

Resource List

Everything you need to ...

Plan

Teacher One Stop

✓ Lesson Plans
✓ Teacher Resources
✓ Audio and Video

Present

Interactive Whiteboard Lessons

Teacher One Stop with Projectable Transparencies

Power Presentations

AnimatedGrammar

Assess

Online Assessment

✓ Assessments for on-level, modified, pre-AP, and heritage learners
✓ Create customized tests with **Examview Assessment Suite**
✓ **performance space**
✓ *Generate Success* Rubric Generator

Print

Plan	Present	Practice	Assess
URB 4 • Video Scripts pp. 71–72 • Family Involvement Activity p. 92 • Absent Student Copymasters pp. 101–111 **Best Practices Toolkit**	**URB 4** • Video Activities pp. 59–66	• *Cuaderno* pp. 171–196 • *Cuaderno para hispanohablantes* pp. 171–196 • *Lecturas para todos* pp. 37–41 • *Lecturas para hispanohablantes* • *¡AvanzaCómics! SúperBruno y Nati,* Episodio 2 **URB 4** • Practice Games pp. 39–46 • Audio Scripts pp. 77–82 • Fine Art Activities pp. 88–89	**Differentiated Assessment Program** **URB 4** • Did you get it? Reteaching and Practice Copymasters pp. 13–24

Projectable Transparencies (Teacher One Stop, my.hrw.com)

Culture	Presentation and Practice	Classroom Management
• Atlas Maps 1–6 • Map of Spain 1 • Fine Art Transparencies 4, 5	• Vocabulary Transparencies 8, 9 • Grammar Presentation Transparencies 12, 13 • Situational Transparencies and label overlay 14, 15 • Situational Student Copymasters pp. 1, 2	• Warm Up Transparencies 20–23 • Student Book Answer Transparencies 28–31

Audio and Video

Audio	Video	¡AvanzaRap! DVD
• Student Book Audio CD 4 Tracks 12–24 • Workbook Audio CD 2 Tracks 31–40 • Heritage Learners Audio CD 1 Tracks 29–32, CD 3 Tracks 23–28 • Assessment Audio CD 1 Tracks 23–28 • *Lecturas para todos* Audio CD 1 Track 8, CD 2 Tracks 1–6 • Sing-along Songs Audio CD	• Vocabulary Video DVD 1 • *Telehistoria* DVD 1 Escena 1 Escena 2 Escena 3 Completa • Culture Video DVD 1	• Video animations of all **¡AvanzaRap!** songs (with Karaoke track) • Interactive DVD Activities • Teaching Suggestions • **¡AvanzaRap!** Activity Masters • **¡AvanzaRap!** video scripts and answers

Online and Media Resources

Student	Teacher
Available online at my.hrw.com • Online Student Edition • News Networking • performance space • @HOMETUTOR • Cultura Interactiva • WebQuests • Interactive Flashcards • Review Games • Self-Check Quiz **Student One Stop** **Holt McDougal Spanish Apps**	**Teacher One Stop (also available at my.hrw.com)** • Interactive Teacher's Edition • All print, audio, and video resources • Projectable Transparencies • Lesson Plans • TPRS • Examview Assessment Suite **Available online at my.hrw.com** *Generate Success* Rubric Generator and Graphic Organizers **Power Presentations**

Differentiated Assessment

On-level	Modified	Pre-AP	Heritage Learners
• Vocabulary Recognition Quiz p. 166 • Vocabulary Production Quiz p. 167 • Grammar Quizzes pp. 168–169 • Culture Quiz p. 170 • On-level Lesson Test pp. 171–177 • On-level Unit Test pp. 183–189 • On-level Midterm pp. 195–204	• Modified Lesson Test pp. 131–137 • Modified Unit Test pp. 143–149 • Modified Midterm pp. 155–164	• Pre-AP Lesson Test pp.131–137 • Pre-AP Unit Test pp. 143–149 • Pre-AP Midterm pp. 155–164	• Heritage Learners Lesson Test pp. 137–143 • Heritage Learners Unit Test pp. 149–155 • Heritage Learners Midterm pp. 161–170

Core Pacing Guide

50 Minute (9 Day)

	Objectives/Focus	Teach	Practice	Assess/HW Options
DAY 1	**Culture:** learn about Spain **Vocabulary:** places and events in town • Warm Up OHT 20 5 min	Lesson Opener pp. 216–217 **Presentación de vocabulario** pp. 218–219 • Read A–F • View video DVD 1 • Play audio TXT CD 4 track 12 • *¡A responder!* TXT CD 4 track 13 25 min	Lesson Opener pp. 216–217 **Práctica de vocabulario** p. 220 • Acts.1, 2 15 min	**Assess:** *Para y piensa* p. 220 5 min **Homework:** *Cuaderno* pp. 171–173 @HomeTutor
DAY 2	**Communication:** talking about transportation • Warm Up OHT 20 • Check Homework 5 min	**Vocabulario en contexto** pp. 221–222 • *Telehistoria escena 1* DVD 1 • *Nota gramatical:* **ir a** + infinitive 20 min	**Vocabulario en contexto** pp. 221–222 • Act. 3 TXT CD 4 track 14 • Act. 4 20 min	**Assess:** *Para y piensa* p. 222 5 min **Homework:** *Cuaderno* pp. 171–173 @HomeTutor
DAY 3	**Grammar:** stem-changing verbs: **o → ue** • Warm Up OHT 21 • Check Homework 5 min	**Presentación de gramática** p. 223 • stem-changing verbs: **o → ue** **Práctica de gramática** pp. 224–225 20 min	**Práctica de gramática** pp. 224–225 • Acts. 5, 6, 7, 8 20 min	**Assess:** *Para y piensa* p. 225 5 min **Homework:** *Cuaderno* pp. 174–176 @HomeTutor
DAY 4	**Communication:** use stem-changing verbs: **o → ue** to talk about things to do in the city • Warm Up OHT 21 • Check Homework 5 min	**Gramática en contexto** pp. 226–227 • *Telehistoria escena 2* DVD 1 15 min	**Gramática en contexto** pp. 226–227 • Act. 9 TXT CD 4 track 15 • Act. 10 25 min	**Assess:** *Para y piensa* p. 227 5 min **Homework:** *Cuaderno* pp. 174–176 @HomeTutor
DAY 5	**Grammar:** stem-changing verbs: **e → i** • Warm Up OHT 22 • Check Homework 5 min	**Presentación de gramática** p. 228 • stem-changing verbs: **e → i** **Práctica de gramática** pp. 229–230 • *Pronunciación* CD 4 track 16 **Culture:** *Las meninas* 15 min	**Práctica de gramática** pp. 229–230 • Acts. 11, 12, 14 • Act. 13 TXT CD 4 track 17 25 min	**Assess:** *Para y piensa* p. 230 5 min **Homework:** *Cuaderno* pp. 177–179 @HomeTutor
DAY 6	**Communication:** Culmination: stem-changing verbs, order food • Warm Up OHT 22 • Check Homework 5 min	**Todo junto** p. 231–233 • *Escenas 1, 2: Resumen* • *Telehistoria completa* DVD 1 15 min	**Todo junto** pp. 231–233 • Acts. 15, 16 TXT CD 4 tracks 14, 15, 18 • Acts. 17, 19 • Act. 18 TXT CD 4 tracks 19, 20 25 min	**Assess:** *Para y piensa* p. 233 5 min **Homework:** *Cuaderno* pp. 180–181 @HomeTutor
DAY 7	**Reading:** Weekends in Spain and Chile **Projects:** Paintings of Spain and Chile • Warm Up OHT 23 • Check Homework **Review:** Lesson Review 5 min	**Lectura cultural** pp. 234–235 • *El fin de semana en España y Chile* TXT CD 4 track 21 **Repaso de la lección** pp. 238–239 20 min	**Lectura cultural** pp. 234–235 • *El fin de semana en España y Chile* **Repaso de la lección** pp. 238–239 • Act. 1 TXT CD 4 track 22 • Acts. 2, 3, 4, 5 20 min	**Assess:** *Para y piensa* p. 235 5 min **Repaso de la lección** pp. 238–239 **Homework:** *En resumen* p. 237, *Cuaderno* pp. 182–193 (optional) Review Games Online @HomeTutor
DAY 8	**Assessment**			**Assess:** Lesson 2 Test or Unit 4 Test 50 min
DAY 9	**Unit Culmination** 5 min	**Comparación cultural** pp. 240–241 • TXT CD 4 track 23 **Repaso Inclusivo** pp. 242–243 15 min	**Comparación cultural** pp. 240–241 **Repaso inclusivo** pp. 242–243 • Act. 1 TXT CD 4 track 24 • Acts 2, 3, 4, 5, 6, 7 30 min	**Homework:** *Cuaderno* pp. 194–196

	Objectives/Focus	Teach	Practice	Assess/HW Options
DAY 1	**Culture:** learn about Spain **Vocabulary:** places and events in town • Warm Up OHT 20 **5 min**	Lesson Opener pp. 216–217 **Presentación de vocabulario** pp. 218–219 • Read A–F • View video DVD 1 • Play audio TXT CD 4 track 12 • *¡A responder!* CD 4 track 13 **20 min**	Lesson Opener pp. 216–217 **Práctica de vocabulario** p. 220 • Acts. 1, 2 **20 min**	**Assess:** *Para y piensa* p. 220 **5 min**
	Communication: talking about transportation **5 min**	**Vocabulario en contexto** pp. 221–222 • *Telehistoria escena 1* DVD 1 • *Nota gramatical:* **ir a** + infinitive **15 min**	**Vocabulario en contexto** pp. 221–222 • Act. 3 TXT CD 4 track 14 • Act. 4 **15 min**	**Assess:** *Para y piensa* p. 222 **5 min** **Homework:** *Cuaderno* pp. 171–173 @HomeTutor
DAY 2	**Grammar:** stem-changing verbs: **o → ue** • Warm Up OHT 21 • Check Homework **5 min**	**Presentación de gramática** p. 223 • stem-changing verbs: **o → ue** **Práctica de gramática** pp. 224–225 **20 min**	**Práctica de gramática** pp. 224–225 • Acts. 5, 6, 7, 8 **15 min**	**Assess:** *Para y piensa* p. 225 **5 min**
	Communication: use stem-changing verbs: **o → ue** to talk about things to do in the city **5 min**	**Gramática en contexto** pp. 226–227 • *Telehistoria escena 2* DVD 1 **20 min**	**Gramática en contexto** pp. 226–227 • Act. 9 TXT CD 4 track 15 • Act. 10 **15 min**	**Assess:** *Para y piensa* p. 227 **5 min** **Homework:** *Cuaderno* pp. 174–176 @HomeTutor
DAY 3	**Grammar:** stem-changing verbs: **e → i** • Warm Up OHT 22 • Check Homework **5 min**	**Presentación de gramática** p. 228 • stem-changing verbs: **e → i** **Práctica de gramática** pp. 229–230 • Pronunciación TXT CD 4 track 16 **Culture:** *Las meninas* **15 min**	**Práctica de gramática** pp. 229–230 • Acts. 11, 12, 14 • Act. 13 TXT CD 4 track 17 **20 min**	**Assess:** *Para y piensa* p. 230 **5 min**
	Communication: Culmination: stem-changing verbs, order food **5 min**	**Todo junto** pp. 231–233 • *Escenas 1, 2: Resumen* • *Telehistoria completa* DVD 1 **10 min**	**Todo junto** pp. 231–233 • Acts. 15, 16 TXT CD 4 tracks 14, 15, 18 • Acts. 17, 19 • Act. 18 TXT CD 4 tracks 19, 20 **25 min**	**Assess:** *Para y piensa* p. 233 **5 min** **Homework:** *Cuaderno* pp. 177–181 @HomeTutor
DAY 4	**Reading:** Weekends in Spain and Chile **Projects:** Paintings of Spain and Chile • Warm Up OHT 23 • Check Homework **5 min**	**Lectura cultural** pp. 234–235 • *El fin de semana en España y Chile* TXT CD 4 track 21 **15 min**	**Lectura cultural** pp. 234–235 • *El fin de semana en España y Chile* **15 min**	**Assess:** *Para y piensa* p. 235 **5 min**
	Review: Lesson Review **5 min**	**Repaso de la lección** pp. 238–239 **15 min**	**Repaso de la lección** pp. 238–239 • Act. 1 TXT CD 4 track 22 • Acts. 2, 3, 4, 5 **25 min**	**Assess:** *Repaso de la lección* pp. 238–239 **5 min** **Homework: En resumen** p. 237; *Cuaderno* 182–193 (optional) Review Games Online @HomeTutor
DAY 5	**Assessment**			**Assess:** Lesson 2 Test, Unit 4 Test, or Midterm **45 min**
	Unit Culmination **5 min**	**Comparación cultural** pp. 240–241 • TXT CD 4 track 23 **Repaso Inclusivo** pp. 242–243 **15 min**	**Comparación cultural** pp. 240–241 **Repaso inclusivo** pp. 242–243 • Act. 1 TXT CD 4 track 24 • Acts 2, 3, 4, 5, 6, 7 **30 min**	**Homework:** *Cuaderno* pp. 194–196

¡AVANZA! Objectives

- Introduce lesson theme: **¿Qué hacemos esta noche?**
- **Culture:** Discuss activities teens do on the weekend in different countries.

Presentation Strategies

- Introduce characters' names: Maribel and Enrique.
- Have students make a list of their favorite places and events in town.
- Have students talk about their favorite weekend activities and the foods they like to eat.

STANDARDS

2.2 Compare products and perspectives
4.2 Compare cultures
21st Century **Social and Cross-Cultural Skills,** Comparación cultural

Warm Up Projectable Transparencies, 4-20

Direct Object Pronouns Complete the following sentences with the correct direct object pronoun attached to the infinitive.

1. ¿El vestido? No quiero llevar _____.
2. ¿Los pantalones? ¿Vas a comprar _____ mañana?
3. ¿La camiseta? Voy a comprar _____ en la tienda de ropa.
4. ¿El gorro? Voy a necesitar _____ para practicar el beísbol.
5. ¿Las blusas? Quiero comprar _____ en el centro comercial.

Answers: 1. llevarlo; 2. comprarlos; 3. comprarla; 4. necesitarlo; 5. comprarlas

Comparación cultural

Ask the following:

1. Are there theaters in or near your town or city? What productions can you see there?
2. Are there historic buildings in your community?
3. What places do you like to visit in your spare time?

¿Qué ves? Possible answers include:

- Sí, el teatro es viejo.
- Maribel lleva un vestido.
- La camisa de Enrique es roja.

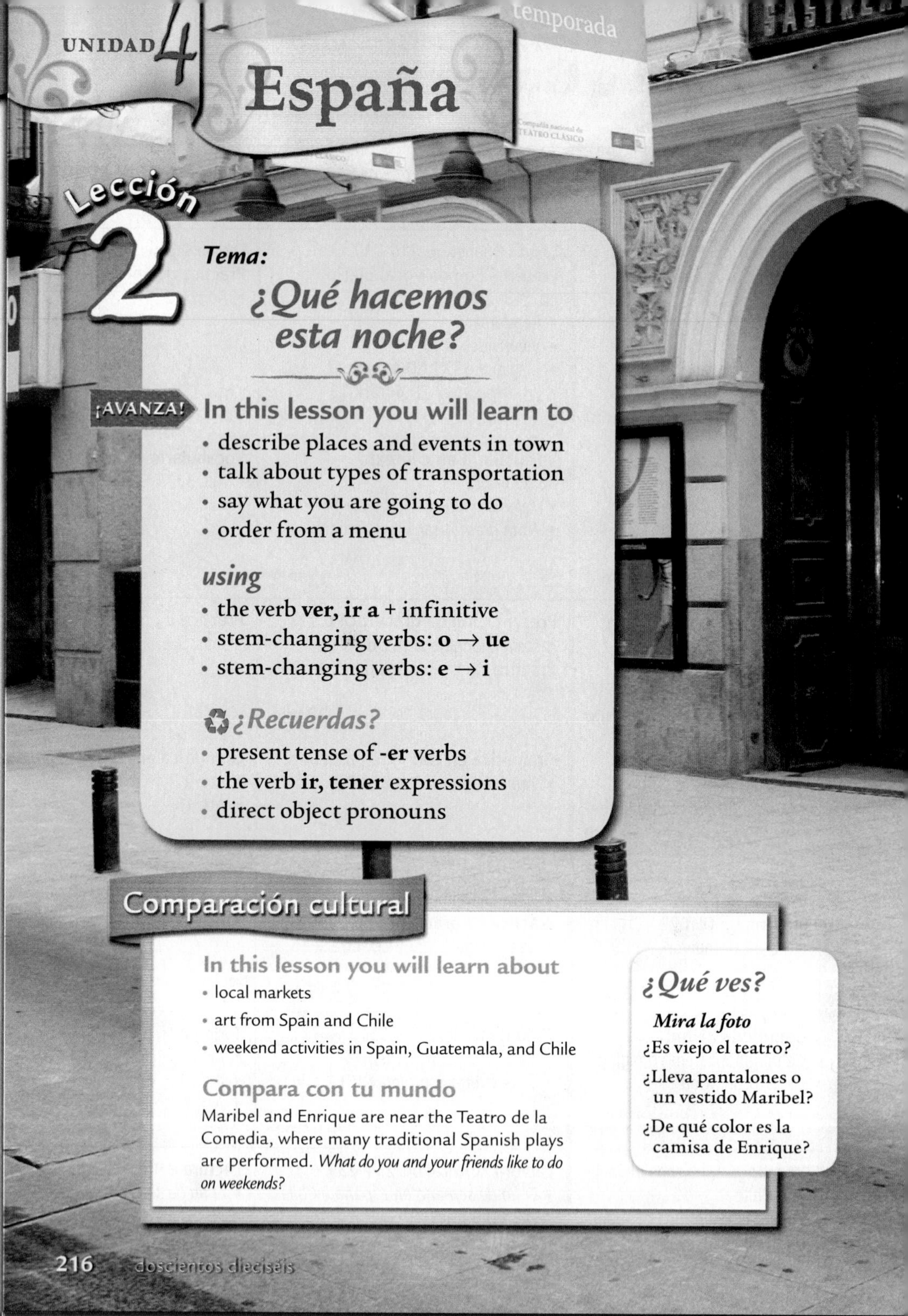

UNIDAD 4 España

Lección 2

Tema:

¿Qué hacemos esta noche?

¡AVANZA! In this lesson you will learn to

- describe places and events in town
- talk about types of transportation
- say what you are going to do
- order from a menu

using

- the verb **ver, ir a** + infinitive
- stem-changing verbs: **o → ue**
- stem-changing verbs: **e → i**

¿Recuerdas?

- present tense of **-er** verbs
- the verb **ir, tener** expressions
- direct object pronouns

Comparación cultural

In this lesson you will learn about

- local markets
- art from Spain and Chile
- weekend activities in Spain, Guatemala, and Chile

Compara con tu mundo

Maribel and Enrique are near the Teatro de la Comedia, where many traditional Spanish plays are performed. *What do you and your friends like to do on weekends?*

¿Qué ves?

Mira la foto

¿Es viejo el teatro?

¿Lleva pantalones o un vestido Maribel?

¿De qué color es la camisa de Enrique?

Differentiating Instruction

English Learners

Build Background Ask students if they have been to a concert, play, or movie. What did they see? Did they like it? Ask them to describe the event and the building where it took place. Ask them how to say *concert, theatre,* or *movies* in their language. Give them time to share experiences and say what they know.

Multiple Intelligences

Kinesthetic Collect an assortment of funny clothes to use as costumes. Write a number of expressions related to emotions and activities on separate index cards, like **triste, contento, ir de compras, jugar al fútbol.** Invite a volunteer to choose a costume and a card to act out. The group needs to describe the costume, as well as guess the activity or emotion being portrayed.

El Teatro de la Comedia en la calle Príncipe
Madrid, España

DIGITAL SPANISH my.hrw.com
ONLINE STUDENT EDITION with...

- performance space
- News + Networking
- @HOMETUTOR
- CULTURA Interactiva

- Audio and Video Resources
- Interactive Flashcards
- Review Activities
- WebQuest
- Conjuguemos.com

PRACTICE SPANISH WITH HOLT MCDOUGAL APPS!

DIGITAL SPANISH

TEACHER TOOLS

- Interactive Whiteboard Lessons
- Generate Success!

ALSO AVAILABLE...

- Online Workbook
- Spanish InterActive Reader

SPANISH ON THE GO!

- Performance Space
- Holt McDougal Spanish Apps
- ¡Avancemos! eTextbook

Using the Photo

Location Information

Teatro de la Comedia is located in downtown Madrid. It was inaugurated on September 18, 1875 by King Alfonso XII and his sister Princess Isabel. At that time it was able to seat 1,000 spectators. Each season (September to June) includes three to four performances of the Spanish classical repertoire by playwrights such as Calderón de la Barca and Lope de Vega, to name a couple.

Expanded Information

Teatro Español is another well-known theater that performs works by both classic and modern Spanish playwrights, among them Federico García Lorca and Jardiel Poncela. It is located in the **Plaza de Santa Ana,** not too far from the **Puerta del Sol.**

Differentiating Instruction

Inclusion

Cumulative Instruction Use limited choice questions about the photo to help students review vocabulary related to clothing, colors, and emotions. Here are a few possibilities:
¿Lleva Maribel un vestido o unos jeans?
¿Tiene Enrique zapatos blancos o zapatos marrones?
¿Está contenta o está triste Maribel?

Heritage Language Learners

Support What They Know Have students watch a Spanish-language comedy. It might be a television show or a movie. Have them describe the characters involved, their names, what they look like, their personalities, and what they wear.

Long-term Retention

Recycle

Ask students **¿Qué llevan Maribel y Enrique?** to see how many items of clothing they can identify.

¡AVANZA! Objectives

- Present vocabulary: places to go in town, means of transportation, ordering a meal.
- Discuss regional variations in vocabulary.

Core Resources

- Video Program: DVD 1
- Audio Program: TXT CD 4 tracks 12, 13

Presentation Strategies

- Point to the items illustrated on pp. 218–219, say each word and have students repeat it after you.
- Play the audio as students read A–F.
- Play the video.

STANDARDS

1.2 Understand language
4.1 Compare languages
21st Century **Creativity and Innovation,** Multiple Intelligences

Communication
Group Work

Prepare props in advance and have students work in pairs or small groups to pantomime scenes that take place in various locations in the city: **el restaurante, el parque, el teatro, el café, el concierto**. The class guesses the location.

Communication
Common Error Alert

Point out that the adjective **bueno** becomes **buen** when it comes before a masculine noun: **Un buen restaurante.** However, it does not change when the noun is feminine: **Una buena película.**

Long-term Retention
Recycle

Review food vocabulary from Unidad 3, Lección 1. Ask the following questions: **¿Qué te gusta comer en la mañana? ¿Qué te gusta comer en el almuerzo? ¿Qué te gusta comer en la noche?**

Presentación de VOCABULARIO

¡AVANZA! Goal: Learn about what Enrique and Maribel do when they go out. Then practice what you have learned to describe places and events in town. ***Actividades 1–2***

¿Recuerdas? Present tense of **-er** verbs p. 150

VIDEO DVD
AUDIO

A En **el centro** de Madrid hay muchos **lugares** para comer. Maribel y yo queremos ir a **la calle** de Alcalá para **encontrar** un buen **restaurante**. ¿**Vamos a pie, en coche** o **en autobús**?

B En **el menú** hay muchos **platos principales.** Si te gusta **la carne,** hay **bistec.** Si no, también hay **pescado.**

C **La cuenta** es veinticinco euros. ¿Cuánto dinero necesitamos para **la propina**?

En España se dice...
In Spain the word for *cake* is **la tarta.** The word for *beans* is **las alubias.**

Differentiating Instruction

Slower-paced Learners

Yes/No Questions Check students' comprehension by pointing to the photos on pp. 218–219. For example, point to the fish and ask, **¿Es el pescado?** Then point to the salad and ask, **¿Es el pollo?**

Multiple Intelligences

Visual Learners Organize students into small groups, and provide each group with a piece of poster board. Instruct each group to create a city plan for an ideal city center. Have them label each location in their city center, and provide as much detail as possible. Encourage students to review vocabulary from previous lessons to include perhaps a school, a shopping center, or a store.

D Tomamos el autobús para ir al **cine.** Vamos al Cine Ideal para **ver una película.**

el cine

la ventanilla

las entradas

Más vocabulario

allí *there*
almorzar *to eat lunch*
costar *to cost*
los frijoles *beans*
la música rock *rock music*
poder *to be able, can*
servir *to serve*
tal vez *perhaps, maybe*
volver *to return, to come back*
Expansión de vocabulario p. R5

E Aquí en Madrid también hay **teatros** y **parques** pero yo prefiero ir a **un concierto** para escuchar música.

el teatro

el parque

el concierto

F Vamos a **un café. De postre** nos gusta **pedir un pastel.** Después, Maribel está muy cansada. Es la hora de **dormir.**

el café
la mesa

dormir

@HOMETUTOR my.hrw.com Interactive Flashcards

¡A responder! Escuchar

Escucha a la camarera. Escribe la comida que menciona.
(Listen to the server. Write the food that she mentions.)

TEACHER to TEACHER

Elizabeth Parks
Dover, NJ

Tips for Presenting Vocabulary

*Whenever I teach vocabulary for places in the city, I use a map transparency with street names and names of various places in the city (stores, museums, theaters, parks, restaurants, etc.). I also include vocabulary terms for different types of transportation. In addition to teaching vocabulary, the map can also be used to teach the verb **ir**, prepositions of locations and for giving directions.*

Go online for more tips!

Long-term Retention

Recycle

Have student groups create a list of activities that are usually done in each of the places mentioned on pp. 218–219. For example: **el café: beber refrescos; el parque: correr, pasear; el teatro: escuchar música,** and so on. Ask groups to share their lists with the rest of the class.

Long-term Retention

Critical Thinking

Analyze Have students arrange the vocabulary on pp. 218–219 in the following category groups: **Comidas, Lugares, Transporte.** Have them write their lists and exchange them with a partner to correct and add items as needed.

Differentiating Instruction

Heritage Language Learners

Regional Variations Ask students to read En España se dice, on p. 218. Ask if they know different ways to say any other words on pp. 218–219? Mention a few other variations of how Spanish words are said throughout Latin America, for example, **coche** is **carro, auto, automóvil.** Also, the word **patatas** is **papas,** and **entradas** is **boletos.**

Pre-AP

Relate Opinions Ask students to share their opinions about the foods and places presented on pp. 218 and 219. Encourage them to use the phrase **porque** to provide more detail. **Me gusta el cine porque me gusta ver películas. No como bistec porque no me gusta comer carne.** Have students continue providing other phrases.

Answers Projectable Transparencies, 4-28

¡A responder! Audio Script, TE p. 215b

Students should point to the following photos:

1. salad
2. fish
3. potatoes
4. steak
5. chicken
6. vegetables
7. rice
8. cake

Objectives
- Practice vocabulary: places in town and items in a restaurant.
- Recycle: present tense of **-er** verbs.

Core Resource
- *Cuaderno,* pp. 171–173

Practice Sequence
- **Activity 1:** Vocabulary recognition: places in town, food
- **Activity 2:** Vocabulary production: the verb **ver,** restaurant-related vocabulary

STANDARDS
1.1 Engage in conversation, Act. 2, PYP
1.3 Present information, Acts. 1–2, PYP
21st Century **Communication,** Act. 2; **Creativity and Innovation,** Act. 2: Expansión

Ongoing Assessment
Get Help Online
More Practice
my.hrw.com

PARA Y PIENSA **Quick Check** If students have difficulties supplying answers in the Para y piensa, have them review the vocabulary spread on pp. 218–219. For additional practice, use Reteaching & Practice Copymasters URB 4, pp. 13, 14, 22.

Communication
Common Error Alert
Students may try to use **ver** with a direct object that is a person or a pet. Tell students that when doing this, they must use an **a** after the verb. They will learn the personal **a** in Unit 6, Lesson 1.

Answers Projectable Transparencies, 4-28
Activity 1 **1.** c; **2.** b; **3.** e; **4.** d; **5.** f; **6.** a

Activity 2 Answers should follow the format:
1. **A.** ¿Qué ves en el restaurante? **B.** Veo un postre.
2. **A.** ¿Qué ves... ? **B.** Veo el menú.
3. **A.** ¿Qué ves... ? **B.** Veo la propina.
4. **A.** ¿Qué ves... ? **B.** Veo la cuenta.
5. **A.** ¿Qué ves... ? **B.** Veo una mesa.
6. **A.** ¿Qué ves... ? **B.** Veo agua.

Para y piensa Answers will vary. Answers may include:
1. el camarero, el menu, la propina
2. el teatro, el parque, el cine

Práctica de VOCABULARIO

1 Diversiones en el centro

Leer Empareja cada palabra con la descripción correspondiente. *(Match each word with its definition.)*

1. Es una persona que trabaja en un café.	**a.** la ventanilla
2. Es el lugar adonde vas para comer.	**b.** el restaurante
3. Vas aquí para ver una película.	**c.** la camarera
4. La necesitas para ir a un concierto.	**d.** la entrada
5. Lo comes después del plato principal.	**e.** el cine
6. Compras entradas aquí.	**f.** el postre

Expansión: Teacher Edition Only
Ask students to write two additional descriptions of new vocabulary words.

Nota gramatical ¿Recuerdas? Present tense of **-er** verbs p. 150

Ver has an irregular **yo** form in the present tense: **veo.**

Veo muchos autobuses en el centro. — ***I see** a lot of buses downtown.*

2 ¿Qué ves en el restaurante?

Hablar Los señores Ortiz están en el restaurante Los Reyes. Pregúntale a otro(a) estudiante qué ve. *(Ask a partner what he or she sees in the restaurant.)*

Expansión
Create a menu for your own café. Include prices.

Más práctica Cuaderno *pp. 171–173* Cuaderno para hispanohablantes *pp. 171–174*

Get Help Online
my.hrw.com

PARA Y PIENSA
Did you get it?
1. Name three things you would find in a restaurant.
2. Name three places where you and your friends might go to have fun.

Differentiating Instruction

Multiple Intelligences
Kinesthetic Ask the class to play a charade game with the questions in Activity 1. For example, have a volunteer mimic a place where you go to see a movie, and other students guess it is **el cine**. Once all six questions have been done, have students continue playing charades with other vocabulary words.

Inclusion
Frequent Review/Repetition Before doing Activity 2, help students write a list of the people and items they see in the illustration. Go over their list to correct and add words as needed. Check pronunciation before starting the activity.

VOCABULARIO en contexto

¡AVANZA! **Goal:** Focus on how Maribel and Enrique talk about where they go and how they get there. Then practice these words and **ir a** + infinitive to talk about types of transportation and what you are going to do. ***Actividades 3–4***

¿Recuerdas? The verb **ir** p. 120

Telehistoria escena 1

@HOMETUTOR my.hrw.com **View, Read and Record**

STRATEGIES

Cuando lees
Think about timing Consider timing while reading. How long will Enrique's plan take? Will they see Trini? Why or why not?

Cuando escuchas
Enter the scene As you listen to Enrique's travel plan, enter the scene. If you were Maribel, would you feel calm or nervous about Enrique's ideas? Why?

VIDEO DVD

AUDIO

Enrique: ¿Trini Salgado está en el centro comercial del Parque de las Avenidas a las doce?

Maribel: Sí. Y ya es tarde. Enrique, ¡por favor!

Enrique: ¡Vale! ¿Y cómo vamos a llegar allí? ¿En autobús?

Enrique puts the T-shirt in his bag so that Maribel can open the map.

Maribel: Podemos empezar aquí en el parque. El centro comercial está allí. ¿Cuál es la calle?

Enrique: Calle Poveda. ¡Es fácil! Tomamos el autobús al centro. Vamos a pie a la biblioteca —aquí. Mi madre está allí. Ella tiene coche. ¡Llegamos al centro comercial en coche!

Maribel: ¡Pero, Enrique! Son las once y cuarenta y cinco. Vamos a llegar tarde. ¿Qué voy a hacer?

Enrique: ¡Ah! El autobús setenta y cuatro va al centro comercial. Llega aquí a las doce y llega al centro comercial a las doce y media.

Maribel: ¡Vale!

Continuará... p. 226

También se dice

España Enrique says **el autobús** to talk about taking the bus. In other Spanish-speaking countries you might hear:
- **Puerto Rico, República Dominicana, Cuba la guagua**
- **México el camión**
- **muchos países el colectivo, el micro**

¡AVANZA! Objective
- Understand activity vocabulary in context.

Core Resources
- Video Program: DVD 1
- Audio Program: TXT CD 4 track 14

Presentation Strategies
- Have students look at the photo and ask them either/or questions: **¿Quién lleva la mochila, Enrique o Maribel? ¿Dónde están los chicos, en la calle o en el restaurante?**
- Have students scan the dialogue to find how many means of transportation are mentioned.
- Play audio or video while students follow the script in their text.

STANDARDS
1.2 Understand languages
4.1 Compare languages

Warm Up
Projectable Transparencies, 4-20

Vocabulary Complete each sentence.

mesas pastel cuenta coche

1. La _____ es treinta euros.
2. El _____ es un postre.
3. Hay muchas _____ en el café.
4. No voy en autobús, voy en _____.

Answers: 1. cuenta; 2. pastel; 3. mesas; 4. coche

Video Summary

@HOMETUTOR VideoPlus my.hrw.com

Maribel is eager to get to the shopping center to see Trini by twelve o'clock. Enrique wonders how they will get there. He suggests they take a bus into town, walk to the library, and from there get a ride to the shopping center with his mother. When Maribel worries they will arrive late, Enrique discovers that a number 74 bus will soon go to the shopping center, arriving at 12:30 P.M. Maribel agrees with Enrique's plan.

Differentiating Instruction

Slower-paced Learners
Read Before Listening Have students preview the Telehistoria silently paying particular attention to information about locations. Then divide the group into two teams to read the parts of Maribel and Enrique. Tell students to raise their hand each time they say or hear the name of a specific place.

Pre-AP
Sequence Information Ask students to write on index cards, in sequential order, Enrique's initial transportation plan to the **centro comercial.**
Tomamos el autobús al centro.
Vamos a pie a la biblioteca.
Llegamos al centro comercial en coche.

Objectives
- Practice using the vocabulary in context.
- Recycle: the verb **ir.**
- Practice **ir a** + infinitive to talk about what you are going to do.

Core Resource
Audio Program: TXT CD 4 track 14

Practice Sequence
- **Activity 3:** Telehistoria comprehension
- **Activity 4:** Vocabulary production: **ir a** + infinitive, foods

STANDARDS
1.1 Engage in conversation, Act. 4
1.2 Understand language, Act. 3
1.3 Present information, Act. 4, PYP
Communication, Act. 4/Heritage Language Learners

Nota gramatical
Make sure students can make the distinction between **ir a** + place to tell where someone is going and **ir a** + infinitive to tell what someone is going to do. Ask questions starting with **¿Adónde vas?** and **¿Qué vas a hacer?** to elicit correct responses.

Get Help Online
More Practice
my.hrw.com

Ongoing Assessment
PARA Y PIENSA **Quick Check** Show illustrations of each mode of transportation and have students say the correponding words. For additional practice, use Reteaching & Practice Copymasters URB 4, pp. 13–15, 22.

Answers Projectable Transparencies, 4-28
Activity 3
1. Falso **2.** Cierto **3.** Cierto
4. Falso **5.** Falso

Activity 4
1. ¿Vas a comer frijoles? Sí, voy (No, no voy) a comer frijoles.
2. ... Sí, voy (No, no voy) a comer bistec.
3. ... Sí, voy (No, no voy) a comer pescado y arroz.
4. ... Sí, voy (No, no voy) a comer verduras.
5. ... Sí, voy (No, no voy) a comer pastel.
6. ... Sí, voy (No, no voy) a comer brócoli.
7. ... Sí, voy (No, no voy) a comer tomates.
8. ... Sí, voy (No, no voy) a comer pollo.

Para y piensa
1. en autobús; **2.** a pie; **3.** en coche

3 *Comprensión del episodio* ¿Cómo piensan llegar?

Escuchar
Leer

Lee las oraciones y decide si son ciertas o falsas. *(Read the sentences and tell whether they are true or false.)*

1. Maribel y Enrique no tienen mapa.
2. La madre de Enrique está en la biblioteca.
3. El centro comercial está en la calle Poveda.
4. Enrique quiere ir a pie al centro comercial.
5. El autobús llega al centro comercial a las doce.

Expansión:
Teacher Edition Only
Have students write two additional true/false statements.

Nota gramatical
¿Recuerdas? The verb **ir** p. 120

To talk about what you are going to do, use a form of **ir a + infinitive.**

¿Qué **van a hacer** ustedes?
*What **are you going to do?***

Vamos a mirar una película.
***We're going to watch** a movie.*

Vamos a can also mean *Let's.*

4 ¿Qué vas a comer?

Hablar

Pregúntale a otro(a) estudiante qué va a comer esta semana. *(Ask a partner what he or she is going to eat this week.)*

A ¿Vas a comer carne?

B Sí, voy a comer carne. Es rica. (No, no voy a comer carne. Es horrible.)

1. 
2. 
3. 
4. 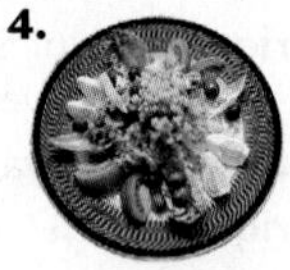
5. 
6. 
7. 
8. 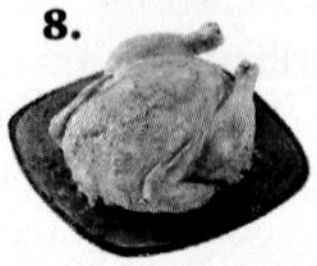

Expansión
Organize this list of foods from your favorite to your least favorite. Compare it with a classmate's.

Get Help Online
my.hrw.com

PARA Y PIENSA

Did you get it? Complete each sentence with the correct phrase to tell what form of transportation is used.
1. Maribel va a la escuela _____ ; va a tomar el cuarenta y dos.
2. Enrique y su hermano van a ir _____ al parque; les gusta pasear.
3. Maribel y su mamá van al concierto _____ porque no quieren llegar tarde.

Differentiating Instruction

Slower-paced Learners
Peer-Study Support Review the forms of **ir.** Then have students brainstorm a list of activities while a volunteer writes them on the board. Encourage them to review previous lessons to refresh their memories. Then have students work in pairs to ask and answer the question **¿Qué vas a hacer mañana?** using the ideas on the board for reference.

Heritage Language Learners
Writing Skills Invite students to develop the question **¿Qué vas a hacer el sábado?** into a full paragraph. Have them make a list to use as a graphic organizer. Encourage them to use time and sequence words, such as **antes** and **después** to link their sentences together.

Presentación de GRAMÁTICA

¡AVANZA! **Goal:** Learn how to form **o → ue** stem-changing verbs. Then practice using these verbs to talk about going out with friends. ***Actividades 5–8***

English Grammar Connection: Remember that there are no stem-changing verbs in the present tense of English (see p. 199). In Spanish, **o → ue** stem changes happen in all three classes of verbs: **-ar, -er,** and **-ir.**

Stem-Changing Verbs: o → ue

ANIMATED GRAMMAR my.hrw.com

Some verbs have an **o → ue** stem change in the present tense. How do you form the present tense of these verbs?

Here's how:

Remember that stem-changing verbs have regular **-ar, -er,** and **-ir** endings. For **o → ue** stem-changing verbs, the last **o** of the stem changes to **ue** in all forms except **nosotros(as)** and **vosotros(as).**

poder *to be able, can*	
puedo	**podemos**
puedes	**podéis**
puede	**pueden**

Carmen **puede** ir al concierto.
*Carmen **can** go to the concert.*

Other verbs you know that have this stem change are **almorzar, costar, dormir, encontrar,** and **volver.**

Almuerzo a la una.
***I eat lunch** at one o'clock.*

Antonio, ¿cuándo **vuelves**?
*Antonio, when **are you coming back**?*

Más práctica
Cuaderno *pp. 174–176*
Cuaderno para hispanohablantes *pp. 175–177*

@HOMETUTOR my.hrw.com
Leveled Practice
Conjuguemos.com

Differentiating Instruction

Pre-AP

Self-correct Allow students to hear and say the different forms of stem-changing verbs. Have them ask and answer everyday classroom questions using **poder, almorzar,** and **encontrar.** It may be easier to recognize that **puedo** sounds right, while **podo** doesn't, rather than always remembering to change the **o** to **ue** before adding the appropriate ending.

Inclusion

Clear Structure Organize students into small groups. Provide each group with six pieces of paper. Have the groups create a chart of the forms for each stem-changing verb: **almorzar, costar, dormir, encontrar,** and **volver**. Tell students to model their charts on the one for **poder** on p. 223.

¡AVANZA! **Objective**

- Present stem-changing verbs: **o → ue.**

Core Resource

- *Cuaderno,* pp. 174–176

Presentation Strategies

- Write the forms of the verb **poder** on the board. Call on a student to underline the **o → ue** stem changes. Ask students which forms don't undergo a stem change.
- Monitor correct usage of forms by saying a pronoun followed by an infinitive and asking students to provide you with the correct form. For example **él: almorzar → él almuerza.**

STANDARD
4.1 Compare languages

Warm Up
Projectable Transparencies, 4-21

ir a + infinitive Complete the sentences with an appropriate phrase.

a. vamos a pedir **b.** van a dormir
c. vas a comer **d.** voy a pagar

1. Yo _____ la cuenta.
2. Nosotros _____ pastel y café.
3. Los chicos _____ a las ocho.
4. Tú _____ carne.

Answers: 1. d; 2. a; 3. b; 4. c

Communication

Interpersonal Mode

Point out that when **poder** is followed by another verb, the second verb is in the infinitive: **Puedo ir al cine.** Ask students whether they can do certain activities or not. Example: **¿Puedes dibujar bien? Sí, puedo dibujar bien** or **No, no puedo dibujar bien.**

Verbs Students Know

Students have learned the following **o → ue** stem-changing verbs in this lesson:

almorzar	**encontrar**
costar	**poder**
dormir	**volver**

Objectives

- Practice using **o → ue** stem-changing verbs and lesson vocabulary.
- **Culture:** the local markets of **El Rastro** and **Chichicastenango.**
- Write about activities in town.
- Give excuses for things you cannot do.

Core Resource

- *Cuaderno,* pp. 174–176

Practice Sequence

- **Activity 5:** Controlled practice: poder
- **Activity 6:** Transitional practice: **o → ue**
- **Activity 7:** Transitional practice: **ir a** + infinitive; **o → ue** stem-changing verbs
- **Activity 8:** Open-ended practice: **o → ue** stem-changing verbs

STANDARDS

1.1 Engage in conversation, Acts. 7–8
1.3 Present information, Acts. 5–8, PYP
2.2 Products and perspectives, Act. 8
4.2 Compare cultures, Act. 8
21st Century **Communication,** Act. 7; **Social and Cross-Cultural Skills,** Comparación cultural

Connections

Las matemáticas

When doing Activity 5, have students notice the date and time in the poster. Remind them that in Spanish-speaking countries the day goes before the month as shown in the poster: **22-23 de abril.** Also remind students that in many countries the official time is written using the 24-hour clock, as in **19:00** (7:00 P.M.), **22:00** (10:00 P.M.), **14:00** (2:00 P.M.), and **21:00** (9:00 P.M.).

Answers Projectable Transparencies, 4-28 and 4-29

Activity 5

1. puedo; **2.** puede; **3.** pueden; **4.** pueden; **5.** puedes; **6.** podemos

Activity 6

1. Las entradas para el concierto cuestan quince euros.
2. Yo almuerzo en el café con mi familia.
3. Vosotros encontráis la calle en el mapa.
4. Tú puedes jugar al fútbol con amigos en el parque.
5. Usted duerme bien después de comer mucho.
6. Nosotros volvemos al centro en autobús.

Práctica de GRAMÁTICA

5 Un concierto de música rock

Leer Escribir

Maribel habla con su amiga, Toni, sobre cuándo pueden ir a un concierto. Completa lo que dice con formas de **poder.** Usa el póster para contestar su pregunta. *(Complete what Maribel says with forms of **poder** and answer her question, based on the poster.)*

Nosotros queremos ir a un concierto el viernes o el sábado, pero ¿cuándo? Yo no __**1.**__ ir el viernes en la noche porque tengo que trabajar. Manolo no __**2.**__ ir el sábado en la noche. Ana y Miguel no __**3.**__ ir el viernes en la noche y el sábado en la tarde no van a estar aquí. Enrique y su hermano no __**4.**__ ir el sábado en la tarde porque van a un restaurante con su primo. Y Toni, tú no __**5.**__ ir el sábado en la noche. ¿Cuándo __**6.**__ ir todos nosotros?

6 Las actividades en el centro

Escribir

Combina frases de las dos columnas con la forma correcta del verbo para describir las actividades de estas personas en el centro. *(Write sentences by conjugating the verbs and combining the phrases.)*

modelo: el camarero / no poder trabajar / en el restaurante
El camarero no puede trabajar en el restaurante.

las entradas para el concierto / costar	en el mapa
yo / almorzar	con amigos en el parque
vosotros / encontrar la calle	después de comer mucho
tú / poder jugar al fútbol	quince euros
usted / dormir bien	en el café con mi familia
nosotros / volver al centro	en autobús

Expansión
Choose three verbs from this activity and write three sentences about yourself.

Differentiating Instruction

Inclusion

Clear Structure Before students complete Activity 5, have them preview the text noting on a separate piece of paper the noun or pronoun associated with the verb in each sentence. Based on what they write, have students choose the correct form of the verb to complete the sentence.

Slower-paced Learners

Peer-study Support After students complete Activity 6, have them read their responses aloud to a partner with stronger skills. Instruct students to listen for the correct stem change in the verb. If a verb does not sound correct, such as **las entradas costan,** rather than **las entradas cuestan,** have students refer back to p. 223 to verify the form.

7 Todos tienen excusas

Hablar

Habla con otro(a) estudiante sobre las actividades que ustedes no pueden hacer este fin de semana. Di que no puedes e inventa una excusa. *(Give excuses for what you cannot do.)*

modelo: ir a un concierto

A: ¿Vas a ir a un concierto?

B: No, no puedo ir a un concierto. Voy a ir al cine con mi hermano.

1. ir al teatro
2. dormir diez horas
3. practicar deportes
4. almorzar en un café
5. pasar un rato con los amigos
6. ver una película en el cine
7. ir al centro
8. comprar ropa

Expansión
Compare with a classmate which of these activities you are going to do this weekend.

8 ¡Vamos a ir de compras!

Hablar

Comparación cultural

Los mercados

Chichicastenango, Guatemala

El Rastro en Madrid, España

How do local markets reflect the culture of an area? Every Sunday, tourists and locals head to El Rastro, one of the oldest flea markets in Madrid, **Spain,** to search for bargains amid the hundreds of stalls. Vendors offer a wide variety of items such as antiques, secondhand clothing, CDs, books, maps, and art. In **Guatemala,** the town of Chichicastenango hosts a popular market in which you can find handicrafts from the Maya-Quiché culture. Many vendors wear the traditional dress of their region and sell colorful textiles, including Mayan blouses called *huipiles*. Other common items include fruits and vegetables, masks, baskets, candles, and flowers.

Compara con tu mundo *What type of souvenir might a visitor to your community purchase?*

Pregúntale a otro(a) estudiante dónde puedes encontrar **libros, discos compactos, fruta, arte, verduras, mapas,** y **huipiles.** *(Ask your partner where you can find these items.)*

A: ¿Dónde puedo encontrar libros?

B: Encuentras libros en El Rastro.

Expansión:
Teacher Edition Only
Have students think of other souvenirs to add to the list of items.

Más práctica Cuaderno *pp. 174–176* Cuaderno para hispanohablantes *pp. 175–177*

Get Help Online my.hrw.com

PARA Y PIENSA

Did you get it? Complete each sentence with the correct form of the appropriate verb: **poder, costar, almorzar,** or **dormir.**

1. El pescado _____ diez dólares.
2. Nosotros _____ a la una en el café.
3. Yo _____ ocho horas.
4. Ellos no _____ contestar.

Differentiating Instruction

Multiple Intelligences

Kinesthetic Invite students to create their own version of **El Rastro**. Ask them to bring in one or two items they would like to sell. Then have them organize their wares into different categories, such as **ropa, frutas, unos libros,** etc., and assign prices. Finally, open up the market. Have students take turns being shoppers and vendors.

Heritage Language Learners

Regional Variations Ask students to share the names for items that would typically be for sale in a **mercado** in their country or region of origin. For example, a **güipil,** a Guatamalan indigenous dress; a Panamenian **mola** which is a hand-sewn tapestry; or native jewelry. If possible, have students bring in examples from home, or create a sample by drawing or using craft supplies.

Comparación cultural

Essential Question

Suggested Answer Goods sold in food and craft markets reflect local agriculture and native materials, eating habits and cuisine, artistic talent and traditions, and various interests and needs of people in the community. Have kids practice saying the name of this market: Chi-chi-cas-te-nan-go. Also practice saying huipiles (1st syllable *hui* is pronounced *wee*).

Expanded Information

Indigenous Markets Other well-known indigenous markets in the Spanish-speaking Americas include those in **Silvia, Colombia; Otavalo, Ecuador;** and **Pisac, Perú.** The **Mercado Guajiro** in **Venezuela,** has a collection of 30 shops featuring indigenous and other typical arts and crafts.

Ongoing Assessment

Get Help Online
More Practice
my.hrw.com

PARA Y PIENSA

Intervention If students have difficulty answering the questionsin the Para y piensa, ask them to review stem-changing verbs on p. 223. For additional practice, use Reteaching & Practice Copymasters URB 4, pp. 16, 17.

Answers Projectable Transparencies, 4-29

Activity 7 Answers will vary. Sample answers include:

1. ¿Vas a ir al teatro? No, no puedo ir al teatro. Tengo que estudiar.
2. ¿Vas a dormir diez horas? No, no puedo dormir diez horas. Tengo que estudiar.
3. ¿Vas a practicer deportes? No, no puedo practicar deportes. No me gustan los deportes.
4. ¿Vas a almorzar en un café? No, no puedo almorzar en un café. Voy a comer en un restaurante.
5. ¿Vas a pasar un rato con los amigos? No, no puedo pasar un rato con los amigos. Estoy muy cansado.
6. ¿Vas a ver una película en el cine? No, no puedo ver una película en el cine. Voy a ir al teatro.
7. ¿Vas a ir al centro? No, no puedo ir al centro. Tengo que estudiar.
8. Vas a comprar ropa? No, no puedo comprar ropa. No tengo dinero.

Activity 8 Answers should follow the pattern: ¿Dónde puedo encontrar...? Encuentras... en...

Para y piensa **1.** cuesta; **2.** almorzamos; **3.** duermo; **4.** pueden

¡AVANZA! Objectives

- Identify **o → ue** stem-changing verbs in context.
- Talk about places around town and what you find there.

Core Resources

- Video Program: DVD 1
- Audio Program: TXT CD 4 track 15

Presentation Strategies

- Have students read the Telehistoria and discuss Enrique's behavior.
- Play the audio.
- Show the video. Point to the Spanish intonation and the use of the word **¡Vale!**

Practice Sequence

- **Activity 9:** Telehistoria comprehension
- **Activity 10:** Transitional practice: **o → ue** verbs

STANDARDS

1.1 Engage in conversation, Act. 10
1.2 Understand language, Telehistoria, Act. 9
1.3 Present information, Act. 9, PYP
21st Century **Communication,** Role-Playing and Skits

Warm Up Projectable Transparencies, 4-21

o → ue Stem-changing Verbs Complete the following sentences with the correct verb form.

1. Los chicos _____ a casa a las siete de la noche. (volver)
2. La entrada _____ veinte euros. (costar)
3. Nosotros _____ en la cafetería. (almorzar)
4. Susana _____ hablar bien el español. (poder)
5. Yo _____ en la noche. (dormir)

Answers: 1. vuelven; 2. cuesta; 3. almorzamos; 4. puede; 5. duermo

Video Summary

@HOMETUTOR VideoPlus my.hrw.com

Enrique and Maribel discuss what to do in the afternoon after going shopping. Maribel says she wants to return to town to hear a rock concert, to go to the movies, or to the theater. After some discussion, they decide to go to the concert. Enrique offers to go quickly to the ticket window to buy the tickets; the bus arrives while he is gone. Maribel is about to board the bus alone, but realizes that she does not have the T-shirt.

GRAMÁTICA en contexto

¡AVANZA! **Goal:** Identify the **o → ue** stem-changing verbs Enrique and Maribel use to talk about things to do in the city. Then practice using these verbs to talk about where you go. ***Actividades 9–10***

Telehistoria escena 2

@HOMETUTOR my.hrw.com View, Read and Record

STRATEGIES

Cuando lees
Compare scenes As you read this scene, compare it to Scene 1. How are these scenes alike in terms of Enrique's promises and his behavior? What trends do you find?

Cuando escuchas
Identify causes A negative feeling can have more than one cause. Listen for the causes of Maribel's anxiety and concerns. How many causes are there? What are they?

VIDEO DVD

AUDIO

Enrique: ¿Qué vas a hacer hoy por la tarde?
Maribel: Después de ir de compras, quiero volver al centro. Hay un concierto de música rock, o puedo ir al cine a ver una película... ¡o puedo ir al teatro!
Enrique: ¡Un concierto de rock! ¿Puedo ir?
Maribel: Mmm... ¡quiero ir al teatro! Vamos al teatro.
Enrique: ¿Al teatro? Pero las entradas cuestan mucho, y...
After the trouble he caused, Enrique decides to go along with Maribel's idea.
Enrique: ¡Vale! Vamos al teatro.
Maribel: *(amused)* No, vamos al concierto.
Enrique: ¡Muy bien! Voy a comprar las entradas.
Maribel: ¡Pero, Enrique! El autobús...
Enrique: La ventanilla está allí, cerca del café. Vuelvo en dos minutos.
As he runs to buy the tickets, Maribel sees the bus approaching. She decides to go alone, but realizes she no longer has the T-shirt.
Maribel: ¡La camiseta! ¡No encuentro la camiseta! ¡Enrique!

Continuará... p. 231

Differentiating Instruction

Slower-paced Learners

Sentence Completion Write the following sentence starters on the board.
Después de _____, quiero _____.
Después de _____, puedo _____.
Después de _____, voy a _____.
Then ask students to complete the sentences based on their own interests and their own daily schedule.

Inclusion

Frequent Review/Repetition Ask pairs of students to read the Telehistoria and write in their notebooks forms of **poder, volver,** and **encontrar.** Have each pair read aloud the sentences containing the verb forms. Check students' pronunciation. **Hay un concierto de música rock, o puedo ir al cine. ¿Puedo ir? Vuelvo en dos minutos. ¡No encuentro la camiseta!**

9 *Comprensión del episodio* Planes para la tarde

Escuchar
Leer

Completa las oraciones con la frase que corresponde. *(Complete the sentences with the corresponding phrase.)*

1. Después de ir de compras, Maribel quiere...
2. Enrique no quiere ir al teatro porque...
3. Maribel y Enrique van...
4. El autobús llega...
5. Enrique va a comprar las entradas...

a. cuando Enrique va a comprar las entradas.
b. volver al centro.
c. a un concierto de música rock en la tarde.
d. y tiene la camiseta.
e. las entradas cuestan mucho.

Expansión: Teacher Edition Only
Ask students to write one additional incomplete statement followed by three possible phrases.

10 ¿Qué encuentras?

Hablar

Habla con otro(a) estudiante sobre qué encuentras en estos lugares. *(Talk about what you find in these places.)*

A ¿Qué encuentras en una biblioteca?

B Encuentro libros y computadoras allí.

1. 

2. 

3. 

4. 

5. 

6. 

Expansión
Write a description of what people can do in each of these places.

Get Help Online
my.hrw.com

PARA Y PIENSA

Did you get it? Complete each sentence based on the Telehistoria with the correct form of the verb in parentheses.
1. Maribel _____ ir al cine o al teatro. (poder)
2. Maribel no _____ la camiseta. (encontrar)
3. Enrique _____ tarde y los dos no van al centro comercial. (volver)

Communication
Role-Playing and Skits

Have students act out a scene at the ticket window of a movie theater. Encourage students to ask questions about movie times and the cost of the tickets. For example:
¿A qué hora empieza la película? La película empieza a las tres de la tarde. ¿Cuánto cuestan las entradas? Las entradas cuestan cinco euros.

Communication
Pair Work

Have students complete answers to Activity 10 in writing. Have students correct each other's work in pairs or small groups.

Ongoing Assessment

Get Help Online
More Practice
my.hrw.com

PARA Y PIENSA **Quick Check** If students have difficulty completing the sentences, practice with them the conjugation of the verbs. For additional practice, use Reteaching & Practice Copymasters URB 4 pp. 16, 18.

Differentiating Instruction

Slower-paced Learners

Memory Aids Before students begin Activity 10, give them this pre-speaking activity. Draw six circles on the board. Elicit from students the name of each location presented, and write one name in the center of each circle. Then have students brainstorm words and phrases associated with each place. Write these words around the appropriate circle.

Pre-AP

Expand and Elaborate After choosing the correct answers in Activity 9, have students brainstorm a follow-up sentence. The second sentence should provide an explanation of the first or tell what will happen next. Here is a possible elaboration for sentence 1.
Ella quiere ir a un concierto, al cine o al teatro.

Answers Projectable Transparencies, 4-29

Activity 9
1. b; **2.** e; **3.** c; **4.** a; **5.** d

Activity 10 Answers will vary. Sample answers include:
1. ¿Qué encuentras en un centro comercial? Encuentro tiendas y ropa allí.
2. ¿Qué encuentras en un restaurante? Encuentro mesas y comida allí.
3. ¿Qué encuentras en una tienda de ropa? Encuentro camisas y pantalones allí.
4. ¿Qué encuentras en una escuela? Encuentro estudiantes y maestros allí.
5. ¿Qué encuentras en un café? Encuentro camareros y amigos allí.
6. ¿Qué encuentras en una calle? Encuentro coches y autobuses allí.

Para y piensa
1. puede; **2.** encuentra; **3.** vuelve

¡AVANZA! **Objective**

- Present **e → i** stem-changing verbs

Core Resource

- *Cuaderno*, pp. 177–179

Presentation Strategy

- Write the full conjugation of the verb **servir** on the board. Ask students to say what the stem change is and in what forms it occurs.

STANDARD

4.1 Compare languages

Warm Up
Projectable Transparencies, 4-22

Vocabulary Complete the sentences with the appropriate location.

la ventanilla **el autobús** **el cine**
el restaurante **el parque**

1. Vamos a comer pollo en ____.
2. Queremos ver una película en ____.
3. ¿Por qué no paseamos en ____?
4. Puedes comprar entradas en ____.
5. Tomamos ____ para ir al teatro.

Answers: 1. el restaurante; 2. el cine; 3. el parque; 4. la ventanilla; 5. el autobús

Communication
Common Error Alert

Remind students of the Spanish pronunciation of the vowels **e** and **i**. The **e** has an *ay* sound and the **i** has an *ee* sound. This may help them correctly spell forms of the verb **servir.**

Verbs Students Know

Students have learned the following **e → i** stem-changing verbs in this lesson: **pedir** and **servir.** They will learn another one in Unit 8: **vestirse.** Remind students that stem-changing verbs are also called boot verbs.

Presentación de GRAMÁTICA

¡AVANZA! **Goal:** Learn how to form **e → i** stem-changing verbs. Then practice using these verbs to order from a menu. ***Actividades 11–14***

¿Recuerdas? Direct object pronouns p. 204, **tener** expressions p. 198

English Grammar Connection: Remember that there are no stem-changing verbs in the present tense of English (see p. 199). There are, however, a number of stem-changing verbs in Spanish.

Stem-Changing Verbs: e → i

ANIMATEDGRAMMAR my.hrw.com

Some **-ir** verbs have an **e → i** stem change in the present tense. How do you form the present tense of these verbs?

Here's how:

For **e → i** stem-changing verbs, the last **e** of the stem changes to **i** in all forms except **nosotros(as)** and **vosotros(as).**

servir *to serve*	
sirvo	**servimos**
sirves	**servís**
sirve	**sirven**

El camarero **sirve** la comida.
*The waiter **serves** the food.*

Another verb you know with this stem change is **pedir.**

¿**Pides** una ensalada?
***Are you ordering** a salad?*

Siempre **pedimos** pollo.
*We always **order** chicken.*

Más práctica
Cuaderno *pp. 177–179*
Cuaderno para hispanohablantes *pp. 178–181*

@HOMETUTOR my.hrw.com
Leveled Practice
Conjuguemos.com

Differentiating Instruction

Heritage Language Learners

Support What They Know Ask students to model the present-tense forms of the verbs **servir** and **pedir** by using each form in a sentence. **Tú pides pollo. Nosotros pedimos pollo.** Then ask students to discuss what they notice about the stem change in each case. It changes from **e** to **i** in all conjugated forms except for **nosotros** and **vosotros.**

Multiple Intelligences

Musical/Rhythmic Have students join in a call-and-response chant to help practice the forms of stem-changing verbs. This will provide them with opportunities to hear the vowel change from **e** to **i**, for example.

Maestro(a)	Estudiantes
¡Yo sirvo!	**¡Yo sirvo!**
¡Tú sirves!	**¡Tú sirves!**
¡Nosotros servimos!	**¡Nosotros servimos!**

Práctica de GRAMÁTICA

11 ¿Qué piden?

Escribir
Hablar

Describe qué piden las personas. *(Tell what these people are ordering.)*

modelo: yo
Yo pido carne.

1. tú

2. mis amigas
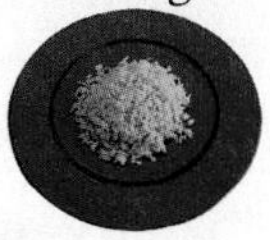

3. yo

4. vosotros

5. mi madre

6. Maribel

7. mis abuelos y yo

8. ustedes

Expansión:
Teacher Edition Only
Ask students to say what their family's favorite foods are.

12 ¿Quién sirve la comida?

¿Recuerdas? Direct object pronouns p. 204

Escribir
Hablar

Describe qué piden estas personas y quién sirve la comida. *(Tell what these people ask for and who serves it.)*

modelo: Maribel: bebida (la camarera)
Maribel pide una bebida y la camarera la sirve.

1. yo: ensalada (Enrique)
2. mi amigo: pollo (sus padres)
3. tú: pescado (yo)
4. mis amigas y yo: verduras (vosotros)
5. usted: patatas (nosotros)
6. vosotros: postre (el camarero)

Expansión
Talk about what you ask for and what your family serves for breakfast, lunch, and dinner.

AUDIO

Pronunciación La letra c con e, i

Before **e** and **i**, the Spanish **c** is pronounced like the *c* in *city*.

Listen and repeat.

ce	→	**cero**	**centro**	**cerrar**	**quince**
ci	→	**cien**	**cine**	**precio**	**estación**

In many regions of Spain, the **c** before **e** and **i** is pronounced like the *th* of the English word *think*.

Differentiating Instruction

Pre-AP

Expand and Elaborate Ask students to write a note to a friend who is coming to visit him or her. The e-mail should mention what time to arrive, a description of what they will eat, and what they will do. **Vienes el sábado a las doce. Vamos a almorzar pescado con ensalada y un buen postre. Después vamos al cine.**

Inclusion

Clear Structure Have students work in groups to create restaurant menus including pictures and prices in euros. Allow them to use their imagination in creating the menu. Then ask each group to read aloud their menus and prices. **En nuestro restaurante el pollo cuesta nueve euros. El pescado cuesta quince euros.** Have students compete for the best menu and presentation.

Objectives

- Practice present tense of **e → i** stem-changing verbs.
- Practice lesson vocabulary: foods
- Recycle: Direct object pronouns.
- Pronunciation: Practice pronouncing the letter **c** before **e** and **i**.

Core Resource

- Audio Program: TXT CD 4, track 16

Practice Sequence

- **Activity 11:** Controlled practice: **e → i** stem-changing verbs.
- **Activity 12:** Controlled practice: **e → i** stem-changing verbs; Recycle: direct object pronouns
- Pronunciation: Oral comprehension and production of the letter **c** before **e** and **i**.

STANDARDS

1.2 Understand language, Pronunciación
1.3 Present information, Acts. 11-12
21st Century **Creativity and Innovation,** Inclusion

Ongoing Assessment

Dictation Have students write the following dictation with the letter combinations **ce** and **ci: Cecilia y Francisco montan en bicicleta en el centro a las cinco.**

Answers Projectable Transparencies, 4-29

Activity 11

1. Tú pides pollo
2. Mis amigas piden arroz.
3. Yo pido pastel.
4. Vosotros pedís ensalada.
5. Mi madre pide bistec.
6. Maribel pide patatas.
7. Mis abuelos y yo pedimos verduras.
8. Ustedes piden pescado y arroz.

Activity 12

1. Yo pido una ensalada y Enrique la sirve.
2. Mi amigo pide pollo y sus padres lo sirven.
3. Tú pides pescado y yo lo sirvo.
4. Mis amigas y yo pedimos verduras y vosotros las servís.
5. Usted pide patatas y nosotros las servimos.
6. Vosotros pedís un postre y el camarero lo sirve.

Objectives

- Practice the present tense of **e → i** stem-changing verbs.
- **Culture:** Compare Velázquez's *Las meninas* to a re-creation of it by Picasso.
- Practice food-related vocabulary.
- Recycle: **tener** expressions

Core Resources

- *Cuaderno,* pp. 177–179
- Audio Program: TXT CD 4, track 17

Practice Sequence

- **Activity 13:** Transitional practice: **e → i** verbs
- **Activity 14:** Transitional practice: **e → i** verbs, food vocabulary; Recycle: **tener** expressions

STANDARDS

1.1 Engage in conversation, Act. 14
1.2 Understand language, Act. 13
1.3 Present information, Act. 14, PYP
21st Century **Communication,** Act. 14

Comparación cultural

Essential Question

Suggested Answer An artist might recreate a famous artwork to honor the work of the artist who created the original work or to continue a particular art or historical tradition.

About the Artist

Diego Velázquez (1599–1660), born in Seville, Spain, was a noted portrait artist. He created many portraits of the Spanish royal family, other notable European figures, and commoners, culminating in the production of his masterpiece, **Las meninas.**

Ongoing Assessment

Get Help Online
More Practice
my.hrw.com

PARA Y PIENSA **Remediation** If students have problems completing the Para y piensa, have them review p. 228 and repeat Activities 11 and 12 on p. 229. For additional practice, use Reteaching & Practice Copymasters URB 4, pp. 19, 20, 23, 24.

See activity answers on p. 231.

13 ¿Qué sirven en el café?

Escuchar
Escribir

Enrique está en un café y habla con los camareros. Escribe oraciones para explicar qué sirven estas personas. *(Listen and write sentences to tell what these people are serving.)*

1. los camareros	**3.** el camarero	**5.** Luis y José
2. el señor Fuentes	**4.** la camarera	**6.** Ana

Audio Program
TXT CD 4 Track 1
Audio Script, TE p. 215b

14 ¿Qué pides del menú?

¿*Recuerdas?* **tener** expressions p. 198

Hablar

Pregúntale a otro(a) estudiante qué pide en un restaurante en las siguientes situaciones. *(Ask a partner what he or she orders in a restaurant in the following situations.)*

modelo: bebida / en el almuerzo

A ¿Qué bebida pides en el almuerzo?

B Pido leche o un refresco.

1. comida / en el almuerzo
2. bebida / cuando tienes frío
3. bebida / en el desayuno
4. comida / cuando tienes calor
5. comida / cuando tienes hambre
6. bebida / cuando tienes mucha sed

Expansión
Write about other things that you ask for at home and at school.

Comparación cultural

Las meninas

Why might an artist create a version of another artist's masterpiece? Diego Velázquez served as the official painter for King Philip IV of **Spain** and painted many portraits of the royal family. *Las meninas* shows the *Infanta* (princess) and her attendants. Velázquez included himself in the painting. Three centuries later, Pablo Picasso, also from Spain, completed 58 interpretations of this painting. What similarities and differences do you notice?

Las meninas *(1656), Diego Velázquez*

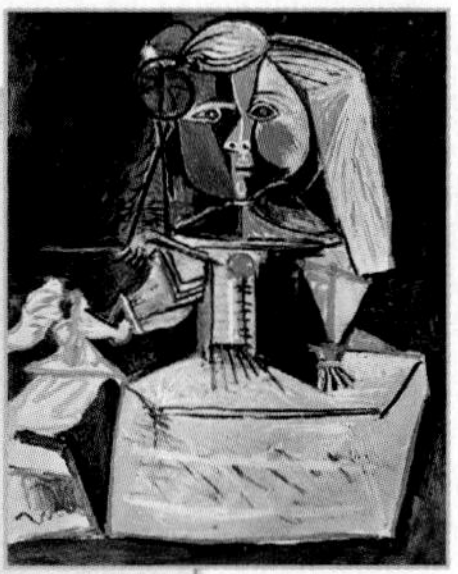

Las meninas (Infanta Margarita) *(1957), Pablo Picasso*

Compara con tu mundo *What famous artwork would you like to try to re-create and why?*

Más práctica Cuaderno *pp. 177–179* Cuaderno para hispanohablantes *pp. 178–181*

Get Help Online
my.hrw.com

PARA Y PIENSA

Did you get it? Complete each sentence with the correct form of **pedir** or **servir.**

1. En la cena los camareros ____ arroz con pollo.
2. Mi madre hace un pastel y lo ____ de postre.
3. Nosotros no ____ mucho porque no tenemos mucha hambre.

Differentiating Instruction

Multiple Intelligences

Interpersonal Have students practice ordering food. Have a few advanced students act as **camareros** writing the orders from other students acting as **clientes.** Be ready to correct pronunciation. Student A: **Tengo calor. Yo pido una ensalada.** Student B: **Yo quiero pollo y ensalada.** When all students have ordered, have the **camareros** show what they wrote and correct if necessary.

Heritage Language Learners

Writing Skills Have students create a Venn diagram with the heading **Las meninas, Diego Velázquez** on one side, and **Las meninas, Pablo Picasso** on the other. Have them record details describing how the two works are similar and different. Allow them to share their observations, and then develop their organizers into a brief compare/contrast paragraph.

Todo junto

¡AVANZA! **Goal:** ***Show what you know*** Pay attention to how Maribel and Enrique tell the waiter what they would like to eat. Then practice using **o → ue** and **e → i** stem-changing verbs to order food and give your opinion on restaurants. ***Actividades 15–19***

Telehistoria completa

@HOMETUTOR my.hrw.com View, Read and Record

STRATEGIES

Cuando lees

Analyze the communication Analyze this scene's communication by answering these questions: Why does Maribel order so much food? What is the effect?

Cuando escuchar

Listen for contrasts Listen for contrasts during the scene. Examples: What do Maribel and Enrique order? Who promises to pay, and who actually pays?

Escena 1 *Resumen*
Enrique y Maribel pueden tomar el autobús setenta y cuatro al centro comercial. Piensan llegar a las doce y media.

Escena 2 *Resumen*
Enrique va a comprar las entradas para un concierto. El autobús llega pero Enrique no está. Maribel no tiene la camiseta.

Escena 3

VIDEO DVD

AUDIO

They arrive at an outdoor restaurant.

Enrique: Es un restaurante muy bonito.

Maribel: Pero no tengo el autógrafo de Trini.

Enrique: Vamos a pedir la comida. ¡Yo pago!

Maribel: Ah, ¿pagas tú? Ahora pido toda la comida del menú.

The waiter arrives.

Maribel: Señor, ¿sirven pescado hoy?

Camarero: No, hoy no tenemos pescado.

Maribel: Quiero empezar con una ensalada. De plato principal quiero el pollo con verduras y... Sí, y filete con patatas.

Camarero: ¿Dos platos principales? ¿Filete y pollo?

Enrique: Es mucho, ¿no?

Maribel: Sí. Y de postre quiero un arroz con leche.

Enrique: *(nervously)* Pan y agua, por favor.

Maribel: Él va a pagar la cuenta.

Enrique: *(nods, then remembers)* ¡Maribel! ¡Mi mochila! ¡No tengo dinero!

Maribel: *(smiling)* Ay, Enrique, yo sí tengo dinero.

Differentiating Instruction

Pre-AP

Sequence Information Have students make a written summary of what happened in **Escena 3.** For example: 1. **Enrique y Maribel llegan al restaurante.** 2. **Ellos piden la comida.** 3. **Enrique no puede pagar porque no tiene su mochila.** 4. **Maribel paga. Ella sí tiene dinero.** Have students read aloud their summaries. Check for misspellings and pronunciation.

Inclusion

Frequent Review/Repetition Assign students one line from the Telehistoria to focus on. Give them time to interpret the line's meaning, and rehearse saying it aloud. Remind students to read with intonation when they see exclamation points and question marks. **¡Yo pago!** and **Ah, ¿pagas tú?** After students are prepared, read through the script, pointing to each reader in turn.

¡AVANZA! **Objectives**
- Integrate lesson content.

Core Resources
- Video Program: DVD 1
- Audio Program: TXT CD 4 track 18

Presentation Strategies
- Ask students to describe the photo for Escena 3 by asking: **¿Dónde están Enrique y Maribel ahora? ¿Quién más está en la foto?**
- Show the video and/or play the audio.

STANDARD
1.1 Understand language

Warm Up
Projectable Transparencies, 4-22

e → i Stem-changing Verbs Complete the sentences with appropriate forms of **pedir** or **servir.**

1. El camarero _____ la comida.
2. Ana Luisa _____ una ensalada porque no tiene mucha hambre.
3. Nosotros preparamos un pastel y lo _____.

Answers: 1. sirve; 2. pide; 3. servimos

Video Summary
@HOMETUTOR VideoPlus my.hrw.com

Later, at a café, Maribel is disappointed not to have Trini's autograph. Enrique offers to pay for the meal. When the waiter arrives, Maribel orders a big meal. Enrique is alarmed. He then realizes his backpack (and money) are still missing. Maribel offers to pay.

Answers
Projectable Transparencies, 4-29 and 4-30

Answers for Activities on p. 230.

Activity 13

1. Sirven pollo y arroz. **2.** Sirve bistec y patatas. **3.** Sirve brócoli. **4.** Sirve pescado. **5.** Sirven verduras. **6.** Sirve pastel de frutas.

Activity 14 Answers will vary. Sample answers include:

1. A. ¿Qué comida pides en el almuerzo? **B.** Pido una ensalada.
2. A. ¿... cuando tienes frío? **B.** Pido un café.
3. A. ¿... en el desayuno? **B.** Pido leche.
4. A. ¿... cuando tienes calor? **B.** Pido una ensalada.
5. A. ¿... cuando tienes hambre? **B.** Pido carne.
6. A. ¿... cuando tienes mucha sed? **B.** Pido un refresco.

Para y piensa **1.** sirven; **2.** sirve; **3.** pedimos

TODO JUNTO

Objective
- Practice using and integrating lesson vocabulary and grammar.

Core Resources
- *Cuaderno,* pp. 180–181
- Audio Program: TXT CD 4 tracks 14, 15, 18, 19, 20

Practice Sequence
- **Activities 15, 16:** Telehistoria comprehension
- **Activity 17:** Transitional practice: speaking
- **Activity 18:** Open-ended practice: reading, listening, speaking
- **Activity 19:** Open-ended practice: writing

STANDARDS
1.1 Engage in conversation, Act. 17
1.2 Understand language, Acts. 15–16, 18
1.3 Present infomation, Acts. 15–19, PYP
21st Century **Communication,** Act. 17/Heritage Language Learners

Answers Projectable Transparencies, 4-30

Activity 15

1. Maribel **2.** Enrique **3.** Maribel **4.** Enrique **5.** Maribel

Activity 16

1. Maribel y Enrique quieren ir al centro comercial en autobús.
2. El autobús setenta y cuatro va al centro comercial.
3. Enrique no quiere ir al teatro porque las entradas cuestan mucho.
4. Maribel está enojada porque no tiene la camiseta. Enrique la tiene en su mochila.
5. Maribel pide una ensalada, pollo con verduras, filete con patatas, y arroz con leche.

Activity 17 Answers should follow this pattern:

Camarero(a): Buenas tardes (noches). ¿Quieren ver el menú? Pueden pedir...

Cliente(s): Yo quiero... or Tengo ganas de comer... or Tengo hambre, voy a pedir...

15 *Comprensión de los episodios* ¿Quién lo hace?

Escuchar Leer

Lee estas oraciones e indica a quién se refieren—a Enrique o a Maribel. *(Read these sentences and tell to whom they refer—Enrique or Maribel.)*

1. Quiere volver al centro después de ir de compras.
2. Piensa que las entradas cuestan mucho.
3. No encuentra la camiseta.
4. Piensa que el restaurante es muy bonito.
5. Pide mucha comida.

Expansión:
Teacher Edition Only
Ask students to create two sentences that refer to both Enrique and Maribel.

16 *Comprensión de los episodios* Problemas en el centro

Escuchar Leer

Contesta las preguntas según los episodios. *(Answer the questions according to the episodes.)*

1. ¿Cómo quieren ir Maribel y Enrique al centro comercial?
2. ¿Adónde va el autobús setenta y cuatro?
3. ¿Por qué no quiere ir al teatro Enrique?
4. ¿Por qué está enojada Maribel?
5. ¿Qué pide Maribel en el restaurante?

Expansión:
Teacher Edition Only
Ask students to summarize aloud what has happened in the Telehistoria so far.

17 Clientes y camareros

Digital performance space

Hablar

STRATEGY **Hablar**
Plan the whole scene Plan the whole scene from start to finish. What would the waiter or waitress say before, during, and after the meal? What would the customers say at each stage?

Trabaja en un grupo de tres. Preparen una escena en un café con un(a) camarero(a) y clientes. *(Prepare a scene in a café.)*

Para organizarte:
- qué comidas y bebidas piden
- qué sirve el (la) camarero(a)
- cuánto cuesta la comida (la cuenta y la propina)

Camarero(a) Buenas tardes. ¿Quieren ver el menú?

Cliente 1 Buenas tardes. Sí, por favor. Tenemos mucha hambre.

Ustedes pueden pedir el pollo con patatas. Es mucha comida.

Cliente 2 Tal vez, pero hoy tengo ganas de comer...

Expansión:
Teacher Edition Only
Ask students to write what they would order at a restaurant.

Differentiating Instruction

Pre-AP

Expand and Elaborate Read aloud the sentences in the Telehistoria where **servir** and **pedir** are used: **Vamos a pedir la comida.** and **¿Sirven pescado?** Ask each student to expand those two sentences by using other verb forms. For example, **Yo pido ensalada, nosotros pedimos pollo.** Continue with **Nosotros servimos. Tú sirves frutas.** Continue until all students have participated.

Heritage Language Learners

Support What They Know Encourage students to add a complication to their scene in Activity 17. Have them create a problem at the restaurant that needs to be resolved. Perhaps the kitchen has run out of a certain dish. Perhaps the client has forgotten his or her wallet. As students plan their scenes, have them brainstorm how the problem will be resolved.

18 Integración

Digital performance space

Leer
Escuchar
Hablar

Lee el folleto y escucha al guía turístico. Describe cinco actividades que vas a hacer, adónde vas a ir y cómo puedes llegar. *(Describe five activities you are going to do, where, and how you can get there.)*

Fuente 1 Folleto del hotel

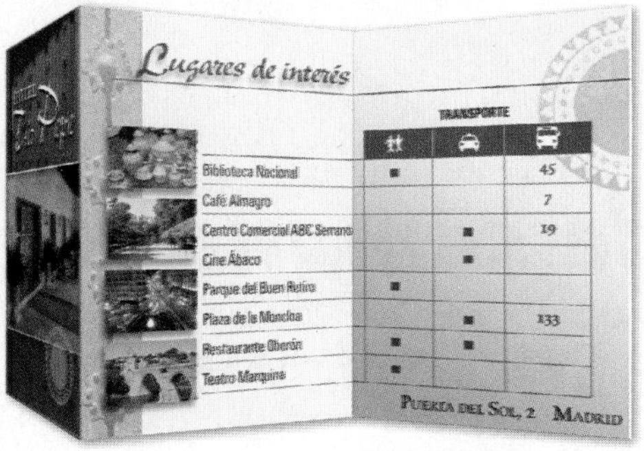

Fuente 2 Anuncio del guía turístico

Listen and take notes

- ¿Qué actividades menciona el guía?
- ¿En qué lugares puedes hacer las actividades?

modelo: Voy a comer pescado. Voy al Restaurante Oberón. Puedo ir a pie o en coche...

Audio Program
TXT CD 4 Tracks 19, 20
Audio Script, TE p. 215b

19 Una crítica culinaria

Digital performance space

Escribir

Escribes críticas para la sección de restaurantes del periódico. Escribe un párrafo sobre tu restaurante favorito. Explica qué sirven, qué pides, cómo es la comida, cómo son los camareros y cuánto cuesta la comida. *(Write a review of your favorite restaurant.)*

modelo: El restaurante Salazar es muy bueno. Los camareros son trabajadores. De plato principal sirven...

Writing Criteria	Excellent	Good	Needs Work
Content	Your review includes a lot of information.	Your review includes some information.	Your review includes little information.
Communication	Most of your review is organized and easy to follow.	Parts of your review are organized and easy to follow.	Your review is disorganized and hard to follow.
Accuracy	Your review has few mistakes in grammar and vocabulary.	Your review has some mistakes in grammar and vocabulary.	Your review has many mistakes in grammar and vocabulary.

Expansión:
Teacher Edition Only
Ask students to read aloud their critiques, and then ask the class to select the best critique.

Más práctica Cuaderno *pp. 180–181* Cuaderno para hispanohablantes *pp. 182–183*

Get Help Online
my.hrw.com

PARA Y PIENSA

Did you get it? Choose the correct verb to make each sentence logical according to the Telehistoria.

1. Maribel y Enrique (almuerzan / encuentran) en un restaurante bonito.
2. Maribel (sirve / pide) mucha comida.
3. Enrique no (puede / vuelve) pagar.

Differentiating Instruction

Multiple Intelligences

Interpersonal Organize students into pairs. Then have them perform Activity 18 in the form of a role-play. One student is the tour guide, and the other is the traveler. Encourage students to think about how their characters would feel at each stage of the situation.

Slower-paced Learners

Peer-study Support Make copies of the Writing Criteria Rubric for each student. Have them exchange their restaurant reviews with a partner. Instruct students to read their partner's work, and circle what they feel is the appropriate box for each criterion. Require students to justify their evaluations with concrete examples, as well as provide advice for improvement.

Long-term Retention

Pre-AP Integration

Activity 18 can be used as a model for a short writing assignment. Have students write a paragraph in which they describe five activities they are going to do, where, and how they are going to get there.

Ongoing Assessment

Rubric Activity 18
Listening/Speaking

Proficient	Not There Yet
Students' notes and oral description reflect comprehension of the materials.	Students' notes and oral description do not reflect comprehension of the materials.

To customize your own rubrics, use the ***Generate Success** Rubric Generator and Graphic Organizers.*

Communication

Motivating with Music

The **¡AvanzaRap!** song for this unit targets vocabulary from Lección 2. To reinforce this vocabulary, play the **¡AvanzaRap!** animated video to students and have them identify the food terms they see and hear. For extra practice, have them complete the Activity Master for Unidad 4.

Ongoing Assessment

Get Help Online
More Practice
my.hrw.com

PARA Y PIENSA **Quick Check** If students have difficulties choosing the correct verb form, review pp. 223, 228. For additional practice, use Reteaching & Practice Copymaster URB 4, pp. 19, 21.

Answers Projectable Transparencies, 4-30

Activity 18 Answers will vary. Sample answers include: Voy a buscar libros. Voy a la Biblioteca Nacional. Puedo ir a pie o en autobús.

Activity 19 Answers will vary. Sample answers include: Mi restaurante favorito se llama Sevilla. Allí sirven pollo con arroz y ensalada, y postres muy ricos. Siempre pido pollo y una ensalada y de postre arroz con leche...

Para y piensa **1.** almuerzan; **2.** pide; **3.** puede

¡AVANZA! Objectives

- Read about weekend activities in Spain and Chile.
- Compare weekend activities in Spain, Chile, and the U.S.
- Find out about popular places and attractions in Madrid and Santiago de Chile.

Core Resource

- Audio Program: TXT CD 4 track 21

Presentation Strategies

- Ask a volunteer to read the ¡Avanza! out loud to the class
- Discuss students' favorite weekend activities briefly before listening to the audio.

STANDARD

1.2 Understand language
1.3 Present information
3.2 Acquire information
4.2 Compare cultures
21st Century **Collaboration,** Multiple Intelligences; **Communication,** Pair Work

Warm Up Projectable Transparencies, 4-23

e → i Verbs Complete each sentence with the correct form of **pedir.**

1. Jorge _____ carne.
2. Yo _____ verduras.
3. Carlos y José _____ patatas.
4. Emilia y yo _____ pollo.
5. Vosotros _____ postre.

Answers: 1. pide; 2. pido; 3. piden; 4. pedimos; 5. pedís

Comparación cultural

Background Information

El Parque del Buen Retiro was originally the site of a royal palace built in 1632 for King Philip IV. Most of the palace was destroyed during the Napoleonic Wars, but its site was opened to the public in 1868. Within the park is the **Estanque del Retiro**, a large artificial lake. Next to it is the Mausoleum of King Alfonso XII, which features a statue of the king on horseback. King Alfonso XII reigned between 1874 and 1885.

Lectura cultural

Additional readings at my.hrw.com SPANISH InterActive Reader

¡AVANZA! Goal: Read about weekend activities in Spain and Chile. Then talk about what each city offers and compare these activities with what you do on weekends.

Comparación cultural

AUDIO

El fin de semana en España y Chile

STRATEGY Leer
List attractions and places
Use a table like the one below to list attractions and the places where they can be found.

	conciertos	zoológico	botes
Madrid	Parque del Buen Retiro		
Santiago de Chile			

Los habitantes de Madrid, España, y Santiago de Chile hacen muchas actividades en el fin de semana. Van a parques, restaurantes, teatros, cines y otros lugares divertidos. También van de compras.

En Madrid hay muchos lugares interesantes para pasar los fines de semana. La Plaza Mayor tiene muchos cafés y restaurantes. Hay un mercado de sellos[1] los domingos. El Parque del Buen Retiro es un lugar perfecto para descansar y pasear. En este parque hay jardines[2], cafés y un lago[3] donde las personas pueden alquilar botes. Hay conciertos allí en el verano. Otro parque popular es la Casa de Campo. Hay un zoológico, una piscina[4], un parque de diversiones[5] y un lago para botes.

Hay muchas tiendas en el centro. El almacén[6] más grande es El Corte Inglés: allí los madrileños[7] pueden comprar ropa, comida y mucho más.

[1] **mercado...** stamp market [2] gardens [3] lake
[4] swimming pool [5] **parque...** amusement park
[6] department store [7] people of Madrid

El Parque del Buen Retiro en Madrid

Differentiating Instruction

Pre-AP

Sequence Information Ask students to work in pairs, telling each other about favorite weekend activities. Ask them to put them in chronological order. **For example: Los sábados a las once practico básquetbol. A la una voy a un restaurante.**

Multiple Intelligences

Interpersonal Divide the class into groups of four. Ask each group to decide on a weekend activity they all like, and where they like to take part in this activity. Have them work collaboratively to create a collage that illustrates what they want to do, where they want to do it, how they will get there, and what they will wear. Their collages should include sentences and phrases in Spanish.

En Santiago de Chile las personas pasan los fines de semana en muchos lugares. Siempre hay mucha actividad en la Plaza de Armas, la parte histórica de Santiago. Hay conciertos allí los domingos.

El parque del Cerro Santa Lucía es perfecto para pasear. Los santiaguinos[8] pueden ver jardines y el panorama de Santiago. El Cerro San Cristóbal en el Parque Metropolitano es un lugar favorito para comer, correr y montar en bicicleta. Hay jardines, piscinas, un zoológico, cafés y restaurantes en el parque.

Los santiaguinos van a tiendas en el centro y a centros comerciales como Alto Las Condes. En el Mercado Central pueden comprar pescado y frutas y comer en restaurantes con precios baratos[9].

[8] people of Santiago, Chile [9] inexpensive

Chile

La Plaza de Armas

Cerro San Cristóbal

PARA Y PIENSA

¿Comprendiste?

1. ¿Qué hay en la Plaza Mayor y la Plaza de Armas los domingos?
2. ¿A qué parques van los madrileños y los santiaguinos?
3. ¿Dónde pueden ir de compras los habitantes de Madrid y Santiago?

¿Y tú?

¿Cuál(es) de estos lugares en Madrid y Santiago quieres visitar? ¿Adónde vas los fines de semana donde vives? ¿Qué haces allí?

Communication
Pair Work

Assign student pairs to talk about a weekend at one of the parks mentioned in the reading. Their conversation should include a place, mode of transportation, what to wear, when to go, and what to do there. For example: **A: ¿Vamos al Parque del Buen Retiro? B: Vale. ¿Vamos a pie o en autobús? A: Vamos en autobús. ¿Qué vas a llevar? B: Jeans y una camiseta porque hace calor. A: ¿Quieres montar en bicicleta? B: No, prefiero...** Ask them to rehearse the conversation before presenting it to the class.

Comparisons
English Language Connections

Call students' attention to the construction: **pasar los fines de semana.** Ask them to compare the grammar and word order to the English: *to spend the weekends.* Point out that in the Spanish construction, a preposition *a* is not used.

Long-term Retention
Personalize It

Ask students to choose a place they would like to visit in Madrid or Santiago. Ask them to imagine themselves in that place and write a short description of it. What time of day is it? What are the people doing? What are they wearing? Encourage them to add as many details as possible.

Differentiating Instruction

Multiple Intelligences

Logical/Mathematical Ask students to list three of their favorite weekend activities, and think about how much time they need to take part in them. Ask them to create a schedule that will show whether they can do all three activities in a Saturday or Sunday afternoon. They should be sure to include time to get ready and transportation time.

Slower-paced Learners

Yes/no questions Ask students yes/no questions to evaluate their understanding of the readings. Examples: **¿Hay muchos cafés y restaurantes en la Plaza Mayor? ¿Hay un lago en el Parque del Buen Retiro? ¿Hay conciertos en la Plaza de Armas? ¿Está el Cerro San Cristóbal en el Parque Metropolitano?**

Answers

Para y piensa ¿Comprendiste?

1. Hay un mercado de sellos en la Plaza Mayor y hay conciertos en la Plaza de Armas.
2. Las madrileños van al Parque del Buen Retiro y a la Casa de Campo. Los santiaguinos van al parque del Cerro Santa Lucía y al Parque Metropolitano.
3. Los habitantes de Madrid pueden ir a El Corte Inglés y los habitantes de Santiago pueden ir a centros comerciales como Alto Las Condes.

¿Y tú? Answers will vary but should follow the model: Quiero visitar... Yo voy a... Voy a las tiendas. Como en restaurantes. Escucho conciertos.

Objectives
- Read about paintings from Spain and from Chile.
- **Culture:** Discuss how to interpret an artist's painting.
- **Community:** Investigate sources of Spanish or Latin American art in the community.
- Create an original landscape painting.

Presentation Strategies
- Ask students if they have ever seen landscape paintings by Spanish or Latin American artists.
- Draw students' attention to the two paintings and to the essential question.
- Ask students to think of the subjects and the colors of the paintings.

STANDARDS
1.3 Present information
2.1 Practices and perspectives
2.2 Products and perspectives
4.2 Compare cultures
5.1 Spanish in the community

Comparación cultural

Essential Question
Suggested Answer An artist can communicate a wide range of messages through a work of art. Artists can express many emotions, from anger to sadness, from love to hatred. They can express the harmony or fury of nature, and they can communicate their opinions of historical events.

Expanded Information
Pedro Lira is considered to be one of the most accomplished Chilean painters of the 19th century. **Ignacio Zuloaga y Zabaleta** traveled widely during his life, returning to Spain to create a personal vision of his country.

Communities

Spanish in the Marketplace
Visit a museum or a poster store in your area. Can you find works of art from Spanish-speaking countries? If so, which artists are represented and what are the titles of their paintings?

Proyectos culturales

Comparación cultural

Pinturas de España y Chile

What messages can an artist communicate through a painting? When you look at a painting, you might see something different than what the artist originally intended when he or she painted it. In fact, a single work of art can have a number of different interpretations.

España Landscape near El Escorial *(1932), Ignacio Zuloaga y Zabaleta*

Chile La Siesta *(1872), Pedro Lira*

Proyecto 1 *Interpret and investigate*
Interpreting the two paintings above from **Spain** and **Chile.**

Instructions
1. After looking at each painting, describe it to yourself. What message do you get from it? As you scan the painting, does any particular point draw your attention?
2. Use the Internet or your school's library to learn more about the two paintings. You might look up information about the artists and whether the paintings reflect personal events in their lives.

Proyecto 2 *Your own painting*
Now try your hand at being an artist.

Materials for your own painting
Construction paper
Charcoal pencil, colored pencils or pens, watercolor paint, paintbrushes

Instructions
Create a landscape scene on construction paper. Use the paintings above as an inspiration.

En tu comunidad
Visit the website of a museum in your part of the country that contains works of art from a Spanish-speaking country. What can you learn about that country by examining the artwork? Record your impressions in a journal.

Differentiating Instruction

Multiple Intelligences
Naturalist Ask students to look at the two paintings for clues to the time of year and the climate of the environment. Ask: **¿Qué estación es? ¿Qué tiempo hace?** What can they tell about the trees? Can they identify the species? In what climates do these trees grow?

English Learners
Build Background Look for landscapes depicting the countryside in the home countries of English learners. Using gestures and simple directions, ask students to find similarities between the paintings of their first countries with those of Lira and Zuloaga.

En resumen
Vocabulario y gramática

ANIMATED GRAMMAR
Interactive Flashcards
my.hrw.com

Vocabulario

Describe Places in Town	
el café	*café*
el centro	*center, downtown*
el cine	*movie theater; the movies*
el parque	*park*
el restaurante	*restaurant*
el teatro	*theater*

Describe Events in Town	
el concierto	*concert*
las entradas	*tickets*
la música rock	*rock music*
la película	*movie*
la ventanilla	*ticket window*

Getting Around Town	
a pie	*by foot*
la calle	*street*
en autobús	*by bus*
en coche	*by car*
encontrar (ue)	*to find*
tomar	*to take*

In a Restaurant

el (la) camarero(a)	*(food) server*
costar (ue)	*to cost*
la cuenta	*bill*
de postre	*for dessert*
el menú	*menu*
la mesa	*table*
el plato principal	*main course*
la propina	*tip*

Ordering from a Menu

pedir (i)	*to order, to ask for*
servir (i)	*to serve*

For Dinner

el arroz	*rice*
el bistec	*beef*
el brócoli	*broccoli*
la carne	*meat*
la ensalada	*salad*
los frijoles	*beans*
el pastel	*cake*
la patata	*potato*
el pescado	*fish*
el pollo	*chicken*
el tomate	*tomato*
las verduras	*vegetables*

Other Words and Phrases	
allí	*there*
almorzar (ue)	*to eat lunch*
aquí	*here*
dormir (ue)	*to sleep*
el lugar	*place*
poder (ue)	*to be able, can*
tal vez	*perhaps, maybe*
ver	*to see*
volver (ue)	*to return, to come back*

Gramática

Notas gramaticales: The verb **ver** *p. 220,* **ir a** + infinitive *p. 222*

Stem-Changing Verbs: o → ue

For o → ue stem-changing verbs, the last o of the stem changes to ue in all forms except **nosotros(as)** and **vosotros(as).**

poder *to be able, can*	
puedo	**podemos**
puedes	**podéis**
puede	**pueden**

Stem-Changing Verbs: e → i

For e → i stem-changing verbs, the last e of the stem changes to i in all forms except **nosotros(as)** and **vosotros(as).**

servir *to serve*	
sirvo	**servimos**
sirves	**servís**
sirve	**sirven**

Practice Spanish with Holt McDougal Apps!

Objective
- Review lesson vocabulary and grammar.

DIGITAL SPANISH

Interactive Flashcards Students can hear every target vocabulary word pronounced in authentic Spanish. Flashcards have Spanish on one side, and a picture or a translation on the other.
Review Games Matching, concentration, hangman, and word search are just a sampling of the fun, interactive games students can play to review for the test.

performance space
News Networking
@HOMETUTOR
CULTURA Interactiva

- Audio and Video Resources
- Interactive Flashcards
- Review Activities
- WebQuest
- Conjuguemos.com

Long-term Retention
Study Tips
Encourage students to list new vocabulary in groups that will help them remember the words later. For example, they could list food vocabulary under meats and vegetables. They could list places and events in town in order of preference.

Communication

Pair Work
Ask students to take turns practicing stem-changing verbs. One student starts a pattern sentence like **Yo puedo ir a la escuela,** and takes turns with his or her partner repeating it using other subject pronouns.

Communication
Humor and Creativity
Ask students to draw cartoons illustrating a visit to a restaurant. They should also create a dialogue between waiter (waitress) and client(s), using the vocabulary words, and write it in balloons over the characters' heads.

Differentiating Instruction

Inclusion
Multisensory Input/Output Ask students to act out going to a concert, and to narrate what they're doing. For example: **Vamos en coche al concierto. Voy a la ventanilla para comprar las entradas. Escuchamos música rock.**

Slower-paced Learners
Memory Aids Ask students to work in groups to create murals on butcher paper. One mural should show a group of friends going out to dinner at a restaurant. The other should show a group of friends going to a concert. The murals should show as much of the activity as possible, and each part should be labeled with the appropriate vocabulary words.

Objective
- Review lesson grammar and vocabulary.

Core Resources
- *Cuaderno,* pp 182–193
- Audio Program: TXT CD 4 track 22

Presentation Strategies
- Before playing the audio for Activity 1, ask students to listen to it carefully, especially to the dishes that are mentioned.
- Before doing Activity 2, have students identify the modes of transportation in the photos.
- Monitor use of correct forms of **o → ue** and **e → i** stem-changing verbs in Activities 3–4.
- Read the Comparación cultural with students and clarify any questions that arise.
- Review may be done in class or given as homework.
- Students can also access the review activities online at my.hrw.com.

STANDARDS
1.2 Understand language, Acts. 1, 3
1.3 Present information, Acts. 2, 4
4.2 Compare cultures, Act. 5
21st Century Creativity and Innovation, Multiple Intelligences

Warm Up
Projectable Transparencies, 4-23

Vocabulary Identify the following as either **carne** or **verdura.**

1. el bistec
2. el brócoli
3. el pescado
4. los frijoles
5. el pollo

Answers: 1. carne; 2. verdura; 3. carne; 4. verdura; 5. carne

Ongoing Assessment
Get Help Online
More Practice
my.hrw.com

Remediation If students achieve less than 85% accuracy with the activities, direct them to pp. 216, 222, 223, 225, 228, 230, 234–235 and to get help online at my.hrw.com.

See Activity answers on p. 239.

Lección 2 Repaso de la lección

@HOMETUTOR
my.hrw.com

¡LLEGADA!

¡AvanzaRap! DVD
Sing and Learn

Now you can
- describe places and events in town
- talk about types of transportation
- say what you are going to do
- order from a menu

Using
- **ir a** + infinitive
- stem-changing verbs: **o → ue**
- stem-changing verbs: **e → i**

To review
- stem-changing verbs: **o → ue** p. 223
- **ir a** + infinitive p. 222
- stem-changing verbs: **e → i** p. 228

1 Listen and understand

AUDIO

Escucha la conversación en un restaurante. Luego contesta las preguntas. *(Listen to the conversation in a restaurant and answer the questions.)*

1. ¿Cuántas personas van a comer?
2. ¿Cómo son los platos principales?
3. ¿Qué pide Raúl con el bistec?
4. ¿Qué pide Raúl para beber?
5. ¿Qué pide Tere de plato principal?
6. ¿Quién pide el pastel de postre?

Audio Program
TXT CD 4 Track 22
Audio Script, TE p. 215b

To review
- **ir a** + infinitive p. 222

2 Say what you are going to do

¿Qué van a hacer estas personas el sábado? ¿Cómo van a ir? *(Tell what people are going to do on Saturday and how they plan to go there.)*

modelo: Angélica / almorzar en un restaurante
Angélica va a almorzar en un restaurante.
Va a ir en autobús.

1. Gilberto / pasear en el parque

2. yo / volver al centro

3. las chicas / beber refrescos en un café

4. tú / ver una película en el cine

5. nosotros / escuchar música rock

6. vosotros / ir al teatro

Differentiating Instruction

Slower-paced Learners
Read Before Listening Before listening to the audio for Activity 1, provide students with the script. Ask student pairs to identify the main characters. Then ask them to read the roles of Raúl and the waiter. Check comprehension as students read: **¿Es la mesa para dos personas? (Sí.) ¿Ven los platos principales en el pizarrón? (No.)**

Pre-AP
Circumlocution Ask students to use an English-Spanish dictionary to find as many different kinds of vegetables as they can and to write them in Spanish and English in their notebooks. Ask them to name the vegetables to the class and to describe them using terms they know. For example: **Las espinacas son verduras verdes. A Popeye le gustan mucho.**

To review
stem-changing verbs: o → ue
p. 223

3 | Describe places and events in town

Tomás describe sus actividades. Completa su mensaje con la forma correcta del verbo apropiado. *(Complete the e-mail message with the correct form of the appropriate verb.)*

encontrar	almorzar
poder	volver
costar	dormir

Los domingos por la tarde, yo __1.__ en el restaurante Casa Serrano con mi familia. Nosotros __2.__ platos muy buenos en el menú y la comida no __3.__ mucho. Yo nunca __4.__ comer todo porque sirven mucha comida. Nosotros __5.__ a casa a las tres o a las cuatro. Muchas veces mis hermanos menores están cansados y __6.__ dos horas. Me gusta pasar los domingos con mi familia. Es un día muy tranquilo.

To review
stem-changing verbs: e → i
p. 228

4 | Order from a menu

Describe los problemas en el restaurante. *(Describe the problems in the restaurant.)*

modelo: Leonor: carne / el camarero: pescado
Leonor pide carne, pero el camarero sirve pescado.

1. tú: agua / la camarera: leche
2. yo: brócoli / el camarero: patatas
3. ustedes: bistec / los camareros: pollo
4. Nicolás: ensalada / el camarero: tomates
5. nosotros: arroz / los camareros: verduras
6. vosotros: pastel / la camarera: helado

To review
Comparación cultural pp. 216, 225, 230
Lectura cultural pp. 234–235

5 | Spain, Guatemala, and Chile

Comparación cultural

Answer these culture questions.

1. What is featured at Madrid's Teatro de la Comedia?
2. What can you find at Madrid's Rastro and Chichicastenango's market?
3. Who is depicted in *Las meninas*?
4. What can you see and do in Madrid's Parque del Buen Retiro and Santiago's Parque Metropolitano?

Más práctica Cuaderno *pp. 182–193* Cuaderno para hispanohablantes *pp. 184–193*

Get Help Online my.hrw.com

Differentiating Instruction

Multiple Intelligences

Visual Learners Ask students to work in groups to make a brochure of a park, real or imaginary. The brochure should include the park's location, days open, opening and closing times, main attractions, and activities for each place. It should include a map of the park with the sites labeled as well as pictures with captions of main attractions.

Heritage Language Learners

Support What They Know Elicit recommendations from students about traditional restaurants and/or foods one would try when visiting their home communities. What do the restaurants look like? When do they open for lunch and for dinner? What items would be found on the menu?

✓ Ongoing Assessment

Get Help Online
More Practice
my.hrw.com

Peer Assessment Have students read their completed e-mail from Activity 3 to a partner, who will correct any errors.

Answers Projectable Transparencies, 4-31

Answers for Activities on p. 238.

Activity 1

1. Dos personas van a comer.
2. Los platos principales son ricos.
3. Raúl pide arroz con el bistec.
4. Raúl pide un refresco para beber.
5. Tere pide el pescado con una ensalada.
6. Raúl pide el pastel.

Activity 2

1. Gilberto va a pasear.... Va a ir a pie.
2. Yo voy a volver al centro. Voy a ir en coche.
3. Las chicas van a beber refrescos en un café. van a ir en autobús.
4. Tú vas a ver.... Vas a ir a pie.
5. Nosotros vamos a escuchar música rock. Vamos a ir en autobús.
6. Vosotros vais a ir.... Vais a ir en coche.

Activity 3

1. almuerzo
2. encontramos
3. cuesta
4. puedo
5. volvemos
6. duermen

Activity 4

1. Tú pides agua, pero la camarera sirve leche.
2. Yo pido brócoli, pero el camerero sirve patatas.
3. Ustedes piden bistec, pero los camareros sirven pollo.
4. Nicolás pide ensalada, pero el camarero sirve tomates.
5. Nosotros pedimos arroz, pero los camareros sirven verduras.
6. Vosotros pedís pastel, pero... sirve helado.

Activity 5

1. Many traditional Spanish plays are featured at Madrid's Teatro de la Comedia.
2. At El Rastro fleamarket in Madrid one can find antiques, secondhand clothing, CDs, books, maps and art. In Chichicastenango's market one can find handicrafts from the Maya-Quiché culture, such as *traditional dresses,* colorful textiles, *huipiles* and other items such as fruits, vegetables, masks, baskets, candles, and flowers.
3. *Las Meninas* shows the *Infanta* (princess) and her attendants.
4. In Madrid's Parque del Buen Retiro there are gardens, cafés, and a lake. You can go there for walks, row on the lake, have refreshments at a café, or listen to concerts during the summer. Santiago's Parque Metropolitano has gardens, swimming pools, a zoo, cafés, and restaurants. You can eat, run, ride bikes, swim, look at the animals in the zoo, and take walks in the gardens.

Objectives
- Read three personal narratives about weekend activities in three different countries.
- Have students compare their favorite activities with one of the three students in the text.
- Write a paragraph about favorite Saturday activities.

Core Resources
- *Cuaderno,* pp. 194–196
- Audio Program: TXT CD 4 track 23
- Video Program: DVD 1

Presentation Strategies
- Ask students to look at the photos on pp. 240 and 241 and describe what they see.
- Instruct students to follow the text in the book as they listen to the audio.
- Tell students to think about their own favorite activities while they are reading about those of Anita, Rodrigo, and Armando.

STANDARDS
1.2 Understand language
1.3 Present information
2.1 Practices and perspectives
2.2 Products and perspectives
4.2 Compare cultures
21st Century **Communication,** Personalize It/ Group Work

Long-term Retention

Personalize It
Ask students to respond to a student on p. 241, as if they were pen pals. Have them include a brief description of themselves, where they go on weekends, what activities they do, and what type of clothes they wear.

Comparación cultural
Exploring the Theme
In many towns and cities, young people like to spend leisure time at local shopping malls. Whether they visit a two-story mall with 100 shops and a food court or a place like Xanadú in Madrid, where they can not only shop, but take ski lessons and practice with artificial snow, **centros comerciales** are a favorite for teens. They can be found in nearly every corner of the world.

Comparación cultural

AUDIO

¿Adónde vamos el sábado?

Lectura y escritura

WebQuest my.hrw.com

1. **Leer** Activities that young people do vary around the world. Read what Anita, Rodrigo, and Armando do for fun on Saturdays.
2. **Escribir** Using the three descriptions as models, write a short paragraph about what you like to do on Saturdays.

STRATEGY **Escribir**
Create an activity chart
To write about what you do for fun on Saturdays, use an activity chart like the one shown.

Categoría	Detalles
lugares	
ropa	
actividades	

Step 1 Complete the chart with details about where you go, what you wear, and what you do for fun on Saturdays.

Step 2 Write your paragraph. Make sure to include all the information from your chart. Check your writing by yourself or with help from a friend. Make final corrections.

Compara con tu mundo
Use the paragraph you wrote to compare the activities you do for fun to the activities described by *one* of the three students. How are the activities similar? How are they different?

Cuaderno *pp. 194–196* Cuaderno para hispanohablantes *pp. 194–196*

Differentiating Instruction

Slower-paced Learners
Read Before Listening Prepare a list of statements related to each of the people in the narratives. After students read the narratives, read the statements and have them say the name of the person to whom it refers. For example: **Necesito comprar camisetas y calcetines. (Rodrigo) Quiero llevar un sombrero de vaquero. (Armando)**

Multiple Intelligences
Logical/Mathematical Have students calculate the distance between: their town/city and Madrid; Madrid and Santiago; and Santiago and Guatemala. Have them figure out the flight time between these cities. Have them write out the statistics they find in Spanish. Example: **De Madrid a Santiago de Chile–cinco mil kilómetros. Llegas en trece horas y media en avión** (plane).

CULTURA Interactiva my.hrw.com *See these pages come alive!*

Guatemala

Anita

¿Qué tal? Soy Anita y me gusta escuchar música folklórica. El sábado mis amigos y yo pensamos ir a un concierto de marimba[1] en el centro. Las entradas no cuestan mucho y los conciertos son muy buenos. ¿Qué ropa voy a llevar? Quiero llevar un vestido porque es primavera y hace calor. Mis amigos prefieren llevar camisetas y jeans.

[1] musical instrument resembling a xylophone

España

Rodrigo

¡Hola! Me llamo Rodrigo y vivo en Madrid. El sábado quiero ir de compras con mi hermano. Siempre necesito comprar camisetas y calcetines. Muchas veces los encuentro en el centro comercial. Se llama Xanadú y tiene tiendas, restaurantes y ¡un parque de nieve! Allí puedes practicar deportes de invierno durante todo el año. A mi hermano le gusta la nieve en el verano, pero a mí no. En el verano ¡prefiero tener calor!

Chile

Armando

¡Hola! Me llamo Armando y soy de Santiago, Chile. En septiembre puedes ir a muchos rodeos porque hay muchas fiestas nacionales en Chile. El sábado voy a ir a un rodeo con mis amigos para ver a los huasos[2]. Pienso llevar unos jeans nuevos y una chaqueta porque no quiero tener frío. Quiero llevar un sombrero de vaquero[3], pero no puedo. ¡Cuestan mucho!

[2] Chilean cowboys [3] cowboy

Differentiating Instruction

Pre-AP

Draw conclusions Ask students to write a short paragraph in which they explain why shopping malls have become so popular. For example: **A muchas personas les gustan los centros comerciales. Pueden hacer muchas cosas allí: pueden comprar ropa, comer y pasar un rato con los amigos.** After they've written their paragraphs, ask them to share their thoughts with the class.

Heritage Language Learners

Writing Skills Ask students to choose Anita, Rodrigo, or Armando as the subject of a fictional story they will write. The story should be at least two paragraphs long and should describe in greater detail the activities they discuss here. Students should be creative.

Communication

Group Work

Divide the class into groups of three. One student plays the role of Anita, Rodrigo, or Armando and the other two are students from the U.S. The students from the U.S. write a list of questions in Spanish based on the narratives. They use these questions to conduct an interview with one of the three teenagers and report the results to the class. Sample questions to Anita: **¿Qué te gusta escuchar? ¿Adónde piensas ir el sábado? ¿Qué ropa vas a llevar?**

✓ Ongoing Assessment

Quick Check Ask students yes/no questions to assess comprehension about each of the three narrations, and write their responses on the board. **¿Quiere Armando llevar un sombrero de vaquero? ¿A Rodrigo le gusta tener frío? ¿Piensa Anita llevar un vestido?**

✓ Ongoing Assessment

Rubric Lectura y escritura

Writing Criteria	Excellent	Good	Needs Work
Content	Paragraph contains a lot of information.	Paragraph contains some information.	Paragraph lacks information.
Communication	Paragraph is organized and easy to follow.	Paragraph is fairly well organized and easy to follow.	Paragraph is disorganized and hard to follow.
Accuracy	Paragraph has few mistakes in vocabulary and grammar.	Paragraph has some mistakes in vocabulary and grammar.	Paragraph has many mistakes in vocabulary and grammar.

To customize your own rubrics, use the ***Generate Success*** *Rubric Generator and Graphic Organizers.*

Objective
- Cumulative review

Core Resource
- Audio Program: TXT CD 4 track 24

Review Options
- **Activity 1:** Listening
- **Activities 2, 3:** Speaking
- **Activity 4:** Writing
- **Activity 5:** Speaking
- **Activity 6:** Speaking and writing
- **Activity 7:** Reading and writing

STANDARDS
1.1 Engage in conversation, Acts. 3, 5, 6
1.2 Understand language, Acts. 1, 7
1.3 Present information, Acts. 2–7
21st Century **Communication,** Act. 3/Heritage Language Learners; **Creativity and Innovation,** Act. 4; **Technology Literacy,** Act. 7

Long-term Retention
Study Tips
Have students review the vocabulary for Unidad 4. Ask them to list the cognates. Then tell students to make a second list for words that are not cognates. Discuss the best ways for them to organize this list.

UNIDADES 1-4

Repaso inclusivo
Options for Review

¡AvanzaRap! DVD Sing and Learn

Digital performance space

1 Listen, understand, and compare
Escuchar

Listen to Mrs. Estrada and her son, Carlitos, order a meal at a restaurant. Then answer the questions.

1. ¿Qué tiene ganas de comer Carlitos?
2. ¿Qué pide para empezar? ¿Y de plato principal?
3. ¿Qué plato pide la señora Estrada para empezar?
4. ¿Qué no sirven hoy en el restaurante?
5. ¿Qué van a beber ellos?

Audio Program
TXT CD 4 Track 24
Audio Script, TE p. 215b

Which order most resembles what you like to eat? What foods and drinks do you order when you go to restaurants?

2 Present a family outing
Hablar

Prepare a presentation about a family outing to a restaurant. Bring in a photo of your own or one from a magazine. Talk about the clothes each person is wearing, what food the restaurant serves, what each person orders, and how much it costs. You should talk for at least three minutes.

3 Compare school days
Hablar

Interview a partner about his or her day at school. Ask about the classes your partner prefers, what he or she eats for lunch and at what time, and what he or she is going to do after school today. Finish by comparing your days. Your conversation should be at least four minutes long.

4 Make a flier
Escribir

As president of the Spanish club, you have been put in charge of a booth at the upcoming international food fair. You have decided to serve breakfast dishes from Spain and Mexico. Use the Internet to learn about Spanish and Mexican cuisine. Create a flier to advertise what food and beverages you will serve, at what time you will be serving them, and how much the tickets cost. Your flier should have illustrations and describe in detail each dish.

Answers
Activity 1
1. Carlitos tiene ganas de comer papas fritas.
2. Para empezar, pide sopa y de plato principal pollo con papas fritas.
3. Para empezar, la señora Estrada pide una ensalada de tomates.
4. Hoy no sirven pescado en el restaurante.
5. Carlitos va a beber un refresco y la señora Estrada va a beber agua.

Differentiating Instruction

Pre-AP
Main Idea Ask students to review pp. 242 and 243. Give them the following questions to guide their review: What are the common themes in all the activities? How will these activities help students learn more successfully? In other words, what is the main idea? Have them write their answers in Spanish.

Multiple Intelligences
Kinesthetic Ask students to help set up stations around the room at which they will find a variety of props they might want to use to do the activities. For example, they might want to put mirrors, fashion show costumes, and makeup in one area; art supplies and materials needed to create scenery for Activity 5 in another; and the fliers for Activity 4 in a third area.

5 Help find a lost child

Hablar

Role-play a situation in which you are a mall employee in customer service. Your partner is shopping at the mall with a younger cousin, but can't find him or her. Interview your partner to find out as much descriptive information as possible, including age, physical characteristics, and clothing. Your conversation should be at least three minutes long.

6 Create a fashion show

Hablar
Escribir

Work in a group of five. Individually, write a detailed description of the clothes you are wearing. Include color, where the clothes are from, where you can buy each item, how much they cost, and in what season(s) you can wear them. Your description should have at least eight sentences. Then perform the fashion show for the class, reading each other's descriptions as each "model" walks down the runway.

7 Plan a weekend with family

Leer
Escribir

You are studying in Barcelona, Spain, for the summer and your parents are coming to visit. Read this newspaper supplement to find out about the weekend's events. Then write an e-mail to your parents, and suggest what you can do and where you can go together or separately during the weekend. Keep in mind everyone's likes and dislikes. Your e-mail should have at least six suggestions.

Suplemento especial – fin de semana

GUÍA DEL OCIO - BARCELONA

VIERNES

Cena especial
Comida española típica, con música de flamenco.
Restaurante Casals (de las 21.30 a las 23.30 h)

Concierto
Los hermanos Pujols tocan música rock.
Plaza Cataluña (a las 14.30 h)

SÁBADO

Películas
Terror en el centro
Hollywood. Película de terror. Dos chicos de Nueva York van en autobús cuando llegan unos extraterrestres horribles.
Cines Maremagnum (a las 16.00 y 18.30 h)
Mi tía loca
España. Película cómica. La historia de una chica y su tía favorita.
Cine Diagonal Mar (a las 13.30 y 21.00 h)

Comprar y pasear
La calle que lo tiene todo: libros, ropa, comida ¡y más!
Las Ramblas (todo el día)

DOMINGO

Eliminar el cáncer
Puedes pasear y donar dinero para combatir el cáncer.
Parque Güell (a las 10.00 h)

Compras
Los mejores precios del verano en las tiendas de ropa.
Centro Comercial Barcelona Glorias (de las 10.30 a las 20.30 h)

Concierto de Beethoven
La orquesta de Barcelona toca música clásica. Un concierto para toda la familia.
Teatro Liceu (a las 20.00 h)

Communication
Group Work

Assign students to work in groups to create summaries of each section in Unit 4. When the summaries are all completed, make multiple copies and have students bind them into booklets for each class member.

✓ Ongoing Assessment

Integrated Performance Assessment Rubric Oral Activities 2, 3, 5, 6 Written Activities 4, 6, 7

Very Good	Proficient	Not There Yet
The student thoroughly develops all requirements of the task.	The student develops most requirements of the task.	The student does not develop the requirements of the task.
The student demonstrates excellent control of verb forms.	The student demonstrates good to fair control of verb forms.	The student demonstrates poor control of verb forms.
Good variety of appropriate vocabulary.	Adequate variety of appropriate vocabulary.	The vocabulary is not appropriate.
The pronunciation is very good to excellent.	The pronunciation is fair to good.	The pronunciation is poor.

To customize your own rubrics, use the ***Generate Success** Rubric Generator and Graphic Organizers.*

Differentiating Instruction

Inclusion

Metacognitive Support For Activity 5, students will need to review descriptive information including age, physical characteristics, and clothing. Refer them to the En resumen, pp. 75, 183, and 213 and ask them to copy the vocabulary for each topic in their notebooks, using different colored pencils or markers and saying the words as they write them.

Heritage Language Learners

Writing Skills Have students write an e-mail to a friend from another state or country making suggestions about what to do on the weekend in their own city or town. Suggestions should include going to a restaurant, going to a movie, play or concert, and going shopping. Students should check their work for correct spelling, punctuation, and grammar.

Proyectos adicionales

Planning Ahead

Projects **Plan a birthday party.** Have students work together to plan a birthday party for a friend. Divide the class into five committees:

1. Food: plan and prepare the menu, arrange for plates, silverware, etc.
2. Presents: plan and assemble party favors and gifts for the birthday person
3. Music: plan and arrange the music to be played
4. Activities: plan games or dances for during the party
5. Decorations: plan and assemble balloons, paper chains, or other decorations

Committees will need to consult with each other, and work together to prepare their aspect of the party. Each group should take notes for their plans in Spanish.

Then they are responsible for securing the items necessary to make the party a success.

PACING SUGGESTION: Have students begin discussing their plans at the beginning of the unit. Provide a schedule with "milestones" to encourage timely progress. Then set the actual party date!

21st Century **Collaboration**

Web Research

Go online to learn more about real estate in Quito, Ecuador. A simple search such as "Quito and real estate" or "Ecuador and houses" will yield many results. Once students have found a selection of Web listings, instruct them to find one particularly interesting home or apartment for sale or rent. Have them draw a picture of the locale, and take notes about the home on an index card. Give students the opportunity to browse through listings that others have found. Discuss with students which offers look like the nicest homes, the best locations, the most value for the price, etc.

PACING SUGGESTION: Throughout the unit as time allows.

21st Century **Information Literacy**

(Virtual) Bulletin Board

Create a bulletin board with the title **La casa ideal.** Organize students into groups of three or four, and provide each group with a large piece of poster board, markers, and a selection of home decorating magazines. Assign each group a certain room of the house to design and decorate. They should create a floor plan of their room that answers the following questions:

- What types of furniture are in the room?
- What is the design motif or color scheme?
- Where are the windows, doors, and closets in the room?

Once groups have completed their rooms, arrange all of the rooms together on a wall to create an entire house. Discuss with students which rooms should go where.

PACING SUGGESTION: After **Lección 1** to reinforce vocabulary related to homes and furniture.

Create a bulletin board with the title **¡A vender!** Invite students to bring in a photograph or create a drawing of a house or apartment that could be for sale. Assemble all of the pictures on a bulletin board, and use them to spark discussions and questions about houses and homes. You can ask students yes or no questions about the different homes, or have students ask each other questions about what they see. Encourage students to refer to these photos and pictures to write their classified ads in Activity 21. As a tech alternative, you may wish to have students create their projects on a class wiki page.

PACING SUGGESTION: After **Lección 1** to reinforce vocabulary related to houses and furniture. Also, to provide a visual resource for Lesson 1, Activity 21.

21st Century **Creativity and Innovation** (Business Literacy)

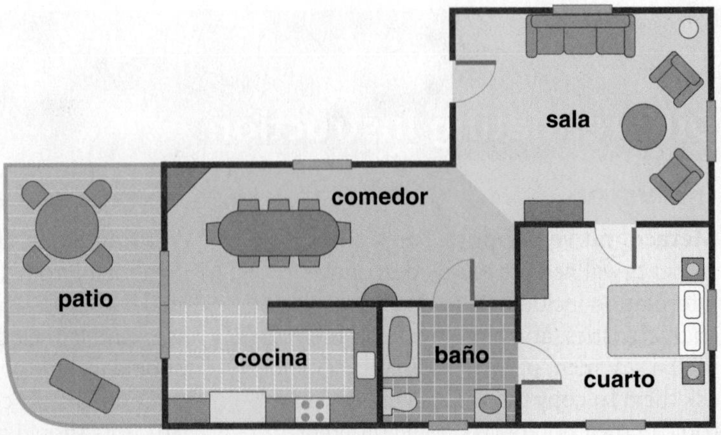

Games

Dibujarama

In advance, gather a timer, an easel, a large drawing pad, and markers. Prepare ten to twenty index cards with commands familiar to students. These might be commands related to household chores or classroom activities. Each card should include one command.

Divide the class into two or three teams. Give a card to a volunteer from the first team. This student must read the card silently. He or she then has thirty seconds to draw the command for the other members of the team. When guessing, only Spanish may be used, or the team forfeits its turn. The artist may not use words or gestures when giving clues. If the team guesses the correct command, it gets a point. The next team then gets a turn.

PACING SUGGESTION: After **Lección 2** to reinforce vocabulary related to household chores and to practice familiar commands.

Pantomimas

Divide the class into two teams. Then have each student write a command on a slip of paper. The command might have to do with household chores, school activities, or even sports. Collect the commands and place them in a separate box for each team. A player from one team picks a slip of paper from the other team's box. That player must pantomime the command written until someone on his or her team guesses it. Place a 30-second time limit, and let students know that using English disqualifies their team for that round.

PACING SUGGESTION: After **Lección 2** to reinforce vocabulary related to household chores and to practice familiar commands.

¡AvanzaRap! DVD

- Video animations of all **¡AvanzaRap!** songs (with Karaoke track)
- Teaching Suggestions
- **¡AvanzaRap!** Activity Masters
- **¡AvanzaRap!** Video Scripts and Answers

Also available on the Teacher One Stop

Recipe

Ecuador is known for its wide variety of food. Fruits, vegetables, meat, seafood, and grains like **quinoa** are all used. Soups and stews are especially common. This salad recipe features another common ingredient of Ecuadorian cooking—corn.

Ensalada de maíz ecuatoriana

Ingredientes

2 latas de maíz
1 lata de chiles verdes
1 pimentón rojo
1 cucharadita de mostaza
1/2 cucharada de mayonesa
1 cucharadita de jugo de limón
3 cebollas verdes

Instrucciones

Corte los chiles, el pimentón rojo y la cebolla. Póngalos a un lado. Mezcle la mostaza, la mayonesa y el jugo de limón en un tazón. Añada el maíz y los vegetales. Mezcle todos los ingredientes. Sazónelo con sal y pimienta.

Music

Direct students to reread the description of the **sanjuanito** on pp. 288 and 289. Main points include:

- The dancers form a circle.
- The dancers wave scarves in the air.
- The music is upbeat and rhythmic.

Then have interested students learn more about this traditional dance via the Internet. Once they have a clear idea about the dance's rhythms, costumes, and special features, have small groups prepare a performance of the **sanjuanito.** Invite students who are not interested in dancing to participate in a rhythm orchestra.

UNIT THEME
Welcome to our house!

UNIT STANDARDS
COMMUNICATION
- Describe a house and household items
- Indicate the order of things
- Describe people and locations
- Plan a party
- Talk about chores and responsibilities
- Tell someone what to do
- Say what you just did

CULTURES
- The art of Targelia Toaquiza
- The Mitad del Mundo monument and the Argentine city of Ushuaia
- Houses and apartments in Ecuador
- Fiestas de Quito
- Otavalo textiles and textile market
- Textile art in Ecuador and Panama
- Celebrations in Spanish-speaking countries

CONNECTIONS
- Mathematics: Comparing shapes used in Incan structures
- Social Studies: Researching Incan construction methods
- History: Learning about all aspects of the Incan empire
- Language: Finding Quechua words that are used in Spanish

COMPARISONS
- Types of houses and apartments around the world
- Accenting in Spanish and English words
- Important geographical locations
- Birthday parties
- Community celebrations
- Traditional crafts in Ecuador and the U.S.
- Folk dances of Ecuador and Panama
- Otavalan tapestries in Ecuador and Kuna women's mola tapestries in Panama
- Party celebrations in Panama, Argentina, Ecuador, and the U.S.

COMMUNITIES
- Where local artists sell their work and how speaking Spanish can help them.

UNIDAD 5

Ecuador

¡Bienvenido a nuestra casa!

Lección 1
Tema: ***Vivimos aquí***

Lección 2
Tema: ***Una fiesta en casa***

«¡Hola!
Somos Fernando y Elena.
Somos de Quito, Ecuador.»

Población: 13.927.650

Área: 109.483 millas cuadradas

Capital: Quito

Moneda: el dólar estadounidense, desde *(since)* el año 2000

Idiomas: español, quechua y otras lenguas indígenas

Comida típica: locro, fritada, llapingachos

Gente famosa: Alexandra Ayala Marín (periodista), Gilda Holst (escritora), Julio Jaramillo (cantante), Jefferson Pérez (atleta)

Canguil, tostado, chifles

244 doscientos cuarenta y cuatro

Cultural Geography

Setting the Scene
- **¿Es Quito la capital de Ecuador? (Sí.)**
- **¿Es fritada una comida típica de Ecuador? (Sí.)**
- **¿Hay más un idioma en Ecuador? (Sí, español, quechua y otras lenguas indígenas)**

Teaching with Maps
- **¿Qué países tienen fronteras con Ecuador? (Colombia y Perú)**
- **¿Qué islas son parte de Ecuador? (las Islas Galápagos)**
- **¿En qué océano está la costa de Ecuador? (el Océano Pacífico)**

CULTURA Interactiva
my.hrw.com
See these pages come alive!

Jóvenes ecuatorianos aplauden al equipo nacional

◀ **Nuestra pasión: el fútbol** In Ecuador, major-league soccer games are played on weekends in the cities of Quito and Guayaquil, while informal games are played at any time, in every city, town, and village. These fans of the **Selección Nacional** team hope for an appearance at the World Cup (**Copa Mundial**). *Where and when is your favorite sport played?*

Las montañas de los Andes Not far from the capital city of Quito lies the 19,347-foot Cotopaxi, the world's highest active volcano. The Andes mountain range, which stretches 4,500 miles north to south along the western coast of South America, has many mountains that reach 20,000 feet or more. *What mountain ranges in the United States are you familiar with?*▶

El volcán Cotopaxi y la ciudad de Quito

Las floristas *(1916), Camilo Egas*

◀ **La ropa tradicional** In *Las floristas*, Camilo Egas shows indigenous women from the market town of Otavalo, north of Quito. They are wearing traditional clothing: white blouses and layered white and black skirts with red sashes, along with gold or red coral jewelry. *How do people in the United States express themselves through the clothing they wear?*

Bridging Cultures

Heritage Language Learners

Support What They Know Invite students who have a personal or family connection to Ecuador to add to the information presented on pp. 244 and 245. What are their memories and/or impressions of Ecuador? How would they compare houses and schools in Ecuador with those in the United States?

English Learners

Build Background Help English learners make connections between the information on Ecuador and that of their own country of origin. After reading each paragraph on p. 245 aloud, ask students whether their home country is similar or different. Is soccer a passion of the country? Is there a typical traditional dress in their country?

CULTURA Interactiva
my.hrw.com

Send your students to my.hrw.com to explore authentic Ecuadorian culture. Tell them to click on Cultura interactiva to see these pages come alive!

Cultures

About the Photos

- Ecuadorians of all ages are completely involved in the world of soccer. Ecuadorians enjoy following the careers of their favorite athletes.
- The **Cotopaxi** volcano dominates the backdrop of Quito. Every year, experienced mountaineers and glacier climbers enjoy the thrill of seeing the view of the city below from a high point on the volcano.
- Camilo Egas (1889–1962) did much through his art to make people aware of the pride and beauty of Ecuador's indigenous people. Many of his paintings can be seen at the Museo Nacional del Banco Central in Quito.

Expanded Information

- The **Selección Nacional,** Ecuador's national team, won 24th place in the World Cup in 2002.
- Although **Cotopaxi** is an active volcano, it has been more than 100 years since it destroyed the nearby city of Latacunga. The volcano is not expected to erupt again for the next several decades.
- The traditional clothing of the Otavalo people is not restricted to women. Men have their own ensemble, which includes a blue poncho, white knickers, a felt fedora, and of course, the long braid, called a **shimba**.

Video Character Guide

Fernando is a friend of Elena and her brother, Manuel. The three of them enjoy playing video games.

Lesson Overview

Culture at a Glance

Topic & Activity	Essential Question
Houses in Ecuador pp. 246–247	Do you live in an apartment building or a house?
Ecuadorian houses p. 255	How do landscapes reflect the way of life in a community?
Geographical locations p. 260	How does a country's location in the world make it unique?
Living in Ecuador pp. 264–265	Where would you prefer to live?
Culture review p. 269	How do Ecuador and Argentina have unique geographical sites?

COMPARISON COUNTRIES Ecuador Argentina Panamá

Practice at a Glance

	Objective	Activity & Skill
Vocabulary	A house	1: Writing/Speaking; 3: Listening/Reading; 5: Writing; 6: Writing; 7: Reading/Writing; 10: Speaking; 13: Speaking; 19: Speaking; 20: Reading/Listening, Speaking; 21: Writing; Repaso 1: Listening
	Household items	2: Writing, Speaking; 16: Speaking; 4: Speaking; Repaso 2: Writing
Grammar	Ser or estar	6: Writing; 7: Reading/Writing; 8: Listening/Writing; 9: Writing; 10: Speaking; 12: Writing; 13: Speaking; 18: Listening/Reading; 19: Speaking; 21: Writing; Repaso 3: Writing; Repaso 4: Writing
	Ordinal numbers	14: Writing; 15: Speaking; 16: Speaking; 20: Reading/Listening/Speaking; 21: Writing; Repaso 3: Writing
Communication	Describe a house and household items	1: Writing/Speaking; 2: Writing/Speaking; 3: Listening/Reading; 4: Speaking; 5: Writing; 6: Writing; 10: Speaking; 19: Speaking; Repaso 2: Writing
	Indicate the order of things	14: Writing; 15: Speaking; 16: Speaking; 17: Listening, Reading; Repaso 2: Writing
	Describe people and locations	7: Reading/Writing; 8: Listening/Writing; 9: Writing; 10: Speaking; 11: Listening/Reading; 12: Writing; 13: Speaking; 18: Listening/Reading; Repaso 4: Writing
	Pronunciation: Accents	*Pronunciación: La acentuación* p. 259: Listening/Speaking
Recycle	Stem-changing verbs: **o** → **ue**	1: Writing/Speaking
	Location words	6: Writing
	Colors	10: Speaking
	Clothing	15: Speaking

The following presentations are recorded in the Audio Program for ***¡Avancemos!***

- **¡A responder!** *page 249*
- **8: Los amigos de Manuel** *page 254*
- **20: Integración** *page 263*
- **Repaso de la lección** *page 268*
  1: Listen and understand

For **¡AvanzaRap!** scripts, see the **¡AvanzaRap! DVD.**

¡A responder! TXT CD 5 track 2

1. Hay una alfombra.
2. Hay una cómoda.
3. Hay una lámpara.
4. Hay un espejo.
5. Hay un sillón.
6. Hay una cama.
7. Hay un sofá.
8. Hay unas cortinas.

8 | Los amigos de Manuel

TXT CD 5 track 4

Estoy contento hoy porque voy a hablar por teléfono con mis amigos. Mi amiga Rosa es de Chile. Es cómica y muy inteligente. Su casa está cerca del centro comercial. Mis amigos José y Carlos son de Estados Unidos. Son altos y cómicos. Son hermanos. Su apartamento está cerca de la escuela. Es grande y muy bonito.

20 | Integración TXT CD 5 tracks 8, 9

¡Hola! Soy el señor Chávez. Si usted y su familia quieren alquilar un apartamento en el centro de Quito, tengo un apartamento muy bonito. Está en la calle Venezuela. No es muy grande, pero no es tan pequeño como mi apartamento. Tiene cuatro cuartos y dos baños. La sala es grande y tiene muchas ventanas. La cocina es un poco pequeña. El apartamento no tiene patio, pero está al lado del parque y cerca del centro comercial. El apartamento está en el quinto piso y pueden ver el parque. Está un poco lejos de la escuela, pero pueden tomar el autobús. ¡Ah!... una cosa más. No cuesta mucho; ustedes pueden alquilarlo por 1.150 dólares al mes. Bueno, hablamos más tarde. Adiós.

Repaso de la lección TXT CD 5 track 11

1 Listen and understand

Vivo en una casa muy bonita. La sala es grande y tiene muchas ventanas. En la sala hay un televisor, un sofá y tres lámparas. El comedor está al lado de la sala. Los muebles del comedor son una mesa grande y seis sillas. También hay unas cortinas azules. Detrás del comedor está la cocina. Cuando subimos la escalera, encontramos tres cuartos. En los cuartos hay cómodas, armarios y lámparas. Mi cuarto es amarillo. También hay dos baños en el segundo piso. Vamos a bajar la escalera ahora para ir al patio. Tenemos un patio grande y un jardín bonito. Mi casa es la casa ideal, ¿no?

Resource List

Everything you need to ...

Plan	Present	Assess
Teacher One Stop ✓Lesson Plans ✓Teacher Resources ✓Audio and Video	**Interactive Whiteboard Lessons** **Teacher One Stop with Projectable Transparencies** **Power Presentations** **AnimatedGrammar**	**Online Assessment** ✓ Assessments for on-level, modified, pre-AP, and heritage learners ✓ Create customized tests with **Examview Assessment Suite** ✓ **performance space** ✓ *Generate Success* Rubric Generator

Print

Plan	Present	Practice	Assess
URB 5 • Video Scripts pp. 69–70 • Family Letter p. 91 • Absent Student Copymasters pp. 93–100 **Best Practices Toolkit**	**URB 5** • Video Activities pp. 51–58	• *Cuaderno* pp. 197–219 • *Cuaderno para hispanohablantes* pp. 197–219 • *Lecturas para todos* pp. 42–46 • *Lecturas para hispanohablantes* • *¡AvanzaCómics! SuperBruno y Nati,* Episodio 3 **URB 5** • Practice Games pp. 31–38 • Audio Scripts pp. 73–77 • Map/Culture Activities pp. 83–84 • Fine Art Activities pp. 86–87	**Differentiated Assessment Program** **URB 5** • Did you get it? Reteaching and Practice Copymasters pp. 1–12

Projectable Transparencies (Teacher One Stop, my.hrw.com)

Culture	Presentation and Practice	Classroom Management
• Atlas Maps 1–6 • Map of Ecuador 1 • Fine Art Transparencies 2, 3	• Vocabulary Transparencies 6, 7 • Grammar Presentation Transparencies 10, 11	• Warm Up Transparencies 16–19 • Student Book Answer Transparencies 24–27

Audio and Video

Audio	Video	¡AvanzaRap! DVD
• Student Book Audio CD 5 Tracks 1–11 • Workbook Audio CD 3 Tracks 1–10 • Heritage Learners Audio CD 2 Tracks 1–4, CD 4 Tracks 1–2 • Assessment Audio CD 2 Tracks 1–2 • *Lecturas para todos* Audio CD 1 Track 9, CD 2 Tracks 1–6 • Sing-along Songs Audio CD	• Vocabulary Video DVD 2 • *Telehistoria* DVD 2 Escena 1 Escena 2 Escena 3 Completa	• Video animations of all **¡AvanzaRap!** songs (with Karaoke track) • Interactive DVD Activities • Teaching Suggestions • **¡AvanzaRap!** Activity Masters • **¡AvanzaRap!** video scripts and answers

Online and Media Resources

Student	Teacher
Available online at my.hrw.com • Online Student Edition • News + Networking • performance space • @HOMETUTOR • CULTURA Interactiva • WebQuests • Interactive Flashcards • Review Games • Self-Check Quiz **Student One Stop** **Holt McDougal Spanish Apps**	**Teacher One Stop (also available at my.hrw.com)** • Interactive Teacher's Edition • All print, audio, and video resources • Projectable Transparencies • Lesson Plans • TPRS • Examview Assessment Suite **Available online at my.hrw.com** *Generate Success* Rubric Generator and Graphic Organizers **Power Presentations**

Differentiated Assessment

On-level	Modified	Pre-AP	Heritage Learners
• Vocabulary Recognition Quiz p. 210 • Vocabulary Production Quiz p. 211 • Grammar Quizzes pp. 212–213 • Culture Quiz p. 214 • On-level Lesson Test pp. 215–221	• Modified Lesson Test pp. 170–176	• Pre-AP Lesson Test pp. 170–176	• Heritage Learners Lesson Test pp. 176–182

Core Pacing Guide

50 Minute (9 Day)

	Objectives/Focus	Teach	Practice	Assess/HW Options
DAY 1	**Culture:** learn about Ecuador **Vocabulary:** house and household items • Warm Up OHT 16 **5 min**	Unit Opener pp. 244–245 Lesson Opener pp. 246–247 **Presentación de vocabulario** pp. 248–249 • Read A–E • View video DVD 2 • Play Audio TXT CD 5 track 1 • *¡A responder!* CD 5 track 2 **25 min**	Lesson Opener pp. 246–247 **Práctica de vocabulario** p. 250 • Activities 1, 2 **15 min**	**Assess:** *Para y piensa* p. 250 **5 min** **Homework:** *Cuaderno* pp. 197–199 @HomeTutor
DAY 2	**Communication:** rooms and household items • Warm Up OHT 16 • Check Homework **5 min**	**Vocabulario en contexto** pp. 251–252 • *Telehistoria escena 1* DVD 2 **20 min**	**Vocabulario en contexto** pp. 251–252 • Act. 3 TXT CD 5 track 3 • Activities 4, 5 **20 min**	**Assess:** *Para y piensa* p. 252 **5 min** **Homework:** *Cuaderno* pp. 197–199
DAY 3	**Grammar:** **ser** or **estar** • Warm Up OHT 17 • Check Homework **5 min**	**Presentación de gramática** p. 253 • **Ser** or **estar** **20 min**	**Práctica de gramática** pp. 254–255 • Acts. 6, 7, 9, 10 • Act. 8 TXT CD 5 track 4 **20 min**	**Assess:** *Para y piensa* p. 255 **5 min** **Homework:** *Cuaderno* pp. 200–202 @HomeTutor
DAY 4	**Communication:** Use **ser** or **estar** to talk about people and things in your life • Warm Up OHT 17 • Check Homework **5 min**	**Gramática en contexto** pp. 256–257 • *Telehistoria escena 2* DVD 2 **15 min**	**Gramática en contexto** pp. 256–257 • Act. 11 TXT CD 5 track 5 • Acts. 12, 13 **25 min**	**Assess:** *Para y piensa* p. 257 **5 min** **Homework:** *Cuaderno* pp. 200–202 @HomeTutor
DAY 5	**Grammar:** ordinal numbers • Warm Up OHT 18 **5 min**	**Presentación de gramática** p. 258 • Ordinal numbers **Práctica de gramática** pp. 259–260 • *Pronunciación* TXT CD 5 track 6 **Culture:** *Sitios geográficos* **15 min**	**Práctica de gramática** pp. 259–260 • Acts. 14, 15, 16 **25 min**	**Assess:** *Para y piensa* p. 260 **5 min** **Homework:** *Cuaderno* pp. 203–205 @HomeTutor
DAY 6	**Communication:** Culmination: **Ser** and **estar**, ordinal numbers, household items • Warm Up OHT 18 • Check Homework **5 min**	**Todo junto** pp. 261–263 • *Escenas 1, 2: Resumen* • *Telehistoria completa* DVD 2 **15 min**	**Todo junto** pp. 261–263 • Acts. 17, 18 TXT CD 5 tracks 3, 5, 7 • Acts. 19, 21 • Act. 20 TXT CD 5 tracks 8, 9 **25 min**	**Assess:** *Para y piensa* p. 263 **5 min** **Homework:** *Cuaderno* pp. 206–207 @HomeTutor
DAY 7	**Reading:** Living in Ecuador **Connections:** Math • Warm Up OHT 19 • Check Homework **5 min**	**Lectura** pp. 264–265 *Vivir en Ecuador* TXT CD 5 track 10 **Conexiones** p. 266 • *Las matemáticas* **20 min**	**Lectura** pp. 264–265 *Vivir en Ecuador* **Conexiones** p. 266 • *Proyectos 1, 2, 3* **20 min**	**Assess:** *Para y piensa* p. 265 **5 min** **Homework:** *Cuaderno* pp. 211–213 @HomeTutor
DAY 8	**Review:** Lesson Review • Warm Up OHT 19 **5 min**	**Repaso de la lección** pp. 268–269 **15 min**	**Repaso de la lección** pp. 268–269 • Act. 1 TXT CD 5 track 11 • Activities 2, 3, 4, 5 **20 min**	**Assess:** *Repaso de la lección* pp. 268–269 **10 min** **Homework:** *En resumen* p. 267; *Cuaderno* pp. 208–210, 214–219 (optional) Review Games Online @HomeTutor
DAY 9	**Assessment**			**Assess:** Lesson 1 Test **50 min**

	Objectives/Focus	Teach	Practice	Assess/HW Options
DAY 1	**Culture:** learn about Ecuador **Vocabulary:** house and household items • Warm Up OHT 16 **5 min**	Unit Opener pp. 244–245 Lesson Opener pp. 246–247 **Presentación de vocabulario** pp. 248–249 • Read A–E • View video DVD 2 • Play Audio TXT CD 5 track 1 • *¡A responder!* CD 5 track 2 **20 min**	Lesson Opener pp. 246–247 **Práctica de vocabulario** p. 250 • Activities 1–2 **20 min**	**Assess:** *Para y piensa* p. 250 **5 min**
	Communication: rooms and household items **5 min**	**Vocabulario en contexto** pp. 251–252 • *Telehistoria escena 1* DVD 2 **15 min**	**Vocabulario en contexto** pp. 251–252 • Act. 3 TXT CD 5 track 3 • Acts. 4, 5 **15 min**	**Assess:** *Para y piensa* p. 252 **5 min** **Homework:** *Cuaderno* pp. 197–199 @HomeTutor
DAY 2	**Grammar: ser** or **estar** • Warm Up OHT 17 • Check Homework **5 min**	**Presentación de gramática** p. 253 • **Ser** or **estar** **20 min**	**Práctica de gramática** pp. 254–255 • Activities 6, 7, 9, 10 • Act. 8 TXT CD 5 track 4 **15 min**	**Assess:** *Para y piensa* p. 255 **5 min**
	Communication: Use **ser** or **estar** to talk about people and things in your life **5 min**	**Gramática en contexto** pp. 256–257 • *Telehistoria escena 2* DVD 2 **20 min**	**Gramática en contexto** pp. 256–257 • Act. 11 TXT CD 5 track 5 • Acts. 12, 13 **15 min**	**Assess:** *Para y piensa* p. 257 **5 min** **Homework:** *Cuaderno* pp. 200–202 @HomeTutor
DAY 3	**Grammar:** ordinal numbers • Warm Up OHT 18 • Check Homework **5 min**	**Presentación de gramática** pp. 258 • **ordinal numbers** **Práctica de gramática** pp. 259–260 • *Pronunciación* TXT CD 5 track 6 **Culture:** *Sitios geográficos* **15 min**	**Práctica de gramática** pp. 259–260 • Acts. 14, 15, 16 **20 min**	**Assess:** *Para y piensa* p. 260 **5 min**
	Communication: Culmination: **Ser** and **estar**, ordinal numbers, household items **5 min**	**Todo junto** pp. 261–263 • *Escenas 1, 2: Resumen* • *Telehistoria completa* DVD 2 **10 min**	**Todo junto** pp. 261–263 • Acts. 17, 18 TXT CD 5 tracks 3, 5, 7 • Acts. 19, 21 • Act. 20 TXT CD 5 tracks 8, 9 **25 min**	**Assess:** *Para y piensa* p. 263 **5 min** **Homework:** *Cuaderno* pp. 203–205 @HomeTutor
DAY 4	**Reading:** Living in Ecuador • Warm Up OHT 19 • Check Homework **5 min**	**Lectura** pp. 264–265 *Vivir en Ecuador* TXT CD 5 track 10 **15 min**	**Lectura** pp. 264–265 *Vivir en Ecuador* **15 min**	**Assess:** *Para y piensa* p. 265 **5 min**
	Review: Lesson Review **5 min**	**Repaso de la lección** pp. 268–269 **15 min**	**Repaso de la lección** pp. 268–269 • Act. 1 TXT CD 5 track 11 • Acts. 2, 3, 4, 5 **25 min**	**Assess:** *Repaso de la lección* pp. 268–269 **5 min** **Homework:** *En resumen* p. 267; *Cuaderno* pp. 208–219 (optional) Review Games Online @HomeTutor
DAY 5	**Assessment**			**Assess:** Lesson 1 Test **45 min**
	Connections: Math **5 min**	**Conexiones** p. 266 • *Las matemáticas* **10 min**	**Conexiones** p. 266 • *Proyectos 1,2,3* **30 min**	

¡AVANZA! Objectives

- Introduce lesson theme: **Vivimos aquí.**
- **Culture:** Discover different types of houses in Spanish-speaking countries.

Presentation Strategies

- Introduce the characters' names: Manuel, Elena, and Fernando.
- Have students describe the people in the photo and what they are wearing.
- Have students talk about the types of buildings in their neighborhood.

STANDARDS

2.2 Products and perspectives
4.2 Compare cultures
21st Century **Creativity and Innovation,** Multiple Intelligences; **Critical Thinking and Problem Solving,** Heritage Language Learners

Warm Up

Projectable Transparencies, 5-16

Ir a Fill in the missing form of **ir** and the preposition **a.**

1. Yo _____ _____ pedir pescado.
2. Usted _____ _____ pedir pollo.
3. Los chicos _____ _____ almorzar en la cafetería.
4. El camarero _____ _____ servir el plato principal.
5. De postre, nosotros _____ _____ pedir pastel.

Answers: 1. voy a; 2. va a; 3. van a; 4. va a; 5. vamos a

Comparación cultural

Exploring the Theme

Ask the following:

1. How is this house similar to or different from those in your home town?
2. How many stories (levels) are in the house in the photo?
3. What similarities and differences do you see in the landscaping?

¿Qué ves? Possible answers include:

- Sí, vive en un lugar tranquilo.
- Hay más chicos.
- La chica lleva pantalones y blusa. Los chicos llevan pantalones y camiseta. Un chico lleva una mochila. Todos llevan zapatos.

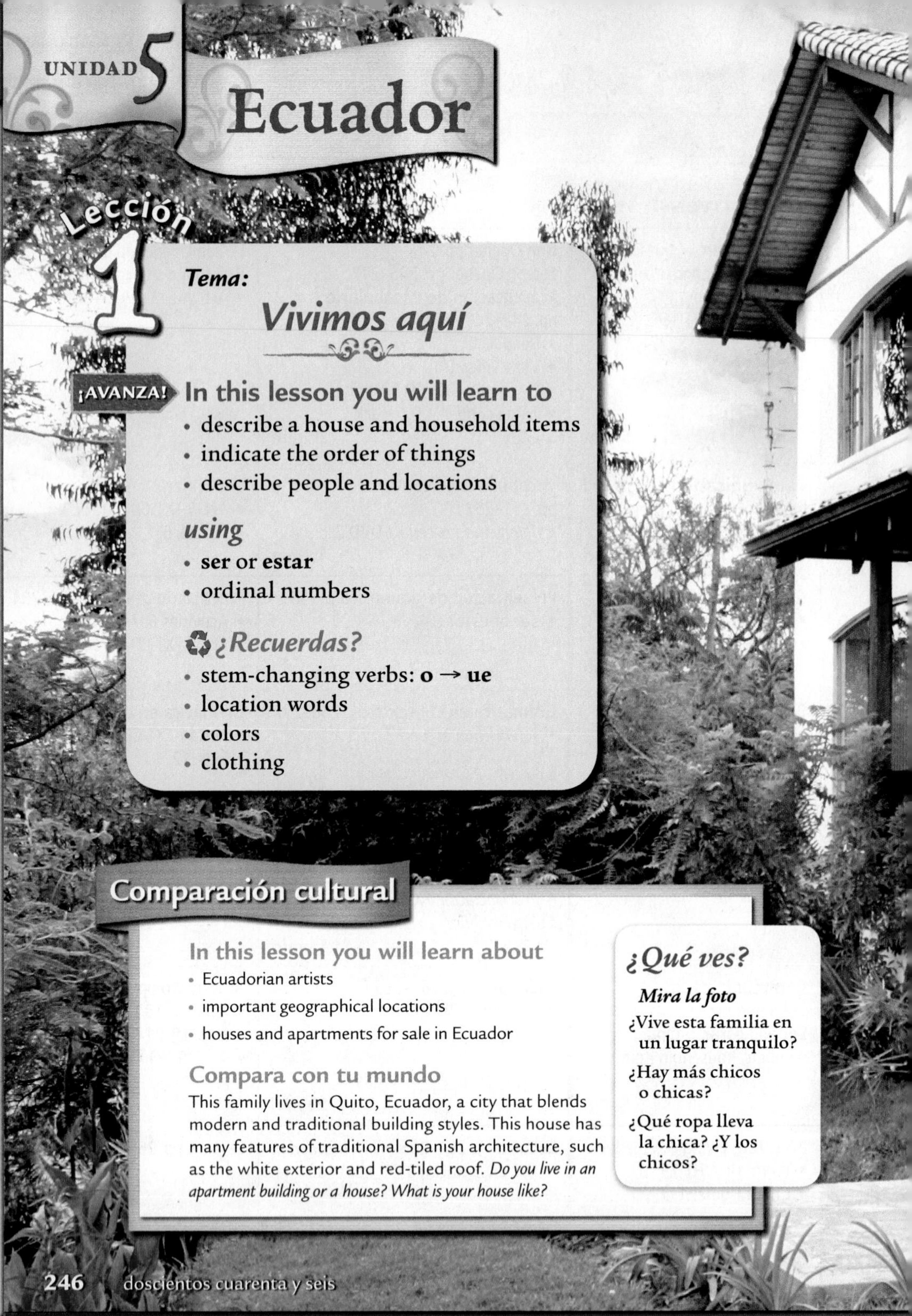

UNIDAD 5 Ecuador

Lección 1

Tema:

Vivimos aquí

¡AVANZA! In this lesson you will learn to

- describe a house and household items
- indicate the order of things
- describe people and locations

using

- **ser** or **estar**
- ordinal numbers

¿Recuerdas?

- stem-changing verbs: **o → ue**
- location words
- colors
- clothing

Comparación cultural

In this lesson you will learn about

- Ecuadorian artists
- important geographical locations
- houses and apartments for sale in Ecuador

Compara con tu mundo

This family lives in Quito, Ecuador, a city that blends modern and traditional building styles. This house has many features of traditional Spanish architecture, such as the white exterior and red-tiled roof. *Do you live in an apartment building or a house? What is your house like?*

¿Qué ves?

Mira la foto

¿Vive esta familia en un lugar tranquilo?

¿Hay más chicos o chicas?

¿Qué ropa lleva la chica? ¿Y los chicos?

Differentiating Instruction

Inclusion

Cumulative Instruction Draw a simple house and an apartment building on the board. Write **mi casa** inside the house, and **mi apartamento** inside the building. Then ask students to brainstorm words and phrases to describe a house or apartment. These could include words that indicate color and location. **Mi casa es verde. Está cerca de la biblioteca.**

Heritage Language Learners

Literacy Skills Ask students to use the library or Internet to research information about Quito and their own home town. Instruct them to find two similarities and two differences between the two locations. Ask them to share their findings with the class.

DIGITAL SPANISH my.hrw.com
ONLINE STUDENT EDITION with...

performance space
News + Networking
@HOMETUTOR
CULTURA Interactiva

- Audio and Video Resources
- Interactive Flashcards
- Review Activities
- WebQuest
- Conjuguemos.com

PRACTICE SPANISH WITH HOLT MCDOUGAL APPS!

Una casa tradicional con jardín
Quito, Ecuador

Ecuador
doscientos cuarenta y siete 247

DIGITAL SPANISH

TEACHER TOOLS
- Interactive Whiteboard Lessons
- Generate Success!

ALSO AVAILABLE...
- Online Workbook
- Spanish InterActive Reader

SPANISH ON THE GO!
- Performance Space
- Holt McDougal Spanish Apps
- ¡Avancemos! eTextbook

Using the Photo

Location Information
Ecuador means *equator* in English. The imaginary line slices through this relatively small South American country that lies just southwest of Colombia. The famous Galapagos Islands in the Pacific Ocean belong to Ecuador.

Expanded Information
Quito, the capital of Ecuador, is 9,300 feet above sea level and is the second highest capital city in the world after La Paz, Bolivia. Although Quito is located 22 miles south of the equator, its climate is not tropical; instead, it is mild to cool and fairly constant throughout the year. Guayaquil is the largest city in Ecuador.

Differentiating Instruction

Multiple Intelligences
Naturalist Using photos from magazines, have students create a collage of an ideal outdoor space for a house or apartment. As they learn vocabulary related to the home, have them label their outdoor spaces. Also, encourage students to use a dictionary to find the names of specific plants or flowers they might want to add to their landscapes.

Slower-paced Learners
Yes/No Questions Have students work in pairs to draft two yes/no questions based on the photo. Encourage students to begin one question with **¿Ves...?** and the other with **¿Hay...?** Then give students the opportunity to ask their peers questions. **¿Hay una casa? ¿Ves a unos chicos?**

Communication
Interpersonal Mode
Display a large classroom map or overhead transparency of Ecuador. Have students work in pairs. Have pairs take turns coming up to the front. One student randomly locates and reads aloud the name of a city on the map, and the other writes the name of that city on the board.

¡AVANZA! Objectives

- Present vocabulary: rooms of a house, furniture, household items.
- Check for recognition.

Core Resources

- Video Program: DVD 2
- Audio Program: TXT CD 5 tracks 1, 2

Presentation Strategies

- Point to the photos on pp. 248–249, say the words and have students repeat after you.
- Play the audio as students read A–E.
- Play the video.

STANDARDS

1.2 Understand language

21st Century **Communication,** Personalize It

Communication
Interpersonal Mode

As a homework assignment, ask students to bring at least five pictures from magazines or catalogues that relate to the vocabulary on this spread: **un sillón, el suelo.** In groups of four or five, have students take turns saying aloud the name of the object in each picture.

Long-term Retention
Personalize It

Ask students to describe in full sentences the furniture they have in their homes or bedrooms. For example, **En mi casa hay una lámpara azul. Mi casa no tiene escalera. El suelo de mi cuarto tiene una alfombra.**

Presentación de VOCABULARIO

¡AVANZA! **Goal:** Learn about what Manuel's house is like. Then practice what you have learned to describe a house and household items. ***Actividades 1–2***

¿Recuerdas? Stem-changing verbs: **o → ue** p. 223

VIDEO DVD

AUDIO

A ¡Hola! Me llamo Manuel. Vivo en **una casa** grande. Tiene dos **pisos.** Hay **un patio** y **un jardín** detrás de la casa.

B A Elena y a mí nos gusta jugar **videojuegos** en **la sala.** En **la cocina** preparamos la comida y en **el comedor** comemos todos los días.

Differentiating Instruction

Inclusion

Alphabetic/Phonetic Awareness Encourage students to scan new vocabulary for words that look and sound familiar. These words might be similar to their English counterparts, or similar to other Spanish words. For example, **sofá** and **televisor** are both very close to their English translations. The room **comedor** is similar to the related verb in Spanish, **comer.**

Heritage Language Learners

Regional Variations Point to the photos on pp. 248–249, and ask students if they know of another name for the items shown. Students might use different words for **cuarto** as explained on p. 251, or **armario** as explained on p. 256. Ask students if they know any other word for **armario** (**ropero**).

C Cuando **subimos la escalera,** llegamos a mi **cuarto.** Allí me gusta estudiar, escuchar mis **discos compactos** y descansar.

D En mi cuarto tengo **un tocadiscos compactos, un radio** y otras **cosas.**

E Mi amigo Fernando piensa que vivir en **un apartamento** es **ideal.** Prefiere vivir en un apartamento donde puede ver el centro de Quito.

Más vocabulario

el armario *closet*
bajar *to descend*
el lector DVD *DVD player*
los muebles *furniture*
Expansión de vocabulario p. R6

@HOMETUTOR my.hrw.com Interactive Flashcards

¡A responder! Escuchar

Escucha la lista de las cosas que hay en la casa. Indica la foto del cuarto donde se encuentra cada cosa. *(Listen to the list of items found in a house and point to the photo of the room in which each item is found.)*

TEACHER to TEACHER

Monica McFadden
Long Island, New York

Tips for Presenting Vocabulary

Places in a house *I usually bring to class several house plans or apartment plans from magazines and I post them on the board. I use the plans to have my students practice saying the names of the rooms in a house or apartment. I also use them to review prepositions of location such as* **el dormitorio está al lado del pasillo, el pasillo está al lado del baño.** *If I have a student with talent, I ask him/her to draw a house plan and label the rooms in it.*

Go online for more tips!

Comparisons

English Language Connection

In many Spanish-speaking countries, the ground floor is not considered as the first floor but as **planta baja.** The first floor, or what in the U.S. is considered to be the second floor, is the **primer piso.**

Communication

Regionalisms

Just as the British refer to an apartment as a *flat,* Spanish speakers also have different words for *apartment.* In Mexico, Peru and Cuba, people use **departamento;** in Spain people say **piso.**

Long-term Retention

Recycle

Ask students to name the family member being described.

1. El padre de mi padre es mi ______.
2. La hermana de mi madre es mi ______.
3. Los hijos de mis tíos son mis ______.
4. El hijo de mis padres es mi ______.

Answers: 1. abuelo; 2. tía; 3. primos; 4. hermano

Differentiating Instruction

Multiple Intelligences

Visual Learners Ask students to draw a picture of their favorite room in their house or apartment. Encourage them to add as much detail as possible. Then have students exchange pictures with a partner. Tell them to make a list of all of the items that they see in their partner's picture.

Slower-paced Learners

Memory Aids Have students create a set of flashcards to help practice vocabulary related to house and home. Using index cards, have them write the vocabulary word or phrase on one side, and draw a simple picture on the other. Encourage students to use their cards individually or with a partner.

Answers Projectable Transparencies, 5-24

¡A responder! AudioScript, TE p. 245b

Students will point to the folowing photos:

1. la sala	**5.** la sala
2. el cuarto	**6.** el cuarto
3. el cuarto	**7.** la sala
4. el cuarto	**8.** el cuarto

VOCABULARIO

Objectives
- Practice vocabulary: rooms in a house, furniture, household items.
- Recycle: stem-changing verbs: **o → ue**.

Core Resource
- *Cuaderno,* pp. 197–199

Practice Sequence
- **Activity 1:** Vocabulary recognition: items in a house, the verb **encontrar**
- **Activity 2:** Vocabulary production: items in a house

STANDARDS
1.3 Present information, Acts. 1–2, PYP

21st Century **Communication,** Multiple Intelligences; **Social and Cross-Cultural Skills,** English Learners

✓ Ongoing Assessment
Get Help Online
More Practice
my.hrw.com

PARA Y PIENSA **Assessment** Have pairs of students say the three items in the Para y piensa and correct each other, as needed. For additional practice, use Reteaching & Practice Copymaster URB 5, pp. 1, 2, 10.

Answers Projectable Transparencies, 5-24

Activity 1
1. Encuentro una cama en el cuarto.
2. Encuentro una mesa y unas sillas en el comedor.
3. Encuentro un sofá en la sala.
4. Encuentro un espejo en el baño.
5. Encuentro una cómoda en el cuarto.
6. Encuentro un sillón en la sala.

Activity 2
1. Son las cortinas.
2. Es la escalera.
3. Es la alfombra.
4. Es el lector DVD.
5. Es la lámpara.
6. Es el tocadiscos compactos.

Para y piensa

Possible answers include: **1.** el sofá, el sillón, el televisor; **2.** la cama, las cortinas, la lámpara

Práctica de VOCABULARIO

1 ¿Dónde encuentras...?
¿Recuerdas? Stem-changing verbs: **o → ue** p. 223

Escribir Hablar

Indica dónde encuentras estas cosas. *(Indicate where you would find these items.)*

modelo: ¿sala o jardín?
Encuentro **un televisor** en **la sala.**

1. ¿cuarto o cocina?

2. ¿comedor o baño?

3. ¿cocina o sala?

4. ¿baño o patio?

5. ¿jardín o cuarto?

6. ¿comedor o sala?

Expansión:
Teacher Edition Only
Ask students to ask each other two more questions about where they would find other items in the house.

2 ¿Qué es?

Escribir Hablar

Lee las descripciones de cosas o lugares en la casa. Identifica la cosa o el lugar. *(Read the clues to identify things and places in a house.)*

modelo: Hay una mesa y sillas, y la familia come aquí pero no prepara la comida aquí.
Es el comedor.

1. Son para las ventanas y las cierras en la noche.
2. La necesitas para bajar al primer piso.
3. Está en el suelo de una sala.
4. Lo usas para ver un DVD.
5. La usas para leer en la noche.
6. Lo usas para escuchar discos compactos.

Expansión
Write your own clues for other parts of the house for a partner to guess.

Más práctica Cuaderno *pp. 197–199* Cuaderno para hispanohablantes *pp. 197–200*

Get Help Online
my.hrw.com

PARA Y PIENSA **Did you get it?** Name three items that can be found in . . .
1. la sala **2.** el cuarto

Differentiating Instruction

English Learners
Build Background Ask students to share information about houses in their country of origin. Have them explain the similarities and differences in the way buildings and neighborhoods are organized. Ask them to talk about furniture. Are television, videogames, and DVDs popular?

Pre-AP
Timed Answer Organize students into two teams to play **¿Qué es?** Invite one player from each team to the front. Then read one of the descriptions aloud from Activity 2. The first student to name the word indicated earns a point for his or her team. Expand the game by creating additional descriptions.

VOCABULARIO en contexto

¡AVANZA! **Goal:** Notice the words Fernando and the Cuevas family use to talk about the rooms in their house. Then practice what you have learned to talk about rooms and other things in a house. ***Actividades 3–5***

Telehistoria escena 1

@HOMETUTOR my.hrw.com View, Read and Record

STRATEGIES

Cuando lees
Compare uses of the verb This scene contains **Voy a...** and **¿Van a...?** What do they mean? Is this different from the meaning in **¿Y vas al gimnasio?** (Unit 2, Lesson 2)?

Cuando escuchas
Draw a map Draw a map showing the places Fernando goes in this scene. To whom is he talking in each place? What are they talking about?

VIDEO DVD

AUDIO

Mrs. Cuevas is working in the garden when Fernando arrives.

Fernando: ¿Cómo está, señora Cuevas? ¿Está Manuel?

Sra. Cuevas: ¿Qué tal, Fernando? Sí, escucha discos compactos en su cuarto...

Fernando: Ah, gracias. Voy a subir.

Sra. Cuevas: ...o está en la sala. Le gusta mucho jugar videojuegos con Elena. ¿Van a estudiar?

Fernando: Sí.

Sra. Cuevas: Bueno. ¡Ah! *(She hands him a package.)* Fernando, es para Manuel.

Fernando takes it and walks inside, where Elena and Manuel are playing videogames in the living room.

Fernando: Hola.

Manuel: *(distracted)* Hola, Fernando.

Elena: Hola, Fernando. ¿Van a estudiar aquí en la sala, en el comedor o en el cuarto de Manuel?

Fernando: *(shrugging his shoulders)* ¿Manuel?

Elena: ¡Manuel! *(She turns off the television to get his attention.)*

Manuel: ¡OK! ¿Qué tal si estudiamos en mi cuarto?

Continuará... p. 256

También se dice

Ecuador To say where Manuel is, Mrs. Cuevas uses the word **cuarto.** In other Spanish-speaking countries you might hear:

- **España** **la habitación**
- **Argentina, Chile** **la pieza**
- **México** **la recámara**
- **muchos países** **la alcoba, el dormitorio**

Differentiating Instruction

Slower-paced Learners

Read Before Listening Before listening to the Telehistoria, have students silently preview the text looking specifically for names of rooms. Then have volunteers read aloud the roles of Fernando, Mrs. Cuevas, Manuel, and Elena. Instruct students to raise their hands when they hear the name of a room. Pause and ask for volunteers to talk about the room mentioned. What furniture might it have?

Multiple Intelligences

Interpersonal Have students work in groups of three or four. Have students in each group take turns asking one question about their own homes, habits, and interests. Each student in the group should answer individually. Sample questions: **¿Les gusta más jugar videojuegos o escuchar discos compactos? ¿En qué lugar de la casa/del apartamento les gusta estudiar?**

¡AVANZA! **Objective**

- Understand activity vocabulary in c

Core Resources

- Video Program: DVD 2
- Audio Program: TXT CD 5 track 3

Presentation Strategies

- Have students identify the location of the first and the second photo.
- As students listen to the audio, ask them to write down the rooms of the house that are mentioned.
- Play the video.

STANDARDS

1.2 Understand language

Warm Up
Projectable Transparencies, 5-16

Vocabulary Write the room or part of the house in which you would find the following items:

1. una mesa y seis sillas
2. un sillón
3. una cama
4. un sofá
5. un armario

Answers: 1. el comedor; 2. la sala; 3. el cuarto; 4. la sala; 5. el cuarto

Video Summary

@HOMETUTOR VideoPlus my.hrw.com

Manuel's mother is working in the garden when Fernando arrives. Manuel is with Elena in the living room playing videogames. Manuel's mother hands Fernando a package to give to Manuel. Fernando goes inside and says hello, but Manuel's attention is on the game. Elena asks where they should study: in the dining room or in Manuel's room. Manuel is still distracted, so Elena turns off the television. Manuel then suggests that they study in his room.

RIO

ary in context.
erring to places or
rtment.

...gram: TXT CD 5 track 3

Practice Sequence
- **Activity 3:** Telehistoria comprehension
- **Activity 4:** Vocabulary production: rooms in a house, household items, direct object pronouns, stem-changing verbs: **o → ue**
- **Activity 5:** Vocabulary production: rooms in a house, descriptive adjectives

STANDARDS
- **1.1** Engage in conversation, Act. 4
- **1.2** Understand language, Act. 3
- **1.3** Present information, Acts. 4–5, PYP
- 21st Century **Communication,** Act. 4/English Learners

Get Help Online
More Practice
my.hrw.com

✓ Ongoing Assessment

PARA Y PIENSA **Alternative Strategy** Say the names of four household items and ask students to explain what they are for. For example: **un radio → lo usas para escuchar música.** For additional practice, use Reteaching & Practice Copymasters URB 5, p. 1, 3.

Answers Projectable Transparencies, 5-24

Activity 3

1. Fernando; **2.** Manuel; **3.** La señora Cuevas; **4.** Elena

Activity 4

Answers will vary. Sample answers:

A: Puedes encontrarla en el comedor. La usas para comer. **B:** Es una mesa.

A: Puedes encontrarlo en la sala. Lo usas para ver películas. **B:** Es un televisor.

A: Puedes encontrarlo en la sala. Necesitas un tocadiscos compactos. **B:** Es un disco compacto.

A: La encuentras en el cuarto. La usas para dormir. **B:** Es una cama.

Answers continue on p. 253.

3 *Comprensión del episodio* La casa de la familia Cuevas

Escuchar
Leer

Lee las oraciones y decide quién lo hace: ¿Fernando, la señora Cuevas, Manuel y/o Elena? *(Read the sentences and tell who is being described.)*

modelo: Van a estudiar.
Manuel y Fernando van a estudiar.

1. Va a subir la escalera para ver a Manuel.
2. Le gusta mucho jugar videojuegos con Elena.
3. Habla con Fernando cuando él llega a la casa.
4. Habla con Fernando porque Manuel no escucha.

Expansión:
Teacher Edition Only
Have volunteers present an oral summary of the last chapter of the Telehistoria.

4 Las cosas que hay en la casa

Hablar

Describe las cosas en la casa. Otro(a) estudiante tiene que adivinarlas. *(Describe these household items for a partner to guess.)*

una mesa	un disco compacto
un televisor	una cama
una cómoda	un radio

A Puedes encontrarlo en muchos lugares: la sala, la cocina, tu cuarto. Lo usas para escuchar música o deportes.

B Es un radio.

Expansión:
Teacher Edition Only
Ask students to write a list of the furniture items they have in their homes.

5 El apartamento ideal

Escribir

Escribe una descripción del apartamento ideal. *(Describe an ideal apartment.)*

modelo: El apartamento ideal es grande.
En la sala hay...

Expansión
Read your description to a partner, who will draw a floor plan of your ideal apartment.

Get Help Online
my.hrw.com

PARA Y PIENSA **Did you get it?** Name items Manuel may use to do the following.
1. escuchar música **2.** estudiar **3.** jugar videojuegos

Differentiating Instruction

English Learners

Provide Comprehensible Input Before doing Activity 4, give students this pre-speaking activity. Organize students into small groups, and assign each group one of the words in the box. Instruct them to list as many words and phrases related to their word as they can. Have each group display their list on a piece of chart paper for everyone to use during the activity.

Multiple Intelligences

Interpersonal Give students the opportunity to change their descriptions in Activity 5 into the first person. Tell them to imagine they have been asked to lead a tour through their ideal apartment. Encourage students to use descriptions of their personality and hobbies to explain the importance of certain rooms. **Soy una persona muy estudiosa. Leo libros en el jadín todos los días.**

Presentación de GRAMÁTICA

¡AVANZA! **Goal:** Learn the differences between **ser** and **estar.** Then practice using these two verbs to describe people and locations. ***Actividades 6–10***

¿Recuerdas? Location words p. 115, colors p. 195

English Grammar Connection: Remember that there are two ways to say the English verb *to be* in Spanish: **ser** and **estar** (see pp. 37 and 115).

Ser or estar

ANIMATED GRAMMAR my.hrw.com

Ser and **estar** both mean *to be.* How do you know which verb to use?

Here's how:

Use **ser** to indicate origin: where someone or something is from.

Soy de Quito.
***I'm** from Quito.*

Use **ser** to describe personal traits and physical characteristics.

Los estudiantes **son** inteligentes.
*The students **are** intelligent.*

Ser is also used to indicate professions.

La señora Ramírez **es** maestra.
*Mrs. Ramírez **is** a teacher.*

Remember that you also use **ser** to identify people or things and to give the time and the date.

Use **estar** to indicate location: where someone or something is.

Quito **está** en Ecuador.
*Quito **is** in Ecuador.*

Estar is also used to describe conditions, such as how someone feels.

physical:	¿Cómo **estás**? *How **are you**?*	**Estoy** bien. ***I'm** fine.*
emotional:	**Estamos** contentos. ***We are** happy.*	**Están** enojados. ***They are** angry.*

Más práctica

Cuaderno *pp. 200–202*

Cuaderno para hispanohablantes *pp. 201–203*

@HOMETUTOR my.hrw.com
Leveled Practice
Conjuguemos.com

Differentiating Instruction

Inclusion

Frequent Review/Repetition Write the following headings on the board: *to indicate origin, to describe traits, to indicate profession, to identify people or things, to indicate location,* and *to describe conditions*. Then ask each student to write a sentence to serve as an example of the different uses of **ser** and **estar.** Have students record their sentences under the appropriate heading.

Slower-paced Learners

Memory Aids If students get confused between the use of **ser** to describe traits, and the use of **estar** to describe conditions, give them this tip. Remind them that a *trait* does not easily change. A *condition*, on the other hand, is easily changed. That's why you would say **Los estudiantes son inteligentes**, but **Los estudiantes están contentos.**

¡AVANZA! **Objective**

- Present the different uses of **ser** and **estar.**

Core Resource

- *Cuaderno*, pp. 200–202

Presentation Strategies

- Remind students that **ser** and **estar** both mean *to be* but their use depends on the context.
- Review uses of **ser** and **estar** from previous lessons.
- Present the different uses of **ser** and **estar.**

STANDARDS

4.1 Compare language

Warm Up
Projectable Transparencies, 5-17

Vocabulary Match the items in the left column with the room where you would find them in the right column. The rooms may be used more than once.

1. cama	**a.** comedor
2. espejo	**b.** cuarto
3. alfombra	**c.** sala
4. mesa y sillas	
5. cómoda	
6. sillón	

Answers: 1. b; 2. b; 3. c; 4. a; 5. b; 6. c

Answers
Projectable Transparencies, 5-24

Answers continued from p. 252.

Activity 5 Answers will vary. Sample answers:

El apartamento ideal es grande. En la sala hay un sofá, dos sillones y una mesa. El comedor está al lado de la sala. En el comedor hay una mesa y ocho sillas. La cocina es grande. El baño está al lado de la cocina y el cuarto. El cuarto es grande. Tiene una cama y una cómoda. También hay un patio. En el patio hay una mesa y cuatro sillas.

Para y piensa

1. el radio, el tocadiscos compactos; **2.** la lámpara, la mesa; **3.** los videojuegos, el televisor

Objectives

- Practice using **ser** and **estar**.
- Recycle: location words and colors.
- **Culture:** How landscapes reflect the way of life in a community.
- Practice using lesson vocabulary in context.

Core Resources

- *Cuaderno,* pp. 200–202
- Audio Program: TXT CD 5 track 4

Practice Sequences

- **Activity 6:** Controlled practice: uses of **ser** and **estar**; Recycle: location words
- **Activity 7:** Controlled practice: uses of **ser** and **estar**
- **Activity 8:** Transitional practice: uses of **ser** and **estar**
- **Activity 9:** Open-ended practice: using **ser** and **estar** to describe where one lives
- **Activity 10:** Open-ended practice: uses of **ser** and **estar**

STANDARDS

1.1 Engage in conversation, Act. 10
1.2 Understand language, Act. 8
1.3 Present information, Acts. 6–10, PYP
4.2 Compare cultures, Act. 9
21st Century **Communication,** Act. 10; **Initiative and Self-Direction,** Pre-AP

Communication
Common Error Alert

Monitor how students pronounce the forms of **estar.** Remind them that the letter with the written accent mark indicates that this is the syllable to stress, as in: **estás, está, están.**

Answers Projectable Transparencies, 5-24 and 5-25

Activity 6

1. es, Está; **2.** son, Están; **3.** es, Está; **4.** es, Está; **5.** son, Están; **6.** es, Está; **7.** es, Está; **8.** es, Está

Activity 7

1. estoy; **2.** están; **3.** es; **4.** es; **5.** es; **6.** están; **7.** son; **8.** es; **9.** estamos; **10.** somos

Answers continue on p. 255.

Práctica de GRAMÁTICA

6 El apartamento de Fernando

¿Recuerdas? Location words p. 115

Escribir

Ayuda a Fernando a describir su apartamento. Escribe oraciones con esta información, utilizando **ser** y **estar.** *(Using the information given, write sentences with **ser** and **estar.**)*

modelo: el apartamento: grande / cerca de la escuela
El apartamento es grande. Está cerca de la escuela.

1. la sala: marrón / lejos de la escalera
2. las cortinas: nuevo / delante de las ventanas
3. el cuarto: pequeño / en la planta baja
4. el sillón: blanco / cerca del sofá
5. las lámparas: feo / encima de las mesas
6. el jardín: bonito / en el patio
7. la cómoda: grande / en el cuarto
8. la alfombra: viejo / debajo del sofá

Expansión
Describe these items in your home.

7 Un sábado con la familia

Leer
Escribir

Manuel describe un sábado por la mañana en su casa. Completa lo que dice con la forma correcta de **ser** o **estar.** *(Complete the description with the correct form of **ser** or **estar.**)*

Los sábados yo no __1.__ cansado porque duermo mucho. Bajo a la cocina a las diez; mis padres y Elena ya __2.__ allí. Elena __3.__ mi hermana. Ella __4.__ un poco perezosa. Mi padre y yo preparamos el desayuno. La cocina __5.__ grande y amarilla. La mesa y las sillas __6.__ cerca de la ventana. Las cortinas __7.__ blancas. La alfombra __8.__ de Otavalo, en Ecuador. Después del desayuno, mi familia y yo __9.__ contentos porque vamos a jugar al fútbol. Nosotros __10.__ muy atléticos.

Expansión:
Teacher Edition Only
Ask students to compare Manuel's description to a typical Saturday for them.

8 Los amigos de Manuel

Escuchar
Escribir

Manuel describe a varias personas. Escucha su descripción y toma apuntes. Contesta las preguntas. *(Listen to Manuel's description and take notes. Then answer the questions.)*

1. ¿Cómo está Manuel hoy?
2. ¿De dónde es Rosa?
3. ¿Cómo es ella?
4. ¿Dónde está su casa?
5. ¿De dónde son José y Carlos?
6. ¿Cómo son ellos?
7. ¿Dónde está su apartamento?
8. ¿Cómo es su apartamento?

Audio Program
TXT CD 5 Track 4
Audio Script, TE p. 245b

Differentiating Instruction

Inclusion

Metacognitive Support After students complete Activities 6 and 7, ask them to explain in English why they chose **ser** or **estar** in each case. Advise them to refer to p. 253 to choose the most appropriate category.

Slower-paced Learners

Read Before Listening Before listening to Manuel's description in Activity 8, advise students to preview the questions. Have them convert each question into a sentence starter, and then fill in the blanks as they listen. For example: **¿Cómo está Manuel hoy? Hoy Manuel está _____.**
¿De dónde es Rosa? Rosa es de _____.
¿Cómo es ella? Ella es _____.

9 Mi casa

Escribir

Comparación cultural

Nochebuena *(alrededor de 1990),* *Targelia Toaquiza*

Casas ecuatorianas

How do landscapes reflect a community's way of life? The Tigua artists from the **Ecuadorian Andes** are known for their colorful paintings, created with chicken feather brushes on sheephide. Their artwork shows the world around them: mountains, valleys, farms, and livestock. Tigua paintings, such as *Nochebuena* by Targelia Toaquiza, are typically landscapes that show scenes of community life, such as festivals, indigenous traditions, harvests, and everyday rural activities.

Compara con tu mundo *What would a painting showing community life in your area include?*

Escribe una descripción del lugar donde tú vives. Explica dónde está y cómo es. *(Write a description of where you live.)*

modelo: Mi casa está cerca de la escuela. Es blanca y está al lado de una casa amarilla. También está cerca del parque...

10 ¡A jugar! ¿Cómo es? *¿Recuerdas?* Colors p. 195

Hablar

Trabaja en un grupo de tres y túrnense para describir los dibujos. La última persona que tiene una descripción original gana. *(In a group of three, take turns describing each drawing. Try to be the last person who can add something new without repeating.)*

A: Es una sala.
B: La mesa está cerca del sofá.
C: La sala es verde...

1.

2.

Expansión:
Teacher Edition Only
Ask students to write a short description of their homes using the vocabulary words they know.

Más práctica Cuaderno *pp. 200–202* Cuaderno para hispanohablantes *pp. 201–203*

Get Help Online my.hrw.com

PARA Y PIENSA

Did you get it? Complete each sentence with the correct form of **ser** or **estar.**

1. Nosotros ____ en la cocina.
2. Voy a mi cuarto porque ____ cansado.
3. El espejo ____ de Bogotá.
4. Los jardines ____ bonitos.

Comparación cultural

Essential Question

Suggested Answer Landscapes can indicate the economic level of a community and the type of terrain that surrounds it. Students may wish to go into detail about what outsiders can know about their community by looking at the neighborhood or landscapes of the area.

✓ Ongoing Assessment

Get Help Online More Practice my.hrw.com

PARA Y PIENSA **Quick Check** Assign one student to write the answers for Para y piensa on the board. Ask students to explain the use of **ser** or **estar** in each sentence. For additional practice, use Reteaching & Practice Copymasters URB 5, pp. 4, 5, 11, 12.

Differentiating Instruction

Heritage Language Learners

Support What They Know Have students draft a paragraph describing their own neighborhood. Then have students exchange paragraphs with a partner, and working together, create a Venn diagram comparing and contrasting the two neighborhoods. If students live in basically the same neighborhood, have them work together to combine and elaborate on their description.

Pre-AP

Self-correct As students converse in Activity 10, tell them to pay careful attention to their partner's choice of **ser** or **estar.** If a sentence does not sound right, tell students to raise their hand. This indicates that the speaker should stop, think, and repeat the sentence.

Answers Projectable Transparencies, 5-25

Answers continued from p. 254.

Activity 8 **1.** Está contento. **2.** Es de Chile. **3.** Es cómica y muy inteligente. **4.** Está cerca del centro comercial. **5.** Son de Estados Unidos. **6.** Son altos y cómicos. **7.** Está cerca de la escuela. **8.** Es grande y muy bonito.

Activity 9 Answers will vary. Sample answers include: Mi casa está lejos del centro. Está cerca de un parque. Es grande y tiene un jardín muy bonito. Es amarilla y las ventanas son blancas. Tiene dos pisos.

Activity 10 Answers will vary. Sample answers include:
A: Es un cuarto. **B:** La cama está encima de la alfombra. **C:** La lámpara está al lado de la ventana.

Para y piensa **1.** estamos; **2.** estoy; **3.** es; **4.** son

¡AVANZA! Objective

- Practice **ser** and **estar** and new vocabulary in context.

Core Resources

- Video Program: DVD 2
- Audio Program: TXT CD 5 track 5

Presentation Strategies

- Ask students to describe what they see in the two photos. **¿Quiénes son los chicos? ¿Dónde están?**
- Have students preview the video activities before watching the video.
- Show the video and/or play the audio.

Practice Sequence

- **Activity 11:** Telehistoria comprehension
- **Activity 12:** Transitional practice: **ser** and **estar**
- **Activity 13:** Open-ended practice: **ser** and **estar**

STANDARDS

1.1 Engage in conversation, Act. 13
1.2 Understand language, Act. 11
1.3 Present information, Acts. 12–13, PYP
21st Century **Communication,** Act. 12/ Presentational Mode

Warm Up Projectable Transparencies, 5-17

Ser and estar Complete each sentence with the correct form of **ser** or **estar.**

1. Mi cuarto _____ al lado de la sala.
2. Manuel y Fernando _____ en el centro comercial.
3. Mi cuarto _____ grande y bonito.
4. Yo _____ estudiante.
5. Nosotros _____ contentos.

Answers: 1. está; 2. están; 3. es; 4. soy; 5. estamos

Video Summary

@HOMETUTOR VideoPlus my.hrw.com

Manuel cannot find his notebook. Fernando finds it and tells him that he is disorganized. While downstairs, Elena gives Manuel Alicia's package. Manuel reads the letter and drops the T-shirt. Manuel decides to go downtown to get Trini's autograph. Fernando notices that Manuel forgot the T-shirt.

GRAMÁTICA en contexto

¡AVANZA! **Goal:** Identify the ways **ser** and **estar** are used in Manuel and Fernando's conversation about themselves and things in the house. Then use these verbs to talk about people and things in your life. ***Actividades 11–13***

Telehistoria escena 2

@HOMETUTOR my.hrw.com View, Read and Record

STRATEGIES

Cuando lees
Consider the influence of the setting Early in this scene, you find out whether Manuel's bedroom is neat or messy. This has a big influence on the action in the scene. How and why?

Cuando escuchas
Find the real feelings How does Elena describe Manuel? Is she sincere, or is she saying the opposite of what she feels? How can you tell?

VIDEO DVD
AUDIO

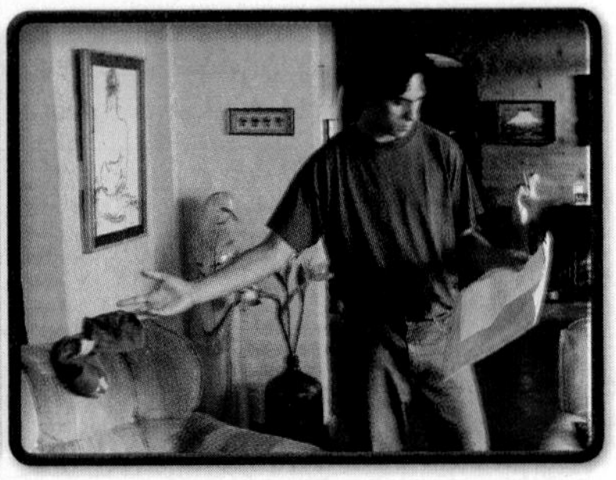

Manuel: ¡Mi cuaderno no está aquí!
Fernando: *(distracted)* Y, ¿encima de la cama? ¿Y cerca de la lámpara? ¿Y en el armario? ¿En la cómoda?
Manuel looks around, but Fernando finds the notebook on the floor.
Fernando: Manuel, ¡eres muy desorganizado! ¡Todas tus cosas están en el suelo!
Meanwhile, Elena sees the package from Alicia in the living room and calls upstairs.
Elena: ¡Manuel! ¡Manueeeel!
Manuel: *(He goes downstairs.)* ¿Qué quieres? Estoy muy ocupado.
Elena: Sí, tú eres muy estudioso.
She gives him the package. Manuel opens it, dropping the T-shirt on the floor to read the letter. He goes back to his room.
Fernando: *(reading the letter)* ¿Tienes que ir al centro de Quito? ¿A ver a Trini Salgado?
Manuel: Sí. ¡Alicia quiere el autógrafo de Trini! Es importante. Tenemos que ir.
As they leave, Fernando realizes that Manuel forgot the T-shirt.
Fernando: Manuel... ¿y la camiseta? **Continuará...** p. 261

También se dice

Ecuador When asking where Manuel's notebook is, Fernando uses the word **el armario.** In other Spanish-speaking countries you might hear:
- **España** **el armario empotrado**
- **muchos países** **el clóset**

Differentiating Instruction

Multiple Intelligences

Interpersonal Mode Invite three volunteers to play the parts of Manuel, Fernando, and Elena. As these students read the script, encourage them to emphasize the facial expressions and tone of voice appropriate to each character. When Manuel says, **¡Mi cuaderno no está aquí!** what might he be feeling? Elena says, **¡Sí, eres muy estudioso!** What might her expression be?

Inclusion

Cumulative Instruction Advise students to revisit Unit 2, Lesson 2 to review words and phrases that express location. Then have students scan this scene of the Telehistoria for the use of these words and phrases. Ask for a volunteer to draw a simple sketch on the board to represent each location word or phrase used.

11 *Comprensión del episodio* Los problemas de Manuel

Escuchar Leer

Di si las siguientes oraciones son ciertas o falsas. Corrige las oraciones falsas. *(Tell whether the following sentences are true or false. Correct the false sentences.)*

1. Manuel es muy organizado.
2. Manuel está tranquilo.
3. Manuel no puede encontrar su calculadora.
4. Todas las cosas de Manuel están en el suelo.
5. Fernando y Manuel tienen que ir al centro comercial.
6. Quieren ver a Trini.
7. Fernando quiere el autógrafo de Trini Salgado.
8. Fernando y Manuel tienen que ir, y Manuel tiene la camiseta.

Expansión: Teacher Edition Only
Have students write one question about the conversation between Manuel, Fernando and Elena, and provide an answer.

12 Una persona importante

Escribir

Escribe una descripción de una persona importante en tu vida. Usa las siguientes preguntas. *(Write about someone special in your life. Use the following questions.)*

Para organizarte:

- ¿Quién es?
- ¿Cómo es?
- ¿De dónde es?
- ¿Dónde está ahora?
- ¿Cómo estás cuando pasas un rato con él o ella?

modelo: Mi madre es simpática y trabajadora. Es más alta que mi padre. Es de Seattle, Washington, pero está en Portland ahora...

Expansión: Teacher Edition Only
Ask students to give a brief description of a famous person they admire.

13 Mi cuarto

Hablar

Descríbele tu cuarto a otro(a) estudiante. Él o ella va a dibujarlo. *(Describe your room to a partner. He or she will draw it.)*

modelo: Mi cuarto es grande. La puerta está al lado de la cómoda. El televisor y los videojuegos están encima de la cómoda...

Expansión
Write a description of someone else's drawing.

Get Help Online
my.hrw.com

PARA Y PIENSA

Did you get it? Choose the correct verb in each sentence based on the Telehistoria.

1. Manuel (es / está) muy desorganizado.
2. Todas las cosas (son / están) en el suelo.
3. El cuaderno no (está / es) encima de la cama.

Communication
Presentational Mode

Have students design plans for a dream house and label all the rooms in Spanish. They should use poster board and make the plan large enough for the class to see. Ask students to choose a location for their dream home and prepare a description in Spanish of the home. They will present their project to the class, pointing out each room as they describe it. A sample speech:

Mi casa es grande. Tiene cinco cuartos, dos salas, una cocina grande, un comedor grande y tres baños. Mi casa está en Miami, cerca de la playa. Hay un jardín al lado del patio. Mi casa es bonita.

✓ Ongoing Assessment

Get Help Online
More Practice
my.hrw.com

PARA Y PIENSA **Peer Assessment** Have students check each other's papers as you call out the correct answers. For additional practice, use Reteaching & Practice Copymasters URB 5, pp. 4, 6.

Differentiating Instruction

Pre-AP

Expand and Elaborate After students make their determination of true or false in Activity 11, have them add a phrase or sentence of explanation. Here are a few examples:

- **Manuel no es muy organizado. Es muy desorganizado. Todas sus cosas están en el suelo.**
- **Manuel no está tranquilo. No encuentra su cuaderno y tiene que estudiar.**

Slower-paced Learners

Peer-study Support Have students pair up to peer-edit their descriptions in Activity 12. Instruct students to read their partner's description three times, focusing on the following aspects during each reading: 1. organization, 2. grammar, 3. spelling. After each reading, direct students to provide one positive piece of feedback and one piece of constructive criticism.

Answers Projectable Transparencies, 5-25

Activity 11

1. Falsa: Manuel es muy desorganizado.
2. Falsa: Manuel está ocupado.
3. Falsa: Manuel no puede encontrar su cuaderno.
4. Cierta
5. Falsa: Manuel tiene que ir al centro de Quito.
6. Cierta
7. Falsa: Alicia quiere el autógrafo de Trini Salgado.
8. Falsa: Manuel no tiene la camiseta.

Activity 12 Answers will vary. Sample answers include: Mi hermano es alto y atlético. Es muy simpático. Es de Portland, Maine. Ahora está en casa de mis tíos. Estoy contento cuando paso un rato con él.

Activity 13 Answers will vary. Sample answers include: Mi cuarto es pequeño. La cómoda está delante de la cama. Los libros y la lámpara están encima de la cómoda...

Para y piensa **1.** es; **2.** están; **3.** está

¡AVANZA! Objective
- Present ordinal numbers.

Core Resource
- *Cuaderno*, pp. 203–205

Presentation Strategies
- Review numbers 1-10.
- Explain that ordinal numbers represent a position in a series.
- Point out that ordinal numbers must agree in number and gender with the noun that follows them.

STANDARDS
4.1 Compare languages

Warm Up Projectable Transparencies, 5-18

Estar Write the correct form of **estar** for each subject:

1. Manuel ____
2. yo ____
3. el gato ____
4. tú ____
5. nosotros ____
6. ustedes ____

Answers: 1. está; 2. estoy; 3. está; 4. estás; 5. estamos; 6. están

Communication — Common Error Alert

Point out that the **-o** is dropped from **primero** and **tercero** only before masculine singular nouns. The other numbers do not drop the **-o** before a masculine singular noun. For example, **el tercer piso** but **el quinto piso.** The **-a** is never dropped from the feminine form.

Communication — Grammar Activity

After writing the sentences that follow on the board, have students circle the ordinal number and the noun that follows.

1. **Vivimos en el noveno piso.**
2. **El arte es la segunda clase del día.**
3. **Mi amigo vive en el primero piso.**

Answers: 1. noveno piso; 2. segunda/clase; 3. primer/piso

Presentación de GRAMÁTICA

¡AVANZA! **Goal:** Learn how to use ordinal numbers. Then practice them to indicate the order of things, and to talk about the floors of a house or building. ***Actividades 14–16***

¿Recuerdas? Clothing p. 194

English Grammar Connection: In both English and Spanish, **ordinal numbers** indicate position in a series or the order of items.

in **second** place — en **segundo** lugar

Ordinal Numbers

ANIMATEDGRAMMAR my.hrw.com

When used with a noun, an **ordinal number** must agree in number and gender with that noun.

Here's how:

Ordinal Numbers			
primero(a)	*first*	**sexto(a)**	*sixth*
segundo(a)	*second*	**séptimo(a)**	*seventh*
tercero(a)	*third*	**octavo(a)**	*eighth*
cuarto(a)	*fourth*	**noveno(a)**	*ninth*
quinto(a)	*fifth*	**décimo(a)**	*tenth*

Ordinals are placed before **nouns.**

before the noun — *agrees*

Es la **primera película** de María Conchita Alonso.
*It's the **first** movie of María Conchita Alonso.*

agrees

Nuestro apartamento está en el **octavo piso.**
*Our apartment is on the **eighth** floor.*

Primero and **tercero** drop the **o** before a **masculine singular noun.**

drops the o

Enero es el **primer mes** del año.
*January is the **first** month of the year.*

Más práctica
Cuaderno *pp. 203–205*
Cuaderno para hispanohablantes *pp. 204–207*

@HOMETUTOR my.hrw.com Leveled Practice

Differentiating Instruction

Multiple Intelligences

Kinesthetic In advance, teach students to recognize and respond to a few simple commands, such as **levanta la mano** or **siéntate.** Then invite ten students to the front of the room to stand in a line. Use ordinal numbers to indicate which students you want to follow your directions. For example, **el cuarto estudiante levanta la mano.**

Inclusion

Synthetic/Analytic Support Provide each student with two self-sticking notes. Instruct them to write **a** on one note, and a **o** on the other. Then write phrases regarding ordinal numbers on the board. Invite volunteers to come attach the appropriate ending. Here are a few possible examples: **el segund ____ piso; la tercer ____ casa.**

Answers: segundo; tercera

Práctica de GRAMÁTICA

14 ¿En qué piso?

Escribir

Escribe en qué piso vive cada familia. *(Tell on which floor each family lives.)*

modelo: Gutiérrez (2)
La familia Gutiérrez vive en **el segundo piso.**

1. Díaz (7)
2. Granados (5)
3. Santiago (10)
4. Ponce (1)
5. Romero (9)
6. Sánchez (6)
7. García (3)
8. Martínez (8)
9. Cabral (4)

Expansión:
Teacher Edition Only
Ask students to give the order in which they take their daily classes in school using ordinal numbers. **Mi primera clase es español, la segunda clase es ciencias...**

15 La primera persona lleva...

¿Recuerdas? Clothing p. 194

Hablar

Estas personas hacen cola. Pregúntale a otro(a) estudiante qué llevan, usando números ordinales. *(Use ordinal numbers to ask what the people in line are wearing.)*

A ¿Qué lleva la **primera** persona?

B La **primera** persona lleva **jeans, una camiseta marrón y...**

Expansión
Ask your partner about the physical appearance of the people in the line.

Pronunciación La acentuación

AUDIO

In Spanish, just like in English, certain syllables are stressed more than others. If a word ends in a vowel, **n,** or **s,** and there is no written accent, the next-to-last syllable is stressed.

sala **suben** **cortinas** **apartamento**

If a word ends in a consonant other than **n** or **s,** the natural stress falls on the last syllable of the word.

mujer **reloj** **bajar** **ideal** **televisor**

Words that have written accents are stressed on the syllable with the accent.

jardín **sillón** **lámpara** **sofá** **décimo**

Differentiating Instruction

Slower-paced Learners

Personalize It Have students draft two sentences about themselves that utilize ordinal numbers. Encourage them to think about their classes, hobbies, and family, such as: **Mi apartamento está en el tercer piso. Todos los días mi primera clase es inglés. Mañana tenemos el sexto examen de español.** Ask them to read their sentences aloud.

English Learners

Provide Comprehensible Input To familiarize students with the concept of stressed syllables, say the following English words aloud: *student, convince,* and *semester.* Have students repeat. Tell students that whenever they see an accent mark **(´)** in a Spanish word, that syllable receives the stress.

Objectives

- Practice using ordinal numbers.
- Recycle: clothes.
- Practice stressing syllables in Spanish.

Core Resource

- Audio Program: TXT CD 5 track 6

Practice Sequence

- **Activity 11:** Controlled practice: ordinal numbers.
- **Activity 12:** Transitional practice: ordinal numbers, clothes, colors.

STANDARDS

1.1 Engage in conversation, Act. 15
1.3 Present information, Acts. 14–15
4.1 Compare languages, Pronunciación
21st Century **Communication,** Slower-paced Learners

Comparisons

English Language Connection

Write the following words on the board or on an OHT:

suben	**jardín**	**sillón**
reloj	**cama**	**escalera**
ideal	**bajar**	**lámpara**

Call on individual students to read aloud one word and point out where the accent falls.

Answers Projectable Transparencies, 5-25 and 5-26

Activity 14

1. La familia Díaz vive en el séptimo piso.
2. La familia Granados vive en el quinto piso.
3. La familia Santiago vive en el décimo piso.
4. La familia Ponce vive en el primer piso.
5. La familia Romero vive en el noveno piso.
6. La familia Sánchez vive en el sexto piso.
7. La familia García vive en el tercer piso.
8. La familia Martínez vive en el octavo piso.
9. La familia Cabral vive en el cuarto piso.

Activity 15

Answers will vary. Answers should follow the pattern: **A.** ¿Qué lleva la primera persona? **B.** La primera persona lleva jeans y una camiseta marrón.

Objectives
- Practice using ordinal numbers and lesson vocabulary.
- **Culture:** Discuss how a country's location makes it unique.

Core Resource
- *Cuaderno,* pp. 203–205

Practice Sequence
- **Activity 16:** Transitional practice: ordinal numbers and lesson vocabulary

STANDARDS
1.1 Engage in conversation, Act. 16
1.3 Present information, Act. 16, PYP
4.2 Compare cultures, CC
21st Century **Communication,** Act. 16/Multiple Intelligences

Comparación cultural

Essential Question
Suggested Answer The place in which each country is geographically located is unique due to various factors including landscape, climate, and physical characteristics. The Grand Canyon and the Amazon jungle are examples of features that lend a uniqueness to the countries in which they are located.

✓ Ongoing Assessment

Get Help Online
More Practice
my.hrw.com

PARA Y PIENSA **Quick Check** Have students write the missing ordinal numbers in the series: **primero, _____, _____, cuarto, _____.** For additional practice, use Reteaching & Practice Copymasters URB 5, pp. 7, 8, 12.

Answers: segundo; tercero; quinto

Answers Projectable Transparencies, 5-26

Activity 16
1. **A:** ¿A qué piso voy para comprar un vestido?
   B: Necesitas ir al segundo piso para comprar un vestido.
2. **A:** ¿... un televisor? **B:** ... al tercer piso...
3. **A:** ¿... una cómoda? **B:** ... al quinto piso...
4. **A:** ¿... un espejo? **B:** ... al cuarto piso...
5. **A:** ¿... una lámpara? **B:** ... al cuarto piso...
6. **A:** ¿... unos zapatos? **B:** ... al primer piso...

Para y piensa **1.** Estoy en el sexto piso. **2.** Estoy en el noveno piso. **3.** Estoy en el segundo piso. **4.** Estoy en el tercer piso.

16 Los pisos del almacén

Hablar

Pregúntale a otro(a) estudiante a qué piso del almacén vas para encontrar las siguientes cosas. *(Ask a partner to what floor you go to find the following items.)*

A: ¿A qué piso voy para comprar sopa?

B: Necesitas ir a la planta baja para comprar sopa.

1. 
2. 
3. 
4. 
5. 
6. 

Expansión:
Teacher Edition Only
Ask students to describe what they do on the weekends using ordinal numbers. **Primero como el desayuno. Segundo...**

Comparación cultural

Mitad del Mundo

Sitios geográficos
How does a country's location in the world make it unique? **Ecuador** is located on the equator, which divides the northern and southern hemispheres. The Mitad del Mundo monument marks the location of the equator. There you can stand with one foot in each hemisphere. Ushuaia, in the province of Tierra del Fuego in **Argentina,** is the southernmost city in the world. It is known as *la ciudad del fin del mundo* (the city at the end of the earth). Located a little over 600 miles from Antarctica, it is a common starting point for arctic explorations.

Ushuaia, Argentina

Compara con tu mundo *What geographical locations are important in the United States and why?*

Más práctica Cuaderno *pp. 203–205* Cuaderno para hispanohablantes *pp. 204–207*

Get Help Online
my.hrw.com

PARA Y PIENSA **Did you get it?** Say that you are on the following floors.
1. sixth **2.** ninth **3.** second **4.** third

Differentiating Instruction

Multiple Intelligences
Linguistic/Verbal Have students add another turn to their conversations in Activity 16. After receiving their directions, have **Estudiante A** ask a follow-up question. **¿Qué más puedo comprar en el segundo piso? Estudiante B** should respond, for example, **Puedes comprar una blusa.**

English Learners
Provide Comprehensible Input Use a map or atlas to help clarify the meaning of the Comparación cultural for English learners. Physically point out the following places: Ecuador, the equator, Tierra del Fuego, Ushuaia, Argentina, and Antarctica. Encourage students to repeat each place name after you say it.

Todo junto

¡AVANZA! **Goal:** ***Show what you know*** Identify how Manuel, his mother, and Fernando use **ser** and **estar** to talk about different places in the house. Then practice these verbs and ordinal numbers to describe houses and apartments. ***Actividades 17–21***

Telehistoria completa

@HOMETUTOR my.hrw.com **View, Read and Record**

STRATEGIES

Cuando lees
Read to know whether and where You already know that Manuel has lost the T-shirt. Read to find out whether he finds it. If so, where?

Cuando escuchas
Notice reactions As you listen, consider the reactions of Manuel, his mother, and Fernando to the T-shirt dilemma. How does each one react? How can you tell?

Escena 1 *Resumen*
Fernando va a la casa de Manuel porque necesitan estudiar. Pero a Manuel le gusta más jugar videojuegos.

Escena 2 *Resumen*
Manuel no puede encontrar su cuaderno. Fernando piensa que Manuel es muy desorganizado.

VIDEO DVD

AUDIO

Escena 3

Manuel: ¡Mamá! ¡La camiseta! ¿Dónde está?

Sra. Cuevas: ¿Qué camiseta?

Manuel: La camiseta de Alicia, mi amiga de Miami.

Sra. Cuevas: Ay, hijo. Aquí en el jardín no está. Tiene que estar en la casa.

Manuel: ¡Mamá! ¡Por favor!

Sra. Cuevas: Manuel, estoy ocupada.

Manuel goes back inside, where Fernando is waiting in the living room.

Manuel: ¿Dónde está? Aquí en la mesa no está.

Fernando: No está encima de la mesa. No está en tu cuarto.

Manuel: ¡No, tiene que estar aquí!

Fernando: ¿En el comedor? ¿En la cocina?

Fernando notices something next to his chair.

Fernando: Manuel, aquí hay un gato al lado del sillón.

Manuel: Sí, es Fígaro, el gato de Elena. ¿Y qué?

Fernando: El gato está encima de ¡una camiseta!

Differentiating Instruction

Pre-AP

Summarize Working in small groups, have students divide this scene into three sections. What do they consider to be the beginning, middle, and end? Then have groups work together to summarize each section into a single sentence. **1. La camiseta no está en el jardín. 2. Fernando y Manuel no encuentran la camiseta en la casa. 3. La camiseta está debajo del gato.**

Inclusion

Cumulative Instruction Create a two-column chart on the board with the headings **Lugar** and **¿Está la camiseta?** Then have students preview the Telehistoria. Ask for volunteers to write in the first column the name of each place mentioned in the scene, and **sí** or **no** in the second column.

¡AVANZA! **Objective**
- Integrate lesson content.

Core Resources
- Video Program: DVD 2
- Audio Program: TXT CD 5 track 7

Presentation Strategies
- Have students skim the Resumen from Escena 1 and Escena 2 to review background information.
- Point to the photos and ask either/or type questions. For example: **¿Dónde están Manuel y su mamá, en la casa o en el jardín? ¿Quién está al lado del sillón, el gato o el perro?**
- Show the video or play the audio.

STANDARDS
1.2 Understand language

Warm Up Projectable Transparencies, 5-18

Ordinal Numbers Write a numeral before each ordinal number below.

_____ tercero _____ octavo
_____ décimo _____ sexto
_____ primero _____ cuarto

Answers: 3; 10; 1; 8; 6; 4

Video Summary @HOMETUTOR VideoPlus my.hrw.com

Manuel asks his mother where Alicia's T-shirt is. Mrs. Cuevas says it is not in the garden and that it has to be in the house. When he tries to get her attention again, she tells him that she is busy. Manuel and Fernando look for the T-shirt on the table, in his room, in the dining room, and in the kitchen, but they don't find it. Finally, Fernando sees Elena's cat. He discovers that the cat is sitting on the T-shirt.

TODO JUNTO

Objective
- Practice using and integrating lesson vocabulary and grammar.

Core Resources
- *Cuaderno,* pp. 206–207
- Audio Program: TXT CD 5 tracks 3, 5, 7, 8, 9

Practice Sequence
- **Activity 17:** Telehistoria comprehension
- **Activity 18:** Telehistoria comprehension
- **Activity 19:** Open-ended practice: speaking
- **Activity 20:** Open-ended practice: reading, listening, speaking
- **Activity 21:** Open-ended practice: writing

STANDARDS
1.1 Engage in conversation, Acts. 19–20
1.2 Understand language, Acts. 17–19
1.3 Present information, Acts. 18–21, PYP
21st Century **Communication,** Heritage Language Learners/Act. 21 (Business Literacy)/Inclusion

✓ Ongoing Assessment

Rubric **Activity 19**

Speaking Criteria	Maximum Credit	Partial Credit	Minimum Credit
Content	The description includes a lot of information.	The description includes some information	The description includes little information
Communication	Most of your description is well organized.	Some of your description is well organized.	The description is disorganized.
Accuracy	There are few mistakes in grammar and vocabulary.	There are some mistakes in grammar and vocabulary.	There are many mistakes in grammar and vocabulary.

Answers Projectable Transparencies, 5-26 and 5-27

Activity 17 c, g, b, f, d, h, e, a

Activity 18

1. **a.** Son Manuel y Fernando. **b.** Son jóvenes y guapos. **c.** Están en la sala. **d.** Están nerviosos. **2. a.** Es la señora Cuevas. **b.** Es simpática y trabajadora. **c.** Está en el jardín. **d.** Está tranquila y contenta.

Answers continue on p. 263.

17 *Comprensión de los episodios* ¿En qué orden?

Escuchar Leer

Pon las oraciones en orden para describir los episodios. *(Put the sentences in order according to the episodes.)*

a. La camiseta está debajo del gato.
b. Manuel y Elena están en la sala.
c. Fernando llega a la casa de Manuel.
d. Manuel no encuentra su cuaderno.
e. La camiseta de Alicia no está en el jardín.
f. Fernando y Manuel van a estudiar en el cuarto de Manuel.
g. Fernando habla con la señora Cuevas.
h. Manuel habla con la señora Cuevas.

Expansión: Teacher Edition Only
Have students work in pairs to write a paragraph about what is happening in the Telehistoria.

18 *Comprensión de los episodios* Descríbelos

Escuchar Leer

Contesta las preguntas según las fotos. *(Answer the questions.)*

1.
a. ¿Quiénes son?
b. ¿Cómo son?
c. ¿Dónde están?
d. ¿Cómo están?

2.
a. ¿Quién es?
b. ¿Cómo es?
c. ¿Dónde está?
d. ¿Cómo está?

Expansión: Teacher Edition Only
Have students describe their favorite friend.

19 Una visita a tu casa

Digital performance space

Hablar

STRATEGY Hablar
Use graphics while you talk For your current or ideal house or apartment, take photos, find photos in magazines or on the Internet, or make detailed drawings with objects' colors shown in each room. Use the graphics while talking with your partner.

Descríbele tu apartamento, tu casa o la casa ideal a otro(a) estudiante. Dile cómo es cada cuarto y qué hay en los cuartos. *(Describe your home or your dream house to a partner.)*

modelo: Vivo en un apartamento. Está en el décimo piso. Hay una sala grande con muchos muebles. En la sala hay un sofá negro...

Expansión
Tell which rooms you like the most and why.

Differentiating Instruction

Multiple Intelligences

Logical Write the numbers 1 through 10 on the board in order to review ordinal numbers. Then, after students have placed the sentences in Activity 17 in sequential order, have them use ordinal numbers to talk about their work. **La primera oración es... El segundo episodio es...**

Heritage Language Learners

Support What They Know Encourage students to think about **la casa ideal** in a broader sense. Ask them to not only describe their ideal house, but also to discuss the advantages and disadvantages of the features they include. How would their ideal house affect the environment, family life, or society in general?

20 Integración

Digital performance space

Leer
Escuchar
Hablar

Tú y tu familia van a vivir un año en Quito y necesitan un apartamento. Mira la lista de una agencia de alquiler y escucha el mensaje telefónico de un agente. Describe cuál es el mejor apartamento para ustedes. *(Describe which apartment is best for you and your family.)*

Fuente 1 Lista de apartamentos

Calle Olmedo, 38 Apartamento en el centro de Quito. Cuesta 1.300 dólares al mes. Está en el tercer piso. Tiene tres cuartos con muchos armarios y dos baños. La sala es un poco pequeña pero la cocina es muy grande. Hay un patio pequeño. Está cerca de tiendas y restaurantes.

Calle de los Olivos, 45 Apartamento lejos del centro. Cuesta 1.050 dólares al mes. Está en el primer piso. Tiene cinco cuartos y tres baños. La cocina es grande y la sala es bonita. El apartamento tiene muchas ventanas y armarios grandes. No tiene patio, pero hay un parque cerca.

Calle Simón Bolívar, 76 Apartamento cerca del centro. Cuesta 1.125 dólares al mes. Está en el décimo piso y puedes ver todo el centro. Tiene dos cuartos y un baño. La sala es grande y la cocina también. También hay un patio bonito. Está cerca de los cines y los teatros.

Fuente 2 Mensaje telefónico

Listen and take notes
- ¿Cómo es el apartamento y dónde está?
- ¿Cuánto cuesta?

modelo: Quiero vivir en el apartamento de la calle... porque...

Audio Program
TXT CD 5 Tracks 8, 9
Audio Script, TE p. 245b

21 Una casa increíble

Digital performance space

Escribir

Escribe un anuncio para vender una casa. Di dónde está, cómo es, y qué cuartos y muebles tiene. *(Write a detailed ad that you would use to sell a house.)*

modelo:

¡Casa bonita! Está cerca del centro. Es grande y tiene cinco cuartos y cuatro baños. La escalera es muy bonita. Ya tiene muebles. En la sala hay un sofá y dos sillones.

Writing Criteria	Excellent	Good	Needs Work
Content	Your ad includes a lot of information.	Your ad includes some information.	Your ad includes little information.
Communication	Most of your ad is organized and easy to follow.	Parts of your ad are organized and easy to follow.	Your ad is disorganized and hard to follow.
Accuracy	Your ad has few mistakes in grammar and vocabulary.	Your ad has some mistakes in grammar and vocabulary.	Your ad has many mistakes in grammar and vocabulary.

Expansión
Present your house ad to the class as if you were a real estate agent trying to sell it.

Más práctica Cuaderno *pp. 206–207* Cuaderno para hispanohablantes *pp. 208–209*

Get Help Online
my.hrw.com

PARA Y PIENSA

Did you get it? Use **ser, estar,** and an ordinal number to complete the sentences.
1. Fígaro _____ el gato de Elena. No _____ tranquilo.
2. Fígaro vive en el _____ piso. (7)

Differentiating Instruction

Slower-paced Learners

Read Before Listening Have students divide a piece of paper into thirds. At the top of each section tell them to write one of the addresses listed in Activity 20. Then guide students through a preview of the text. Read each sentence aloud pausing to let students take notes.

Inclusion

Clear Structure Remind students to follow the steps of the writing process in order to create their ads in Activity 21. Have them brainstorm important vocabulary including words related to rooms, colors, location, numbers, and furniture. Then have them draft complete sentences, revise, and proofread before turning in their final drafts.

Long-term Retention

Pre-AP Integration

Activity 20 Assign a group of students to write three apartment ads using the examples in Activity 20 as models. Assign a second group to evaluate the ads, decide which one is the best for them, and explain why.

✓ Ongoing Assessment

Rubric Activity 20

Listening/Speaking

Proficient	Not There Yet
Student uses correct forms of **ser** and **estar**, and ordinal numbers.	Student uses incorrect forms of **ser** and **estar,** and ordinal numbers.

To customize your own rubrics, use the ***Generate Success*** *Rubric Generator and Graphic Organizers.*

✓ Ongoing Assessment

Get Help Online
More Practice
my.hrw.com

PARA Y PIENSA If students have difficulties completing the sentences, ask them to review p. 253. For additional practice, use Reteaching & Practice Copymasters URB 5 pp. 7, 9.

Answers Projectable Transparencies, 5-26 and 5-27

Answers for Activity 19 from p. 262

Activity 19 Answers will vary. Sample answers include: Vivo en una casa grande. Tiene tres cuartos, una sala, una cocina, un comedor y dos baños. En la sala hay un sofá verde y dos sillones. La mesa del comedor es grande y tiene ocho sillas.

Activity 20 Answers will vary. Sample answers include: Quiero vivir en el apartamento de la Calle de los Olivos porque me gusta estar lejos del centro. Mi familia es grande y necesitamos cinco cuartos. La cocina es grande. No tiene patio, pero hay un parque cerca.

Activity 21 Answers will vary. Sample answers include: ¡La casa ideal! Está cerca del centro y de un parque. Tiene dos pisos. En el primer piso hay el comedor grande, la sala con muchas ventanas, la cocina y un baño. En el segundo piso encuentras tres cuartos y otro baño. Tiene un patio muy bonito.

Para y piensa **1.** es, está; **2.** séptimo

¡AVANZA! Objectives

- Learn about real estate in Ecuador.
- Compare houses and apartments for sale.

Core Resource

- Audio Program: TXT CD 5 track 10

Presentation Strategies

- Ask students to read the title **Vivir en Ecuador.**
- Ask for predictions, based on the title and the illustrations.

STANDARDS

1.2 Understand language
2.1 Practices and perspectives
2.2 Products and perspectives
4.2 Compare cultures
21st Century **Critical Thinking and Problem Solving,** Pre-AP; **Media Literacy,** Presentational Mode

Warm Up Projectable Transparencies, 5-19

Ser and estar Fill in the blanks with **ser** or **estar.**

1. Nosotros _____ maestros.
2. El disco compacto _____ aquí.
3. Tú _____ triste.
4. Ustedes _____ de Ecuador.
5. Ellos _____ en la cafetería.

Answers: 1. somos; 2. está; 3. estás; 4. son; 5. están.

Culture

Background Information

The ancient city of Quito was once inhabited by the Quitus, an indigenous group, who gave the city its name. In 1533, Inca leader Rumiñahui destroyed Quito to prevent its takeover by the conquistadors. Just a year later, though, the Spanish began rebuilding it.

Comparación cultural

The Old City and the New City Today Quito is actually two cities, the Old City and the New City. The Old City seems untouched, almost preserved intact from colonial days. The New City is bustling and modern. Some cities in the U.S. also maintain two profiles. One is Old Town, nestled in the midst of modern Chicago.

Lectura

Additional readings at my.hrw.com SPANISH InterActive Reader

¡AVANZA! Goal: Read advertisements for houses and apartments for sale in Ecuador. Then compare the two places and talk about where you prefer to live.

AUDIO

Vivir en Ecuador

The following are an apartment brochure from Quito and a real-estate ad from Guayaquil.

STRATEGY Leer

Use a checklist and explain Make a checklist showing which place—apartment or house—is more useful for a single person, a small family, and a large family. List reasons.

	el apartamento	la casa	¿Por qué?
una persona			
una familia pequeña			
una familia grande			

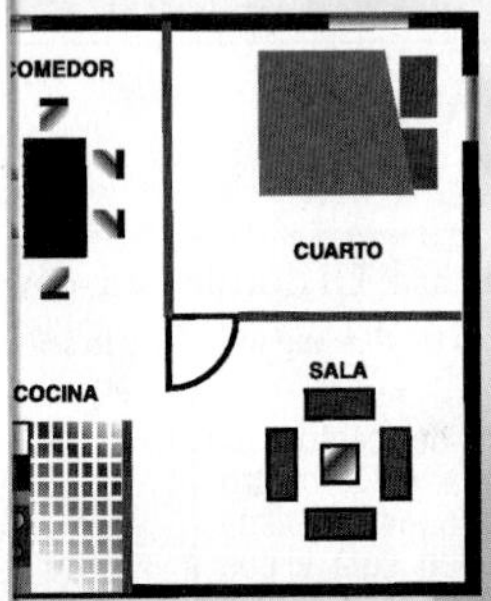

LAS CAMELIAS

COMUNIDAD RESIDENCIAL

EL QUITEÑO MODERNO

- Construcción antisísmica[1]
- Jardines comunales
- Sauna
- Gimnasio
- Portero[2] de 24 horas
- Áreas verdes y recreativas
- Cerca de tiendas, supermercados y restaurantes

[1] earthquake-proof [2] Doorman [3] From [4] square

Differentiating Instruction

Pre-AP

Support Opinions Divide students into two groups—**Las Camelias** and **Cerro Santa Ana.** Give each group a large piece of paper with a line down the middle to create two columns. Then have students work together to list both the pros of their housing, and the cons of the other group's housing. Finally, have representatives from each group take turns debating which is the better choice.

Heritage Language Learners

Writing Skills Have students write a short persuasive essay describing whether, in their opinion, it is better to live in a house or an apartment. Advise students to begin with a graphic organizer. They might draw a simple outline of a house and apartment, and list their ideas inside of each. Remind students to support their opinions with specific details.

Cerro Santa Ana

Comunidad privada de 18 residencias

Aquí puedes ir de compras o al cine y en unos minutos volver a tu casa cerca del río[5] Guayas. Cerro Santa Ana es para las personas a quienes les gusta el aire puro tanto como un lugar urbano.

$130.000

Casa ultramoderna de dos pisos con acceso fácil a Guayaquil

- 4 cuartos
- sala-comedor
- cocina
- oficina
- de lavar[6]
- 2 garajes

La casa está en un lugar tranquilo pero no está muy lejos de Guayaquil. Puedes preparar la comida en el patio y hay zonas para practicar deportes.

Cerro Santa Ana | Escalón 68 | Teléfono 231-6687

[5] river [6] washing machines

PARA Y PIENSA

¿Comprendiste?

1. ¿Cómo es el apartamento y dónde está? ¿Y la casa?
2. ¿Qué puedes hacer en los dos lugares?
3. ¿Cuál es mejor para una familia, el apartamento o la casa? ¿Por qué?

¿Y tú?

Explícale a otro(a) estudiante dónde prefieres vivir y por qué.

Communication

Presentational Mode

Ask students to search their local papers for real-estate ads, looking for illustrated ads that are similar to those on pp. 264 and 265. Then tell them to re-create the local ads, using the Spanish vocabulary they've learned in this lesson. Ask them to use a Venn diagram to compare and contrast the properties advertised in Ecuador and those advertised in their hometowns. Finally, have students present their local ads to the class.

Comparisons

English Language Connection

Grammar and Syntax Ask students to read the ads on pp. 264–265 carefully, paying attention to word choice and order. Then ask them to make comparisons with similar phrases in English. For instance, **puedes ir de compras** is correct in Spanish, but in English we say *you can go shopping.*

Differentiating Instruction

Slower-paced Learners

Yes/No Questions Ask students yes or no questions to assess their comprehension of the readings on pp. 264–265. If the answer to a question is no, ask students to supply the correct information. For example:

¿Tienen dos baños las casas de Cerro Santa Ana?

No, las casas tienen tres baños.

Multiple Intelligences

Visual Learners Ask students to choose either the apartment or the house described on pp. 264–265. Then have students create a sketch of their choice, based on the description they read. Encourage students to provide additional details on their sketches. Give students the opportunity to share and describe their drawings.

Answers

Para y piensa

¿Comprendiste?

1. El apartamento es pequeño y está en el centro de la ciudad. La casa es ultramoderna y está en un lugar tranquilo no muy lejos de Guayaquil.
2. En Las Camelias puedo usar las áreas recreativas y puedo ir a las tiendas y a los restaurantes. En Cerro Santa Ana puedo preparar la comida en el patio y practicar deportes.
3. La casa es mejor para una familia porque tiene más cuartos.

¿Y tu?

Answers will vary. Sample answers:

Prefiero el apartamento porque me gusta vivir en la ciudad.

Prefiero vivir en la casa porque yo tengo dos gatos, y ellos pueden ir al patio.

Objectives
- Learn about an Inca settlement.
- Understand how the Incas developed ways to make their buildings earthquake-proof.
- Use perspectives from social sciences, history, and language arts to gain a fuller understanding of the Incas.

Presentation Strategies
- Ask what students know about the Incan civilization.
- Ask for four volunteers: one to read the title of the Conexiones and three to read the titles of the Proyectos.
- When discussing the shapes of **El Templo del Sol** and the ruins of Sacsayhuaman, draw students' attention to the pictures.

STANDARDS
1.3 Present information
2.1 Practices and perspectives
2.2 Products and perspectives
3.1 Knowledge of other disciplines
Information Literacy, Proyecto 1, 2, 3

Connections
La historia
Cusco, which was once capital of the Incan empire, is now a city of some 300,000 inhabitants. Ancient Cusco was constructed in four quarters, each corresponding to a part of the empire. A road stretched from each quarter into its related region, where that region's governor lived.

Answers
Proyecto 1
Students should use their imaginations, while remaining realistic.

Proyecto 2
The Incan empire lasted from A.D. 1438–1533; its center was in what is now Peru. It was called Tawantinsuya by the indigenous people, a term that means "the four united regions" in Quechua. It was ruled by emperors, the last of whom was put to death at the command of Francisco Pizarro.

Proyecto 3
Lists should include some of the following: **cóndor, llama, pampa, puma,** and **gaucho**. The French word *lagniappe* also comes from the Quechua language.

Conexiones *Las matemáticas*

Las ruinas de Ingapirca

At one time, the Incan empire stretched from modern-day Colombia to Chile. At Ingapirca, an important settlement in Ecuador, the Incas built a majestic temple called El Templo del Sol (Temple of the Sun). Carved into a steep rocky cliff, the temple served as a fortress and place of worship.

Many Incan buildings have withstood centuries of earthquakes. The Incas used large stone blocks of different shapes for building. Often the blocks, as well as the doors and windows, were wider at the base and narrower at the top.

Look at the images below. Write two paragraphs comparing the shapes you see in the buildings to other shapes such as circles, squares, and triangles. Give the names and a description of the shapes you discuss. Make an illustration for each shape.

El Templo del Sol

Las ruinas de Sacsayhuaman, Perú

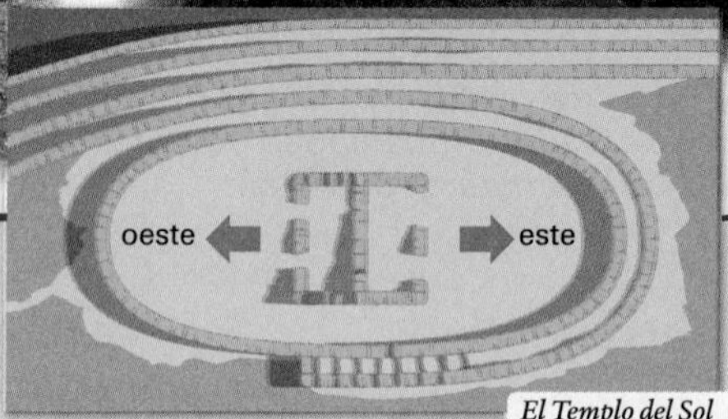

El Templo del Sol

Proyecto 1 *Las ciencias sociales*
The external walls of the buildings at Ingapirca were made of chiseled blocks that fit together so precisely that no mortar was needed to hold them. Research and report on how the Incas may have cut, transported, and fit these huge blocks without the use of iron tools or wheels.

Proyecto 2 *La historia*
Research the Incan empire and create a map showing its size. Then write a paragraph about its population, duration, and political structure.

Proyecto 3 *El lenguaje*
There are many different indigenous groups and languages in Ecuador. The most common indigenous language, Quechua, was also spoken by the Incas. Spanish and English have borrowed many words from Quechua. Use the Internet or a library to find four or five Quechua words that are used in Spanish. Write the words in Spanish, then explain what they mean in English.

Differentiating Instruction

Pre-AP
Draw Conclusions Discuss with students the conclusions they can draw about the history of the Incas, and Ecuador in general, based on the information presented in the reading. Do they believe the Incas were powerful? What leads them to that conclusion? Do they think the Incas had enemies? Why? Does it seem that earthquakes were prevalent? What leads them to that conclusion?

Inclusion
Clear Structure If students choose Proyecto 1 or Proyecto 2, remind them to follow the steps of the writing process. Provide students with an appropriate graphic organizer to record the information they find through their research, as well as their own thoughts and opinions. Then have them draft complete sentences, revise, and proofread before turning in their final drafts.

Lección 1

En resumen

Vocabulario y gramática

ANIMATED GRAMMAR
Interactive Flashcards
my.hrw.com

Vocabulario

Describe a House

el apartamento	*apartment*	el jardín (*pl.* los jardines)	*garden*
el armario	*closet; armoire*	el patio	*patio*
bajar	*to descend*	el piso	*floor (of a building)*
la casa	*house*	la planta baja	*ground floor*
la cocina	*kitchen*	la sala	*living room*
el comedor	*dining room*	subir	*to go up*
el cuarto	*room; bedroom*	el suelo	*floor (of a room)*
la escalera	*stairs*		
ideal	*ideal*		

Describe Household Items

la cosa	*thing*
el disco compacto	*compact disc*
el lector DVD	*DVD player*
el radio	*radio*
el televisor	*television set*
el tocadiscos compactos	*CD player*
los videojuegos	*video games*

Furniture

la alfombra	*rug*	la lámpara	*lamp*
la cama	*bed*	los muebles	*furniture*
la cómoda	*dresser*	el sillón (*pl.* los sillones)	*armchair*
las cortinas	*curtains*	el sofá	*sofa, couch*
el espejo	*mirror*		

Ordinal Numbers

primero(a)	*first*
segundo(a)	*second*
tercero(a)	*third*
cuarto(a)	*fourth*
quinto(a)	*fifth*
sexto(a)	*sixth*
séptimo(a)	*seventh*
octavo(a)	*eighth*
noveno(a)	*ninth*
décimo(a)	*tenth*

Gramática

Ser or estar

Ser and **estar** both mean *to be.*

- Use **ser** to indicate origin.
- Use **ser** to describe personal traits and physical characteristics.
- **Ser** is also used to indicate professions.
- You also use **ser** to express possession and to give the time and the date.

- Use **estar** to indicate location.
- **Estar** is also used to describe conditions, both physical and emotional.

Ordinal Numbers

When used with a noun, an **ordinal number** must agree in number and gender with that noun.

- **Ordinals** are placed before nouns.
- **Primero** and **tercero** drop the **o** before a masculine singular noun.

Practice Spanish with Holt McDougal Apps!

Differentiating Instruction

Multiple Intelligences

Visual Learners In advance, collect a number of home design and decorating magazines. Then give students the opportunity to skim through the magazines, labeling and commenting on the dwellings and furniture they see. For example: **Me gusta el apartamento. Tiene una cocina muy grande. Prefiero vivir en la planta baja.**

Slower-paced Learners

Sentence Completion Provide students with additional examples to help them sort the different uses of **ser** and **estar.** Write a number of sentences on the board with the verb missing. For example: **Mi madre _____ maestra. El apartamento _____ cerca del centro.** Invite volunteers to fill in the blank with the correct verb. Then have students provide additional examples for their peers.

Objective

- Review lesson vocabulary and grammar.

DIGITAL SPANISH

Interactive Flashcards Students can hear every target vocabulary word pronounced in authentic Spanish. Flashcards have Spanish on one side, and a picture or a translation on the other.

Review Games Matching, concentration, hangman, and word search are just a sampling of the fun, interactive games students can play to review for the test.

performance space
News Networking
@HOMETUTOR
CULTURA Interactiva

- **Audio and Video Resources**
- **Interactive Flashcards**
- **Review Activities**
- **WebQuest**
- **Conjuguemos.com**

Communication

Group Work

Organize students into small groups. Each group is assigned one room in a house. Have students make a list of the items that can be found in that room. Students will draw the room showing and labeling all of the items found in the room, as well as labeling an activity a person in the room is doing. Refer them to the Expansión de vocabulario for more items. Students can present their drawings to the class.

Objective
- Review lesson grammar and vocabulary.

Core Resources
- *Cuaderno,* pp. 208–219
- Audio Program: TXT CD 5 track 11

Presentation Strategies
- Before listening to the audio, explain to students that they will hear Rebeca describe her house and that they will be answering questions about it.
- Ask each student to describe one thing in their house that they do not like, and say what they would rather have. Example: **Mi cuarto es pequeño. Quiero un cuarto más grande.**
- Before doing the verb-related activities, ask students to review the uses of **ser** and **estar.** In which situations would each verb apply?
- Ask students to make use of ordinal numbers and vocabulary by describing a fictitious department store, and tell what kinds of items are on each floor. Example: **En el primer piso hay ropa para mujeres. En el segundo piso hay discos compactos.**
- Ask students to generate two questions to ask their classmates, based on the Comparación cultural.

STANDARDS
1.2 Understand language, Act. 1
1.3 Present information, Acts. 2–5
4.2 Compare cultures, Act. 5

Warm Up Projectable Transparencies, 5-19

Vocabulary Complete each sentence with the correct vocabulary word.

1. Yo duermo en mi _____ en mi cuarto.
2. Mi hermana siempre prepara la comida en _____.
3. Nosotros comemos la cena en _____.
4. Tengo que subir _____ para ir al segundo piso.
5. _____ está detrás de la casa.

Answers: 1. cama; 2. la cocina; 3. el comedor; 4. la escalera; 5. El jardín

✓ Ongoing Assessment

Get Help Online
More Practice
my.hrw.com

Remediation If students achieve less than 80% accuracy with the activities, direct them to the review pp. 246, 253, 255, 258, 260, 267 and to get help online at my.hrw.com.

See activity answers on p. 269.

Lección 1

Repaso de la lección

@HOMETUTOR my.hrw.com

¡LLEGADA!

Now you can
- describe a house and household items
- indicate the order of things
- describe people and locations

Using
- **ser** or **estar**
- ordinal numbers

To review
- **ser** or **estar** p. 253

1 Listen and understand

AUDIO

Escucha a Rebeca describir su casa. Indica si las oraciones son ciertas o falsas.
(Listen to Rebeca describe her house and tell whether the statements are true or false.)

1. La casa es muy bonita.
2. Hay un sillón en la sala.
3. En el comedor hay diez sillas.
4. El baño está detrás del comedor.
5. En el segundo piso hay tres cuartos y dos baños.
6. El cuarto de Rebeca es azul.

Audio Program
TXT CD 5 Track 11
Audio Script, TE p. 245b

To review
- ordinal numbers p. 258

2 Indicate the order of things

El señor Cabrera tiene que ayudar a los residentes de su edificio de apartamentos a mover unos muebles. Indica en qué piso están estas cosas.
(Tell on what floor of the apartment building these items are.)

modelo: PB
Las alfombras están en la planta baja.

1. 4°

2. 5°

3. 6°

4. 3°

5. 7°

6. 1°

7. 2°

8. 8°

Differentiating Instruction

Multiple Intelligences

Intrapersonal Divide the class into pairs. One student in each pair pretends that he/she is talking with an exchange student who has come to spend a month at his/her house. The host gives the guest a tour of the house, explaining something about each room. For example: **Aquí está la sala donde miramos la televisión.** Then the students switch roles.

Slower-paced Learners

Sentence Completion Have students fill in missing information about an item in each room. For example: **En la sala hay _____. (un televisor) En mi cuarto tengo _____. (un tocadiscos) En el armario tengo _____. (mi ropa)** There can be several answers that are correct.

To review
- **ser** or **estar** p. 253

3 Describe a house and household items

Joaquín describe su casa en un correo electrónico. Completa su mensaje con la forma correcta de **ser** o **estar.** *(Complete the email message with the correct form of* ***ser*** *or* ***estar.****)*

```
Hola, amigo. Aquí __1.__ yo en mi casa. Nuestra casa
__2.__ al lado del parque. La casa __3.__ blanca y muy
bonita. Ahora mi hermano y yo __4.__ en nuestro cuarto.
Muchos discos compactos __5.__ en el suelo porque
nosotros no __6.__ muy organizados. ¿Y tú? ¿Tú __7.__
organizado o desorganizado? El cuarto de nuestros padres
__8.__ al lado de nuestro cuarto. Su cuarto __9.__ más
grande que nuestro cuarto. ¿Cómo __10.__ tu casa?
```

To review
- **ser** or **estar** p. 253

4 Describe people and locations

Describe a estas personas y explica dónde y cómo están. *(Describe these people, their locations, and how they feel.)*

modelo: Ernesto (artístico / en el parque / tranquilo)
Ernesto es artístico. Está en el parque. Está tranquilo.

1. las maestras (simpáticas / en la escuela / contentas)
2. tú (estudioso / en la biblioteca / nervioso)
3. la señora Moreno (seria / deprimida / en el pasillo)
4. nosotros (cómicos / en el teatro / emocionados)
5. mi hermano menor (malo / en su cuarto / enojado)
6. yo (inteligente / en clase / ocupado)

To review
- Comparación cultural pp. 246, 255, 260

5 Ecuador and Argentina

Comparación cultural

Answer these culture questions.

1. What are some characteristics of traditional Spanish architecture?
2. What are some features found in Tigua paintings?
3. What does Ecuador's **Mitad del Mundo** monument mark?
4. Why is Ushuaia, Argentina, known as **la ciudad del fin del mundo**?

Más práctica Cuaderno *pp. 208–219* Cuaderno para hispanohablantes *pp. 210–219*

Get Help Online my.hrw.com

Differentiating Instruction

Inclusion

Frequent Review/Repetition To practice **ser** and **estar,** have students write at least two facts about themselves and/or family members using each of the verbs. For example: **Ser: Mi hermano es maestro. Mi hermana y yo somos estudiantes. Estar: Nosotros estamos en Chicago. Nuestra casa está en la ciudad. Mis padres siempre están ocupados.**

Pre-AP

Expand and Elaborate Students can tell about their families by using ordinal numbers, verbs, and vocabulary. For example: **Mi hermana es la primera hija. Ella es maestra y es muy simpática. Yo soy el segundo hijo de la familia. Yo soy estudiante.**

✓ Ongoing Assessment

Peer Assessment Ask students to work in pairs to write e-mails to each other, using the e-mail from Joaquín in Activity 3 as a model. They should read each other's e-mail messages and edit them if necessary.

Answers Projectable Transparencies, 5-27

Answers for activities on p. 268.

Activity 1
1. cierto
2. falso
3. falso
4. falso
5. cierto
6. falso

Activity 2
1. La cómoda está en el cuarto piso.
2. El televisor está en el quinto piso.
3. La cama está en el sexto piso.
4. El sillón está en el tercer piso.
5. La mesa y las sillas están en el séptimo piso.
6. Las cortinas están en el primer piso.
7. El sofá está en el segundo piso.
8. La lámpara está en el octavo piso.

Activity 3
1. estoy
2. está
3. es
4. estamos
5. están
6. somos
7. eres
8. está
9. es
10. es

Activity 4
1. Las maestras son simpáticas. Están en la escuela. Están contentas.
2. Tú eres estudioso. Estás en la biblioteca. Estás nervioso.
3. La señora Moreno es seria. Está deprimida. Está en el pasillo.
4. Nosotros estamos emocionados. Estamos en el teatro. Somos cómicos.
5. Mi hermano menor es malo. Está enojado. Está en su cuarto.
6. Yo estoy ocupado. Soy inteligente. Estoy en clase.

Activity 5
1. Houses have a white exterior and a red-tiled roof.
2. Tigua paintings are typically landscapes that show scenes of community life.
3. It marks the location of the equator line.
4. It is the southernmost city in the world.

Lesson Overview

Culture at a Glance

Topic & Activity	Essential Question
A brithday party pp. 270–271	Where and with whom do you like to celebrate your birthday?
Festival in Quito p. 278	How do people show pride for their community?
Otavalo's textiles p. 284	Why are traditional crafts important to a culture?
Traditional dances of Ecuador and Panama pp. 288–289	How would you compare the **sanjuanito** and the **tamborito** dances?
Textile art of Ecuador and Panama p. 290	How do different cultures express themselves through crafts?
Culture review p. 293	How do Ecuador and Panama celebrate?

COMPARISON COUNTRIES  **Ecuador**  **Argentina**  **Panamá**

Practice at a Glance

	Objective	Activity & Skill
Vocabulary	Parties	1: Reading; 3: Listening/Reading; 5: Speaking/Writing; 6: Reading/Writing; 7: Speaking; 8: Speaking; 9: Listening/Reading; 11: Writing; 13:Speaking; 18: Speaking; Repaso 1: Listening; Repaso 2: Writing
Vocabulary	Chores	2: Writing/Speaking; 4: Speaking; 12: Writing; 14: Listening; 15: Speaking; 18: Speaking; 19: Reading/Listening/Speaking; 20: Writing; Repaso 4: Writing
Grammar	Irregular verbs	5: Speaking/Writing; 6: Reading/Writing; 7:Speaking; 8: Speaking; 10: Speaking; Repaso 2: Writing
Grammar	Affirmative **tú** commands	12: Writing; 13: Speaking; 14:Listening; 15: Speaking; 18: Speaking; 20: Writing; Repaso 3: Writing
Grammar	**Acabar de** and infinitive	15: Speaking; 18: Speaking; 20: Writing; Repaso 4: Writing
Communication	Plan a party	1: Reading; 3: Listening/Reading; 5: Speaking/Writing; 7: Speaking; 8: Speaking; 9: Listening/Reading; 13: Speaking; 18: Speaking; Repaso 2: Writing
Communication	Talk about chores and responsibilities	2: Writing/Speaking; 4: Speaking; 14: Listening; 15: Speaking; 18: Speaking; 20: Writing; Repaso 4: Writing
Communication	Tell someone what to do	12: Writing; 13: Speaking; 14: Listening; 15: Speaking; 18: Speaking; 19: Reading/Listening/Speaking; 20: Writing; Repaso 3: Writing
Communication	Say what you just did	15: Speaking; 18: Speaking; 20: Writing; Repaso 4: Writing
Communication	Pronunciation: the letters **b** and **v**	**Pronunciación:** Las letras ***b*** y ***v*** p. 283: Listening/Speaking
Recycle	**Tener que**	4: Speaking
Recycle	Interrogative words	8: Speaking
Recycle	Expressions of frequency	10: Speaking
Recycle	Direct object pronouns	13: Speaking

The following presentations are recorded in the Audio Program for ¡Avancemos!

- **¡A responder!** *page 273*
- **14: Una casa sucia** *page 284*
- **19: Integración** *page 287*
- **Repaso de la lección** *page 292*
  1: Listen and understand
- **Repaso Inclusivo** *page 296*
  1: Listen, understand, and compare

For **¡AvanzaRap!** scripts, see the **¡AvanzaRap! DVD.**

¡A responder! TXT CD 5 track 13

1. planchar la ropa
2. bailar
3. barrer el suelo
4. poner la mesa
5. envolver el regalo
6. cocinar
7. lavar los platos
8. pasar la aspiradora

14 Una casa sucia TXT CD 5 track 17

1. Elena, la alfombra está muy sucia. Todavía necesitas pasar la aspiradora.
2. Ay, ¿qué pasa en la cocina? Todavía necesitas barrer el suelo.
3. Todavía hay que sacar la basura en la cocina.
4. Hay que lavar los platos. Están muy sucios. ¿Me ayudas, mi hija?
5. Tus abuelos vienen hoy. Necesitas hacer la cama.
6. Vamos a comer temprano. Todavía hay que poner la mesa.

19 Integración TXT CD 5 tracks 19, 20

Hola y bienvenidos al programa. Si limpian la casa en dos horas reciben dos coches nuevos y cinco mil dólares. Pero no es fácil. Hay que ser organizados. Tienen que limpiar todos los cuartos y baños. Deben hacer las camas; hay siete camas. También necesitan limpiar la cocina. En la cocina hay que sacar la basura, lavar los platos y barrer el suelo. En la sala hay una alfombra sucia y encima del sofá está toda la ropa sucia de la familia. Deben pasar la aspiradora, lavar y planchar la ropa. Hay que poner la mesa del comedor. En el jardín, necesitan cortar el césped. Buena suerte y... ¡Limpia ya!

Repaso de la lección TXT CD 5 track 22

1 Listen and understand

Sr. Robles:
Chicos, la fiesta para la directora es una sorpresa. Todos ustedes van a ayudar, ¿no?

Chicos:
Sí. Yo, sí. Sí, señor.

Sr. Robles:
Andrés, trae los globos, por favor.

Andrés:
Sí, señor. Los traigo mañana.

Sr. Robles:
Samuel, ayuda a limpiar el cuarto.

Samuel:
Está bien. Mañana vengo temprano.

Sr. Robles:
Carla, ven temprano también y pon las decoraciones.

Carla:
Sí, señor Robles. Me gusta decorar.

Sr. Robles:
Y yo traigo pizza para todos.

Chicos:
¡Qué bien! ¡Buena idea!

Repaso inclusivo TXT CD 5 track 24

1 Listen, understand, and compare

¿Dónde estás? Son las cinco y media y acabo de volver a mi casa. La fiesta de sorpresa para Elisa es a las seis y media. Hay mucho que hacer. Tú vas a ayudarme, ¿verdad? Tengo que ir a la tienda para comprar comida. Sirvo pollo con patatas y una ensalada. Por favor, trae los tomates de tu jardín. Si llegas antes de las seis y media, ve al apartamento de la señora Domínguez, en el cuarto piso. Ella tiene el pastel de cumpleaños. Después, baja al segundo piso y habla con Jorge y Marlene. Ellos tienen los discos compactos que necesito para la fiesta. Si los invitados llegan temprano y no estoy, sirve los refrescos. Gracias. Hasta luego.

Resource List

Everything you need to ...

Plan	Present	Assess
TEACHER ONE STOP ✓Lesson Plans ✓Teacher Resources ✓Audio and Video	**INTERACTIVE WHITEBOARD LESSONS** **TEACHER ONE STOP WITH PROJECTABLE TRANSPARENCIES** **POWER PRESENTATIONS** **ANIMATEDGRAMMAR**	**ONLINE ASSESSMENT** ✓ Assessments for on-level, modified, pre-AP, and heritage learners ✓ Create customized tests with **Examview Assessment Suite** ✓ **performance space** ✓ *Generate Success* Rubric Generator

Print

Plan	Present	Practice	Assess
URB 5 • Video Scripts pp. 71–72 • Family Involvement Activity p. 92 • Absent Student Copymasters pp. 101–111 **Best Practices Toolkit**	**URB 5** • Video Activities pp. 59–66	• *Cuaderno* pp. 220–245 • *Cuaderno para hispanohablantes* pp. 220–245 • *Lecturas para todos* pp. 47–51 • *Lecturas para hispanohablantes* • *¡AvanzaCómics! SuperBruno y Nati,* Episodio 3 **URB 5** • Practice Games pp. 39–46 • Audio Scripts pp. 78–82 • Fine Art Activities pp. 88–89	**Differentiated Assessment Program** **URB 5** • Did you get it? Reteaching and Practice Copymasters pp. 13–24

Projectable Transparencies (Teacher One Stop, my.hrw.com)

Culture	Presentation and Practice	Classroom Management
• Atlas Maps 1–6 • Fine Art Transparencies 4, 5	• Vocabulary Transparencies 8, 9 • Grammar Presentation Transparencies 12, 13 • Situational Transparencies and label overlay 14, 15 • Situational Student Copymasters pp. 1, 2	• Warm Up Transparencies 20–23 • Student Book Answer Transparencies 28–31

Audio and Video

Audio	Video	¡AvanzaRap! DVD
• Student Book Audio CD 5 Tracks 12–24 • Workbook Audio CD 3 Tracks 11–20 • Heritage Learners Audio CD 2 Tracks 5–8, CD 4 Tracks 3–6 • Assessment Audio CD 2 Tracks 3–6 • *Lecturas para todos* Audio CD 1 Track 10, CD 2 Tracks 1–6 • Sing-along Songs Audio CD	• Vocabulary Video DVD 2 • *Telehistoria* DVD 2 Escena 1 Escena 2 Escena 3 Completa • Culture Video DVD 2	• Video animations of all **¡AvanzaRap!** songs (with Karaoke track) • Interactive DVD Activities • Teaching Suggestions • **¡AvanzaRap!** Activity Masters • **¡AvanzaRap!** video scripts and answers

Online and Media Resources

Student	Teacher
Available online at my.hrw.com • Online Student Edition • News + Networking • performance space • @HOMETUTOR • CULTURA Interactiva • WebQuests • Interactive Flashcards • Review Games • Self-Check Quiz **Student One Stop** **Holt McDougal Spanish Apps**	**Teacher One Stop (also available at my.hrw.com)** • Interactive Teacher's Edition • All print, audio, and video resources • Projectable Transparencies • Lesson Plans • TPRS • Examview Assessment Suite **Available online at my.hrw.com** *Generate Success* Rubric Generator and Graphic Organizers **Power Presentations**

Differentiated Assessment

On-level	Modified	Pre-AP	Heritage Learners
• Vocabulary Recognition Quiz p. 227 • Vocabulary Production Quiz p. 228 • Grammar Quizzes pp. 229–230 • Culture Quiz p. 231 • On-level Lesson Test pp. 232–238 • On-level Unit Test pp. 244–250	• Modified Lesson Test pp. 182–188 • Modified Unit Test pp. 194–200	• Pre-AP Lesson Test pp. 182–188 • Pre-AP Unit Test pp. 194–200	• Heritage Learners Lesson Test pp. 188–194 • Heritage Learners Unit Test pp. 200–206

Core Pacing Guide

50 Minute (9 Day)

	Objectives/Focus	Teach	Practice	Assess/HW Options
DAY 1	**Culture:** learn about Ecuador **Vocabulary:** Vocabulary: planning a party • Warm Up OHT 20 **5 min**	Lesson Opener pp. 270–271 **Presentación de vocabulario** pp. 272–273 • Read A–E • View video DVD 2 • Play audio TXT CD 5 track 12 • *¡A responder!* TXT CD 5 track 13 **25 min**	Lesson Opener pp. 270–271 **Práctica de vocabulario** p. 274 • Acts. 1, 2 **15 min**	**Assess:** *Para y piensa* p. 274 **5 min** **Homework:** *Cuaderno* pp. 220–222 @HomeTutor
DAY 2	**Communication:** talking about chores and responsibilities • Warm Up OHT 20 • Check Homework **5 min**	**Vocabulario en contexto** pp. 275–276 • *Telehistoria escena 1* DVD 2 **20 min**	**Vocabulario en contexto** pp. 275–276 • Act. 3 TXT CD 5 track 14 • Act. 4 **20 min**	**Assess:** *Para y piensa* p. 276 **5 min** **Homework:** *Cuaderno* pp. 220–222 @HomeTutor
DAY 3	**Grammar:** more irregular verbs • Warm Up OHT 21 • Check Homework **5 min**	**Presentación de gramática** p. 277 • more irregular verbs **20 min**	**Práctica de gramática** pp. 278–279 • Acts. 5, 6, 7, 8 **20 min**	**Assess:** *Para y piensa* p. 279 **5 min** **Homework:** *Cuaderno* pp. 223–225 @HomeTutor
DAY 4	**Communication:** talk about what you and others do at parties • Warm Up OHT 21 • Check Homework **5 min**	**Gramática en contexto** pp. 280–281 • *Telehistoria escena 2* DVD 2 **15 min**	**Gramática en contexto** pp. 280–281 • Act. 9 TXT CD 5 track 15 • Acts. 10, 11 **25 min**	**Assess:** *Para y piensa* p. 281 **5 min** **Homework:** *Cuaderno* pp. 223–225 @HomeTutor
DAY 5	**Grammar:** affirmative **tú** commands • Warm Up OHT 22 **5 min**	**Presentación de gramática** p. 282 • affirmative **tú** commands **Práctica de gramática** pp. 283–284 • *Pronunciación* TXT CD 5 track 16 • *Nota gramatical:* **acabar de** + infinitive **Culture:** *Los textiles de Otavalo* **15 min**	**Práctica de gramática** pp. 283–284 • Acts. 12, 13, 15 • Act. 14 TXT CD 5 track 17 **25 min**	**Assess:** *Para y piensa* p. 284 **5 min** **Homework:** *Cuaderno* pp. 226–228 @HomeTutor
DAY 6	**Communication:** Culmination: Affirmative **tú** commands, irregular verbs, parties and chores • Warm Up OHT 22 • Check Homework **5 min**	**Todo junto** pp. 285–287 • *Escenas 1, 2: Resumen* • *Telehistoria completa* DVD 2 **15 min**	**Todo junto** pp. 285–287 • Acts. 16, 17 TXT CD 5 tracks 14, 15, 18 • Acts. 18, 20 • Act. 19 TXT CD 5 tracks 19, 20 **25 min**	**Assess:** *Para y piensa* p. 287 **5 min** **Homework:** *Cuaderno* pp. 229, 230 @HomeTutor
DAY 7	**Reading:** Traditional dances in Ecuador and Panama **Review:** Lesson Review • Warm Up OHT 23 • Check Homework **5 min**	**Lectura cultural** pp. 288–289 *Bailes folklóricos de Ecuador y Panamá* TXT CD 5 track 21 **Repaso de la lección** pp. 292–293 **20 min**	**Lectura cultural** pp. 288–289 *Bailes folklóricos de Ecuador y Panamá* **Repaso de la lección** pp. 292–293 • Act. 1 TXT CD 5 track 22 • Acts. 2, 3, 4, 5 **20 min**	**Assess:** *Para y piensa* p. 289 **5 min** *Repaso de la lección* pp. 292–293 **Homework:** *En resumen* p. 291; *Cuaderno* pp. 231–242 (optional) Review Games Online @HomeTutor
DAY 8	**Assessment**			**Assess:** Lesson 2 test or Unit 5 test **50 min**
DAY 9	**Unit Culmination** **5 min**	**Comparación cultural** pp. 294–295 • TXT CD 5 track 23 • View culture video DVD 2 **Repaso inclusivo** pp. 296–297 **15 min**	**Comparación cultural** pp. 294–295 **Repaso inclusivo** pp. 296–297 • Act. 1 TXT CD 5 track 24 • Acts. 2, 3, 4, 5, 6, 7 **25 min**	**Homework:** *Cuaderno* pp. 243–245 **5 min**

	Objectives/Focus	Teach	Practice	Assess/HW Options
DAY 1	**Culture:** learn about Ecuador **Vocabulary:** planning a party • Warm Up OHT 20 5 min	Lesson Opener pp. 270–271 **Presentación de vocabulario** pp. 272–273 • Read A–E • View video DVD 2 • Play audio TXT CD 5 track 12 • *¡A responder!* TXT CD 5 track 13 20 min	**Práctica de vocabulario** p. 274 • Acts. 1, 2 20 min	**Assess:** *Para y piensa* p. 274 5 min
	Communication: talking about chores and responsibilities 5 min	**Vocabulario en contexto** pp. 275–276 • *Telehistoria escena 1* DVD 2 15 min	**Vocabulario en contexto** pp. 275–276 • Act. 3 TXT CD 5 track 14 • Act. 4 15 min	**Assess:** *Para y piensa* p. 276 5 min **Homework:** *Cuaderno* 220–222 @HomeTutor
DAY 2	**Grammar:** more irregular verbs • Warm Up OHT 21 • Check Homework 5 min	**Presentación de gramática** p. 277 • More irregular verbs 20 min	**Práctica de gramática** pp. 278–279 • Acts. 5, 6, 7, 8 15 min	**Assess:** *Para y piensa* p. 279 5 min
	Communication: talk about what you and others do at parties 5 min	**Gramática en contexto** pp. 280–281 • *Telehistoria escena 2* DVD 2 • *También se dice* 20 min	**Gramática en contexto** pp. 280–281 • Act. 9 TXT CD 5 track 15 • Acts. 10, 11 15 min	**Assess:** *Para y piensa* p. 281 5 min **Homework:** *Cuaderno* pp. 223–225 @HomeTutor
DAY 3	**Grammar:** affirmative **tú** commands • Warm Up OHT 22 • Check Homework 5 min	**Presentación de gramática** p. 282 • affirmative **tú** commands **Práctica de gramática** pp. 283–284 • *Pronunciación* TXT CD 5 track 16 • *Nota gramatical:* **acabar de** + infinitive **Culture:** Los textiles de Otavalo 15 min	**Práctica de gramática** pp. 283–284 • Acts. 12, 13, 15 • Act. 14 TXT CD 5 track 17 20 min	**Assess:** *Para y piensa* p. 284 5 min
	Communication: Culmination: Affirmative **tú** commands, irregular verbs, parties and chores 5 min	**Todo junto** pp. 285–287 • *Escenas 1, 2: Resumen* • *Telehistoria completa* DVD 2 15 min	**Todo junto** pp. 285–287 • Acts. 16, 17 TXT CD 5 tracks 14, 15, 18 • Acts. 18, 20 • Act. 19 TXT CD 5 tracks 19, 20 20 min	**Assess:** *Para y piensa* p. 287 5 min **Homework:** *Cuaderno* pp. 226–228 @HomeTutor
DAY 4	**Reading:** Traditional dances of Ecuador and Panama • Warm Up OHT 23 • Check Homework 5 min	**Lectura cultural** pp. 288–289 *Bailes folklóricos de Ecuador y Panamá* TXT CD 5 track 21 15 min	**Lectura cultural** pp. 288–289 *Bailes folklóricos de Ecuador y Panamá* 15 min	**Assess:** *Para y piensa* p. 289 5 min
	Review: Lesson Review 5 min	**Repaso de la lección** pp. 292–293 15 min	**Repaso de la lección** pp. 292–293 • Act. 1 TXT CD 5 track 22 • Acts. 2, 3, 4, 5 25 min	**Assess:** *Repaso de la lección* pp. 292–293 5 min **Homework:** *En resumen* p. 291; *Cuaderno* pp. 231–242 (optional) Review Games online @HomeTutor
DAY 5	**Assessment**			**Assess:** Lesson 2 test or Unit 5 test 45 min
	Unit Culmination 5 min	**Comparación cultural pp. 294–295** CD 5 track 23 • View culture video DVD 2 **Repaso inclusivo pp. 296–297** 20 min	**Comparación cultural pp. 294–295** CD 5 track 23 **Repaso inclusivo pp. 296–297** • Act. 1 TXT CD 5 track 24 • Acts. 2, 3, 4, 5, 6, 7 20 min	**Homework:** *Cuaderno* pp. 243–245

¡AVANZA! Objectives

- Introduce lesson theme: **Una fiesta en casa.**
- **Culture:** Learn how family parties are celebrated in different countries.

Presentation Strategies

- Ask students to describe the people in the photo and talk about what they are doing.
- Have students talk about family parties:who attends, where they take place, what people wear, and what foods are served.

STANDARDS

2.2 Products and perspectives
4.2 Compare cultures
21st Century **Social and Cross-Cultural Skills,** Comparación cultural

Warm Up
Projectable Transparencies, 5-20

Vocabulary Write the room or rooms of the house in which you would find:

1. una cama
2. un sillón
3. un espejo
4. una mesa
5. un sofá

Answers: 1. el cuarto; 2. la sala; 3. el baño, el cuarto; 4. el comedor, la cocina; 5. la sala

Comparación cultural

Exploring the Theme

Ask the following:

1. How do teenagers celebrate birthday parties in the United States?
2. Do grandparents usually attend parties and dance with their grandchildren or grandchildren's friends?
3. What are other types of parties in the U.S.?

¿Qué ves? Possible answers include:

1. No, están en un patio.
2. Elena sirve el pastel.
3. Hay dos mesas y una silla.

UNIDAD 5

Ecuador

Lección 2

Tema:

Una fiesta en casa

¡AVANZA! In this lesson you will learn to

- plan a party
- talk about chores and responsibilities
- tell someone what to do
- say what you just did

using

- more irregular verbs
- affirmative **tú** commands
- **acabar de** + infinitive

¿Recuerdas?

- **tener que,** interrogative words
- expressions of frequency
- direct object pronouns

Comparación cultural

In this lesson you will learn about

- a festival honoring Quito, and textiles in Otavalo
- folk dances and traditional crafts, like **tapices** and **molas**
- throwing parties in Ecuador, Argentina, and Panama

Compara con tu mundo

This photo shows a teenager's birthday party in Quito, Ecuador. In Latin America it is common to celebrate with family and perhaps a few close friends. *Where and with whom do you like to celebrate your birthday?*

¿Qué ves?

Mira la foto

¿Están en un parque las personas?

¿Elena sirve pastel o una pizza?

¿Qué muebles hay?

270 doscientos setenta

Differentiating Instruction

Slower-paced Learners

Personalize It Ask students to share their own personal thoughts and feelings about parties. Possible questions: **¿Te gustan las fiestas de cumpleaños? ¿Qué haces en las fiestas? ¿Con quiénes celebras tu cumpleaños?**

Multiple Intelligences

Visual Learners Ask students to bring in photographs of a party scene. Alternatively, students could draw photos of a memorable party they attended. Instruct students to tape their photos to a piece of drawing paper. Then, as they proceed through Lección 2, have them label the people and items in their photos.

DIGITAL SPANISH my.hrw.com
ONLINE STUDENT EDITION with...

performance space
News Networking
@HOMETUTOR
CULTURA Interactiva

- Audio and Video Resources
- Interactive Flashcards
- Review Activities
- WebQuest
- Conjuguemos.com

PRACTICE SPANISH WITH HOLT MCDOUGAL APPS!

Una fiesta de cumpleaños
Quito, Ecuador

DIGITAL SPANISH

TEACHER TOOLS

- Interactive Whiteboard Lessons
- Generate Success!

ALSO AVAILABLE...

- Online Workbook
- Spanish InterActive Reader

SPANISH ON THE GO!

- Performance Space
- Holt McDougal Spanish Apps
- ¡Avancemos! eTextbook

Using the Photo

Expanded Information

In this photo you will notice fruit juice and a platter of fruit on the table. Many tropical fruits are commonly found in Ecuador, and are often made into juice. Popular juices includes **mora** (blackberry), **maracuya** (passion fruit), and the orange-like **naranjilla.**

Long-term Retention

Recycle

Have students list in Spanish outdoor activities that could be done in a backyard. Have them exchange lists with a neighbor and place a check beside the activities they would enjoy doing. Exchange again and count how many activities they have in common.

Communication

Reluctant Speakers

Write the following *A* and *B* phrases on index cards. **A. Un sofá azul y dos/ B. sillones están en la sala. A. Mis amigos escuchan/ B. música en sus cuartos. A. Yo miro la televisión/ B. en la sala.** Tell students that three complete sentences can be formed by putting together the correct *A* and *B* parts. Distribute the cards. Ask a student who has the *A* part to read it aloud. The student with the *B* phrase that correctly forms the sentence reads his or her phrase. Continue until all sentences are put together.

Differentiating Instruction

Inclusion

Cumulative Instruction Write the word **fiesta** in the center of a concept web. Then have students brainstorm words and phrases they already know that could be applied to the theme of parties. Responses might include vocabulary related to the home, furniture, food, music, and favorite activities.

Heritage Language Learners

Support What They Know Ask students to describe the photo on pp. 270 and 271 in as much detail as possible. If they do not know the exact word for an item, ask them to describe the item. Then ask students to compare the party in the photo to a party they have attended. What features are similar and different?

¡AVANZA! **Objectives**
- Present vocabulary: household chores, party activities.
- Check for recognition.

Core Resources
- Video Program: DVD 2
- Audio Program: TXT CD 5 tracks 12, 13

Presentation Strategies
- Say the words illustrated on pp. 272–273 at random and ask students to tell you whether they refer to **quehaceres** or **una fiesta.**
- Play the audio as students read A–E.
- Play the video.

STANDARDS
1.2 Understand language
21st Century **Communication,** Pre-AP

Communication
TPR Activity

Bring the following props to class: a broom, a dishcloth, an iron, a trash can. Select a student to come to the front and do the commanded activity, using the appropriate prop.
Activities: **Barre el suelo. Lava los platos. Plancha la ropa. Saca la basura.**

Long-term Retention
Recycle

Write the following verbs on the board: **planchar, sacar, pasar, hacer, lavar.** Also provide students with a variety of subjects, for example: **Mi mamá, Yo, Mi hermano, Uds., Mi hermana y yo.** Have students form sentences using the information, making sure that the verb agrees with the subject in each sentence.

Presentación de VOCABULARIO

¡AVANZA! **Goal:** Learn about how Elena and others get ready for Manuel's surprise party. Then practice what you have learned to talk about how you plan a party. ***Actividades 1–2***

VIDEO DVD
AUDIO

A ¡Hola! Soy Elena. Vamos a **dar una fiesta** porque es el cumpleaños de Manuel, pero es **un secreto.** Antes de **celebrar, hay que limpiar** la cocina porque está **sucia.**

B **Acabamos de** limpiar la cocina pero **todavía** tenemos que trabajar. Toda la casa **debe** estar **limpia.**

Más vocabulario

abrir *to open*	**salir** *to leave, to go out*
buscar *to look for*	**si** *if*
invitar a *to invite (someone)*	**traer** *to bring*
recibir *to receive*	

Expansión de vocabulario p. R6

Differentiating Instruction

Slower-paced Learners

Yes/No Questions Ask students yes or no questions about the vocabulary related to household chores. **¿Tienes que lavar los platos? ¿Tienes que pasar la aspiradora?** After students answer **sí** or **no,** encourage them to add a complete sentence of explanation. **Sí, tengo que lavar los platos todos los días. No, no tengo que pasar la aspiradora pero tengo que barrer el suelo.**

Inclusion

Synthetic/Analytic Support Write the phrases on p. 272 on the board. Ask volunteers to circle the verb and underline the direct object in each. Have students use the expression **tener que** to explain what chores they have to do, using direct object pronouns to replace the direct objects. For example: **Tengo que hacer la cama → Tengo que hacerla.**

C Mi papá quiere **ayudar** con **los quehaceres** pero no **cocina** muy bien. Prefiere **poner la mesa.**

D Son las cuatro y **los invitados** van a **venir** a las cinco. Papá **pone las decoraciones** y Fernando **envuelve un regalo** para Manuel.

E Cuando Manuel llega, todos **dicen** «¡Sorpresa!» Yo **canto** «Feliz cumpleaños» y mis padres **bailan.**

@HOMETUTOR my.hrw.com Interactive Flashcards

¡A responder! Escuchar

Escucha la lista de actividades. Mientras escuchas, representa las actividades. *(Listen to the list of activities. Act out the activities as you hear them.)*

Teacher to Teacher

Jennifer Swender
Brooklyn, New York

Tips for Presenting Vocabulary

To review parts of the house and chores, I have my students draw a floor plan on a large piece of paper. I then ask them to draw or glue pictures of people doing chores on index cards. Under each picture I ask them to write a sentence such as Tengo que planchar la ropa. *I put the index cards face down on a table. I ask a student to pick a card, read the sentence, and place it in the floor plan room where the chore would most likely be done. Then I ask the student to say the sentence aloud, adding the name of the room.* Tengo que planchar la ropa en el cuarto.

Go online for more tips!

Communication

Pair Work

Read the following statements as a dictation exercise. Once finished, have students work in pairs to read each sentence aloud and correct the illogical ones.

1. **Hay que limpiar la aspiradora.**
2. **Hay que cortar los platos.**
3. **Hay que limpiar la cocina.**
4. **Hay que darle de comer al padre.**
5. **Hay que envolver a los invitados.**

Answers: 1. Hay que pasar la aspiradora./ Hay que limpiar la cocina. 2. Hay que lavar los platos./Hay que cortar el césped. 3. logical 4. Hay que darle de comer al perro. 5. Hay que envolver el regalo (los regalos)./ Hay que invitar a los invitados.

Differentiating Instruction

Multiple Intelligences

Kinesthetic Instruct students to choose one of the tasks presented in this lesson's vocabulary. Then ask for a volunteer to act out his or her task for the group without using words. The other students must name the activity being performed, and put the phrase into a sentence. **Mario hace la cama.**

Pre-AP

Relate Opinions Ask students to share their opinions about the tasks presented on pp. 272–273. Encourage them to use adjectives such as **fácil, difícil,** as well as the phrases **más que** and **menos que. Me gusta envolver regalos porque es fácil. No me gusta cortar el césped porque es difícil. Me gusta bailar más que cortar el césped.**

Answers

Projectable Transparencies, 5-28

¡A responder! AudioScript, TE p. 269b

Students act out the following activities:

1. to iron
2. to dance
3. to sweep the floor
4. to set the table
5. to wrap a present
6. to cook
7. to wash the dishes
8. to vacuum

Objective
- Practice vocabulary: household chores, party preparations.

Core Resource
- *Cuaderno,* pp. 220–222

Practice Sequence
- **Activity 1:** Vocabulary recognition: party preparations
- **Activity 2:** Vocabulary production: household chores

STANDARDS
1.3 Present information, Acts. 1-2, PYP

Communication
Pair Work
Have students work with a partner to write a list of things they must do to prepare for a birthday party and the activities that might take place at that party. Ask them to use at least two phrases or sentences from previous lessons.

✓ Ongoing Assessment
Get Help Online
More Practice
my.hrw.com

PARA Y PIENSA **Peer Assessment** Before writing the correct answers on the board, have students exchange papers and correct each other's statements. For additional practice, use Reteaching & Practice Copymasters URB 5, pp. 13, 14.

Answers Projectable Transparencies, 5-28
Activity 1
1. decoraciones
2. invitados
3. regalo
4. globos
5. secreto
6. papel de regalo

Activity 2 Answers should follow the format: Hay que + chore: **1.** lavar los platos. **2.** cortar el césped. **3.** pasar la aspiradora. **4.** cocinar (preparar la comida). **5.** hacer la cama. **6.** planchar la ropa.

Para y piensa Answers will vary but may include:
1. Limpiar la casa. **2.** Poner las decoraciones. **3.** Lavar los platos. **4.** Envolver los regalos.

Práctica de VOCABULARIO

1 La fiesta de cumpleaños
Leer

Lee las pistas que describen una fiesta de cumpleaños. Identifica las palabras de la lista. *(Read the clues to identify the words.)*

papel de regalo	invitados	globos
regalo	decoraciones	secreto

1. Las usas para decorar la casa.
2. Son las personas en la fiesta.
3. Lo abres si celebras tu cumpleaños.
4. Son decoraciones de colores.
5. Hay una fiesta de sorpresa y no debes decirlo.
6. Lo usas para envolver un regalo.

Expansión:
Teacher Edition Only
Have students create two more clues for other vocabulary words and exchange with a partner.

2 ¿Qué hay que hacer?
Escribir
Hablar

Mira las fotos e identifica qué hay que hacer para limpiar la casa. *(Identify what must be done.)*

modelo: Hay que limpiar la cocina.

1.

2.

3.

4.

5.
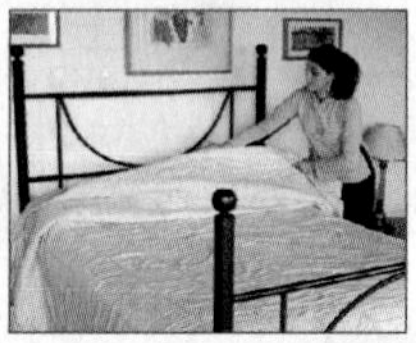
6.

Expansión
Write about the two chores you like to do most and least.

Más práctica Cuaderno *pp. 220–222* Cuaderno para hispanohablantes *pp. 220–223*

Get Help Online
my.hrw.com

PARA Y PIENSA **Did you get it?** Name four things you do before having a party at your house.

Differentiating Instruction

Inclusion
Metacognitive Support Write a few sentences involving the word **hay** on the board. **Hay muchos estudiantes. Hay una fiesta.** Remind students that this word can be translated into the two-word phrase **There is (are)** in English. Then direct students to the title of Activity 2 **¿Qué hay que hacer?** Elicit that this question can be translated as *What is there to do?*

Heritage Language Learners
Regional Variations Ask students to share the songs they would sing at a birthday party or other type of celebration. Some students might sing «Cumpleaños feliz». Others might sing «Las mañanitas» or other traditional songs. Ask for volunteers to write out the words on a poster for the whole group to follow.

VOCABULARIO en contexto

¡AVANZA! **Goal:** Identify the words Fernando and the Cuevas family use to talk about the preparations they have to do before Manuel's party. Then use what you have learned to talk about your chores and responsibilities. ***Actividades 3–4***

¿Recuerdas? **tener que** p. 91

Telehistoria escena 1

@HOMETUTOR my.hrw.com **View, Read and Record**

STRATEGIES

Cuando lees

Consider cultural customs How do Manuel's family and friends prepare for his birthday party? How are teenagers' birthdays usually celebrated in the United States? What are some differences and similarities?

Cuando escuchas

Listen for cognates This scene has several cognates, including **sorpresa.** Listen for them. Which ones do you recognize? How do they help you with understanding?

VIDEO DVD

AUDIO

The Cuevas family is preparing for a party. Fernando arrives with a gift.

Fernando: ¿Y los regalos? ¿Dónde...?

Sra. Cuevas: En la mesa.

Elena: Fernando, ¿qué regalo traes para Manuel?

Fernando: Un videojuego. Lo acabo de envolver.

Sr. Cuevas: Un videojuego. ¡Qué sorpresa!

Fernando: ¿Puedo ayudar?

Elena: Sí, puedes abrir la puerta a los invitados.

Fernando: Ay, prefiero preparar la comida. ¡Me gusta cocinar!

Sr. Cuevas: Bueno. Puedes ayudar en la cocina.

Guests begin to arrive, and everyone starts to wonder when Manuel is coming.

Sra. Cuevas: ¿Qué hora es? *(to Elena)* ¿Dónde está tu hermano?

Fernando: Acabo de hablar por teléfono con Manuel. Va a venir.

Continuará... p. 280

¡AVANZA! **Objective**

- Understand activity vocabulary in context.

Core Resources

- Video Program: DVD 2
- Audio Program: TXT CD 5 track 14

Presentation Strategies

- Have students describe what the people in the photo are doing.
- Play the audio as students follow the script in the text.
- Play the video.

STANDARDS

1.2 Understand language

Warm Up

Projectable Transparencies, 5-20

Vocabulary Complete each sentence using the appropriate vocabulary word.

1. Hay que _____ la aspiradora.
2. Hay que cortar _____.
3. Hay que _____ los platos.
4. Hay que envolver _____.
5. Hay que _____ la mesa.

Answers: 1. pasar; 2. el césped; 3. lavar; 4. el regalo; 5. poner.

Communication

Interpretive Mode

Telehistoria Ask students to keep the following questions in mind:

1. Whose birthday party is it?
2. What is Fernando bringing as a gift?
3. What does Fernando prefer to do?

Video Summary

@HOMETUTOR VideoPlus my.hrw.com

Fernando arrives at the party and asks where the gifts are. He says his gift for Manuel is a videogame. Fernando offers to help in the kitchen because he likes to cook. Guests arrive and Mrs. Cuevas wonders where Manuel is. Fernando reassures her that Manuel is coming.

Differentiating Instruction

Slower-paced Learners

Sentence Completion Organize students into small groups and instruct them to write two sentence starters on note cards based on information presented in the Telehistoria. For example: **Los regalos están... Fernando acaba de... A Fernando le gusta...**
Have groups exchange note cards and complete the starters they receive.

Pre-AP

Summarize Ask students to write three sentences summarizing the Telehistoria Escena 1. When they finish, have volunteers read the summary aloud. Ask the other students to correct pronunciation and to check if the summary is accurate.

Objectives
- Practice using vocabulary in context.
- Recycle: **tener que.**

Core Resource
- Audio Program: TXT CD 5 track 14

Practice Sequence
- **Activity 3:** Telehistoria comprehension
- **Activity 4:** Vocabulary production: household chores, Recycle: **tener que**

STANDARDS
1.1 Engage in conversation, Act. 4
1.2 Understand language, Act. 3
1.3 Present information, Act. 4, PYP
21st Century **Communication,** Act. 4

3 *Comprensión del episodio* Preparan una celebración

Escuchar Leer

Escoge la respuesta correcta. *(Choose the correct answer.)*

1. Los regalos están
a. en la cocina.
b. en el comedor.
c. en la mesa.

2. Fernando acaba de
a. envolver el regalo.
b. ayudar en la cocina.
c. abrir la puerta a los invitados.

3. Fernando trae
a. un DVD para Manuel.
b. un disco compacto para Manuel.
c. un videojuego para Manuel.

4. Fernando prefiere
a. abrir la puerta a los invitados.
b. jugar videojuegos.
c. preparar la comida.

Expansión: Teacher Edition Only
Ask students to summarize the Telehistoria, escena 1.

4 Las obligaciones en casa

¿*Recuerdas?* **tener que** p. 91

Hablar

Pregúntale a otro(a) estudiante si tiene que hacer estos quehaceres en casa. Si no, ¿quién los tiene que hacer? *(Ask a classmate if he or she has to do these chores. If not, who has to do them?)*

A ¿Tienes que barrer el suelo?

B Sí, tengo que barrer el suelo. (No, no tengo que barrer el suelo. Mi padre tiene que hacerlo.)

1. 
2. 
3. 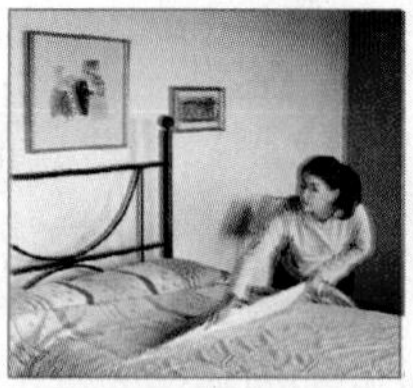
4. 
5. 
6. 

Expansión
Compare your chores with a partner's. Which do you have in common?

Communication
Group Work

Divide the class into small groups. Have each group write a list of ten activities on note cards in Spanish. Students in one group will use the note cards supplied by another group and vice versa. Students will take turns acting out the phrases and the group guessing will have 15 seconds to come up with the correct answer in Spanish. If the answer is correct, the group receives a point.

✓ Ongoing Assessment

Get Help Online
More Practice
my.hrw.com

PARA Y PIENSA **Alternative Strategy** When students finish the Para y piensa, have three volunteers each write one of the sentences. Ask other volunteers to read each sentence aloud and the class to correct the sentence if necessary. For additional practice, use Reteaching & Practice Copymasters URB 5, pp. 13, 15, 22.

PARA Y PIENSA

Get Help Online
my.hrw.com

Did you get it? Complete each sentence with the appropriate vocabulary word.
1. Manuel saca _____ antes de ir a la escuela.
2. El señor Cuevas corta _____ los sábados.
3. Fernando necesita pasar _____ porque sus abuelos van a venir.

Answers Projectable Transparencies, 5-28

Activity 3 **1.** c; **2.** a; **3.** c; **4.** c

Activity 4 Answers should follow the format: ¿Tienes que (chore)? Sí, tengo que (chore). (No, no tengo que (chore). (Person) tiene que hacerlo.)
1. sacar la basura; **2.** lavar los platos; **3.** hacer la cama; **4.** cortar el césped; **5.** darle de comer al perro; **6.** cocinar

Para y piensa **1.** la basura; **2.** el césped; **3.** la aspiradora

Differentiating Instruction

Inclusion

Synthetic/Analytic Support Remind students of the many different and correct ways they can answer questions in Activity 4. For the question **¿Tienes que barrer el suelo?** they might answer with any of the following: **Sí, tengo que barrer el suelo. No, no tengo que barrer el suelo. Sí, tengo que barrerlo. No, no tengo que barrerlo. Sí, lo tengo que barrer. No, no lo tengo que barrer.**

English Learners

Build Background Some of the household chores presented in Lección 2 may be culturally or regionally based, such as mowing the lawn or feeding a pet dog. Give students the opportunity to ask any questions they might have, as well as compare and contrast the household chores shown with those typical in their country of origin.

Presentación de GRAMÁTICA

¡AVANZA! **Goal:** Learn the forms of six more irregular verbs. Then practice using these verbs to talk about parties. ***Actividades 5–8***

¿Recuerdas? Interrogative words p. 140

English Grammar Connection: Just as the English verb *to be* does not follow a pattern in the present tense (*I am, you are, he/she/it is,* etc.), **irregular verbs** in Spanish do not follow the pattern of regular or stem-changing verbs.

More Irregular Verbs

ANIMATED GRAMMAR my.hrw.com

Dar, decir, poner, salir, traer, and **venir** are all irregular. How do you form the present tense of these verbs?

Here's how:

Decir has several irregular forms. Only the **nosotros(as)** and **vosotros(as)** forms are regular.

Dicen que es una fiesta de sorpresa.
They say *that it is a surprise party.*

decir *to say, to tell*	
digo	decimos
dices	decís
dice	dicen

Venir is similar to **tener,** except that the **nosotros(as)** and **vosotros(as)** forms have -ir endings, while **tener** uses **-er** endings.

¿De dónde **vienes**?
Where ***are you coming*** *from?*

venir *to come*	
vengo	venimos
vienes	venís
viene	vienen

Some verbs are irregular only in the **yo** form of the present tense.

Doy una fiesta.
I am giving *a party.*

dar	*to give*	**doy**
poner	*to put, to place*	**pongo**
salir	*to leave, to go out*	**salgo**
traer	*to bring*	**traigo**

Más práctica
Cuaderno *pp. 223–225*
Cuaderno para hispanohablantes *pp. 224–226*

@HOMETUTOR my.hrw.com
Leveled Practice
Conjuguemos.com

¡AVANZA! **Objective**
- Present more irregular verbs.

Core Resource
- *Cuaderno,* pp. 223–225

Presentation Strategies
- Point out that irregular verbs in Spanish do not follow the pattern of regular or stem-changing verbs.
- Write on the board or OHT the paradigms of **decir** and **hacer.** Ask students to explain why they are irregular.
- Ask a volunteer to come to the board and underline the verb parts that are irregular.
- Say the forms of **decir** and **hacer** and have students repeat after you.
- After presenting the verbs **dar, poner, salir** and **traer,** say sentences using forms of these verbs and have students provide you with the corresponding subject pronoun: **Pongo el pastel en la mesa. → yo.**

STANDARDS
4.1 Compare languages
Creativity and Innovation, Heritage Language Learners

Warm Up Projectable Transparencies, 5-21

Vocabulary Write a chore or activity that you would do in each of the following rooms or places.

1. el cuarto
2. el jardín
3. la cocina
4. la sala
5. el comedor

Answers: 1. hacer la cama; 2. cortar el césped; 3. lavar los platos; 4. pasar la aspiradora, mirar la televisión; 5. comer

Differentiating Instruction

Slower-paced Learners

Memory Aids Have students add the irregular verbs presented on p. 277 to their set of verb reference cards. On each card, have them copy the forms of the verb for each pronoun. Remind students to write a capital *I* in the upper right-hand corner of each card to indicate that these are all *irregular* verbs.

Heritage Language Learners

Writing Skills Give students this writing challenge. Have them create a short story about a party that involves all of the verbs listed on p. 277. Give students the opportunity to read their stories aloud to the whole group.

Communication
Common Error Alert

Explain to students that the verb **poner** can be used in different ways. For example, **poner la mesa** means *to set the table.* **Poner las decoraciones** means *to put up the decorations.* Remind students that the addition of a preposition is not necessary.

Objectives
- Practice irregular verbs.
- **Culture:** Discuss how people show pride for their community.
- Review lesson vocabulary.
- Recycle: Interrogative words.

Core Resource
- *Cuaderno,* pp. 223–225

Practice Sequence
- **Activity 5:** Controlled practice: irregular verbs
- **Activity 6:** Transitional practice: irregular verbs
- **Activity 7:** Transitional practice: **traer**
- **Activity 8:** Open-ended practice: irregular verbs; Recycle: Interrogative words.

STANDARDS
1.1 Engage in conversation, Acts. 7–8
1.3 Present information, Acts. 5–8, PYP
2.1 Practices and perspectives, Act. 6
4.2 Compare culture, Act. 6
21st Century Social and Cross-Cultural Skills, Heritage Language Learners/ Comparación cultural

Comparación cultural

Essential Question
Suggested Answer People show pride for their community by celebrating their culture in various ways. Examples of celebrating one's culture include traditional festivals and parades. Being proud of one's community also means taking care of one's surroundings by keeping them clean and working together in ways that benefit the community as a whole.

Background Information
Quito The official name of Quito is San Francisco de Quito. The city served as an important center for the Incas. When the Spaniards arrived, however, the Incas destroyed the city and left the ruins to the explorers. Quito flourished until social unrest in the early 1800s led Ecuador into a war against Spain. Once their independence was established, Quito blossomed once more. Today, Quito consists of Old Quito, with its rich colonial heritage, and New Quito.

See Activity answers on p. 279.

Práctica de GRAMÁTICA

5 ¿Lo haces?

Hablar Escribir

Di si haces estas cosas en una fiesta de sorpresa. *(Tell whether you do the following at a surprise party.)*

modelo: salir con amigos antes de la fiesta
(No) Salgo con amigos antes de la fiesta.

1. poner la mesa con platos bonitos
2. dar diez regalos
3. salir de la fiesta muy temprano
4. venir a la fiesta con amigos
5. traer libros de historia
6. decir «¡Feliz cumpleaños!»

Expansión
Describe in 3–4 sentences a typical birthday celebration in your family.

6 ¡Vamos a celebrar!

Leer Escribir

Comparación cultural

Preparan los carritos de madera (wooden cars) *para las fiestas.*

Fiestas de Quito
How do people show pride for their community? On December 6, *quiteños* celebrate Fiestas de Quito, a festival honoring the anniversary of the founding of Quito, **Ecuador,** in 1534. The week-long celebration includes many parades, concerts, and dances. Some residents perform *serenatas quiteñas,* musical tributes to their city. Other popular activities are fireworks displays and the Reina de Quito beauty pageant. Many young people build and decorate wooden cars to race in competitions for their age level.

Compara con tu mundo *Is there an event that celebrates your area or region?*

Manuel y Fernando hablan por teléfono. Completa su conversación con la forma correcta del verbo apropiado. *(Complete the conversation with the correct form of the appropriate verb.)*

dar	traer
decir	poner
salir	venir

Manuel: ¿Cuándo __1.__ a mi casa? Tenemos que decorar los carritos para las Fiestas de Quito.
Fernando: __2.__ de aquí en quince minutos y llego en media hora.
Manuel: Elena __3.__ que la carrera (*race*) empieza a las dos.
Fernando: Hay un desfile (*parade*) después. ¿Vas a traer tu guitarra?
Manuel: Sí, yo la __4.__. Quiero tocar una serenata quiteña.
Fernando: ¡Y yo voy a cantar! ¿Qué hacemos después del desfile?
Manuel: Elena y yo __5.__ una fiesta en casa. Ahora ella prepara la ensalada y yo __6.__ la mesa.
Fernando: Bueno, llego en media hora. ¡Hasta luego!

Expansión: Teacher Edition Only
Have students write a brief summary of the conversation between Manuel and Fernando. Have them read it aloud and select the best summary.

Differentiating Instruction

Heritage Language Learners
Support What They Know Ask students to share information about traditional celebrations in their country or region of origin. Possibilities might include **Cinco de mayo** in Mexico, or **la quinceañera** in many countries. Have students describe their celebrations in as much detail as possible. What do people wear, eat, and do?

Inclusion
Clear Structure Students should follow these steps to fill in the blanks in Activity 6.
1. List the meanings of the verbs in the box.
2. Read the sentence for content, skipping over the blank.
3. Choose the best verb based on context.
4. Decide on the correct form of the verb based on context.
5. Read the complete sentence to yourself.

7 Una fiesta en la clase

Hablar

Hay una fiesta en la clase de español. Pregúntale a otro(a) estudiante si trae estas cosas a la fiesta y por qué. *(Ask a partner whether he or she is bringing these things to the class party, and why or why not.)*

A ¿Traes DVDs a la fiesta?

B Sí, traigo DVDs porque quiero ver películas. (No, no traigo DVDs porque no quiero ver películas.)

1. 
2. 
3. 
4. 
5. 

6. 

Expansión: Teacher Edition Only
Have students write a summary of what their partners are bringing to the party.

8 Hay que preparar

¿Recuerdas? Interrogative words p. 140

Hablar

Tu amigo(a) ayuda a organizar una fiesta de cumpleaños. Pregúntale a otro(a) estudiante sobre los preparativos. *(Ask a partner about a party he or she is helping organize.)*

modelo: ¿cuándo? / dar la fiesta

A ¿Cuándo das la fiesta?

B Doy la fiesta el sábado.

1. ¿cuántos(as)? / venir a la fiesta
2. ¿qué? / traer a la fiesta
3. ¿dónde? / poner las decoraciones
4. ¿qué? / servir para comer y beber
5. ¿por qué? / dar la fiesta
6. ¿qué? / cantar los invitados
7. ¿qué? / decir los invitados
8. ¿cuándo? / salir los invitados

Expansión
Write down the description of the party and present it to the class.

Más práctica Cuaderno *pp. 223–225* Cuaderno para hispanohablantes *pp. 224–226*

Get Help Online my.hrw.com

PARA Y PIENSA

Did you get it? Complete each sentence with the correct form of one of the irregular verbs you just learned.

1. Yo _____ la mesa porque los invitados van a llegar.
2. Isabel _____ que el pastel es muy rico.
3. Yo _____ los regalos a la fiesta.

Long-term Retention

Personalize It

Have students write about a party they might give. Tell them to describe what they will do to prepare, how many guests will come, and what they will do at the party. When they finish writing, divide them into small groups to read their descriptions aloud. Walk around the room and pause by each group several times to make sure they are speaking Spanish and staying on task.

✓ Ongoing Assessment

Get Help Online
More Practice
my.hrw.com

PARA Y PIENSA **Intervention** If students have problems completing the sentences in Para y piensa, have them review p. 277. For additional practice, use Reteaching & Practice Copymasters URB 5, pp. 16, 17, 22.

Differentiating Instruction

Multiple Intelligences

Interpersonal After students complete Activity 7, ask the whole group to imagine that they are planning a party. Ask students to assign tasks based on their peers' personalities and talents. **Javier va a preparar la comida porque le gusta cocinar. Marisa y Linda van a hacer las decoraciones porque son muy artísticas.**

Pre-AP

Expand and Elaborate As students ask and answer the questions indicated in Activity 8, encourage **Estudiante A** to pose a follow-up question for **Estudiante B** to answer. Here is an example based on the model.

A: ¿Por qué das la fiesta el sábado?
B: Porque el lunes tengo un examen y el domingo tengo que estudiar.

Answers Projectable Transparencies, 5-28 and 5-29

Answers for Activities on pp. 278, 279.

Activity 5

1. (No) Pongo la mesa con platos bonitos.
2. (No) Doy diez regalos.
3. (No) Salgo de la fiesta muy temprano.
4. (No) Vengo a la fiesta con amigos.
5. (No) Traigo libros de historia.
6. (No) Digo «¡Feliz cumpleaños!»

Activity 6 **1.** vienes; **2.** Salgo; **3.** dice; **4.** traigo; **5.** damos; **6.** pongo

Activity 7 Answers will vary. Answers should follow the format: ¿Traes (*item*) a la fiesta? Sí, traigo (No, no traigo) (*item*) porque (*reason*).

1. globos, decoraciones; **2.** discos compactos; **3.** ensalada; **4.** pastel; **5.** refrescos; **6.** regalo

Activity 8 Answers will vary. Sample answers include:

1. ¿Cuántas personas vienen a la fiesta? Vienen diez personas.
2. ¿Qué traes a la fiesta? Traigo refrescos.
3. ¿Dónde pones las decoraciones? Las pongo en la mesa.
4. ¿Qué sirves para comer y beber? Sirvo pastel y refrescos.
5. ¿Por qué das la fiesta? Doy la fiesta porque es el cumpleaños de mi hermana.
6. ¿Qué cantan los invitados? Cantan «Cumpleaños feliz».
7. ¿Qué dicen los invitados? Dicen ¡Sorpresa!
8. ¿Cuándo salen los invitados? Salen después de la fiesta.

Para y piensa **1.** pongo; **2.** dice; **3.** traigo

¡AVANZA! Objectives

- Practice irregular verbs and new vocabulary in context.
- Recycle: expressions of frequency.

Core Resources

- Video Program: DVD 2
- Audio Program: TXT CD 5 track 15

Presentation Strategies

- Ask students to describe what they see in the two photos. **¿Quién es el chico? ¿Qué tiene?**
- Have students preview the video activities before watching the video.
- Show the video and/or play the audio.

Practice Sequence

- **Activity 9:** Telehistoria comprehension
- **Activity 10:** Transitional practice: **salir;** Recycle: expressions of frequency
- **Activity 11:** Open-ended practice: irregular verbs, household chores, party activities, telling time

STANDARDS

1.2 Understand language
4.1 Compare languages
21st Century **Information Literacy,** Multiple Intelligences

Warm Up Projectable Transparencies, 5-21

Irregular verbs Write the **yo** and **nosotros** forms of the following verbs:

1. dar	**4.** hacer
2. tener	**5.** poner
3. venir	**6.** traer

Answers: 1. doy, damos; 2. tengo, tenemos; 3. vengo, venimos; 4. hago, hacemos; 5. pongo, ponemos; 6. traigo, traemos

Video Summary

@HOMETUTOR VideoPlus my.hrw.com

Manuel finally arrives with Alicia's T-shirt with Trini's autograph. He is very surprised as he comes into the yard. They sing to him as he blows out the candles. Then Manuel opens the gifts. Finally, Mr. Cuevas suggests that everybody dance.

GRAMÁTICA en contexto

¡AVANZA! **Goal:** Pay attention to the irregular verbs that Manuel, his family, and his friends use to talk about what to do at his party. Then use them to talk about what you and others do at parties. ***Actividades 9–11***

¿Recuerdas? Expressions of frequency p. 93

Telehistoria escena 2

@HOMETUTOR my.hrw.com **View, Read and Record**

STRATEGIES

Cuando lees
Predict based on visuals Predict what might happen, based on the photos. Does Manuel get the T-shirt signed? Was Manuel surprised, or did he know about the party?

Cuando escuchas
Consider two kinds of language Notice feelings based on both spoken language and body language, such as facial expressions, posture, and gestures. How does Manuel feel about Fernando's present? How do you know?

VIDEO DVD
AUDIO

Manuel arrives home with Alicia's T-shirt, admiring the autograph.

Manuel: ¡El autógrafo de Trini Salgado!
Elena: *(in the backyard)* ¡Allí viene Manuel!

Manuel enters the yard.

Todos: ¡Sorpresa!
Sra. Cuevas: ¡Feliz cumpleaños, hijo!
Elena: ¡Aquí viene el pastel!

Manuel blows out the candles while people clap.

Manuel: Y, ¿qué hago ahora?
Fernando: ¡Abrir los regalos! Yo los traigo.
Manuel: *(opening a gift)* ¡Qué sorpresa! ¡Un videojuego! No lo tengo. Muchas gracias, Fernando.
Fernando: Hmmm... Y, ¿qué hacemos ahora?
Sr. Cuevas: ¡A bailar todos!

Continuará... p. 285

También se dice

Ecuador When serving the cake, Elena uses the word **el pastel.** In other Spanish-speaking countries you might hear:
- **España** **la tarta**
- **Puerto Rico** **el bizcocho**
- **muchos países** **el queque, la torta**

Differentiating Instruction

Slower-paced Learners

Read Before Listening Have students preview the Telehistoria, focusing specifically on punctuation. Then read the script aloud in chorus. Instruct students to raise their hands each time they come to a **signo de interrogación** or a **signo de admiración.** Discuss with students what these punctuation marks say about the tone and energy level of the scene.

Multiple Intelligences

Musical/Rhythmic Have students research popular music in Ecuador. If possible have them bring to class two or three Ecuadorian pop songs that teenagers might dance to at a party. Then play the songs and have students sing or dance along.

9 *Comprensión del episodio* Muchas sorpresas

Escuchar
Leer

Contesta las preguntas. *(Answer the questions.)*

1. ¿Quiénes dan la fiesta?
2. ¿Quién viene?
3. ¿Quién trae los regalos?
4. ¿Quiénes dicen «¡Sorpresa!»?
5. ¿Qué recibe Manuel de Fernando?
6. ¿Qué quiere hacer el señor Cuevas?

Expansión:
Teacher Edition Only
Ask students to use the vocabulary words to talk about a party they attended.

10 ¿Con qué frecuencia?

¿Recuerdas? Expressions of frequency p. 93

Hablar

Habla con otros(as) estudiantes sobre la frecuencia con que haces las siguientes actividades. *(Tell how often you do these activities.)*

A ¿Con qué frecuencia sales con amigos?

B Salgo con amigos de vez en cuando.

C Nunca salgo con amigos.

1. 
2. 
3. 
4. 
5. 
6. 

Expansión
Write a summary of your group's responses and present it.

11 ¿Y tú?

Escribir

Contesta las preguntas. *(Answer the questions.)*

1. ¿Das muchas fiestas? ¿A quién(es) invitas?
2. ¿Quién pone la mesa en tu casa?
3. ¿Qué traes a tus clases?
4. ¿A qué hora sales de la casa en la mañana?
5. ¿A qué hora vienes a la escuela?
6. ¿Qué dices cuando recibes un regalo?

Expansión:
Teacher Edition Only
Ask students to write 3 sentences about what they like to do most at a party.

Get Help Online
my.hrw.com

PARA Y PIENSA

Did you get it? Complete each sentence based on the Telehistoria with the correct form of **venir, traer,** or **decir.**

1. Elena _____ que Manuel _____ a la fiesta.
2. Fernando _____ un regalo.

Differentiating Instruction

Inclusion

Frequent Review/Repetition Have students write a brief paragraph talking about how often they do their favorite activities. **Yo practico el fútbol todos los días. Mis amigos y yo vamos al cine de vez en cuando.**

Slower-paced Learners

Peer-study Support After completing their written answers to Activity 11, have students exchange papers with a partner. Instruct them to read their partner's answers twice, asking themselves if they understand the sentences and if there are mistakes. Then have partners share their responses with each other, and correct errors they find.

Long-term Retention

Connect to Previous Learning

Activity 10 Before doing the activity, refer students to p. 93 of Unidad 2 Lección 1 to review expressions of frequency. Have student pairs ask each other questions starting with: **¿Con qué frecuencia...?** and respond using an expression of frequency. For example: **¿Con qué frecuencia vas al cine? Voy al cine de vez en cuando.**

Expressions of Frequency Students Know

de vez en cuando	**nunca**	**siempre**
muchas veces	**mucho**	**todos los días**

✓ Ongoing Assessment

Get Help Online
More Practice
my.hrw.com

PARA Y PIENSA **Intervention** If students can't complete the sentences, suggest that they review irregular verbs on p. 277 and repeat Activities 5 and 6 on p. 278. For additional practice, use Reteaching & Practice Copymasters URB 5, pp. 16, 18, 23.

Answers Projectable Transparencies, 5-29

Activity 9

1. La familia de Manuel da la fiesta.
2. Los amigos vienen a la fiesta.
3. Los amigos y la familia traen los regalos.
4. Todos dicen ¡Sorpresa!
5. Manuel recibe un videojuego de Fernando.
6. El señor Cuevas quiere bailar.

Activity 10 Answers will vary. Sample answers:

1. **A:** ¿Con qué frecuencia pones la mesa?
   B: Pongo la mesa todos los días.
   C: Nunca pongo la mesa.
2. **A:** ¿Con qué frecuencia bailas?
   B: Bailo de vez en cuando.
   C: Bailo todos los sábados.
3. **A:** ¿Con qué frecuencia das regalos?
   B: Nunca doy regalos.
   C: Doy regalos de vez en cuando.
4. **A:** ¿Con qué frecuencia dices un secreto?
   B: Nunca digo secretos.
   C: Siempre digo secretos.
5. **A:** ¿Con qué frecuencia pones las decoraciones?
   B: Nunca pongo las decoraciones.
   C: Pongo las decoraciones de vez en cuando.
6. **A:** ¿Con qué frecuencia envuelves regalos?
   B: Siempre envuelvo regalos.
   C: Envuelvo regalos muchas veces.

Activity 11 Answers will vary. Sample answers:

1. Doy muchas fiestas. Invito a mis amigos.
2. Yo pongo la mesa.
3. Traigo libros a mis clases.
4. Salgo de la casa a las siete.
5. Vengo a la escuela a las ocho.
6. Digo gracias cuando recibo un regalo.

Para y piensa **1.** dice, viene; **2.** trae

¡AVANZA! **Objective**
- Present affirmative **tú** commands.

Core Resource
- *Cuaderno,* pp. 226–228

Presentation Strategies
- Point out that affirmative **tú** commands are used to address a friend or family member.
- Explain how to form affirmative **tú** commands.
- Present irregular affirmative **tú** commands.
- Explain how to attach a pronoun to a command.

STANDARDS
4.1 Compare languages

Warm Up Projectable Transparencies, 5-22

Verbs Complete each sentence with the appropriate verb.

1. Él siempre (barrer) la sala.
2. Nosotros (ir) al cine de vez en cuando.
3. Ellos nunca (dar) fiestas.
4. Yo siempre (tener) buenas notas.
5. Tú nunca (querer) cerrar la puerta.

Answers: 1. barre; 2. vamos; 3. dan; 4. tengo; 5. quieres

Communication

Grammar Activity

Have students respond with the infinitive for each of these command forms:

1. haz	6. barre
2. lava	7. sé
3. sal	8. ven
4. limpia	9. di
5. pon	10. ten

Answers: 1. hacer 2. lavar 3. salir 4. limpiar 5. poner 6. barrer 7. ser 8. venir 9. decir 10. tener

Presentación de GRAMÁTICA

¡AVANZA! **Goal:** Learn how to give affirmative **tú** commands and use **acabar de** + infinitive. Then tell someone what to do and say what you just did. ***Actividades 12–15***

¿Recuerdas? Direct object pronouns p. 204

English Grammar Connection: In both English and Spanish, **affirmative commands** are used to tell someone to do something.

Clean the kitchen! → **command**
¡**Limpia** la cocina! → **command**

Affirmative tú Commands

ANIMATEDGRAMMAR my.hrw.com

Use **affirmative tú commands** with a friend or a family member.

Here's how:

Regular **affirmative tú commands** are the same as the **él/ella** forms in the present tense.

Infinitive	Present Tense	Affirmative tú Command
lavar	(él, ella) **lava**	¡**Lava** los platos!
barrer	(él, ella) **barre**	¡**Barre** el suelo!
abrir	(él, ella) **abre**	¡**Abre** la puerta!

Some verbs you know have irregular **affirmative tú commands.**

Infinitive	decir	hacer	ir	poner	salir	ser	tener	venir
Affirmative tú Command	di	haz	ve	pon	sal	sé	ten	ven

If you use an **affirmative command** with a **direct object pronoun,** attach the pronoun to the end. Add an accent when you attach a pronoun to a command of two or more syllables to retain the original stress (see p. 259).

¡**Cierra** la ventana! *becomes* ¡**Ciérrala**!
***Close** the window!* ***Close** it!*

¡**Pon** la mesa ahora! *becomes* ¡**Ponla** ahora!
***Set** the table now!* ***Set** it now!*

Más práctica
Cuaderno *pp. 226–228*
Cuaderno para hispanohablantes *pp. 227–230*

@HOMETUTOR my.hrw.com
Leveled Practice
Conjuguemos.com

Differentiating Instruction

English Learners

Build Background Review the concept of commands with English learners by discussing commands they might hear or use often. Some examples might include *come here, sit down,* or *open the door.* Ask students to define the term *command* in their own words. Also, ask students to share some of these commands in their language of origin.

Multiple Intelligences

Kinesthetic Ask students to stand up. Then give them a list of affirmative **tú** commands, such as **abre la puerta, barre el suelo,** or **cierra la ventana.** Instruct students to pantomime each action indicated. After a few rounds, give volunteers the opportunity to call out the command.

Práctica de GRAMÁTICA

12 ¿Quién tiene que hacerlo?

Escribir

Manuel siempre le dice a Elena lo que tiene que hacer. Usa los mandatos para escribir lo que le dice. *(Write Manuel's commands to Elena.)*

modelo: limpiar la cocina
Limpia la cocina, por favor.

1. lavar los platos
2. planchar la ropa
3. venir a casa
4. barrer el suelo
5. salir temprano
6. hacer la cama
7. cortar el césped
8. ser buena
9. sacar la basura
10. traer el pastel
11. ir a la tienda
12. poner la mesa

Expansión
Write five commands you would hear in the classroom.

13 ¿Debo hacerlo?

¿Recuerdas? Direct object pronouns p. 204

Hablar

Tú y otro(a) estudiante preparan una fiesta de cumpleaños. Pregúntale lo que debes hacer. Sigue el modelo. *(Ask a partner what you should do to prepare for a party. Follow the model.)*

modelo: comprar el papel de regalo

A: ¿Debo comprar el papel de regalo?

B: Sí, cómpralo.

1. traer las bebidas
2. preparar la comida
3. buscar los globos
4. poner las decoraciones
5. limpiar la cocina
6. envolver los regalos
7. abrir la puerta a los invitados
8. servir el pastel
9. pasar la aspiradora
10. sacar la basura

Expansión: Teacher Edition Only
Ask students to write a list in sequential order of the steps they should take to prepare a party.

Pronunciación — Las letras b y v

AUDIO

In Spanish, the **b** and **v** are pronounced almost the same. As the first letter of a word, at the beginning of a sentence or after the letters **m** and **n, b** and **v** are pronounced like the hard *b* in the English word *boy.*

In the middle of a word, **b** and **v** have a softer sound, made by keeping the lips slightly apart.

Listen and repeat.

basura	**venir**	**alfombra**	**invitar**
deber	**todavía**	**globo**	**acabar**

Bárbara baila la cumbia en Colombia.
Debes subir al octavo piso.

Objectives

- Practice affirmative **tú** commands.
- Review vocabulary for household chores and planning a party.
- Recycle: direct object pronouns.
- Pronunciation: Compare pronunciation of the letters **b** and **v.**

Core Resource

- Audio Program: TXT CD 5 track 16

Practice Sequence

- **Activity 12:** Controlled practice: affirmative **tú** commands, household chores
- **Activity 13:** Transitional practice: affirmative **tú** commands, Recycle: direct object pronouns
- **Pronunciation:** Oral comprehension and production of the letters **b** and **v.**

STANDARDS

1.1 Engage in conversation, Act. 13
1.3 Present information, Acts. 12–13
4.1 Compare languages, Pronunciación

Differentiating Instruction

Inclusion

Clear Structure Suggest that students use the following questions as a guide to help construct their commands in Activity 12:

1. Is the verb regular or irregular in the command form?
2. If regular, what is the **él/ella** form?
3. If irregular, consult p. 282.
4. Say your command!

Heritage Language Learners

Increase Accuracy Create two columns on the board, one with the heading **B,** and the other with the heading **V.** Remind students that since these letters represent similar sounds, they can create spelling problems. Next, say a number of words containing **b** or **v** aloud. Have students write each on an index card. Then have students place each word in the correct column.

Answers Projectable Transparencies, 5-29 and 5-30

Activity 12

1. Lava los platos, por favor.
2. Plancha la ropa, por favor.
3. Ven a casa.
4. Barre el suelo.
5. Sal temprano.
6. Haz la cama.
7. Corta el césped.
8. Sé buena.
9. Saca la basura.
10. Trae el pastel.
11. Ve a la tienda.
12. Pon la mesa.

Activity 13 Answers should follow the format: ¿Debo comprar el papel de regalo? Sí, cómpralo.

1. Sí, tráelas.
2. Sí, prepárala.
3. Sí, búscalos.
4. Sí, ponlas.
5. Sí, límpiala.
6. Sí, envuélvelos.
7. Sí, ábrela.
8. Sí, sírvelo.
9. Sí, pásala.
10. Sí, sácala.

Objectives
- Practice affirmative **tú** commands.
- **Culture:** Learn about the textiles of Otavalo.
- Practice **acabar de** + infinitive.
- Review direct object pronouns.

Core Resources
- *Cuaderno,* pp. 226–228
- Audio Program: TXT CD 5 track 17

Practice Sequence
- **Activity 14:** Transitional practice: affirmative **tú** commands
- **Activity 15:** Transitional practice: affirmative tú commands; **acabar de** + infinitive; direct object pronouns

STANDARDS
1.1 Engage in conversation, Act. 15
1.2 Understand language, Act. 14
1.3 Present information, Act. 15, CC, PYP
2.2 Products and perspectives, CC
4.2 Compare cultures, CC
21st Century **Communication,** Act. 14/Slower paced Learners

Comparación cultural

Essential Question
Suggested Answer Throughout history, crafts have represented a very important form of cultural expression. Traditionally, handmade works created to serve a function, such as quilting that provided warmth in the winter, today are considered an art form.

Background Information
Otavalo The Otavalos are a very prosperous indigenous group of South America. The town of Otavalo is at 9,000 feet above sea level. Approximately 50,000 indigenous people live in this area.

Get Help Online More Practice my.hrw.com

✓ Ongoing Assessment
PARA Y PIENSA **Peer Assessment** Have pairs of students say their sentences aloud and then correct each other. For additional practice, use Reteaching & Practice Copymasters URB 5, pp. 19, 20, 24.

See Activity answers on p. 285.

14 Una casa sucia

Escuchar

La casa de Elena está sucia y su madre necesita ayuda. Escucha las situaciones y escribe un mandato para cada una. *(Write the mother's commands to Elena.)*

Audio Program
TXT CD 5 Track 17
Audio Script, TE p. 269b

Nota gramatical
When you want to say that something has just happened, use the verb phrase **acabar de + infinitive.**

Acabamos de comprar el pastel para la fiesta. ***We just bought*** *the cake for the party.*
Acaban de cortar el césped. ***They just cut*** *the grass.*

15 ¿Ayudas?

Hablar

Tú y otro(a) estudiante tienen muchos quehaceres. Usa un mandato para decirle lo que tiene que hacer. Él o ella va a contestar que acaba de hacerlo. *(Tell a partner what chores to do. Your partner will answer that he or she just did them.)*

A: Limpia la cocina.
B: La acabo de limpiar. (Acabo de limpiarla.)

Expansión:
Teacher Edition Only
Ask students to write a list in command form of the chores they have to do on the weekend.

Comparación cultural

Los textiles de Otavalo
Why are traditional crafts important to a culture? Many tourists visit the town of Otavalo for its Saturday market to find woven sweaters, rugs, and other items. The Otavalos, an indigenous group from **Ecuador,** have practiced weaving for centuries and are famous worldwide for their textiles. Common designs include landscapes, animals, and geometric patterns. The Otavalos take pride in their heritage and have achieved economic success selling their work both locally and internationally.

Textiles en el mercado de Otavalo

Compara con tu mundo *What are some traditional U.S. crafts?*

Más práctica Cuaderno *pp. 226–228* Cuaderno para hispanohablantes *pp. 227–230*

Get Help Online my.hrw.com

PARA Y PIENSA **Did you get it?** Give the affirmative **tú** command of each verb. Then say you just did it.
1. decorar la sala **2.** hacer los quehaceres **3.** cortar el césped

Differentiating Instruction

Inclusion

Metacognitive Support Assure students that using the verb **acabar** to express the idea that something *just happened* does not require the past tense. Even though they would say *I just wrapped the present* in the past tense in English, the verb **acabar** remains in the present. **Acabo de envolver el regalo.**

Slower-paced Learners

Read Before Listening Before students listen to Elena's mother's situations in Activity 14, have them brainstorm possible commands. What are some of the chores Elena's mother might need help with? Create a list on the board, and have students copy it onto their own papers. As students listen, have them circle the appropriate commands.

Todo junto

¡AVANZA! **Goal:** ***Show what you know*** Identify the affirmative **tú** commands and irregular verbs the Cuevas family uses in their discussion of after-party chores. Then say what chores need to be done, using irregular verbs and commands. ***Actividades 16–20***

Telehistoria completa

@HOMETUTOR my.hrw.com View, Read and Record

STRATEGIES

Cuando lees
Find the key event A key event at the end of this scene causes big trouble. What is this event? Why is it important? What hints do you find earlier in the scene?

Cuando escuchas
Listen for commands What are the family members doing? Why wasn't the catastrophe at the end prevented?

Escena 1 ***Resumen***
Fernando trae un regalo a la fiesta de sorpresa para Manuel y quiere ayudar a la familia. Manuel todavía no está en casa.

Escena 2 ***Resumen***
Manuel llega a la fiesta con el autógrafo de Trini Salgado. Hay pastel, y él abre los regalos de los invitados.

Escena 3

VIDEO DVD

AUDIO

After the party, the family begins to clean up.

Sra. Cuevas: *(to Elena)* Pon los platos sucios allí.

Sr. Cuevas: Elena, barre el suelo, saca la basura y yo lavo la ropa.

Elena: ¿Y Manuel? ¿Por qué no ayuda?

Sra. Cuevas: Acaba de celebrar su cumpleaños. Hoy no tiene que limpiar.

Elena: *(to Manuel)* ¿Vienes a ayudar? Toma. *(She tries to hand him the broom.)*

Manuel: ¡Elena! Ahora, ¡no! Tengo que buscar la camiseta de Alicia. ¿Dónde está? ¿Mamá...?

Manuel and Elena go into the laundry room and find their father.

Elena: La camiseta de Alicia... ¿Dónde está?

Sr. Cuevas: ¡Ahh! ¡Acabo de lavarla!

Differentiating Instruction

Pre-AP

Draw Conclusions Present students with discussion questions that require them to draw conclusions based on the information in the Telehistoria. Here are a few possibilities:

- **¿Por qué la familia tiene que limpiar?**
- **¿Por qué no tiene que ayudar Manuel?**
- **¿Cómo está Elena? ¿Contenta?**

Multiple Intelligences

Interpersonal Divide students into four groups. Assign each group to play the part of **la señora Cuevas, el señor Cuevas, Elena,** or **Manuel.** As students read the script aloud, encourage them to emphasize the facial expressions and tone of voice appropriate to each character. Then have groups switch parts, and read the script again.

¡AVANZA! **Objective**
- Integrate lesson content.

Core Resources
- Video Program DVD 2
- Audio Program: TXT CD 5 track 18

Presentation Strategies
- Ask students what they remember about the Telehistoria so far.
- Have students look at the photos and predict what will happen at the end.
- Show the video or play the audio.

STANDARDS
1.2 Understand language
21st Century **Communication,** Multiple Intelligences

Warm Up Projectable Transparencies, 5-22

Commands Write **sí** if the command is logical and **no** if it is not.

1. Saca la basura.
2. Haz la cama.
3. Barre la basura.
4. Limpia los globos.
5. Pon la mesa.
6. Ven a la fiesta.

Answers: 1. sí; 2. sí; 3. no; 4. no; 5. sí; 6. sí

Video Summary

@HOMETUTOR VideoPlus my.hrw.com

Mrs. Cuevas asks Elena to help with the chores. Manuel doesn't have to help because it's his birthday. Manuel and Elena look for Alicia's T-shirt, and they find out that Mr. Cuevas has just washed it.

Answers Projectable Transparencies, 5-30

Answers for Activities on p. 284.

Activity 14
1. Pasa la aspiradora.
2. Barre el suelo.
3. Saca la basura.
4. Lava los platos.
5. Haz la cama.
6. Pon la mesa.

Activity 15 Answers will vary. Sample answers include: Haz la cama. Acabo de hacerla. (La acabo de hacer.)

Para y piensa
1. Decora la sala. Acabo de decorarla. /La acabo de decorar.
2. Haz los quehaceres. Acabo de hacerlos. /Los acabo de hacer.
3. Corta el césped. Acabo de cortarlo. /Lo acabo de cortar.

TODO JUNTO

Objective

- Practice using and integrating lesson vocabulary and grammar.

Core Resources

- *Cuaderno,* pp. 229–230
- Audio Program: TXT CD 5 tracks 14, 15, 18, 19, 20

Practice Sequence

- **Activities 16, 17:** Telehistoria comprehension
- **Activity 18:** Open-ended practice: speaking
- **Activity 19:** Open-ended practice: reading, listening, speaking
- **Activity 20:** Open-ended practice: writing

STANDARDS

1.1 Engage in conversation, Act. 18
1.2 Understand language, Acts. 16–17, Act. 19
1.3 Present information, Acts. 18–20, PYP
21st Century **Communication,** Acts. 18, 19, 20/ Heritage Language Learners

Communication
Motivating with Music

The **¡AvanzaRap!** song for this unit targets party preparations and chores. To reinforce these concepts, play the **¡AvanzaRap!** animated video song for students and have them complete the Activity Master for this unit. Activity masters and teaching suggestions can be found on the **¡AvanzaRap!** DVD.

Answers Projectable Transparencies, 5-30

Activity 16

1. El padre de Manuel dice que quiere bailar en la fiesta.
2. Fernando prepara la comida./Fernando ayuda en la cocina.
3. El padre de Elena lava la ropa.
4. Manuel no tiene que ayudar.
5. El padre de Manuel tiene la camiseta de Alicia.
6. El padre de Manuel acaba de lavar la camiseta.

Activity 17

1. Manuel recibe un videojuego.
2. Fernando no quiere abrir la puerta a los invitados.
3. El señor Cuevas lava la camiseta y Manuel busca la camiseta.
4. Los invitados comen pastel y bailan.
5. Elena tiene que barrer el suelo y sacar la basura.
6. El señor Cuevas lava la ropa.

Answers continue on p. 287.

16 *Comprensión de los episodios* No es cierto

Escuchar
Leer

Todas estas oraciones son falsas. Corrígelas. *(Correct these false statements.)*

1. El padre de Manuel dice que quiere cantar en la fiesta.
2. Fernando abre la puerta a los invitados.
3. La madre de Elena lava la ropa.
4. Manuel tiene que ayudar.
5. Los padres de Manuel tienen la camiseta de Alicia.
6. El padre de Manuel acaba de planchar la camiseta.

Expansión
Once correct, put these sentences in the order in which they occur.

17 *Comprensión de los episodios* ¡A buscar!

Escuchar
Leer

Busca la información en los episodios y escríbela en una hoja de papel. *(Look for the following in the episodes and write down the information on a piece of paper.)*

modelo: un quehacer que Fernando hace
Fernando ayuda en la cocina.

1. un regalo que Manuel recibe
2. un quehacer que Fernando no quiere hacer
3. dos cosas que hacen con la camiseta
4. dos actividades que hacen en la fiesta
5. dos quehaceres que Elena tiene que hacer
6. un quehacer que el señor Cuevas hace

Expansión:
Teacher Edition Only
When students have finished Activity 17, ask them to read aloud their answers in a group to check for wrong answers.

18 ¡Qué organizados!

Digital performance space

Hablar

STRATEGY **Hablar**
Combine imagination with organization Think creatively while organizing. To do this, consider questions like these: Is the party for a special occasion? Will it be inside or outside? When will it be? How many guests will there be? Is there a theme for party activities, decorations, and food?

Trabaja con un grupo para planear una fiesta. Habla sobre la comida, las decoraciones y los quehaceres. Todos son muy organizados. Dile a otro(a) estudiante lo que tiene que hacer. Él o ella va a decir que lo acaba de hacer. *(You are planning a party with a group. Tell another student to do something. He or she will say that he or she just did it.)*

A: Ve a la tienda para comprar un pastel.

B: Acabo de ir a la tienda. Ya tengo el pastel. Pon la mesa.

C: Acabo de poner la mesa. Barre el suelo.

Expansión:
Teacher Edition Only
After finishing Activity 18, ask each group to summarize in writing what they will do to organize the party.

Differentiating Instruction

Slower-paced Learners

Read Before Listening Before listening to the Telehistoria, ask students to read the script on p. 285. Ask them to pay attention to their own pronunciation and to repeat several times the words they find difficult to pronounce. If they still have difficulties, model the pronunciation for them. Remind students of the /r/ and /rr/ sounds in words like **barre, basura, ropa.**

Multiple Intelligences

Linguistic/Verbal Have students work in groups to prepare a skit about a family getting ready for a party. The parents give the children orders: **Limpia la cocina. Haz las camas.** The children respond: **Acabo de limpiarla. Acabo de hacerlas.** Encourage them to use vocabulary for household chores, rooms of the house, as well as **tú** commands and **acabar de** + infinitive.

19 Integración

Digital performance space

Leer
Escuchar
Hablar

Tú y tu amigo(a) son participantes en un programa de televisión, **¡Limpia ya!** Escucha el mensaje para aprender cuál es tu misión y mira los planos de la casa. Luego, explica lo que tú haces y dile a tu amigo(a) qué hacer. *(Explain which rooms you are cleaning and what chores you are doing and tell your friend what to do.)*

Fuente 1 Los planos de la casa

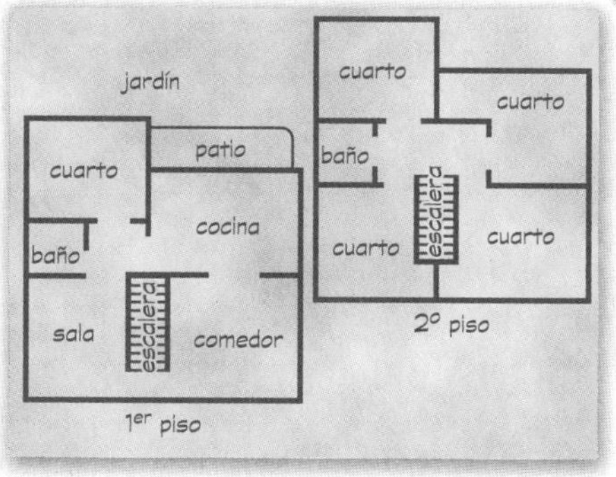

Fuente 2 Instrucciones para la misión

Listen and take notes
- ¿Qué quehaceres tienen que hacer?
- ¿Donde tienen que hacerlos?

modelo: Yo subo al segundo piso y... Roberto, sal al jardín y...

Audio Program
TXT CD 5 Tracks 19, 20
Audio Script, TE p. 269b

20 Una casa bonita y limpia

Digital performance space

Escribir

Para darle una sorpresa a tu familia, quieres limpiar toda la casa. Necesitas la ayuda de tu hermano(a), pero no está en casa. Escríbele una nota para decirle qué acabas de hacer y qué debe hacer él o ella. *(Write a note to your sibling, telling him or her what to do and what you just did.)*

modelo: ¡Queremos una casa limpia! En el baño, acabo de sacar la basura. Barre el suelo, por favor. En la sala...

Writing Criteria	Excellent	Good	Needs Work
Content	Your note includes a lot of information.	Your note includes some information.	Your note includes little information.
Communication	Most of your note is organized and easy to follow.	Parts of your note are organized and easy to follow.	Your note is disorganized and hard to follow.
Accuracy	Your note has few mistakes in grammar and vocabulary.	Your note has some mistakes in grammar and vocabulary.	Your note has many mistakes in grammar and vocabulary.

Expansión:
Teacher Edition Only
Ask students to read aloud their notes.

Más práctica Cuaderno *pp. 229–230* Cuaderno para hispanohablantes *pp. 231–232*

Get Help Online
my.hrw.com

PARA Y PIENSA

Did you get it? Give Elena three more commands for chores to do around the house.

Differentiating Instruction

Heritage Language Learners

Writing Skills Have students write a short paragraph about who among their family members has to do house chores and who does most of the work. Encourage them to include excuses for not doing the job. For example: **Mi hermano Julián nunca quiere lavar los platos porque está ocupado. Mi hermana menor dice que no puede poner la mesa porque tiene que hacer la tarea.**

Inclusion

Clear Structure Advise students to use the graphic in Activity 19 to help them brainstorm their notes in Activity 20. Have them write down one idea for each of the rooms presented. Then have them continue the writing process by developing their ideas into complete sentences, revising, editing, and then creating a final copy.

Long-term Retention

Pre-AP Integration

Activity 19 Ask students to share with the class the chores and activities he or she has to do at home on weekends. Ask them to recreate what their parents might say. For example: **¡Come el desayuno! ¡Limpia tu cuarto! ¡Haz la cama!**

✓ Ongoing Assessment

Rubric Activity 19

Listening/Speaking

Proficient	Not There Yet
Student responds correctly to the instructions and can explain their chores as well as instruct a friend on what to do.	Student cannot respond correctly to the instructions and cannot explain their chores or instruct a friend on what to do.

To customize your own rubrics, use the ***Generate Success** Rubric Generator and Graphic Organizers.*

✓ Ongoing Assessment

Get Help Online
More Practice
my.hrw.com

PARA Y PIENSA

Peer Assessment Ask students to work in pairs to practice the commands with each other. For additional practice, use Reteaching & Practice Copymasters URB 5 pp. 19, 21.

Answers Projectable Transparencies, 5-30 and 5-31

Answers continued from p. 286.

Activity 18 Answers will vary. Sample answer:
A. Ve a la tienda para comprar globos.
B. Acabo de comprar los globos. Pon la mesa.
C. Acabo de poner la mesa. Barre el patio.

Activity 19 Answers will vary. Sample answers: Voy a la cocina porque tengo que lavar los platos. Ve a la sala y pasa la aspiradora.

Activity 20 Answers will vary. Sample answers include: Acabo de sacar la basura de la cocina. También acabo de pasar la aspiradora en la sala. Por favor haz la cama...

Para y piensa Answers will vary but may include:
Elena, plancha la ropa. Pasa la aspiradora. Haz la cama.

¡AVANZA! Objectives

- Read about folk dances in **Ecuador** and **Panamá.**
- Learn about the origins of the **sanjuanito** and **tamborito** and compare them in terms of music and costumes.
- Compare folk dances in Latin America to folk dances in the U.S.

Core Resource

- Audio Program: TXT CD 5 track 21

Presentation Strategies

- Have students think about the traditional dances of the U.S. and other countries. Have they seen Native American dancing? Have they seen a square dance?
- Ask students to look at the photos. Ask quick comprehension questions: **¿Dónde bailan las personas en Ecuador? ¿De qué color es la ropa de la mujer en Panamá? ¿Quién tiene un sombrero?**
- Play the audio as students read the text.

STANDARDS

1.2 Understand language
1.3 Present information, PYP
2.1 Practices and perspectives, PYP
4.2 Compare cultures, PYP
21st Century Social and Cross-Cultural Skills, Heritage Language Learners

Warm Up Projectable Transparencies, 5-23

Acabar de + infinitive. Read the commands and write that you just did them using **acabar de** + infinitive and the correct object pronoun.

1. ¡Barre la sala! _____.
2. ¡Corta el césped! _____.
3. ¡Limpia la cocina! _____.
4. ¡Lava los platos! _____.
5. ¡Pon la mesa! _____.

Answers: 1. Acabo de barrerla. 2. Acabo de cortarlo. 3. Acabo de limpiarla. 4. Acabo de lavarlos. 5. Acabo de ponerla.

Culture

Background Information

Every culture has its folkloric dances, complete with layers of history and tradition. In folk dancing, each article of clothing, from the headdress to the shoes, has meaning. Now performed as entertainment, folk dances were once performed by local people for the joy of celebration.

Lectura cultural

Additional readings at my.hrw.com SPANISH InterActive Reader

¡AVANZA! **Goal:** Read about two traditional dances of Ecuador and Panama. Then compare the two dances and talk about when you go dancing.

Comparación cultural

AUDIO

Bailes folklóricos de Ecuador y Panamá

STRATEGY Leer
Draw key aspects Draw pictures of the **sanjuanito** and the **tamborito.** Label key aspects of your drawings. Then add more details by writing captions describing each dance.

Los bailes folklóricos de Latinoamérica representan una combinación de culturas. Ayudan a formar una identidad nacional y continuar las tradiciones de las personas que viven allí. A muchas personas de Ecuador y Panamá les gusta bailar cuando celebran fiestas.

Hay muchos bailes de influencia indígena[1] en Ecuador. Uno de los bailes más populares se llama el sanjuanito. El sanjuanito tiene un ritmo alegre[2] y es una buena representación de la fusión de culturas indígenas y españolas.

Ecuador

Para bailar, chicos y chicas forman un círculo y muchas veces bailan con pañuelos[3] en las manos[4]. Es posible ver el baile del sanjuanito todo el año en celebraciones en casa, pero es más común durante el festival de San Juan en junio.

[1] indigenous [2] **ritmo...** upbeat rhythm
[3] scarves [4] hands

Un baile tradicional en Mitad del Mundo, Ecuador

Differentiating Instruction

Heritage Language Learners

Support What They Know Ask students to talk about traditional dances in their country or region of origin. How are they similar to, or different from, the **sanjuanito** and **tamborito?** Remind students to think about all aspects of the dance—the music, the costumes, and where and when the dances are performed.

Multiple Intelligences

Visual Learners Instruct students to cover up the photos on pp. 288 and 289 with a piece of paper. Then have them create their own illustrations for the two dances based on the reading. Remind students to include each detail they read about in their drawings.

Panamá

Un baile folklórico, Ciudad de Panamá

En Panamá, es muy popular bailar salsa en fiestas o discotecas[5], pero el baile nacional es el tamborito. El tamborito usa ritmos de influencia africana, pero también tiene orígenes indígenas y españoles.

Las personas bailan con el sonido[6] de palmadas[7] y tambores[8] africanos. El tamborito es popular durante fiestas grandes y celebraciones regionales, como Carnaval. Para bailar en los festivales, las chicas llevan polleras (los vestidos tradicionales de Panamá) y los chicos llevan el dominguero (pantalones negros con una camisa blanca).

[5] nightclubs [6] sound [7] handclaps [8] drums

PARA Y PIENSA

¿Comprendiste?

1. ¿Qué influencias culturales forman el baile del sanjuanito? ¿Y el tamborito?
2. ¿Qué artículos de ropa usan para bailar en Ecuador? ¿Y en Panamá?
3. ¿En qué tipo de fiestas bailan el sanjuanito y el tamborito?

¿Y tú?

¿Te gusta bailar en fiestas? ¿Sales para bailar o bailas en casa? ¿Qué ropa llevas cuando bailas? Si no bailas, ¿quieres aprender?

Differentiating Instruction

Slower-paced Learners

Peer-study Support Organize students into pairs to read the Lectura cultural. Instruct them to take turns reading sentences aloud. After each sentence, have students stop and talk about what they have read. Also, have students work together to use context clues to deduce the meaning of unfamiliar words.

Inclusion

Clear Structure On the board, create two concept webs. Write **el sanjuanito** in the center of one, and **el tamborito** in the center of the other. Then have students supply details about each of the dances around the appropriate web. As an alternative, provide students with details written on cards, and have students place the cards around the appropriate web.

Comparisons

English Language Connection

Ask students to skim the reading on pp. 288–289 and write a list of cognates. The list should include: **folklóricos, representan, combinación, culturas, formar, identidad, nacional, continuar, tradiciones, personas, celebran, durante, influencia, indígena, populares, ritmo, fusión, círculo, posible.** Have students share the list with the class.

Communication

Group Work

Have students make lists of key words/phrases that pertain to each dance and help define it. For example, for **el sanjuanito,** relevant words/phrases would be: **identidad nacional, tradiciones, influencia indígena, ritmo alegre,** and **pañuelo.** These words should be recorded in a notebook. Point out that students do not have to know the full meaning of the words to understand the context.

Communities

Spanish in the Arts

Ask students if they have ever participated in a folk dance or watched a folk dance performance. What country was the dance from? What were some of the key elements, such as costume, instruments, or special steps/skills? Do they know the name(s) of any dance(s) from their own ethnic background?

Answers

Para y piensa

¿Comprendiste?

1. Las culturas indígenas y españolas forman el baile del sanjuanito. El tamborito tiene orígenes indígenas y españoles, con ritmos de influencia africana.
2. Para bailar en Ecuador, usan pañuelos. En Panamá las chicas llevan polleras y los chicos llevan el dominguero.
3. El tamborito es popular durante fiestas grandes y celebraciones regionales. El sanjuanito es más común durante el festival de San Juan en junio.

¿Y tú?

Answers will vary but should follow the model: Sí, me gusta bailar en fiestas. Salgo para bailar. Prefiero llevar jeans y una camiseta cuando bailo.

Objectives

- Learn about the tapestries of **Ecuador** and the **molas** of **Panamá.**
- **Culture:** Discuss how different cultures express themselves through crafts.
- **Community:** Investigate where you can find samples of crafts from Ecuador and Panama in your community.

Presentation Strategies

- Discuss with students different forms of handmade artwork. Have students give examples (jewelry, tapestries, ceramics, etc.).
- If available, show a **mola** or Otavalan tapestry or point to the pictures. Emphasize that these items are still handmade.
- Show on a map of Central and South America the location of Otavalo in Ecuador and the San Blas Islands in Panama.
- Have students read the text and make a list of words they do not understand. Encourage them to use context clues to find their meanings.

STANDARDS

2.1 Practices and perspectives
2.2 Products and perspectives
4.2 Compare cultures
21st CENTURY **Communication,** Slower-paced Learners

Comparación cultural

Essential Question

Suggested Answer Because they are made by hand, and because they are made of locally available materials, traditional crafts embody much of what the culture is based on. In addition, each culture has its own rich symbols, which can include colors as well as shapes, and these symbols form a kind of language in traditional crafts.

Communities

Spanish in the Marketplace

Because **molas** are well-known, they can often be bought in gift shops. Another place to look for **molas** is in the shops of art or natural history museums. The technique used to make **molas** is called reverse appliqué: several layers of brightly colored cloth are held together and designs are created by cutting away parts of each layer.

Proyectos culturales

Comparación cultural

Arte textil de Ecuador y Panamá

How do different cultures express themselves through crafts? Indigenous Otavalans are famous for the beautiful woolen textiles sold in a weekly market in Otavalo, **Ecuador.** In the San Blas Islands of **Panama,** women from the Kuna culture design and produce **molas,** which are pieces of fabric art that are traditionally sewn onto women's blouses. The crafts from both the Otavalan and the Kuna cultures are colorful, unique creations that have become representative of the people that make them.

Proyecto 1 *Tapestry design*

Ecuador Otavalan tapestries often use a design of geometric shapes and can depict people, objects of everyday life, and scenes of nature. Create a tapestry design in the Otavalan style.

Materials for making a tapestry design
Construction paper
Colored pens and pencils

Instructions
Think about the variety of objects the Otavalans weave. Then draw your own design using construction paper and colored pens or pencils.

Proyecto 2 *Las molas*

Panamá The Kuna women make **molas** out of several layers of colorful fabric. Make a **mola** out of paper.

Materials for making a mola
Construction paper (3 colors)
Piece of plain paper
Scissors
Glue

Instructions
1. Cut out a shape on plain paper to use as the pattern for your **mola.**
2. Trace the pattern onto a sheet of construction paper. Cut out the shape and set aside the sheet of paper.
3. Use scissors to trim your original pattern to make it smaller. Repeat step two on a second piece of construction paper.
4. Layer the two pieces of construction paper into a third one so that all the colors are visible.

En tu comunidad

Where can local artists in your community sell their work? What advantages would an artist have who is able to communicate with potential customers in Spanish?

Differentiating Instruction

Multiple Intelligences

Logical/Mathematical Direct students' attention to the description of textiles at the top of p. 290. Then ask for volunteers to draw geometric shapes on the board, such as a circle, square, triangle, trapezoid, etc. Provide students with the Spanish names for these shapes. Later, encourage them to use this vocabulary in talking about their designs.

Slower-paced Learners

Personalize It After students have created their tapestry or **mola** designs, give them the opportunity to talk about their inspiration. Why did they choose the figures, shapes, and colors they did? What is the personal significance of their design?

Lección 2

En resumen

Vocabulario y gramática

ANIMATEDGRAMMAR
Interactive Flashcards
my.hrw.com

Vocabulario

Plan a Party

bailar	*to dance*	el globo	*balloon*
cantar	*to sing*	los invitados	*guests*
celebrar	*to celebrate*	invitar a	*to invite (someone)*
dar una fiesta	*to give a party*	salir	*to leave, to go out*
las decoraciones	*decorations*	el secreto	*secret*
decorar	*to decorate*	venir	*to come*
la fiesta de sorpresa	*surprise party*		

Talk About Gifts

abrir	*to open*
buscar	*to look for*
envolver (ue)	*to wrap*
el papel de regalo	*wrapping paper*
recibir	*to receive*
el regalo	*gift*
traer	*to bring*

Talk About Chores and Responsibilities

acabar de...	*to have just . . .*	limpiar (la cocina)	*to clean the kitchen*
ayudar	*to help*	limpio(a)	*clean*
barrer el suelo	*to sweep the floor*	pasar la aspiradora	*to vacuum*
cocinar	*to cook*	planchar la ropa	*to iron*
cortar el césped	*to cut the grass*	poner la mesa	*to set the table*
darle de comer al perro	*to feed the dog*	los quehaceres	*chores*
deber	*should, ought to*	sacar la basura	*to take out the trash*
hacer la cama	*to make the bed*	sucio(a)	*dirty*
lavar los platos	*to wash the dishes*		

Other Words and Phrases

decir	*to say, to tell*
hay que	*one has to, one must*
poner	*to put, to place*
si	*if*
todavía	*still; yet*

Gramática

Nota gramatical: **acabar de** + infinitive *p. 284*

More Irregular Verbs

Dar, decir, poner, salir, traer, and **venir** are all irregular.

decir *to say, to tell*	
digo	decimos
dices	decís
dice	dicen

venir *to come*	
vengo	venimos
vienes	venís
viene	vienen

Some verbs are irregular only in the **yo** form of the present tense.

dar	poner	salir	traer
doy	pongo	salgo	traigo

Affirmative tú Commands

Regular **affirmative tú commands** are the same as the **él/ella** forms in the present tense.

Infinitive	Present Tense	Affirmative tú Command
lavar	(él, ella) **lava**	¡Lava los platos!
barrer	(él, ella) **barre**	¡Barre el suelo!
abrir	(él, ella) **abre**	¡Abre la puerta!

There are irregular **affirmative tú commands.**

decir	hacer	ir	poner	salir	ser	tener	venir
di	haz	ve	pon	sal	sé	ten	ven

Practice Spanish with Holt McDougal Apps!

Differentiating Instruction

Inclusion

Multisensory Input/Output Help students review vocabulary by playing this game. Invite a volunteer to act out one of the words or phrases from Lección 2. The other students must:

1. Guess the name of the word or phrase.
2. Find it on p. 291.
3. Mimic the action.
4. Write down the word or phrase on a separate piece of paper.

Slower-paced Learners

Memory Aids Encourage students to create "pop-up" flashcards to review the **tú** command forms from Unidad 5. Have students fold an index card in half to form a small book. On the outside, have them write the infinitive of a verb, such as **lavar.** On the inside, have them write the command form of the verb.

Objective

- Review lesson vocabulary and grammar.

DIGITAL SPANISH

Interactive Flashcards Students can hear every target vocabulary word pronounced in authentic Spanish. Flashcards have Spanish on one side, and a picture or a translation on the other.

Review Games Matching, concentration, hangman, and word search are just a sampling of the fun, interactive games students can play to review for the test.

performance space
News Networking
@HOMETUTOR
CULTURA Interactiva

- Audio and Video Resources
- Interactive Flashcards
- Review Activities
- WebQuest
- Conjuguemos.com

Long-term Retention

Critical Thinking

Synthesize Ask students to use the vocabulary about chores to create a one-week calendar for **los quehaceres,** assigning them to members of a fictional family. They should also describe the family, giving names and ages for each member. The completed calendar should list at least one job for each family member for each day.

Communication

Pair Work

Have pairs plan a party. Ask them to create a chart and write what activities they will want to do, what food they will serve, what music they will play, and how they will decorate. Students will use their charts and discuss their party plans with another pair.

Objective
- Review lesson vocabulary and grammar.

Core Resources
- *Cuaderno,* pp. 231–242
- Audio Program: TXT CD 5 track 22

Presentation Strategies
- Before starting the audio for Activity 1, ask students to listen to it carefully and pay special attention to the chores that each person is supposed to do.
- Review irregular verb forms by saying a subject pronoun and infinitive and asking students to supply the correct verb form. For example: **tú: decir → tú dices**
- Point out that in Activity 3 some of the commands that students will elicit have irregular forms. Go over irregular command forms before doing the activity.
- Go over the Comparación cultural with students and clarify any questions that arise.
- Review may be done in class or given as homework. You may want students to access the review online.

STANDARDS
1.2 Understand language, Act. 1
1.3 Present information, Acts. 2–5
4.2 Compare cultures, Act. 5
21st Century **Communication,** English Learners; **Creativity and Innovation,** Multiple Intelligences

Warm Up
Projectable Transparencies, 5-23

Irregular verbs Fill in the blanks with the correct form of the verb in parentheses:
1. ¿Qué _____ tú? (decir)
2. Yo _____ los platos en la mesa. (poner)
3. Ella _____ aquí. (venir)
4. Nosotros _____ a su casa. (venir)
5. ¿ _____ ustedes a mi casa? (venir)
6. Yo _____ dos regalos. (dar)

Answers: 1. dices; 2. pongo; 3. viene; 4. venimos; 5. Vienen; 6. doy

Ongoing Assessment
Get Help Online
More Practice
my.hrw.com

PARA Y PIENSA **Remediation** If students achieve less than 85% accuracy with the activities, direct them to pp. 245, 277–278, 282, 284, 288–289 and to get help online at my.hrw.com.

See Activity answers on p. 293.

Lección 2

Repaso de la lección

@HOMETUTOR
my.hrw.com

¡LLEGADA!

¡AvanzaRap! DVD
Sing and Learn

Now you can
- plan a party
- talk about chores and responsibilities
- tell someone what to do
- say what you just did

Using
- more irregular verbs
- affirmative **tú** commands
- **acabar de** + infinitive

To review
- more irregular verbs p. 277
- affirmative **tú** commands p. 282
- **acabar de** + infinitive p. 284

1 Listen and understand

AUDIO

El señor Robles y sus estudiantes hablan de una fiesta. Escucha la conversación y empareja las personas con las oraciones correspondientes. *(Listen to Mr. Robles and his students. Then match each person with the appropriate sentence.)*

1. La fiesta es para ella.	**a.** Andrés
2. No deben hablar de la fiesta.	**b.** Carla
3. Va a traer los globos.	**c.** Samuel
4. Va a ayudar a limpiar.	**d.** el señor Robles
5. Va a poner las decoraciones.	**e.** la directora
6. Va a traer pizza.	**f.** los estudiantes

Audio Progra[m]
TXT CD 5 Track [22]
Audio Script, TE 269b

To review
- more irregular verbs p. 277

2 Plan a party

Natalia da una fiesta para su hermano y habla con Catalina, una amiga. Completa sus mensajes instantáneos con la forma correcta del verbo apropiado. *(Complete the instant messages with the correct form of the appropriate verb.)*

dar	salir
decir	traer
poner	ven

mensajero instantáneo

chica_cómica: Catalina, yo __1.__ una fiesta de sorpresa para Hugo el sábado. Hay mucho que hacer.
Cati268: El sábado llego a tu casa temprano para ayudar. También yo __2.__ los refrescos.
chica_cómica: Yo decoro la casa y mamá __3.__ la mesa.
Cati268: ¿Cuándo __4.__ Hugo?
chica_cómica: A las dos. Los invitados __5.__ «¡Feliz cumpleaños!», y él abre los regalos.
Cati268: Y después de comer el almuerzo, todos nosotros __6.__ de la casa para comer pastel en un café.

Differentiating Instruction

Pre-AP
Summarize Have the students create two lists of tasks: those that are done before a party and those done afterwards. They can choose from a list of tasks such as: **poner las decoraciones, lavar los platos, preparar la comida,** etc. Ask them to recite their lists: **Antes de la fiesta, yo..., Después de la fiesta, yo...** Call their attention to the fact that some tasks go on both lists.

English Learners
Build Background Divide the class into pairs. Ask one student in each pair to come up with some questions to ask the other student about the way household tasks are handled in his or her home. Some questions might be **¿En tu casa, quién saca la basura?** or **¿Cuándo limpias tu cuarto?** Answers should be given in full sentences: **En mi casa, mi hermano saca la basura.**

REPASO DE LA LECCIÓN

To review
- affirmative **tú** commands p. 282

3 Tell someone what to do

Alfredo es muy perezoso. Usa mandatos para escribir lo que él le dice a su hermana. *(Write Alfredo's commands to his sister.)*

modelo: venir a mi cuarto
Ven a mi cuarto.

1. traer mi mochila
2. buscar mi libro de ciencias
3. envolver el regalo para mamá
4. ponerlo en el escritorio
5. ir a la tienda
6. hacer todos mis quehaceres

To review
- **acabar de** + infinitive p. 284

4 Talk about chores and responsibilities

Escribe qué acaban de hacer Fernando y otros. *(Write what these people have just done.)*

modelo: Elena
Elena acaba de barrer el suelo.

1. mamá

2. yo

3. papá

4. ellos

5. Elena

6. Elena y yo

To review
- **las montañas** p. 245
- Comparación cultural pp. 278, 284
- Lectura cultural pp. 288–289

5 Ecuador and Panama

Comparación cultural

Answer these culture questions.

1. What is the world's highest active volcano? Where is it located?
2. What is celebrated during **Fiestas de Quito**? How?
3. Who are the Otavalos and what are they known for?
4. How do you dance **el sanjuanito**? What instruments are used in **el tamborito**? Where are these dances popular?

Más práctica Cuaderno *pp. 231–242* Cuaderno para hispanohablantes *pp. 233–242*

Get Help Online my.hrw.com

✓ Ongoing Assessment

Alternative Assessment Ask students to give **tú** commands to each other in a round robin fashion, with each issuing a command to the person behind him or her. To encourage the use of a range of verbs, write the following on the board, and ask students to choose from the list: **bailar, cantar, celebrar, dar, decorar, ayudar, poner, cocinar, lavar, limpiar, envolver.**

Answers Projectable Transparencies, 5-31

Answers for Activities on pp. 292–293.

Activity 1
1. e; **2.** f; **3.** a; **4.** c; **5.** b; **6.** d

Activity 2
1. doy; **2.** traigo; **3.** pone; **4.** viene; **5.** dicen; **6.** salimos

Activity 3
1. Trae mi mochila.
2. Busca mi libro de ciencias.
3. Envuelve el regalo para mamá.
4. Ponlo en el escritorio.
5. Ve a la tienda.
6. Haz todos mis quehaceres.

Activity 4
1. Mamá acaba de cocinar.
2. Yo acabo de pasar la aspiradora.
3. Papá acaba de planchar.
4. Ellos acaban de lavar los platos, barrer el suelo y sacar la basura.
5. Elena acaba de hacer la cama.
6. Elena y yo acabamos de cortar el césped.

Activity 5
1. Cotopaxi is the world's highest active volcano. It is located near the capital city of Quito.
2. Fiestas de Quito celebrate the anniversary of the founding of Quito, Ecuador, in 1534. The celebration includes parades, concerts, dances and musical tributes.
3. The Otavalos are an indigenous group from Ecuador. They are known for their textiles and weaving designs.
4. To dance **el sanjuanito,** boys and girls form a circle and dance holding scarves in their hands. **El tamborito** uses African drums. **El sanjuanito** is popular in Ecuador and **el tamborito** is popular in Panama.

Differentiating Instruction

Multiple Intelligences

Musical/Rhythmic Ask student groups to create a rhyme or rap song using chore vocabulary and command forms with **tú.** For example: **Lava los platos. Barre el piso. Pon la mesa. ¡Qué sorpresa!** As the piece is recited, make students aware of its specific cadence by having them tap or clap. As other pieces are shared, point out to students how the cadences and rhyme schemes may vary.

Slower-paced Learners

Sentence Completion To help with Activity 2, give students a choice of two infinitives from the verb bank to complete each sentence. Ask, **¿Qué verbo completa mejor la oración: Yo ____ una fiesta de sorpresa. ¿Dar o decir?** Continue in this manner with the rest of the sentences. After students have chosen the correct infinitive, have them come up with the correct verb form.

Objectives
- Read what three teens have to say about celebrations in their countries.
- Compare your family celebrations with those in Panama, Argentina, and Ecuador.

Core Resources
- *Cuaderno* pp. 243–245
- Audio Program: TXT CD 5 track 23
- Video Program: DVD 2

Presentation Strategies
- Ask students to name their favorite holidays.
- Have students read the text in the book as they listen to the audio.
- Ask student volunteers to take turns reading the descriptions Daniel, Carla, and María Elena give of their favorite holidays. Correct pronunciation as needed.

STANDARDS
1.2 Understand language
1.3 Present information
2.1 Practices and perspectives
4.2 Compare cultures
21st Century **Social and Cross-Cultural Skills,** Lectura y escritura/Heritage Language Learners

Communication
Group Work
Have student groups bring in a photo or a magazine cutout of a family celebration. Have students brainstorm what they could say to describe the scene. Display the photo and have the class ask questions about what is happening in the photo. For example: **¿Qué celebran? ¿Dónde es la fiesta? ¿Quiénes están en la fiesta? ¿Qué ropa llevan los invitados? ¿Qué hacen los invitados?**

Comparación cultural

AUDIO
¡Así celebramos!

Lectura y escritura

WebQuest my.hrw.com

1. **Leer** Party celebrations vary around the world. Read how María Elena, Carla, and Daniel enjoy parties and celebrations.
2. **Escribir** Using the three descriptions as models, write a short paragraph about a celebration of your own.

STRATEGY **Escribir**
Use a chart To write about a celebration, complete a chart like the one shown.

tipo de fiesta			
lugar	invitados	comida	actividades

Step 1 Complete the chart with details about the type of celebration, location, guests, food, and activities.

Step 2 Write your paragraph. Make sure to include all the information from the chart. Check your writing by yourself or with help from a friend. Make final corrections.

Compara con tu mundo
Use the paragraph you wrote to compare your celebration to a celebration described by *one* of the three students. What is similar? What is different?

Cuaderno *pp. 243–245* Cuaderno para hispanohablantes *pp. 243–245*

Differentiating Instruction

Slower-paced Learners
Personalize It Based on the descriptions they read, ask students to share information about their own experiences with parties and celebrations. For example, after they read the sentence: **El 24 de diciembre es muy importante en Panamá,** you might ask: **¿Es el 24 de diciembre muy importante en tu casa?**

Pre-AP
Self-correct After students have finished writing about their own party or celebration, have them read their paragraphs aloud to a partner. Remind students to listen to themselves as they read aloud to catch any mistakes in their writing. Also, instruct the partners to make note of sentences or phrases that do not sound correct due to problems with agreement or verb forms.

CULTURA Interactiva my.hrw.com *See these pages come alive!*

Panamá *María Elena*

¡Saludos desde Panamá! Me llamo María Elena. Mi familia y yo acabamos de decorar la casa para celebrar la Navidad[1]. El 24 de diciembre es muy importante en Panamá. Las familias comen la cena tarde y a las doce de la noche abren los regalos. Mis hermanos y yo siempre decoramos el árbol de Navidad[2]. También me gusta envolver regalos con papel. Quiero dar y recibir muchos regalos este año.

[1] Christmas [2] **árbol...** Christmas tree

Argentina *Carla*

¡Hola! Me llamo Carla y vivo en el norte de Argentina. Todos los años celebramos un gran festival. En el festival podemos ver a los gauchos[3] con sus caballos[4], escuchar música típica y comer comida rica. Siempre llevo un vestido bonito para participar en los bailes típicos con otros chicos y chicas.

[3] Argentinean cowboys [4] horses

Ecuador *Daniel*

¡Hola! Me llamo Daniel y vivo en Cuenca, Ecuador. Para la fiesta del año nuevo, muchas personas hacen figuras grandes de papel maché. Las figuras son de muchos colores y muchas veces son muy cómicas. La noche del 31 de diciembre mis padres dan una fiesta. Invitan a muchas personas. Limpiamos toda la casa, ponemos la mesa y compartimos una cena rica con nuestra familia y los otros invitados.

Ecuador

Comparación cultural

Exploring the Theme

Christmas is celebrated in many different ways around the world. Although the Panamanian Christmas includes many of the same elements we find in other Christmas celebrations (special foods, gifts, the Christmas tree), Panama also has its own individual rituals. Regional variations on Christmas are almost always the result of that region's own traditions, geography, and even its weather.

✓ Ongoing Assessment

PARA Y PIENSA **Quick Check** Have students say two sentences about each of the three narratives and record their responses on the board.

✓ Ongoing Assessment

Rubric Lectura y escritura

Writing Criteria	Excellent	Good	Needs Work
Content	Paragraph contains a lot of information.	Paragraph contains some information.	Paragraph lacks information.
Communication	Paragraph is organized and easy to follow.	Paragraph is fairly well organized and easy to follow.	Paragraph is disorganized and hard to follow.
Accuracy	Paragraph has few mistakes in vocabulary and grammar.	Paragraph has some mistakes in vocabulary and grammar.	Paragraph has many mistakes in vocabulary and grammar.

To customize your own rubrics, use the ***Generate Success*** *Rubric Generator and Graphic Organizers.*

Differentiating Instruction

Inclusion

Clear Structure Before students read the celebration descriptions on p. 295, have them copy this list onto three separate pieces of paper.

País:
Nombre:
Celebración:
Actividades:
Otros detalles:

Instruct students to fill in the information as they read the three paragraphs.

Heritage Language Learners

Support What They Know Ask students to discuss how the celebrations described by Daniel, Carla, and María Elena compare to those in their country or region of origin. How are Christmas, birthdays, and New Year's Eve/Day traditionally celebrated? What are some of the other major holidays or celebrations in their culture?

Objective
- Cumulative review.

Core Resource
- Audio Program: TXT CD 5 track 24

Review Options
- **Activity 1:** Listening
- **Activity 2:** Speaking
- **Activity 3:** Speaking
- **Activity 4:** Writing
- **Activity 5:** Speaking
- **Activity 6:** Speaking and writing
- **Activity 7:** Reading and writing

STANDARDS
1.1 Engage in conversation, Acts. 2-5
1.2 Understand language, Act. 1
1.3 Present information, Acts. 2-7
21st Century **Collaboration,** Plan a surprise party; **Communication,** Act. 6

Long-term Retention
Study Tips
To reinforce the irregular **yo** forms of **dar, poner, traer,** and **salir,** ask students to work in pairs or small groups to create chants using the words **doy, pongo, traigo,** and **salgo.**

Answers
Activity 1
1. Gabriela acaba de volver a su casa.
2. Gabriela sirve pollo con patatas y una ensalada.
3. Yo traigo los tomates.
4. La señora Domínguez vive en el cuarto piso. Jorge y Marlene viven en el segundo piso.
5. La señora Domínguez tiene el pastel de cumpleaños. Jorge y Marlene tienen los discos compactos.
6. Si los invitados llegan temprano, debo servir los refrescos.

UNIDADES 1-5

Repaso inclusivo
Options for Review

¡AvanzaRap! DVD Sing and Learn

Digital performance space

1 Listen, understand, and compare
Escuchar

Gabriela is giving a surprise party. Listen to her phone message. Then answer the following questions.

1. ¿Qué acaba de hacer Gabriela?
2. ¿Qué sirve Gabriela?
3. ¿Qué traes tú a la fiesta?
4. ¿Dónde vive la señora Domínguez? ¿Y Jorge y Marlene?
5. ¿Qué tiene la señora Domínguez? ¿Y Jorge y Marlene?
6. ¿Qué debes hacer si los invitados llegan temprano?

Have you ever given or gone to a surprise party? How did others help prepare for the party?

Audio Program
TXT CD 5 Track 24
Audio Script, TE p. 269b

2 Give orders
Hablar

You have designed a personal robot to perform your everyday tasks for you. Your friend asks if he or she can borrow your robot for a day, but your robot only listens to you. Your friend tells you what his or her schedule is and what has to be done, and you give the commands to your robot.

3 Plan a surprise party
Hablar

Work in a group of four to plan a surprise party for a close friend or family member. Each member of your group should take on a role: food coordinator, invitation designer, guest list creator, and activities organizer. Present your party plans to the class.

4 Have a yard sale
Escribir

You want to earn some extra money by holding a yard sale. Make a flier to advertise what you are selling: books, personal items, clothing, and furniture. Include information such as the date, time, and location of the sale.

Differentiating Instruction

Slower-paced Learners
Read Before Listening Before students listen to Gabriela's phone message in Activity 1, have them preview the questions presented. Advise them to turn each question into a sentence starter for its answer. **¿Cuándo llega Gabriela? Gabriela llega a ____.** As they listen to the message, students can fill in the blanks they have created.

Inclusion
Cumulative Instruction Before discussing Activity 2 with a partner, have students review the formation of **tú** command forms. Refer students to p. 282 in Lesson 2 or **En resumen** on p. 291. Also, give students time to practice with any flashcards or other memory aids they have created during Unidad 5.

5 Furnish a dorm room

Hablar

Role-play a conversation between college roommates. You and your partner need to furnish your dorm room. Discuss with your partner the items that you want to have in your room, where those items will go, and what color your room should be. Once you come to an agreement on what your room will look like, draw a sketch and present it to the class.

6 Design a family home

Hablar
Escribir

Your partner has contracted you to design a floor plan for a house that will fit his or her family's personalities and lifestyles. Interview your partner to find out what his or her family is like and what they like to do. Also find out what they like and dislike about where they live now. Take notes and use the information to write a proposal. Present it to your partner.

7 Prepare a dinner

Leer
Escribir

Your family has invited your Spanish teacher home for dinner tonight. Your parents left you this note telling you to do some dinner preparations. Read the note and write another note saying that you have just done certain tasks and make excuses as to why you can't do the other items.

Necesitamos ir a trabajar y no podemos preparar todo. Por favor:

haz la tarea temprano
ve a la tienda para comprar el postre
prepara la ensalada
cocina el pollo y las patatas
limpia la cocina
lava los platos
saca la basura
pon la mesa

Hablamos más tarde. ¡Gracias!

Communication
Group Work

Place students in small groups and ask them to discuss what they've learned in Unidad 5. Then ask them to categorize their learning into "most interesting," "most helpful," "most memorable," and "most fun." Ask each group to share with the class.

✓ Ongoing Assessment

Integrated Performance Assessment Rubric **Oral Activities 2, 3, 5, 6**
Written Activities 4, 7

Very Good	Proficient	Not There Yet
The student thoroughly develops all requirements of the task.	The student develops most requirements of the task.	The student does not develop the requirements of the task.
The student demonstrates excellent control of verb forms.	The student demonstrates good to fair control of verb forms.	The student demonstrates poor control of verb forms.
Good variety of appropriate vocabulary.	Adequate variety of appropriate vocabulary.	The vocabulary is not appropriate.
The pronunciation is excellent to very good.	The pronunciation is good to fair.	The pronunciation is poor.

To customize your own rubrics, use the ***Generate Success*** *Rubric Generator and Graphic Organizers.*

Differentiating Instruction

Slower-paced Learners

Yes/No Questions Help get students talking in Actividad 5 by asking yes or no questions about typical dorm room items. Model questions that students might ask to find out what their partners do and do not want in the room. **¿Quieres un tocadiscos? ¿Te gusta tener un sofá? ¿Cuántas lámparas necesitas?**

Multiple Intelligences

Visual Learners Before designing a house for their partner's family in Actividad 6, suggest that students organize their ideas in the form of a drawing. After interviewing their partner about his or her family and their preferences, have students translate the information they have acquired into a visual floor plan. They can then show the drawing to their partner for approval before moving ahead and writing the proposal.

Proyectos adicionales

Planning Ahead

Projects **Create a brochure for a health resort.** With a partner, have students create a brochure describing a typical day at a health resort. The brochure should include a schedule of a day's activities and descriptions of breakfast, lunch, and dinner. Photos and/or drawings should accompany descriptions of the meals and possible activities. Encourage students to work in pencil first, and to try different layouts before drawing pictures or gluing magazine clippings. Once they have a final version, give partners the opportunity to present their brochures to the whole group as if they were sales representatives from the resort.

PACING SUGGESTION: Upon completion of **Lección 2** to review vocabulary related to healthy living. Students will also need to recall vocabulary related to food, sports, and daily activities.

21st Century **Creativity and Innovation**

(Virtual) Bulletin Board

Create a bulletin board with the title **Mi deporte favorito.** Ask students to bring in photos of themselves playing their favorite sport. They might bring in photos from school sports events, photos from casual family games, or team photos. If students do not have a photo, have them draw a picture of themselves playing their favorite sport. Then have students write a caption for their photo. The caption should name the sport, and say something about why it is their favorite. As a tech alternative, you may wish to have students create their projects on a class wiki page.

Soy Melissa. Mi deporte favorito es el béisbol. Mi equipo se llama Los Tigres. Siempre ganamos.

PACING SUGGESTION: After vocabulary is presented in **Lección 1** to reinforce sports vocabulary. Students will also need to review phrases related to describing activities, and expressing preferences.

21st Century **Creativity and Innovation**

Web Research

Go online to learn more about baseball in the Dominican Republic. Students might focus their research on one particular star, such as Miguel Tejada, Pedro Martínez or David Ortiz. These students should present the information they learn in the form of a short biography and timeline of the player's life and career. Other students might choose to focus on one particular team, such as **los Tigres de Licey** from Santo Domingo or **las Águilas de Cibao** from Santiago. These students should present their information in the form of a team profile, describing the team's history and style.

PACING SUGGESTION: Throughout **Lección 1** as time allows.

21st Century **Technology Literacy**

Games

Escucha y dibuja

For homework, have students write a description of past sports experience. Here is one example:

Ayer jugué al básquetbol. Caminé al gimnasio con mis amigos. Llegué a la cancha a las cinco de la tarde. Jugué bien pero no ganamos.

Have volunteers take turns reading their sentences aloud. As they listen, students should sketch what they hear. They might put all of the activities in one scene, or use a comic book format to show the different activities separately. Let the reader choose his or her favorite depiction of the story.

PACING SUGGESTION: After **Lección 1** to reinforce sports vocabulary, as well as preterite forms of regular **-ar** verbs.

¿Eres atleta?

Gather pictures that represent different sports. Glue or tape them to individual index cards. Then place the cards facedown in a pile.

Divide the class into two teams. One team member chooses a card, and acts out the sport for his or her teammates to guess. The player may talk about what he or she is doing, but must not name the sport. For example, students might talk about where they play the sport or the equipment they use. If the team guesses the sport correctly, it gets a point. The other team then gets a turn.

PACING SUGGESTION: After vocabulary has been presented in **Lección 2.**

¡AvanzaRap! DVD

- Video animations of all **¡AvanzaRap!** songs (with Karaoke track)
- Teaching Suggestions
- **¡AvanzaRap!** Activity Masters
- **¡AvanzaRap!** Video Scripts and Answers

Also available on the **Teacher One Stop**

Recipe

Mangú is a Dominican favorite that is also popular throughout Central America. It is often eaten in the morning with breakfast, but can accompany any meal. Its main ingredient is the plantain, a starchy banana often prepared and used similar to a potato.

Mangú

Ingredientes

2 plátanos verdes
3 tazas de agua
3 cucharadas de aceite de cocinar o de mantequilla
1/2 taza de cebolla morada

Instrucciones

Corte la cebolla en rodajas delgadas y pele los plátanos. Hierva los plátanos en el agua hasta que estén suaves. Retire los plátanos del agua y guarde el agua. Maje los plátanos como lo hace con las papas. Añada suficiente agua y las tres cucharadas de aceite de cocinar o de mantequilla hasta que el mangú adquiera la consistencia de puré. Añada sal al gusto. Adórnelo con la cebolla.

Music

Have students bring in materials to create their own **maracas.** Some possibilities might include empty film canisters, yogurt containers, or paper towel tubes. The shakers can then be filled with dried beans, rice, or beads. Have students seal their shakers with packing tape. Finally, have students go to a music store or to an online music store to find examples of **merengue.** Play some of the music they find. Encourage students to use their newly created instruments to play along with the music they hear.

UNIT THEME
Staying healthy

UNIT STANDARDS

COMMUNICATION
- Talk about sports
- Talk about whom you know
- Talk about what you know
- Talk about parts of the body
- Make excuses
- Say what you did
- Talk about staying healthy

CULTURES
- The *Serie del Caribe*
- Dominican artist Juan Medina
- Sports clubs in Santo Domingo
- Healthy habits when spending time doing outdoor sports
- The art of Amaya Salazar
- The Merengue Festival of Santo Domingo
- The meanings of gestures and proverbs from Spanish-speaking countries
- Popular sports

CONNECTIONS
- Social Studies: Researching the Dominican flag and coat of arms
- History: Researching the Dominican struggle for independence
- Art: Designing a flag for the school
- Physical Education: Writing about the role of flags and anthems in sports

COMPARISONS
- Sports in the Dominican Republic and the U.S.
- The *Serie del Caribe* and other championships
- The Spanish letter **g** with **a, o,** and **u** and with **e** and **i**
- Outdoor activities and staying healthy
- The Merengue Festival, music festivals in the U.S.
- World-class Dominican and Venezuelan atheletes
- Gestures and proverbs in Spanish-speaking countries
- Students' favorite sports in the Dominican Republic, Honduras, Venezuela, and the U.S.

COMMUNITIES
- Variations in the meaning of gestures, especially in the business world

UNIDAD 6

República Dominicana

Mantener un cuerpo sano

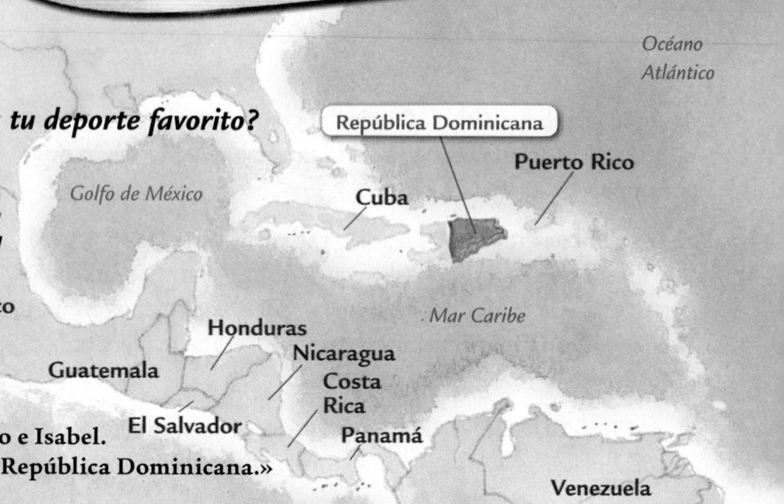

Lección 1
Tema: ***¿Cuál es tu deporte favorito?***

Lección 2
Tema: ***La salud***

«¡Hola!
**Somos Mario e Isabel.
Somos de la República Dominicana.»**

Población: 9.507.133

Área: 18.815 millas cuadradas; comparte la isla de La Española con Haití

Capital: Santo Domingo

Moneda: el peso dominicano

Idioma: español

Comida típica: mangú, cazabe, la bandera

Gente famosa: Julia Álvarez (escritora), Juan Luis Guerra (cantante), Pedro Martínez (beisbolista), Oscar de la Renta (diseñador)

Frutas tropicales

298 doscientos noventa y ocho

Cultural Geography

Setting the Scene
- ¿Cuál es el deporte nacional de la República Dominicana? (el béisbol)
- ¿Cuántas personas viven en este país? (9.507.133)
- ¿Cuál es la capital del país? (Santo Domingo)

Teaching with Maps
- ¿En qué isla está la República Dominicana? (La Española)
- ¿Qué país tiene frontera con la República Dominicana? (Haití)
- ¿Qué países están cerca de la República Dominicana? (Cuba y Puerto Rico)

Cultura Interactiva my.hrw.com *See these pages come alive!*

Una familia de pescadores en una playa de Pedernales

La importancia del Mar Caribe The white sand beaches of the Dominican Republic are popular with Dominican and international tourists. The clear blue waters and coral reefs are ideal for snorkeling and diving. *What can tourists enjoy in your area?*

El deporte nacional Baseball is considered the Dominican Republic's national sport. It can be played throughout the year because of the country's warm climate, and fans can see professional games from October through February. *What sports are popular where you live?*

Juegan al deporte nacional en Santo Domingo

El Altar de la Patria en la capital

Un monumento de la Independencia Santo Domingo's **Altar de la Patria** (Altar of the Nation) is a memorial dedicated to the heroes of the Dominican Republic's fight for freedom from Haiti in 1844. The monument's walkway contains a 32-point nautical star, considered kilometer one, from which all distances within the country are measured. *How are heroes honored in your country's capital?*

Bridging Cultures

Heritage Language Learners

Literacy Skills Have students use the library or Internet to learn more about the life and work of Julia Álvarez. Encourage interested students to read Álvarez's work in either Spanish or English. Then have students comment on the role of Dominican history and culture in the author's work.

English Learners

Build Background Help students organize the information presented on page 299 by creating three concept webs. After reading the paragraphs, ask students to propose one word to represent the main idea of each, such as *beaches, baseball,* and *monument*. Then have students re-read the paragraphs, adding details to each web. Finally, have students draw comparisons to their home country.

Cultura Interactiva my.hrw.com

Send your students to my.hrw.com to explore authentic Dominican culture. Tell them to click on Cultura interactiva to see these pages come alive!

Culture

About the Photos

- Apart from its many beaches, the Dominican Republic offers visitors exciting, close-up views of nature. Adventurous tourists may enjoy exploring the rain forests or going whale watching.
- Baseball is universally popular in the Dominican Republic. Even the smallest towns have their own teams and take pride in practicing the national sport.
- The **Altar de la Patria** is not just a monument. It is also a tomb in which many of the country's heroes are buried. Among them is Juan Pablo Duarte, who is considered the father of the country.

Expanded Information

- The Dominican Republic, which shares the island of Hispaniola with Haiti, is a country of contrasts. It is the home of the Caribbean's highest mountains and the lowest point, a million-year-old lake.
- Baseball was brought to the Dominican Republic from Cuba more than 100 years ago. American sailors working in Cuba's sugar fields migrated to the Dominican Republic when the sugar season was slow, and introduced the sport to the people.
- The capital city of Santo Domingo has a colonial quarter which houses many well preserved and restored landmarks such as mansions and churches. Some of the structures date from the 17th century.

Video Character Guide

Mario and Isabel both like sports, but baseball is their favorite. Isabel's team is usually the winner, but Mario hopes his team will rise to the level of champion.

Lesson Overview

Culture at a Glance

Topic & Activity	Essential Question
Baseball in the Dominican Republic pp. 300–301	Do you like to play or watch sports with your friends?
Caribbean Series p. 308	How do professional athletes support their home countries?
Representative art p. 314	How can artists reflect the people of their country through their artwork?
A sports club pp. 318–319	What are some of the activities that you can enjoy at the Palacio de los Deportes?
Culture review, p. 323	What sport is popular in the Dominican Republic and Venezuela?

COMPARISON COUNTRIES República Dominicana · Honduras · Venezuela

Practice at a Glance

	Objective	Activity & Skill
Vocabulary	Sports	3: Listening/Reading; 4: Speaking; 5: Reading/Writing; 6: Listening/Writing; 8: Speaking; 9: Speaking; 10: Listening/Reading; 11: Speaking; 14: Speaking; 16: Listening/Reading; 17: Listening/Reading; 18: Writing/Speaking; 19: Reading/Listening/Speaking; 20: Writing; Repaso 1: Listening
Vocabulary	Sports equipment	1: Reading; 2: Writing/Speaking; 18: Writing/Speaking; Repaso 2: Writing
Grammar	Using the verb **jugar**	5: Reading/Writing; 6: Listening/Writing; 7: Speaking; 8: Speaking; 9: Speaking; 10: Listening/Reading; 11: Speaking; 14: Speaking; 17: Listening/Reading; 19: Reading/Listening/Speaking; 20: Writing; Repaso 2: Writing
Grammar	Using the verbs **saber** and **conocer**	12: Reading; 13: Writing; 14: Speaking; 15: Writing; 16: Listening/Reading; Repaso 3: Writing
Grammar	The personal **a**	13: Writing; 14: Speaking; Repaso 4: Writing
Communication	Talk about sports	1: Reading; 2: Writing/Speaking; 3: Listening/Reading; 4: Speaking; 5: Reading/Writing; 6: Listening/Writing; 8: Speaking; 9: Speaking; 11: Speaking; 14: Speaking; 16: Listening/Reading; 17: Listening/Reading; 19: Reading/Listening/Speaking; 20: Writing; Repaso 2: Writing; Repaso 4: Writing
Communication	Talk about whom and what you know	13: Writing; 14: Speaking; 15: Writing; Repaso 3: Writing
Communication	Pronunciation: The letter **g** with **a, o, u**	**Pronunciación:** *La letra* **g** *con* ***a, o, u,*** p. 311, Listening/Speaking
Recycle	Numbers from 200 to 1,000,000	2: Writing/Speaking
Recycle	**Gustar** with nouns	4: Speaking
Recycle	Comparatives	9: Speaking

The following presentations are recorded in the Audio Program for ***¡Avancemos!***

- **¡A responder!** *page 303*
- **6: ¿A qué juegan?** *page 308*
- **19: Integración** *page 317*
- **Repaso de la lección** *page 322*
  1: Listen and understand

For **¡AvanzaRap!** scripts, see the **¡AvanzaRap! DVD.**

¡A responder! TXT CD 6 track 2

1. la raqueta
2. el guante
3. la pelota
4. los patines en línea
5. el bate
6. la piscina
7. el casco
8. el campo

6 | ¿A qué juegan? TXT CD 6 track 4

Elena: Hola, soy Elena. Soy jugadora de fútbol. Es mi deporte favorito. Juego todos los días en el campo.

Rogelio: Me llamo Rogelio. Mi amigo José y yo jugamos en la cancha de voleibol.

Sr. Morales: Pero, ¿dónde están los bates y los guantes? Hoy el equipo juega en el campo de béisbol...

Elena: Señor Morales, ¿qué hacen los maestros después de las clases?

Sr. Morales: Jugamos en la cancha de básquetbol. Tenemos un partido a las cinco.

Rogelio: Tomás, ¿a qué juegas?

Tomás: Soy jugador de fútbol americano... Juego todas las tardes en el campo de la escuela.

Atleta profesional: Soy atleta profesional. Tengo mi raqueta de tenis y pelotas... Juego en la cancha cerca de mi casa.

19 | Integración TXT CD 6 tracks 8, 9

Antonio: Buenas tardes. Aquí estamos en el Centro de Deportes Solimar. Soy Antonio y les presento a mi compañera, Rosa.

Rosa: Gracias, Antonio. Hoy juegan dos equipos muy buenos: Los Cometas y Los Pumas.

Antonio: Es cierto. Conozco a Los Cometas. Los jugadores siempre vienen a la cancha muy tranquilos porque saben practicar muy bien antes del partido. Practican todos los días y son muy serios.

Rosa: Hmmm... tienes razón. Los Pumas saben jugar pero no saben practicar bien antes de los partidos. No practican, no comen bien y no duermen. Ya están cansados antes de empezar a jugar.

Antonio: Bueno, ahora los dos equipos están en la cancha...

Repaso de la lección TXT CD 6 track 11

1 Listen and understand

Tina: Hola, señor Martínez. Usted es jugador de fútbol americano. ¿Practica otros deportes?

Sergio: Sí, juego al básquetbol y al tenis con mis amigos.

Tina: El fútbol americano es peligroso, ¿no?

Sergio: Sí, es un poco peligroso, pero también es divertido.

Tina: ¿Conoce usted a muchos de sus aficionados?

Sergio: No, no conozco a muchos, pero son todos muy simpáticos.

Tina: ¿Le gusta hacer otras actividades?

Sergio: Sí, yo nado mucho. También sé dibujar muy bien.

Tina: ¿Ah, sí? Usted es un atleta muy interesante.

Sergio: Gracias, señorita.

Resource List

Everything you need to ...

Plan

TEACHER ONE STOP

- ✓Lesson Plans
- ✓Teacher Resources
- ✓Audio and Video

Present

INTERACTIVE WHITEBOARD LESSONS

TEACHER ONE STOP WITH PROJECTABLE TRANSPARENCIES

POWER PRESENTATIONS

ANIMATEDGRAMMAR

Assess

ONLINE ASSESSMENT

- ✓ Assessments for on-level, modified, pre-AP, and heritage learners
- ✓ Create customized tests with **Examview Assessment Suite**
- ✓ **performance space**
- ✓ *Generate Success* Rubric Generator

Print

Plan	Present	Practice	Assess
URB 6 • Video Scripts pp. 69–70 • Family Letter p. 91 • Absent Student Copymasters pp. 93–100 **Best Practices Toolkit**	**URB 6** • Video Activities pp. 51–58	• *Cuaderno* pp. 246–268 • *Cuaderno para hispanohablantes* pp. 246–268 • *Lecturas para todos* pp. 52–56 • *Lecturas para hispanohablantes* • *¡AvanzaCómics! SuperBruno y Nati,* Episodio 3 **URB 6** • Practice Games pp. 31–38 • Audio Scripts pp. 73–77 • Map/Culture Activities pp. 83–84 • Fine Art Activities pp. 86–87	**Differentiated Assessment Program** **URB 6** • Did you get it? Reteaching and Practice Copymasters pp. 1–12

Projectable Transparencies (Teacher One Stop, my.hrw.com)

Culture	Presentation and Practice	Classroom Management
• Atlas Maps 1–6 • Map of Dominican Republic 1 • Fine Art Transparencies 2, 3	• Vocabulary Transparencies 6, 7 • Grammar Presentation Transparencies 10, 11	• Warm Up Transparencies 16–19 • Student Book Answer Transparencies 24–27

Audio and Video

Audio	Video	¡AvanzaRap! DVD
• Student Book Audio CD 6 Tracks 1–11 • Workbook Audio CD 3 Tracks 21–30 • Heritage Learner Audio CD 2 Tracks 9–12, CD 4 Tracks 7–8 • Assessment Audio CD 2 Tracks 7–8 • *Lecturas para todos* Audio CD 1 Track 11, CD 2 Tracks 1–6 • Sing-along Songs Audio CD	• Vocabulary Video DVD 2 • *Telehistoria* DVD 2 Escena 1 Escena 2 Escena 3 Completa	• Video animations of all **¡AvanzaRap!** songs (with Karaoke track) • Interactive DVD Activities • Teaching Suggestions • **¡AvanzaRap!** Activity Masters • **¡AvanzaRap!** video scripts and answers

Online and Media Resources

Student	Teacher
Available online at my.hrw.com • Online Student Edition • News + Networking • performance space • @HOMETUTOR • CULTURA Interactiva • WebQuests • Interactive Flashcards • Review Games • Self-Check Quiz **Student One Stop** **Holt McDougal Spanish Apps**	**Teacher One Stop (also available at my.hrw.com)** • Interactive Teacher's Edition • All print, audio, and video resources • Projectable Transparencies • Lesson Plans • TPRS • Examview Assessment Suite **Available online at my.hrw.com** *Generate Success* Rubric Generator and Graphic Organizers **Power Presentations**

Differentiated Assessment

On-level	Modified	Pre-AP	Heritage Learners
• Vocabulary Recognition Quiz p. 256 • Vocabulary Production Quiz p. 257 • Grammar Quizzes pp. 258–259 • Culture Quiz p. 260 • On-level Lesson Test pp. 261–267	• Modified Lesson Test pp. 206–212	• Pre-AP Lesson Test pp. 206–212	• Heritage Learners Lesson Test pp. 212–218

Core Pacing Guide

50 Minute (9 Day)

	Objectives/Focus	Teach	Practice	Assess/HW Options
DAY 1	**Culture:** learn about the Dominican Republic **Vocabulary:** sports and sports equipment • Warm Up OHT 16 **5 min**	Unit Opener pp. 298–299 Lesson Opener pp. 300–301 **Presentación de vocabulario** pp. 302–303 • Read A–D • Play Audio TXT CD 6 track 1 View video DVD 2 • *¡A responder!* TXT CD 6 track 2 **25 min**	Lesson Opener pp. 300–301 **Práctica de vocabulario** p. 304 • Acts. 1, 2 **15 min**	**Assess:** *Para y piensa* p. 304 **5 min** **Homework:** *Cuaderno* pp. 246–248 @HomeTutor
DAY 2	**Communication:** sports and sports equipment • Warm Up OHT 16 • Check Homework **5 min**	**Vocabulario en contexto** pp. 305–306 • *Telehistoria escena 1* DVD 2 **20 min**	**Vocabulario en contexto** pp. 305–306 • Act. 3 TXT CD 6 track 3 • Act. 4 **20 min**	**Assess:** *Para y piensa* p. 306 **5 min** **Homework:** *Cuaderno* pp. 246–248 @HomeTutor
DAY 3	**Grammar:** the verb **jugar** • Warm Up OHT 17 • Check Homework **5 min**	**Presentación de gramática** p. 307 • the verb **jugar** **20 min**	**Práctica de gramática** pp. 308–309 • Acts. 5, 7, 8, 9 • Act. 6 TXT CD 6 track 4 **20 min**	**Assess:** *Para y piensa* p. 309 **5 min** **Homework:** *Cuaderno* pp. 249–251 @HomeTutor
DAY 4	**Communication:** use the verb **jugar** to say what sports people play • Warm Up OHT 17 • Check Homework **5 min**	**Gramática en contexto** pp. 310–311 • *Telehistoria escena 2* DVD 2 • *Pronunciación* TXT CD 6 track 6 **15 min**	**Gramática en contexto** p. 310–311 • Act. 10 TXT CD 6 track 5 • Act. 11 **25 min**	**Assess:** *Para y piensa* p. 311 **5 min** **Homework:** *Cuaderno* pp. 249–251 @HomeTutor
DAY 5	**Grammar:** the verbs **saber** and **conocer** • Warm Up OHT 18 • Check Homework **5 min**	**Presentación de gramática** p. 312 • the verbs **saber** and **conocer** **Práctica de gramática** pp. 313–314 • *Nota gramatical:* the personal a **Culture:** *El arte representativo*	**Práctica de gramática** pp. 313–314 • Acts. 12, 13, 14, 15 **25 min**	**Assess:** *Para y piensa* p. 314 **5 min** **Homework:** *Cuaderno* pp. 252–254 @HomeTutor
DAY 6	**Communication:** Culmination: the verbs **jugar, saber** and **conocer** • Warm Up OHT 18 • Check Homework **5 min**	**Todo junto** pp. 315–317 • *Escenas 1, 2: Resumen* • *Telehistoria completa* DVD 2 **20 min**	**Todo junto** pp. 315–317 • Acts. 16, 17 TXT CD 6 tracks 3, 5, 7 • Acts. 18, 20 • Act. 19 TXT CD 6 tracks 8, 9 **20 min**	**Assess:** *Para y piensa* p. 317 **5 min** **Homework:** *Cuaderno* pp. 255–256 @HomeTutor
DAY 7	**Reading:** A sports club **Connections:** Social Sciences • Warm Up OHT 19 • Check Homework **5 min**	**Lectura** pp. 318–319 • *Un club de deportes* TXT CD 6 track 10 **Conexiones** p. 320 • *Las ciencias sociales* **15 min**	**Lectura** pp. 318–319 • *Un club de deportes* **Conexiones** p. 320 • *Proyectos* 1, 2, 3 **25 min**	**Assess:** *Para y piensa* p. 319 **5 min** **Homework:** *Cuaderno* pp. 260–262 @HomeTutor
DAY 8	**Review:** Lesson Review • Warm Up OHT 19 **5 min**	**Repaso de la lección** pp. 322–323 **15 min**	**Repaso de la lección** pp. 322–323 • Act. 1 TXT CD 6 track 11 • Acts. 2, 3, 4, 5 **25 min**	**Assess: Repaso de la lección** pp. 322–323 **5 min** **Homework:** *En resumen* p. 321; *Cuaderno* pp. 257–259, 263–268 (optional) Review Games Online @HomeTutor
DAY 9	Assessment			**Assess:** Lesson 1 test **50 min**

Day	Objectives/Focus	Teach	Practice	Assess/HW Options
DAY 1	**Culture:** learn about the Dominican Republic **Vocabulary:** sports and sports equipment • Warm Up OHT 16 **5 min**	Unit Opener pp. 298–299 Lesson Opener pp. 300–301 **Presentación de vocabulario** pp. 302–303 • Read A–D • Play Audio TXT CD 6 track 1 View video DVD 2 • *¡A responder!* TXT CD 6 track 2 **20 min**	Lesson Opener pp. 300–301 **Práctica de vocabulario** p. 304 • Acts. 1, 2 **20 min**	**Assess:** *Para y piensa* p. 304 **5 min**
	Communication: sports and sports equipment **5 min**	**Vocabulario en contexto** pp. 305–306 • *Telehistoria escena 1* DVD 2 **15 min**	**Vocabulario en contexto** pp. 305–306 • Act. 3 TXT CD 6 track 3 • Act. 4 **15 min**	**Assess:** *Para y piensa* p. 306 **5 min** **Homework:** *Cuaderno* pp. 246–248 @HomeTutor
DAY 2	**Grammar:** the verb **jugar** • Warm Up OHT 17 • Check Homework **5 min**	**Presentación de gramática** p. 307 • the verb **jugar** **20 min**	**Práctica de gramática** pp. 308–309 • Acts. 5, 7, 8, 9 • Act. 6 TXT CD 6 track 4 **15 min**	**Assess:** *Para y piensa* p. 309 **5 min**
	Communication: use the verb **jugar** to say what sports people play **5 min**	**Gramática en contexto** pp. 310–311 • *Telehistoria escena 2* DVD 2 • *Pronunciación* TXT CD 6 track 6 **20 min**	**Gramática en contexto** pp. 310–311 • Act. 10 TXT CD 6 track 5 • Act. 11 **15 min**	**Assess:** *Para y piensa* p. 311 **5 min** **Homework:** *Cuaderno* pp. 249–251 @HomeTutor
DAY 3	**Grammar:** the verbs **saber** and **conocer** • Warm Up OHT 18 • Check Homework **5 min**	**Presentación de gramática** p. 312 • the verbs **saber** and **conocer** **Práctica de gramática** pp. 313–314 • *Nota gramatical:* the personal **a** **Culture:** *El arte representativo* **15 min**	**Práctica de gramática** pp. 313–314 • Acts. 12, 13, 14, 15 **20 min**	**Assess:** *Para y piensa* p. 314 **5 min**
	Communication: Culmination: the verbs **jugar, saber** and **conocer** **5 min**	**Todo junto** pp. 315–317 • *Escenas 1, 2: Resumen* • *Telehistoria completa* DVD 2 **15 min**	**Todo junto** pp. 315–317 • Acts. 16, 17 TXT CD 6 tracks 3, 5, 7 • Acts. 18, 20 • Act. 19 TXT CD 6 tracks 8, 9 **20 min**	**Assess:** *Para y piensa* p. 317 **5 min** **Homework:** *Cuaderno* pp. 252–256 @HomeTutor
DAY 4	**Reading:** A sports club • Warm Up OHT 19 • Check Homework **5 min**	**Lectura** pp. 318–319 • *Un club de deportes* TXT CD 6 track 10 **15 min**	**Lectura** pp. 318–319 • *Un club de deportes* **15 min**	**Assess:** *Para y piensa* p. 319 **5 min**
	Review: Lesson review **5 min**	**Repaso de la lección** pp. 322–323 **15 min**	**Repaso de la lección** pp. 322–323 • Act. 1 TXT CD 6 track 11 • Acts. 2, 3, 4, 5 **25 min**	**Assess: Repaso de la lección** pp. 322–323 **5 min** **Homework:** *En resumen* p. 321; *Cuaderno* pp. 257–268 (optional) Review Games Online @HomeTutor
DAY 5	**Assessment**			**Assess:** Lesson 1 Test **45 min**
	Connections: Social Sciences **5 min**	**Conexiones** p. 320 • *Las ciencias sociales* **10 min**	**Conexiones** p. 320 • *Proyectos 1, 2, 3* **30 min**	

¡AVANZA! Objectives

- Introduce lesson theme: **¿Cuál es tu deporte favorito?**
- **Culture:** Compare students' favorite sports with sports played in other parts of the world.

Presentation Strategies

- Introduce characters' names: Mario and Isabel.
- Ask students to make a list of their favorite sports. Have students talk about where they go to watch these sports and with whom.
- Ask students to write down a list of their favorite activities. Then as a group discuss them with the class.

STANDARDS

4.2 Compare cultures

21st Century **Social and Cross-Cultural Skills,** Comparación cultural

Warm Up Projectable Transparencies, 6-16

Tú commands Complete the following sentences.

1.	¡ _____ la aspiradora, Mariana!	**a.** Pon
2.	¡ _____ la mesa, Enrique!	**b.** Barre
3.	¡ _____ la cama, Pablo!	**c.** Corta
4.	¡ _____ el césped, Alicia!	**d.** Pasa
5.	¡ _____ el suelo, Manuel!	**e.** Haz

Answers: 1. d; 2. a; 3. e; 4. c; 5. b

Comparación cultural

Exploring the Theme

Ask the following:

1. Are certain sports particularly popular in your community?
2. In what season are different sports played in your community?
3. Do you prefer individual or team sports? Why?

¿Qué ves? Possible answers include:

- Sí, practican el béisbol.
- Son atléticas.
- Siete personas llevan camisetas rojas.

UNIDAD 6 República Dominicana

Lección 1

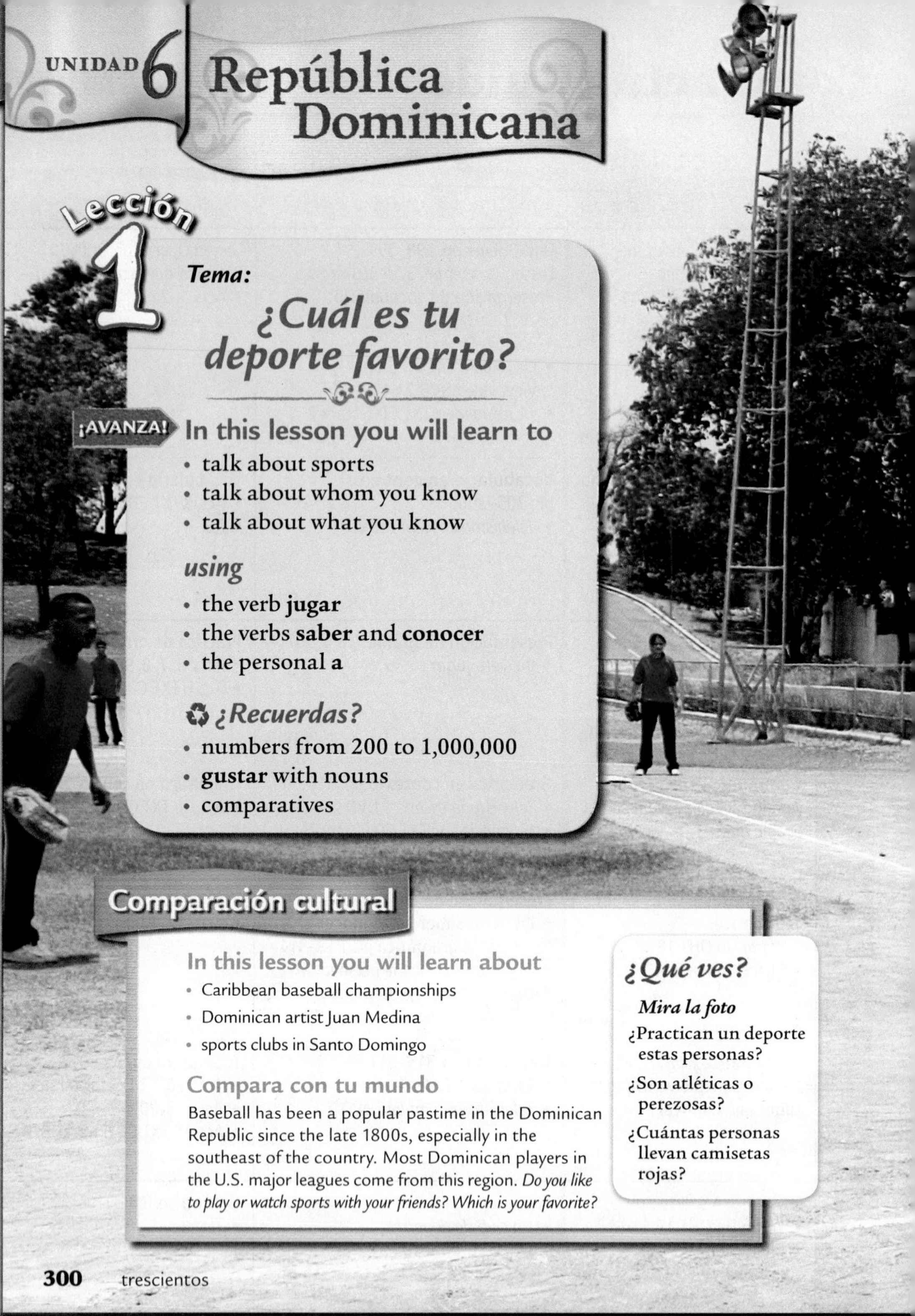

Tema:

¿Cuál es tu deporte favorito?

¡AVANZA! In this lesson you will learn to

- talk about sports
- talk about whom you know
- talk about what you know

using

- the verb **jugar**
- the verbs **saber** and **conocer**
- the personal **a**

¿Recuerdas?

- numbers from 200 to 1,000,000
- **gustar** with nouns
- comparatives

Comparación cultural

In this lesson you will learn about

- Caribbean baseball championships
- Dominican artist Juan Medina
- sports clubs in Santo Domingo

Compara con tu mundo

Baseball has been a popular pastime in the Dominican Republic since the late 1800s, especially in the southeast of the country. Most Dominican players in the U.S. major leagues come from this region. *Do you like to play or watch sports with your friends? Which is your favorite?*

¿Qué ves?

Mira la foto

¿Practican un deporte estas personas?

¿Son atléticas o perezosas?

¿Cuántas personas llevan camisetas rojas?

Differentiating Instruction

Heritage Language Learners

Support What They Know Ask students which sports are most popular in their country of origin. Group students with the same sport together. Then have them explain the rules for that sport. Is it an individual or team sport? What kind of equipment is needed? How does play begin? How does one player or team win?

English Learners

Build Background Ask students to share information about sports in their country of origin. Which sports are the most popular? How are these sports played? Are they similar to or different from popular sports in the United States? Who are some of the biggest sports stars or favorite sports teams?

DIGITAL SPANISH my.hrw.com
ONLINE STUDENT EDITION with...

- performance space
- News + Networking
- @HOMETUTOR
- CULTURA Interactiva

- Audio and Video Resources
- Interactive Flashcards
- Review Activities
- WebQuest
- Conjuguemos.com

PRACTICE SPANISH WITH HOLT MCDOUGAL APPS!

Un partido en la escuela
Santo Domingo, República Dominicana

DIGITAL SPANISH

TEACHER TOOLS
- Interactive Whiteboard Lessons
- Generate Success!

ALSO AVAILABLE...
- Online Workbook
- Spanish InterActive Reader

SPANISH ON THE GO!
- Performance Space
- Holt McDougal Spanish Apps
- ¡Avancemos! eTextbook

Using the Photo

Expanded Information

Baseball Season In the Dominican Republic, the regular baseball season opens at the end of October and runs through the first week of February. In February, the winner of the Winter Professional Baseball Championship represents the country in the Caribbean Series. The series is also referred to as the Caribbean World Series. It is hosted by a different country each year and usually involves 12 games. It is very popular with fans, who dance, cheer, and wave flags to support their teams.

Location Information

National Sport The national sport and passion of the Dominican Republic is baseball. No matter where you go on the island you will find a baseball stadium or park, even in the smallest communities. Today more than one in six players in the American league is from Latin America, the majority of them coming from the towns located on the southeastern coast of the Dominican Republic.

Differentiating Instruction

Inclusion

Cumulative Instruction On the board, create a concept web around the word **deportes.** Then have students brainstorm words and phrases they already know that can be applied to the theme of sports. They might think of places, such as **gimnasio** and **escuela,** adjectives, such as **atlético(a),** or expressions of frequency, such as **todos los días.**

Slower-paced Learners

Yes/No Questions Tell students they are going to draft two questions about the photo on pp. 300 and 301. The answer to one question should be *yes,* and the answer to the other should be *no.* Advise students to begin their questions with **¿Ves...?** or **¿Hay...?** For example, **¿Ves unos chicos? ¿Hay un autobús?** Give students the opportunity to read their questions aloud to the group.

Long-term Retention

Recycle

Ask students **¿Qué llevan los chicos?** to see how many items of clothing they can identify.

¡AVANZA! Objectives

- Present vocabulary: sports, places where sports are played, sports equipment.
- Identify regional variations of sports vocabulary.

Core Resources

- Video Program: DVD 2
- Audio Program: TXT CD 6 tracks 1, 2

Presentation Strategies

- Point to the items on pp. 302–303, say the words and have students repeat after you.
- Play the audio as students read A–D.
- Play the video.

STANDARDS

1.2 Understand language

21st Century **Communication,** Pre-AP

Communication — TPR Activity

Read the following statements aloud. Ask students to raise their hand if the statement is true.

1. **Mario es atleta.** (T)
2. **Mario lleva un casco.** (T)
3. **Mario no tiene un guante.** (F)
4. **Los aficionados están emocionados.** (T)
5. **Hay chicos y chicas en el equipo de béisbol.** (T)
6. **El equipo azul acaba de ganar el partido.** (F)

Communication — Regionalisms

In this lesson students learn that **aficionado(a)** is the Spanish equivalent for *fan*. Point out that in the Dominican Republic the preferred term is **fanático(a): Soy una fanática del béisbol.**

Presentación de VOCABULARIO

¡AVANZA! **Goal:** Learn what sports Mario and Isabel like to play. Then use what you have learned to talk about sports. ***Actividades 1–2***

¿Recuerdas? Numbers from 200 to 1,000,000 p. 165

VIDEO DVD

AUDIO

A ¡Hola! Me llamo Mario. Soy **atleta** y mi deporte **favorito** es **el béisbol.** Hoy tenemos **un partido** con **el equipo** rojo.

B Acabamos de **perder** el partido, cuatro a cinco. Mi amiga Isabel y su equipo son **los ganadores.** Tal vez debo practicar otro deporte.

Más vocabulario

el estadio *stadium*
patinar *to skate*
Expansión de vocabulario p. R7

En la República Dominicana se dice...
In the Dominican Republic the word for *baseball game* is **el juego de pelota.**

Differentiating Instruction

Inclusion

Alphabetic/Phonetic Awareness Help students differentiate between the English and Spanish pronunciations of sports names that may be cognates. Say the words **béisbol, fútbol, básquetbol, tenis,** and **voleibol** aloud, and have students repeat. Discuss with students the sounds that each letter is representing.

Multiple Intelligences

Logical/Mathematical Create two columns on the board: **jugadores** and **aficionados.** Then say the name of a sport aloud as you write it on the board. Ask students to raise their hands first, if they play the sport, and second, if they are fans. Record your findings in the appropriate column. Have students present the information in the form of a bar graph.

C Me gusta **nadar,** pero **la piscina** está lejos de mi casa. **El voleibol** es divertido, pero prefiero el béisbol.

D De vez en cuando voy al **campo** para jugar al **fútbol americano,** pero es difícil **comprender las reglas.** Me gusta **el básquetbol,** pero nunca **gano.** También voy a **la cancha** de **tenis,** pero siempre hay muchas personas allí. Puedo **patinar en línea,** pero es **peligroso.** ¡Es mejor jugar al béisbol!

@HOMETUTOR my.hrw.com Interactive Flashcards

¡A responder! Escuchar

Escucha la lista de palabras asociadas con los deportes. Si es una palabra que asocias con el béisbol, levanta la mano. *(Raise your hand if the word you hear is associated with baseball.)*

TEACHER to TEACHER

Janirah Figueroa
New York, New York

Tips for Presenting Vocabulary

I like to play a game called Matamoscas (Fly swatter) with my students to review the illustrated vocabulary words. I write the same Spanish vocabulary words at random on two separate boards. I then divide the class into two groups. As I say one word in Spanish, one member of each group uses the fly swatter to identify the word. The first student that touches the word with the fly swatter wins a point. The group with the most points is the winner.

Go online for more tips!

Communication

Common Error Alert

Point out that the singular masculine form of **campeones** is **campeón** and carries written accent on the last syllable.The singular form of **patines** also carries a written accent on the last syllable: **patín.**

Verbs Students Know

Students have learned the following sports-related verbs:

andar en patineta	**jugar al fútbol**
correr	**montar en bicicleta**

Ongoing Assessment

Dictation Dictate the vocabulary words on pp. 302 and 303 to students. When finished, ask volunteers to write the words on the board. The class should correct any spelling mistakes.

Differentiating Instruction

Inclusion

Multisensory Input/Output Have students follow this sequence of activities to help learn new vocabulary related to sports. Begin by writing a word or phrase on the board, such as **la natación.**

1. Read it and say it.
2. Write it and say it.
3. Act it out and say it.
4. Draw it and say it.

Pre-AP

Communicate Preferences Have students ask each other questions about the sports they prefer. **¿Te gusta más el fútbol americano o el tenis? ¿Prefieres el voleibol o el básquetbol?** Then have them explain their choices. Write the adjectives **divertido(a), interesante, difícil, fácil,** and **peligroso(a)** on the board for reference. **El fútbol americano es más peligroso que el tenis.**

Answers Projectable Transparencies, 6-24

¡A responder! Audio Script TE p. 299b

Students should raise their hand after hearing **el guante, la pelota, el bate, el casco,** and **el campo.**

Objectives
- Practice vocabulary: sports, places where sports are played, sports equipment.
- Recycle: numbers from 200 to 1,000,000.

Core Resource
- *Cuaderno,* pp. 246–248

Practice Sequence
- **Activity 1:** Vocabulary recognition: places where sports are played, sports equipment.
- **Activity 2:** Vocabulary production: sports equipment; Recycle: numbers from 200 to 1,000,000

STANDARDS
1.2 Understand language, Act. 1
1.3 Present information, Act. 2
21st Century **Communication,** Act. 2/Multiple Intelligences

✓ Ongoing Assessment
Get Help Online
More Practice
my.hrw.com

PARA Y PIENSA **Quick Check** Say aloud vocabulary words from pp. 302–303. Ask students to raise their hand if the word represents a sport that can be played: **el béisbol, el fútbol americano, la natación, la piscina, los patines, el tenis, la raqueta, el básquetbol.**
For additional practice, use Reteaching & Practice Copymasters URB 6 pp. 1, 2, 10.

Answers Projectable Transparencies, 6-24
Activity 1
1. Necesita una raqueta.
2. Necesita un bate.
3. Necesita unos patines en línea.
4. Necesita un casco.
5. Necesita una piscina.
6. Necesita una pelota.

Activity 2
1. Un guante cuesta tres mil doscientos pesos.
2. Tres pelotas de tenis cuestan ciento ochenta pesos.
3. Un casco cuesta dos mil seiscientos veinte pesos.
4. Una raqueta cuesta dos mil trescientos pesos.
5. Unos patines en línea cuestan cinco mil cuatrocientos setenta y cinco pesos.
6. Una pelota de básquetbol cuesta cuatrocientos treinta y cinco pesos.

Para y piensa **1.** una pelota, una cancha; **2.** una pelota, un bate, un casco, un guante, un campo; **3.** una pelota, una raqueta, una cancha

Práctica de VOCABULARIO

1 ¿Qué necesitan?

Leer

Isabel describe los artículos deportivos que sus amigos tienen y/o los deportes que quieren practicar. Identifica la cosa que necesita. *(For each situation, identify the sports-related item that Isabel's friend needs.)*

bate
casco
patines en línea
pelota
piscina
raqueta

1. Ya tiene una pelota y quiere jugar al tenis.
2. Ya tiene una pelota y un guante y quiere jugar al béisbol.
3. Tiene un casco y quiere patinar en línea.
4. Ya tiene una pelota y va a jugar al fútbol americano.
5. Quiere nadar.
6. Está en la cancha y quiere jugar al básquetbol.

Expansión:
Teacher Edition Only
Ask students to write two similar sentences to identify the following items: **guante** and **cancha.**

2 La tienda de deportes

¿Recuerdas? Numbers from 200 to 1,000,000 p. 165

Escribir
Hablar

La tienda Mundo de Deportes, en Santo Domingo, vende muchos artículos deportivos. Di cuánto cuestan estas cosas. *(Tell how much these items cost.)*

modelo: Un bate cuesta tres mil setecientos treinta pesos.

Expansión
Write four sentences comparing the cost of these items.

Más práctica Cuaderno *pp. 246–248* Cuaderno para hispanohablantes *pp. 246–249*

Get Help Online
my.hrw.com

PARA Y PIENSA **Did you get it?** Say what you would need to play the following sports.
1. el básquetbol **2.** el béisbol **3.** el tenis

Differentiating Instruction

Pre-AP
Circumlocution Before students begin Activity 1, have them preview the words in the box. Present students with the challenge of explaining each word without using the word itself or its English translation. For example: **Es como un gorro y lo necesitas para patinar. Tiene mucha agua y puede estar en un gimnasio.**

Multiple Intelligences
Visual Learners Give students the opportunity to create their own advertising posters for a sports store. Advise them to choose two or three items, and write two or three sentences about each item. Their sentences should communicate the price, as well as something about the quality of the item.

VOCABULARIO en contexto

¡AVANZA! **Goal:** Identify the words Isabel and Mario use to talk about sports. Then practice what you have learned to talk about sports. ***Actividades 3–4***

¿Recuerdas? **gustar** with nouns p. 145

Telehistoria escena 1

@HOMETUTOR my.hrw.com View, Read and Record

STRATEGIES

Cuando lees
Brainstorm before reading
Brainstorm English words for equipment used in baseball, swimming, in-line skating, tennis, football, and other sports. Which items on your list are in the Telehistoria?

Cuando escuchas
Listen for non-responses Some statements or questions don't receive responses. Listen for Mario's last questions to Isabel. Does she respond? Does Mario expect a response? Why or why not?

VIDEO DVD

AUDIO

Isabel is on first base, where Mario is playing.

Isabel: Hoy tu equipo va a perder el partido, Mario. Mi equipo siempre gana.

Mario: Sí, Isabel, eres muy buena jugadora de béisbol. Pero hoy nosotros vamos a ser los campeones.

Isabel: ¿Qué vas a hacer después de las clases? ¿Vamos al café?

Mario: Tengo que comprar un regalo. Es el cumpleaños de mi hermano.

Isabel: ¿Qué vas a comprar? Es un atleta. Le gusta el béisbol, ¿no?

Mario: Sí, pero tiene un bate y pelotas de béisbol.

Isabel: ¿Le gusta patinar en línea?

Mario: Sí, pero los patines en línea cuestan mucho dinero.

Isabel: ¿Le gusta el fútbol americano? ¿El tenis? La natación, ¿le gusta?

Mario: Sí, le gusta nadar pero, ¿qué puedo comprar? ¿Una piscina? ¿Agua?

Isabel's teammate hits a home run, and Mario's team loses.

Continuará... p. 310

También se dice

República Dominicana Mario uses the word **piscina** to joke about buying a swimming pool. In other Spanish-speaking countries you might hear:
- **México** la alberca
- **Argentina** la pileta

¡AVANZA! Objectives
- Understand and practice using the vocabulary in context.
- Recycle: using **gustar** with nouns.

Core Resources
- Video Program: DVD 2
- Audio Program: TXT CD 6 track 3

Presentation Strategies
- Have students look at the photo and ask brief comprehension questions such as **¿Dónde están Isabel y Mario? ¿Qué lleva Isabel? ¿Quién tiene el guante?**
- Have students scan the dialogue to find out how many sports are mentioned.
- Play the audio or video while students follow the script in their textbooks.

STANDARDS
1.2 Understand language

Warm Up
Projectable Transparencies, 6-16

Vocabulary Complete the sentences with the appropriate word or phrase.

la cancha la natación un guante una raqueta los campeones

1. Mi deporte favorito es _____.
2. La jugadora de béisbol tiene _____.
3. Isabel y su equipo son _____.
4. Voy a _____ para jugar al básquetbol.
5. Necesito _____ para practicar el tenis.

Answers: 1. la natación; 2. un guante; 3. los campeones; 4. la cancha; 5. una raqueta

Video Summary

@HOMETUTOR VideoPlus my.hrw.com

Isabel and Mario are chatting while at base. They are discussing which team will win. After the game, Mario has to buy a gift for his brother. They talk about various sports the brother likes, and what Mario could get him. At the end of the game, Mario's team loses.

Differentiating Instruction

Slower-paced Learners

Read Before Listening Before listening to the Telehistoria, have students preview the text silently. Instruct them to make a note each time they see a sentence using the construction **ir a...**, such as Isabel's first line, **Hoy tu equipo va a perder.** Review with students the purpose of this construction—to express future time.

Heritage Language Learners

Regional Variations Direct students to the También se dice box at the bottom of the page. Ask students to comment on the various ways to say *swimming pool.* Which of these expressions is the most familiar to them? Are there other variations for the names of sports or sports equipment in their country or region of origin?

Objectives
- Practice using the vocabulary in context.
- Recycle: using **gustar** with nouns.

Core Resource
- Audio Program: TXT CD 6 track 3

Practice Sequence
- **Activity 3:** Telehistoria comprehension
- **Activity 4:** Vocabulary production: sports; Recycle: **gustar** with nouns

STANDARDS
1.1 Engage in conversation, Act. 4. PYP
1.2 Understand language, Act. 3
21st Century **Communication,** Act. 4/Pre-AP

Communication
Common Error Alert
Remind students of the two Spanish verbs that mean *to play* in English. **Tocar** means to play an instrument, while **jugar** means to play a sport or a game.

Get Help Online
More Practice
my.hrw.com

Ongoing Assessment
PARA Y PIENSA **Quick Check** Ask students to name sports played on a field (**en un campo**) and those on a court (**en una cancha**). For additional practice, use Reteaching & Practice Copymasters URB 6 pp. 1, 3, 11.

Answers Projectable Transparencies, 6-24 and 6-25
Activity 3 **1.** ganar; **2.** los campeones; **3.** jugadora de béisbol; **4.** un regalo; **5.** un bate; **6.** patines en línea

Activity 4
1. ¿Te gusta el béisbol?
   Sí, me gusta (No, no me gusta) el béisbol.
2. ¿Te gusta patinar en línea?
   Sí, me gusta (No, no me gusta) patinar en línea.
3. ¿Te gusta la natación?
   Sí, me gusta (No, no me gusta) la natación.
4. ¿Te gusta el fútbol americano?
   Sí, me gusta (No, no me gusta) el fútbol americano.
5. ¿Te gusta el tenis?
   Sí, me gusta (No, no me gusta) el tenis.
6. ¿Te gusta el voleibol?
   Sí, me gusta (No, no me gusta) el voleibol.

Para y piensa **1.** la ganadora; **2.** la natación; **3.** un casco

3 *Comprensión del episodio* ¿Quién gana?
Escuchar Leer

Completa las oraciones con información del episodio. *(Complete the sentences.)*

un bate	los campeones	ganar
jugadora de béisbol	patines en línea	un regalo

1. Isabel piensa que su equipo va a ____ .
2. Mario piensa que él y su equipo van a ser ____ .
3. Isabel es una buena ____ .
4. Mario tiene que comprar ____ después de las clases.
5. El hermano de Mario no necesita ____ .
6. Mario no quiere comprar ____ porque cuestan mucho.

Expansión:
Teacher Edition Only
Have students complete the sentences using other words that make sense. Have them exchange their papers with a partner and correct each other's sentences.

4 ¿Te gustan los deportes?
¿Recuerdas? **gustar** with nouns p. 145

Hablar

Pregúntale a otro(a) estudiante si le gustan estos deportes. *(Ask a partner whether he or she likes the following sports.)*

A ¿Te gusta el fútbol?

B Sí, me gusta el fútbol. (No, no me gusta el fútbol.)

1. 
2. 
3. 
4. 
5. 
6. 

Expansión
Use a Venn diagram to compare your sports preferences with a partner's.

Get Help Online
my.hrw.com

PARA Y PIENSA

Did you get it? Complete each sentence with the appropriate vocabulary word.
1. Cuando Isabel gana un partido, ella es ____ .
2. Al hermano de Mario le gusta nadar; su deporte favorito es ____ .
3. Mario lleva ____ porque el béisbol puede ser peligroso.

Differentiating Instruction

Slower-paced Learners
Sentence Completion Have students try this strategy to complete Activity 3. Have a volunteer read the first sentence aloud six times, each time trying out a different word or phrase in the blank. When the sentence makes sense, have the group give the sentence a thumbs-up. Repeat with the remaining sentences. Have a different student read the sentence each time in order to practice pronunciation as well.

Pre-AP
Expand and Elaborate As students do Activity 4, encourage **Estudiante A** to say a follow-up question for **Estudiante B** to answer. Here is an example based on the model.

A. ¿Te gusta el fútbol?
B. Sí, me gusta el fútbol.
A. ¿Juegas en un equipo?
B. Sí, mi equipo se llama *Los valientes*.

Presentación de GRAMÁTICA

¡AVANZA! **Goal:** Learn how to form the verb **jugar.** Then practice using **jugar** to talk about playing sports. ***Actividades 5–9***

¿Recuerdas? Comparatives p. 174

English Grammar Connection: There is more than one way to say the English verb *to play* in Spanish. Use **jugar** when you mean playing a sport or a game; use **tocar** when you mean playing a musical instrument or a CD.

The Verb jugar

ANIMATEDGRAMMAR my.hrw.com

Use **jugar** to talk about playing a sport or a game. How do you form the present tense of this verb?

Here's how:

Jugar is a stem-changing verb in which the **u** changes to **ue** in all forms except **nosotros(as)** and **vosotros(as).**

jugar *to play*	
juego	**jugamos**
juegas	**jugáis**
juega	**juegan**

When you use **jugar** with the name of a sport, use **jugar a** + **sport.**

Mi primo **juega al fútbol.**
*My cousin **plays soccer.***

Jugamos al fútbol americano.
We play football.

Juegan al béisbol en la República Dominicana.
***They play baseball** in the Dominican Republic.*

Más práctica
Cuaderno *pp. 249–251*
Cuaderno para hispanohablantes *pp. 250–252*

@HOMETUTOR my.hrw.com
Leveled Practice
Conjuguemos.com

¡AVANZA! Objective
- Present the verb **jugar.**

Core Resource
- *Cuaderno,* pp. 249–251

Presentation Strategies
- Write the forms of **jugar** on the board and underline stem changes with a different color.
- Check understanding by asking one student to say a pronoun and another student to give the corresponding verb form.
- Write examples of **jugar a** + sport. Remind students that when **a** is followed by **el**, the two words combine to form **al**. **Juego al tenis.**

STANDARDS
4.1 Compare languages

Warm Up
Projectable Transparencies, 6-17

Vocabulary Complete the sentences with the letter of the appropriate word or phrase.
a. Los campeones **b.** nadar **c.** una cancha **d.** peligroso **e.** Las reglas

1. A mí, me gusta _____ en la piscina.
2. Patinar en línea puede ser _____.
3. _____ a veces son difíciles.
4. _____ ganan el partido.
5. Practicamos el básquetbol en _____.

Answers: 1. b; 2. d; 3. e; 4. a; 5. c

Communication
Common Error Alert
The Spanish equivalent of *to play a sport* follows the construction **jugar** + **a** + definite article + sport. Remind students that any masculine sport used in this construction (**el béisbol, el fúbol americano, el baloncesto**) will need to employ the construction **al** (**a** + **el**). Example: **Yo no juego al tenis, pero yo juego al básquetbol.**

Differentiating Instruction

Multiple Intelligences
Kinesthetic Write the words **jugar** and **tocar** on opposite sides of the board. Then invite a volunteer to the front to act out an activity related to one of these verbs, such as playing the guitar or playing soccer. Instruct the whole group to point to the appropriate verb. Then have the group come up with a sentence describing the activity. **Mariela toca la guitarra.**

Inclusion
Clear Structure Have students write sentences in a logical order to state what sports different people play and where they practice that sport. Write the following sentence structure on the board as a model: Subject + **jugar** + sport + place. Invite students to write sentences with **jugar** using different subjects and places. For example: **Nosotros jugamos al béisbol en el campo.**

Objectives
- Practice using **jugar** and lesson vocabulary.
- **Culture:** Find out how professional athletes support their home countries.
- Recycle: Comparatives

Core Resources
- *Cuaderno,* pp. 249–251
- Audio Program: TXT CD 6 track 4

Practice Sequence
- **Activity 5:** Controlled practice: **jugar**
- **Activity 6:** Transitional practice: **jugar**, sports vocabulary
- **Activity 7:** Open-ended practice: **jugar**, sports
- **Activity 8:** Transitional practice: **jugar**, places to play sports
- **Activity 9:** Open-ended practice: **jugar**, sports; Recycle: comparatives

STANDARDS
1.1 Engage in conversation, Acts. 7–9
1.2 Understand language, Act. 6
1.3 Present information, Acts. 7–9
2.1 Practices and perspectives, Act.7
4.2 Compare cultures, Act.7
21st Century **Communication,** Acts. 7, 8, 9/ Slower-paced Learners

Comparación cultural

Essential Question
Suggested Answer Many famous baseball players play on their country's national team in competitions. They also make donations to provide educational and work opportunities for young people.

Background Information
Professional baseball in the Dominican Republic has evolved dramatically in its 100-year history. Originally there were two professional teams in the entire country; today the league consists of five teams. **Santo Domingo: Tigres del Licey** and **Leones del Escogido; San Pedro de Macorís: Estrellas Orientales; Santiago: Águilas del Cibao** and **La Romana: Azucareros del Este.**

See Activity answers on p. 309.

Práctica de GRAMÁTICA

5 Una familia activa

Leer / Escribir

La familia de Mario es muy atlética. Completa su descripción con formas de **jugar** y luego contesta la pregunta. *(Complete Mario's description of his family with forms of **jugar**. Then answer his question.)*

Mi familia practica muchos deportes. Yo __1.__ al béisbol en un equipo. Mi hermano __2.__ también. Él y mi hermana __3.__ al voleibol los sábados. Mis padres __4.__ mucho al tenis. Ellos __5.__ casi todos los días. Nosotros no __6.__ al fútbol americano, pero lo miramos en la televisión. ¿Y tú? ¿A qué deportes __7.__ ?

Expansión
List your family members and tell what sports they play or like to watch.

6 ¿A qué juegan?

Escuchar / Escribir

Estos atletas hablan de los lugares donde juegan. Escucha las descripciones y escribe a qué juegan estas personas. *(Listen to the descriptions and write what sports these people play.)*

1. Elena	**3.** el equipo	**5.** Tomás
2. Rogelio y José	**4.** los maestros	**6.** la atleta

Audio Program
TXT CD 6 Track 4
Audio Script, TE p. 299b

7 ¿Para qué equipo?

Hablar

Comparación cultural

La Serie del Caribe
How do professional athletes support their home countries? Every February, Winter League championship teams from four countries compete in baseball's *Serie del Caribe,* or Caribbean Series. Many major league ballplayers have taken part in the Winter Leagues. Miguel Tejada and David Ortiz have represented the **Dominican Republic.** Other players include Johan Santana and Miguel Cabrera for **Venezuela,** Oliver Pérez and Vinny Castilla for **Mexico,** and Carlos Beltrán and Iván Rodríguez for **Puerto Rico.**

Miguel Tejada juega para el equipo de la República Dominicana durante la Serie del Caribe.

Compara con tu mundo ***How does the Serie del Caribe compare to other sports championships you are familiar with?***

Pregúntale a otro(a) estudiante para qué equipo juegan los jugadores de las Ligas de Invierno. *(Ask what team each player plays for.)*

A ¿Para qué equipo juega Oliver Pérez?

B Pérez juega para el equipo de México.

Differentiating Instruction

Slower-paced Learners
Personalize It Have students write on separate index cards the names of favorite sports or activities. They will use the cards to interview a partner on how often he/she engages in this activity. Students should record their partner's answers on the back of the card. For example: **¿Juegas al voleibol? Sí, juego al voleibol todos los días.** Follow up by asking the class what other students like to do.

Heritage Language Learners
Literacy Skills Invite students to talk about a favorite sports figure from their country of origin. Students create a list of five or six important facts such as birth date, hometown, current team and position, etc. Students record the information they find for each question on a separate index card. Give students the opportunity to present what they know to the group.

8 ¿Dónde juegas?

Hablar Mira las fotos de estos deportes. Pregúntale a otro(a) estudiante dónde los juega. *(Ask a partner where he or she plays these sports.)*

Expansión
Quiz a partner on sports that famous athletes play.

9 ¿A qué juegas mejor?

¿Recuerdas? Comparatives p. 174

Hablar Habla con otro(a) estudiante sobre a qué juegas mejor. *(Tell what sports you play better than others.)*

Expansión:
Teacher Edition Only
Ask students to write their answers in their notebooks, then have them compare answers as a group to check spelling.

Más práctica Cuaderno *pp. 249–251* Cuaderno para hispanohablantes *pp. 250–252*

Get Help Online
my.hrw.com

PARA Y PIENSA

Did you get it? Create sentences that tell the sports each of the following people play, using **jugar.**

1. Ana y yo / el béisbol
2. ustedes / el básquetbol
3. el hermano de Rosa / el voleibol
4. yo / el tenis

Differentiating Instruction

Pre-AP

Vary Vocabulary Provide students with additional verbs that may be used when talking about playing sports. Some examples might include **golpear, recibir, tirar,** and **correr.** Have students create a chart outlining the present-tense forms of each verb. Encourage students to incorporate these verbs into Activity 9 where possible.

Inclusion

Multisensory Input/Output Collect real examples of the balls shown in Activity 9. Then ask a volunteer **¿Juegas mejor al béisbol o al fútbol?** When the student responds **Juego mejor al fútbol,** toss him or her the appropriate ball. After the student catches the ball, he or she chooses another ball and poses a question to another student and the game continues.

✓ Ongoing Assessment

Get Help Online
More Practice
my.hrw.com

PARA Y PIENSA **Peer Assessment** Have students complete the Para y piensa sentences in writing. In pairs, have students correct each other's work. For additional practice, use Reteaching & Practice Copymasters URB 6 pp. 4, 5, 12.

Answers Projectable Transparencies, 6-25

Answers for Activities on pp. 308, 309.

Activity 5
1. juego; **2.** juega; **3.** juegan; **4.** juegan; **5.** juegan; **6.** jugamos; **7.** juegas

Activity 6
1. Elena juega al fútbol.
2. Rogelio y José juegan al voleibol.
3. El equipo juega al béisbol.
4. Los maestros juegan al básquetbol.
5. Tomás juega al fútbol americano.
6. La atleta juega al tenis.

Activity 7 Answers will vary. Sample answers include:
1. ¿Para qué equipo juegan Miguel Tejada y David Ortiz?
   Tejada y Ortiz juegan para el equipo de la República Dominicana.
2. ¿Para qué equipo juegan Johan Santana y Miguel Cabrera?
   Santana y Cabrera juegan para el equipo de Venezuela.
3. ¿Para qué equipo juega Vinny Castilla?
   Castilla juega para el equipo de México.
4. ¿Para qué equipo juegan Carlos Beltrán e Iván Rodríguez?
   Beltrán y Rodríguez juegan para el equipo de Puerto Rico.

Activity 8
1. ¿Dónde juegas al voleibol?
   Juego al voleibol en una cancha.
2. ¿Dónde juegas al fútbol americano?
   Juego al fútbol americano en un campo.
3. ¿Dónde juegas al fútbol?
   Juego al fútbol en un campo.
4. ¿Dónde juegas al béisbol?
   Juego al béisbol en un campo.
5. ¿Dónde juegas al tenis?
   Juego al tenis en una cancha.
6. ¿Dónde juegas al básquetbol?
   Juego al básquetbol en una cancha.

Activity 9 Answers will vary. Sample answers include:
A. ¿Juegas mejor al béisbol o al tenis?
B. Juego mejor al tenis. Me gusta más.

Para y piensa
1. Ana y yo jugamos al béisbol.
2. Ustedes juegan al básquetbol.
3. El hermano de Rosa juega al voleibol.
4. Yo juego al tenis.

¡AVANZA! Objectives

- Practice **jugar** and lesson vocabulary in context.
- **Pronunciation:** Practice pronunciation of the letter **g** before **a**, **o**, **u**.

Core Resources

- Video Program: DVD 2
- Audio Program: TXT CD 6 tracks 5, 6

Presentation Strategies

- Have students identify the sports equipment in the photo.
- Play the audio and have students follow it in their texts.
- Show the video

Practice Sequence

- **Activity 10:** Telehistoria comprehension: **jugar**, sports equipment
- **Activity 11:** Transitional practice: **jugar**, sports-related vocabulary

STANDARDS

1.1 Engage in conversation, Act. 11
1.2 Understand language, Act. 10, PYP
4.1 Compare languages, Pronunciación
21st Century **Flexibility and Adaptability,** Act. 11/Role-Playing and Skits

Warm Up Projectable Transparencies, 6-17

Jugar Complete the following sentences with the correct form of **jugar.**

1. Mamá y Papá _____ al tenis.
2. Álvaro _____ bien al voleibol.
3. Yo _____ al básquetbol.
4. Mercedes y yo _____ al fútbol por la tarde.
5. ¿A qué deportes _____ tú?

Answers: 1. juegan; 2. juega; 3. juego; 4. jugamos; 5. juegas

Video Summary

@HOMETUTOR VideoPlus my.hrw.com

In a sporting goods store, Isabel suggests several pieces of sports equipment for Mario's brother. Mario rejects Isabel's suggestions, but he doesn't know what to buy.

GRAMÁTICA en contexto

¡AVANZA! **Goal:** Pay attention to the forms of **jugar** that Isabel and Mario use to talk about sports and sports equipment. Then use **jugar** to say what sports people play. ***Actividades 10–11***

Telehistoria escena 2

@HOMETUTOR my.hrw.com View, Read and Record

STRATEGIES

Cuando lees
Make a mindmap for related words Write the name of a piece of sports equipment, such as **el casco,** in the center circle. In outside circles, write as many sports as possible that use that piece of equipment.

Cuando escuchas
Listen for stressed words When Mario and Isabel talk about possible gifts, listen for the way they stress or emphasize certain words to show their preferences.

VIDEO DVD
AUDIO

Isabel and Mario are in a sporting goods store, looking for a gift.

Isabel: Un guante de béisbol. Me gusta para tu hermano.

Mario takes the glove and puts it back on the shelf.

Isabel: Me gusta la raqueta.

He also takes the racket and puts it back. Isabel picks up a basketball.

Mario: No, una bola de básquetbol, no. Es un regalo para mi hermano; no es tu cumpleaños.

Isabel: ¿Necesita un casco?

Mario: No, pero necesito un casco para jugar al tenis.

Isabel: ¡Un partido de tenis no es peligroso!

Mario: Tú no juegas al tenis con mi hermano.

Isabel: *(laughing)* No, no juego al tenis. Pero me gusta el voleibol. ¿Tu hermano juega al voleibol?

Continuará... p. 315

También se dice

República Dominicana Mario uses the word **bola** to talk about the ball. In other Spanish-speaking countries you might hear:
- **muchos países** el balón

Differentiating Instruction

Multiple Intelligences

Kinesthetic Have students bring to class the sports equipment props that appear in the Telehistoria: a baseball glove, a helmet, a ball, rackets, and so on. Ask students to act out the Telehistoria scene, using the props and appropriate gestures. Encourage them to use humor in their presentation.

Slower-paced Learners

Personalize It Copy Isabel's first line on the board: **Un guante de béisbol. Me gusta para tu hermano.** Then erase the phrases **un guante de béisbol** and **tu hermano.** Now, ask students to imagine they are shopping for a present for a friend or family member. Have them use this structure to create their own sentences. **Una raqueta de tenis. Me gusta para mi hermana.**

10 Comprensión del episodio Buscan un regalo

Escuchar
Leer

Di si la oración es cierta o falsa. Si es falsa, escribe lo que es cierto. *(Tell whether it is true or false. Correct the false statements.)*

1. Isabel piensa que un guante de béisbol es un buen regalo.
2. Mario quiere comprar una pelota de básquetbol.
3. Es el cumpleaños de Isabel.
4. Mario necesita un bate para jugar al tenis con su hermano.
5. Es peligroso cuando Mario juega al tenis con su hermano.
6. Isabel juega al tenis.

Expansión:
Teacher Edition Only
Assign student pairs to write a false statement about the Telehistoria. Have them exchange papers and correct it.

11 Un atleta famoso

Hablar

Eres reportero(a) y tu amigo(a) es un(a) atleta famoso(a). Entrevista a otro(a) estudiante, usando estas preguntas. *(Interview a partner.)*

1. ¿A qué deporte juegas?
2. ¿Dónde juegas?
3. ¿Qué necesitas hacer para ser campeón (campeona) en tu deporte?
4. ¿Qué prefieres, ser jugador(a) o aficionado(a)? ¿Por qué?
5. ¿Quién es tu atleta favorito(a)? ¿A qué deporte juega?
6. ¿Qué te gusta hacer después de un partido? ¿Qué haces cuando pierdes?

Expansión
Use the answers to write an article.

AUDIO

Pronunciación La letra g con a, o, u

Before **a, o, u,** and consonants, the Spanish **g** is pronounced like the *g* in the English word *game*.

Listen and repeat.

ga	**go**	**gu**	**g** + consonant
ganar	**tengo**	**guante**	**reglas**

A Gregorio le gusta jugar al béisbol en agosto.

Get Help Online
my.hrw.com

PARA Y PIENSA

Did you get it? Complete each sentence based on the Telehistoria with the appropriate form of the verb **jugar.**

1. Isabel no _____ al tenis.
2. Cuando Mario y su hermano _____ al tenis, Mario necesita un casco.
3. A Isabel le gusta _____ al básquetbol.

Communication

Role-Playing and Skits

In pairs, have students practice Telehistoria escena 2 on p. 310. Later, regroup pairs and have students present dialogues with props in front of the class.

✓ Ongoing Assessment

Get Help Online
More Practice
my.hrw.com

PARA Y PIENSA

Intervention If students can't complete the sentences, refer them to p. 307 and ask them to do Activities 5 and 6 on p. 308 again. For additional practice, use Reteaching & Practice Copymasters URB 6, pp. 4, 6.

Differentiating Instruction

Heritage Language Learners

Writing Skills Have students combine their answers from Activity 11 to create a feature story for a sports magazine. Students may want to begin with a question to spark interest. **¿Quién es el jugador de béisbol más famoso del mundo?** Anticipate the reader's follow-up questions and provide that information.

Inclusion

Alphabetic/Phonetic Awareness Ask students to brainstorm as many words as they can containing the letter **g.** Some examples might include **grande, regalo, inglés, globo, jugo, yogur,** and **hamburguesa.** Next, add the words **gimnasio, gigante, general** and **gente** to the board. Read each aloud, and discuss with students the sound the letter **g** represents in these words.

Answers Projectable Transparencies, 6-25 and 6-26

Activity 10

1. Cierto.
2. Falso. Mario no quiere comprar una pelota de básquetbol.
3. Falso. Es el cumpleaños del hermano de Mario.
4. Falso. Mario necesita un casco para jugar al tenis.
5. Cierto.
6. Falso. Isabel no juega al tenis.

Activity 11 Answers will vary. Sample answers include:

1. Juego al béisbol.
2. Juego en una cancha.
3. Necesito practicar mucho.
4. Prefiero ser jugador. Me gusta correr mucho.
5. Mi atleta favorito es Manny Ramírez. Juega al béisbol.
6. Después de un partido, descanso. Cuando pierdo, practico más.

Para y piensa **1.** juega; **2.** juegan; **3.** jugar

¡AVANZA! **Objective**

- Present **saber** and **conocer**.

Core Resource

- *Cuaderno,* pp. 252–254

Presentation Strategies

- Write the conjugations of **saber** and **conocer** on the board. Circle the irregular **yo** forms **sé** and **conozco**.
- Explain that **saber** means to know facts, whereas **conocer** means to be acquainted with people or places. Provide examples.

STANDARDS

4.1 Compare languages

Warm Up Projectable Transparencies, 6-18

Vocabulary Complete each sentence with one of these words.

peligroso campeón guante pelota reglas

1. Necesito un _____ de béisbol.
2. No comprendo las _____ del juego.
3. No llevar casco es _____.
4. Voy a comprar una _____ de básquetbol.
5. Quiero ser un _____ de natación.

Answers: 1. guante; 2. reglas; 3. peligroso; 4. pelota; 5. campeón

Ongoing Assessment

Alternative Strategy Ask students questions using **saber, conocer** and vocabulary words. **¿Tú sabes jugar al básquetbol?** The student should answer: **Yo (no) sé jugar al básquetbol.** Ask: **¿Conocen ustedes a un equipo de béisbol?** Students could either answer individually or as a group: **Nosotros (no) conocemos a un equipo.** Create other questions using different forms of the verbs.

Presentación de GRAMÁTICA

¡AVANZA! **Goal:** Learn how to form **saber** and **conocer,** as well as use the personal **a.** Then use them to talk about whom and what you know. ***Actividades 12–15***

English Grammar Connection: There are two ways to say the English verb *to know* in Spanish: **saber** and **conocer.**

The Verbs saber and conocer

ANIMATEDGRAMMAR my.hrw.com

In Spanish, there are two verbs that mean *to know.* How do you form the present tense of **saber** and **conocer** and use them correctly?

Here's how: Both **saber** and **conocer** have irregular **yo** forms in the present tense.

saber *to know*	
sé	sabemos
sabes	sabéis
sabe	saben

conocer *to know*	
conozco	conocemos
conoces	conocéis
conoce	conocen

Use **saber** to talk about factual information you know.

Sé cuánto cuesta el bate.
I know *how much the bat costs.*

¿Sabes a qué hora empieza el partido?
Do you know *what time the game begins?*

You can also use **saber** + **infinitive** to say that you know how to do something.

Nicolás sabe **patinar** muy bien.
Nicolás ***knows*** *how to skate very well.*

Use **conocer** when you want to say that you are familiar with a person or place.

Conozco a tu hermano David.
I know *your brother David.*

Mi prima conoce Santo Domingo.
My cousin ***knows (is familiar with)*** *Santo Domingo.*

You also use **conocer** to talk about meeting someone for the first time.

Queremos conocer a los jugadores.
We want ***to meet*** *the players.*

Más práctica
Cuaderno *pp. 252–254*
Cuaderno para hispanohablantes *pp. 253–256*

@HOMETUTOR my.hrw.com
Leveled Practice
Conjuguemos.com

Differentiating Instruction

English Learners

Provide Comprehensible Input Review the verb *to know* and its various meanings with English learners. Have students brainstorm sentences using the verb *to know.* Record each sentence on a sentence strip. Organize the strips into two columns—one with sentences that correspond to the Spanish verb **saber,** and the other with sentences that correspond to the Spanish verb **conocer.**

Heritage Language Learners

Support What They Know Ask students to model the use of the verbs **saber** and **conocer.** Then present them with this challenge—tell a short story that uses the two verbs as many times as possible. The story could be on the theme of sports, for example. **¿Conoces a mi amiga Ana? Ella sabe jugar al tenis muy bien. Sus padres conocen a una campeona de tenis...**

Práctica de GRAMÁTICA

12 Un correo electrónico de Alicia

Leer

Alicia le escribe un correo electrónico a Mario. Escoge el verbo correcto entre paréntesis. *(Complete Alicia's e-mail to Mario by choosing the correct verb in parentheses.)*

Hola, Mario:

¿Qué tal? ¿ **1.** (Sabes / Conoces) tú que Trini Salgado acaba de ganar otro partido de fútbol? Ella **2.** (sabe / conoce) jugar muy bien. Es campeona. Ella **3.** (sabe / conoce) a muchos campeones de deportes también. Yo **4.** (sé / conozco) que ella va a ir a la capital de tu país. ¿La **5.** (sabes / conoces) tú? Yo no la **6.** (sé / conozco) todavía, pero es mi jugadora favorita y tú y yo **7.** (sabemos / conocemos) que la quiero **8.** (saber / conocer). Mario, yo no **9.** (sé / conozco) dónde está la camiseta. **10.** ¿(Saben/ Conocen) Isabel y tú dónde está la camiseta?

Tu amiga, Alicia

Expansión: Teacher Edition Only
Instruct students to respond to Alicia's e-mail.

Nota gramatical

When a specific person is the direct object of a sentence, use the personal **a** *after* the verb and *before* the person.

No conozco **a** Raúl.	Ayudo **a** la maestra.
I don't know Raúl.	*I am helping the teacher.*

13 ¿Qué saben? ¿Qué conocen?

Escribir

¿Qué saben y conocen estas personas? Escribe oraciones con **saber** o **conocer.** *(Write about what and whom these people know, using **saber** or **conocer.**)*

modelo: mi madre (cuándo empieza el partido)
Mi madre sabe cuándo empieza el partido.

1. las campeonas (nadar muy bien)
2. yo (un jugador de béisbol)
3. el equipo (el estadio de fútbol)
4. tú (dónde está la cancha)
5. mis amigos y yo (la República Dominicana)
6. los jugadores (Trini Salgado)
7. yo (qué equipo va a ganar)
8. Ana (cuánto cuesta el casco)
9. tú (las ganadoras)
10. nosotros (patinar en línea)
11. ustedes (quién es el campeón)

Expansión
Write three things you know how to do well and three things you don't.

Objectives

- Practice forms and uses of the verbs **saber** and **conocer**.
- Practice lesson vocabulary: sports.
- Practice the personal **a** after verbs like **conocer.**

Practice Sequence

- **Activity 12:** Controlled practice: uses of **saber** and **conocer**
- **Activity 13:** Controlled practice: forms and uses of **saber** and **conocer**, personal **a**

STANDARDS

1.3 Present information, Act. 12–13

21st Century **Communication,** Group Work

Nota gramatical

When using the verb **conocer** to speak about knowing a person, the personal **a** must be used. It is also often used when speaking about animals that are pets. Example: **Conozco a Carmen, pero no conozco a su papá Francisco. No conozco (a) su perro Beto.**

Communication
Group Work

Have pairs of students ask each other whether they know (are familiar with) certain people and locations in their community (for a place). Questions should begin with **¿Conoces...?** (for a place) or **¿Conoces a...?** (for a person or pet).

Answers Projectable Transparencies, 6-26

Activity 12 **1.** Sabes; **2.** sabe; **3.** conoce; **4.** sé; **5.** conoces; **6.** conozco; **7.** sabemos; **8.** conocer; **9.** sé; **10.** Saben

Activity 13
1. Las campeonas saben nadar muy bien.
2. Yo conozco a un jugador de béisbol.
3. El equipo conoce el estadio de fútbol.
4. Tú sabes dónde está la cancha.
5. Mis amigos y yo conocemos la República Dominicana.
6. Los jugadores conocen a Trini Salgado.
7. Yo sé qué equipo va a ganar.
8. Ana sabe cuánto cuesta el casco.
9. Tú conoces a las ganadoras.
10. Nosotros sabemos patinar en línea.
11. Ustedes saben quién es el campeón.

Differentiating Instruction

Inclusion

Synthetic/Analytic Support Instruct students to write the letter **a** on a blank self-sticking note. Direct their attention to the Nota gramatical. Write sentences on the board, omitting the personal **a** and leaving space between each word.

Yo conozco Isabel.
Nosotros invitamos Marco.

Invite volunteers to come place their **a** notes in the appropriate place in each sentence.

Pre-AP

Expand and Elaborate Provide students with the following model sentences to explain their choice of **conocer** or **saber** in Activity 13.

- **Uso el verbo *conocer* porque la oración habla de una persona.**
- **Uso el verbo *saber* porque la oración da información.**

Have students follow up each of their sentences with one of these explanations.

Objectives
- Practice forms and uses of **saber** and **conocer**.
- **Culture:** Discuss how an artist's work can reflect his or her own country.
- Practice sports-related vocabulary.

Core Resource
- *Cuaderno,* pp. 252–254

Practice Sequence
- **Activity 14:** Transitional practice: forms and uses of **saber** and **conocer**, sports-related vocabulary
- **Activity 15:** Open-ended practice: forms of **saber**

STANDARDS
1.1 Engage in conversation, Act. 14
1.3 Present information, Act. 15
3.1 Knowledge of other disciplines, CC
4.2 Compare cultures, CC
21st Century **Communication,** Acts. 14, 15; **Social and Cross-Cultural Skills,** Comparación cultural

Comparación cultural
Essential Question
Suggested Answer An artist reflects the people of his country by showing their clothing, homes, families, places of work, etc.

✓ Ongoing Assessment
Get Help Online
More Practice
my.hrw.com

PARA Y PIENSA **Peer Assessment** Ask students to complete the Para y piensa answers in writing. Then have students correct each other's work in pairs or small groups. For additional practice, use Reteaching & Practice Copymasters URB 6, pp. 7, 8.

See Activity answers on p. 315.

14 ¡A charlar!
Hablar

Trabaja en un grupo de tres. Habla de lo que sabes y conoces en el mundo de los deportes. *(Talk with a group of three about what and whom you know in sports.)*

A ¿Saben jugar al voleibol ustedes?
B Sí, sé jugar al voleibol. Juego los sábados con mis hermanos.
C No, no sé jugar al voleibol. No comprendo las reglas...

1. las reglas de...
2. un lugar donde juegan al...
3. unos aficionados de...
4. el (la) atleta...
5. un lugar donde... es muy popular
6. ¿ ?

Expansión
Ask your group three more questions about a topic other than sports. Use **saber** or **conocer.**

15 ¿Qué saben hacer tus amigos?
Escribir

Escribe un párrafo sobre tus amigos u otras personas y lo que ellos saben hacer. *(Write a paragraph about friends or other people you know and what they know how to do.)*

modelo: Mi amigo Sean sabe tocar la guitarra. Toca todos los días...

Expansión: Teacher Edition Only
Ask students to read their paragraphs aloud.

Comparación cultural
El arte representativo
How can artists represent the people of their country through their artwork? Juan Medina, an artist from the **Dominican Republic**, has experimented with different styles of art, combining traditional and modern techniques. Some of his paintings are inspired by his Dominican heritage, showing the history, people, and social and political issues of his country. *Vendedora de flores* shows a flower vendor. Vendors and their carts are found throughout Santo Domingo, selling everything from shaved ice to coffee to flowers to newspapers.

Vendedora de flores
(alrededor de 1990), Juan Medina

Compara con tu mundo *How would you represent a typical sight or activity in your community through artwork?*

Más práctica Cuaderno *pp. 252–254* Cuaderno para hispanohablantes *pp. 253–256*

Get Help Online
my.hrw.com

PARA Y PIENSA **Did you get it?** Complete each sentence with the correct form of **saber** or **conocer.** Use the personal **a** if necessary.
1. ¿ _____ ustedes jugar al voleibol?
2. Yo _____ María muy bien porque es mi amiga.
3. Nosotros _____ que el fútbol americano puede ser peligroso.

Differentiating Instruction

Inclusion
Clear Structure Remind students to follow the steps of the writing process in order to create their paragraphs in Activity 15. Have them record their thoughts using a graphic organizer, such as a concept web around the person's name. Then have them draft complete sentences, revise, and proofread before turning in their final drafts.

English Learners
Provide Comprehensible Input Ask English learners the following questions to help them interpret the meaning of the information presented in the Comparación cultural. When students learn the answer to one of the questions, record it on the board. **¿Quién?** *Who?;* **¿Qué?** *What?;* **¿Dónde?** *Where?;* **¿Cuándo?** *When?;* **¿Por qué?** *Why?*

Todo junto

¡AVANZA! **Goal:** ***Show what you know*** Notice how Mario and Isabel use **saber** and **conocer** to talk about people and things they know in the world of sports. Then use these verbs and **jugar** to talk about athletes and sports.
Actividades 16–20

Telehistoria completa

@HOMETUTOR my.hrw.com **View, Read and Record**

STRATEGIES

Cuando lees
Scan for the details Before reading carefully, scan the scene for these details: Who is Trini Salgado? What is she doing today? Who is a bigger fan of Trini: Alicia or Mario's brother?

Cuando escuchas
Go for the goals While listening, consider Mario's two goals in this scene. What are they? Does he fulfill both goals during the scene?

Escena 1 ***Resumen***
En un partido de béisbol, Mario habla con Isabel. Él tiene que comprar un regalo para el cumpleaños de su hermano.

Escena 2 ***Resumen***
Isabel y Mario buscan un regalo en una tienda de deportes. Mario no sabe qué va a comprar.

Escena 3

VIDEO DVD

AUDIO

Mario points to a soccer jersey.

Mario: ¡Es como la camiseta de Alicia! ¿Conoces a Trini Salgado? Ella está aquí, en Santo Domingo.

Isabel: Lo sé. ¿Alicia la conoce?

Mario: No, pero Trini es su jugadora de fútbol favorita. Alicia quiere un autógrafo en la camiseta. Y yo debo encontrar a Trini...

Vendedor: ¿Buscan a Trini Salgado? *(Mario and Isabel nod.)* ¿Saben dónde encontrar a Trini Salgado?

Mario and Isabel shake their heads, and the clerk turns up the radio.

«La jugadora de fútbol Trini Salgado va a estar en el estadio hoy a las seis de la tarde. Los primeros quinientos aficionados pueden conocer a Trini.»

Mario: ¡Vamos! *(He buys the jersey.)*

Isabel: ¿A tu hermano le gusta Trini Salgado?

Mario: No sé. ¡Pero sé que le gustan las camisetas con autógrafos de atletas importantes!

Differentiating Instruction

Multiple Intelligences

Kinesthetic Divide the class into groups of three. Have each group choose a portion of the Telehistoria and retell it in their own words, using gestures as necessary to communicate meaning.

Slower-paced Learners

Read Before Listening Have students take turns reading the Telehistoria script. As they read, point out the uses of **saber** and **conocer** in the story. Help students decode any words or structures that seem familiar to them. Have them make a list of words that present difficulties and ask them to keep it for later reference. After everyone has had a chance to read the script, play the audio or video.

¡AVANZA! **Objective**
- Integrate lesson content.

Core Resources
- Video Program: DVD 2
- Audio Program: TXT CD 6 track 7

Presentation Strategies
- Ask students what they remember about the Telehistoria so far.
- Ask students to describe the photos of Escena 3 **¿Dónde están los chicos? ¿Qué va a comprar Mario?**
- Show the video or play the audio.

STANDARDS
1.2 Understand language
21st Century **Communication,** Multiple Intelligences

Warm Up Projectable Transparencies, 6-18

Saber and conocer Complete the sentences with appropriate forms of **saber** or **conocer.**

1. El jugador _____ que necesita un casco.
2. Juan Carlos no _____ a mi amigo.
3. ¿ _____ tú Santo Domingo?

Answers: 1. sabe; 2. conoce; 3. Conoces

Video Summary

@HOMETUTOR VideoPlus my.hrw.com

While looking at a soccer jersey, Mario and Isabel talk about Trini Salgado. They want to find Trini to get her autograph on a jersey for Alicia. They learn that Trini will be at a stadium that afternoon. Mario buys the jersey and plans to have it autographed for his brother.

Answers Projectable Transparencies, 6-26

Answers for Activities on p. 314.

Activity 14 Answers will vary. Sample answers include:

1. ¿Conoces tú las reglas del fútbol americano? No, no las conozco todas.
2. ¿... juegan al voleibol? Sí, conozco una cancha.
3. ¿... de tenis? Sí, conozco a tres aficionados.
4. ¿... Tiger Woods? No, no lo conozco.
5. ¿... el béisbol es muy popular? No, no conozco un lugar donde...

Activity 15 Answers will vary. Sample answers include: Mi amiga María sabe jugar al tenis. Ella juega ocho horas al día.

Para y piensa **1.** Saben; **2.** conozco a; **3.** sabemos

Objective
- Practice using and integrating lesson vocabulary and grammar.

Core Resources
- *Cuaderno,* pp. 255–256
- Audio Program: TXT CD 6 tracks 3, 5, 7, 8, 9

Practice Sequence
- **Activities 16, 17:** Telehistoria comprehension
- **Activity 18:** Open-ended practice: writing, speaking
- **Activity 19:** Open-ended practice: listening, reading, speaking
- **Activity 20:** Open-ended practice: writing

STANDARDS
1.1 Engage in conversation, Acts. 18–19
1.2 Understand language, Acts. 16–17, Act. 19
1.3 Present information, Acts. 18–20
21st Century **Communication,** Act. 20; **Creativity and Innovation,** Act. 18/ Pre-AP

✓ Ongoing Assessment

Rubric Activity 18

Speaking Criteria	Maximum Credit	Partial Credit	Minimum Credit
Content	Radio ad is well planned.	Parts of the radio ad are well planned.	Radio ad is not well planned.
Communi-cation	Most of the dialogue is under-stood.	Parts of the dialogue are understood.	Dialogue is very hard to understand.
Accuracy	There are few mistakes in grammar and vocabulary.	There are some mistakes in grammar and vocabulary.	There are many mistakes in grammar and vocabulary.

Answers Projectable Transparencies 6-26

Activity 16 **1.** Isabel y Mario; **2.** Isabel; **3.** Mario; **4.** Isabel y Mario; **5.** Mario; **6.** Mario

Activity 17
1. Isabel y Mario juegan al béisbol.
2. Mario tiene que comprar un regalo para su hermano.
3. Sí, el hermano de Mario necesita un casco.
4. Trini va a estar en el estadio a las seis.

Answers continue on p. 317.

16 *Comprensión de los episodios* ¿A quién(es) describen?

Escuchar
Leer

Identifica a quién(es) describen estas oraciones: a Mario, a Isabel o a los dos. *(Tell whom these sentences describe: Mario, Isabel, or both.)*

1. Piensa que va a ganar el partido de béisbol.
2. Su equipo de béisbol siempre gana.
3. Dice que el tenis es peligroso.
4. Va a una tienda de deportes.
5. Compra una camiseta de fútbol.
6. Dice que debe encontrar a Trini.

Expansión:
Teacher Edition Only
Have students write two additional sentences abou the Telehistoria characters and exchange them with a partner who will identif the character.

17 *Comprensión de los episodios* Regalo para un atleta

Escuchar
Leer

Contesta las preguntas, según los episodios. *(Answer the questions, based on the Telehistoria.)*

1. ¿A qué juegan Isabel y Mario?
2. ¿Qué tiene que hacer Mario después de las clases?
3. ¿Necesita un casco el hermano de Mario?
4. ¿Dónde va a estar Trini a las seis?
5. ¿Quiénes pueden conocer a Trini?
6. ¿Qué compra Mario para su hermano?

Expansión:
Teacher Edition Onl
Have students reac their answers alou and have a partner suggest corrections if necessary.

18 Un anuncio de radio

Digital performance space

Escribir
Hablar

STRATEGY Hablar
Use logical steps to meet the goal Use logical steps to create a radio ad, such as: (a) make a chart containing types of key information, like **qué hay en la tienda,** in column 1 and specific examples for each type in column 2; (b) choose the best examples; (c) write an exciting ad; and (d) record and present it.

Trabaja en un grupo de tres. Escriban un anuncio de radio para una tienda de deportes. Preséntenlo a la clase. Deben incluir el nombre de un deporte y un(a) atleta famoso(a), lo que venden en la tienda y los precios. *(Work in a group of three. Create a radio ad and present it to the class.)*

A Si quieres conocer a Trini Salgado, ven a la tienda El Deportista el sábado.

B Tenemos pelotas de fútbol, ropa... ¡y mucho más!

C El sábado, las pelotas de fútbol cuestan setecientos pesos. Puedes recibir un autógrafo de la jugadora...

Expansión
Create a radio ad for a professional sports game.

Differentiating Instruction

Inclusion
Clear Structure Have students copy the sentences from Activity 16 onto a piece of paper. Underneath, have them create two concept webs—one around the name **Isabel**, and the other around the name **Mario.** Then have students reread each scene of the Telehistoria. As they find reference to one of the sentences, have them draw a line between that sentence and the appropriate web.

Pre-AP
Persuade As students create their radio ads in Activity 18, remind them they are trying to persuade their listeners. Before creating their ads, have students brainstorm words and phrases that will be useful for persuasion, such as **mejor, más, precios bajos, grande, fantástico(a),** etc. Also, remind students to use an enthusiastic and persuasive tone of voice while presenting their ads.

19 Integración

Digital performance space

Leer
Escuchar
Hablar

Lee el anuncio de un partido y escucha a los comentaristas. Luego di qué equipo va a ganar y por qué. *(Read the ad and listen to the sports broadcasters' commentary. Then tell which team you think will win and why.)*

Fuente 1 Anuncio

Fuente 2 Comentarios

Listen and take notes
- ¿Cómo juegan los equipos?
- ¿Cómo practican antes de los partidos?

modelo: El equipo de Los... va a ganar el partido porque...

Audio Program
TXT CD 6
Tracks 8, 9
Audio Script, TE p. 299b

20 Tus ideas sobre los deportes

Digital performance space

Escribir

Hay chicas que quieren jugar en los equipos con los chicos, por ejemplo, en los equipos de fútbol americano. ¿Piensas que es buena o mala idea? ¿Por qué? *(Do you think it's a good or bad idea for boys and girls to play on the same sports teams? Explain your answer.)*

modelo: Es una buena idea. Si las chicas pueden jugar al fútbol americano, deben jugar en el equipo de los chicos. Conozco a unas chicas que juegan...

Writing Criteria	Excellent	Good	Needs Work
Content	Your argument is supported with many reasons.	Your argument is supported with some reasons.	Your argument is supported with few reasons.
Communication	Your argument is organized and easy to follow.	Your argument is somewhat organized and easy to follow.	Your argument is disorganized and hard to follow.
Accuracy	Your argument has few mistakes in grammar and vocabulary.	Your argument has some mistakes in grammar and vocabulary.	Your argument has many mistakes in grammar and vocabulary.

Expansión:
Teacher Edition Only
Have students exchange essays with a partner and write a paragraph in response to their partner's essay.

Más práctica Cuaderno *pp. 255–256* Cuaderno para hispanohablantes *pp. 257–258*

Get Help Online
my.hrw.com

PARA Y PIENSA

Did you get it? Fill in the paragraph with the correct form of **saber** or **conocer.**

Trini Salgado _____ jugar al fútbol muy bien. Alicia y sus amigos la _____, y ellos _____ que ella va a estar en el estadio en Santo Domingo.

Differentiating Instruction

Inclusion

Clear Structure If students have difficulty beginning their stories in Activity 19, advise them to ask the following information questions.

¿Quién?	**un chico—Jorge**
¿Qué?	**juega al básquetbol**
¿Dónde?	**en la cancha de la escuela**
¿Cuándo?	**todos los días**
¿Cómo?	**mal, no juega bien**

Heritage Language Learners

Writing Skills Give students the opportunity to choose their own sports debate for Activity 20. Some possibilities might include the benefits of team sports versus individual sports, or the high salaries of sports stars. In addition to stating and supporting their own opinion, have students acknowledge how people on the other side feel. **Hay personas que dicen... pero yo pienso que...**

Long-term Retention

Pre-AP Integration

Have students use Activity 19 as a model to write two radio ads about upcoming sporting events. Have them record or read their ads to the class to initiate a discussion about which team will win and why.

✓ Ongoing Assessment

Rubric Activity 19

Listening/Speaking

Proficient	Not There Yet
Student notes and oral description reflect some comprehension of the written and oral information.	Student notes and oral description do not reflect comprehension of the written and oral information.

To customize your own rubrics, use the ***Generate Success*** *Rubric Generator and Graphic Organizers.*

✓ Ongoing Assessment

Get Help Online
More Practice
my.hrw.com

PARA Y PIENSA **Intervention** If students have difficulty answering the questions ask them to review p. 312. For additional practice, use Reteaching & Practice Copymasters URB 6 pp. 7, 9.

Answers Projectable Transparencies, 6-26 and 6-27

Answers continued from p. 316.

5. Los primeros quinientos aficionados pueden conocer a Trini.
6. Mario compra una camiseta para su hermano.

Activity 18 Answers will vary. Sample answer: Ven a la tienda Mundo del Béisbol el domingo para conocer a David Ortiz. Vendemos bates, cascos, pelotas y más. Los bates cuestan dos mil pesos y las pelotas cien pesos.

Activity 19 Answers will vary. Sample answers include: El equipo de Los Cometas va a ganar el partido porque los jugadores practican muy bien antes del partido.

Activity 20 Answers will vary. Sample answers include: Me parece buena idea. Si las chicas pueden jugar en el mismo equipo, las chicas pueden aprender de los chicos. Los chicos también pueden aprender de las chicas.

Para y piensa sabe, conocen, saben

Objectives
- Read about a sports club in the Dominican Republic
- Compare sports facilities in the Dominican Republic and in the U.S.

Core Resources
- Audio Program: TXT CD 6 track 10

Presentation Strategies
- Ask students to discuss briefly what they would expect from a sports facility.
- Have students take turns reading the brochure. Correct pronunciation as needed.
- Ask students to examine the photos and compare what they see with their initial discussion.
- Play the audio.

STANDARDS
1.2 Understand language
2.1 Practices and perspectives
2.2 Products and perspectives
4.2 Compare cultures
21st Century Creativity and Innovation, Multiple Intelligences; **Technology Media,** Physical Education

Warm Up
Projectable Transparencies, 6-19

Vocabulary Fill in the blank with an appropriate word from the word bank.

equipos bate pelota conocer sabe

1. Necesitamos un _____ para jugar al béisbol.
2. Ella _____ dónde es el partido.
3. Para jugar al tenis, fútbol, o básquetbol, necesitas una _____.
4. Dos _____ juegan en un partido.
5. ¿Tú quieres _____ a mi amigo?

Answers: 1. bate; 2. sabe; 3. pelota; 4. equipos; 5. conocer

Culture
Background Information
Both small and large towns in the Dominican Republic have baseball stadiums and sports clubs. The Dominican Republic's Director of Sports, Juan Marichal, once played in the U.S. major leagues, and, due to his superb pitching record for the San Francisco Giants, has a place of honor in the National Baseball Hall of Fame.

Lectura

Additional readings at my.hrw.com SPANISH InterActive Reader

¡AVANZA! **Goal:** Read a flier for a sports club in the Dominican Republic. Then describe the club and compare it with any sports facilities you know.

AUDIO

Un club de deportes

This is a brochure for a sports club in Santo Domingo.

STRATEGY Leer
Make a mind map Make a mind map of the sports club in Santo Domingo, showing everything the club offers. Add circles! Highlight the features you like most.

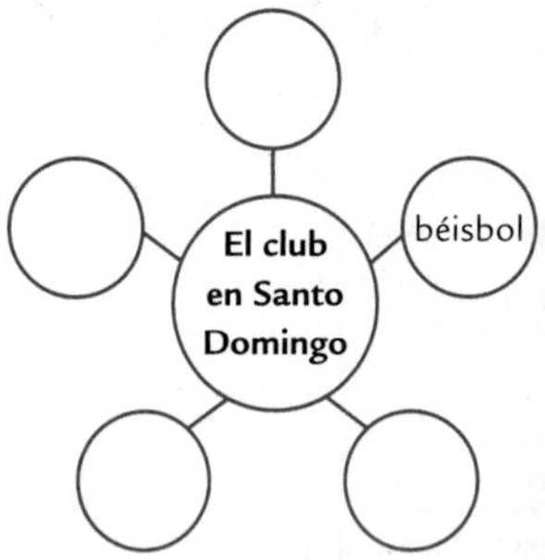

Differentiating Instruction

Slower-paced Learners
Personalize It Organize students into pairs. Then have partners ask each other the questions on the brochure. Instruct students to answer from their own perspective.

Estudiante A: ¿Eres atlético?
Estudiante B: Sí, soy atlético.
Estudiante A: ¿Te gusta practicar deportes?
Estudiante B: Sí, pero también me gusta leer.

Multiple Intelligences
Visual Learners In small groups, have students design a brochure for a competitor sports club. Advise them to give their clubs catchy names, and to try to offer more activities and longer hours than **Palacio de los Deportes.** Remind students to design their brochures in a way that is attractive and easy to read. Display the completed brochures for all to see.

Palacio
de los Deportes

Para nuestros socios [1]**...**

Si no sabes practicar los siguientes deportes, tenemos clases de...

- natación
- tenis
- artes marciales
- ejercicios aeróbicos

Si quieres jugar con otras personas, hay equipos de...

- básquetbol
- béisbol
- voleibol

Horas

lunes a viernes	6:00 de la mañana a 9:00 de la noche
sábado	7:00 de la mañana a 6:00 de la tarde

Membresías [2]
Hay membresías personales y familiares [3]. Puedes pedir la lista de los precios.

Dirección [4]
Calle Mella, 100
Santo Domingo

Teléfono
(809) 583-1492

Palacio
de los Deportes

[1] members [2] memberships [3] family [4] address

PARA Y PIENSA

¿Comprendiste?

1. ¿A qué puedes jugar en el Palacio de los Deportes?
2. ¿Qué puedes hacer si no sabes nadar?
3. Si quieres jugar con un equipo, ¿a qué puedes jugar?

¿Y tú?

Si eres socio(a) de un club de deportes, compara tu club con el Palacio de los Deportes. Si no, ¿quieres ser socio(a) del Palacio de los Deportes? Explica.

Connections

Physical Education

Ask students to search the Internet for information on the many athletic possibilities enjoyed by tourists who visit the Dominican Republic. Have students create a one-week sports vacation for a U.S. family visiting the Dominican Republic. Their plans should include activities for a mother who enjoys tennis, a father who likes hiking, a teenage son who is an avid baseball player, and a teenage daughter who swims competitively.

Comparisons

English Language Connection

Have students read the brochure for **El Palacio de los Deportes** carefully, looking for examples of **gustar.** Remind them that **gustar** constructions translate literally as "it is pleasing." Then ask them how many examples they can find of the use of an implied subject, for example: **"Si no sabes hacer los..."**

Differentiating Instruction

Pre-AP

Support Opinions Write the heading **deportes** on the board. Underneath, add the subheadings: **individuales** and **equipos**. Ask students to think about which is better—individual or team sports? Then divide students into two groups. Instruct each group to come up with two or three sentences supporting their side of the argument.

Heritage Language Learners

Support What They Know Ask students who belong to or have visited a sports club to describe the facility in as much detail as possible. Encourage students to use specific vocabulary to describe the activities and resources at the club. If students do not know the exact Spanish term for a particular piece of equipment or activity, encourage them to circumlocute to explain what they mean.

Answers

Para y piensa

¿Comprendiste?

1. Answers will vary but should follow the model: Puedo jugar al tenis, béisbol y básquetbol en el Palacio de los Deportes.
2. Answers may vary, but should follow the model: En el Palacio de los Deportes hay clases de natación.
3. Si quiero jugar con un equipo puedo jugar al básquetbol, béisbol y voleibol.

¿Y tu?

Answers will vary but should follow the model: Soy socio(a) de un club de deportes, hay una piscina olímpica y cuatro canchas de tenis, pero no hay campo de béisbol. Sí, quiero ser socio(a) de un club como el Palacio de los Deportes. Quiero nadar y jugar al tenis.

Objectives
- Learn about the Dominican flag.
- Understand the symbolism of the colors in the flag.
- Identify and discuss elements in the coat of arms.

Presentation Strategies
- Ask what students know about symbolism in national flags.
- Ask students to think about how the four disciplines: Social sciences, History, Art, and Physical education relate to a country's flag.

STANDARDS
1.3 Present information
2.1 Practices and perspectives
3.1 Knowledge of other disciplines
3.2 Acquire information
21st Century **Creativity and Innovation,** Proyecto 2; **Critical Thinking and Problem Solving,** Heritage Language Learners; **Information Literacy,** Proyecto 1

Connections
La historia
In 1492, Columbus discovered a small island in the Caribbean and named it La Española. The country's first viceroy was Columbus' own son, Diego. In English, the island is called Hispaniola, and it is shared by two countries: the Dominican Republic and Haiti. Sugar is the Dominican Republic's main crop, along with coffee, bananas, and rice.

Answers
Conexiones The laurel branch represents honor and glory and the palm branch represents victory and success.

Proyecto 1
In 1795 France took over the Dominican Republic from Spain. Spain regained control of the Dominican Republic in 1809. A group of Dominicans drove out the Spanish governor and claimed independence from Spain in 1821. Shortly thereafter, Haiti invaded, and the Dominican Republic was occupied by Haiti from 1822 to 1844.

Proyecto 2
Students should label the flag and write their explanation of it in Spanish.

Answers continue on page 321.

Conexiones *Las ciencias sociales*

La bandera dominicana

The colors and symbols of the Dominican flag reflect the country's long struggle for independence from France, Spain, and Haiti. It was not until 1844 that the Dominican Republic finally gained its independence.

On the Dominican flag, blue stands for liberty (**libertad**), red for the fire and blood of the fight for independence (**independencia**), and white for faith and sacrifice (**sacrificio**).

Write a description of the coat of arms (**el escudo de armas**). Research and explain the symbolism of the laurel branch (**rama de laurel**) and the palm branch (**rama de palma**).

El simbolismo de la bandera dominicana

Proyecto 1 *La historia*
Research and write about the Dominican struggle for independence from 1800 to 1844. Include specific facts such as dates, countries that were involved, and important people.

Proyecto 2 *El arte*
Flags combine geometric shapes, colors, symbols, and mottos. Design a flag for your school and explain the meaning of each element you use. Include a motto and labels in Spanish.

Proyecto 3 *La educación física*
In many countries, people fly their flag and sing their national anthem at sporting events. Write a paragraph about the role of flags and anthems in sports. Why do you think this tradition started?

El equipo nacional de voleibol femenino en los Juegos Panamericanos de 2003

Differentiating Instruction

English Learners
Build Background Ask students to find and point to the color words in the description of the Dominican flag: blue, red, white. Write these words on the board. Then ask students to scan the text to find what each of these colors represents. Give students specific examples to help concretize the meaning of abstract concepts, such as liberty, independence, faith, and sacrifice.

Heritage Language Learners
Writing Skills Have students use a Venn diagram to compare the flag of the Dominican Republic to the flag of another country. Remind students to think about symbolism as well as design features. After they have noted similarities and differences in the graphic organizer, have students develop their ideas into a compare and contrast essay.

En resumen

Vocabulario y gramática

ANIMATED GRAMMAR
Interactive Flashcards
my.hrw.com

Vocabulario

Sports	
el básquetbol	*basketball*
el béisbol	*baseball*
el fútbol americano	*football*
nadar	*to swim*
la natación	*swimming*
patinar	*to skate*
patinar en línea	*to in-line skate*
el tenis	*tennis*
el voleibol	*volleyball*

Sports Equipment	
el bate	*bat*
el casco	*helmet*
el guante	*glove*
los patines en línea	*in-line skates*
la pelota	*ball*
la raqueta	*racket*

Talk About Sports	
comprender las reglas	*to understand the rules*
favorito(a)	*favorite*
ganar	*to win*
el partido	*game*
peligroso(a)	*dangerous*
perder (ie)	*to lose*

Locations and People			
los aficionados	*fans*	el equipo	*team*
el (la) atleta	*athlete*	el estadio	*stadium*
el campeón (*pl.* los campeones), la campeona	*champion*	el (la) ganador(a)	*winner*
el campo	*field*	el (la) jugador(a)	*player*
la cancha	*court*	la piscina	*swimming pool*

Gramática

Nota gramatical: The personal **a** *p. 313*

The Verb jugar

Jugar is a stem-changing verb in which the **u** changes to **ue** in all forms except **nosotros(as)** and **vosotros(as)**.

jugar *to play*	
juego	jugamos
juegas	jugáis
juega	juegan

When you use **jugar** with the name of a sport, use **jugar a + sport.**

The Verbs saber and conocer

Both **saber** and **conocer** mean to know and have irregular **yo** forms in the present tense.

saber *to know*	
sé	sabemos
sabes	sabéis
sabe	saben

conocer *to know*	
conozco	conocemos
conoces	conocéis
conoce	conocen

- Use **saber** to talk about factual information you know. You can also use **saber + infinitive** to say that you know how to do something.
- Use **conocer** when you want to say that you are familiar with a person or place. You also use **conocer** to talk about meeting someone for the first time.

Practice Spanish with Holt McDougal Apps!

Differentiating Instruction

Inclusion

Alphabetic/Phonetic Awareness Have students write the infinitives **jugar, saber,** and **conocer** on separate index cards. In groups of three, each student chooses a card, writes the **yo** form of the verb and passes their card to the partner on the right. Next, each person writes the **tú** form and passes the card again. Repeat until all conjugations are written.

Multiple Intelligences

Visual Learners Organize students into small groups. Provide each group with a sports magazine or sports section of a newspaper. Have students flip through the periodical, and label as many images as they can. Then have them choose one photo to describe in detail. Have students post the photo and share their description with the group.

Objective

- Review lesson vocabulary and grammar.

DIGITAL SPANISH

Interactive Flashcards Students can hear every target vocabulary word pronounced in authentic Spanish. Flashcards have Spanish on one side, and a picture or a translation on the other.

Review Games Matching, concentration, hangman, and word search are just a sampling of the fun, interactive games students can play to review for the test.

performance space
News Networking
@HOMETUTOR
CULTURA Interactiva

- Audio and Video Resources
- Interactive Flashcards
- Review Activities
- WebQuest
- Conjuguemos.com

Long-term Retention

Critical Thinking

Analyze Ask students to make charts with a list of sports and the equipment used for each sport. Have them identify how many sports use one kind of equipment, for example, **una pelota.**

Communication

Humor/Creativity

Have students create comic strips in which a character takes the wrong equipment to compete in a sports event or goes to a place wearing the wrong outfit. For example, a character could go to **la piscina,** carrying **una raqueta.** Have students write a dialogue to accompany their drawings and describe them to the class.

Answers

Answers continued from page 320

Proyecto 3
Answers will vary, sample answers include: The tradition started as a way for people to show their pride in their country and their patriotism.

Objective
- Review vocabulary and grammar.

Core Resources
- *Cuaderno*, pp 257–268
- Audio Program: TXT CD 6 track 11

Presentation Strategies
- Before starting the audio for Activity 1, ask students to listen to it carefully and pay special attention to what Sergio replies.
- Before doing Activity 2, ask students to identify the equipment illustrations.
- Monitor correct use of **saber** and **conocer** as students do Activity 3.
- Go over the Comparación cultural with students and clarify any questions that arise.
- Review may be done in class or given as homework.
- You may want students to access the review online.

STANDARDS
1.2 Understand language, Act. 1
1.3 Present information, Acts. 2–5
4.2 Compare cultures, Act. 5
21st Century **Collaboration,** Multiple Intelligences

Warm Up
Projectable Transparencies, 6-19

Jugar, saber, and conocer Fill in the blanks with the correct form of **jugar, conocer,** or **saber.**

1. Nosotros _____ (jugar) al béisbol.
2. Yo _____ (saber) jugar al tenis.
3. María _____ (jugar) al fútbol americano.
4. Ustedes _____ (conocer) a Trini Salgado.
5. Ellos _____ (jugar) en el partido.
6. Irma y Teresa _____ (saber) las reglas.

Answers: 1. jugamos; 2. sé; 3. juega; 4. conocen; 5. juegan; 6. saben.

Ongoing Assessment
Get Help Online
More Practice
my.hrw.com

Remediation If students achieve less than 80% accuracy with the activities, direct them to pp. 299, 307–308, 312–314 and to get help online at my.hrw.com.

See Activity answers on page 323.

Lección 1 Repaso de la lección

@HOMETUTOR
my.hrw.com

¡LLEGADA!

Now you can
- talk about sports
- talk about whom you know
- talk about what you know

Using
- the verb **jugar**
- the verbs **saber** and **conocer**
- the personal **a**

To review
- the verb **jugar** p. 307
- the verbs **saber** and **conocer** p. 312
- the personal **a** p. 313

1 Listen and understand

AUDIO

Escucha una entrevista entre Tina y Sergio Martínez, un atleta famoso. Luego escoge la respuesta correcta. *(Listen as Tina interviews the famous athlete Sergio Martínez. Then choose the correct answer.)*

1. Sergio es jugador de...
   a. fútbol americano.
   b. béisbol.
2. También Sergio sabe jugar...
   a. al voleibol.
   b. al tenis.
3. Sergio dice que el fútbol americano es un poco...
   a. aburrido.
   b. peligroso.
4. Sergio no conoce a...
   a. muchos de sus aficionados.
   b. muchos jugadores.
5. Sergio...
   a. corre mucho.
   b. nada mucho.
6. Sergio sabe...
   a. patinar en línea.
   b. dibujar bien.

Audio Pro
TXT CD 6 Tra
Audio Script,
p. 299b

To review
- the verb **jugar** p. 307

2 Talk about sports

Escribe a qué juegan estas personas y qué artículos usan. *(Write what sports these people play and what equipment they use.)*

modelo: Adriana
Adriana juega al béisbol con un bate.

1.  tú
2.  Horacio y Mercedes
3.  Santiago
4.  nosotros
5.  yo
6.  ustedes

Differentiating Instruction

Slower-paced Learners
Read Before Listening Before doing Activity 1, have students read the possible answers, then copy them in their notebook. Next to each possible answer, have students make a quick sketch of the sports mentioned. Then ask them to refer to their drawings while listening to the audio.

Multiple Intelligences
Interpersonal Break students into small groups and assign each group a country in which baseball is played. The groups will report to each other and compare their findings on how baseball is played in "their" country. Students should include facts such as the baseball season, what uniforms look like, fans' customs, etc.

To review
- the verbs **saber** and **conocer** p. 312

3 Talk about whom and what you know

Completa el correo electrónico con la forma correcta de **saber** o **conocer.** *(Complete the e-mail message with the correct form of **saber** or **conocer.**)*

Hola, Norma.
Yo no __1.__ qué voy a hacer el sábado. Quiero jugar al tenis. Yo __2.__ a una chica que juega muy bien. Se llama Ana. ¿Y tú? ¿ __3.__ jugar al tenis? ¿Por qué no jugamos el sábado con Ana? Nosotras __4.__ un parque con muchas canchas. ¿Tú __5.__ el Parque Miraflores? Está cerca de mi casa. ¿Tú __6.__ dónde está la calle Olmeda? Allí está el parque. Hablamos esta noche.
Hasta luego,
Estela

To review
- the personal **a** p. 313

4 Talk about sports

Escribe oraciones para describir la importancia de los deportes en tu vida diaria. Usa la **a** personal si es necesario. *(Write sentences describing the importance of sports in your daily life. Use the personal **a**, if needed.)*

modelo: ver / mis atletas favoritos en la televisión
(No) Veo a mis atletas favoritos en la televisión.

1. comprender / las reglas de muchos deportes
2. invitar / mis amigos a los partidos de fútbol americano
3. practicar / dos o tres deportes
4. mirar / muchos deportes en la televisión
5. ayudar / mis amigos a aprender las reglas de fútbol
6. conocer / muchos jugadores de mi equipo favorito

To review
- **El deporte nacional** p. 299
- **Altar de la Patria** p. 299
- Comparación cultural pp. 308, 314

5 Dominican Republic and Venezuela

Comparación cultural

Answer these culture questions.

1. When is professional baseball played in the Dominican Republic?
2. What does the **Altar de la Patria** monument commemorate?
3. What is the **Serie del Caribe**? Which countries participate?
4. What is featured in Juan Medina's painting *Vendedora de flores?*

Get Help Online
my.hrw.com

Más práctica Cuaderno *pp. 257–268* Cuaderno para hispanohablantes *pp. 259–268*

Differentiating Instruction

Heritage Language Learners

Support What They Know Ask students if they can name an important monument in their country of origin. What does it represent? Have they ever visited it? Have they ever visited one of the U.S.'s monuments, and if so, what do they remember about it?

Inclusion

Frequent Review/Repetition Before assigning Activity 3, review the conjugation of the verbs **saber** and **conocer** with students. Have students repeat the forms as you say them, then ask volunteers to write the forms on the board.

✓ Ongoing Assessment

Peer Assessment Once students have completed Activity 4, have them exchange their sentences with a partner. They should compare their work and discuss what changes, if any, need to be made.

Answers Projectable Transparencies, 6-27

Answers for Activities on pp. 322 and 323.

Activity 1

1. a **2.** b **3.** b **4.** a **5.** b **6.** b

Activity 2

1. Tú juegas al fútbol con una pelota.
2. Horacio y Mercedes juegan al tenis con una raqueta.
3. Santiago juega al voleibol con una pelota.
4. Nosotros jugamos al béisbol con un guante.
5. Yo juego al básquetbol con una pelota.
6. Ustedes juegan al fútbol americano con un casco.

Activity 3

1. sé **2.** conozco **3.** sabes **4.** conocemos **5.** conoces **6.** sabes

Activity 4

1. Yo comprendo las reglas de muchos deportes.
2. Yo invito a mis amigos a los partidos de fútbol americano.
3. Yo practico dos o tres deportes.
4. Yo miro muchos deportes en la televisión.
5. Yo ayudo a mis amigos a aprender las reglas de fútbol.
6. Yo conozco a muchos jugadores de mi equipo favorito.

Activity 5

1. Professional baseball in the Dominican Republic is played from October through February.
2. The **Altar de la Patria** commemorates the Dominican Republic's fight for freedom from Haiti in 1844.
3. The **Serie del Caribe** is the Caribbean's baseball championship. The participating countries are the Dominican Republic, Venezuela, Mexico, and Puerto Rico.
4. The painting *Vendedora de flores* features a flower vendor. Flower vendors are common in Santo Domingo.

Lesson Overview

Culture at a Glance

Topic & Activity	Essential Question
Dominican beaches pp. 324-325	What outdoor activities do you like to do to stay healthy?
The Festival del Merengue p. 338	How do music and dance reflect the culture of a country?
Two world-class athletes pp. 342–343	Who are two world-class athletes representing the Dominican Republic and Venezuela?
Gestures and proverbs p. 344	How can gestures and proverbs facilitate communication?
Culture Review p. 347	What are some elements of Dominican culture?

COMPARISON COUNTRIES República Dominicana Honduras Venezuela

Practice at a Glance

	Objective	Activity & Skill
Vocabulary	Parts of the body	1: Writing/Speaking; 2: Writing/Speaking; 4: Speaking; 9: Listening/Reading; 14: Speaking; Repaso 2: Writing
	Staying healthy	7: Speaking; 8: Speaking 18: Speaking
	Outdoor activities	3: Listening/Reading; 4: Speaking; 7: Speaking; 9: Listening/Reading; 20: Writing
Grammar	Using **doler**	3: Listening/Reading; 4: Speaking; 9: Listening/Reading; 14: Speaking; 16: Listening/Speaking; 17: Listening/Speaking; Repaso 2: Writing
	Preterite of **-ar** verbs	5: Writing/Speaking; 6: Reading/Writing; 7: Speaking; 8: Speaking; 10: Writing; 11: Writing/Speaking;
	Preterite of **-car, -gar, -zar** verbs	12: Writing; 13: Listening/Writing; 14: Speaking; 15: Writing; 17: Listening; 18: Speaking; 19: Reading/Listening/Speaking; Repaso 1: Listening; Repaso 4: Writing;
Communication	Make excuses	3: Listening/Reading; 4: Speaking; 14: Speaking
	Say what you did	5: Writing/Speaking; 6: Reading/Writing; 7: Speaking; 8: Speaking; 10: Writing; 11: Writing/Speaking; 12: Writing; 13: Listening/Writing; 14: Speaking; 18: Speaking; Repaso 1: Listening; Repaso 4: Writing
	Talk about staying healthy	2: Writing/Speaking; 6: Reading/Writing; 8: Speaking; 9: ListeningReading; 18: Speaking; 19: Reading/Listening/Speaking; Repaso 3: Writing
	Pronunciation: the letter **g** with **e, i**	*Pronunciación: La letra g con e, i*, p. 337: Listening/Speaking
Recycle	Stem-changing verbs: **o → ue**	4: Speaking
	Telling time	5: Writing/Speaking

The following presentations are recorded in the Audio Program for ***¡Avancemos!***

- **¡A responder!** *page 327*
- **13: Muchas preguntas** *page 337*
- **19: Integración** *page 341*
- **Repaso de la lección** *page 346*
  1: Listen and understand
- **Repaso inclusivo** *page 350*
  1: Listen, understand, and compare

For **¡AvanzaRap!** scripts, see the **¡AvanzaRap! DVD.**

¡A responder! TXT CD 6 track 13

1. Me duele el brazo.
2. Me duele el tobillo.
3. Me duele la mano.
4. Me duele la rodilla.
5. Me duele la pierna.
6. Me duele la nariz.
7. Me duele el pie.

13 | Muchas preguntas TXT CD 6 track 16

Mario: ¿Pagaste el almuerzo?

Chica 1: Sí, pagué el almuerzo.
No, no pagué el almuerzo.

Mario: ¿A qué hora llegaste a la escuela ayer?

Mario: ¿Sacaste buenas o malas notas?

Mario: ¿A qué hora almorzaste?

Mario: ¿Comenzaste la tarea?

Mario: ¿Buscaste ropa nueva?

Mario: ¿A qué jugaste?

19 | Integración TXT CD 6 tracks 19, 20

¿Qué hiciste durante la semana para la salud?
Durante la semana practiqué muchos deportes. El lunes y el miércoles jugué al tenis con mi hermana. También caminé a la escuela. Normalmente tomo el autobús pero el lunes empecé a caminar. El sábado jugué al fútbol. Comer comida sana es difícil. ¡Me gusta mucho comer! Hoy almorcé pizza con jamón y de postre, helado de chocolate.

Repaso de la lección TXT CD 6 track 22

1 Listen and understand

Ayer pasé un rato con mi familia en la playa. Mi hermana y yo usamos mucho bloqueador porque tomamos el sol. Nuestro hermano buceó en el mar. Nuestros padres caminaron, y yo almorcé con mis hermanos. Otras personas jugaron al voleibol. Yo jugué un poco con ellos. Después yo descansé. En la noche unos chicos tocaron la guitarra y nosotros cantamos con ellos. Pasamos un día muy divertido en la playa.

Repaso inclusivo TXT CD 6 track 24

1 Listen, understand, and compare

Carlos: Hace sol y un poco de calor aquí en el campo de béisbol. Yo soy Carlos Pérez y estoy aquí con Luis Alomar.

Luis: Gracias, Carlos. Allí en el campo está Mariano Sandoval y tengo que decir que no hay mejor atleta en todos los equipos de Latinoamérica.

Carlos: Tienes razón, Luis. Sandoval es de San Pedro de Macorís y allí saben jugar. Él juega tan bien con el bate como juega con el guante.

Luis: ¡Sí, señor! Ayer él me explicó por qué es un jugador tan bueno. Vamos a escuchar lo que dice Mariano.

Mariano Sandoval: Sabes, no siempre tenemos guantes nuevos o cascos pero tenemos mucho corazón. No pienso que soy más fuerte que los otros jugadores o que corro más que ellos. Pero sé que trabajo más que ellos.

Carlos: Sí, Luis... Mariano es un ganador de primera clase.

Resource List

Everything you need to ...

Plan

TEACHER ONE STOP

✓Lesson Plans
✓Teacher Resources
✓Audio and Video

Present

INTERACTIVE WHITEBOARD LESSONS

TEACHER ONE STOP WITH PROJECTABLE TRANSPARENCIES

POWER PRESENTATIONS

ANIMATEDGRAMMAR

Assess

ONLINE ASSESSMENT

✓ Assessments for on-level, modified, pre-AP, and heritage learners
✓ Create customized tests with **Examview Assessment Suite**
✓ **performance space**
✓ *Generate Success* Rubric Generator

Print

Plan	Present	Practice	Assess
URB 6 • Video Scripts pp. 71–72 • Family Involvement Activity p. 92 • Absent Student Copymasters pp. 101–111 **Best Practices Toolkit**	**URB 6** • Video Activities pp. 59–66	• *Cuaderno* pp. 269–294 • *Cuaderno para hispanohablantes* pp. 269–294 • *Lecturas para todos* pp. 57–61 • *Lectura para hispanohablantes* • *¡AvanzaCómics! SuperBruno y Nati*, Episodio 3 **URB 6** • Practice Games pp. 39–46 • Audio Scripts pp. 78–82 • Fine Art Activities pp. 88–89	**Differentiated Assessment Program** **URB 6** • Did you get it? Reteaching and Practice Copymasters pp. 13–24

Projectable Transparencies (Teacher One Stop, my.hrw.com)

Culture	Presentation and Practice	Classroom Management
• Atlas Maps 1–6 • Map of Dominican Republic 1 • Fine Art Transparencies 4, 5	• Vocabulary Transparencies 8, 9 • Grammar Presentation Transparencies 12, 13 • Situational Transparencies and label overlay 14, 15 • Situational Student Copymasters pp. 1, 2	• Warm Up Transparencies 20–23 • Student Book Answer Transparencies 28–31

Audio and Video

Audio	Video	¡AvanzaRap! DVD
• Student Book Audio CD 6 Tracks 12–24 • Workbook Audio CD 3 Tracks 31–40 • Heritage Learners Audio CD 2 Tracks 13–16, CD 4 Tracks 9–12 • Assessment Audio CD 2 Tracks 9–12 • *Lecturas para todos* Audio CD 1 Track 12, CD 2 Tracks 1–6 • Sing-along Songs Audio CD	• Vocabulary Video DVD 2 • *Telehistoria* DVD 2 Escena 1 Escena 2 Escena 3 Completa • Culture Video DVD 2	• Video animations of all **¡AvanzaRap!** songs (with Karaoke track) • Interactive DVD Activities • Teaching Suggestions • **¡AvanzaRap!** Activity Masters • **¡AvanzaRap!** video scripts and answers

Online and Media Resources

Student	Teacher
Available online at my.hrw.com • Online Student Edition • News + Networking • performance space • @HOMETUTOR • CULTURA Interactiva • WebQuests • Interactive Flashcards • Review Games • Self-Check Quiz **Student One Stop** **Holt McDougal Spanish Apps**	**Teacher One Stop (also available at my.hrw.com)** • Interactive Teacher's Edition • All print, audio, and video resources • Projectable Transparencies • Lesson Plans • TPRS • Examview Assessment Suite **Available online at my.hrw.com** *Generate Success* Rubric Generator and Graphic Organizers **Power Presentations**

Differentiated Assessment

On-level	Modified	Pre-AP	Heritage Learners
• Vocabulary Recognition Quiz p. 273 • Vocabulary Production Quiz p. 274 • Grammar Quizzes pp. 275–276 • Culture Quiz p. 277 • On-level Lesson Test pp. 278–284 • On-level Unit Test pp. 290–296	• Modified Lesson Test pp. 218–224 • Modified Unit Test pp. 230–236	• Pre-AP Lesson Test pp. 218–224 • Pre-AP Unit Test pp. 230–236	• Heritage Learners Lesson Test pp. 224–230 • Heritage Learners Unit Test pp. 236–242

Core Pacing Guide

50 Minute (9 Day)

	Objectives/Focus	Teach	Practice	Assess/HW Options
DAY 1	**Culture:** learn about the Dominican Republic **Vocabulary:** parts of the body • Warm Up OHT 20 **5 min**	Lesson Opener pp. 324–325 **Presentación de vocabulario** pp. 326–327 • Read A–E • View video DVD 2 • Play Audio TXT CD 6 track 12 • *¡A responder!* TXT CD 6 track 13 **25 min**	Lesson opener pp. 324–325 **Práctica de vocabulario** p. 328 • Acts. 1, 2 **15 min**	**Assess:** *Para y piensa* p. 328 **5 min** **Homework:** *Cuaderno* pp. 269–271 @HomeTutor
DAY 2	**Communication:** parts of the body • Warm Up OHT 20 • Check Homework **5 min**	**Vocabulario en contexto** pp. 329–330 • *Telehistoria escena 1* DVD 2 • *Nota gramatical:* **doler** **20 min**	**Vocabulario en contexto** pp. 329–330 • Act. 3 TXT CD 6 track 14 • Act. 4 **20 min**	**Assess:** *Para y piensa* p. 330 **5 min** **Homework:** *Cuaderno* pp. 269–271 @HomeTutor
DAY 3	**Grammar:** preterite of regular **-ar** verbs • Warm Up OHT 21 • Check Homework **5 min**	**Presentación de gramática** p. 331 • preterite of regular **-ar** verbs **Práctica de gramática** pp. 332–333 **Culture:** *La artista y su estilo* **20 min**	**Práctica de gramática** pp. 332–333 • Acts. 5, 6, 7, 8 **20 min**	**Assess:** *Para y piensa* p. 333 **5 min** **Homework:** *Cuaderno* pp. 272–274 @HomeTutor
DAY 4	**Communication:** staying healthy • Warm Up OHT 21 • Check Homework **5 min**	**Gramática en contexto** pp. 334–335 • *Telehistoria escena 2* DVD 2 **15 min**	**Gramática en contexto** pp. 334–335 • Act. 9 TXT CD 6 track 15 • Acts. 10, 11 **25 min**	**Assess:** *Para y piensa* p. 335 **5 min** **Homework:** *Cuaderno* pp. 272–274 @HomeTutor
DAY 5	**Grammar:** preterite of **-car, -gar, -zar** verbs • Warm Up OHT 22 • Check Homework **5 min**	**Presentación de gramática** p. 336 • preterite of **-car, -gar, -zar** verbs **Práctica de gramática** pp. 337–338 • *Pronunciación* TXT CD 6 track 17 **15 min**	**Práctica de gramática** pp. 337–338 • Acts. 12, 14, 15 • Act. 13 TXT CD 6 track 16 **25 min**	**Assess:** *Para y piensa* p. 338 **5 min** **Homework:** *Cuaderno* pp. 275–277 @HomeTutor
DAY 6	**Communication:** Culmination: parts of the body, preterite of regular **-ar** verbs, preterite of **-car , -gar, -zar** verbs • Warm Up OHT 22 • Check Homework **5 min**	**Todo junto** pp. 339–341 • *Escenas 1, 2: Resumen* • *Telehistoria completa* DVD 2 **15 min**	**Todo junto** pp. 339–341 • Acts. 16, 17 TXT CD 6 tracks 14, 15, 18 • Acts. 18, 20 • Act. 19 TXT CD 6 tracks 19, 20 **25 min**	**Assess:** *Para y piensa* p. 341 **5 min** **Homework:** *Cuaderno* pp. 278–279 @HomeTutor
DAY 7	**Reading:** Two high-speed athletes **Review:** Lesson review • Warm Up OHT 23 • Check Homework **5 min**	**Lectura cultural** pp. 342–343 • *Dos atletas de alta velocidad* TXT CD 6 track 21 **Repaso de la lección** pp. 346–347 **15 min**	**Lectura cultural** pp. 342–343 • *Dos atletas de alta velocidad* **Repaso de la lección** pp. 346–347 • Act. 1 TXT CD 6 track 22 • Acts. 2, 3, 4, 5 **20 min**	**Assess:** *Para y piensa* p. 343 **Repaso de la leccion** pp. 346–347 **10 min** **Homework:** *En resumen* p. 345; *Cuaderno* pp. 280–291 (optional) Review Games Online @HomeTutor
DAY 8	**Assessment**			**Assess:** Lesson 2 Test or Unit 6 Test **50 min**
DAY 9	**Unit Culmination** **5 min**	**Comparación cultural** pp. 348–349 TXT CD 6 track 23 • View culture video DVD 2 **Repaso inclusivo** pp. 350–351 **15 min**	**Comparación cultural** pp. 348–349 **Repaso inclusivo** pp. 350–351 • Act. 1 TXT CD 6 track 24 • Acts. 2, 3, 4, 5, 6, 7 **25 min**	**Homework:** *Cuaderno* pp. 292–294 **5 min**

	Objectives/Focus	Teach	Practice	Assess/HW Options
DAY 1	**Culture:** learn about the Dominican Republic **Vocabulary:** parts of the body • Warm Up OHT 20 **5 min**	Lesson Opener pp. 324–325 **Presentación de vocabulario** pp. 326–327 • Read A–E • View video DVD 2 • Play audio TXT CD 6 track 12 • *¡A responder!* TXT CD 6 track 13 **20 min**	Lesson opener pp. 324–325 **Práctica de vocabulario** p. 328 • Acts. 1, 2 **20 min**	**Assess:** *Para y piensa* p. 328 **5 min**
	Communication: parts of the body **5 min**	**Vocabulario en contexto** pp. 329–330 • *Telehistoria escena 1* DVD 2 • *Nota gramatical:* **doler** **15 min**	**Vocabulario en contexto** pp. 329–330 • Act. 3 TXT CD 6 track 14 • Act. 4 **15 min**	**Assess:** *Para y piensa* p. 330 **5 min** **Homework:** *Cuaderno* pp. 269–271 @HomeTutor
DAY 2	**Grammar:** preterite of regular **-ar** verbs • Warm Up OHT 21 • Check Homework **5 min**	**Presentación de gramática** p. 331 • preterite of regular **-ar** verbs **Práctica de gramática** pp. 332–333 **Culture:** *La artista y su estilo* **20 min**	**Práctica de gramática** pp. 332–333 • Acts. 5, 6, 7, 8 **15 min**	**Assess:** *Para y piensa* p. 333 **5 min**
	Communication: staying healthy **5 min**	**Gramática en contexto** pp. 334–335 • *Telehistoria escena 2* DVD 2 **20 min**	**Gramática en contexto** pp. 334–335 • Act. 9 TXT CD 6 track 15 • Acts. 10, 11 **15 min**	**Assess:** *Para y piensa* p. 335 **5 min** **Homework:** *Cuaderno* pp. 272–274 @HomeTutor
DAY 3	**Grammar:** preterite of **-car, -gar, -zar** verbs • Warm Up OHT 22 • Check Homework **5 min**	**Presentación de gramática** p. 336 • preterite of **-car, -gar, -zar** verbs **Práctica de gramática** pp. 337-338 • *Pronunciación* TXT CD 6 track 17 **15 min**	**Práctica de gramática** pp. 337–338 • Acts. 12, 14, 15 • Act. 13 TXT CD 6 track 16 **20 min**	**Assess:** *Para y piensa* p. 338 **5 min**
	Communication: Culmination: parts of the body, preterite of regular **-ar** verbs, preterite of **-car, -gar, -zar** verbs **5 min**	**Todo junto** pp. 339–341 • *Escenas 1, 2: Resumen* • *Telehistoria completa* DVD 2 **15 min**	**Todo junto** pp. 339–341 • Acts. 16, 17 TXT CD 6 tracks 14, 15, 18 • Acts. 18, 20 • Act. 19 TXT CD 6 tracks 19, 20 **20 min**	**Assess:** *Para y piensa* p. 341 **5 min** **Homework:** *Cuaderno* pp. 275–279 @HomeTutor
DAY 4	**Reading:** Two high-speed athletes • Warm Up OHT 23 • Check Homework **5 min**	**Lectura cultural** pp. 342–343 • *Dos atletas de alta velocidad* • TXT CD 6 track 21 **15 min**	**Lectura cultural** pp. 342–343 • *Dos atletas de alta velocidad* **20 min**	**Assess:** *Para y piensa* p. 343 **5 min**
	Review: Lesson review **5 min**	**Repaso de la lección** pp. 346–347 **15 min**	**Repaso de la lección** pp. 346–347 • Act. 1 TXT CD 6 track 22 • Acts. 2, 3, 4, 5 **20 min**	**Assess: Repaso de la lección** pp. 346–347 **5 min** **Homework:** *En resumen* p. 345; *Cuaderno* pp. 280–291 (optional) Review Games Online @HomeTutor
DAY 5	**Assessment:** Lesson Test			**Assess:** Lesson 2 test or Unit 6 Test **45 min**
	Unit Culmination **5 min**	**Comparación cultural** pp. 348–349 TXT CD 6 track 23 • View culture video DVD 2 **Repaso inclusivo** pp. 350–351 **15 min**	**Comparación cultural** pp. 348–349 **Repaso inclusivo** pp. 350–351 • Act. 1 TXT CD 6 track 24 • Acts. 2, 3, 4, 5, 6, 7 **20 min**	**Homework:** *Cuaderno* pp. 292–294 **5 min**

¡AVANZA! Objectives

- Introduce lesson theme: **La salud.**
- **Culture:** Compare healthy outdoor activities with activities teens do in other parts of the world.

Presentation Strategies

- Introduce the characters' names again: Isabel and Mario.
- Create a conversation about students' favorite outdoor places.
- Ask students what they like to do to stay healthy.

STANDARDS

2.2 Products and perspectives
4.2 Compare cultures
21st Century **Communication,** Interpersonal Mode; **Social and Cross-Cultural Skills,** Heritage Language Learners

Warm Up Projectable Transparencies, 6-20

Verbs Complete the sentences with a form of **saber** or **conocer.**

1. ¿_____ tú cuánto cuestan los gorros?
2. ¿ _____ ellas las playas del Caribe?
3. Liliana y yo no _____ jugar al béisbol.
4. ¿Vamos a _____ Santo Domingo este marzo?
5. ¿ _____ usted la hora, por favor?

Answers: 1. Sabes; 2. Conocen; 3. sabemos; 4. conocer; 5. Sabe

Comparación cultural

Exploring the Theme

Ask the following:

1. Do you like to go to the beach? When?
2. Are there beaches close to where you live? What can you do there?
3. What other natural attractions do you like to visit?

¿Qué ves? Possible answers include:

- No, no hace frío.
- Los dos chicos llevan camisetas.
- Isabel y Mario juegan en la playa.

UNIDAD 6 República Dominicana

Lección 2

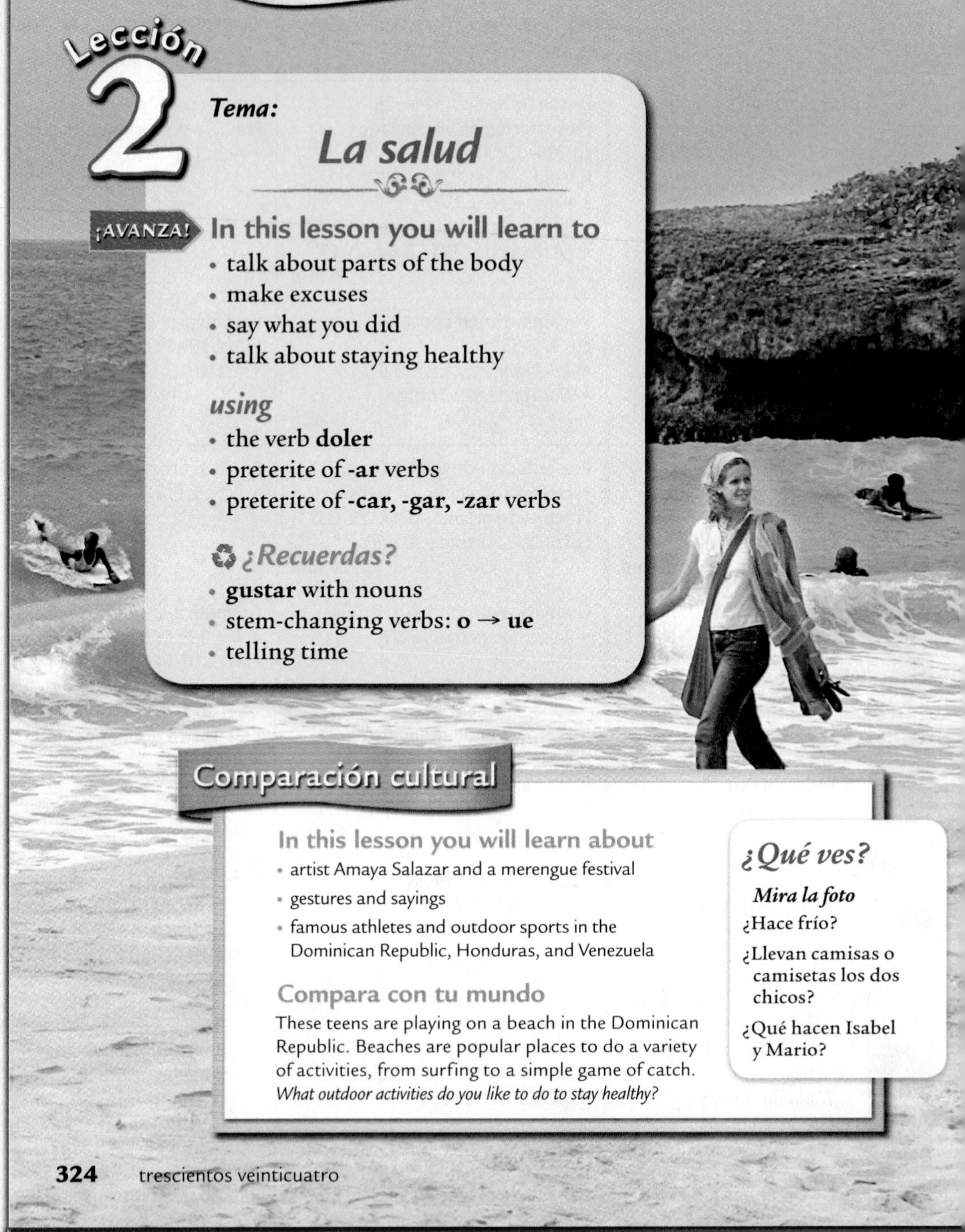

Tema: *La salud*

¡AVANZA! **In this lesson you will learn to**

- talk about parts of the body
- make excuses
- say what you did
- talk about staying healthy

using

- the verb **doler**
- preterite of **-ar** verbs
- preterite of **-car, -gar, -zar** verbs

¿Recuerdas?

- **gustar** with nouns
- stem-changing verbs: **o → ue**
- telling time

Comparación cultural

In this lesson you will learn about

- artist Amaya Salazar and a merengue festival
- gestures and sayings
- famous athletes and outdoor sports in the Dominican Republic, Honduras, and Venezuela

Compara con tu mundo

These teens are playing on a beach in the Dominican Republic. Beaches are popular places to do a variety of activities, from surfing to a simple game of catch. *What outdoor activities do you like to do to stay healthy?*

¿Qué ves?

Mira la foto

¿Hace frío?

¿Llevan camisas o camisetas los dos chicos?

¿Qué hacen Isabel y Mario?

324 trescientos veinticuatro

Differentiating Instruction

Inclusion

Cumulative Instruction Have students brainstorm a list of topics that relate to the photo on pp. 324 and 325. For example: colors, sports, clothing, personal adjectives, and place names. Divide students into small groups and assign each group one topic. Each group should list as many words and phrases as possible related to their topic.

Multiple Intelligences

Naturalist Using their own drawings or photos from magazines, have students create a depiction of a favorite outdoor location. Instruct them to include people engaged in outdoor activities, such as walking or water-skiing. As students learn vocabulary throughout Lección 2, have them label the people and objects in their illustrations.

DIGITAL SPANISH my.hrw.com
ONLINE STUDENT EDITION with...

performance space
News Networking
@HOMETUTOR
CULTURA Interactiva

- Audio and Video Resources
- Interactive Flashcards
- Review Activities
- WebQuest
- Conjuguemos.com

PRACTICE SPANISH WITH HOLT MCDOUGAL APPS!

Un día en la Playa Caribe
Juan Dolio, República Dominicana

DIGITAL SPANISH

TEACHER TOOLS
- Interactive Whiteboard Lessons
- Generate Success!

ALSO AVAILABLE...
- Online Workbook
- Spanish InterActive Reader

SPANISH ON THE GO!
- Performance Space
- Holt McDougal Spanish Apps
- ¡Avancemos! eTextbook

Using the Photo

Location Information

Natural Attractions The Dominican Republic is home to many internationally renowned beach resort communities, including the **Playa Juan Dolio** in the south, Punta Cana in the east, and Puerto Plata and Las Terrenas in the north.

Expanded Information

The Dominican Republic occupies the eastern part of the Caribbean island of Hispaniola. Haiti, a French-speaking country, occupies the western part of the island.

Long-term Retention

Recycle

Have students say or write sentences describing cities or countries they have visited or activities they know how to do. Sentences should begin with **Yo conozco** or **Yo sé.**

Communication

Interpersonal Mode

Have students work in pairs. One student asks **¿Qué puedes hacer en la playa?** The other answers. Switch and repeat to see how many answers they can come up with.

Differentiating Instruction

Slower-paced Learners

Yes/No Questions Ask students yes or no questions about what they see in the photo. **¿Ves a tres chicos? ¿Lleva la chica pantalones cortos?** Have students correct the sentence when the answer is no. **¿Están cansados los chicos? No, los chicos están contentos.**

Heritage Language Learners

Support What They Know Ask students to share some popular outdoor activities from their place of origin. If you have students of Dominican descent, ask them to share information about the country and its culture. Or, generate a list of outdoor activities like **nadar, patinar,** etc., and let students add other activities and talk about their favorite ones.

¡AVANZA! Objective
- Present vocabulary: activities to stay healthy, parts of the body.

Core Resources
- Video Program: DVD 2
- Audio Program: TXT CD 6 tracks 12, 13

Presentation Strategies
- Ask students to read aloud the Más vocabulario words, paying attention to the pronunciation of the words.
- Point at random to the photos on pp. 326–327, and have students say the words. Correct pronunciation as needed.
- Play the audio as students read A–E.
- Play the video.

STANDARDS
1.2 Understand language

21st Century **Communication,** Role-Playing and Skits

Long-term Retention
Connect to Previous Learning
Using vocabulary from the lesson, read statements about activities that could be done at the beach. Ask students to raise their hand if the statement is true. Example: **Puedo tomar el sol en la playa. Puedo patinar en línea en la playa.**

Long-term Retention
Recycle
Review sports vocabulary from Unit 6, Lesson 1. Ask the following questions: **¿Qué deportes te gustan? ¿Qué deporte te gusta practicar en el verano? ¿Qué deporte te gusta practicar en el invierno?**

Communication
Common Error Alert
Remind students of the **e → ie** stem-changing verbs. Write on the board: **yo comienzo, tú comienzas, usted/él/ella comienza, nosotros comenzamos, ellos/ellas comienzan.** Have students notice the changes on the second syllable: it changes from **e** to **ie.**

Presentación de VOCABULARIO

¡AVANZA! **Goal:** Learn about what Mario and Isabel do to stay healthy. Then use what you have learned to talk about parts of the body. ***Actividades 1–2***

VIDEO DVD

AUDIO

A Soy Isabel. En **la playa** Mario y yo siempre usamos **bloqueador de sol.** Si no lo usamos, **tomar el sol** puede ser malo para **la piel.**

B En la República Dominicana hay muchas actividades que son buenas para **la salud.** Yo **camino,** pero también puedes **hacer esquí acuático** o **bucear.** A Mario le gusta **levantar pesas.**

Más vocabulario
anoche *last night*
ayer *yesterday*
comenzar *to begin*
terminar *to end*
Lo siento. *I'm sorry.*
¿Qué hiciste (tú)? *What did you do?*
¿Qué hicieron ustedes? *What did you do?*
Expansión de vocabulario p. R7

Differentiating Instruction

Inclusion
Multisensory Input/Output Help students internalize new vocabulary through this series of activities. Begin by writing a word or phrase on the board, such as **levantar pesas.** Then give students the following instructions:
1. Read the phrase aloud.
2. Repeat the phrase as you act it out.
3. Repeat the phrase as you write it down.

Slower-paced Learners
Memory Aids Have students create a set of flashcards for the vocabulary on pp. 326 and 327. Ask them to write a word or phrase on the front of a card, and draw a picture on the back. Have students organize their cards into categories such as activities, parts of the body, and adjectives.

C Si hacemos actividades en la playa, usamos bloqueador de sol en todo el cuerpo: la nariz, las orejas, los brazos, las piernas...

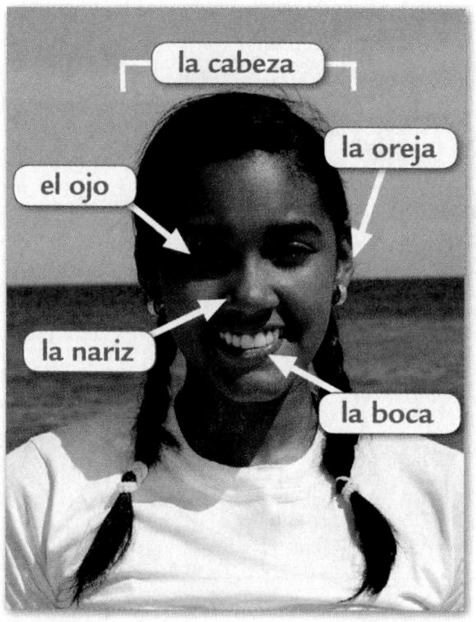

D Mario es **fuerte** pero ahora está **herido**. **Le duele** mucho **el tobillo.**

E Yo soy muy **sana** pero de vez en cuando estoy **enferma.**

@HOMETUTOR my.hrw.com Interactive Flashcards

¡A responder! Escuchar

Levántate. Escucha al atleta profesional hablar de lo que le duele. Señala las partes del cuerpo que menciona. *(Stand up. Point to each part of the body as it is mentioned.)*

TEACHER to TEACHER

Mercedes Roffé
New York, New York

Tips for Presenting Vocabulary

I often bring to class Spanish-language sports or leisure magazines. I show photos of the different sports to my students to encourage a discussion about how these sports compare with those that they do and enjoy. I always ask my students to skim the magazines to identify cognates in the headlines, captions, and articles.

Go online for more tips!

Communication

Common Error Alert

- Remind students that the word **la mano**, although ending in **-o**, is feminine.
- Remind them also that the plural of **la nariz** is **las narices.**

Long-term Retention

Study Tips

Have students make a two-column chart. One column should include parts of the body and the other column should include activities associated with that part. Example: **la boca: hablar, comer, cantar**

Communication

Role-Playing and Skits

Have students prepare and perform skits in which they discuss events that take place during a day at the beach. Encourage students to include the vocabulary introduced in this lesson.

Differentiating Instruction

Multiple Intelligences

Visual Learners Have students draw the outline of a person on a piece of paper and label the parts of the body.

Heritage Language Speakers

Standard Spanish Have students read aloud the **D** and **E** sentences. Discuss why the adjective **fuerte** follows the verb **ser,** while **herido** follows the verb **estar,** and why **sana** follows **ser,** while **enferma** follows **estar.** Use these examples to address errors in the use of **ser** and **estar.** Remind students that **ser** indicates a quality of the person, and **estar** a condition that may change.

Answers

Projectable Transparencies, 6-28

¡A responder! Audio Script, TE p. 323b

Students should indicate the arm, ankle, hand, knee, leg, nose, and foot.

Objective
- Practice vocabulary: parts of the body.

Core Resource
- *Cuaderno,* pp. 269–271

Practice Sequence
- **Activity 1:** Vocabulary recognition: parts of the body
- **Activity 2:** Vocabulary production: **usar**, parts of the body, sports, activities

STANDARDS
1.2 Understand language, Act. 1
1.3 Present information, Act. 2
21st Century **Communication,** Act. 2/Slower-paced Learners

Communication
Common Error Alert
Explain to students that when naming parts of the body in Spanish, the article **el, la, los, las** is used instead of the possessive adjectives.

Ongoing Assessment
Get Help Online
More Practice
my.hrw.com

PARA Y PIENSA **Quick Check** If students have difficulties naming parts of the face and legs, have them review p. 327. For additional practice, use Reteaching & Practice Copymasters URB 6 pp. 13, 14.

Answers Projectable Transparencies, 6-28
Activity 1 **a.** el ojo; **b.** la cabeza; **c.** la oreja; **d.** la boca; **e.** la nariz; **f.** el brazo; **g.** el corazón; **h.** el estómago; **i.** la rodilla; **j.** la mano; **k.** el cuerpo

Activity 2 Answers will vary. Sample answers:
1. Cuando camino, uso las piernas y los pies.
2. Cuando como, uso la boca y los dientes
3. Cuando buceo, uso los brazos y las piernas.
4. Cuando dibujo, uso la mano.
5. Cuando levanto pesas, uso los brazos y las manos.
6. Cuando patino, uso las piernas y los pies.
7. Cuando juego al fútbol, uso la cabeza, las piernas y los pies.
8. Cuando bailo, uso todo el cuerpo.
9. Cuando miro la televisión, uso los ojos.
10. Cuando hago esquí acuático, uso las manos, los brazos y las piernas.

Para y piensa Answers will vary. Sample answers:
1. los ojos, la boca, la nariz
2. la rodilla, el tobillo, el pie

Práctica de VOCABULARIO

1 Las partes del cuerpo
Escribir
Hablar

Identifica las partes del cuerpo. *(Identify the body parts.)*

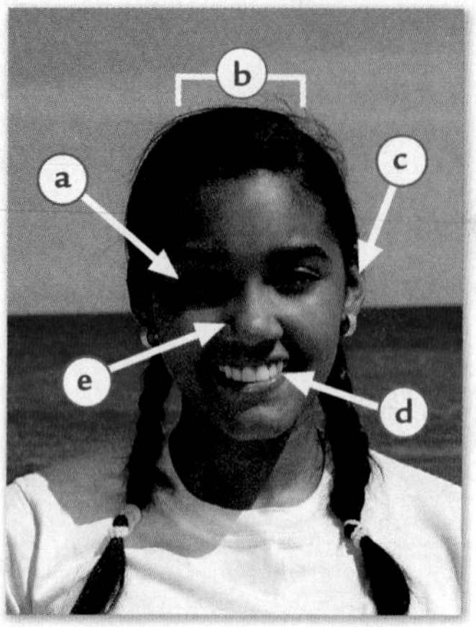

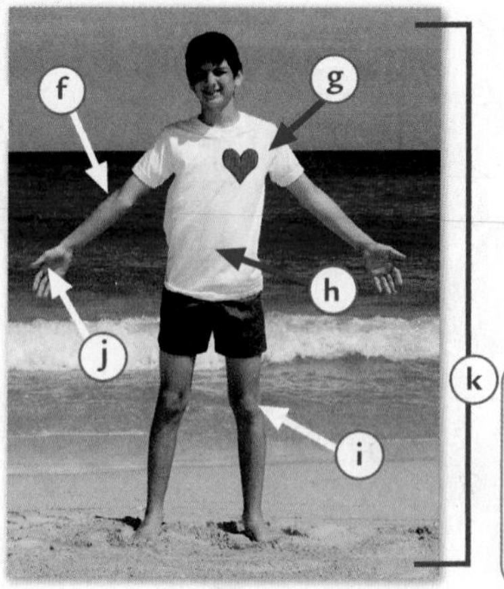

Expansión:
Teacher Edition Only
Have students write activities associated with 5 body parts.

2 ¿Qué usas?
Escribir
Hablar

Identifica qué partes del cuerpo usas cuando haces estas actividades. *(Tell what parts of the body you use to do these activities.)*

la boca	las manos	los ojos	los pies
los brazos	la cabeza	las piernas	¿ ?

modelo: nadar
Cuando nado, uso los brazos, las piernas, las manos y los pies.

1. caminar
2. comer
3. bucear
4. dibujar
5. levantar pesas
6. patinar
7. jugar al fútbol
8. bailar
9. mirar la televisión
10. hacer esquí acuático

Expansión
Write a description of an alien. Read your description to a partner, who will draw it.

Más práctica Cuaderno *pp. 269–271* Cuaderno para hispanohablantes *pp. 269–272*

Get Help Online
my.hrw.com

PARA Y PIENSA
Did you get it?
1. Name three parts of your face.
2. Name three parts of your leg.

Differentiating Instruction

Slower-paced Learners
Peer-study Support Have students work with a partner to review the parts of the body. Have one student point to a body part, and ask a yes or no question. **¿Es la nariz?** If the answer is no, the partner should correct the statement. **No, es el ojo.** Have partners change roles after each turn.

Inclusion
Clear Structure Provide students with the following sentence framework to structure their responses for Activity 2. **Cuando** _____ **uso** _____. After filling in the first blank with the name of the activity, ask students to fill in the second blank with the name(s) of the body part(s).

VOCABULARIO en contexto

¡AVANZA! **Goal:** Notice the words Isabel and Mario use to talk about what happens to Mario. Then use **doler** to say what hurts and make excuses. ***Actividades 3–4***

¿Recuerdas? **gustar** with nouns p. 145, stem-changing verbs: **o → ue** p. 223

Telehistoria escena 1

@HOMETUTOR my.hrw.com View, Read and Record

VIDEO DVD
AUDIO

STRATEGIES

Cuando lees
Draw and label Draw an outline of a body. Label the body parts that Mario and Isabel mention in this scene. Which others do you know?

Cuando escuchas
Listen for the action This scene has a lot of action. Listen to what happens to Mario. What does Isabel do and say in response? Will they go to their planned destination?

Mario and Isabel get on their bicycles.

Mario: ¡Tenemos que ser los primeros aficionados en el estadio!
Isabel: Mario, ¿sabes montar en bicicleta?
Mario: Sí, sí, ¡es fácil!
Isabel: ¡Necesitas el casco!
Mario wobbles on his bicycle and crashes into a fruit cart.
Mario: ¡No estoy herido!
Isabel: Pero, ¿y el tobillo? ¿Y la pierna?
Mario: Soy fuerte y sano...
Isabel: Y la cabeza, ¿Mario? ¡Tienes la piel muy roja! ¡La nariz! Abre la boca. ¿Puedes caminar?
Mario: Sí. Me duele un poco el pie... pero puedo caminar.
Isabel: No, no debes caminar.
Mario: Pero... ¡Y Trini Salgado!
Isabel: ¿Trini Salgado? ¡Un autógrafo no es importante! Vamos... **Continuará...** p. 334

También se dice

República Dominicana Mario uses the common phrase **es fácil** to describe riding a bike. In other Spanish-speaking countries you might hear:
- **Puerto Rico** es un guame
- **España** está tirado
- **muchos países** es pan comido, es coser y cantar

¡AVANZA! Objective
- Understand activity vocabulary in context.

Core Resources
- Video Program: DVD 2
- Audio Program: TXT CD 6 track 14

Presentation Strategies
- Have students look at the photo. Ask quick comprehension questions such as the following: **¿Qué llevan los chicos en la cabeza? ¿Quién está herido?**
- Ask students to scan the dialogue to find out how many parts of the body are mentioned.
- Play audio and/or show video while students follow the script in their text.

STANDARDS
1.2 Understand language

Warm Up
Projectable Transparencies, 6-20

Vocabulary Complete the following sentences.

a. bucear
b. las piernas
c. el bloqueador de sol
d. la piel
e. fuerte

1. Siempre uso ____ en la playa.
2. Tomar el sol puede ser malo para ____.
3. Juan levanta muchas pesas. Es ____.
4. Una actividad acuática es ____.
5. Usamos ____ para correr.

Answers: 1. c; 2. d; 3. e; 4. a; 5. b

Communication

Interpretive Mode

Telehistoria Ask students to keep the following questions in mind:
1. ¿Quién dice que es fácil montar en bicicleta?
2. ¿Quién no lleva casco?
3. ¿Quién dice que el autógrafo de Trini no es importante?

Video Summary
@HOMETUTOR VideoPlus my.hrw.com

Mario is eager to get to the stadium to meet Trini. On the way he has a bicycle accident and hurts his ankle and leg.

Differentiating Instruction

Heritage Language Learners
Regional Variations Direct students to the También se dice box. Ask students to comment on the various ways to say that something is easy. Which expression is most familiar to them? Have students translate some of these expressions directly, such as **es pan comido.** Are any of these similar to expressions in English, such as *easy as pie*?

Pre-AP
Sequence Information Copy the following Telehistoria lines onto separate sentence strips.
- **¿Sabes montar en bicicleta?**
- **¡Pero el tobillo y la pierna!**
- **No debes caminar.**
- **¡Un autógrafo no es importante!**

Scramble the sentences. Then ask students to place the strips in sequential order. Which comes first, second, third, and fourth?

Objectives
- Practice using vocabulary in context.
- Practice using **doler** to say what hurts.
- Recycle: stem-changing **o → ue** verbs.
- Practice giving excuses.

Core Resource
- Audio Program: TXT CD 6 track 14

Practice Sequence
- **Activity 3:** Telehistoria comprehension
- **Activity 4:** Vocabulary production: beach activities, stem-changing **o → ue** verbs

STANDARDS
1.1 Engage in conversation, Act. 4
1.2 Understand language, Act. 3, PYP

Nota gramatical
Remind students that the verb **doler** is an **o → ue** stem-changing verb. Other **o → ue** verbs students have learned are **encontrar** and **poder.**

✓ Ongoing Assessment
Get Help Online
More Practice
my.hrw.com

PARA Y PIENSA **Dictation** Dictate some sentences from Telehistoria escena 1 and check students' spelling. For additional practice, use Reteaching & Practice Copymasters URB 6 pp. 13, 15, 22, 23.

Answers Projectable Transparencies, 6-28
Activity 3 **1.** d; **2.** c; **3.** e; **4.** a; **5.** b

Activity 4 Answers will vary. Each response should be preceded by Lo siento, pero no puedo. Sample answers include:
1. ¿Quieres hacer esquí acuático?
   Me duelen las piernas.
2. ¿Quieres jugar al voleibol?
   Me duele la rodilla.
3. ¿Quieres caminar en la playa?
   Me duelen los pies.
4. ¿Quieres nadar?
   Me duele la mano.
5. ¿Quieres leer?
   Me duelen los ojos.
6. ¿Quieres levantar pesas?
   Me duele el brazo.

Para y piensa **1.** le duele **2.** le duelen

3 *Comprensión del episodio* Un accidente

Escuchar
Leer

Combina las frases para describir el episodio. *(Match phrases from the two columns to form sentences about the episode.)*

1. Van en bicicleta porque	**a.** la piel muy roja.
2. Mario piensa que	**b.** más importante que un autógrafo.
3. Mario no debe caminar	**c.** montar en bicicleta es fácil.
4. Mario tiene	**d.** quieren ser los primeros en el estadio.
5. La salud de Mario es	**e.** porque está herido.

Expansión:
Teacher Edition Only
Have students write two more sentences related to the episode.

Nota gramatical
¿*Recuerdas?* **gustar** with nouns p. 145

When you want to say what hurts, use **doler (ue).** This verb functions like **gustar.**

agrees **Me duele la cabeza.** *My head hurts.* *agrees* **Le duelen los brazos.** *His arms hurt.*

With **doler,** you use a definite article with parts of the body.

4 ¿Quieres ir a la playa?
¿*Recuerdas?* Stem-changing verbs: **o → ue** p. 223

Hablar

Pregúntale a otro(a) estudiante si quiere hacer estas actividades en la playa. Él o ella va a decir que no puede porque le duele una parte del cuerpo. *(Ask a partner if he or she wants to do these activities. Your partner will decline, saying something hurts.)*

A ¿Quieres tomar el sol en la playa?

B Lo siento, pero no puedo. Me duele la piel.

1. 
2. 
3. 
4. 
5. 
6. 

Expansión
Say whether you like to do these activities and why.

Get Help Online
my.hrw.com

PARA Y PIENSA **Did you get it?** Complete each sentence based on the Telehistoria with the correct form of **doler.**
1. A Mario _____ la cabeza. **2.** También a él _____ el pie y la pierna.

Differentiating Instruction

Slower-paced Learners
Sentence Completion Before beginning Activity 3, have students complete these sentence starters.
1. **Van en bicicleta porque quieren ser los primeros en el _____.**
2. **Mario piensa que montar en bicicleta es _____.**
3. **Mario no debe caminar porque está _____.**
4. **Mario tiene la piel muy _____.**

Inclusion
Metacognitive Support Write the following sentences on the board. Have students read them aloud.

Me gusta nadar.	**Me duele la cabeza.**
¿Te gusta la playa?	**¿Te duelen los pies?**
Le gustan las uvas.	**Le duele la rodilla.**

Discuss with students the similarity in sentence structure when using the verbs **doler** and **gustar.**

Presentación de GRAMÁTICA

¡AVANZA! **Goal:** Learn how to form the preterite of **-ar** verbs. Then practice using the verbs to say what you did and talk about staying healthy. ***Actividades 5–8***

¿Recuerdas? Telling time p. 90

English Grammar Connection: The **preterite** is a tense used to express an action completed at a definite time in the past. This tense is usually referred to as the past tense in English. In English, regular verbs in the past tense end in *-ed*.

You **lifted** weights yesterday. → **past tense**

Usted **levantó** pesas ayer. → **preterite**

Preterite of Regular -ar Verbs

ANIMATEDGRAMMAR my.hrw.com

Use the preterite tense to talk about actions completed in the past. How do you form the **preterite** of regular **-ar** verbs?

Here's how: To form the **preterite** of a regular **-ar** verb, add the appropriate preterite ending to the verb's stem.

nadar *to swim*	
nadé	**nadamos**
nadaste	**nadasteis**
nadó	**nadaron**

Notice that the **yo** and **usted/él/ella** forms have an accent over the final vowel.

Nadé en el mar. *I **swam** in the sea.*

Mariana **patinó.** *Mariana **skated.***

The **nosotros(as)** form is the same in the preterite as in the present tense. Use the context to determine the tense of the verb

Caminamos en la playa anoche. *We **walked** on the beach last night.*

Más práctica

Cuaderno *pp. 272–274*

Cuaderno para hispanohablantes *pp. 273–275*

@HOMETUTOR my.hrw.com Leveled Practice

Conjuguemos.com

Differentiating Instruction

English Learners

Build Background Write several regular English verbs on the board under the heading *Today.* Then review with English learners how to create the past tense form of these verbs by adding *-ed.* Record these forms under the heading *Yesterday.* Tell students that in many languages the ending of the verbs in the preterite always changes in each form. Ask students to read aloud p. 331.

Heritage Language Learners

Support What They Know Ask students to share an informal story about an exciting or memorable outdoor experience. Instruct other students to raise their hands when they hear a verb in the preterite.

¡AVANZA! Objective

- Present the preterite of regular **-ar** verbs.

Core Resource

- *Cuaderno,* pp. 272–274

Presentation Strategies

- Write the preterite tense of an **-ar** verb such as **caminar** on the board. Underline the preterite endings with a different color chalk. Discuss why the accent is on the first and third person singular verb forms.
- Say the preterite forms of **caminar** and have students repeat after you.

STANDARDS

4.1 Compare languages

21st Century **Communication,** Heritage Language Learners

Warm Up

Projectable Transparencies, 6-21

Vocabulary Complete the sentences.

a. la piel **b.** las piernas **c.** los ojos **d.** la mano **e.** el estómago

1. No quiero escribir. Me duele ____.
2. ¿Por qué no quieres leer? ¿Te duelen ____?
3. Marta no quiere correr. Le duelen ____.
4. Papá no quiere comer. Le duele ____.
5. No queremos tomar el sol. Nos duele ____.

Answers: 1. d; 2. c; 3. b; 4. e; 5. a

Communication

Grammar Activity

Read the following statements aloud. Ask students to raise their hand if the verb is in the preterite tense.

1. **Hablé con Felipe anoche. (preterite)**
2. **Clara toma el sol en la playa. (present)**
3. **Pablo nada en la piscina. (present)**
4. **Carlos buceó ayer por la tarde. (preterite)**
5. **¿Usaste bloqueador de sol? (preterite)**

Ongoing Assessment

Peer Assessment Have students read the English Grammar Connection individually. Then ask pairs of students to read aloud the verbs and check each other's pronunciation.

Objectives

- Practice using the preterite of regular **-ar** verbs.
- Recycle: telling time.
- **Culture:** Discuss how artists reflect their style through their paintings.

Core Resource

- *Cuaderno,* pp. 272–274

Practice Sequence

- **Activity 5:** Controlled practice: preterite of **terminar;** Recycle: telling time
- **Activity 6:** Controlled practice: preterite of **-ar** verbs
- **Activity 7:** Transitional practice: preterite of **-ar** verbs
- **Activity 8:** Open-ended practice: preterite of **-ar** verbs

STANDARDS

1.1 Engage in conversation, Acts. 7–8
1.3 Present information, Acts. 5–8, PYP
2.2 Products and perspectives, CC
4.2 Compare cultures, CC
21st Century **Communication,** Acts. 7, 8; **Flexibility and Adaptability,** Multiple Intelligences; **Initiative and Self-Direction,** Pre-AP: Self-correct

Comparación cultural

Essential Question

Suggested Answer The style that an artist uses can represent his or her ideas and emotions.

About the Artist

Amaya Salazar was born in the Dominican Republic in 1951. She is inspired by the female form and by mother and child images. As shown in the painting *Bosque escondido,* light and flora play an important role in Salazar's work.

Answers Projectable Transparencies, 6-28

Activity 5
1. Yo terminé a las once menos cuarto.
2. Mario y un amigo terminaron a las doce y veinte.
3. Tú terminaste a la una y cuarto.

Answers continue on page 333.

Práctica de GRAMÁTICA

5 ¿Cuándo terminaron? ¿Recuerdas? Telling time p. 90

Escribir Hablar

Ayer Isabel y otros caminaron. ¿Qué dice Isabel sobre cuándo terminaron? *(Indicate when these people finished their walks.)*

11:30 **modelo:** mi madre
Mi madre terminó a las once y media.

1. yo 10:45
2. Mario y un amigo 12:20
3. tú 1:15
4. Carlota 9:50
5. ustedes 10:10
6. nosotros 3:40
7. mis hermanas 1:55
8. mi padre 9:30

Expansión: Teacher Edition Only
Have students rewrite the sentences using other **-ar** verbs and verb phrases such as **estudiar, trabajar, mirar la televisión, levantar pesas.**

6 Una playa en la República Dominicana

Leer Escribir

Fernando y su familia fueron a la playa ayer. Completa su descripción de lo que hicieron. Escribe la forma apropiada en el pretérito del verbo correcto entre paréntesis. *(Write the appropriate preterite form of the correct verb in parentheses.)*

Ayer mi familia y yo __1.__ (decorar / pasar) un rato en la playa de Boca Chica. Mis padres __2.__ (invitar / celebrar) a mis abuelos también. Mi madre __3.__ (trabajar / preparar) sándwiches y yo __4.__ (limpiar / ayudar) con las bebidas. Mis hermanos __5.__ (usar / bucear) en el mar y yo __6.__ (tomar / usar) el sol. Después, toda la familia __7.__ (nadar / ganar). Y tú, ¿ __8.__ (caminar / nadar) en el mar ayer?

Expansión
Write a paragraph about a trip you and someone you know took to the beach.

Comparación cultural

La artista y su estilo

How do artists reflect a distinctive style in their painting? Bright pastel colors, glowing light, and abstract images that reveal hidden figures are common elements in Amaya Salazar's work. This painter from the **Dominican Republic** is also a sculptor and muralist. Many consider her painting to have a magical or dreamlike quality. What images can you find hidden in this painting of a tropical forest?

Bosque escondido *(2005), Amaya Salazar*

Compara con tu mundo *How would you describe the style, colors, and images used by your favorite artist? How does his or her work compare to that of Amaya Salazar?*

Differentiating Instruction

Inclusion

Clear Structure Have students fold a piece of paper in three columns. Provide them with the following steps to complete Activity 5.
1. In column 1, copy the subject.
2. In column 2, write the corresponding preterite form of the verb **terminar.**
3. In column 3, write the time shown on the clock in words.
4. Read the completed sentence aloud.

Pre-AP

Self-correct After students complete Activity 6, have them read each sentence aloud to a partner. Remind students to make sure that each verb choice makes sense in context, and that each preterite form is correct given the subject of the sentence.

7 ¿Lo hiciste?

Hablar

Habla con otro(a) estudiante sobre lo que hiciste la semana pasada. *(Talk about what activities you did last week.)*

A ¿Montaste en bicicleta?

B Sí, monté en bicicleta en el parque. (No, no monté en bicicleta.)

1. 
2. 
3. 
4. 
5. 
6. 

Expansión
Create a Venn diagram to compare your answers with your partner's.

8 Durante el fin de semana

Hablar

Trabaja en un grupo de tres. Habla de lo que hicieron el fin de semana pasado. *(In a group of three, talk about what you did last weekend.)*

comprar un almuerzo sano	caminar en la playa
estudiar	mirar la televisión
levantar pesas	trabajar
nadar en una piscina	¿ ?

A ¿Compraron ustedes un almuerzo sano?

B Sí, compré una ensalada.

C No, mis amigos y yo compramos papas fritas.

Expansión:
Teacher Edition Only
Have students conduct a class survey about activities they did last weekend.

Más práctica Cuaderno *pp. 272–274* Cuaderno para hispanohablantes *pp. 273–275*

Get Help Online
my.hrw.com

PARA Y PIENSA

Did you get it? Complete each sentence with the preterite form of the verb in parentheses.
1. Ayer mis amigos y yo ____ en el mar. (bucear)
2. Tú ____ el sol mucho y ahora tu piel está roja. (tomar)
3. José y Ricardo ____ pesas para ser más fuertes. (levantar)

Differentiating Instruction

Multiple Intelligences

Interpersonal After students complete Activity 7, have each pair create a role-play based on two or three of the questions and answers they just discussed. Tell students to pretend they are talking with a friend at school, on the street, or on the phone. Encourage them to use body language to support the meaning of their statements.

Pre-AP

Expand and Elaborate Before doing Activity 8, write each word or phrase found in the word box in the center of a concept web. Divide the class into small groups, and assign each group one web. Instruct students to add as much vocabulary around the web as they can that could be used to talk about their word or phrase.

Communication

Grammar Activity

Ask students to write ten questions that include regular **-ar** verbs in the preterite. Have students ask and answer the questions aloud. Example: **¿Caminaste a la escuela hoy? No, no caminé a la escuela.**

Long-term Retention

Recycle

On the board, list activities that someone could do on a day at the beach. Ask students at what time they did each activity. Example: **¿A qué hora nadaste? Nadé a las tres.**

✓ Ongoing Assessment

Get Help Online
More Practice
my.hrw.com

Peer Assessment Ask students to work in pairs to complete the sentences and correct each other. For additional practice, use Reteaching & Practice Copymasters URB 6 pp. 16, 17, 24.

Answers Projectable Transparencies, 6-28 and 6-29

Answers continued from page 332

4. Carlota terminó a las diez menos diez.
5. Ustedes terminaron a las diez y diez.
6. Nosotros terminamos a las cuatro menos veinte.
7. Mis hermanas terminaron a las dos menos cinco.
8. Mi padre terminó a las nueve y media.

Activity 6
1. pasamos
2. invitaron
3. preparó
4. ayudé
5. bucearon
6. tomé
7. nadó
8. nadaste

Activity 7
1. ¿Caminaste en la playa?
Sí, (No, no) caminé en la playa.
2. ¿Nadaste?
Sí, (No, no) nadé.
3. ¿Levantaste pesas?
Sí, (No, no) levanté pesas.
4. ¿Usaste bloqueador de sol?
Sí, (No, no) usé bloqueador de sol.
5. ¿Preparaste la comida?
Sí, (No, no) preparé la comida.
6. ¿Tomaste el sol?
Sí, (No, no) tomé el sol.

Activity 8 Answers will vary. Sample answers: ¿Estudiaron ustedes? No, no estudiamos. Miramos un DVD.

Para y piensa **1.** buceamos **2.** tomaste **3.** levantaron

¡AVANZA! Objectives

- Practice using the preterite of regular **-ar** verbs in context.
- Identify lesson vocabulary in context.

Core Resources

- Video Program: DVD 2
- Audio Program: TXT CD 6 track 15

Presentation Strategies

- Have students scan the conversation with the doctor. Ask them to look for examples of preterite tense forms.
- Play the audio.
- Show the video. Point to the Spanish use of the word **¡Pum!** Ask them what its English equivalent might be.

Practice Sequence

- **Activity 9:** Telehistoria comprehension
- **Activity 10:** Transitional practice: preterite of **-ar** verbs, beach activities
- **Activity 11:** Transitional practice: preterite of **-ar** verbs

STANDARDS

1.2 Understand language, Acts. 9, 11
1.3 Present information, Acts. 10–11, PYP
21st Century **Creativity and Innovation,** Multiple Intelligences: Interpersonal/ Heritage Language Learners

Warm Up Projectable Transparencies, 6-21

Preterite of -ar verbs Complete the sentences using the preterite of the given verb.

1. Ana y Teresa _____ el sol ayer. (tomar)
2. Yo _____ en el mar. (bucear)
3. Nosotros _____ bloqueador de sol. (usar)
4. ¿Tú _____ pesas en el gimnasio? (levantar)
5. Felipe _____ en la oficina. (trabajar)

Answers: 1. tomaron; 2. buceé; 3. usamos; 4. levantaste; 5. trabajó

Video Summary

@HOMETUTOR VideoPlus my.hrw.com

Isabel helps Mario walk to the doctor's office. Isabel answers all the questions the doctor asks Mario about the accident. Mario avoids admitting his fault in the crash.

GRAMÁTICA en contexto

¡AVANZA! **Goal:** Pay attention to how Mario and Isabel use the preterite to tell the doctor about Mario's accident. Then use the preterite of regular **-ar** verbs to talk about past actions. ***Actividades 9–11***

Telehistoria escena 2

@HOMETUTOR my.hrw.com **View, Read and Record**

STRATEGIES

Cuando lees
Read for excuses Read the conversation involving Mario, Isabel, and the doctor. What excuse does Mario use to avoid admitting his fault in the crash?

Cuando escuchas
Listen for incomplete sentences Listen for the sentence that Mario starts, but does not complete. Finish his sentence using previous knowledge gained in scene 1.

VIDEO DVD

AUDIO

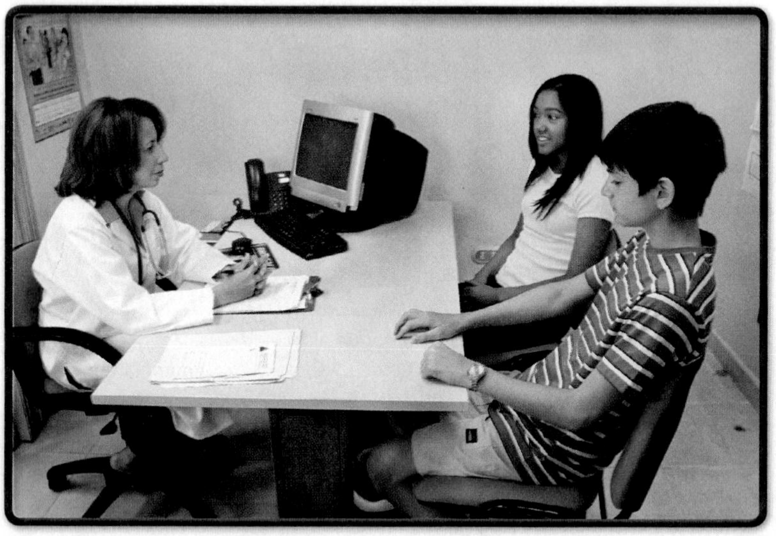

Isabel takes Mario to the doctor's office.

Doctora: ¿Mario Álvarez? ¿Está usted enfermo?

Isabel: Le duelen la pierna y la cabeza. Lo ayudé a caminar.

Doctora: *(to Mario)* ¿Qué hiciste?

Isabel: Pues, montó en su bicicleta... ¡cerca de unas frutas!

Mario: Monté en mi bicicleta...

Doctora: ¿Llevaste un casco?

Isabel: Sí, ¡pero Mario piensa que es Lance Armstrong!

Mario: Isabel, ¡el señor de las frutas caminó delante de mi bicicleta!

Isabel: Y allí... ¡Pum!

Doctora: Mario, ¿sabes montar en bicicleta?

Mario: Sí, es fácil.

Doctora: ¿Te gustó?

Mario: Ahora estoy herido, ¡pero me gustó!

Doctora: *(to Isabel)* Para la salud de tu amigo, no más bicicletas, ¡por favor!

Continuará... p. 339

Differentiating Instruction

Slower-paced Learners

Read Before Listening Before listening to the Telehistoria, have students scan the text silently. Ask them to copy each verb they find onto a separate index card. Have students divide the verbs into two groups—present tense and preterite tense. Discuss why each verb is in the present or preterite tense based on the context.

Multiple Intelligences

Interpersonal Have volunteers play the parts of Isabel, Mario, and la doctora. As students read the script, encourage them to emphasize the facial expressions appropriate to each character's part. When Isabel says, **¡Pero Mario piensa que es Lance Armstrong!** what might her expression be? What about Mario's?

9 *Comprensión del episodio* Hablan con la doctora

Escuchar
Leer

Indica si estas oraciones son ciertas o falsas según el episodio. Corrige las oraciones falsas. *(Tell whether these sentences are true or false. Correct the false statements.)*

1. A Mario le duelen la cabeza y los brazos.
2. El señor de las frutas caminó detrás de Mario.
3. Mario llevó casco.
4. La doctora piensa que Mario es Lance Armstrong.
5. A Mario le gustó montar en bicicleta.
6. Ahora Isabel está herida.

Expansión:
Teacher Edition Only
Have students write two or more false statements about the Telehistoria, exchange them with a partner, and correct each other.

10 De vacaciones con tu familia

Escribir

Estás de vacaciones en la playa con tu familia y le escribes una tarjeta postal a un(a) amigo(a). Describe lo que hicieron ayer. *(Write a postcard about what you and your family did yesterday on vacation at the beach.)*

modelo:

Expansión:
Teacher Edition Only
Have students write a short e-mail to a friend, describing what they did at the park during the weekend.

11 ¿Qué hicieron tú y tus amigos?

Escribir
Hablar

Describe lo que tú y tus amigos hicieron recientemente. *(Describe what you and your friends did recently.)*

1. ¿Alquilaron ustedes un DVD interesante?
2. ¿Con quién hablaste por teléfono ayer?
3. ¿Qué hiciste tú en la biblioteca ayer?
4. ¿Dónde escucharon ustedes buena música?
5. ¿Qué miraste en la televisión anoche?
6. ¿Qué hicieron ustedes en el centro comercial?

Expansión
Write three original questions and ask them to a partner.

Get Help Online
my.hrw.com

PARA Y PIENSA

Did you get it? Create sentences using each verb in the preterite tense.
1. Isabel y Mario / llevar cascos
2. Mario / no montar en bicicleta muy bien
3. El señor de las frutas / caminar delante de Mario

Communication

Common Error Alert

Remind students that the verb **bucear** is a regular **-ar** verb. The **yo** form of **bucear** in the preterite tense is **buceé.**

Long-term Retention

Study Tips

Have students practice subject-verb agreement by writing the verb in the preterite form with the subject. Give them a few verbs to practice, such as **llevar: yo llevé, tú llevaste, usted/él/ella llevó, nosotros(as) llevamos, ellos/ellas llevaron.**

Ongoing Assessment

Get Help Online
More Practice
my.hrw.com

PARA Y PIENSA

Peer Assessment Ask students to complete the Para y piensa sentences. Then have students correct each other's work in pairs or small groups. For additional practice, use Reteaching & Practice Copymasters URB 6 pp. 16, 18.

Answers Projectable Transparencies, 6-29

Activity 9
1. Falso. A Mario le duelen la cabeza y la pierna.
2. Falso. El señor de las frutas caminó delante de Mario.
3. Cierto.
4. Falso. Mario piensa que él es Lance Armstrong.
5. Cierto.
6. Falso. Ahora Mario está herido.

Activity 10 Answers will vary. Sample answers include: Un saludo desde la playa. Ayer tomamos el sol. Yo nadé un rato en la tarde.

Activity 11 Answers will vary. Sample answers include:
1. Sí, alquilamos un DVD interesante.
2. Hablé con un amigo.
3. Estudié en la biblioteca.
4. Escuchamos buena música en la escuela.
5. Miré una película en la televisión anoche.
6. Compramos ropa nueva en el centro comercial.

Para y piensa
1. Isabel y Mario llevaron cascos.
2. Mario no montó en bicicleta muy bien.
3. El señor de las frutas caminó delante de Mario.

Differentiating Instruction

Multiple Intelligences

Visual Learners Provide students with pieces of cardstock to design their own postcards for Activity 10. After drafting the message for their card, have students design the front with a beach scene that reflects the information they have written. Students might also research Dominican stamps, and draw one in the upper right-hand corner.

Heritage Language Learners

Writing Skills Have students choose one of the questions from Activity 11 to develop into a longer paragraph. Encourage them to recount the whole story related to the question they choose. What happened first, next, and last? Also, remind students to proofread their writing for the use of accents in the preterite.

¡AVANZA! Objective

- Present the preterite of verbs ending in **-car**, **-gar**, **-zar**

Core Resource

- *Cuaderno,* pp. 275–277

Presentation Strategies

- Review the preterite endings of regular **-ar** verbs by writing on the board or OHT the preterite forms of **sacar**, **pagar**, and **empezar**.
- Underline the spelling change in the **yo** forms: **saqué**, **pagué**, **empecé**.
- Say a subject pronoun followed by a **-car**, **-gar**, **-zar** infinitive and call on students to say the appropriate preterite form.

STANDARDS

4.1 Compare languages

Warm Up Projectable Transparencies, 6-22

Preterite of -ar verbs Complete the sentences.

a. enseñó **b.** buceamos **c.** usaste
d. escucharon **e.** tomó

1. El maestro ____ la lección.
2. Los estudiantes ____.
3. Carlos ____ apuntes.
4. Tú ____ la computadora.
5. Francisco y yo ____ en el mar.

Answers: 1. a; 2. d; 3. e; 4. c; 5. b

Verbs Students Know

Students have learned the following **-car, -gar,** and **-zar** verbs: **practicar, tocar, sacar, buscar, jugar, llegar, pagar, empezar, almorzar,** and **comenzar.**

Communication

Grammar Activity

Prepare a list of sentences with **-ar** verbs in the **yo** form of the preterite tense, including several from verbs ending in **-car, -gar,** and **-zar.** Read the list aloud and have students raise their hand when they hear a verb that requires a spelling change in the preterite **yo** form.

Presentación de GRAMÁTICA

¡AVANZA! **Goal:** Learn how to form the preterite of verbs ending in **-car, -gar,** and **-zar.** Then use these verbs to say what people did. ***Actividades 12–15***

English Grammar Connection: The spelling of some verbs in English changes in the past tense when *-ed* is added: for example, *admit → admitted, stop → stopped, picnic → picnicked.* Spanish also has verbs that change their spelling in the preterite.

Preterite of -car, -gar, -zar Verbs

ANIMATEDGRAMMAR my.hrw.com

There is a spelling change in the preterite of regular verbs that end in **-car, -gar,** or **-zar.** How do you write the verb forms that have a change in spelling?

Here's how:

Regular verbs that end in **-car, -gar,** or **-zar** have a spelling change in the **yo** form of the preterite. This change allows these words to maintain their original sound.

buscar	c	*becomes*	qu	**(yo) busqué**
jugar	g	*becomes*	gu	**(yo) jugué**
almorzar	z	*becomes*	c	**(yo) almorcé**

Busqué el bloqueador de sol. Él **buscó** las toallas.
I looked for *the sunscreen. He* ***looked for*** *the towels.*

Jugué al béisbol. Ellas **jugaron** al fútbol.
I played *baseball. They* ***played*** *soccer.*

Almorcé a la una. ¿A qué hora **almorzaste** tú?
I ate lunch *at one o'clock. What time* ***did you eat lunch****?*

Más práctica
Cuaderno *pp. 275–277*
Cuaderno para hispanohablantes *pp. 276–279*

@HOMETUTOR my.hrw.com
Leveled Practice
Conjuguemos.com

Differentiating Instruction

Slower-paced Learners

Memory Aids Have students add to their set of verb reference cards. On separate index cards, have students copy the preterite forms of the verbs presented in Lección 2. Instruct students to staple each preterite card to the card for the verb's present tense. Students should write **presente** or **pretérito** at the top of each card.

Inclusion

Alphabetic/Phonetic Awareness Direct students' attention to preterite forms that have an accent over the final syllable, such as **pagué** and **montó.** Say several examples aloud, and have students repeat. Tell students to clap when they say the syllable in the word that receives the stress. Discuss how these words would be pronounced with no accent.

Práctica de GRAMÁTICA

12 La agenda de Isabel

Escribir

Mira la agenda de Isabel y completa lo que dice ella sobre las actividades de la semana pasada. Sigue el modelo. *(Complete what Isabel says she did last week. Follow the model.)*

modelo: «_____ a las cuatro el martes.»
«Practiqué el piano a las cuatro el martes.»

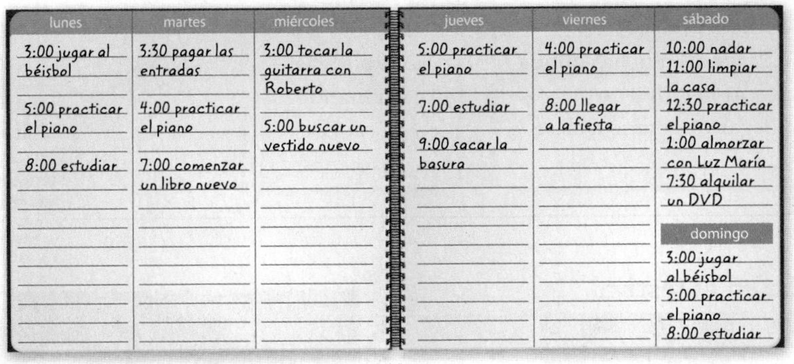

1. «_____ a la una el sábado.»
2. «_____ a las ocho el viernes.»
3. «_____ a las siete el martes.»
4. «_____ a las tres y media el martes.»
5. «_____ a las tres el miércoles.»
6. «_____ a las cinco el miércoles.»
7. «_____ a las tres el domingo.»
8. «_____ a las nueve el jueves.»

Expansión:
Teacher Edition Only
Have students add three more items to Isabel's agenda, exchange them with a partner, and write sentences based on what she said.

Audio Program
TXT CD 6 Track 16
Audio Script, TE p. 323b

13 Muchas preguntas

Escuchar
Escribir

Mario quiere saber lo que hiciste ayer. Escucha sus preguntas y escribe tus respuestas. *(Listen to Mario's questions and then write your answers.)*

modelo: ¿Pagaste el almuerzo?
Sí, pagué el almuerzo. (No, no pagué el almuerzo.)

Expansión
Explain why, where, and/or with whom you did these activities.

AUDIO

Pronunciación La letra g con e, i

Before **e** and **i**, the **g** in Spanish is pronounced like the Spanish **j,** or **jota.** Listen and repeat.

ge	→	**inteligente**	**Argentina**	**Jorge**	**general**
gi	→	**gimnasio**	**digital**	**página**	**Sergio**

Jorge corre en el gimnasio. **Regina tiene una cámara digital.**

Objectives
- Practice using the preterite of **-car**, **-gar**, **-zar** verbs.
- **Pronunciation:** Practice pronouncing the letter **g** before **e** and **i**.

Core Resource
- Audio Program: TXT CD 6 tracks 16, 17

Practice Sequence
- **Activity 12:** Controlled practice: preterite of **-car**, **-gar**, **-zar** verbs
- **Activity 13:** Transitional practice: preterite of **-car**, **-gar**, **-zar** verbs

STANDARDS
1.2 Understand language, Act. 13, Pronunciación
1.3 Present information, Acts. 12, 13
4.1 Compare languages, Pronunciación
21st Century **Communication,** Slower-paced Learners

Ongoing Assessment
Dictation Have students write the following dictation with the letter combination **ge** and **gi: Gerardo, el chico de Argentina, es muy inteligente pero no sabe usar la cámara digital.**

Differentiating Instruction

Multiple Intelligences
Intrapersonal Throughout Lección 2, have students make journal entries about what they did the day before. Encourage students to choose from the verbs they know in preterite forms, and write two or three sentences about their recent activities. In addition, students might reflect on past events using specific dates and times.

Slower-paced Learners
Yes/No Questions After completing Activity 12, have students work in pairs to ask each other yes or no questions based on Isabel's planner. One student pretends the planner is his or hers, while the other student asks questions. **¿Practicaste la guitarra el viernes? Sí, practiqué la guitarra el viernes.** Then have partners change roles.

Answers Projectable Transparencies, 6-29 and 6-30

Activity 12
1. Almorcé con Luz María a la una el sábado.
2. Llegué a la fiesta a las ocho el viernes.
3. Comencé un libro nuevo a las siete el martes.
4. Pagué las entradas a las tres y media el martes.
5. Toqué la guitarra con Roberto a las tres el miércoles.
6. Busqué un vestido nuevo a las cinco el miércoles.
7. Jugué al béisbol a las tres el domingo.
8. Saqué la basura a las nueve el jueves.

Activity 13 Answers will vary. Sample answers include:
1. Llegué a la escuela a las ocho.
2. Saqué buenas notas.
3. Almorcé a las doce.
4. No comencé la tarea.
5. Sí, busqué ropa nueva.
6. Jugué al fútbol.

Objectives
- Practice using the preterite of **-car**, **-gar**, **-zar** verbs.
- **Culture:** Learn about a merengue festival.

Core Resource
- *Cuaderno,* pp. 275–277

Practice Sequence
- **Activity 14:** Transitional practice: preterite of **-car**, **-gar**, **-zar** verbs, parts of the body, **doler**
- **Activity 15:** Open-ended practice: preterite of **-car, -gar, -zar** verbs

STANDARDS
1.1 Engage in conversation, Act. 14
2.1 Practices and perspectives, Act. 15
3.1 Knowledge of other disciplines, Act. 15
4.2 Compare cultures, Act. 15
21st Century **Information Literacy,** Multiple Intelligences

Comparación cultural

Essential Question
Suggested Answer Music and dance can reflect the ethnic background and character of a country.

Background Information
The main venue for musical performances during the **Festival del Merengue** is a large, open-air stage facing the Caribbean Sea. Performances are free and open to the public.

✓ Ongoing Assessment
Get Help Online
More Practice
my.hrw.com

PARA Y PIENSA **Peer Assessment** After completing the Para y piensa, have students correct each other's work in pairs. For additional practice, use Reteaching & Practice Copymasters URB 6 pp. 19, 20.

Answers Projectable Transparencies, 6-30
Activity 14 Answers will vary, but should follow the model and include these verb forms:
1. A. jugaste B. jugué
2. A. practicaste B. practiqué
3. A. almorzaste B. almorcé
4. A. tocaste B. toqué
5. A. llegaste B. llegué

Activity 15 Answers will vary. Sample answers: Llegué a las diez. Tocaron música alegre…

Para y piensa **1.** llegué **2.** jugaron **3.** comenzó **4.** practiqué

14 Me duele...
Hablar

Pregúntale a otro(a) estudiante por qué no hizo estas cosas hoy. Él o ella va a decir que le duele una parte del cuerpo. *(Ask a partner why he or she didn't do these things today. Your partner will answer by saying something hurts.)*

modelo: sacar una buena nota

A: ¿Por qué no sacaste una buena nota?

B: No saqué una buena nota porque me duele la cabeza.

Estudiante A	Estudiante B
1. jugar al ¿ ?	los pies
2. practicar deportes	el estómago
3. almorzar mucha comida	las piernas
4. tocar la guitarra	la mano
5. llegar temprano a clase	la cabeza
6. ¿ ?	¿ ?

Expansión
Tell about activities you can't do when something hurts.

15 Un día en el festival
Escribir

Comparación cultural
El Festival del Merengue
How do music and dance reflect the culture of a country? Merengue is a lively style of music and dance that many consider a symbol of the **Dominican Republic.** Musicians use instruments such as the *güiro,* maracas, accordion, saxophone, and drums to play its characteristic rhythm. The Festival del Merengue takes place every summer in Santo Domingo. The ten-day event includes music, parades, arts and crafts fairs, cart races, and a wide variety of Dominican foods.

El Festival del Merengue

Compara con tu mundo *Do you know of any similar festivals in your area?*

Fuiste al Festival del Merengue. Describe el día. *(Describe your day at the festival.)*

pistas: llegar, tocar, almorzar, comenzar, escuchar, bailar

modelo: El festival comenzó a las diez...

Más práctica Cuaderno *pp. 275–277* Cuaderno para hispanohablantes *pp. 276–279*

Get Help Online
my.hrw.com

PARA Y PIENSA **Did you get it?** Complete each sentence with the preterite form of the appropriate verb: **comenzar, jugar, llegar,** or **practicar.**
1. Yo _____ a casa temprano.
2. ¿Ustedes _____ al tenis ayer?
3. El partido _____ a las siete.
4. Yo _____ deportes anoche.

Differentiating Instruction

Pre-AP
Expand and Elaborate Encourage students to add another turn to their conversations in Activity 14. Have **Estudiante A** ask a follow-up question about why that specific part of the body hurts. **Estudiante B** should explain.
A: ¿Por qué te duele la cabeza?
B: Porque no dormí bien.

Multiple Intelligences
Musical/Rhythmic Have students choose one of the instruments mentioned in the Comparación cultural to research. They might look for information about the history of the instrument, how it is played, what it is made of, or famous musicians who play it.

Todo junto

¡AVANZA! **Goal:** ***Show what you know*** Pay attention to the doctor's advice to Mario. Then use the preterite of regular **-ar** verbs and verbs ending in **-car, -gar,** and **-zar** to talk about your health. ***Actividades 16–20***

Telehistoria completa

@HOMETUTOR my.hrw.com View, Read and Record

STRATEGIES

Cuando lees
Find the topics While reading, find at least two or three topics in this scene. One is the doctor's suggestions for Mario's health. What other topics can you identify?

Cuando escuchas
Listen for the implied meaning Listen for the unstated meaning to answer these questions: Will Mario ever get Trini's autograph? Is Mario strong and healthy now?

Escena 1 *Resumen*
Mario está herido y no puede ir con Isabel al estadio para ver a Trini Salgado.

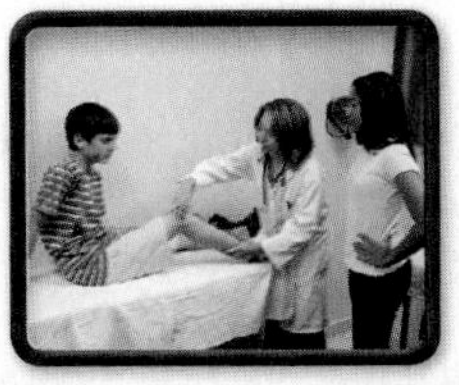

Escena 2 *Resumen*
Isabel ayuda a Mario a caminar. A él le duelen la pierna y la cabeza. Ellos hablan con una doctora.

Escena 3

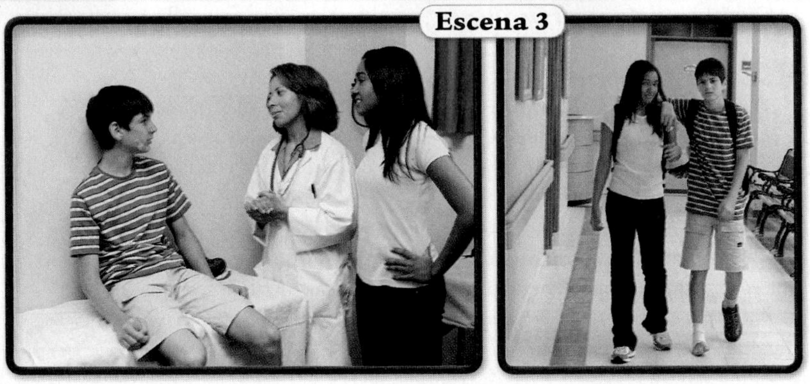

VIDEO DVD

AUDIO

Doctora: El tobillo está bien. ¿Te duele la rodilla?

Mario: No. *(The doctor touches Mario's knee, and he yelps.)* Un poco.

Doctora: No puedes jugar al fútbol, y no puedes jugar al béisbol por cuatro semanas.

Mario: ¿Puedo levantar pesas?

Doctora: Levantar pesas, sí, con los brazos. Con las piernas, no...

Isabel: Muchas gracias, doctora. Adiós.

The doctor leaves. Mario turns to Isabel.

Mario: ¡Ay, el autógrafo para Alicia! Comencé a...

Isabel: Sí, Mario, lo siento. Comenzaste a buscar a Trini, pero ¿qué podemos hacer? *(They stand to leave.)*

Isabel: ¿Vamos a la playa mañana? El mar es bueno para los enfermos.

Mario: ¡No estoy enfermo!

Differentiating Instruction

Pre-AP

Draw Conclusions Ask students questions about the Telehistoria that begin with **¿Por qué?** Remind students that the answers might not be explicitly stated in the text. Here are a few possibilities:
¿Por qué Mario no puede jugar al fútbol?
¿Por qué Mario puede levantar pesas solamente con los brazos?

Heritage Language Learners

Support What They Know Ask students to share stories of minor injuries they have encountered. Have they ever fallen off a bike, or been injured playing a sport? Ask students to describe what happened, and how they resolved the problem.

¡AVANZA! **Objective**
- Integrate lesson content.

Core Resources
- Video Program: DVD 2
- Audio Program: TXT CD 6 track 18

Presentation Strategies
- Ask students to summarize Escenas 1 and 2.
- Ask students to describe the photos for Escena 3 by asking quick comprehension questions such as: **¿Dónde están Isabel y Mario ahora? ¿Quién más está en la foto?**
- Show the video or play the audio.

STANDARDS
1.2 Understand language

Warm Up
Projectable Transparencies, 6-22

Preterite of -car, -gar, -zar verbs Complete the sentences with the preterite of the verb indicated.

1. El verano pasado, nosotros _____ muchos deportes. (practicar)
2. Mónica _____ a jugar al voleibol. (comenzar)
3. Yo _____ al béisbol con mi equipo. (jugar)
4. Y tú, ¿cuándo _____? (almorzar)

Answers: 1. practicamos; 2. comenzó; 3. jugué; 4. almorzaste

Long-term Retention
Recycle

Remind students that **doler** is an **o** to **ue** stem-changing verb. Remind them that stem-changing verbs have regular **-ar, -er,** and **-ir** endings. Have them read p. 223 again.

Video Summary
@HOMETUTOR VideoPlus my.hrw.com

The doctor discovers that Mario's knee is injured. She tells him he cannot play certain sports for some time. He asks if he can lift weights, and the doctor says—only hand weights. Upon leaving the doctor's office, Mario worries about getting Trini's autograph. Instead, Isabel suggests going to the beach the next day because the sea is good for sick people.

TODO JUNTO

Objective

- Practice using and integrating lesson content.

Core Resources

- *Cuaderno,* pp. 278–279
- Audio Program: TXT CD 6 tracks 14, 15, 18, 19, 20

Practice Sequence

- **Activities 16, 17:** Telehistoria comprehension
- **Activity 18:** Open-ended practice: speaking
- **Activity 19:** Open-ended practice: listening, reading, speaking
- **Activity 20:** Open-ended practice: writing

STANDARDS

1.1 Engage in conversation, Act. 18
1.2 Understand language, Acts. 16–17, PYP
1.3 Present information, Acts. 18–20
Communication, Act. 18; **Creativity and Innovation,** Act. 20/ Slower-paced Learners: Peer-study Support

✓ Ongoing Assessment

Get Help Online
More Practice
my.hrw.com

Rubric Activity 18

Speaking Criteria	Maximum Credit	Partial Credit	Minimum Credit
Content	Dialogue includes all of the information.	Dialogue includes some of the information.	Dialogue includes little information.
Communication	Most of the conversation is well organized and easy to follow.	Parts of the conversation are well organized and easy to follow.	The conversation is disorganized and hard to follow.
Accuracy	There are few mistakes in grammar and vocabulary.	There are some mistakes in grammar and vocabulary.	There are many mistakes in grammar and vocabulary.

Answers Projectable Transparencies, 6-30

Activity 16
1. ...aficionados en el estadio.
2. ...le duelen la cabeza y la pierna.
3. ...quieren su autógrafo.
4. ...caminó delante de la bicicleta de Mario.
5. ...jugar al fútbol y al béisbol.
6. ...con los brazos y no con las piernas.

Answers continue on page 341.

16 *Comprensión de los episodios* ¡A completar!

Escuchar
Leer

Completa las oraciones para describir lo que pasó en los episodios. *(Complete the sentences.)*

1. Isabel y Mario quieren ser los primeros...
2. Mario no está enfermo, pero...
3. Isabel y Mario buscaron a Trini Salgado porque...
4. El señor de las frutas...
5. A Mario le duele la rodilla y no puede...
6. Mario puede levantar pesas, pero...

Expansión:
Teacher Edition Only
Have students make an oral summary of the Telehistoria.

17 *Comprensión de los episodios* ¿Qué pasó?

Escuchar
Leer

Contesta las preguntas sobre los episodios. *(Answer the questions.)*

1. ¿Qué buscaron Isabel y Mario?
2. ¿Qué llevó Mario?
3. ¿Le gustó a Mario montar en bicicleta?
4. ¿Qué le duele a Mario?

Expansión:
Teacher Edition Only
Have students write three more questions about each episode, exchange them with a partner, and answer each other's questions.

18 ¿Qué hiciste para la salud?

Digital performance space

Hablar

STRATEGY Hablar
Draw a Venn diagram for similarities and differences While talking, make a Venn diagram. In one circle list healthy things *you* did that your partner did not. In the other circle, list what *your partner* did that you did not. In the overlap, list what *you both* did.

Habla con otro(a) estudiante sobre las actividades sanas que hiciste el mes pasado. Explícale qué beneficios tienen, dónde las hiciste y con quién. *(Talk with a partner about the healthy activities you did last month. Explain what benefits the activities have for your health, where you did them, and with whom.)*

caminar	levantar pesas
jugar al ¿ ?	nadar
practicar deportes	almorzar bien

A ¿Levantaste pesas?

B Sí, levanté pesas porque es bueno para los brazos. Levanté pesas en el gimnasio con mi amigo Fernando...

Expansión:
Teacher Edition Only
Have student pairs play the roles of doctor and patient. The patient talks about the activities he/she did during the week. The doctor explains why they are healthy or not.

Differentiating Instruction

Slower-paced Learners

Sentence Completion Organize students into pairs, and provide each pair with a blank sentence strip. Then instruct students to review the three scenes of the Telehistoria to draft the beginning of a sentence. Have pairs pass their sentence starter to another group for that group to complete.

Multiple Intelligences

Linguistic/Verbal Write names of activities on index cards. Write these headings on the board: **Es sano** and **No es sano.** Invite a volunteer to the front to stand under one of the headings. Give him or her one of the activity cards. The student must give a sentence supporting the position. **No es sano no tomar desayuno. Es sano comer cereal y fruta.**

19 Integración

Digital performance space

Leer
Escuchar
Hablar

Lee el artículo y escucha la entrevista. Compara lo que tú hiciste durante la semana para la salud con lo que estas personas hicieron. Decide si eres tan sano(a) como ellos. *(Compare what you did last week to stay healthy to what these people did.)*

Fuente 1 Artículo del periódico

Ricardo, ¿qué hiciste para ganar?

Ricardo Núñez es el campeón olímpico de natación. Él nos explicó cómo ganó el año pasado. Es un atleta muy trabajador. «Yo soy una persona muy seria. Practico todos los días. Este fin de semana nadé por dos horas el sábado y el domingo levanté pesas en el gimnasio por tres horas». Para él, la comida es muy importante. «Ayer preparé un desayuno muy sano... cereal, jugo de naranja y pan. Hoy almorcé una ensalada y sopa de pollo». Núñez también tiene que descansar. «También descanso. Ayer alquilé una película muy buena... una película de natación».

Fuente 2 Entrevista de radio

Listen and take notes
- ¿Qué deportes practicó la chica?
- ¿Qué almorzó?

modelo: Durante la semana yo...

Audio Program
TXT CD 6
Tracks 19, 20.
Audio Script, TE p. 323b

20 Un poema diamante

Digital performance space

Escribir

Escribe un poema diamante sobre algo que te hace sentir sano(a). *(Write a diamond poem about something that makes you feel healthy.)*

Para organizarte: modelo:
- *el nombre del lugar o de la actividad* → la playa
- *una descripción* → agua bonita
- *tres cosas que hiciste* → tomé el sol, caminé, miré el agua
- *otra descripción* → agua tranquila
- *otro nombre* → el mar Caribe

Writing Criteria	Excellent	Good	Needs Work
Content	Your poem includes most of the required elements.	Your poem includes some of the required elements.	Your poem includes few of the required elements.
Communication	Most of your poem is organized and easy to follow.	Parts of your poem are organized and easy to follow.	Your poem is disorganized and hard to follow.
Accuracy	Your poem has few mistakes in grammar and vocabulary.	Your poem has some mistakes in grammar and vocabulary.	Your poem has many mistakes in grammar and vocabulary.

Expansión:
Teacher Edition Only
Have students write a diamond poem about another topic

Más práctica Cuaderno *pp. 278–279* Cuaderno para hispanohablantes *pp. 280–281*

Get Help Online my.hrw.com

PARA Y PIENSA

Did you get it? Complete each sentence based on the Telehistoria with the preterite form of the verb in parentheses.
1. Mario _____ a buscar a Trini. (comenzar)
2. Isabel y Mario no la _____ . (encontrar)

Differentiating Instruction

Inclusion

Cumulative Instruction Have students tell their stories in Activity 19 twice. First, have them recount the events in the present tense. This round should give them a chance to compile vocabulary, construct sentences, and create a storyline without worrying about preterite forms. Next, have students retell their stories in the past.

Slower-paced Learners

Peer-study Support Before completing Activity 20, organize students into small groups. Each group should work together to create a poem following the organizational structure. Provide each group with a piece of chart paper or poster board to display their work. Encourage students to use these models for reference as they work on their poems individually.

Long-term Retention

Pre-AP Integration

Activity 19 Have students write short essays in which they discuss events from the past week at school. Have students write a rough draft and ask them to correct their errors.

Ongoing Assessment

Get Help Online
More Practice
my.hrw.com

Rubric Activity 19

Listening/Speaking

Proficient	Not There Yet
Student takes notes and answers the questions correctly in preterite tense form.	Student takes notes and answers some of the questions correctly in preterite tense form.

Communication

Motivating with Music

The **¡AvanzaRap!** song targets content from Lección 1 and Lección 2. To reinforce these concepts, play the **¡AvanzaRap!** video song for students and have them complete the Activity Master.

Ongoing Assessment

Get Help Online
More Practice
my.hrw.com

PARA Y PIENSA **Intervention** If students have difficulties in completing the sentences, have them review pp. 331, 336. For additional practice, use Reteaching & Practice Copymasters URB 6 pp. 19, 21.

Answers Projectable Transparencies, 6-30

Answers continued from page 340.

Activity 17
1. Isabel y Mario buscaron el autógrafo de Trini Salgado.
2. Mario llevó un casco.
3. Sí, a Mario le gustó montar en bicicleta.
4. A Mario le duelen la cabeza y la pierna.

Activity 18 Answers will vary. Sample answers include: ¿Caminaste? Sí, caminé porque es bueno para el corazón.

Activity 19 Answers will vary. Sample answers include: Durante la semana, yo practiqué fútbol con mi equipo. Almorcé hamburguesas y refrescos. No soy tan sano como ellos.

Activity 20 Answers will vary. Sample answers include: Santo Domingo
al lado del mar Caribe
escuché música, canté, bailé
mucha emoción
Festival del Merengue

Para y piensa **1.** comenzó **2.** encontraron

Objectives
- Read about two world-class athletes representing the Dominican Republic and Venezuela.
- Compare their careers and achievements.
- Talk about the sports you play.

Core Resource
- Audio Program: TXT CD 6 track 21

Presentation Strategies
- Ask students to look at the photos on pp. 342–343. Ask: **¿Qué hacen los atletas? ¿Qué ropa llevan?**
- Ask students to think about how athletes train. What kind of discipline does it take to becomes an Olympian?
- Ask students if they can name important competitions in the United States in the fields of track and bicycle racing.

STANDARDS
1.2 Understand language
1.3 Present information
2.1 Practices and perspectives
4.2 Compare cultures
Communication, Pair Work; **Information Literacy,** Heritage Language Learners: Literacy Skills/English Language Connections

Lectura cultural

Additional readings at my.hrw.com SPANISH InterActive Reader

¡AVANZA! **Goal:** Read about two world-class athletes from the Dominican Republic and Venezuela. Then compare them and talk about the sports you play.

Comparación cultural

AUDIO

Dos atletas de alta velocidad

STRATEGY Leer
Chart the data In a chart, record the following data for Félix and for Daniela.

	país	deporte	medallas	año(s) que ganó
Félix				
Daniela				

Latinoamérica tiene una gran historia de deportes y de atletas ganadores. Algunos[1] practican su deporte día y noche, en las calles y pistas[2] que están muy lejos de los aficionados y cámaras de televisión.

Félix Sánchez es uno de los atletas más dominantes en los 400 metros de vallas[3]. Estadounidense de nacimiento, Sánchez decidió representar a la República Dominicana, el país de sus padres, en competiciones internacionales. En los Juegos Olímpicos del 2000 en Sydney, Australia, Félix Sánchez llegó en cuarto lugar. Para tener motivación, Sánchez prometió[4] llevar el brazalete que llevó en Sydney hasta[5] ganar una medalla de

[1] Some [2] tracks [3] hurdles [4] promised [5] until

Félix Sánchez con la bandera dominicana

República Dominicana

Differentiating Instruction

Heritage Language Learners
Support What They Know Ask students to describe their favorite sports hero in detail. Who is the person? What sport does he/she play? Why is this person a hero? Then ask students to recount a particularly memorable event related to their hero.

Inclusion
Alphabetic/Phonetic Awareness Have students preview the text silently before reading it aloud. Encourage them to practice sounding out long or unfamiliar words. Also, remind students that the accent indicates where the stress falls. Write a few words from the reading on the board, such as **Latinoamérica, llegó,** and **Olímpicos.** Model how to use the accent as a guide to pronunciation.

Warm Up
Projectable Transparencies, 6-23

Preterite of -car, -gar, -zar Verbs Complete the sentences with the preterite of the verb in parentheses.
1. Nosotros _____ el almuerzo. (pagar)
2. Yo _____ a las doce y media. (almorzar)
3. Ellos _____ al fútbol. (jugar)
4. Ella no _____ una buena nota. (sacar)
5. Yo _____ a la escuela tarde. (llegar)

Answers: 1. pagamos; 2. almorcé; 3. jugaron; 4. sacó; 5. llegué

oro[6]. Lo llevó por cuatro años. En los Juegos Olímpicos del 2004, ganó la primera medalla de oro para la República Dominicana y se hizo[7] héroe nacional. Después de ganar, el triunfante Sánchez caminó delante de los aficionados con la bandera[8] dominicana en las manos.

Daniela Larreal y su medalla de oro

Muchas personas montan en bicicleta pero pocos van tan rápido como la ciclista venezolana Daniela Larreal. Ella ganó tres medallas de oro en los Juegos Bolivarianos en el 2001. En el 2003, se hizo campeona de la Copa Mundial[9] de Ciclismo de Pista. En agosto del 2005, ella ganó otra medalla de oro en los Juegos Bolivarianos. Llegó a los 500 metros con un tiempo de 35,56 segundos. «Qué rico es volver a estar en unos Bolivarianos y ganar nuevamente otra medalla», comentó la campeona.

[6] gold [7] became [8] flag [9] **Copa...** World Cup

PARA Y PIENSA

¿Comprendiste?

1. ¿Qué deporte practica Félix Sánchez? ¿Y Daniela Larreal?
2. ¿Qué ganó Sánchez? ¿Y Larreal?
3. Haz una comparación de los dos atletas. ¿Qué hacen? ¿De dónde son?

¿Y tú?

¿Practicas un deporte? ¿Cuál? ¿Ganaste medallas?

Communication

Grammar Activity

Assign individual students to take turns reading the text on pp. 342–343 to the class. Before they start reading, tell the class to pay special attention to the many examples of preterite verb forms. Instruct them to raise their hands every time they hear a verb in the preterite form. Examples: **decidió, llegó, prometió, llevó, ganó, caminó, comentó.**

Comparisons

English Language Connections

Tell students to look for the origin of the word *champion,* or **campeona.** They may look in an etymological dictionary online, and should find that the word derives from the Latin word *campus,* and related originally to military victory.

Communication

Pair Work

Assign students pairs the roles of interviewer and of Daniela Larreal or Félix Sánchez. Ask them to write in advance a short interview (three to four questions) based on the reading. For example: Interviewer: **¿Qué país representas en las competencias? Félix: Represento a la República Dominicana.**

Differentiating Instruction

Slower-paced Learners

Sentence Completion In advance, draft a page of sentence starters based on the reading. Distribute these to students. Then have them reread the selection to complete each sentence. Here are a few possibilities:
Félix Sánchez es uno de los atletas más dominantes en ____.
En el año 2000, Sánchez llegó en ____.
Daniela Larreal es de ____.

Heritage Language Learners

Literacy Skills Have students use the library or Internet to research a news story from the most recent Olympic Games. Give students five index cards, and have them write one of the following question words on each: **¿Quién? ¿Qué? ¿Cuándo? ¿Dónde?** and **¿Cómo?** Give students the chance to report on their news story to the class.

Answers

Para y piensa

¿Comprendiste?

1. Félix Sánchez practica los 400 metros de vallas. Daniela Larreal practica el ciclismo de pista.
2. Sánchez ganó la primera medalla de oro de los Juegos Olímpicos para la República Dominicana. Larreal ganó una medalla de oro en los Juegos Bolivarianos.
3. Los dos atletas ganaron medallas para sus países. Sánchez es de Estados Unidos pero representa a la República Dominicana. Larreal es de Venezuela.

¿Y tú?
Answers will vary but should follow the model: Sí, practico la natación. Este año gané una medalla de oro y ahora soy una campeona.

Objectives

- **Culture:** Learn about the gestures that are uniquely those of Spanish-speaking countries.
- **Culture:** Read about proverbs that are used in Spanish.
- **Community:** Learn that gestures are very important in different cultures.

Presentation Strategies

- Ask students to look at the photos and to consider the essential question.
- Ask students to think about American Sign Language as a language that uses only gestures, and no sound.
- Ask students to think about proverbs, and mention *an inch is as good as a mile* as an example. What does it mean? Why do people create proverbs?

STANDARDS

1.3 Present information
2.1 Practices and perspectives
4.1 Compare languages
4.2 Compare cultures
5.1 Spanish in the community
21st Century **Creativity and Innovation,** Heritage Language Learners

Comparación cultural

Essential Question

Suggested Answer Gestures often emphasize what is being said and proverbs can sometimes facilitate communication by using a simple saying to get across a complicated idea.

Communities

Spanish in the Marketplace

If there are Spanish stores in your area, visit one and observe owners and employees, looking for any of the gestures illustrated on p. 344.

Proyectos culturales

Comparación cultural

Gestos y refranes

How can gestures and proverbs facilitate communication? When you speak, you communicate with more than just words. When you move your hands, face, or body while you speak, you are using gestures. You can also use gestures to communicate without words. Some gestures are universally understood, yet others are only understood within one language or cultural group. **Refranes,** or proverbs, are short, well-known sayings that express a basic truth or idea. Like gestures, some **refranes** are unique to one language, while others are similar in many languages.

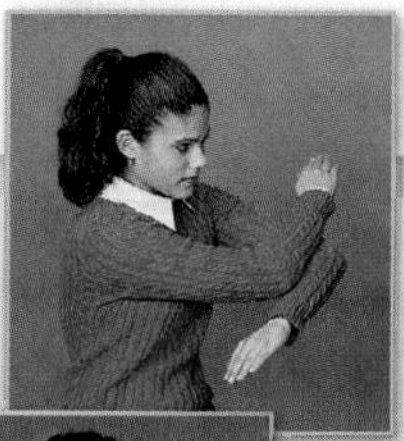

¡En absoluto!
To show "No way!" start with your forearms crossed. Uncross your arms quickly and straighten them completely.

¡Qué loco!
To show that someone is being silly, place your finger against your temple and rotate your wrist back and forth.

¡Mucha gente!
To show that a place is crowded with people, bunch the fingers of both your hands together and then straighten your fingers. Repeat.

¡Ojo!
To show "Watch out!" use your finger to point to your eye. Tug lightly on the skin below your eye.

Proyecto 1 *Los gestos*

With a partner, practice using gestures common in Spanish-speaking countries.

Instructions
1. Study the photos that illustrate some of the gestures used in Spanish-speaking countries.
2. Make one of the gestures on the page and have your partner say its meaning aloud. Take turns.

¡En absoluto!

Proyecto 2 *Los refranes*

Illustrate one of these **refranes** and explain what it means.
1. El que busca, encuentra.
2. Quien va a Sevilla pierde su silla.
3. Donde una puerta se cierra, otra se abre.

Materials for illustrating los refranes
Colored pens or pencils
Paper

Instructions
On a piece of paper, draw the **refrán** that you selected.

En tu comunidad

It is important to understand the meanings of gestures in different cultures. Why would this be especially useful in the business world?

Differentiating Instruction

Multiple Intelligences

Kinesthetic Have students act out the gestures shown at the top of p. 344. Discuss whether these gestures are similar to or different from gestures with the same meaning in the United States. Then ask students to brainstorm other gestures that they know and use. Have the class try each gesture. Does the physical movement support the meaning?

Heritage Language Learners

Writing Skills Ask students to share other proverbs they have heard. Then give them the challenge of writing their own proverb. Advise students to start with a lesson or moral they wish to convey. Then give them time to draft a poetic sentence that expresses their meaning. Have students share their proverbs with the whole group.

Lección 2

En resumen

Vocabulario y gramática

ANIMATEDGRAMMAR
Interactive Flashcards
my.hrw.com

Vocabulario

Talk About Staying Healthy

enfermo(a)	*sick*	levantar pesas	*to lift weights*
fuerte	*strong*	la salud	*health*
herido(a)	*hurt*	sano(a)	*healthy*

Parts of the Body

la boca	*mouth*	la nariz (*pl.* las narices)	*nose*
el brazo	*arm*	el ojo	*eye*
la cabeza	*head*	la oreja	*ear*
el corazón (*pl.* los corazones)	*heart*	el pie	*foot*
el cuerpo	*body*	la piel	*skin*
el estómago	*stomach*	la pierna	*leg*
la mano	*hand*	la rodilla	*knee*
		el tobillo	*ankle*

Outdoor Activities

el bloqueador de sol	*sunscreen*	hacer esquí acuático	*to water-ski*
bucear	*to scuba-dive*	el mar	*sea*
caminar	*to walk*	la playa	*beach*
		tomar el sol	*to sunbathe*

Make Excuses

doler (ue)	*to hurt, to ache*
Lo siento.	*I'm sorry.*

Other Words and Phrases

anoche	*last night*
ayer	*yesterday*
comenzar (ie)	*to begin*
terminar	*to end*
¿Qué hiciste (tú)?	*What did you do?*
¿Qué hicieron ustedes?	*What did you do?*

Gramática

Nota gramatical: The verb **doler** p. 330

Preterite of Regular -ar Verbs

To form the **preterite** of a regular **-ar** verb, add the appropriate preterite ending to the verb's stem.

nadar to swim	
nadé	nadamos
nadaste	nadasteis
nadó	nadaron

Preterite of -car, -gar, -zar Verbs

Regular verbs that end in **-car, -gar,** or **-zar** have a spelling change in the **yo** form of the preterite.

buscar	c	*becomes*	qu	(yo)	**busqué**
jugar	g	*becomes*	gu	(yo)	**jugué**
almorzar	z	*becomes*	c	(yo)	**almorcé**

Practice Spanish with Holt McDougal Apps!

Objective

- Review lesson vocabulary and grammar.

DIGITAL SPANISH

Interactive Flashcards Students can hear every target vocabulary word pronounced in authentic Spanish. Flashcards have Spanish on one side, and a picture or a translation on the other.

performance space
News Networking
@HOMETUTOR
CULTURA Interactiva

- **Audio and Video Resources**
- **Interactive Flashcards**
- **Review Activities**
- **WebQuest**
- **Conjuguemos.com**

Long-term Retention

Critical Thinking

Analyze Ask students to choose their favorite outdoor activity from the list on p. 345. Then ask them to list the parts of the body that benefit from those exercises.

Communication

Pair Work

Ask students to list favorite activities and pastimes that are expressed with **-ar** verbs. Then place them in pairs, and ask them to interview each other about what they did during the previous week. Ask them to write each other's answers. After the interviews, ask them to discuss and evaluate their use of the preterite.

Communication

Humor/Creativity

Following a game show format, ask one student to take the part of the master of ceremonies, another to act as the game show assistant, and the rest of the class to take turns being contestants. The MC will announce a subject and a verb; the assistant will hold up a sign that says **hoy, ayer,** or **anoche.** The first contestant to answer with an appropriate form of the verb will win a point.

Differentiating Instruction

Slower-paced Learners

Peer-study Support Organize students in pairs. Instruct partners to ask each other three or four questions based on the vocabulary reviewed on p. 345. Possible questions might include parts of the body that hurt, or what someone did yesterday.
¿Te duele la rodilla? Sí, me duele la rodilla. ¿Qué hiciste ayer? Nadé en el mar.

Inclusion

Synthetic/Analytic Support Write the preterite endings for regular **-ar** verbs on separate self-sticking notes: **é, aste, ó,** etc. Next, write a regular **-ar** verb on the board, such as **terminar.** Say a pronoun aloud, such as **tú.** Then have a volunteer place the correct note at the end of the verb. Ask the class to read the form aloud: **tú terminaste.**

Objective
- Review lesson grammar and vocabulary.

Core Resources
- *Cuaderno,* pp 280–291
- Audio Program: TXT CD 6 track 22

Presentation Strategies
- Before playing the audio for Activity 1, ask students to listen to it carefully, especially to the preterite verb forms.
- Before doing Activity 2, remind students that the verb form **duele** precedes a singular noun, whereas **duelen** precedes a plural noun. Give examples: **Me duele la cabeza. Me duelen las piernas**.
- Monitor correct use of preterite forms of **-car, -gar, -zar** verbs by asking questions starting with **¿Jugaste...? ¿Almorzaste...? ¿Pagaste...?** to elicit responses with the correct **yo** form: **Jugué..., Almorcé..., Pagué...**
- Read the Comparación cultural with students and clarify questions.
- Review may be done in class or given as homework.

STANDARDS

1.2 Understand language, Act. 1
1.3 Present information, Acts. 2–5
4.2 Compare cultures, Act. 5
21st Century **Information Literacy,** Heritage Language Learners

Warm Up Projectable Transparencies, 6-23

Vocabulary Complete each sentence with the correct word.

piel ojos playa estómago fuerte

1. Me gusta ir a la _____.
2. Siempre uso bloqueador de sol para la _____.
3. Cuando como mucho, después me duele el _____.
4. Mario es _____ porque levanta pesas.
5. Me duelen los _____ y no puedo ver bien.

Answers: 1. playa; 2. piel; 3. estómago; 4. fuerte; 5. ojos

Ongoing Assessment

Get Help Online
More Practice
my.hrw.com

Remediation If students achieve less than 85% accuracy with the activities, direct them to review pp. 299, 330–332, 336, 338, 342–343 and to get help online at my.hrw.com.

Lección 2 Repaso de la lección

@HOMETUTOR
my.hrw.com

¡LLEGADA!

Now you can
- talk about parts of the body
- make excuses
- say what you did
- talk about staying healthy

Using
- the verb **doler**
- preterite of regular **-ar** verbs
- preterite of **-car, -gar, -zar** verbs

To review
- preterite of regular **-ar** verbs p. 331
- preterite of **-car, -gar, -zar** verbs p. 336

1 Listen and understand

AUDIO

Elisa describe un día en la playa. Escucha y escribe si ella hizo o no las siguientes actividades. *(Listen to Elisa's description. Then write whether or not she did the following activities.)*

modelo: usar bloqueador de sol
Elisa usó bloqueador de sol.

1. tomar el sol	**5.** jugar al voleibol
2. bucear	**6.** descansar
3. caminar	**7.** tocar la guitarra
4. almorzar	**8.** cantar

Audio Program
TXT CD 6 Track 22
Audio Script, TE p. 323b

To review
- the verb **doler** p. 330

2 Talk about parts of the body

Estas personas van a la enfermería de la escuela. Explica qué les duele. *(Explain why these people are going to the school nurse.)*

modelo: Andrés
A Andrés le duele la cabeza.

1.  Esteban

2. 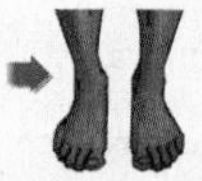 Amalia y Patricio

3. 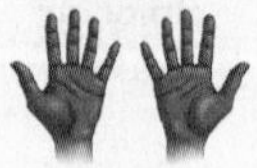 yo

4.  usted

5. 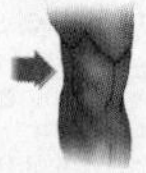 nosotros

6. 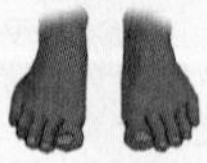 tú

Differentiating Instruction

Multiple Intelligences

Intrapersonal Students can use the Festival del Merengue as an example, and plan a fictitious festival for their school. Incorporating the same elements present in the Festival del Merengue, they can decide upon a theme, music, crafts, food, and dances that they would have at the event. Various committees could be formed to plan each aspect of the festival.

Heritage Language Learners

Support What They Know Ask students from other Spanish-speaking countries to research an artist who, like Juan Medina, represents the folkloric aspect of that country's life. See if they can find an example, either in postcard, print, or electronic form, of that artist's work to share with the class.

To review
- preterite of regular **-ar** verbs p. 331

3 Talk about staying healthy

Todas las personas en la familia de Guillermo son sanas. ¿Qué hicieron ayer? Completa el párrafo con la forma correcta del verbo apropiado. *(Complete the paragraph with the correct form of the appropriate verb.)*

preparar	patinar	levantar
bucear	montar	nadar

A mi familia y a mí nos gusta ser sanos. Ayer mi hermano Marcos y yo __1.__ pesas antes de jugar al fútbol. Mi papá __2.__ en la piscina, y mi mamá y mi tía __3.__ en el mar. Mi hermana Carlota __4.__ una ensalada para todos nosotros. Después del almuerzo, yo __5.__ en bicicleta y mis hermanos __6.__ en línea en el parque.

To review
- preterite of **-car, -gar, -zar** verbs p. 336

4 Say what you did

Lee lo que hizo Carolina ayer y escribe si también lo hiciste tú. *(Read what Carolina did yesterday and write whether or not you did the same thing.)*

modelo: Carolina sacó la basura.
Yo también saqué la basura. (Yo no saqué la basura.)

1. Llegó tarde a la escuela.
2. Tocó la guitarra.
3. Comenzó a leer un libro.
4. Practicó deportes.
5. Jugó al voleibol.
6. Almorzó a las doce y media.
7. Pagó la cuenta en un restaurante.
8. Empezó la tarea.

To review
- Beaches p. 299
- Comparación cultural pp. 332, 338
- Lectura cultural pp. 342–343

5 Dominican Republic and Venezuela

Comparación cultural

Answer these culture questions.

1. What are beaches in the Dominican Republic known for?
2. What are some common themes of Amaya Salazar's artwork?
3. What can you see and do at Santo Domingo's **Festival del Merengue**?
4. Where are Félix Sánchez and Daniela Larreal from and what sports do they play? What competitions have they participated in?

Más práctica Cuaderno *pp. 280–291* Cuaderno para hispanohablantes *pp. 282–291*

Get Help Online my.hrw.com

Differentiating Instruction

Pre-AP

Expand and Elaborate Reinforce students' knowledge of the vocabulary by having them look up the Spanish words for the following: finger, toe, hip, lungs, back, shoulder, etc. They may use the words to expand upon their activity answers.

Slower-paced Learners

Peer-study Support Teaming the students in pairs, have them write the first person preterite of some unfamiliar **-car, -gar,** and **-zar** verbs, such as **calzar, colocar, avanzar, lanzar, juzgar, pegar.**

✓ Ongoing Assessment

Alternative Assessment Assign students to play the role of the students and school nurse using Activity 2. Have each student tell the nurse what hurts.

Answers Projectable Transparencies, 6-30 and 6-31

Answers for Activities on p. 346–347.

Activity 1
1. Elisa tomó el sol.
2. Elisa no buceó.
3. Elisa no caminó.
4. Elisa almorzó.
5. Elisa jugó al voleibol.
6. Elisa descansó.
7. Elisa no tocó la guitarra.
8. Elisa cantó.

Activity 2
1. A Esteban le duele el brazo.
2. A Amalia y a Patricio les duelen los tobillos.
3. A mí me duelen las manos.
4. A usted le duelen los ojos.
5. A nosotros nos duelen las rodillas.
6. A ti te duelen los pies.

Activity 3
1. levantamos
2. nadó
3. bucearon
4. preparó
5. monté
6. patinaron

Activity 4
1. Yo también llegué tarde a la escuela. (Yo no llegué tarde a la escuela.)
2. Yo también toqué la guitarra. (Yo no toqué la guitarra.)
3. Yo también comencé a leer un libro. (Yo no comencé a leer un libro.)
4. Yo también practiqué deportes. (Yo no practiqué deportes.)
5. Yo también jugué al voleibol. (Yo no jugué al voleibol.)
6. Yo también almorcé a las doce y media. (Yo no almorcé a las doce y media.)
7. Yo también pagué la cuenta en un restaurante. (Yo no pagué la cuenta en un restaurante.)
8. Yo también empecé la tarea. (Yo no empecé la tarea.)

Activity 5
1. Beaches in the Dominican Republic are known for their white sand, clear blue waters, and coral reefs.
2. Bright colors and flora and fauna are some common themes of Amaya Salazar's work.
3. The Festival del Merengue in Santo Domingo includes music, parades, arts and crafts fairs, cart races, and a wide variety of Dominican foods.
4. Félix Sánchez is from the United States but represents the Dominican Republic when he competes. He runs hurdles. Daniela Larreal is from Venezuela and competes in bicycle races. Félix took part in the 2000 and the 2004 Olympic Games. Daniela Larreal raced in the Juegos Bolivarianos in 2001 and 2005.

Objectives

- Read about the favorite sports of teens from the Dominican Republic, Honduras, and Venezuela.
- Compare their favorite sports with your own.
- Write a paragraph about your favorite sport.

Core Resource

- *Cuaderno,* pp. 292–294
- Audio Program: TXT CD 6 track 23
- Video Program DVD 2

Presentation Strategies

- Ask students to look at the photos on pp. 348–349 and describe what they see.
- Have students take turns reading each narration as their classmates follow it in the text. Correct pronunciation as needed.
- Play the audio.

STANDARDS

1.2 Understand language
1.3 Present information
2.1 Practices and perspectives
4.2 Compare cultures

21st Century **Communication,** Pre-AP; **Critical Thinking and Problem Solving,** Compara con tu mundo

Long-term Retention

Critical Thinking

Conceptualize Sports history assignment: Have students choose any sport they like and find out something about its origins. Where was this sport first practiced and by whom? How did people dress for it? How did it become a popular pastime? Students will be surprised to learn how some sports actually date from ancient times.

Comparación cultural

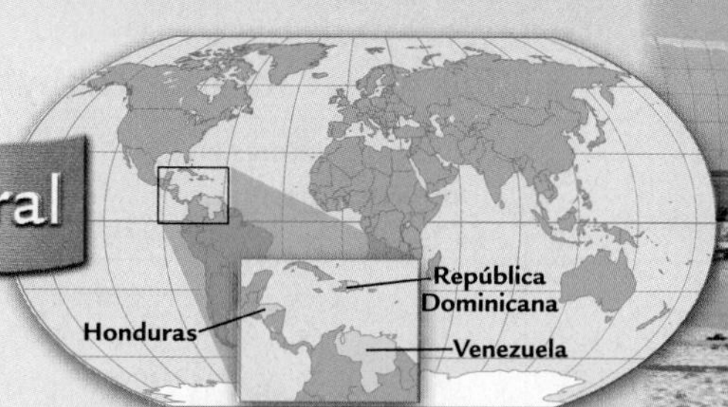

AUDIO

Deportes favoritos

Lectura y escritura

WebQuest my.hrw.com

❶ **Leer** Choices of favorite sports vary around the world. Read what Felipe, Gloria, and Agustín say about their favorite sports.

❷ **Escribir** Using the three descriptions as models, write a short paragraph about your favorite sport.

STRATEGY **Escribir**
Use a sports chart
To write about your favorite sport, complete a chart like the one shown.

Categoría	Detalles
nombre del deporte	
lugar	
participantes	
equipo necesario	
ropa apropiada	

Step 1 Complete the chart with information about your sport. Include details about where it is played, who participates, what equipment is needed, and what clothes should be worn.

Step 2 Write your paragraph. Make sure to include all the information from your chart. Check your writing by yourself or with help from a friend. Make final corrections.

Compara con tu mundo

Use the paragraph you wrote to compare your favorite sport to a sport described by *one* of the three students. How are they similar? How are they different?

Cuaderno *pp. 292–294* Cuaderno para hispanohablantes *pp. 292–294*

Differentiating Instruction

Multiple Intelligences

Visual Learners Distribute three large index cards to each student. Then based on the descriptions they read, have students create three postcards. Instruct them to include all of the details they read about in their illustrations.

Inclusion

Clear Structure Choose sentences from the three descriptions, and copy them onto separate sentence strips. Then write the names Felipe, Gloria, and Agustín on the board. Have students choose a sentence to read aloud, and place it under the appropriate name.

Cultura Interactiva my.hrw.com

See these pages come alive!

República Dominicana

Felipe

¡Hola! Me llamo Felipe y vivo en Punta Cana, cerca del mar. Ayer pasé el día en la playa con mis amigos. Después de nadar un rato, jugamos un partido de voleibol con ocho jugadores. Mi equipo comprende las reglas pero ayer no ganó el partido. El voleibol es mi deporte favorito porque puedo jugar con mis amigos y no es peligroso.

Honduras

Gloria

¿Qué tal? Me llamo Gloria y vivo en La Ceiba, el lugar perfecto para practicar deportes acuáticos. Mi deporte favorito es el rafting. Uno de los mejores ríos para practicar rafting en Honduras es el río Cangreja. La semana pasada, mis hermanos y yo alquilamos una balsa[1] para navegar el río. Es una actividad muy divertida.

[1] raft

Venezuela

Agustín

¡Hola! Me llamo Agustín. Soy aficionado de los deportes. Me gusta mucho el béisbol, pero me gusta más el básquetbol porque soy alto y tengo las piernas y los brazos largos[2]. También me gusta correr y saltar[3]. Mis amigos y yo jugamos casi todos los días en una cancha cerca de mi casa en Caracas.

[2] long [3] to jump

Comparación cultural

Exploring the Theme

Gloria says that white-water rafting is fun. But she has not mentioned that it requires a great amount of teamwork, cooperation, and an ability to follow instructions. Rafting is a risky sport that can only be fun when all the members aboard the raft are working together as a whole, making sure everyone is safe enough to enjoy the thrill of the river ride.

✓ Ongoing Assessment

Quick Check Ask students quick comprehension questions about each of the three narrations and write their answers on the board. For example: **¿Dónde vive Felipe? ¿Cuál es su deporte favorito? ¿Cuál es uno de los mejores ríos en Honduras para practicar rafting? ¿Por qué a Agustín le gusta el básquetbol?**

✓ Ongoing Assessment

Rubric Lectura y escritura

Writing Criteria	Excellent	Good	Needs Work
Content	Paragraph contains a lot of information about sport.	Paragraph contains some information about sport.	Paragraph lacks information about sport.
Communi-cation	Paragraph is organized and easy to follow.	Paragraph is fairly well organized and easy to follow.	Paragraph is disorga-nized and hard to follow.
Accuracy	Paragraph has few mistakes in vocabulary and grammar.	Paragraph has some mistakes in vocabulary and grammar.	Paragraph has many mistakes in vocabulary and grammar.

To customize your own rubrics, use the ***Generate Success*** *Rubric Generator and Graphic Organizers.*

Differentiating Instruction

Pre-AP

Communicate Preferences Give students the opportunity to read their paragraphs about their favorite sport aloud. Then facilitate a discussion wherein students talk about their preferences regarding sports. Which sports are their favorites, and why? Are there any sports they do not like?

Heritage Language Learners

Increase Accuracy Encourage students to use verbs in the preterite to express memorable events related to their favorite sports. Review the use of accents in spelling verbs in the preterite tense. Also, have students review the spelling of verbs that are irregular in the preterite.

Objective
- Review vocabulary and grammar.

Core Resource
- Audio Program: TXT CD 6 track 24

Review Options
- **Activity 1:** Listening activity
- **Activity 2:** Speaking activity
- **Activity 3:** Speaking activity
- **Activity 4:** Writing activity
- **Activity 5:** Speaking activity
- **Activity 6:** Speaking and writing activity
- **Activity 7:** Reading and writing activity

STANDARDS

1.1 Engage in conversation, Acts. 3, 5, 6
1.2 Understand language, Act. 1
1.3 Present information, Acts. 2–7
21st Century **Collaboration,** Act. 6/Multiple Intelligences; **Creativity and Innovation,** Act. 4; **Flexibility and Adaptability,** Acts. 2, 3

Long-term Retention
Study Tips

To reinforce the **yo** preterite form of **-ar** verbs, ask students to create a calendar that shows the current date and the two weeks preceding it. Ask them to brainstorm as many **-ar** verbs as they can think of, then use them to note on their calendars what they did on those days.

Answers

Activity 1
1. Hace sol y un poco de calor en el campo.
2. Mariano Sandoval juega al béisbol.
3. Sandoval es de San Pedro de Macorís.
4. Él juega tan bien con el bate como con el guante.
5. Sandoval dice que es un buen jugador porque él trabaja más que los otros.

UNIDADES 1-6

Repaso inclusivo
Options for Review

¡AvanzaRap! DVD Sing and Learn

Digital performance space

1 Listen, understand, and compare

Escuchar

Listen to a sports broadcast from the Dominican Republic. Then answer the following questions.
1. ¿Qué tiempo hace en el campo?
2. ¿A qué juega Mariano Sandoval?
3. ¿De dónde es Sandoval?
4. ¿Cómo juega él?
5. ¿Por qué dice Sandoval que es un buen jugador?

Have you ever excelled at something? Who influenced you and how?

Audio Program
TXT CD 6 Track 24
Audio Script, TE p. 323b

2 Be a sports commentator

Hablar

You have been asked to present a student's view on sports for a Spanish-language channel on television. Prepare a commentary on your favorite sport. Include when and where it is played, why it is important to you, and information on teams and/or athletes. You may want to videotape your commentary or present it live to the class.

3 Talk with the school nurse

Hablar

Role-play a conversation with the school nurse. You are injured and you decide to go to the nurse's office. Tell your partner what hurts and name three activities that you did recently. He or she will make a connection between the activities and your injuries and make some recommendations for getting better. Your conversation should be at least four minutes long.

4 Write a Web article

Escribir

Write a Web article about the sports and activities that visitors to your area can participate in. Mention at least three activities for each season of the year and explain where people should go to take part in these activities. Be sure to mention what the weather is like during different times of the year. Your article should be at least seven sentences long.

Differentiating Instruction

Pre-AP

Expand and Elaborate Organize students into small groups based on the sport they choose to discuss in Activity 2. Have each group create a concept web around the name of their sport. Then have students work together to brainstorm as many details as they can to answer the questions presented. When and where is the sport played? Why is it important? Who are some famous athletes?

Slower-paced Learners

Peer-study Support After students have completed their Web articles for Activity 4, have them exchange papers with a partner. Instruct students to look for areas where their partner could add more details to make the article more informative and interesting.

5 Agree on what to watch

Hablar

You and a partner have to decide what to watch on television. Choose a sporting event and compare it to the sporting event that your partner chose. Try to convince your partner to watch what you want to watch. Your conversation should be at least four minutes long.

6 Plan a class reunion

Hablar
Escribir

Work in a group of four to plan your ten-year class reunion in Punta Cana, Dominican Republic. Plan how long the reunion will be, what activities people can participate in, and what food will be served. Create an invitation and present it to the class. After looking at all of the invitations, vote for the plan that you want to use for your class reunion.

7 Compare classes

Leer
Escribir

Silvia is in her second year of high school. Read her report cards from last year and this year. Write a paragraph about what she studied and did during her first year and the classes she has and activities she does now. Then compare her grades and give possible reasons for why her grades are different from one year to the next. Your paragraph should have at least six sentences.

Escuela Secundaria de Santo Domingo

Silvia Ibáñez
Primer año

Clase	Nota final
Matemáticas - Álgebra I	A
Arte	B
Inglés I	B
Ciencias Naturales	C
Literatura	A
Música	B

Actividades extracurriculares:
Equipo de natación
Equipo de voleibol

Escuela Secundaria de Santo Domingo

Silvia Ibáñez
Segundo año

Clase	Nota final
Ciencias - Biología	B
Historia	A
Música	A
Matemáticas - Geometría	A
Literatura	B
Inglés II	A

Actividades extracurriculares:
Banda musical (trompeta)
Equipo de voleibol

Communication

Group Work

Create a Round-robin Review Take a large piece of paper and tape it to the wall. Write "Unit 6" at the top, and ask students to think for three or four minutes of several things they've learned while studying this unit. Distribute colored markers and one by one, have students come to the wall and write their thoughts on the paper. Then allow the class ten minutes to view and comment on their collaborative review.

✓ Ongoing Assessment

Integrated Performance Assessment Rubric Oral Activities 2, 3, 5
Written Activities 4, 6, 7

Very Good	Proficient	Not There Yet
The student thoroughly develops all requirements of the task.	The student develops most requirements of the task.	The student does not develop the requirements of the task.
The student demonstrates excellent control of verb forms.	The student demonstrates good to fair control of verb forms.	The student demonstrates poor control of verb forms.
Good variety of appropriate vocabulary.	Adequate variety of appropriate vocabulary.	The vocabulary is not appropriate.
The pronunciation is excellent to very good.	The pronunciation is good to fair.	The pronunciation is poor.

To customize your own rubrics, use the ***Generate Success*** *Rubric Generator and Graphic Organizers.*

Differentiating Instruction

Multiple Intelligences

Interpersonal Before students begin Activity 6, help them organize their groups of four. Create a different assignment for each member of the group. For example, one student can be in charge of designing the schedule, two students in charge of describing activities, and the fourth student in charge of planning the food. Each team member must present his or her ideas for the group to discuss.

Slower-paced Learners

Personalize It Ask students to compare Silvia's class schedule in Activity 7 with their own. What classes or activities do they have in common? How are their schedules different? Also, ask students to comment on a time when their grades improved. What did they do to bring about the change?

Proyectos adicionales

Planning Ahead

Projects Organize a technology fair. Have pairs create a display board for a technology fair. The board should illustrate two or three technologies, and instructions on how to use them. Students might choose taking digital photos and sending instant messages. The titles and captions must be in Spanish. More detailed instructions about how to use the technology may be in English. After students' display boards are complete, set a date for the fair. Have students take turns to stay by the board and circulate to view the other displays. Encourage them to ask and answer questions as they browse the different displays.

PACING SUGGESTION: Upon completion of **Lección 1** to review vocabulary related to computers and technology.

21st Century **Technology Literacy**

(Virtual) Bulletin Board

Create a bulletin board with the title **La computadora.** Have students cut out photos or advertisements from computer or technology magazines. They should assemble multiple examples of different parts of the computer, such as the mouse, screen, keyboard, as well as things used with the computer, such as CDs and digital cameras. Organize like objects in the same section of the bulletin board. Then have students practice labeling the different groups of objects that they see.

PACING SUGGESTION: After vocabulary is presented in **Lección 1.**

Create a bulletin board with the title **Un día fabuloso.** Organize students into small groups, and have each group choose one of the special locations presented in **Lección 2,** such as **la feria, el museo,** or **el parque de diversiones.** Have groups create a front door or front gate to their special location. Encourage them to use pieces of cardboard, folded paper, or even clay to give their doors a three-dimensional effect. Advise students to add as many Spanish words and phrases to their doors as possible. Use the doors and gates to ask questions about what people do at these locations. Also, ask students about their personal preferences for the best place to spend a fabulous day. As a tech alternative, you may wish to have students create their projects on a class wiki page.

PACING SUGGESTION: After vocabulary is presented in **Lección 2.**

21st Century **Creativity and Innovation**

Web Research

Design a personal homepage. Have students create their own personal homepage that includes information about themselves that they would like to share. They might include information about their school and studies, sports and hobbies, or a special interest. Have students create a prototype for their homepage on a large piece of paper. Encourage them to think about possible links to other sites related to their interests.

PACING SUGGESTION: Upon completion of **Lección 1** to utilize vocabulary related to computers and technology. Students will also need to review phrases related to personal descriptions, activities, and preferences from previous units.

21st Century **Technology Literacy**

Games

Pregúntame

In advance, have each student write a series of sentences describing one vocabulary word or phrase from the unit. Their sentences should not name the object described, and should read like a riddle. Here is one example: **Está en un parque de diversiones. Es muy divertido. Es un círculo muy grande.** Students should write their descriptions on an index card. Collect all of the cards, and place them in a box or a bowl.

Next, divide the class into two teams, and decide which team will go first. Invite one player from this team to the front to choose a card and read it aloud. The team then has ten seconds to confer and respond with a question appropriate to the description on the card. For example, **¿Qué es la vuelta al mundo?** If the question is correct, the team earns a point. Then the other team takes a turn. The team with the most points wins.

PACING SUGGESTION: At the end of the unit to review vocabulary related to technology and exciting destinations.

Tesoros en el Web

Organize an Internet treasure hunt. In advance, create a list of questions about Argentina. Questions should be information related with clear and definitive answers. Here are a few possibilities:

¿Cuántas personas viven en Buenos Aires?
¿Por qué es especial la Avenida 9 de Julio en Buenos Aires?

Working with partners or in small groups, give students a set amount of time to investigate their treasure hunts. This time might be split up among different class periods. Alternately, if students need to visit a computer lab to access the Internet, allow different pairs or groups to work on their hunts at different times. The main concern is that all students have the same amount of time to research. The team with the most correct answers at the end of the time period wins.

PACING SUGGESTION: Throughout the unit as time allows.

Recipe

No Argentine **asado** would be complete without **chimichurri,** a marinade or sauce that can be used over just about anything—grilled meat, poultry, seafood, vegetables, even bread.

Chimichurri

Ingredientes

1 taza de perejil
4 dientes de ajo
1/2 cucharadita de pimienta
2 cucharadas de orégano
2 cucharadas de cebolla picada
3/4 de taza de aceite de oliva
2 cucharadas de jugo de limón

Instrucciones

Corte el perejil y el ajo. Ponga todos los ingredientes en una licuadora o procesador de comida. La salsa debe estar picada pero no en pedacitos muy pequeños.

Music

Have interested students do additional research on the Argentine **tango.** Advise students to begin by brainstorming a list of things they already know about this music and dance style. Then have students choose a specific topic to research. Students might focus on one particular singer, such as Carlos Gardel, on the history of the musical form, or on the specific steps of the dance. Have students share the information they learn in the form of a lecture/demonstration using live or recorded music.

¡AvanzaRap! DVD

- Video animations of all **¡AvanzaRap!** songs (with Karaoke track)
- Teaching Suggestions
- **¡AvanzaRap!** Activity Masters
- **¡AvanzaRap!** Video Scripts and Answers

Also available on the **Teacher One Stop**

UNIT THEME
A Terrific Week!

UNIT STANDARDS

COMMUNICATION
- Talk about technology
- Talk about a series of events
- Say what you did
- Talk about indefinite or negative situations
- Talk on the phone
- Say where you went, what you did, and how it was
- Extend invitations

CULTURE
- The use of **lunfardo** in Argentina
- The Mar del Plata beach
- A Spanish-language virus-protection questionnaire
- The port of La Boca and artist Benito Quinquela Martín
- Argentinean cuisine
- Places to have fun in Latin America
- Last names, family trees, and photo albums

CONNECTIONS
- Language: Learning the language game **jeringozo**.
- Social Studies: Discussing the origin and purpose of language games
- Geography: determining how geographical location affects the cultures of Chile and Argentina
- Science: Researching the characteristics and value of silver

COMPARISONS
- **Mate** and regional foods and beverages
- Slang terms in Argentina and the U.S.
- The sound of Spanish **qu**
- Amusement parks
- The Spanish letters **ll** and **y**
- Summertime activities and places
- Port cities in Agentina and the U.S.
- Foods in Argentina and the U.S.
- Museums around the world
- Comparing last names
- Fun places to visit in Argentina, Bolivia, Nicaragua, and the U.S.

COMMUNITIES
- Inquiring about family names of Spanish-speaking members of the community

UNIDAD 7

Argentina

¡Una semana fenomenal!

Lección 1
Tema: ***En el cibercafé***

Lección 2
Tema: ***Un día en el parque de diversiones***

«¡Hola!
Somos Florencia y Mariano.
Vivimos en Argentina.»

Población: 40.482.000

Área: 1.068.302 millas cuadradas, el país hispanohablante más grande del mundo

Capital: Buenos Aires

Moneda: el peso argentino

Idioma: español

Comida típica: asado, matambre, dulce de leche

Gente famosa: Norma Aleandro (actriz), Jorge Luis Borges (escritor), César Milstein (biólogo), Mercedes Sosa (cantante)

Cultural Geography

Setting the Scene
- ¿Cuál es la capital de Argentina? (Buenos Aires)
- ¿Cómo se llama la moneda de Argentina? (el peso argentino)
- ¿Qué son los gauchos? (cowboys)

Teaching with Maps
- ¿Qué países tienen frontera con Argentina? (Chile, Bolivia, Paraguay, Brasil y Uruguay)
- ¿Qué está al este de Argentina? (el Océano Atlántico)
- ¿En qué continente está Argentina? (Sudamérica)

Cultura Interactiva my.hrw.com *See these pages come alive!*

El Obelisco en la Plaza de la República, Buenos Aires

◀ **Modernidad y tradición** Buenos Aires is often called "Paris of the Americas," in part due to its European-style architecture mixed with modern elements, such as **El Obelisco** (Obelisk) in the Plaza de la República. At 400 feet across, the Avenida 9 de Julio leading up to the plaza is considered the widest avenue in the world. *What landmarks does your community have?*

La identidad nacional y el gaucho **Los gauchos** are considered cultural icons in Argentina. They lead an independent and simple life, raising cattle on the plains (**las pampas**). *How do **gauchos** compare to the cowboys of the western United States?* ▶

Gauchos y sus caballos en un bosque petrificado cerca de Sarmiento, Argentina

◀ **Un baile muy popular** On Sundays in Barrio de San Telmo, you can see **tango** dancers and hear the accordion-like instrument **el bandoneón.** Most agree that the now-famous **tango** originated in working-class neighborhoods of Buenos Aires at the end of the 19th century. *What are some popular dances in the U.S.?*

El Barrio de San Telmo, Buenos Aires

Bridging Cultures

Heritage Language Learners

Making Connections Have students do more research on Buenos Aires and Paris to determine why Buenos Aires is known as the "Paris of the Americas." Have them present examples of landmarks of both cities to the class.

English Learners

Increase Interaction Point out that each of the paragraphs on p. 353 contains a comparison. Have students work in pairs to find the comparison made in each paragraph (Buenos Aires and Paris; **gauchos** and cowboys; the accordion and **el bandoneón**). Then ask for volunteers to draw comparisons to their own country of origin.

Cultura Interactiva my.hrw.com

Send your students to my.hrw.com to explore authentic Argentinian culture. Tell them to click on Cultura interactiva to see these pages come alive!

Culture

About the Photos

- The obelisk, built in 1936, commemorates four important moments in the history of Argentina. Perhaps the most significant of these moments is the one in which the country's flag was flown for the first time.
- Like American cowboys, **gauchos** have become something of a legend. Once solitary and nomadic, they inherited their name from the Quechua word **huachu,** which means "orphan" or "vagabond."
- The San Telmo district is densely packed with authentic bohemian culture. Music, local art, food, antiques, and street life are plentiful in this quaint, colonial labyrinth.

Expanded Information

- Buenos Aires has an inexhaustible wealth of artistic and cultural activities. But more extraordinary is the population, which seemingly never goes to sleep. Even late at night, restaurants and theaters are lively, noisy places.
- **Gauchos** are responsible for Argentina's tradition of the **asado**, or outdoor meat roasting. Since **gauchos** once lived directly off the land, their meals consisted of freshly roasted meat accompanied by **yerba mate**.
- The tango was originally a 19th century country dance. After its introduction to life in Paris in the 1920's, it grew into the glamorous ballroom dance it is today.

Video Character Guide

Florencia and Mariano are friends who like to use computers. They communicate with their friends via e-mail, search the Internet, and send digital photos.

Lesson Overview

Culture at a Glance

Topic & Activity	Essential Question
Mate pp. 354–355	Does your region have a special beverage or food?
El lunfardo, p. 362	How do slang words develop?
A computer virus questionnaire p. 372	What happens when a virus infects your computer?
Culture review p. 377	What are some aspects of Argentine culture?

COMPARISON COUNTRIES Argentina Bolivia Nicaragua

Practice at a Glance

	Objective	Activity & Skill
Vocabulary	Technology words	1: Reading; 2: Speaking / Writing; 5: Speaking; 19: Reading / Listening / Speaking; 20: Writing
	Sequence vocabulary	3: Listening / Reading; 4: Listening; 8: Speaking; 17: Listening / Reading; Repaso 2: Writing
Grammar	Preterite of regular **-er** and **-ir** verbs	6: Speaking / Writing; 7: Reading / Writing; 8: Speaking; 9: Speaking / Writing; 10: Listening / Reading; 11: Reading; 13: Speaking; 16: Listening / Reading; 20: Writing; Repaso 2: Writing; Repaso 3: Writing
	Affirmative and negative words	12: Speaking / Writing; 13: Speaking; 14: Speaking / Writing; 15: Speaking; 16: Listening / Reading; Repaso 1: Listening
Communication	Talk about technology	1: Reading; 2: Speaking / Writing; 5: Speaking; 19: Reading / Listening / Speaking; 20: Writing
	Talk about a series of events	3: Listening / Reading; 4: Listening; 10: Listening / Reading; 16: Listening / Reading; 17: Listening / Reading
	Say what you did	6: Speaking / Writing; 7: Reading / Writing; 8: Speaking; 9: Speaking / Writing; 10: Listening / Reading; 11: Reading; 14: Speaking / Writing; 18: Speaking; 20: Writing; Repaso 1: Listening
	Talk about indefinite or negative situations	12: Speaking / Writing; 13: Speaking; 15: Speaking; 19: Reading / Listening / Speaking; Repaso 4: Writing
	Pronunciation: The combination **qu**	*Pronunciación: La combinación qu,* p. 363: Listening / Speaking
Recycle	Affirmative commands	16: Listening / Reading
	Telling time	6: Speaking / Writing
	Foods and beverages	9: Speaking / Writing
	Preterite of regular **-ar** verbs	14: Speaking / Writing

The following presentations are recorded in the Audio Program for **¡Avancemos!**

- **¡A responder!** *page 357*
- **4: ¿En qué orden?** *page 360*
- **19: Integración** *page 371*
- **Repaso de la lección** *page 376*
  1: Listen and understand

For **¡AvanzaRap!** scripts, see the **¡AvanzaRap! DVD.**

¡A responder! TXT CD 7 track 2

1. la pantalla
2. el sitio Web
3. el teclado
4. el icono
5. la dirección electrónica
6. el ratón

4 | ¿En qué orden? TXT CD 7 track 4

El año pasado compré una cámara digital. La semana pasada tomé fotos de mis amigas en una fiesta. Anteayer quemé un disco compacto con las fotos. Anoche busqué las direcciones electrónicas de mis amigas. Hoy conecté a Internet. Por fin mandé las fotos por correo electrónico.

19 | Integración TXT CD 7 tracks 8, 9

¡Hola! Soy yo, Raquel Cabrera. Ayer busqué un cibercafé y encontré el Cibercafé Ratoncito. Tienen 25 computadoras nuevas y todas tienen conexión a Internet. Primero usé el mensajero instantáneo. Luego abrí el correo electrónico. ¡Alguien me mandó fotos! Abrí el mensaje, pero nunca vi las fotos. En el cibercafé no hay nadie para ayudar con el correo. Y la tarea... Es difícil pensar allí porque muchas personas hablan por teléfono. Más tarde, comí pizza. En total, pagué nueve pesos. Para pasar una tarde divertida, el Cibercafé Ratoncito es el lugar perfecto.

Repaso de la lección TXT CD 7 track 11

1: Listen and understand

Ramiro: ¿Piensas que hay algún problema con tu computadora?

Diana: Sí. No recibí ningún correo electrónico ayer. No recibí nada.

Ramiro: ¿Y siempre recibes algo?

Diana: Sí. Mis amigos y yo siempre usamos Internet para mandar mensajes y fotos. También usamos el mensajero instantáneo. Pero ayer no recibí ni un correo electrónico ni una foto. Nada.

Ramiro: ¿Qué hiciste anteayer?

Diana: Anteayer yo quemé algunos discos compactos y navegué por Internet.

Ramiro: Pues, yo no encuentro ningún problema con la computadora. Tal vez tus amigos están ocupados con otras actividades.

Resource List

Everything you need to ...

Plan

TEACHER ONE STOP

✓Lesson Plans
✓Teacher Resources
✓Audio and Video

Present

INTERACTIVE WHITEBOARD LESSONS
TEACHER ONE STOP WITH PROJECTABLE TRANSPARENCIES
POWER PRESENTATIONS
ANIMATEDGRAMMAR

Assess

ONLINE ASSESSMENT

✓ Assessments for on-level, modified, pre-AP, and heritage learners
✓ Create customized tests with **Examview Assessment Suite**
✓ **performance space**
✓ *Generate Success* Rubric Generator

Print

Plan	Present	Practice	Assess
URB 7 • Video Scripts pp. 69–70 • Family Letter p. 91 • Absent Student Copymasters pp. 93–100 **Best Practices Toolkit**	**URB 7** • Video Activities pp. 51–58	• *Cuaderno* pp. 295–317 • *Cuaderno para hispanohablantes* pp. 295–317 • *Lecturas para todos* pp. 62–66 • *Lecturas para hispanohablantes* • *¡AvanzaCómics! SuperBruno y Nati,* Episodio 4 **URB 7** • Practice Games pp. 31–38 • Audio Scripts pp. 73–77 • Map/Culture Activities pp. 83–84 • Fine Art Activities pp. 86–87	**Differentiated Assessment Program** **URB 7** • Did you get it? Reteaching and Practice Copymasters pp. 1–12

Projectable Transparencies (Teacher One Stop, my.hrw.com)

Culture	Presentation and Practice	Classroom Management
• Atlas Maps 1–6 • Argentina Map 1 • Fine Art Transparencies 2, 3	• Vocabulary Transparencies 6, 7 • Grammar Presentation Transparencies 10, 11	• Warm Up Transparencies 16–19 • Student Book Answer Transparencies 24–27

Audio and Video

Audio	Video	¡AvanzaRap! DVD
• Student Book Audio CD 7 Tracks 1–11 • Workbook Audio CD 4 Tracks 1–10 • Heritage Learners Audio CD 2 Tracks 17–20, CD 4 Tracks 13–14 • Assessment Audio CD 2 Tracks 13–14 • *Lecturas para todos* Audio CD 1 Track 13, CD 2 Tracks 1–6 • Sing-along Songs Audio CD	• Vocabulary Video DVD 2 • *Telehistoria* DVD 2 Escena 1 Escena 2 Escena 3 Completa	• Video animations of all **¡AvanzaRap!** songs (with Karaoke track) • Interactive DVD Activities • Teaching Suggestions • **¡AvanzaRap!** Activity Masters • **¡AvanzaRap!** video scripts and answers

Online and Media Resources

Student	Teacher
Available online at my.hrw.com • Online Student Edition • News + Networking • performance space • @HOMETUTOR • CULTURA Interactiva • WebQuests • Interactive Flashcards • Review Games • Self-Check Quiz **Student One Stop** **Holt McDougal Spanish Apps**	**Teacher One Stop (also available at my.hrw.com)** • Interactive Teacher's Edition • All print, audio, and video resources • Projectable Transparencies • Lesson Plans • TPRS • Examview Assessment Suite **Available online at my.hrw.com** *Generate Success* Rubric Generator and Graphic Organizers **Power Presentations**

Differentiated Assessment

On-level	Modified	Pre-AP	Heritage Learners
• Vocabulary Recognition Quiz p. 302 • Vocabulary Production Quiz p. 303 • Grammar Quizzes pp. 304–305 • Culture Quiz p. 306 • On-level Lesson Test pp. 307–313	• Modified Lesson Test pp. 242–248	• Pre-AP Lesson Test pp. 242–248	• Heritage Learners Lesson Test pp. 248–254

Core Pacing Guide

50 Minute (9 Day)

	Objectives/Focus	Teach	Practice	Assess/HW Options
DAY 1	**Culture:** learn about Argentina **Vocabulary:** Technology • Warm Up OHT 16 **5 min**	Unit Opener pp. 352–353 Lesson Opener pp. 354–355 **Presentación de vocabulario** pp. 356–357 • Read A–C • View video DVD 2 • Play audio TXT CD 7 track 1 • *¡A responder!* TXT CD 7 track 2 **25 min**	Lesson Opener pp. 354–355 **Práctica de vocabulario** p. 358 • Acts. 1, 2 **15 min**	**Assess:** *Para y piensa* p. 358 **5 min** **Homework:** *Cuaderno* pp. 295–297 @HomeTutor
DAY 2	**Communication:** Technology • Warm Up OHT 16 • Check Homework **5 min**	**Vocabulario en contexto** pp. 359–360 • *Telehistoria escena 1* DVD 2 **20 min**	**Vocabulario en contexto** pp. 359–360 • Acts. 3, 4 TXT CD 7 tracks 3, 4 • Act. 5 **20 min**	**Assess:** *Para y piensa* p. 360 **5 min** **Homework:** *Cuaderno* pp. 295–297 @HomeTutor
DAY 3	**Grammar:** preterite of regular **-er** and **-ir** verbs • Warm Up OHT 17 • Check Homework **5 min**	**Presentación de gramática** p. 361 • preterite of regular **-er** and **-ir** verbs **Práctica de gramática** pp. 362–363 **Cultura:** *El lunfardo* • *Pronunciación* TXT CD 7 track 5 **20 min**	**Práctica de gramática** pp. 362–363 • Acts. 6, 7, 8, 9 **20 min**	**Assess:** *Para y piensa* p. 363 **5 min** **Homework:** *Cuaderno* pp. 298–300 @HomeTutor
DAY 4	**Communication:** talk about the past • Warm Up OHT 17 • Check Homework **5 min**	**Gramática en contexto** pp. 364–365 • *Telehistoria escena 2* DVD 2 **15 min**	**Gramática en contexto** p. 364 • Act. 10 TXT CD 7 track 6 • Act. 11 **25 min**	**Assess:** *Para y piensa* p. 365 **5 min** **Homework:** *Cuaderno* pp. 298–300 @HomeTutor
DAY 5	**Grammar:** affirmative and negative words • Warm Up OHT 18 • Check Homework **5 min**	**Presentación de gramática** p. 366 • affirmative and negative words **Práctica de gramática** pp. 367–368 • *Nota gramatical: Ningunos* **15 min**	**Práctica de gramática** pp. 367–368 • Acts. 12, 13, 14, 15 **25 min**	**Assess:** *Para y piensa* p. 368 **5 min** **Homework:** *Cuaderno* pp. 301–303 @HomeTutor
DAY 6	**Communication:** Culmination: Technology, preterite of regular **-er** and **-ir** verbs, affirmative and negative words • Warm Up OHT 18 • Check Homework **5 min**	**Todo junto** pp. 369–371 • *Escenas 1, 2: Resumen* • *Telehistoria completa* DVD 2 **20 min**	**Todo junto** pp. 369–371 • Acts. 16, 17 TXT CD 7 tracks 3, 6, 7 • Act. 19 TXT CD 7 tracks 8, 9 • Acts. 18, 20 **20 min**	**Assess:** *Para y piensa* p. 371 **5 min** **Homework:** *Cuaderno* pp. 304–305 @HomeTutor
DAY 7	**Reading:** Computer questionnaire **Connections:** Language • Warm Up OHT 19 • Check Homework **5 min**	**Lectura** pp. 372–373 • *Un cuestionario sobre las computadoras* • TXT CD 7 track 10 **Conexiones** p. 374 • *El lenguaje* **15 min**	**Lectura** pp. 372–373 • *Un cuestionario sobre las computadoras* **Conexiones** p. 374 • *Proyectos* 1, 2, 3 **25 min**	**Assess:** *Para y piensa* p. 373 **5 min** **Homework:** *Cuaderno* pp. 309–311 @HomeTutor
DAY 8	**Review:** Lesson Review • Warm Up OHT 19 **5 min**	**Repaso de la lección** pp. 376–377 **15 min**	**Repaso de la lección** pp. 376–377 • Act. 1 TXT CD 7 track 11 • Acts. 2, 3, 4, 5 **20 min**	**Assess: Repaso de la lección** pp. 376–377 **10 min** **Homework:** *En resumen* p. 375; *Cuaderno* pp. 306–308, 312–317 (optional) Review Games Online @HomeTutor
DAY 9	**Assessment**			**Assess:** Lesson 1 Test **50 min**

Core Pacing Guide 90 Minute (5 Day) Unidad 7 Lección 1

	Objectives/Focus	Teach	Practice	Assess/HW Options
DAY 1	**Culture:** learn about Argentina **Vocabulary:** Technology • Warm Up OHT 16 **5 min**	Unit Opener pp. 352–353 Lesson Opener pp. 354–355 **Presentación de vocabulario** pp. 356–357 • Read A–C • View video DVD 2 • Play audio TXT CD 7 track 1 • *¡A responder!* TXT CD 7 track 2 **20 min**	Lesson Opener pp. 354–355 **Práctica de vocabulario** p. 358 • Acts. 1–2 **20 min**	**Assess:** *Para y piensa* p. 358 **5 min**
	Communication: Technology **5 min**	**Vocabulario en contexto** pp. 359–360 • *Telehistoria escena 1* DVD 2 **15 min**	**Vocabulario en contexto** pp. 359–360 • Acts. 3, 4 TXT CD 7 tracks 3, 4 • Act. 5 **15 min**	**Assess:** *Para y piensa* p. 360 **5 min** **Homework:** *Cuaderno* pp. 295–297 @HomeTutor
DAY 2	**Grammar:** preterite of regular **-er** and **-ir** verbs • Warm Up OHT 17 • Check Homework **5 min**	**Presentación de gramática** p. 361 • preterite of regular **-er** and **-ir** verbs **Práctica de gramática** pp. 362–363 **Cultura:** *El lunfardo* • *Pronunciación* TXT CD 7 track 5 **20 min**	**Práctica de gramática** pp. 362–363 • Acts. 6, 7, 8, 9 **15 min**	**Assess:** *Para y piensa* p. 363 **5 min**
	Communication: talk about the past **5 min**	**Gramática en contexto** pp. 364–365 • *Telehistoria escena 2* DVD 2 **20 min**	**Gramática en contexto** p. 364 • Act. 10 TXT CD 7 track 6 • Act. 11 **15 min**	**Assess:** *Para y piensa* p. 365 **5 min** **Homework:** *Cuaderno* pp. 298–300 @HomeTutor
DAY 3	**Grammar:** affirmative and negative words • Warm Up OHT 18 • Check Homework **5 min**	**Presentación de gramática** p. 366 • affirmative and negative words **Práctica de gramática** pp. 367–368 • *Nota gramatical:* Ningunos **15 min**	**Práctica de gramática** pp. 367–368 • Acts. 12, 13, 14, 15 **20 min**	**Assess:** *Para y piensa* p. 368 **5 min**
	Communication: Culmination: Technology, preterite of regular **-er** and **-ir** verbs, affirmative and negative words **5 min**	**Todo junto** pp. 369–371 • *Escenas 1, 2: Resumen* • *Telehistoria completa* DVD 2 **15 min**	**Todo junto** pp. 369–371 • Acts. 16, 17 TXT CD 7 tracks 3, 6, 7 • Act. 19 TXT CD 7 tracks 8, 9 • Acts. 18, 20 **20 min**	**Assess:** *Para y piensa* p. 371 **5 min** **Homework:** *Cuaderno* pp. 301–305 @HomeTutor
DAY 4	**Reading:** Computer questionnaire • Warm Up OHT 19 • Check Homework **5 min**	**Lectura** pp. 372–373 • *Un cuestionario sobre las computadoras* • TXT CD 7 track 10 **15 min**	**Lectura** pp. 372–373 • *Un cuestionario sobre las computadoras* **15 min**	**Assess:** *Para y piensa* p. 373 **5 min**
	Review: Lesson Review **5 min**	**Repaso de la lección** pp. 376–377 **15 min**	**Repaso de la lección** pp. 376–377 • Act. 1 TXT CD 7 track 11 • Acts. 2, 3, 4, 5 **25 min**	**Assess: Repaso de la lección** pp. 376–377 **5 min** **Homework:** *En resumen* p. 375; *Cuaderno* pp. 306–317 (optional) @HomeTutor
DAY 5	**Assessment**			**Assess:** Lesson 1 Test **45 min**
	Connections: Language **5 min**	**Conexiones** p. 374 • *El lenguaje* **10 min**	**Conexiones** p. 374 • *Proyectos* 1, 2, 3 **30 min**	

¡AVANZA! Objectives

- Introduce lesson theme: **En el cibercafé.**
- **Culture:** Special beverages or foods in different regions of the world.

Presentation Strategies

- Introduce characters' names: Florencia, Mariano, and Luciana.
- Ask students to make a list of favorite landmarks in their city or town. Have them talk about how often they go there and with whom.

STANDARDS

4.2 Compare cultures

21st Century **Social and Cross-Cultural Skills,** Compara con tu mundo/Exploring the Theme/English Learners

Warm Up Projectable Transparencies, 7-16

Preterite of -car, -gar, -zar Verbs Complete each sentence using the preterite of the verb in parentheses.

1. Ayer Felipe _____ una A en español y yo _____ una B. (sacar)
2. El lunes ustedes _____ a aprender el español pero yo _____ ayer. (empezar)
3. El sábado tú _____ al fútbol pero yo _____ al básquetbol. (jugar)

Answers: 1. sacó, saqué; 2. empezaron, empecé; 3. jugaste, jugué

Comparación cultural

Exploring the Theme

Ask the following:

- What does the Casa Rosada look like? Does it remind you of any buildings that you know?
- Based on the teens' clothing, what season could it be? During what months is that season in Argentina?

¿Qué ves? Possible answers include:

- Sí, son amigos.
- Tienen sed.
- Sirve una bebida.

UNIDAD 7 Argentina

Lección 1

Tema:

En el cibercafé

¡AVANZA! In this lesson you will learn to

- talk about technology
- talk about a series of events
- say what you did
- talk about indefinite or negative situations

using

- preterite of regular **-er** and **-ir** verbs
- affirmative and negative words

¿Recuerdas?

- affirmative **tú** commands
- telling time
- foods and beverages
- preterite of regular **-ar** verbs

Comparación cultural

In this lesson you will learn about

- the use of **lunfardo** in Argentina
- the city of Mar del Plata
- protecting your computer

Compara con tu mundo

These teens are drinking a tea-like beverage called **mate.** Drinking **mate** involves a special cup, often made out of a dried, decorated gourd, with a metal or wood straw, called a **bombilla.** *Does your region have a special beverage or food? What is it?*

¿Qué ves?

Mira la foto

¿Son amigos estas personas?

¿Tienen sed o tienen hambre?

¿Qué hace la chica de la blusa roja?

Differentiating Instruction

Inclusion

Cumulative Instruction Organize students into four groups and give each a piece of poster board. Assign each group one of the ¿Recuerdas? topics on p. 354. Instruct students to create a poster that will help their peers review the details of that topic. They might design a chart, list examples, or create an exercise.

English Learners

Build Background Explain to students that La Casa Rosada in Buenos Aires can be compared to the White House in Washington, D.C. Ask students to share what the equivalent would be in their country of origin. Is there a famous house for the country's leader? Or is there another famous building that represents the government?

DIGITAL SPANISH my.hrw.com

ONLINE STUDENT EDITION with...

performance space
News + Networking
@HOMETUTOR
CULTURA Interactiva

- Audio and Video Resources
- Interactive Flashcards
- Review Activities
- WebQuest
- Conjuguemos.com

PRACTICE SPANISH WITH HOLT MCDOUGAL APPS!

La Casa Rosada
Buenos Aires, Argentina

DIGITAL SPANISH

TEACHER TOOLS

- Interactive Whiteboard Lessons
- Generate Success!

ALSO AVAILABLE...

- Online Workbook
- Spanish InterActive Reader

SPANISH ON THE GO!

- Performance Space
- Holt McDougal Spanish Apps
- ¡Avancemos! eTextbook

Using the Photo

Location Information

Argentina The country lies south of the equator, so the seasons are opposite of ours. Buenos Aires, the capital, is a bustling metropolis located in Río de la Plata. Argentina is the eighth largest country in the world.

Expanded Information

La Casa Rosada (the Pink House) is located in downtown Buenos Aires. It houses a museum, which is open to the public. It is said that in 1873, one of Argentina's presidents chose to paint the building in a pink color to defuse political tension by blending the red and white colors of the country's political parties. Since then it is called **la Casa Rosada.**

Long-term Retention

Recycle

Review vocabulary by asking either/or questions about the photo.

1. **¿Dónde están los chicos, delante o detrás de la Casa Rosada?**
2. **¿Qué llevan los chicos, pantalones o jeans?**
3. **¿Qué van a hacer el chico y la chica de la blusa roja?**
4. **¿Qué tiempo hace, frío o calor?**

Differentiating Instruction

Pre-AP

Support Opinions Ask students to write a paragraph about the photo. Ask them to write what is happening, using descriptive words they have already learned. For example, **Los tres chicos están contentos. Los chicos llevan jeans. El chico lleva una camiseta verde. Una chica lleva blusa roja y la otra chica lleva blusa azul.**

Heritage Language Learners

Literacy Skills Have students form two groups. Ask both groups to brainstorm information about Argentina. Ask each group to write about the country, which could be focused on its cuisine, music, history, or famous people. Tell them to consult the encyclopedia if necessary. Then have the groups give an oral presentation to the class.

¡AVANZA! Objectives

- Present vocabulary: technology-related activities, parts of a computer.
- Present sequence words.

Core Resources

- Video Program: DVD 2
- Audio Program: TXT CD 7 tracks 1, 2

Presentation Strategies

- Point to the items on pp. 356–357, or use a class computer to review parts of a computer. Say the words and have students repeat after you.
- Use a classroom computer to explain the steps for sending an e-mail. Include sequence words.
- Play the audio as students read A–C.
- Play the video.

STANDARDS

1.2 Understand language

21st Century **Communication,** Slower-paced Learners; **Technology Literacy,** TPR Activity

Long-term Retention
Personalize It

Encourage students to say what they did yesterday by starting a sentence with the word **ayer.** For example: **Ayer tomé fotos de mi familia.** Write each sentence on the board until everyone has finished. Then continue by asking students to dictate sentences starting with **Anteayer** and **La semana pasada.**

Communication
TPR Activity

Bring in a computer to your classroom to identify computer parts while students follow your commands. Introduce the commands **Señala** and **Toca.**

- **Señala la pantalla.**
- **Toca el teclado.**
- **Pon el disco debajo del ratón.**
- **Conecta a Internet.**
- **Haz clic con el ratón.**
- **Busca un sitio Web.**

Presentación de VOCABULARIO

¡AVANZA! **Goal:** Learn about how Florencia and her friends use the computer to send photos. Then practice what you have learned to talk about how you and others use the computer. ***Actividades 1–2***

VIDEO DVD

AUDIO

A ¡Hola! Me llamo Florencia. **Anteayer** pasé un rato con mis amigos Mariano y Luciana. **Tomamos fotos** delante de la Casa Rosada.

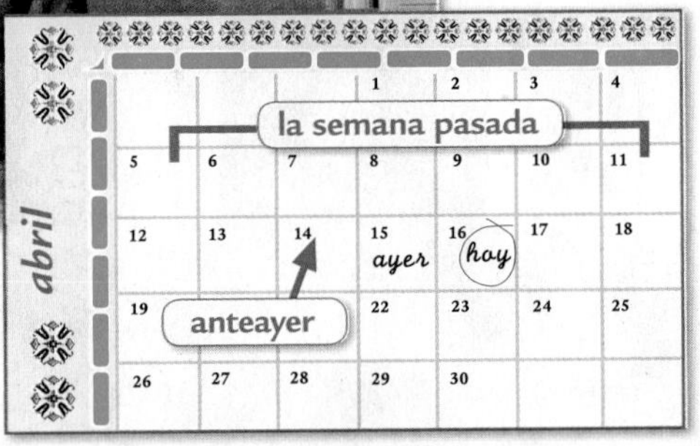

B Hoy, Mariano y yo estamos en la biblioteca. Aquí **navegamos por Internet,** usamos **el mensajero instantáneo** y **mandamos** correos electrónicos. Quiero mandar las fotos que tomé anteayer.

Differentiating Instruction

Inclusion

Alphabetic/Phonetic Awareness Ask students to locate technology terms that are the same in Spanish and English (**Web, Internet, digital**). Discuss the pronunciation of these words in each language. For example, the *g* in the English word *digital* makes a /j/ sound, while the **g** in the Spanish word **digital** makes an /h/ sound.

Slower-paced Learners

Personalize It Ask students questions about their own experiences with computers and technology. Questions might use the verbs **gustar, saber,** or **tener.** Here are a few possibilities:

- **¿Te gusta navegar por Internet?**
- **¿Sabes usar una cámara digital?**
- **¿Tienes una computadora con una pantalla y un teclado?**

C Es fácil mandarlas y no cuesta **nada**. Primero **conecto a Internet.** Cuando **estoy en línea**, escribo un correo electrónico con las fotos. **Por fin**, pongo **la dirección electrónica** de mi amiga y **hago clic en el icono** para mandarlas.

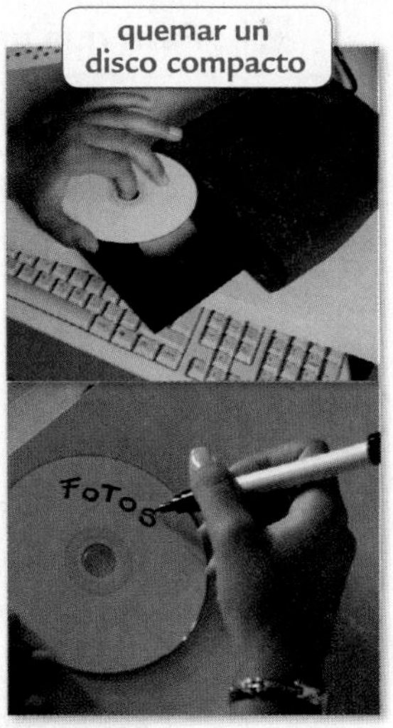

Más vocabulario

el año pasado *last year*
entonces *then, so*
luego *later, then*
más tarde *later on*
Expansión de vocabulario p. R8

@HOMETUTOR my.hrw.com Interactive Flashcards

¡A responder! Escuchar

Florencia compró una computadora nueva. Escucha la lista de palabras y levanta la mano si la palabra es parte de su computadora. *(Listen to the list of words. Raise your hand if the word is part of a computer.)*

TEACHER to TEACHER

Elizabeth Uhlig
Queens, New York

Tips for Presenting Vocabulary

When I teach computer-related vocabulary, I use one of the school computers or bring in my own laptop to class. I point to the different parts of the computer, say the word aloud, and ask students to repeat after me. Once I confirm that students have learned the words, I expand the activity by asking them to say a word or expression related to a particular computer part. For example, ***el teclado*** *might elicit answers from students such as* ***tocar el teclado, mandar correos electrónicos,*** *or* ***la cámara digital*** *may elicit* ***tomar fotos.***

Go online for more tips!

Communication
Group Work

Game Divide the class into two groups. Each group has two minutes to write a list of computer-related words. After the time limit, a member of each group reads his or her list to the rest of the class. The group with the longest list wins.

Long-term Retention
Study Tips

To help remember new vocabulary, have students group the words on pp. 356–357 and list them into categories such as computer-related activities: **navegar, quemar, mandar, hacer clic;** parts of the computer: **el teclado, el ratón, la pantalla;** and computer applications: **el sitio Web, la dirección electrónica.**

Differentiating Instruction

Heritage Language Learners

Regional Variations Ask students to share other words they know to talk about computers and technology. For example, some people use **la red** to refer to the Web; others might use the English term *e-mail* instead of **correo electrónico.** Also, what are some of the slang computer terms that teenagers use?

Multiple Intelligences

Visual Learners Make copies of a one-month calendar for students. Have them listen to your directions and circle the appropriate day(s) on their calendars. Tell them to circle the appropriate day for **hoy, ayer, anteayer,** and the week for **la semana pasada.** Have students say each term as they circle it.

Answers Projectable Transparencies, 7-24

¡A responder! Audio Script, TE p. 353B
Students should raise their hands when they hear **la pantalla, el teclado, el ratón.**

Objective
- Practice vocabulary: technology-related activities, parts of a computer.

Core Resource
- *Cuaderno,* pp. 295–297

Practice Sequence
- **Activity 1:** Vocabulary recognition: computer-related words
- **Activity 2:** Vocabulary production

STANDARDS
1.2 Understand language, Act. 1
1.3 Present information, Act. 2, PYP
21st Century **Communication,** Act. 2

Communication — Pair Work
Have students write false statements in Spanish describing how to use the computer. For example: **Haz clic con el teclado.** Exchange with a partner and correct the false statements to make them true.

✓ Ongoing Assessment
Get Help Online
More Practice
my.hrw.com

PARA Y PIENSA **Quick Check** Say aloud vocabulary words from pp. 356–357. Ask students to raise their right hand if they refer to a computer part and their left hand if they refer to an Internet-related activity. For additional practice, use Reteaching and Practice Copymasters URB 7, pp. 1, 2.

Answers Projectable Transparencies, 7-24
Activity 1 **1.** b; **2.** d; **3.** e; **4.** a; **5.** f; **6.** c

Activity 2
1. Uso la cámara digital para tomar fotos.
2. Uso el mensajero instantáneo para hablar con amigos.
3. Uso la dirección electrónica para mandar correos electrónicos.
4. Uso la pantalla para mirar fotos.
5. Uso el teclado para escribir en la computadora.
6. Uso el ratón para hacer clic.

Para y piensa
1. la pantalla, el ratón, el teclado
2. Possible answers include: mandar correos electrónicos, navegar por Internet, mandar fotos

Práctica de VOCABULARIO

1 El mundo digital
Leer

Empareja las frases para describir computadoras. *(Match the phrases.)*

1. Florencia toma fotos	**a.** por Internet en la biblioteca.
2. Conectamos a Internet	**b.** con su cámara digital.
3. Hago clic	**c.** un disco compacto.
4. Mariano navega	**d.** para estar en línea.
5. Uso el ratón	**e.** en el icono para abrir un sitio Web.
6. Voy a quemar	**f.** para hacer clic en los iconos.

Expansión
Draw a computer and label as many parts as you can.

2 ¿Para qué usas...?
Hablar
Escribir

Describe para qué usas cada cosa que ves en las fotos. *(Tell how you use the items pictured below.)*

escribir en la computadora	hacer clic
tomar fotos	mirar fotos
buscar una película	hablar con amigos
mandar correos electrónicos	

modelo: Uso **el sitio Web** para **buscar una película.**

1. 
2. 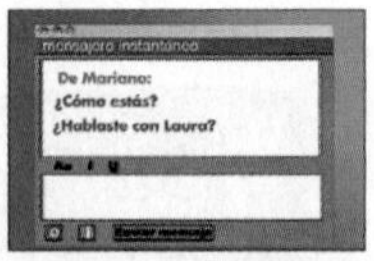
3. 
4. 
5. 
6. 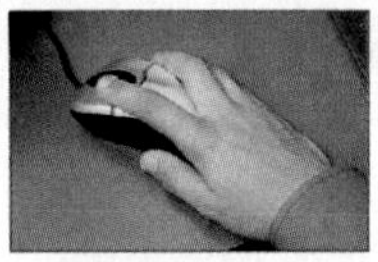

Expansión:
Teacher Edition Only
Have students say what they can't do with each item.

Más práctica Cuaderno *pp. 295–297* Cuaderno para hispanohablantes *pp. 295–298*

Get Help Online
my.hrw.com

PARA Y PIENSA **Did you get it?** 1. Name three parts of a computer.
2. Name three things you can do on the Internet.

Differentiating Instruction

Inclusion
Frequent Review/Repetition Organize students into pairs to discuss Activity 1. Give each student six index cards. One student should copy the phrases **1** through **6** onto his or her cards, while the other copies the phrases **a** through **f.** Have partners work together to match each sentence beginning with its ending.

Slower-paced Learners
Yes/No Questions Before starting Activity 2, ask students yes/no questions about each photo. Ask two or three no questions before asking the yes question. Here is an example for photo 1.
¿Usas una cámara digital para escribir en la computadora?
¿Usas una cámara digital para buscar una película?

VOCABULARIO en contexto

¡AVANZA! **Goal:** Pay attention to the words Florencia uses to put events in order. Then practice these words to talk about a series of events. ***Actividades 3–5***

¿Recuerdas? Affirmative **tú** commands p. 282

Telehistoria escena 1

@HOMETUTOR my.hrw.com **View, Read and Record**

STRATEGIES

Cuando lees

List related words This conversation includes several expressions for time-sequencing, such as **luego.** While reading, list them and add any others you know.

Cuando escuchas

Listen for sequences Listen for places Alicia's T-shirt has been. Write the names of cities, states, and countries, using arrows for sequencing.

VIDEO DVD

AUDIO

Florencia: ¡Mariano! Mira, tengo un correo electrónico de Alicia.

Mariano: ¿Qué dice, Florencia? No puedo ver la pantalla.

Florencia: Alicia quiere el autógrafo de Trini Salgado en su camiseta.

Mariano: ¡Qué bárbaro tener el autógrafo de una jugadora de fútbol famosa como Trini Salgado!

Florencia: Alicia mandó la camiseta a Sandra, una amiga que vive en Texas. Después, Sandra la mandó a un amigo de Puebla, en México, pero tampoco la encontró.

Mariano: ¿Y entonces?

Florencia: Luego, su amigo de México mandó la camiseta a Puerto Rico. Más tarde, sus amigos mandaron la camiseta a España, y entonces a Ecuador y a la República Dominicana. Y por fin, anteayer la mandaron aquí a Buenos Aires. ¡Porque Trini está aquí!

Continuará... p. 364

También se dice

Argentina Mariano uses the phrase **¡Qué bárbaro!** to say *Cool!* In other Spanish-speaking countries you might hear:

- **Perú, Chile, Ecuador** **¡Qué bacán!**
- **México** **¡Qué padre!**
- **España** **¡Qué guay!**
- **muchos países** **¡Qué chévere!**

Differentiating Instruction

Heritage Language Learners

Writing Skills Ask students to draft two or three comprehension questions based on the Telehistoria. Have volunteers choose one question to write on the board, and pose to the group. Then have all students write their answers for the questions presented. Monitor correct spelling and grammar.

Multiple Intelligences

Visual Learners Use a world map or globe to help students visualize the T-shirt's travels as explained by Florencia in the Telehistoria. Mark each stop with a pin or sticker. Then discuss with students the sequence of the shirt's journey using **después, luego, más tarde, entonces,** and **por fin.**

¡AVANZA! Objective

- Understand activity vocabulary in context.

Core Resources

- Video Program: DVD 2
- Audio Program: TXT CD 7 track 3

Presentation Strategies

- As students look at the photo, ask comprehension questions such as **¿Qué hacen Florencia y Mariano? ¿Quién tiene la mano en el teclado?**
- Ask students to scan the dialogue to find out how many time-sequencing expressions are mentioned.
- Play the audio or video while students follow the script in their text.

STANDARDS

1.2 Understand language

Warm Up Projectable Transparencies, 7-16

Vocabulary Write **sí** if the statement is logical and **no** if it is illogical.

1. Hago clic con la pantalla.
2. Quemo un disco compacto.
3. Escribo con el teclado.
4. Tomo fotos con un ratón.

Answers: 1. no; 2. sí; 3. sí; 4. no

Communication

Grammar Activity

Telehistoria Have students listen to the Telehistoria with their books closed. Ask them to write on a separate sheet of paper the verbs they hear in the preterite tense. Then ask them to compare the list with a classmate's.

Video Summary

@HOMETUTOR VideoPlus my.hrw.com

Florencia receives an e-mail from Alicia. Trini Salgado is in Buenos Aires, and Alicia wants her autograph on a T-shirt. Florencia explains to Mariano all of the places that Alicia's T-shirt has been sent so far.

Objectives
- Practice using the vocabulary in context.
- Recycle: affirmative **tú** commands.

Core Resource
Audio program: TXT CD 7 tracks 3, 4

Practice Sequence
- **Activity 3:** Telehistoria comprehension: time-sequencing expressions
- **Activity 4:** Vocabulary production: technology-related activities, time-sequencing expressions
- **Activity 5:** Vocabulary production: technology-related activities; Recycle: affirmative **tú** commands.

STANDARDS
1.1 Engage in conversation, Act. 5
1.2 Understand language, Acts. 3–4, PYP
1.3 Present information, Act. 5
Communication, Act. 5

✓ Ongoing Assessment
Get Help Online
More Practice
my.hrw.com

PARA Y PIENSA **Peer Assessment** When students finish putting the sentences in order, ask them to verify their answers with a partner. Then have a volunteer write the answer on the board. For additional practice, use Reteaching & Practice Copymasters URB 7, pp. 1, 3, 10.

Answers Projectable Transparencies, 7-24
Activity 3 ...Luego, su amiga Sandra la mandó a Puebla, México. Después, el amigo de Puebla la mandó a Puerto Rico. Más tarde, sus amigos de Puerto Rico la mandaron a España, y entonces a Ecuador y a la República Dominicana. Por fin, la mandaron a Buenos Aires.
Activity 4 f; d; b; a; e; c
Activity 5 Answers will vary. Sample answers include: ¿Cómo mando fotos? Quema un disco compacto con las fotos. Luego, conecta a Internet y manda las fotos por correo electrónico.
Para y piensa d; b; a; c

3 *Comprensión del episodio* ¿Adónde la mandaron?
Escuchar Leer

Usa las palabras de la lista para indicar el orden y los lugares adonde mandaron la camiseta de Alicia. *(Use the words in the list to write the order of the places where they sent Alicia's T-shirt.)*

entonces	más tarde
luego	por fin

modelo: Primero, Alicia mandó la camiseta de Miami a Texas. Luego...

4 ¿En qué orden?
Escuchar

Escucha la descripción de cómo Florencia tomó fotos y se las mandó a sus amigas. Luego indica el orden correcto de los dibujos. *(Listen to the description and put the drawings in order.)*

a.

b.

c.

d.

e.

f.

5 ¿Cómo lo hago?
¿Recuerdas? Affirmative **tú** commands p. 282

Hablar

Pregúntale a otro(a) estudiante cómo hacer varias cosas en la computadora. *(Ask a partner how to do these things.)*

- navegar por Internet
- usar una cámara digital
- mandar fotos
- usar el mensajero instantáneo
- mandar un correo electrónico
- ¿ ?

A ¿Cómo uso una cámara digital?

B Toma fotos. Luego ponlas en la computadora y míralas en la pantalla.

Get Help Online
my.hrw.com

PARA Y PIENSA

Did you get it? Put the following sentences in order.
a. Más tarde, Trini va a Puerto Rico y a España.
b. Luego, Trini está en Puebla, México.
c. Por fin, Trini está en Buenos Aires.
d. Primero, Trini llega a San Antonio.

Expansión:
Teacher Edition Only
Have students write about something they did recently using the preterite tense and at least three time-sequencing expressions.

Audio Program
TXT CD 7, Track 4
Audio Script, TE p. 353b

Expansión
Write five sentences to tell how you use the computer at home or at school.

Expansión:
Teacher Edition Only
Ask students to write step-by-step instructions on how to send an e-mail.

Differentiating Instruction

Pre-AP
Sequence Information Provide each student with six index cards. They should label the cards **a** through **f**. Before listening to Florencia's description in Activity 4, have students describe what they see in each drawing on a card. As students listen to the description, instruct them to physically arrange their cards in the correct order.

Inclusion
Frequent Review/Repetition Have students preview Activity 5 to compile a list of verbs that they might find useful. Some examples might include **tomar, poner, hacer, usar,** and **escribir.** Then review with students the affirmative **tú** command for each of these verbs. Play a game where you state the verb, and students call out the affirmative **tú** command form.

Presentación de GRAMÁTICA

¡AVANZA! **Goal:** Learn about the preterite forms of **-er** and **-ir** verbs. Then practice using these verbs to say what you and others did. ***Actividades 6–9***

¿Recuerdas? Telling time p. 90, foods and beverages pp. 33, 140, 218

English Grammar Connection: Remember that the **preterite** is a tense used to express an action completed at a definite time in the past (see p. 331). In English, regular verbs in the past tense end in *-ed*.

Preterite of Regular -er and -ir Verbs

ANIMATEDGRAMMAR my.hrw.com

Regular **-er** and **-ir** verbs follow a pattern similar to regular **-ar** verbs in the **preterite.** How do you form the **preterite** of regular **-er** and **-ir** verbs?

Here's how:

In the preterite, **-er** and **-ir** verb endings are identical.

vender *to sell*	
vendí	**vendimos**
vendiste	**vendisteis**
vendió	**vendieron**

escribir *to write*	
escribí	**escribimos**
escribiste	**escribisteis**
escribió	**escribieron**

The **yo** forms and the **usted/él/ella** forms take accents.

Vendí la computadora.
***I sold** the computer.*

Tomás **escribió** un correo electrónico.
*Tomás **wrote** an e-mail.*

The **nosotros(as)** form of regular **-ir** verbs is the same in both the present and the preterite. Use context clues to determine the tense of the verb.

Salimos a las ocho **anoche.**
We left** at eight o'clock **last night.

The word **anoche** tells you that **salimos** is in the preterite tense.

Más práctica
Cuaderno *pp. 298–300*
Cuaderno para hispanohablantes *pp. 299–301*

@HOMETUTOR my.hrw.com
Leveled Practice
Conjuguemos.com

¡AVANZA! **Objective**
- Present the preterite of **-er** and **-ir** verbs.

Core Resource
- *Cuaderno,* pp. 298–300

Presentation Strategies
- Write the forms of **vender** and **escribir** on the board or OHT and underline the verb endings with a different color.
- Ask students to point out which forms take accents.
- Ask students to copy these paradigms in their notebooks.
- Check comprehension of present and preterite forms by saying sentences in the present and the preterite in random order. Have students raise their hands when they hear a sentence in the preterite.

STANDARDS
4.1 Compare languages

Warm Up Projectable Transparencies, 7-17

Vocabulary Arrange these expressions in order from first to final:
por fin, primero, más tarde
Answers: primero; más tarde; por fin

Long-term Retention
Study Tips

The ending **-imos** may indicate the present tense as well as the preterite tense of **-ir** verbs. Tell students to look for context clues and adverbial expressions to help them determine if the tense being used is present or preterite.

Differentiating Instruction

Slower-paced Learners

Peer-study Support Create a three-column chart on the board. List the pronouns **yo, tú,** etc. down the left-hand column. Write **-ar** at the top of the middle column, and **-er/-ir** on the top of the right-hand column. Discuss how the preterite endings for these three types of verbs compare. Ask students to work in pairs to give examples for each pronoun.

Multiple Intelligences

Linguistic/Verbal Give students several sentences with **-er** and **-ir** verbs following the pronoun **nosotros.** For example: **Ayer escribimos muchos correos electrónicos. Siempre escribimos la dirección electrónica.** Based on context clues, ask students to explain which verbs are in the preterite and which are in the present.

Verbs Students Know

Students have learned the following verbs that follow the pattern of the regular preterite tense: **escribir, compartir, vivir, subir, salir, abrir, recibir, aprender, beber, comer, correr, vender, deber, entender, perder, barrer, comprender, volver, envolver, conocer.** The preterite of **ver** also follows this pattern except that there are no accents.

Objectives

- Practice using the preterite of regular **-er** and **-ir** verbs.
- Recycle: telling time, foods and beverages.
- **Culture:** Find out how slang words develop.
- Pronunciación: Practice pronouncing **qu** before **e** and **i.**

Core Resources

- *Cuaderno,* pp. 298–300
- Audio Program: TXT CD 7 track 5

Practice Sequence

- **Activity 6:** Controlled practice: preterite of **-er** and **-ir** verbs; Recycle: telling time
- **Activity 7:** Controlled practice: preterite of **-er** and **-ir** verbs
- **Activity 8:** Transitional practice: preterite of **-er** and **-ir** verbs
- **Activity 9:** Open-ended practice: preterite of **-er** verbs; Recycle: foods and beverages

STANDARDS

1.1 Engage in conversation, Acts. 8–9
1.3 Present information, Acts. 6–9, CC, PYP
2.1 Practices and perspectives, CC
4.1 Compare languages, CC, Pronunciación

21st Century **Critical Thinking and Problem Solving,** Multiple Intelligences; **Social and Cross-Cultural Skills,** English Learners; **Technology Literacy,** Heritage Language Learners

Comparación cultural

Essential Question

Suggested Answer Slang develops as people make up or modify words and others pick them up. Slang may include metaphors, similes, words with new meanings, words borrowed from other languages, abbreviated words, and so on.

Background Information

The word **lunfardo** is a deformation of the Italian word *lombardo,* which has the additional meaning of "outlaw." Many **lunfardo** words derive from Italian, French, Polish, and Portuguese and include many words used by the **gauchos** (Argentine cowboys). As a class activity, write the following **lunfardo** terms and ask students to guess what they mean: **gotán = tango; laburar = trabajar; broli = libro; feca = café.**

See Activity answers on p. 363.

Práctica de GRAMÁTICA

6 ¿Cuándo volvieron? ¿Recuerdas? Telling time p. 90

Hablar
Escribir

Mariano y sus amigos salieron ayer. Indica cuándo volvieron, según la hora a la que salieron y cuántas horas pasaron fuera de casa. *(Tell when these people came home, according to the time they left and how long they were out.)*

modelo: **Mariano / 4:00 (dos horas)**
Mariano salió a las cuatro y volvió a las seis.

1. Mariano y yo / 8:30 (siete horas)
2. usted / 9:20 (dos horas)
3. yo / 6:40 (una hora)
4. Florencia y Ana / 10:05 (cuatro horas)
5. tú / 1:15 (tres horas)
6. Florencia / 2:45 (seis horas)

Expansión
Tell what time you went out and came home yesterday and the day before.

7 Mariano y su familia

Leer
Escribir

Mariano le escribió un correo electrónico a Luciana. Complétalo con la forma correcta del pretérito del verbo apropiado. *(Complete Mariano's e-mail.)*

Yo te __1.__ (escribir / correr) un correo electrónico ayer y mandé unas fotos. ¿Tú las __2.__ (vivir / recibir)? Mi familia y yo __3.__ (perder / salir) a un restaurante. Mis padres __4.__ (comer / deber) churrasco, el bistec de Argentina. De postre mi hermana y yo __5.__ (abrir / compartir) un pastel y mi padre __6.__ (subir / beber) un café. Luego nosotros __7.__ (volver / ver) a casa.

Expansión: Teacher Edition Only
Have students respond to Mariano's e-mail.

Comparación cultural

El famoso Carlos Gardel

El lunfardo

How do slang words develop? Lunfardo is a variety of slang that originated among the immigrant populations of Buenos Aires, **Argentina,** during the early 20th century. Many words were influenced by other languages, especially Italian, while others were created by reversing the syllables of Spanish terms. For example, *amigos* became *gomías* and *pizza* became *zapi. Lunfardo* appeared in many tango lyrics, such as those popularized by Carlos Gardel. His music helped introduce *lunfardo* to the general public. Many people in Argentina still use some of these words in their informal speech, often in a playful or humorous manner.

Compara con tu mundo *What slang terms do you know that mean "Great!"?*

Differentiating Instruction

English Learners

Increase Interaction Write **lunfardo** in the center of a concept web. Have students read the Comparación cultural twice to find examples and definitions of this word. Record the words *slang, Italian,* **gomías,** and **zapi** around the web. Define the word *slang* by giving examples in English. Ask students to share appropriate slang terms from their language of origin.

Heritage Language Learners

Literacy Skills Assign students the task of researching the life and work of Carlos Gardel or the tango in general. Encourage students to use technology in their research, as well as their presentations. They might print photos from the Web, list interesting Web sites, or download music samples to play for the group.

8 La semana pasada

Hablar

Habla con otro(a) estudiante sobre las actividades que hizo la semana pasada. *(Talk with a partner about activities he or she did last week.)*

salir	recibir	escribir
barrer	comer	correr
beber		

A ¿Saliste con tus amigos la semana pasada?

B Sí, salí con mis amigos al cine. (No, no salí con mis amigos.)

1. 
2. 
3. 
4. 
5. 
6. 

Expansión:
Teacher Edition Only
Have students talk about the house chores they did last week. Encourage them to use time-sequencing expressions.

9 Una encuesta

¿Recuerdas? Foods and beverages pp. 33, 140, 218

Hablar
Escribir

Haz una encuesta sobre qué comieron y bebieron los estudiantes de tu clase ayer. Presenta los resultados a la clase. *(Take a survey of what your classmates ate and drank yesterday. Report your findings to the class.)*

Expansión:
Teacher Edition Only
Expand the survey to include where the students ate and drank yesterday.

Pronunciación La combinación qu

AUDIO

You already know that **c** before **a, o, u,** and consonants makes the sound of the English *k*. To make this sound before **e** and **i** in Spanish, use **qu.**

Listen and repeat.

que	→	**queso**	**pequeño**	**raqueta**	**quemar**
qui	→	**tranquilo**	**quince**	**quiero**	**equipo**

¿Quién tiene que hacer los quehaceres? ¿Quieres ir al parque?

Más práctica Cuaderno *pp. 298–300* Cuaderno para hispanohablantes *pp. 299–301*

Get Help Online
my.hrw.com

PARA Y PIENSA

Did you get it? Fill in the preterite form of the verb in parentheses.

1. Anteayer yo _____ la cena con mi amiga Teresa. (comer)
2. ¿ _____ tú muchos regalos para tu cumpleaños? (recibir)

Differentiating Instruction

Multiple Intelligences

Logical/Mathematical After completing Activity 9, have students present their data in the form of a bar graph. Instruct students to label the x-axis with the names of foods and drinks, and the y-axis with numbers, starting with zero. Have students compare their findings. Do all of the graphs look the same?

Inclusion

Alphabetic/Phonetic Awareness Have students work in groups. Organize an informal spelling bee to help students remember **que-** and **qui-** words, as opposed to **ca-, co-,** and **cu-** words. Say a word such as **que, queso, cuando** (not the question words) and ask a volunteer to write it on the board. If the volunteer spells the word correctly, he or she earns a point for his or her group.

Long-term Retention

Recycle

Activity 9 Make flashcards using pictures cut from magazines for the following foods: **el brócoli, la ensalada, los frijoles, el tomate, el pescado, el pollo.** Show each card and have students say the corresponding Spanish word.

Ongoing Assessment

Get Help Online
More Practice
my.hrw.com

PARA Y PIENSA **Quick Check** Ask students to write a short paragraph telling what they did in school yesterday and the day before yesterday. For additional practice, use Reteaching & Practice Copymasters URB 7, pp. 4, 5, 11.

Answers Projectable Transparencies, 7-24 and 7-25

Answers for Activities on pp. 362–363.

Activity 6

1. Mariano y yo salimos a las ocho y media y volvimos a las tres y media.
2. Usted salió a las nueve y veinte y volvió a las once y veinte.
3. Yo salí a las siete menos veinte y volví a las ocho menos veinte.
4. Florencia y Ana salieron a las diez y cinco y volvieron a las dos y cinco.
5. Tú saliste a la una y cuarto y volviste a las cuatro y cuarto.
6. Florencia salió a las tres menos cuarto y volvió a las nueve menos cuarto.

Activity 7 **1.** escribí; **2.** recibiste; **3.** salimos; **4.** comieron; **5.** compartimos; **6.** bebió; **7.** volvimos

Activity 8

1. A. ¿Recibiste un regalo la semana pasada?
   B. Sí, (No, no) recibí un regalo.
2. A. ¿Corriste la semana pasada?
   B. Sí, (No, no) corrí.
3. A. ¿Bebiste un refresco la semana pasada?
   B. Sí, (No, no) bebí un refresco.
4. A. ¿Escribiste en la computadora la semana pasada?
   B. Sí, (No, no) escribí en la computadora.
5. A. ¿Barriste el suelo la semana pasada?
   B. Sí, (No, no) barrí el suelo.
6. A. ¿Comiste en un restaurante la semana pasada?
   B. Sí, (No, no) comí en un restaurante.

Activity 9 Answers will vary. Sample answers: Juana bebió leche. Raúl comió pollo.

Para y piensa **1.** comí; **2.** Recibiste

¡AVANZA! Objectives

- Identify preterite forms of regular **-er** and **-ir** verbs in context.
- Identify lesson vocabulary in context.

Core Resources

- Video Program: DVD 2
- Audio Program: TXT CD 7 track 6

Presentation Strategies

- Have students scan the dialogue, looking for examples of preterite tense forms. Ask students to write these preterite forms along with the corresponding infinitive for future reference.
- Play the audio as students follow in their textbooks.
- Show the video.

Practice Sequence

- **Activity 10:** Telehistoria comprehension
- **Activity 11:** Transitional practice: preterite of **-er** and **-ir** verbs

STANDARDS

1.2 Understand language, Acts. 10–11, PYP

21st Century **Communication,** Group Work/ Personalize It; **Critical Thinking and Problem Solving,** Act. 11: Expansión

Warm Up Projectable Transparencies, 7-17

Preterite of -er and -ir Verbs Complete the sentences with the correct preterite form of the verb.

1. Usted _____ la puerta. (abrir)
2. Nosotros ____ la camiseta. (perder)
3. Yo _____ un correo electrónico. (recibir)
4. Tú _____ una carta. (escribir)
5. Ellas _____ refrescos. (beber)

Answers: 1. abrió; 2. perdimos; 3. recibí; 4. escribiste; 5. bebieron

Video Summary

HOMETUTOR VideoPlus my.hrw.com

Florencia received another e-mail from Alicia stating that they should look for Trini at the stadium. Mariano and Florencia have to search the Internet to find out the date and time.

GRAMÁTICA en contexto

¡AVANZA! **Goal:** Listen to Florencia and Mariano talk about what happened the day before. Then use the preterite of **-er** and **-ir** verbs to describe what you did recently. ***Actividades 10–11***

Telehistoria escena 2

HOMETUTOR my.hrw.com View, Read and Record

STRATEGIES

Cuando lees
Locate and practice key phrases
Read the scene, finding phrases about the Internet and writing or receiving e-mails. Repeat each one (aloud or to yourself) until you know it and can use it in conversation.

Cuando escuchas
Use visual clues while listening
While listening to the video, search for visual clues that tell you where Trini is going to be. How do the characters' movements keep them from finding out?

VIDEO DVD

AUDIO

Mariano: Florencia, ¿ahora qué va a pasar con la camiseta de Alicia?

Florencia: Anoche cuando volví a casa, recibí otro correo electrónico de Alicia.

Florencia takes a printout of the e-mail from her bag.

Florencia: Aquí está. Compartimos muchas ideas anoche. Escribió que debemos buscar a Trini en el estadio.

Mariano: Pero, ¿cuándo?

Florencia: No sé. No recibí mucha información. Tenemos que navegar por Internet para buscar la fecha y la hora. ¿Salimos para el cibercafé?

As they leave, Florencia leaves her camera on the table in the restaurant.

Continuará... p. 369

Differentiating Instruction

Multiple Intelligences

Linguistic/Verbal Ask students to preview the Telehistoria, looking for verbs in the preterite tense. Ask for volunteers to read the parts of Mariano and Florencia aloud. Have students raise their hand when they hear a verb in the preterite. Discuss the verbs **compartimos** and **salimos** in particular. Are they in the preterite or present?

Pre-AP

Identify the Main Idea Have students summarize this scene of the Telehistoria in two sentences. In the first sentence, tell them to write about what Mariano and Florencia know. In the second sentence, have them write about what Mariano and Florencia don't know. **Mariano y Florencia saben que deben buscar a Trini en el estadio. No saben cuándo Trini va a estar allí.**

10 *Comprensión del episodio* ¿Qué necesitan saber?

Escuchar Leer

Contesta las preguntas. *(Answer the questions.)*

1. ¿Qué recibió Florencia anoche?
2. ¿Quiénes compartieron ideas?
3. ¿Quién escribió que deben buscar a Trini en el estadio?
4. ¿Cómo van a buscar información Florencia y Mariano sobre la fecha y la hora?
5. ¿Adónde van ellos después?

Expansión:
Teacher Edition Only
Have students write a summary of the episode using the questions as a guide.

11 ¿Pasaste una semana fenomenal?

Leer

Completa este cuestionario para saber si acabas de pasar una semana fenomenal. *(Take this magazine quiz to see if you had a great week.)*

¿Una semana fenomenal?

1 ¿Qué perdiste?
a. ropa
b. dinero
c. nada

2 ¿Dónde comiste el viernes por la noche?
a. en casa
b. en un café
c. en un restaurante fantástico

3 ¿Con quién saliste?
a. con familia
b. con mi mejor amigo(a)
c. con familia y amigos

4 ¿Qué recibiste?
a. un regalo
b. un correo electrónico
c. nada

5 ¿Qué compartiste?
a. dinero
b. comida
c. nada

6 ¿A quién conociste?
a. a una persona simpática
b. a una persona mala
c. a un actor de Hollywood

Clave: Cuenta los puntos para ver qué tipo de semana pasaste.

puntos	1	2	3
★1	b	a	c
★2	a	b	c
★3	a	c	b
★4	c	b	a
★5	c	b	a
★6	b	a	c

6–9 puntos: Pasaste una semana normal. Mejor suerte en el futuro.
10–14 puntos: Pasaste una semana interesante.
15–18 puntos: *¡Felicidades!* Pasaste una semana fenomenal.

Expansión
Compare and contrast your answers with a classmate's.

Get Help Online
my.hrw.com

PARA Y PIENSA

Did you get it? Complete each sentence with the preterite form of the appropriate verb: **salir, compartir,** or **recibir.**
1. Florencia _____ un correo electrónico de Alicia.
2. Alicia y Florencia _____ muchas ideas.
3. Florencia y Mariano _____ para el cibercafé.

Communication
Group Work

Activity 11 Divide the class into small groups. Ask each group to write their own questionnaire about a great weekend. Have them use the questionnaire in Activity 11 as a model, but change some of the questions and options. Ask groups to exchange questionnaires and complete them.

Long-term Retention
Personalize It

Ask students to write a short paragraph about computer-related activities they did this week. They can use these questions as a guide: **¿Qué escribiste? ¿Qué recibiste? ¿Qué mandaste? ¿Qué buscaste en Internet?**

✓ Ongoing Assessment

Get Help Online
More Practice
my.hrw.com

PARA Y PIENSA **Intervention** If students have problems completing the sentences in Para y piensa, have them review p. 361 and repeat Activities 6 and 7 on p. 362. For additional practice, use Reteaching & Practice Copymasters URB 7, pp. 4, 6.

Differentiating Instruction

Inclusion

Frequent Review/Repetition Before completing Activity 10, model how to turn each question into a sentence starter for its answer. For example, **¿Qué recibió Florencia anoche?** becomes **Anoche Florencia recibió** _____. Once students have converted all of the questions, have them find and insert the answers.

Slower-paced Learners

Peer-study Support Have students work with a partner to complete Activity 11. Have partners ask each other the questions, and record each other's answers. When necessary, have students identify the infinitive of the preterite forms used to help recall their meanings. For example, **perdiste** comes from the verb **perder**, **comiste** from the verb **comer**.

Answers Projectable Transparencies, 7-25

Activity 10
1. Florencia recibió un correo electrónico de Alicia.
2. Florencia y Alicia compartieron ideas.
3. Alicia escribió que deben buscar a Trini en el estadio.
4. Mariano y Florencia van a navegar por Internet.
5. Después ellos van a un cibercafé.

Activity 11 Answers will vary.

Para y piensa **1.** recibió; **2.** compartieron; **3.** salieron

¡AVANZA! **Objective**

- Present affirmative and negative words.

Core Resource

- *Cuaderno,* pp. 301–303

Presentation Strategies

- Write on the board or OHT the lists of affirmative and negative words. Say each word and its opposite and have students repeat after you.
- Give several examples for words like **algún/alguno(a)** and **ningún/ninguno(a)**, then check students' comprehension by asking them to complete sentences such as: **¿Conoces _____ tienda de cámaras digitales? (alguna) No tengo _____ amigo de Puerto Rico. (ningún)**

STANDARDS

4.1 Compare languages

Warm Up Projectable Transparencies, 7-18

Preterite of -er Verbs Write the preterite of the verbs in parentheses.

1. Yo _____ un refresco. (beber)
2. Ana _____ mucho ayer. (aprender)
3. Tú _____ el partido. (perder)
4. Rosa _____ el suelo. (barrer)

Answers: 1. bebí; 2. aprendió; 3. perdiste; 4. barrió

TEACHER to TEACHER

Giuliana Vera
Verona, New Jersey

Tips for Presenting Grammar

You can present structures that operate in pairs by using the round-robin approach. For example, have the first student in a row say an affirmative word: **algo.** *The second student gives its opposite:* **nada,** *and says another word to a third student:* **nunca,** *and so on.*

Go online for more tips!

Communication

Pair Work

Have students make flashcards, writing an affirmative word on one side of an index card, and the negative word on the other. Have students work with a partner to practice all the words.

Presentación de GRAMÁTICA

¡AVANZA! **Goal:** Learn how to use affirmative and negative words. Then practice them to talk about indefinite or negative situations. ***Actividades 12–15***

¿Recuerdas? Preterite of regular **-ar** verbs p. 331

English Grammar Connection: A **double negative** is the use of two negative words to express a negative idea. Double negatives are considered incorrect in English. In Spanish, they are often required.

There's nobody at the door. — No hay nadie en la puerta.

Affirmative and Negative Words

ANIMATEDGRAMMAR my.hrw.com

Use an **affirmative** or a negative word when you want to talk about an indefinite or negative situation.

Here's how:

Affirmative Words		Negative Words	
algo	*something*	**nada**	*nothing*
alguien	*someone*	**nadie**	*no one, nobody*
algún/alguno(a)	*some, any*	**ningún/ninguno(a)**	*none, not any*
o... o	*either . . . or*	**ni... ni**	*neither . . . nor*
siempre	*always*	**nunca**	*never*
también	*also*	**tampoco**	*neither, not either*

Alguno(a) and **ninguno(a)** must match the gender of the noun they replace or modify. They have different forms when used before masculine singular nouns.

alguno *becomes* **algún** — **ninguno** *becomes* **ningún**

¿Conoces **algún** sitio Web cómico?
*Do you know **any** funny Web sites?*

No conozco **ningún** sitio Web cómico.
*I do **not** know **any** funny Web sites.*

If a verb is preceded by **no,** words that follow must be negative. A double negative is required in Spanish when **no** precedes the verb.

No queremos **nada.**
*We do **not** want **anything.***

No me gusta **ninguna** cámara digital.
*I do **not** like **any** digital cameras.*

However, if the negative word comes before the verb, there is no need to use **no.**

Mi padre **nunca** usa la computadora.
*My father **never** uses the computer.*

Nadie navega por Internet ahora.
***No one** is surfing the Web now.*

Más práctica

Cuaderno *pp. 301–303*
Cuaderno para hispanohablantes *pp. 302–305*

@HOMETUTOR my.hrw.com
Leveled Practice

Differentiating Instruction

Inclusion

Clear Structure Write each of the affirmative and negative words from p. 366 on a separate self-sticking note. Create a poster with two columns: *Affirmative Words* and *Negative Words.* Distribute the words at random, and have students post each note in the appropriate column. As they do, model a sample sentence using that word.

Heritage Language Learners

Writing Skills Explain to students that when **alguno, ninguno, alguien, nadie** are used referring to a person as a direct object, whether the person is known or not, the personal **a** is almost always used. For example, **¿Conoces a alguien en la escuela? No veo a nadie en el parque. No conozco a ningún jugador de fútbol.** Ask students to write the sentences in their notebooks, and to create other sentences on their own.

Práctica de GRAMÁTICA

12 ¡Qué negativa!

Hablar
Escribir

Florencia no quiere hacer nada hoy. Completa la conversación con las formas correctas de palabras afirmativas y negativas. *(Complete the conversation with affirmative and negative words.)*

Mariano

Florencia

Mariano	Florencia
¿Quieres ver __1.__ película en el cine Rex?	No, no quiero ver __2.__ película en el cine Rex.
¿Quieres comprar __3.__ en la tienda?	No, no quiero comprar __4.__ en la tienda.
¿Quieres pasar un rato con __5.__?	No, no quiero pasar un rato con __6.__.
¿Quieres practicar __7.__ deporte?	No, no quiero practicar __8.__ deporte.

Expansión
Give your own answers for Mariano's questions.

Nota gramatical

Ningunos(as) is used only with nouns that are not typically singular, such as **jeans.**

No compro ningunos jeans. *I'm **not** buying **any jeans.***

13 El domingo pasado

Hablar

Pregúntale a otro(a) estudiante si hizo estas cosas el domingo pasado. Te va a decir que no las hizo. *(Ask a partner whether he or she did these things last Sunday. He or she will say no.)*

1. beber algunos refrescos
2. usar el mensajero instantáneo con alguien
3. recibir algo especial de un amigo
4. tomar algunas fotos con una cámara digital
5. salir con alguien
6. escribir algún correo electrónico
7. vender algo
8. quemar algún disco compacto

A ¿Comiste pizza y papas fritas?

B No, no comí ni pizza ni papas fritas.

Expansión: Teacher Edition Only
Have students write a summary of what their partner said.

Differentiating Instruction

Slower-paced Learners

Peer-study Support Have students work in pairs to write **afirmativa** on the front of an index card, and **negativa** on the back. Read a sentence from Activity 12. Ask students if the sentence is affirmative or negative; instruct them to hold up the appropriate side of their cards. Then have them pick an appropriate word from the chart on p. 366.

Pre-AP

Expand and Elaborate Encourage students to add another turn to their conversations in Activity 13. Have **Estudiante A** ask a follow-up question about what his or her partner did eat. **Estudiante B** should explain.

A: Entonces, ¿qué comiste? B: Comí una hamburguesa y una ensalada también.

Objectives

- Practice affirmative and negative words.
- Explain the negative form **ningunos(as).**
- Review preterite of **-ar, -er, -ir** verbs.

Practice Sequence

- **Activity 12:** Controlled practice: affirmative and negative words
- **Activity 13:** Transitional practice: preterite tense of **-ar, -er, -ir** verbs, negative words

STANDARDS

1.2 Understand language, Act. 12
1.3 Present information, Act. 13

Communication

Grammar Activity

Read the following statements aloud. Ask students to respond with **yo también** if they hear an affirmative statement; or with **yo tampoco** if they hear a negative statement.

1. **Quiero hablar con alguien en la escuela.**
2. **No quiero escuchar a nadie.**
3. **Nunca estudio en la mañana.**
4. **Quiero comprar algo en la tienda.**

Answers: 1. yo también; 2. yo tampoco; 3. yo tampoco; 4. yo también

Answers Projectable Transparencies, 7-25 and 7-26

Activity 12 **1.** alguna; **2.** ninguna; **3.** algo; **4.** nada; **5.** alguien; **6.** nadie; **7.** algún; **8.** ningún

Activity 13

1. A. ¿Bebiste algunos refrescos?
   B. No, no bebí ningún refresco.
2. A. ¿Usaste el mensajero instantáneo con alguien?
   B. No, no usé el mensajero instantáneo con nadie.
3. A. ¿Recibiste algo especial de un amigo?
   B. No, no recibí nada especial de un amigo.
4. A. ¿Tomaste algunas fotos con una cámara digital?
   B. No, no tomé ninguna foto con una cámara digital.
5. A. ¿Saliste con alguien?
   B. No, no salí con nadie.
6. A. ¿Escribiste algún correo electrónico?
   B. No, no escribí ningún correo electrónico.
7. A. ¿Vendiste algo?
   B. No, no vendí nada.
8. A. ¿Quemaste algún disco compacto?
   B. No, no quemé ningún disco compacto.

Objectives

- Practice affirmative and negative words.
- Practice the preterite tense of **-er, -ir** verbs.
- Recycle: Preterite of regular **-ar** verbs
- **Culture:** Discuss popular vacation destinations.

Core Resource

- *Cuaderno,* pp. 301–303

Practice Sequence

- **Activity 14:** Transitional practice: preterite tense of **-er, -ir** verbs, affirmative and negative words; Recycle: Preterite of regular **-ar** verbs
- **Activity 15:** Open-ended practice: affirmative and negative words

STANDARDS

1.1 Engage in conversation, Act. 15
1.3 Present information, Act. 14, PYP
2.1 Practices and perspectives, CC
3.1 Knowledge of other disciplines, CC
4.2 Compare cultures, CC

Comparación cultural

Essential Question

Suggested Answer Tourists often seek warm climates, beaches, and other such features for travel.

Location Information

Mar del Plata, a relatively young city, was established in 1874 as an industrial center. Today, its wealth lies in tourism as thousands flock to its beaches. It is near dunes and cliffs.

✓ Ongoing Assessment

Get Help Online
More Practice
my.hrw.com

PARA Y PIENSA **Peer Assessment** Have students check each other's work in Para y piensa and correct each other's mistakes. For additional practice, use Reteaching & Practice Copymasters URB 7, pp. 7, 8, 12.

See Activity answers on p. 369.

14 ¿Y tú?

♻ ***¿Recuerdas?*** Preterite of regular **-ar** verbs p. 331

Hablar
Escribir

Contesta las preguntas sobre lo que hiciste. Explica tus respuestas si es posible. *(Answer the questions about what you did. Explain your answers whenever possible.)*

modelo: **¿Aprendiste algo en la clase de español la semana pasada?**
Sí, aprendí algo la semana pasada. Aprendí el vocabulario nuevo. (No, no aprendí nada.)

1. ¿Estudiaste con alguien anteayer?
2. ¿Comiste algunas galletas anoche?
3. ¿Perdiste algo el año pasado?
4. ¿Compraste algo la semana pasada?
5. ¿Ayudaste a alguien el sábado pasado?
6. ¿Practicaste algún deporte ayer?
7. ¿Escribiste algo anoche?
8. ¿Compartiste algo con alguien ayer?

Expansión
Ask a partner these questions and write down the answers.

15 ¿Qué hay en la playa?

Hablar

Comparación cultural

Las playas de Mar del Plata

What features and attractions are most popular for tourists? Mar del Plata is a city with miles of beaches along the Atlantic Ocean. It is a popular destination for Buenos Aires residents and other tourists during the summer, especially between December and February. Visitors can participate in a variety of activities such as sunbathing, surfing, scuba diving, and fishing.

Las playas de Mar del Plata

Compara con tu mundo *During the summer months, what are popular destinations in your area? What are common activities in these places?*

Pregúntale a otro(a) estudiante sobre la foto. Usa palabras afirmativas y negativas. *(Ask your partner about the photo. Use affirmative and negative words.)*

A ¿Hay alguien con un sombrero en la playa?

B No, no hay nadie con un sombrero. ¿Hay algo azul?

Más práctica Cuaderno *pp. 301–303* Cuaderno para hispanohablantes *pp. 302–305*

Get Help Online
my.hrw.com

PARA Y PIENSA

Did you get it? Write the opposite of these sentences.

1. Siempre recibo algunos correos electrónicos.
2. Nadie escribe nada con el mensajero instantáneo.
3. A Beatriz le gusta navegar por Internet y estar en línea.

Differentiating Instruction

Multiple Intelligences

Naturalist Have students create their own a painting or drawing of the Mar del Plata beaches. They might also research an outdoor location in Argentina, or use a natural resource closer to home as their subject matter. Have students ask and answer questions about their work.

Inclusion

Frequent Review/Repetition Organize a round-robin interview wherein students ask each question in Activity 14 to a different person. After the activity, give students the opportunity to report on what they learned. Remind them that they should relate their answers using the third person. **Roberto estudió con Elena anteayer.**

Todo junto

¡AVANZA! **Goal:** ***Show what you know*** Notice the affirmative and negative words used to talk about Trini in Buenos Aires. Then use these words and the preterite of **-er** and **-ir** verbs to talk about past actions. ***Actividades 16–20***

Telehistoria completa

@HOMETUTOR my.hrw.com **View, Read and Record**

STRATEGIES

Cuando lees
Notice the information exchange
While reading, notice the information exchange. What does the waiter tell Mariano and Florencia? How does he help them solve their problem?

Cuando escuchas
Practice what you hear Listen to how the speakers emphasize negative expressions (**no, nada, nadie, ni... ni**). After listening, say these sentences with proper emphasis. Remember this for future communication.

Escena 1 *Resumen*
Florencia recibe un correo electrónico de Alicia porque Trini Salgado va a estar en Buenos Aires. Sus amigos mandan la camiseta a Argentina.

Escena 2 *Resumen*
Alicia escribe que Trini va a estar en el estadio. Pero Florencia y Mariano tienen que navegar por Internet para buscar más información.

VIDEO DVD

AUDIO

Escena 3

Florencia: ¡Señor, por favor! ¿Tiene usted mi cámara?

Camarero: Sí, sí, tranquila. Aquí está. ¿Qué pasa? ¿Necesitan algo?

Mariano: No, nada. Gracias. Queremos ir al estadio para ver a Trini Salgado, pero no sabemos ni la fecha ni la hora. Nadie sabe cuándo va a llegar ella.

Florencia: Usted tampoco sabe, ¿no?

Camarero: No sé nada del estadio, pero sé que Trini Salgado va a estar en el Parque de la Costa en El Tigre, el sábado.

Florencia: ¿Sí? ¿Cómo lo sabe?

Camarero: Mira, allí dice. *(He points to a poster in the restaurant's window.)*

Mariano: ¡Florencia! Nadie encontró a Trini... ni en Estados Unidos... ni en Puerto Rico... tampoco en España. Pero ahora, tú vas a tener el autógrafo.

Differentiating Instruction

Slower-paced Learners

Read Before Listening Have students preview the Telehistoria silently, paying particular attention to negative words, such as **nada, ni, tampoco,** and **nadie.** Then ask for volunteers to read the parts of Florencia, Mariano, and **el camarero** aloud. Tell students to write down each negative word they hear.

Heritage Language Learners

Support What They Know Ask students to share an anecdote about a time when they left something important behind. What did they forget, and how did they get it back? Remind students to use words such as **luego, después, entonces,** and **por fin** to accurately explain the sequence of events.

¡AVANZA! **Objective**
- Integrate lesson content.

Core Resources
- Video Program: DVD 2
- Audio Program: TXT CD 7 track 7

Presentation Strategies
- Ask students to read aloud the Resumen for Escena 1 and Escena 2.
- Have them skim the Telehistoria script for examples of negative expressions.
- Show the video or play the audio.

STANDARDS
1.2 Understand language
21st Century **Communication,** Heritage Language Learners

Warm Up Projectable Transparencies, 7-18

Negative Words Answer the questions, using negative words.
1. ¿Jugaste algunos videojuegos ayer?
2. ¿Bebiste algo en la mañana?
3. ¿Siempre estudias después de las clases?
4. ¿Compraste algo en la tienda?

Answers:
1. **No, no jugué ningún videojuego ayer.**
2. **No, no bebí nada en la mañana.**
3. **No, nunca estudio después de las clases.**
4. **No, no compré nada en la tienda.**

Video Summary @HOMETUTOR VideoPlus my.hrw.com

Florencia and Mariano come back to the restaurant, looking for Florencia's camera. The waiter directs them to information on the whereabouts of Trini.

Answers Projectable Transparencies, 7-26

Answers for Activities on p. 368.

Activity 14 Answers will vary. Sample answers:
1. Sí, estudié con alguien.... Estudié con Alex.
2. Sí, comí algunas galletas anoche.
3. No, no perdí nada el año pasado.
4. Sí, compré... Compré un cuaderno.
5. No, no ayudé a nadie el sábado pasado.
6. Sí, practiqué algún deporte ayer. Jugué al tenis.
7. No, no escribí nada anoche.
8. No, no compartí nada con nadie ayer.

Para y piensa
1. Nunca recibo ningún correo electrónico.
2. Alguien escribe algo con...
3. A Beatriz no le gusta ni navegar por Internet ni estar en línea.

TODO JUNTO

Objective

- Practice using and integrating lesson vocabulary and grammar.

Core Resources

- *Cuaderno*, pp. 304-305
- Audio Program: TXT CD 7 tracks 3, 6, 7, 8, 9

Practice Sequence

- **Activities 16, 17:** Telehistoria comprehension
- **Activity 17:** Transitional practice: listening, reading
- **Activity 18:** Open-ended practice: speaking
- **Activity 19:** Open-ended practice: listening, reading, speaking
- **Activity 20:** Open-ended practice: writing

STANDARDS

1.1 Engage in conversation, Act. 18
1.2 Understand language, Acts. 16–17, 19 PYP
1.4 Present information, Acts. 18–20
21st Century **Communication,** Act. 20/Heritage Language Learners; **Flexibility and Adaptability,** Act. 18

Answers Projectable Transparencies, 7-26

Activity 16

1. Cierto.
2. Falso. Van a buscar a alguien en el estadio.
3. Falso. El camarero tiene algo de Florencia.
4. Falso. El camarero no sabe nada de Trini en el estadio.
5. Cierto.
6. Falso. Tampoco la encontraron en España.

Activity 17

1. La mandaron anteayer porque Trini está allí.
2. Florencia recibió otro correo electrónico de Alicia.
3. Florencia compartió ideas con Alicia.
4. Florencia perdió su cámara.
5. Nadie sabe cuándo Trini va a llegar al estadio.
6. Florencia y Mariano no saben ni la fecha ni la hora en que Trini va a llegar al estadio.

Answers continue on page 371.

16 *Comprensión de los episodios* ¿Estás seguro(a)?

Escuchar
Leer

Indica si estas oraciones son ciertas o falsas. Corrige las oraciones falsas con palabras afirmativas o negativas. *(Tell if these sentences are true or false. Correct the false sentences, using affirmative or negative words.)*

1. Florencia recibió algo de Alicia.
2. No van a buscar a nadie en el estadio.
3. El camarero no tiene nada de Florencia.
4. El camarero sabe algo de Trini en el estadio.
5. Nadie encontró a Trini en Estados Unidos.
6. También la encontraron en España.

Expansión: Teacher Edition Only
Have students write three sentences based on the three episodes, using negative expressions.

17 *Comprensión de los episodios* ¿Lo sabes?

Escuchar
Leer

Contesta las preguntas. *(Answer the questions.)*

1. ¿Cuándo mandaron la camiseta a Argentina? ¿Por qué?
2. ¿Qué recibió Florencia cuando volvió a casa?
3. ¿Con quién compartió ideas Florencia?
4. ¿Qué perdió Florencia?
5. ¿Alguien sabe cuándo Trini va a llegar al estadio?
6. ¿Qué no saben Florencia y Mariano?

Expansión: Teacher Edition Only
Have students write a summary of the episodes using the questions as a guide.

18 Los reporteros

Digital performance space

Hablar

STRATEGY **Hablar**
Choose an interesting topic Decide with your partner whether to talk about something interesting that actually occurred or something amazing that you can pretend happened. That way, whatever you choose to talk about in your interview will be of interest to listeners.

Eres reportero(a). Entrevista a otro(a) estudiante sobre algo que pasó en la escuela. *(Interview a partner about something that happened at school.)*

A Estamos aquí en la cafetería. Alguien habló con el director de la escuela y ya no sirven refrescos. ¿Qué piensas, Víctor?

B ¡No me gusta! No hay nada bueno para beber. Ayer bebí leche...

Expansión
Turn your interview into an article.

Differentiating Instruction

Inclusion

Clear Structure Before starting Activity 18, ask each pair of students to draw a large concept web. Have them write their topic in the center, and record useful vocabulary around the web. Have them draw a secondary circle around each verb, and list the preterite forms of useful verbs on the outside. Students should refer to their webs as they talk.

Heritage Language Learners

Writing Skills Have students develop their interviews from Activity 18 into a short newsletter piece about a school event or issue. If possible, have students interview other Spanish speakers in your school and community to get their perspectives on the event or issue.

19 Integración

Digital performance space

Leer
Escuchar
Hablar

Lee la página Web y escucha el programa de radio. Explica a qué lugar prefieres ir después de las clases y por qué. *(Read the Web page and listen to the radio program. Then tell where you prefer to go after school and why.)*

Fuente 1 Página Web

Escuela del Arce
Laboratorio de Computadoras

Nuestros servicios no cuestan nada:
- 15 computadoras
- 5 computadoras con conexión a Internet
- Acceso al correo electrónico de la escuela
- Discos compactos para quemar

Hay algunas reglas:
- No permitimos ni comidas ni bebidas dentro del laboratorio
- No pueden hablar por teléfono celular
- No pueden usar el mensajero instantáneo

¿Necesitas sacar buenas notas? Podemos ayudarte. Todos los días, de las 4:00 a las 7:00 de la tarde, hay maestros aquí para contestar tus preguntas.

Fuente 2 Programa de radio

Listen and take notes
- ¿Qué lugar buscó Raquel?
- ¿Qué hay allí?
- ¿Qué pasó allí?

modelo: Después de las clases prefiero ir al... porque...

Audio Program
TXT CD 7 Tracks 8, 9
Audio Script, TE p. 353b

20 Teclados y ratones

Digital performance space

Escribir

Escribe un artículo para una revista sobre computadoras. Di cómo usaste la tecnología ayer y cómo usas la computadora en tu vida diaria. *(Write an article for a computer magazine about your computer use.)*

modelo: Me gusta usar la computadora. Ayer navegué por Internet, pero no escribí ningún correo electrónico. Siempre uso el mensajero instantáneo para...

Writing Criteria	Excellent	Good	Needs Work
Content	Your article includes a lot of information.	Your article includes some information.	Your article includes little information.
Communication	Most of your article is organized and easy to follow.	Parts of your article are organized and easy to follow.	Your article is disorganized and hard to follow.
Accuracy	Your article has few mistakes in grammar and vocabulary.	Your article has some mistakes in grammar and vocabulary.	Your article has many mistakes in grammar and vocabulary.

Expansión
Compare your article with a classmate's.

Más práctica Cuaderno *pp. 304–305* Cuaderno para hispanohablantes *pp. 306–307*

Get Help Online
my.hrw.com

PARA Y PIENSA

Did you get it? Answer the following questions negatively.

1. ¿Perdió algo Mariano?
2. ¿Recibió Florencia la fecha o la hora?
3. ¿Escribió Mariano algún correo electrónico?

Differentiating Instruction

Pre-AP

Vary Vocabulary Organize students into groups of three or four to brainstorm ideas for Activity 19. Have each team member offer at least one sentence.

Slower-paced Learners

Peer-study Support Distribute a copy of the Writing Criteria Rubric (Act. 20) to each student. Have students exchange their technology articles with a partner, read their partner's work, and circle the appropriate box for each criterion. Ask students to justify their evaluations with concrete examples, and provide advice for improvement.

Long-term Retention

Pre-AP Integration

Activity 19 Have students name two places where they like to go after school and give at least three reasons why they like to go there.

✓ Ongoing Assessment

Rubric Activity 19

Listening/Speaking	
Proficient	**Not There Yet**
Student takes detailed notes answering the questions and writes a well-organized and detailed explanation of where he or she likes to go.	Student takes few notes answering some or no questions and writes an explanation lacking organization and key information.

To customize your own rubrics, use the ***Generate Success** Rubric Generator and Graphic Organizers.*

✓ Ongoing Assessment

Get Help Online
More Practice
my.hrw.com

PARA Y PIENSA **Peer Assessment** Ask students to work in pairs to ask and answer the Para y piensa questions. Ask them to review the affirmative and negative words on p. 366. For additional practice, use Reteaching & Practice Copymasters URB 7 pp. 7, 9.

Answers Projectable Transparencies, 7-26 and 7-27

Answers continued from p. 370.

Activity 18 Sample answer: A: Hoy hay un concierto de música en la biblioteca. ¿Qué piensas, María? B: ¡Qué bueno! Me gusta mucho la música y podemos descansar un rato.

Activity 19 Answers will vary. Sample answers:

Después de las clases prefiero ir al cibercafé porque puedo usar el mensajero instantáneo para hablar con mis amigos.

Activity 20 Students should be instructed to use an introduction, three main points, and a conclusion when writing their articles.

Para y piensa
1. No, Mariano no perdió nada.
2. No, Florencia no recibió ni la fecha ni la hora.
3. No, Mariano no escribió ningún correo electrónico.

Objectives
- Read about how to protect a computer from viruses.
- Take a virus-protection questionnaire.
- Compare antivirus measures mentioned in the questionnaire with the measures you take.

Core Resource
- Audio Program: TXT CD 7 track 10

Presentation Strategies
- Ask students about the antivirus measures they are familiar with.
- Have students read the questionnaire and make a list of words they don't know. Encourage them to find their meaning through context clues or cognates before checking the glosses or consulting a dictionary.
- After students have taken the questionnaire, conduct a class survey to find out how many had perfect scores.

STANDARDS
1.2 Understand language
1.3 Present information
3.1 Knowledge of other disciplines
21st Century Social and Cross-Cultural Skills, English Language Connection/English Learners

Warm Up
Projectable Transparencies, 7-19

Affirmative and Negative Words Complete the sentences with the correct word.

algún algo nunca nada ningún siempre

1. ¿Conoces ____ sitio Web de historia?
2. No, no conozco ____ sitio Web de historia.
3. ¿ ____ estudias con Ernesto?
4. No, ____ estudio con él.
5. ¿Quieres comer ____ ahora?
6. No, no quiero comer ____.

Answers: 1. algún; 2. ningún; 3. Siempre; 4. nunca; 5. algo; 6. nada

Culture
Expanded Information
Many students in Latin America go to local Internet cafés. At the cafés they e-mail friends, write school papers, and do research projects on the Internet.

Lectura

Additional readings at my.hrw.com SPANISH InterActive Reader

¡AVANZA! **Goal:** Take this virus-protection questionnaire. Then talk about computer viruses and how you protect your computer.

AUDIO

Un cuestionario sobre las computadoras

Cuestionario: Protección para tu PC

STRATEGY Leer
Use a cause-and-effect chart Make a cause-and-effect chart for computer viruses.

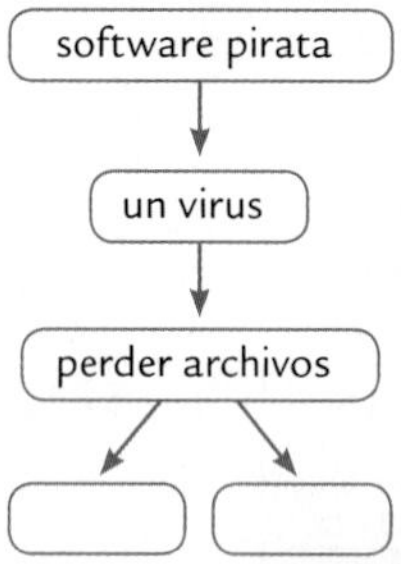

www.antivirus.ar

Cuestionario: Protección para tu PC

¿Qué pasa cuando un virus infecta tu computadora? El virus funciona como un borrador. Puede destruir tus archivos[1]. Puede afectar tu acceso a Internet y el sistema del correo electrónico. Otras personas pueden ver tus datos[2] personales. ¿Conoces las medidas[3] básicas que debes tomar como protección contra[4] los virus? Toma este cuestionario para saber.

1. ¿Cuál de los siguientes *no* es un método típico de propagación de los virus?

A. programas que se descargan[5] de Internet
B. archivos adjuntos[6] a correos electrónicos
C. la provisión de datos personales en un sitio Web no seguro[7]
D. software pirata

[1] files [2] information [3] measures [4] against
[5] are downloaded [6] attached [7] secure, safe

Differentiating Instruction

Inclusion
Alphabetic/Phonetic Awareness Direct students to preview **Un cuestionario sobre las computadoras** to look for cognates. Some examples include **virus, infectar, pirata,** and **instalar.** Model for students how to pronounce these terms in Spanish. For example, the **i** in the Spanish **virus** is pronounced as a long *e,* while the *i* in the English *virus* is pronounced as a long *i.*

Slower-paced Learners
Sentence Completion Remind students to preview the **¿Comprendiste?** questions prior to reading the text. Have them convert each question into a sentence starter for its answer. For example, **¿Por qué son peligrosos los virus?** becomes **Los virus son peligrosos porque...**

Cuestionario: Protección para tu PC

www.antivirus.ar

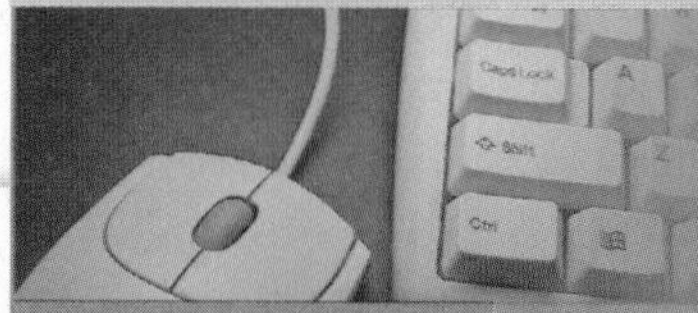

Cuestionario: Protección para tu PC

Centro de Protección

Introducción
Protege tu equipo
Recursos

2. Cierto o falso: Después de instalar software antivirus, la computadora está completamente protegida[8].

A. cierto
B. falso

3. ¿Qué es un firewall de Internet?

A. una contraseña[9] segura
B. un artículo de asbesto que protege la computadora de las llamas[10]
C. un candado[11] que puedes poner en la computadora para impedir acceso no autorizado
D. software o hardware que ayuda a proteger la computadora contra ataques como los virus

HAZ CLIC

Respuestas correctas

1. *C:* la provisión de datos personales en un sitio Web no seguro
2. *B:* falso
3. *D:* software o hardware que ayuda a proteger la computadora contra ataques como los virus

[8] protected [9] password [10] flames [11] padlock

PARA Y PIENSA

¿Comprendiste?

1. ¿Por qué son peligrosos los virus?
2. ¿Cuáles son los métodos típicos de propagación de los virus?
3. ¿Cómo se llama el software o hardware que ayuda a proteger la computadora contra ataques como los virus?

¿Y tú?

¿Qué medidas antivirus tomas cuando usas la computadora?

Differentiating Instruction

Heritage Language Learners

Support What They Know Ask students to share a story about a time when they ran into a computer problem. What were they doing on the computer when the problem occurred? What was the effect of the problem? How were they able to resolve the situation?

English Learners

Build Background Ask students to consider why many English words related to computers and technology are used in Spanish. Some examples include *software, hardware, Internet,* and *firewall.* Ask students if they can describe these words, and if they use these words in their native language.

Communication

Pair Work

Have pairs of students interview classmates about computers. Write the following questions on the board: **¿En casa tienes una computadora? ¿Tienes problemas con los virus en la computadora? ¿Tienes software antivirus en tu computadora?** Have students keep a tally of how many students say **Sí** and how many say **No.**

Comparisons

English Language Connection

Ask students to go through the questionnaire and make a list of all the English words. Ask: Why are so many of these words in English? Possible answer: For practical reasons, Spanish has borrowed many English computer-related words, rather than inventing a new computer-based language. English computer terminology is used globally.

Communities

Spanish in the Media

Bring to class computer magazines in Spanish. Ask students to scan the articles for computer-related words that appeared in the questionnaire. Have them circle the words and read them to the class.

Answers

Para y piensa ¿Comprendiste?

1. Los virus son peligrosos porque pueden destruir los archivos, y pueden afectar el acceso a Internet y el sistema del correo electrónico. Otras personas pueden ver tus datos personales.
2. Los métodos típicos de propagación de los virus son programas que se descargan de Internet, los archivos adjuntos a correos electrónicos y software pirata.
3. El software o hardware que ayuda a proteger la computadora contra ataques como los virus se llama el firewall.

¿Y tú? Answers will vary. Sample answers include:

Yo uso software que ayuda a proteger la computadora contra ataques como los virus.

Objectives

- Read about a language game played by children in Argentina.
- Talk about similar language games that children play in English.
- Find out how the geography of Chile and Argentina may affect their culture.
- Find out about the origin of the word *Argentina*.

Presentation Strategies

- Before reading **Los juegos de lenguaje,** ask students what the title means in English. (Language games)
- Ask students if they are familiar with language games that children play.
- Discuss with students how to divide words into syllables in Spanish before converting words into **jeringozo.**

STANDARDS

1.3 Present information
3.1 Knowledge of other disciplines
3.2 Acquire information
21st Century **Communication,** Proyecto 3; **Social and Cross-Cultural Skills,** Proyectos 1, 2/El lenguaje/English Learners

Connections

El lenguaje

In English, children also play a version of **jeringozo.** It's called pig Latin. To create pig Latin, add *ay* to any word that begins with a vowel. For example, *apple* becomes *appleay* or *elephant* becomes *elephantay*. For words that don't begin with a vowel, remove the first letter of the word and attach it and *ay* to the end of the word. Hello becomes *ellohay*.

Conexiones *El lenguaje*

Los juegos de lenguaje

Jeringozo is a language game played by children in Argentina. To say a word in **jeringozo,** divide the word into syllables. After each one, add a syllable consisting of **p** and the vowel sound of the original syllable. For example:

tarde	mesa
tar + *pa* | de + *pe* = tar*pa*de*pe*	me + *pe* | sa + *pa* = me*pe*sa*pa*
(Pronounced tárpa-dépe)	(Pronounced mépe-sápa)

If a syllable has more than one vowel, the stressed vowel is used: **bueno** = **bue*pe*no*po*** *(buépe-nópo)*. Accents are omitted when writing in **jeringozo.** Try saying and writing the following words in **jeringozo:**

Argentina **semana** **durante** **favorito**

Now that you have mastered it, try saying **República Dominicana**!

El juego de jeringozo

Proyecto 1 *Las ciencias sociales*

Can you think of a game children play in English that is similar to **jeringozo**? Describe the game. How do you think these language games are invented? What purpose do they serve?

Proyecto 2 *La geografía*

Children in Chile play a variation of **jeringozo.** Look at the map of South America on page xlii. Examine the location and geographical features of Argentina and Chile. Write a paragraph about how you think geography affects the cultures of these two countries. Why would they have cultural similarities? Why might they also have cultural differences?

Proyecto 3 *Las ciencias*

The word *Argentina* comes from *argentum*, the Latin word for silver. It has this name because Spanish explorers hoped to find silver there. Research and write about this valuable metal. What characteristics does it have that make it desirable?

Espuelas de plata (Silver spurs)

Answers

Conexiones Have students create short lists of Spanish words to be practiced in **jeringozo.**

Proyecto 1 Pig Latin is one similar game in English.

Proyecto 2 They may have similarities because they are adjacent and share a long border. However, they might have differences because they are separated by the Andes.

Proyecto 3 Silver does not tarnish or rust easily. It can be shaped into jewelry.

Differentiating Instruction

Inclusion

Clear Structure Have students create diagrams to figure out how to say **Argentina, semana, durante,** and **favorito** in **jeringozo.** Give students these steps:

1. Write the word down.
2. Divide the word into syllables.
3. Rewrite the word, leaving a space between each syllable.
4. Add a **p** and vowel sound after each syllable.

English Learners

Build Background Introduce English learners to the English language game pig Latin. Ask students familiar with the game to explain the rules, and offer examples of translated words. Then invite students to describe language games played by children in their country of origin. What are the rules?

En resumen

Vocabulario y gramática

ANIMATED GRAMMAR
Interactive Flashcards
my.hrw.com

Vocabulario

Talk About Technology

la cámara digital	*digital camera*	navegar por Internet	*to surf the Internet*
conectar a Internet	*to connect to the Internet*	la pantalla	*screen*
la dirección (*pl.* las direcciones) electrónica	*e-mail address*	quemar un disco compacto	*to burn a CD*
estar en línea	*to be online*	el ratón (*pl.* los ratones)	*mouse*
hacer clic en	*to click on*	el sitio Web	*Web site*
el icono	*icon*	el teclado	*keyboard*
mandar	*to send*	tomar fotos	*to take photos*
el mensajero instantáneo	*instant messaging*		

Talk About Events

anteayer	*the day before yesterday*
el año pasado	*last year*
entonces	*then, so*
luego	*later, then*
más tarde	*later on*
por fin	*finally*
la semana pasada	*last week*

Talk About Negative or Indefinite Situations

algo	*something*	ni... ni	*neither . . . nor*
alguien	*someone*	ningún / ninguno(a)	*none, not any*
algún / alguno(a)	*some, any*	o... o	*either . . . or*
nada	*nothing*	tampoco	*neither, not either*
nadie	*no one, nobody*		

Gramática

Nota gramatical: ningunos(as) *p. 367*

Preterite of Regular -er and -ir Verbs

In the preterite, **-er** and **-ir** verb endings are identical.

vender *to sell*	
vendí	**vendimos**
vendiste	**vendisteis**
vendió	**vendieron**

escribir *to write*	
escribí	**escribimos**
escribiste	**escribisteis**
escribió	**escribieron**

Affirmative and Negative Words

Affirmative Words		Negative Words	
algo	*something*	nada	*nothing*
alguien	*someone*	nadie	*no one, nobody*
algún/alguno(a)	*some, any*	ningún/ninguno(a)	*none, not any*
o... o	*either . . . or*	ni... ni	*neither . . . nor*
siempre	*always*	nunca	*never*
también	*also*	tampoco	*neither, not either*

Alguno(a) and ninguno(a) must match the gender of the noun they replace or modify. They have different forms when used before masculine singular nouns.

Practice Spanish with Holt McDougal Apps!

Objective

- Review lesson vocabulary and grammar.

DIGITAL SPANISH

Interactive Flashcards Students can hear every target vocabulary word pronounced in authentic Spanish. Flashcards have Spanish on one side, and a picture or a translation on the other.

Review Games Matching, concentration, hangman, and word search are just a sampling of the fun, interactive games students can play to review for the test.

performance space
News + Networking
@HOMETUTOR
CULTURA Interactiva

- Audio and Video Resources
- Interactive Flashcards
- Review Activities
- WebQuest
- Conjuguemos.com

Long-term Retention

Study Tips

Have student pairs quiz each other on affirmative and negative words. They can create flashcards, writing the affirmative word on one side and the negative word on the other.

Communication

Pair Work

Have students write eight sentences about what they did last week, using verbs ending in **-er** and **-ir.** Four sentences should be true and four sentences should be false. Working in pairs, students read each sentence. The partner must guess if the statement is **cierto** or **falso.** For example: **Ayer comí cien hamburguesas. Falso. Anteayer estudié en la biblioteca. Cierto.**

Differentiating Instruction

Pre-AP

Vary Vocabulary In groups of three or four, have students draft a short story about a computer. For each word or phrase they include from the **Vocabulario** on p. 375, their group will earn one point. Encourage students to use as many words as possible. Then have each group share their story. **Anteayer usé el mensajero instantáneo. Pero ahora cuando hago clic para conectar a Internet...**

Inclusion

Frequent Review/Repetition Brainstorm with students **-er** and **-ir** verbs that they already know. Create a list on the board. Then organize students into pairs to review the preterite forms of these verbs. Have each pair choose a verb. One partner says a subject pronoun; the other partner responds with the correct preterite form.

Objective
- Review lesson grammar and vocabulary.

Core resources
- *Cuaderno*, pp. 306–317
- Audio Program: TXT CD 7 track 11

Presentation Strategies
- Before starting the audio for Activity 1, ask students to pay special attention to the uses of the preterite forms.
- Before starting Activities 2 and 3, review preterite forms of regular **-er** and **-ir** verbs. Give students a subject pronoun and a verb and ask students to respond with the correct preterite form of that verb.
- Review affirmative and negative words by giving students a negative statement and having them give you an opposite response.
- Go over the Comparación cultural with students and clarify any questions.

STANDARDS
1.2 Understand language, Act. 1
1.3 Present information, Acts. 2–5
4.2 Compare cultures, Act. 5
21st Century **Communication,** Heritage Language Learners

Warm Up
Projectable Transparencies, 7-19

Vocabulary Tell whether the following statements are logical (**lógico**) or illogical (**ilógico**).
1. Cuando estoy en línea, escribo un correo electrónico.
2. Usamos el mensajero instantáneo para tomar fotos.
3. Voy a quemar un disco compacto.
4. Hago clic en la pantalla para buscar una película.
5. Conectamos a Internet para estar en línea.

Answers: 1. lógico; 2. ilógico; 3. lógico; 4. ilógico; 5. lógico

✓ Ongoing Assessment
Get Help Online
More Practice
my.hrw.com

Intervention and Remediation If students achieve less than 80% accuracy with the activities, direct them to pp. 353–354, 361–362, 366, 368 and to get help online at my.hrw.com.

See Activity answers on p. 377.

Lección 1

Repaso de la lección

@HOMETUTOR
my.hrw.com

¡LLEGADA!

Now you can
- talk about technology
- talk about a series of events
- say what you did
- talk about indefinite or negative situations

Using
- preterite of regular **-er** and **-ir** verbs
- affirmative and negative words

To review
- preterite of regular **-er** and **-ir** verbs p. 361
- affirmative and negative words p. 366

1 Listen and understand

AUDIO

Diana habla con Ramiro sobre su computadora. Escucha y escribe si las oraciones son ciertas o falsas. *(Listen and write whether the statements are true or false.)*

1. Diana piensa que hay algún problema con su computadora.
2. Diana recibió correos electrónicos ayer.
3. A Diana y a sus amigos les gusta usar Internet.
4. Ramiro no encontró ningún problema con la computadora.
5. Diana recibió fotos de sus amigos ayer.
6. Diana no quemó ningún disco compacto anteayer.

Audio Program
TXT CD 7 Track 11
Audio Script TE, p. 353b

To review
- preterite of regular **-er** and **-ir** verbs p. 361

2 Talk about a series of events

Completa el correo electrónico con la forma correcta del pretérito del verbo apropiado. *(Complete the e-mail with the correct preterite form of the appropriate verb.)*

abrir	recibir
comer	salir
compartir	subir
envolver	volver

Hola, Inés. ¿Qué tal? La semana pasada celebré mi cumpleaños. Primero mi familia y yo __**1.**__ a comer en un restaurante. De primer plato mi hermana __**2.**__ pescado. Nunca como mucha carne, entonces yo __**3.**__ un bistec grande con mi padre. Más tarde nosotros __**4.**__ a casa y cuando yo __**5.**__ las escaleras, vi una sorpresa: ¡unos regalos! Entonces yo los __**6.**__: un videojuego de mi hermana y una cámara de mi madre. Después mi padre me explicó que él no __**7.**__ su regalo con papel. ¡De mi padre, yo __**8.**__ un perro! ¡Qué bárbaro!

Differentiating Instruction

Heritage Language Learners
Writing Skills Have students write a paragraph describing what they did over the weekend. The sentences must use the preterite of **-er** and **-ir** verbs as well as some affirmative and negative words. Encourage them to use different subject pronouns. Have them check their spelling, punctuation, and grammar.

Slower-paced Learners
Personalize It Have students use the verbs in Activity 2 to talk about a birthday party they recently attended. Encourage each student to provide a sentence in the preterite for each verb, using the paragraph as a guide. **Yo comí un postre muy rico. Mi amigo abrió su regalo.**

REPASO DE LA LECCIÓN

To review
- preterite of regular **-er** and **-ir** verbs p. 361

3 Say what you did

Escribe lo que hicieron estas personas la semana pasada. Luego escribe si tú lo hiciste o no. *(Write what people did last week. Then write whether or not you did that activity.)*

modelo: el señor Cruz / a casa tarde.
El señor Cruz volvió a casa tarde.
Yo no volví a casa tarde.
(Yo también volví a casa tarde.)

barrer	recibir
beber	correr
aprender	escribir
volver	perder
comer	

1. tú / un correo electrónico
2. mis amigos y yo / una pizza
3. Marta / refrescos
4. el jugador / el partido
5. Paca y Teresa / al parque
6. usted / el suelo
7. Isabel / regalos
8. mis hermanos / español

To review
- affirmative and negative words p. 366

4 Talk about indefinite or negative situations

Juan y Juana son hermanos muy diferentes. Lee lo que dice Juan y escribe lo que responde Juana. Usa palabras afirmativas y negativas. *(Use affirmative or negative words to give Juana's opposite responses to her brother Juan's statements.)*

modelo: Conozco algunos sitios Web muy interesantes.
No conozco ningún sitio Web muy interesante.

1. Siempre recibo correos electrónicos de mis amigos.
2. No mandé nada por Internet anteayer.
3. No hay ningún problema con mi computadora.
4. Los sábados quemo un disco compacto o navego por Internet.
5. Ayer tomé fotos de alguien.
6. Nunca uso cámaras digitales.

To review
- **gauchos** p. 353
- Comparación cultural pp. 354, 362, 368

5 Argentina

Comparación cultural

Answer these culture questions.

1. What do **gauchos** do?
2. What is **mate** and how is it served?
3. What is **lunfardo**? Give an example of a **lunfardo** word.
4. When and why do many people go to Mar del Plata, Argentina?

Más práctica Cuaderno *pp. 306–317* Cuaderno para hispanohablantes *pp. 308–317*

Get Help Online my.hrw.com

Differentiating Instruction

Inclusion

Synthetic/Analytic Support Divide the board into two columns: **Palabras afirmativas** and **Palabras negativas.** Then have students come to the board and write examples under each column. Using these lists as a guide, have students create sentences to talk about indefinite or negative situations.

Slower-paced Learners

Peer-study Support After students complete the paragraph in Activity 2, have them read it aloud to a partner. Remind students to listen to themselves as they read aloud to catch any mistakes in the use of preterite verb forms. Also, instruct the partners to make note of sentences or phrases that do not sound correct because of problems with verb forms.

✓ Ongoing Assessment

Quick Check Using the list of verbs in Activity 2, ask students to talk about five things they did on their last birthday. For example: **Abrí muchos regalos. Comí pastel.**

Answers Projectable Transparencies, 7-27

Answers for Activities on pp. 376–377.

Activity 1

1. cierto; **2.** falso; **3.** cierto; **4.** cierto; **5.** falso; **6.** falso

Activity 2

1. salimos; **2.** comió; **3.** compartí; **4.** volvimos; **5.** subí; **6.** abrí; **7.** envolvió; **8.** recibí

Activity 3

1. Tú escribiste un correo electrónico. Yo también (Yo no) escribí un correo electrónico.
2. Mis amigos y yo comimos una pizza. Yo también (Yo no) comí una pizza.
3. Marta bebió refrescos. Yo también (Yo no) bebí refrescos.
4. El jugador perdió el partido. Yo también (Yo no) perdí el partido.
5. Paca y Teresa corrieron al parque. Yo también (Yo no) corrí al parque.
6. Usted barrió el suelo. Yo también (Yo no) barrí el suelo.
7. Isabel recibió regalos. Yo también (Yo no) recibí regalos.
8. Mis hermanos aprendieron el español. Yo también (Yo no) aprendí el español.

Activity 4

1. Nunca recibo correos electrónicos de mis amigos.
2. Yo mandé algo por Internet anteayer.
3. Hay algún problema con mi computadora.
4. Los sábados ni quemo ningún disco compacto ni navego por Internet.
5. Ayer no tomé fotos de nadie.
6. Siempre uso cámaras digitales.

Activity 5

1. **Gauchos** are like U. S. cowboys: they live on the plains and raise cattle.
2. **Mate** is a tea-like drink that is served in a gourd, with a straw called a **bombilla.**
3. **Lunfardo** is a type of slang that is spoken in Argentina. An example is **gomías.**
4. Many people go to Mar del Plata between December and February for the wonderful beaches and availability of opportunities to do water sports.

Lesson Overview

Culture at a Glance

Topic & Activity	Essential Question
El Parque de la Costa pp. 378–379	Have you visited an amusement park?
El puerto de La Boca p. 386	How do paintings reflect a city's character?
Argentinean food, p. 392	What factors influence a country's cuisine?
Non-traditional museums in Argentina and Bolivia p. 396	What do you imagine when you think of a museum?
Names p. 398	How do last names show family ties across generations?
Culture review p. 401	What are some elements of Argentine culture?

COMPARISON COUNTRIES Argentina Bolivia Nicaragua

Practice at a Glance

	Objective	Activity & Skill
Vocabulary	Amusement parks and places of interest	1: Reading; 2: Speaking / Writing; 3: Listening / Reading; 4: Speaking; 5: Reading / Writing; 9: Listening / Reading; 13: Speaking / Writing; Repaso 2: Writing
	Phone etiquette	1: Reading; 3: Listening / Reading; 12: Speaking; 13: Speaking / Writing; 17: Speaking; 18: Reading / Listening / Speaking; Repaso 1: Listening; Repaso 3: Writing
	Invitations	1: Reading; 4: Speaking; 11: Writing; 12: Speaking; 13: Speaking / Writing; 18: Reading / Listening / Speaking; Repaso 2: Writing
Grammar	Preterite of **–ir, ser** and **hacer**	5: Reading / Writing; 6: Speaking / Writing; 7: Listening / Writing; 8: Speaking; 9: Listening / Reading; 10: Speaking; 13: Speaking / Writing; 15: Listening / Reading; 16: Listening / Reading; 19: Writing; Repaso 4: Writing
	Pronouns after prepositions	11: Writing; 12: Speaking; 13: Speaking / Writing
Communication	Talk on the phone	1: Reading; 5: Reading / Writing; 12: Speaking; 17: Speaking; 18: Reading / Listening / Speaking; Repaso 3: Writing
	Extend invitations	1: Reading; 4: Speaking; 5: Reading / Writing; 11: Writing; 12: Speaking; 19: Writing; Repaso 1: Listening
	Say where you went, how it was, and what you did	6: Speaking / Writing; 7: Listening / Writing; 8: Speaking; 10: Speaking; 14: Writing; 15: Listening / Reading; 19: Writing; Repaso 4: Writing
	Pronunciation: The letters **ll** and **y**	*Pronunciación: Las letras* ***ll*** *y* ***y***, p. 389: Listening
Recycle	Places around town	10: Speaking
	Stem-changing verbs: **e –> i**	14: Writing

The following presentations are recorded in the Audio Program for **¡Avancemos!**

For **¡AvanzaRap!** scripts, see the **¡AvanzaRap! DVD.**

¡A responder! TXT CD 7 track 13

1. Me gustaría ir al museo.
2. ¡Qué lástima!
3. ¡Claro que sí!
4. Sí, me encantaría.

7 | Fueron a diferentes lugares

TXT CD 7 track 15

Florencia: Soy Florencia. Fui al parque de diversiones con mi amiga. Subimos a la montaña rusa pero no me gustó. Tengo miedo de las montañas rusas. ¡Fue horrible!

Luciana: Me llamo Luciana. Mi hermano y yo fuimos a la feria del libro. Compré tres libros nuevos. ¡Qué interesante!

Mariano: Soy Mariano. Florencia me invitó al museo. Pasamos todo el día allí. Vimos un Picasso. Nos gustó mucho. ¡Qué divertido!

18 | Integración TXT CD 7 tracks 19, 20

Carlos: Hola. Soy yo, Carlos. Si no tienes planes para mañana a la una y media, tengo una idea. Escucha: anteayer fui al estadio de fútbol. Compré boletos para el partido; un boleto para mi hermana y uno para mí. Pagué 50 pesos por los dos boletos. Es mucho dinero, pero las sillas están muy cerca del campo. Ahora tengo un problema... ¡mi hermana está enferma! Ella no puede ir conmigo. ¿Quieres acompañarme tú? Puedes pagarme los 25 pesos después. Llámame al teléfono celular. Adiós.

Repaso de la lección TXT CD 7 track 22

1: Listen and Understand

Male: ¿Quieres acompañarme al museo el sábado?
Female: Lo siento. Fui al museo anteayer y fue un poco aburrido.

Female:¿Te gustaría ir al zoológico conmigo?
Male: Sí, me encantaría ir al zoológico. ¿A qué hora salimos?

Male: Voy a la feria el viernes. ¿Quieres acompañarme?
Female: ¿La feria? ¡Qué divertido! Hasta el viernes.

Female: Tengo dos boletos para ir al acuario el domingo. Te invito.
Male:¡Qué lástima! Voy a salir con mi familia el domingo.

Male:¿Quieres hacer algo este fin de semana?
Female:¡Claro que sí! ¿Adónde vamos?

Female: Fui al parque de diversiones anoche. La montaña rusa fue muy divertida. Voy a volver hoy. ¿Te gustaría ir conmigo?
Male: ¿La montaña rusa? ¡Qué miedo! Prefiero ir al zoológico.

Repaso inclusivo TXT CD 7 track 24

1: Listen, Understand and Compare

Sra. Palomar: ¿Aló?

Teresa: Buenas tardes. ¿Puedo hablar con Jaime?

Sra. Palomar: ¿Quién habla?

Teresa: Perdón... habla Teresa, Teresa Rodríguez. Soy una amiga de Jaime.

Sra. Palomar: Ah, claro... ¡Teresa! Soy la madrastra de Jaime. Lo siento, pero él no está aquí en casa. Salió al parque. Fue con unos amigos. ¿Quieres dejar un mensaje?

Teresa: No, gracias. Quiero ir a la feria con él pero yo...

Sra. Palomar: O, si quieres hablar con él ahora, puedes llamarlo a su teléfono celular.

Teresa: Muy bien. El número es 335-9064, ¿no?

Sra. Palomar: No, no. Es 335-9074.

Teresa: Muchas gracias, Señora Palomar.

Sra. Palomar: Adiós.

Resource List

Everything you need to ...

Plan	Present	Assess
Teacher One Stop ✓Lesson Plans ✓Teacher Resources ✓Audio and Video	**Interactive Whiteboard Lessons** **Teacher One Stop with Projectable Transparencies** **Power Presentations** **AnimatedGrammar**	**Online Assessment** ✓ Assessments for on-level, modified, pre-AP, and heritage learners ✓ Create customized tests with **Examview Assessment Suite** ✓ **performance space** ✓ *Generate Success* Rubric Generator

Print

Plan	Present	Practice	Assess
URB 7 • Video Scripts pp. 71–72 • Family Involvement Activity p. 92 • Absent Student Copymasters pp. 101–111 **Best Practices Toolkit**	**URB 7** • Video Activities pp. 59–66	• *Cuaderno* pp. 318–343 • *Cuaderno para hispanohablantes* pp. 318–343 • *Lecturas para todos* pp. 67–71 • *Lecturas para hispanohablantes* • *¡AvanzaCómics! SuperBruno y Nati,* Episodio 4 **URB 7** • Practice Games pp. 39–46 • Audio Scripts pp. 78–82 • Fine Art Activities pp. 88–89	**Differentiated Assessment Program** **URB 7** • Did you get it? Reteaching and Practice Copymasters pp. 13–24

Projectable Transparencies (Teacher One Stop, my.hrw.com)

Culture	Presentation and Practice	Classroom Management
• Atlas Maps 1 1–6 • Argentina Map 1 • Fine Art Transparencies 4, 5	• Vocabulary Transparencies 8, 9 • Grammar Presentation Transparencies 12, 13 • Situational Transparency and label overlay 14, 15 • Situational Student Copymaster pp. 1, 2	• Warm Up Transparencies 20–23 • Student Book Answer Transparencies 28–31

Audio and Video

Audio	Video	¡AvanzaRap! DVD
• Student Book Audio CD 7 Tracks 12–24 • Workbook Audio CD 4 Tracks 11–20 • Heritage Learners Audio CD 2 Tracks 21–24, CD 4 Tracks 15–18 • Assessment Audio CD 2 Tracks 15–18 • *Lecturas para todos* Audio CD 1 Track 14, CD 2 Tracks 1–6 • Sing-along Songs Audio CD	• Vocabulary Video DVD 2 • *Telehistoria* DVD 2 Escena 1 Escena 2 Escena 3 Completa • Culture Video DVD 2	• Video animations of all **¡AvanzaRap!** songs (with Karaoke track) • Interactive DVD Activities • Teaching Suggestions • **¡AvanzaRap!** Activity Masters • **¡AvanzaRap!** video scripts and answers

Online and Media Resources

Student	Teacher
Available online at my.hrw.com • Online Student Edition • News + Networking • performance space • @HOMETUTOR • CulTura Interactiva • WebQuests • Interactive Flashcards • Review Games • Self-Check Quiz **Student One Stop** **Holt McDougal Spanish Apps**	**Teacher One Stop (also available at my.hrw.com)** • Interactive Teacher's Edition • All print, audio, and video resources • Projectable Transparencies • Lesson Plans • TPRS • Examview Assessment Suite **Available online at my.hrw.com** *Generate Success* Rubric Generator and Graphic Organizers **Power Presentations**

Differentiated Assessment

On-level	Modified	Pre-AP	Heritage Learners
• Vocabulary Recognition Quiz p. 319 • Vocabulary Production Quiz p. 320 • Grammar Quizzes pp. 321–322 • Culture Quiz p. 323 • On-level Lesson Test pp. 324–330 • On-level Unit Test pp. 336–342	• Modified Lesson Test pp. 254–260 • Modified Unit Test pp. 266–272	• Pre-AP Lesson Test pp. 254–260 • Pre-AP Unit Test pp. 266–272	• Heritage Learners Lesson Test pp. 260–266 • Heritage Learners Unit Test pp. 272–278

Core Pacing Guide

50 Minute (9 Day)

	Objectives/Focus	Teach	Practice	Assess/HW Options
DAY 1	**Culture:** learn about Argentina **Vocabulary:** amusement parks • Warm Up OHT 20 **5 min**	Lesson Opener pp. 378–379 **Presentación de vocabulario** pp. 380–381 • Read A–D • View video DVD 2 • Play audio TXT CD 7 track 12 • *¡A responder!* TXT CD 7 track 13 **25 min**	Lesson Opener pp. 378–379 **Práctica de vocabulario** p. 382 • Acts. 1, 2 **15 min**	**Assess:** *Para y piensa* p. 382 **5 min** **Homework:** *Cuaderno* pp. 318–320 @HomeTutor
DAY 2	**Communication:** amusement parks • Warm Up OHT 20 • Check Homework **5 min**	**Vocabulario en contexto** pp. 383–384 • *Telehistoria escena 1* DVD 2 • *Nota gramatical: Noun-adjective agreement* **20 min**	**Vocabulario en contexto** p. 383 • Act. 3 TXT CD 7 track 14 • Act. 4 **20 min**	**Assess:** *Para y piensa* p. 384 **5 min** **Homework:** *Cuaderno* pp. 318–320 @HomeTutor
DAY 3	**Grammar:** preterite of **ir, ser** and **hacer** • Warm Up OHT 21 • Check Homework **5 min**	**Presentación de gramática** p. 385 • preterite of **ir, ser** and **hacer** **Práctica de gramática** p. 386 **Culture:** El puerto de La Boca **20 min**	**Práctica de gramática** pp. 386–387 • Acts. 5, 6, 8 • Act. 7 TXT CD 7 track 15 **20 min**	**Assess:** *Para y piensa* p. 387 **5 min** **Homework:** *Cuaderno* pp. 321–323 @HomeTutor
DAY 4	**Communication:** talking about the past • Warm Up OHT 21 • Check Homework **5 min**	**Gramática en contexto** pp. 388–389 • *Telehistoria escena 2* DVD 2 • *Pronunciación* TXT CD 7 track 17 **15 min**	**Gramática en contexto** pp. 388–389 • Act. 9 TXT CD 7 track 16 • Act. 10 **25 min**	**Assess:** *Para y piensa* p. 389 **5 min** **Homework:** *Cuaderno* pp. 321–323 @HomeTutor
DAY 5	**Grammar:** pronouns after prepositions • Warm Up OHT 22 • Check Homework **5 min**	**Presentación de gramática** p. 390 • pronouns after prepositions **Práctica de gramática** pp. 391–392 **15 min**	**Práctica de gramática** pp. 391–392 • Acts. 11, 12, 13, 14 **25 min**	**Assess:** *Para y piensa* p. 392 **5 min** **Homework:** *Cuaderno* pp. 324–326 @HomeTutor
DAY 6	**Communication:** Culmination: amusement parks, preterite of **ir, ser** and **hacer,** pronouns after prepositions • Warm Up OHT 22 • Check Homework **5 min**	**Todo junto** pp. 393–395 • *Escenas 1, 2: Resumen* • *Telehistoria completa* DVD 2 **20 min**	**Todo junto** pp. 393–395 • Acts. 15, 16 TXT CD 7 tracks 14, 16, 18 • Acts. 17, 19 • Act. 18 TXT CD 7 tracks 19, 20 **20 min**	**Assess:** *Para y piensa* p. 395 **5 min** **Homework:** *Cuaderno* pp. 327–328 @HomeTutor
DAY 7	**Reading:** Unique museums **Review:** Lesson Review • Warm Up OHT 23 • Check Homework **5 min**	**Lectura cultural** pp. 396–397 • Museos excepcionales • TXT CD 7 track 21 **Repaso de la lección** pp. 400–401 **15 min**	**Lectura cultural** pp. 396–397 • Museos excepcionales **Repaso de la lección** pp. 400–401 • Act. 1 TXT CD 7 track 22 • Acts. 2, 3, 4, 5 **20 min**	**Assess: Repaso de la lección** pp. 400–401 **10 min** **Homework:** *En resumen* p. 399; *Cuaderno* pp. 329–340 (optional) Review Games Online @HomeTutor
DAY 8	**Assessment**			**Assess:** Lesson 2 Test or Unit 7 Test **50 min**
DAY 9	**Unit Culmination** **5 min**	**Comparación cultural** pp. 402–403 • TXT CD 7 track 23 **Repaso inclusivo** pp. 404–405 **20 min**	**Comparación cultural** pp. 402–403 **Repaso inclusivo** pp. 404–405 • Act. 1 TXT CD 7 track 24 • Acts. 2, 3, 4, 5, 6, 7 **25 min**	**Homework:** *Cuaderno* pp. 341–343

	Objectives/Focus	Teach	Practice	Assess/HW Options
DAY 1	**Culture:** learn about Argentina **Vocabulary:** amusement parks • Warm Up OHT 20 5 min	Lesson Opener pp. 378–379 **Presentación de vocabulario** pp. 380–381 • Read A–D • View video DVD 2 • Play audio TXT CD 7 track 12 • *¡A responder!* TXT CD 7 track 13 20 min	Lesson Opener pp. 378–379 **Práctica de vocabulario** p. 382 • Acts. 1, 2 20 min	**Assess:** *Para y piensa* p. 382 5 min
	Communication: amusement parks 5 min	**Vocabulario en contexto** pp. 383–384 • *Telehistoria escena 1* DVD 2 • *Nota gramatical:* Noun-adjective agreement 15 min	**Vocabulario en contexto** p. 383 • Act. 3 TXT CD 7 track 14 • Act. 4 15 min	**Assess:** *Para y piensa* p. 384 5 min **Homework:** *Cuaderno* pp. 318–320 @HomeTutor
DAY 2	**Grammar:** preterite of **ir, ser** and **hacer** • Warm Up OHT 21 • Check Homework 5 min	**Presentación de gramática** p. 385 • preterite of **ir, ser** and **hacer** **Práctica de gramática** p. 386 **Culture:** *El puerto de La Boca* 20 min	**Práctica de gramática** pp. 386–387 • Acts. 5, 6, 8 • Act. 7 TXT CD 7 track 15 15 min	**Assess:** *Para y piensa* p. 387 5 min
	Communication: talking about the past 5 min	**Gramática en contexto** pp. 388–389 • *Telehistoria escena 2* DVD 2 • *Pronunciación* TXT CD 7 track 17 20 min	**Gramática en contexto** pp. 388–389 • Act. 9 TXT CD 7 track 16 • Act. 10 15 min	**Assess:** *Para y piensa* p. 389 5 min **Homework:** *Cuaderno* pp. 321–323 @HomeTutor
DAY 3	**Grammar:** pronouns after prepositions • Warm Up OHT 22 • Check Homework 5 min	**Presentación de gramática** p. 390 • pronouns after prepositions **Práctica de gramática** pp. 391–392 15 min	**Práctica de gramática** pp. 391–392 • Acts. 11, 12, 13, 14 20 min	**Assess:** *Para y piensa* p. 392 5 min
	Communication: Culmination: amusement parks, preterite of **ir, ser** and **hacer,** pronouns after prepositions 5 min	**Todo junto** pp. 393–395 • *Escenas 1, 2: Resumen* • *Telehistoria completa* DVD 2 15 min	**Todo junto** pp. 393–395 • Acts. 15, 16 TXT CD 7 tracks 14, 16, 18 • Acts. 17, 19 • Act. 18 TXT CD 7 tracks 19, 20 20 min	**Assess:** *Para y piensa* p. 395 5 min **Homework:** *Cuaderno* pp. 324–328 @HomeTutor
DAY 4	**Reading:** Unique museums • Warm Up OHT 23 • Check Homework 5 min	**Lectura cultural** pp. 396–397 • *Museos excepcionales* • TXT CD 7 track 21 15 min	**Lectura cultural** pp. 396–397 • *Museos excepcionales* 15 min	**Assess:** *Para y piensa* p. 397 5 min
	Review: Lesson Review 5 min	**Repaso de la lección** pp. 400–401 15 min	**Repaso de la lección** pp. 400–401 • Act. 1 TXT CD 7 track 22 • Acts. 2, 3, 4, 5 25 min	**Assess: Repaso de la lección** pp. 400–401 5 min **Homework:** *En resumen* p. 399; *Cuaderno* pp. 329–340 (optional) Review Games Online @HomeTutor
DAY 5	**Assessment**			**Assess:** Lesson 2 Test or Unit 7 Test 50 min
	Unit Culmination 5 min	**Comparación cultural** pp. 402–403 • TXT CD 7 track 23 **Repaso inclusivo** pp. 404–405 15 min	**Comparación cultural** pp. 402–403 **Repaso inclusivo** pp. 404–405 • Act. 1 TXT CD 7 track 24 • Acts. 2, 3, 4, 5, 6, 7 20 min	**Homework:** *Cuaderno* pp. 341–343

¡AVANZA! **Objectives**
- Introduce lesson theme: **Un día en el parque de diversiones.**
- **Culture:** Learn about amusement parks in different parts of the world.

Presentation Strategies
- Remind students of the characters' names: Florencia, Mariano, and Luciana.
- Have students make a list of amusement parks they have visited or heard about. Have them talk about the rides visitors can find there.

STANDARDS
4.2 Compare cultures
21st Century **Flexibility and Adaptability,** Multiple Intelligences

Warm Up Projectable Transparencies, 7-20

Affirmative and negative words Complete each sentence with the correct affirmative or negative word.
1. Nunca mando correos electrónicos, pero ____ uso el mensajero instantáneo.
2. ¿No tienes una cámara digital? Yo ____.
3. A Juan no le gusta mandar ____ fotos ____ correos electrónicos.
4. ¿Conocen ____ tienda de computadoras?

Answers: 1. siempre; 2. tampoco; 3. ni... ni; 4. alguna

Comparación cultural

Exploring the Theme
Ask the following:
1. What are the names of some well-known amusement parks in the United States?
2. Is there an amusement park close to where you live? If so, what is it?
3. What are some things to do besides going on the rides?

¿Qué ves? Possible answers include:
1. No, no están delante del cine.
2. Tiene una mochila.
3. Florencia tiene un mapa del parque.

UNIDAD 7
Argentina

Lección 2

Tema:
Un día en el parque de diversiones

¡AVANZA! **In this lesson you will learn to**
- talk on the phone
- say where you went, how it was, and what you did
- extend invitations

using
- **¡Qué** + adjective!
- preterite of **ir, ser,** and **hacer**
- pronouns after prepositions

¿Recuerdas?
- noun-adjective agreement
- places around town
- stem-changing verbs: **e → i**

Comparación cultural

In this lesson you will learn about
- family names
- artist Benito Quinquela Martín and Argentinean cuisine
- places to visit in Argentina, Bolivia, and Nicaragua

Compara con tu mundo
El Parque de la Costa is near Buenos Aires. With over 50 rides, it is the largest amusement park in South America. *Have you visited an amusement park? What rides do you like? If you haven't, would you like to go?*

¿Qué ves?
Mira la foto
¿Están delante del cine los amigos?
¿Tiene Mariano una mochila o una chaqueta?
¿Qué tiene Florencia en las manos?

Differentiating Instruction

Heritage Language Learners
Support What They Know Ask students to describe the photo on pp. 378 and 379 in as much detail as possible. Ask them to draw conclusions about certain items in the photo in order to describe them. For example, what does the map probably show? What does the sign behind the people probably say?

English Learners
Build Background Discuss with students the concept of an amusement park or theme park. Ask them if there are any famous amusement parks in their country of origin, or if there are other kinds of outdoor attractions that people visit.

DIGITAL SPANISH my.hrw.com
ONLINE STUDENT EDITION with...

performance space
News + Networking
@HOMETUTOR
CULTURA Interactiva

- Audio and Video Resources
- Interactive Flashcards
- Review Activities
- WebQuest
- Conjuguemos.com

PRACTICE SPANISH WITH HOLT MCDOUGAL APPS!

El Parque de la Costa
El Tigre, Argentina

Differentiating Instruction

Pre-AP

Timed Response Organize students into two teams. One player from each team stands up. Players have thirty seconds to create a sentence about the photo. They may get assistance from their teammates. After thirty seconds, each player presents his or her sentence. Appropriate responses earn the team a point; sentences can not be repeated.

Multiple Intelligences

Interpersonal Organize students into groups of three. Tell each group to imagine that they are the friends shown on p. 379. Have each group draft a short role-play about what these friends might be talking about. Each person must say at least two lines. Give students the chance to share their role-plays with the group.

DIGITAL SPANISH

TEACHER TOOLS
- Interactive Whiteboard Lessons
- Generate Success!

ALSO AVAILABLE...
- Online Workbook
- Spanish InterActive Reader

SPANISH ON THE GO!
- Performance Space
- Holt McDougal Spanish Apps
- ¡Avancemos! eTextbook

Using the Photo

Location Information

El Tigre The city of El Tigre is located approximately one hour north of Buenos Aires and is considered to be a resort city. It is in the delta region along the Paraná River and is built on an island.

Long-term Retention

Recycle

Ask questions about the photos that elicit vocabulary and grammar from previous units. For example: **¿Alguien lleva un gorro? No, nadie lleva un gorro. ¿Hace sol? Sí, hace sol. ¿Quién lleva una mochila? Mariano lleva una mochila.**

¡AVANZA! Objective

- Present lesson vocabulary: amusement parks, places of interest and special events, extending and declining invitations, talking on the phone.

Core Resources

- Video Program: DVD 2
- Audio Program: TXT CD 7 tracks 12, 13

Presentation Strategies

- Point to the places of interest on pp. 380-381, say the words and have students repeat after you.
- Point to the expressions for extending and declining invitations. Ask students: If I say **me encantaría,** am I accepting or declining an invitation? Continue with other expressions.
- Play the audio as students read A–D.
- Play the video.

STANDARDS

1.2 Understand language

21st Century **Communication,** Pair Work

Communication

Grammar Activity

Ask a volunteer to read aloud the Presentación de vocabulario. Ask other students to raise their hands every time they hear a cognate. Remind them that cognates are words that are written similarly and have the same meaning in two languages. Answers: **el teléfono celular; invitar(la); acompañar(me); el zoológico; la feria; el museo; el acuario; el parque**

Long-term Retention

Recycle

Have students summarize the dialogue on p. 380 in a short paragraph, using third-person pronouns. A possible paragraph is: **Mariano habla con Florencia. Mariano la invita al zoológico. A Florencia no le gusta ir al zoológico. Entonces Mariano la invita a la feria del libro. Florencia no puede el sábado, pero le gustaría hacer algo el domingo. Mariano la invita al parque de diversiones con Luciana.**

Presentación de VOCABULARIO

¡AVANZA! **Goal:** Learn about Mariano's trip to the amusement park with his friends. Then practice what you have learned to talk on the phone about where you like to go with your friends. ***Actividades 1–2***

VIDEO DVD

AUDIO

A Voy a **llamar** a Florencia para invitarla a hacer algo este **fin de semana.**

llamar
el teléfono celular
Mariano
Florencia

B
Mariano: ¿**Aló?** ¿**Puedo hablar con** Florencia?
Florencia: Hola, Mariano. Soy yo, Florencia.
Mariano: Hola, Florencia. **¿Quieres acompañarme al zoológico? Te invito.**
Florencia: Lo siento. No me gusta mucho ir al zoológico.
Mariano: ¿**Te gustaría** ir a **la feria** del libro el sábado?
Florencia: ¡**Qué lástima!** El sábado no puedo, pero **me gustaría** hacer algo el domingo.
Mariano: Voy a ir al **parque de diversiones con** Luciana. ¿Quieres ir?
Florencia: ¡**Claro que sí!** Hasta el domingo.

el zoológico

la feria

el acuario

el museo

Differentiating Instruction

Pre-AP

Communicate Preferences Use the verbs **gustar** and **preferir** to ask students about the places and activities shown on pp. 380 and 381. When students answer **sí** or **no**, ask them to explain why. **¿Te gusta el zoológico? Sí, me gusta mucho. Es muy interesante y divertido.**

Slower-paced Learners

Yes/No Questions Ask students yes/no questions to assess their understanding of Florencia's responses during the telephone conversation presented on p. 380. Here are a few possible questions:
¿Quiere acompañar a Mariano al zoológico?
¿A ella le gusta ir a zoológico?
¿Puede ir ella a la feria del libro el sábado?

C Hola, Florencia. Hola, Luciana. Vamos a comprar **los boletos.** Primero quiero **subir a la vuelta al mundo.**

D No voy a subir a **la montaña rusa** porque **tengo miedo.** Luciana y yo preferimos **los autitos chocadores.** Son más divertidos.

Más vocabulario

dejar un mensaje *to leave a message*
la llamada *phone call*
¿Está...? *Is . . . there?*
No, no está. *No, he's/she's not here.*
Sí, me encantaría. *Yes, I would love to.*
Un momento. *One moment.*
Expansión de vocabulario p. R8

@HOMETUTOR my.hrw.com Interactive Flashcards

¡A responder! Escuchar

Mariano invita a Luciana al museo. Escucha sus respuestas y señala con el pulgar hacia arriba si ella acepta la invitación o con el pulgar hacia abajo si no la acepta. *(Listen to Luciana's responses to Mariano's invitation. Make a thumbs-up sign if she accepts or a thumbs-down sign if she declines.)*

Differentiating Instruction

Heritage Language Learners

Support What They Know Ask students to share other expressions they might use beginning with **¡Qué...!** Have students demonstrate what the expression means by giving an example of a time they have used it, or acting out a situation in which they would use it.

Inclusion

Cumulative Instruction Brainstorm with students a list of adjectives they already know that could be combined with **Qué** to form expressions. Suggest that students think in terms of opposites. Here are a few examples:

¡Qué interesante!	**¡Qué aburrido!**
¡Qué fácil!	**¡Qué difícil!**
¡Qué bonito!	**¡Qué feo!**

TEACHER to TEACHER
Laura Cantor
New York, New York

Tips for Presenting Vocabulary

I often bring to class brochures and maps from zoos, botanical gardens, and amusement parks I've visited abroad. I share these items with my students to encourage them to talk about these places and the activities they might enjoy doing there. I pass these brochures around the class and ask students to note particular details such as opening and closing times, ways to get there, entrance fees, etc. I also encourage them to identify cognates in the headlines, captions, and articles.

Go online for more tips!

Communication
Pair Work

In Spain, someone may answer the phone by saying **Diga.** Other expressions used in various countries are **aló, hola** and **bueno.** Have students work with a partner to make phone calls inviting each other to go to the amusement park. Encourage them to use the expressions above. Ask them to ask their partner if he/she likes to go on the rides pictured on this page.

Long-term Retention
Learning Tips

To facilitate learning vocabulary about extending invitations ask students to make a three-column chart. Label column one: Ways of extending invitations, column two: Ways of accepting invitations, and column three: Ways of refusing invitations. After they have completed the chart, ask student pairs to prepare short dialogues using the information they have collected. For example, **¿Te gustaría ir al zoológico el sábado? Qué lástima, el sábado no puedo.** Or, **Sí, me encantaría.**

Answers Projectable Transparencies, 7-28

¡A responder! Audio Script, TE p. 377B
Students signal thumbs up for numbers 1, 3, 4 and thumbs down for number 2.

Objective

- Practice vocabulary: talking on the phone, extending and declining invitations, places of interest, amusement park.

Core Resource

- *Cuaderno,* pp. 318–320

Practice Sequence

- **Activity 1:** Vocabulary recognition: talking on the phone, extending and declining invitations, places of interest, sports
- **Activity 2:** Vocabulary production: amusement park, places of interest

STANDARDS

1.2 Understand language, Act. 1
1.3 Present information, Act. 2, PYP
21st Century **Communication,** Humor/Creativity; **Creativity and Innovation,** Multiple Intelligences

Communication

Humor/Creativity

Ask students to work in pairs to extend invitations to five different places. Remind them to start the invitation with phrases such as: **¿Quieres acompañarme...? ¿Te gustaría ir...?** Responses should include humorous excuses. For example: **Lo siento, no puedo porque tengo que salir con mi gato.**

Ongoing Assessment

Get Help Online
More Practice
my.hrw.com

PARA Y PIENSA **Quick Check** If students have trouble completing Para y piensa, refer them to pp. 380 and 381 and have them review the vocabulary. For additional practice, use Reteaching & Practice Copymasters URB 7, pp. 13, 14.

Answers Projectable Transparencies, 7-28

Activity 1
1. b; **2.** a; **3.** c; **4.** b; **5.** b; **6.** b

Activity 2 Answers should follow the format:El boleto es para (name of place).
1. ...el zoológico
2. ...la montaña rusa
3. ...el acuario
4. ...los autitos chocadores
5. ...el museo
6. ...la vuelta al mundo

Para y piensa
1. la montaña rusa, la vuelta al mundo;
2. el museo, el parque de diversiones, el zoológico, el acuario

Práctica de VOCABULARIO

1 Conversaciones por teléfono

Leer

Completa las conversaciones. *(Complete these phone conversations.)*

1. ¿Quieres acompañarme a la feria?
a. ¿Aló?
b. ¡Claro que sí!
c. Tienes una llamada.

2. ¿Puedo hablar con Julieta?
a. No, no está.
b. Sí, me encantaría.
c. ¡Qué lástima!

3. ¿Está Manuel?
a. ¿Puedo hablar con él?
b. Te invito.
c. Un momento.

4. ¿Aló?
a. Un momento.
b. ¿Puedo hablar con Rafael?
c. ¿Puedo dejar un mensaje?

5. No, no está.
a. ¡Claro que sí!
b. Me gustaría dejar un mensaje.
c. ¿Te gustaría ir a la feria?

6. ¿Te gustaría ir al museo?
a. ¡Qué miedo!
b. Lo siento, pero no puedo.
c. ¿Quieres dejar un mensaje?

Expansión
Write the next part of each conversatic

2 Los boletos

Hablar
Escribir

Mariano tiene boletos para las atracciones del parque de diversiones y otros lugares. Mira el boleto e identifica para qué es. *(Identify what each ticket is for.)*

modelo: El boleto es para **la feria** del libro.

1.

2.

3.

4.
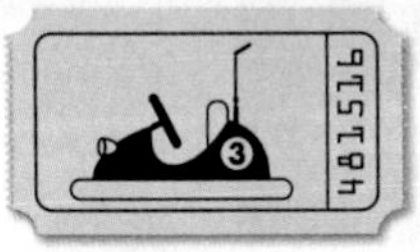

5.

6.

Expansión:
Teacher Edition
Have students invite their par to each of the places mention

Más práctica Cuaderno *pp. 318–320* Cuaderno para hispanohablantes *pp. 318–321*

Get Help Online
my.hrw.com

PARA Y PIENSA

Did you get it?
1. Name two amusement park rides.
2. Name four places that might require you to buy tickets.

Differentiating Instruction

Slower-paced Learners

Peer-study Support Have students work with a partner to complete Activity 1. Instruct one partner to read the question aloud, and the other partner to read all three choices in response. Then have students discuss which sounds the most logical. Students should switch roles after each question.

Multiple Intelligences

Visual Learners After students have completed Activity 2, give them the opportunity to design their own tickets. Encourage them to include information such as the price and the date. Students can then use their tickets to play a question and answer game to review vocabulary.

VOCABULARIO en contexto

¡AVANZA! **Goal:** Listen to Florencia and Mariano talk about the things they see at an amusement park. Then use **Qué** + adjective to describe the different activities you do. ***Actividades 3–4***

¿Recuerdas? Noun-adjective agreement p. 66

Telehistoria escena 1

@HOMETUTOR my.hrw.com View, Read and Record

STRATEGIES

Cuando lees
Map the scene Draw a map of the park, using arrows and the initials **M, L,** and **F** for the characters' changing locations. Then use location expressions, such as **cerca de...**, to write sentences describing where they are.

Cuando escuchas
Link words and visual images Match the location expressions you hear with visual images. For example, when you hear **la montaña rusa,** visualize the roller coaster.

VIDEO DVD

AUDIO

Florencia: *(muttering to herself)* ¿Dónde está Mariano? Tengo que llamarlo a su teléfono celular.

Mariano is also at the amusement park, with his friend Luciana.

Mariano: *(answering phone)* Hola, Florencia. Sí, Luciana y yo estamos en el Parque de la Costa. Compramos nuestros boletos.

Florencia: Yo también. ¿Pueden ver la montaña rusa?

Mariano: Sí, pero estamos más cerca de la vuelta al mundo.

Florencia: Ahora veo la vuelta al mundo. Ustedes deben estar cerca.

Mariano: Sí, sí. Veo la montaña rusa, pero no te veo.

Florencia and Mariano both walk backward, looking for each other.

Luciana: ¿Por qué no encontramos a Florencia delante de los autitos chocadores?

As she says this, Mariano and Florencia suddenly bump into each other.

Continuará... p. 388

También se dice

Argentina To say that he and Luciana are near the Ferris wheel, Mariano uses the words **la vuelta al mundo.** In other Spanish-speaking countries you might hear:
- **España** **la noria**
- **México** **la rueda de la fortuna**
- **Puerto Rico** **la estrella**
- **Perú, Colombia y otros países** **la rueda de Chicago**

Differentiating Instruction

Slower-paced Learners

Memory Aids Have students create posters advertising different amusement park attractions, such as **la vuelta al mundo, la montaña rusa, los autitos chocadores.** Each poster should include the name of the attraction and an illustration. Display the posters. Read the Telehistoria aloud and have students point to the posters for the different places they hear.

Heritage Language Learners

Regional Variations Direct students to the También se dice box at the bottom of the page. Have students comment on the various ways to say *Ferris wheel.* Which expression is most familiar to them? Students might find it interesting that the English name comes from the ride's inventor, a bridge-builder named George W. Ferris.

¡AVANZA! Objective
- Understand activity vocabulary in context.

Core Resources
- Video Program: DVD 2
- Audio Program: TXT CD 7 track 14

Presentation Strategies
- Have students look at the photo and ask comprehension questions such as **¿Dónde están Luciana y Mariano? ¿Qué hace Mariano?**
- Have students scan the dialogue to find out how many amusement rides are mentioned.
- Play the audio or video while students follow the script in their text.

STANDARDS
1.2 Understand language
4.1 Compare languages

Warm Up
Projectable Transparencies, 7-20

Vocabulary In Spanish, write the name of the place where you would find:
1. el arte de Picasso
2. libros para comprar
3. una montaña rusa
4. muchos animales

Answers: 1. un museo; 2. una feria; 3. el parque de diversiones; 4. un zoológico

Communication

Pair Work

Ask students to use the Telehistoria to create a dialogue about visiting an amusement park and the things they can see there. Have them mention at least four places they can go to and use the expression **¡Qué** + adjective! to express their reaction to each place.

Video Summary

@HOMETUTOR VideoPlus my.hrw.com

Florencia can't find Mariano at the amusement park, so she calls him on her cell phone. As they talk on the phone, they bump into each other.

Objectives
- Practice using vocabulary in context.
- Recycle noun/adjective agreement.

Core Resource
- Audio Program: TXT CD 7 track 14

Practice Sequence
- **Activity 3:** Telehistoria comprehension
- **Activity 4:** Vocabulary production: accepting or declining invitations.

STANDARDS
1.1 Engage in conversation, Act. 4
1.2 Understand language, Acts. 3–4, PYP
1.3 Present information, PYP
21st Century **Flexibility and Adaptability,** Act. 4

Nota gramatical
Use a masculine form when a masculine noun or an action is described: **(el zoológico) ¡Qué divertido!** Use a feminine adjective when a feminine noun is being described: **(la montaña rusa) ¡Qué divertida!**

✓ Ongoing Assessment
Get Help Online
More Practice
my.hrw.com

PARA Y PIENSA **Quick Check** Review adjectives from previous lessons that go with **qué** such as **limpio, sucio, fuerte,** etc. Remind students that **qué** can also be used with a noun, such as **¡Qué miedo!** and **¡Qué lástima!** For additional practice, use Reteaching & Practice Copymasters URB 7 pp. 13, 15, 22.

Communication
Motivating with Music
The **¡AvanzaRap!** song for this unit targets vocabulary from both Lección 1 and Lección 2. To reinforce these concepts, play the **¡AvanzaRap!** animated video song for the students and have them complete the Activity Master for this unit.

Answers Projectable Transparencies, 7-28
Activity 3
1. d; **2.** e; **3.** b; **4.** a; **5.** c
Activity 4 Answers will vary. Sample answers include:
¿Te gustaría ir al zoológico? ¡Qué divertido! Me gustan los animales.
Para y piensa
1. ¡Qué divertido! **3.** ¡Qué interesante!
2. ¡Qué pequeña! **4.** ¡Qué grandes!

3 *Comprensión del episodio* ¿Dónde están?
Escuchar
Leer

Empareja las frases para describir el episodio. *(Match the following sentence starters with logical endings according to the episode.)*

1. Florencia y Mariano hablan por
2. Florencia, Luciana y Mariano están
3. Luciana y Mariano compran
4. Todos pueden ver
5. Mariano y Luciana están

a. la montaña rusa.
b. sus boletos.
c. cerca de la vuelta al mundo.
d. teléfono celular.
e. en el parque de diversiones.

Expansión
Predict what will happen in the next episode of the Telehistoria.

Nota gramatical
¿Recuerdas? Noun-adjective agreement p. 66

To express *How* + **adjective,** use **Qué** + **adjective** in the masculine singular form.

¡**Qué divertido**! ¡**Qué aburrido**!
***How** fun!* ***How** boring!*

Use the feminine form only when a feminine noun is being described.

4 Invitaciones
Hablar

Estás en Argentina con un(a) amigo(a). Invita a otro(a) estudiante a varios lugares y atracciones. Él o ella va a dar su opinión y aceptar o no tu invitación. *(Invite a classmate to various places and attractions. He or she will give an opinion and accept or decline your invitation.)*

A ¿Te gustaría subir a la montaña rusa?

B ¡Qué peligroso! No, no me gustaría.

Expansión:
Teacher Edition Only
Have students ask about two other places or attractions and their partners will give an opinion and decline the invitation.

Get Help Online
my.hrw.com

PARA Y PIENSA
Did you get it? Describe the following, using **Qué** + an adjective.
1. Ir al parque es divertido.
2. La pantalla es pequeña.
3. El museo es interesante.
4. Las fotos son grandes.

Differentiating Instruction

Slower-paced Learners
Sentence Completion Have students try this strategy to complete Activity 3. Have a volunteer read the first sentence aloud five times, each time trying out a different word or phrase in the blank. When the sentence makes sense, have the group give the sentence a thumbs-up. Repeat with the remaining sentences.

Inclusion
Metacognitive Support Remind students that expressions that might begin with the word *how* in English, such as *How interesting!* start with the word **Qué,** not **Cómo,** in Spanish. Give students this tip. Tell them to think of the phrases **¡Qué divertido!** and **¡Qué lástima!** In English, you might also say *What fun!* or *What a shame!*

Presentación de GRAMÁTICA

¡AVANZA! **Goal:** Learn about the irregular preterite forms of **ir, ser,** and **hacer.** Then practice these forms to say where you went and what you did, and tell how it was. ***Actividades 5–8***

English Grammar Connection: **Irregular verbs** do not follow the pattern of regular verbs. In English, irregular verbs in the past tense do not end in *-ed*.

She **went** to the aquarium. (↑ irregular verb) — Ella **fue** al acuario. (↑ irregular verb)

Preterite of ir, ser, and hacer

ANIMATEDGRAMMAR my.hrw.com

Ir, ser, and **hacer** are irregular in the preterite tense. How do you form the preterite of these verbs?

Here's how: The preterite forms of **ir** and **ser** are exactly the same.

ir *to go* / **ser** *to be*	
fui	fuimos
fuiste	fuisteis
fue	fueron

Use context clues to determine which verb is being used.

Fuimos a la feria.
***We went** to the fair.*

¡**Fue** un día divertido!
***It was** a fun day!*

Like **ir** and **ser,** the preterite forms of **hacer** have no accents.

hacer *to do, to make*	
hice	hicimos
hiciste	hicisteis
hizo	hicieron

Notice that the **c** *becomes* **z** *before* **o.**

¿Qué **hiciste** ayer?
*What **did you do** yesterday?*

Él **hizo** la tarea.
*He **did** homework.*

Más práctica
Cuaderno *pp. 321–323*
Cuaderno para hispanohablantes *pp. 322–324*

@HOMETUTOR my.hrw.com
Leveled Practice
Conjuguemos.com

Differentiating Instruction

English Learners

Build Background Remind students that English also has verbs that are irregular in the past tense. Provide these examples:
Today I have... Yesterday I had...
Today I go... Yesterday I went...
Ask students to comment on how the past is constructed in their language of origin. Are there verbs that don't follow the pattern?

Inclusion

Alphabetic/Phonetic Awareness Write the preterite forms of **ser, ir,** and **hacer** on the board. Have students break each word into its individual phonetic components to figure out its pronunciation. For example, for the word **hice,** the **h** is silent, the **i** makes a long **e** sound, the **c** is soft, the **e** sounds similar to the long **a** in English.

¡AVANZA! Objective

- Present the preterite of **ir, ser,** and **hacer.**

Core Resource

- *Cuaderno,* pp. 321–323

Presentation Strategies

- Write the preterite forms of **ir** on the board or OHT. Point out that they do not have accent marks. Say the forms and have students repeat after you.
- Say sentences using preterite forms of **ir** and **ser** and have students tell you which verb you're using based on the context clues. For example: **Fui al zoológico. (ir) La montaña rusa fue muy divertida. (ser)**
- Write the preterite forms of **hacer.** Point out that the **h** at the beginning is silent.

STANDARDS

4.1 Compare languages
21st Century **Social and Cross-Cultural Skills,** English Learners

Warm Up Projectable Transparencies, 7-21

Qué + adjective Create an exclamation using **¡qué** + adjective! for each sentence.

1. El chico es muy alto.
2. La fiesta es divertida.
3. Paco es muy cómico.
4. El videojuego es muy interesante.

Answers: 1. ¡Qué alto! 2. ¡Qué divertida! 3. ¡Qué cómico! 4. ¡Qué interesante!

Communication

Grammar Activity

Have students listen to each sentence. They will raise their right hand if the sentence is in the present tense and raise their left hand if the sentence is in the preterite tense.

1. Ayer los amigos fueron al parque. (preterite)
2. Siempre hago mi tarea. (present)
3. El día fue muy aburrido. (preterite)

Communication

Common Error Alert

When working with the verb **hacer,** tell students to pay extra attention to the **usted/él/ella** that changes the *c* for a *z* in the preterite form: **hizo.** Have students practice writing sentences using **hizo,** for example, **Ella hizo la tarea muy bien.**

Objectives

- Practice using the preterite of **ir, ser,** and **hacer.**
- **Culture**: Discuss how paintings reflect a city's character.
- Practice places of interest and attractions; weekend activities

Core Resources

- *Cuaderno,* pp. 321–323
- Audio Program: TXT CD 7, track 15

Practice Sequence

- **Activity 5:** Controlled practice: preterite of **hacer**
- **Activity 6:** Controlled practice: preterite of **ser** and **ir,** places of interest, adjectives
- **Activity 7:** Transitional practice: preterite of **hacer, ser,** and **ir**
- **Activity 8:** Open-ended practice: preterite of **ir, hacer, -ar, -er, -ir** verbs, places of interest, weekend activities

STANDARDS

1.1 Engage in conversation, Acts. 6–8
1.2 Present information, Acts. 5–8, CC, PYP
2.1 Practices and perspectives, CC
4.1 Compare cultures, CC
21st Century **Communication,** Act. 8

Comparación cultural

Essential Question

Suggested Answer Many paintings reflect specific characteristics of a place, its political leaders, modes of transportation, and culture during a certain period of time.

About the Artist

Benito Quinquela Martín was born in Buenos Aires. He began taking art classes at the age of 14. In 1938, he opened the Museo de Bellas Artes de la Boca museum located in La Boca—the home and studio where he worked. It is now also known as Museo Quinquela Martín.

See Activity answers on p. 387

Práctica de GRAMÁTICA

5 Muchísimas llamadas

Leer Escribir

El sábado y el domingo Florencia, Mariano y Luciana hicieron 40 llamadas por teléfono. Completa la descripción de Mariano con la forma apropiada del pretérito de **hacer.** Luego contesta las preguntas 7 y 8. *(Complete Mariano's description with the correct preterite form of **hacer.** Then answer questions 7 and 8.)*

El fin de semana pasado, mis amigas y yo __1.__ 40 llamadas por teléfono. ¡Qué bárbaro! Luciana __2.__ cinco llamadas el sábado. Luciana y Florencia __3.__ el mismo (*same*) número de llamadas el domingo. Yo __4.__ dos más que ellas el domingo. Una persona en el grupo __5.__ ocho llamadas cada (*each*) día. Florencia __6.__ dos más que Luciana el sábado. ¿Cuántas llamadas __7.__ cada persona? ¿Cuántas llamadas __8.__ tú el fin de semana pasado?

Expansión:
Teacher Edition Only
Have students create three questions using the preterite of **hacer,** exchange them with a partner and answer each other's questions.

6 ¿Cómo fue el día?

Hablar Escribir

Muchas personas salieron ayer. Explica adónde fueron y si fue divertido o aburrido. *(Tell where these people went and if it was fun or boring.)*

modelo: nosotros / parque de diversiones / ☺
Fuimos al parque de diversiones. Fue divertido.

1. yo / museo / ☺	**4.** Florencia / centro / ☺
2. ustedes / acuario / ☹	**5.** tú / zoológico / ☺
3. mis amigos y yo / cine / ☹	**6.** mis padres / feria / ☹

Expansión
Interview your classmates to find out where they went yesterday and how it was.

Comparación cultural

El puerto de La Boca

How do paintings reflect a city's character? People from Buenos Aires, **Argentina,** are called *porteños,* meaning "people of the port." This reflects the essential role of the port in the nation's development. La Boca, the city's first port, is a famous neighborhood of Buenos Aires known for its brightly colored buildings. The artist Benito Quinquela Martín grew up in La Boca in the early 20th century, during the height of the port's development. His paintings capture the neighborhood's color and port activities.

Día de Trabajo *(1948),*
Benito Quinquela Martín

Compara con tu mundo *What are some port cities in the United States?*

Differentiating Instruction

Inclusion

Clear Structure Suggest that students follow these steps to complete Activity 5.
1. Read the sentence for content, skipping over the blank.
2. Point to the subject. If it is not a pronoun, determine the corresponding pronoun.
3. Find the correct preterite form of **hacer.**
4. Read the completed sentence aloud.

Multiple Intelligences

Visual Learners Have students use the Internet to find visual images of Argentina and Buenos Aires. Then have students use these images to repeat Activity 6. Direct them to replace the destination given in the prompt with a new destination.
Modelo: Fuimos a La Boca en Buenos Aires. Fue divertido.

7 Fueron a diferentes lugares

Escuchar
Escribir

Escucha las descripciones y contesta las preguntas. *(Listen and answer the questions.)*

1.

a. ¿Quiénes fueron?
b. ¿Qué hicieron?
c. ¿Cómo fue?

2.

a. ¿Quiénes fueron?
b. ¿Qué hicieron?
c. ¿Cómo fue?

3.

a. ¿Quiénes fueron?
b. ¿Qué hicieron?
c. ¿Cómo fue?

Audio Program
TXT CD 7 Track 15
Audio Script, TE p. 377b

8 ¡Qué divertido!

Hablar

Habla con otro(a) estudiante sobre adónde fuiste y qué hiciste el fin de semana pasado. *(Talk with a partner about where you went and what you did last weekend.)*

A ¿Fuiste al centro?
B Sí, fui al centro con mi familia.
A ¿Qué hicieron ustedes allí?
B Fuimos al cine y...

Estudiante A	Estudiante B
1. el parque de diversiones	ir de compras
2. el centro	mirar...
3. el museo	hacer esquí acuático
4. la playa	subir a...
5. el zoológico	pasar un rato
6. el estadio	comer
7. el restaurante	pasear
8. ¿ ?	¿ ?

Expansión
Write a summary of where you went and what you did last weekend.

Más práctica Cuaderno *pp. 321–323* Cuaderno para hispanohablantes *pp. 322–324*

Get Help Online
my.hrw.com

PARA Y PIENSA

Did you get it? Complete the following sentences with the correct preterite form of **hacer** and **ir** or **ser.** Then tell whether you used **ir** or **ser.**

1. Nosotros _____ la tarea; _____ muy fácil.
2. Yo _____ a la playa. _____ esquí acuático.
3. ¿ _____ ellos al parque? ¿Y qué _____ allí?

Differentiating Instruction

Slower-paced Learners

Read Before Listening Before listening to the descriptions in Activity 7, remind students to preview the questions and the photos. For each question, have students jot down notes regarding their predictions for the answer. **¿Quiénes fueron?** Describe who is on the picture. **¿Qué hicieron?** Look at the place where they are. **¿Cómo fue?** Look at the expressions on the people's faces.

Pre-AP

Expand and Elaborate As students complete Activity 8, tell them they should do all they can to keep the conversation going. Here is a possible continuation of the model:
Estudiante A: ¿Fue interesante la película?
Estudiante B: No, fue aburrida.
Estudiante A: ¡Qué lástima! ¿Qué hiciste después?
Estudiante B: Fui a comer con Sonia.

Communication

Grammar Activity

Have students write **Singular** on one index card and **Plural** on another. Call out the following verbs and have them hold up the correct card corresponding to the verb indicating a singular subject or a plural subject.

1. hizo
2. fueron
3. fui
4. hiciste
5. hicimos
6. hice

Answers: 1. singular; 2. plural; 3. singular; 4. singular; 5. plural; 6. singular

✓ Ongoing Assessment

Get Help Online
More Practice
my.hrw.com

PARA Y PIENSA

Peer Assessment Have pairs of students say their sentences aloud and correct each other. For additional practice, use Reteaching & Practice Copymasters URB 7, pp. 16, 17.

Answers Projectable Transparencies, 7-28 and 7-29

Answers for Activities on pp. 386, 387.

Activity 5
1. hicimos; **2.** hizo; **3.** hicieron; **4.** hice; **5.** hizo; **6.** hizo; **7.** hizo; **8.** hiciste

Activity 6
1. Fui al museo. Fue divertido.
2. Ustedes fueron al acuario. Fue aburrido.
3. Fuimos al cine. Fue aburrido.
4. Florencia fue al centro. Fue divertido.
5. Fuiste al zoológico. Fue divertido.
6. Mis padres fueron a la feria. Fue aburrido.

Activity 7
1. a. Florencia y su amiga fueron al parque de diversiones.
b. Subieron a la montaña rusa.
c. Fue horrible.
2. a. Luciana y su hermano fueron a la feria del libro.
b. Luciana compró tres libros.
c. Fue interesante.
3. a. Mariano y Florencia fueron al museo.
b. Pasaron todo el día allí y vieron un Picasso.
c. Fue divertido.

Activity 8 Answers will vary. Sample answers include:
1. A: ¿Fuiste al parque de diversiones? **B:** Sí, fui con mi prima. **A:** ¿Qué hicieron ustedes allí? **B:** Subimos a la montaña rusa.

Para y piensa
1. hicimos, fue (ser); **2.** fui (ir), Hice; **3.** Fueron (ir), hicieron

¡AVANZA! **Objectives**
- Identify preterite forms of **ir, ser,** and **hacer** in context.
- Identify lesson vocabulary in context.
- Recycle: places around town.
- Pronunciation: Practice the letters **ll** and **y.**

Core Resources
- Video Program: DVD 2
- Audio Program: TXT CD 7 tracks 16, 17

Presentation Strategies
- Have students scan the dialogue, looking for examples of preterite forms of **ir, ser,** and **hacer**.
- Play the audio as students follow in their textbooks.
- Show the video.

Practice Sequence
- **Activity 9:** Telehistoria comprehension
- **Activity 10:** Transitional practice: preterite of regular verbs and **ir**; Recycle: places around town

STANDARDS
1.1 Engage in conversation, Act. 10, PYP
1.2 Understand language, Acts. 9-10, PYP
4.1 Compare languages, Pronunciación
21st Century **Communication,** Act. 10

Warm Up
Projectable Transparencies, 7-21

Preterite of ir, ser, hacer Complete the sentences with the correct preterite form of the verb.
1. Ayer yo _____ al acuario. (ir)
2. ¿Qué _____ tú en el museo? (hacer)
3. La feria _____ muy interesante. (ser)
4. ¿Adónde _____ ustedes ayer? (ir)
5. Yo no _____ nada. (hacer)

Answers: 1. fui; 2. hiciste; 3. fue; 4. fueron; 5. hice

Video Summary
@HOMETUTOR VideoPlus my.hrw.com

A man behind a ticket counter tells Mariano that Trini went to the Ferris wheel. Then another man tells Florencia that Trini went to eat. When they arrive at the food court, Trini is not there.

GRAMÁTICA en contexto

¡AVANZA! **Goal:** Notice how Mariano, Florencia, and Luciana use the preterite tense to talk about what they and others did. Then use **ir, ser,** and **hacer** in the preterite to ask about what others did. ***Actividades 9–10***

¿Recuerdas? Places around town p. 219

Telehistoria escena 2

@HOMETUTOR my.hrw.com View, Read and Record

STRATEGIES

Cuando lees
Identify verb forms in context Identify preterite-tense forms of **ir** in this scene. For each, find out where the character(s) went and why.

Cuando escuchas
Sort out the speakers In this scene, characters use **dice que...** to report what another person says. Listen for who reports what was said. What information do they report?

VIDEO DVD
AUDIO

Luciana: ¡Ay! Che, Mariano, ¿adónde fuiste?
Mariano: Yo fui a ver dónde podemos encontrar a Trini. Sé dónde está.
Luciana: ¿Cómo lo sabes?
Mariano: Fue el señor de la ventanilla. Él dice que Trini fue a la vuelta al mundo.
Florencia: Mariano, ¡qué bárbaro! ¡Vamos!

They start to walk. Florencia stops to speak to someone, then catches up.

Florencia: El señor dice que Trini y sus amigos fueron a comer.
Mariano: ¿Trini fue a comer? ¡Ay, no! ¿Qué podemos hacer? Tenemos que ir a buscarla.

They reach the food court but don't see Trini.

Luciana: Fuimos a la vuelta al mundo, fuimos al restaurante. ¿Dónde está Trini? Nunca la vamos a encontrar.

Continuará... p. 393

También se dice

Argentina Luciana uses the word **che** to greet Mariano in a friendly way. In other Spanish-speaking countries you might hear:
- **México cuate**
- **España tío(a), colega**
- **Colombia llave**
- **Puerto Rico, Venezuela y otros países pana**

Differentiating Instruction

Pre-AP

Identify the Main Idea Ask students to pick one character from the Telehistoria. Have them read their character's lines several times to determine what their character knows, and how their character gets his or her information. Invite three volunteers to act out the scene without using their books.

Multiple Intelligences

Interpersonal Have students read through Telehistoria Escena 2 twice silently. The first time, instruct them to read the script for meaning. The second time, tell them to read it for emotion. Ask volunteers to take turns reading lines aloud, emphasizing the emotional tone. Have students name some emotions Mariano and Florencia go through.

9 *Comprensión del episodio* Fueron a buscarla

Escuchar Leer

Contesta las preguntas. *(Answer the questions.)*

1. ¿Quién habló con el señor de la ventanilla?
2. ¿Quién fue a la vuelta al mundo?
3. ¿Quién habló con otro señor en el parque?
4. ¿Qué dice el señor?
5. ¿Por qué fueron al restaurante los chicos?
6. ¿Quién dice que nunca van a encontrar a Trini?

Expansión:
Teacher Edition Only
Ask students to write a short summary of the Episodio, using the questions in Activity 9 as a guide.

10 ¡A jugar! Adivina

¿Recuerdas? Places around town p. 219

Hablar

Trabaja con otros estudiantes. Sin decir adónde fuiste, explícales que hiciste. Ellos tienen que adivinar el lugar. *(Give clues about what you did so your partners can guess where you went.)*

un partido de...	el parque de diversiones
el cine	un concierto
el centro comercial	¿ ?
la playa	
el museo	

A Compré bloqueador de sol y nadé en el mar.

B ¿Fuiste a la piscina?

C ¿Fuiste a la playa?

Expansión
For each place, tell how you got there and how it was.

AUDIO

Pronunciación Las letras LL y Y

The letter combination **ll** in Spanish sounds like the English *y* in *yet*. The **y** has the same sound unless it stands alone or is at the end of a word, in which case the **y** is pronounced like the *ee* in the English word *see*.

Listen and repeat.

llamar	**tobillo**	**rodilla**	**ella**	**galleta**
yo	**ayer**	**playa**	**mayo**	**desayuno**
y	**hay**	**muy**	**hoy**	

Yo me llamo Marco y ella es Yolanda.

Hoy voy a la playa de Marbella. Es muy bonita.

Get Help Online
my.hrw.com

PARA Y PIENSA

Did you get it? Ask Mariano the questions to which he would provide these statements as answers. Use **ir, ser,** and **hacer.**

1. Florencia, Luciana y yo fuimos al restaurante.
2. Yo hablé con el señor de la ventanilla.
3. El día fue divertido.

Differentiating Instruction

Heritage Language Learners

Increase Accuracy Create two columns on the board, one with the heading **y,** the other with the heading **ll.** Remind students that since these letters represent similar sounds, they can create spelling problems. Say a number of words containing **y** or **ll** aloud. Ask volunteers to write each word in the correct column.

Inclusion

Clear Structure To help students organize their thoughts in Activity 10, have them create a concept web around the name of the place they went to. Have them add ideas to the outside to help construct their clues. Finally, have students cover up the center with a self-sticking note so their partner can't see the answer.

Communication

Intrapersonal Mode

Telehistoria After reading the Telehistoria, have students respond to the following statements by writing **sí** if true and **no** if false.

1. Mariano dice que sabe donde está Trini. (sí)
2. Trini fue a la montaña rusa. (no)
3. Trini fue a la ventanilla. (no)
4. Trini fue a comer. (sí)

Get Help Online
More Practice
my.hrw.com

✓ Ongoing Assessment

PARA Y PIENSA

Peer Assessment Ask students to work in pairs to write the questions for the Para y piensa, and also to write the answers. Then, ask them to correct spelling and punctuation. For additional practice, use Reteaching & Practice Copymasters URB 7 pp. 16, 18, 23.

Answers Projectable Transparencies, 7-29

Activity 9

1. Mariano
2. Mariano, Luciana, Florencia
3. Florencia
4. El señor dice que Trini fue a comer.
5. Fueron a buscar a Trini.
6. Luciana

Activity 10 Answers will vary. Sample answers:

A. Compré un boleto y fui al estadio.
B. ¿Viste un partido de fútbol?
C. ¿Viste un partido de básquetbol?
A. Compré un boleto y fui al cine.
B. ¿Viste una película?
C. ¿Viste un concierto?
A. Compré una falda.
B. ¿Fuiste al centro comercial?
C. ¿Fuiste de compras?
A. Compré un bloqueador de sol y fui a nadar.
B. ¿Fuiste a la playa?
C. ¿Fuiste a la piscina?
A. Compré un boleto y fui al museo.
B. ¿Viste el arte de Picasso?
C. ¿Viste muchos libros?
A. Compré un boleto y fui al parque de diversiones.
B. ¿Fuiste a la montaña rusa?
C. ¿Fuiste a los autitos chocadores?
A. Compré un boleto y fui a escuchar música.
B. ¿Fuiste a un concierto?
C. ¿Fuiste a una fiesta?

Para y piensa

1. ¿Quiénes fueron al restaurante? / ¿Adónde fueron Florencia, Luciana y tú?
2. ¿Qué hiciste?
3. ¿Cómo fue el día?

¡AVANZA! **Objective**

- Present pronouns after prepositions.

Core Resource

- *Cuaderno*, pp. 324-326

Presentation Strategies

- Write the pronouns used after prepositions on the board or on a transparency.
- Remind students that they have already learned these pronouns with **gustar.**
- Check comprehension of pronouns by pointing to yourself or other people to elicit the correct pronoun.
- Write several sentences using **conmigo** and **contigo.** Ask students to copy them in their notebooks and to present additional examples to the class.

STANDARDS

4.1 Compare languages

Warm Up Projectable Transparencies, 7-22

Preterite of ir, ser and hacer Write the preterite form of the verb indicated for each subject:

1. tú (ir) **4.** nosotros (ir)
2. ella (hacer) **5.** ustedes (hacer)
3. yo (ser) **6.** usted (ser)

Answers: 1. fuiste; 2. hizo; 3. fui; 4. fuimos; 5. hicieron; 6. fue

Comparisons
English Grammar Connection

Point out that in English, the only prepositional pronoun that is the same as a subject pronoun is **you.** In Spanish, however, all of the prepositional pronouns are the same as the subject pronouns except for **mí** and **ti.** Emphasize to students the use of the accented "i" in **mí.** The accent serves to distinguish **mí (me)** from **mi (my).**

Communication
Common Error Alert

Monitor students closely for correct use of **conmigo** and **contigo.** Point out that the preposition and the pronoun form one word.

Presentación de GRAMÁTICA

¡AVANZA! **Goal:** Learn what pronouns are used after prepositions. Then practice them to give and accept or decline invitations. ***Actividades 11–14***
¿Recuerdas? Stem-changing verbs: **e → i** p. 228

English Grammar Connection: Prepositions (such as *at, for, in, on,* and *with* in English) link a noun or a **pronoun** with another word in a sentence. In both English and Spanish, some of the pronouns that follow these prepositions are different from the subject pronouns.

I have a ticket. The ticket is **for me.** **Yo** tengo un boleto. El boleto es **para mí.**

Pronouns After Prepositions

ANIMATEDGRAMMAR my.hrw.com

Use **pronouns** after **prepositions** like **a, con, de,** and **para.**

Here's how: **Pronouns** that follow prepositions are the same as the subject pronouns in all forms except **mí** (**yo**) and **ti** (**tú**).

Pronouns After Prepositions	
mí	nosotros(as)
ti	vosotros(as)
usted, él, ella	ustedes, ellos(as)

La montaña rusa está **detrás de mí.**
*The roller coaster is **behind me.***

El teléfono celular está **cerca de ti.**
*The cellular phone is **near you.***

When you use **mí** and **ti** after the preposition **con,** they combine with **con** to form the words **conmigo** and **contigo.**

¿Vas al museo **conmigo**?
*Are you going to the museum **with me**?*

Sí, voy **contigo.**
*Yes, I'm going **with you.***

¿Recuerdas? You use these pronouns with verbs like **gustar** to emphasize or clarify which person you are talking about (see p. 42).

A **él** le **gusta** ir al zoológico. *He likes to go to the zoo.*
A **ella** le **gusta** ir al zoológico. *She likes to go to the zoo.*
A **usted** le **gusta** ir al zoológico. *You like to go to the zoo.*

Más práctica
Cuaderno *pp. 324–326*
Cuaderno para hispanohablantes *pp. 325–328*

HOMETUTOR my.hrw.com
Leveled Practice

Differentiating Instruction

Inclusion

Cumulative Instruction Review with students prepositions they already know. Remind them that in Unit 2, Lesson 2 they learned many prepositions used to talk about location. Direct students to p. 115 to review them.

Multiple Intelligences

Kinesthetic On the board, write a number of prepositions, such as **detrás de, cerca de, para, de,** and **con.** Have students pass around an object. Each time the object gets moved, ask a volunteer to describe where it is using a pronoun. **El lápiz está detrás de mí. El lápiz está cerca de ella.**

Práctica de GRAMÁTICA

11 Invitaciones para ella

Escribir

Hoy hace sol y Luciana prefiere hacer algo al aire libre. Sus amigos la invitan a varios lugares. Escribe sus respuestas, usando pronombres. *(Luciana wants to do something outdoors. Write her responses to these invitations, using pronouns.)*

modelo: ¿Quieres ir al cine con nosotros?
No, no quiero ir al cine con ustedes.

1. ¿Te gustaría ir a la playa conmigo?
2. ¿Quieres comprar ropa para ti en el centro comercial?
3. ¿Quieres tomar fotos de nosotros en el parque?
4. ¿Te gustaría ir al Café Internet con Mariano y Florencia?
5. ¿Puedes preparar la comida para mí y para mi hermano?
6. ¿Puedo ir al zoológico contigo?

Expansión:
Teacher Edition Only
Have students ask and answer two more questions about what outdoor activities Luciana wants to do.

12 Te invito

Hablar

Llama a otro(a) estudiante por teléfono para hacerle invitaciones a estos lugares. Él o ella va a decir que va con otra(s) persona(s). *(Make phone calls to invite a classmate to go to these places. Your partner will say that he or she is going with someone else.)*

modelo: mis tíos

A ¿Aló? ¿Puedo hablar con Ana?

B Hola, Laura. Soy yo. ¿Cómo estás?

A Bien. ¿Te gustaría ir al museo conmigo?

B Lo siento, pero no puedo ir contigo. Voy a ir con mis tíos.

1. él

2. ellas

3. mi hermano

4. ellos

5. mis padres

6. ella

Expansión
Invite your partner to three more places.

Objective

- Practice using pronouns after prepositions.

Practice Sequence

- **Activity 11:** Transitional practice: pronouns after prepositions, making invitations
- **Activity 12:** Open-ended practice: pronouns after prepositions, extending, accepting and declining invitations

STANDARDS

1.1 Engage in conversation, Act. 12
1.3 Present information, Act. 11
21st Century **Communication,** Act. 12/Heritage Language Learners/Personalize It

Long-term Retention

Personalize It

Have each student write a letter to a classmate (draw names to decide who writes to whom). Tell them to pretend their classmate is coming for a visit. They should ask what the person wants to do (**quieres**), what he/she is able to do (**puedes**), and what he/she would like to do (**te gustaría**). Once completed, deliver the letter to the appropriate person and respond.

Differentiating Instruction

Slower-paced Learners

Peer-study Support Have students work on Activity 11 with a partner. Students should take turns asking the questions as if they were inviting their partner to the activity mentioned. The partner should then answer the question. Finally, both students should work together to write the answer.

Heritage Language Learners

Support What They Know Ask students to share other helpful phrases for talking on the telephone. How would they ask to take or leave a message? How might they say that someone will be right back, or is on the other line? What are some informal phrases to say hello and goodbye on the phone?

Answers Projectable Transparencies, 7-29 and 7-30

Activity 11

1. Sí, me gustaría ir a la playa contigo.
2. No, no quiero comprar ropa para mí en el centro comercial.
3. Sí, quiero tomar fotos de ustedes en el parque.
4. No, no me gustaría ir al Café Internet con ellos.
5. No, no puedo preparar la comida para ustedes.
6. Sí, puedes ir al zoológico conmigo.

Activity 12 Answers should follow the format:
¿Aló? Puedo hablar con... ¿Te gustaría ir (place) conmigo? Lo siento, pero no puedo ir contigo. Voy a ir con (person).

1. al zoológico; con él
2. a la feria; con ellas
3. al acuario; con mi hermano
4. al parque de diversiones; con ellos
5. a la biblioteca; con mis padres
6. al restaurante; con ella

Objectives
- Practice using pronouns after prepositions.
- **Culture:** Learn about food from Argentina.
- Recycle: stem-changing verbs: **e → i**

Core Resource
- *Cuaderno,* pp. 324–326

Practice Sequence
- **Activity 13:** Open-ended: pronouns after prepositions
- **Activity 14:** Open-ended: pronouns after prepositions, foods; Recycle: **e → i** stem-changing verbs.

STANDARDS
1.2 Understand language, Act. 13, PYP
1.3 Present information, Act. 13
4.2 Compare cultures, Act. 14 CC
21st Century **Information Literacy,** Multiple Intelligences

Comparación cultural

Essential Question
Suggested Answer The location of a region often determines the foods that are eaten there. For example, people living along the coast are likely to eat more seafood.

Expanded Information
The Argentine **asado** begins with **chorizo** (sausage) and **morcilla** (blood sausage) and is followed by **bife.** The classic **asado** sauce is **chimichurri,** which consists of garlic, red pepper, parsley, oregano, peppers, onion, thyme, laurel, olive oil, and balsamic vinegar. In Argentina, **bife de chorizo** is a very thick cut of beef (sirloin). It should *not* be confused with the term **chorizo**, whick refers to pork.

✓ Ongoing Assessment
Get Help Online
More Practice
my.hrw.com

PARA Y PIENSA **Intervention** If students have problems completing the sentences in Para y piensa, have them review p. 390 and repeat Activity 11 on p. 391. For additional practice, use Reteaching & Practice Copymasters URB 7 pp. 19, 20, 24.

See Activity answers on p. 393.

13 ¿Y tú?

Hablar
Escribir

Contesta las preguntas. Usa pronombres en tus respuestas. *(Answer the questions, using pronouns.)*

1. ¿Te gustaría subir a una montaña rusa con tus amigos?
2. ¿Tienes miedo cuando no hay nadie contigo?
3. ¿Qué hay delante de ti ahora?
4. ¿A qué museo te gustaría ir con los estudiantes de tu clase?
5. ¿Qué te gusta hacer con tus amigos durante el fin de semana?
6. ¿Cómo contestas el teléfono cuando hay una llamada para ti?

Expansión
Write five original questions using prepositions for your classmates to answer.

14 En un restaurante argentino

¿Recuerdas? Stem-changing verbs: **e → i** p. 228

Escribir

Comparación cultural

La comida argentina
What factors influence a country's cuisine? In the late 18th century, many *estancias,* or ranches, were developed on the sprawling grasslands, or *pampas,* of **Argentina.** More beef is eaten per person in Argentina than in any other country. Some people may have *bife,* or steak, twice a day. A traditional weekend activity of many Argentines is an *asado,* or outdoor barbecue with family and friends. Steakhouses, known as *parrillas,* are also common. Argentinean cuisine is not limited to meat, however. Because of Argentina's many Italian immigrants, dishes such as pizza and pasta are also popular.

Un gaucho prepara bife en una estancia

Compara con tu mundo *What has influenced the common foods available in your area?*

Restaurante
Mirasol

Parrilla	
Bife de chorizo	$11,00
Bife de lomo	$12,00
Pastas	
Ravioles de ricota	$9,00
Canelones	$9,00
Pizzas	
Cuatro quesos	
Vegetariana *(espinaca y tomates)*	
mediana: $11,50	grande: $15,00

Escribe sobre una visita a este restaurante. Di quiénes van contigo y describe qué piden y por qué. *(Write about a trip to this restaurant. Tell who goes with you, what they order, and why.)*

modelo: Mis padres y mi hermano van conmigo al Restaurante Mirasol. Mi padre pide el bife de chorizo porque a él le gusta la carne...

Más práctica Cuaderno *pp. 324–326* Cuaderno para hispanohablantes *pp. 325–328*

Get Help Online
my.hrw.com

PARA Y PIENSA

Did you get it? Complete the sentences with the correct pronoun according to the hint in parentheses.
1. ¿Te gustaría ir con ____ ? (Simón y yo)
2. El boleto es para ____ . (tú)
3. Quiero ir con ____ . (mis amigos)

Differentiating Instruction

Inclusion
Synthetic/Analytic Support Have students copy the questions from Activity 13 onto sentence strips. Instruct them to separate each word by cutting the strip into pieces. Discuss with students which words will change to form the answer. For example, **Te** becomes **Me,** and **tus amigos** becomes **ellos.** Have them reassemble the pieces, and copy the response.

Multiple Intelligences
Naturalist Have students work in small groups to research the **pampas** of Argentina. Inform students that they will use the information they find to construct a diorama of this geographic area. What plants, animals, and other natural resources will they include?

Todo junto

¡AVANZA! **Goal:** ***Show what you know*** Pay attention to the different characters and their roles in this scene. Then practice using the preterite forms of **ir, ser,** and **hacer** and prepositions after pronouns to tell a friend what activities you did. ***Actividades 15–19***

Telehistoria completa

@HOMETUTOR my.hrw.com View, Read and Record

STRATEGIES

Cuando lees

Recall and reason As you read, recall the previous scenes to understand how hard the teenagers have tried to find Trini Salgado. Analyze why another woman shows up at the information booth.

Cuando escuchas

Compare characters' approaches Listen for how Florencia assigns tasks and compare it with how the announcer calls for Trini. What differences do you hear in their approaches to making something happen?

Escena 1 *Resumen*
Florencia va al parque de diversiones para buscar a Trini Salgado, pero primero necesita encontrar a Mariano y a su amiga, Luciana.

Escena 2 *Resumen*
Los amigos van a la vuelta al mundo y al restaurante para buscar a Trini Salgado, pero no la encuentran.

Escena 3

VIDEO DVD

AUDIO

Luciana: *(eyeing a food stand)* Empanadas, ¡qué ricas! Voy a comprar unas.

Florencia: Gracias, Luciana. ¿Por qué no compras un refresco para mí, y unas empanadas para nosotros dos? Y Mariano, ¿te gustaría venir conmigo a buscar a Trini a los autitos chocadores?

Luciana speaks with a manager, who makes an announcement over the loudspeaker.

(crackling) «Atención, por favor, señorita Trini Salgado, por favor, la esperan en la puerta, señorita Trini Salgado».

Florencia y Mariano: ¡Vamos!

A woman, not the famous soccer player, arrives at the booth.

Mujer: Señor, ¡yo soy Trini Salgado!

Florencia: ¿Trini Salgado? ¿La jugadora de fútbol?

Mujer: *(confused)* ¿La jugadora de fútbol?

Differentiating Instruction

Pre-AP

Support Ideas with Details Copy Luciana's last line from Telehistoria escena 2 on the board. **Nunca la vamos a encontrar.** Ask students to recall events from the Telehistoria that support Luciana's feeling that they will never find Trini Salgado.

Heritage Language Learners

Support What They Know Ask students if they have ever experienced a mix-up because two people had the same or similar names. Who were the people, what were their names, and what was the confusion?

¡AVANZA! **Objective**
- Integrate lesson content.

Core Resources
- Video Program: DVD 2
- Audio Program: TXT CD 7 track 18

Presentation Strategies
- Ask students what they remember about the Telehistoria so far.
- Have students listen to the audio paying special attention to the uses of pronouns before prepositions.
- Show the video.

STANDARDS
1.2 Understand language

Warm Up Projectable Transparencies, 7-22

Pronouns After Prepositions Complete the phrase using the correct prepositional pronoun:
1. detrás de ____ (las estudiantes)
2. con ____ (yo)
3. para ____ (tú)

Answers: 1. ellas; 2. conmigo; 3. ti

Video Summary

@HOMETUTOR VideoPlus my.hrw.com

Luciana goes to a food stand and buys empanadas and drinks for herself and Florencia. Then Luciana has a manager make an announcement calling Trini Salgado to the gate. A woman named Trini Salgado comes to the booth, but she is not the famous soccer player.

Answers Projectable Transparencies, 7-30

Answers for Activities on p. 392.

Activity 13
1. Sí, (No, no) me gustaría subir a una montaña rusa con ellos.
2. Sí, (No, no) tengo miedo cuando no hay nadie conmigo.
3. Hay ____ delante de mí ahora.
4. Me gustaría ir a (name of a museum) con ellos.
5. Me gusta (activity) con ellos el fin de semana.
6. Cuando hay una llamada para mí, digo ____.

Activity 14 Answers will vary. Sample answers include:

Mi prima va conmigo al Restaurante Mirasol. Ella pide canelones porque tiene hambre.

Para y piensa **1.** nosotros; **2.** ti; **3.** ellos

Objective
- Practice using and integrating lesson vocabulary and grammar.

Core Resources
- *Cuaderno,* pp 327–328
- Audio Program: TXT CD 7 tracks 14, 16, 18, 19, 20

Practice Sequence
- **Activities 15, 16:** Telehistoria comprehension
- **Activity 17:** Open-ended practice: speaking
- **Activity 18:** Open-ended practice: reading, listening, speaking
- **Activity 19:** Open-ended practice: writing

STANDARDS
1.1 Engage in conversation, Acts. 17–18
1.2 Understand language, Acts. 15–18, PYP
1.3 Present Information, Act. 16, Acts. 18–19
21st Century **Creativity and Innovation,** Multiple Intelligences

✓ Ongoing Assessment

Rubric Activity 17

Speaking Criteria	Maximum Credit	Partial Credit	Minimum Credit
Content	Conversation contains many ideas.	Conversation contains some ideas.	Conversation contains few ideas.
Communication	Conversation is well organized.	Parts of the conversation are well organized.	Conversation is disorganized.
Accuracy	Conversation has few mistakes in grammar and vocabulary.	Conversation has some mistakes in grammar and vocabulary.	Conversation has many mistakes in grammar and vocabulary.

Answers Projectable Transparencies, 7-30

Activity 15
1. ...para el parque de diversiones.
2. Florencia y Mariano hablaron por teléfono.
3. Mariano habló con el señor de la ventanilla.
4. ...comprar empanadas y un refresco.
5. ...a los autitos chocadores para ...
6. Los amigos encontraron a Trini Salgado, pero no es la jugadora de fútbol.

Answers continue on p. 395.

15 *Comprensión de los episodios* ¡No es cierto!

Escuchar
Leer

Corrige los errores en estas oraciones. *(Correct the errors.)*

1. Luciana y Mariano compraron boletos para el zoológico.
2. Luciana y Mariano hablaron por teléfono.
3. Florencia habló con el señor de la ventanilla.
4. Luciana fue a comprar hamburguesas y un café.
5. Florencia invitó a Mariano a acompañarla a la montaña rusa para buscar a Trini.
6. Los amigos encontraron a Trini Salgado, la jugadora de fútbol.

Expansión:
Teacher Edition Onl
Have students write three false sentences based o the three episodes and exchange them with another student. Students correct each other's sentences.

16 *Comprensión de los episodios* ¿Qué pasó?

Escuchar
Leer

Explica lo que pasó en los episodios. Menciona como mínimo dos cosas para cada foto. *(Tell what happened in the episodes. Mention at least two things for each.)*

1.

2.

3.

Expansión:
Teacher Edition Only
Have students writ a different ending for the last episode of the Telehistoria.

17 Unas llamadas telefónicas

Digital performance space

Hablar

STRATEGY Hablar
Expand and use the list The list contains an open topic, signified by **¿ ?** Expand the list by including three or four new ideas of your own. Use as many ideas as possible during the phone conversation, making them understandable to your partner.

Trabaja con otro(a) estudiante. Haz varias llamadas por teléfono, usando las ideas de la lista. Presenta la mejor conversación a la clase. *(Have phone conversations with a partner, using the ideas on the list. Share your best conversation with the class.)*

Para organizarte:
- Invita a la persona al parque de diversiones o a otro lugar.
- Habla sobre adónde fuiste y qué hiciste durante la semana pasada.
- ¿ ?

A ¿Aló?
B Buenas tardes. ¿Puedo hablar con Andrew, por favor?

Expansión
Leave a phone message for a friend who is not at home.

Differentiating Instruction

Slower-paced Learners

Sentence Completion Have students copy each of the sentences from Activity 15 onto a piece of paper. Instruct them to cross out the incorrect information, and replace it with a blank. They should fill in the blank with the correct information. Example:
Luciano y Mariano compraron boletos para *el parque de diversiones.*

Pre-AP

Expand and Elaborate Before starting Activity 17, give students this "pre-speaking" exercise. Have each pair decide on a topic and write it at the top of a large sheet of paper. Have them divide the paper into two columns. Tell students to take turns writing down notes and ideas for their half of the conversation.

18 Integración

Digital performance space

Leer
Escuchar
Hablar

Lee la nota y escucha el mensaje telefónico. Decide qué invitación quieres aceptar, y deja un mensaje para Álvaro y después para Carlos para decirles si vas a ir o no. *(Decide which invitation you want to accept and then respond to both invitations.)*

Fuente 1 Nota

3 P.M.

Llamó Álvaro. Ayer fue a la ventanilla del zoológico y compró dos boletos. Tienen una exhibición con elefantes y gorilas de África. Quiere saber si te gustaría ir con él mañana, a la una y media de la tarde. Álvaro te invita; no necesitas dinero. Llámalo a su casa, y si no está allí, deja un mensaje en su teléfono celular.

Fuente 2 Mensaje telefónico

Listen and take notes
- ¿Qué hizo Carlos anteayer?
- ¿Qué quiere hacer mañana?
- ¿Cuál es el problema?

modelo: Hola,... Me gustaría...
(Hola,... Lo siento...)

Audio Program
TXT CD 7 Tracks 19, 20
Audio Script, TE p. 377b

Expansión:
Teacher Edition Only
Have students work with a partner to practice extending an invitation to go somewhere and accepting or declining the invitation.

19 Una carta para un(a) amigo(a)

Digital performance space

Escribir

Escribe una carta sobre adónde fuiste durante la semana pasada y qué hiciste. También incluye una invitación. *(Write a letter about where you went and what you did last week. Also include an invitation.)*

modelo: ¿Sabes qué? La semana pasada fui a la feria con mis amigos. Compré helados para ellos y...

Writing Criteria	Excellent	Good	Needs Work
Content	Your letter includes a lot of information.	Your letter includes some information.	Your letter includes little information.
Communication	Most of your letter is organized and easy to follow.	Parts of your letter are organized and easy to follow.	Your letter is disorganized and hard to follow.
Accuracy	Your letter has few mistakes in grammar and vocabulary.	Your letter has some mistakes in grammar and vocabulary.	Your letter has many mistakes in grammar and vocabulary.

Expansión
Write your friend's response to your invitation.

Más práctica Cuaderno *pp. 327–328* Cuaderno para hispanohablantes *pp. 329–330*

Get Help Online
my.hrw.com

PARA Y PIENSA

Did you get it? Create sentences using the preterite form of each verb and the correct pronoun after each preposition.
1. Florencia / hacer / una cena para (Mariano)
2. Las empanadas / ser / para (Florencia y Mariano)
3. Mariano / ir / con (Florencia) a los autitos chocadores

Long-term Retention

Pre-AP Integration

Activity 18 Ask students to work in pairs to write a description of a visit to an amusement park, zoo, or aquarium. They may use a glossary or a Spanish/English dictionary. Have them correct each other's writing.

✓ Ongoing Assessment

Rubric Activity 18
Listening/Speaking

Proficient	Not There Yet
Student takes detailed notes, decides which invitation to accept, and responds correctly.	Student takes few notes and has difficulty responding correctly to the invitation.

To customize your own rubrics, use the ***Generate Success*** *Rubric Generator and Graphic Organizers.*

✓ Ongoing Assessment

Get Help Online
More Practice
my.hrw.com

PARA Y PIENSA

Quick Check If students have difficulty in answering the questions, have them review p. 385. For additional practice, use Reteaching & Practice Copymasters URB 7 pp. 19, 21.

Differentiating Instruction

Multiple Intelligences

Visual Learners Encourage interested students to convert the pictures and their stories in Telehistoria completa on p. 393 into a comic book format. Students can redraw the pictures using word balloons and thought bubbles to show each character's words and thoughts. Give students the chance to share their creations with the group.

Heritage Language Learners

Writing Skills Before completing Activity 19, review the standard form of a friendly letter with students. Provide a model that shows proper placement of the date, greeting, and closing. Remind students to tailor the tone of their language to their audience. Are they writing this letter and invitation to a best friend or a grandparent? For example, **Querido... Atentamente... con afecto...**

Answers Projectable Transparencies, 7-30 and 7-31

Answers continued from p. 394.

Activity 16 Answers will vary. Sample answer: Florencia va al parque de diversiones. Habla por teléfono con Mariano...

Activity 17 Answers will vary. Sample answers:
A. Hola Marcos. ¿Quieres ir a la feria mañana?
B. No puedo. Tengo que estudiar.

Activity 18 Answers will vary. Sample answers: Hola Álvaro, es Marta. Me gustaría acompañarte al zoológico. Llámame esta noche. ¡Gracias!

Activity 19 Answers will vary. Sample answers:Hola. La semana pasada fui al museo con Juana. Vimos muchos cuadros...

Para y piensa
1. Florencia hizo una cena para él.
2. Las empanadas fueron para ellos.
3. Mariano fue con ella a los autitos chocadores.

Objectives
- **Culture:** Read about two unusual museums in Argentina and Bolivia.
- Compare the two museums in terms of name, location, focus, and exhibits.
- Talk about museums you have visited.

Core Resources
- Audio Program: TXT CD 7 track 21

Presentation Strategies
- Ask students to look at the photos on pp. 396 and 397. Ask quick comprehension questions: **¿El Museo al Aire Libre está en una calle? ¿Qué hay en el museo? ¿Qué hay en el museo de La Paz, Bolivia?**
- Have students read the text, listing any words they don't know. Ask them to see if they might be able to guess the meaning of the words on their lists. Go over context clues to help them with any they still don't know.
- Have students listen to the audio, paying special attention to the topics listed in the strategy.

STANDARDS
1.2 Understand language
2.2 Products and perspectives
4.2 Compare cultures
21st Century **Creativity and Innovation,** Multiple Intelligencies: Musical/Rythmic/Group Work

Warm Up
Projectable Transparencies, 7-23

Pronouns After Prepositions Complete the answers with the correct pronoun.

1. ¿Quieres comer con nosotros? Sí, quiero comer con ____.
2. ¿Puedes preparar la comida para mí? No, no puedo preparar la comida para ____.
3. ¿Quieres comprar ropa para ti? No, no quiero comprar ropa para ____.
4. ¿Te gustaría salir con Julia y Marisa? No, no me gustaría salir con ____.

Answers: 1. ustedes; 2. ti; 3. mí; 4. ellas

Culture
Background Information
La Boca is also home to the famous soccer team, Boca Juniors. Their stadium, La Bombonera, is located there.

Lectura cultural

Additional readings at my.hrw.com SPANISH InterActive Reader

¡AVANZA! **Goal:** Read about non-traditional museums in Argentina and Bolivia. Then compare the two museums and talk about museums that you have visited.

Comparación cultural

AUDIO

Museos excepcionales

STRATEGY Leer
Compare museums Make a table to compare the two museums by name (**nombre**), location (**ubicación**), focus (**enfoque**), and exhibits (**exhibiciones**).

	1.	2.
nombre		
ubicación		
enfoque		
exhibiciones		

¿Qué imaginas cuando piensas en un museo? Muchas personas imaginan cuartos formales con obras[1] de arte. Hay museos en Latinoamérica que celebran su cultura y también dan una experiencia diferente, sin[2] tantas restricciones como un museo tradicional.

El Museo al Aire Libre[3] no tiene ni puertas ni paredes[4], pero es uno de los museos más populares de Buenos Aires. Está en el corazón de La Boca, una sección de Buenos Aires cerca del mar, en una calle pequeña que se llama el Caminito. Allí viven muchos artistas argentinos en sus famosas casas multicolores.

[1] works [2] without [3] Open-air [4] walls

Argentina

El Museo al Aire Libre en Buenos Aires, Argentina

Differentiating Instruction

Slower-paced Learners
Peer-study Support Have students work with a partner to read the selection together. Instruct partners to take turns reading and repeating sentences aloud.

Multiple Intelligences
Visual Learners Have interested students set up their own **Museo al Aire Libre** in a public space at your school such as a courtyard, entryway, or hallway. Ask for volunteers to contribute samples of their own artwork of various media. Each artist should also prepare a card with the work's title and a short description.

El Museo de Instrumentos Musicales en La Paz, Bolivia

El Caminito sirve como un marco[5] natural para diversas obras de arte: pinturas[6], esculturas y murales. Es posible caminar por la calle, ver obras de arte, comer en cafés, escuchar música y mirar a personas que bailan el tango.

La cultura boliviana, especialmente la música, tiene dos orígenes: indígena[7] y español. En el centro de La Paz, Bolivia, la calle Jaén tiene varios museos de arte donde puedes ver obras indígenas. El Museo de Instrumentos Musicales es un poco diferente de los otros. En este museo interactivo, ¡puedes tocar algunos de los instrumentos! Allí hay exhibiciones de instrumentos precolombinos, instrumentos de viento y tambores[8]. Puedes tocar instrumentos como el charango, una guitarra pequeña de influencia española.

[5] frame [6] paintings [7] indigenous [8] drums

PARA Y PIENSA

¿Comprendiste?

1. ¿Dónde está el Museo al Aire Libre? ¿Y el Museo de Instrumentos Musicales?
2. ¿Qué hay en los dos museos?
3. ¿Por qué no es tradicional el museo de Buenos Aires? ¿Y el museo de La Paz?

¿Y tú?

¿Alguna vez fuiste a un museo? ¿Con quién? ¿Te gustaría visitar el Museo al Aire Libre o el Museo de Instrumentos Musicales? ¿Por qué?

Differentiating Instruction

Inclusion

Clear Structure In advance, copy details from the reading selection onto separate sentence strips. Here are a few possibilities: **No tiene ni puertas ni paredes. Es un museo interactivo.** Then write the headings **Museo al Aire Libre** and **Museo de Instrumentos Musicales** on the board. Have students place each detail under the correct heading.

Multiple Intelligences

Musical/Rhythmic Have students create their own **Museo de Instrumentos Musicales**. First, have each student choose an instrument to research. These might be traditional Bolivian instruments, or instruments from a different part of the world. Have students locate a picture, make a model, and write a short description of their instrument for your museum.

Community

Spanish in the Arts

Have students think of two museums or exhibition spaces in your geographic area. If possible, ask them to search for places that may include samples of Spanish or Latin American art. Ask them to use the chart on p. 396 to compare the entities by **nombre, ubicación, enfoque,** and **exhibiciones.**

Communication

Group Work

Divide the class in small groups. Assign each group to create a postcard about **el Museo al Aire Libre.** They can download images from the Internet, use magazine cutouts, or their own drawings. Ask them to brainstorm ideas for the images and words they want to include. Each group must present its postcard to the class and explain the images represented on it.

Answers

Para y piensa

¿Comprendiste?

1. El Museo al Aire Libre está en una calle pequeña de La Boca, Buenos Aires, que se llama el Caminito. El Museo de Instrumentos Musicales está en La Paz, Bolivia, en la calle Jaén.
2. El Museo al Aire Libre tiene varias obras de arte, como pinturas, esculturas y murales. El Museo de Intrumentos Musicales tiene instrumentos precolombinos, instrumentos de viento y tambores.
3. El Museo al Aire Libre no es tradicional porque no tiene ni puertas ni paredes. El Museo de Instrumentos Musicales tampoco es tradicional porque es interactivo: las personas pueden tocar los instrumentos.

¿Y tú?

Answers will vary. Sample answers will follow this format: Sí, la semana pasada fui a un museo con mi clase de arte. Me gustaría visitar el Museo al Aire Libre porque está en una calle con casas muy bonitas de muchos colores y porque me gusta mucho el arte. También me gustaría visitar el Museo de Instrumentos Musicales porque es interactivo y puedo tocar los instrumentos.

Objectives

- Read about how last names are inherited in Spanish-speaking countries.
- **Culture:** Discuss the importance of carrying two last names in the Spanish-speaking world.
- **Community:** Find out whether Spanish speakers in the United States follow the tradition of carrying two last names.

Presentation Strategies

- Have students read the Comparación cultural. Ask if they know people who use two last names, where they come from.
- Initiate a class discussion about the use of both last names. Would they like to use both parents' last names? How do they feel about this tradition?

STANDARDS

3.1 Knowledge of other disciplines
5.1 Spanish in the community
21st Century **Flexibility and Adaptability,** Multiple Intelligencies; **Social and Cross-Cultural Skills,** Nombres y apellidos/Spanish in Public Information

Comparación cultural

Essential Question

Suggested Answer In Spanish-speaking countries, a person's first last name (**apellido paterno**) comes from the father. A person's second last name (**apellido materno**) comes from the mother. For example, in the chart on the right, the son of Alejandro and Guadalupe is Gregorio García Saavedra.

Expanded Information

In Latin American countries, when a woman marries, she may drop her mother's last name and adopts her husband's paternal last name, with a **de** inserted between. Thus if Silvia Durante Guillén marries Luis Moreno Roldán, she may call herself Silvia Durante de Moreno.

Communities

Spanish in Public Information

Look through your local phone book for listings where two Spanish last names are presented. In the U.S., how does the phone company treat the issue of two last names?

Proyectos culturales

Comparación cultural

Nombres y apellidos

How do last names show family ties across generations? In English-speaking countries, people traditionally inherit one last name, from their father. In Spanish-speaking countries, many people inherit two last names (**apellidos**); the first is the father's, the second is the mother's. Look at the chart to see how this works. Which names represent the father and which ones represent the mother?

Proyecto 1 *Family tree*

Make a family tree of your family or a family you know.

Instructions for family tree
Draw a family tree chart like the one above to show how the family names of you, your parents, and grandparents would change using the Spanish tradition of two last names.

Proyecto 2 *Photo album*

Make a photo album of your immediate family or one you know. Use two last names to label the people in your photos.

Materials for photo album
Photos or copies of photos
Construction paper
Glue or tape
Cardboard and cord or ribbon

Instructions
1. Make a page for each person you want to include in your album, using construction paper. Label the page with his or her name or write a caption below each photo. Use the two last names. You may include the date of birth or words that describe the person's interests and personality.
2. Make a cover for your family album. Punch holes in the cover and pages. Bind them together with cord or ribbon.

En tu comunidad

If you know any native speakers of Spanish, ask them about their own last names. Do they have two surnames? If so, do they ordinarily use both of them?

Differentiating Instruction

Heritage Language Learners

Support What They Know Ask students if they or any members of their family use both last names. Ask them to give examples. Do they know of any other traditions having to do with names? For example, sons named after their father often add the word **Hijo** after their last name, as in **José Domínguez Gómez, Hijo,** an equivalent to *Jr.* in English.

English Learners

Build Background Before doing Proyecto 1, review with English learners the vocabulary required to assemble the family tree. Then invite students to describe their own family tree. How are last names inherited in their country of origin? Which family name is dominant?

En resumen

Vocabulario y gramática

ANIMATEDGRAMMAR
Interactive Flashcards
my.hrw.com

Vocabulario

At the Amusement Park

los autitos chocadores	*bumper cars*	¡Qué divertido!	*How fun!*
el boleto	*ticket*	¡Qué miedo!	*How scary!*
la montaña rusa	*roller coaster*	tener miedo	*to be afraid*
subir a	*to ride*	la vuelta al mundo	*Ferris wheel*

Places of Interest

el acuario	*aquarium*
la feria	*fair*
el museo	*museum*
el parque de diversiones	*amusement park*
el zoológico	*zoo*

Make a Phone Call

dejar un mensaje	*to leave a message*
la llamada	*phone call*
llamar	*to call (by phone)*
el teléfono celular	*cellular phone*

Talk on the Phone

¿Aló?	*Hello?*
¿Está...?	*Is . . . there?*
No, no está.	*No, he's / she's not.*
¿Puedo hablar con...?	*May I speak with . . . ?*
Un momento.	*One moment.*

Extend Invitations

¿Quieres acompañarme a...?	*Would you like to come with me to . . . ?*
¿Te gustaría...?	*Would you like . . . ?*
Te invito.	*I'll treat you. / I invite you.*

Accept

¡Claro que sí!	*Of course!*
Me gustaría...	*I would like . . .*
Sí, me encantaría.	*Yes, I would love to.*

Decline

¡Qué lástima!	*What a shame!*

Other Words and Phrases

con	*with*
el fin de semana	*weekend*

Gramática

Nota gramatical: **¡Qué** + adjective! *p.384*

Preterite of ir, ser, and hacer

Ir, ser, and **hacer** are irregular in the preterite tense. The preterite forms of **ir** and **ser** are exactly the same.

ir *to go* / **ser** *to be*	
fui	fuimos
fuiste	fuisteis
fue	fueron

hacer *to do, to make*	
hice	hicimos
hiciste	hicisteis
hizo	hicieron

Pronouns After Prepositions

Pronouns that follow prepositions are the same as the subject pronouns except **mí (yo)** and **ti (tú)**.

Pronouns After Prepositions	
mí	nosotros(as)
ti	vosotros(as)
usted, él, ella	ustedes, ellos(as)

The preposition **con** combines with **mí** and **ti** to form the words **conmigo** and **contigo**.

Practice Spanish with Holt McDougal Apps!

Objective

- Review lesson vocabulary and grammar.

DIGITAL SPANISH

Interactive Flashcards Students can hear every target vocabulary word pronounced in authentic Spanish. Flashcards have Spanish on one side, and a picture or a translation on the other.
Review Games Matching, concentration, hangman, and word search are just a sampling of the fun, interactive games students can play to review for the test.

performance space
News Networking
@HOMETUTOR
CULTURA Interactiva

- **Audio and Video Resources**
- **Interactive Flashcards**
- **Review Activities**
- **WebQuest**
- **Conjuguemos.com**

Long-term Retention

Recycle

Ask students to brainstorm words from other units that they could add to the categories listed in En resumen. For example, under Places of Interest they could write **el cine, el parque, el teatro.** Under At the Amusement Park: **¡Qué bonito! ¡Qué aburrido! ¡Qué peligroso!** Under Talk on the Phone: **¿Qué tal? ¿Cómo estás?** Have them share their lists with other students and add other examples for further reference.

Communication

Pair Work

Have pairs of students make up a word search or crossword puzzle using the En resumen vocabulary. Then have them exchange puzzles with another pair. After finding the words, they must write sentences using them.

Differentiating Instruction

Multiple Intelligences

Interpersonal Working in pairs, have students role-play the following situation: one friend calls another on the phone to extend an invitation. Students may choose what the invitation is for, and whether to accept or decline. Remind students to use appropriate manners and polite expressions as they extend or respond to the invitation.

Inclusion

Multisensory Input/Output Review pronouns after prepositions by playing this game. Place a book or another item behind a student. Then make a false statement, such as **El libro está delante de ella.** Students must correct the statement. **No, el libro está detrás de ella.** Next, have a volunteer move the object and make the next false statement.

Objective
- Review lesson grammar and vocabulary.

Core Resources
- *Cuaderno*, pp. 329–340
- Audio Program: TXT CD 7 track 22

Presentation Strategies
- As students listen to Activity 1, instruct them to pay special attention to the expressions used for extending, accepting, and declining invitations.
- Before doing Activity 2, ask students to identify the places in the photos.
- Review preterite forms of **hacer, ir,** and **ser** by saying a subject pronoun and asking students to provide the correct preterite form of these verbs.
- Go over the Comparación cultural with students and clarify any questions that arise.
- Review may be done in class or given as homework.
- You may want students to access the review online.

STANDARDS
1.2 Understand language, Act. 1
1.3 Present information, Acts. 2–4
4.2 Compare cultures, Act. 5
21st Century **Communication,** Multiple Intelligences,

Warm Up Projectable Transparencies, 7-23

Preterite of ir, ser, and hacer Complete the sentences with the correct preterite form of the verb in parentheses.

1. Ayer mi hermano y yo _____ al zoológico. (ir)
2. ¿Qué _____ ustedes en el museo? (hacer)
3. El fin de semana _____ muy aburrido. (ser)
4. Marisa _____ cinco llamadas esta tarde. (hacer)
5. ¿Con quién _____ tú a la feria? (ir)

Answers: 1. fuimos; 2. hicieron; 3. fue; 4. hizo; 5. fuiste

Ongoing Assessment
Get Help Online
More Practice
my.hrw.com

Intervention and Remediation If students achieve less than 80% accuracy on each activity, direct them to review pp. 378, 384–386, 390, 392, 396–397 and to get help online at my.hrw.com.

See Activity answers on p. 401.

Lección 2 Repaso de la lección

@HOMETUTOR my.hrw.com

¡LLEGADA!

¡AvanzaRap! DVD Sing and Learn

Now you can
- talk on the phone
- say where you went, how it was, and what you did
- extend invitations

Using
- ¡**Qué** + adjective!
- preterite of **ir, ser,** and **hacer**
- pronouns after prepositions

Audio Program
TXT CD 7 Track 22
Audio Script, TE p. 377b

To review
- ¡**Qué** + adjective! p. 384
- pronouns after prepositions p. 390

1 Listen and understand

AUDIO

Escucha las conversaciones. En una hoja de papel, escribe **sí** si el (la) invitado(a) acepta la invitación, o **no** si no la acepta. *(Listen to the conversations. On a separate sheet of paper, write **sí** or **no** to tell whether or not each invitation is accepted.)*

To review
- ¡**Qué** + adjective! p. 384

2 Extend invitations

Jaime invita a Laura a salir con él. Escribe sus invitaciones y las respuestas de Laura. *(Write Jaime's invitations to Laura. Then write her responses.)*

modelo: no / horrible
Jaime: ¿Quieres acompañarme a la feria?
Laura: No. ¡Qué horrible!

1. sí / interesante

2. sí / bonito

3. no / aburrido

4. sí / divertido

5. no / peligroso

6. sí / bueno

Differentiating Instruction

Pre-AP
Communicate Preferences Ask students to use the expressions **¿Te gustaría?** or **¿Quieres acompañarme a...?** to invite a partner to the things shown on p. 400. Students must accept or decline and explain why. **¿Te gustaría subir a la montaña rusa? Sí, me encantaría. La montaña rusa es muy divertida.** or **No, no quiero subir a la montaña rusa porque tengo miedo.**

Slower-paced Learners
Peer-study Support Have students work with a partner to complete the conversation in Activity 3. Have them discuss which preposition and pronoun sound the most logical. Then have them take the roles of Manuel and Guillermo and read their lines.

review
ronouns after
repositions
. 390

3 Talk on the phone

Completa esta conversación. Usa **con** o **para** y el pronombre correcto. *(Complete the conversation with **con** or **para** and the correct pronoun.)*

—¿Bueno?

—¿Está Manuel?

—Sí, soy yo.

—Manuel, soy Guillermo. ¿Te gustaría ir al acuario __1.__ ? Te invito. Ya tengo un boleto __2.__ , y si quieres acompañarme, puedo comprar un boleto __3.__ .

—Lo siento, Guillermo, pero no puedo ir __4.__ . Carlos y Beatriz quieren ir al museo y voy __5.__ . ¿Por qué no vienes __6.__ ? Vamos a salir a las diez.

—Mi hermano también quiere ir. Voy a hablar __7.__ para ver si puede.

—Está bien. Hasta luego.

review
reterite of **ir, ser,**
nd **hacer** p. 385

4 Say where you went, how it was, and what you did

Luisa habla con Gregorio. Lee las respuestas de Gregorio y escribe las preguntas de Luisa. Usa los verbos **ir, ser** y **hacer.** *(Write Luisa's questions based on Gregorio's answers. Use **ir, ser,** and **hacer.**)*

modelo: Hice muchas cosas el sábado. (¿Qué?)
¿Qué hiciste el sábado?

1. El viernes fui al cine. (¿Adónde?)
2. La película fue muy interesante. (¿Cómo?)
3. Lucas fue conmigo. (¿Quién?)
4. Hicimos algo muy divertido después. (¿Qué?)
5. Fuimos al nuevo café. (¿Adónde?)
6. La comida fue buena. (¿Cómo?)

review
Comparación cultural pp. 378, 386, 392
Lectura cultural pp. 396-397

5 Argentina and Bolivia

Comparación cultural

Answer these culture questions.

1. Where is El Parque de la Costa and what can you do there?
2. To whom does the term **porteños** refer and why?
3. What foods are popular in Argentina and why? What is an **asado**?
4. Describe what you can find on **el Caminito** in Buenos Aires and **calle Jaén** in La Paz.

ás práctica Cuaderno *pp. 329–340* Cuaderno para hispanohablantes *pp. 331–340*

Get Help Online my.hrw.com

✓ Ongoing Assessment

Peer Assessment Have student pairs exchange the completed conversation in Activity 3 and check each other's work.

✓ Ongoing Assessment

Alternative Strategy To review the interrogative words in Activity 4, have students write four questions using **¿Adónde?, ¿Qué?, ¿Cómo?, ¿Quién?** and the preterite of **ir, ser,** and **hacer** to ask their classmates. Check for correct questions and answers.

Answers Projectable Transparencies, 7-31

Answers for Activities on pp. 400–401.

Activity 1 **1.** no; **2.** sí; **3.** sí; **4.** no; **5.** sí; **6.** no

Activity 2
1. ¿Quieres acompañarme al museo? Sí. ¡Qué interesante!
2. ¿Quieres acompañarme al zoológico? Sí. ¡Qué bonito!
3. ¿Quieres acompañarme al acuario? No. ¡Qué aburrido!
4. ¿Quieres acompañarme al parque de diversiones? Sí. ¡Qué divertido!
5. ¿Quieres acompañarme a la montaña rusa? No. ¡Qué peligroso!
6. ¿Quieres acompañarme a la vuelta al mundo? Sí. ¡Qué bueno!

Activity 3 **1.** conmigo; **2.** para mí; **3.** para ti; **4.** contigo; **5.** con ellos; **6.** con nosotros; **7.** con él

Activity 4
1. ¿Adónde fuiste el viernes?
2. ¿Cómo fue la película?
3. ¿Quién fue contigo?
4. ¿Qué hicieron después?
5. ¿Adónde fueron?
6. ¿Cómo fue la comida?

Activity 5
1. El Parque de la Costa is near Buenos Aires. It is an amusement park where visitors can go on a wide variety of rides.
2. The term **porteños** refers to the residents of Buenos Aires, which is a port city. It means "people of the port."
3. Meat is popular in Argentina because of Argentina's plentiful supply of cattle. An **asado** is an outdoor barbecue.
4. On **el Caminito** you can find the **Museo al Aire Libre,** cafés, and places where you can listen to music and watch people dancing the tango. On **calle Jaén,** you can see the **Museo de Instrumentos Musicales.**

Differentiating Instruction

Multiple Intelligences

Interpersonal Have students circulate around the room asking each other where they went, with whom, and what they did yesterday. Students should also ask follow-up questions. For example: **¿Adónde fuiste ayer? Fui al parque de diversiones. ¿Con quién fuiste? Fui con mis amigos. ¿Qué hiciste allí? Subí a la montaña rusa y a la vuelta al mundo.**

Inclusion

Cumulative Instruction Before doing Activity 3, review with students pronouns they already know. Remind them that in Unit 1, Lesson 1, they learned pronouns with **gustar.** Direct students to p. 42 to review.

Objectives

- Read about places where teens like to go to have fun.
- Compare favorite places of teens in Bolivia, Argentina, and Nicaragua with favorite places of teens in the U.S.
- Write about a place you visited recently.

Core Resources

- *Cuaderno,* pp. 341–343
- Audio Program: TXT CD 7 track 23
- Video Program: DVD 2

Presentation Strategies

- Draw students' attention to the photos on p. 403 and ask them to predict what the text will be about.
- Have students take turns reading each description as their classmates follow it in the text. Correct pronunciation as needed.
- Play the audio.

STANDARDS

1.2 Understand language
1.3 Present information
2.1 Practices and perspectives
4.2 Compare cultures
21st Century **Critical Thinking and Problem Solving,** Compara con tu mundo/ Interpersonal Mode

Communication

Group Work

Ask students to read the three descriptions in groups of three. Each student will prepare an activity timeline for one of the three descriptions, using the timeline on p. 402 as a model. Students should check each other's work for accuracy.

Communication

Interpersonal Mode

Conduct a class survey of the places and activities mentioned by Luis, Liliana, and Eva. Ask students to prepare a chart with the following column headings: **¡Qué divertido! ¡Qué aburrido! ¡Qué miedo!** In the left margin of the paper ask them to make a list of the places and things mentioned in the three narratives. Students then switch papers with a partner and the partner checks off what they find fun, boring, scary.

Comparación cultural

AUDIO

¿Conoces un lugar divertido?

Lectura y escritura

WebQuest
my.hrw.com

1. **Leer** People like to go to different places to have fun. Read about the places that Luis, Liliana, and Eva visited.
2. **Escribir** Using the three descriptions as models, write a short paragraph about a place you recently visited.

STRATEGY **Escribir**
Make an activity timeline Make a timeline of your activities. What did you do first, second, third, and so on? Use the timeline to guide your writing.

Primero — Segundo — Tercero →

Step 1 Complete the timeline, showing what you did first, second, third, and so on.

Step 2 Write your paragraph, including all the activities on your timeline. Check your writing by yourself or with help from a friend. Make final corrections.

Compara con tu mundo

Use the paragraph you wrote to compare your visit to a visit described by *one* of the three students. Are the activities similar? In what ways are they different?

Cuaderno *pp. 341–343* Cuaderno para hispanohablantes *pp. 341–343*

Differentiating Instruction

Heritage Language Learners

Increase Accuracy Have students take turns reading each paragraph on p. 403 aloud to a partner. Remind students to use punctuation and accent marks to help guide their reading.

Inclusion

Clear Structure Provide students with a graphic organizer to record their ideas for the paragraphs they will write. For example:

Fui a _____.
Primero:
Después:
Más tarde:
Por fin:

CULTURA Interactiva my.hrw.com *See these pages come alive!*

Bolivia *Luis*

¿Qué tal? Soy Luis y vivo en La Paz, en las montañas de los Andes. Anteayer mis amigos y yo hicimos algo divertido. Primero fuimos al Paseo el Prado, una calle divertida. Allí caminamos y miramos los restaurantes y las tiendas. Por fin llegamos a la Plaza del Estudiante. Encontramos a otros amigos allí. Hizo buen tiempo, entonces hablamos y paseamos en la plaza. ¡Qué bonito!

Argentina *Liliana*

¡Hola! Me llamo Liliana y soy de Buenos Aires. Ayer mi hermana y yo fuimos a un parque de diversiones cerca de mi casa. Primero nosotras subimos a la montaña rusa, pero a mí no me gustó. ¡Qué miedo! Me gustaron más los autitos chocadores. Más tarde comimos unas hamburguesas. Luego miramos un espectáculo de láser[1]. Volvimos a casa en la noche, cuando cerró el parque. ¡Qué bárbaro!

[1] **espectáculo...** laser show

Nicaragua *Eva*

Me llamo Eva y soy de Managua. El jueves pasado mis padres y yo fuimos a Masaya, el centro folklórico de Nicaragua. Todos los jueves, en el Mercado Nacional de Artesanías[2] celebran las Verbenas de Masaya: un festival folklórico de danza y música. Los artistas llevan trajes[3] de muchos colores. ¡Tomé unas fotos fabulosas! Después compramos artesanías y comimos comidas típicas de Nicaragua. ¡Fue muy divertido!

[2] **Mercado...** National Handicraft Market [3] costumes

Comparación cultural

Exploring the Theme

The **Parque de la Costa** is about an hour from Buenos Aires by car or train. There are rides for both children and adults. Apart from the roller coaster, the park's scariest ride is the Vértigo Xtremo. Those who dare jump from a high tower attached by a bungee cord. When the rides close, parkgoers can watch a laser light show synchronized to music. The **Parque de la Costa** is a popular destination spot for families on a day trip, celebrating a reunion or a birthday.

✓ Ongoing Assessment

Quick Check Ask students quick comprehension questions about each of the three descriptions and write their responses on the board. For example: **¿Qué hicieron Luis y sus amigos en el Paseo el Prado? ¿Quién fue a un parque de diversiones? ¿Le gustó a Liliana subir a la montaña rusa? ¿Qué son las Verbenas de Masaya?**

✓ Ongoing Assessment

Rubric **Lectura y escritura**

Writing Criteria	Excellent	Good	Needs Work
Content	Paragraph contains a lot of information.	Paragraph contains some information.	Paragraph lacks information.
Communication	Paragraph is organized and easy to follow.	Paragraph is fairly well-organized and easy to follow.	Paragraph is disorganized and hard to follow.
Accuracy	Paragraph has few mistakes in vocabulary and grammar.	Paragraph has some mistakes in vocabulary and grammar.	Paragraph has many mistakes in vocabulary and grammar.

To customize your own rubrics, use the ***Generate Success*** *Rubric Generator and Graphic Organizers.*

Differentiating Instruction

Pre-AP

Communicate Preferences Discuss with students which of the excursions described on p. 403 they would most like to join. Encourage students to use the phrase **Me gustaría...** to begin their statements.

Slower-paced Learners

Sentence Completion Have students choose one of the paragraphs to use as a model. Instruct them to copy one of the paragraphs onto another piece of paper in pencil. Then have them erase specific information and replace it with their own. **Me llamo Eva ____ y soy de Managua ____.**

Objective
- Cumulative review

Core Resource
- Audio Program: TXT CD 7 track 24

Review Options
- **Activity 1:** Listening
- **Activity 2:** Speaking
- **Activity 3:** Speaking
- **Activity 4:** Writing
- **Activity 5:** Speaking
- **Activity 6:** Speaking and writing
- **Activity 7:** Reading and writing

STANDARDS
1.1 Engage in conversation, Acts. 3, 5-6
1.2 Understand language, Act. 1
1.3 Present information, Acts. 2-7
21st Century **Communication,** Acts. 2, 3, 4, 5/ Heritage Language Learners; **Creativity and Innovation,** Act. 6

Long-term Retention
Study Tips
Encourage students to prepare in advance vocabulary lists or graphic organizers that will help them complete the activities in Repaso inclusivo.

UNIDADES 1-7

Repaso inclusivo
Options for Review

¡AvanzaRap! DVD Sing and Learn

Digital performance space

1 Listen, understand, and compare
Escuchar

Listen to the phone conversation. Then answer the following questions.

1. ¿Quién llama a Jaime?
2. ¿Quién contesta el teléfono en la casa de Jaime?
3. ¿Adónde fue Jaime?
4. ¿Quiere dejar un mensaje Teresa?
5. ¿Qué quiere hacer Teresa hoy? ¿Con quién?
6. ¿Cuál es el número del teléfono celular de Jaime?

Who do you like to do things with on the weekends? Where do you go?

Audio Pr
TXT CD 7 Tr
Audio Script
p. 377b

2 Present a trip
Hablar

Prepare a presentation about the last trip or outing that you took. Make a poster out of your own photos or magazine clippings and give your poster a title. Use it as a visual cue while you talk about where you went and with whom, when and how you got there, and what you did. Your presentation should be at least three minutes long.

3 Talk with a fellow passenger
Hablar

You are on a plane returning home after a long weekend trip. You strike up a conversation with the teen sitting next to you. Find out as much as you can about him or her: name, age, where he or she is from, where he or she is going, and what he or she is going to do there. Your partner will also ask where you went and what you did there. Your conversation should be at least three minutes long.

Differentiating Instruction

Slower-paced Learners
Read Before Listening Before students listen to the phone conversation in Activity 1, have them preview the questions presented. Encourage students to brainstorm possible logical answers to each question. As they listen to the conversation, have students circle or write down the correct answer.

Pre-AP
Expand and Elaborate Before students begin Activity 2 or 3, have them create a vocabulary reference list as a whole group. Have students brainstorm words and phrases related to trips and outings. Once students have compiled a list, guide them to organize the vocabulary into categories, such as places, actions, and descriptions.

Answers
Activity 1
1. Teresa llama a Jaime.
2. La señora Palomar, la madrastra de Jaime, contesta el teléfono.
3. Jaime fue al parque con unos amigos.
4. No, Teresa no quiere dejar un mensaje.
5. Teresa quiere ir a la feria con Jaime.
6. El número de teléfono celular de Jaime es 335-9074.

Activities 2–7 Answers will vary.

4 | Write a computer guide

scribir

While working at your summer job in a cybercafé, you are asked to create a guide for Spanish-speaking customers. Include the café's name, location, hours, and prices. Explain what kinds of computers the café has and what customers are able to do there, and give step-by-step instructions for those who are unfamiliar with Internet activities. Your guide should have illustrations and at least eight sentences.

5 | Tell what is true or false

Hablar

Work in a group of three. Take turns making statements about things you or someone you know did or about your life now. Most of the statements should be true but some should be made-up. The other members of your group will say whether they think each statement is true or false. The winner is the person who guessed correctly the most.

6 | Create a TV ad

Hablar

Work with a partner. Use the Internet to research an amusement park in a Spanish-speaking country. Then write the script for a TV ad for the park, mentioning the name, days and hours of operation, prices, and rides, including any special facts or features. Also tell people how they can get there from the nearest city. Record the ad or present it to the class.

7 | Give advice to another teen

Leer
scribir

You run an advice column on the Web for other teens. Read this e-mail that a student sent to you and write a response, telling him what to do. Use affirmative **tú** commands, **deber,** and **tener que** in your response. Your e-mail should include at least six pieces of advice.

> Hola. Soy estudiante del primer año de español. Tengo un problema y necesito tu ayuda. Me gusta aprender el español, pero muchas veces saco malas notas en los exámenes. La clase es interesante y escucho a la maestra, pero no entiendo nada. ¿Qué debo hacer?
>
> Muchas gracias.
>
> Estudiante nervioso

✓ Ongoing Assessment

Peer Assessment Have student pairs exchange the completed computer guide in Activity 4 and check each other's work.

✓ Ongoing Assessment

Rubric Integrated Performance Assessment Rubric
Oral Activities 2, 3, 5, 6
Written Activities 4, 6, 7

Very Good	Proficient	Not There Yet
The student thoroughly develops all requirements of the task.	The student develops most requirements of the task.	The student does not develop the requirements of the task.
The student demonstrates excellent control of verb forms.	The student demonstrates good to fair control of verb forms.	The student demonstrates poor control of verb forms.
Good variety of appropriate vocabulary.	Adequate variety of appropriate vocabulary.	The vocabulary is not appropriate.
The pronunciation is excellent to very good.	The pronunciation is good to fair.	The pronunciation is poor.

To customize your own rubrics, use the ***Generate Success*** *Rubric Generator and Graphic Organizers.*

Differentiating Instruction

Multiple Intelligences

Visual Learners Encourage students to pay attention to the design of their guides in Activity 4. Perhaps their guide will be in the form of a card, a folded brochure, or a poster. Remind students to include clear and helpful illustrations or photographs to support the meaning of their words.

Heritage Language Learners

Writing Skills Have students draft their own e-mail messages to a student advice column. They might ask for help with a real problem, or create a fictional situation. Have students write their messages on index cards. Then shuffle the cards, and redistribute them. Have students respond to the problem they receive on the back of the card.

Proyectos adicionales

Planning ahead...

Projects **Create a scrapbook.** Tell students that they have just returned from a wonderful vacation to Costa Rica. Using a large piece of paper, magic markers, drawings, photos from travel magazines, or photographs from the web, have students design a page for a travel scrapbook. Students should write a caption for each photo or drawing explaining what is happening in the picture. Remind students to use the preterite to talk about actions completed in the past. Also, encourage students to use sequence words to help explain what happened when. Once they have arranged their pictures and captions, students might also add decorations or small "souvenirs" that they may have bought at the market in Costa Rica.

After their scrapbook pages are complete, organize students into pairs to share their work. Encourage students to discuss what is similar and different about their pages and the trips they represent. Display all of the scrapbook pages.

PACING SUGGESTION: Upon completion of **Lección 2** to use vocabulary related to vacation activities, as well as to practice the preterite forms of regular **-ar, -er,** and **-ir** verbs.

Creativity and Innovation

(Virtual) Bulletin Board

Create a bulletin board highlighting life **En el bosque tropical lluvioso.** Assign each student the task of identifying and researching one plant or animal from the Costa Rican rain forest. Students will then create a model using construction paper, cardboard, or even clay. Once all of the models are complete, arrange them on the bulletin board. Ask students to share what they know about their plants and animals as you decide on a logical arrangement for all of the species.

Create a bulletin board with the title **Antes de las clases.** Have each student create a poster illustrating his or her daily routine before getting to school each morning. Encourage students to take photos or draw pictures of themselves engaged in different morning activities. Instruct students to divide their poster into two columns. On the left, they should write a specific time and/or show a clock representing that time. On the right, they should show the picture of an activity with a caption explaining what is happening. Display all of the completed posters. As a tech alternative, you may wish to have students create their projects on a class wiki page.

PACING SUGGESTION: After **Lección 1** to review reflexive verbs.

Creativity and Innovation

Web Research

Go online to research possible eco-tours in Costa Rica. Have students work in pairs or small groups to design an eco-vacation itinerary in Costa Rica. They might locate a package deal, or find different activities from different resources. Tell students to imagine that they have only three days to spend in Costa Rica, and they want to see as much of the natural life as possible. Remind them, however, that they are on a budget.

Have students present their itinerary in the form of three daily schedules—Day 1, Day 2, and Day 3. The schedules should outline what it happening, when, how long the activity lasts, and how much it costs. Remind students not to forget about important activities like eating and sleeping. Have each pair or group present their itinerary to the whole class. Then have students discuss which sounds like the best eco-vacation.

PACING SUGGESTION: Research can be done through the unit as time allows. Presentations should be done in Spanish after vocabulary is presented in **Lección 2.**

Technology Literacy

Games

Juego de mesa

Have students create their own buy-and-sell board games based on a trip to Costa Rica. To create their games, students will need pieces of cardboard for the game boards, slips of paper to create fake **colones,** and odds and ends for tokens. Organize students into small groups to create their board games. Encourage them to be creative with the kinds of spaces they create for the board: a souvenir at the market, a meal at a restaurant, a windsurfing lesson, a walking tour through the rain forest. Students should also include spaces with fines or prizes. Each group can make up their own rules for buying, selling, and winning, but advise them to keep the rules simple. After the games are complete, give each group time to play. Also, let groups switch to play the game another group has created.

PACING SUGGESTION: As time allows throughout the unit.

Pantomimas

Divide students into two teams. After reviewing the vocabulary from **Lección 1** and **Lección 2,** have each student write a sentence on a slip of paper. The sentence should express something they did on their last vacation. **Monté a caballo. Comí al aire libre.** The sentence may be true, but it can also be fictional. Have all students place their sentences into a hat or a bowl.

Invite two players from one team to the front to choose a sentence. Working together, the players have thirty seconds to act out the sentence so that their teammates can guess it. The players may not talk. If their team guesses the sentence correctly, it earns a point.

PACING SUGGESTION: Upon completion of **Lección 2** to review vacation activities and preterite verb forms.

¡AvanzaRap! DVD

- Video animations of all **¡AvanzaRap!** songs (with Karaoke track)
- Teaching Suggestions
- **¡AvanzaRap!** Activity Masters
- **¡AvanzaRap!** Video Scripts and Answers

Also available on the **Teacher One Stop**

Recipe

Frescos are refreshing shakes made out of fresh fruit and water or milk. Tropical flavors include **tamarindo** (tamarind), **maracuyá** (passion fruit), **carambola** (star fruit), and **guanábana** (soursop). In Costa Rica, a **fresco** often accompanies a **casado,** an inexpensive lunch or dinner plate that usually includes rice, beans, meat, and a salad.

Fresco de Melón

Ingredientes

1 melón

1/2 taza de agua

2 cucharadas de jugo de limón

1 cucharada de azúcar

Instrucciones

Corte el melón en pedazos de tamaño mediano. Pélelo y sáquele las semillas. Coloque todos los ingredientes en la licuadora y hágalo en puré hasta que adquiera una consistencia suave. Puede servirse con o sin hielo.

Music

Organize a Costa Rican style **peña.** Discuss with students the Costa Rican tradition of **la peña.** Explain that this tradition of sharing songs and poetry at a café originally traveled from Chile and Argentina. A **peña** is a time for friends to gather over music and stories, or a combination of the two. Have students plan their own music or literary performance. Students may work individually or in small groups. Also, arrange for refreshments to be served at your café while students share the artistic work they have prepared.

UNIT THEME
- A different routine

UNIT STANDARDS

COMMUNICATION
- Talk about a typical day
- Talk about what you are doing
- Talk about your daily routine while on vacation
- Talk about buying souvenirs on vacation
- Talk about vacation activities

CULTURES
- The use of **usted, tú** and **vos**
- Vacation spots in Costa Rica
- Transportation in Costa Rica
- The coffee industry
- Travel destinations in Costa Rica, Ecuador and Uruguay

CONNECTIONS
- Science: Sections of the La Salle Museum
- Mathematics: Museum entry fee in **colones** and dollars
- Language Arts: Latin and Greek roots of some Spanish words
- Art: Animals or insects found in the museum

COMPARISONS
- Plant life in Costa Rica and the U.S.
- Features of landscapes in various countries
- Diphthongs vs. separately pronounced pairs of vowels
- Variations in language in different situations
- Modes of transportation in Costa Rica and the U.S.
- Ecotourism and other vacation activities
- Linking words together in Spanish
- Important industries in Costa Rica and the U.S.
- Market places in Costa Rica, Uruguay, and the U.S.
- Desserts in Costa Rica and Uruguay
- Vacations of students from Costa Rica, Ecuador, Uruguay, and the U.S.

COMMUNITIES
- How knowledge of other languages and cultures would be an asset to a professional chef

UNIDAD 8

Costa Rica

Una rutina diferente

Lección 1

Tema: ***Pensando en las vacaciones***

Lección 2

Tema: ***¡Vamos de vacaciones!***

«¡Hola!

Somos Jorge y Susana.
Vivimos en San José, Costa Rica.»

Población: 4.195.914

Área: 19.730 millas cuadradas

Capital: San José

Moneda: el colón (por Cristóbal Colón)

Idioma: español

Comida típica: gallo pinto, casado, sopa negra

Gente famosa: Óscar Arias Sánchez (político), José Figueres Ferrer (político), Claudia Poll (atleta), Francisco Zúñiga (artista)

Casado

Cultural Geography

Setting the Scene

- ¿Cuál es la población de Costa Rica? (4.195.914)
- ¿Quién es un político famoso de Costa Rica? (José Figueres Ferrer)
- ¿Cómo se llama la moneda de Costa Rica? (el colón) ¿Por qué? (por Cristóbal Colón)

Teaching with Maps

- ¿Qué país está al norte de Costa Rica? (Nicaragua) ¿Al sur? (Panamá)
- ¿En qué océanos o mares tiene costa Costa Rica? (Océano Pacífico, Mar Caribe)
- ¿Está Costa Rica en Sudamérica o Centroamérica? (Centroamérica)

CULTURA Interactiva my.hrw.com *See these pages come alive!*

La naturaleza: un lugar para relajarse The active Arenal Volcano provides immense heat to the waters nearby, which creates the Tabacón hot springs. Costa Ricans and other tourists come here to relax and enjoy the health benefits of the springs' mineral water pools. *Where can people go to relax and experience nature in your area?*

Las aguas termales de Tabacón y el Volcán Arenal

Un competidor de surf kayac en Puntarenas

Los deportes acuáticos Costa Rica's Pacific coast has dozens of beaches where tourists come to sunbathe and swim. More daring water sports, especially surfing, are also very popular. Costa Rica recently hosted the World Surf Kayak Championship. *Where can people practice water sports where you live?*

Las artesanías de madera The town of Sarchí holds an annual festival for their **carretas,** or wooden oxcarts. The carts were used to transport coffee in Costa Rica in the 1800s, before the construction of the railroad. Today's **carretas** are elaborately painted by hand, often have musical wheels, and can be found in all sizes, even as miniature souvenirs. *What typical handicrafts are made in the United States?*

Las carretas, artesanías típicas de Sarchí

CULTURA Interactiva my.hrw.com

Send your students to my.hrw.com to explore authentic Costa Rican culture. Tell them to click on Cultura interactiva to see these pages come alive!

Culture

About the Photos

- The Arenal Volcano, which is less than 3,000 years old, has had major eruptions several times in recent years. The first eruption was in 1968, when the villages of Pueblo Nuevo and Tabacón were completely destroyed.
- **Puntarenas** offers the tourist several beaches for outdoor sports and leisure. Wildlife lovers will enjoy observing the scarlet macaws that nest in the foliage there.
- The designs on the carretas evolved for practical reasons. In the days of coffee transport, each farming region had its own motif. Today, these painted oxcarts are strictly decorative.

Expanded Information

- The Arenal hot springs were long considered a rejuvenating venue for nature-loving tourists. Recently, though, this area has been classified as dangerous because of volcanic eruptions. Tourists now enjoy the safer Baldi hot springs.
- Costa Rica has many bodies of water: beaches, lakes, rivers, bays, and lagoons. Pavones Beach is known by surfers for having the longest waves in the world.
- The first place to construct **carretas** was the Joaquín Chaverri Oxcart Factory, built in 1902. Today there are many places in the town of Sarchí that produce these carts, which are sold to tourists.

Bridging Cultures

Heritage Language Learners

Support What They Know Give students the opportunity to design and construct their own **carretas.** Have them start with a cardboard box as the base. They might choose a shoebox, a larger box, or a small jewelry box to make a miniature. Then have students cut out and attach wheels, and decorate their **carretas** with images and symbols from their country of origin.

English Learners

Build Background Write statements on the board, such as:
Costa Rica is an ideal ecotourism location.
Costa Rica has a diverse ecology.
Next, have students find details on page 407 to support each statement. Can the same statements be made about students' countries and cultures of origin?

Video Character Guide

Jorge and Susana are siblings who both have elaborate routines as they get ready for school. When on vacation, their routines are a lot more relaxed.

Lesson Overview

Culture at a Glance

Topic & Activity	Essential Question
Plant life in Costa Rica pp. 408-409	What plants and trees are native to your region?
The use of **usted, tú,** and **vos** p. 422	How do forms of address differ among countries?
A trip to Costa Rica pp. 426–427	What do you like to do in Costa Rica?
Culture review p. 431	What are some aspects of culture in Costa Rica, Ecuador, and Uruguay?

COMPARISON COUNTRIES Costa Rica Ecuador Uruguay

Practice at a Glance

	Objective	Activity & Skill
Vocabulary	Daily routine	1: Reading; 5: Speaking/Writing; 6: Speaking/Writing; 7: Speaking/Writing; 8: Speaking; 10: Listening/Writing; 13: Speaking; Repaso 2: Writing
	Talk about grooming	1: Reading; 4: Speaking; 7: Speaking/Writing; 8: Speaking; Repaso 1: Listening; Repaso 3: Writing
	Vacation words	2: Speaking; 3: Listening/Reading; 11: Speaking/Writing; 12: Writing
Grammar	Using reflexive verbs	1: Reading; 6: Speaking/Writing; 7:Speaking/Writing; 8: Speaking; 9: Listening/Reading; 10: Listening/Writing; 12: Writing; 13: Speaking; 17: Speaking; Repaso 1:Listening; Repaso 2: Writing; Repaso 3: Writing
	Using present progressive	11: Speaking/Writing; 12: Writing; 13: Speaking; 14: Speaking; 19: Writing; Repaso 4: Writing
Communication	Talk about a typical day	5: Speaking/Writing; 6: Speaking/Writing; 8: Speaking; 9: Listening/Reading; 10: Listening/Writing; 11: Speaking/Writing; 13: Speaking; 15: Listening/Reading; 17: Speaking; 18: Reading/Listening/Speaking; Repaso 2: Writing
	Talk about what you are doing	7: Speaking/Writing; 11: Speaking/Writing; 12: Writing; 13: Speaking; 14: Speaking; 16: Listening/Reading; Repaso 4: Writing
	Talk about your daily routine while on vacation	2: Speaking; 11: Speaking/Writing; 12: Writing; 19: Writing; Repaso 3: Writing
	Pronunciation: diphthongs	Pronunciación: *Los diptongos,* p. 419: Listening/Speaking
Recycle	Preterite of **hacer**, chores, houses	2: Speaking; 11: Speaking/Writing; 13: Speaking
	Direct object pronouns	4: Speaking;
	Parts of the body, telling time	5: Speaking/Writing; 17: Speaking

The following presentations are recorded in the Audio Program for *¡Avancemos!*

For **¡AvanzaRap!** scripts, see the **¡AvanzaRap! DVD.**

¡A responder! TXT CD 8 track 2

1. Voy a despertarme temprano.
2. Voy a levantarme.
3. Voy a lavarme la cara.
4. Voy a afeitarme la cara.
5. Voy a lavarme el pelo.
6. Voy a peinarme.
7. Voy a cepillarme los dientes.
8. Voy a ponerme los zapatos.

10 | La rutina de Susana TXT CD 8 track 5

Hola, soy Susana. Me gustan los sábados porque no tengo que ir a la escuela. Generalmente me despierto tarde, a las once. Me gusta ducharme, pero los sábados normalmente me baño. Después, me seco la cara. Luego, me cepillo los dientes. Por fin, me maquillo y salgo con los amigos. Los sábados me acuesto muy tarde, a las doce de la noche.

18 | Integración TXT CD 8 tracks 8, 9

¡Hola! Soy yo, Carmen. Vamos a estar en línea mañana, ¿no? Bueno... hoy, como siempre, me levanté a las seis menos diez. Me duché por veinte minutos y después de vestirme, preparé el almuerzo. Ahora me estoy cepillando el pelo y también me estoy maquillando un poco. Ya son las siete menos veinte. A las siete menos cuarto voy a caminar cuarenta y cinco minutos con mi perro. Tengo que salir a las ocho menos cuarto, y mis clases empiezan a las ocho. ¿Y tú? ¿Cuándo puedes estar en línea?

Repaso de la lección TXT CD 8 track 11

1 Listen and understand

Silvia: Mamá...
Mamá: ¿Qué necesitas, Silvia?
Silvia: Estoy lavándome el pelo y necesito algo.

Roberto: Mamá...
Mamá: ¿Qué necesitas, Roberto?
Roberto: Me estoy secando la cara. Necesito algo.

Anita: Mamá...
Mamá: ¿Qué necesitas, Anita?
Anita: Voy a cepillarme los dientes pero necesito algo.

Juan: Mamá...
Mamá: ¿Qué, Juan?
Juan: No puedo secarme el pelo. Necesito algo.

Tomás: Mamá...
Mamá: ¿Qué, Tomás?
Tomás: Estoy lavándome la cara y necesito algo.

Laura: Mamá...
Mamá: ¿Qué necesitas, Laura?
Laura: Tengo que peinarme, pero necesito algo.

Resource List

Everything you need to ...

Plan

TEACHER ONE STOP

- ✓Lesson Plans
- ✓Teacher Resources
- ✓Audio and Video

Present

INTERACTIVE WHITEBOARD LESSONS

TEACHER ONE STOP WITH PROJECTABLE TRANSPARENCIES

POWER PRESENTATIONS

ANIMATEDGRAMMAR

Assess

ONLINE ASSESSMENT

- ✓ Assessments for on-level, modified, pre-AP, and heritage learners
- ✓ Create customized tests with **Examview Assessment Suite**
- ✓ **performance space**
- ✓ *Generate Success* Rubric Generator

Print

Plan	Present	Practice	Assess
URB 8 • Video Scripts pp. 69–70 • Family Letter p. 91 • Absent Student Copymasters pp. 93–100 **Best Practices Toolkit**	**URB 8** • Video Activities pp. 51–58	• *Cuaderno* pp. 344–366 • *Cuaderno para hispanohablantes* pp. 344–366 • *Lecturas para todos* pp. 72–76 • *Lecturas para hispanohablantes* • *¡AvanzaCómics! SuperBruno y Nati*, Episodio 4 **URB 8** • Practice Games pp. 31–38 • Audio Scripts pp. 73–77 • Map/Culture Activities pp. 83–84 • Fine Art Activities pp. 86–87	**Differentiated Assessment Program** **URB 8** • Did you get it? Reteaching and Practice Copymasters pp. 1–12

Projectable Transparencies (Teacher One Stop, my.hrw.com)

Culture	Presentation and Practice	Classroom Management
• Atlas Maps 1–6 • Map of Costa Rica 1 • Fine Art Transparencies 2, 3	• Vocabulary Transparencies 6, 7 • Grammar Presentation Transparencies 10, 11	• Warm Up Transparencies 16–19 • Student Book Answer Transparencies 24–27

Audio and Video

Audio	Video	¡AvanzaRap! DVD
• Student Book Audio CD 8 Tracks 1–11 • Workbook Audio CD 4 Tracks 21–30 • Heritage Learners Audio CD 2 Tracks 25–28, CD 4 Tracks 19–20 • Assessment Audio CD 2 Tracks 19–20 • *Lecturas para todos* Audio CD 1 Track 15, CD 2 Tracks 1–6 • Sing-along Songs Audio CD	• Vocabulary Video DVD 2 • *Telehistoria* DVD 2 Escena 1 Escena 2 Escena 3 Completa	• Video animations of all **¡AvanzaRap!** songs (with Karaoke track) • Interactive DVD Activities • Teaching Suggestions • **¡AvanzaRap!** Activity Masters • **¡AvanzaRap!** video scripts and answers

Online and Media Resources

Student	Teacher
Available online at my.hrw.com • Online Student Edition • News Networking • performance space • @HOMETUTOR • CULTURA Interactiva • WebQuests • Interactive Flashcards • Review Games • Self-Check Quiz **Student One Stop** **Holt McDougal Spanish Apps**	**Teacher One Stop (also available at my.hrw.com)** • Interactive Teacher's Edition • All print, audio, and video resources • Projectable Transparencies • Lesson Plans • TPRS • Examview Assessment Suite **Available online at my.hrw.com** *Generate Success* Rubric Generator and Graphic Organizers **Power Presentations**

Differentiated Assessment

On-level	Modified	Pre-AP	Heritage Learners
• Vocabulary Recognition Quiz p. 348 • Vocabulary Production Quiz p. 349 • Grammar Quizzes pp. 350–351 • Culture Quiz p. 352 • On-level Lesson Test pp. 353–359	• Modified Lesson Test pp. 278–284	• Pre-AP Lesson Test pp. 278–284	• Heritage Learners Lesson Test pp. 284–290

Core Pacing Guide

50 Minute (9 Day)

	Objectives/Focus	Teach	Practice	Assess/HW Options
DAY 1	**Culture:** learn about Costa Rica **Vocabulary:** Daily routines • Warm Up OHT 16 **5 min**	Unit Opener pp. 406–407 Lesson Opener pp. 408–409 **Presentación de vocabulario** pp. 410–411 • Read A–E • View video DVD 2 • Play audio TXT CD 8 track 1 • *¡A responder!* TXT CD 8 track 2 **25 min**	Lesson opener pp. 408–409 **Práctica de vocabulario** p. 412 • Acts. 1, 2 **15 min**	**Assess:** *Para y piensa* p. 412 **5 min** **Homework:** *Cuaderno* pp. 344–346 @HomeTutor
DAY 2	**Communication:** daily routines • Warm Up OHT 16 • Check Homework **5 min**	**Vocabulario en contexto** pp. 413–414 • *Telehistoria escena 1* DVD 2 **20 min**	**Vocabulario en contexto** pp. 413–414 • Act. 3 TXT CD 8 track 3 • Act. 4 **20 min**	**Assess:** *Para y piensa* p. 414 **5 min** **Homework:** *Cuaderno* pp. 344–346 @HomeTutor
DAY 3	**Grammar:** reflexive verbs • Warm Up OHT 17 • Check Homework **5 min**	**Presentación de gramática** p. 415 • reflexive verbs **Práctica de gramática** pp. 416–417 **Culture:** *El paisaje de Costa Rica* **20 min**	**Práctica de gramática** pp. 416–417 • Acts. 5, 6, 7, 8 **20 min**	**Assess:** *Para y piensa* p. 417 **5 min** **Homework:** *Cuaderno* pp. 347–349 @HomeTutor
DAY 4	**Communication:** vacation schedules • Warm Up OHT 17 • Check Homework **5 min**	**Gramática en contexto** pp. 418–419 • *Telehistoria escena 2* DVD 2 • *Pronunciación* TXT CD 8 track 6 **15 min**	**Gramática en contexto** pp. 418–419 • Act. 9 TXT CD 8 track 4 • Act. 10 TXT CD 8 track 5 **25 min**	**Assess:** *Para y piensa* p. 419 **5 min** **Homework:** *Cuaderno* pp. 347–349 @HomeTutor
DAY 5	**Grammar:** present progressive • Warm Up OHT 18 • Check Homework **5 min**	**Presentación de gramática** p. 420 • present progressive **Práctica de gramática** pp. 421–422 **15 min**	**Práctica de gramática** pp. 421–422 • Acts. 11, 12, 13, 14 **25 min**	**Assess:** *Para y piensa* p. 422 **5 min** **Homework:** *Cuaderno* pp. 350–352 @HomeTutor
DAY 6	**Communication:** Culmination: daily routines, reflexive verbs, present progressive • Warm Up OHT 18 • Check Homework **5 min**	**Todo junto** pp. 423–425 • *Escenas 1, 2: Resumen* • *Telehistoria completa* DVD 2 **20 min**	**Todo junto** pp. 423–425 • Acts. 15, 16 TXT CD 8 tracks 3, 4, 7 • Acts. 17, 19 • Act. 18 TXT CD 8 tracks 8, 9 **20 min**	**Assess:** *Para y piensa* p. 425 **5 min** **Homework:** *Cuaderno* pp. 353–354 @HomeTutor
DAY 7	**Reading:** My trip to Costa Rica **Connections:** Science • Warm Up OHT 19 • Check Homework **5 min**	**Lectura** pp. 426–427 • *Mi viaje a Costa Rica* TXT CD 8 track 10 **Conexiones** p. 428 • *Las ciencias* **15 min**	**Lectura** pp. 426–427 • *Mi viaje a Costa Rica* **Conexiones** p. 428 • *Proyectos* 1, 2, 3 **25 min**	**Assess:** *Para y piensa* p. 427 **5 min** **Homework:** *Cuaderno* pp. 358–360 @HomeTutor
DAY 8	**Review:** Lesson review • Warm Up OHT 19 **5 min**	**Repaso de la lección** pp. 430–431 **15 min**	**Repaso de la lección** pp. 430–431 • Act. 1 TXT CD 8 track 11 • Acts. 2, 3, 4, 5 **20 min**	**Assess: Repaso de la lección,** pp. 430–431 **10 min** **Homework:** *En resumen* p. 429; *Cuaderno* pp. 355–357, 361–366 (optional) Review Games Online @HomeTutor
DAY 9	**Assessment**			**Assess:** Lesson 1 Test **50 min**

	Objectives/Focus	Teach	Practice	Assess/HW Options
DAY 1	**Culture:** learn about Costa Rica **Vocabulary:** Daily routines • Warm Up OHT 16 **5 min**	Unit Opener pp. 406–407 Lesson Opener pp. 408–409 **Presentación de vocabulario** pp. 410–411 • Read A–E • View video DVD 2 • Play audio TXT CD 8 track 1 • *¡A responder!* TXT CD 8 track 2 **20 min**	Lesson Opener pp. 408–409 **Práctica de vocabulario** p. 412 • Acts. 1, 2 **20 min**	**Assess:** *Para y piensa* p. 412 **5 min** @HomeTutor
	Communication: daily routines **5 min**	**Vocabulario en contexto** pp. 413–414 • *Telehistoria escena 1* DVD 2 **15 min**	**Vocabulario en contexto** pp. 413–414 • Act. 3 TXT CD 8 track 3 • Act. 4 **15 min**	**Assess:** *Para y piensa* p. 414 **5 min** **Homework:** *Cuaderno* pp. 344–346 @HomeTutor
DAY 2	**Grammar:** reflexive verbs • Warm Up OHT 17 • Check Homework **5 min**	**Presentación de gramática** p. 415 • reflexive verbs **Práctica de gramática** pp. 416–417 **Culture:** *El paisaje de Costa Rica* **20 min**	**Práctica de gramática** pp. 416–417 • Acts. 5, 6, 7, 8 **15 min**	**Assess:** *Para y piensa* p. 417 **5 min**
	Communication: vacation schedules **5 min**	**Gramática en contexto** pp. 418–419 • *Telehistoria escena 2* DVD 2 • *Pronunciación* TXT CD 8 track 6 **20 min**	**Gramática en contexto** pp. 418 • Act. 9 TXT CD 8 track 4 • Act. 10 TXT CD 8 track 5 **15 min**	**Assess:** *Para y piensa* p. 419 **5 min** **Homework:** *Cuaderno* pp. 347–349 @HomeTutor
DAY 3	**Grammar:** present progressive • Warm Up OHT 18 • Check Homework **5 min**	**Presentación de gramática** p. 420 • present progressive **Práctica de gramática** pp. 421–422 **15 min**	**Práctica de gramática** pp. 421–422 • Acts. 11, 12, 13, 14 **20 min**	**Assess:** *Para y piensa* p. 422 **5 min**
	Communication: Culmination: daily routines, reflexive verbs, present progressive **5 min**	**Todo junto** pp. 423–425 • *Escenas 1, 2: Resumen* • *Telehistoria completa* DVD 2 **15 min**	**Todo junto** pp. 423–425 • Acts. 15, 16 TXT CD 8 tracks 3, 4, 7 • Acts. 17, 19 • Act. 18 TXT CD 8 tracks 8, 9 **20 min**	**Assess:** *Para y piensa* p. 425 **5 min** **Homework:** *Cuaderno* pp. 350–354 @HomeTutor
DAY 4	**Reading:** My trip to Costa Rica • Warm Up OHT 19 • Check Homework **5 min**	**Lectura** pp. 426–427 • *Mi viaje a Costa Rica* TXT CD 8 track 10 **15 min**	**Lectura** pp. 426–427 • *Mi viaje a Costa Rica* **15 min**	**Assess:** *Para y piensa* p. 427 **5 min**
	Review: Lesson review **5 min**	**Repaso de la lección** pp. 430–431 **15 min**	**Repaso de la lección** pp. 430–431 • Act. 1 TXT CD 8 track 11 • Acts. 2, 3, 4, 5 **20 min**	**Assess: Repaso de la lección** pp. 430–431 **10 min** **Homework:** *En resumen* p. 429; *Cuaderno* pp. 355–366 (optional) Review Games Online @HomeTutor
DAY 5	**Assessment**			**Assess:** Lesson 1 Test **45 min**
	Connections: Science **5 min**	**Conexiones** p. 428 • *Las ciencias* **10 min**	**Conexiones** p. 428 • *Proyectos* 1, 2, 3 **30 min**	

¡AVANZA! Objectives

- Introduce lesson theme: **Pensando en las vacaciones.**
- **Culture:** Discuss landscapes in other parts of the world with those that students know.

Presentation Strategies

- Introduce the characters' names: Susana and Jorge.
- Ask students to make a list of their daily routine.
- Ask students where they would like to go on vacation.

STANDARDS

2.2 Products and perspectives
4.2 Compare cultures
21st Century **Communication,** Slower-paced Learners; **Social and Cross-Cultural Skills,** Compara con tu mundo

Warm Up Projectable Transparencies, 8-16

Pronouns after Prepositions Complete the sentences with the appropriate word.

ella   ti   conmigo   contigo

1. ¿Te gustaría ir ____ a la playa?
2. ¿Está Ana en casa? ¿Puedo hablar con ____?
3. Lo siento, no puedo ir al cine ____.
4. ¡Feliz cumpleaños, Carlos! Este regalo es para ____.

Answers: 1. conmigo; 2. ella; 3. contigo; 4. ti

Comparación cultural

Exploring the Theme

Ask the following:

1. What is the climate in your region? Are there seasonal differences?
2. Are there vacation spots in your region? What sorts of activities can you do there?
3. Have you had the opportunity to take a vacation abroad? Where?

¿Qué ves? Possible answers include:

- Sí, hace sol.
- Hay fruta en la mesa.
- La familia está en el patio de su casa.

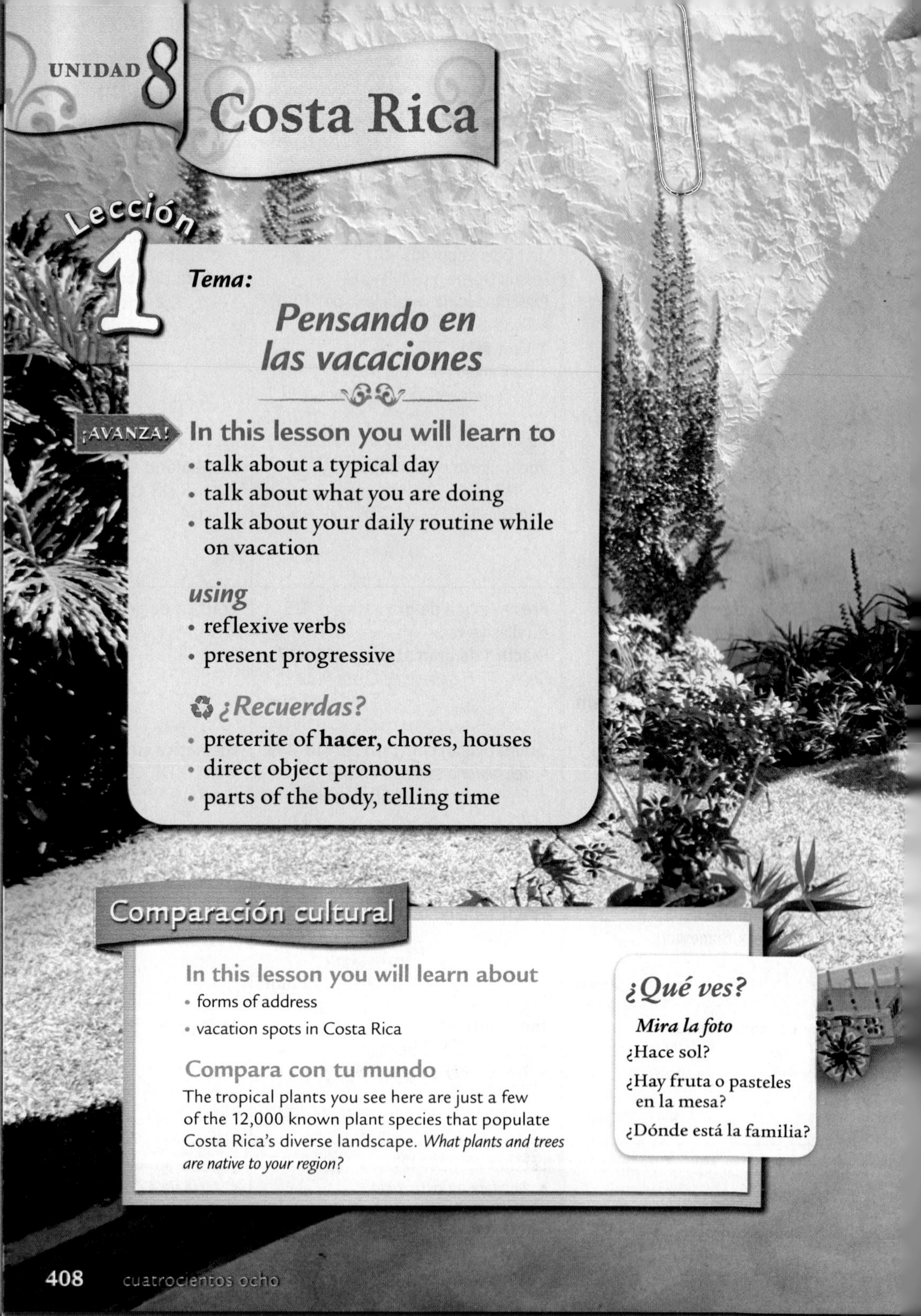

UNIDAD 8 Costa Rica

Lección 1

Tema:

Pensando en las vacaciones

¡AVANZA! In this lesson you will learn to

- talk about a typical day
- talk about what you are doing
- talk about your daily routine while on vacation

using

- reflexive verbs
- present progressive

¿Recuerdas?

- preterite of **hacer,** chores, houses
- direct object pronouns
- parts of the body, telling time

Comparación cultural

In this lesson you will learn about

- forms of address
- vacation spots in Costa Rica

Compara con tu mundo

The tropical plants you see here are just a few of the 12,000 known plant species that populate Costa Rica's diverse landscape. *What plants and trees are native to your region?*

¿Qué ves?

Mira la foto

¿Hace sol?

¿Hay fruta o pasteles en la mesa?

¿Dónde está la familia?

408 cuatrocientos ocho

Differentiating Instruction

Multiple Intelligences

Kinesthetic Review parts of the body by playing a modified Simon Says game. Say the name of a body part aloud, and instruct students to point to that body part. Then give volunteers the opportunity to lead the game. As a challenge, ask students to say something about each body part indicated. **Me duele la rodilla. Levanto pesas con los brazos.**

Inclusion

Cumulative Instruction Organize students into four groups. Give each group a piece of chart paper or poster board. Then direct students' attention to the topics under the ¿Recuerdas? title on p. 408. Assign each group one of the topics. Instruct them to create a poster that will help their peers review the details of that topic. They might design a chart, list examples, or create an exercise.

DIGITAL SPANISH my.hrw.com
ONLINE STUDENT EDITION with...

performance space
News + Networking
@HOMETUTOR
CULTURA Interactiva

- Audio and Video Resources
- Interactive Flashcards
- Review Activities
- WebQuest
- Conjuguemos.com

PRACTICE SPANISH WITH HOLT MCDOUGAL APPS!

Una familia habla de las vacaciones
San José, Costa Rica

Differentiating Instruction

Slower-paced Learners

Personalize It Ask students to talk about places they have visited or vacations they have taken with their families. Encourage them to use the preterite of the verb **ir** to express where they went. Tell them they can use specific place names, such as **Los Ángeles** or **España**, or general place names, such as **la playa** or **la ciudad**.

Heritage Language Learners

Support What They Know Ask students to share the story of a memorable family vacation or trip. Where did they go and what did they do there? Why was this vacation or trip special? Encourage students to use as much detail as possible in their description and narration.

DIGITAL SPANISH

TEACHER TOOLS
- Interactive Whiteboard Lessons
- Generate Success!

ALSO AVAILABLE...
- Online Workbook
- Spanish InterActive Reader

SPANISH ON THE GO!
- Performance Space
- Holt McDougal Spanish Apps
- ¡Avancemos! eTextbook

Using the Photo

About the Photo

In **San José**, the temperature is around 70 to 75 degrees year round. Because of its temperate climate, many San José homes have walled-in backyards with cozy patios and lush vegetation.

Expanded Information

The National Conservation Areas System of Costa Rica (SINAC) protects more than 186 areas, including 32 national parks, 8 biological reserves, 13 forest reserves, and 51 wildlife refuges.

The lure for 90 percent of all visitors to the park system is these parks: Manuel Antonio, with its beautiful beaches; Braulio Carrillo, a rain forest located beside a highway; Tortuguero, a watery, forested world teeming with wildlife; Irazú, where on a clear day there are views of the Caribbean and the Pacific; and Poás, noted for its steaming crater allowing visitors to see the earth's crust.

Long-term Retention

Recycle

Ask students questions about the photo. For example: **¿Hay tres o cuatro personas? (cuatro) ¿Están contentos o tristes? (contentos) ¿Hablan de las vacaciones o de la escuela? (vacaciones)**

¡AVANZA! **Objective**

- Present vocabulary: daily routine, personal-care items, vacation destinations, ways to travel.

Core Resources

- Video Program: DVD 2
- Audio Program: TXT CD 8 tracks 1, 2

Presentation Strategies

- Point to the photos on pp. 410–411, say the words, and have students repeat after you. Correct pronunciation as needed.
- Play the audio as students read A–E.
- Play the video.

STANDARDS

1.2 Understand language

21st Century **Critical Thinking and Problem Solving,** Multiple Intelligences

Communication

TPR Activity

Using vocabulary from the lesson, read expressions about activities that are usually part of the daily routine and other statements not part of the daily routine. Ask students to stand up if the expressions refer to part of the daily routine. Example: **Secarse el pelo (sí), levantarse (sí), nadar (no), jugar al básquetbol (no), ir a un museo (no).**

Long-term Retention

Critical Thinking

Categorize Write on the board categories for the words on pp. 410–411. For example: **rutina diaria** (daily routine), **cuidado personal** (personal-care items), **transporte** (transportation), **lugar** (place). Say a word and ask students to give you the corresponding category. For example: **cepillo de dientes → cuidado personal; campo → lugar.**

Communication

Common Error Alert

Remind students that when using reflexive verbs and a direct object, Spanish speakers use the definite articles **el, la, los, las** as opposed to possessive adjectives. Example: **Me lavo la cara. Me cepillo los dientes.**

Presentación de VOCABULARIO

¡AVANZA! **Goal:** Learn about the daily routines of Susana and Jorge and where they would like to go on vacation. Then practice what you have learned to talk about your daily routine and trips you've taken. ***Actividades 1–2***

¿Recuerdas? Preterite of **hacer** p. 385

VIDEO DVD

AUDIO

A ¡Hola! Me llamo Susana. En los días de escuela **me acuesto** muy temprano. **Normalmente** tengo que **despertarme** a las seis. Antes del desayuno voy al baño para **lavarme la cara** y **maquillarme.**

B **Generalmente** mi hermano Jorge **se levanta** tarde y pasa mucho tiempo en el baño. **Se afeita, se ducha** y usa **el secador de pelo** para **secarse el pelo.** Siempre usa mi **pasta de dientes** para **cepillarse los dientes.** No es fácil vivir con él.

Differentiating Instruction

Pre-AP

Sequence Information Distribute nine index cards to each student. On each card, have students write the infinitive for each reflexive verb presented on pp. 410 and 411. Then have students put their cards in order based on their own daily routine.

Slower-paced Learners

Yes/No Questions Ask students yes/no questions about their daily routines. Use qualifying words, such as **normalmente** and **generalmente** in your questions. **¿Normalmente te levantas después de las siete? ¿Generalmente te pones una chaqueta?**

C Después de **peinarse** y **vestirse,** Jorge se **pone** una chaqueta para ir a la escuela. Está contento porque mañana vamos **de vacaciones.**

peinarse

vestirse

ponerse la chaqueta

D Para **las vacaciones,** mi familia y yo vamos a **hacer un viaje.** A mí me gustaría ir a **la ciudad,** pero Jorge quiere ir al **campo.**

la ciudad

el campo

E Mamá prefiere hacer un viaje **en tren** y papá quiere hacer un viaje **en barco.**

en tren

en barco

Más vocabulario

en avión *by plane*
el hotel *hotel*
esperar *to wait (for)*
quedarse en *to stay in*
la rutina *routine*
bañarse *to take a bath*
lavarse *to wash oneself*
secarse *to dry oneself*
Expansión de vocabulario p. R9

@HOMETUTOR my.hrw.com Interactive Flashcards

¡A responder! Escuchar

Escucha la rutina de Jorge. Mientras escuchas, representa las acciones.
(Listen to Jorge's routine and act out the verbs as you hear them.)

Communication

Common Error Alert

1. Inform students of the following stem-changing verbs:
   - **acostarse** an **o → ue** stem-changing verb
   - **despertarse** an **e → ie** stem-changing verb
   - **vestirse** an **e → i** stem-changing verb
2. Explain to students that the plural of nouns ending in **-ón**, like **avión**, **jabón**, is formed by adding **-es** at the end. In the plural form, the accent is dropped: **aviones**, **jabones.**

Long-term Retention

Study Tips

Suggest that students group the reflexive verbs presented in this lesson by type. One group should include the **-ar** verbs, a second the **-er** verbs, and a third the **-ir** verbs.

Long-term Retention

Personalize It

Ask students **¿Qué te gusta hacer durante las vacaciones?** to see how many vacation-related activities they can produce.

Differentiating Instruction

Slower-paced Learners

Memory Aids Have students create their own set of flashcards for the vocabulary presented on pp. 410 and 411. Encourage them to use magazines to find ads or photos representative of each word or phrase. Then have them glue the photo to the front of the card, and write the word or phrase on the back.

Multiple Intelligences

Logical/Mathematical As a group, take a survey of students' vacation preferences. **¿La ciudad o el campo? ¿En tren, en barco, en coche o en avión?** Record the results in a chart. Then have students present the data in the form of a bar graph or pie chart. Ask questions about the findings. **¿Cuál es más popular—un viaje a la ciudad o un viaje al campo?**

Answers Projectable Transparencies, 8-24

¡A responder! Audio Script, TE p. 407B

Students should pantomime the following:

1. Waking up
2. Getting up
3. Washing their face
4. Shaving
5. Washing their hair
6. Combing their hair
7. Brushing their teeth
8. Putting on their shoes

Objectives
- Practice vocabulary: daily routine, personal-care items, ways to travel, vacation destinations.
- Recycle: preterite of **hacer.**

Core Resource
- *Cuaderno,* pp. 344–346

Practice Sequence
- **Activity 1**: Vocabulary recognition: daily routine, personal-care items
- **Activity 2:** Vocabulary production; modes of transportation, vacation destinations; Recycle: preterite of **hacer**

STANDARDS
1.1 Engage in conversation, Act. 2
1.3 Present information, Acts. 1-2, PYP

✓ Ongoing Assessment
Get Help Online
More Practice
my.hrw.com

PARA Y PIENSA **Intervention** If students miss more than two items in each Para y piensa question, suggest that they review pp. 410-411. For additional practice, use Reteaching & Practice Copymasters URB 8, pp. 1, 2, 10.

Answers Projectable Transparencies, 8-24
Activity 1 **1.** d; **2.** f; **3.** c; **4.** h; **5.** g; **6.** a; **7.** b; **8.** e

Activity 2
1. **A:** ¿Hiciste un viaje en tren?
   B: Sí, hice un viaje en tren. (No, no hice un viaje en tren.)
2. **A:** ¿... en avión?
   B: Sí, hice un viaje en avión. (No, no hice un viaje en avión.)
3. **A:** ¿... en barco?
   B: Sí, hice un viaje en barco. (No, no hice un viaje en barco.)
4. **A:** ¿... a la ciudad?
   B: Sí, hice un viaje a la ciudad. (No, no hice un viaje a la ciudad.)
5. **A:** ¿... al campo?
   B: Sí, hice un viaje al campo. (No, no hice un viaje al campo.)
6. **A:** ¿... a la playa?
   B: Sí, hice un viaje a la playa. (No, no hice un viaje a la playa.)

Para y piensa Answers will vary. Sample answers include:
1. Me levanto, me baño, me seco el pelo. Me cepillo los dientes, me acuesto, me duermo.
2. en tren, en avión, en barco

Práctica de VOCABULARIO

1 ¿Qué usas?

Leer

Empareja cada actividad con el objeto correspondiente. *(Match each activity with the item that someone would need to do the activity.)*

1. secarse el cuerpo	**a.** el cepillo de dientes
2. bañarse	**b.** la ropa
3. lavarse el pelo	**c.** el champú
4. secarse el pelo	**d.** la toalla
5. peinarse	**e.** el espejo
6. cepillarse los dientes	**f.** el jabón
7. vestirse	**g.** el peine
8. maquillarse	**h.** el secador de pelo

Expansión
Make a list of the items you used while getting ready for school this morning.

2 Las vacaciones

¿Recuerdas? Preterite of **hacer** p. 385

Hablar

Pregúntale a otro(a) estudiante si hizo estas cosas durante las vacaciones. *(Ask a partner if he or she did the following things during vacation.)*

modelo: hacer un viaje en

A ¿Hiciste un viaje en coche?

B Sí, hice un viaje en coche el año pasado.

1. hacer un viaje en

2. hacer un viaje en

3. hacer un viaje en

4. hacer un viaje a

5. hacer un viaje a

6. hacer un viaje a

Expansión:
Teacher Edition Only
Ask students to write three sentences about where they went during the last year and what means of transportation they used.

Más práctica Cuaderno *pp. 344–346* Cuaderno para hispanohablantes *pp. 344–347*

Get Help Online
my.hrw.com

PARA Y PIENSA

Did you get it?
1. Name three morning activities and three nighttime activities in your daily routine.
2. Name three ways to travel.

Differentiating Instruction

Multiple Intelligences

Kinesthetic In advance, collect examples of the objects listed in Activity 1. Review with students the name of each. Then invite a student to act out one of the actions from the left-hand column. Another student must then collect the items necessary for that activity and give them to the first student. Encourage students to narrate their choices. **Para secarse el cuerpo, Ángel necesita una toalla.**

Inclusion

Frequent Review/Repetition Before beginning Activity 2, have students review the preterite forms of the verb **hacer**. Say each pronoun aloud, and have students respond with the preterite form. **Yo... hice, Tú... hiciste,** etc. Encourage students to change the pronouns in their questions and answers. **¿Hizo tu madre un viaje en tren? Sí, ella hizo un viaje en tren.**

VOCABULARIO en contexto

¡AVANZA! **Goal:** Identify the words Susana uses to talk about what she would like to do on vacation. Then use the words to talk about being on vacation. ***Actividades 3–4***

¿Recuerdas? Direct object pronouns p. 204

Telehistoria escena 1

@HOMETUTOR my.hrw.com **View, Read and Record**

STRATEGIES

Cuando lees
Group the travel expressions While reading, group the scene's expressions for vacation destinations and modes of transportation. What are some other destinations and modes of transportation?

Cuando escuchas
Understand the interruption Notice the interruption. Who interrupts whom? What is each person doing at the time? What is the response? How do you think the parents feel when they arrive?

VIDEO DVD

AUDIO

Susana reads about vacations as she waits for her brother so they can leave for school.

Susana: *(daydreaming)* Voy a hacer un viaje con mi familia. Podemos ir en avión, en barco...

Jorge: *(yelling from the other room)* ¡Susana!

Susana: *(ignoring him)* ¿Voy al campo o a la ciudad? El año pasado mi familia y yo fuimos al campo. Pero yo generalmente prefiero...

Jorge: ¡Susana! ¿Qué haces?

She goes to the kitchen. Jorge is sitting calmly at the table, shaking an empty milk carton.

Jorge: Susana, ¿dónde está la leche?

Susana: ¡Mamá, papá!

Their parents come running into the kitchen.

Mamá: Susana, ¿qué?

Susana: Mi hermano es imposible. ¡Me voy a quedar en un hotel!

Continuará... p. 418

Differentiating Instruction

Pre-AP

Expand and Elaborate Point out that Susana's lines in the Telehistoria end with an ellipses twice. She stops talking aloud, but her thoughts continue. Have students draft one or two sentences to continue Susana's thoughts.

Heritage Language Learners

Writing Skills In small groups, have students create a travel brochure like the one Susana is reading in the Telehistoria. Instruct students to include information about means of travel, schedule, hotel, and pricing, as well as more general information about the destination and its activities. Advise students to present the information in a way that is well-organized and engaging.

¡AVANZA! **Objective**

- Understand activity vocabulary in context.

Core Resources

- Video Program: DVD 2
- Audio Program: TXT CD 8 track 3

Presentation Strategies

- Have students look at the photos and ask simple answer questions such as: **¿Quién quiere beber leche? ¿Quién lee de las vacaciones? ¿Qué lleva la mamá, una camiseta azul o una camiseta verde?**
- Have students scan the dialogue to find out how many modes of transportation are mentioned.
- Play audio or video while students follow the script in their text.

STANDARDS

1.2 Understand language

21st Century Creativity and Innovation, Heritage Language Learners

Warm Up Projectable Transparencies, 8-16

Vocabulary Write the item needed for each activity.

1. cepillarse los dientes
2. secarse el cuerpo
3. peinarse
4. lavarse la cara
5. vestirse

Answers: 1. el cepillo de dientes; 2. la toalla; 3. el peine; 4. el jabón; 5. la ropa

Video Summary

@HOMETUTOR VideoPlus my.hrw.com

While waiting for her brother, Susana dreams about a trip she will take with her family. While Jorge calls out her name, Susana continues to think about last year's vacation and about options for a trip this year. Susana finally goes to the kitchen to discover that Jorge wants to know where the milk has gone. Susana calls their parents into the kitchen, and says her brother is impossible and that she wants to stay in a hotel.

Objectives
- Practice using the vocabulary in context.
- Recycle: direct object pronouns.

Core Resource
- Audio Program: TXT CD 8 track 3

Practice Sequence
- **Activity 3:** Telehistoria comprehension
- **Activity 4:** Vocabulary production: personal-care items; Recycle: direct object pronouns

STANDARDS
1.1 Engage in conversation, Act. 4
1.2 Understand language, Act. 3
1.3 Present information, Act. 4, PYP

✓ Ongoing Assessment

Get Help Online
More Practice
my.hrw.com

PARA Y PIENSA **Peer Assessment** Have pairs of students complete the Para y piensa sentences and correct each other's work. For additional practice, use Reteaching & Practice Copymasters URB 8, pp. 1, 3, 11.

Answers Projectable Transparencies, 8-24

Activity 3
1. Susana va a hacer un viaje.
2. Quiere ir de vacaciones con su familia.
3. Pueden hacer el viaje en avión o en barco.
4. Pueden ir al campo o a la ciudad.
5. Fueron al campo el año pasado.
6. Jorge es el hermano de Susana.
7. Jorge es imposible.

Activity 4
1. No tengo la toalla.
   Está bien. En el hotel la tienen.
2. No tengo la pasta de dientes.
   En el hotel no la tienen.
3. No tengo el cepillo.
   En el hotel no lo tienen.
4. No tengo el secador de pelo.
   Está bien. En el hotel lo tienen.
5. No tengo el champú.
   Está bien. En el hotel lo tienen.
6. No tengo el jabón.
   Está bien. En el hotel lo tienen.
7. No tengo el peine.
   Está bien. En el hotel lo tienen.
8. No tengo el cepillo de dientes.
   En el hotel no lo tienen.

Para y piensa **1.** unas vacaciones; **2.** la ciudad; **3.** un hotel

3 *Comprensión del episodio* Las vacaciones de Susana

Escuchar
Leer

Contesta las preguntas. *(Answer the questions.)*

1. ¿Qué va a hacer Susana?
2. ¿Con quién quiere ir de vacaciones?
3. ¿Cómo pueden hacer el viaje?
4. ¿Adónde pueden ir de vacaciones?
5. ¿Adónde fueron el año pasado?
6. ¿Quién es Jorge?
7. ¿Cómo es Jorge?

Expansión:
Teacher Edition Only
Ask students to write a brief summary of the Telehistoria episode using the Activity questions as a guide.

4 En el hotel

¿Recuerdas? Direct object pronouns p. 204

Hablar

Estás de vacaciones y perdiste la maleta. Dile a otro(a) estudiante las cosas que no tienes. Basado en la tarjeta, él o ella te va a decir si en el hotel las tienen o no. *(Tell your partner the items that you don't have. He or she will tell you if they are available at the hotel.)*

A No tengo el reloj.

B Está bien. En el hotel lo tienen.

1. 
2. 

3. 
4. 
5. 
6. 
7. 
8. 

Expansión
Write a list of items you would pack to stay overnight at a friend's house. Compare your list with a partner's.

Get Help Online
my.hrw.com

PARA Y PIENSA

Did you get it? Complete each sentence with the most logical word, based on the Telehistoria: **la ciudad, unas vacaciones,** or **un hotel.**
1. Susana quiere tomar ____ .
2. Susana no quiere ir al campo; prefiere ir a ____ .
3. Susana quiere quedarse en ____ para estar lejos de Jorge.

Differentiating Instruction

Slower-paced Learners

Peer-study Support Organize students into pairs to complete Activity 3. Assign one partner the even-numbered questions, and the other the odd-numbered questions. Instruct pairs to come up with two answer choices for each question. **¿Qué va a hacer Susana? ¿Va a hacer un viaje con su familia o va a pasar un rato con sus amigos?**

Inclusion

Synthetic/Analytic Support Write the direct object pronouns **lo, la, los,** and **las** on separate self-sticking notes. Then ask for a volunteer to write the word for each picture in Activity 4 on the board. Review with students the direct object pronoun that corresponds with each noun, for example, **lo** for **el jabón**. Ask for a volunteer to place the correct note in front of each word.

Presentación de GRAMÁTICA

¡AVANZA! **Goal:** Learn how to form and use reflexive verbs. Then use these verbs to describe the daily routines of yourself and others. ***Actividades 5–8***

¿Recuerdas? Parts of the body p. 327

English Grammar Connection: Reflexive verbs and **reflexive pronouns** show that the subject of a sentence both does and receives the action of the verb. The reflexive pronouns in English end in *-self* or *-selves.*

She **dried herself** with a towel. Ella **se secó** con una toalla.

Reflexive Verbs

ANIMATEDGRAMMAR my.hrw.com

Use **reflexive pronouns** with **reflexive verbs** when the subject in a sentence is the same as its object.

Here's how:

lavar**se** *to wash oneself*	
me lavo	**nos** lavamos
te lavas	**os** laváis
se lava	**se** lavan

Many verbs can be used with or without reflexive pronouns. When there is no reflexive pronoun, the person doing the action does not receive the action.

reflexive
Anita **se** lava.
*Anita **washes herself.***

not reflexive
Anita lava los platos.
*Anita **washes** the dishes.*

Do *not* use possessive adjectives with **reflexive verbs.** Use the **definite article** instead.

Anita **se** lava la cara. *Anita **is washing** her face.*

When an infinitive follows a conjugated verb, the **reflexive pronoun** can be placed before the **conjugated verb** or attached to the **infinitive.**

Me voy a **acostar** a las once. *I'm going **to go to bed** at eleven.*
or Voy a **acostarme** a las once.

Some verbs have different meanings when used reflexively.

dormir *to sleep* → **dormirse** *to fall asleep*
poner *to put* → **ponerse** *to put on (clothes)*

Más práctica
Cuaderno *pp. 347–349*
Cuaderno para hispanohablantes *pp. 348–350*

@HOMETUTOR my.hrw.com
Leveled Practice
Conjuguemos.com

¡AVANZA! **Objective**
- Present reflexive pronouns and reflexive verbs.

Core Resource
- *Cuaderno,* pp. 347–349

Presentation Strategies
- Ask students what a reflexive verb is.
- Write the paradigm of **lavarse** on the board or on an OHT.
- Say a subject pronoun and call on students to give you the corresponding reflexive form of **lavarse.** For example: **nosotros → nos lavamos.**
- Explain both ways of using infinitives with reflexive verbs. Give several examples and check comprehension. For example, say: **Me voy a levantar**. Ask students to give you the alternate form: **Voy a levantarme.**

STANDARDS
4.1 Compare languages

Warm Up
Projectable Transparencies, 8-17

Vocabulary Complete the sentences with the correct word.

hotel **viaje** **campo**
acostarte **vacaciones**

1. Mis padres quieren tomar unas _____.
2. Yo quiero quedarme en un _____ cerca de la playa.
3. Podemos hacer el _____ en avión.
4. Alicia no quiere ir a la ciudad, prefiere ir al _____.
5. Debes _____ temprano esta noche.

Answers: 1. vacaciones; 2. hotel; 3. viaje; 4. campo; 5. acostarte

Differentiating Instruction

Multiple Intelligences

Linguistic/Verbal Write on the board, **levantar, lavar.** Ask students to write in their notebooks two sentences using the given verbs, the vocabulary words previously learned, and the reflexive pronouns **me, te.** For example, **Yo me levanto temprano. Tú te lavas las manos.** Ask a volunteer to read aloud his/her sentences and the other students to correct pronunciation.

English Learners

Build Background Write a selection of reflexive English verbs on the board in complete sentences. *I dry myself. She washes herself.* Review with students the words *myself, yourself, himself, herself,* etc. Then draw a circular arrow from the subject to the reflexive pronoun and back again to illustrate that these words refer to the same person.

Objectives
- Practice using reflexive verbs and reflexive pronouns.
- Recycle: parts of the body.
- **Culture:** Learn about Volcán Arenal.

Core Resource
- *Cuaderno,* pp. 347–349

Practice Sequence
- **Activity 5:** Controlled practice: **lavarse**; Recycle: parts of the body
- **Activity 6:** Controlled practice: reflexive verbs, time-sequence words
- **Activity 7:** Transitional practice: use of reflexive and non-reflexive verbs
- **Activity 8:** Open-ended practice: reflexive verbs, frequency words

STANDARDS
1.1 Engage in conversation, Act. 8
1.3 Present information, Acts. 5–7, PYP
2.2 Products and perspectives, CC
21st Century **Critical Thinking and Problem Solving,** Act. 6: Expansión; **Information Literacy,** Multiple Intelligences; **Social and Cross-Cultural Skills,** Comparación cultural

Comparación cultural
Essential Question
Suggested Answer Costa Rica's varied topography: volcanic mountains, rain forests, waterfalls, lakes, beaches, etc. attracts tourists and impacts agriculture.

Práctica de GRAMÁTICA

5 ¡Se lavan!
¿Recuerdas? Parts of the body p. 327

Hablar
Escribir

Explica qué se lavan estas personas. *(Tell what these people wash.)*

1. tú

2. nosotros
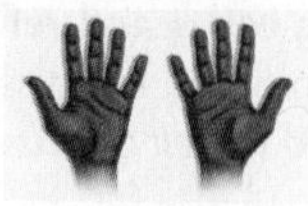
3. Jorge
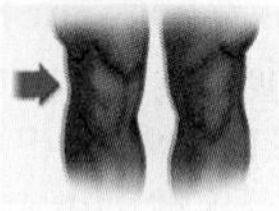
4. yo
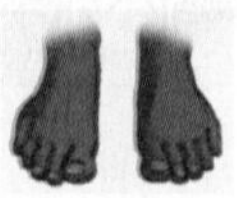
5. ustedes
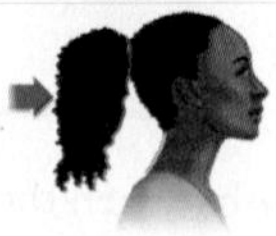
6. los chicos

Expansión: Teacher Edition Only
Ask students to write five more sentences with the verb **lavarse** and different subjects.

6 ¿Qué hacen primero?

Hablar
Escribir

Explica el orden lógico en que las siguientes personas hacen estas actividades. *(Explain the logical order in which the following people do these activities.)*

modelo: yo (dormirse / acostarse)
Primero me acuesto y luego me duermo.

1. mi familia y yo (despertarse / levantarse)
2. tú (vestirse / ducharse)
3. mis amigas (maquillarse / bañarse)
4. usted (secarse / ponerse la ropa)
5. mi padre (afeitarse / secarse la cara)
6. yo (cepillarse los dientes / acostarse)

Expansión
Compare the order of your regular morning or nighttime activities with those of a partner.

Comparación cultural

Volcán Arenal, Costa Rica

El paisaje de Costa Rica
How can a country's geography affect daily life? **Costa Rica's** varied landscape includes mountain ranges, active volcanoes, tropical rain forests, rivers, and sandy beaches. Volcán Arenal is one of the ten most active volcanoes in the world, producing glowing red lava and ash columns almost every day. After a major eruption in 1968 which buried several communities, the town of La Fortuna became the area's main village. The volcano heats several hot springs in the area and has become a major tourist attraction.

Compara con tu mundo *How does the landscape of your area compare to Costa Rica? What features are similar or different?*

Differentiating Instruction

Inclusion
Sequential Organization Provide students with the following directions to help organize their responses in Activity 5.
1. Write the corresponding reflexive pronoun.
2. Write the correct form of the verb **lavar**.
3. Write the definite article for the body part.
4. Write the name of the body part.

Multiple Intelligences
Naturalist Assign students the task of researching one of the geographic areas of Costa Rica. Encourage them to find five interesting facts about the region. Also, have them create illustrations or find photographs that represent the landscape. Have students present their findings in the form of a poster.

Answers Projectable Transparencies, 8-25

Activity 5
1. Tú te lavas la cara.
2. Nosotros nos lavamos las manos.
3. Jorge se lava las rodillas.
4. Yo me lavo los pies.

Answers continue on p. 417.

7 Lorena y Napoleón

Hablar
Escribir

Describe el día de Lorena y su perro Napoleón. Usa la forma reflexiva si es necesario. *(Describe Lorena and Napoleón's day, using reflexive verbs when needed.)*

modelo: Lorena despierta a Napoleón.

Expansión: Teacher Edition Only
Ask students to describe their day using reflexive and non-reflexive verbs as needed.

8 ¿Cuándo lo hacen?

Hablar

Habla con otros(as) estudiantes sobre cuándo haces estas actividades. *(Talk about when you generally do these activities.)*

modelo: afeitarse

A ¿Cuándo se afeitan ustedes generalmente?

B Me afeito la cara cuando voy a una fiesta.

C Nunca me afeito.

cuando...
nunca
antes de...
después de...
a la(s)...
¿ ?

1. cepillarse los dientes
2. mirarse en el espejo
3. ducharse
4. levantarse
5. secarse el pelo
6. maquillarse
7. bañarse
8. acostarse
9. lavarse las manos

Expansión
Report the activities you have in common to the class.

Más práctica Cuaderno *pp. 347–349* Cuaderno para hispanohablantes *pp. 348–350*

Get Help Online
my.hrw.com

PARA Y PIENSA

Did you get it? Create sentences using the following information. Use reflexive pronouns only when necessary.

1. yo / lavar(se) / las manos
2. los chicos / secar(se) / el perro
3. Juana y yo / poner(se) / la mesa
4. mi abuelo / afeitar(se) / la cara

Communication

Pair Work

Have students ask each other what items they need in order to complete their daily morning routine. Example: **¿Qué necesitas para despertarte? Para despertarme, necesito un reloj.**

✓ Ongoing Assessment

Get Help Online
More Practice
my.hrw.com

PARA Y PIENSA **Peer Assessment** Have students work in pairs to read answers aloud and check each other's written work. For additional practice, use Reteaching & Practice Copymasters URB 8, pp. 4, 5, 12.

Answers Projectable Transparencies, 8-25

Answers continued from p. 416.

5. Ustedes se lavan el pelo.
6. Los chicos se lavan las piernas.

Activity 6

1. Primero mi familia y yo nos despertamos y luego nos levantamos.
2. Primero tú te duchas y luego te vistes.
3. Primero mis amigas se bañan y luego se maquillan.
4. Primero usted se seca y luego se pone la ropa.
5. Primero mi padre se afeita y luego se seca la cara.
6. Primero me cepillo los dientes y luego me acuesto.

Activity 7

1. Lorena se cepilla el pelo.
2. Lorena cepilla a Napoleón.
3. Lorena se lava la cara.
4. Lorena lava a Napoleón.
5. Lorena seca a Napoleón.
6. Lorena se acuesta.

Activity 8 Answers will vary. Answers must follow this pattern:

1. ¿Cuándo se cepillan los dientes? Me cepillo los dientes después de comer.
2. ¿Cuándo se miran en el espejo? Me miro...
3. ¿Cuándo se duchan? Me ducho...
4. ¿Cuándo se levantan? Me levanto...
5. ¿Cuando se secan...? Me seco...
6. ¿Cuándo se maquillan? Me maquillo...
7. ¿Cuándo se bañan? Me baño...
8. ¿Cuándo se acuestan? Me acuesto...
9. ¿Cuándo se lavan...? Me lavo...

Para y piensa

1. Me lavo las manos.
2. Los chicos secan al perro.
3. Juana y yo ponemos la mesa.
4. Mi abuelo se afeita la cara.

Differentiating Instruction

Pre-AP

Sequence Information Have students add to their descriptions in Activity 7 by using time words, such as **primero, luego, después,** and **entonces**. Also, students can use specific times to express what Lorena does and when. **Lorena se lava la cara a las ocho de la mañana.**

Slower-paced Learners

Sentence Completion Provide students with the following sentence starters to help structure their conversations in Activity 8. Provide the beginning of a response for each activity listed. Here are a few examples.
Me cepillo los dientes antes de...
Me miro en el espejo después de...
Me ducho cuando...

¡AVANZA! Objective

- Identify lesson vocabulary and reflexive verbs in context.
- Learn about and practice the pronunciation of diphthongs in Spanish.

Core Resources

- Video Program: DVD 2
- Audio Program: TXT CD 8 tracks 4, 5, 6

Presentation Strategies

- Have students scan the dialogue looking for examples of reflexive verbs. Ask what they notice about the placement of reflexive pronouns.
- Play the audio while students follow the script.
- Show the video.

Practice Sequence

- **Activity 9:** Telehistoria comprehension
- **Activity 10:** Transitional practice: reflexive verbs

STANDARDS

1.2 Understand language, Acts. 9–10, Pronunciación
1.3 Present information, Acts. 9–10
21st Century **Creativity and Innovation,** Group Work

Warm Up Projectable Transparencies, 8-17

Reflexive Verbs Complete the following sentences.

a. lavan **b.** secamos **c.** Me seco

1. Mis hermanos _____ el carro.
2. _____ el pelo con un secador de pelo.
3. Nosotros _____ los platos.

Answers: 1. a; 2. c; 3. b

Video Summary

@HOMETUTOR VideoPlus my.hrw.com

During lunch, Susana and Jorge talk with their father about vacation plans. Jorge asks if they can go to the beach on Saturday. His father says yes, but adds that Jorge will have to get up at 6 a.m. in order to get to the first bus for Playa Jacó. Jorge asks if they can go to the beach by car, but his father has to work on Saturday. Jorge asks if he can use the car.

GRAMÁTICA en contexto

¡AVANZA! **Goal:** Focus on the reflexive verbs Susana, Jorge, and their father use to talk about their vacation schedules. Then use these reflexive verbs to talk about different routines. ***Actividades 9–10***

Telehistoria escena 2

@HOMETUTOR my.hrw.com View, Read and Record

STRATEGIES

Cuando lees
Compare daily routines While reading, make a note of Jorge's regular daily routine. How do you think his routine will change when he is on vacation?

Cuando escuchas
Listen for persuasion Jorge repeatedly asks his father about going to the beach. Listen to how Jorge tries to persuade him and how his father responds each time. What persuasive techniques would you try?

VIDEO DVD
AUDIO

Susana and Jorge are at home eating lunch with their father.

Susana: ¿Y mamá? ¿Dónde está?
Papá: En la oficina. Ahora ustedes tienen vacaciones, ¿no? ¿Qué planes tienen?
Jorge: Queremos ir a la playa el sábado. ¿Podemos?
Papá: Sí, pero el primer autobús a Playa Jacó sale a las nueve. Con tu rutina, Jorge, debes acostarte a las diez, para levantarte a las seis de la mañana. Necesitas tiempo para ducharte, lavarte el pelo, secarte el pelo, peinarte, ponerte la ropa...
Jorge: *(with a horrified look)* ¿Despertarme a las seis? Normalmente me levanto temprano y me visto rápidamente para ir a la escuela, pero ¡estoy de vacaciones! Papá, ¿podemos ir a la playa en carro?
Papá: No, tengo que ir a la oficina el sábado.
Jorge: *(mischievously)* ¿Puedo usar yo el carro?

Susana and their father look at Jorge in amazement. **Continuará...** p. 423

También se dice

Costa Rica To ask his father about using the car, Jorge says **el carro.** In other Spanish-speaking countries you might hear:
- **España** **el coche**
- **México** **la nave**
- **Venezuela, Cuba** **la máquina**
- **muchos países** **el auto, el automóvil, el vehículo**

Differentiating Instruction

Heritage Language Learners

Support What They Know Point out the description of Jorge's morning routine in the Telehistoria. Then ask students to share a summary of their own morning routines on a school day, and then on a weekend or vacation day. How do they compare? Have all students listen and raise their hands each time they hear the use of a reflexive verb.

Pre-AP

Draw Conclusions Ask students questions about the Telehistoria that begin with the question word **¿por qué?** Remind them that the answers might not be explicitly stated in the text. Here are a few possibilities:
¿Por qué mamá está en la oficina?
¿Por qué Jorge debe acostarse a las diez?
¿Por qué quiere ir en carro a la playa?

9 *Comprensión del episodio* Planes para el sábado

Escuchar
Leer

Empareja las frases para describir el episodio. *(Match phrases from the columns to create accurate sentences according to the episode.)*

1. La madre está **a.** se levanta temprano.
2. Jorge y Susana quieren ir **b.** en la oficina.
3. Normalmente Jorge **c.** más tarde el sábado.
4. Jorge quiere despertarse **d.** porque su padre tiene que trabajar.
5. No pueden ir en coche **e.** a la playa.

Expansión:
Teacher Edition Only
Ask students to write three false statements about the episode, exchange them with a partner, and correct each other's statements.

10 La rutina de Susana

Escuchar
Escribir

Susana habla de lo que hace los sábados. Escucha la descripción y pon las fotos en orden según lo que dice. Luego escribe un párrafo para describir su rutina. *(Listen to Susana's description and put the drawings in order. Then write a paragraph.)*

Audio Program
TXT CD 8 Track 5
Audio Script, TE p. 407b

a.

b.

c.

d.

e.

f.

Expansión
Write about what you did last Saturday.

AUDIO

Pronunciación Los diptongos

In Spanish, vowels are divided into two categories: strong and weak. **A, e,** and **o** are the strong vowels; **i** and **u** are weak. A weak vowel with another vowel forms one sound, called a diphthong.

igualmente **demasiado** **afeitarse** **ciudad**

If there are two consecutive vowels, and one has an accent mark, then each vowel is pronounced separately. The same is true for two strong vowels.

día **país** **frío** **leí** **toalla** **zoológico** **peor** **leer**

Get Help Online
my.hrw.com

PARA Y PIENSA

Did you get it? Complete these sentences with the correct form of **acostarse** or **levantarse,** based on the Telehistoria.
1. Jorge debe _____ a las diez si quiere tomar el autobús a las nueve.
2. Cuando está de vacaciones, Jorge no _____ a las seis.

Communication
Group Work

Have students work in small groups to make up a story about their daily routine using at least five reflexive verbs. Groups then present their stories to the class using props and gestures if possible.

✓ Ongoing Assessment

Dictation Dictate the following sentences to students to check comprehension and correct spelling of diphthongs. **Leí que hace frío en la ciudad. Mi tío se afeita con agua fría todos los días.**

✓ Ongoing Assessment

Get Help Online
More Practice
my.hrw.com

PARA Y PIENSA

Peer Assessment If students have difficulties in completing the sentences, have them review the reflexive pronouns on p. 415. For additional practice, use Reteaching & Practice Copymasters URB 8, pp. 4, 6.

Differentiating Instruction

Multiple Intelligences

Visual Learners Instruct students to divide a piece of paper into six sections, *a* through *f*. In each section, have them draw a simple sketch of the activity shown in the photo in Activity 10. As they listen to Susana, have students take notes in the appropriate section. Finally, have them cut the sections apart, and put them in order.

Inclusion

Alphabetic/Phonetic Awareness Write the words **ciudad** and **frío** on the board. Direct students' attention to the two vowels that are next to each other. When the two vowels blend, such as the **iu** in **ciudad**, have a volunteer circle the two letters together. When the two vowels are distinct, have a volunteer draw a line between the two. Repeat the activity with other examples.

Answers Projectable Transparencies, 8-25

Activity 9 **1.** b; **2.** e; **3.** a; **4.** c; **5.** d

Activity 10 Order of drawings: **e**; **d**; **c**; **a**; **f**; **b**

Suggested Answer: Los sábados, Susana se despierta a las once. Se baña y después se seca la cara. Luego se cepilla los dientes y por fin se maquilla. Los sábados se acuesta muy tarde.

Para y piensa **1.** acostarse; **2.** se levanta

¡AVANZA! **Objective**
- Present the present progressive tense.

Core Resource
- *Cuaderno,* pp. 350–352

Presentation Strategies
- Explain what a present participle is. Ask students for examples in English.
- Point out the present participles of **-ar, -er,** and **-ir** verbs. Give examples of infinitives with these three endings and ask students to say the corresponding present participle. Include stem-changing verbs and the verbs **leer** and **traer.** For example: **estudiar → estudiando, pedir → pidiendo, leer → leyendo.**
- Point out placement of pronouns with the present progressive.

STANDARDS
4.1 Compare languages

Warm Up Projectable Transparencies, 8-18

Reflexive Verbs Complete the sentences.

a. vestirnos **b.** maquillarse **c.** lavarte
d. bañarme **e.** levantarse

1. Jorge no quiere _____ temprano.
2. A mí me gusta _____ por la noche.
3. Preferimos _____ después del desayuno.
4. ¿Necesitas _____ las manos?
5. Mamá y Julia van a _____ para la fiesta.

Answers: 1. e; 2. d; 3. a; 4. c; 5. b

Communication
Common Error Alert

In Spanish, the present progressive is used only to say that an action is in progress at this exact moment. It cannot be used for an action that is not currently in progress; the simple present tense would be used instead.

Presentación de GRAMÁTICA

¡AVANZA! **Goal:** Learn how to form the present progressive tense of the verbs you know. Then practice this tense to talk about what people are doing right now. ***Actividades 11–14***

¿Recuerdas? Chores p. 272, houses p. 248

English Grammar Connection: In both English and Spanish, the **present progressive** tense is used to say that an action is in progress at this moment.

Roberto **is skating** in the park. Roberto **está patinando** en el parque.

Present Progressive

ANIMATEDGRAMMAR my.hrw.com

To form the present progressive in Spanish, use the present tense of **estar** + a **present participle.**

Here's how: To form the **present participle** of a verb, drop the ending of the infinitive and add **-ando** or **-iendo.**

-ar verbs	-er verbs	-ir verbs
caminar ← ando (~~ar~~)	poner ← iendo (~~er~~)	abrir ← iendo (~~ir~~)
caminando	poniendo	abriendo

Estamos poniendo la mesa. ***We are setting*** *the table.*

When the stem of an **-er** or **-ir** verb ends in a vowel, change the **-iendo** to **-yendo.**

leer → leyendo **traer → trayendo**

The **e → i** stem-changing verbs have a vowel change in the stem.

pedir → pidiendo **servir → sirviendo** **vestir → vistiendo**

Some other verbs also have a vowel change in the stem.

decir → diciendo **venir → viniendo** **dormir → durmiendo**

Place **pronouns** before the conjugated form of **estar** or attach them to the end of the **present participle.** Add an **accent** when you attach a pronoun.

Me estoy vistiendo. *or* **Estoy vistiéndome.** *I'm getting dressed.*
before *attached*

Más práctica
Cuaderno *pp. 350–352*
Cuaderno para hispanohablantes *pp. 351–354*

@HOMETUTOR my.hrw.com
Leveled Practice
Conjuguemos.com

Differentiating Instruction

Heritage Language Learners

Increase Accuracy Review with students the spelling of irregular present participles. Give students infinitives with irregular present participles. Have them say and spell the participles aloud.

Inclusion

Synthetic/Analytic Support Provide each student with two self-sticking notes. Instruct them to write the ending **-ando** on one, and the ending **-iendo** on the other. Then write a number of regular verbs on the board. Have students take turns choosing and applying the correct ending to create the present participle.

Práctica de GRAMÁTICA

11 ¿De vacaciones o no?

¿Recuerdas? Chores p. 272

Hablar
Escribir

Completa las siguientes oraciones y decide si estas personas están de vacaciones o no. *(Complete the sentences and decide who is on vacation.)*

modelo: Jorge ____ la basura. (sacar)
Jorge **está sacando** la basura. No está de vacaciones.

1. Susana y Jorge ____ el sol en la playa. (tomar)
2. Nosotros ____ el autobús para ir a la escuela. (esperar)
3. Mi amigo ____ un viaje al campo. (hacer)
4. Tú ____ la mesa. (poner)
5. Yo ____ el suelo. (barrer)
6. Ustedes ____ un libro en la playa. (leer)

Expansión
Write three sentences about what people in your class are doing right now.

12 ¿Qué están haciendo?

Escribir

Mira las fotos de las vacaciones y escribe lo que están haciendo estas personas. *(Write what these people are doing.)*

levantarse tarde	ponerse bloqueador de sol
hacer un viaje en barco	servir comida
nadar en la piscina	quedarse en un buen hotel
hacer esquí acuático	

modelo: mi madre
Mi madre se está poniendo bloqueador de sol. (Mi madre está poniéndose bloqueador de sol.)

1. nosotros

2. yo

3. mis amigos

4. usted

5. el camarero

6. mi padre

Expansión:
Teacher Edition Only
Ask students to write two more vacation activities using the present progressive.

Differentiating Instruction

Multiple Intelligences

Visual Learners Have students illustrate each of the sentences in Activity 11 on a small piece of paper. Then have them write the sentence underneath as a caption. After they finish completing the sentences, instruct students to divide a larger piece of paper into two sections—**Está de vacaciones** and **No está de vacaciones**. Have students glue each picture in the correct section.

Slower-paced Learners

Yes/No Questions Preview Activity 12 with students by asking them yes questions about the pictures. After answering yes, have students reformulate the question into a complete sentence.
Maestro(a): ¿Está mi madre poniéndose bloqueador de sol?
Estudiante: Sí, su madre está poniéndose bloqueador de sol.

Objectives

- Practice using the present progressive.
- Recycle: chores.

Practice Sequence

- **Activity 11:** Controlled practice: present progressive
- **Activity 12:** Transitional practice: present progressive, present progressive with reflexive pronouns

STANDARDS

1.3 Present information, Acts. 11–12
21st Century **Communication,** Act. 11: Expansión

Long-term Retention

Study Tips

Activity 12 Before doing the activity, review placement of reflexive pronouns with present participles. Say: **Se está levantando tarde.** Then ask students to attach the pronoun to the participle: **Está levantándose tarde.** Repeat with **ponerse** and **quedarse.**

Answers Projectable Transparencies, 8-25 and 8-26

Activity 11

1. Susana y Jorge están tomando el sol. Están de vacaciones.
2. Nosotros estamos esperando el autobús para ir a la escuela. No estamos de vacaciones.
3. Mi amigo está haciendo un viaje al campo. Está de vacaciones.
4. Tú estás poniendo la mesa. No estás de vacaciones.
5. Yo estoy barriendo el suelo. No estoy de vacaciones.
6. Ustedes están leyendo un libro en la playa. Están de vacaciones.

Activity 12

1. Nos estamos quedando en un buen hotel. (Estamos quedándonos en un buen hotel.)
2. Me estoy levantando tarde. (Estoy levantándome tarde.)
3. Mis amigos están nadando en la piscina.
4. Usted está haciendo un viaje en barco.
5. El camarero está sirviendo la comida.
6. Mi padre está haciendo esquí acuático.

Objectives

- Practice using the present progressive.
- Recycle: parts of a house.
- **Culture**: Learn about and practice the use of **usted, tú,** and **vos.**

Core Resource

- *Cuaderno,* pp. 350–352

Practice Sequence

- **Activity 13:** Transitional practice: present progressive; Recycle: houses
- **Activity 14:** Open-ended practice: uses of **usted, tú,** and **vos,** present progressive

STANDARDS

1.1 Engage in conversation, Acts. 13–14
1.3 Present information, PYP
2.1 Practices and perspectives, Act. 14
4.1 Compare languages, Act. 14
21st Century Flexibility and Adaptability, Act. 14; **Social and Cross-Cultural Skills,** Heritage Language Learners

Comparación cultural

Essential Question

Suggested Answer In some countries, forms of address may be more formal than in others. When talking to someone who is older or to someone you don't know very well, you may need to use a formal form of address.

Background Information

Tú or Vos? Point out that in the comic strip from Costa Rica, the superhero used **vos** (informal) with his assistant, while the assistant uses **usted** to address his boss. Mention that **vos sos** has the same meaning as **tú eres. Recordá** is the *vos* command form equivalent to **recuerda** (remember).

In all three countries, students use **usted** with teachers and authority figures, while the informal **vos** or **tú** is used among friends.

✓ Ongoing Assessment

Get Help Online
More Practice
my.hrw.com

PARA Y PIENSA **Peer Assessment** Ask students to complete the answers in writing. Have students correct each other's work. For additional practice, use Reteaching & Practice Copymasters URB 8, pp. 7, 8, 10.

See Activity answers on p. 423.

13 ¿Dónde estoy? ¿Recuerdas? Houses p. 248

Hablar

Describe qué estás haciendo y otro(a) estudiante va a adivinar dónde estás en la casa. *(Tell what you are doing so that a partner can guess where you are in the house.)*

modelo: cepillarse

A: Me estoy cepillando los dientes.
B: Estás en el baño.

Estudiante A

1. cocinar	**5.** ducharse
2. leer	**6.** vestirse
3. dormirse	**7.** jugar...
4. mirar...	**8.** ¿ ?

Estudiante B

la sala
el baño
el cuarto
la cocina
el jardín
¿ ?

Expansión
Say what items you are using for each activity.

14 Por teléfono

Hablar

Comparación cultural

El uso de usted, tú y vos

How do forms of address differ among countries? Informal and formal address vary in the Spanish-speaking world. In both **Costa Rica** and **Uruguay,** *vos* is used rather than *tú.* In Costa Rica, family members often use *usted;* however, in Uruguay, *usted* is rarely used within a family. In **Ecuador,** some families may use *usted* as a sign of respect, but many families use *tú.*

Una tira cómica de Francisco Munguía

Compara con tu mundo *How does your language change depending on the situation you are in?*

Eres de Costa Rica y hablas por teléfono con tu hermano(a). Usa la forma **usted.** *(Role-play a telephone conversation. Use* **usted.***)*

A: Hola, Diego. ¿Qué está haciendo?
B: Estoy estudiando. ¿Y usted?

Más práctica Cuaderno *pp. 350–352* Cuaderno para hispanohablantes *pp. 351–354*

Get Help Online
my.hrw.com

PARA Y PIENSA

Did you get it? Complete each sentence with the correct present progressive form of the verb in parentheses.

1. Todos los días a las ocho de la mañana yo ____ . (ducharse)
2. Tú siempre ____ cuando queremos ir a la playa. (dormir)
3. Nosotros ____ para ir a la escuela. (vestirse)

Differentiating Instruction

Pre-AP

Expand and Elaborate Have students expand on their conversations in Activity 13 by describing what they have and what they see during the activity. Here is a possible follow-up based on the model.

Estudiante A: Sí, tengo mi cepillo de dientes y la pasta. Veo un espejo.

Heritage Language Learners

Support What They Know Ask students to comment on their own use of the words **usted, tú,** and **vos.** Which words do they use, and in what situations? Ask students to create a simple three-column chart with each word at the top of a column. Then have them list the people they refer to using that word.

Todo junto

¡AVANZA! **Goal:** ***Show what you know*** Notice how Susana and Jorge use the present progressive in their conversation. Then use this tense and reflexive verbs to talk about your daily routine while on vacation. ***Actividades 15–19***

¿Recuerdas? Telling time p. 90

Telehistoria completa

@HOMETUTOR my.hrw.com **View, Read and Record**

STRATEGIES

Cuando lees

Analyze differences in behavior While reading, discover the differences in behavior between Jorge and Susana. How do they react to being late?

Cuando escuchas

Listen for attempts to control Listen for differences in intonation as Jorge and Susana each try to gain control over the situation. How does each person sound? Why? What is their father's role?

Escena 1 *Resumen*

Susana va a hacer un viaje con su familia, pero su hermano, Jorge, es imposible.

Escena 2 *Resumen*

Jorge y Susana quieren ir a la playa en coche el sábado, pero su padre tiene que ir a la oficina.

Escena 3

VIDEO DVD

AUDIO

Susana and Jorge are finishing breakfast in the kitchen. Their father waits in the car.

Susana: *(impatiently)* Jorge, estás comiendo y comiendo. ¡Por favor! ¿Quieres ir al centro comercial o no? Papá nos está esperando. Tiene que ir a la oficina.

Jorge keeps eating and ignores his sister.

Susana: Jorge, ¿no me escuchas? ¡Nos está llamando papá!

Jorge: Pero estoy comiendo el desayuno...

Susana wraps up his breakfast.

Susana: ¡Vamos, ahora! ¿No me estás escuchando? Papá está esperando. ¡Toma la mochila!

Jorge: Un momento, hay algo... Necesito algo importante. Pero, ¿qué puede ser?

Jorge unknowingly leaves Alicia's T-shirt behind.

Differentiating Instruction

Multiple Intelligences

Interpersonal Invite volunteers to play the parts of Susana and Jorge. As these students read the script, encourage them to emphasize the facial expressions appropriate to each character's part. When Susana asks, **¿Quieres ir al centro comercial o no?** what emotion might she be feeling? When Jorge says, **Pero, ¿qué puede ser?** what might his expression be? What about Susana's?

Inclusion

Metacognitive Support Have students review the Telehistoria making a list of each verb or verb phrase they find. Discuss whether verbs are in the present, present progressive, or command form, and why.

¡AVANZA! **Objective**

- Integrate lesson content.

Core Resources

- Video Program: DVD 2
- Audio Program: TXT CD 8 track 7

Presentation Strategies

- Ask students to scan the script and list all the verbs that are in the present progressive.
- Show the video or play the audio.

STANDARDS

1.2 Understand languages

21st Century **Flexibility and Adaptability,** Multiple Intelligences

Warm Up Projectable Transparencies, 8-18

Present Progressive Complete the sentences with the correct form of the verb.

1. Manuel _____ deportes. (practicar)
2. Los niños _____ en el mar. (bucear)
3. Yo _____ una carta. (escribir)

Answers: 1. está practicando; 2. están buceando; 3. estoy escribiendo

Video Summary

@HOMETUTOR VideoPlus my.hrw.com

While their father waits in the car, Susana hurries Jorge to finish his breakfast so they can go to the mall. Susana wraps up his breakfast, and tells him to take his backpack. Jorge needs a moment to think of an important thing he needs, but can't remember it. He leaves Alicia's T-shirt behind.

Answers Projectable Transparencies, 8-26

Answers for Activities on p. 422.

Activity 13 Answers will vary. Sample answers:
1. **A.** Estoy cocinando. **B.** Estás en la cocina.
2. **A.** Estoy leyendo. **B.** Estás en la sala.
3. **A.** Me estoy durmiendo. **B.** Estás en el cuarto.
4. **A.** Estoy mirando la televisión. **B.** Estás en la sala.
5. **A.** Me estoy duchando. **B.** Estás en el baño.
6. **A.** Me estoy vistiendo. **B.** Estás en el cuarto.
7. **A.** Estoy jugando... **B.** Estás en el jardín.
8. **A.** Estoy... **B.** Estás...

Activity 14 Answers will vary. Sample answers:
A. Hola, Nora. ¿Qué está haciendo? **B.** Estoy estudiando.

Para y piensa **1.** me estoy duchando/estoy duchándome; **2.** estás durmiendo; **3.** nos estamos vistiendo/estamos vistiéndonos

TODO JUNTO

Objective
- Practice using and integrating lesson vocabulary and grammar.

Core Resources
- *Cuaderno*, pp 353–354
- Audio Program: TXT CD 8 tracks 3, 4, 7, 8, 9

Practice Sequence
- **Activities 15, 16:** Telehistoria comprehension
- **Activity 17:** Open-ended practice: speaking
- **Activity 19:** Open-ended practice: reading, listening, speaking
- **Activity 20:** Open-ended practice: writing

STANDARDS
1.1 Engage in conversation, Act. 17
1.2 Understand language, Acts. 15–16
1.3 Present information, Acts. 16–19, PYP
21st Century **Communication,** Acts. 17, 19/ Heritage Language Learners; **Creativity and Innovation,** Multiple Intelligences; **Technology Literacy,** Integration

Answers Projectable Transparencies, 8-26

Activity 15
1. Falso. Susana va a hacer un viaje con su familia.
2. Cierto.
3. Cierto.
4. Falso. Susana y Jorge tienen que ir en autobús porque su padre tiene que trabajar.
5. Cierto.
6. Falso. Jorge no sabe qué necesita para ir al centro comercial.

Activity 16
1. Susana está hablando de las vacaciones y Jorge está preguntando ¿dónde está la leche?
2. Susana y Jorge están comiendo el almuerzo con su papá. Jorge quiere saber si puede ir a la playa.
3. Jorge está comiendo y comiendo.

Answers continue on p. 425.

15 *Comprensión de los episodios* ¿Cierto o falso?

Escuchar Leer

Decide si estas oraciones son ciertas o falsas. Corrige las falsas. *(Tell if these sentences are true or false. Correct the false ones.)*

1. Susana va a hacer un viaje con sus amigas.
2. Jorge y Susana quieren ir a la playa el sábado.
3. Su padre piensa que Jorge debe levantarse temprano para hacer su rutina.
4. Susana y Jorge pueden ir en coche a la playa porque su padre no tiene que trabajar el sábado.
5. Susana y Jorge necesitan salir porque su padre los está esperando.
6. Jorge sabe qué necesita para ir al centro comercial.

Expansión:
Teacher Edition On
Ask students to write about a trip to the beach. Tell them to include when they want to go, at what time they're going to ge up, how and with whom they are going to go.

16 *Comprensión de los episodios* ¿Qué está pasando?

Escuchar Leer

Describe qué está pasando en cada foto, según los episodios. *(Tell what is happening in each picture, according to the episodes.)*

modelo: Susana está pensando en unas vacaciones. No está escuchando a Jorge.

1. 
2. 
3. 

Expansión:
Teacher Edition Onl
Distribute photos of people doing different activities and have students describe them to their partners usin the present progressive.

17 ¿Quién está de vacaciones?

¿Recuerdas? Telling time p. 90

Digital performance space

Hablar

STRATEGY Hablar
Use clock faces to link times and activities Organize your drawings by including clock faces with your daily routine. Practice narrating your routine using the clocks, then get together with your partner to ask and answer questions.

En una hoja de papel, dibuja tu rutina diaria cuando estás de vacaciones. Otro(a) estudiante va a dibujar su rutina diaria durante un día escolar típico. Haz preguntas sobre los dibujos. *(Draw your daily routine while on vacation. Your partner will draw his or her daily routine during a typical school day. Ask questions about the drawings.)*

A ¿A qué hora te levantas?

B Me levanto a las seis porque tengo que ir a la escuela.

Expansión
Choose different destinations for your vacations and compare your activities.

Differentiating Instruction

Pre-AP
Identify Main Idea Have students fold a piece of paper lengthwise. Then have them write **Susana** at the top of one half, and **Jorge** at the top of the other. Direct students to reread each scene of the Telehistoria, jotting down important notes about what each character says, does, or feels. Have students turn these notes into a summary of the entire Telehistoria.

Heritage Language Learners
Writing Skills Have students develop their conversations from Activity 17 into a compare and contrast essay. First, have them create a Venn diagram to organize the similarities and differences between their school day routine and vacation routine. Then have them develop the notes from their diagram into complete sentences, and organize these sentences into paragraphs.

18 Integración

Digital performance space

Leer
Escuchar
Hablar

Quieres hablar por Internet antes de las clases con dos amigos de Costa Rica. Lee el correo electrónico y escucha el mensaje telefónico. Decide si pueden hacerlo y explica por qué. *(Decide if the three of you can be online together before school. Explain why or why not.)*

Audio Program
TXT CD 8 Tracks 8, 9. Audio Script, TE p. 407b

Fuente 1 Correo electrónico

Hola, ¿qué tal? Tenemos que decidir a qué hora vamos a estar en línea mañana. Normalmente me levanto a las siete menos veinte de la mañana. Me lavo la cara y luego me visto. Entonces voy a la sala para ver un programa de televisión a las siete. Termina a las siete y media. A las ocho menos cuarto me pongo los zapatos y la chaqueta y salgo para la escuela. ¿Y tú? ¿Qué haces antes de las clases?
Ignacio

Fuente 2 Mensaje telefónico

Listen and take notes
- ¿A qué hora se levantó hoy Carmen?
- ¿Cuándo está ocupada?
- ¿Cuándo puede estar en línea?

modelo: Ignacio, Carmen y yo podemos estar en línea a las... porque... (No podemos estar en línea porque...)

Expansión:
Teacher Edition Only
Ask students to write an e-mail to a friend describing what he or she did during the school day and setting up a time to meet after school.

19 Un viaje fenomenal

Digital performance space

Escribir

Haces un viaje fenomenal. Escribe un diario para describir dónde estás, cómo es tu rutina y qué estás haciendo en el viaje. *(You are on a great trip. Write a diary that describes where you are, what your daily routine is, and what you are doing on your trip.)*

modelo: sábado, 12 de junio 10:00
Estoy en Guanacaste. Acabo de levantarme y estoy comiendo el desayuno y bebiendo jugo al lado de la playa. Voy a...

Writing Criteria	Excellent	Good	Needs Work
Content	Your diary includes a lot of information.	Your diary includes some information.	Your diary includes little information.
Communication	Most of your diary is organized and easy to follow.	Parts of your diary are organized and easy to follow.	Your diary is disorganized and hard to follow.
Accuracy	Your diary has few mistakes in grammar and vocabulary.	Your diary has some mistakes in grammar and vocabulary.	Your diary has many mistakes in grammar and vocabulary.

Expansión:
Teacher Edition Only
Ask students to write about their daily routine on weekends.

Más práctica Cuaderno *pp. 353–354* Cuaderno para hispanohablantes *pp. 355–356*

Get Help Online my.hrw.com

PARA Y PIENSA

Did you get it? Tell what Jorge and Susana are doing before going to the mall, using this information and the present progressive.
1. Jorge / peinarse
2. Susana / maquillarse
3. los hermanos / cepillarse los dientes
4. Jorge / ponerse la chaqueta

Long-term Retention

Pre-AP Integration

Activity 18 Assign three students to e-mail each other their Saturday schedule. After students read each other's e-mails, have them set up a time when they can go to an event such as a movie, a play, or a concert.

✓ Ongoing Assessment

Rubric Activity 18
Listening/Speaking

Proficient	Not There Yet
Student answers all questions and explains why he/she can be online at a certain time.	Student answers some questions and cannot explain why he/she can be online at a certain time.

To customize your own rubrics, use the ***Generate Success*** *Rubric Generator and Graphic Organizers.*

✓ Ongoing Assessment

Get Help Online More Practice my.hrw.com

PARA Y PIENSA **Peer Assessment** Ask students to write the sentences and check spelling with a classmate. For additional practice, use Reteaching & Practice Copymasters URB 8 pp. 7, 9, 10.

Differentiating Instruction

Slower-paced Learners

Peer-study Support Have students work with a partner to complete Activity 18. First, have them work together to create a timeline of the information presented in the e-mail. Instruct them to write each time in numbers, followed by a short description of the activity, for example: **6:40AM – se levanta**. Have students do the same for the telephone message, and compare the information.

Multiple Intelligences

Visual Learners Encourage students to develop their travel diaries into a page for a travel scrapbook. They might include photos, tickets, mementos, etc. These might be real objects from an actual trip, or created objects from an imaginary vacation. Remind students that their writing, however, must still be full and complete.

Answers Projectable Transparencies, 8-26 and 8-27

Answers continued from p. 424

Activity 17 Answers will vary. Answers should follow the pattern:
A: ¿A qué hora te duchas? **B:** Me ducho a las seis y cuarto porque tengo que salir temprano.

Activity 18
Answers to the voice mail include:
Carmen se levantó a las seis menos diez.

Activity 19 Answers will vary. Sample answers: Estoy en Punta Cana. Durante las vacaciones, me gusta levantarme tarde. Luego, me ducho, me afeito y me visto...

Para y piensa
1. Jorge se está peinando/está peinándose.
2. Susana se está maquillando/está maquillándose.
3. Los hermanos se están cepillando/están cepillándose los dientes.
4. Jorge se está poniendo/está poniéndose la chaqueta.

Objectives
- Read about a vacation to Costa Rica.
- **Culture:** Learn about Monteverde, a nature reserve in Costa Rica.
- Talk about Sara's vacation and compare it with what you like to do on vacation.

Core Resources
- Audio Program: TXT CD 8 track 10

Presentation Strategies
- Ask students if they ever visited a nature reserve and what their impressions were.
- Have students look at the photos on pp. 426 and 427 and ask: **¿Qué lugar les gusta más? ¿Por qué?**
- Have students read the captions and make a list of words they don't know. Encourage them to find their meaning through context clues or cognates before checking the glosses or consulting a dictionary.
- Play the audio.

STANDARDS
1.2 Understand language
2.1 Practices and perspectives
21st Century **Communication,** Presentational Mode; **Creativity and Innovation,** Multiple Intelligences/Pre-AP; **Information Literacy,** Heritage Language Learners

Warm Up
Projectable Transparencies, 8-19

Present Progressive Write sentences using the present progressive
1. yo / cepillarse los dientes
2. Marta y Elena / limpiar el cuarto
3. nosotras / peinarse
4. Estela / mirar la televisión
5. tú / ponerse los guantes

Answers: 1. Yo me estoy cepillando los dientes. 2. Marta y Elena están limpiando el cuarto. 3. Nosotras nos estamos peinando. 4. Estela está mirando la televisión. 5. Tú te estás poniendo los guantes.

Culture
Expanded Information
Land purchased for dairy farming in the 1950s was set aside to create the Monteverde Cloud Reserve in Costa Rica. Because of its high altitude, Monteverde is known as a cloud forest, which is different from a rain forest. A cloud forest will generally receive less rain than a rain forest on an annual basis.

Lectura

Additional readings at my.hrw.com SPANISH InterActive Reader

¡AVANZA! **Goal:** Read the captions from the scrapbook of a student who went on vacation to Costa Rica. Then talk about her vacation and compare it with what you would like to do.

Mi viaje a Costa Rica

AUDIO

STRATEGY Leer
Use an "L" to link place and event Draw L's like the ones below. On the tall part, write the name of the place. On the low part, write events and activities.

El año pasado Sara y su familia hicieron un viaje a Costa Rica. Cuando volvieron a Miami, Sara hizo un álbum con fotos y recuerdos de sus experiencias.

Fuimos todos al bosque nuboso[1] en Monteverde. Es una reserva biológica con muchos tipos de árboles[2] y pájaros[3]. Es un lugar ideal para caminar y tomar fotos.

¿Qué están mirando mi mamá y mis hermanos? No es un pájaro y no es un avión... Es Papá.

¡Papá nunca tiene miedo! Aquí está en un zip line. Aquí va de árbol en árbol en un cable de metal.

Vimos un tucán. Es un pájaro bonito de muchos colores. Es típico de Costa Rica. Allí hay más de 850 especies de pájaros.

[1] **bosque...** cloud forest [2] trees [3] birds

Differentiating Instruction

Multiple Intelligences
Visual Learners Ask students to create two pages of their own photo album of a vacation they took recently. They can also use magazine cutouts to illustrate an imaginary trip. Under each photo they should write a caption identifying the location and describing what happened. Have students display their albums in class.

Pre-AP
Persuade Ask students to write a travel brochure that includes the places mentioned in the reading. Their aim will be to persuade travelers to visit these places. Encourage them to use commands. For example: **Haz un viaje a Monteverde. Camina por esta maravillosa reserva biológica y toma fotos de sus árboles y pájaros.**

Un día fuimos a Escazú. Estoy comprando regalos para mis amigos en Miami. También compré una pequeña máscara de barro[4].

En San José, nos quedamos en un hotel en el centro. El hotel está cerca de la Plaza Central y la Catedral Metropolitana.

Hicimos un viaje en avión de San José a Tambor (en la costa del Pacífico de Costa Rica). Pasamos tres días en Montezuma. Descansamos en la playa, tomamos el sol y buceamos. ¡Fue mi parte favorita de las vacaciones!

[4] **máscara...** clay mask

PARA Y PIENSA

¿Comprendiste?

1. ¿Adónde fueron Sara y su famila en Monteverde? Si te gusta ver pájaros, ¿es Costa Rica un buen lugar? ¿Por qué?
2. ¿Dónde está el hotel donde se quedaron Sara y su familia?
3. ¿Qué hizo Sara en Escazú?
4. ¿Está Tambor cerca o lejos de San José? ¿Cómo lo sabes?

¿Y tú?

¿Qué te gustaría hacer de vacaciones en Costa Rica?

Communication
Pair Work

Ask student pairs to take turns describing each picture on pp. 426–427. One student should point to the photo while the other speaks. For example, using the first picture on p. 426, students might say: **Es la familia de Sara. La familia mira a su padre. La familia está en Monteverde.** For the second picture: **Papá nunca tiene miedo.** Then have students switch roles.

Communication
Presentational Mode

Ask students to think of an area in their community that has been set aside for preservation purposes such as a town, state, or national park. Ask them to write a short description in Spanish of what one can see and do there. What kinds of animals are there? What kinds of trees and plants are there? What can you do in the park: swim, ski, take a walk? Encourage them to use an English-Spanish dictionary to find terms that will enhance their description. If possible, ask them to bring photos to illustrate their presentation.

Differentiating Instruction

Differentiating Instruction

Yes/No Questions Tell students they are going to write two questions about each photo on pp. 426–427. The answer to one question should be **sí**, and the answer to the other should be **no.** Advise students to begin their questions with the preterite form of one of the verbs used in the caption. Give students the opportunity to read their questions aloud to the class.

Heritage Language Learners

Writing Skills Invite students to research another Costa Rican nature reserve using the library or Internet. Have students create a list of five or six questions that they would like to have answered. Advise students to record the information they find for each question on a separate index card and to check their punctuation, spelling, and grammar.

Answers

Para y piensa

¿Comprendiste?

1. En Monteverde, Sara y su familia fueron al bosque nuboso. Sí, Costa Rica es un buen lugar para ver pájaros, porque allí hay muchas especies.
2. El hotel donde Sara y su familia se quedaron está en el centro, cerca de la Plaza Central y la Catedral Metropolitana.
3 En Escazú, Sara compró regalos para sus amigos en Miami y compró una máscara de barro.
4. Tambor está lejos de San José. Ellos hicieron un viaje en avión de San José a Tambor.

¿Y tú?

Answers will vary. Sample answers include: En Costa Rica, me gustaría ir al bosque nuboso en Monteverde.

Objectives
- Read about a natural science museum in Costa Rica, its sections and exhibits.
- Investigate the Greek and Latin roots of scientific terms.
- Calculate how much something costs in **colones,** the currency of Costa Rica.

Presentation Strategies
- Ask students about the last time they visited a museum of natural history. Encourage them to describe the museum's sections and the kinds of exhibits that were on display.
- Ask students to find cognates for the names of the museum's various sections.
- Ask quick comprehension questions about the exhibit's poster: **¿Cuánto cuestan los boletos para adultos? ¿Y para niños?**

STANDARDS
1.3 Present information
3.1 Knowledge of other disciplines
3.2 Acquire information
21st Century **Creativity and Innovation,** English Learners; **Critical Thinking and Problem Solving,** Proyecto 1 (Financial Literacy)

Connections
La historia
Costa Rica has many fine museums including **El Museo de Oro.** It houses over 2,000 gold objects dating back to as early as 500 B.C.

Answers
Conexiones

minerales y rocas: minerals and rocks
paleontología: paleontology, the study of prehistoric life forms
invertebrados: invertebrates, animals with no spines/backbones
malacología: study of mollusks
artrópodos: arthropods, single-celled organisms
insectos: insects - six legs, exoskeleton, head/thorax/abdomen body
vertebrados: vertebrates, animals with spines
ornitología: study of birds
mamíferos: mammals
esqueletos: skeletons

Proyecto 1 Have students do this assignment by looking up a current exchange rate online, or supply them with one.

Proyecto 2 logy-study, discourse; zoo-living being; paleo-ancient, prehistoric; orni-bird

Proyecto 3 Answers will vary: Sample answers: elefantes, arañas, hormigas, langostas.

Conexiones *Las ciencias*

¡Vamos al museo!

In addition to outdoor activities, visitors at **Parque La Sabana** in Costa Rica can enjoy **el Museo de Ciencias Naturales La Salle,** a museum dedicated to nature and science located in the southwest corner of the park. The museum is divided into various sections: **minerales y rocas, paleontología, invertebrados, malacología, artrópodos, insectos, vertebrados, ornitología, mamíferos,** and **esqueletos.** There are more than 55,000 exhibits on permanent display.

Choose five sections of the museum and find their meanings in a dictionary. Then make a list of two or three items you might see on exhibit for each of the five sections.

Museo de Ciencias Naturales La Salle

¡Ve el esqueleto de un mamut enorme en la exhibición de paleontología!
lunes a sábado, 8 a.m.–4 p.m.
domingo, 9 a.m.–5 p.m.
adultos ¢400, niños ¢300

Para más información llama:
Teléfono: 232-4876 **Fax:** 231-1920
o visita nuestro sitio Web

Proyecto 1 *Las matemáticas*
Your Spanish class has taken a trip to Costa Rica. Calculate how much it will cost in **colones** (symbol ¢) for everyone in your class to visit the museum. Then use a current exchange rate to calculate the cost in U.S. dollars. Write out your calculations in Spanish.

Proyecto 2 *El lenguaje*
Many scientific terms in Spanish and English are similar due in part to their common Latin and Greek roots. Research the Latin and Greek roots of the following words:

zoología paleontología ornitología

Proyecto 3 *El arte*
Make a list of six to ten animals or insects that may be found in **Parque La Sabana** or **el Museo de Ciencias Naturales La Salle.** If you need more animal names, see page R8. Make a poster containing illustrations of each with captions in Spanish.

Una mariposa

Differentiating Instruction

English Learners
Build Background Students may not be familiar with specific scientific terms. Have students read through the Conexiones to find terms they don't know. Then have them work with a partner to use a dictionary to create a scientific glossary with explanations of each of these terms.

Multiple Intelligences
Visual Learners After students complete the reading and search for the meanings for the sections in the **Museo de Ciencias Naturales La Salle,** ask them to create icons for each of the sections. Students will display their icons and the class will guess what section the icons represent.

Lección 1

En resumen

Vocabulario y gramática

ANIMATEDGRAMMAR
Interactive Flashcards
my.hrw.com

Vocabulario

Talk About a Daily Routine

acostarse (ue)	*to go to bed*	lavarse la cara	*to wash one's face*
afeitarse	*to shave oneself*	levantarse	*to get up*
bañarse	*to take a bath*	maquillarse	*to put on makeup*
cepillarse los dientes	*to brush one's teeth*	peinarse	*to comb one's hair*
despertarse (ie)	*to wake up*	ponerse (la ropa)	*to put on (clothes), to get dressed*
dormirse (ue)	*to fall asleep*	secarse	*to dry oneself*
ducharse	*to take a shower*	secarse el pelo	*to dry one's hair*
lavarse	*to wash oneself*	vestirse (i)	*to get dressed*

Talk About Grooming

el cepillo (de dientes)	*brush (toothbrush)*	el peine	*comb*
el champú	*shampoo*	el secador de pelo	*hair dryer*
el jabón	*soap*	la toalla	*towel*
la pasta de dientes	*toothpaste*		

Talk About a Typical Day

generalmente	*generally*
normalmente	*normally*
la rutina	*routine*

Other Words and Phrases

el campo	*the country, countryside*
la ciudad	*city*
esperar	*to wait (for)*
hacer un viaje	*to take a trip*
en avión	*by plane*
en barco	*by boat*
en tren	*by train*
el hotel	*hotel*
quedarse en	*to stay in*
las vacaciones	*vacation*
de vacaciones	*on vacation*

Gramática

Reflexive Verbs

Use **reflexive pronouns** with **reflexive verbs** when the subject in a sentence is the same as its object.

lavar**se** *to wash oneself*	
me lavo	**nos** lavamos
te lavas	**os** laváis
se lava	**se** lavan

Present Progressive

To form the present progressive in Spanish, use the present tense of **estar** + **present participle.**

-ar verbs	**-er** verbs	**-ir** verbs
caminar ← ando	poner ← iendo	abrir ← iendo
caminando	poniendo	abriendo

Some verbs have a spelling change or a stem change in the present participle.

Practice Spanish with Holt McDougal Apps!

Objective

- Review lesson vocabulary and grammar.

DIGITAL SPANISH

Interactive Flashcards Students can hear every target vocabulary word pronounced in authentic Spanish. Flashcards have Spanish on one side, and a picture or a translation on the other.

Review Games Matching, concentration, hangman, and word search are just a sampling of the fun, interactive games students can play to review for the test.

performance space
News Networking
@HOMETUTOR
CULTURA Interactiva

- **Audio and Video Resources**
- **Interactive Flashcards**
- **Review Activities**
- **WebQuest**
- **Conjuguemos.com**

Long-term Retention

Study Tips

Help students think of other ways of grouping the words in En resumen, for easy recall. For example, they could group words related to a specific action such as **cepillarse los dientes: el cepillo de dientes, la pasta de dientes** or **lavarse: el jabón, la toalla,** and so on.

Communication

Pair Work

Ask students to work in small groups to brainstorm ideas about a typical day **en la ciudad** and **en el campo.** Encourage them to use a graphic organizer such as a Venn diagram to organize their ideas. Have them use the information in the organizer to write sentences for each category. Remind them that some sentences might fall under both **ciudad** and **campo.** Sample sentences: **Generalmente, cuando voy al campo me levanto a las seis de la mañana. Normalmente, cuando estoy en la ciudad me acuesto a las once de la noche.**

Differentiating Instruction

Slower-paced Learners

Memory Aids Have students create a flashcard for each of the reflexive verbs presented on p. 429 under Talk About a Daily Routine. On the front of each card, have them glue a magazine photo or draw an illustration of the verb's meaning. On the back of the card, have them list all of the verb's present tense forms.

Inclusion

Synthetic/Analytic Support Write each of the following reflexive pronouns on a separate self-sticking note: **me, te, se, nos**. On the board, present students with the infinitive of a reflexive verb, such as **bañarse**. Then give students a subject pronoun, such as **tú**. Have a volunteer choose the correct reflexive pronoun, place it in front of the verb, and then erase and correct the verb's ending.

Objective
- Review lesson grammar and vocabulary.

Core Resources
- *Cuaderno,* pp. 355–366
- Audio Program: TXT CD 8 track 11

Presentation Strategies
- Before starting the audio for Activity 1, ask student to pay special attention to what each character needs.
- Before starting Activity 2, review telling time. Write on the board **11:15; 1:30; 7:45: 12:40** and ask students to read the time in Spanish.
- Go over the Comparación cultural with students and clarify any questions that arise.
- Review may be done in class or given as homework.
- You may want students to access the review online.

STANDARDS
1.2 Understand language, Act. 1
1.3 Present information, Acts. 2–4
4.2 Compare cultures, Act. 5
21st Century **Initiative and Self-Direction,** Pre-AP

Warm Up Projectable Transparencies, 8-19
Vocabulary Choose the correct word to complete each sentence.
1. Me lavo las manos con (peine/ jabón).
2. Uso (el champú/el peine) para lavarme el pelo.
3. Normalmente (me acuesto/me levanto) a las siete de la mañana.
4. Necesito (la toalla/la pasta de dientes) para secarme la cara.
5. Siempre (me quedo/me pongo) en un hotel cuando voy de vacaciones.

Answers: 1. jabón; 2. el champú; 3. me levanto; 4. la toalla; 5. me quedo

✓ Ongoing Assessment
Get Help Online
More Practice
my.hrw.com

Intervention and Remediation If students achieve less than 80% accuracy with the activities, direct them to pp. 407, 415–416, 420, 422 and to get help online at my.hrw.com.

See Activity answers on p. 431.

Lección 1
Repaso de la lección

@HOMETUTOR
my.hrw.com

¡LLEGADA!

Now you can
- talk about a typical day
- talk about what you are doing
- talk about your daily routine while on vacation

Using
- reflexive verbs
- present progressive

To review
- reflexive verbs p. 415
- present progressive p. 420

1 Listen and understand

AUDIO

Escucha a Silvia y a sus hermanos mientras se preparan para ir a la escuela. Indica lo que necesitan y explica por qué. *(Listen to Silvia and her brothers and sisters. Tell what they need and why.)*

a. 
b. 
c. 
d. 
e. 
f. 

1. Silvia
2. Roberto
3. Anita
4. Juan
5. Tomás
6. Laura

Audio Progra
TXT CD 8 Track 1
Audio Script, TE
407b

To review
- reflexive verbs p. 415

2 Talk about a typical day

Escribe a qué hora las siguientes personas hacen estas actividades. *(Write when the following people do these activities.)*

modelo: Pancho / acostarse / 10:00 p.m.
Pancho se acuesta a las diez de la noche.

1. yo / dormirse / 10:50 p.m.
2. nosotros / cepillarse los dientes / 9:15 p.m.
3. Papá / afeitarse / 6:40 a.m.
4. mi hermana / ducharse / 8:20 a.m.
5. Ignacio y Pablo / levantarse / 7:10 a.m.
6. tú / peinarse / 8:45 a.m.

Differentiating Instruction

Heritage Language Learners
Writing Skills Have students write a paragraph describing what their daily routine is like. Have them use expressions such as **normalmente, generalmente**. Encourage them to use different subjects and reflexive pronouns. Have them check their spelling, punctuation, and grammar before they hand in their work.

Slower-paced Learners
Personalize It Have students use the reflexive verbs in Activity 2 to talk about their own daily routine. Encourage each student to provide a sentence with each verb, using a different time. For example: **Yo me duermo a las diez y media. Yo me cepillo los dientes a las siete y cuarto.**

To review
- reflexive verbs p. 415

3 Talk about your daily routine while on vacation

Julia describe sus vacaciones. Completa la carta con la forma correcta del verbo apropiado. *(Complete the letter with the correct form of the appropriate verb.)*

> Hola, Beatriz.
>
> ¿Qué pasa? Estoy en un hotel bonito en San José. Mi rutina es muy diferente aquí. Mis padres prefieren __1.__ (maquillarse / levantarse) temprano para ir de compras. Yo __2.__ (ponerse / despertarse) más tarde, a las diez de la mañana. Después mi hermana y yo __3.__ (acostarse / vestirse). Luego salimos a conocer la ciudad.
>
> Mis padres __4.__ (acostarse / despertarse) a las diez y media de la noche. Mi hermana y yo __5.__ (cepillarse / levantarse) los dientes, y después ella siempre __6.__ (ducharse / lavarse) el pelo. Yo leo mi libro y __7.__ (dormirse / ponerse) a las doce. ¿Y tú? ¿También __8.__ (quedarse / ponerse) en un hotel cuando vas de vacaciones?

To review
- present progressive p. 420

4 Talk about what you are doing

Estas personas no pueden salir porque están ocupadas. Escribe lo que están haciendo. *(Write what the following people are doing right now.)*

modelo: Alberto / correr
Alberto está corriendo.

1. mamá y papá / comer
2. Adriana / hablar por teléfono
3. tú / hacer la tarea
4. ustedes / escribir correos electrónicos
5. yo / cocinar
6. nosotros / envolver un regalo

To review
- **carretas** p. 407
- **Tabacón** p. 407
- Comparación cultural pp. 416, 422

5 Costa Rica, Ecuador, and Uruguay

Comparación cultural

Answer these culture questions.

1. What are **carretas**? Describe them.
2. Where are the Tabacón hot springs and what can you do there?
3. What types of land features are found in Costa Rica?
4. How do family members address each other in Costa Rica, Ecuador, and Uruguay?

Más práctica Cuaderno *pp. 355–366* Cuaderno para hispanohablantes *pp. 357–366*

Get Help Online my.hrw.com

✓ Ongoing Assessment

Alternative Strategy Ask student pairs to write five questions and answers about the activities and times in Activity 2. For example: **¿A qué hora se levantan Ignacio y Pablo? Ignacio y Pablo se levantan a las siete y diez.**

Answers Projectable Transparencies, 8-27

Answers for Activities on pp. 430–431.

Activity 1
1. Silvia necesita el champú porque está lavándose el pelo.
2. Roberto necesita una toalla porque está secándose la cara.
3. Anita necesita un cepillo de dientes porque va a cepillarse los dientes.
4. Juan necesita el secador de pelo porque va a secarse el pelo.
5. Tomás necesita el jabón porque se está lavando la cara.
6. Laura necesita un peine porque tiene que peinarse.

Activity 2
1. Yo me duermo a las once menos diez de la noche.
2. Nosotros nos cepillamos los dientes a las nueve y cuarto de la noche.
3. Papá se afeita a las siete menos veinte de la mañana.
4. Mi hermana se ducha a las ocho y veinte de la mañana.
5. Ignacio y Pablo se levantan a las siete y diez de la mañana.
6. Tú te peinas a las nueve menos cuarto de la mañana.

Activity 3
1. levantarse; **2.** me despierto; **3.** nos vestimos; **4.** se acuestan; **5.** nos cepillamos; **6.** se lava; **7.** me duermo; **8.** te quedas

Activity 4
1. Mamá y papá están comiendo.
2. Adriana está hablando por teléfono.
3. Tú estás haciendo la tarea.
4. Ustedes están escribiendo correos electrónicos.
5. Yo estoy cocinando.
6. Nosotros estamos envolviendo un regalo.

Activity 5
1. **Carretas** are oxcarts that were once used to transport coffee. They are brightly painted.
2. The Tabacón hot springs are near the Arenal Volcano. You can relax in the mineral water pools.
3. Costa Rica has beaches, rivers, volcanoes, mountains, and tropical rain forests.
4. In Costa Rica family members often address each other as **usted.** In Ecuador, families use **tú** or **usted.** In Uruguay, they use **vos.**

Differentiating Instruction

Inclusion

Synthetic/Analytic Support Divide the board into three columns: **-ando, -iendo,** and **-yendo.** Next to the columns write a list of the following infinitives: **cocinar, comer, hacer, escribir, leer, traer, pedir, servir, envolver,** and **dormir.** Then have students come to the board and write the present participle of a verb in the appropriate column.

Pre-AP

Self-correct After students complete the paragraph in Activity 3, have them read it aloud to a partner. Remind students to listen to themselves as they read aloud to catch any mistakes in the choice of verb and correct reflexive verb form. Also, instruct the partners to make note of sentences that do not sound correct because of problems with verb forms.

Lesson Overview

Culture at a Glance

Topic & Activity	Essential Question
Let's go on vacation! pp. 432–433	Where do you like to go and what do you like to do during vacation?
Transportation, p. 440	How is transportation important to a country?
Coffee production, p. 446	How does Costa Rica's climate impact its leading exports?
Local markets in Costa Rica and Uruguay, pp. 450–451	How can you bargain in Costa Rica and Uruguay?
Culture review, p. 455	What are some cultural elements of Costa Rica and Uruguay?

COMPARISON COUNTRIES Costa Rica Ecuador Uruguay

Practice at a Glance

	Objective	Activity & Skill
Vocabulary	Leisure and vacation activities	4: Speaking; 10: Speaking; 18: Reading/Listening/Speaking; 19: Writing; Repaso 3: Writing
	Shopping and bargaining	2: Reading/Writing; 3:Listening/Reading; 5: Reading; 7: Speaking/Writing; 8: Speaking; 11: Reading/Writing; 12: Listening/Writing; 15: Listening/Reading; 16: Listening/Reading; 17: Speaking; Repaso 1: Listening; Repaso 2: Writing
	Jewelry and handicrafts	1: Speaking/Writing; 6: Writing; 8: Speaking; 9: Listening/Reading; Repaso 1: Listening
Grammar	Indirect object pronouns	5: Reading; 6: Writing; 7: Speaking/Writing; 8: Speaking; 10: Speaking; 18: Reading/Listening/Speaking; 19: Writing; Repaso 2: Writing
	Demonstrative adjectives	11: Reading/Writing; 12: Listening/Writing; 13: Speaking; 14: Speaking; 17: Speaking; Repaso 3: Writing
Communication	Talk about buying souvenirs on vacation	5: Reading; 6: Writing; 7: Speaking/Writing; 8: Speaking; 12: Listening/Writing; 18: Reading/Listening/Speaking; Repaso 2: Writing
	Bargain at a market	2: Reading/Writing; 17: Speaking; Repaso 2: Writing
	Talk about vacation activities	4: Speaking; 10: Speaking; 18: Reading/Listening/Speaking; 19: Writing; Repaso 3: Writing
	Pronunciation: Linking words	*Pronunciación: Unir las palabras;* p. 443: Listening/Speaking
Recycle	Family, classroom objects	5: Reading; 14: Speaking
	Numbers from 200 to 1,000,000	7: Speaking/Writing
	Gustar with an infinitive	10: Speaking
	Present progressive	12: Listening/Writing

The following presentations are recorded in the Audio Program for ***¡Avancemos!***

- **¡A responder!** *page 435*
- **12: ¿Qué están haciendo?** *page 445*
- **18: Integración** *page 449*
- **Repaso de la lección** *page 454*
  1 Listen and understand
- **Repaso inclusivo** *page 458*
  1 Listen, understand, and compare

¡A responder! CD 8 track 13

1. Me gustaría dar una caminata.
2. Quisiera hacer surfing.
3. Quisiera acampar.
4. Me gustaría hacer surf de vela.
5 Me gustaría hacer una parrillada.
6. Quisiera comer al aire libre.
7. Me gustaría montar a caballo.

12 | ¿Qué están haciendo? CD 8 track 17

1. Estas chicas están comprando collares.
2. Aquella señora está buscando un libro.
3. Esos señores están comprando cerámica.
4. Estas chicas están mirando ropa.
5. Aquel chico está comiendo helado.
6. Esa señora está vendiendo fruta.

18 | Integración TXT CD 8 tracks 19, 20

¿Necesitas descansar en un lugar tranquilo? ¿O prefieres ir de compras y practicar deportes? En Playa Tamarindo vas a encontrar todo esto... y mucho más. Esta ciudad pequeña, con sus playas bonitas, es perfecta para las personas a quienes les gusta el mar. Aquí puedes estar en la playa todo el día: nadar y tomar el sol, y luego hacer una parrillada y comer al aire libre. Las personas más atléticas pueden hacer surfing, bucear o hacer surf de vela. Pero Tamarindo es más que una playa en el mar. Muchas personas vienen aquí para acampar y montar a caballo. ¡Hay actividades para todos! Llama a tu agente de viajes y ¡compra los boletos de avión ahora! Nos vemos... en Playa Tamarindo.

For **¡AvanzaRap!** scripts, see the **¡AvanzaRap! DVD.**

Repaso de la lección TXT CD 8 track 22

1 Listen and understand

César: Buenas tardes, señora. Busco un recuerdo para una buena amiga.
Vendedora: ¿A ella le gustan las artesanías?
César: No. Prefiere las joyas. ¿Me deja ver aquellos anillos?
Vendedora: Claro que sí... Este anillo de oro es mi favorito.
César: Es muy bonito. ¿Cuánto cuesta?
Vendedora: Cuesta veinte mil colones.
César: ¡Uy! Es demasiado caro.
Vendedora: ¿Le gusta ese anillo de plata? Es bonito.
César: No, gracias. Mi amiga prefiere las joyas de oro.
Vendedora: Tengo unos aretes de oro de buena calidad. Le dejo los aretes en quince mil.
César: Está bien. Los voy a comprar.

Repaso inclusivo TXT CD 8 track 24

1 Listen, understand, and compare

Sra. Daza: Hola, Alberto. Te llamo porque todavía estoy trabajando en la oficina. Voy a llegar tarde a casa.
Sr. Daza: ¡Pero son las siete! ¿Qué pasó?
Sra. Daza: Hmmm... nada. Hay algunos problemas con el artículo que estoy escribiendo. Bueno... y tú, ¿qué hiciste hoy?
Sr. Daza: Después de trabajar, fui al mercado para comprar verduras. Cuando llegué a casa, preparé la cena: pescado, arroz con verduras...
Sra. Daza: ¿Ya terminaste la cena? ¿Y qué estás haciendo ahora?
Sr. Daza: Estoy escuchando música. ¡Pero aquí en casa... no hay nadie!
Sra. Daza: ¿No hay nadie? ¿Luisa y David no están allí?
Sr. Daza: No... aquí en la mesa hay un mensaje de David. Dice que está en la biblioteca.
Sra. Daza: Ah, entonces está estudiando. Debe llegar a las siete y media.
Sr. Daza: Y Luisa... no sé. Aquí no hay ningún mensaje de ella.
Sra. Daza: ¡Ah! Es verdad. Ella me llamó por teléfono a las cinco. Está en el teatro y está comprando las entradas. Vamos a ir todos este sábado, ¿no?
Sr. Daza: ¡¿Cómo?! ¡Pero yo las compré ayer!

Resource List

Everything you need to ...

Plan

TEACHER ONE STOP

- ✓Lesson Plans
- ✓Teacher Resources
- ✓Audio and Video

Present

INTERACTIVE WHITEBOARD LESSONS

TEACHER ONE STOP WITH PROJECTABLE TRANSPARENCIES

POWER PRESENTATIONS

ANIMATEDGRAMMAR

Assess

ONLINE ASSESSMENT

- ✓Assessments for on-level, modified, pre-AP, and heritage learners
- ✓ Create customized tests with **Examview Assessment Suite**
- ✓ **performance space**
- ✓ *Generate Success* Rubric Generator

Print

Plan	Present	Practice	Assess
URB 8 • Video Scripts pp. 71–72 • Family Involvement Activity p. 92 • Absent Student Copymasters pp. 101–111 **Best Practices Toolkit**	**URB 8** • Video Activities pp. 59–66	• *Cuaderno* pp. 367–392 • *Cuaderno para hispanohablantes* pp. 367–392 • *Lecturas para todos* pp. 183–187 • *Lecturas para hispanohablantes* • *¡AvanzaCómics! SuperBruno y Nati, Episodio 4* **URB 8** • Practice Games pp. 39–46 • Audio Scripts pp. 78–82 • Fine Art Activities pp. 88–89	**Differentiated Assessment Program** **URB 8** • Did you get it? Reteaching and Practice Copymasters pp. 13–24

Projectable Transparencies (Teacher One Stop, my.hrw.com)

Presentation and Practice	Classroom Management
• Vocabulary Transparencies 8, 9 • Grammar Presentation Transparencies 12, 13 • Situational Transparencies and label overlay 14, 15 • Situational Student Copymasters pp. 1, 2	• Warm Up Transparencies 20–23 • Student Book Answer Transparencies 28–31

Audio and Video

Audio	Video	¡AvanzaRap! DVD
• Student Book Audio CD 8 Tracks 12–24 • Workbook Audio CD 4 Tracks 31–40 • Heritage Learners Audio CD 2 Tracks 29–32, CD 4 Tracks 21–26 • Assessment Audio CD 2 Tracks 21–26 • *Lecturas para todos* Audio CD 1 Track 16, CD 2 Tracks 1–6 • Sing-along Songs Audio CD	• Vocabulary Video DVD 2 • *Telehistoria* DVD 2 Escena 1 Escena 2 Escena 3 Completa • Culture Video DVD 2	• Video animations of all **¡AvanzaRap!** songs (with Karaoke track) • Interactive DVD Activities • Teaching Suggestions • **¡AvanzaRap!** Activity Masters • **¡AvanzaRap!** video scripts and answers

Online and Media Resources

Student	Teacher
Available online at my.hrw.com • Online Student Edition • **News** Networking • **performance space** • @HOMETUTOR • Cultura Interactiva • WebQuests • Interactive Flashcards • Review Games • Self-Check Quiz **Student One Stop** **Holt McDougal Spanish Apps**	**Teacher One Stop (also available at my.hrw.com)** • Interactive Teacher's Edition • All print, audio, and video resources • Projectable Transparencies • Lesson Plans • TPRS • Examview Assessment Suite **Available online at my.hrw.com** *Generate Success* Rubric Generator and Graphic Organizers **Power Presentations**

Differentiated Assessment

On-level	Modified	Pre-AP	Heritage Learners
• Vocabulary Recognition Quiz p. 365 • Vocabulary Production Quiz p. 366 • Grammar Quizzes pp. 367–368 • Culture Quiz p. 369 • On-level Lesson Test pp. 370–376 • On-level Unit Test pp. 382–388 • On-level Final Exam pp. 394–403	• Modified Lesson Test pp. 290–296 • Modified Unit Test pp. 302–308 • Modified Final Exam pp. 314–323	• Pre-AP Lesson Test pp. 290–296 • Pre-AP Unit Test pp. 302–308 • Pre-AP Final Exam pp. 314–323	• Heritage Learners Lesson Test pp. 296–302 • Heritage Learners Unit Test pp. 308–314 • Heritage Learners Final Exam pp. 320–329

Core Pacing Guide

50 Minute (9 Day)

	Objectives/Focus	Teach	Practice	Assess/HW Options
DAY 1	**Culture:** Learn about Costa Rica **Vocabulary:** vacation activities • Warm Up OHT 20 **5 min**	Lesson Opener pp. 432–433 **Presentación de vocabulario** pp. 434–435 • Read A–D • View video DVD 2 • *¡A responder!* TXT CD 8 track 13 **25 min**	Lesson Opener pp. 432–433 **Práctica de vocabulario** p. 436 • Acts. 1, 2 **15 min**	**Assess:** *Para y piensa* p. 436 **5 min** **Homework:** *Cuaderno* pp. 367–369 @HomeTutor
DAY 2	**Communication:** vacation activities • Warm Up OHT 20 • Check Homework **5 min**	**Vocabulario en contexto** pp. 437–438 • *Telehistoria escena* 1 DVD 2 **20 min**	**Vocabulario en contexto** pp. 437–438 • Act. 3 TXT CD 8 track 14 • Act. 4 **20 min**	**Assess:** *Para y piensa* p. 438 **5 min** **Homework:** *Cuaderno* pp. 367–369 @HomeTutor
DAY 3	**Grammar:** indirect object pronouns • Warm Up OHT 21 • Check Homework **5 min**	**Presentación de gramática** p. 439 • indirect object pronouns **Práctica de gramática** pp. 440–441 **Culture:** *El transporte* **20 min**	**Práctica de gramática** pp. 440–441 • Acts. 5, 6, 7, 8 **20 min**	**Assess:** *Para y piensa* p. 441 **5 min** **Homework:** *Cuaderno* pp. 370–372 @HomeTutor
DAY 4	**Communication:** use indirect object pronouns to talk about vacation activities • Warm Up OHT 21 • Check Homework **5 min**	**Gramática en contexto** pp. 442–443 • *Telehistoria escena* 2 DVD 2 • *Pronunciación* TXT CD 8 track 16 **15 min**	**Gramática en contexto** pp. 442–443 • Act. 9 TXT CD 8 track 15 • Act. 10 **25 min**	**Assess:** *Para y piensa* p. 443 **5 min** **Homework:** *Cuaderno* pp. 370–372 @HomeTutor
DAY 5	**Grammar:** demonstrative adjectives • Warm Up OHT 22 • Check Homework **5 min**	**Presentación de gramática** p. 444 • demonstrative adjectives **Práctica de gramática** pp. 445–446 **15 min**	**Práctica de gramática** pp. 445–446 • Acts. 11, 13, 14 • Act. 12 TXT CD 8 track 17 **25 min**	**Assess:** *Para y piensa* p. 446 **5 min** **Homework:** *Cuaderno* pp. 373–375 @HomeTutor
DAY 6	**Communication:** Culmination: vacation activities, indirect object pronouns, demonstrative adjectives • Warm Up OHT 22 • Check Homework **5 min**	**Todo junto** pp. 447–449 • *Escenas 1, 2: Resumen* • *Telehistoria completa* DVD 2 **20 min**	**Todo junto** pp. 447–449 • Acts. 15, 16 TXT CD 8 tracks 14, 15, 18 • Act. 17, 19 • Act. 18, TXT CD 8 tracks 19, 20 **20 min**	**Assess:** *Para y piensa* p. 449 **5 min** **Homework:** *Cuaderno* pp. 376–377 @HomeTutor
DAY 7	**Reading:** Local markets in Costa Rica and Uruguay **Review:** Lesson Review • Warm Up OHT 23 • Check Homework **5 min**	**Lectura cultural** pp. 450–451 • *Mercados en Costa Rica y Uruguay* TXT CD 8 track 21 **Repaso de la lección** pp. 454–455 **15 min**	**Lectura cultural** pp. 450–451 • *Mercados en Costa Rica y Uruguay* **Repaso de la lección** pp. 454–455 • Act. 1 TXT CD 8 track 22 • Acts. 2, 3, 4 **20 min**	**Assess:** *Para y piensa* p. 451 **Repaso de la lección** pp. 454–455 **10 min** **Homework:** *En resumen* p. 453; *Cuaderno* pp. 378–389 (optional) Review Games Online @HomeTutor
DAY 8	**Assessment**			**Assess:** Lesson 2 test, Unit 8 Test, or Final Exam **50 min**
DAY 9	**Unit Culmination** **5 min**	**Comparación cultural** pp. 456–457 TXT CD 8 track 23 **Repaso inclusivo** pp. 458–459 **20 min**	**Comparación cultural** pp. 456–457 **Repaso inclusivo** pp. 458–459 • Act. 1 TXT CD 8 track 24 • Acts. 2, 3, 4, 5, 6, 7 **25 min**	**Homework:** *Cuaderno* pp. 390–392

	Objectives/Focus	Teach	Practice	Assess/HW Options
DAY 1	**Culture:** Learn about Costa Rica **Vocabulary:** vacation activities • Warm Up OHT 20 **5 min**	Lesson Opener pp. 432–433 **Presentación de vocabulario** pp. 434–435 • Read A–D • View video DVD 2 • *¡A responder!* TXT CD 8 track 13 **20 min**	Lesson Opener pp. 432–433 **Práctica de vocabulario** p. 436 • Acts. 1, 2 **20 min**	**Assess:** *Para y piensa* p. 436 **5 min**
	Communication: vacation activities **5 min**	**Vocabulario en contexto** pp. 437–438 • *Telehistoria escena* 1 DVD 2 **15 min**	**Vocabulario en contexto** pp. 437–438 • Act. 3 TXT CD 8 track 14 • Act. 4 **15 min**	**Assess:** *Para y piensa* p. 438 **5 min** **Homework:** *Cuaderno* pp. 367–369 @HomeTutor
DAY 2	**Grammar:** indirect object pronouns • Warm Up OHT 21 • Check Homework **5 min**	**Presentación de gramática** p. 439 • indirect object pronouns **Práctica de gramática** pp. 440–441 **Culture:** *El transporte* **20 min**	**Práctica de gramática** pp. 440–441 • Acts. 5, 6, 7, 8 **15 min**	**Assess:** *Para y piensa* p. 441 **5 min**
	Communication: Use indirect object pronouns to talk about vacation activities **5 min**	**Gramática en contexto** pp. 442–443 • *Telehistoria escena* 2 DVD 2 • *Pronunciación* TXT CD 8 track 16 **20 min**	**Gramática en contexto** pp. 442–443 • Act. 9 TXT CD 8 track 15 • Act. 10 **15 min**	**Assess:** *Para y piensa* p. 443 **5 min** **Homework:** *Cuaderno* pp. 370–372 @HomeTutor
DAY 3	**Grammar:** demonstrative adjectives • Warm Up OHT 22 • Check Homework **5 min**	**Presentación de gramática** p. 444 • demonstrative adjectives **Práctica de gramática** pp. 445–446 **15 min**	**Práctica de gramática** pp. 445–446 • Acts. 11, 13, 14, 15 • Act. 12 TXT CD 8 track 17 **20 min**	**Assess:** *Para y piensa* p. 446 **5 min**
	Communication: Culmination: vacation activities, indirect object pronouns, demonstrative adjectives **5 min**	**Todo junto** pp. 447–449 • *Escenas* 1, 2: *Resumen* • *Telehistoria completa* DVD 2 **15 min**	**Todo junto** pp. 447–449 • Acts. 15, 16 TXT CD 8 tracks 14, 15, 18 • Act. 17, 19 • Act. 18 TXT CD 8 tracks 19, 20 **20 min**	**Assess:** *Para y piensa* p. 449 **5 min** **Homework:** *Cuaderno* pp. 373–377 @HomeTutor
DAY 4	**Reading:** Local markets in Costa Rica and Uruguay • Warm Up OHT 23 • Check Homework **5 min**	**Lectura cultural** pp. 450–451 • *Mercados en Costa Rica y Uruguay* TXT CD 8 track 21 **15 min**	**Lectura cultural** pp. 450–451 • *Mercados en Costa Rica y Uruguay* **15 min**	**Assess:** *Para y piensa* p. 451 **5 min**
	Review: Lesson Review **5 min**	**Repaso de la lección** pp. 454–455 **15 min**	**Repaso de la lección** pp. 454–455 • Act. 1 TXT CD 8 track 22 • Acts. 2, 3, 4 **25 min**	**Assess: Repaso de la lección** pp. 454–455 **5 min** **Homework:** *En resumen* p. 453; *Cuaderno* pp. 378–389 @HomeTutor
DAY 5	**Assessment**			**Assess:** Lesson 2 Test, Unit 8 Test, or Final Exam **45 min**
	Unit Culmination **5 min**	**Comparación cultural** pp. 456–457 TXT CD 8 track 23 **Repaso inclusivo** pp. 458–459 **20 min**	**Comparación cultural** pp. 456–457 **Repaso inclusivo** pp. 458–459 • Act. 1 TXT CD 8 track 24 • Acts. 2, 3, 4, 5, 6, 7 **20 min**	**Homework:** *Cuaderno* pp. 390–392

¡AVANZA! Objectives

- Introduce lesson theme: **Vamos de vacaciones.**
- **Culture:** Discuss vacation activities in other parts of the world and those in your region.

Presentation Strategies

- Introduce again the characters' names: Susana and Jorge.
- Ask students to make a list of vacation activities they like to do.
- Ask students what kinds of souvenirs they like to buy on vacation.

STANDARDS

2.2 Products and perspectives
4.2 Compare cultures
21st Century **Communication,** Slower-paced Learners

Warm Up Projectable Transparencies, 8-20

Present Progressive Write sentences with the present progressive form of the given verb.

1. yo / peinarse
2. María y Julieta / maquillarse
3. tú / levantarse
4. mis hermanos / vestirse
5. nosotros / cepillarse los dientes

Answers: 1. Yo me estoy peinando (estoy peinándome). 2. María y Julieta se están maquillando (están maquillándose). 3. Tú te estás levantando (estás levantándote). 4. Mis hermanos se están vistiendo (están vistiéndose). 5. Nosotros nos estamos cepillando (estamos cepillándonos) los dientes.

Comparación cultural

Exploring the Theme

Ask the following:

1. What national parks in the United States would you like to visit?
2. Which souvenir items in the photo would you find in your region?
3. Which souvenir items in the photo would you like to buy?

¿Qué ves? Possible answers include:

- No, Susana y Jorge están contentos.
- La tienda es verde.
- Pueden comprar regalos.

UNIDAD 8 Costa Rica

Lección 2

Tema:

¡Vamos de vacaciones!

¡AVANZA! In this lesson you will learn to

- talk about buying souvenirs on vacation
- talk about vacation activities

using

- indirect object pronouns
- demonstrative adjectives

¿Recuerdas?

- family, classroom objects
- numbers from 200 to 1,000,000
- **gustar** with an infinitive
- present progressive

Comparación cultural

In this lesson you will learn about

- transportation and marketplaces
- the coffee industry and desserts from Costa Rica and Uruguay
- travel destinations in Costa Rica, Ecuador, and Uruguay

Compara con tu mundo

This shop has several items depicting tropical birds, such as the **quetzal** and the **tucán.** Costa Rica is home to about five percent of the world's plant and animal species, making it an ideal place for ecotourism. *Where do you like to go and what do you like to do during vacation?*

¿Qué ves?

Mira la foto

¿Están enojados Susana y Jorge?

¿De qué color es la tienda?

¿Qué pueden comprar aquí?

Differentiating Instruction

Multiple Intelligences

Naturalist Create a web on the board around the word *ecotourism*. Ask students to share their understanding of this word, as well as any experiences they have had with ecotourism. What do they see as its benefits and drawbacks?

Inclusion

Cumulative Instruction Organize students into four groups. Give each group a piece of chart paper or poster board. Then direct students' attention to the topics under the *¿Recuerdas?* title on p. 432. Assign each group one of the topics. Instruct them to create a poster that will help their peers review the details of that topic. They might draw pictures, design a chart, list examples, or create a review exercise.

DIGITAL SPANISH my.hrw.com
ONLINE STUDENT EDITION with...

performance space
News + Networking
@HOMETUTOR
CULTURA Interactiva

- Audio and Video Resources
- Interactive Flashcards
- Review Activities
- WebQuest
- Conjuguemos.com

PRACTICE SPANISH WITH HOLT MCDOUGAL APPS!

Una tienda de artesanías y recuerdos
San José, Costa Rica

DIGITAL SPANISH

TEACHER TOOLS
- Interactive Whiteboard Lessons
- Generate Success!

ALSO AVAILABLE...
- Online Workbook
- Spanish InterActive Reader

SPANISH ON THE GO!
- Performance Space
- Holt McDougal Spanish Apps
- ¡Avancemos! eTextbook

Using the Photo

Location Information

Handicraft Shops in San José offer an extensive choice of native crafts. Typical items include boxes, bowls, and frames made of tropical wood; ceramic replicas of pre-Columbian figures; ceramic bowls, vases, and coffee mugs; and typical tourist items such as T-shirts, posters, and postcards. The making and selling of handicrafts encourages the retention of artistic traditions and offers economic opportunity for local artisans and businesses.

Expanded Information

Arts and Crafts Many of the best crafts in Costa Rica come from Sarchí, in the province of Alajuela, where they produce full-size and miniature versions of wooden **carretas** (ox-carts) handpainted in colorful designs. They are also noted for their leather satchels and purses.

Differentiating Instruction

Slower-paced Learners

Personalize It Ask students to bring in a souvenir from a trip or vacation or something someone brought back for them from a trip. Give students the opportunity to talk about their souvenirs. Here are a few possible sentences starters:
Es de..., Me gusta porque..., Lo/La compré porque..., Me lo compró...

Heritage Language Learners

Support What They Know Encourage students to describe the photo on pp. 432–433 in as much detail as possible. How would they describe the windows, the floor, and the objects in the store?

Long-term Retention

Personalize It

Ask students to look at the photo on pp. 432–433 for several minutes. With books closed, ask **¿Qué te gustaría comprar en la tienda de artesanías y recuerdos?** Ask them to mention at least 3 items.

¡AVANZA! Objective

- Present vocabulary: vacation activities, handicrafts, jewelry, bargaining expressions.

Core Resources

- Video Program: DVD 2
- Audio Program: TXT CD 8 tracks 12, 13

Presentation Strategies

- Point to the photos on pp. 434–435, say the words, and have students repeat after you. Correct pronunciation as needed.
- Ask **cierto/falso** questions to verify comprehension. For example: **El anillo es una joya. (cierto) Podemos dar una caminata en el mar. (falso)**
- Play the audio as students read A–D.
- Show the video.

STANDARDS

1.2 Understand language

21st Century **Flexibility and Adaptability,** Multiple Intelligences; **Social and Cross-Cultural Skills,** English Learners

Long-term Retention — Recycle

Using vocabulary from the lesson, read statements about activities that are generally done outdoors. Add other statements to the list. Ask students to raise their hands if the statements refers to an outdoor activity. Example: **Me gusta comer al aire libre. Me gustaría hacer surfing. Este verano, voy a acampar. Me afeito a las ocho. Quiero montar a caballo. Me acuesto a las diez de la noche. Es divertido dar una caminata. Vamos a hacer una parrillada.**

Communication — TPR Activity

After presenting the vocabulary, say the following activities and ask students to act them out.

- **acampar**
- **hacer surfing**
- **montar a caballo**
- **hacer surf de vela**
- **dar una caminata**

Presentación de VOCABULARIO

¡AVANZA! **Goal:** Learn about the activities Susana likes to do on vacation. Then practice what you have learned to talk about buying souvenirs. ***Actividades 1–2***

VIDEO DVD
AUDIO

A **Estoy comiendo al aire libre** con mi amiga. Es divertido, pero yo **quisiera** hacer un viaje al campo o al mar.

B Me gustaría **hacer surfing, hacer surf de vela, acampar** o **montar a caballo.**

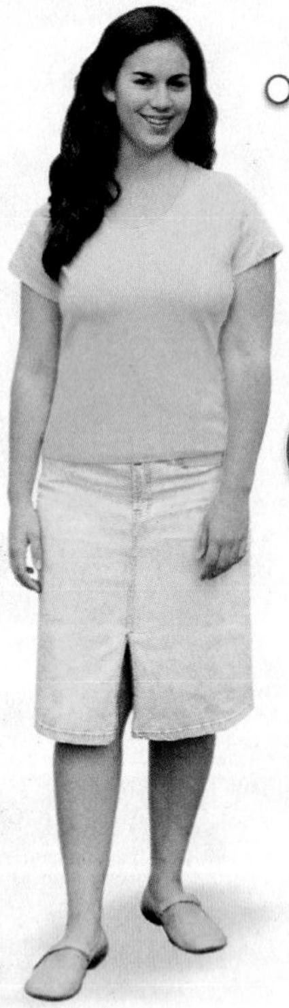

Más vocabulario

el tiempo libre *free time*	**¿Me deja ver...?** *May I see. . .?*
Le dejo... en... *I'll give. . . to you for. . .*	**¡Qué caro(a)!** *How expensive!*
Le puedo ofrecer... *I can offer you. . .*	**¿Qué es esto?** *What is this?*

Expansión de vocabulario p. R9

Differentiating Instruction

Pre-AP

Communicate Preferences Use the verbs **gustar** and **preferir** to ask students about the vacation activities shown on pp. 434–435. When students answer **sí** or **no**, ask them to explain why.

¿Te gusta acampar? No, prefiero un hotel.
¿Te gusta hacer surfing? Sí, pero me gusta más hacer surf de vela.

Slower-paced Learners

Yes/No Questions Ask students to think about the last trip or vacation they went on. Then ask yes or no questions related to the activities presented.

Cuando fuiste de vacaciones, ¿hiciste surf de vela?
Cuando fuiste de vacaciones, ¿montaste a caballo?

C Cuando estoy de vacaciones siempre compro **recuerdos** en **el mercado.** Allí puedes **regatear** y las cosas son más **baratas.**

D Hay **artesanías** y **joyas** de buena **calidad.** Quiero comprar **un anillo de oro** pero cuesta **demasiado.** Hay **unos aretes de plata** menos **caros.**

las artesanías

las joyas

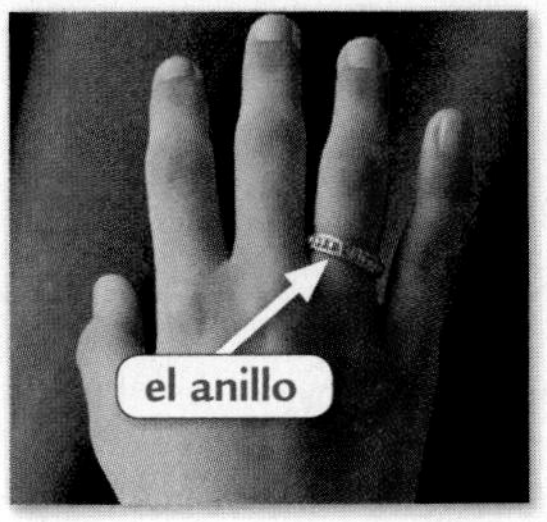

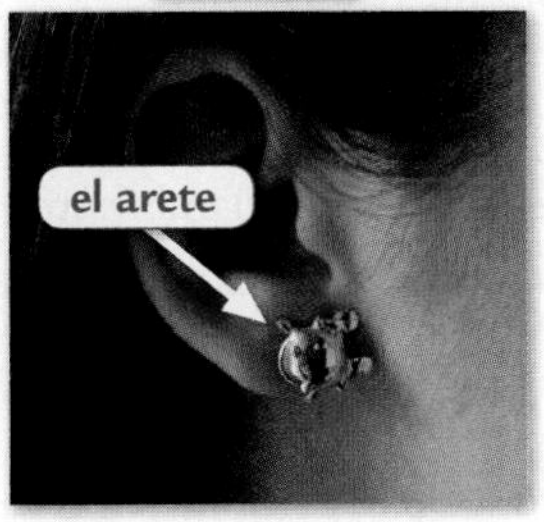

@HOMETUTOR my.hrw.com Interactive Flashcards

¡A responder! Escuchar

Escucha la lista de actividades que Susana quisiera hacer durante las vacaciones. Señala la foto correcta para cada actividad que menciona.
(Point to the photo of each activity that Susana mentions.)

TEACHER to TEACHER

Teresa M. Suárez
Coral Gables, Florida

Tips for Presenting Vocabulary

I try to reinforce travel vocabulary by bringing to class travel brochures, posters, photos, and maps of places I've visited. I have a collection of interesting items that I use over and over to stimulate my students' imagination as we talk about travel and related subjects. These include train tickets; tickets to theaters, museums, stadiums; brochures for ski and beach resorts, hotels, camping gear, shopping mall guides... Though small, these items provide the class with a fascinating window to the Spanish-speaking world.

Go online for more tips!

Long-term Retention

Personalize It

Say the activities on pp. 434–435 and ask students to qualify them using the following expressions: **Es divertido, Es aburrido, Es fácil, Es difícil.** For example: **Es difícil hacer surf de vela. Es aburrido hacer una parrillada.** Write the answers on the board.

Communication

Regionalisms

Explain to students that there are regional variations for some of the words and phrases on pp. 434–435. For example: **acampar** (Costa Rica); **ir de camping** (Argentina, Chile), **hacer surfing** (México, Costa Rica), **surfear** (Puerto Rico), **hacer surf** (España).

Differentiating Instruction

English Learners

Build Background Discuss with students the concept of bargaining. Is this a custom in their country of origin? If so, are there places where it is and is not appropriate? Also, ask students to describe typical crafts or jewelry from their home country.

Multiple Intelligences

Interpersonal Organize students in pairs. Have each pair draft the script for a role play that involves buying something **en el mercado**. Refer students to the box entitled Más vocabulario on p. 434 for helpful phrases. Tell students that their role play should involve some bargaining over the price of the item.

Answers Projectable Transparencies, 8-28

¡A responder! Audio Script, TE p. 431B

Students should point to the following photos: hiking, surfing, camping, windsurfing, barbecuing, eating outdoors, and horseback riding.

Objective
- Practice vocabulary: jewelry, handicrafts, bargaining expressions.

Core Resource
- *Cuaderno,* pp. 367–369

Practice Sequence
- **Activity 1:** Vocabulary recognition: jewelry, handicrafts
- **Activity 2:** Vocabulary production: jewelry, bargaining expressions

STANDARDS
1.3 Present information, Acts. 1–2
21st Century **Creativity and Innovation,** Multiple Intelligences

Communication
Common Error Alert
Remind students that the phrases **de oro** and **de plata** are used to describe what items are made of. Other examples could include **de piedra** *(stone)*, **de madera** *(wood)*, **de cuero** *(leather)*, **de vidrio** *(glass)*, **de barro** *(clay)*, and **de mimbre** *(wicker)*.

✓ Ongoing Assessment
Get Help Online
More Practice
my.hrw.com

PARA Y PIENSA **Peer Assessment** Have pairs of students take turns asking for the items in Para y piensa and correct each other. For additional practice, use Reteaching & Practice Copymasters URB 8, pp. 13, 14.

Answers Projectable Transparencies, 8-28

Activity 1
1. Hay artículos de madera en la tienda.
2. Hay joyas en la tienda.
3. Hay cerámica en la tienda.
4. Hay anillos de oro en la tienda.
5. No hay collares de madera en la tienda.
6. Hay aretes de plata en la tienda.
7. Hay artesanías en la tienda.
8. No hay anillos de plata en la tienda.

Activity 2
1. Quisiera
2. Me deja ver
3. Le dejo
4. caro
5. ofrecer
6. demasiado

Para y piensa
1. ¿Me deja ver los aretes?
2. ¿Me deja ver el collar de plata?
3. ¿Me deja ver el anillo de oro?
4. ¿Me deja ver las artesanías de madera?

Práctica de VOCABULARIO

Expansión: Teacher Edition Only
Ask students to write three other items that they would find in a **tienda de artesanías.**

1 ¿Qué hay en la tienda?

Hablar
Escribir

Indica qué hay en la tienda, según el anuncio.
(Indicate what items the store has, according to the ad.)

modelo: **collares de plata**
No hay collares de plata en la tienda.

1. artículos de madera
2. joyas
3. cerámica
4. anillos de oro
5. collares de madera
6. aretes de plata
7. artesanías
8. anillos de plata

2 Unos aretes de plata

Leer
Escribir

Susana quiere comprar algo en el mercado. Completa la conversación.
(Complete the conversation.)

le dejo	me deja ver	caro
demasiado	quisiera	ofrecer

Susana: Buenas tardes. __1.__ comprar un regalo para mi madre. ¿ __2.__ los aretes de plata?
Vendedor: Sí, claro. Son muy bonitos.
Susana: ¿Cuánto cuestan?
Vendedor: __3.__ los aretes en quince mil quinientos colones.
Susana: ¡Quince mil quinientos! ¡Qué __4.__ ! Le puedo __5.__ trece mil quinientos.
Vendedor: Lo siento. Son de buena calidad. Le dejo los aretes en catorce mil.
Susana: ¿Catorce mil? Es __6.__ , pero me gustan mucho. Los compro.

Expansión
Talk with a partner about which of these items you would like to buy for yourself.

Más práctica Cuaderno *pp. 367–369* Cuaderno para hispanohablantes *pp. 367–370*

Get Help Online
my.hrw.com

PARA Y PIENSA **Did you get it?** Ask to see the following items.
1. earrings
2. silver necklace
3. gold ring
4. wooden handicrafts

Differentiating Instruction

Multiple Intelligences

Visual Learners Have students create their own store ads like the one pictured in Activity 1. Students might draw pictures of the available items, or cut out pictures from magazines. Once students have completed their ads, have them switch with a partner, and repeat Activity 1 using the new material to form sentences.

Inclusion

Frequent Review/Repetition Have students work in pairs as they read Activity 2 aloud and fill in the blanks. Instruct them to try out each possible answer in each blank until they find the one that sounds the most logical.

VOCABULARIO en contexto

¡AVANZA! **Goal:** Pay attention to the words Susana uses to talk about items in a store. Then practice these words to talk about shopping and what you would and would not like to do in your free time. ***Actividades 3–4***

@HOMETUTOR my.hrw.com View, Read and Record

Telehistoria escena 1

STRATEGIES

Cuando lees
Find the hidden reasons Read between the lines to understand hidden reasons. Why does Susana ask her father to buy a blue car?

Cuando escuchas
Identify teasing Susana is embarrassed twice in this scene. Identify who says things to embarrass her, when it happens, and what the differences are.

VIDEO DVD

AUDIO

Susana and Jorge's father drops them off at a store in his red car that looks like a taxi. One of Susana's classmates is standing outside.

Susana: Gracias, Papi. Pero, ¿por qué no compras un carro nuevo? ¿Un carro azul?

Amiga: Eh, Susanita, ¡qué divertido viajar en taxi todos los días!

Embarrassed, Susana smiles, and she and Jorge enter the shop quickly.

Vendedora: ¿Quiere usted ver algo en especial?

Susana: A ver... ¿este anillo de oro?

Vendedora: Claro que sí.

Susana tries on the ring.

Susana: ¿Cuánto cuesta?

Vendedora: Veinte mil colones.

Susana: ¡Qué caro! Tengo diez mil colones, nada más.

Vendedora: Señorita, no estamos en el mercado. Aquí no regateamos.

A little embarrassed, Susana leaves.

Continuará... p. 442

¡AVANZA! Objective

- Understand activity vocabulary in context.

Core Resources

- Video Program: DVD 2
- Audio Program: TXT CD 8 track 14

Presentation Strategies

- Have students look at the photos. Ask simple questions such as: **¿De qué color es el carro del papá de Susana? ¿Qué venden en la tienda? ¿Con quién habla Susana?**
- Ask students to scan the dialogue to find out what Susana wants to buy.
- Play audio or video while students follow the script in their text.

STANDARDS

1.2 Understand language

21st Century **Technology Literacy,** Multiple Intelligences (Financial Literacy)

Warm Up Projectable Transparencies, 8-20

Vocabulary Complete the following sentences.

a. comer al aire libre **b.** hacer surf de vela
c. acampar **d.** regatear
e. hacer una parrillada

1. A Patricia le gusta _____ en el mar.
2. Vamos a _____ y comer hamburguesas.
3. Quisiera _____ en el mercado.
4. A los chicos les gusta _____ para dormir en el campo.
5. ¿Prefieres comer en el restaurante o _____?

Answers: 1. b; 2. e; 3. d; 4. c; 5. a

Video Summary

@HOMETUTOR VideoPlus my.hrw.com

Susana and Jorge arrive at a store in their father's old red car. In the store, Susana tries on a gold ring and then learns that it costs 20,000 colones. When Susana says she only has 10,000 colones, the salesperson says they are not in a market and that bargaining isn't done in the store.

Differentiating Instruction

Multiple Intelligences

Logical/Mathematical Have students use the Internet to research the current value of the Costa Rican **colón** as compared to the U.S. dollar. Have students do the conversion to get a sense of how much the ring that Susana likes costs, and how much money Susana has to spend.

Slower-paced Learners

Sentence Completion Beginning with the clerk's line **¿Quiere usted ver algo en especial?**, copy the script of the Telehistoria on the board. Erase pieces of information, such as the material the ring is made out of, or its price. Then have students fill in the blanks with new information to create a new version of the scene.

Objective
- Practice using the vocabulary in context.

Core Resource
- Audio Program: TXT CD 8 track 14

Practice Sequence
- **Activity 3:** Telehistoria comprehension
- **Activity 4:** Vocabulary production: outdoor activities

STANDARDS

1.1 Engage in conversation, Act. 4
1.2 Understand language, Act. 3
1.3 Present information, Act. 4, PYP

✓ Ongoing Assessment

Get Help Online
More Practice
my.hrw.com

PARA Y PIENSA **Quick Check** Have students say the sentences in Para y piensa aloud and write them on the board. For additional practice, use Reteaching & Practice Copymasters URB 8, pp. 13, 15.

Answers Projectable Transparencies, 8-28

Activity 3
1. A Susana no le gusta el coche de su papá porque es rojo.
2. Susana va a la tienda con Jorge.
3. Susana quiere ver el anillo de oro.
4. El anillo cuesta veinte mil colones.
5. Susana tiene diez mil colones.
6. La vendedora no regatea porque no están en un mercado.

Activity 4 Answers will vary. Sample answers:
1. A. ¿Te gustaría montar a caballo en tu tiempo libre?
   B. Sí, me gustaría montar a caballo.
   C. No, no me gustaría montar a caballo.
2. A. ¿Te gustaría dar una caminata en tu tiempo libre?
   B. Sí, me gustaría dar una caminata.
   C. No, no me gustaría dar una caminata.
3. A. ¿Te gustaría hacer surf de vela en tu tiempo libre?
   B. Sí, me gustaría hacer surf de vela.
   C. No, no me gustaría hacer surf de vela.
4. A. ¿Te gustaría comer al aire libre en tu tiempo libre?
   B. Sí, me gustaría comer al aire libre.
   C. No, no me gustaría comer al aire libre.

3 *Comprensión del episodio* En una tienda

Escuchar Leer

Contesta las preguntas. *(Answer the questions.)*

1. ¿A Susana le gusta el coche de su papá? ¿Por qué?
2. ¿Con quién va Susana a la tienda?
3. ¿Qué anillo quiere ver Susana?
4. ¿Cuánto cuesta el anillo?
5. ¿Cuánto dinero tiene Susana?
6. ¿Por qué no regatea la vendedora?

Expansión:
Teacher Edition Only
Ask students to write a short summary of the Telehistoria using questions 1–6 as a guide.

4 ¡Qué divertido!

Hablar

Pregúntales a otros estudiantes si les gustaría hacer las siguientes actividades en su tiempo libre. *(Ask if your partners would like to do these activities.)*

A ¿Te gustaría acampar en tu tiempo libre?
B Sí, me gustaría acampar.
C No, no me gustaría acampar.

1. 
2. 
3. 
4. 
5. 
6. 

Expansión
Tell how often you do these activities.

Get Help Online
my.hrw.com

PARA Y PIENSA

Did you get it? Create logical sentences by choosing the correct word.
1. Susana está contenta porque el collar es muy (caro / barato).
2. A ella le gustan (la cerámica / los aretes) de madera.
3. Ella puede regatear en (las artesanías / el mercado).

Differentiating Instruction

Slower-paced Learners

Yes/No Questions Help students understand Telehistoria, escena 1 by changing the questions in Activity 3 to yes/no questions. For example: **¿Va Susana a la tienda con su padre? ¿Quiere Susana ver el anillo de plata?**

Pre-AP

Expand and Elaborate Encourage students to elaborate on their responses to Activity 4. Ask them to explain why they do or do not like a certain activity. Here is a possible extension for the model.
Sí, me gustaría acampar. Me gusta pasar un rato en el campo.
No, no me gustaría acampar. Prefiero quedarme en un hotel.

Presentación de GRAMÁTICA

¡AVANZA! **Goal:** Learn how to use indirect object pronouns. Then practice using these pronouns to talk about buying things for people. ***Actividades 5–8***

¿Recuerdas? Family p. 164, numbers from 200 to 1,000,000 p. 165

English Grammar Connection: In both English and Spanish, **indirect objects** are nouns or pronouns that tell *to whom* or *for whom* the action takes place in a sentence.

Aunt Lola sends **us** gifts. (us = indirect object pronoun)

Tía Lola **nos** manda regalos. (nos = indirect object pronoun)

Indirect Object Pronouns

ANIMATEDGRAMMAR my.hrw.com

Use **indirect object pronouns** to clarify to whom or for whom an action takes place.

Here's how: **Indirect object pronouns** use the same words as direct object pronouns except for **le** and **les.**

Singular		Plural	
me	*me*	**nos**	*us*
te	*you (familiar)*	**os**	*you (familiar)*
le	*you (formal), him, her*	**les**	*you, them*

The pronouns **le** and **les** can refer to a variety of people. To clarify what they mean, they are often accompanied by **a** + **noun** or **pronoun.**

Le doy las joyas.
I'm giving the jewelry ***to him/her/you.***

Le doy las joyas **a Juana.**
I'm giving the jewelry ***to Juana.***

When a conjugated verb is followed by an infinitive, the same rules for placement apply as for direct object pronouns. The **pronoun** can be placed before the **conjugated verb** or attached to the end of the **infinitive.**

Les voy a **comprar** recuerdos a mis amigos.
or Voy a **comprarles** recuerdos a mis amigos.
I'm going to buy souvenirs for my friends.

Más práctica
Cuaderno *pp. 370–372*
Cuaderno para hispanohablantes *pp. 371–373*

@HOMETUTOR my.hrw.com
Leveled Practice

¡AVANZA! **Objective**
- Present indirect object pronouns.

Core Resource
- *Cuaderno,* pp. 370–372

Presentation Strategies
- Remind students that they have used indirect object pronouns with the verbs **gustar** and **doler.**
- Distribute classroom objects to students, describing as you go. For example, **Le doy el libro a Pedro. Les doy las plumas a Jorge y a Esteban.** Reach for someone's notebook and ask: **¿Me das tu cuaderno?** Ask students to pass items to other students and describe: **Celia le da el lápiz a Juan Carlos.**
- Explain both ways of placing indirect objects with infinitives. Give several examples and check comprehension. For example, say: **Le voy a dar un anillo de oro a mi mamá.** Ask students to give you the alternate form: **Voy a darle un anillo de oro a mi mamá.**

STANDARDS
4.1 Compare languages

Warm Up Projectable Transparencies, 8-21

Vocabulary Complete the sentences.

a. recuerdos **b.** aretes **c.** barato
d. calidad **e.** demasiado

1. El collar no es caro. Es ______.
2. Los ______ son de plata y no de oro.
3. Cuando estoy de vacaciones, siempre compro ______.
4. Susana y Jorge no quieren pagar ______ por la artesanía.
5. Las joyas son de muy buena ______.

Answers: **1.** c; **2.** b; **3.** a; **4.** e; **5.** d

Answers Projectable Transparencies, 8-28 and 8-29

Answers continued from p. 438

5. A: ¿Te gustaría hacer una parrillada en tu tiempo libre?
B: Sí, me gustaría hacer una parrillada.
C: No, no me gustaría hacer una parrillada.

6. A: ¿Te gustaría hacer surfing en tu tiempo libre?
B: Sí, me gustaría hacer surfing.
C: No, no me gustaría hacer surfing.

Para y piensa **1.** barato; **2.** los aretes; **3.** el mercado

Differentiating Instruction

Inclusion

Multisensory Input/Output You will need a box wrapped to look like a present. Write the verbs **dar** and **comprar** on the board. Then create sentences that utilize indirect object pronouns. **Le doy el regalo a Manuel.** Use gestures and the prop to clarify that something is being given *to*, sent *to*, or bought *for* someone. Have students repeat your words and gestures.

Slower-paced Learners

Memory Aids Have students create a chart that compares indirect object pronouns with the direct object pronouns they have already learned. Then have them discuss their observations. Which forms are the same? **(me, te; nos, os)** Which are different? **(lo, la; le/los, las; les)**

Objectives
- Practice using indirect object pronouns.
- **Culture**: Discuss means of transportation in different countries.
- Practice lesson vocabulary: jewelry, handicrafts, what things are made of.
- Recycle: family members, numbers from 200 to 1,000,000.

Core Resource
- *Cuaderno,* pp. 370–372

Practice Sequence
- **Activity 5:** Controlled practice: indirect object pronouns, jewelry, handicrafts, gift items; Recycle: family
- **Activity 6:** Controlled practice: indirect object pronouns, gift items, family members
- **Activity 7:** Transitional practice: indirect object pronouns, gift items; Recycle: numbers from 200 to 1,000,000
- **Activity 8:** Transitional practice: indirect object pronouns, gift items, family members

STANDARDS
1.1 Engage in conversation, Act. 8
1.3 Present information, Acts. 5–7, PYP
2.2 Products and perspectives, CC
21st Century **Flexibility and Adaptability,** Group Work; **Social and Cross-Cultural Skills,** Comparación cultural

Comparación cultural

Essential Question
Suggested Answer Public transportation as well as a wide network of public roads is essential to the development and economy of a country. It allows inexpensive access to all areas.

Expanded Information
Public Transportation Taxis provide an excellent service and are much cheaper in Costa Rica than in other countries. All taxis have a meter, which is turned on when you enter the cab. Tipping taxi drivers is not a common practice in Costa Rica. Buses are another option. They are inexpensive and easily available. The ICT (Tourism Bureau) gives out information on bus schedules, fares, stops, and major terminals.

See Activity answers on p. 441.

Práctica de GRAMÁTICA

5 De compras
¿Recuerdas? Family p. 164

Leer

Susana le explica a Jorge qué compran sus padres. Escoge el pronombre de objeto indirecto apropiado (**me, te, le, nos, les**). *(Choose the appropriate indirect object pronoun.)*

modelo: Mamá y papá (te / le) compran un sombrero a nuestra tía.
Mamá y papá **le** compran un sombrero **a nuestra tía.**

1. Mamá y papá (nos / les) compran un DVD a nosotros.
2. (Le / Les) compran aretes a nuestra abuela.
3. A nuestros primos (le / les) compran un disco compacto.
4. (Me / Te) compran un collar de madera a ti.
5. A mí también (me / les) compran un collar, pero es de plata.
6. (Le / Les) compran artículos de cerámica a su amigo.

Expansión:
Teacher Edition Only
Ask students to think of five gifts they would like to buy and for whom. Have them use this information to write five sentences using **comprar** and indirect object pronouns.

6 ¿Qué les compró?

Escribir

Durante las vacaciones, Susana compró recuerdos. Escribe oraciones para indicar a quiénes les compró estas cosas. *(Write sentences to tell for whom Susana bought these souvenirs.)*

modelo: artículo de madera / padre
Le compró un artículo de madera **a su padre.**

1. collar de madera / madre
2. aretes de plata / yo
3. cerámica / nosotros
4. anillo de oro / tú
5. joyas / amigas
6. aretes de oro / abuelas

Expansión
Tell for whom you have bought gifts recently.

Comparación cultural

Taxis en el Parque Central en San José

El transporte
How is transportation important to a country? In **Costa Rica,** taxis are generally inexpensive and easy to find, especially in larger cities. You can recognize Costa Rican taxis by their color: airport taxis are orange, while all other taxis are red. Traveling by bus is also common. The capital, San José, has extensive bus lines and almost all areas of the country can be reached by bus. Many travelers also use local airlines to reach popular destinations, such as coastal cities and beaches.

Compara con tu mundo *How does transportation in your area compare to that of Costa Rica?*

Differentiating Instruction

Inclusion
Clear Structure Suggest that students follow these steps to choose the correct pronoun in Activity 5.
1. Write the sentences on a sheet of paper.
2. Underline the noun or pronoun following **a**.
3. Find the corresponding indirect object pronoun.
4. Circle the correct choice.
5. Read the completed sentence aloud.

English Learners
Build Background Create a concept web around the heading *transportation in Costa Rica*. Then, as students read the information presented in the Comparación cultural, have them add ideas to the web. Some responses might include *taxis, buses,* and *airlines*. Then encourage students to find details about each of these topics at the library.

7 La vendedora

¿Recuerdas? Numbers from 200 to 1,000,000 p. 165

Hablar
Escribir

Ayer una vendedora vendió muchas cosas en el mercado. Indica a quiénes les vendió estos artículos, según lo que pagaron. *(Based on the amount each person paid, indicate to whom the salesclerk sold these items.)*

modelo: Tú pagaste dieciséis mil cuatrocientos colones.
Ella **te** vendió **un collar de plata.**

1. Jorge pagó quince mil seiscientos colones.
2. Mis amigos y yo pagamos cinco mil novecientos colones.
3. Susana y su madre pagaron dos mil colones.
4. Yo pagué treinta mil ochocientos colones.
5. La maestra de español pagó veinte mil colones.
6. Ustedes pagaron nueve mil trescientos colones.

Ventas, el 6 de junio

Artículo	Precio
aretes de oro	20.000
recuerdos de madera	15.600
collar de plata	16.400
platos de cerámica	5.900
libro de Costa Rica	2.000
anillo de plata	9.300
collares de oro	30.800

Expansión:
Teacher Edition Only
To review numbers above 1,000, ask students to write another list of articles and prices (between 1,000 and 50,000 colones). Ask them to read their lists.

8 ¿Qué les das a otros?

Hablar

Di qué regalos les das a otras personas. *(Tell what gifts you give to whom.)*

modelo:

A ¿A quién le das artesanías?

B Le doy artesanías a mi abuela.

1. 
2. 
3. 
4. 
5. 
6. 

Expansión
Describe what gifts people gave you last year.

Más práctica Cuaderno *pp. 370–372* Cuaderno para hispanohablantes *pp. 371–373*

Get Help Online
my.hrw.com

PARA Y PIENSA

Did you get it? Give the correct indirect object pronoun.
1. Nosotros ____ damos los recuerdos a nuestros hermanos.
2. A ti ____ quiero comprar un collar de oro.
3. Carlos ____ pide 2.000 colones a nosotros.

Differentiating Instruction

Slower-paced Learners

Yes/No Questions Help students preview Activity 7 by asking yes or no questions about the price of the items sold.
¿Cuesta veinte mil colones el collar de plata?
¿Cuesta dos mil colones el libro de Costa Rica?

Heritage Language Learners

Support What They Know Ask students to share a story about a great gift they either gave or received. What was the item, what was it made of, whom did it come from or go to, and why was it so special?

Communication

Group Work

Have students create skits in which they shop for handicrafts in a store or in a market. Encourage students to bargain if their skit takes place in a market.

Communication

Common Error Alert

Activity 7 Remind students that the **yo** form of **pagar** in the preterite is **pagué.**

✓ Ongoing Assessment

Get Help Online
More Practice
my.hrw.com

PARA Y PIENSA **Peer Assessment** Have students complete the sentences individually. Then ask pairs of students to read their answers aloud and check each other's written work. For additional practice, use Reteaching & Practice Copymasters URB 8, pp. 16, 17, 22, 23.

Answers Projectable Transparencies, 8-29

Answers for Activities on pp. 440, 441.

Activity 5 **1.** nos; **2.** Le; **3.** les; **4.** Te; **5.** me; **6.** Le

Activity 6
1. Le compró un collar de madera a su madre.
2. Me compró unos aretes de plata a mí.
3. Nos compró cerámica a nosotros.
4. Te compró un anillo de oro a ti.
5. Les compró unas joyas a sus amigas.
6. Les compró unos aretes de oro a sus abuelas.

Activity 7
1. Ella le vendió unos recuerdos de madera.
2. Ella nos vendió unos platos de cerámica.
3. Ella les vendió un libro de Costa Rica.
4. Ella me vendió unos collares de oro.
5. Ella le vendió unos aretes de oro.
6. Ella les vendió un anillo de plata.

Activity 8 Answers will vary. Sample answers include:
1. **A:** ¿A quién le das un collar? **B:** Le doy un collar a mi mamá.
2. **A:** ...anillos
3. **A:** ...un artículo de madera
4. **A:** ...cerámica
5. **A:** ...discos compactos
6. **A:** ...aretes

Para y piensa **1.** les; **2.** te; **3.** nos

¡AVANZA! Objectives

- Identify lesson vocabulary and indirect object pronouns in context.
- Recycle: **gustar** with an infinitive.
- Pronunciation: Linking words in Spanish.

Core Resources

- Video Program: DVD 2
- Audio Program: TXT CD 8 tracks 15, 16

Presentation Strategies

- Have students scan the dialogue, looking for examples of indirect object pronouns with **gustar.**
- Play the audio while students follow the script.
- Show the video.

Practice Sequence

- **Activity 9:** Telehistoria comprehension
- **Activity 10:** Transitional practice: indirect object pronouns, vacation activities, vacation locations; Recycle: **gustar** with an infinitive

STANDARDS

1.1 Engage in conversation, Act. 10
1.2 Understand language, Act. 9, Pronunciación
1.3 Present information, Act. 10, PYP
21st Century **Flexibility and Adaptability,** Role-Playing and Skits

Warm Up Projectable Transparencies, 8-21

Indirect Object Pronouns Complete the following sentences with one of the following indirect object pronouns. **le nos me te les**

1. Mis hermanos ___ dan los aretes a mamá.
2. Yo ___ doy el collar a ti.
3. Nosotros ___ damos el plato a nuestros abuelos.

Answers: 1. le; 2. te; 3. les

Video Summary

@HOMETUTOR VideoPlus my.hrw.com

In another store, Susana looks at some necklaces made of wood, but they are too expensive. The salesperson asks Susana if he can help her; she asks to see a piece of jewelry and its cost. At 50,000 colones, it is a little expensive, but Jorge says Susana likes all expensive things. The salesperson asks if Susana likes silver earrings, as Jorge notices someone has entered the store.

GRAMÁTICA en contexto

¡AVANZA! **Goal:** Listen to Susana's conversation with the salesclerk. Then use indirect object pronouns to talk about vacation activities and shopping for yourself and others. ***Actividades 9–10***

¿Recuerdas? **gustar** with an infinitive p. 42

Telehistoria escena 2

@HOMETUTOR my.hrw.com View, Read and Record

STRATEGIES

Cuando lees
Focus on shopping expressions
While reading, notice at least four expressions normally used in stores. Reread the scene, then write these expressions in new sentences.

Cuando escuchas
Listen for "turn-taking" tactics
Listen for how the salesclerk greets Susana and how Susana asks for something. How does Jorge enter the conversation?

VIDEO DVD
AUDIO

Susana and Jorge enter another shop.

Susana: ¡A mí me gustan los collares de madera! *(She looks at a price tag.)* ¡Qué caro!
Vendedor: ¡Buenos días! ¿Los puedo ayudar?
Susana: ¿Me deja ver esa joya? ¿Cuánto cuesta?
Vendedor: Cuesta cincuenta mil colones. Es un poco cara, ¿verdad?
Jorge: A ti te gustan todas las cosas caras.
Vendedor: *(to Susana)* ¿A usted le gustan los aretes de plata?
As Susana looks at the earrings, Jorge turns to see who has just entered the store.
Jorge: Susana...
Susana: *(impatiently)* Y ahora, ¿qué te pasa a ti?

Continuará... p. 447

También se dice

Costa Rica To ask Susana if she likes the earrings, the salesclerk uses **los aretes.** In other Spanish-speaking countries you might hear:
- **Argentina los aros**
- **España los pendientes, los zarcillos**
- **Puerto Rico las pantallas**

Differentiating Instruction

Multiple Intelligences

Interpersonal Have students read through Telehistoria escena 2 twice silently. The first time, instruct them to read the script for meaning. The second time, tell them to read the script for emotion. Then have volunteers take turns reading lines aloud, emphasizing the appropriate tone.

Pre-AP

Vary Vocabulary In small groups, have students work to rewrite the Telehistoria so that different words convey the same meaning. For example, instead of saying, **¿Los puedo ayudar?** the sales clerk might say, **¿Quieres ver esta joya?** Instead of asking, **¿Me deja ver esa joya?** Susana might say, **Me gustaría ver un collar de madera.**

9 | *Comprensión del episodio* Unas joyas

Escuchar Leer

Todas estas oraciones son falsas. Corrígelas, según el episodio. *(Correct these false statements.)*

1. A Susana le gustan mucho los aretes de madera.
2. Los collares son muy baratos.
3. Susana quiere ver un recuerdo.
4. El vendedor dice que la joya no es cara.
5. Jorge dice que a Susana le gustan las cosas baratas.

Expansión:
Teacher Edition Only
Ask students to write two more false statements, exchange them with a partner, and correct each other's statements.

10 | El viaje ideal

¿Recuerdas? **gustar** with an infinitive p. 42

Hablar

Habla con un(a) agente de viajes sobre las personas a quienes les gusta hacer estas actividades. Él o ella te va a ofrecer un viaje ideal. *(Tell a travel agent who likes to do these activities. He or she will offer an ideal trip.)*

modelo: hacer un viaje en barco

A: A mi hermano le gusta hacer un viaje en barco.

B: A él le puedo ofrecer un viaje al mar.

Estudiante A

1. hacer surfing
2. montar a caballo
3. ir de compras
4. dar caminatas
5. acampar
6. ¿ ?

Estudiante B

la ciudad
la playa
el campo
el mar
¿ ?

Expansión
Find out what activities both you and a partner like to do. Agree on an ideal trip to take.

Pronunciación Unir las palabras

AUDIO

Native speakers may seem to speak quickly when they link their words in breath groups. Instead of pronouncing each word separately, they run some words together. This is common in all languages.

Listen and repeat.

¿A qué hora empieza el almuerzo?

Quisiera el anillo de oro y el artículo de madera.

Ella no puede acampar porque está ocupada.

Get Help Online
my.hrw.com

PARA Y PIENSA

Did you get it? Complete each sentence with the correct indirect object pronoun, based on the Telehistoria.

1. A Susana _____ gustan los collares de madera.
2. El vendedor _____ pregunta a Jorge y a Susana si los puede ayudar.
3. Susana quiere saber qué _____ pasa a Jorge.

Differentiating Instruction

Inclusion

Clear Structure Before students begin their conversations in Activity 10, help them organize their thoughts. Have each pair of students create a three-column chart with the headings **persona, actividad,** and **viaje a...** Instruct them to add the information presented in the prompt, as well as additional ideas. Remind students to refer to their charts as they converse.

Inclusion

Alphabetic/Phonetic Awareness Read the sentences in the Pronunciación box aloud. Have students repeat. Emphasize the linking of two words together by gesturing as if you were conducting a held note in music. Throughout the remainder of the lesson, have students focus on this key to fluency. Also, discuss with students how they naturally link words together in English.

Communication
Role-Playing and Skits

Telehistoria Have students play the roles in Escena 2. Ask them to use different gift items and prices. Ask them to repeat the scene several times until they feel ready to present it to the class.

Communication
Group Work

Have students make two sets of cards. The first will consist of subjects: **yo, mi amiga, ustedes, nosotros, mi mamá, el maestro de español,** etc. The second set will include names or pictures of gift items. In small groups, students take turns turning over one card from each stack and telling what they are buying for that person: **mi mamá/un collar de plata. Le compro un collar de plata.**

✓ Ongoing Assessment

Get Help Online
More Practice
my.hrw.com

PARA Y PIENSA

Intervention If students cannot complete the Para y piensa sentences with the correct indirect object pronoun, refer them to p. 439 and ask them to repeat Activities 5 and 6 on p. 440. For additional practice, use Reteaching & Practice Copymasters URB 8 pp. 16, 18, 23.

Answers Projectable Transparencies, 8-29

Activity 9

1. A Susana le gustan los collares de madera.
2. Los collares son muy caros.
3. Susana quiere ver una joya.
4. El vendedor dice que la joya es cara.
5. Jorge dice que a Susana le gustan las cosas caras.

Activity 10 Answers will vary. Sample answers include:

1. **A.** A mi tío le gusta hacer surfing.
   B. A él le puedo ofrecer un viaje a la playa.
2. **A.** A mi tía le gusta montar a caballo.
   B. A ella le puedo ofrecer un viaje al campo.
3. **A.** A mi madre le gusta ir de compras.
   B. A ella le puedo ofrecer un viaje a la ciudad.
4. **A.** A mi hermano le gusta dar caminatas.
   B. A él le puedo ofrecer un viaje al campo.
5. **A.** A mi padre le gusta acampar.
   B. A él le puedo ofrecer un viaje al campo.
6. **A.** A... le gusta...
   B. A... le puedo ofrecer un viaje a...

Para y piensa **1.** le; **2.** les; **3.** le

¡AVANZA! **Objectives**
- Present demonstrative adjectives.

Core Resource
- *Cuaderno,* pp. 373–375

Presentation Strategies
- Ask students to tell you what a demonstrative adjective is.
- Point to items near and far around the room and identify them using demonstrative adjectives. For example, point to a book on your desk and say: **este libro.** Point to the windows and say: **esas ventanas.** Point to an object that's far away and say: **aquel reloj.** Ask students to do the same, identifying objects near and far.

STANDARDS
4.1 Compare languages

Warm Up Projectable Transparencies, 8-22

Indirect Object Pronouns Complete the sentences with the correct indirect object pronoun.

a. te **b.** nos **c.** le **d.** me **e.** les

1. A Bárbara _____ gusta hacer surf de vela.
2. A mí _____ duele la cabeza.
3. A los estudiantes no _____ gustan los exámenes.
4. ¿Qué _____ duele a ti?
5. A nosotros _____ gusta comprar recuerdos.

Answers: 1. c; 2. d; 3. e; 4. a; 5. b

Long-term Retention
Study Tips

The following is a way to remember the demonstrative adjectives: **este, esta, estos, estas;** *this* and *these* both have **t**'s.

Presentación de GRAMÁTICA

¡AVANZA! **Goal:** Learn how to point out specific things by using demonstrative adjectives. Then use these words to identify objects. ***Actividades 11–14***

¿Recuerdas? Present progressive p. 420, classroom objects p. 110

English Grammar Connection: Demonstrative adjectives indicate the location of a person or thing in relation to the speaker. They go before the noun in both English and Spanish.

This necklace is expensive. ↑ **demonstrative adjective**

Este collar es caro. ↑ **demonstrative adjective**

Demonstrative Adjectives

ANIMATED GRAMMAR my.hrw.com

In Spanish, **demonstrative adjectives** must match the nouns they modify in gender and number.

Here's how:

Masculine

Singular		Plural	
este anillo	*this ring*	**estos** anillos	*these rings*
ese anillo	*that ring*	**esos** anillos	*those rings*
aquel anillo	*that ring (over there)*	**aquellos** anillos	*those rings (over there)*

Feminine

Singular		Plural	
esta camiseta	*this T-shirt*	**estas** camisetas	*these T-shirts*
esa camiseta	*that T-shirt*	**esas** camisetas	*those T-shirts*
aquella camiseta	*that T-shirt (over there)*	**aquellas** camisetas	*those T-shirts (over there)*

No sé si debo comprar **estos** aretes de aquí o **esos** aretes de allí.
*I don't know if I should buy **these** earrings here or **those** earrings there.*

Aquellas cerámicas son muy baratas.
***Those** ceramics **(over there)** are very inexpensive.*

Más práctica
Cuaderno *pp. 373–375*
Cuaderno para hispanohablantes *pp. 374–377*

@HOMETUTOR my.hrw.com
Leveled Practice

Differentiating Instruction

Multiple Intelligences

Kinesthetic Direct students' attention to three books in the classroom—one close to you, one on another table, and one across the room. Then point to each book as you model **este libro, ese libro,** and **aquel libro**. Have students choose and arrange their own objects, and then describe them using gestures and demonstrative adjectives.

Inclusion

Alphabetic/Phonetic Awareness Discuss with students the correct pronunciation of demonstrative adjectives. Remind them that the final *e* in **este** and **ese** is pronounced similar to a long *a* in English; the *qu* in **aquel** is pronounced as /k/, not /kw/; and the *ll* in **aquellos** is similar to a /y/ in English.

Práctica de GRAMÁTICA

11 En el mercado

Leer
Escribir

Susana está en el mercado. Escoge el adjetivo demostrativo correcto para completar la conversación. Luego pon las joyas en orden según su proximidad a Susana, empezando con la más cercana. *(Choose the correct demonstrative adjective. Then write a list of the jewelry items in order from the closest to the farthest in relation to Susana.)*

Susana: Me gustan las joyas de plata. ¿Me deja ver __1.__ (aquella / aquel) collar?

Vendedora: Sí, le dejo __2.__ (aquel / aquellos) collar en treinta mil colones.

Susana: Es caro. ¿Y __3.__ (estas / estos) aretes de aquí? ¿Cuánto cuestan?

Vendedora: __4.__ (Esos / Esas) aretes de plata cuestan veinticinco mil colones. Son de buena calidad.

Susana: Me gustan __5.__ (esas / esos) joyas de allí, pero cuestan demasiado.

Vendedora: ¿Le gustaría __6.__ (ese / esa) anillo de plata? Sólo cuesta dieciocho mil colones.

Susana: ¡Está bien! Quisiera comprar __7.__ (esa / ese) anillo.

Expansión:
Teacher Edition Only
Ask students to write a dialogue based on Activity 11, using different items and prices.

12 ¿Qué están haciendo?

¿Recuerdas? Present progressive p. 420

Escuchar
Escribir

Hay muchas personas en el mercado hoy. Mira el dibujo y escucha las oraciones sobre qué están haciendo. Indica si cada oración es cierta o falsa. *(Listen to the sentences and tell whether they are true or false, according to the drawing.)*

Audio Program
TXT CD 8 Track 17
Audio Script, TE p. 431b

Expansión
Write four true sentences based on the drawing.

Differentiating Instruction

Inclusion

Metacognitive Support Ask students to explain their choice of demonstrative adjectives in Activity 11. Remind them to consider both masculine vs. feminine, and singular vs. plural.

1. Es aquel collar porque collar es masculino y singular.
3. Es estos aretes porques aretes es masculino y plural.

Slower-paced Learners

Read Before Listening In small groups, have students closely observe the picture in Activity 12 before listening to the true or false sentences. Then have students work together to predict five true sentences they might hear about what is happening in the picture. Instruct them to write these sentences on a piece of paper.

Objective

- Practice demonstrative adjectives, jewelry items, handicrafts.
- Recycle: the present progressive

Core Resource

- Audio Program: TXT CD 8 track 17

Practice Sequence

- **Activity 11:** Controlled practice: demonstrative adjectives
- **Activity 12:** Transitional practice: demonstrative adjectives; Recycle: present progressive

STANDARDS

1.2 Understand language, Act. 12
1.3 Present information, Acts. 11–12

Communication

Grammar Activity

Point out that the word **aquí** indicates that the demonstrative adjective **este(a)** should be used. The word **allí** indicates that the demonstrative adjective **ese(a)** should be used. The word **allá** (which students do not know yet) indicates that the demonstrative adjective **aquel(la)** should be used. Have students write on separate index cards the words **aquí, allí, allá.** As you say several sentences with demonstrative adjectives, ask them to hold up the appropriate card.

Answers Projectable Transparencies, 8-30

Activity 11

1. aquel; **2.** aquel; **3.** estos; **4.** Esos; **5.** esas; **6.** ese; **7.** ese
Closest: **aretes,** mid-distance: **anillo,** farthest: **collar**

Activity 12

1. Falso. Aquellas chicas están comprando collares.
2. Cierto.
3. Falso. Estos señores están comprando cerámica.
4. Cierto.
5. Falso. Este chico está comiendo helado.
6. Cierto.

Objectives
- Practice demonstrative adjectives, jewelry items, handicrafts.
- **Culture:** Discuss how climate can impact important industries of a country.
- Recycle: classroom objects

Core Resource
- *Cuaderno,* pp. 373-375

Practice Sequence
- **Activity 12:** Transitional practice: demonstrative adjectives
- **Activity 13:** Open-ended practice: demonstrative adjectives; Recycle: classroom objects

STANDARDS
1.1 Engage in conversation, Acts. 13-14
1.3 Present information, Acts. 13-14, PYP
21st Century **Information Literacy,** Heritage Language Learners; **Social and Cross-Cultural Skills,** Comparación cultural

Comparación cultural

Essential Question
Suggested Answer Costa Rica's climate and rich soil are ideal for coffee harvests. Coffee production is extremely important to Costa Rica's economy.

Background Information
The Coffee Industry Coffee was brought to Costa Rica during the late eighteenth century. Costa Rica became the first Central American country to establish coffee as an industry. Costa Rican soil and coffee were made for each other. The soils have a slight degree of acidity enriched by volcanic ashes, rich in organic matter. This characteristic invigorates the plant and is one of the factors that contribute to the quality of this coffee.

✓ Ongoing Assessment
Get Help Online
More Practice
my.hrw.com

PARA Y PIENSA **Peer Assessment** Ask students to complete the answers to Para y piensa in writing. Have students correct each other's work in pairs or small groups. For additional practice, use Reteaching & Practice Copymasters URB 8, pp. 19, 20, 22, 24.

See Activity answers on p. 447.

13 Hablando del café
Hablar

Comparación cultural

Coffee plantation, *Costa Rica*

El café
How does Costa Rica's climate impact its leading exports? Coffee is one of **Costa Rica's** leading exports. It grows well due to the country's high altitudes, rich soils, and warm temperatures. The coffee harvest takes place between November and January. Workers carefully handpick and sort the berries of the coffee plants, placing only the ripe, red ones in their baskets. The berries are then brought to mills so that the beans can be removed and processed.

Compara con tu mundo *What is an important industry in your area?*

Elena: __1.__ café de Costa Rica me gusta más que __2.__ café que toma Daniel, que es de Indonesia.

Rodrigo: Mi favorito fue __3.__ café que nos sirvió Alejandra la semana pasada.

Alicia: Estoy de acuerdo con Elena. En casa estamos tomando __4.__ cafés que nos compraron mis padres en San José el año pasado, y creo que los de Costa Rica son más sabrosos.

14 ¡A jugar! Veo, veo
♻ ***¿Recuerdas?*** Classroom objects p. 110

Hablar

Habla con otro(a) estudiante. Describe objetos que ves en la clase. Él o ella va a adivinar qué son, usando adjetivos demonstrativos. *(Describe classroom objects for a partner to guess.)*

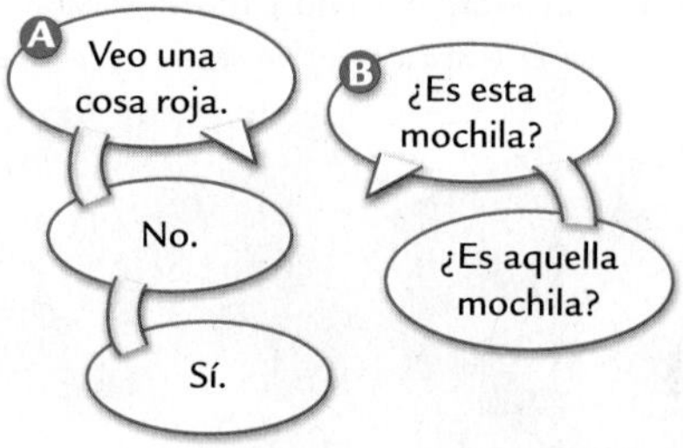

Expansión
Point out six classroom objects to a partner. He or she will describe them.

Más práctica Cuaderno *pp. 373–375* Cuaderno para hispanohablantes *pp. 374–377*

Get Help Online
my.hrw.com

PARA Y PIENSA

Did you get it? Complete each sentence with the correct demonstrative adjective: **esas, aquellos,** or **este.**
1. _____ aretes son más bonitos que esos aretes.
2. _____ anillo es de oro.
3. La calidad de _____ artesanías es muy buena.

Differentiating Instruction

Heritage Language Learners
Literacy Skills Assign students the task of researching one of Costa Rica's prominent industries, such as coffee, textiles, or tourism. Encourage them to use the library or Internet to find five interesting facts and figures about that industry. How many people are involved? How much money does it generate each year? Ask them to report their findings back to the class.

Multiple Intelligences
Visual Learners Have students create a drawing or painting of a scene showing people at work in Costa Rica. Encourage students to use the Internet, library, or other information they have learned in Unit 8 as the basis for their images.

Todo junto

¡AVANZA! **Goal:** ***Show what you know*** Identify the demonstrative adjectives used to indicate items in a store. Then practice using demonstrative adjectives and indirect object pronouns to bargain and describe vacations. ***Actividades 15–19***

Telehistoria completa

@HOMETUTOR my.hrw.com View, Read and Record

STRATEGIES

Cuando lees
Find the dramatic turn Read the scene slowly, trying to discover the dramatic "turn" or change. Why do the teens stop paying attention to the salesclerk? What happens after that?

Cuando escuchas
Listen to problems and imagine solutions Listen to and observe the problems. What are they? How does Jorge respond? What are the possible solutions, if any?

Escena 1 *Resumen*
Jorge y Susana llegan al centro comercial. Susana quiere comprar un anillo, pero es muy caro.

Escena 2 *Resumen*
Susana está hablando con el vendedor en la tienda cuando Jorge ve a alguien.

Escena 3

VIDEO DVD

AUDIO

Vendedor: ¿Y a usted no le gustan aquellos aretes de oro? ¿Ese collar de plata? ¿Estos anillos?

The salesclerk sees that Jorge and Susana have stopped paying attention and leaves.

Jorge: *(excited)* Susana, ¡allí está Trini Salgado, la jugadora de fútbol! Es ella, ¿no? ¿Qué está haciendo?

Susana: Sí, sí, es ella. Está comprando unos aretes.

Jorge: ¡Vamos! Necesito su autógrafo para Alicia. *(He opens his backpack but can't find the T-shirt.)* ¿Dónde está la camiseta de Alicia?

Susana: No sé...

While he looks through his backpack, Trini leaves the store.

Differentiating Instruction

Inclusion

Multisensory Input/Output Have students read the final scene of the Telehistoria aloud as a group. As they encounter demonstrative adjectives or other words that indicate the location of something, instruct students to point to an appropriate place in the room. For example, when they read **aquellos aretes**, they should point to something far away.

Slower-paced Learners

Personalization Ask students if they have ever seen a famous person in public. Help students describe their experience by providing the following structure. Allow students to narrate using the present.

Estoy en... cuando veo a...
Él/Ella está... Estoy muy...

¡AVANZA! **Objective**
- Integrate lesson content.

Core Resources
- Video Program: DVD 2
- Audio Program: TXT CD 8 track 18

Presentation Strategies
- Ask students what they remember about the Telehistoria so far.
- Ask students to scan the script and list all jewelry items they find.
- Show the video or play the audio as students follow the script.

STANDARDS
1.2 Understand language
21st Century **Communication,** Slower-paced Learners

Warm Up
Projectable Transparencies, 8-22

Demonstrative Adjectives Complete the sentences with the correct demonstrative adjective.

a. esas **b.** esta **c.** este **d.** esos

1. ¿Prefieres estos anillos de aquí o _____ de allí?
2. Me gusta _____ collar.
3. _____ cerámica es barata.
4. _____ artesanías son caras.

Answers: 1. d; 2. c; 3. b; 4. a

Video Summary
@HOMETUTOR VideoPlus my.hrw.com

The salesperson asks whether Susana likes various items of jewelery, but she and Jorge have noticed that the soccer player Trini Salgado is buying earrings. Jorge hopes to get Trini's autograph for Alicia, but he cannot find her T-shirt in his backpack and does not know where it is.

Answers
Projectable Transparencies, 8-30

Answers for Activities on p. 446.

Activity 13
1. Este
2. ese
3. aquel
4. aquellos (esos)

Activity 14 Answers will vary. Sample answers:
A. Veo una cosa azul.
B. ¿Es este libro?

Para y piensa **1.** Aquellos; **2.** Este; **3.** esas

Objectives
- Practice using and integrating lesson vocabulary and grammar.

Core Resources
- *Cuaderno,* pp. 376–377
- Audio Program: TXT CD 8 tracks 14, 15, 18, 19, 20

Practice Sequence
- **Activities 15, 16:** Telehistoria comprehension
- **Activity 17:** Open-ended practice: speaking
- **Activity 18:** Open-ended practice: reading, listening, speaking
- **Activity 19:** Open-ended practice: writing

STANDARDS
1.1 Engage in conversation, Act. 17
1.2 Understand language, Acts. 15–16, 18
1.3 Present information, Acts. 15–19, PYP
21st Century **Communication,** Acts. 17, 18, 19; **Creativity and Innovation,** Act. 19/ Inclusion

Communication
Motivating with Music
The **¡AvanzaRap!** song for this unit targets vocabulary from Lección 2. To reinforce this vocabulary, play the **¡AvanzaRap!** animated video to students. For extra practice, have them complete the Activity Master for Unidad 8.

Answers Projectable Transparencies, 8-30
Activity 15
d, a, c, f, e, b

Activity 16
Answers will vary. Sample answers include:
1. Susana le dice a su papá: ¿Por qué no compras un carro nuevo? ¿Un carro azul?
2. Susana dice que el anillo de oro es muy caro pero la vendedora no quiere regatear.
3. Susana quiere comprar un collar de madera, pero es muy caro también.
4. Jorge busca la camiseta de Alicia en su mochila pero no la encuentra.

Activity 17
Answers will vary. Sample answers:
A: Buenos días. ¿Me deja ver esos aretes de oro?
B: Sí, son muy buenos. Le dejo estos aretes en...

15 *Comprensión de los episodios* ¿En qué orden?
Escuchar
Leer

Pon estas oraciones en orden para describir los episodios. *(Put the sentences in order.)*

a. Susana empieza a regatear, pero ella no está en el mercado.
b. Jorge no puede encontrar la camiseta.
c. Jorge le dice a Susana que a ella le gustan las cosas caras.
d. A Susana no le gusta llegar en el coche de su papá.
e. Jorge le dice a Susana que ve a Trini Salgado.
f. Susana le pregunta a Jorge qué le pasa a él.

Expansión:
Teacher Edition Only
Ask students to write a short summary of what happened in Escena 3.

16 *Comprensión de los episodios* ¿Qué pasó?
Escuchar
Leer

Mira las fotos y describe lo que pasó en los episodios. *(Describe what happened in the episodes.)*

1.

2.

3.

4.

Expansión:
Teacher Edition Only
Ask students to write a short dialogue for each picture in Activity 16.

17 ¡A regatear!
Digital performance space

Hablar

STRATEGY Hablar
Be realistic Make your drawings of items as clear as possible. Add details and colors, so that the bargaining can be realistic. If you have time to prepare in advance, bring actual items from home to use while you bargain.

Regatea con otro(a) estudiante. Dibuja los artículos que quieres vender y trata de recibir el mejor precio posible. *(Bargain with your classmates.)*

A Buenas tardes. ¿Me deja ver aquel tocadiscos compactos?

B Sí. Es de buena calidad. Le dejo este tocadiscos compactos en treinta dólares...

Expansión
Tell the class what you bought, including the original price and final purchase price. The class will decide if it was a fair deal.

Differentiating Instruction

Pre-AP
Sequence Information Organize students in small groups. Have groups work together to copy each sentence from Activity 15 on separate sentence strips. Instruct them to arrange the strips in the correct order based on the events in the Telehistoria. Have each group create two or three more sentences. They should then scramble all of the sentences, and pass them to another group to sequence.

Pre-AP
Expand and Elaborate Before students begin their bargaining in Activity 17, give them this pre-speaking exercise. As a group, brainstorm names of objects that might be sold at the market, things a vendor might say, and things a buyer might say. Write students' answers on the board. Encourage them to refer to the list during their conversations.

18 Integración

Digital performance space

Leer
Escuchar
Hablar

Lee la guía y escucha el anuncio. Luego di qué te gustaría hacer allí y qué les vas a comprar a tu familia y amigos. *(Read the guide and listen to the ad. Then tell what you would like to do there and what you are going to buy for your family and friends.)*

Fuente 1 Guía turística

TamarindoPlayaTamarindoPlaya

De compras en
Playa Tamarindo

Mercado Costeño En este mercado al aire libre, encuentras ropa, artículos de madera, joyas de madera y café orgánico. Puedes regatear.

Artesanías Iguana Verde Esta tienda tiene artesanías de buena calidad, pero son un poco caras. Venden cerámica, platos de madera y joyas de oro.

Librería Sol Tico Aquí venden libros, discos compactos y mapas decorativos.

Tienda Colibrí En esta tienda hay anillos y aretes de plata, y collares de madera. También venden camisetas y sombreros. Precios baratos.

Fuente 2 Anuncio de radio

Listen and take notes
- ¿Qué actividades hay en la playa?
- ¿Qué puedes hacer si no te gusta el mar?

modelo: En Playa Tamarindo me gustaría...
A... le voy a comprar...

Audio Program
TXT CD 8 Tracks 19, 20. Audio Script, TE p.431b

19 ¡Ya llegan las vacaciones!

Digital performance space

Escribir

Escribe un artículo comparando dos viajes para un sitio Web. Describe a quién le gustaría cada viaje, qué hace la gente durante su tiempo libre, y qué puede comprar y para quién. *(Write an article for a Web site comparing two trips.)*

modelo: Tenemos dos viajes fenomenales. Si a usted le gusta el mar, le podemos ofrecer un viaje a Playa del Coco. Usted puede...

Writing Criteria	Excellent	Good	Needs Work
Content	Your article includes a lot of information.	Your article includes some information.	Your article includes little information.
Communication	Most of your article is organized and easy to follow.	Parts of your article are organized and easy to follow.	Your article is disorganized and hard to follow.
Accuracy	Your article has few mistakes in grammar and vocabulary.	Your article has some mistakes in grammar and vocabulary.	Your article has many mistakes in grammar and vocabulary.

Expansión
Tell which trip you prefer and why.

Más práctica Cuaderno *pp. 376–377* Cuaderno para hispanohablantes *pp. 378–379*

Get Help Online
my.hrw.com

PARA Y PIENSA

Did you get it? Complete each sentence with the correct indirect object pronoun and demonstrative adjective, based on the Telehistoria.

1. Jorge ____ pregunta a Susana si ____ mujer allí es Trini Salgado.
2. El hombre ____ quiere vender a Jorge y a Susana ____ anillos de aquí.

Long-term Retention

Pre-AP Integration

Activity 18 Have students discuss various activities they could do on a vacation in Costa Rica. Encourage students to persuade classmates to do one activity over another.

✓ Ongoing Assessment

Get Help Online
More Practice
my.hrw.com

Rubric Activity 18
Listening/Speaking

Proficient	Not There Yet
Student takes notes and answers all questions. They explain what they would like to do and the items they are going to buy.	Student takes few notes and has difficulty answering the questions. They do not explain what they would like to do or the items they are going to buy.

To customize your own rubrics, use the ***Generate Success*** *Rubric Generator and Graphic Organizers.*

✓ Ongoing Assessment

Get Help Online
More Practice
my.hrw.com

PARA Y PIENSA

Intervention If students miss more than one or two of the Para y piensa answers, suggest that they review pp. 439 and 444. For additional practice, use Reteaching & Practice Copymasters URB 8, pp. 19, 21.

Answers Projectable Transparencies, 8-30

Activity 18 Answers will vary. Sample answers include: En Playa Tamarindo me gustaría ir a la playa, nadar, tomar el sol y descansar todo el día. También quisiera ir de compras al mercado, donde los precios son baratos y puedo regatear. A mi hermana le voy a comprar unas joyas de madera.

Activity 19 Answers will vary. Sample answers include:

Ofrecemos muchos viajes interesantes. Si a usted le gusta ir de compras, le ofrecemos un viaje a Sarchí. Allí puede comprar artesanías de madera y cerámica.

Para y piensa
1. le, esa; **2.** les, estos

Differentiating Instruction

Slower-paced Learners

Read Before Listening Before listening to the radio ad in Activity 18, encourage students to read the tourist guide, as well as the questions under the heading *Listen and take notes.* Also, advise students to look at the model for their responses. Remind students that all of this information will help them decide what kind of information they should be listening for.

Inclusion

Clear Structure Advise students to use a graphic organizer, such as a Venn diagram, to help organize their thoughts in Activity 19. Have them write down the name of each trip at the top of a circle. Then have them record similarities between the two trips in the center of the diagram, and differences on either side. They can then develop these ideas into complete sentences.

Objectives

- **Culture:** Read about markets in Costa Rica and Uruguay.
- Learn what these markets sell and why people go there.
- Compare markets and bargaining in Costa Rica, Uruguay, and the U.S.

Core Resource

- Audio Program: TXT CD 8 track 21

Presentation Strategies

- Ask students if there are markets in their region like the markets shown here. Ask volunteers to describe local markets and the items they sell.
- Have students read the text, and make a list of cognates they encounter. Then have student volunteers read the selection aloud or listen to the audio.
- Stop after each paragraph and ask students to summarize the main idea.

STANDARDS

1.1 Engage in conversation
1.2 Understand language
2.1 Practices and perspectives
4.2 Compare cultures
21st Century **Flexibility and Adaptability,** Pair Work/Multiple Intelligences

Warm Up Projectable Transparencies, 8-23

Demonstrative Adjectives Complete the sentences with the correct demonstrative adjective.

1. ¿Me deja ver (aquella / aquel) camiseta?
2. ¿Te gustan (ese / esos) anillos de plata?
3. ¿Cuánto cuesta (este / esa) collar?
4. Quisiera comprar (aquellos / aquella) aretes.
5. Quiero ver (esas / esos) artículos de cerámica.

Answers: 1. aquella; 2. esos; 3. este; 4. aquellos; 5. esos

Long-term Retention
Study Tips

Have pairs of students work together to compile a list of key words used in the reading. Then have them make flashcards of the words and quiz each other. In addition, they could work together to write original sentences using these words.

Lectura cultural

Additional readings at my.hrw.com SPANISH InterActive Reader

¡AVANZA! **Goal:** Read about markets in Costa Rica and Uruguay. Then compare markets and bargaining in Costa Rica, Uruguay, and the United States.

Comparación cultural

Mercados en Costa Rica y Uruguay

AUDIO

STRATEGY **Leer**
Diagram comparisons
Use a Venn diagram to compare markets and bargaining in Costa Rica, Uruguay, and the U.S.

En Latinoamérica, muchas ciudades tienen mercados al aire libre, donde puedes ir de compras y encontrar artículos interesantes y de buena calidad. Es muy común regatear en los puestos[1] de estos mercados. Si quieres regatear, hay algunas recomendaciones. Cuando escuchas el primer precio, puedes contestar: «¡Es demasiado!» También es importante ir a varios puestos para encontrar el precio más barato.

[1] stalls

Costa Rica

Representación de un mercado, San José, Costa Rica

Differentiating Instruction

Pre-AP

Summarize Provide pairs of students with three index cards. Instruct partners to read the **Lectura cultural** together. After the first paragraph, tell them to discuss and identify the main idea of that paragraph. Have them write the main idea in a one-sentence summary on one card. Then have them repeat with the remaining two paragraphs.

Inclusion

Clear Structure Present students with a Venn diagram to compare and contrast **El Mercado Central de San José** and **El Mercado del Puerto**. Then have them reread the second and third paragraphs of the **Lectura cultural.** Direct them to look for things that the two markets have in common, as well as things that are different.

LECTURA CULTURAL

Mercado de fruta, Montevideo, Uruguay

Uruguay

El Mercado Central de San José, Costa Rica, se fundó en el año 1880. En los puestos, venden una variedad de cosas, como café, frutas, verduras, pescado, carne, flores[2] y plantas medicinales. También puedes comprar recuerdos. Hay camisetas, joyas y artículos de madera y de cuero[3]. Si tienes hambre, hay restaurantes pequeños que se llaman sodas.

El Mercado del Puerto está cerca del mar en Montevideo, la capital de Uruguay. Se inauguró[4] en 1868. Allí hay artistas locales que venden sus artículos y puedes comprar artesanías en las tiendas. También puedes comer en los restaurantes, donde sirven carne y pescado. La parrillada, un plato con diferentes tipos de carne, es muy popular. Los sábados, muchas personas van a este mercado para almorzar y escuchar música.

[2] flowers [3] leather [4] opened

PARA Y PIENSA

¿Comprendiste?

1. ¿Qué puedes comprar en el Mercado Central? ¿En el Mercado del Puerto?
2. ¿Cuál de los mercados es más viejo?
3. ¿Qué recuerdos hay en el Mercado Central?
4. ¿En qué mercado es popular la parrillada?

¿Y tú?

¿Hay un mercado donde tú vives? Si hay, ¿cómo es? ¿Puedes regatear allí? ¿Dónde puedes regatear en Estados Unidos?

Communication

Pair Work

Assign student pairs the roles of an American exchange student in Costa Rica and a vendor in a local market. The exchange student wants to prepare a simple meal for his or her host family. The merchant sells everything needed to make this meal. Ask students to use the foods mentioned in the reading as well as food items they have learned in other units and make a list of what they will need. Then have them ask the vendor for the different items and negotiate a fair price. After they have worked out their transactions orally have them write down their dialogue.

Culture

Background Information

The open air market in Latin America can trace its roots to pre-Columbian times. Today, markets continue to play an important role economically and socially throughout the region. Socially they are also important places to see friends and acquaintances and hear local news. Bargaining is expected in many situations. The buyer wants the lowest price and the seller the highest. A rule of thumb is to offer about half of the first price named by the vendor. If the vendor wants 20 pesos offer 10. Next, the vendor may say 18 pesos and you offer 12. The dialogue can continue until you agree on a fair amount.

Differentiating Instruction

Slower-paced Learners

Sentence Completion Before reading about **Mercados en Costa Rica y Uruguay**, have students preview the questions under **¿Comprendiste?** Then have them convert each question into a sentence starter for its answer. Remind students to look for the information to complete these sentences as they read the selection.

Multiple Intelligences

Interpersonal In pairs, have students create a short role-play in which one student is a market vendor, and the other is an interested buyer. Remind students to follow the bargaining advice presented in the reading. Encourage them to use phrases, such as **¡Es demasiado!** Or, **Soy estudiante. No tengo mucho dinero.**

Answers

Para y piensa

¿Comprendiste?

1. En el Mercado Central, puedo comprar una variedad de comidas, flores y plantas medicinales. En el Mercado del Puerto, puedo comprar artículos de arte y artesanías.
2. El Mercado del Puerto es más viejo.
3. En el Mercado Central, tienen recuerdos, como camisetas, joyas y artículos de madera y de cuero.
4. La parrillada es popular en el Mercado del Puerto.

¿Y tú?

Answers will vary.

Objectives

- Read about traditional desserts from Costa Rica and Uruguay.
- **Culture:** Discuss how foods from Spanish-speaking countries are enjoyed in the United States.
- **Community:** Find out about the importance of knowing other languages in the art of cooking.

Presentation Strategies

- Ask students to describe desserts from Spanish-speaking countries they have tasted.
- Have they eaten **arroz con leche, dulce de leche,** or **flan?**
- Assign students to look up the ingredients of both recipes in an English-Spanish dictionary and come up with a list of ingredients in Spanish.

STANDARDS

3.1 Knowledge of other disciplines
5.1 Spanish in the community
21st Century **Communication,** Spanish in the Kitchen/Pre-AP; **Social and Cross-Cultural Skills,** Comparación cultural/Heritage Language Learners

Comparación cultural

Essential Question

Suggested Answer In order to enjoy foods from Spanish-speaking countries in the United States, students can check the yellow pages or Internet for restaurants in their area. In addition, many local supermarkets have aisles dedicated to foods from Spanish-speaking countries. There are many food fairs that are generally sponsored by cultural agencies from Spain and Latin America. Finally, many cities and towns in the United States have open air markets which sell foods from Spain and Latin America.

Communities

Spanish in the Kitchen

Ask students to interview a bilingual professional cook or a Spanish-speaking person they know who likes to cook. Ask the interviewee what kinds of foods they like to cook. Ask them how knowing both Spanish and English helps them in their cooking. How does knowing two cultures and geographic areas improve their meals?

Proyectos culturales

Comparación cultural

Postres en Costa Rica y Uruguay

How can foods from other Spanish-speaking countries be enjoyed here in the U.S.? Desserts in Spanish-speaking countries may appear to be different from the desserts that you are used to, but if you read the ingredients you'll see that these recipes from **Costa Rica** and **Uruguay** contain foods you could find in your own kitchen or the supermarket. **Plátanos horneados** and **dulce de leche** are prepared in slightly different ways throughout Latin America.

Proyecto 1 *Plátanos horneados*

Costa Rica **Plátanos,** or plantains, grow in abundance in Latin America and are a dietary staple. This fruit resembles a banana, but it is typically not eaten raw. You know a plantain is ripe when its outer skin has turned from green to black. Ripe plantains are called **maduros.**

Ingredients for plátanos horneados
6 ripe plantains
1 stick of butter
1/2 cup honey
1/4 teaspoon ground cloves

Instructions
Preheat a toaster oven to 300 degrees. Remove the peels of the plantains and cut them in half lengthwise. Place them in a rectangular glass pan and pour the honey over them. Cut the butter into six pieces and place them on top of every other plantain, then sprinkle with the cloves. Cover the pan with aluminum foil and bake for 30 minutes or until the plantains are golden brown.
Optional: Once you remove the plantains from the oven, sprinkle them with cinnamon.

Proyecto 2 *Dulce de leche*

Uruguay **Dulce de leche** has a sweet, caramel flavor and a texture that resembles fudge. It is often used as a filling for pastries and desserts, but can also be eaten by itself.

Ingredients for dulce de leche
4 cups whole milk
2 cups sugar
1 teaspoon baking soda
1/2 teaspoon vanilla extract

Instructions
Place all the ingredients in a heavy-bottomed saucepan. Bring the liquid to a boil and then reduce to medium heat, stirring frequently until the mixture thickens and turns caramel in color. Cool to room temperature.
Optional: Serve with cookies, bread, or fruit.

En tu comunidad

The work of a professional chef often brings him or her in contact with foods and people from other countries. How would knowing about other languages and cultures help you to be a better chef?

Differentiating Instruction

Heritage Language Learners

Support What They Know Ask students familiar with **plátanos horneados** or **dulce de leche** to talk about these desserts. Who in their family prepares them? How would they describe the taste? Is it similar to other tastes that students might be familiar with? Also, ask students to talk about some other traditional desserts or sweets from their country or region of origin.

Pre-AP

Communicate Preferences Ask students to talk about their favorite desserts. First, have them name and describe a dish in as much detail as possible. Then have them express why it is their favorite. If possible, have volunteers prepare and bring in **plátanos horneados** and **dulce de leche** to share with the group. Students can then express their opinions about these dishes as well.

Lección 2

En resumen

Vocabulario y gramática

ANIMATEDGRAMMAR
Interactive Flashcards
my.hrw.com

Vocabulario

Talk About Vacation Activities

acampar	*to camp*	hacer surf de vela	*to windsurf*
comer al aire libre	*to picnic, to eat outside*	hacer surfing	*to surf*
dar una caminata	*to hike*	montar a caballo	*to ride a horse*
hacer una parrillada	*to barbecue*	el tiempo libre	*free time*

Indicate Position

aquel(aquella)	*that (over there)*
aquellos(as)	*those (over there)*
ese(a)	*that*
esos(as)	*those*
este(a)	*this*
estos(as)	*these*
¿Qué es esto?	*What is this?*

Talk About Buying Souvenirs

barato(a)	*inexpensive*
la calidad	*quality*
caro(a)	*expensive*
demasiado	*too much*
el mercado	*market*
el recuerdo	*souvenir*

Jewelry and Handicrafts

el anillo	*ring*
el arete	*earring*
las artesanías	*handicrafts*
los artículos	*goods*
de madera	*wood*
de oro	*gold*
de plata	*silver*
la cerámica	*ceramics*
el collar	*necklace*
las joyas	*jewelry*

Bargaining

Le dejo... en...	*I'll give . . . to you for . . .*
Le puedo ofrecer...	*I can offer you . . .*
¿Me deja ver...?	*May I see . . . ?*
¡Qué caro(a)!	*How expensive!*
Quisiera...	*I would like . . .*
regatear	*to bargain*

Gramática

Indirect Object Pronouns

Indirect object pronouns use the same words as direct object pronouns except for **le** and **les**.

Singular		Plural	
me	*me*	nos	*us*
te	*you (familiar)*	os	*you (familiar)*
le	*you (formal), him, her*	les	*you, them*

Demonstrative Adjectives

In Spanish, **demonstrative adjectives** must match the nouns they modify in gender and number.

Masculine

Singular	Plural
este anillo	estos anillos
ese anillo	esos anillos
aquel anillo	aquellos anillos

Feminine

Singular	Plural
esta camiseta	estas camisetas
esa camiseta	esas camisetas
aquella camiseta	aquellas camisetas

Practice Spanish with Holt McDougal Apps!

Differentiating Instruction

Multiple Intelligences

Interpersonal Working in pairs, have students draft a role-play involving a client buying jewelry or handicrafts and a vendor. Students may choose what they want to buy and for how much. Remind students to use bargaining expressions to negotiate their purchase.

Inclusion

Multisensory Input/Output Help students review demonstrative adjectives by asking them to place different objects around the room and generate questions to ask their partners. For example, Student A might point to a notebook close to him or her and ask: **¿Necesitas este cuaderno?** Student B might respond: **Sí, necesito ese cuaderno.**

Objective

· Review lesson vocabulary and grammar.

DIGITAL SPANISH

Interactive Flashcards Students can hear every target vocabulary word pronounced in authentic Spanish. Flashcards have Spanish on one side, and a picture or a translation on the other.
Review Games Matching, concentration, hangman, and word search are just a sampling of the fun, interactive games students can play to review for the test.

performance space
News Networking
@HOMETUTOR
CULTURA Interactiva

- Audio and Video Resources
- Interactive Flashcards
- Review Activities
- WebQuest
- Conjuguemos.com

Long-term Retention
Personalize It

Ask students to create a personal illustrated Spanish glossary of words listed in En Resumen. Good illustration choices would be vacation activities and souvenirs. Have them write the word in Spanish and draw the corresponding picture next to it.

Long-term Retention
Recycle

Ask student groups to brainstorm words from other units that they could add to the categories listed in En resumen. For example, under vacation activities they could write: **nadar, hacer el esquí acuático, montar en bicicleta.** Under expressions for buying souvenirs: **¿Te gustaría...? Me encantaría...** Have them share their lists with other groups and add other examples for further reference.

Objective
- Review lesson grammar and vocabulary.

Core Resources
- *Cuaderno*, pp. 378-389
- Audio Program, TXT CD 8 track 22

Presentation Strategies
- As students listen to Activity 1, instruct them to pay special attention to the gift items mentioned in the script.
- Before doing Activity 2, review indirect object pronouns by starting a phrase with **a mí... a ti... a él/ella/usted...; a nosotros/as..., a ellos/ellas/ustedes...** and asking students to complete it using the corresponding indirect object pronoun. **A ella le doy un regalo.**
- Before doing Activity 3, remind students that items close to the speaker require a form of **este,** items farther a form of **ese,** and items farthest a form of **aquel.**
- Go over the Comparación cultural with students and clarify any questions.
- Review may be done in class or at home.
- Students can also access the review online.

STANDARDS
1.2 Understand language, Act. 1
1.3 Present information, Acts. 2-4
4.2 Compare cultures, Act. 5
21st Century **Communication,** Pre-AP; **Flexibility and Adaptability,** Multiple Intelligences

Warm Up
Projectable Transparencies, 8-23

Vocabulary Find the word that corresponds to each definition.

hacer surfing mercado aretes caro

1. Una joya que se pone en las orejas.
2. Un lugar al aire libre donde puedes comprar comida, ropa y artesanías.
3. No es barato.
4. Un deporte que puedes practicar en el mar.

Answers: 1. aretes; 2. mercado; 3. caro; 4. hacer surfing

✓ Ongoing Assessment
Get Help Online
More Practice
my.hrw.com

Intervention/Remediation If students achieve less than 80% accuracy on each activity, direct them to review pp. 432, 439-440, 444, 446, 450-451 and to get help online at my.hrw.com.

Lección 2

Repaso de la lección

@HOMETUTOR
my.hrw.com

¡LLEGADA!

¡AvanzaRap! DVD
Sing and Learn

Now you can
- talk about buying souvenirs on vacation
- talk about vacation activities

Using
- indirect object pronouns
- demonstrative adjectives

To review
- indirect object pronouns p. 439
- demonstrative adjectives p. 444

1 Listen and understand

AUDIO

Escucha la conversación entre César y una vendedora. Luego escoge la respuesta correcta. *(Listen and choose the correct word to complete each sentence.)*

1. César busca (un recuerdo / un artículo de madera) para su amiga.
2. La amiga prefiere (las artesanías / las joyas).
3. César piensa que el anillo de (oro / plata) es bonito.
4. El anillo es muy (caro / barato).
5. La amiga de César prefiere las joyas de (oro / plata).
6. La vendedora le deja (los aretes / los anillos) en quince mil.

Audio Program
TXT CD 8 Track 22
Audio Script, TE p. 431b

To review
- indirect object pronouns p. 439

2 Talk about buying souvenirs on vacation

Soledad y su amiga Ana están regateando en un mercado. Completa la conversación con el pronombre de objeto indirecto apropiado.
(Complete the conversation with the appropriate indirect object pronoun.)

Soledad: Buenos días, señor. ¿ __1.__ deja ver los collares de oro?
Vendedor: ¡Claro que sí! A usted __2.__ dejo el collar más bonito en quince mil colones.
Soledad: ¡Qué caro! Mi amiga también quiere comprar un collar. ¿ __3.__ deja ver a nosotras los collares de plata?
Vendedor: Sí, señoritas. A ustedes __4.__ dejo dos collares en veinticinco mil colones.
Soledad: Todavía son caros.
Vendedor: Está bien. A usted __5.__ dejo los dos collares en veinticuatro mil.
Ana: ¡Gracias, Soledad! ¿Quieres ir al café? __6.__ invito.

Differentiating Instruction

Slower-paced Learners
Read Before Listening Before students listen to the conversation in Activity 1, change the statements to questions and write them on the board. Then write the choices given in parentheses. Ask students to come to the board and underline a key word in each question, and discuss the possible answers. **¿Qué busca César para su amiga? un recuerdo/un artículo de madera**

Multiple Intelligences
Interpersonal After students complete Activity 2, invite two volunteers to play the parts of Soledad and Vendedor. Encourage them to emphasize the facial expressions appropriate to each character's emotions. When the Vendedor says, **¡Claro que sí!** what might his expression be? When Soledad says, **¡Qué caro!** what emotions might she be feeling?

To review
- demonstrative adjectives p. 444

3 Talk about vacation activities

Estás de vacaciones y ves a muchas personas en la playa. Indica quiénes están haciendo las siguientes actividades. Usa adjetivos demostrativos. *(Use demonstrative adjectives to indicate who is doing the following activities.)*

modelo: acampar
Estos chicos están acampando.

1. hacer surfing
2. montar a caballo
3. comer al aire libre
4. vender refrescos
5. caminar en la playa
6. hacer surf de vela
7. hacer una parrillada
8. comprar un refresco

To review
- Comparación cultural pp. 432, 440, 446
- Lectura cultural pp. 450–451

4 Costa Rica and Uruguay

Comparación cultural

Answer these culture questions.

1. Why is Costa Rica a good destination for ecotourism?
2. What are some transportation options in Costa Rica? Describe them.
3. How is coffee harvested in Costa Rica? Why does it grow well there?
4. Where are **el Mercado Central** and **el Mercado del Puerto** located? What foods can you buy at these markets?

Más práctica Cuaderno *pp. 378–389* Cuaderno para hispanohablantes *pp. 380–389*

Get Help Online my.hrw.com

✓ Ongoing Assessment

Peer Assessment Have student pairs exchange the completed conversation in Activity 2 and check each other's work.

✓ Ongoing Assessment

Alternative Strategy To review the demonstrative adjectives in Activity 3 have students write 4 questions using forms of **este, ese and aquel** to ask their classmates. For example, **¿Quieres esta camisa azul? No, prefiero esa camisa verde.** Check for correct questions and answers.

Answers Projectable Transparencies, 8-30 and 8-31

Activity 1
1. un recuerdo; **2.** las joyas; **3.** oro; **4.** caro; **5.** oro; **6.** los aretes

Activity 2 **1.** Me; **2.** le; **3.** Nos ; **4.** les; **5.** le; **6.** Te

Activity 3
1. Aquel chico está haciendo surfing.
2. Esos chicos están montando a caballo.
3. Estas chicas están comiendo al aire libre.
4. Ese chico está vendiendo refrescos.
5. Aquellas chicas están caminando...
6. Aquellos chicos están haciendo surf de vela.
7. Este chico está haciendo una parillada.
8. Esa chica está comprando un refresco.

Activity 4
1. Costa Rica is a good destination for ecotourism because with its abundance of plant and animal life, many of its vacation activities center around nature.
2. Taxis are readily available and cheap. Normal taxis are red, and airport taxis are orange. In town, there is plenty of bus service. To get to farther destinations, travelers go by plane.
3. Coffee is harvested between November and January. The harvesters gather the beans in baskets, and are careful to choose the ripest, reddest ones. The berries are brought to mills for processing. Coffee grows well in Costa Rica because of the moderate climate and the quality of the soil.
4. The Mercado Central is located in San José, Costa Rica. In this market, you can buy coffee, fruit, vegetables, fish, and meat. The Mercado del Puerto is near the sea in Montevideo, Uruguay. This market serves foods such as meat and fish in its restaurants. Especially popular is the parrillada, which is an assortment of cooked meats.

Differentiating Instruction

Pre-AP

Relate Opinions Draw a picture of a jewelry item or souvenir on the board, such as a gold ring. Then review with students the different strategies they now have for expressing their opinions about the item. They might begin their sentences with **Prefiero..., Quiero..., Me gusta...,** or **Pienso que...** Encourage them to use demonstrative pronouns. **Pienso que estos aretes de plata son muy bonitos.**

Inclusion

Clear Structure Before students complete Activity 3, have them draw a chart with the headings **este, ese, aquel.** Then ask them to write the activities under the appropriate heading. For example, **hacer surfing** would be under **aquel; montar a caballo** under **ese;** and **hacer una parillada** under **este**. Then have students write the present participle of each infinitive. For example: **vender: vendiendo.**

Objectives

- Read about travel destinations in Uruguay, Ecuador and Costa Rica.
- Compare favorite vacation spots of teens in Uruguay, Ecuador, Costa Rica, and the U.S.
- Write about a real or imaginary vacation.

Core Resources

- *Cuaderno*, pp. 390–392
- Audio Program: TXT CD 8 track 23
- Video Program: DVD 2

Presentation Strategies

- Draw students' attention to the photos on p. 457 and ask them to predict what the text will be about.
- Have students take turns reading each description as their classmates follow it in the text. Correct pronunciation as needed.
- Play the audio. After each account, encourage students to say if they also would like to visit these places.

STANDARDS

1.2 Understand language
1.3 Present information
2.1 Practices and perspectives
4.2 Compare cultures
21st Century **Critical Thinking and Problem Solving,** Compara con tu mundo; **Initiative and Self-Direction,** Pre-AP; **Social and Cross-Cultural Skills,** Heritage Language Learners

Communication
Group Work

Put these sentences on the board and ask students to write them on a piece of paper. Then allow them to circulate around the class asking the following questions. Students should keep a tally of how many respondents there are for each question. **¿Prefieres pasar las vacaciones en la playa, en la ciudad o en las montañas? ¿Prefieres visitar otros países o quedarte en los Estados Unidos? ¿Tu estación favorita para ir de vacaciones es el invierno, la primavera, el verano o el otoño? ¿Cuando estás de vacaciones te gusta comprar recuerdos o prefieres no comprar nada? ¿Cuando estás de vacaciones prefieres estar solo/a, estar con tu familia o ir con tus amigos?** Keep a tally of class responses and record the information on the board.

Comparación cultural

¡De vacaciones!

AUDIO

Lectura y escritura

WebQuest my.hrw.com

1. **Leer** Travel destinations vary around the world. Read and compare where and how Ernesto, Isabel, and Osvaldo are spending their vacations.

2. **Escribir** Using the three descriptions as models, write a short paragraph about a real or imaginary vacation.

STRATEGY **Escribir**
Use three boxes Use three boxes to help you describe the vacation.

Lugar	Actividades	Opinión

Step 1 Complete the boxes. In the first box write information about the place, in the second box write details about what you usually do there, and in the third box give your opinion about the location.

Step 2 Write your paragraph. Make sure to include all the information from the boxes. Check your writing by yourself or with help from a friend. Make final corrections.

Compara con tu mundo

Use the paragraph you wrote to compare your vacation with a vacation described by *one* of the three students. How are they similar? How are they different?

Cuaderno *pp. 390–392* Cuaderno para hispanohablantes *pp. 390–392*

Differentiating Instruction

Heritage Language Learners

Support What They Know Ask students to discuss how the vacations described by Ernesto, Isabel, and Osvaldo compare to typical vacations in their country or region of origin. What are some popular tourist or vacation destinations? What kinds of activities do people do there?

Inclusion

Clear Structure Before students read the vacation descriptions on p. 457, have them copy these headings onto a piece of paper.
País: **Vacaciones en:**
Nombre: **Actividades:**
Instruct students to fill in the information as they read the three paragraphs.

CULTURA Interactiva my.hrw.com *See these pages come alive!*

Uruguay *Ernesto*

¡Hola! Me llamo Ernesto y vivo en Montevideo. Es febrero, y mis padres y yo estamos de vacaciones en Punta del Este. Generalmente nos quedamos con mi abuela. Su casa está muy cerca de Playa Mansa. Es una playa donde el mar es muy tranquilo. Es ideal para nadar o tomar el sol. Yo prefiero ir a Playa Brava porque tiene más olas[1] y es perfecta para hacer surfing. En las tardes me gusta pasear por el Mercado de los Artesanos. Allí les compro recuerdos a mis amigos.

[1] waves

Ecuador *Isabel*

¿Qué tal? Me llamo Isabel y soy de Quito. Mi familia y yo estamos pasando unos días de vacaciones en Baños, una ciudad que está en un valle[2], al lado de un volcán. Nos estamos quedando en un hotel que está muy cerca de las cascadas[3] y de las aguas termales[4]. Aquí puedes hacer muchas actividades al aire libre: montar a caballo, dar caminatas por la ruta de las cascadas y montar en bicicleta. ¡Es un lugar fenomenal!

[2] valley [3] waterfalls [4] hot springs

Costa Rica *Osvaldo*

¡Hola! Me llamo Osvaldo y soy de Costa Rica. Estoy pasando las vacaciones de julio en el Parque Nacional Manuel Antonio. El hotel está en un bosque tropical lluvioso[5] pero también tiene una playa en la costa del océano Pacífico. Todas las mañanas, mis padres y yo nos levantamos muy temprano y salimos a dar caminatas en el parque. Allí hay plantas y animales muy exóticos. ¡Me gusta estar en la naturaleza![6]

[5] **bosque...** tropical rain forest [6] nature

Comparación cultural

Exploring the Theme

Costa Rica, the size of West Virginia, has managed to preserve a larger proportion of its land than any country in the world. In 1970 the country began setting aside acreage for preservation purposes. It now boasts thirty-two national parks, eight biological reserves, 13 forest reserves and 51 wildlife refuges. These areas represent a section of all major habitats and ecosystems in the nation. The most visited place in the country's park system is Manuel Antonio. This national park lies on Costa Rica's Pacific coast. Although it is the smallest park in the system it is considered the most beautiful. The park has four lovely beaches and a tropical rainforest brimming with monkeys, sloths, ocelots and toucans. Visitors can hike trails, whitewater raft, fish, and sea kayak.

✓ Ongoing Assessment

Quick Check Ask students quick comprehension questions and write their responses on the board. **¿En qué mes van Ernesto y su familia de vacaciones? ¿Dónde pasa Isabel sus vacaciones? ¿Dónde puedes montar a caballo?**

✓ Ongoing Assessment

Rubric Lectura y escritura

Writing Criteria	Excellent	Good	Needs Work
Content	Paragraph contains a lot of informa-tion.	Paragraph contains some informa-tion.	Paragraph lacks informa-tion.
Communi-cation	Paragraph is orga-nized and easy to follow.	Paragraph is fairly well-orga-nized.	Paragraph is disorga-nized and hard to follow.
Accuracy	Few mistakes in vocabulary and grammar.	Some mistakes in vocabulary and grammar.	Many mistakes in vocabulary and grammar.

To customize your own rubrics, use the ***Generate Success** Rubric Generator and Graphic Organizers.*

Differentiating Instruction

Slower-paced Learners

Personalize It Based on the descriptions they read, ask students to share information about their own experiences with family vacations. For example, after they read the sentence: **En febrero, vamos de vacaciones en Punta del Este**, you might ask: **¿Va tu familia de vacaciones en febrero? ¿Adónde van a ir? ¿Qué van a hacer allí?**

Pre-AP

Self-correct After students finish writing about their own family vacation, have them read their paragraphs aloud to a partner. Remind them to listen to themselves as they read aloud to catch any mistakes in their writing. Also, instruct partners to make note of sentences or phrases that do not sound correct because of problems with agreement or verb forms.

Objective
- Cumulative review.

Core Resource
- Audio Program: TXT CD 8 track 24

Review Options
- **Activity 1:** Listening
- **Activity 2:** Speaking
- **Activity 3:** Speaking
- **Activity 4:** Writing
- **Activity 5:** Speaking
- **Activity 6:** Speaking
- **Activity 7:** Reading and Writing

STANDARDS
1.1 Engage in conversation, Acts. 2-3, 5-6
1.2 Understand language, Act. 1
1.3 Present information, Acts. 2-7
21st Century **Communication,** Acts. 2, 5/ Heritage Language Learners; **Creativity and Innovation,** Act. 4; **Flexibility and Adaptability,** Act. 3 (Health Literacy)/ Act. 6

Long-term Retention
Study Tips
Encourage students to generate a list of words associated with going on vacation. Have them group the words under the following categories: **sustantivos, verbos, adjetivos, expresiones.** Tell students to refer to this list when doing the activities for Repaso Inclusivo.

Answers
Activity 1
1. La señora Daza está trabajando en su oficina. Va a llegar tarde porque hay algunos problemas con el artículo que está escribiendo.
2. Después de trabajar, el señor Daza fue al mercado para comprar verduras.
3. Ahora, él está escuchando música.
4. David está estudiando en la biblioteca y Luisa está en el teatro, comprando entradas para el teatro.
5. La familia Daza va al teatro este sábado. El problema es que el señor Daza ya compró las entradas ayer.

UNIDADES 1-8

Repaso inclusivo
Options for Review

¡AvanzaRap! DVD Sing and Learn

Digital performance space

1 Listen, understand, and compare
Escuchar

Listen to the telephone conversation between Mrs. Daza and her husband. Then answer the following questions.

1. ¿Dónde está la señora Daza y qué está haciendo? ¿Por qué va a llegar tarde?
2. ¿Qué hizo el señor Daza después de trabajar?
3. ¿Qué está haciendo él ahora?
4. ¿Dónde están Luisa y David? ¿Qué están haciendo?
5. ¿Qué va a hacer la familia Daza este sábado? ¿Cuál es el problema?

Does your family eat dinner together? At what time? What do you do as a group on weekends?

Audio Program
TXT CD 8 Track 24
Audio Script, TE p. 431b

2 Talk about your ideal routine
Hablar

Prepare a presentation about your ideal daily routine. Include what time you get up, the sequence of your morning activities, what your school day is like, and what you do after school. Also include as many details as possible about your perfect day: what you eat, with whom you do different activities, and what the weather is like. Your presentation should be about four minutes long.

3 Talk about your health
Hablar

You are at the doctor's office for a checkup. You should tell your partner about your general health routine, including when you go to bed, what time you get up, what you eat and drink throughout the day, and what your activities are. Your partner will make recommendations about what you should do differently. Your conversation should be about five minutes long.

4 Create a tourist booklet
Escribir

You are an intern at a travel agency and have been asked to plan a one-week trip for a family of four to a Spanish-speaking country. Research a destination and map out a route. Create a booklet describing places of interest along the route, transportation, and costs. Include other tourist information, such as cuisine, festivals, or souvenirs that can be bought there. Use illustrations and at least eight sentences.

Differentiating Instruction

Multiple Intelligences
Visual Learners Have students create a poster to accompany their presentations about an ideal daily routine in Activity 2. Encourage them to use pictures of clocks showing different times in conjunction with magazine photos or illustrations of people engaged in different activities. Have students use their posters for reference as they give their presentations to the group.

Slower-paced Learners
Yes/No Questions As a whole group, have students brainstorm yes or no questions that can be used in Activity 3. Create two columns on the board—**doctor** and **paciente**. Then have students contribute questions for each role. Here are a few possibilities:
¿Te duele la rodilla? ¿Puedo levantar pesas?
Encourage students to refer to these lists during their conversations.

5 Interview a potential roommate

Hablar

Work in a group of four. Three of you room together at soccer camp and the fourth is a potential roommate. Ask questions to find out about your new roommate's personality, likes, dislikes, and daily routine. The potential roommate should give as much detail as possible about himself or herself and also ask questions. Each person should speak for at least two minutes.

6 Mingle at a party

Hablar

In a group of six, role-play a dinner party in which you mingle with other guests. Walk around and introduce yourself to others. Talk about the people that you know in common, what you are studying, what you like to do in your free time, and anything else you find out about the person you are talking to, such as plans for summer vacation. You should spend at least two minutes talking to each person.

7 Decide where to study

Leer
Escribir

This summer you want to study Spanish for a month in Costa Rica. Your Spanish teacher gave you the following information to help you decide which program to choose. Read the descriptions and write a note to your teacher, explaining where you would like to study and why. Offer comparisons of the two programs.

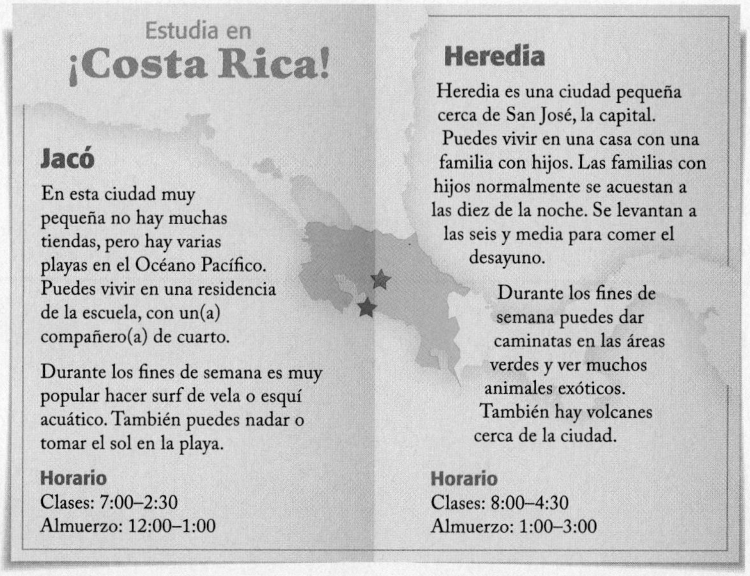

✓ Ongoing Assessment

Integrated Performance Assessment Rubric

Oral Activities 2, 3, 5, 6
Written Activities 4, 7

Very Good	Proficient	Not There Yet
The student thoroughly develops all requirements of the task.	The student develops most requirements of the task.	The student does not develop the requirements of the task.
The student demonstrates excellent control of verb forms.	The student demonstrates good to fair control of verb forms.	The student demonstrates poor control of verb forms.
Good variety of appropriate vocabulary.	Adequate variety of appropriate vocabulary.	The vocabulary is not appropriate.
The pronunciation is excellent to very good.	The pronunciation is good to fair.	The pronunciation is poor.

To customize your own rubrics, use the ***Generate Success** Rubric Generator and Graphic Organizers.*

Differentiating Instruction

Pre-AP

Expand and Elaborate Before students begin Activity 5, give them this "pre-speaking" activity. Have each group draw four concept webs on a large piece of paper. Instruct them to write **cuarto** in the center of one, and the name of one roommate in the center of the others. Have students add vocabulary around each web to describe the room or the roommates.

Heritage Language Learners

Writing Skills Have students use the information presented in Activity 7 to write an article for a school newsletter. Instruct them to write an article for their peers comparing and contrasting two study-abroad programs in Costa Rica. Advise students to use a Venn diagram to organize their ideas.

¿?Entre dos

Pair Activities

Objectives
- Talk about activities
- **Gustar** with an infinitive

Core Resources
- Conversation cards, Teacher One Stop

STANDARDS
1.1 Engage in conversation

Possible Answer

A: A Ricardo le gusta jugar al fútbol. ¿Y a Isabel?

B: A Isabel también le gusta jugar al fútbol. Y a ella le gusta hablar por teléfono. ¿A Ricardo le gusta hablar por teléfono?

A: No. A él le gusta escribir correos electrónicos. ¿A Isabel le gusta escribir correos electrónicos?

B: Sí. A Isabel le gusta leer libros. ¿Y a Ricardo?

A: No, a Ricardo no le gusta leer libros. A él le gusta andar en patineta. ¿Y a Isabel?

B: A Isabel no le gusta andar en patineta. Le gusta montar en bicicleta. ¿A Ricardo le gusta montar en bicicleta?

A: Sí, a Ricardo le gusta montar en bicicleta. También le gusta preparar la comida. ¿A Isabel le gusta preparar la comida?

B: No. A ella le gusta dibujar. ¿Y a Ricardo?

A: A Ricardo no le gusta dibujar. A él le gusta tocar la guitarra. ¿A Isabel le gusta tocar la guitarra?

B: No, a Isabel no le gusta tocar la guitarra.

Answer:
jugar al fútbol, escribir correos electrónicos, montar en bicicleta

¿Qué les gusta hacer?

Ricardo and Isabel like to do many things. Look at the pictures on the right to find out what Ricardo likes to do. (Your partner has pictures showing what Isabel likes to do.) Take turns asking each other questions to discover what Ricardo and Isabel like to do.

Estudiante A: **A Ricardo le gusta... ¿Y a Isabel?**

Estudiante B: **A Isabel también le gusta... ¿A Ricardo le gusta...?**

What activities do Ricardo and Isabel both like to do?

Estudiante A

Ricardo

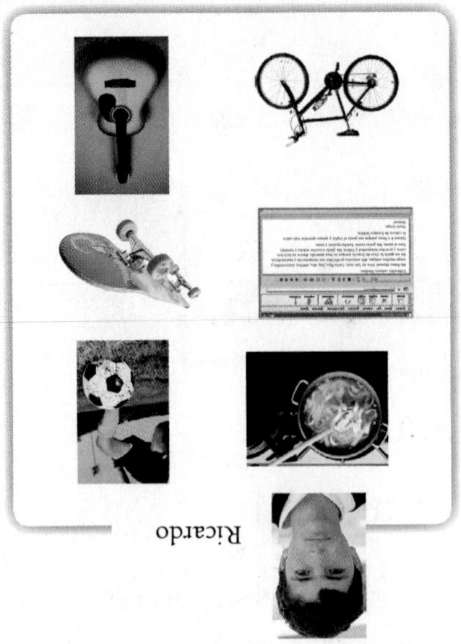

¿Qué les gusta hacer?

Estudiante B

Ricardo and Isabel like to do many things. Look at the pictures on the right to find out what Isabel likes to do. (Your partner has pictures showing what Ricardo likes to do.) Take turns asking each other questions to discover what Ricardo and Isabel like to do.

Estudiante A: **A Ricardo le gusta... ¿Y a Isabel?**

Estudiante B: **A Isabel también le gusta... ¿A Ricardo le gusta...?**

Isabel

What activities do Ricardo and Isabel both like to do?

Differentiating Instruction – Lección 1

Pre-AP

Expand and Elaborate Have students circulate around the class and find out which of the items pictured their classmates like and dislike. After students have polled their classmates, have them work in small groups and compile their results in a table or graph. Have each group present its findings to the class.

Inclusion

Clear Structure On their own sheet of paper, have students make a numbered list of the six images they have on their sheet. As they proceed through the activity, they should add a check for items that Ricardo and Isabel like and an X by the items that they dislike.

Entre dos • Lección 2

¿Cómo se llaman?

Estudiante A

You and your partner want to know the names of the people in the picture. Your picture has the names of three people and your partner's picture has the names of three other people. Take turns asking each other questions and describing people to find out the names of all the people.

Estudiante A: ¿Cómo se llama la chica rubia?

Estudiante B: ¿La chica pequeña y joven?

Estudiante A: Sí.

Estudiante B: Se llama Gabi.

¿Cómo se llama...?

Who in the picture do you think is ***artístico(a)****? Why?*

¿Cómo se llaman?

Estudiante B

You and your partner want to know the names of the people in the picture. Your picture has the names of three people and your partner's picture has the names of three other people. Take turns asking each other questions and describing people to find out the names of all the people.

Estudiante A: ¿Cómo se llama la chica rubia?

Estudiante B: ¿La chica pequeña y joven?

Estudiante A: Sí.

Estudiante B: Se llama Gabi.

¿Cómo se llama...?

Who in the picture do you think is ***artístico(a)****? Why?*

Objectives

- Identify people and things
- Noun-adjective agreement

Core Resources

- Conversation cards, Teacher One Stop

STANDARDS

1.1 Engage in conversation

UNIDAD 1

Possible Answer

A: ¿Cómo se llama la chica rubia?
B: ¿La chica pequeña y joven?
A: Sí.
B: Se llama Gabi. ¿Cómo se llama el hombre viejo?
A: Se llama Lorenzo. ¿Cómo se llama el hombre alto?
B: ¿Tiene pelo castaño?
A: Sí.
B: Se llama Tomás. ¿Cómo se llama el chico?
A: Se llama Mateo. ¿Cómo se llama la mujer? Tiene pelo rubio.
B: Se llama Marta. ¿Cómo se llama la chica joven?
A: ¿Tiene pelo castaño?
B: Sí.
A: Se llama Lupe.

Answers will vary. Possible answer: Mateo es artístico porque tiene pelo verde.

Differentiating Instruction – Lección 2

Heritage Language Learners

Writing Skills After students have completed their conversations, have them write a note to a friend describing all the people in the picture. Have them exchange their notes with a partner to check for spelling and accuracy.

Multiple Intelligences

Visual Learners Have students create a chart with two columns. In the first column, they should include the names of all six people. In the second column, they should fill in the description of that person. When students have finished the activity, have partners compare their charts to make sure they have included the same information.

Communication

Pair Work

Have pairs of students collect pictures of celebrities and take turns describing the celebrities to a partner. Each will try to identify the celebrity.

Objectives
- Talk about daily schedules
- Ask and tell time
- The verb **tener**

Core Resources
- Conversation cards, Teacher One Stop

STANDARDS
1.1 Engage in conversation
1.2 Understand language

Possible Answer
A: A las ocho de la mañana tengo la clase de español. ¿Y tú?
B: Yo también tengo la clase de español a las ocho. ¿Qué clase tienes a las nueve menos diez?
A: Tengo la clase de matemáticas. ¿Y tú?
B: Yo tengo la clase de historia. A las diez menos veinte tengo la clase de ciencias. ¿Y tú?
A: Yo también. ¿Qué clase tienes a las diez y media?
B: Tengo la clase de arte.
A: Yo también tengo la clase de arte. ¿Tienes clase a las once y veinte?
B: Sí, tengo la clase de inglés. ¿Y tú?
A: No tengo clase a las once y veinte. Tengo la clase de inglés a las doce y diez. ¿Qué clase tienes a las doce y diez?
B: No tengo clase a las doce y diez. ¿Qué clase tienes a la una?
A: A la una tengo la clase de historia. ¿Y tú?
B: Tengo la clase de matemáticas. ¿Qué clase tienes a las dos menos diez?
A: Tengo la clase de música. ¿Y tú?
B: Yo también tengo la clase de música.

Answer:
a las 8:00, a las 9:40, a las 10:30 y a las 1:50

UNIDAD 2 Entre dos • Lección 1

Horario de clases

You and your partner want to compare class schedules. Look at your class schedule on the right. Your partner has a different schedule. Ask each other questions to find out what classes you have at various times of the day.

Estudiante A: A las... tengo... ¿Y tú?
Estudiante B: Yo (también) tengo... ¿Qué clase tienes a las...?

Estudiante A

Horario

8:00 – 8:45	español
8:50 – 9:35	matemáticas
9:40 – 10:25	ciencias
10:30 – 11:15	arte
11:20 – 12:05	———
12:10 – 12:55	inglés
1:00 – 1:45	historia
1:50 – 2:35	música

What classes do you and your partner have at the same time?

Horario de clases

Estudiante B

You and your partner want to compare class schedules. Look at your class schedule on the right. Your partner has a different schedule. Ask each other questions to find out what classes you have at various times of the day.

Estudiante A las... tengo... ¿Y tú?
Estudiante B: Yo (también) tengo... ¿Qué clase tienes a las...?

Horario

8:00 – 8:45	*español*
8:50 – 9:35	*historia*
9:40 – 10:25	*ciencias*
10:30 – 11:15	*arte*
11:20 – 12:05	*inglés*
12:10 – 12:55	———
1:00 – 1:45	*matemáticas*
1:50 – 2:35	*música*

What classes do you and your partner have at the same time?

Differentiating Instruction – Lección 1

Slower-Pace Learners
Personalize It Instead of using the class schedules provided, have students create a conversation based on their own class schedules. Allow students a few minutes before beginning the activity to make notes about their schedule on a separate piece of paper.

Multiple Intelligences
Mathematical-Logical After completing the activity, have students calculate the total number of minutes they spent in classes using these schedules. Have them compare this number with the amount of time they spend in class using their own schedules. Ask them to share their results with the class.

Entre dos • Lección 2

Estudiante A

¿Dónde están?

You and your partner have borrowed some school supplies from friends but have forgotten them at different places in school. Ask your partner where the following friends' supplies are:

Alejo's and Marta's calculators

Sergio's paper

Julia's pencil

Then, answer your partner's questions based on the images and cues. Take turns doing this activity.

Estudiante A: ¿Dónde está el borrador de la maestra?

Estudiante B: Está en la clase.

Did you and your partner leave some of the supplies in the same places? ?

Estudiante B

¿Dónde están?

You and your partner have borrowed some school supplies from friends but have forgotten them at different places in school. Ask your partner where the following friends' supplies are:

Daniel's backpack

Florencia's and Luis's pens

Félix's notebook

Then, answer your partner's questions based on the images and cues. Take turns doing this activity.

Estudiante A: ¿Dónde está el borrador de la maestra?

Estudiante B: Está en la clase.

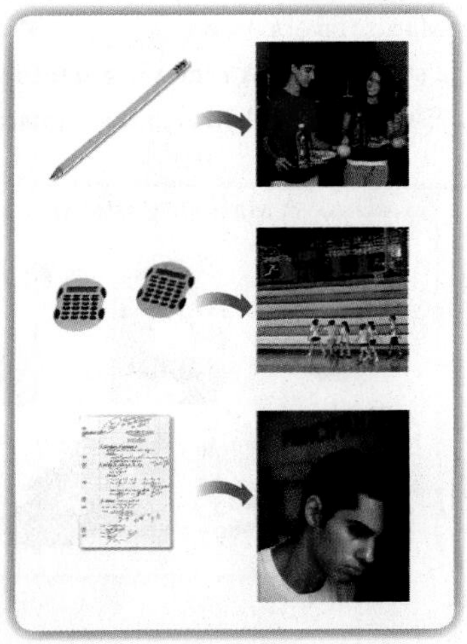

Did you and your partner leave some of the supplies in the same places? ?

UNIDAD 2

Objectives
- Describe classes and classoom objects
- The verb **estar**

Core Resources
- Conversation cards, Teacher One Stop

STANDARDS

1.1 Engage in conversation

Possible Answer

A: Dónde están las calculadoras de Alejo y Marta?

B: Están en el gimnasio. ¿Dónde está la mochila de Daniel?

A: Está en el pasillo. ¿Dónde está el papel de Sergio?

B: Está en la oficina del director. ¿Dónde están las plumas de Florencia y Luis?

A: Están en la cafetería. ¿Dónde está el lápiz de Julia?

B: Está en la cafetería. ¿Dónde está el cuaderno de Félix?

A: Está en la biblioteca.

Answer:
Sí, en la cafetería

Differentiating Instruction – Lección 2

Inclusion

Activity Preparation Before starting this activity, review the instructions with students. Explain to them that they are to ask questions about the three items listed in italics. They answer their partner's questions by using the images. Have students identify each school supply item and each school area in Spanish for their section before they begin the activity.

Pre-AP

Support Ideas with Details For each school location pictured, have students provide a list of the different supplies or school items they would logically find in each area. Ask them to identify the items used in more than one location.

Long-term Retention

Personalize It

After students complete the activity, have them find a school supply ad online in Spanish. Have them make a list of the items available that they would use for their own classes. Which items would they not use and why?

Objectives
- Say which foods you like and dislike
- **Gustar** with nouns

Core Resources
- Conversation cards, Teacher One Stop

STANDARDS
1.1 Engage in conversation

Possible Answer

A: A Elena le gusta la sopa pero no le gusta el jugo de naranja. ¿Y a Mario?

B: A Mario no le gusta la sopa pero le gustan las manzanas. ¿A Elena le gustan las manzanas?

A: No, a Elena no le gustan las manzanas pero le gustan las uvas y las bananas.

B: A Mario le gustan las uvas pero no le gustan las bananas y no le gustan las hamburguesas.

A: A Elena no le gustan las hamburguesas pero le gusta el yogur. ¿Y a Mario, le gusta el yogur?

B: Sí, a Mario le gusta mucho el yogur y le gustan mucho los sándwiches también.

A: A Elena no le gustan los sándwiches pero le gusta el pan. Y a ella no le gusta el café. ¿Y a Mario?

B: A Mario no le gusta el café pero le gusta la leche.

Answer:
A los dos les gustan las uvas y el yogur, pero no les gusta el café.

Long-term Retention
Personalize It

After students complete their conversations, have them talk about their own food preferences using the items pictured for Mario and Elena.

¿Qué le gusta comer?

Estudiante A

You and your partner are discussing what Elena and Mario like and don't like to eat. Look at the pictures below to find out what Elena likes and dislikes. (Your partner has pictures showing what Mario likes and dislikes.) Talk to your partner about Elena's and Mario's favorite foods.

Estudiante A: **A Elena le gusta(n)..., pero no le gusta(n)... ¿Y a Mario?**

Estudiante B: **A Mario no le gusta(n)..., pero le gusta(n)... ¿A Elena le gusta(n)...?**

A Elena le gusta(n)...

A Elena no le gusta(n)...

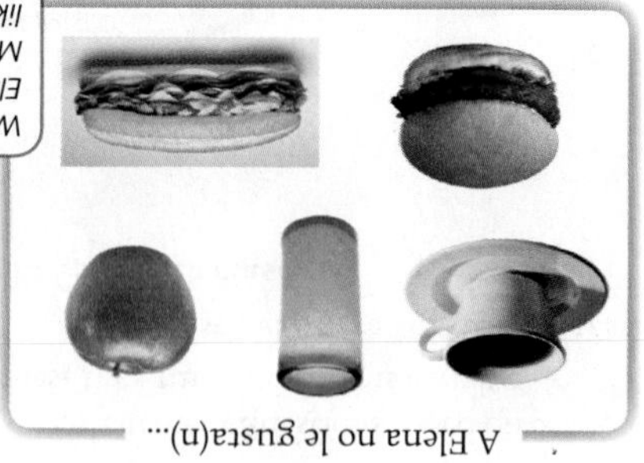

What foods do Elena and Mario both like? What foods do they both dislike?

¿Qué le gusta comer?

Estudiante B

You and your partner are discussing what Elena and Mario like and don't like to eat. Look at the pictures below to find out what Mario likes and dislikes. (Your partner has pictures showing what Elena likes and dislikes.) Talk to your partner about Elena's and Mario's favorite foods.

Estudiante A: **A Elena le gusta(n)..., pero no le gusta(n)... ¿Y a Mario?**

Estudiante B: **A Mario no le gusta(n)..., pero le gusta(n)... ¿A Elena le gusta(n)...?**

A Mario le gusta(n)...

A Mario no le gusta(n)...

What foods do Elena and Mario both like? What foods do they both dislike?

Differentiating Instruction – Lección 1

Slower-Pace Learners

Sentence Completion Before starting this activity, make a list of singular and plural nouns that the students have learned. Then, have students say whether they like or dislike each item you listed using **(no) me gusta(n).** Have them explain why they chose the form they used.

Multiple Intelligences

Logical/Mathematical Have students use the model to ask five classmates about their preferences. Students should tally the responses and assign percentages for the items most liked and disliked by the students. Have them report their findings to the class.

¿Cuántos años tienen?

Estudiante A

You and your partner are looking at Pedro's family tree. You know the age of some of Pedro's family members and your partner knows the age of the other members of Pedro's family. Take turns asking each other how old Pedro's family members are.

Estudiante A: **¿Cuántos años tiene su...?**

Estudiante B: **Su... tiene...**

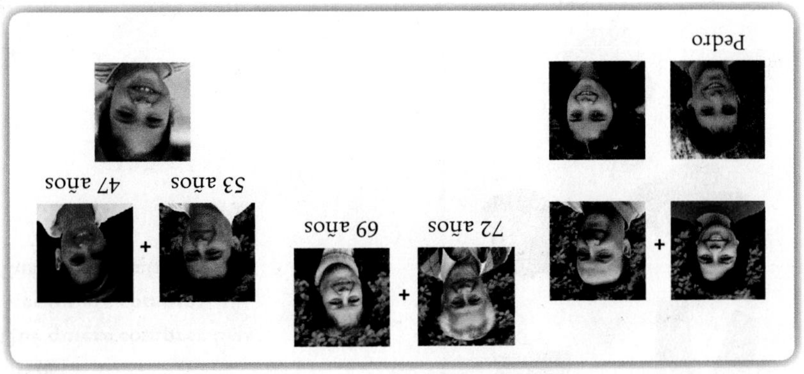

Which family members are the same age?

¿Cuántos años tienen?

Estudiante B

You and your partner are looking at Pedro's family tree. You know the age of some of Pedro's family members and your partner knows the age of the other members of Pedro's family. Take turns asking each other how old Pedro's family members are.

Estudiante A: **¿Cuántos años tiene su...?**

Estudiante B: **Su... tiene...**

Which family members are the same age?

Objectives

- Talk about family
- Ask and tell ages
- Possessive adjectives

Core Resources

- Conversation cards, Teacher One Stop

STANDARDS

1.1 Engage in conversation

Possible Answer

A: ¿Cuántos años tiene su hermana?

B: Su hermana tiene once años. ¿Cuántos años tiene su abuelo?

A: Su abuelo tiene setenta y dos años. ¿Cuántos años tiene su madre?

B: Su madre tiene cuarenta y siete años. ¿Cuántos años tiene su abuela?

A: Su abuela tiene sesenta y nueve años. ¿Cuántos años tiene su padre?

B: Su padre tiene cincuenta y tres años. ¿Cuántos años tiene su tío?

A: Su tío tiene cincuenta y tres años. ¿Cuántos años tiene su prima?

B: Su prima tiene cuatro años. ¿Cuántos años tiene su tía?

A: Su tía tiene cuarenta y siete años.

Answer:
La madre de Pedro y la tía tienen 47 años. El padre de Pedro y el tío tienen 53 años.

Differentiating Instruction – Lección 2

Multiple Intelligences

Visual Learners Before help students complete this activity, have them sketch a larger version of the family tree on their own paper, adding captions as needed. As an extension, have students pick a different member of the family and relabel everyone to show the new relationships.

Pre-AP

Expand and Elaborate Once students have completed identifying the ages of the different family members, have them compare the ages of the various family members using **mayor** and **menor.**

Objectives
- Talk about clothes you want to buy
- Stem-changing verbs: e to ie

Core Resources
- Conversation cards, Teacher One Stop

STANDARDS
1.1 Engage in conversation

Possible Answer

A: ¿Qué quiere comprar Éster?

B: Éster quiere comprar un vestido azul, un sombrero amarillo, unos zapatos rojos, una blusa verde, y una camiseta roja.

A: ¿Cuánto cuestan?

B: El vestido azul cuesta ochenta y nueve euros, el sombrero amarillo cuesta treinta y tres euros, los zapatos rojos cuestan cuarenta y nueve euros, la blusa verde cuesta treinta y ocho euros y la camiseta roja cuesta nueve euros. ¿Qué quiere comprar Eduardo?

A: Eduardo quiere comprar unos zapatos negros, una chaqueta roja y blanca, unos pantalones azules, una camisa roja y un gorro rojo y negro.

B: ¿Cuánto cuesta la ropa de Eduardo?

A: Los zapatos negros cuestan ciento trece euros, la chaqueta roja y blanca cuesta ciento cuarenta y cinco euros, los pantalones azules cuestan treinta y cinco euros, el gorro rojo y negro cuesta doce euros y la camisa roja cuesta veintitrés euros.

Answer:
La ropa de Éster cuesta 218 euros y la ropa de Eduardo cuesta 328 euros.

UNIDAD 4

Entre dos • Lección 1

En la tienda de ropa

Estudiante A

Eduardo and Éster are shopping for clothes. Look at the pictures on the right to find out what Eduardo wants to buy. (Your partner has pictures showing what Éster wants to buy.) Take turns asking each other what Éster and Eduardo are buying, in what color, and how much each item costs. Note the cost of each item.

Estudiante A: **¿Qué quiere comprar Éster?**
Estudiante B: **Éster quiere comprar...**
Estudiante A: **¿Cuánto cuesta(n)...?**

¿Cuánto cuesta la ropa de Éster en total? ¿Y de Eduardo?

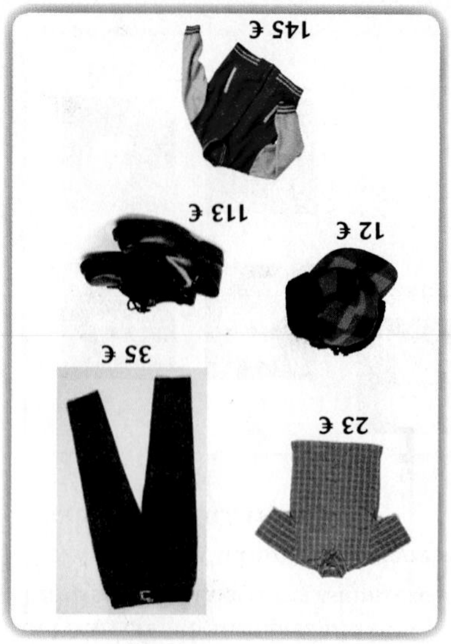

En la tienda de ropa

Estudiante B

Eduardo and Éster are shopping for clothes. Look at the pictures on the right to find out what Éster wants to buy. (Your partner has pictures showing what Eduardo wants to buy.) Take turns asking each other what Éster and Eduardo are buying, in what color, and how much each item costs. Note the cost of each item.

Estudiante A: **¿Qué quiere comprar Eduardo?**
Estudiante B: **Eduardo quiere comprar...**
Estudiante A: **¿Cuánto cuesta(n)...?**

¿Cuánto cuesta la ropa de Éster en total? ¿Y de Eduardo?

Differentiating Instruction – Lección 1

Pre-AP

Relate Opinions After students have completed their conversation, have them discuss what they think of the clothing items pictured. They should mention if they would prefer certain items in another color or if there are items that they would like to buy that are not pictured on the page.

Multiple Intelligences

Kinesthetic Learners Bring in clothing items similar to the items pictured in the activity and have pairs take turns using the real items. Include price labels similar to the ones in the activity. Have students complete the activity using the real clothing items, adding as many details as they can.

Are any of your friends ordering the same thing?

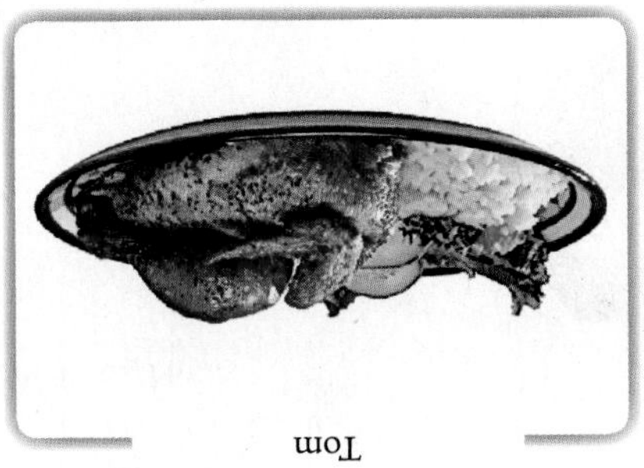

Tom

Julie

Estudiante A

¿Qué van a pedir?

You and your partner are supposed to meet some friends at a restaurant. They are late and they asked you to order for them. Take turns asking each other what your friends are going to order.

Estudiante A: **¿Qué va a pedir Tom?**

Estudiante B: **Tom va a pedir...**

¿Qué van a pedir?

Estudiante B

You and your partner are supposed to meet some friends at a restaurant. They are late and they asked you to order for them. Take turns asking each other what your friends are going to order.

Estudiante A: **¿Qué va a pedir Sara?**

Estudiante B: **Sara va a pedir...**

Sara

Sam

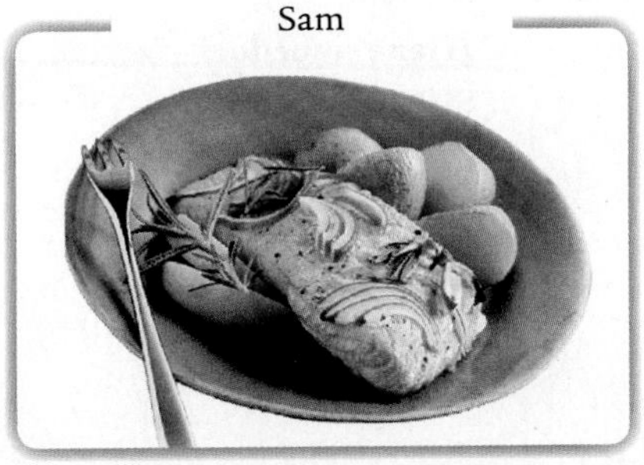

Are any of your friends ordering the same thing?

UNIDAD 4

Objectives

- Order from a menu
- The verb **ir a** + infinitive

Core Resources

- Conversation cards, Teacher One Stop

STANDARDS

1.1 Engage in conversation

Possible Answer

A: ¿Qué va a pedir Sara?

B: Sara va a pedir frijoles con arroz y una ensalada con tomates. ¿Qué va a pedir Julie?

A: Julie va a pedir un bistec con brócoli, verduras y patatas. ¿Qué va a pedir Sam?

B: Sam va a pedir pescado con patatas. ¿Qué va a pedir Tom?

A: Tom va a pedir pollo con arroz y verduras.

Answer:
Sara y Tom van a pedir arroz. Julie y Sam van a pedir patatas.

Differentiating Instruction – Lección 2

Heritage Language Learners

Regional Variations After completing this conversation, have students create a menu containing all the items pictured on the page. If they use different vocabulary for the items, encourage them to include it. They should include prices for each item. They should also add descriptions of regional dishes they like to their menus.

Slower-paced Learners

Activity Preparation Review the names of each person and food item pictured before beginning the activity. As an alternative to using the dinners pictured, you might want to have students use individual food item pictures (from a magazine or clip art) to simplify the activity.

Communication

Presentational Mode

Have students research restaurant menus online from various Spanish-speaking countries. Have them present their favorite menu to the class and tell what they would order if they could eat at that restaurant.

Objectives
- Describe a house and household items

Core Resources
- Conversation cards, Teacher One Stop

STANDARDS
1.1 Engage in conversation

Possible Answer

B: ¿La casa tiene dos pisos?
A: Sí, tiene dos pisos.
B: ¿Tiene comedor?
A: Sí, tiene un comedor cerca de la cocina.
B: ¿Cuántos cuartos hay en la casa?
A: Hay tres cuartos, pero no tienen armarios.
B: ¿Hay sala?
A: Sí, hay una sala con sofá.
B: ¿Tiene patio o jardín?
A: No sé. Y tu casa, ¿tiene dos pisos?
B: No, tiene uno...

Answers will vary on home selection.
Answer:
Las dos casas tienen una cocina, un comedor y una sala.

Communication
Role-Playing and Skits

Have students role-play a conversation between a real-estate agent and a client. The real-estate agent shows each of the houses pictured to the client, and the client indicates which house he or she prefers and why. Ask partners to act out their skit for the class.

Which features do both homes have in common?

Estudiante A: **¿La casa tiene dos pisos?**
Estudiante B: **Sí/No...**
Estudiante A: **¿Tiene comedor?**
Estudiante B: **Sí/No...**

Imagine that you and your family are going to rent a vacation home. You and your partner each found a home that would be available. First, answer your partner's questions about the home you found. Then, ask your partner at least five questions about his or her home. Decide which one you would select and why.

Estudiante A

Un hogar para las vacaciones

Un hogar para las vacaciones

Estudiante B

Imagine that you and your family are going to rent a vacation home. You and your partner each found a home that would be available. First, ask your partner at least five questions about the home he or she found. Then, answer your partner's questions about the home you found. Decide which one you would select and why.

Estudiante A: **¿La casa tiene dos pisos?**
Estudiante B: **Sí/No...**
Estudiante A: **¿Tiene comedor?**
Estudiante B: **Sí/No...**

Which features do both homes have in common?

Differentiating Instruction – Lección 1

Inclusion

Clear Structure Before students begin the activity, have them spend a minute or two looking at the home they found and making notes on that home. Then, students should take a few minutes to write down the questions they want to ask about their partner's home. Students can then use their notes and questions to complete the activity.

Multiple Intelligences

Visual Learners Have students sketch an imaginary floor plan of a house and label each room or home feature. Then, have students present their floor plan to the rest of the class.

Entre dos • Lección 2

Antes de celebrar, hay que limpiar

Estudiante A

Imagine that you and a family member (your partner) want to have a party. You are allowed to have the party as long as you both complete your chores. Take turns asking each other what you are going to do today. First, ask your partner if he or she plans to set the table, wash the dishes, make the bed, cook, and mow the lawn. Then, answer your partner's questions based on the images and clues below.

Estudiante A: **¿Vas a hacer la cama?**

Estudiante B: **Sí/No...**

√

X

√

√

X

What are two chores you and your partner still need to do tomorrow?

Antes de celebrar, hay que limpiar

Estudiante B

Imagine that you and a family member (your partner) want to have a party. You are allowed to have the party as long as you both complete your chores. Take turns asking each other what you are going to do today. First, answer your partner's questions based on the images and clues below. Then, ask your partner if he or she plans to sweep, feed the cat, take out the trash, iron, and vacuum.

Estudiante A: **¿Vas a planchar la ropa?**

Estudiante B: **Sí/No...**

X

√

√

X

√

What are two chores you and your partner still need to do tomorrow?

UNIT 5

ENTRE DOS

Objectives
- Talk about chores and responsibilities

Core Resources
- Conversation cards, Teacher One Stop

STANDARDS
1.1 Engage in conversation

Possible Answer

A: ¿Vas a poner la mesa?

B: No, no voy a poner la mesa. ¿Vas a barrer el suelo?

A: Sí, voy a barrer. ¿Vas a lavar los platos?

B: Sí, voy a lavar los platos ahora. ¿Vas a darle de comer al gato?

A: No, no voy a darle de comer al gato ahora. ¿Vas a hacer la cama?

B: Sí, voy a hacer la cama. ¿Y vas a sacar la basura?

A: Sí, voy a sacar la basura. ¿Vas a cocinar para la fiesta?

B: No, no voy a cocinar. ¿Vas a planchar la ropa?

A: Sí, voy a planchar. ¿Vas a cortar el césped?

B: Sí, voy a cortar el césped. ¿Vas a pasar la aspiradora?

A: No, no voy a pasar la aspiradora.

Answer:
darle de comer al gato, pasar la aspiradora, poner la mesa, cocinar

Differentiating Instruction – Lección 2

Slower-paced Learners

Personalize It Instead of using the chores pictured, have students talk with their partner about the chores they have to do in their own homes. Have partners identify which chores they have in common. Ask them which chores are the most important to complete if they were going to have a party.

Pre-AP

Support Ideas with Details When students are responding yes or no about the chores they have done or not done, have them also explain why or why not or in what order they are going to complete the chores. Ask them to create as many details as possible to expand their responses.

Objectives

- Talk about sports
- The verb **jugar**

Core Resources

- Conversation cards, Teacher One Stop

STANDARDS

1.1 Engage in conversation

Possible Answer

A: Enrique juega al fútbol americano. ¿Y Carolina?

B: Ella no juega al fútbol americano, pero patina. ¿Enrique patina?

A: No, Enrique no patina, pero le gusta nadar. ¿Y a Carolina?

B: Sí, a ella le gusta nadar. ¿Enrique juega al tenis?

A: No, Enrique no juega al tenis, pero juega al básquetbol. ¿Y Carolina?

B: Sí, ella también juega al básquetbol. ¿Enrique juega al voleibol?

A: No, él no juega al voleibol, pero juega al fútbol. ¿Y Carolina?

B: Sí, ella también juega al fútbol. A ella no le gusta el béisbol. ¿Y a Enrique?

A: Sí, a Enrique le gusta al béisbol.

Answer:
nadar, jugar al básquetbol, jugar al fútbol

Entre dos • Lección 1

Los deportes

You and your partner are talking about what sports Enrique and Carolina like to play. Look at Enrique's equipment to see the sports he enjoys. With a partner, talk about what sports Enrique and Carolina do.

Estudiante A: **Enrique juega al fútbol americano. ¿Y Carolina?**

Estudiante B: **Ella no juega al fútbol americano, pero patina.**

Which sports do Carolina and Enrique have in common?

Enrique

Estudiante A

Los deportes

Estudiante B

You and your partner are talking about what sports Enrique and Carolina like to play. Look at Carolina's equipment to see the sports she enjoys. With a partner, talk about what sports Carolina and Enrique do.

Estudiante A: **Enrique juega al fútbol americano. ¿Y Carolina?**

Estudiante B: **Ella no juega al fútbol americano, pero patina.**

Which sports do Carolina and Enrique have in common?

Carolina

Long-term Retention

Interest Inventory

Ask students whether they like or dislike the activities Enrique and Carolina enjoy. Have students raise their right hand if they like an activity, or their left hand if they don't. Keep track of their responses, and group students with similar answers together. Have them discuss why they like or dislike an activity.

Differentiating Instruction – Lección 1

Pre-AP

Expand and Elaborate As students complete the activity, have them expand their answers. Have them tell how often Enrique and Carolina do these activities, where they do these activities, and why they like or don't like these activities.

Multiple Intelligences

Kinesthetic Learners Instead of asking partners about the items pictured, have one student pantomime various sports. The other students will confirm whether or not Enrique (or Carolina) likes the activity.

¡Ay, me duele...!

Estudiante A

You and your partner are doctors. Each of you has information about some patients. Ask each other about patients on your charts. Use the images to tell your partner what the medical problems are. Then, imagine what each patient did to cause that problem.

Estudiante A: **¿Qué le duele a Ana?**

Estudiante B: **Le duele el tobillo. Ayer caminó mucho.**

	Le duele...	*¿Por qué?*
Patricia		
Esteban		
Mario		

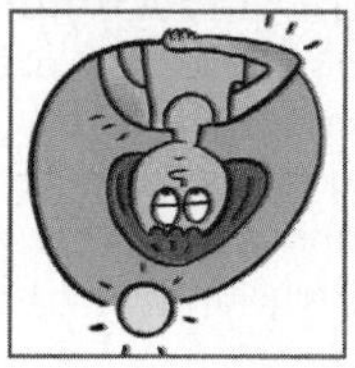

Daniela

Carlos

Sarita

What would you advise these patients to do to get better?

¡Ay, me duele...!

Estudiante B

You and your partner are doctors. Each of you has information about some patients. Ask each other about patients on your charts. Use the images to tell your partner what the medical problems are. Then, imagine what each patient did to cause that problem.

Estudiante A: **¿Qué le duele a Ana?**

Estudiante B: **Le duele el tobillo. Ayer caminó mucho.**

	Le duele...	*¿Por qué?*
Daniela		
Carlos		
Sarita		

Patricia

Esteban

Mario

What would you advise these patients to do to get better?

Differentiating Instruction – Lección 2

Heritage Language Learners

Writing Skills Have students imagine that they are doctors and that the six students on this page are patients. Have them create a medical chart. The chart should include a description of each person's problem along with suggestions for curing them.

Inclusion

Clear Structure In order for students to provide an explanation for why each student is complaining about a problem, they will be producing the preterite of verbs they know. Review the forms of the preterite and list the infinitives of verbs they could use to complete the activity on the board.

UNIDAD 6

Objectives

- Talk about parts of the body
- The verb **doler**

Core Resources

- Conversation cards, Teacher One Stop

STANDARDS

1.1 Engage in conversation

Possible Answer

A: ¿Qué le duele a Patricia?

B: A Patricia le duele el brazo. Jugó mucho al tenis. ¿Qué le duele a Daniela?

A: A Daniela le duele todo el cuerpo. Ayer tomó el sol sin bloqueador. ¿Qué le duele a Esteban?

B: A Esteban le duele la cabeza. Escuchó música fuerte. ¿Qué le duele a Carlos?

A: A Carlos le duele la mano. Ayer dibujó mucho. ¿Qué le duele a Sarita?

B: A Sarita le duele la pierna. Ayer patinó en el parque. ¿Qué le duele a Mario?

A: A Mario le duele el estómago. Almorzó muchas hamburguesas.

Answer:
descansar, hablar con un doctor

Objectives
- Talk about technology
- Affirmative and negative words

Core Resources
- Conversation cards, Teacher One Stop

STANDARDS
1.1 Engage in conversation

Possible Answer
A: ¿Quién usó el mensajero instantáneo?
B: Marcelo usó el mensajero instantáneo. ¿Quién tomó fotos?
A: Luisa y Andrea tomaron fotos. ¿Quién quemó discos compactos?
B: Teresa y yo quemamos discos compactos. ¿Quién buscó los libros en la biblioteca?
A: Nadie. ¿Quién navegó por Internet?
B: Juan y Cristina navegaron por Internet. ¿Quién mandó correos electrónicos?
A: Roberto mandó correos electrónicos. ¿Quién compró un ratón nuevo?
B: Nadie. ¿Quién mandó las fotos?
A: Rita mandó las fotos.

Answer:
Buscar libros en la biblioteca y comprar un ratón nuevo.

El proyecto

Estudiante A

You and your partner are in charge of a class project and you want to make sure that all your team members have completed their tasks. Ask your partner who did the tasks listed below. Answer your partner's questions based on the images. Take turns doing this activity.

- Use instant messaging
- Burn compact discs
- Surf the Internet
- Buy a new mouse

Estudiante A: **¿Quién habló con el profesor?**
Estudiante B: **... habló con el profesor./ Nadie.**

Which tasks have not yet been completed?

Luisa y Andrea

Rita

Roberto

El proyecto

Estudiante B

You and your partner are in charge of a class project and you want to make sure that all your team members have completed their tasks. Ask your partner who did the tasks listed below. Answer your partner's questions based on the images. Take turns doing this activity.

- Take photos
- Send photos
- Look for books in the library
- Send e-mails

Estudiante A: **¿Quién habló con el profesor?**
Estudiante B: **... habló con el professor./ Nadie.**

Which tasks have not yet been completed?

Juan y Cristina

Marcelo

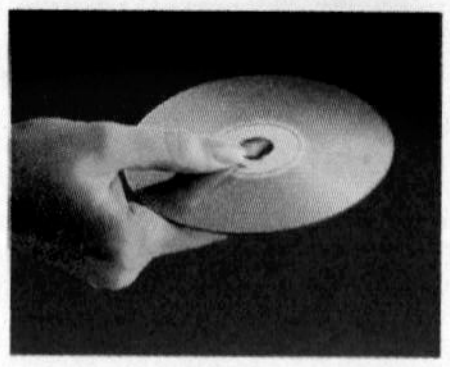
Teresa y yo

Differentiating Instruction – Lección 1

Pre-AP
Summarize After students have completed the activity, have them write a paragraph summarizing their findings. They should include the tasks that were completed, mention who completed them, and also identify which ones need to still be done. Have them use the preterite as needed in their paragraphs.

Multiple Intelligences
Linguistic Verbal After students complete the activity, have them work in pairs to see if they can repeat who did what, starting with Marcelo, and adding a subject each round. For example: Student 1: Marcelo usó el mensajero instantáneo. Student 2: Marcelo usó el mensajero instantáneo. Luisa y Ana tomaron fotos., etc. Call on volunteers to repeat the entire list to the class.

Entre dos • Lección 2

El fin de semana pasado

Estudiante A

You and your partner are talking about what you did last weekend. Take turns asking and telling each other where you went and whether it was fun or boring.

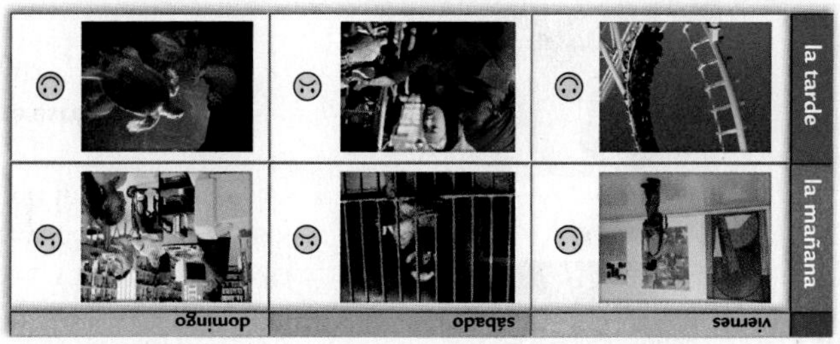

Estudiante A: **¿Adónde fuiste el viernes pasado?**
Estudiante B: **Por la mañana, ... y por la tarde...**
Estudiante A: **¿Cómo fue?**
Estudiante B: **... divertido(a)/aburrido(a). Y tú, ¿qué hiciste?**

What did you both enjoy doing?

El fin de semana pasado

Estudiante B

You and your partner are talking about what you did last weekend. Take turns asking and telling each other where you went and whether it was fun or boring.

Estudiante A: **¿Adónde fuiste el viernes pasado?**
Estudiante B: **Por la mañana, ... y por la tarde...**
Estudiante A: **¿Cómo fue?**
Estudiante B: **... divertido(a)/aburrido(a). Y tú, ¿qué hiciste?**

What did you both enjoy doing?

Objectives
- Say where you went, how it was, and what you did
- Preterite if **ir, ser,** and **hacer**

Core Resources
- Conversation cards, Teacher One Stop

STANDARDS
1.1 Engage in conversation

UNIT 7

Possible Answer
A: ¿Adónde fuiste el viernes pasado?
B: Por la mañana, fui al parque y por la tarde fui a los autitos chocadores.
A: ¿Cómo fue?
B: El parque fue aburrido pero los autitos chocadores fueron divertidos. Y tú, ¿qué hiciste?
A: Por la mañana, fui al museo y por la tarde fui al parque de diversiones.
B: ¿Cómo fue?
A: El museo y el parque de diversiones fueron divertidos.
B: ¿Adónde fuiste el sábado pasado?
A: Por la mañana, fui al zoológico y por la tarde fui al centro comercial.
B: ¿Cómo fue?
A: El zoológico y el centro comercial fueron aburridos. Y tú, ¿qué hiciste?
B: Por la mañana, fui al parque de diversiones y por la tarde fui a la feria del libro.
A: ¿Cómo fue?
B: El parque de diversiones fue divertido pero la feria del libro fue aburrida.
A: ¿Adónde fuiste el domingo pasado?
B: Por la mañana, fui al restaurante y por la tarde fui a un concierto.
A: ¿Cómo fue?
B: El restaurante fue divertido pero el concierto fue aburrido. Y tú, ¿qué hiciste?
A: Por la mañana, fui a la biblioteca y por la tarde fui al acuario.
B: ¿Cómo fue?
A: La biblioteca fue aburrida pero el acuario fue divertido.

Answer:
Going to the amusement park

Differentiating Instruction – Lección 2

Inclusion
Frequent Review/Repetition Before students begin the activity, review the preterite forms of the verbs **ir, ser,** and **hacer.** Have students also think of some adjectives they could use to give opinions about certain activities. Have them use these notes to complete the activity.

Slower-pace Learners
Yes-No Questions Preview the activity by writing all the places students could go on the board. Have them use the cues to answer simple yes-no questions as a warm-up. For example: ¿Fuiste al (a la) _____? ¿Fue divertido?

Objectives
- Talk about your daily routine while on vacation
- Present progressive
- Reflexive verbs

Core Resources
- Conversation cards, Teacher One Stop

STANDARDS
1.1 Engage in conversation

Possible Answer

A: ¿Qué está haciendo el Sr. Costas?
B: Está afeitándose.
A: ¿Qué está haciendo Cris?
B: Se está lavando la cara.
A: ¿Qué está haciendo la Sra. Vásquez?
B: Está bañándose.
A: ¿Qué está haciendo Rafael?
B: Se está vistiendo.
A: ¿Qué está haciendo Rita?
B: Está despertándose.
A: ¿Qué está haciendo Elena?
B: Está durmiendo.
B: ¿Qué está haciendo Rosa?
A: Está maquillándose.
B: ¿Qué está haciendo Sofía?
A: Se está peinando.
B: ¿Qué está haciendo Mateo?
A: Está levantándose.
B: ¿Qué está haciendo Sergio?
A: Está duchándose.
B: ¿Qué está haciendo Isabel?
A: Está secándose el pelo.
B: ¿Qué está haciendo Diego?
A: Se está cepillando los dientes.

Answer:
Rafael or Sofía

Entre dos • Lección 1

¡Date prisa!

Estudiante A

Your class is leaving for a trip to Spain today. You and your partner are trying to make sure that everyone gets to the airport on time. Ask your partner what the following people are doing: el Sr. Costas, Cris, la Sra. Vásquez, Rafael, Rita, and Elena. Then, answer your partner's questions about what the people in the images below are doing.

Estudiante A: **¿Qué está haciendo...?**
Estudiante B: **Está...**

Rosa · Sofía · Mateo · Sergio · Isabel · Diego

Who is almost ready to leave?

¡Date prisa!

Estudiante B

Your class is leaving today for a trip to Spain. You and your partner are trying to make sure that everyone gets to the airport on time. Answer your partner's questions about what the people in the images are doing. Then, ask your partner what these people are doing: Rosa, Sofía, Mateo, Sergio, Isabel, and Diego.

Estudiante A: **¿Qué está haciendo...?**
Estudiante B: **Está...**

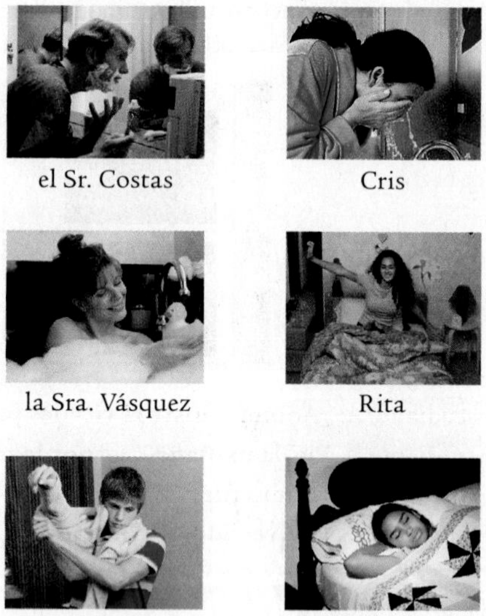

el Sr. Costas · Cris · la Sra. Vásquez · Rita · Rafael · Elena

Who is almost ready to leave?

Differentiating Instruction – Lección 1

Heritage Learners

Support What They Know Ask heritage students to work together to describe their daily routine in the morning and in the evening. Encourage them to add details, such as at what time they do certain things, what takes them longer, etc. Between them, who gets ready for school faster? Who stays up later? Ask volunteers to share their schedule with the class.

Multiple Intelligences

Kinesthetic Learners When students ask what each person is doing, have partners act out their response instead of answering orally. Students should confirm that they understood the action correctly by stating the Spanish term for the action. Partners will confirm their guesses to be correct or incorrect.

De vacaciones

Estudiante A

You and your partner are organizing a summer camp and are trying to decide what activities to include. Ask your partner what the teens on your list would like to do. Answer your partner's questions based on the images. Take turns doing the activity.

Estudiante A: **¿Qué le gustaría hacer a Miguel?**

Estudiante B: **A Miguel le gustaría...**

Miguel	*Pablo*
Susana	*Jorge*
María	*Carlos*

Gabi

Ana

Rosa

Juan

Paloma

Raquel

What are the two activities that more than one person would like?

De vacaciones

Estudiante B

You and your partner are organizing a summer camp and are trying to decide what activities to include. Ask your partner what the teens on your list would like to do. Answer your partner's questions based on the images. Take turns doing the activity.

Estudiante A: **¿Qué le gustaría hacer a Miguel?**

Estudiante B: **A Miguel le gustaría...**

Gabi	*Ana*
Rosa	*Juan*
Paloma	*Raquel*

Miguel

Pablo

Susana

Jorge

Maria

Carlos

What are the two activities that more than one person would like?

UNIT 8

Objectives
- Talk about vacation activities

Core Resources
- Conversation cards, Teacher One Stop

STANDARDS
1.1 Engage in conversation

Possible Answer

A: ¿Qué le gustaría hacer a Miguel?

B: A Miguel le gustaría hacer surfing. ¿Qué le gustaría hacer a Gabi?

A: A Gabi le gustaría nadar. ¿Qué le gustaría hacer a Pablo?

B: A Pablo le gustaría montar a caballo. ¿Qué le gustaría hacer a Ana?

A: A Ana le gustaría dar una caminata. ¿Qué le gustaría hacer a Susana?

B: A Susana le gustaría hacer surf de vela. ¿Qué le gustaría hacer a Rosa?

A: A Rosa le gustaría montar en bicicleta. ¿Qué le gustaría hacer a Jorge?

B: A Jorge le gustaría jugar al voleibol. ¿Qué le gustaría hacer a Juan?

A: A Juan le gustaría patinar en línea. ¿Qué le gustaría hacer a María?

B: A María le gustaría montar en bicicleta. ¿Qué le gustaría hacer a Paloma?

A: A Paloma le gustaría acampar. ¿Qué le gustaría hacer a Carlos?

B: A Carlos le gustaría comer al aire libre. ¿Qué le gustaría hacer a Raquel?

A: A Raquel le gustaría montar a caballo.

Answer:
Cycling and horseback riding

Differentiating Instruction – Lección 2

Multiple Intelligences

Linguistic-Verbal Student should take the activities on this page and create a TV or radio commercial advertising a summer camp that features these activities. Students should provide details about the activities and persuade their viewers or listeners that this camp is special. Ask them to present their commercials to the class.

Pre-AP

Support with Details When students share what the campers enjoy doing, they should provide details in their responses. Why do they like the activity? When do they do the activity? They could also expand by telling whether or not they personally like the same activities the campers like.

Recursos

R1

Unidad 1 Expansión de vocabulario

Lección 1
¿Qué te gusta hacer?

Talk About Activities

cuidar niños	to baby-sit
pintar	to paint
la reunión	meeting
el club	club
manejar	to drive
trabajar a tiempo parcial	to work part-time
trabajar de voluntario	to volunteer
tocar un instrumento	to play an instrument
Instruments	
el piano	piano
el clarinete	clarinet
la flauta	flute
el saxofón	saxophone
el tambor	drum
la trompeta	trumpet
la viola	viola
el violín	violin

Snack Foods and Beverages

la merienda	snack
las papitas	chips
las galletas saladas	crackers
las galletitas	cookies
el chicle	chewing gum
los dulces	candy
la limonada	lemonade

Lección 2
Mis amigos y yo

Describe Yourself and Others

Personality	
listo(a)	clever / smart
callado(a)	quiet
extrovertido(a)	outgoing
tímido(a)	shy
sincero(a)	sincere
tonto(a)	silly
travieso(a)	mischievous
paciente	patient
talentoso(a)	talented
creativo(a)	creative
ambicioso(a)	ambitious
Appearance	
el pelo oscuro	dark hair
el pelo rizado	curly hair
el pelo lacio	straight hair
calvo(a)	bald
los frenillos	braces

People

el (la) policía	police officer
el actor	actor
la actriz	actress
el (la) compañero(a) de clase	classmate
el (la) bombero(a)	firefighter
el (la) secretario(a)	secretary
el jefe, la jefa	boss

Unidad 2 Expansión de vocabulario

Lección 1
Somos estudiantes

Tell Time and Discuss Daily Schedules

la medianoche	midnight
el mediodía	noon

Describing Classes

School Subjects	
la asignatura	school subject
la educación física	physical education
las ciencias sociales	social studies
la geometría	geometry
la geografía	geography
el álgebra	algebra
la lengua, el idioma	language
la literatura	literature
la biología	biology
la química	chemistry
la banda	band
el coro	choir
la orquesta	orchestra
la hora de estudio	study hall
In School	
la asamblea	assembly
el recreo	recess, break
Classroom Activities	
preguntar	to ask
la respuesta	answer
la prueba	test, quiz

Describe Frequency

cada	each
a veces	sometimes
¿Con qué frecuencia...?	How often. . . ?
rara vez	rarely

Other Words and Phrases

terminar	to finish
esperar	to wait (for)
mientras	while
otra vez	again

Lección 2
En la escuela

Describe Classroom Objects

la carpeta	folder
las tijeras	scissors
la regla	ruler
el diccionario	dictionary
la impresora	printer
la bandera	flag
el globo	globe

Places in School

la sala de clase	classroom
el casillero	locker
el auditorio	auditorium

Say Where Things Are Located

entre	between
fuera (de)	out / outside (of)
(a la) derecha (de)	(to the) right (of)
(a la) izquierda (de)	(to the) left (of)
aquí	here
allí	there
enfrente (de)	across from, facing

Talk About How You Feel

feliz, alegre	happy
preocupado(a)	worried
listo(a)	ready
Estoy de acuerdo.	I agree.

Other Words and Phrases

mismo(a)	same
según	according to
creer	to think, to believe
especialmente	especially
olvidar	to forget
sobre	about
además	besides, further
suficiente, bastante	enough
sin	without

Unidad 3

Expansión de vocabulario

Lección 1
Mi comida favorita

Talk About Foods and Beverages

For Breakfast	
desayunar	to have breakfast
la mantequilla	butter
la miel	honey
el pan tostado	toast
el batido	milkshake, smoothie
For Lunch	
la bolsa	bag
la mantequilla de cacahuate	peanut butter
la jalea	jelly
el atún	tuna
la ensalada	salad
Fruit	
el plátano	banana; plantain
la toronja	grapefruit
la piña	pineapple
el durazno	peach
el limón	lemon
la sandía	watermelon

Lección 2
En mi familia

Talk About Family

el esposo	husband
la esposa	wife
la hermanastra	stepsister
el hermanastro	stepbrother
la media hermana	half-sister
el medio hermano	half-brother
el nieto	grandson
la nieta	granddaughter
el sobrino	nephew
la sobrina	niece
el (la) bebé	baby

Pets

el pájaro	bird
el pez (*pl.* los peces)	fish
el conejo	rabbit
el lagarto	lizard
la rana	frog
el hámster	hamster

Unidad 4 Expansión de vocabulario

Lección 1
¡Vamos de compras!

Describe Clothing

las botas	boots
el impermeable	raincoat
la falda	skirt
el suéter	sweater
la sudadera (con capucha)	(hooded) sweatshirt
los pantalones deportivos	sweatpants
el abrigo	coat
los zapatos de tenis	tennis shoes, sneakers
el pijama	pajamas
las sandalias	sandals
la gorra	baseball cap
las gafas de sol	sunglasses
los guantes	gloves
la bufanda	scarf
el paraguas	umbrella
la bolsa	bag, purse
Colors	
morado(a)	purple
rosado(a)	pink
gris	gray

Discuss Seasons

el norte	north
el sur	south
el este	east
el oeste	west

Lección 2
¿Qué hacemos esta noche?

Describe Places In Town

la iglesia	church
el edificio	building
el centro de videojuegos	arcade
la piscina	pool
la acera	sidewalk
el correo	post office
la librería	bookstore
la zapatería	shoe store
el templo	temple
la tienda de discos	music store
Music	
el rap	rap
alternativa	alternative
la música electrónica	electronic music, techno
la canción	song
la letra	lyrics

In a Restaurant

la cuchara	spoon
el cuchillo	knife
el tenedor	fork
el vaso	glass
la servilleta	napkin
el tazón	bowl
la taza	cup
For Dinner	
el puerco	pork
el pavo	turkey
los fideos	noodles
la salsa	sauce
la pimienta	pepper
la sal	salt
los mariscos	seafood
Vegetables	
la zanahoria	carrot
la lechuga	lettuce
el maíz	corn

Unidad 5

Expansión de vocabulario

Lección 1
Vivimos aquí

Describe A House

el garaje	garage
la pared	wall
el traspatio	back yard
antiguo(a)	old, ancient
la cerca	fence

Describe Household Items

el congelador	freezer
la estufa	stove
el refrigerador	refrigerator
el lavaplatos	dishwasher
el microondas	microwave
la videograbadora	VCR
el teléfono celular	cellular phone
los audífonos	headphones

Lección 2
Una fiesta en casa

Plan a Party

sorprender	to surprise
el aniversario	anniversary
el confeti	confetti
la celebración	celebration
el día festivo	holiday
el ponche	punch
los juegos	games
los premios	prizes

Holidays/Celebrations

el bautizo	baptism
la graduación	graduation
la Navidad	Christmas
la Nochebuena	Christmas Eve
la Pascua Florida	Easter
el Ramadán	Ramadan
Rosh Hashaná	Rosh Hashanah
la Jánuca	Hanukkah
la Nochevieja	New Year's Eve
el día de Año Nuevo	New Year's Day
la confirmación	confirmation
el bar / bat mitzvá	bar / bat mitzvah

Talk About Gifts

la tarjeta de cumpleaños	birthday card
la tarjeta de regalo	gift card
el certificado de regalo	gift certificate

Talk About Chores and Responsibilities

quitar la mesa	to clear the table
el estipendio	allowance

Unidad 6 Expansión de vocabulario

Lección 1
¿Cuál es tu deporte favorito?

Sports	
esquiar	to ski
hacer snowboard	to snowboard
el gol	goal
el hockey	hockey
el golf	golf
la gimnasia	gymnastics
el jonrón	homerun
los deportes de pista y campo	track and field
correr a campo traviesa	to run cross country
el (la) porrista	cheerleader
la carrera	race
las artes marciales	martial arts
caerse	to fall
saltar	to jump
hacer trucos	to do tricks
Locations and People	
la pista	track
el (la) entrenador(a)	coach
el (la) capitán del equipo	team captain
el árbitro	referee, umpire

Lección 2
La salud

Talking About Staying Healthy	
el (la) doctor(a)	doctor
el (la) paciente	patient
el consultorio	doctor's office
tener una cita	to have an appointment
la alergia	allergy
la gripe	flu
el resfriado	cold
estornudar	to sneeze
toser	to cough
la medicina	medicine
Parts of the Body	
el dedo	finger
el dedo de pie	toe
el cuello	neck
la espalda	back
la garganta	throat
el hombro	shoulder
el oído	inner ear
la muñeca	wrist
Outdoor activities	
las máquinas para hacer ejercicio	exercise machines
remar	to row
hacer aeróbicos	to do aerobics
The Beach	
la arena	sand
el traje de baño	bathing suit
el tiburón	shark
el delfín	dolphin
la toalla	towel
las olas	waves
el (la) salvavidas	lifeguard

Unidad 7 Expansión de vocabulario

Lección 1
En el cibercafé

Talk About Technology

el apodo	screen name
la contraseña	password
cortar y pegar	to cut and paste
borrar	to delete
el archivo adjunto	attachment
la sonrisa, la carita feliz (emoticono)	smiley face (emoticon)
escribir a máquina	to type
charlar en línea	to chat
la cadena de e-mail	e-mail chain (forward)
arroba	@ (at)
punto com	.com (dot com)
el enlace	link
el blog	blog
bajar música	to download music
el tocador de mp3 (eme pe tres)	mp3 player
comenzar / terminar la sesión	to log on / to log off

Lección 2
Un día en el parque de diversiones

At the Amusement Park

el carrusel	carousel
el tobogán acuático	water slide
el espectáculo	show

Places of Interest

At the Aquarium	
la ballena	whale
el pez (pl. los peces)	fish
la tortuga	turtle
la foca	seal
At the Fair	
los juegos mecánicos	rides
el algodón de azúcar	cotton candy
los animales de peluche	stuffed animals
At the Zoo	
el león	lion
el tigre	tiger
el oso	bear
el canguro	kangaroo
el pingüino	penguin
el mono	monkey
el hipopótamo	hippopotamus
la jirafa	giraffe
la jaula	cage

Extend Invitations

Decline	
¿Quizás otra vez?	Maybe another time?

Make a Phone Call

¿De parte de quién?	Who's calling?
¿Puedo tomar un mensaje?	Can I take a message?
Puedo llamar más tarde.	I can call back later.

Unidad 8 Expansión de vocabulario

Lección 1
Pensando en las vacaciones

Talk About a Daily Routine

el despertador	alarm clock
rizarse el pelo	to curl one's hair
alisarse el pelo	to straighten one's hair
Talk About Grooming	
el desodorante	deodorant
la seda dental	dental floss
el acondicionador	conditioner
la loción	lotion
el gel	hair gel
el lápiz labial	lipstick
el rímel	mascara
la sombra de ojos	eye shadow
el perfume	perfume
la colonia	cologne

Discussing a Vacation

el lago	lake
el río	river
hacer / tener una reservación	to make / have a reservation
el aeropuerto	airport

Lección 2
¡Vamos de vacaciones!

Talk About Vacation Activities

la tienda de campaña	tent
la cabaña	cabin
ver las atracciones	to go sightseeing
pescar	to go fishing
mandar tarjetas postales	to send postcards
el (la) turista	tourist

Talk About Shopping

el dinero en efectivo	cash
la tarjeta de crédito	credit card
probarse la ropa	to try on clothing
el probador	fitting room
el recibo	receipt
la moneda	coin
la talla	(clothing) size
la vitrina	store window
gastar	to spend
la caja	cash register
la billetera	wallet
el cajero automático	automatic teller machine
Jewelry and Handicrafts	
la pulsera	bracelet
la joyería	jewelry store
brillante	shiny
el diamante	diamond
Bargaining	
¿Tiene otros(as)?	Do you have others?

Para y piensa
Self-Check Answers

Lección preliminar

p. 5
1. Buenos días.
2. ¿Cómo estás?

Answers may vary but can include:
3. Adiós, hasta mañana, hasta luego.

p. 9
1. c.
2. a.
3. b.

p. 11
1. See p. 10

p. 15
1. b.
2. a.
3. c.

p. 17
1. seis - dos - cinco - uno - cuatro - dos - cero - nueve
2. tres - siete - cero - ocho - nueve - dos - seis - tres
3. cuatro - uno - ocho - cinco - dos - siete - seis - cero

p. 19
1. lunes
2. mañana

p. 21
1. b.
2. a.
3. c.

p. 24
1. ¿Cómo se dice *please*?
2. ¿Comprendes?

Unidad 1 Estados Unidos

Lección 1

p. 34 Práctica de vocabulario
1. escuchar música
2. hacer la tarea

p. 36 Vocabulario en contexto
1. jugar
2. música
3. comer

p. 39 Práctica de gramática
1. Cristóbal y yo somos de Honduras.
2. Tomás es de la República Dominicana.
3. Yo soy de México.

p. 41 Gramática en contexto
1. El Sr. Costas es de la Florida.
2. Alicia es de Miami.
3. Teresa y Miguel son de Honduras y Cuba.

p. 44 Práctica de gramática
1. Le gusta
2. Te gusta
3. Nos gusta

p. 47 Todo junto
1. Teresa es de Honduras. Le gusta tocar la guitarra.
2. Alicia es de Miami. Le gusta comer.
3. Miguel es de Cuba. Le gusta mirar la televisión.

Lección 2

p. 58 Práctica de vocabulario
1. Juan es bajo.
2. David es artístico.
3. Carlos es serio.

p. 60 Vocabulario en contexto
1. perezoso
2. atlético
3. estudioso

p. 63 Práctica de gramática
1. la televisión
2. unas frutas
3. el libro
4. unos hombres

p. 65 Gramática en contexto
1. Ricardo es un amigo de Alberto.
2. Marta y Carla son unas chicas de una clase de español.
3. Ana es una chica muy inteligente.

p. 68 Práctica de gramática
1. una estudiante desorganizada
2. unos chicos simpáticos
3. unas mujeres trabajadoras
4. un hombre grande

p. 71 Todo junto
1. Alberto es un chico simpático.
2. Ricardo es un estudiante trabajado
3. Sandra es una persona organizada.

Unidad 2 México

Lección 1

p. 88 Práctica de vocabulario

1. Me gusta dibujar en la clase de arte.
2. Hay veintitrés chicos en la clase de matemáticas.

p. 90 Vocabulario en contexto

1. a las diez y cuarto (a las diez y quince)
2. las ocho y veinte
3. a las siete

p. 93 Práctica de gramática

1. Juan nunca tiene que preparar la comida.
2. Tenemos la clase de inglés todos los días.
3. Siempre tengo que usar la computadora.

p. 95 Gramática en contexto

1. tienen
2. tiene que
3. tienen

p. 98 Práctica de gramática

1. usamos
2. preparo
3. dibujan
4. Necesitas

p. 101 Todo junto

1. toma
2. practicar
3. estudian

Lección 2

p. 112 Práctica de vocabulario

Answers may vary but can include:

1. el baño, el gimnasio, la cafetería, la biblioteca, etc.
2. el mapa, el escritorio, la silla, el reloj, etc.

p. 114 Vocabulario en contexto

1. la biblioteca
2. el gimnasio
3. la biblioteca

p. 117 Práctica de gramática

1. Estoy cerca de las ventanas.
2. Pablo, ¿estás nervioso?

p. 119 Gramática en contexto

Answers may vary but can include:

1. Pablo y Claudia están en la biblioteca.
2. Pablo está nervioso.
3. Pablo tiene que estar en el gimnasio a las cinco.

p. 122 Práctica de gramática

1. Teresa va a la cafetería.
2. Los estudiantes van a la oficina del director.
3. Nosotros vamos al gimnasio.
4. Yo voy a la clase de matemáticas.

p. 125 Todo junto

1. está; va a
2. están; van a
3. está; va a

Unidad 3 Puerto Rico

Lección 1

p. 142 Práctica de vocabulario

Answers may vary but can include:

1. los huevos, el cereal, el yogur, la fruta
2. el sándwich, la sopa, la hamburguesa

p. 144 Vocabulario en contexto

1. Quiénes
2. Cuándo
3. Por qué

p. 147 Práctica de gramática

1. Me gustan los huevos para el desayuno.
2. A José le gusta la pizza con jamón.
3. ¿Por qué no te gusta la fruta?

p. 149 Gramática en contexto

1. gusta
2. gusta
3. gustan

p. 152 Práctica de gramática

1. hacen; comen
2. haces; leo
3. hace; bebe

p. 155 Todo junto

1. gusta; come
2. gustan; comparten

Lección 2

p. 166 Práctica de vocabulario

1. hijo
2. padres
3. hermanas

p. 168 Vocabulario en contexto

1. Marisol tiene catorce años.
2. El gato de la familia Vélez tiene ocho años.
3. Los padres de Marisol tienen cincuenta y dos años.

p. 171 Práctica de gramática

1. mi; el seis de septiembre
2. nuestro; el veinticinco de enero.
3. su; el diecisiete de abril.

p. 173 Gramática en contexto

1. El cumpleaños de Camila es el doce de junio.
2. El cumpleaños de Éster es el primero de octubre.
3. El cumpleaños de Tito es el veintiocho de marzo.
4. El cumpleaños de Celia es el diecisiete de enero.

p. 176 Práctica de gramática

1. Mi hermano es más alto que mi padre.
2. Me gustan las manzanas tanto como las bananas.
3. La clase de matemáticas es mejor que la clase de arte.

p. 179 Todo junto

1. Sus perros son tan grandes como Marisol.
2. Su primo es menor que él.
3. Sus perros son más perezosos que los gatos.

Unidad 4 España

Lección 1

p. 196 Práctica de vocabulario

1. ¿Cuánto cuestan los calcetines blancos?
2. ¿Cuánto cuesta el vestido azul?
3. ¿Cuánto cuesta la chaqueta anaranjada?
4. ¿Cuánto cuestan los pantalones cortos rojos?

p. 198 Vocabulario en contexto

1. tiene frío
2. tiene calor
3. tiene frío

p. 201 Práctica de gramática

1. pienso
2. empieza
3. cierra

p. 203 Gramática en contexto

1. entiende
2. prefiere
3. quiere

p. 206 Práctica de gramática

1. los
2. La
3. Las

p. 209 Todo junto

1. Sí, Enrique la necesita.
2. Sí, Enrique lo prefiere.
3. Sí, Enrique la quiere comprar. (Sí, Enrique quiere comprarla.)

Lección 2

p. 220 Práctica de vocabulario

Answers may vary but can include:

1. El menú, el (la) camarero(a), la cuenta, los platos principales, etc.
2. El teatro, el parque, el cine, etc.

p. 222 Vocabulario en contexto

1. en autobús
2. a pie
3. en coche

p. 225 Práctica de gramática

1. cuesta
2. almorzamos
3. duermo
4. pueden

p. 227 Gramática en contexto

1. puede
2. encuentra
3. vuelve

p. 230 Práctica de gramática

1. sirven
2. sirve
3. pedimos

p. 233 Todo junto

1. almuerzan
2. pide
3. puede

Unidad 5 Ecuador

Lección 1

p. 250 Práctica de vocabulario

Answers may vary but can include:

1. el sillón, el sofá, el televisor, la alfombra
2. la cama, el armario, la lámpara, la cómoda

p. 252 Vocabulario en contexto

Answers may vary but can include:

1. el disco compacto, el tocadiscos compactos, el radio
2. la lámpara, el sillón
3. el sofá, el televisor

p. 255 Práctica de gramática

1. estamos
2. estoy
3. es
4. son

p. 257 Gramática en contexto

1. es
2. están
3. está

p. 260 Práctica de gramática

1. Estoy en el sexto piso.
2. Estoy en el noveno piso.
3. Estoy en el segundo piso.
4. Estoy en el tercer piso.

p. 263 Todo junto

1. es; está
2. séptimo

Lección 2

p. 274 Práctica de vocabulario

Answers may vary but can include:

Cocinar, poner la mesa, decorar, limpiar la cocina

p. 276 Vocabulario en contexto

1. la basura
2. el césped
3. la aspiradora

p. 279 Práctica de gramática

1. pongo
2. dice
3. traigo

p. 281 Gramática en contexto

1. dice; viene
2. trae

p. 284 Práctica de gramática

1. Decora la sala. Acabo de decorarla. (La acabo de decorar.)
2. Haz los quehaceres. Acabo de hacerlos. (Los acabo de hacer.)
3. Corta el césped. Acabo de cortarlo. (Lo acabo de cortar.)

p. 287 Todo junto

Answers may vary but can include:

Pasa la aspiradora. Lava los platos. Limpia la cocina.

Unidad 6 República Dominicana

Lección 1

p. 304 Práctica de vocabulario
1. una cancha, una bola
2. un campo, un bate, un guante, un casco, una pelota
3. una cancha, una pelota, una raqueta

p. 306 Vocabulario en contexto
1. la ganadora
2. la natación
3. un casco

p. 309 Práctica de gramática
1. Ana y yo jugamos al béisbol.
2. Ustedes juegan al básquetbol.
3. El hermano de Rosa juega al voleibol.
4. Yo juego al tenis.

p. 311 Gramática en contexto
1. juega
2. juegan
3. jugar

p. 314 Práctica de gramática
1. Saben
2. conozco a
3. sabemos

p. 317 Todo junto
sabe; conocen; saben

Lección 2

p. 328 Práctica de vocabulario
Answers may vary but can include:
1. la boca, la nariz, los ojos, las orejas
2. el tobillo, el pie, la rodilla

p. 330 Vocabulario en contexto
1. le duele
2. le duelen

p. 333 Práctica de gramática
1. buceamos
2. tomaste
3. levantaron

p. 335 Gramática en contexto
1. Isabel y Mario llevaron cascos.
2. Mario no montó en bicicleta muy bien.
3. El señor de las frutas caminó delante de Mario.

p. 338 Práctica de gramática
1. llegué
2. jugaron
3. comenzó
4. practiqué

p. 341 Todo junto
1. comenzó
2. encontraron

Unidad 7 Argentina

Lección 1

p. 358 Práctica de vocabulario
Answers may vary but can include:
1. la pantalla, el ratón, el teclado
2. usar el mensajero instantáneo, navegar por Internet, mandar fotos, buscar un sitio Web

p. 360 Vocabulario en contexto
1. Primero, Trini llega a San Antonio.
2. Luego, Trini está en Puebla, México.
3. Más tarde, Trini va a Puerto Rico y a España.
4. Por fin, Trini está en Buenos Aires.

p. 363 Práctica de gramática
1. comí
2. Recibiste

p. 365 Gramática en contexto
1. recibió
2. compartieron
3. salieron

p. 368 Práctica de gramática
1. Nunca recibo ningún correo electrónico.
2. Alguien escribe algo con el mensajero instantáneo.
3. A Beatriz no le gusta ni navegar por Internet ni estar en línea.

p. 371 Todo junto
1. No, Mariano no perdió nada.
2. No, Florencia no recibió ni la fecha ni la hora.
3. No, Mariano no le escribió ningún correo electrónico a Alicia.

Lección 2

p. 382 Práctica de vocabulario
Answers may vary but can include:
1. la vuelta al mundo, la montaña rusa, los autitos chocadores
2. el zoológico, el museo, el acuario, el parque de diversiones

p. 384 Vocabulario en contexto
1. ¡Qué divertido!
2. ¡Qué pequeña!
3. ¡Qué interesante!
4. ¡Qué grandes!

p. 387 Práctica de gramática
1. hicimos; fue (ser)
2. fui (ir); Hice
3. Fueron (ir); hicieron

p. 389 Gramática en contexto
1. ¿Adónde fueron Florencia, Luciana y tú?
2. ¿Qué hiciste?
3. ¿Cómo fue el día?

p. 392 Práctica de gramática
1. nosotros
2. ti
3. ellos

p. 395 Todo junto
1. Florencia hizo una cena para él.
2. Las empanadas fueron para ellos.
3. Mariano fue con ella a los autitos chocadores.

Unidad 8 Costa Rica

Lección 1

p. 412 Práctica de vocabulario

Answers may vary but can include:

1. levantarse, lavarse la cara, maquillarse, lavarse el pelo, secarse el pelo, ducharse, afeitarse, cepillarse los dientes, vestirse
2. en barco, en tren, en avión

p. 414 Vocabulario en contexto

1. unas vacaciones
2. la ciudad
3. un hotel

p. 417 Práctica de gramática

1. Yo me lavo las manos.
2. Los chicos secan al perro.
3. Juana y yo ponemos la mesa.
4. Mi abuelo se afeita la cara.

p. 419 Gramática en contexto

1. acostarse
2. se levanta

p. 422 Práctica de gramática

1. me estoy duchando (estoy duchándome)
2. estás durmiendo
3. nos estamos vistiendo (estamos vistiéndonos)

p. 425 Todo junto

1. Jorge se está peinando. (Jorge está peinándose.)
2. Susana se está maquillando. (Susana está maquillándose.)
3. Los hermanos se están cepillando los dientes. (Los hermanos están cepillándose los dientes.)
4. Jorge se está poniendo la chaqueta. (Jorge está poniéndose la chaqueta.)

Lección 2

p. 436 Práctica de vocabulario

1. ¿Me deja ver los aretes?
2. ¿Me deja ver el collar de plata?
3. ¿Me deja ver el anillo de oro?
4. ¿Me deja ver las artesanías de madera?

p. 438 Vocabulario en contexto

1. barato
2. los aretes
3. el mercado

p. 441 Práctica de gramática

1. les
2. te
3. nos

p. 443 Gramática en contexto

1. le
2. les
3. le

p. 446 Práctica de gramática

1. Aquellos
2. Este
3. esas

p. 449 Todo junto

1. le; esa
2. les; estos

Resumen de gramática

Nouns, Articles, and Pronouns

Nouns

Nouns identify people, animals, places, and things. All Spanish nouns, even if they refer to objects, are either **masculine** or **feminine.** They are also either **singular** or **plural.**
Nouns ending in **-o** are usually masculine; nouns ending in **-a** are usually feminine.

To form the **plural** of a noun, add **-s** if the noun ends in a vowel; add **-es** if it ends in a consonant.

Singular Nouns

Masculine	Feminine
abuelo	abuela
chico	chica
hombre	mujer
papel	pluma
zapato	blusa

Plural Nouns

Masculine	Feminine
abuelo**s**	abuela**s**
chico**s**	chica**s**
hombre**s**	mujer**es**
papel**es**	pluma**s**
zapato**s**	blusa**s**

Articles

Articles identify the class of a noun: masculine or feminine, singular or plural. **Definite articles** are the equivalent of the English word *the.* **Indefinite articles** are the equivalent of *a, an,* or *some.*

Definite Articles

	Masculine	Feminine
Singular	**el** chico	**la** chica
Plural	**los** chicos	**las** chicas

Indefinite Articles

	Masculine	Feminine
Singular	**un** chico	**una** chica
Plural	**unos** chicos	**unas** chicas

Resumen de gramática

Pronouns

Pronouns take the place of nouns. The pronoun used is determined by its function or purpose in a sentence.

Subject Pronouns

yo	nosotros(as)
tú	vosotros(as)
usted	ustedes
él, ella	ellos(as)

Direct Object Pronouns

me	nos
te	os
lo, la	los, las

Indirect Object Pronouns

me	nos
te	os
le	les

Pronouns After Prepositions

mí	nosotros(as)
ti	vosotros(as)
usted	ustedes
él, ella	ellos(as)

Reflexive Pronouns

me	nos
te	os
se	se

Adjectives

Adjectives describe nouns. In Spanish, adjectives match the **gender** and **number** of the nouns they describe. To make an adjective plural, add **-s** if it ends in a vowel; add **-es** if it ends in a consonant. The adjective usually comes after the noun in Spanish.

Adjectives

	Masculine	Feminine
Singular	el chico alt**o**	la chica alt**a**
	el chico inteligente	la chica inteligente
	el chico joven	la chica joven
	el chico trabajador	la chica trabajador**a**
Plural	los chicos alto**s**	las chicas alta**s**
	los chicos inteligente**s**	las chicas inteligente**s**
	los chicos jóven**es**	las chicas jóven**es**
	los chicos trabajador**es**	las chicas trabajadora**s**

Adjectives (continued)

Sometimes adjectives are shortened when they are placed in front of a masculine singular noun.

Shortened Forms

alguno	**algún** chico
bueno	**buen** chico
malo	**mal** chico
ninguno	**ningún** chico
primero	**primer** chico
tercero	**tercer** chico

Possessive adjectives indicate who owns something or describe a relationship between people or things. They agree in number with the nouns they describe. **Nuestro(a)** and **vuestro(a)** must also agree in gender with the nouns they describe.

Possessive Adjectives

	Masculine		Feminine	
Singular	**mi** amigo	**nuestro** amigo	**mi** amiga	**nuestra** amiga
	tu amigo	**vuestro** amigo	**tu** amiga	**vuestra** amiga
	su amigo	**su** amigo	**su** amiga	**su** amiga
Plural	**mis** amigos	**nuestros** amigos	**mis** amigas	**nuestras** amigas
	tus amigos	**vuestros** amigos	**tus** amigas	**vuestras** amigas
	sus amigos	**sus** amigos	**sus** amigas	**sus** amigas

Demonstrative adjectives describe the location of a person or a thing in relation to the speaker. Their English equivalents are *this, that, these,* and *those*.

Demonstrative Adjectives

	Masculine	Feminine
Singular	**este** chico	**esta** chica
	ese chico	**esa** chica
	aquel chico	**aquella** chica
Plural	**estos** chicos	**estas** chicas
	esos chicos	**esas** chicas
	aquellos chicos	**aquellas** chicas

Comparatives

Comparatives are used to compare two people or things.

Comparatives

más (+)	**menos (–)**	**tan, tanto (=)**
más serio **que...**	**menos** serio **que...**	**tan** serio **como...**
Me gusta leer **más que** pasear.	Me gusta pasear **menos que** leer.	Me gusta hablar **tanto como** escuchar.

There are a few irregular comparative words. When talking about the age of people, use **mayor** and **menor.** When talking about qualities, use **mejor** and **peor.**

Age	Quality
mayor	mejor
menor	peor

Affirmative and Negative Words

Affirmative or **negative** words are used to talk about indefinite or negative situations.

Affirmative Words	Negative Words
algo	nada
alguien	nadie
algún/alguno(a)	ningún/ninguno(a)
o... o	ni... ni
siempre	nunca
también	tampoco

Verbs: Present Tense

Regular Verbs

Regular verbs ending in **-ar, -er,** or **-ir** always have regular endings in the present tense.

-ar Verbs

habl**o**	habl**amos**
habl**as**	habl**áis**
habl**a**	habl**an**

-er Verbs

vend**o**	vend**emos**
vend**es**	vend**éis**
vend**e**	vend**en**

-ir Verbs

compart**o**	compart**imos**
compart**es**	compart**ís**
compart**e**	compart**en**

RESUMEN DE GRAMÁTICA

Verbs with Irregular yo Forms

Some verbs have regular forms in the present tense except for the **yo** form.

conocer

cono**zco**	conocemos
conoces	conocéis
conoce	conocen

dar

d**oy**	damos
das	dais
da	dan

hacer

ha**go**	hacemos
haces	hacéis
hace	hacen

poner

pon**go**	ponemos
pones	ponéis
pone	ponen

saber

sé	sabemos
sabes	sabéis
sabe	saben

salir

sal**go**	salimos
sales	salís
sale	salen

traer

tra**igo**	traemos
traes	traéis
trae	traen

ver

v**eo**	vemos
ves	veis
ve	ven

Verbs: Present Tense (continued)

Stem-Changing Verbs

e → ie

qu**ie**ro	queremos
qu**ie**res	queréis
qu**ie**re	qu**ie**ren

Other **e → ie** stem-changing verbs are **cerrar, comenzar, despertarse, empezar, entender, pensar, perder,** and **preferir.**

o → ue

p**ue**do	podemos
p**ue**des	podéis
p**ue**de	p**ue**den

Other **o → ue** stem-changing verbs are **acostarse, almorzar, costar, doler, dormir, encontrar, envolver,** and **volver.**

e → i

s**i**rvo	servimos
s**i**rves	servís
s**i**rve	s**i**rven

Other **e → i** stem-changing verbs are **pedir** and **vestirse.**

u → ue

j**ue**go	jugamos
j**ue**gas	jugáis
j**ue**ga	j**ue**gan

Jugar is the only verb with a **u → ue** stem change.

Irregular Verbs

The following verbs are irregular in the present tense.

decir

digo	decimos
dices	decís
dice	dicen

estar

estoy	estamos
estás	estáis
está	están

ir

voy	vamos
vas	vais
va	van

ser

soy	somos
eres	sois
es	son

tener

tengo	tenemos
tienes	tenéis
tiene	tienen

venir

vengo	venimos
vienes	venís
viene	vienen

Verbs: Present Participles

Present participles are used with a form of **estar** to say that an action is in progress at this moment.

Regular Participles

-ar Verbs	-er Verbs	-ir Verbs
camin**ando**	hac**iendo**	abr**iendo**
habl**ando**	pon**iendo**	compart**iendo**
jug**ando**	vend**iendo**	sal**iendo**

Stem Changes

decir	d**i**ciendo
dormir	d**u**rmiendo
pedir	p**i**diendo
servir	s**i**rviendo
venir	v**i**niendo
vestir	v**i**stiendo

y Spelling Change

leer	le**y**endo
traer	tra**y**endo

Resumen de gramática

Verbs: Affirmative tú Commands

Affirmative tú commands are used to tell a friend or family member to do something. Regular affirmative **tú** commands are the same as the **él/ella forms** in the present tense.

Regular Affirmative tú Commands

-ar Verbs	-er Verbs	-ir Verbs
lava	barre	abre
cierra	entiende	duerme
almuerza	vuelve	pide

Irregular Affirmative tú Commands

Infinitive	Affirmative tú Command
decir	**di**
hacer	**haz**
ir	**ve**
poner	**pon**
salir	**sal**
ser	**sé**
tener	**ten**
venir	**ven**

Verbs: Preterite Tense

Regular Verbs

Regular preterite verbs ending in **-ar, -er,** or **-ir** have regular endings.

-ar Verbs

nad**é**	nad**amos**
nad**aste**	nad**asteis**
nad**ó**	nad**aron**

-er Verbs

vend**í**	vend**imos**
vend**iste**	vend**isteis**
vend**ió**	vend**ieron**

-ir Verbs

escrib**í**	escrib**imos**
escrib**iste**	escrib**isteis**
escrib**ió**	escrib**ieron**

Verbs with Spelling Changes

-car Verbs

bus**qu**é	buscamos
buscaste	buscasteis
buscó	buscaron

-gar Verbs

ju**gu**é	jugamos
jugaste	jugasteis
jugó	jugaron

-zar Verbs

almor**c**é	almorzamos
almorzaste	almorzasteis
almorzó	almorzaron

Note: The verb **leer** also has a spelling change in the preterite. You will learn about this in Level 2.

R22

Irregular Verbs

hacer

hice	hicimos
hiciste	hicisteis
hizo	hicieron

ir

fui	fuimos
fuiste	fuisteis
fue	fueron

ser

fui	fuimos
fuiste	fuisteis
fue	fueron

Note: The verbs **dormir, pedir, preferir,** and **servir** have a stem change in the preterite tense. The verbs **dar, decir, estar, poner, querer, saber, tener,** and **traer** are irregular in the preterite tense. You will learn about the preterite of these verbs in Level 2.

Glosario
español-inglés

This Spanish-English glossary contains all the active vocabulary words that appear in the text as well as passive vocabulary lists.

A

a to, at
A la(s)... At... o'clock. **2.1**
a pie on foot **4.2**
¿A qué hora es/son...? At what time is/are...? **2.1**
abril April **3.2**
abrir to open **5.2**
la abuela grandmother **3.2**
el abuelo grandfather **3.2**
los abuelos grandparents **3.2**
aburrido(a) boring **2.2**
acabar de... to have just... **5.2**
acampar to camp **8.2**
acompañar to go *or* come with
¿Quieres acompañarme a...? Would you like to come with me to...? **7.2**
acostarse (ue) to go to bed **8.1**
la actividad activity **1.1**
el acuario aquarium **7.2**
Adiós. Goodbye. **LP**
adivinar to guess
adjunto(a) attached
adónde (to) where **2.2**
¿Adónde vas? Where are you going? **2.2**
afeitarse to shave oneself **8.1**
el (la) aficionado(a) fan, sports fan **6.1**
agosto August **3.2**
el agua (fem.) water **1.1**
las aguas termales hot springs
ahora now **3.1**
el aire air
al aire libre outside; open-air **8.2**
al to the **2.2**
al aire libre outside; open-air **8.2**
al lado (de) next to **2.2**
alegre happy; upbeat
la alfombra rug **5.1**
algo something **7.1**
alguien someone **7.1**
alguno(a) some, any **7.1**
allí there **4.2**
el almacén (*pl.* los almacenes) department store
almorzar (ue) to eat lunch **4.2**
el almuerzo lunch **3.1**
¿Aló? Hello? (on telephone) **7.2**
alquilar to rent **1.1**
alquilar un DVD to rent a DVD **1.1**
alto(a) tall **1.2**
amarillo(a) yellow **4.1**
el (la) amigo(a) friend **1.2**
anaranjado(a) orange (color) **4.1**
andar en patineta to skateboard **1.1**
el anillo ring **8.2**
el ánimo spirit
anoche last night **6.2**
anteayer the day before yesterday **7.1**
antes (de) before **1.1**
la antorcha torch
el anuncio advertisement; announcement
el año year **3.2**
el Año Nuevo New Year
el año pasado last year **7.1**
¿Cuántos años tienes? How old are you? **3.2**
tener... años to be... years old **3.2**
el apartamento apartment **5.1**
aprender to learn **1.1**
aprender el español to learn Spanish **1.1**
los apuntes notes **2.1**
tomar apuntes to take notes **2.1**
aquel (aquella) that (over there) **8.2**
aquellos(as) those (over there) **8.2**
aquí here **4.2**
el árbol tree
el árbol de Navidad Christmas tree
el archivo file
el arete earring **8.2**
el armario closet; armoire **5.1**
el arrecife de coral coral reef
el arroz rice **4.2**
el arte art **2.1**
las artes marciales martial arts
las artesanías handicrafts **8.2**
el artículo article
los artículos goods **8.2**
los artículos deportivos sporting goods
artístico(a) artistic **1.2**
la aspiradora vacuum cleaner **5.2**
el (la) atleta athlete **6.1**
atlético(a) athletic **1.2**
los autitos chocadores bumper cars **7.2**
el autobús (*pl.* los autobuses) bus **4.2**
en autobús by bus **4.2**
avanzar to advance, to move ahead
¡Avanza! Advance!, Move ahead!
avancemos let's advance, let's move ahead
el avión (*pl.* los aviones) airplane **8.1**
en avión by plane **8.1**
ayer yesterday **6.2**
el aymara indigenous language of Bolivia and Peru
ayudar to help **5.2**
azul blue **4.1**

B

bailar to dance **5.2**
el (la) bailarín(ina) (*pl.* los bailarines) dancer
el baile dance
bajar to descend **5.1**
bajo(a) short (height) **1.2**

la balsa raft
la banana banana **3.1**
la banda musical band
la bandera flag
bañarse to take a bath **8.1**
el baño bathroom **2.2**
barato(a) inexpensive **8.2**
el barco boat **8.1**
  en barco by boat **8.1**
barrer to sweep **5.2**
  barrer el suelo to sweep the floor **5.2**
el básquetbol basketball (the sport) **6.1**
la basura trash, garbage **5.2**
la batalla battle
el bate (baseball) bat **6.1**
beber to drink **1.1**
la bebida beverage, drink **3.1**
el béisbol baseball (the sport) **6.1**
la biblioteca library **2.2**
la bicicleta bicycle **1.1**
bien well, fine **LP**
  Bien. ¿Y tú/usted? Fine. And you? (familiar/formal) **LP**
  Muy bien. ¿Y tú/usted? Very well. And you? (familiar/formal) **LP**
el bistec beef **4.2**
blanco(a) white **4.1**
el bloqueador de sol sunscreen **6.2**
la blusa blouse **4.1**
la boca mouth **6.2**
el boleto ticket **7.2**
bonito(a) pretty **1.2**
el borrador eraser **2.2**
el bosque forest
  el bosque nuboso cloud forest
  el bosque tropical lluvioso tropical rain forest
el bote boat
el brazo arm **6.2**
el brindis celebratory toast
el brócoli broccoli **4.2**
bucear to scuba-dive **6.2**
bueno(a) good **1.2**
  Buenos días. Good morning. **LP**
  Buenas noches. Good evening; Good night. **LP**
  Buenas tardes. Good afternoon. **LP**
buscar to look for **5.2**

C

el caballo horse
  montar a caballo to ride horses **8.2**
la cabeza head **6.2**
cada each; every
el café coffee; café **3.1, 4.2**
la cafetería cafeteria **2.2**
la calavera skull
el calcetín (*pl.* los calcetines) sock **4.1**
la calculadora calculator **2.2**
la calidad quality **8.2**
caliente hot
la calle street **4.2**
el calor heat
  Hace calor. It is hot. **LP**
  tener calor to be hot (person) **4.1**
la cama bed **5.1**
  hacer la cama to make the bed **5.2**
la cámara camera **7.1**
  la cámara digital digital camera **7.1**
el (la) camarero(a) (food) server **4.2**
el cambio change
caminar to walk **6.2**
la caminata hike **8.2**
  dar una caminata to hike **8.2**
la camisa shirt **4.1**
la camiseta T-shirt **4.1**
el campeón (*pl.* los campeones), la campeona champion **6.1**
el campo field (sports) **6.1**; the country, countryside **8.1**
la cancha court (sports) **6.1**
cansado(a) tired **2.2**
cantar to sing **5.2**
carnaval carnival
la carne meat **4.2**
caro(a) expensive **8.2**
  ¡Qué caro(a)! How expensive! **8.2**
la carrera (sports) race
la carreta horse-drawn carriage
el carro car
la casa house **5.1**
la cascada waterfall
el cascarón (*pl.* los cascarones) confetti-filled egg
el casco helmet **6.1**
la caseta small house or tent
casi almost **2.1**
castaño(a) brown (hair) **1.2**
catorce fourteen **2.1**
celebrar to celebrate **5.2**
el cementerio cemetery
la cena dinner **3.1**
el centro center, downtown **4.2**
  el centro comercial shopping center, mall **4.1**
cepillar to brush **8.1**
  cepillarse los dientes to brush one's teeth **8.1**
el cepillo brush **8.1**
  el cepillo de dientes toothbrush **8.1**
la cerámica ceramics **8.2**
cerca (de) near (to) **2.2**
el cereal cereal **3.1**
cero zero **LP**
cerrar (ie) to close **4.1**
el césped grass, lawn **5.2**
el champú shampoo **8.1**
la chaqueta jacket **4.1**
la chica girl **1.2**
el chico boy **1.2**
cien one hundred **2.1**
las ciencias science **2.1**
ciento(a) one hundred **3.2**
cierto(a) true
cinco five **LP**
cincuenta fifty **2.1**
el cine movie theater; the movies **4.2**
la ciudad city **8.1**
¡Claro que sí! Of course! **7.2**
la clase class, classroom **LP**; kind, type
el coche car **4.2**
  en coche by car **4.2**
la cocina kitchen **5.1**
cocinar to cook **5.2**
el colegio high school
el collar necklace **8.2**
el color color
  ¿De qué color es/son...? What color is/are...?
el comedor dining room **5.1**
comenzar (ie) to begin **6.2**
comer to eat **1.1**
  comer al aire libre to picnic, to eat outside **8.2**
cómico(a) funny **1.2**
la comida meal; food **1.1, 3.1**
como as, like
¿Cómo...? How...? **3.1**
  ¿Cómo eres? What are you like? **1.2**
  ¿Cómo estás? How are you? (familiar) **LP**

Glosario español-inglés

¿Cómo está usted? How are you?
(formal) **LP**
¿Cómo se llama? What's his/her/
your (formal) name? **LP**
¿Cómo te llamas? What's your name? (familiar) **LP**
la cómoda dresser **5.1**
comparar to compare
compartir to share **3.1**
comprar to buy **1.1**
comprender to understand **6.1**
¿Comprendiste? Did you understand?
la computación computer studies
la computadora computer **2.1**
común common
con with **7.2**
el concierto concert **4.2**
conectar to connect **7.1**
conectar a Internet to connect to the Internet **7.1**
conmigo with me **7.2**
conocer (conozco) to know, to be familiar with; to meet **6.1**
contento(a) happy **2.2**
contestar to answer **2.1**
contigo with you **7.2**
contra against
la contraseña password
el corazón (*pl.* los corazones) heart **6.2**
corregir to correct
el correo electrónico e-mail **1.1**
correr to run **1.1**
cortar to cut **5.2**
cortar el césped to cut the grass **5.2**
la cortina curtain **5.1**
la cosa thing **5.1**
costar (ue) to cost **4.2**
¿Cuánto cuesta(n)? How much does it (do they) cost? **4.1**
Cuesta(n)... It (They) cost... **4.1**
la Cremà burning of papier-mâché figures during Las Fallas
el cuaderno notebook **2.2**
el cuadro painting
¿Cuál(es)? Which?; What? **3.1**
¿Cuál es la fecha? What is the date? **3.2**
¿Cuál es tu/su número de teléfono? What is your phone number? (familiar/formal) **LP**
cuando when **2.2**
¿Cuándo? When? **2.2**
cuánto(a) how much **3.2**
¿Cuánto cuesta(n)? How much does it (do they) cost? **4.1**
cuántos(as) how many **3.2**
¿Cuántos(as)...? How many...? **2.1**
¿Cuántos años tienes? How old are you? **3.2**
cuarenta forty **2.1**
cuarto quarter **2.1**
... y cuarto quarter past... (the hour) **2.1**
el cuarto room; bedroom **5.1**
cuarto(a) fourth **5.1**
cuatro four **LP**
cuatrocientos(as) four hundred **3.2**
la cuenta bill (in a restaurant) **4.2**
el cuero leather
el cuerpo body **6.2**
el cumpleaños birthday **3.2**
¡Feliz cumpleaños! Happy birthday! **3.2**

D

dar (doy) to give **5.2**
dar una caminata to hike **8.2**
dar una fiesta to give a party **5.2**
darle de comer al perro to feed the dog **5.2**
los datos information
de of, from **1.1**
de madera wood (made of wood) **8.2**
de la mañana in the morning (with a time) **2.1**
De nada. You're welcome. **LP**
de la noche at night (with a time) **2.1**
de oro gold (made of gold) **8.2**
de plata silver (made of silver) **8.2**
¿De qué color es/son...? What color is/are...?
de la tarde in the afternoon (with a time) **2.1**
de vacaciones on vacation **8.1**
de vez en cuando once in a while **2.1**
debajo (de) underneath, under **2.2**
deber should, ought to **5.2**
décimo(a) tenth **5.1**
decir to say **5.2**
también se dice... you can also say...
la decoración (*pl.* las decoraciones) decoration **5.2**
decorar to decorate **5.2**
dejar to leave
dejar un mensaje to leave a message **7.2**
Le dejo... en... I'll give... to you for... (a price) **8.2**
¿Me deja ver...? May I see...? **8.2**
del (de la) of *or* from the **2.2**
delante (de) in front (of) **2.2**
demasiado too much **8.2**
dentro (de) inside (of) **2.2**
los deportes sports **1.1**
deprimido(a) depressed **2.2**
derecho(a) right
el desayuno breakfast **3.1**
descansar to rest **1.1**
descargar to download
desde from
desear to wish, to want
el desfile parade
desorganizado(a) disorganized **1.2**
despertarse (ie) to wake up **8.1**
después (de) afterward; after **1.1**
destruir to destroy
detrás (de) behind **2.2**
el día day **LP**
Buenos días. Good morning. **LP**
¿Qué día es hoy? What day is today? **LP**
todos los días every day **2.1**
dibujar to draw **1.1**
el dibujo drawing
diciembre December **3.2**
diecinueve nineteen **2.1**
dieciocho eighteen **2.1**
dieciséis sixteen **2.1**
diecisiete seventeen **2.1**
diez ten **LP**
diferente different
difícil difficult **2.1**
el difunto deceased
el dinero money **4.1**
la dirección (*pl.* las direcciones) address **7.1**
la dirección electrónica e-mail address **7.1**
el (la) director(a) principal **2.2**

el disco compacto compact disc **5.1**
quemar un disco compacto to burn a CD **7.1**
el disfraz (*pl.* los disfraces) costume
divertido(a) fun **2.2**
¡Qué divertido! How fun! **7.2**
doce twelve **2.1**
el (la) doctor(a) doctor
el dólar dollar **4.1**
doler (ue) to hurt, to ache **6.2**
domingo Sunday **LP**
donde where
¿De dónde eres? Where are you from? (familiar) **LP**
¿De dónde es? Where is he/she from? **LP**
¿De dónde es usted? Where are you from? (formal) **LP**
¿Dónde? Where? **2.2**
dormir (ue) to sleep **4.2**
dormirse (ue) to fall asleep **8.1**
dos two **LP**
doscientos(as) two hundred **3.2**
ducharse to take a shower **8.1**
durante during **4.1**
el DVD DVD **1.1**

E

el ecoturismo ecotourism
el ejercicio exercise
el ejército army
él he **1.1**; him **7.2**
ella she **1.1**; her **7.2**
ellos(as) they **1.1**; them **7.2**
emocionado(a) excited **2.2**
emparejar to match
empezar (ie) to begin **4.1**
en in **2.1**; on
en autobús by bus **4.2**
en avión by plane **8.1**
en barco by boat **8.1**
en coche by car **4.2**
en línea online **7.1**
en tren by train **8.1**
Encantado(a). Delighted; Pleased to meet you. **LP**
encima (de) on top (of) **2.2**
encontrar (ue) to find **4.2**
la encuesta survey
enero January **3.2**
enfermo(a) sick **6.2**
enojado(a) angry **2.2**
la ensalada salad **4.2**
enseñar to teach **2.1**
entender (ie) to understand **4.1**
entonces then, so **7.1**
la entrada ticket **4.2**
entrar to enter
la entrevista interview
entrevistar to interview
envolver (ue) to wrap **5.2**
el equipo team **6.1**
la escalera stairs **5.1**
la escena scene
escribir to write **1.1**
escribir correos electrónicos to write e-mails **1.1**
el escritorio desk **2.2**
la escritura writing
escuchar to listen (to) **1.1**
escuchar música to listen to music **1.1**
la escuela school **1.1**
la escuela secundaria high school
ese(a) that **8.2**
esos(as) those **8.2**
el español Spanish **2.1**
especial special
el espejo mirror **5.1**
esperar to wait (for) **8.1**
el esqueleto skeleton
la estación (*pl.* las estaciones) season **4.1**
el estadio stadium **6.1**
la estancia ranch
estar to be **2.2**
¿Está...? Is... there? **7.2**
¿Está bien? OK?
estar en línea to be online **7.1**
No, no está. No, he's/she's not here. **7.2**
este(a) this **8.2**
el estómago stomach **6.2**
estos(as) these **8.2**
el (la) estudiante student **1.2**
estudiar to study **1.1**
estudioso(a) studious **1.2**
el euro euro **4.1**
el examen (*pl.* los exámenes) test, exam **2.1**

F

fácil easy **2.1**
falso(a) false
las fallas displays of large papier-mâché figures
el (la) fallero(a) celebrant of *Las Fallas*
la familia family **3.2**
favorito(a) favorite **6.1**
febrero February **3.2**
la fecha date **3.2**
¿Cuál es la fecha? What is the date? **3.2**
la fecha de nacimiento birth date **3.2**
feliz happy
¡Feliz cumpleaños! Happy birthday! **3.2**
feo(a) ugly **4.1**
la feria fair **7.2**
la fiesta party; holiday
la fiesta de sorpresa surprise party **5.2**
la fiesta nacional national holiday
la fiesta patria patriotic holiday
el fin end
el fin de semana weekend **7.2**
por fin finally **7.1**
la flor flower
la foto photo, picture **7.1**
tomar fotos to take photos **7.1**
el (la) francés(esa) (*pl.* los franceses) French
los frijoles beans **4.2**
el frío cold
Hace frío. It is cold. **LP**
tener frío to be cold **4.1**
la fruta fruit **1.1**
los fuegos artificiales fireworks
la fuente source; fountain
fuerte strong **6.2**
el fútbol soccer (the sport) **1.1**
el fútbol americano football (the sport) **6.1**

G

la galleta cookie **1.1**
ganador(a) winning
el (la) ganador(a) winner **6.1**
ganar to win **6.1**
el (la) gato(a) cat **3.2**
generalmente generally **8.1**
el gimnasio gymnasium **2.2**
el globo balloon **5.2**
el gorro winter hat **4.1**
Gracias. Thank you. **LP**
Muchas gracias. Thank you very much. **LP**

R27

la gramática grammar
grande big, large; great **1.2**
el grito shout
el guante glove **6.1**
guapo(a) good-looking **1.2**
la guitarra guitar **1.1**
gustar
  Me gusta... I like... **1.1**
  Me gustaría... I would like... **7.2**
  No me gusta... I don't like... **1.1**
  ¿Qué te gusta hacer? What do you like to do? **1.1**
  ¿Te gusta...? Do you like...? **1.1**
  ¿Te gustaría...? Would you like...? **7.2**
el gusto pleasure
  El gusto es mío. The pleasure is mine. **LP**
  Mucho gusto. Nice to meet you. **LP**

H

hablar to talk, to speak **1.1**
  hablar por teléfono to talk on the phone **1.1**
  ¿Puedo hablar con...? May I speak with...? **7.2**
hacer (hago) to make, to do **3.1**
  Hace calor. It is hot. **LP**
  Hace frío. It is cold. **LP**
  Hace sol. It is sunny. **LP**
  Hace viento. It is windy. **LP**
  hacer la cama to make the bed **5.2**
  hacer clic en to click on **7.1**
  hacer esquí acuático to water-ski **6.2**
  hacer una parrillada to barbecue **8.2**
  hacer surf de vela to windsurf **8.2**
  hacer surfing to surf **8.2**
  hacer la tarea to do homework **1.1**
  hacer un viaje to take a trip **8.1**
  ¿Qué hicieron ustedes? What did you do? (pl., formal) **6.2**
  ¿Qué hiciste tú? What did you do? (sing., familiar) **6.2**
  ¿Qué tiempo hace? What is the weather like? **LP**
hacerse to become
el hambre hunger
  tener hambre to be hungry **3.1**
la hamburguesa hamburger **3.1**
hasta until
  Hasta luego. See you later. **LP**
  Hasta mañana. See you tomorrow. **LP**
hay... there is/are... **2.1**
  hay que... one has to..., one must... **5.2**
el helado ice cream **1.1**
herido(a) hurt **6.2**
la hermana sister **3.2**
el hermano brother **3.2**
los hermanos brothers, brother(s) and sister(s) **3.2**
la hija daughter **3.2**
el hijo son **3.2**
los hijos children, son(s) and daughter(s) **3.2**
la hispanidad cultural community of Spanish speakers
la historia history **2.1**
Hola. Hello; Hi. **LP**
el hombre man **1.2**
la hora hour; time **2.1**
  ¿A qué hora es/son...? At what time is/are...? **2.1**
  ¿Qué hora es? What time is it? **2.1**
el horario schedule **2.1**
horrible horrible **3.1**
el hotel hotel **8.1**
hoy today **LP**
  ¿Qué día es hoy? What day is today? **LP**
  Hoy es... Today is... **LP**
el huevo egg **3.1**

I

el icono icon **7.1**
ideal ideal **5.1**
el idioma language
Igualmente. Same here; Likewise. **LP**
importante important **3.1**
  Es importante. It's important. **3.1**
los incas Incas, an indigenous South American people
la independencia independence
la información information
el inglés English **2.1**
inteligente intelligent **1.2**
interesante interesting **2.2**
Internet Internet **7.1**
  conectar a Internet to connect to the Internet **7.1**
  navegar por Internet to surf the Web **7.1**
el invierno winter **4.1**
los invitados guests **5.2**
invitar to invite **5.2**
  invitar a to invite (someone) **5.2**
  Te invito. I invite you; I'll treat you. **7.2**
ir to go **2.2**
  ir a... to be going to... **4.2**
  ir de compras to go shopping **4.1**
  Vamos a... Let's... **4.2**
izquierdo(a) left

J

el jabón (*pl.* los jabones) soap **8.1**
el jamón (*pl.* los jamones) ham **3.1**
el jardín (*pl.* los jardines) garden **5.1**
los jeans jeans **4.1**
joven (*pl.* jóvenes) young **1.2**
las joyas jewelry **8.2**
jueves Thursday **LP**
el (la) jugador(a) player **6.1**
jugar (ue) to play (sports or games) **1.1**
  jugar al fútbol to play soccer **1.1**
el jugo juice **1.1**
  el jugo de naranja orange juice **3.1**
julio July **3.2**
junio June **3.2**

L

el lado side
  al lado (de) next to **2.2**
el lago lake
la lámpara lamp **5.1**
el lápiz (*pl.* los lápices) pencil **2.2**
largo(a) long
lavar to wash **5.2**
  lavarse to wash oneself **8.1**

lavarse la cara to wash one's face **8.1**
lavar los platos to wash the dishes **5.2**
la lección (*pl.* las lecciones) lesson
la leche milk **3.1**
el lector DVD DVD player **5.1**
la lectura reading
leer to read **1.1**
leer un libro to read a book **1.1**
lejos (de) far (from) **2.2**
las lentejas lentils
levantar to lift **6.2**; to raise
levantar pesas to lift weights **6.2**
levantarse to get up **8.1**
el libertador liberator
el libro book **1.1**
limpiar to clean **5.2**
limpiar la cocina to clean the kitchen **5.2**
limpio(a) clean **5.2**
la llamada phone call **7.2**
llamar to call (by phone) **7.2**
llamarse to be called
¿Cómo se llama? What's his/her/your (formal) name? **LP**
¿Cómo te llamas? What's your name? (familiar) **LP**
Me llamo... My name is... **LP**
Se llama... His/Her name is... **LP**
la llegada arrival
llegar to arrive **2.1**
llevar to wear **4.1**
llover (ue) to rain **LP**
Llueve. It is raining. **LP**
Lo siento. I'm sorry. **6.2**
luego later, then **7.1**
Hasta luego. See you later. **LP**
el lugar place **4.2**
lunes Monday **LP**

M

la madera wood **8.2**
de madera wood (made of wood) **8.2**
la madrastra stepmother **3.2**
la madre mother **3.2**
el (la) maestro(a) teacher **LP**
malo(a) bad **1.2**
Mal. ¿Y tú/usted? Bad. And you? (familiar/formal) **LP**
mandar to send **7.1**
la mano hand **6.2**
la manzana apple **3.1**
mañana tomorrow **LP**
Hasta mañana. See you tomorrow. **LP**
Mañana es... Tomorrow is... **LP**
la mañana morning **2.1**
de la mañana in the morning (with a time) **2.1**
el mapa map **2.2**
maquillarse to put on makeup **8.1**
el mar sea **6.2**
marrón (*pl.* marrones) brown **4.1**
martes Tuesday **LP**
marzo March **3.2**
la mascletà firecracker explosions during *Las Fallas*
más more **1.1**
Más o menos. ¿Y tú/usted? So-so. And you? (familiar/formal) **LP**
más que... more than... **3.2**
más... que more... than **3.2**
más tarde later (on) **7.1**
la máscara mask
las matemáticas math **2.1**
mayo May **3.2**
mayor older **3.2**
la medianoche midnight
medio(a) half
...y media half past... (the hour) **2.1**
mejor better **3.2**
menor younger **3.2**
menos less
...menos (diez) (ten) to/before... (the hour) **2.1**
menos que... less than... **3.2**
menos... que less... than **3.2**
el mensaje message **7.2**
dejar un mensaje to leave a message **7.2**
el mensaje instantáneo instant message
el mensajero instantáneo instant messaging **7.1**
el menú menu **4.2**
el mercado market **8.2**
el mercado al aire libre open-air market
el mes month **3.2**
la mesa table **4.2**
poner la mesa to set the table **5.2**
el metro meter
mí me **7.2**
mi my **3.2**
el miedo fear
¡Qué miedo! How scary! **7.2**
tener miedo to be afraid **7.2**
miércoles Wednesday **LP**
mil thousand, one thousand **3.2**
un millón (de) million, one million **3.2**
el minuto minute **2.1**
mirar to watch **1.1**; to look at
mirar la televisión to watch television **1.1**
mismo(a) same
la mochila backpack **2.2**
el momento moment
Un momento. One moment. **7.2**
la montaña rusa roller coaster **7.2**
montar to ride **1.1**
montar a caballo to ride a horse **8.2**
montar en bicicleta to ride a bike **1.1**
mucho a lot **2.1**
Mucho gusto. Nice to meet you. **LP**
muchos(as) many **2.1**
muchas veces often, many times **2.1**
los muebles furniture **5.1**
la mujer woman **1.2**
el mundo world
el museo museum **7.2**
la música music **1.1**
la música folklórica folk music
la música rock rock music **4.2**
el (la) músico(a) musician
muy very **1.2**
Muy bien. ¿Y tú/usted? Very well. And you? (familiar/formal) **LP**

N

nacer to be born
nada nothing **7.1**
De nada. You're welcome. **LP**
nadar to swim **6.1**
nadie no one, nobody **7.1**
la naranja orange (fruit) **3.1**
la nariz (*pl.* las narices) nose **6.2**
la natación swimming **6.1**
la naturaleza nature
navegar por Internet to surf the Web **7.1**
la Navidad Christmas

necesitar to need **2.1**
negro(a) black **4.1**
nervioso(a) nervous **2.2**
nevar (ie) to snow **LP**
  Nieva. It is snowing. **LP**
ni... ni neither... nor **7.1**
la nieve snow
ninguno(a) none, not any **7.1**
el ninot (*pl.* los ninots) large papier-mâché figure
no no **LP**
la noche night **2.1**; evening **LP**
  Buenas noches. Good evening; Good night. **LP**
  de la noche at night (with a time) **2.1**
la Nochebuena Christmas Eve
la Nochevieja New Year's Eve
el nombre name
normalmente normally **8.1**
nosotros(as) we **1.1**; us **7.2**
la nota grade (on a test) **2.1**
  sacar una buena/mala nota to get a good/bad grade **2.1**
novecientos(as) nine hundred **3.2**
noveno(a) ninth **5.1**
noventa ninety **2.1**
noviembre November **3.2**
nuestro(a) our **3.2**
nueve nine **LP**
nuevo(a) new **4.1**
el número number **LP**
  el número de teléfono phone number **LP**
nunca never **2.1**
nutritivo(a) nutritious **3.1**

O

o or **1.1**
  o... o either... or **7.1**
la obra work (of art)
ocho eight **LP**
ochocientos(as) eight hundred **3.2**
octavo(a) eighth **5.1**
octubre October **3.2**
ocupado(a) busy **2.2**
la oficina office **2.2**
  la oficina del (de la) director(a) principal's office **2.2**
ofrecer (ofrezco) to offer
  Le puedo ofrecer... I can offer you... (a price) **8.2**
el ojo eye **6.2**
once eleven **2.1**
la oración (*pl.* las oraciones) sentence
la oreja ear **6.2**
organizado(a) organized **1.2**
el oro gold
  de oro gold (made of gold) **8.2**
el otoño autumn, fall **4.1**
otro(a) other **3.1**

P

el padrastro stepfather **3.2**
el padre father **3.2**
los padres parents **3.2**
pagar to pay **4.1**
la página page
el país country, nation **LP**
el pájaro bird
el pan bread **3.1**
  el pan de muertos special bread made for *Día de los Muertos*
la pantalla screen **7.1**
los pantalones pants **4.1**
  los pantalones cortos shorts **4.1**
la papa potato **1.1**
  las papas fritas French fries **1.1**
el papel paper **2.2**
  el papel de regalo wrapping paper **5.2**
  el papel picado paper cutouts
para for; in order to **3.1**
parar to stop
  Para y piensa. Stop and think.
la pared wall
la pareja pair
el párrafo paragraph
la parrillada barbecue **8.2**
  hacer una parrillada to barbecue **8.2**
el parque park **4.2**
  el parque de diversiones amusement park **7.2**
la parte part
el partido game (in sports) **6.1**
el pasado the past
pasado(a) past **7.1**
  el año pasado last year **7.1**
  la semana pasada last week **7.1**
pasar to happen
  pasar la aspiradora to vacuum **5.2**
  pasar un rato con los amigos to spend time with friends **1.1**
  ¿Qué pasa? What's happening? **LP**
  ¿Qué te pasa (a ti)? What's the matter (with you)?
pasear to go for a walk **1.1**
el paseo walk, stroll; ride
el pasillo hall **2.2**
la pasta de dientes toothpaste **8.1**
el pastel cake **4.2**
la patata potato **4.2**
patinar to skate **6.1**
  patinar en línea to in-line skate **6.1**
los patines en línea in-line skates **6.1**
el patio patio **5.1**
pedir (i) to order, to ask for **4.2**
peinarse to comb one's hair **8.1**
el peine comb **8.1**
la película movie **4.2**
peligroso(a) dangerous **6.1**
pelirrojo(a) red-haired **1.2**
el pelo hair **1.2**
  el pelo castaño/rubio brown/blond hair **1.2**
la pelota ball **6.1**
pensar (ie) to think; to plan **4.1**
peor worse **3.2**
pequeño(a) little, small **1.2**
perder (ie) to lose **6.1**
Perdón. Excuse me. **LP**
perezoso(a) lazy **1.2**
el periódico newspaper
  el periódico escolar student newspaper
pero but **1.1**
el (la) perro(a) dog **3.2**
la persona person **1.2**
el pescado fish (as food) **4.2**
el pie foot **6.2**
  a pie on foot **4.2**
la piel skin **6.2**
la pierna leg **6.2**
la pintura painting
la piscina swimming pool **6.1**
el piso floor (of a building) **5.1**
  primer piso second floor (first floor above ground floor) **5.1**
la pista track; clue
el pizarrón (*pl.* los pizarrones) chalkboard, board **2.2**
la pizza pizza **1.1**
planchar to iron **5.2**
la planta plant
la planta baja first floor, ground

floor **5.1**
la plata silver
de plata silver (made of silver) **8.2**
el plato plate; dish; course
el plato principal main course **4.2**
la playa beach **6.2**
la pluma pen **2.2**
un poco a little **1.2**
pocos(as) few
poder (ue) to be able, can **4.2**
Le puedo ofrecer... I can offer you... **8.2**
¿Puedo hablar con...? May I speak with...? **7.2**
el pollo chicken **4.2**
poner (pongo) to put, to place **5.2**
poner la mesa to set the table **5.2**
ponerse (me pongo) to put on **8.1**
ponerse la ropa to put one's clothes on, to get dressed **8.1**
por for, per
Por favor. Please. **LP**
por fin finally **7.1**
¿Por qué? Why? **3.1**
porque because **1.2**
el postre dessert **4.2**
de postre for dessert **4.2**
practicar to practice **1.1**
practicar deportes to play or practice sports **1.1**
el precio price **4.1**
preferir (ie) to prefer **4.1**
la pregunta question
el premio award
preparar to prepare **1.1**
preparar la comida to prepare food, to make a meal **1.1**
presentar to introduce **LP**
Te/Le presento a... Let me introduce you to... (familiar/formal) **LP**
la primavera spring **4.1**
primero(a) first **5.1**
el primero de... the first of... (date) **3.2**
el (la) primo(a) cousin **3.2**
los primos cousins **3.2**
el problema problem **2.2**
la procesión (*pl.* las procesiones) procession
proclamar to declare
la propina tip (in a restaurant) **4.2**
proteger (protejo) to protect
el pueblo town
la puerta door **2.2**

Q

¿Qué? What? **3.1**
¿De qué color es/son...? What color is/are...?
¡Qué bárbaro! How cool!
¡Qué caro(a)! How expensive! **8.2**
¡Qué divertido! How fun! **7.2**
¡Qué lástima! What a shame! **7.2**
¡Qué miedo! How scary! **7.2**
¿Qué día es hoy? What day is today? **LP**
¿Qué es esto? What is this? **8.2**
¿Qué hicieron ustedes? What did you do? (pl., formal) **6.2**
¿Qué hiciste tú? What did you do? (sing., familiar) **6.2**
¿Qué hora es? What time is it? **2.1**
¿Qué pasa? What's happening? **LP**
¿Qué tal? How's it going? **LP**
¿Qué te gusta hacer? What do you like to do? **1.1**
¿Qué tiempo hace? What is the weather like? **LP**
el quechua indigenous language from South America
quedarse en to stay in **8.1**
los quehaceres chores **5.2**
quemar to burn
quemar un disco compacto to burn a CD **7.1**
querer (ie) to want **4.1**
¿Quieres acompañarme a...? Would you like to come with me to...? **7.2**
Quisiera... I would like... **8.2**
el queso cheese **3.1**
el queso crema cream cheese
¿Quién(es)? Who? **3.1**
¿Quién es? Who is he/she/it? **LP**
quince fifteen **2.1**
quinientos(as) five hundred **3.2**
quinto(a) fifth **5.1**

R

el radio radio **5.1**
rápido(a) fast
la raqueta racket (in sports) **6.1**
un rato a while, a short time
el ratón (*pl.* los ratones) mouse **7.1**
la raza (human) race
la razón (*pl.* las razones) reason
tener razón to be right **4.1**
recibir to receive **5.2**
la reconstrucción (*pl.* las reconstrucciones) reenactment
recordar (ue) to remember
¿Recuerdas? Do you remember?
el recorrido run, journey
el recreo recess
el recuerdo souvenir **8.2**
el refresco soft drink **1.1**
regalar to give (a gift)
el regalo present, gift **5.2**
regatear to bargain **8.2**
la regla rule
regular OK **LP**
Regular. ¿Y tú/usted? OK. And you? (familiar/formal) **LP**
el reloj watch; clock **2.2**
el repaso review
responder to reply
la respuesta answer
el restaurante restaurant **4.2**
el resultado result
el resumen summary
en resumen in summary
los Reyes Magos Three Kings
rico(a) tasty, delicious; rich **3.1**
la rodilla knee **6.2**
rojo(a) red **4.1**
la ropa clothing **4.1**
la rosca de reyes sweet bread eaten on January 6
rubio(a) blond **1.2**
la rutina routine **8.1**

S

sábado Saturday **LP**
saber (sé) to know (a fact, how to do something) **6.1**
sacar to take out
sacar la basura to take out the trash **5.2**
sacar una buena/mala nota to get a good/bad grade **2.1**
la sala living room **5.1**
salir (salgo) to leave, to go out **5.2**

Glosario español-inglés

la salud health **6.2**
¡Saludos! Greetings!
Saludos desde... Greetings from...
el sándwich sandwich **3.1**
el sándwich de jamón y queso ham and cheese sandwich **3.1**
sano(a) healthy **6.2**
el santo saint
el secador de pelo to hair dryer **8.1**
secar to dry
secarse to dry oneself **8.1**
secarse el pelo to dry one's hair **8.1**
el secreto secret **5.2**
la sed thirst
tener sed to be thirsty **3.1**
según according to
segundo(a) second **5.1**
seguro(a) secure, safe
seis six **LP**
seiscientos(as) six hundred **3.2**
la semana week **LP**
el fin de semana weekend **7.2**
la semana pasada last week **7.1**
Semana Santa Holy Week
Señor (Sr.) Mr. **LP**
Señora (Sra.) Mrs. **LP**
Señorita (Srta.) Miss **LP**
sentir to feel
Lo siento. I'm sorry. **6.2**
septiembre September **3.2**
séptimo(a) seventh **5.1**
ser to be **1.1**
Es de... He/She is from... **LP**
Es el... de... It's the... of... (day and month) **3.2**
Es la.../Son las... It is... o'clock. **2.1**
Soy de... I'm from... **LP**
serio(a) serious **1.2**
servir (i) to serve **4.2**
sesenta sixty **2.1**
setecientos(as) seven hundred **3.2**
setenta seventy **2.1**
sexto(a) sixth **5.1**
si if **5.2**
sí yes **LP**
¡Claro que sí! Of course! **7.2**
Sí, me encantaría. Yes, I would love to. **7.2**
siempre always **2.1**
siete seven **LP**
siguiente following
la silla chair **2.2**
el sillón (*pl.* los sillones) armchair **5.1**
simpático(a) nice, friendly **1.2**
sin without
el sitio Web Web site **7.1**
sobre about; on
el sofá sofa, couch **5.1**
el sol sun **LP**
el bloqueador de sol sunscreen **6.2**
Hace sol. It is sunny. **LP**
tomar el sol to sunbathe **6.2**
el sombrero hat **4.1**
la sopa soup **3.1**
la sorpresa surprise **5.2**
su his, her, its, their, your (formal) **3.2**
subir to go up **5.1**
subir a la vuelta al mundo/la montaña rusa to ride the Ferris wheel/roller coaster **7.2**
sucio(a) dirty **5.2**
el suelo floor (of a room) **5.1**
la suerte luck
tener suerte to be lucky **4.1**
el supermercado supermarket

T

tal vez perhaps, maybe **4.2**
también also, too **1.1**
también se dice... you can also say...
tampoco neither, not either **7.1**
tan... como as... as **3.2**
tanto como... as much as... **3.2**
tanto(a) so much
tantos(as) so many
tarde late **2.1**
la tarde afternoon **2.1**
Buenas tardes. Good afternoon. **LP**
de la tarde in the afternoon (with a time) **2.1**
más tarde later (on) **7.1**
la tarea homework **1.1**
la tarjeta postal postcard
el teatro theater **4.2**
el teclado keyboard **7.1**
el teléfono telephone **7.2**
¿Cuál es tu/su número de teléfono? What is your phone number? (familiar/formal) **LP**
Mi número de teléfono es... My phone number is... **LP**
el teléfono celular cellular telephone **7.2**
la televisión television **1.1**
el televisor television set **5.1**
el tema theme
temprano early **2.1**
tener to have **2.1**
¿Cuántos años tienes? How old are you? **3.2**
tener... años to be... years old **3.2**
tener calor to be hot **4.1**
tener frío to be cold **4.1**
tener ganas de... to feel like... **3.1**
tener hambre to be hungry **3.1**
tener miedo to be afraid **7.2**
tener que... to have to... **2.1**
tener razón to be right **4.1**
tener sed to be thirsty **3.1**
tener suerte to be lucky **4.1**
el tenis tennis **6.1**
tercero(a) third **5.1**
terminar to end **6.2**
ti you (sing., familiar) **7.2**
la tía aunt **3.2**
el tiempo weather **LP**; time **8.2**
el tiempo libre free time **8.2**
¿Qué tiempo hace? What is the weather like? **LP**
la tienda store **4.1**
el tío uncle **3.2**
los tíos uncles, uncle(s) and aunt(s) **3.2**
típico(a) typical
el tipo type
la tiza chalk **2.2**
la toalla towel **8.1**
el tobillo ankle **6.2**
el tocadiscos compactos CD player **5.1**
tocar to play (an instrument) **1.1**
tocar la guitarra to play the guitar **1.1**
todavía still; yet **5.2**
todo junto all together
todos(as) all **1.2**
todos los días every day **2.1**
tomar to take **4.2**
tomar apuntes to take notes **2.1**

tomar fotos to take photos **7.1**
tomar el sol to sunbathe **6.2**
el tomate tomato **4.2**
trabajador(a) hard-working **1.2**
trabajar to work **1.1**
traer (traigo) to bring **5.2**
el traje costume
tranquilo(a) calm **2.2**
trece thirteen **2.1**
treinta thirty **2.1**
treinta y uno thirty-one **2.1**
el tren train **8.1**
en tren by train **8.1**
tres three **LP**
trescientos(as) three hundred **3.2**
triste sad **2.2**
tu your (sing., familiar) **3.2**
tú you (sing., familiar) **1.1**
el turismo tourism
el turrón (*pl.* los turrones) almond nougat candy

U

último(a) last
la unidad unit
uno one **LP**
usar to use **2.1**
usar la computadora to use the computer **2.1**
usted you (sing., formal) **1.1, 7.2**
ustedes you (pl.) **1.1**
la uva grape **3.1**
las doce uvas twelve grapes (eaten on New Year's Eve)

V

las vacaciones vacation **8.1**
de vacaciones on vacation **8.1**
¡Vale! OK!
el valle valley
varios(as) various
veinte twenty **2.1**
veintiuno twenty-one **2.1**
el (la) vendedor(a) salesclerk
vender to sell **3.1**
venir to come **5.2**
la ventana window **2.2**
la ventanilla ticket window **4.2**
ver (veo) to see **4.2**
¿Me deja ver...? May I see...? **8.2**
el verano summer **4.1**
la verdad truth
¿Verdad? Really?; Right? **LP**
verde green **4.1**
las verduras vegetables **4.2**
el vestido dress **4.1**
vestirse (i) to get dressed **8.1**
la vez (*pl.* las veces) time
a veces sometimes
de vez en cuando once in a while **2.1**
muchas veces often, many times **2.1**
tal vez maybe **4.2**
el viaje trip, journey
hacer un viaje to take a trip **8.1**
la vida life
el videojuego video game **5.1**
viejo(a) old **1.2**
el viento wind
Hace viento. It is windy. **LP**
viernes Friday **LP**
el villancico seasonal children's song
visitar to visit
vivir to live **3.2**
el vocabulario vocabulary
el voleibol volleyball (the sport) **6.1**
volver (ue) to return, to come back **4.2**
vosotros(as) you (pl. familiar) **1.1, 7.2**
la vuelta al mundo Ferris wheel **7.2**
vuestro(a) your (pl., familiar) **3.2**

Y

y and
...y (diez) (ten) past... (the hour) **2.1**
...y cuarto quarter past... (the hour) **2.1**
...y media half past... (the hour) **2.1**
¿Y tú? And you? (familiar) **LP**
¿Y usted? And you? (formal) **LP**
ya already **3.2**
yo I **1.1**
el yogur yogurt **3.1**

Z

el zapato shoe **4.1**
el zoológico zoo **7.2**

Glosario inglés-español

This Spanish-English glossary contains all the active vocabulary words that appear in the text as well as passive vocabulary lists.

A

about sobre
to accompany acompañar **7.2**
according to según
to ache doler (ue) **6.2**
activity la actividad **1.1**
address la dirección (*pl.* las direcciones) **7.1**
  e-mail address la dirección electrónica **7.1**
to advance avanzar
advertisement el anuncio
afraid: to be afraid tener miedo **7.2**
after después (de) **1.1**
afternoon la tarde **2.1**
  Good afternoon. Buenas tardes. **LP**
  in the afternoon de la tarde **2.1**
afterward después **1.1**
against contra
air el aire
airplane el avión (*pl.* los aviones) **8.1**
  by plane en avión **8.1**
all todos(as) **1.2**
all together todo junto
almost casi **2.1**
already ya **3.2**
also también **1.1**
always siempre **2.1**
and y
angry enojado(a) **2.2**
ankle el tobillo **6.2**
announcement el anuncio
answer la respuesta
to answer contestar **2.1**
any alguno(a) **7.1**
  not any ninguno(a) **7.1**
apartment el apartamento **5.1**
apple la manzana **3.1**
April abril **3.2**
aquarium el acuario **7.2**
arm el brazo **6.2**
armchair el sillón (*pl.* los sillones) **5.1**
armoire el armario **5.1**
arrival la llegada
to arrive llegar **2.1**
art el arte **2.1**
  martial arts las artes marciales
article el artículo
artistic artístico(a) **1.2**
as como
  as... as tan... como **3.2**
  as much as... tanto como... **3.2**
to ask for pedir (i) **4.2**
at a
  at night de la noche **2.1**
  At... o'clock. A la(s)... **2.1**
  At what time is/are...? ¿A qué hora es/son...? **2.1**
athlete el (la) atleta **6.1**
athletic atlético(a) **1.2**
attached adjunto(a)
August agosto **3.2**
aunt la tía **3.2**
autumn el otoño **4.1**
award el premio

B

backpack la mochila **2.2**
bad malo(a) **1.2**
  Bad. And you? (familiar/formal) Mal. ¿Y tú/usted? **LP**
ball la pelota **6.1**
balloon el globo **5.2**
banana la banana **3.1**
barbecue la parrillada **8.2**
to barbecue hacer una parrillada **8.2**
to bargain regatear **8.2**
baseball el béisbol **6.1**
  (baseball) bat el bate **6.1**
basketball el básquetbol **6.1**
bathroom el baño **2.2**
to be ser **1.1**; estar **2.2**
  to be able poder (ue) **4.2**
  to be afraid tener miedo **7.2**
  to be called llamarse
  to be cold tener frío **4.1**
  to be familiar with conocer (conozco) **6.1**
  to be hot tener calor **4.1**
  to be hungry tener hambre **3.1**
  to be lucky tener suerte **4.1**
  to be online estar en línea **7.1**
  to be right tener razón **4.1**
  to be thirsty tener sed **3.1**
  to be... years old tener... años **3.2**
beach la playa **6.2**
beans los frijoles **4.2**
because porque **1.2**
to become hacerse
bed la cama **5.1**
  to go to bed acostarse (ue) **8.1**
  to make the bed hacer la cama **5.2**
bedroom el cuarto **5.1**
beef el bistec **4.2**
before antes (de) **1.1**; menos (with a time) **2.1**
to begin empezar (ie) **4.1**, comenzar (ie) **6.2**
behind detrás (de) **2.2**
better mejor **3.2**
beverage la bebida **3.1**
bicycle la bicicleta **1.1**
big grande **1.2**
bill (in a restaurant) la cuenta **4.2**
bird el pájaro
birth date la fecha de nacimiento **3.2**
birthday el cumpleaños **3.2**
  Happy birthday! ¡Feliz cumpleaños! **3.2**
black negro(a) **4.1**
blond rubio(a) **1.2**
blouse la blusa **4.1**
blue azul **4.1**

board el pizarrón (*pl.* los pizarrones) **2.2**
boat el barco **8.1**, el bote
  by boat en barco **8.1**
body el cuerpo **6.2**
book el libro **1.1**
boring aburrido(a) **2.2**
boy el chico **1.2**
bread el pan **3.1**
breakfast el desayuno **3.1**
to bring traer (traigo) **5.2**
broccoli el brócoli **4.2**
brother el hermano **3.2**
brown marrón (*pl.* marrones) **4.1**
  brown hair el pelo castaño **1.2**
brush el cepillo **8.1**
to brush cepillar
  to brush one's teeth cepillarse los dientes **8.1**
bumper cars los autitos chocadores **7.2**
burn: to burn a CD quemar un disco compacto **7.1**
bus el autobús (*pl.* los autobuses) **4.2**
  by bus en autobús **4.2**
busy ocupado(a) **2.2**
but pero **1.1**
to buy comprar **1.1**

C

café el café **4.2**
cafeteria la cafetería **2.2**
cake el pastel **4.2**
calculator la calculadora **2.2**
call la llamada **7.2**
to call llamar **7.2**
calm tranquilo(a) **2.2**
camera la cámara **7.1**
  digital camera la cámara digital **7.1**
to camp acampar **8.2**
can (to be able) poder (ue) **4.2**
  I can offer you... Le puedo ofrecer... **8.2**
car el coche **4.2**; el carro
  by car en coche **4.2**
cat el (la) gato(a) **3.2**
CD player el tocadiscos compactos **5.1**
to celebrate celebrar **5.2**
cellular phone el teléfono celular **7.2**
center el centro **4.2**
ceramics la cerámica **8.2**
cereal el cereal **3.1**
chair la silla **2.2**
chalk la tiza **2.2**
chalkboard el pizarrón (*pl.* los pizarrones) **2.2**
champion el campeón (*pl.* los campeones), la campeona **6.1**
change el cambio
cheese el queso **3.1**
  cream cheese el queso crema
chicken el pollo **4.2**
children los hijos **3.2**
chores los quehaceres **5.2**
Christmas la Navidad
  Christmas tree el árbol de Navidad
city la ciudad **8.1**
class la clase **LP**
classroom la clase **LP**
clean limpio(a) **5.2**
to clean limpiar **5.2**
to click on hacer clic en **7.1**
clock el reloj **2.2**
to close cerrar (ie) **4.1**
closet el armario **5.1**
clothing la ropa **4.1**
clue la pista
coffee el café **3.1**
cold el frío **4.1**
  It is cold. Hace frío. **LP**
  to be cold tener frío **4.1**
color el color
  What color is/are...? ¿De qué color es/son...?
comb el peine **8.1**
  to comb one's hair peinarse **8.1**
to come venir **5.2**
  to come back volver (ue) **4.2**
  to come with acompañar **7.2**
common común
compact disc el disco compacto **5.1**
to compare comparar
computer la computadora **2.1**
  computer studies la computación
concert el concierto **4.2**
to connect conectar **7.1**
  to connect to the Internet conectar a Internet **7.1**
to cook cocinar **5.2**
cookie la galleta **1.1**
coral reef el arrecife de coral
to correct corregir
to cost costar (ue) **4.2**
  How much does it (do they) cost? ¿Cuánto cuesta(n)? **4.1**
  It (They) cost... Cuesta(n)... **4.1**
costume el disfraz (*pl.* los disfraces), el traje
couch el sofá **5.1**
country el campo **8.1**; el país **LP**
course el plato
  main course el plato principal **4.2**
court la cancha **6.1**
cousin el (la) primo(a) **3.2**
curtain la cortina **5.1**
to cut cortar **5.2**
  to cut the grass cortar el césped **5.2**

D

dance el baile
to dance bailar **5.2**
dangerous peligroso(a) **6.1**
date la fecha **3.2**
  birth date la fecha de nacimiento **3.2**
  What is the date? ¿Cuál es la fecha? **3.2**
daughter la hija **3.2**
day el día **LP**
  the day before yesterday anteayer **7.1**
  every day todos los días **2.1**
  What day is today? ¿Qué día es hoy? **LP**
December diciembre **3.2**
to decorate decorar **5.2**
decoration la decoración (*pl.* las decoraciones) **5.2**
delicious rico(a) **3.1**
Delighted. Encantado(a). **LP**
department store el almacén (*pl.* los almacenes)
depressed deprimido(a) **2.2**
to descend bajar **5.1**
desk el escritorio **2.2**
dessert el postre **4.2**
  for dessert de postre **4.2**
to destroy destruir
different diferente
difficult difícil **2.1**
dining room el comedor **5.1**
dinner la cena **3.1**
dirty sucio(a) **5.2**
dish el plato
  main dish el plato principal **4.2**
disorganized desorganizado(a) **1.2**
to do hacer (hago) **3.1**
doctor el (la) doctor(a)
dog el (la) perro(a) **3.2**
dollar el dólar **4.1**

Glosario inglés-español

door la puerta **2.2**
to download descargar
downtown el centro **4.2**
to draw dibujar **1.1**
drawing el dibujo
dress el vestido **4.1**
dresser la cómoda **5.1**
drink la bebida **3.1**
to drink beber **1.1**
to dry secar
  to dry one's hair secarse el pelo **8.1**
  to dry oneself secarse **8.1**
during durante **4.1**
DVD el DVD **1.1**
  DVD player el lector DVD **5.1**

E

each cada
ear la oreja **6.2**
early temprano **2.1**
earring el arete **8.2**
easy fácil **2.1**
to eat comer **1.1**
  to eat lunch almorzar (ue) **4.2**
  to eat outside comer al aire libre **8.2**
ecotourism el ecoturismo
egg el huevo **3.1**
eight ocho **LP**
eight hundred ochocientos(as) **3.2**
eighteen dieciocho **2.1**
eighth octavo(a) **5.1**
either
  either... or o... o **7.1**
  not either tampoco **7.1**
eleven once **2.1**
e-mail el correo electrónico **1.1**
  e-mail address la dirección (*pl.* las direcciones) electrónica **7.1**
to end terminar **6.2**
English el inglés **2.1**
to enter entrar
eraser el borrador **2.2**
euro el euro **4.1**
evening la noche **LP**
  Good evening. Buenas noches. **LP**
every cada
  every day todos los días **2.1**
exam el examen (*pl.* los exámenes) **2.1**
excited emocionado(a) **2.2**
Excuse me. Perdón. **LP**
exercise el ejercicio
expensive caro(a) **8.2**
  How expensive! ¡Qué caro(a)! **8.2**
eye el ojo **6.2**

F

fair la feria **7.2**
fall el otoño **4.1**
to fall asleep dormirse (ue) **8.1**
false falso(a)
family la familia **3.2**
fan el (la) aficionado(a) **6.1**
far (from) lejos (de) **2.2**
fast rápido(a)
father el padre **3.2**
favorite favorito(a) **6.1**
fear el miedo **7.2**
February febrero **3.2**
to feed darle(s) de comer **5.2**
  to feed the dog darle de comer al perro
to feel sentir (ie)
  to feel like... tener ganas de... **3.1**
Ferris wheel la vuelta al mundo **7.2**
few pocos(as)
field el campo **6.1**
fifteen quince **2.1**
fifth quinto(a) **5.1**
fifty cincuenta **2.1**
file el archivo
finally por fin **7.1**
to find encontrar (ue) **4.2**
fine bien **LP**
  Fine. And you? (familiar/formal) Bien. ¿Y tú/usted? **LP**
fireworks los fuegos artificiales
first primero(a) **5.1**
  the first of... el primero de... **3.2**
fish el pescado **4.2**
five cinco **LP**
five hundred quinientos(as) **3.2**
flag la bandera
floor el piso; el suelo **5.1**
  first *or* ground floor la planta baja **5.1**
  second floor (first above ground) el primer piso **5.1**
flower la flor
following siguiente
food la comida **1.1, 3.1**
food server el (la) camarero(a) **4.2**
foot el pie **6.2**
  on foot a pie **4.2**
football el fútbol americano **6.1**
for para **3.1**; por
forest el bosque
  cloud forest el bosque nuboso
  tropical rain forest el bosque tropical lluvioso
forty cuarenta **2.1**
fountain la fuente
four cuatro **LP**
four hundred cuatrocientos(as) **3.2**
fourteen catorce **2.1**
fourth cuarto(a) **5.1**
free time el tiempo libre **8.2**
French fries las papas fritas **1.1**
Friday viernes **LP**
friend el (la) amigo(a) **1.2**
  to spend time with friends pasar un rato con los amigos **1.1**
from de **1.1**; desde
front: in front (of) delante (de) **2.2**
fruit la fruta **1.1**
fun divertido(a) **2.2**
  How fun! ¡Qué divertido! **7.2**
funny cómico(a) **1.2**
furniture los muebles **5.1**

G

game el partido **6.1**
garbage la basura **5.2**
garden el jardín (*pl.* los jardines) **5.1**
generally generalmente **8.1**
to get
  to get dressed vestirse (i) **8.1**
  to get up levantarse **8.1**
gift el regalo **5.2**
girl la chica **1.2**
to give dar (doy) **5.2**; regalar
glove el guante **6.1**
to go ir **2.2**
  to be going to... ir a... **4.2**
  to go for a walk pasear **1.1**
  to go out salir (salgo) **5.2**
  to go shopping ir de

compras **4.1**
to go to bed acostarse (ue) **8.1**
to go up subir **5.1**
to go with acompañar **7.2**
gold el oro
(made of) gold de oro **8.2**
good bueno(a) **1.2**
Good afternoon. Buenas tardes. **LP**
Good evening. Buenas noches. **LP**
Good morning. Buenos días. **LP**
Good night. Buenas noches. **LP**
Goodbye. Adiós. **LP**
good-looking guapo(a) **1.2**
goods los artículos **8.2**
sporting goods los artículos deportivos
grade la nota **2.1**
to get a good/bad grade sacar una buena/mala nota **2.1**
grammar la grámatica
grandfather el abuelo **3.2**
grandmother la abuela **3.2**
grandparents los abuelos **3.2**
grape la uva **3.1**
grass el césped **5.2**
to cut the grass cortar el césped **5.2**
green verde **4.1**
Greetings! ¡Saludos!
Greetings from... Saludos desde...
to guess adivinar
guests los invitados **5.2**
guitar la guitarra **1.1**
gymnasium el gimnasio **2.2**

H

hair el pelo **1.2**
blond hair pelo rubio **1.2**
brown hair pelo castaño **1.2**
hair dryer el secador de pelo **8.1**
half medio(a)
half past... ... y media **2.1**
hall el pasillo **2.2**
ham el jamón (*pl.* los jamones) **3.1**
hamburger la hamburguesa **3.1**
hand la mano **6.2**
handicrafts las artesanías **8.2**
to happen pasar
What's happening? ¿Qué pasa? **LP**
happy contento(a) **2.2**; feliz **3.2**; alegre
Happy birthday! ¡Feliz cumpleaños! **3.2**
hard-working trabajador(a) **1.2**
hat el sombrero **4.1**
winter hat el gorro **4.1**
to have tener **2.1**
one has to... hay que... **5.2**
to have just... acabar de... **5.2**
to have to... tener que... **2.1**
he él **1.1**
head la cabeza **6.2**
health la salud **6.2**
healthy sano(a) **6.2**
heart el corazón (*pl.* los corazones) **6.2**
heat el calor
Hello. Hola. **LP**
Hello? ¿Aló? **7.2**
helmet el casco **6.1**
to help ayudar **5.2**
her su **3.2**; ella **7.2**
here aquí **4.2**
Hi. Hola. **LP**
high school el colegio, la escuela secundaria
hike la caminata **8.2**
to hike dar una caminata **8.2**
him él **7.2**
his su **3.2**
history la historia **2.1**
homework la tarea **1.1**
to do homework hacer la tarea **1.1**
horrible horrible **3.1**
horse el caballo **8.2**
to ride a horse montar a caballo **8.2**
hot caliente
It is hot. Hace calor. **LP**
to be hot tener calor **4.1**
hotel el hotel **8.1**
hour la hora **2.1**
house la casa **5.1**
How...? ¿Cómo...? **3.1**
How are you? ¿Cómo estás? (familiar); ¿Cómo está usted? (formal) **LP**
How cool! ¡Qué bárbaro!
How expensive! ¡Qué caro(a)! **8.2**
How fun! ¡Qué divertido! **7.2**
How many...? ¿Cuántos(as)...? **2.1**
How old are you? ¿Cuántos años tienes? **3.2**
How scary! ¡Qué miedo! **7.2**
How's it going? ¿Qué tal? **LP**
how many cuántos(as) **3.2**
how much cuánto(a) **3.2**
How much does it (do they) cost? ¿Cuánto cuesta(n)? **4.1**
hungry: to be hungry tener hambre **3.1**
hurt herido(a) **6.2**
to hurt doler (ue) **6.2**

I

I yo **1.1**
I'm sorry. Lo siento. **6.2**
ice cream el helado **1.1**
icon el icono **7.1**
ideal ideal **5.1**
if si **5.2**
important importante **3.1**
It's imporant. Es importante. **3.1**
in en **2.1**
in front (of) delante (de) **2.2**
in order to para **3.1**
in the afternoon de la tarde **2.1**
in the morning de la mañana **2.1**
inexpensive barato(a) **8.2**
information la información; los datos
in-line skates los patines en línea **6.1**
to in-line skate patinar en línea **6.1**
inside (of) dentro (de) **2.2**
instant message el mensaje instantáneo
instant messaging el mensajero instantáneo **7.1**
intelligent inteligente **1.2**
interesting interesante **2.2**
Internet Internet **7.1**
to connect to the Internet conectar a Internet **7.1**
interview la entrevista
to interview entrevistar
to introduce presentar **LP**
Let me introduce you to... Te/Le presento a... (familiar/formal) **LP**
to invite invitar **5.2**
I invite you. Te invito. **7.2**
to iron planchar **5.2**
its su **3.2**

J

jacket la chaqueta **4.1**
January enero **3.2**
jeans los jeans **4.1**
jewelry las joyas **8.2**
juice el jugo **1.1**
  orange juice el jugo de naranja **3.1**
July julio **3.2**
June junio **3.2**

K

keyboard el teclado **7.1**
kind la clase
kitchen la cocina **5.1**
knee la rodilla **6.2**
to know
  (a fact; how to do something) saber (sé) **6.1**
  (a person) conocer (conozco) **6.1**

L

lake el lago
lamp la lámpara **5.1**
language el idioma, el lenguaje
large grande **1.2**
last último(a)
  last night anoche **6.2**
  last week la semana pasada **7.1**
  last year el año pasado **7.1**
late tarde **2.1**
later luego **7.1**
  later (on) más tarde **7.1**
  See you later. Hasta luego. **LP**
lawn el césped **5.2**
lazy perezoso(a) **1.2**
to learn aprender **1.1**
  to learn Spanish aprender el español **1.1**
leather el cuero
to leave salir (salgo) **5.2**; dejar **7.2**
left izquierdo(a)
leg la pierna **6.2**
less menos
  less than... menos que... **3.2**
  less... than menos... que **3.2**
lesson la lección
Let's... Vamos a... **4.2**
library la biblioteca **2.2**
life la vida
to lift levantar **6.2**
  to lift weights levantar pesas **6.2**
like como
to like
  Do you like...? ¿Te gusta...? **1.1**
  I don't like... No me gusta... **1.1**
  I like... Me gusta... **1.1**
  I would like... Me gustaría... **7.2**; Quisiera... **8.2**
  What do you like to do? ¿Qué te gusta hacer? **1.1**
  Would you like...? ¿Te gustaría...? **7.2**
Likewise. Igualmente. **LP**
to listen (to) escuchar **1.1**
  to listen to music escuchar música **1.1**
little pequeño(a) **1.2**
  a little un poco **1.2**
to live vivir **3.2**
living room la sala **5.1**
long largo(a)
to look (at) mirar
  to look for buscar **5.2**
to lose perder (ie) **6.1**
a lot mucho **2.1**
luck la suerte
  to be lucky tener suerte **4.1**
lunch el almuerzo **3.1**
  to eat lunch almorzar (ue) **4.2**

M

to make hacer (hago) **3.1**
  to make the bed hacer la cama **5.2**
mall el centro comercial **4.1**
man el hombre **1.2**
many muchos(as) **2.1**
  many times muchas veces **2.1**
map el mapa **2.2**
March marzo **3.2**
market el mercado **8.2**
  open-air market el mercado al aire libre
to match emparejar
math las matemáticas **2.1**
May mayo **3.2**
maybe tal vez **4.2**
me mí **7.2**
meal la comida **1.1, 3.1**
meat la carne **4.2**
to meet conocer (conozco) **6.1**
  Nice to meet you. Mucho gusto. **LP**
menu el menú **4.2**
message el mensaje **7.2**
  instant message el mensaje instantáneo **7.1**
  to leave a message dejar un mensaje **7.2**
meter el metro
milk la leche **3.1**
million un millón (de) **3.2**
minute el minuto **2.1**
mirror el espejo **5.1**
Miss Señorita (Srta.) **LP**
moment el momento **7.2**
  One moment. Un momento. **7.2**
Monday lunes **LP**
money el dinero **4.1**
month el mes **3.2**
more más **1.1**
  more than... más que... **3.2**
  more... than más... que **3.2**
morning la mañana **2.1**
  Good morning. Buenos días. **LP**
  in the morning de la mañana **2.1**
mother la madre **3.2**
mouse el ratón (*pl.* los ratones) **7.1**
mouth la boca **6.2**
movie la película **4.2**
movie theater el cine **4.2**
the movies el cine **4.2**
Mr. Señor (Sr.) **LP**
Mrs. Señora (Sra.) **LP**
museum el museo **7.2**
music la música **1.1**
  folk music la música folklórica
  rock music la música rock **4.2**
must: one must... hay que... **5.2**
my mi **3.2**

N

name el nombre
  His/Her name is... Se llama... **LP**
  My name is... Me llamo... **LP**
  What's his/her/your (formal) name? ¿Cómo se llama? **LP**
  What's your (familiar) name? ¿Cómo te llamas? **LP**
nature la naturaleza

near (to) cerca (de) **2.2**
necklace el collar **8.2**
to need necesitar **2.1**
neither tampoco **7.1**
 neither... nor ni... ni **7.1**
nervous nervioso(a) **2.2**
never nunca **2.1**
new nuevo(a) **4.1**
 New Year el Año Nuevo
newspaper el periódico
 student newspaper el periódico escolar
next to al lado (de) **2.2**
nice simpático(a) **1.2**
 Nice to meet you. Mucho gusto. **LP**
night la noche **2.1**
 at night de la noche **2.1**
 Good night. Buenas noches. **LP**
 last night anoche **6.2**
nine nueve **LP**
nine hundred novecientos(as) **3.2**
nineteen diecinueve **2.1**
ninety noventa **2.1**
ninth noveno(a) **5.1**
no no **LP**
nobody nadie **7.1**
no one nadie **7.1**
none ninguno(a) **7.1**
normally normalmente **8.1**
nose la nariz (*pl.* las narices) **6.2**
notebook el cuaderno **2.2**
notes los apuntes **2.1**
 to take notes tomar apuntes **2.1**
nothing nada **7.1**
November noviembre **3.2**
now ahora **3.1**
number el número **LP**
 phone number el número de teléfono **LP**
nutritious nutritivo(a) **3.1**

O

o'clock: It is... o'clock. Es la.../Son las... **2.1**
October octubre **3.2**
of de **1.1**
 Of course! ¡Claro que sí! **7.2**
to offer ofrecer **8.2**
office la oficina **2.2**
 principal's office la oficina del (de la) director(a) **2.2**
often muchas veces **2.1**
OK
 OK! ¡Vale!
 OK? ¿Está bien?
 OK. And you? Regular. ¿Y tú/usted? (familiar/formal) **LP**
old viejo(a) **1.2**
 How old are you? ¿Cuántos años tienes? **3.2**
 to be... years old tener... años **3.2**
older mayor **3.2**
on en; sobre
 on foot a pie **4.2**
 on top (of) encima (de) **2.2**
 on vacation de vacaciones **8.1**
once: once in a while de vez en cuando **2.1**
one uno **LP**
one hundred cien **2.1**
one thousand mil **3.2**
online en línea **7.1**
to open abrir **5.2**
open-air al aire libre **8.2**
or o **1.1**
orange (color) anaranjado(a) **4.1**
orange (fruit) la naranja **3.1**
to order pedir (i) **4.2**
organized organizado(a) **1.2**
other otro(a) **3.1**
ought to deber **5.2**
our nuestro(a) **3.2**
outside al aire libre **8.2**

P

page la página
painting el cuadro, la pintura
pair la pareja
pants los pantalones **4.1**
paper el papel **2.2**
 wrapping paper el papel de regalo **5.2**
parade el desfile
paragraph el párrafo
parents los padres **3.2**
park el parque **4.2**
 amusement park el parque de diversiones **7.2**
part la parte
party la fiesta
 surprise party la fiesta de sorpresa **5.2**
password la contraseña
past pasado(a) **7.1**
 half past... ...y media **2.1**
 quarter past... ...y cuarto **2.1**
the past el pasado
patio el patio **5.1**
to pay pagar **4.1**
pen la pluma **2.2**
pencil el lápiz (*pl.* los lápices) **2.2**
perhaps tal vez **4.2**
person la persona **1.2**
phone el teléfono **LP**
 phone call la llamada **7.2**
 What is your phone number? ¿Cuál es tu/su número de teléfono? (familiar/formal) **LP**
 My phone number is... Mi número de teléfono es... **LP**
photo la foto **7.1**
 to take photos tomar fotos **7.1**
to picnic comer al aire libre **8.2**
picture la foto **7.1**
pizza la pizza **1.1**
place el lugar **4.2**
to place poner (pongo) **5.2**
to plan pensar (ie) **4.1**
plant la planta
plate el plato
to play
 (an instrument) tocar **1.1**
 (games) jugar (ue) **1.1**
 (sports) jugar (ue), practicar **1.1**
player el (la) jugador(a) **6.1**
Please. Por favor. **LP**
 Pleased to meet you. Encantado(a). **LP**
pleasure el gusto **LP**
 The pleasure is mine. El gusto es mío. **LP**
post card la tarjeta postal
potato la papa **1.1**; la patata **4.2**
to practice practicar **1.1**
to prefer preferir (ie) **4.1**
to prepare preparar **1.1**
 to prepare food/a meal preparar la comida **1.1**
present el regalo **5.2**
pretty bonito(a) **1.2**
price el precio **4.1**
principal el (la) director(a) **2.2**
problem el problema **2.2**
to protect proteger (protejo)
to put poner (pongo) **5.2**
 to put on (clothes) ponerse (me pongo) (la ropa) **8.1**
 to put on makeup maquillarse **8.1**

Q

quality la calidad **8.2**
quarter (to) (menos) cuarto **2.1**
quarter past ... y cuarto **2.1**
question la pregunta

R

race la carrera
racket la raqueta **6.1**
radio el radio **5.1**
raft la balsa
to rain llover (ue) **LP**
  It is raining. Llueve. **LP**
to raise levantar
ranch la estancia
to read leer **1.1**
  to read a book leer un libro **1.1**
reading la lectura
Really? ¿Verdad?
to receive recibir **5.2**
recess el recreo
red rojo(a) **4.1**
red-haired pelirrojo(a) **1.2**
to remember recordar (ue)
to rent alquilar **1.1**
  to rent a DVD alquilar un DVD **1.1**
to reply responder
to rest descansar **1.1**
restaurant el restaurante **4.2**
result el resultado
to return volver (ue) **4.2**
review el repaso
rice el arroz **4.2**
rich rico(a)
to ride montar **1.1**; subir a **7.2**
  to ride a bike montar en bicicleta **1.1**
  to ride a horse montar a caballo **8.2**
  to ride the Ferris wheel/roller coaster subir a la vuelta al mundo/la montaña rusa **7.2**
right derecho(a)
  Right? ¿Verdad? **LP**
  to be right tener razón **4.1**
ring el anillo **8.2**
roller coaster la montaña rusa **7.2**
room el cuarto **5.1**
routine la rutina **8.1**
rug la alfombra **5.1**
rule la regla **6.1**
to run correr **1.1**

S

sad triste **2.2**
safe seguro(a)
salad la ensalada **4.2**
salesclerk el (la) vendedor(a)
same mismo(a)
  Same here. Igualmente. **LP**
sandwich el sándwich **3.1**
  ham and cheese sandwich el sándwich de jamón y queso **3.1**
Saturday sábado **LP**
to say decir **5.2**
scary: How scary! ¡Qué miedo! **7.2**
scene la escena
schedule el horario **2.1**
school la escuela **1.1**
  high school el colegio, la escuela secundaria
science las ciencias **2.1**
screen la pantalla **7.1**
to scuba-dive bucear **6.2**
sea el mar **6.2**
season la estación (*pl.* las estaciones) **4.1**
second segundo(a) **5.1**
secret el secreto **5.2**
secure seguro(a)
to see ver (veo) **4.2**
  May I see...? ¿Me deja ver...? **8.2**
  See you later. Hasta luego. **LP**
  See you tomorrow. Hasta mañana. **LP**
to sell vender **3.1**
to send mandar **7.1**
sentence la oración (*pl.* las oraciones)
September septiembre **3.2**
serious serio(a) **1.2**
to serve servir (i) **4.2**
set: to set the table poner (pongo) la mesa **5.2**
seven siete **LP**
seven hundred setecientos(as) **3.2**
seventeen diecisiete **2.1**
seventh séptimo(a) **5.1**
seventy setenta **2.1**
shame: What a shame! ¡Qué lástima! **7.2**
shampoo el champú **8.1**
to share compartir **3.1**
to shave oneself afeitarse **8.1**
she ella **1.1**
shirt la camisa **4.1**
shoe el zapato **4.1**
shop: to go shopping ir de compras **4.1**
shopping center el centro comercial **4.1**
short (height) bajo(a) **1.2**
shorts los pantalones cortos **4.1**
should deber **5.2**
shower: to take a shower ducharse **8.1**
sick enfermo(a) **6.2**
silver la plata
  (made of) silver de plata **8.2**
to sing cantar **5.2**
sister la hermana **3.2**
six seis **LP**
six hundred seiscientos(as) **3.2**
sixteen dieciséis **2.1**
sixth sexto(a) **5.1**
sixty sesenta **2.1**
to skate patinar **6.1**
  to in-line skate patinar en línea **6.1**
to skateboard andar en patineta **1.1**
skin la piel **6.2**
to sleep dormir (ue) **4.2**
small pequeño(a) **1.2**
snow la nieve
to snow nevar (ie) **LP**
  It is snowing. Nieva. **LP**
so entonces **7.1**
  so many tantos(as)
  so much tanto(a)
soap el jabón (*pl.* los jabones) **8.1**
soccer el fútbol **1.1**
sock el calcetín (*pl.* los calcetines) **4.1**
sofa el sofá **5.1**
soft drink el refresco **1.1**
some alguno(a) **7.1**
someone alguien **7.1**
something algo **7.1**
sometimes a veces
son el hijo **3.2**
sorry: I'm sorry. Lo siento. **6.2**
So-so. And you? Más o menos. ¿Y tú/usted? (familiar/formal) **LP**
soup la sopa **3.1**
source la fuente
souvenir el recuerdo **8.2**

Spanish el español **2.1**
to speak hablar **1.1**
  May I speak with...? ¿Puedo hablar con...? **7.2**
special especial
to spend: to spend time with friends pasar un rato con los amigos **1.1**
spirit el ánimo
sports los deportes **1.1**
spring la primavera **4.1**
stadium el estadio **6.1**
stairs la escalera **5.1**
to stay in quedarse en **8.1**
stepfather el padrastro **3.2**
stepmother la madrastra **3.2**
still todavía **5.2**
stomach el estómago **6.2**
to stop parar
store la tienda **4.1**
street la calle **4.2**
strong fuerte **6.2**
student el (la) estudiante **1.2**
studious estudioso(a) **1.2**
to study estudiar **1.1**
summary el resumen
  in summary en resumen
summer el verano **4.1**
sun el sol **LP**
  It is sunny. Hace sol. **LP**
to sunbathe tomar el sol **6.2**
Sunday domingo **LP**
sunscreen el bloqueador de sol **6.2**
supermarket el supermercado
to surf hacer surfing **8.2**
  to surf the Web navegar por Internet **7.1**
surprise la sorpresa **5.2**
survey la encuesta
to sweep barrer **5.2**
  to sweep the floor barrer el suelo **5.2**
to swim nadar **6.1**
swimming la natación **6.1**
swimming pool la piscina **6.1**

T

table la mesa **4.2**
  to set the table poner la mesa **5.2**
to take tomar **4.2**
  to take a bath bañarse **8.1**
  to take a shower ducharse **8.1**
  to take a trip hacer un viaje **8.1**
  to take notes tomar apuntes **2.1**
  to take out the trash sacar la basura **5.2**
  to take photos tomar fotos **7.1**
to talk hablar **1.1**
  to talk on the phone hablar por teléfono **1.1**
tall alto(a) **1.2**
tasty rico(a) **3.1**
to teach enseñar **2.1**
teacher el (la) maestro(a) **LP**
team el equipo **6.1**
telephone el teléfono **7.2**
  cellular telephone el teléfono celular **7.2**
  My phone number is... Mi número de teléfono es... **LP**
  What is your phone number? (familiar/formal) ¿Cuál es tu/su número de teléfono? **LP**
television la televisión **1.1**
television set el televisor **5.1**
ten diez **LP**
tennis el tenis **6.1**
tenth décimo(a) **5.1**
test el examen (*pl.* los exámenes) **2.1**
Thank you. Gracias. **LP**
  Thank you very much. Muchas gracias. **LP**
that ese(a) **8.2**
  that (over there) aquel (aquella) **8.2**
theater el teatro **4.2**
their su **3.2**
them ellos(as) **7.2**
theme el tema
then luego; entonces **7.1**
there allí **4.2**
  there is/are... hay... **2.1**
these estos(as) **8.2**
they ellos(as) **1.1**
thing la cosa **5.1**
to think pensar (ie) **4.1**
third tercero(a) **5.1**
thirst la sed
  to be thirsty tener sed **3.1**
thirteen trece **2.1**
thirty treinta **2.1**
thirty-one treinta y uno **2.1**
this este(a) **8.2**
those esos(as) **8.2**
  those (over there) aquellos(as) **8.2**
thousand mil **3.2**
three tres **LP**
three hundred trescientos(as) **3.2**
Thursday jueves **LP**
ticket la entrada **4.2**; el boleto **7.2**
time la hora **2.1**; la vez; el tiempo **8.2**
  At what time is/are...? ¿A qué hora es/son...? **2.1**
  free time el tiempo libre **8.2**
  What time is it? ¿Qué hora es? **2.1**
tip la propina **4.2**
tired cansado(a) **2.2**
to menos (with a time) **2.1**; a
today hoy **LP**
  Today is... Hoy es... **LP**
  What day is today? ¿Qué día es hoy? **LP**
tomato el tomate **4.2**
tomorrow mañana **LP**
  See you tomorrow. Hasta mañana. **LP**
  Tomorrow is... Mañana es... **LP**
too también **1.1**
too much demasiado **8.2**
toothbrush el cepillo de dientes **8.1**
toothpaste la pasta de dientes **8.1**
tourism el turismo
towel la toalla **8.1**
town el pueblo
track la pista
train el tren **8.1**
  by train en tren **8.1**
trash la basura **5.2**
tree el árbol
trip el viaje **8.1**
true cierto(a)
truth la verdad
T-shirt la camiseta **4.1**
Tuesday martes **LP**
twelve doce **2.1**
twenty veinte **2.1**
twenty-one veintiuno **2.1**
two dos **LP**
two hundred doscientos(as) **3.2**
type el tipo; la clase
typical típico(a)

U

ugly feo(a) **4.1**
uncle el tío **3.2**
under debajo (de) **2.2**
underneath debajo (de) **2.2**

to understand entender (ie) **4.1**; comprender **6.1**
Did you understand? ¿Comprendiste?
unit la unidad
until hasta
us nosotros(as) **7.2**
to use usar **2.1**
to use the computer usar la computadora **2.1**

V

vacation las vacaciones **8.1**
on vacation de vacaciones **8.1**
to vacuum pasar la aspiradora **5.2**
vacuum cleaner la aspiradora **5.2**
valley el valle
various varios(as)
vegetables las verduras **4.2**
very muy **1.2**
Very well. And you? Muy bien. ¿Y tú/usted? (familiar/formal) **LP**
video game el videojuego **5.1**
to visit visitar
vocabulary vocabulario
volleyball el voleibol **6.1**

W

to wait (for) esperar **8.1**
waiter el camarero **4.2**
waitress la camarera **4.2**
to wake up despertarse (ie) **8.1**
to walk caminar **6.2**
to go for a walk pasear **1.1**
wall la pared
to want querer (ie) **4.1**; desear
to wash lavar **5.2**
to wash one's face lavarse la cara **8.1**
to wash oneself lavarse **8.1**
watch el reloj **2.2**
to watch mirar **1.1**
to watch television mirar la televisión **1.1**
water el agua (fem.) **1.1**
waterfall la cascada
to water-ski hacer esquí acuático **6.2**
we nosotros(as) **1.1**
to wear llevar **4.1**
weather el tiempo **LP**
What is the weather like? ¿Qué tiempo hace? **LP**
Web site el sitio Web **7.1**
Wednesday miércoles **LP**
week la semana **LP**
last week la semana pasada **7.1**
weekend el fin de semana **7.2**
welcome: You're welcome. De nada. **LP**
well bien **LP**
Very well. And you? Muy bien. ¿Y tú/usted? (familiar/formal) **LP**
what qué
What? ¿Qué?; ¿Cuál? **3.1**
What a shame! ¡Qué lástima! **7.2**
What are you like? ¿Cómo eres? **1.2**
What color is/are...? ¿De qué color es/son...?
What day is today? ¿Qué día es hoy? **LP**
What did you do? (pl., formal) ¿Qué hicieron ustedes? **6.2**
What did you do? (sing., familiar) ¿Qué hiciste tú? **6.2**
What do you like to do? ¿Qué te gusta hacer? **1.1**
What is the date? ¿Cuál es la fecha? **3.2**
What is the weather like? ¿Qué tiempo hace? **LP**
What is this? ¿Qué es esto? **8.2**
What is your phone number? (familiar/formal) ¿Cuál es tu/su número de teléfono? **LP**
What time is it? ¿Qué hora es? **2.1**
What's happening? ¿Qué pasa? **LP**
What's his/her/your (formal) name? ¿Cómo se llama? **LP**
What's your (familiar) name? ¿Cómo te llamas? **LP**
when cuando **2.2**
When? ¿Cuándo? **2.2**
where donde
Where? ¿Dónde? **2.2**
(To) Where? ¿Adónde? **2.2**
Where are you from? ¿De dónde eres (familiar)/es usted (formal)? **LP**
Where are you going? ¿Adónde vas? **2.2**
Where is he/she from? ¿De dónde es? **LP**
Which? ¿Cuál(es)? **3.1**
a while un rato
once in a while de vez en cuando **2.1**
white blanco(a) **4.1**
Who? ¿Quién(es)? **3.1**
Who is he/she/it? ¿Quién es? **LP**
Why? ¿Por qué? **3.1**
to win ganar **6.1**
wind el viento
It is windy. Hace viento. **LP**
window la ventana **2.2**
ticket window la ventanilla **4.2**
to windsurf hacer surf de vela **8.2**
winner el (la) ganador(a) **6.1**
winning ganador(a)
winter el invierno **4.1**
to wish desear
with con **7.2**
with me conmigo **7.2**
with you contigo **7.2**
without sin
woman la mujer **1.2**
wood la madera **8**
made of wood de madera **8.2**
work (of art) la obra
to work trabajar **1.1**
world el mundo
worse peor **3.2**
to wrap envolver (ue) **5.2**
wrapping paper el papel de regalo **5.2**
to write escribir **1.1**
to write e-mails escribir correos electrónicos **1.1**
writing la escritura

Y

year el año **3.2**
last year el año pasado **7.1**
New Year el Año Nuevo
to be... years old tener... años **3.2**
yellow amarillo(a) **4.1**
yes sí **LP**

Yes, I would love to. Sí, me encantaría. **7.2**
yesterday ayer **6.2**
the day before yesterday anteayer **7.1**
yet todavía **5.2**
yogurt el yogur **3.1**
you
(sing., familiar) tú **1.1**; ti **7.2**
(sing., formal) usted **1.1**, **7.2**
(pl., familiar) vosotros(as) **1.1**,
(pl.) ustedes **1.1**
young joven (*pl.* jóvenes) **1.2**
younger menor **3.2**
your
(sing., familiar) tu **3.2**
(pl., familiar) vuestro(a) **3.2**
(formal) su **3.2**

Z

zero cero **LP**
zoo el zoológico **7.2**

GLOSARIO inglés-español

Índice

C

ÍNDICE

D

E

F

G

H

I

J

K

L

M

ÍNDICE

N

O

P

Q

T

ÍNDICE

W

Y

Z

ÍNDICE

Créditos

Acknowledgment

"Invierno tardío" by Antonio Colinas. Reprinted by permission of the author.

Photography

Cover *center* Nino H. Photography/Getty Images; *bottom right* H. Sitton/zefa/Corbis; **Title Page** *top* Nino H. Photography/Getty Images; *bottom right* H. Sitton/zefa/Corbis; **Half Title Page** H. Sitton/zefa/Corbis; **iv** *bottom left* Jaime Puebla/AP Images; *bottom right* Alberto Martin/Agencia EFE; **v** *bottom left* Gregory Bull/AP Images; *bottom right* Jennifer Szymaszek/AP Images; **vi-vii** *all* Ann Summa/Holt McDougal/Houghton Mifflin Harcourt; **xxx** *top* Erich Lessing/Art Resource, New York; *bottom* Ann Summa/Holt McDougal/Houghton Mifflin Harcourt.; **xxxi** *both* Ken Karp/Holt McDougal/Houghton Mifflin Harcourt.; **xxxiii** Jay Penni/Holt McDougal/Houghton Mifflin Harcourt.; **xxxix** *both* Jay Penni/Holt McDougal/Houghton Mifflin Harcourt.; **xxxv** *both* Michael Goss/Holt McDougal/Houghton Mifflin Harcourt.; **xxxvi** *top left* Robert Galbraith/Reuters Pictures; *top right* Holt McDougal/Houghton Mifflin Harcourt.; **xxxvii** *top left* Richard Wareham Fotografie/Alamy; *top right* Ann Summa; *center* Edward Hernández/Edward H. Photos; *bottom* Philip Coblentz/Brand X Pictures/Getty Images; **C2** *banner, left to right 1* Jesús Dominguez/Agencia EFE; *2-4* Rafael Diaz/Agencia EFE; *all others* Rafael Diaz/Agencia EFE; **C3** *top left, top right* Rafael Diaz/Agencia EFE; *bottom right* Jesús Dominguez/Agencia EFE; **C4** *banner, left to right* Juan Carlos Ulate/Reuters Pictures; The Brownsville Herald/Anthony Padilla/AP Images; José Luis Magaña/AP Images; Agencia EFE; *bottom left* Héctor López/Agencia EFE; *bottom right* Marco Ugarte/AP Images; **C5** *top right* Kent Gilbert/AP Images; *top left* Daniel LeClair/Reuters Pictures; *bottom right* Juan Carlos Ulate/Reuters Pictures; **C6** *banner, left to right* Greg Smith/Corbis; Eduardo Verdugo/AP Images; Claudia Daut/Landov/Reuters Pictures; Les Stone/NewsCom/Zuma Press; *left* Laura Cano/NewsCom/Agence France Presse; *bottom right* Jacqueline Castellon/NewsCom/Notimex; **C7** *center left* Dennis Callahan/NewsCom/Notimex; *bottom right* Susana Vera/Reuters Pictures; *top right* Claudia Daut/Reuters/Landov LLC; **C8** *banner, left to right* Ann Summa; Lightworks Media/Alamy; Denis Defibaugh; Rodrigo Abd/AP Images; *bottom left* Juan Barreto/Getty Images; *bottom left, inset* Ann Summa; *center left* Charles Bennett/AP Images; *top right* Marco Ugarte/AP Images; **C9** *top left* Glen Allison/Alamy; *top right* Eduardo Verdugo/AP Images; *bottom left* Jaime Puebla/AP Images; **C10** *banner, left to right* Marcelo Del Pozo/Reuters; Enrique Marcarian/Reuters Pictures; Juan Martin/Agencia EFE; Blake Sell/Reuters; *top left* Alberto Lowe/Reuters; *bottom left* Paul Taylor/The Image Bank/Getty Images; *bottom right* Leo La Valle/epa/Corbis; **C11** *top* Silvia Izquierdo/AP Images; *bottom* Desmond Boylan/Reuters; **C12** *banner, left to right* Dolores Ochoa R./AP Images; Marcou/Sipa Press; Denis Doyle/AP Images; Eric L. Weather/Lonely Planet Images; Luis Nereo Bueno Martinez/NewsCom/Reforma; *top left* Silvia Izquierdo/AP Images; *bottom right* Alberto Martin/Agencia EFE; *bottom center* Juanjo Martin/Agencia EFE; *bottom left* Olga Vasilkova/ShutterStock; **C13** *top right* Kryzsztof Dydynki/Lonely Planet Images; *left* Richard I'Anson/Lonely Planet Images; **C14** *banner, left to right* Miguel Vidal/Reuters/Corbis; Pablo Aneli/EPA/Corbis; Miguel Menéndez V./EPA/Corbis; Andrés Leighton/AP Images; *left* Elvira Urquijo A./EPA/Corbis; *bottom right* Martin Crespo/EPA/Corbis; **C15** *top left* Juan Barreto/Staff/Getty Images; *right* David Mercado/Reuters Pictures; *bottom left* Javier Galeano/AP Images; *bottom right* Guy Jarvis/Holt McDougal/Houghton Mifflin Harcourt; **C16** *banner, left to right* **1** Kai Forsterling/Agencia EFE; **2** Hannah Levy/Lonely Planet Images; **3-5** Manuel Bruque/Agencia EFE; *bottom* Hannah Levy/Lonely Planet Images; *left* J.C. Cárdenas/Agencia EFE; **C17** *right* Heino Kalis/Reuters/Corbis; *left* Kai Forsterling/Agencia EFE; **C18** *banner, left to right* Jack Kurtz/NewsCom/Zuma Press; Olneystudio/Alamy; Andres Aguirre/LatinContent/Getty Images; Jack Kurtz/NewsCom/Zuma Press; *bottom right* Luis Romero/AP/Corbis; *left* Ann Summa; **C19** *top left* Pilar Olivares/Reuters Pictures; *bottom right* Luis Romero/AP/Corbis;; *right* Dolores Ochoa R./AP Images; **C20** *banner, left to right* Tyler Hicks/New York Times/Redux Pictures; Joe Raedle/Getty Images; Jorge Uzon/Getty Images; Damian Dovarganes/AP Images; *right, bottom left* Robert Galbraith/Reuters Pictures; **C21** *top right* José Luis Magaña/AP Images; *center* Michael Springer/Zuma Press; **C22** *banner, left to right* **1-2** Keren Su/Corbis; Paolo Aguilar/Agencia EFE; *bottom right, left* Paolo Aguilar/EPA/Corbis; **C23** *right* Guillermo Legaria/Agencia EFE; *left* Christian Lombardi/Agencia EFE; **C24** *banner, left to right* Dado Galdieri/AP Images; Tony Morrison/South American Pictures; Stuart Franklin/Magnum Photos; *left* Daniel Muñoz/Reuters/Corbis; *bottom right* Jupiter Images/Comstock; **C25** *bottom* Pablo Corral V/Corbis; *top left* Stuart Franklin/Magnum Photos; *top right* "Simón Bolívar" (1830), José Gil de Castro. Oil on canvas, 237cm x 167cm (93 5/16" x 65 3/4"). Museo Nacional de Arqueología, Antropología, e Historia del Perú, Instituto Nacional de Cultura, Lima. Photograph by Mireille Vautier/The Art Archive; **1–2** Alan Schein Photography/

Corbis; *bottom left* Gregory Bull/AP Images; *bottom right* Jennifer Szymaszek/AP Images; **2** *all* Ken Karp/Holt McDougal/Houghton Mifflin Harcourt; **3** *all* Ken Karp/Holt McDougal/Houghton Mifflin Harcourt; **5** *both* Ken Karp/Holt McDougal/Houghton Mifflin Harcourt; **6** *all* Ken Karp/Holt McDougal/Houghton Mifflin Harcourt; **7** *all* Ken Karp/Holt McDougal/Houghton Mifflin Harcourt; **8** *bottom* Ken Karp/Holt McDougal/Houghton Mifflin Harcourt; **9** *top left, top right* Ken Karp/Holt McDougal/Houghton Mifflin Harcourt; *bottom* Nikretes/Alamy; **12** *top* Ann Summa/Holt McDougal/Houghton Mifflin Harcourt; **14** *bottom center, bottom right* Ann Summa/Holt McDougal/Houghton Mifflin Harcourt; **16** *all* Ken Karp/Holt McDougal/Houghton Mifflin Harcourt; **18** *both* Ken Karp/Holt McDougal/Houghton Mifflin Harcourt; **20** *all* Jay Penni/Holt McDougal/Houghton Mifflin Harcourt; **21** *left* Clive Watkins/ShutterStock; *center left* Radius Images/Alamy; *center right* WizData, Inc./ShutterStock; *right* Michael Coglianty/Getty Images; **22** *both* Ken Karp/Holt McDougal/Houghton Mifflin Harcourt; **23** *both* Ken Karp/Holt McDougal/Houghton Mifflin Harcourt; **27** *top left* David R. Frazier Photolibrary, Inc./Alamy; *top right* HIRB/Index Stock Imagery; *bottom left* Don Couch/Houghton Mifflin Harcourt; *bottom right* HIRB/Index Stock Imagery; **28** *bottom left* Ann Summa/Holt McDougal/Houghton Mifflin Harcourt; *bottom right* Holt McDougal/Houghton Mifflin Harcourt; *center* Image Club; **29** *top left* Tomas Abad/age fotostock; *center inset* Ann Summa/Holt McDougal/Houghton Mifflin Harcourt; *center right* AFP/Getty Images; *bottom center* Richard Cummins/Lonely Planet Images; *bottom left* Eric Gray/AP Images; **30–31** Ann Summa/Holt McDougal/Houghton Mifflin Harcourt; **32** *all* Ann Summa/Holt McDougal/Houghton Mifflin Harcourt; **33** *fruit* Tina Rencelj/ShutterStock; *ice cream* Comstock; *fries* Royalty-Free/Corbis; *pizza* SuperStock; *cookies* Michael Newman/PhotoEdit; *water* PhotoDisc/Getty Images; *soda* Guy Jarvis/School Division/Houghton Mifflin Harcourt; *all others* Ann Summa/Holt McDougal/Houghton Mifflin Harcourt; **34** *modelo* Guy Jarvis/School Division/Houghton Mifflin Harcourt; *1* Michael Newman/PhotoEdit; *3* Comstock; *4* Royalty-Free/Corbis; *5* PhotoDisc/Getty Images; *6* Tina Rencelj/ShutterStock; **35** *both* Ann Summa/Holt McDougal/Houghton Mifflin Harcourt; **39** *both* Ann Summa/Holt McDougal/Houghton Mifflin Harcourt; **40** Ann Summa/Holt McDougal/Houghton Mifflin Harcourt; **41** *left* Rodrigo Varela/WireImage.com; *right* Orlando García/Getty Images; **43** *all* Ann Summa/Holt McDougal/Houghton Mifflin Harcourt; **44** "Music" (2005), Xavier Cortada. Acrylic on canvas, 60 in. x 96 in. Bridgeman Art Library International; **45** *all* Ann Summa/Holt McDougal/Houghton Mifflin Harcourt; **46** *both* Ann Summa/Holt McDougal/Houghton Mifflin Harcourt; **48** *left* Michael Newman/PhotoEdit; *right* Guy Jarvis/School Division/Houghton Mifflin Harcourt; **49** *top right* PhotoDisc/Getty Images; *top left* Tracy Frankel/Getty Images; *bottom right* Stewart Cohen/Getty Images; *center* Guy Jarvis/School Division/Houghton Mifflin Harcourt; **50** *top* Bettmann/Corbis; *bottom* Vince Bucci /AFP/ Getty Images; **53** *modelo* Paul Costello/Getty Images; *1, 2* David Young-Wolff/PhotoEdit; *3* Stockdisc/Alamy; *4* Jacques Alexandre/age fotostock; *5* Don Hammond/age fotostock; *6* HIRB/Index Stock Imagery; 54–55 Ann Summa/Holt McDougal/Houghton Mifflin Harcourt; 56 *all* Ann Summa/Holt McDougal/Houghton Mifflin Harcourt; **57** *all* Ann Summa/Holt McDougal/Houghton Mifflin Harcourt; **59** Ann Summa/Holt McDougal/Houghton Mifflin Harcourt; **60** *center* Stockbyte Royalty Free; *bottom right* Jim Scherer Photography Inc./StockFood; *bottom center* Jay Penni/Holt McDougal/Houghton Mifflin Harcourt; **62** *modelo* Michael Newman/PhotoEdit; *1* Royalty-Free/Corbis; *2* Guy Jarvis/School Division/Houghton Mifflin Harcourt; *3, 5* FoodCollection/SuperStock; *4, 6* Comstock; *7* Tina Rencelj/ShutterStock; **64** *both* Ann Summa/Holt McDougal/Houghton Mifflin Harcourt; **68** *bottom right* Guy Jarvis/School Division/Houghton Mifflin Harcourt; *top right* Eric Gay/AP Images; **69** *all* Ann Summa/Holt McDougal/Houghton Mifflin Harcourt; **70** *all* Ann Summa/Holt McDougal/Houghton Mifflin Harcourt; **72** Phil Schermeister/Corbis; **73** *background* Royalty-Free/Corbis; *inset* Ryan McVay/PhotoDisc/Getty Images; **74** *top* Jay Penni/Holt McDougal/Houghton Mifflin Harcourt; *bottom left* ShutterStock; *bottom right* Holt McDougal/Houghton Mifflin Harcourt; **78–79** Richard Wareham Fotografie/Alamy; **79** *center* David Young-Wolff/PhotoEdit; *bottom* David Buffington/Getty Images; **82** *whisk* Jay Penni/Holt McDougal/Houghton Mifflin Harcourt; *center* Image Club; *cup* PhotoObjects/Jupiterimages Corp.; *bottom left* Ann Summa/Holt McDougal/Houghton Mifflin Harcourt; **83** *top left* Ann Summa; *center right* Erich Lessing/Art Resource, New York; *bottom left* "The Historical Representation of Culture" (1949), Juan O'Gorman. Mosaic, southeast view of exterior of Biblioteca Central, Universidad Nacional Autónoma de México (UNAM), Mexico City. © 2005 Sandro Landucci, Mexico City/Estate of Juan O'Gorman. Photograph by Ian Pearson/Mexicolore/Bridgeman Art Library; *bottom right* Detail, "The Historical Representation of Culture" (1949), Juan O'Gorman. Exterior of Biblioteca Central, Universidad Nacional Autónoma de México (UNAM), Mexico City. © 2005 Sandro Landucci, Mexico City/Estate of Juan O'Gorman. Photograph by Ian Pearson/Mexicolore/Bridgeman Art Library; **86** *top left* Jay Penni/Holt McDougal/Houghton Mifflin Harcourt; *map inset* Royalty-Free/Corbis; **92** *6, map inset* Royalty-Free/Corbis; **93** *all* Ann Summa/Holt McDougal/Houghton Mifflin Harcourt; **97** © 2009 Artists Rights Society (ARS), New York/SOMAAP, Mexico City. Photo: © Schalkwijk/Art Resource, NY; **110** *paper* Jay Penni/Holt McDougal/Houghton Mifflin Harcourt; *pencil* PhotoDisc; *backpack* Guy Jarvis/School Division/

R57

Houghton Mifflin Harcourt; *clock rim* Willem Bosman/ShutterStock; *clock face* Andrés Rodriguez/ShutterStock; **114** *modelo* PhotoDisc/Getty Images; *1* Ira Block/IPNstock; **116** *3* HIRB/Index Stock Imagery; **122** "Frida Kahlo" (1939), Nickolas Muray. Color photograph, assembly (Carbro) process, 40.1 cm x 29.9 cm. Gift of Mrs. Nickolas Muray. GEH NEG: 40130; 71:0050:0016. George Eastman House; **126** *bottom left* Corbis; *bottom right* Guy Jarvis/School Division/Houghton Mifflin Harcourt; **127** *top left* Guy Jarvis/School Division/Houghton Mifflin Harcourt; *bottom right* Xinhua/Landov; **128** *top* Jay Penni/Holt McDougal/Houghton Mifflin Harcourt; *bottom left* James Lyon/Lonely Planet Images; *bottom right* Lynne Guitar, Ph.D.; **132** *top* David Dudenhoefer/Odyssey Productions, Inc.; **133** *center* HIRB/Index Stock Imagery; *bottom* Dan Gair/Index Stock Imagery; **136** *bottom right* Martha Granger/EDGE Productions/Holt McDougal/Houghton Mifflin Harcourt; *flag* Image Club; **137** *bottom center, inset* Kevin Schafer/Corbis; *center right* Angelo Cavalli/age fotostock; *bottom left* Jason Ross/Alamy; **140** *top right* Comstock; *bottom right* Jay Penni/Holt McDougal/Houghton Mifflin Harcourt; **141** *soup* John A. Rizzo/Getty Images; *apple* Comstock; **142** *modelo left* Royalty-Free/Corbis; *modelo right* SuperStock; *3 left* John A. Rizzo/Getty Images; *4 right* SuperStock; *5 left* Comstock; *6 left* FoodPix/Getty Images; **144** *1* SuperStock; *3* John A. Rizzo/Getty Images; *8* FoodCollection/SuperStock; **146** *bottom* Renee Comet Photography, Inc./StockFood; **152** Rolf Richardson/Alamy; **155** *all* Comstock; **156** *grapes* PhotoObjects/Jupiterimages Corp.; *all others* Guy Jarvis/School Division/Houghton Mifflin Harcourt; **157** *whole pineapple* Jim Jurica/ShutterStock; *halved pineapple* Rudolf Georg/ShutterStock; *bottom left center inset* Holt McDougal/Houghton Mifflin Harcourt; *all others* Guy Jarvis/School Division/Houghton Mifflin Harcourt; **158** *top* NOAA; *bottom* Tony Arruza/Corbis; **160** *modelo* Arau/Cinevista/Aviacsa/The Kobal Collection; *4* Comstock; *6* John A. Rizzo/Getty Images; *8* SuperStock; **170** Kim Karpeles/Alamy; **176** *right* "Smiling Country Girl" (2005), Fernando Sayan Polo. Oil on canvas, 15" x 21". Courtesy of the artist; *left* "Lavandera," Rafael Tufiño (1960). Oil on masonite, 48 x 28 inches (121.9 x 71.1 cm.), Collection El Museo del Barrio, NY, Gift of Edward Bejan, P92.125; Image Courtesy El Museo del Barrio, NY; **179** Comstock; **180** *left* Ed Kashi/Corbis; *right* HIRB/Index Stock Imagery; **181** *bottom center* PhotoDisc; *all others* Edward Hernández/Edward H. Photos; **182** *top* Jay Penni/Holt McDougal/Houghton Mifflin Harcourt; *bottom left* PhotoObjects/Jupiterimages Corp.; *bottom right* David Stares/Alamy; **186–187** Jorgrn Schytte/Peter Arnold, Inc.; **187** *bottom* Terry Harris/Alamy; *center* J Marshall-Tribaleye Images/Alamy; **189** *both* David Sacks/Getty Images; **190** *center* Image Club; *bottom right* Martha Granger/EDGE Productions/Holt McDougal/Houghton Mifflin Harcourt; **191** *top left* Shizuo Kambayashi/AP Images; *center* AP Images; *center right* "Don Quixote" (1955), Pablo Picasso. Gouache on paper. Private collection. © 2007 Estate of Pablo Picasso/Artists Rights Society (ARS), New York. Photograph by Bridgeman Art Library; *bottom left* Anthony Cassidy/Getty Images; **194** *top right* Jon Ivern/age fotostock; **195** *spring* Jonelle Weaver/Getty Images; *t-shirt* Jay Penni/Holt McDougal/Houghton Mifflin Harcourt; *shorts* Guy Jarvis/School Division/Houghton Mifflin Harcourt; *Euros* Gary Conner/PhotoEdit; *summer* José Pascual/age fotostock; *fall* M.A. Otsoa de Alda/age fotostock; *winter* Paco Ayala/age fotostock; **196** *modelo* Jessica Bethke/ShutterStock; *1, 6* Guy Jarvis/School Division/Houghton Mifflin Harcourt; *2, 4, 5, 7* C Squared Studios/Getty Images; *3* Jay Penni/Holt McDougal/Houghton Mifflin Harcourt; *8* PhotoObjects/Jupiterimages Corp.; **200** *shirt* PhotoObjects/Jupiterimages Corp.; *blouse* Jay Penni/Holt McDougal/Houghton Mifflin Harcourt; *socks* Burke/Triolo/Getty Images; *hat* Stockbyte Royalty Free; *shoes* Michael Newman/PhotoEdit; *jeans* C Squared Studios/Getty Images; **201** *top* Stief & Schnare/SuperStock; *1* Burke/Triolo/Getty Images; *2* Siede Preis/Getty Images; *3, 8* Guy Jarvis/School Division/Houghton Mifflin Harcourt; *4* Lara Barrett/ShutterStock; *5, 6* C Squared Studios/Getty Images; *7* Michael Newman/PhotoEdit; **203** *bottom* "The Persistence of Memory" (1931), Salvador Dalí. Oil on canvas, 9 1/2" x 13" (24.1 cm x 33 cm). Museum of Modern Art, New York (162.1934). Given anonymously. © 2007 Salvador Dalí, Gala-Salvador Dalí Foundation/Artists Rights Society (ARS), New York. Digital Image © The Museum of Modern Art/Licensed by SCALA / Art Resource, NY; **206** *bottom right* Francois Gohier/Photo Researchers, Inc.; *bottom left* Michelle Chaplow/Alamy; **209** *right* Getty Images; *left* PhotoSpin; **210** *inset* Victor Lerena/Agencia EFE; background Guy Jarvis/School Division/Houghton Mifflin Harcourt; **211** *left* Yanik Chauvin/ShutterStock; *right* Guy Jarvis/School Division/Houghton Mifflin Harcourt; **212** *top left* Frank Vetere/Alamy; *top center* Royalty-Free/Corbis; *bottom right* F. Damm/Zefa/Corbis; *top right* Victor Kotler/age fotostock; **214** *1* C Squared Studios/Getty Images; *2, 6* Jay Penni/Holt McDougal/Houghton Mifflin Harcourt; *3* Charles Shapiro/ShutterStock; *4* Tracy Siermachesky/ShutterStock; *5* PhotoObjects/Jupiterimages Corp.; **218** *fish* Rusty Hill/StockFood; *cake* Comstock; *all others* Jay Penni/Holt McDougal/Houghton Mifflin Harcourt; **219** *center right* Mauricio-José Schwarz/Alamy; **222** *modelo* Christina Peters/Getty Images; *1* Jay Penni/Holt McDougal/Houghton Mifflin Harcourt; *2* Rita Maas/Getty Images; *3* Rusty Hill/StockFood; *5, 6, 7* Comstock; *8* J.G. Photography/Alamy; **224** *background* Stockbyte Royalty Free; **225** *left* Bruno Perousse/age fotostock; *right* Author's Image Ltd./Alamy; **227** *modelo* Royalty-Free/Corbis; *1* Jon Ivern/age fotostock; *2* Guy Moberly/Lonely Planet Images; *6* Nigel Francis/Corbis; **229** *modelo* Christina Peters/Getty Images; *1* J.G. Photography/Alamy; *2, 7* Jay Penni/Holt McDougal/Houghton Mifflin Harcourt; *3* Comstock; *5* Rita Maas/Getty Images; *6* James Carrier Photography/StockFood; *8* Rusty Hill/StockFood; **230** *right* "Las Meninas

(Infanta Margarita)" (1957), Pablo Picasso. Oil on canvas, 194 cm x 260 cm. Gift of the artist, 1968, Museo Picasso, Barcelona (MPB 70.433)/© 2007 Estate of Pablo Picasso/Artists Rights Society (ARS), New York/Bridgeman Art Library; *left* "Las Meninas" (1656), Diego Rodriguez Velázquez. Oil on canvas, 276 cm x 318 cm. Museo del Prado, Madrid, Spain. Photograph by Erich Lessing/Art Resource, New York; **234** Ken Welsh/age fotostock; **235** *both* Yadid Levy/Alamy; **236** *top right* "Landscape Near El Escorial" (1932), Ignacio Zuloaga y Zabaleta. Oil on canvas, 71 cm x 96 cm. Photograph by Erich Lessing/Art Resource, New York; *bottom right* "Girl Under a Parasol" Lira, Pedro. © Whitford & Hughes, London, UK/The Bridgeman Art Library; *left* Jay Penni/Holt McDougal/Houghton Mifflin Harcourt; **240** *top* David Dudenhoefer/Odyssey Productions, Inc.; **241** *center* Pierre Merimee/Corbis; *bottom* David Noton/Getty Images; **244** *center* Image Club; **245** *top left* Guillermo Granja/Reuters Pictures; *right* Guido Alberto Rossi/Tips Images; *center, inset* Roussel Photography/Alamy; *bottom left* "Las Floristas" (1916), Camilo Egas. Oil on canvas, 97cm x 155cm. Courtesy of Eric Egas.; **250** *4* Salvador Álvaro Nebot/age fotostock; **255** *top* "Christmas Eve" Targelia Toaquiza. Photograph by Pablo Corral V/Corbis; **259** Jay Penni/Holt McDougal/Houghton Mifflin Harcourt; **260** *modelo* John A. Rizzo/Getty Images; *1* Hemera/age fotostock; *4* Salvador Álvaro Nebot/age fotostock; *6* Michael Newman/PhotoEdit; *bottom left* Pablo Corral Vega/Corbis; *bottom right* Sergio Pitamitz/Alamy; **264** *bottom* Larry Luxner/DDB Stock Photography; *background* Guy Jarvis/School Division/Houghton Mifflin Harcourt; *sky* Val Maun/Holt McDougal/Houghton Mifflin Harcourt; **265** Gonzalo Azumendi/age fotostock; *background* Guy Jarvis/School Division/Houghton Mifflin Harcourt; **266** *right* Gary Cook/Alamy; *left* Royalty-Free/Corbis; **278** Pablo Corral V/Corbis; **279** *modelo* Jay Penni/Holt McDougal/Houghton Mifflin Harcourt; *3* PhotoDisc; *5* Guy Jarvis/School Division/Houghton Mifflin Harcourt; **281** *modelo* Michael Newman/PhotoEdit; *4* Tony Freeman/PhotoEdit; **284** Pep Roig/Alamy; **288** Michael Moody/DDB Stock Photography; **289** Danny Lehman/Corbis; **290** *top* Jay Penni/Holt McDougal/Houghton Mifflin Harcourt; *bottom left* David Sanger/Alamy; *bottom right* Danny Lehman/Corbis; **294–295** Bruce Ayers/Getty Images; **295** *bottom* Gary Irvine/Alamy; center Paul Springett/Alamy; **298** *bottom right* Holt McDougal/Houghton Mifflin Harcourt; **299** *top left* Nevada Weir/Corbis; *bottom left* Andre Jenny/Alamy; *center* Image Club; **303** *top left* Markku Lahdesmaki/Corbis; *center* Ryan McVay/Getty Images; *bottom right* S. Andreas/Corbis; **304** *modelo, top left, center left* Royalty-Free/Corbis; *bottom left* C Squared Studios/Getty Images; **306** *2* Leo Dennis/age fotostock; *bottom left* Fotopic/Index Stock Imagery; **308** Claudio Cruz/AP Images; **309** *tennis ball* Royalty-Free/Corbis; *football* PhotoDisc/Getty Images; **314** "Vendadora de Flores" (1998), Juan Medina. Mixed media on paper. Courtesy of the artist.; **318** *top* Jessica L. Archibald/ShutterStock; *top upper center* Galina Barskaya/ShutterStock; *bottom lower center* Paul Yates/ShutterStock; *bottom, bottom left* Spencer Jones/Getty Images; **319** *top left* Royalty-Free/Corbis; *top right, bottom right* LWA-Stephen Welstead/Corbis; *bottom left* Roy Morsch/age fotostock; **320** *modelo* Royalty-Free/Corbis; *4* PhotoObjects/Jupiterimages Corp.; *6* PhotoDisc/Getty Images; *bottom* Ándres Leighton/AP Images; **326** *center right* PhotoDisc/Getty Images; *bottom left* Ron Steiner/Alamy; **330** *1* Bill Losh/Getty Images; *2* Royalty-Free/Corbis; *4* Dennis MacDonald/Alamy; *5* Frank Simonetti/Index Stock Imagery; **332** "Bosque Escondido" ("Hidden Forest") (2005), Amaya Salazar. Oil on canvas, 60" x 80". Courtesy of the artist.; **333** *2* Robert Laberge/Getty Images; *5* Susan Van Etten/PhotoEdit; **338** Hemis/Alamy; **341** Stockbyte/Getty Images; **342** *left* Jorge Silva/Reuters/Corbis; *right* Tim De Waele/Corbis; **343** *both* Reuters/Corbis; **344** *all* Jay Penni/Holt McDougal/Houghton Mifflin Harcourt; **348–349** Tom Bean/Corbis; **349** *center* Doug Scott/*age* fotostock; *bottom* Henry Horenstein/Getty Images; **352** *center* Image Club; **353** *top left* Peter Adams/Getty Images; *center right* Hubert Stadler/Corbis; *bottom left* Imagebroker/SuperStock; *bottom left inset* Daniel García/NewsCom/Agence France Press; **357** *top right* Juncal/Alamy; *bottom center* Juan David Ferrando Subero/ShutterStock; **358** *1* Juan David Ferrando Subero/ShutterStock; **362** Homer Sykes/Alamy; **363** *2, 3, 4* Ann Summa/Holt McDougal/Houghton Mifflin Harcourt; *5* Kayte M. Deioma/PhotoEdit; **368** Craig Pershouse/Lonely Planet Images; **372** *top* Tan Kian Khoon/ShutterStock; *bottom* Dynamic Graphics/Photis/Alamy; **373** Tan Kian Khoon/ShutterStock; **374** *top* Ariel Skelley/Getty Images; *bottom* Barnabas Bosshart/Corbis; **380** *bottom center* Javier Larrea/age fotostock; **384** *top right center* Patrick Hermans/ShutterStock; *left* Javier Pierini/age fotostock; *center right* Joy Fera/ShutterStock; *bottom right* Ernest Manewal/Index Stock Imagery; *bottom left inset* Zina Seletskaya/ShutterStock; **386** "Dia de Trabajo" (1948), Benito Quinquela Martín (1890–1977/Argentinian). Oil on board, Zurbarán Galeria, Buenes Aires. © Zurbarán Galeria/SuperStock; **387** *center* Jeff Greenberg/PhotoEdit; *right* Jorge González/age fotostock; **391** *modelo* Jorge González/age fotostock; *3* Javier Larrea/age fotostock; *5* Jon Ivern/age fotostock; *6* Guy Moberly/Lonely Planet Images; **392** Owen Franken/Corbis; **396** Beryl Goldberg; **397** Agencia EFE; **398** *top right* Jay Penni/Holt McDougal/Houghton Mifflin Harcourt; Alejandro Michael Prince/Getty Images; Lorenzo Ryan McVay/Getty Images; Guadalupe PNC/Getty Images; Esperanza Tony Anderson/Getty Images; Gregorio Giantstep/Getty Images; Margarita Don Couch/HRW Photo; *Background & inset* Jay Penni/Holt McDougal/Houghton Mifflin Harcourt; **400** *modelo* Jeff Greenberg/PhotoEdit; *1* Jorge González/age fotostock; *2* Glenn R. McGloughlin/ShutterStock; *3* Javier Larrea/age fotostock; *5* Ames M. Phelps/ShutterStock; **402–403** Gonzalo Azumendi/age fotostock; **403** *bottom* Alyx Kellington/Index Stock Imagery; **406** *center* Image Club; **407** *top right* Kevin Schafer/Corbis; *center left* Tomas Staragardter/Getty Images; *bottom right* Dave G. Houser/Corbis; **411** *bottom right* Youssouf Cader/ShutterStock; **412** *2* ShutterStock; *3* Bill Gruber/ShutterStock; **414** *modelo* Ray G.

Perreault/ShutterStock; *1* Dorling Kindersley/Getty Images; *2* RMIP/Richards Haynes/Holt McDougal/Houghton Mifflin Harcourt; *3* Joanne and Daniel/ShutterStock; *6* Tina Rencelj/ShutterStock; **416** Dave G. Houser/Corbis; **422** © 2005 Francisco Munguía San José, Costa Rica; **426** *top right* Kevin Schafer/Getty Images; *left* Mitch Diamond/Alamy; *bottom right* Jan Csernoch/Alamy; *background* Guy Jarvis/School Division/Houghton Mifflin Harcourt; **427** *bottom* Jerry Driendl/Getty Images; *bottom left inset* PhotoDisc; *background* Guy Jarvis/School Division/Houghton Mifflin Harcourt; **428** *top right* Jonathan Blair/Corbis; *bottom* Nik Wheeler/Corbis; **430** *b* Dorling Kindersley/Getty Images; *e* Tina Rencelj/ShutterStock; **434** *top center* Sam Diephuis/Zefa/Corbis; *center* Thomas Hoeffgen/Getty Images; *bottom left* Catherine Wessel/Corbis; **436** right Jay Penni/Holt McDougal/Houghton Mifflin Harcourt; **438** modelo Ken Chernus/Getty Images; 2 Luke Hunter/Lonely Planet Images; *3* Ewa Walicka/ShutterStock; **440** Jose Fuste Raga/Corbis; **441** *6* Tony Freeman/PhotoEdit; **446** top right Don Couch/HRW Photo; inset Bob Stefko/Getty Images; **450** *left* Frank Pedrick/The Image Works; *right* Doug Scott/age fotostock; **451** *top* Sonda Dawes/The Image Works; *bottom* PhotoDisc; **452** *top* Jay Penni/Holt McDougal/Houghton Mifflin Harcourt; *bottom right* Guy Jarvis/School Division/Houghton Mifflin Harcourt; **456–457** Raymond Forbes/age fotostock; **457** *center* Insadco Photography/Alamy; *bottom* Paul Costello/Getty Images ; **462** *Ricardo* H&S Graphics, Inc.; *soup, soccer, hand with book, phone* Getty Images/PhotoDisc; *screen* HRW Photo; *skateboard, bike Comstock; guitar, charcoal drawing* Corbis; *Isabel* Holt McDougal; **465** *spiral notebooks* Victoria Smith/HRW Photo; *cafeteria, backpack, loose leaf paper* Don Couch/HRW Photo; *boy and girl talking in hall, pens, calculators* HRW Photo; **466** *bananas, grapes* Jupiter Images; *bread* Corbis; *bowl of soup, apple, sandwich, cup of coffee* Getty Images/PhotoDisc; *milk, yogurt,* juice HRW Photo; *burger* Brand X Pictures; **467** *grandfather, grandmother, father, mother, uncle, Pedro, sister* Don Couch/HRW Photo; *aunt, cousin* Corbis **468** *jeans, shoes, red plaid shirt, blue sundress, women's sandals* HRW Photo; *green button-up shirt* H & S Graphics; *striped t-shirt* Don Couch/HRW Photo; *hunting cap, team jacket* Getty Images/PhotoDisc; *straw hat* Brand X Pictures; **469** *all* HRW Photo; **472** *baseball and bat, football, tennis racket* Getty Images/PhotoDisc; *swim goggles* New England Typographic; *basketball, inline skate, volleyball* Corbis; *soccer ball* HRW Photo; *bike* Stockbyte; **474** *top to bottom* HRW Photo; HRW Photo; Corbis; John Langford/HRW Photo; Getty Images/PhotoDisc; Corbis; **475** *art gallery* Victoria Smith/HRW Photo; *monkey* Don Crouch/HRW Photo; *girl at computer* Sam Dudgeon/HRW Photo; *roller coaster* Corbis; *girls shoe shopping* Getty Images/PhotoDisc; *turtle in aquarium* National Geographic/Punchstock; *San Jose Park* Don Crouch/HRW Photo; *giant swing* Design Pics/Punchstock; *seated at table* HRW Photo; *bumper cars* Sam Dudgeon/HRW Photo; *market stalls* Don Crouch/HRW Photo; *musicians* Goodshoot; **476** *Rosa, Sr. Costas, Sra. Vasquez* Corbis; *Sofia, Mateo, Isabel, Rita* Don Crouch/HRW Photo; *Sergio, Diego* Dennis Fagan/HRW Photo; *Cris, Rafael* HRW Photo; *Elena* H&S Graphics, Inc.; **477** *Gabi, Paloma, Miguel, Maria* Getty Images/PhotoDisc; *Ana, Juan* Corbis; *Rosa* Image Ideas; *Raquel, Pablo* Victoria Smith/HRW Photo; *Susana, Carlos* Don Couch/HRW Photo; *Jorge* image100/Alamy.

All other photography by Jorge Albán/Holt McDougal/Houghton Mifflin Harcourt

Illustration

xxviii–xxxiii Mapquest.com; **4** *top* Anna Veltfort; **10** *all* Vilma Órtiz-Dillon; **12** Mapquest.com; **13** *both* Mapquest.com; **14** Mapquest.com; **15** Mapquest.com; **16** Steve McEntee; **20** Mapquest.com; **24** *all* Anna Veltfort; **26** *all* James Yamasaki; **28** maps Mike Reagan; **38** *all* Vilma Órtiz-Dillon; **43** *all* Steve McEntee; **50** *center* Mapquest.com; **60** Steve McEntee; **63** Vilma Órtiz-Dillon; **65** *both* Anna Veltfort; **67** Anna Veltfort; **76** James Yamasaki; **82–83** Mike Reagan; **86** *clocks* Steve McEntee; **88** Steve McEntee; **90** Steve McEntee; **104** Mapquest.com; **111** Steve McEntee; **112** Steve McEntee; **117** *bottom* Anna Veltfort; **117** *all others* Steve McEntee; **119** *faces* Steve McEntee; **130** Steve McEntee; **131** Vilma Órtiz-Dillon; **135** Steve McEntee; **136–137** Mike Reagan; **142** Vilma Órtiz-Dillon; **147** Steve McEntee; **151** *all* Anna Veltfort; **165** *both* Kenneth Batelman; **171** Steve McEntee; **175** *all* Anna Veltfort; **190–191** Mike Reagan; **196** *top* Anna Veltfort; **220** Vilma Órtiz-Dillon; **244–245** Mike Reagan; **252** Kenneth Batelman; **255** *both* Kenneth Batelman; **260** *top right* Stephen Durke; **266** *top right* Mapquest.com; *bottom* Steve McEntee; **298–299** Mike Reagan; **335** *left* Steve McEntee; **346** *all* Steve McEntee; **352–353** Mike Reagan; **360** *all* Steve McEntee; **386** *all* Steve McEntee; **406–407** Mike Reagan; **416** *all* Steve McEntee; **417** *all* Anna Veltfort; **421** *all* Anna Veltfort; **445** Vilma Órtiz-Dillon; **455** Vilma Órtiz-Dillon.

All other illustrations by Robin Storesund or Chris Wilson/Holt McDougal/Houghton Mifflin Harcourt